D0796775

FIELDING'S CARIBBEAN

Other Fielding Titles

Fielding's Alaska Cruises and the Inside Passage
Fielding's Asia's Top Dive Sites
Fielding's Amazon
Fielding's Australia
Fielding's Bahamas
Fielding's Baja
Fielding's Bermuda
Fielding's Borneo
Fielding's Budget Europe
Fielding's Caribbean
Fielding's Caribbean Cruises
Fielding's Disney World and Orlando
Fielding's Diving Indonesia
Fielding's Eastern Caribbean
Fielding's England
Fielding's Europe
Fielding's European Cruises
Fielding's Far East
Fielding's France
Fielding's Freewheelin' USA
Fielding's Kenya
Fielding's Hawaii
Fielding's Italy
Fielding's Las Vegas Agenda
Fielding's London Agenda
Fielding's Los Angeles
Fielding's Malaysia and Singapore
Fielding's Mexico
Fielding's New Orleans Agenda
Fielding's New York Agenda
Fielding's New Zealand
Fielding's Paradors, Pousadas and Charming Villages of Spain and Portugal
Fielding's Paris Agenda
Fielding's Portugal
Fielding's Rome Agenda
Fielding's San Diego Agenda
Fielding's Southeast Asia
Fielding's Southern Vietnam on Two Wheels
Fielding's Spain
Fielding's Surfing Indonesia
Fielding's Sydney Agenda
Fielding's Thailand, Cambodia, Laos & Myanmar
Fielding's Vacation Places Rated
Fielding's Vietnam
Fielding's Western Caribbean
Fielding's The World's Most Dangerous Places
Fielding's Worldwide Cruises

FIELDING'S CARIBBEAN

By

David Swanson

and

Joyce Wiswell

Fielding Worldwide, Inc.

308 South Catalina Avenue

Redondo Beach, California 90277 U.S.A.

Fielding's Caribbean

Published by Fielding Worldwide, Inc.

Text Copyright ©1997 Fielding Worldwide, Inc.

Maps, Icons & Illustrations Copyright ©1997 Fielding Worldwide, Inc.

Photo Copyrights ©1997 to Individual Photographers

Some maps ©MAGELLAN Geographix, Santa Barbara, California, Telephone (800) 929-4MAP, www.magellangeo.com

FIELDING WORLDWIDE INC.

PUBLISHER AND CEO	**Robert Young Pelton**
GENERAL MANAGER	**John Guillebeaux**
MARKETING DIRECTOR	**Paul T. Snapp**
OPERATIONS DIRECTOR	**George Posanke**
ELECTRONIC PUBLISHING DIRECTOR	**Larry E. Hart**
PUBLIC RELATIONS DIRECTOR	**Beverly Riess**
ACCOUNT SERVICES MANAGER	**Christy Harp**
PROJECT MANAGER	**Chris Snyder**

EDITORS

Kathy Knoles	**Linda Charlton**
Catherine Bruhn	**Reed Parsell**

PRODUCTION

Martin Mancha	**Alfredo Mercado**
Ramses Reynoso	**Craig South**

COVER DESIGNED BY	**Digital Artists, Inc.**
COVER PHOTOGRAPHERS — Front Cover	**Mark Lewis & Donald Nausbaum/Tony Stone Images**
Back Cover	**Julie Houck/Westlight**
INSIDE PHOTOS	**Carol Lee, Benford Associates, Grenada Tourist Office, Karen Weiner, Escalera Associates, Robinson, Yesavich & Pepperdine, Inc., Saba Tourist Office, Trombone Associates, Corel Professional Photos**

Inquiries should be addressed to: Fielding Worldwide, Inc., 308 South Catalina Ave., Redondo Beach, California 90277 U.S.A., ☎ *(310) 372-4474*, Facsimile *(310) 376-8064*, 8:30 a.m.–5:30 p.m. Pacific Standard Time.

Website: http://www.fieldingtravel.com

e-mail: fielding@fieldingtravel.com

ISBN 1-56952-109-3

Printed in the United States of America

Letter from the Publisher

The Caribbean can be a daunting place when it comes to choosing the perfect island getaway. Our focus is making sure you get the best experience for your time and money. To assist you we have created handy comparison tables for accommodations and restaurants complete with best buy and highest rated listings so you can get the most for your money. You'll also find the introductions tighter and with a definite accent on the romantic and adventurous.

Authors Joyce Wiswell and David Swanson, faced with covering and reviewing hundreds of "tropical getaways on white sandy beaches," bring a youthful enthusiasm along with a true love of the Caribbean to this book. They have tackled the daunting task of giving the reader a balanced overview of the region as well as highlighting the unique personality of each island. In these pages you will find the famous, the hidden and the overlooked all rated and reviewed in our new easy-to-use format. Supporting their efforts have been the staff and researchers at Fielding Worldwide who have done an impressive job of gathering, checking, sorting and compiling more than 1500 attractions, hotels and restaurants. Special thanks to our staff for making it all come together. If it helps you find that one perfect place for your once-a-year getaway, then we have done our job.

Today, the concept of independent travel has never been bigger. Our policy of *brutal honesty* and a highly personal point of view has never changed; it just seems the travel world has caught up with us.

Enjoy your Caribbean adventure.

R Y P

Robert Young Pelton
Publisher and CEO
Fielding Worldwide, Inc.

ABOUT THE AUTHORS

Joyce Wiswell

Joyce Wiswell has been writing about travel for more than 15 years. Various writing assignments have taken her to nearly every state in the union, as well as China, Hong Kong, the Philippines, Thailand, Europe and, of course, throughout the Caribbean. Her work has appeared in numerous magazines and newspapers. Wiswell is also the author of *Fielding's Las Vegas Agenda*, *Fielding's Bermuda* and *Fielding's Eastern* and *Western Caribbean*.

A native of New Jersey, she is a magna cum laude graduate of Connecticut's Quinnipiac College. After paying her dues as a magazine writer and editor in New York City for eight years, she fled for life in California, where she lives happily in Santa Barbara. When not traveling, she putters in the garden and pampers her cats, and worries unduly about both when on the road.

David Swanson

David Swanson has been enthusiastically hoofing the globe on a regular basis since his first trip to Europe in 1982. The journals from that trip also represented his first forays into travel writing, a career that blossomed into a full-time profession after abandoning his nine-to-five in 1993. Since then, his writing has appeared in the *Los Angeles Times, San Francisco Examiner, Chicago Sun-Times, Dallas Morning News, Cleveland Plain Dealer, Denver Post, Caribbean Travel and Life, Latitudes* and a number of other newspapers and publications. Swanson is also the author of *Fielding's Walt Disney World and Orlando Area Theme Parks.*

When Swanson isn't writing, he's bicycling, hiking and enjoying obscure movies.

Fielding Rating Icons

The Fielding Rating Icons are highly personal and awarded to help the besieged traveler choose from among the dizzying array of activities, attractions, hotels, restaurants and sights. The awarding of an icon denotes unusual or exceptional qualities in the relevant category.

RATINGS
Fielding Award · Author Selection · Money Saver · Expensive · Quality · Warning · Danger · Inexpensive · Spacious · Cramped · Mild Disapproval

CULTURAL
Museum/Art · Interesting Architecture · History · Book Reference · Artistically Important · Musically Interesting · Cultural Archaeology · Crafts · Theatre · Festivals

SIGHTS
Picturesque · Great Scenery · Market · Beaches/Resorts · Cultural · Fortress · Castles · Church

WHERE TO STAY
Simple · Luxurious · Cottage · Bed & Breakfast · Scenic · Business · Honeymoon · Chateau

TRAVEL TIPS
Arrival/Departure · By Air · By Water · By Train · By Car · Bus/Local Transit · Barge · Riverboat · Calendar · Itinerary · Compass · Kids

ACTIVITIES

Downhill Skiing	X-country Skiing	Watersports	Sailing	Scuba Diving	Snorkeling/ Diving	Deep-sea Fishing	Freshwater Fishing
Swimming	Hiking	Walking	Relaxing	Golf	Tennis	Horseback Riding	General Sports
Cycling	Workout						

SPECIAL INTEREST

Nightlife	Singles	Romantic	Nude Beaches	Lecture	Spectacular Cuisine	Wine Tasting	Shopping
Cafe Stops	Gardening	Pro Sports	Mystery				

What's in the Stars

Fielding's Five Star Rating System for the Caribbean

★ ★ ★ ★ ★ Exceptionally outstanding hotels, resorts, restaurants and attractions.

★ ★ ★ ★   Excellent in most respects.

★ ★ ★   Very good quality and superior value.

★ ★   Meritorious and worth considering.

★   Modest or better than average.

Restaurants are star rated and classified by dollar signs as:

$	Inexpensive	$1–$9
$$	Moderate	$9–$15
$$$	Expensive	$15 and up

A NOTE TO OUR READERS:

If you have had an extraordinary, mediocre or horrific experience we want to hear about it. If something has changed since we have gone to press, please let us know. Those business owners who flood us with shameless self-promotion under the guise of readers' letters will be noted and reviewed more rigorously next time. If you would like to send information for review in next year's edition send it to:

Fielding's Caribbean
308 South Catalina Avenue
Redondo Beach, CA 90277
FAX: (310) 376-8064

TABLE OF CONTENTS

LIST OF MAPS

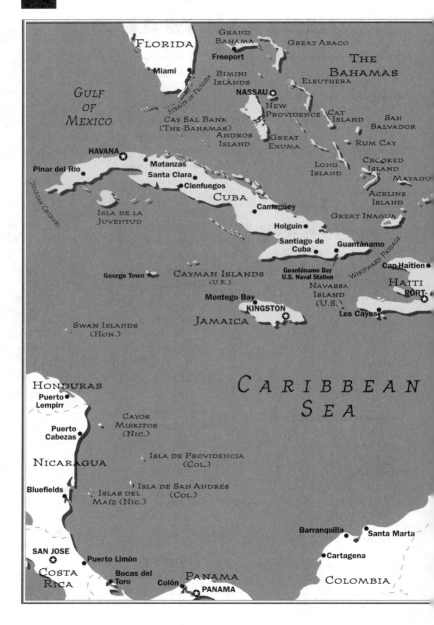

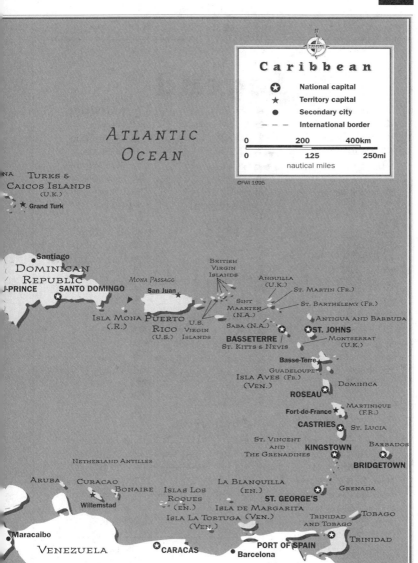

Caribbean

✪ National capital
★ Territory capital
● Secondary city
- - - International border

| 0 | 200 | 400km |
| 0 | 125 | 250mi |

nautical miles

©FWI 1995

ATLANTIC OCEAN

NA   TURKS & CAICOS ISLANDS (U.K.)
★ Grand Turk

● Santiago
DOMINICAN REPUBLIC   MONA PASSAGE
J-PRINCE   ✪ SANTO DOMINGO   ● San Juan ★
ISLA MONA   PUERTO
(.R.)   RICO   U.S. VIRGIN ISLANDS
(U.S.)

BRITISH VIRGIN ISLANDS
ANGUILLA (U.K.)
SINT MAARTEN (N.A.)   ST. MARTIN (FR.)
ST. BARTHÉLEMY (FR.)
SABA (N.A.)   ✪ ANTIGUA AND BARBUDA
BASSETERRE   ✪ ST. JOHNS
ST. KITTS & NEVIS   MONTSERRAT (U.K.)

Basse-Terre ★
GUADELOUPE
ISLA AVES (FR.)   (VEN.)
ROSEAU ✪   DOMINICA

Fort-de-France ★   MARTINIQUE (F.R.)
CASTRIES ✪   ST. LUCIA

ST. VINCENT AND THE GRENADINES   KINGSTOWN ✪   BARBADOS ● BRIDGETOWN

NETHERLAND ANTILLES

ARUBA   CURACAO   La BLANQUILLA (EN.)   GRENADA
BONAIRE   ISLAS LOS ROQUES   ST. GEORGE'S ✪
Willemstad   (EN.)   ISLA DE MARGARITA
ISLA LA TORTUGA (VEN.)   TRINIDAD AND TOBAGO   TOBAGO
(VEN.)

● Maracaibo   TRINIDAD

VENEZUELA   ✪ CARACAS   PORT OF SPAIN ✪
● Barcelona

Legend

Essentials

- 🏨 Hotel
- ♟ Youth Hostel
- ✗ Restaurant
- 💲 Bank
- 📞 Telephone
- ℹ Tourist Info.
- ✚ Hospital
- 🍺 Pub / Bar
- ✉ Post Office
- 🅿 Parking
- 🚕 Taxi
- Ⓢ Subway
- Ⓜ Metro
- Ⓜ Market
- 🛍 Shopping
- 🎬 Cinema
- 🎭 Theatre
- ✈ Int'l Airport
- ✛ Regional Airport
- ★ Police Station
- ⚖ Courthouse
- 🏛 Gov't. Building

Attraction

- ■ Attraction
- Military Airbase
- Army Base
- Naval base
- Fort
- University
- School

Historical

- Archeological Site
- Battleground
- Castle
- Monument
- Museum
- Ruin
- Shipwreck

Religious

- ✝ Church
- Buddhist Temple
- Hindu Temple
- Mosque
- Pagoda
- Synagogue

Activities

- Beach
- ▲ Campground
- Picnic Area
- Golf Course
- Boat Launch
- Diving
- Fishing
- Water Skiing
- Snow Skiing
- Bird Sanctuary
- Wildlife Sanctuary
- Park
- Park Headquarters
- Mine
- Lighthouse
- Windmill
- ⚓ Cruise Port
- View
- Stadium
- Building
- Zoo
- Garden

Physical

— — — · International Boundary	Hiking Trail
- · - · - · County / Regional Boundary	Dirt Road
PARIS ⊙ National Capital	Railroad
Montego Bay ● State / Parish Capital	**R·R** Railroad Station
Los Angeles ● Major City	Ferry Route
Quy Nhon ○ Town / Village	▲ Mountain Peak
—⑤— Motorway / Freeway	Lake
⑯③ Highway	River
Primary Road	Cave
Secondary Road	Coral Reef
— — — — Subway	Waterfall
⚲ Biking Routed	Hot Spring

©FWI 1995

TO OUR READERS

So you're off to the Caribbean—lucky you! Will you spend your days trekking through rainforests and inspecting colonial ruins? Exploring coral reefs teeming with sea creatures? Grooving away the night to the reggae and calypso beats? Or simply in a semi-comatose state of bliss on the beach, striving for the perfect tan?

Whatever your idea of paradise, the Caribbean—and this book—delivers. We know that just as no two beaches are exactly the same, neither are two people's ideas of the perfect vacation. Power to the adventurers among us who wouldn't dream of wasting time just lolling in the sun, and kudos to those who seek nothing more from their Caribbean getaway than the perfect tan. Most folks, we've found, fall somewhere in the middle, and we've provided plenty of information on shopping, attractions and sporting activities to give a clear picture of what each destination offers.

For most of us, alas, monetary restrictions will be the primary consideration when planning a vacation. You'll find this book covers virtually every property on each island, from the poshest of the posh to the lowest of the low. Happily, most islands offer a healthy assortment of mid-range choices, and with our brutally honest ratings system, you'll know just what to expect.

As Paul Simon says, one man's ceiling is another man's floor. For each person thrilled to ecstasy by the idea of giant, free-form pools, structured activities and theme parties, there's another who considers such a resort his or her personal version of hell. You may not go for cold-water showers and large insects as roommates, but the true bohemians among us could just as soon spend cash on other pleasures. And that's the beauty of the Caribbean: it's all there, from snooty country clubs to dependable Holiday Inns to seedy no-tell motels. You'll find it all in these pages.

To use this book in the most efficient way, start by reading the Island Snapshots, which give you thumbnail sketches of what to expect on each destination. From there, read the introduction to each island; "Bird's-Eye View," "History," and "People." "Where to Stay" and Where to Eat" provide details on exactly what to expect—and how much it will cost you. And before you leave, be sure to read the "Island Directory" following each chapter for helpful nuts and bolts information, as well as the sections upfront called "Caribbean Planner" and "Caribbean Culture."

Leave room in your suitcase for this guide, of course, but remember, the best vacation pleasures are often the surprises. While we've obviously written this book to help guide your perfect holiday, we also caution against overplanning. Leave enough time—and an open mind—to let some of the true allure of the Caribbean find you. We promise, it will.

FIELDING'S BEST VALUE ACCOMMODATIONS

Rating	Accommodation	City	Island
★★★	Lloyd's Guest House	The Valley	Anguilla
★★	Lord Nelson's Beach Hotel	St. John's	Antigua
★★★★	Amsterdam Manor Beach	Oranjestad	Aruba
★★★	Ocean View Hotel	Christ Church	Barbados
★★★★	Coco Point Lodge	Codrington	Barbuda
★★★	Divi Flamingo Resort	Kralendijk	Bonaire
★★	Fort Burt Hotel	Road Town	British Virgin Islands
★★	Sleep Inn	Georgetown	Cayman Islands
★★★★★	Lions Dive Hotel & Marina	Willemstad	Curaçao
★★★	Papillotte Wilderness Retreat	Roseau	Dominica
★★★★	Hotel Cayacoa Beach	Santo Domingo	Dominican Republic
★★★	Silver Beach Resort	Hillsborough	Grenada
★★★	Auberge de l'Arbre a Pain	Pointe-a-Pitre	Guadaloupe
★★★	Natania's Guest House	Westmorland	Jamaica
★★★	Martinique Cottages	Lamentin	Martinique
★	Marie's Guest House	Plymouth	Montserrat
★★★	Golden Rock Estate	Gingerland	Nevis
★★★	Villa Esperanza	Vieques	Puerto Rico
★★★	Captain's Quarters	The Bottom	Saba
★★★	Hotel Baie des Flamands	Gustavia	St. Barthélémy
★★★	Hilty House Inn	Christiansted	St. Croix
★★	Airport View Apartments	Oranjestad	Sint Eustatius
★★★	Concordia Eco-Tents	Cruz Bay	St. John
★★★	St. Christopher Club	Basseterre	St. Kitts
★★★	Doolittle's Resort	Castries	St. Lucia
★★	Hevea	Grand Case	St. Martin
★★	Heritage Manor	Charlotte Amalie	St. Thomas
★	Kingston Park Guest House	Kingston	St. Vincent
★★	Hampden Inn	Plymouth	Tobago
★★	Laguna Mar Resort	Port of Spain	Trinidad
★★★	Le Deck Hotel	Grace Bay	Turks & Caicos

CARIBBEAN PLANNER

What is it about the idea of a tropical island that sets our pulses racing and hearts swooning? It's the lure of palm-dotted beaches, no doubt, and a sea so incredibly clear you can inspect your pedicure in five feet of water. It's balmy evenings when trade winds caress your hair, soothe your spirit and make everyone look and feel sensuous. It's the sheer romance of escaping the bills and the boss, not worrying about wind-chill factors and having only to decide if it's time to turn over and tan your back or if you're up to a night dive.

While the many islands of the Eastern Caribbean are strewn closely together as if a giant tossed a handful of land into the sea, those of the West are generally much more spread out, with miles of deep blue sea between landfalls. While the East is generally known for its smashing resorts and excellent shopping, the isles of the West are famed for their superior diving and untamed natural beauty. But that in itself is a huge generalization, as each island has its own treasures and pleasures. With the notable exception of hot, humid weather and that alluring crystalline sea, Aruba has no more in common with St. John than Arkansas has to California. To determine which is right for you, see the chapter called "Island Snapshots."

While a rose may still be a rose no matter what it's called, lumping the Caribbean islands together under one category is, categorically, unfair. Each island has its own history, its own culture, its own personality. Seen one, seen them all is not the reality of the Caribbean. And vive la différence!

By Air

Many airlines fly to the Caribbean, though for island-hoppers, American and American Eagle are probably the best bets, as they service many destinations and give good deals on multi-island tickets. (On one swing, I hopped to eight islands, and the fare was about $1250, including round-trip from California.) On the other hand, many flights connect through San Juan, Puerto Rico, which means it can take many hours to get where a crow can fly in minutes. TACA is also good for short hops between islands. If you do find yourself stuck with a long layover in Puerto Rico, hop a cab to one of the nearby resorts—the El San Juan, in particular, is just a five-minute ride away. Its plush and the spacious lobby is a great place to wile away the hours, and time really flies in the upscale casino—though, alas, your vacation money may too.

Other airlines with service from the United States to the Caribbean are Aeromexico, Air Jamaica, ALM, Avensa, Avianca, BWIA, Cayman Airways, Continental, Delta, Dominicana, Lacsa, LanChile, Mexicana, Northwest, TWA, United, USAir and Viasa.

How much you'll pay depends on how demanding you are. If you're counting pennies, obviously you'll fly coach. If you're willing to spend more, upgrade to business or first-class—but be aware you'll pay dearly for the wider seat and better food, in most cases, several hundred dollars more. When island hopping, you'll invariably be on small craft with no separate classes of service.

To save money, buy your ticket as far in advance as possible, and be on the lookout for special promotions. It's cheaper all the way around to travel to the Caribbean in the summertime—everything from air to hotels are generally discounted. Also consider a package deal that includes air, transfers, hotel accommodations and sometimes meals and a rental car. Charter flights are also worth investigating, but have the distinct disadvantage of extremely limited schedules and a disturbing propensity to cancel flights. Unlike a commercial carrier, if your charter flight is canceled, you're usually left on your own to scramble for an alternate.

The *Affordable Caribbean (P.O. Box 3000, Denville, NJ 07834-9498;* ☎ *[301] 588-2300)* is a monthly newsletter that reports on last-minute deals and other Caribbean bargains. If you travel to the Caribbean frequently and have a flexible schedule, it's well worth the $49 annual subscription cost.

By Sea

There's nothing like a cruise for relaxing and really getting away from it all. These floating hotels pamper guests and provide lots of on-board activities for those who get bored just laying on deck soaking up the rays. Cruise ships stop at virtually every island, and several, such as Princess, have their own private islands where passengers spend the day enjoying watersports and a beach barbecue.

Life at sea is so pleasant it can be hard to drag yourself off the ship at the ports of call. Obviously you're not going to soak up much island flavor in five or six hours, but there's still plenty to do and see—besides the requisite shopping—at each island. (See the chapter on "Cruise Ports" for ideas.) And take note that if you sign up for one of the official cruise line excursions, you'll pay much more than if you venture off alone. The disadvantage is that if you don't get back on time, you're in trouble—ships sail exactly when they say they will, and don't take a head count first. Always bring your passport ashore just in case you—literally—miss the boat.

A cruise can be as short as three days and as long as several weeks; seven-day trips are most popular in the Caribbean. What you pay varies widely upon what type of cabin you snag. The most expensive are the suites with balconies—a true treat if you can afford it—while the cheapest fares go to those who have a tiny inside cabin (no window) on a lower deck. Generally, the higher up you are, the higher the price. Watch the newspapers for deals on last-minute cruises—cruise lines will slash fares a few weeks out rather than sail empty.

Once you cruise with a line, it will try hard to get you back. The major lines reward frequent cruisers with deep discounts and two-for-one fares. While it's fun to try out different cruise lines, these promotions go a long way to assure brand loyalty. Also note the loyalty of your travel agent (cruises are virtually always booked through an agent rather than directly through the line). A good travel agent will send flowers and/or a bottle of wine to your cabin. If you've used the same agent a few times and have not received these perks, it's time to try an agency that will let you know your business is appreciated.

For general information on cruising, contact the **Cruise Lines Association** (*500 Fifth Avenue, New York, NY 10110;* ☎ *[212] 921-0066*). Also see *Fielding's Worldwide Cruises* for frank reviews of each ship and line.

By Land

Some islands are so tiny you'll easily get around on foot. Others use the golf cart as the preferred mode of transportation. Several have excellent bus systems and good taxi fleets—it varies widely by island. For details, see the "Getting Around" section in the directory in the back of each island chapter.

The biggest decision will be whether or not to rent a car. Chain and locally owned rental companies are available on virtually every island, and summer rates are often cheaper than during the prime winter season.

If you're staying at an all-inclusive resort and plan to rarely leave the property, there's no need to rent a car. If, however, you plan to explore and try different restaurants each evening, you're often better off renting a car than paying lots of taxi fares. You'll also be more independent.

Road conditions vary from island to island. Some have modern paved roads, but too often, the roadways are narrow, rutted and filled with hairpin turns. Driving is often on the left side of the road, which can be dangerous if you're not used to it. On the plus side, most islands have few major roads, so getting lost is rarely a problem. Consider renting a convertible so you can soak up every possible ray of sunshine, or a four-wheel-drive to easily navigate the often torturous roads on some islands.

A few tips on car rentals: Always reserve as far in advance as possible, as the cars get snatched up during prime tourist seasons. Check to see if they'll deliver the car to your hotel—many do at no extra charge, and it's a nice perk. Before leaving home, check your car insurance policy to see if rental cars are covered. They often are, and this allows you to refuse the rental company's outrageously priced insurance, which saves big bucks. If you're not covered, seriously consider buying the rental insurance, as island drivers can be wackier than even those in Boston, and, as stated, the roads are often awful.

Taxi service also varies. Some islands have metered cabs, but many more use standardized fares. In those cases, always ask what the trip will cost before you get in. If you're hiring a cabbie for a day's sight-seeing, you'll usually be able to negotiate a fare. On some islands, such as St. Martin, fares increase dramatically at night and on Sundays. In others, cabs disappear by midnight. If you're relying on taxis, be sure you'll be able to catch one if you plan to stay out late. Always treat your cabdriver with courtesy and respect. You should anyway, but it can especially pay off when you hit it off and the cabbie—virtually always a native—turns you on to interesting facts and places you'd never otherwise find. If you're a business traveler on expense account, tote along a small notebook for receipts, as most cabbies don't carry them.

A fun way to get around some islands is via a motor scooter or moped. They are pretty easy to learn, even for first-timers, and you often don't even need a driver's license to rent one. It's probably not worth the time to shop around for the best rates, as prices are usually quite competitive. Always wear your helmet, whether or not local law requires it, and be sure to lock up the bike and take your helmet along when not using it.

Lodging

Some of the world's best resorts are found in the Caribbean. So, alas, are some sleazy and roach-ridden dumps. Most fall in between.

Once you decide on an island—no easy choice in itself—your next task is to choose accommodations. The choices are immense—luxury resorts that cater to every whim, all-inclusive properties where everything from soup to nuts is included in the price, glamorous villas with your own butler and pool, budget motels with limited amenities, atmospheric inns with rich history and often colorful owners, cheap guest houses where you'll get little more than a clean (or not so) room, and apartments and condominiums where you can save money by preparing your own meals.

Many hotels offer the same rates for single and double occupancy, with a surcharge for a third or fourth person in the room. Children under 17 or 12 (it varies by property) often stay and even eat for free. Larger resorts offer supervised children's activities during the high season, and it's often complimentary. They can also arrange for a nighttime baby-sitter for a nominal charge.

Always ascertain if you are paying for the Full American Plan (FAP, three meals), Modified American Plan (MAP, two meals), Breakfast Plan (BP, full breakfast), Continental Plan (CP, continental breakfast) or European Plan (EP, no meals). The latter is the most common. Many resorts offer optional meal plans that for, say, $40 to $60 a day, include three meals. Unless you really have no plans to venture off-site, eschew these deals since it can be terribly dull to eat all your meals at the same spot, no matter how good the food. Also, unless you're a very hardy eater, you can probably save money by dining a la carte. As you spend a few days on your vacation, you'll inevitably hear about some great restaurant you must try, so it's better not to be locked in with a meal plan.

Also be sure exactly what is included in the rates. Watersports are sometimes complimentary, but often not—and that snorkel equipment and float can really add up. Other non-motorized watersports are free, but you'll pay to rent a jet ski or take a sunset cruise. Even the coffeemaker in your room can't be taken for granted. It's usually free to make a cup of joe, but sometimes (and ironically, usually at the most expensive resorts) you'll get a charge tacked onto the room. When it comes to the mini-bar, assume that you're paying (dearly) for anything you use. Some hotels and resorts, however, will tuck a bottle of champagne or wine in your refrigerator as a welcome gift. If in doubt, call the front desk. (I once assumed a delicious box of bon-bons was graciously supplied to each guest, until I saw the $20 charge on my final tab when checking out.)

No matter what class of lodging you choose, you can generally assume you'll pay a premium for an oceanfront room. Slightly less are rooms with a view of the sea, through not necessarily on it. Cheapest are the "garden view" rooms—but beware—that "garden" may actually be a parking lot. In cases where rooms are on multiple levels, request a unit on the upper floor(s) for increased privacy and better views.

Never assume a hotel has air conditioning—it's not nearly as common in the Caribbean as throughout the United States. You can usually count on having a ceiling fan—and trade winds often do a good job in keeping things cool—but if you're set on air, be sure to ask. Some places charge a $10 or $20 daily fee for the use of air-conditioners. Also keep in mind that central air is very rare; most hotels use individual units that can be quite noisy, enough to drown out the soothing sounds of the surf. Television and telephones are also not often available—if it's important to you, ask first.

All-Inclusives

One fast-growing Caribbean trend is the all-inclusive property, which means that for one price, you get lodging, all meals, drinks, activities and entertainment. They also frequently include gratuities and surcharges.

All-inclusives such as Sandals and Couples (the latter's logo, oddly enough, is a copulating pair of lions) accept only couples. Honeymooners and lovers staring dreamily into each other's eyes and making out in the pool is the norm. At the other extreme, the properties that cater to singles, such as Jamaica's Hedonism, are tropical meat markets where scoring with the opposite sex is a top priority. Club Med, which started the whole all-inclusive phenomenon nearly 30 years ago, used to be known as the premiere singles spot, but lately is courting families with lots of special activities for kids.

Several all-inclusives are quite luxurious and cater to the well-heeled crowd. Others are relatively tiny and you'll really get a chance to know the staff and your fellow guests. Most fall in between, with a hundred or so rooms, several restaurants and decent nightlife. Nearly all have well-manicured grounds and a wealth of watersports, arts and crafts activities, talent shows, sports competitions and theme nights. Most also offer diving and sight-seeing excursions that cost extra, and a few don't include alcohol in the price. Be sure to ask exactly what you're getting before making your reservations.

They may sound great, but there are definite disadvantages to such a resort. Generally, as with Club Meds, the rooms are quite basic and nothing to get excited about. There are usually just a few restaurants (and sometimes only one), so meals can become routine. Some can overdo the camaraderie angle to the point where you're made to feel almost guilty if you don't join in corny group activities.

The biggest drawback is that when everything is made so easy and accessible, it can be hard to tear yourself off the grounds. This is fine if you're just looking to escape the world for a while, but if you're interested in really getting to know an island and its people, that won't happen at an all-inclusive. Often they have fences and guards to keep the locals out—good for security but hardly conducive to a cultural exchange. Many times all-inclusives are so generic they could be located anywhere—the same feel on Montserrat as in St. Thomas—two very distinct destinations.

The most important thing to keep in mind when deciding on an all-inclusive is, if you're not interested in socializing, don't stay in one! If, on the other hand, you only have a set amount of money to spend and don't want to worry about carrying cash, an all-inclusive can be perfect for a relaxed, hassle-free holiday.

Lots of properties throughout the Caribbean offer all-inclusive packages in addition to European and American plans. In these cases, you're probably better booking your room under the European Plan (no meals), then seeing how you feel once you check the resort out in person. It's the rare hotel that won't let you switch to an all-inclusive plan—what's really hard to find are the ones that will let you get out of it once you make the commitment.

Packing the Suitcase

First and foremost, try to pack lightly enough so you can carry your luggage on the plane, as opposed to checking it in. That way you'll whisk through customs (where applicable) well ahead of your fellow travelers waiting forlornly at the luggage carousel. Everything goes slower in the Caribbean—and luggage retrieval is certainly no exception. Most airlines will only let you carry on two bags (and sometimes one on a very crowded flight) that measures no more than 62 inches (width plus length plus height). In all cases, carry-ons must fit under your seat or in the overhead compartment. This is impossible on the tiny planes that hop from island to island, but if you hand your bag to them on the runway, rather than check it, you'll still get it back more quickly.

As humidity is quite high throughout the Caribbean, bring natural fabrics; lightweight cotton is the best. Casual clothes are fine just about anywhere both day and night (when it's not, it's noted in the hotel or restaurant description) An exception are historic churches, which generally have a no-shorts rule. Respect this custom; it's especially easy for women, who can wear a light sundress.

The nights are generally warm and sultry, but some clubs and restaurants will invariably overdo the air conditioning, so tuck in a jacket or sweater. If you're going to be trekking through the jungle or rainforest, obviously you want sturdy shoes and raingear. The nicer hotels equip their rooms with umbrellas; you may want to tuck in a small portable one just in case. Don't forget to bring a beach bag to hold your suntan lotion, hat or visor and a few dollars for lunch (your carry-on bag can serve this purpose).

Bring sandals or flip-flops for the beach (the sand gets hot!) and good sneakers or walking shoes for touring around. Lots of villages have cobblestone streets, and the old forts usually have dubious pathways, so you'll appreciate sturdy shoes. Unless you're into tottering around on high heels, you can leave them at home; flat dressy sandals will do even at the finer resorts.

Consider buying a sarong once you arrive. These large, colorful pieces of rectangular cloth can be tied in a variety of ways, from halter dress to shirt, fold up into practically nothing, are easy to handwash and make great souvenirs to boot. You'll find them in all the shops and marketplaces.

You'll also find lots of hats—mainly straw—and it's a good idea to pick one up. The sun is very strong throughout the region, and just because you are dutifully sight-seeing rather than lazing on the beach doesn't mean you won't get burned.

The sunbathers on many islands go topless; whether or not you do too is a personal choice. However, it's considered rude to go to a nude beach and keep your clothes on. In any event, wearing swimsuits anywhere but the pool or beach is generally a no-no, and men, please spare us the sight of your hairy (or otherwise) chest in public places.

Other essentials include mosquito repellant, a portable water bottle, strong sunscreen and film. You'll generally save a lot of money by buying these items stateside rather than on the island. Smokers, on the other hand, can usually score cigarettes much cheaper on the islands, often even compared with the duty-free shops. (Remember you can legally bring only one carton back into the U.S.)

Finer hotels outfit their bathrooms with hair dryers, shampoo, conditioner and body lotion, but these products are usually of a cheap quality, so if you're particular, bring your own. It's well worth checking out the "introductory" or travel sizes of personal care items at the drug store or supermarket, or buying small plastic containers to fill. There's no need to lug your whole bottle of shampoo—just bring what you'll need for your length of stay.

Women should pack a few tampons or sanitary pads. . . just in case. Also bring a small sewing kit, extra eyeglasses, condoms if you're planning to get extra friendly with new acquaintances and motion-travel wristbands or medication if you're prone to seasickness and will be boating. There's nothing like the fit of your own snorkel mask, so bring that along, too. Men who use electric shavers may need an electric converter—see the "directory" at the end of each island chapter for electrical currents. Prescription medications and eyeglasses should always be carried on your person when traveling, not checked with your luggage.

What not to bring: a travel iron (virtually all hotels supply one on request—and besides, this is the Caribbean and wrinkles are acceptable), expensive jewelry (why add to the myth that Americans are all rich, and the possibility of getting ripped off?), cowboy boots (too hot) and beach towels (unless you're staying in the cheapest of guest houses, they are supplied). Rather than dragging your whole address book along—which you'd hate to lose anyway, copy the addresses of friends to whom you plan to send postcards and tuck it into your wallet.

Fanny packs are excellent for carrying your money and camera, and a lot cooler than backpacks. Always lock your passport, extra money, plane ticket and other valuables in the in-room safe or check them at the front desk.

Remember, unless you're extremely fashion conscious, it's inevitable you'll wear the same comfortable clothes again and again, so pack lightly. And be sure to leave room in your suitcase for souvenirs!

Money Managing

Unless you plan to bring huge sums of money with you or are staying a very long time, it's much more convenient to not bring traveler's checks to the Caribbean. There are two reasons for this advice: many establishments tack on at least a 5 percent surcharge when cashing them; and worse, many places don't take at all. On the other hand, you always run a risk when carrying cash, so it basically comes down to a personal decision. If you do opt for traveler's checks, be sure to carry the numbered receipts separately from your money—you'll need them for a refund in the event of loss or theft. Members of the Automobile Club of America (AAA) can get free traveler's checks, as can American Express cardholders.

A credit card is essential, even if you don't plan to use it. Most hotels won't give you a room without a credit card imprint, even if you're paying in cash. The same is true for car rental companies. This may be annoying, but perfectly understandable as hotels get ripped off constantly and with a credit card, at least have a chance of recouping their losses. Also, you never know what emergencies may arise, so always carry a credit card. Visa and Mastercard are the most widely accepted and American Express is often honored, but the still relatively new Discover card has yet to make any inroads in the Caribbean.

Except for Puerto Rico and the U.S. Virgins, each island has its own currency—but U.S. dollars are accepted virtually everywhere. In most cases, you won't even need to change money. If you do want to convert to local dollars, you're best off doing so at a bank, where the rate of exchange is invariably better than at hotels. In all instances, avoid the black market. In poorer nations such as the Dominican Republic, you're setting yourself up for scams or outright robbery.

Unless you're a whiz at division and multiplication, it's a good idea to carry a small calculator when shopping to figure out how prices translate into U.S. dollars. The calculator can also be used to communicate and negotiate when you're dealing with someone who doesn't speak English.

Automatic teller machines (ATMs) are becoming more common throughout most islands, but not so that you can really rely on them—except on San Juan and the U.S. Virgins. If you're island hopping and need cash, seek out the ATM at the San Juan airport. It's also a good idea to tuck a few blank checks into your wallet—if you really get into trouble cash-wise, some major hotels will cash one for you (after a lot of begging). If you're really stuck, you can always get a cash advance on your credit card at a casino—but be warned that the service charges are exorbitant (about $17 for each $100).

When traveling about the island, always carry small bills. They are much more convenient for paying taxi and restaurant fares. Plus, it's rude to dicker over a price at the marketplace, get the seller down from $18 to $9, then present a $20 bill. Keep a supply of singles for tipping doormen and other personnel at your hotel, as necessary.

Above all, use your in-room safe (they are becoming increasingly standard) or check your valuables with the front desk. Nothing will ruin a vacation faster than getting ripped off—it's worth the few minutes of hassle to play it safe.

Documents

Each island requires some sort of identification to enter; details are given in the directory at the back of each chapter. Generally, you're best off with a passport, though some nations accept a photo I.D. such as a driver's license. (Often, expired passports are also acceptable.) Visas are generally not required for citizens of the United States, Canada and the European Economic Community, but again, rules vary by island.

You'll need to show proof that you're just a visitor and are not planning to make the island your new home (a return plane ticket). Sometimes you're even required to prove you have enough funds for the length of your stay.

When you purchase your plane ticket, the agent will inform you of any special documents needed. If he or she fails to volunteer this information, ask. Cruise ship passengers need to bring a passport along, but usually don't need to show it at ports of call. Still, it's a good idea to take it along with you when debarking the ship, just in case.

Customs and Duties

As if coming home from a glorious Caribbean holiday isn't depressing enough, you have to go through customs, unless Puerto Rico is your vacation spot. (In that case, you don't pass through customs and can bring back as much stuff as you want.) You'll fill out a simple form stating how much you spent on goods you're bringing back—if it's more than $400, you'll have to list each item. When shopping in duty-free stores, be sure to save the receipts to show proof of purchase.

Rules vary by region, but here's the general scoop on duty-free shopping:

You can bring $1200 worth of stuff back from the Virgin Islands.

Six hundred dollars for Antigua, Barbuda, Barbados, British Virgin Islands, Dominica, Grenada, Montserrat, Saba, St. Eustatius, St. Kitts, Nevis, St. Lucia, Sint Maarten (the Dutch side), St. Vincent, the Grenadines, Trinidad and Tobago.

Four hundred dollars for Anguilla, Guadeloupe, Martinique, St. Martin (the French side) and St. Barthelemy.

If you stay on an island less than 48 hours or have been outside the United States within 30 days of your current trip, you can only bring back $25 worth of duty-free goods, except, again, for Puerto Rico.

If you've gone over the limit, you'll be taxed at a flat rate of 10 percent (5 percent for the U.S. Virgins) on the first $1000 of merchandise. Except for gifts under $50 sent directly to the recipient, all items shipped home are considered dutiable.

Some people try to beat customs by wearing their new Rolex or emerald earrings and acting as if they've always owned them. This is not especially recommended—you may need to show proof you did indeed leave the U.S. with these expensive items. Conversely, if you're traveling with a Rolex or huge rock on your finger, it's a good idea to bring the receipt along to prove you already owned it.

A NOTE ON DRUGS:

Don't even think of trying to get illegal drugs into an island or back to the United States. It's just not worth the risk, and while few people busted in the Caribbean have Midnight Express-style horror stories to tell, remember you are in a foreign country and you're under its rules. Carry prescription drugs in their original containers to avoid hassles.

For more information on duty-free allowances, contact the U.S. Customs Service *(P.O. Box 7404, Washington, DC 20044; for taped information, call* ☎ *[202] 927-2095).*

Insurance and Refunds

You can insure against everything from your valuables being stolen to your rental car crashing to bad weather ruining your trip—it's up to you and how much of a gambler you are. A must: car rental collision insurance, unless your car owner's policy covers rental cars (many do, and it's well worth checking before you leave home, as this is a big savings).

Always check the small print when booking a hotel and airline ticket. These days most airlines charge anywhere from $30 to $50 (and more) if you change your flight times; if you decide to scrap the whole trip, airline tickets are often nonrefundable. Most hotels require at least 48 hours' notice (and as much as two full weeks in the high season) to refund your deposit. When cruising, consider the optional insurance policy that lets you cancel at the last minute, for any reason, and still get a refund.

When to Go

Islanders know how to throw a party, and festivals full of song and dance occur year-round in the Caribbean. On some islands, there are even more festivals during the off-season, which serves to attract visitors who are keen for off-season bargains. Although Carnival is generally celebrated as the advent of Lent, it can happen anytime in the Caribbean, even during the summer. Throughout the year individual islands celebrate their own arts and crafts traditions, as well as various other religious and folklore celebrations. Sports competitions happen according to the high season for that sport, attracting athletes and fishermen from all over the world. (Singles should note these events as prime times to visit and the chance for meeting someone "tall and tan and young and handsome" soars sky-high.) For more information, check under "When to Go" in the directory of each individual island.

Carnival

Guadeloupe (January-Lent)

Bonaire (February)

Puerto Rico (February)

St. Lucia (February)

St. Maarten (February)

Aruba (mid-late February)

Martinique (for six weeks starting after New Year's)

Trinidad (Monday and Tuesday preceding Ash Wednesday)

St. Thomas (after Easter, sometime in April).

Curaçao (late January-early February)

Cayman Islands (May)

St. John (July)

Antigua (July)

Anguilla (early August)

Turks & Caicos (late August)

Cultural Festivals

Barbados' Hole Town Festival (Feb. 17)

St. Martin Food Festival (May)

Tobago Heritage Festival (July)

Barbados' Crop-Over Festival (August)

St. Bart's Cayman Islands Pirate Week (late October)

Music

Barbados' Caribbean Jazz Festival (May)

Aruba's Jazz and Latin Music Festival (June)

Puerto Rico's Festival Pablo Casals (June)

Dominican Republic's Merengue Festival (10 days in July)

Jamaica's Reggae Sunsplash Music Festival (August)

Statia/America Day (St. Eustatius) Puerto Rico's Hatillo Festival of the Masks (December)

Sports

Grenada's New Year's Fiesta Yacht Race

Antigua's Tennis Week (January)

Jamaica's Classic Golf Tournament (January)

Curaçao Regatta (March)

Antigua's Windsurfing Week (April)

British Virgin Islands Spring Regatta (April)

U.S. Virgin Islands International Rolex Spring Regatta (April)

Anguilla's Boat Racing Day (May 30)

Aruba's High-Winds Pro-Am Windsurfing Tournament (June)

U.S. and British Virgin Islands' Hook In and Hold On Boardsailing Regatta (June and July)

Grenada's Carriacou Regatta (end of July)

Martinique's Tour des Yoles Rondes (yawl race) (early August)

Virgin Islands Open Atlantic Blue Marlin Tournament (August)

Bonaire's Sailing Regatta (October)

Barbados' International Road Race Series (December)

Secret Tips for Caribbean Survival

Duty Free Does Not Necessarily Mean Cheaper

The term "duty free" (a shopper's best friend) means that retailers are not required to pay import taxes on certain items, so can pass these savings directly along to the consumer. Often that translates to prices 30 to 40 percent cheaper than in the United States. Even islands not officially duty free still often have duty-free shops at the airport or around the island, such as St. Lucia's Pointe Seraphine. Furthermore, on your way to an island, you can shop duty free in major U.S. airports by showing your boarding pass.

While most duty-free items are truly a bargain, it ain't always necessarily so. Cigarettes, for example, often cost close to $17 per carton at airport-duty free shops, and you can often do better on the island itself (and even in some

U.S. supermarkets). If you're planning to buy expensive French perfume or a good piece of jewelry, do some comparison shopping before leaving the United States to see how prices stack up. And remember, if the product is defective, you'll have a much easier time getting satisfaction from your local store than a little shop in the Caribbean.

Good duty-free bargains can generally be found on French perfumes, Dutch porcelain, Swiss crystal, fine bone china and woolens from England, linens and gemstones, especially emeralds. Prices are especially good on European-owned territories such as St. Martin. St. Barts, Martinique and Guadeloupe for French items and Anguilla, Antigua, Montserrat, Nevis, St. Kitts, Grenada, St. Lucia, St. Vincent and the British Virgins for goods from England.

Those Damn Surcharges

Most folks are genuinely amazed when checking out of a hotel and seeing their final hotel tab. Where did all these charges come from? What's this government tax? What on earth is a "service charge?"

While it's always a good idea to go over your bill with a fine-tooth comb, most of these charges, alas, are legitimate.

All hotels (even all-inclusives) charge a government tax of anywhere from 5-10 percent of your nightly room rate. The service charge, which averages 10-15 percent, is supposedly for maids and other staff—whether they actually ever see it or not is another matter. Still, don't feel obligated to tip extra if the service charge is included. Many hotels automatically tack on a service charge whenever you charge a meal or drink to your room; and room service checks virtually always include a service charge. In these cases, it's not necessary to tip the bartender or waiter. If you're not sure, ask. Energy surcharges are sometimes added to the bill to help defray the costs of electricity when local prices are quite high. Note that all these charges are rarely, if ever, mentioned in the brochure or when you inquire about rates.

The biggest killers are the telephone surcharges. Ironically, it seems the more expensive the hotel, the higher the telephone rates. Many charge around $1 per local phone call—even if you're calling an 800 number to use your credit card. If you dial direct to the United States, be prepared for exorbitant fees—double or triple the amount of your call. If you must call the States direct, have your party immediately call you back—you'll save a lot of money that way. Also consider buying a phone card, which are springing up all over the United States and on the islands, wherein you pay a flat fee (say, $20) for a prescribed amount of time. These cards, which do not require a credit card to obtain, are often much cheaper per minute than dialing direct from your hotel or a payphone. When you can use your stateside carrier's credit card (such as ATT, Sprint and MCI) you'll invariably save, but note that their 800 access numbers are often not reachable from the Caribbean, even with operator assistance.

Beware of the mini-bar—that tempting bottle of Red Stripe probably costs double or triple the usual price. If you don't trust your will power regarding raiding the fridge and gobbling down all those $5 candy bars (which cost 50 cents in the store) leave the mini-bar key at the front desk.

Cruise Ship Passengers

If you're a drinker, you'll really drop dead when you get your cruise ship bill. (Most lines give you a preliminary statement a few days before the end of the trip to help ease the final shock.) The cruise fare usually doesn't include drinks—alcohol and otherwise—and while the prices are reasonable, they really add up. You'll also pay for port taxes (about $75 per person), any shopping you did aboard, those tempting pictures snapped by the ship's photographers, casino chips charged to your cabin (an especially dangerous habit to fall into) and any ship-run shore excursions.

The biggest expense, and one you must plan for, are the tips given out at the end of the cruise. Most cruise lines hand out printed guidelines and even give formal talks on the art of tipping, but the general rule of thumb is that waiters and cabin stewards get $3 per day per person and busboys (they're rarely female) and wine stewards get $1.50 per day per person. You may be tempted to skip the tips—after all, you're leaving and will never see these people again—but keep in mind that the service staff's salary is virtually nil with tips making up the vast majority of their income. So bring aboard enough cash for tips, then forget about it until the last night, when tips are usually distributed in envelopes provided by the cruise line. You may also want to tip the bartender and mâitre d' if he took special care of you, but that's completely optional. It's never necessary to tip those higher up the chain such as the cruise director and shore excursions manager.

Health Precautions

There are very few health risks throughout the Caribbean. In most cases, the water is safe to drink (even if it doesn't taste so great); always inquire at your hotel if you're not sure. They'll give you an honest answer—the last thing these people want is a bunch of sick guests on their hands.

The biggest health threat in the Caribbean—as, alas, the world over these days—is from AIDS and other sexually transmitted diseases. Use condoms! It's best to bring them from home because they are not always as readily available on smaller islands. Latex condoms offer much more protection than those made of lambskin.

It's always a good idea to carry along a small bottle of stomach medicine such as Mylanta, diarrhea aides such as Pepto Bismol and pain relievers like aspirin or Tylenol. Don't assume you'll be able to find such items on the island. (No problem in Jamaica, but lots of luck on Saba or Cuba.) If you require injections, bring your own sterile syringes and consider buying disposable ones from a U.S. pharmacy before you leave.

Malaria is generally no longer a threat (except possibly in the Dominican Republic and Haiti), which is good news, since you can count on providing lots of free meals for mosquitoes and no-see-ums. For the latest news on Caribbean health conditions, call the Centers for Disease Control's International Travelers' Hotline at ☎ *(404) 332-4559.*

Watch out for the sun—it's going to be a lot stronger than you think, especially on overcast days when you may forget to apply sunscreen. Though getting a killer tan is high on many tourists' list of things to do, start slowly with a strong sunscreen, then once you work up a good base tan, gradually switch to a lower number. (Of course dermatologists recommend no tan at all, but try convincing vacationers of that.)

The high humidity will probably make you perspire more than usual. Drink lots of fluids to avoid dehydration (water is best) to replace the ones you're oozing through your pores.

Guests at all-inclusive properties invariably go wild the first night with all those free drinks—then pay dearly for it the next day. Keep that in mind as you order your fourth pina colada.

Buying prepared food from street vendors is generally safe, but do check out the operation. Is the meat kept refrigerated? Are the utensils clean? When buying bottled water, especially on the street, check that the tamper-proof band is intact. Some unscrupulous vendors will refill bottles with tap water.

Illegal Drugs

If you're a recreational drug user, you'll generally have no problem scoring high-quality marijuana (called ganga on many islands) at prices much cheaper than in the United States. You'll be especially deluged by dealers in Jamaica. We're not endorsing this, but if you are intent on buying drugs, use common sense and stay away from dim alleyways, deserted parking lots and the like. You can often ask your trusty bellboy or bartender where it's okay to score. Bring your own pipe or rolling papers, because they can be hard to find on some islands. It's incredibly stupid to buy anything stronger than pot because heaven only knows what they are lacing cocaine, crystal meth and other potent drugs with. As stated earlier, don't even think of trying to bring drugs into another country or back into the United States—it's just not worth the risk.

Weather—or Not

Californians cope with earthquakes and mudslides, East Coasters deal with blizzards and ice storms and Midwesterners have bitter cold and flash floods. In the Caribbean the enemy is the hurricane.

Hurricane season is an annual event that generally runs from June to September. Most turn out to be little more than pesky rainstorms or dramatic electrical displays, but some are deadly—and should be taken deadly seriously. Heed the warnings of locals, who know of what they speak when it comes to threatening weather. (One French tourist was swept out to sea while photographing the dramatic surf on Guadeloupe during a 1995 hurricane.)

Nineteen ninety-five was a terrible year for hurricanes, especially the month of September, when first Luis and then Marilyn roared through and caused major damage on many Eastern Caribbean islands, including St. Thomas, St. John, both the French and Dutch sides of St. Martin, Antigua and St. Barthelemy. As tourism is the lifeblood of these islands' economies, nearly everything has been rebuilt or put back into place, and even St. Thomas, which was particularly devastated, is just about back to normal.

Mother Nature's other biggest drawback is the high humidity that lingers on the islands all year long and is especially uncomfortable in the summer. It won't kill you (though it sometimes feels like it will) but take care to avoid overexertion and drink lots of water to keep hydrated.

For the latest on worldwide weather conditions, call the Weather Channel Connection (☎ *900-WEATHER*), which costs 95 cents per minute.

Travel for Seniors

Senior citizens are often entitled to great discounts, and should always look into such deals before traveling. The **National Council of Senior Citizens** *(1331 F Street, NW, Washington, D.C. 20004;* ☎ *[202] 347-8800)* is a nonprofit organization that publishes a monthly newsletter that includes travel tips and bargains; it's well worth the $12 per year membership/subscription. Also contact **Grand Circle Travel** *(347 Congress Street, Boston, MA 02210;* ☎ *[617] 350-7500 or [800] 248-3737)* for a free copy of "101 Tips for the Mature Traveler." The agency also offers escorted tours and cruises for older folks. Also catering to people over 50 is **SAGA International Holidays** *(222 Berkeley Street, Boston, MA 02116;* ☎ *[800] 343-0273).*

Island Etiquette

Little girl in Barbados

While some of your best vacation photos will be candid shots of locals, keep in mind that many folks—older ones especially—often don't appreciate being part of your tourist experience. Always ask before snapping someone's photo and take a refusal with grace. (Although it is annoying that the old woman who makes johnnycakes at St. Croix's Whim Plantation refuses photos—rudely at that—since she is part of the attraction and you pay a hefty admission price to get in.) Kids, on the other hand, usually love to get the attention and will often ask you to take their picture. Indulge them, even if you're down to your last shot (better to fake taking the picture than hurt their feelings), and besides, you'll probably get some really cute shots.

Carry small bills when dealing with street vendors and in marketplaces where you'll be negotiating prices.

In museums and restaurants, keep your negative feelings to yourself (or at least whisper them to your companion) about the lousy artwork or greasy food. You may find you just hate conch, but remember that it's a staple in many island diets, so try not to be judgmental. On the other hand, if the food is truly inedible, you have every right to send it back.

No one should have to endure lousy service, but extra patience will be required in the Caribbean. Everything is on a slower pace, and that certainly includes the cooks and waitstaff.

Respect local rules and customs regarding the formality of dress. In most cases shorts and T-shirts are just fine, but most churches ban them, even if you're just ducking in for a quick peek. Bathing suits are nearly always improper anywhere but on the beach or at the pool. If you want to go topless, make sure it's considered acceptable on the island.

Make a genuine effort to speak the language on islands such as Guadeloupe and the Dominican Republic, where English speakers are rare. No matter how terrible your syntax or pronunciation, such efforts are greatly appreciated, and people will be much more apt to help you out than if you just walk up expecting them to speak your language.

Above all, do your fellow countrymen a big favor, and don't act like the Ugly American. It's no wonder everyone thinks we're all rich the way some U.S. travelers flash around large bills and expensive jewelry. (And actually, if we can afford a Caribbean vacation—even on the cheap—we are pretty rich compared with most locals.) Be sensitive to the fact that on most of these islands, life is much simpler and less materialistic. Remember, too, that you are a guest in this foreign land. Sure, you're paying for it, but that doesn't mean you've bought the right to impose your values on people of different cultures. However, it's amazing how far a smile will go.

CARIBBEAN ADVENTURE

Hiking in Little Cayman

On Foot

It surprises many to hear that it actually snows in the Caribbean. Not in quantities that are enough to ski, and certainly not with any regularity, but the lofty, 10,370-foot summit of Pico Duarte in the Dominican Republic usually receives one or two dustings of snow each winter to the delight of islanders. We point this out by way of establishing that hiking in the Caribbean can yield the truly unexpected. The flip side of the multi-day ascent of Pico Duarte might be a visit to flat Barbuda, where mile after mile of rolling, scrub-covered dunes and velvety beaches unfold as far as the eye can see, while several caves beckon the adventurous. Unique Barbudan wildlife includes the magnificent frigate bird, a curious avian with an immense wingspan and a startling mating habit.

The sharp cry of the eco-tourism monster is ringing through the region and, for reasons right and wrong, government tourism offices are groping about blindly to try and cash in on the latest rubbernecking craze. Needless to say, the results are usually positive, and sometimes they are spectacularly successful on a number of levels. But so often it seems that the end result—a better educated visitor and/or direct financial support of local environmental causes—is a mere afterthought in the process. Nonetheless, eco-tourism is a concept whose time has come, even if the path is a little murky in the hands of a few opportunistic governments.

This isn't always the case in the Caribbean: Guadeloupe, Martinique and St. John each furnish literally dozens of trail options; most of these hikes are regularly maintained, with trailhead signs providing distances and directions. At the other extreme is St. Kitts, which has a verdant rainforest and a splendid volcanic summit, but essentially no maintained or marked trails, leaving visitors largely at the beck and call of the very good, but not inexpensive local guide service. The norm is somewhere in between, with island governments slowly integrating nature's bounty into their infrastructure, largely because of the financial dividend eco-tourism offers.

The geographical appearance of islands in the Caribbean falls into two general categories: those which were formed by continuing volcanic evolution, producing steep flanks which climb to the summit of both dormant and active volcanoes, and those which were created by an uplift of coral limestone, creating a gentler, usually drier, landscape of rolling hills, scalloped by coves of white sand. The twin-island nation of Trinidad and Tobago is the exception; they were once linked to South America (Trinidad's mountains are actually an extension of the Andes). As a rule, the volcanic islands have the greatest quantity and diversity of hiking options with ambitious treks through rainforests and over mountains, while the limestone islands offer quieter walks visiting beaches, forts and bird sanctuaries.

A number of the Eastern Caribbean's volcanoes are still very much alive. The most famous eruption during modern times was that of Martinique's Mt. Pelee in 1902, which exploded in a torrent of hot ash and gas, and suffocated the thriving city of Saint-Pierre and its entire population of 30,000.

La Soufriere on St. Vincent erupted in 1979 sending clouds of ash and steam 10 miles into the air, while the like-named Soufriere on Guadeloupe sputtered to life in 1976 and encouraged the evacuation of the island's capital, Basse-Terre. Most recently, English Crater on tiny Montserrat sputtered to life in July 1995 and has subsequently caused multiple evacuations of the island's charming capital—new acreage is being added to the island as we go to press. Otherwise, the region's volcanic summits are generally sleeping peacefully and invite exploration on foot. Details of these hikes, sometimes among the most challenging in the Caribbean, are given in each chapter. (You'll see the term *soufriere* a lot throughout the region; it's a French word for volcanic crater that has found its way into common usage within the Eastern Caribbean).

Most of the hikes we've listed can be made on your own. On occasion, however, there will be recommendations regarding the use of local guides, obtained either through a guide service or, sometimes, by inquiring in the vicinity of the trailhead. The availability of independent guides in the Caribbean is more a by-product of eco-tourism in the region, rather than locals looking for free handouts. On the more impoverished islands, there is less government money to spend on trail upkeep and markers, making guides a prerequisite for first-time visitors. In some areas, however, island tourism offices will strongly encourage using a guide for trails of only moderate difficulty; the hidden agenda, obviously, is indirect support of the local economy. There are at least three main reasons for using a guide:

1. The guide will help lead you through genuinely difficult or dangerously exposed areas.

2. A good guide will add to your trek by explaining the natural environment you are exploring and the historical significance of ruins you may encounter, as well as providing an inside glimpse into the local character of the island.

3. Hiring a guide contributes to the local economy by directly supporting an individual, some of whom spend a good deal of their "spare" time maintaining trails.

Not coincidentally, there are at least three reasons against hiring guides:

1. Many of the trails where guides are recommended by tourist offices are not that difficult for hikers of basic ability.

2. If you're looking for escape and solitude, the well-meaning conversation a guide might engage in may detract from your desired interaction with the natural environment.

3. For those of us visiting the Caribbean on a budget, guides can be expensive; it's not uncommon to spend more than a hundred dollars for a guide on a major trail, which can add up after a few hikes.

CARIBBEAN ADVENTURE

Nonetheless, the unique and varied environments of the Caribbean should not be underestimated. In March 1995, a trio of British travelers to St. Vincent were visiting Trinity Falls when a tragedy occurred during a stream-side stop for a photograph. A sudden downpour in the mountains above lead to an unanticipated flash flood. One minute, the two women were posing for a picture on a rock below the falls, a few minutes later, the water had risen so quickly they were washed downstream to their deaths.

While the quality of guides available on various islands differs greatly, and trail conditions are constantly evolving, we urge you to use your own judgment, keeping in mind that a good guide will do much more than point you to your destination, and can greatly add to the experience of the hike. If you plan to hike several major trails on an island, hire a guide for at least the first day so that you gain a sense of the difficulties you will be encountering, as well as an appreciation for the plant life and history of the area. You may decide that you'll want to use that guide's services for the remainder of your visit.

There are a few precautions hikers should take into account before embarking on any trail. First, carry plenty of fresh water. Rivers, as clean and refreshing as they may appear, are generally not safe to drink from. The parasite bilharziasis is frequently found in slow-moving streams and lakes, and the illness it causes can even result in death (islands to be particularly wary of the parasite are Guadeloupe, Martinique and St. Lucia). Let the heat and humidity of the tropics be a constant reminder to drink bottled water regularly while exercising. If you feel dehydrated at the end of a day, slightly increase the salt in your diet, which will help you retain fluids when exercising.

If you're walking through areas where shade is minimal (the coralline islands in particular), the sun will be intense. Even in moderate doses of an hour or two, it can cause severe sunburns that will crimp your style for an entire vacation and, in extreme cases, can cause sunstroke (and we won't even start on the skin cancer topic). For the former, use sunblock at all times, taking into account that much of the lotion will drip off during sweat-inducing activities. For the latter, minimize your time in the sun, particularly at the start of a trip, wear sunglasses and a wide-brimmed hat and, again, always drink plenty of fluids. If you plan to do more than a day or two of hiking, consider bringing along a Gatorade-style drink (available in powdered form) which will help replace lost electrolytes. For severe cases of dehydration, consult a doctor.

Watch out for the ghastly manchineel tree, amply offered throughout the Caribbean. Its fruit, which looks something like a green crab apple, is very poisonous. But problems with the tree don't end there: if you stand under a manchineel during rainfall, the runoff from the leaves can cause blisters. Like the fruit, the tree's sap is also quite potent and was once used by Carib Indians to dip their arrowheads in before heading out for a missionary slaughter. In more heavily traveled areas, particularly around beaches, locals will frequently post warning signs on the trees (some manchineels are marked with red paint). However, in more remote areas, you're on your own. Have an islander point out the tree shortly after arrival so you can avoid it on your explorations. Also note that the sap from the oleander is also poisonous.

Snakes are not generally a problem in the Caribbean, but one variety, the fer-de-lance, deserves attention; its powerful bite can be deadly or, at least, extremely painful. Fortunately, the snake is found only on Martinique, St. Lucia and Trinidad. The fer-de-lance really doesn't want to have anything to do with us and bites are infrequent, but it's prudent to be aware of its presence. They are most likely to attack when cornered or surprised, so the best way to keep the fer-de-lance away is to tap a stick in front of your feet as you hike. Heavy shoes and long pants are a good idea if you plan to be exploring the bush. Another problematic encounter is that with a scorpion, recognized by the stinger arching over its back. Although generally not fatal, scorpions boast a painful defense strategy and are best avoided. Like the fer-de-lance, they are usually found in hot, dry areas. Finally, two mere nuisances are mosquitoes and sand flies, found principally in areas of stagnant water and on beaches, respectively. They are best combated with insect repellent, although moving out of the afflicted area usually does the trick.

Wear appropriate clothing for your treks. It may be difficult to conceive of in the balmy Caribbean, but temperatures drop dramatically as one climbs into cloud-wrapped mountains. Yes, it actually snows in the region atop Pico Duarte in the Dominican Republic, but the hike to the top of Jamaica's 7402-foot Blue Mountain Peak can also be challenging. While most of the region doesn't experience temperatures to that extreme, mountain conditions can be ideal for hypothermia. For any hike ascending elevations above 3000 feet, we recommend packing a pair of long pants and a light windbreaker jacket. Although heavy hiking boots aren't really necessary in the Caribbean, a sturdy pair of walking shoes, broken in before your trip (to avoid blisters), is generally sufficient. Before you invest a chunk of change on a tasteful pair of new shoes, remember that you may be hiking on muddy paths or through streams that are sure to alter the appearance of the most colorful designs! As appealing as it might be at some points, walking barefoot is not a good idea; hookworms can penetrate skin.

By Pedal

It makes sense that, following the explosion of mountain biking in the United States, it would catch on sooner or later in the Caribbean. And why not? What could be more inviting than riding through charming island villages, past rolling fields of sugarcane and down to silky white beaches? Those interested in more demanding explorations will find an ample quantity of steep hills and challenging forest trails on most islands. Though the sport is still in its nascent stages, there are biking organizations on most of the larger islands, as well as an increasing quantity of rental shops carrying a variety of the better brands known at home.

With more than 1200 paved miles to ride, Guadeloupe is the regional capital of road riding and features the Tour de la Guadeloupe every August, a sort of miniature Tour de France-gone-tropical. Although cars race by on the main roads at breakneck speeds, islanders embrace cyclists enthusiastically. Other islands that encourage road biking include Martinique, Trinidad and Barbados although, again, each of these islands feature their share of heavy vehicular traffic. It's worth noting that the quality of paved roads varies greatly within the region and it's best to check with a local rider or biking outfit before importing a road bike for touring an island.

Mountain biking is spreading throughout the region, from St. Vincent and tiny Montserrat, where old goat paths and plantation trails lace the hillsides, to the British Virgin Islands, where every direction appears to be up or down, except for the ferry which leads to another island and more trails. When off-roading through drier sections—and this includes the lower elevations of virtually all the islands—you'll want to have a patch-kit handy for the ever-present stickers and thorns; they can be a menace.

It is possible to ship your bike into the Caribbean on the same plane you are arriving on, although the disadvantages may far outweigh the relative ease of renting from a local shop. If your bike uses exotic parts, you may want to bring the unique items and a tool kit with you. Don't ship anything fragile (like a top-of-the-line road bike) that you wouldn't want banged around. I watched as one island baggage handler tossed a boxed bicycle onto the airport's baggage conveyer-belt hard enough to have the handlebars puncture the cardboard. Moments later, as the bike turned a corner, it flopped sadly off the belt and onto the floor where it sat unattended while its owner stood trapped in a long customs line.

When renting a bike, check to make sure the seat and handlebars are adjusted for your height. Discovering that your bike doesn't "fit" a few miles from the shop is annoying. Verify that tires are adequately filled and learn how to use the air pump for the bike you are renting (it may be foreign to what you are used to at home). If you don't know how to patch a tire, have someone in the shop spend a few minutes showing you how; if you're planning a long ride, carry a spare tube, if possible.

As with hiking, bicycling comes with some precautions. In addition to carrying plenty of bottled water, hydrate your body by guzzling a quart or two of water before you hit the road. You may find it helpful to bring along energy bars or powdered drinks which help maintain your stamina and replace electrolytes. Heed prior warnings concerning the sun, which can be relentless on some treeless roads (see "On Foot"). Helmets are an essential component of safe riding; although most or all of the shops provide them, bring one from home if you can.

Bike and Cruise Tours

☎ *(503) 667-4053.*

If you are willing to dedicate your entire Caribbean vacation to cycling, Oregon-based Linda Thompson offers biking tours in conjunction with Norwegian Cruise Line sailings out of Puerto Rico. Bikes are provided in Puerto Rico, loaded onto the ship, and a leader and pre-set riding itinerary—averaging 20-25 miles each day—greets cyclists on each island. Group size varies but usually averages a couple dozen riders and prices start at about $1850 (from the East Coast) including airfare, seven-day cruise, bike rental and port taxes.

Underwater

When divers dream, they're probably fantasizing about Bonaire, the Caymans, the Turks and Caicos. Each area has its specialties. Grand Cayman has perfected the dive vacation and offers a well-organized diving infrastructure that appeals to those who are new to the sport; it doesn't hurt that the Caymans have a series of magnificent walls and dozens of sites to tour (and don't forget the region's best animal dive, Sting Ray City). Bonaire is the environmental choice, matching its spectacular reefs with a strictly enforced underwater protection plan. This same island offers one of the world's best collection of shore dives, allowing you to visit Bonaire for a couple weeks, and dive two or three times daily without ever getting into a boat or repeating a site; just park and dive. The Turks and Caicos offer several breathtaking walls, and have the added bonus of being a front-row seat for the annual winter migration of 3000 humpback whales.

CARIBBEAN
ADVENTURE

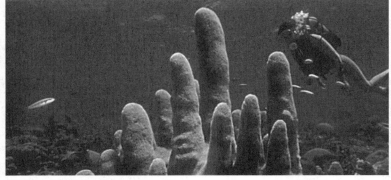

The Caribbean is a diver's paradise.

These are the region's highlights, all located in the Western Caribbean and providing some of the best and most varied diving in the world, but there's plenty to keep divers happily occupied on other islands, too. Wall dives and pinnacles, wrecks and reefs are found throughout the Caribbean and, though the diving can be dramatic and dynamic, the experience tends to be more relaxed, less-crowded on some of the less well-known islands. If the Eastern Caribbean lacks the exciting 6000-foot walls of the Caymans, or the breathtaking walls of the Turks, there's definitely a spirit of adventure to be tapped on many of the islands.

With so many less-heralded destinations to choose from where does one go in the Eastern Caribbean? Wall enthusiasts should head for St. Croix, Saba, Dominica or St. Lucia, where steep drop-offs provide canyons, pinnacles and more. If investigating wrecks is your pleasure, you need look no further than the Virgin Islands, Anguilla or Barbados, destinations which have proven a magnet for both planned and unexpected disasters, creating artificial reefs for the pleasure of divers. And if reefs call to you, the plateau-shaped underwater landscapes of Antigua, the Virgin Islands, and the Grenadines will hit the right notes. Shore diving is not widely available in the Eastern Caribbean, but you'll find opportunities on St. Croix and St. Lucia. Finally, if heading well off the beaten track is your objective, try St. Eustatius or Montserrat, islands with ample sights and few visitors, or better yet, head for Barbuda's desolate shores, where diving on pristine reefs is possible only from the decks of a live-aboard situation.

Or perhaps your dive dreams are simpler; let's say, just trying it, for starters. Learning to dive is a less complicated, and more available exercise, than many people imagine. You've probably heard of hours spent in a classroom obtaining certification. While this in itself probably appeals to no one, you can try diving in a much easier fashion by signing up for a resort course. These half-day introductions into the world of diving are available through most major dive shops, generally for around $75. While there is some classroom-style information, the course culminates, usually in a pool or shallow reef, with actual diving in full regalia. In the French West Indies, a similar overture, referred to as a "Baptism," is available, although their introduction actually takes you down onto the reefs for a short spin, in the hands of an able instructor.

If you are certain that diving is something you're willing to fall in love with, then you'll want to obtain certification—your "C" card—which allows you to dive on your own, without needing an instructor to tag along (although all diving should be done with a buddy). You can take the entire course at home spread out over several weeks or months (usually starting in a pool, graduating to a lake or ocean dive), or you can do it all in the Caribbean, concentrated into five or six days. An increasingly popular option is a combination of the two, allowing you to review the classroom material at home (usually via video), and save the actual water training for your vacation. Another route is to obtain your certification one dive at a time, spread over several vacations and different destinations; NAUI calls this their "Passport Diver" program and it allows you to pick up the course wherever you left off, spread out over a period of months or even years.

Another option is the fleet of "live-aboard" vessels that ply the waters of the Western Caribbean with increasing popularity. The advantage, obviously, is that you can maximize your actual diving time while on vacation (up to four or five dives per day), and minimize the hassle of traveling to and from dive sites. Additionally, live-aboards generally visit more remote areas—like the Blue Hole in Belize, French Cay in the Caicos, or the West Wall of Grand Cayman—which are difficult to reach by day boats. Like a cruise ship, the live-aboards are all-inclusive (though BC, regulators and computers must be rented if you don't bring your own); also like a cruise ship, you are hostage to a fairly strict itinerary and you'll have little or no interaction with island life. However, for divers who just can't get enough, the one-week live-aboard trips are a very popular option. It's also possible to become certified on the live-aboards; for an extra charge, you may obtain open-water certification on the Peter Hughes boats, or the entire classroom and open-water course on the Aggressor trips. The chapters in which you'll find live-aboard choices are the Cayman Islands and the Turks and Caicos Islands.

Diving is a serious, potentially dangerous sport. There are universal risks, which won't be addressed here, and there are those which are fairly unique to the Caribbean. Sharp-toothed creatures, fortunately, are not as great a hazard. The shark activity common in the Bahamas is actually rare in most of the Caribbean. Nurse sharks are spotted throughout the region, but they are typically shy and unproblematic, content to nap under ledges. On rare occasion, hammerheads will be seen where deeper waters approach dive sites, but they tend to stay at a distance. The huge, graceful whale shark—the largest fish in the seas—is rare, but the timid creature is affably tolerant of human interaction. Barracudas and moray eels, both of which can pack a powerful punch, also tend to be shy and won't usually bite unless provoked or cornered.

On the other hand, there are several, more innocuous creatures that do create problems. One is fire coral, which is found throughout the region, and remains most deserving of its name. Although the nasty sting you'll feel after touching it will eventually go away, it can be inflamed by scratching the area of your skin which came into contact (quickly fanning your hands around the affected area while underwater helps to dispel the coral darts that cause the pain). On the same theme, avoid the beautiful fireworm which also defends itself with bunches of tiny daggers. Another tough customer is more obvious: the black sea urchin has dozens of sharp needles protruding from its body like a pincushion. These spines can grow up to a foot long and will back up their sting with a dose of venom. More serious still is the scorpionfish, which frequently appears to be just another rock, until it's stepped on, at which point it releases a potentially fatal toxin; medical attention should be sought immediately.

As a rule, in the Eastern Caribbean, dive sites are clustered on the western coasts of most islands, away from the brisk currents of the Atlantic. A primary exception is around the Virgin Islands, where the numerous tiny islands provide shelter for reefs, and divers. As one continues west, location of dive sites varies from island to island.

The four destinations of the French West Indies adhere to different dive standards than is commonly practiced at PADI or NAUI style outfits. This is not to say these standards are better (or worse) than those you are used to, but you should familiarize yourself with their methods and styles before boarding a boat; a good grasp of conversational French is necessary for some of the shops on Guadeloupe and Martinique (St. Barthelemy and St. Martin dive shops are more fluent in English). One key difference is that while Americans consider 130 feet the depth limit for safe recreational diving, the French allow advanced divers to descend to about 195 feet. Additionally, you will be expected to produce a medical certificate before diving with a French operation. And, instead of a standard resort course, the French offer le baptism, a handheld submersion into the dive experience.

WHAT THE TOURIST MISSES

The simian population of St. Kitts and Nevis is more than 125,000.

Let's face it—in our day-to-day existence, we're all tourists. When we traipse across town for a meal of foreign cuisine produced by a kitchen that knows it first-hand, we're tourists. When we participate in the rituals—a concert, a party—of our children or grandchildren, we're tourists. The gaps that separate us from one another and make us unique are ethnic, social, political, generational, geographical, et al. But for many, when we are on vacation, there's an invisible dividing line that somehow separates tourists from travelers. And of course, almost all of us prefer to assume we're the latter, rather than the former.

When we are on vacation, the line between them and us becomes its most apparent as we fight to experience something that hasn't been prepackaged for the cruise-ship masses. So we head to a beach we are told is secluded, remote, paradisiacal. The line is almost literally drawn in the sand when a catamaran loaded with a few dozen noisy, sunburned, half-drunk day-trippers pulls onto the beach you and your mate thought you would have to yourselves. The paradise we were promised in a brochure is gone—because of tourists.

This book covers the entire Caribbean, from St. Thomas where more than a million visitors each year scatter over its well-developed acres, to St. Eustatius, a quirky destination that's lucky to have its annual visitor arrival count break four digits. But if you're looking for a Caribbean destination that's off the beaten track, where the local population doesn't all work in the tourism sector, where the neon signs of Burger King and Kentucky Fried Chicken are not yet lit, there are a few options. Most of these islands are smaller and less populated, and they're harder to get to. The (now) well-established haunts of the rich and famous such as St. Barthelemy and Anguilla, chic and remote as they may have once been, have been left off. This is a list of islands that your friends haven't heard of yet.

Anegada

This flat, coral outpost sits well apart from the rest of the British Virgin Islands in more ways than one. While some islands focus on the number of beaches they have, 15-square-mile Anegada itself is practically a beach—its highest point is a scrawny 28 feet above sea level. The island is protected by treacherous reefs that are said to contain the carcasses of more than 300 ships, but today are grounds for excellent snorkeling. It's the farthest north of the Lesser Antilles, so when you sit at serene Loblolly Bay and gaze north, the next land mass is Bermuda, almost a thousand miles away, further establishing the isolation. The island is home to only 170 people, all of whom know each other. At the end of a few days or a week at the Anegada Reef Hotel, essentially the only tourist facilities on the island, you'll know almost everyone too.

Barbuda

Another recumbent and coralline backwater, Barbuda (not to be confused with Bermuda or Barbados) lies 28 miles off the shores of sibling island Antigua. The most unique sight is a colony of frigate birds (one of only two in the world), particularly during mating season when males puff up the distinctive red balloon under their beaks to attract mates. Spelunkers will find caves to investigate, many of which are unexplored to this day, indeed, most of the island is void of footprints. The beaches are plush, with a slightly pinkish hue, and long—one alone sprawls an unbroken 14 miles. But lodgings are limited either to ultra-simple guest houses or ultra-pricey resorts catering to the very well-heeled. In spite of the isolation and usual type of visitor, 1100 residents call Barbuda home, and continue a more-traditional life of fishing, farming and hunting.

Bequia

One of the string of islands that queue up off the southern tip of St. Vincent like the tail of a kite, Bequia is small yet vibrant—part of the St. Vincent and the Grenadines. An airport opened only in 1992, but despite local concerns, it doesn't seem to have had tragic consequences for the island's charm, which is legendary. There is no car rental on Bequia, but walking will surround you with the colorful island character and lifestyle, which you can further immerse yourself in at the Harpoon Saloon in quaint Port Elizabeth. The bar is named for the island's whaling industry, which still exists today (in a shadow of its former self) when the animals pass by the island on their annual migration. The whaling station is actually located on Petit Nevis a mile off Bequia's southern coast, and several older gentlemen keep the industry alive in 26-foot cedar boats under power of oar and sail. Sailing remains big (Admiralty Bay is a lovely and popular anchorage), and other island activities include diving, a secluded beach at Industry Bay near the end of the road, and exploring a fine bookstore on the waterfront featuring Caribbean authors and a healthy stock of maps and charts.

Carriacou

The largest of the Grenadines, though politically connected with Grenada to the south, Carriacou has a richer cultural scene than its 6000-strong population might seem to dictate. One of the region's finest painters, Canute Caliste, lives in L'Esterre, and you can visit with him at his house/gallery (just follow the signs). Many of the islanders can trace their African roots to specific tribes, and a tradition known as "Big Drum," African tribal drumming and dancing, is rolled out for all special events—boat launches, among them. The tiny community of Windward appears at first to be a fishing village, but instead, this is where boats are built, much the way they have been for decades, and with renowned results. Not everything produced on Carriacou floats as well, however: the local rum, Jack Iron, is so strong that ice settles to the bottom of a glass. On the other hand, if your glass has that much rum in it to start, maybe you're seeing things?

Cayman Brac

Grand Cayman is a magnet for divers and bankers and served as a major location for *The Firm*, but two other islands make up this British Crown Colony. Little Cayman is a sand pancake with a breathtaking undersea wall that pulls in its share of dive business, but Cayman Brac was awarded all of the above-water character. Brac means "bluff" in Gaelic and a limestone formation at one end of the island rises 140 feet straight up out of the sea, providing what is probably the region's only (admittedly nascent) rock climbing wall with a dozen difficult routes put up in 1995. On top of this plateau is the Brac Parrot Reserve, home to a unique subspecies of the Amazon parrot. With little tourism or local business to stimulate the economy, the population (about 1300) is in decline, making the island a true backwater offering peaceful retreat and perhaps unequaled friendliness.

Culebra

More than a few passengers aboard flights from San Juan to the Virgin Islands have sailed over this spindly outpost and thought about a detour. The first thing they notice is the beaches—at least two, Soni and Flamenco, are sublime. Then there's the scrubby, untouched quality of the interior, thanks in large part to the U.S. Naval Reservation that previously occupied a portion of Culebra. Once on the island, the barren landscape is almost mirrored by the social scene. Culebra is laid back and rustic to the 'nth, accommodations are almost exclusively in guest houses, and activities are mostly of the do-it-yourself kind. But those activities—mountain biking, snorkeling and diving, kayaking among the 20 or so cays, or just lazing on a beach with an extra-thick layer of sun-block (there's little shade)—are unfettered by tour hawkers and cruise-ship arrivals. And despite Culebra's hardscrabble appearance, the ecology is rich in bird life and turtle hatchings, making the island a true delight for eco-sensitive travelers.

Dominica

When Dominica (not to be confused with the Dominican Republic) began a pursuit of eco-tourism in the 1980s, other Caribbean islands scratched their collective heads and wondered, "Why would anyone want to hike through the mud?" A few thousand happy hikers and a decade later, Dominica legitimately calls itself "the Nature Isle" and other countries are trying to attract ecologically oriented visitors. To be sure, Dominica's success has meant a buildup of small hotels and resorts, but the island has doggedly stayed with its eco-sensitive mindset and been rewarded with a tourism infrastructure that nicely complements an agricultural economy of bananas, coconuts and grapefruits. The underwater scene has also been discovered, and divers can swim with the humpback whales that pass close to shore. Plus, the hiking is no small deal. The unforgettable all-day trek to The Boiling Lake, a furiously bubbling caldera cradled in a volcanic gault called the Valley of Desolation, is a classic.

Terre-de-Haut and Marie-Galante

The Iles des Saintes, a small archipelago of a half-dozen islands just off the southern shores of Guadeloupe are known primarily for Terre-de-Haut, a muscular outcrop and home to 1500 residents, many of them fishermen. Daytime activities include mountain biking (steep), sunbathing (nude at Anse Crawen) or appreciation for the island's barren landscape (the most exotic greenery are native succulents). The mountainous island receives a quantity of day-trippers from Guadeloupe, but stick around after dusk and Terre-de-Haut quiets down to a facsimile of what St. Barts might have been like a few decades ago. There's a road and a few cars, but this is one island you can explore entirely on foot if you choose. Much bigger in size, Marie-Galante's sweet landscape rolls along gently, which allows its fields of sugarcane to be carted to distilleries by oxen cart—the most obvious example (among many) of how this island gently embraces an older fashion of life, one still untouched by tourism, despite glorious beaches and wonderful Creole food. Not many of Marie-Galante's 60,000 islanders speak English (nor on somewhat more visited Terre-de-Haut), so you'll arrive with either a firm grasp of the French language, or a good phrasebook in hand.

Montserrat

"Who would want to go to Montserrat?" was the question any reasonable travel agent might ask when queried about this delightful though currently troubled destination. The turmoil caused by a recently reawakened volcano has been enough to reach the pages of *The New York Times*, but careful monitoring by scientists has so far prevented any injuries to the local population, a number of whom have been relocated away from the volcano's slopes. More than half of the island (as we went to press) was considered part of the "safe zone," including its best beach, some tranquil hiking trails and bucolic mountain biking territory, though the occasional ash fall does darken the mood a bit. The situation evolves regularly (you'll need an alternate plan in your back pocket if you head this way, in case things get really serious), but visit Montserrat and you are afforded an opportunity to commune with Mother Nature when she's hard at work building an island.

Saba

Shaped like a green gumdrop and plopped just a few miles off the shores of busy Sint Maarten, the dive world has discovered Saba, anointing it as home to some of the best underwater scenery in the Caribbean. But the island has plenty to offer non-divers, too. Twelve hundred residents are perched in aerie hamlets clinging to the sides of steep Mt. Scenery, and a concrete road weaves and curls its way from one side of the island to the other. There's no real crime, though excessive partying on weekends isn't tolerated, even by the School of Medicine students. A few small inns are found in the village of Windwardside, though many people shack up with the locals who rent their cottages and villas. An attraction of a different sort is found at the airport: the mountainous island could only find space for a quarter-mile-long runway, and cliffs plunge into the ocean at either end—a true E Ticket ride when you land. Just don't come to Saba for the beaches—other than an ephemeral rocky cove, there aren't any.

Sint Eustatius

Nearby Saba is better known for its diving and hiking, but Sint Eustatius, also called Statia, has its fair share, and beaches too. The island is a languid retreat, though it was once the most important slave depot in the West Indies with some 20,000 inhabitants. Blue beads—five-sided and over 200 years old—were once used for slave trading, and can still be found along the shores of Statia by a lucky few. The diving is fine, and surprisingly unknown, though more and more are coming to tour Statia's pristine reefs and walls. For hiking, there's an ancient, classically shaped volcanic cone, The Quill, whose gaping crater contains a verdant rainforest (the island's lushest vegetation) that most visitors make the hike to. Today, just 2100 live on Statia, though more than 20 nationalities are represented.

St. John

As a group, the U.S. Virgin Islands have a reputation for being crowded shopping ports long past their prime as island getaways. Not so on St. John. There's no airstrip and two-thirds of the island is a National Park overseen by kindly gray-haired ladies and rangers with dreadlocks. When you debark at the ferry dock, you'll feel like you're landing at the island out of *Jurassic Park*, but as you head into the mostly undeveloped park, you'll realize instead you've entered paradise. St. John's infamous accommodations swing to two extremes—luxury resorts or eco-sensitive campgrounds with wooden tent structures that overlook sublime ribbons of white sand. In truth, there are also a few guest houses, and several hundred villas for rent, but they might put a filter on the away-from-it-all experience.

St. Vincent

One of the larger and more-populous islands of the Eastern Caribbean, in many ways St. Vincent is the last vestige of the banana economy most of the islands have put behind them. The interior is lush, containing extensive rainforests, and home to the rare, endangered St. Vincent parrot—marvelous in flight—which you can see in the Buccament River Valley. Waterfalls are chief attractions, and one, the Falls of Baleine on the north coast, is reached only by boat. Like a number of the nearby islands, St. Vincent, too, has a gently smoldering volcano (it last erupted in 1979), which provides a thigh-challenging trek. American Eagle began service to this island in late 1996—what are you waiting for?

Trinidad

What's an island with more than 1.2 million residents doing in a list of retreats leading you away from it all? Trinidad is an exotic bridge between cultures that's overlooked by most North Americans. Come here for the tremendous bird-watching, or to see mammoth sea turtles lumber up onto a beach at night and deposit a few dozen eggs. Indulge in some of the most interesting West Indian cooking, courtesy of the diverse racial makeup of the island, and stay in a guest house—both opportunities that make Trinidad one of the Caribbean's best bargains. Or participate in Carnival, the annual, orgiastic revelry that overtakes Port of Spain for two days each February (though the preparations begin months in advance). Other islands claim to produce a carnival each year, but none can hold a candle to this one—the biggest and best in the region, and some say better than Rio's.

WHAT THE TOURIST
MISSES

CRUISE PORTS

Charlotte Amalie in St. Thomas is one of the most popular cruise ship ports.

Cruising can be so addicting that it's sometimes hard to even get off the ship at a port of call. If you do choose to do so, you have several options for exploring that day's island. The cruise company will try hard to get you to take one of its organized shore excursions, which often include lunch. The advantage is that you'll be shown around safely and you'll always be back on time to catch the ship. The drawback, however, is that prices can be quite high, often as much as 100 percent above what you'd pay on your own. If you're adventurous, it's better to explore on your own, but keep a sharp eye on the time, as cruise ships set sail promptly as scheduled with or without straggling passengers.

Antigua

Island Tour

A visit to the island's Interpretation Center focuses on local history, followed by visits to historic sites, notably Nelson's Dockyard National Park and English Harbour, where Horatio Nelson once plied the waters. Day trips are also available to Barbuda, 25 miles away and inaccessible by cruise ship.

Jolly Roger Cruise

On this veritable floating pirate theme park, you can hang out at the open bar, learn the latest Caribbean dances, watch a staged "pirate wedding," snorkel or walk the plank.

Catamaran Cruise

Sail the northwest coast of the island, stopping to snorkel, swim or relax on the beach.

Snorkeling

Various snorkeling adventures are available on the island, notably to Prickly Pear Island, often accompanied by lunch.

Golf

The Cedar Valley Golf Course, a 6142-yard, par-70 facility, welcomes you to its native grass fairways and greens.

Aruba

Island Tour

A tour for landlubbers focusing on the island's markets, historical sites and scenic vistas. Highlights are the Frenchmen Pass and St. Ann's Church in the village of Noord.

Atlantis Submarine

A 30-minute cruise aboard a catamaran takes you to the dive site on the island's southeast coast. A 50-minute tour of the ocean floor follows and includes looks at coral reefs and associated marine life.

Seaworld Explorer

The semi-submarine Seaworld Explorer tours the spectacular Arashi Reef and the wreck of the *Antilla*, a German freighter that went down during World War II, leaving behind the largest shipwreck in the Caribbean. Other tours aboard the vessel also are offered.

Snorkeling

A catamaran takes you from the dock to the snorkeling site of *Arashi*, the west point of the island.

Scuba

Certified divers only are invited to view the wreck of the *Pedernales*, torpedoed during World War II by a German submarine. The dive site may change due to weather conditions.

Barbados

Island Tours

Historic sites and breathtaking vistas are on the agendas of several island tours that emphasize historical sites such as Gun Hill Signal Station, Villa Nova, Sam Lord's Castle, St. John's Church and local plantations. Tours focusing on natural wonders take you to the Flower Forest and/or Andromeda Gardens.

Jolly Roger Tour

Pretend you're a pirate and sail the west coast, anchoring in Holetown Bay to walk the plank, snorkel or land on the beach. Free rum and a staged pirate wedding add to the merriment.

Carlisle Beach Excursion

You'll find everything you need (towels, chairs, showers, lockers) for a day at the beach at the Carlisle Beach Center. A barbecue lunch is included, along with live island music and access to a bar and gift shop.

Pub-Hopping

It's bar-hopping in the English tradition, but with a Caribbean flavor. A guide will accompany you to all the local hot spots such as the Bamboo Beach Bar, Rumors and the Coach House. A complimentary drink is available at each stop. (All pub-hoppers must be 18 or older.)

Photography Tour

Serious photographers will enjoy the many photo opportunities on this excursion, which takes in Bathsheba Beach and Skeete's Bay.

Harrison's Cave

Not for claustrophobics, this tram ride takes you on an underground ride past dramatic waterfalls, tranquil pools and stalactites and stalagmites.

Atlantis Submarine

The air-conditioned *Atlantis II* takes you down more than 100 feet for a look at a shipwreck, coral reefs, sponge gardens and other marine life.

Snorkeling

Explore the waters (and a shipwreck) at Carlisle Bay or sail on a catamaran to Bridgetown Deep Water Harbour for some serious snorkeling.

Scuba

Certified divers are invited to explore parts of the island's western coast, including a coral reef, on this one-tank dive. Equipment and experienced guides provided.

Golf

The Sandy Lane Resort is home to this 18-hole, par-72 course. The cost for a ship excursion includes transportation and greens fees; carts and lunch are extra.

Bonaire

Washington National Park

Nature lovers will be intrigued by this 13,500-acre preserve that offers excellent hiking and birding opportunities.

Bonaire Marine Park

Both snorkelers and divers will enjoy this underwater marine park that descends to a depth of nearly 200 feet. Divers have dubbed it one of the best scuba areas in the world, so you won't be disappointed.

British Virgin Islands

Virgin Gorda

It's a 40-minute boat ride to Virgin Gorda from the Tortola port of Road Town. Once you get there, visit Baths, where you can explore marine caves with equipment provided.

Tortola Island Tour

Visit Tortola's Botanical Gardens, Cane Garden Bay and the island's most panoramic vistas aboard an open-air safari bus.

Mount Sage

One of the island's most famous viewpoints, Mount Sage is the highest mountain in the Virgin Islands. Walk the fairly strenuous trail to the top, enjoying the rainforest flora and fauna on the way up.

Glass-Bottom Boat

Watch marine life from a dry perch in a 21-foot glass-bottom boat.

Snorkeling

Peter Island is one of the most beautiful of Tortola's islands—perfect for snorkeling.

Cayman Islands

Combination Island Tour

It's a trip to Hell and back, but there's nothing remotely evil about this tour, which emphasizes land and sea. Observe marine life at the underwater observatory at Sting Ray City, then visit the Cayman Turtle Farm, local historic sites, and Hell, named for the eerie rock formations that surround it.

Island Tour

See the island's historic sites, the Cayman Turtle Farm, and the unspoiled Seven Mile Beach. Stop at Hell's post office to send that special someone a postcard from Hell.

Seaworld Explorer

View Grand Cayman's underwater world without getting wet aboard the Seaworld Explorer, a semi-submarine (glass-bottomed boat) that allows you to view coral reefs, tropical fish and even a shipwreck in air-conditioned comfort. A guide provides commentary.

Submarine Atlantis

If "semi-submarines" just don't do it for you, dive to depths of 150 feet in the *Atlantis I*, an air-conditioned, pressurized submarine.

Deep-Dive Submarine

This little excursion will put a definite dent in your wallet, but this may be a once-in-a-lifetime adventure. Board a two-passenger research submarine for an 800-foot-deep dive down the Cayman Wall.

Flight Seeing

View Grand Cayman from the air aboard the twin-engine *Otter*.

Catamaran to Stingray City

The *Cockatoo*, a 60-foot racing catamaran, takes you on a 45-minute trip through the North Sound to the Southern Stingray Playground. After you've watched the rays being fed, don snorkeling gear and join the fun.

Jolly Roger Cruise

The *Jolly Roger*, an authentic replica of a 17th century Spanish Galleon, provides a Disneyesque look at pirates as it "attacks" another ship, fires its cannon, and engages its "pirates" in sword fighting and plank walking.

Deep-Sea Fishing

You could find wahoo, tuna or marlin at the end of your line on this excursion. All fishing gear is provided, and an experienced captain will lend a hand.

Snorkeling

Everything is provided on this snorkeling adventure, which takes place just off Parrot's Landing. Other snorkeling adventures take place at the Stingray City Sand Bar and at Cheeseburger and Cemetery reefs.

Scuba

Coral reefs, tropical fish, shipwrecks, and other enticing sights await both certified and noncertified divers at various locations on the island.

Golf

Play the 18-hole, par-57 executive course at the Britannia Golf Course, designed by Jack Nicklaus.

CRUISE PORTS

Curaçao

Island Tour

See the distillery where Curacao liqueur is produced (samples provided), then see the island's historical sites and the fascinating Curacao Seaquarium.

Seaworld Explorer

The semi-submarine *Seaworld Explorer* takes you on a guided tour of the island's coral reefs. Fish feeding makes for great photo ops. Some tours include a stop at the Seaquarium.

Trolley Train Tour

Board the Willemstad Trolley Train for a narrated tour of the island's architectural and historic sites.

Snorkeling

Snorkeling near the Seaquarium provides a colorful look at local marine life around a sunken tugboat. Equipment included.

Scuba

The Curacao National Underwater Park, offering 3000 acres for exploration, is one of the island's most popular dive sites. The Seaquarium also offers scuba diving.

Dominica

Nature Tour

The island's Botanical Gardens, Trois Pitons National Park and the Emerald Pool are the destinations on this nature-lover's tour. Some tours proceed to Trafalgar Falls.

Dominican Republic

Santa Domingo

A bus tour of Santo Domingo acquaints you with the island's historical sites as well as modern buildings. Highlights are the Alcazar, a house built in the 1500s and occupied by Columbus and his bride; Casas Reales, a 16th-century restoration of the tongue-twisting Palacio de la Real Audiencia y Chancilleria de Indias y el Palacio de los Governadores y Capitanes Generales de la Isla Espanola (basically, the house where the governor and captains lived); the city's grand cathedral, and the Columbus Lighthouse.

North Coast

Bus tours are available in the town of Puerto Plata, near the shore where Columbus first landed. Although there's not that much to see here, it's an option if you're interested in local history.

Scuba

There are plenty of opportunities for diving, but most are meant for experienced divers.

Grenada

Island Tour

Driving tour includes a visit to the capital of St. George, Westerhall Point, a sugar factory and Flamboyant Beach, where drinks, swimming and sun are complimentary.

Grand Etang National Park

Everything is uphill on this tour, which takes in Annandale Falls and continues to 1910 feet to Grand Etang National Park. Explore the rainforest, view Grand Etang Lake (set in an extinct volcano) and visit Fort Frederick—built by the French in 1779—on the way down. Naturalists also may enjoy a visit to Bay Gardens, located in St. Paul.

Party Raft

Raft along the coast of Grenada, sip rum punch and stop at a deserted beach for swimming or snorkeling.

Helicopter Tour

See the island from above on a helicopter tour. The pilot narrates; you take the pictures.

St. Pauls/Westerhall

Sugar and spice and everything nice on this tour, which checks on the growing and processing of sugar, cocoa and nutmeg (among other species), then stops briefly at the white-sand Grand Anse Beach.

Catamaran Tour

Aboard the double-deck catamaran *Rhum Runner* your guide will brief you on the history of the island while you drink rum punch. View a coral reef through the glass bottom, then relax or swim at Morne Rouge Beach.

Guadeloupe

Island Tour

Enjoy the gorgeous island scenery, walk up to Crawfish Falls, and tantalize your taste buds with a visit to the Severin Distillery, where you can imbibe on the spot or buy at factory prices for later consumption.

Carbet Falls

This half-day excursion takes in banana plantations, tropical forest, Carbet Falls (the walk to the falls takes approximately one hour), La Soufriere volcano and lunch at a typical Creole restaurant.

Domaine de Valombreuse

Flower enthusiasts won't want to miss an excursion to this stunning floral park, where there are varieties of flowers from all over the world. Birders also may find this a hot spot.

Jamaica

Montego Bay Tour

Take the Howard Cook Highway to the Rose Hall Great Plantation for a tour. Stops at the City Center Shopping Plaza and the Jamaican Craft Market. Other city tours include a visit to the Greenwood Great House, filled with antiques, rare books and musical instruments.

Mountain Valley Rafting

Low-key water rafting from Lethe through the island's lush landscapes.

Freestyle Sailing

Fun in the sun on the trimaran *Freestyle*, where you can snorkel, sail, swim or just enjoy a cruise of the harbor at Montego Bay.

Dunn's River Falls

If you don't take the tour, do Dunn's River Falls on your own. The 600-foot waterfall is stunning—and one of the most famous sights on the island. You're welcome to climb, but be sure to wear rubber-soled shoes.

Ocho Rios

View the local flora and famous historic sites on your journey to Ocho Rios and Dunn's River Falls, which you can climb with the help of an experienced guide. Also available are tours that focus specifically on local plantations.

Rafting on the Martha Brae

Scenic tour includes historical landmarks and rafting two miles down the Martha Brae River aboard a 30-foot bamboo raft. See bamboo groves, staghorn ferns, exotic orchids and tropical birds.

Horseback Riding

A trail guide will accompany you on this horseback excursion, where you'll ride in the saddle until you get to the beach, where the saddle is removed and you'll ride bareback along the edge of the sparkling water.

Sundancer Yacht Cruise

It's all aboard for a cruise along the island's coast on the 75-foot *Sundancer*, which also stops at Dunn's River Falls.

Photography Tour

A professional photographer accompanies you on a photo excursion to Montego Bay's most famous landmarks and scenic overlooks. Highlights include the Rose Hall Great House, St. James Parish Church and a look at the island's various architectural styles.

Helicopter Tour

Tour Montego Bay aboard a helicopter while the pilot narrates your excursion. The view is spectacular, and you'll soar over landmarks such as the Rose Great Hall and the Half Moon Bay Golf Club.

Shop 'Til You Drop

It's duty-free shopping at more than 100 stores in Ocho Rios. Tour buses take you to downtown, Soni's Plaza and Taj Majal, and a shopping map serves as a guide to local shops.

Kingston

Your tour of the Kingston area should include the National Gallery, Devon House, the Bob Marley Museum and St. Peter's Church, located in Port Royal. Also worth a stop is the Archaeological Museum at Fort Charles.

Sportfishing

Deep-sea fishing is available in Montego Bay, where the captain and his mate will help you as much as needed. Fishing gear is provided.

Snorkel

A yacht transports you to Sunset or Sergeant Major reefs for snorkeling (equipment provided) and fish feeding.

Scuba

Both certified and noncertified dives are offered in the area, and all dives are supervised by a certified divemaster or instructor. Dive sites depend on local conditions on the day of the dive.

Golf

Spend the day golfing in the Jamaica hills at the 18-hole, par-72 Runaway Bay Country Club, or opt for a game at the 18-hole Half Moon Bay Golf Club, designed by Robert Trent Jones.

Martinique

Island Tour

An overview of the island and rainforest, plus a stop at St. Pierre, destroyed by the eruption of Mount Pelee in 1902, and various other historical sites. Some island tours include a visit to the Butterfly Farm, set in a beautiful botanic park.

Calypso Tour

This double-deck party boat cruises across the Bay of Fort-de-France, stops at a beach for swimming and allows you to look down on a coral reef through its glass-bottom viewers.

Walking Tour

If you're tired of water-related transportation and are in good physical condition, use your feet to explore the capital's historic and architectural sites. An English-speaking guide accompanies you.

Balata Gardens

Caribbean flora is highlighted at Balata Gardens, where footpaths wind through one of the best collections of native plants and flowers in the islands. Also visit Balata Church, modeled after the Sacred Heart Basilica in Paris, and the Creole House. Other nature-oriented stops worth a look include Les Ombrages and the Parc des Floralies.

St. Pierre/Plantation de Leyritz

Visit St. Pierre and stop at the historic Plantation de Leyritz, a restored sugar plantation converted into an inn and restaurant. Enjoy a complimentary beverage and lunch in the restaurant, do some exploring, or swim in the pool. On the trip back, stop for a look at a local rum factory.

Snorkeling

Equipment and instruction are provided as you explore one of the island's coral reefs.

Golf

The Country Club de la Martinique welcomes you to its par-71 course, designed by Robert Trent Jones. The scenery is as exciting as the game is challenging, and a constant 15- to 20-m.p.h. wind keeps things interesting.

Montserrat

Galaways Plantation

This estate, touted as the only Irish plantation in the New World, is now mostly ruins, but it provides an interesting look at life on the island in the 17th and 18th centuries.

Great Alps Waterfalls

It's a bit of a hike, but there is much tropical flora and fauna to be enjoyed along the way. You may be able to find a guide at Shooter's Hill Village, where the trail begins.

Nevis

Island Tour

There's not all that much to see on Nevis, but you may wish to take in the area around Charlestown and historical sites such as the Montpelier Plantation and the Nelson Museum.

Puerto Rico

City Tour

Both the old and the new San Juan are explored on this tour, which includes El Morro Fort, Carnegie Library, the Capitol, Condado Lagoon and other scenic landmarks.

Museo Pablo Casals

This museum pays homage to the famous cellist, who left Spain to live out most of his later life on the island. Included are tapes, musical scores and the master's cello.

El Yunque Rainforest

It's a one-hour drive to El Yunque Rainforest and Luquillo Beach, each one of the island's natural wonders. A great option for photographers and serious nature lovers.

Arecibo Observatory

Operated by Cornell University, this observatory, about a two-hour drive from San Juan, has an impressive telescope and is part of the National Astronomy and Ionosphere Center. Tours are given on a regular basis.

Parque de las Cavernas del Rio Camuy

This area in the limestone hills on the island's northwest coast is especially popular with spelunkers, who will enjoy exploring the huge caves. Guided tours are available.

Bacardi Rum Distillery

Watch the process whereby sugarcane becomes rum, then sample the results, or visit the Bacardi shops and museum.

Barrachina Center

Whether you take a scheduled excursion or make the trip yourself, you won't want to miss this shopper's paradise. Get good deals on jewelry, perfumes, and other items, with an extra 10 percent discount for ship passengers.

Nightlife Tour

Nightlife tours may include shows at the Sands Hotel or at other locations in the city. Some allow time for a visit to the casino.

Golf

Play either the Cerromar Beach North or Cerromar Beach South course, both par-72 courses nestled amid island scenery.

St. Barthélémy

Island Tour

Tour downtown Gustavia by minibus, then take in the local historical sites and scenic views, with a short shopping stop in La Savone.

Scuba

Many dive sites in the area lend themselves to both scuba diving and snorkeling. Some favorites are Pain de Sucre and Les Petits Saints.

St. Croix

Island Tour

A driver/guide takes you around the island in an air-conditioned van, stopping to tour the Whim Great House and to enjoy the lush rainforest on St. Croix's north shore.

Botanical Gardens

See St. George Village and Botanical Gardens in Christiansted and other scenic and historical highlights—including the 1493 Columbus landing site at Salt River—on this guided tour.

Catamaran Tour

A 52-foot catamaran takes passengers to fabulous Buck Island for snorkeling, and to Coakley Beach for a barbecue lunch prepared by the crew.

Buck Island Snorkeling

Buck Island Reef, part of the Buck Island National Monument, is the destination on this excursion, led by experienced guides and appropriate for snorkelers of all levels. Highly recommended!

Butler Bay Hike

Nature lovers shouldn't miss this hike through 225-acre Butler Bay preserve, which begins at the Ghut Bird Sanctuary and includes the ruins of the Estate Mount Washington Plantation, and panoramic views of Frederiksted Harbor, Sandy Point Beach and the rainforest. Wear comfortable footwear and bring bottled water for this moderately strenuous hike.

Sail and Snorkel

Gear and instruction are provided in this one-hour dive just off the island's coast.

Party Cruise

Complimentary rum and fruit punch add to the party atmosphere on the double-decked, glass-bottomed *Reef Queen*, but you also can look down on shipwrecks, coral reefs and marine life. A stop at Sandy Point Beach for swimming or sunning is included.

Golf

Robert Trent Jones' par-72, 18-hole Carambola course is one of the Caribbean's finest, and was featured on "Shell's Wonderful World of Golf," when Chi Chi Rodriguez burned up the links with a 69.

Sint Eustatius

The Quill

The climb up the side of this volcanic cone yields plenty of birds and other fauna—including an occasional iguana. Degree of difficulty varies, depending on which trail you take.

St. John

Island Tour

A narrated driving/walking tour of the island that departs from the ship's pier. Highlights include island history and panoramic overlooks.

Beach Tour

Tour Virgin Island National Park and other sights of interest, then snorkel or swim at Trunk Bay, which boasts its own underwater snorkel trail.

Island Cruise

Explore the island by sea on this guided tour that takes you around the island and focuses on both history and current events. After the tour, anchor near the beach for swimming and snorkeling.

St. Kitts

Brimstone Hill Tour

Christopher Columbus' 1493 landing site at Old Road Town is just one of the intriguing stops on this tour, which also visits the Romney Estate, an old West Indian plantation home where the Caribelle Batik Industry is now located. The main attraction is Brimstone Hill, site of a 17th-century fortress that houses a museum and offers panoramic views of the coastline.

Rainforest Excursion

After a stop at a Caribelle workshop to watch batiks being created, venture into a rainforest valley for a naturalist-led hike and look at the tropical flora and fauna.

Horseback Riding

What better way to experience the beach than astride a gentle, well-trained horse! After the one-hour ride, enjoy a complimentary cocktail.

Catamaran Adventure

Sail along the southern coast of the island, then disembark for snorkeling—gear and instruction provided.

Golf

The 18-hole Royal St. Kitts Golf Course welcomes you to its 6918-yard championship links.

St. Lucia

Sea Safari

Travel by boat to the Soufriere, where you can peer over the edge into the volcano's hissing abyss (it's dormant, not to worry). Enjoy the gorgeous Diamond Mineral Baths and surrounding botanical garden, then stop at Anse Cochon Beach for a swim.

CRUISE PORTS

Helicopter Tour

Enjoy the view over Castries Harbor, the Pitons (volcanic mountains), Jalousie Plantation and the tropical rainforest.

Plantation Tour

Island history is highlighted on a tour of the restored, 600-acre Invergoil Sugar Mill. See the settlement villages, the stone mill, and hear stories of plantation life. Great photo ops along the way. Variations of this tour include exploration of the local rainforest accompanied by a naturalist.

Rodney Bay/Pigeon Island

Visit Rodney Bay and Pigeon Island, site of Fort Rodney. Tour the fort, then head to Reduit Beach for recreation and relaxation.

Sint Maarten/St. Martin

Island Tour

A bus ride from the capital city of Philipsburg takes you to both the French and Dutch sides of the island, and includes historical sites, shopping and refreshments.

Beach Rendezvous

Get away from it all at Orient Bay, sometimes called the French Riviera of the Caribbean. A barbecue lunch with all the trimmings will be served while you relax in lounge chairs.

Le Privelege

This exclusive resort, located on the French side of the island, overlooks Anse Marcel Bay. Enjoy use of all the resort's sports facilities and have lunch by the pool.

Sun and Sea Cruise

Board the 60-foot *Maison Maru* for a coastal cruise that includes both the French and Dutch sides of the island. The rum punch is on the house.

See and Sea

See the sights on the French part of St. Maarten, then board a semi-submarine for a 45-minute narrated tour of coral reefs and Crole Rock. Watch a diver feed the moray eels, then—if you still have the stomach for it—stop for a complimentary drink, do some shopping and enjoy plenty of photo ops on the way back.

Golden Eagle Sailing

The 76-foot catamaran *Golden Eagle* sweeps you across the shimmering waters to Tintamar, an island where you can swim, snorkel or relax on the beach. A continental champagne breakfast or afternoon snack is included, and there's an open bar for your enjoyment on the return trip.

Champagne Brunch Tour

Board the *Lady Mary* and sip champagne as you sail through Simpson Bay Lagoon. Enjoy authentic Creole dishes, listen to the steel band or watch local artisans on the yacht, who carve and make weavings before your eyes.

Explorer Cruise

See the sights on the Dutch side of the island, then board the *Explorer* for a cruise through a French lagoon and into the Port la Royale Marine. Visit the Explorer's private island for swimming, jet-skiing or parasailing.

America's Cup Sailing

Wannabe America's Cup sailors can get a taste of the action in an actual race aboard 70-foot America's Cup yachts. Go along for the ride or assist the crew if you have the stamina for it.

Pinel Island

Visit the secluded isle de Pinel, where you can swim, snorkel, play volleyball or sunbathe—*au naturel* if you wish.

Deep Sea Fishing

Marlin, sailfish, tuna and shark are a few of the possibilities when you fish onboard one of the island's fishing boats.

Shipwreck Cove

With the help of a professional staff, snorkel your way through a sunken ship, explore the coral or feed the fish.

Scuba

Certified divers only on this shallow water, one-tank dive in the company of a divemaster, who will give you a guided tour. Equipment provided or bring your own.

Golf

The par-70 Mullet Bay Golf Club is more challenging that its 6200 yards would imply. Try out your over-water shots—and watch those tricky greens!

St. Thomas

Island Tour

A driver will take you on a narrated tour to St. Peter's Greathouse, where you can explore the former getaway estate of the "rich and famous." Then enjoy the spectacular view from the island's highest point, Mountain Top, where shopping also is available.

Charlotte Amalie

It takes a couple of hours to walk this historic district, but the beautifully restored homes are worth seeing, and the area is a window into the island's past. See Fort Christian, the oldest building in the Virgin Islands, along with other historic landmarks, and visit the Emancipation Garden, Market Square and the fishing village of Frenchtown. The shopping in picturesque Charlotte Amalie is great.

St. John Island

Take a ferry from the eastern tip of St. Thomas to the St. John Island. Then enjoy the sights on a scenic drive to Trunk Bay, where you can swim or snorkel (there's an underwater trail for snorkeling enthusiasts). Not to be missed!

The Arboretum at Magens' Beach

Although the arboretum is touted as one of St. Thomas' "best-kept secrets," it's no secret to the cruise lines, which regularly list it on their excursion agendas. Highlights include the 100-foot Puerto Rico palms and other magnificent trees planted in the restored arboretum and the opportunity to swim in the crystal clear waters of Magens' Beach.

Skyline Drive

Yo, ho ho! This tour takes you past old hideouts of the notorious Bluebeard the pirate and others of his ilk, then sweeps you up the mountain to the Saint Peter House for dozens of photo ops and a stroll around the estate.

Coral World

A good way for landlubbing tourists to see the marvels of the coral reef without getting wet. A visit to this underwater observatory includes a 90-minute tour. Some excursions also include a ride on a semi-submarine and/or snorkeling at Coki Point.

Windsong Sailing Tour

Get off the boat and into a yacht for this approximately three-hour sailing tour of the island. Lots of scenery and plenty of opportunities for swimming or soaking up the sun.

Sunset Sail

It doesn't get more romantic than this: a sunset, gorgeous scenery and complimentary wine and munchies.

Charter Sail

Have your own private party aboard a 65-foot schooner or 36-foot sloop available for half-day charter. Captain and crew are included, but you plan the trip, with stops for snorkeling if you wish.

Kon Tiki

The Kon Tiki is about as touristy as you can get, offering sight-seeing above and below water (it has glass-bottomed tanks for your viewing pleasure), music for dancing and a never-ending supply of rum punch.

Atlantis Submarine

Moderately expensive as shore excursions go, this one offers a narrated underwater excursion aboard the 65-foot submarine *Atlantis*.

Seaplane Vistaliner

It's up, up and away on the Seaplane Vistaliner, an excursion that will put a bit of a bite in your vacation budget, but allows you to view the island chain from a completely different perspective. The 40-minute flight originates from St. Thomas Harbor. Great views, so bring your camera.

Helicopter Tour

A 25-minute flight takes you over Thatch and Grass cays and past other local landmarks. Some tours combine a helicopter flight with a 90-foot submarine dive into the waters off Charlotte Amalie.

CRUISE PORTS

Snorkeling

Everything is provided for you on this underwater adventure, including snorkeling gear, instructions and food to feed the fish. Weather permitting, the destination is St. John, where you can "snuba" as well as snorkel. Other snorkeling adventures are available to Turtle Cove on Buck Island.

Scuba

If you are a certified diver, board a custom dive boat for a one-tank dive to one of several island locations. Most lines also offer scuba adventures for noncertified divers that involve instruction and a dive to a coral reef.

Golf

Mahogany Run is one of the most famous golf courses in the Caribbean, and also one of the most challenging. The par-70 course is surrounded by gorgeous vistas, which takes your mind off the difficulty you're having staying on the fairways.

St. Vincent/Grenadines

Falls of Baleine

Approximately 20 miles from Kingstown, the falls are accessible by boat. Great scenery and opportunities for swimming, snorkeling and exploring.

Sights around Kingstown include Fort Charlotte, the St. Vincent Museum and the St. Vincent Library.

Mayreau/Palm Island

Sail past the Tabago Cays to Palm Island, where you can swim or explore to your heart's content. Lunch is served aboard the sailboat.

Mayreau/Glass-bottom Boat

View coral reefs from above on this guided tour of local waters.

Catamaran Sailing

Sail past Petit St. Vincent and Palm Island on the *Jetset*, one of the fastest catamarans in the Caribbean.

Snorkeling

Dive at one of the island's most colorful reefs. Equipment and instruction are included.

Scuba

One-tank dives are available for both certified and noncertified divers.

Tobago

Island History and Culture

Survey this island's historical and cultural sites, including Fort King George, Fort James, and plantations of coconut palms. Final stop is the famous Flambeaux Club, where you'll be immersed in the island's cultural side in the form of Tobagonian music and dance.

CRUISE PORTS

Beach Excursion

Spend the day at Mount Irvine Beach, one of the island's most exclusive private beaches. A barbecue lunch is included.

Glass-bottom Boat Tour

View Buccoo Reef and Coral Gardens from above, with a guide pointing out the undersea flora and fauna. Then anchor at Nylon Pool, where you can swim or relax.

Catamaran Cruise

Take a cruise along the coast in the 50-foot catamaran *Loafer*, which makes stops at Nylon Pool and Bon Accord Point. Opportunities for swimming—and an open bar—are available along the way.

Golf

The 18-hole, par-72 championship Mount Irvine course is gorgeous, and your golf excursion includes transportation, greens fees and a shared golf cart.

Trinidad

Island Tour

Begin your island tour at Port of Spain, with stops at the National Museum and Art Gallery and at various historic churches and homes.

Asa Wright Nature Centre

It's an hour's drive from Port of Spain, but both the flora and fauna are worth the trip—especially for birders and other nature lovers. Serious birders may want to visit the Caroni Bird Sanctuary, 10 miles south of Port of Spain.

Turks & Caicos

These islands are generally not on the cruise ship itinerary, but if you elect to visit (access is by plane or boat), you may wish to see the National Museum, housed in the former Guinep Lodge on Grand Turk.

ANGUILLA

The children of Anguilla are polite, proud and friendly.

When you're out on a bitter morning, scraping the snow and ice off your car, struggling to get to work on time, and start dreaming wistfully of sitting on a Caribbean beach instead, it's the beaches of Anguilla you're yearning. The English colony is justifiably proud of its glorious beaches, where the sand is as soft as a baby's bottom and as white as the lace on a wedding gown. They seem to stretch on forever, dipping even so gently into a sea as clear and inviting as the first day of spring.

But, alas, every good thing comes with a price, and the price on Anguilla can be quite high. The island boasts smashing resorts with rates as high as the fashions in Saks Fifth Avenue. Though the beaches and watersports are divine, there is not much in the way on historical or diverting attractions, so any but the true sun worshipper may be a bit bored. There's great gourmet dining but little nightlife, no casinos, not even a movie theater or duty-free shop. What there is, however, exists in glorious abundance: pristine nature, endless beaches, unlimited sunshine, friendly, laid-back locals. And don't forget, those seeking after-sunset fun can always take the ferry that chugs to St. Martin/Sint Maarten in less than a half hour.

Anguilla is the most northernmost of the Caribbean's Leeward Islands and totals just 35 square miles. It's shaped something like an anchovy, and in fact the name in Italian means "eel," a nickname said to have come from Christopher Columbus when he spotted (but did not stop at) the land in 1493. Perhaps he feared that once his crew got the chance to laze on some of the island's 33 pristine beaches, they would never get back on board. You'll feel the same way after spending some time on peaceful Anguilla, and those memories of winter will melt away as quickly as the sun dries your skin.

Though the island took a beating in September 1995 by both hurricanes Luis and Marilyn, it is now essentially recovered. Tourists will notice little damage and no inconvenience from the storms, where winds of 250 miles per hour ripped the roof off virtually every abode and resulted in a three-month loss of power.

Located 190 miles directly east of Puerto Rico and just five miles north of St. Martin/St. Maarten, Anguilla is long, flat and scrubby. It measures 16 miles long by three miles wide and totals 35 square miles of flat coral limestone. The tallest spot, called Crocus Hill, is just 213 square feet above sea level.

The island consists of mostly high craggy shoreline with inland depression. Rolling hills of granite rock are covered with scrubs and there is little cultivation. Anguilla is quite arid, with just about 35 inches of rain per year. The average temperature is around 80 degrees Fahrenheit and average relative humidity just over 70 percent.

The Anguilla Beautification Club, the brainchild of Lidia Shave, wife of Governor Alan W. Shave, is making admirable attempts to add some color to Anguilla's dusty topography. The club plants trees and flowers and tourists are welcome to "adopt" a tree—even receiving a "certificate of proof." If interested, contact ABC Trees, P.O. Box 274, Anguilla, BWI.

The island has no city, just small villages scattered around. The hub, if it can even be called that, is known as the Valley, where you'll find the Depart-

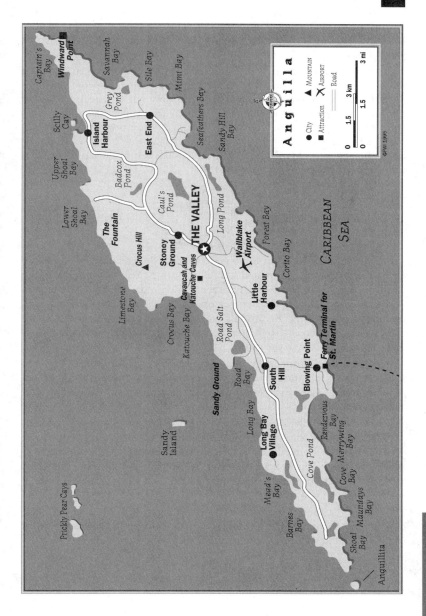

ment of Tourism, a few shops and the Wallblake Airport nearby. Ferry passengers arrive in Blowing Point, straight across from Marigot, St. Martin. Keep in mind you'll go through immigration when arriving by ferry just as plane passengers do.

The sleepy island has just six traffic lights but seemingly as many speed bumps as goats, who roam freely. "We have more goats than people," laughs a tourist board representative, and she's probably not exaggerating. Other creatures you are bound to encounter include lizards, pelicans, frigate birds and bananaquits, a pretty little yellow bird. The once-prevalent hummingbirds had, at presstime, yet to reappear on the island after being wiped out by hurricanes Luis and Marilyn in 1995, though the rest of the island, as far as tourists are concerned, is back to normal.

People

Anguilla is home to about 8000 people who, while technically citizens of Great Britain, have a culture and style all their own. You won't find a strong British influence on other colonies such as Bermuda; the ambience here is pure Caribbean. In fact, the number-one sport is the decidedly non-British pastime of boat racing. Because its limestone land makes for poor agriculture, slavery never really took hold here and there is scant evidence of boggier or tension between the races.

Anguillians are a proud, friendly and polite people; it's considered rude to jump in with a question or statement without first uttering the requisite good morning or good afternoon. Happily, there was very little looting after the 1995 hurricanes.

The island has a British education system in which elementary students graduate to one comprehensive school located in the Valley. For North American grade 12 and 13 equivalencies, students take Caribbean and British exams. There is no college or university on the island, so those interested in higher education attend schools in England, the United States, Jamaica or other Caribbean countries.

The island has both a British governor and deputy governor as well as an elected Legislative Assembly. Crime is quite low, through tourists are urged to take the same common-sense precautions as anywhere.

Fielding Tip:

It's considered rude to meet anyone without the prerequisite greeting: a gentle good morning or good afternoon, or more informally "okay" or "awrigh" (meaning, "hello-how-are-you-everything-okay-all right?"

History

Long before the Europeans arrived in the Caribbean, Arawak Indians inhabited Anguilla's hot and dusty scrubland. Over the past 10 years, some 40,000 Amerindian artifacts have been uncovered by the Anguilla Archaeological and Historical Society from some 50 sites, indicating Anguilla may have been an important ceremonial site, even a pilgrimage, for this native American tribe. By the time the English settled in the 1650s, the Arawaks had vanished—probably decimated by European conquistadors and marauding pirates. When the dry climate foiled all British attempts at farming, their former slaves divided up the land, cultivated pigeon peas and corn, and then finally turned to the sea, building and trading sloops and schooners and fishing in rich waters. In the late '60s, the British forced Anguilla into an uncomfortable tri-island alliance when the Associated State of St. Kitts-Nevis-Anguilla was signed into law. The single act stimulated a determined, if not exactly violent, rebellion, which found Anguillians marching a coffin around the island, burning the Government House and sending its 12 policemen packing. World headlines roared with news of "The Eel that Squeeled" (sic) as the Brits sent in paratroopers, only to be met on the shore by cheering Anguillians singing the British national anthem and waving Union Jacks. Finally the Brits succumbed and gave Anguilla what it really wanted—a benevolent overlord who took the pains to build a badly needed phone system, a new pier and roads. Today Anguilla is a happy British dependent with its own elected governing body.

Lingering in Anguilla

A British-dependent territory, and home to 8500, Anguilla is the northernmost of the leeward islands. The shape of the island may have spawned its name, which in Spanish means "eel." Today, Anguilla is a beach-lover's treasure—the main island is rimmed with long, white sand beaches dotted with stands of picture-postcard palm trees that face bright blue waters. Offshore, the diving is superb.

Fountain Cave

Located near Shoal Bay East, the Fountain is a dome-shaped cavern that shelters several freshwater pools. Discovered in 1979, the cavern contains petroglyphs on the walls. A 16-foot stalagmite has been carved with the image of Jocahu, a Taino Indian god.

Cove Bay

Near Maunday's Bay, you can relax in your own private paradise—provided you bring along your own picnic and towels. This soft-sand beach edged with coconut trees has no facilities.

Shoal Beach

No longer one of the Caribbean's best-kept secrets, this beach is still worth a visit, if only to sit on the powder white sands and watch the waves lap the water. Beach chairs and umbrellas are available.

Anguilla

Flat Cap Point

Wallblake Airport

Sandy Ground

Long Bay

West End

Anguillita Island

Blowing Point Harbor

Crocus Hill Prison

At an elevation of 213 feet, the ruins of the prison occupy the island's highest point.

Island Harbor

This fishing village is set near a long, slender beach that fronts a safe harbor. Local fishermen put out to sea in handmade boats. You can hire a boat to head to tranquil Scilly Cay.

Scilly Cay

From the water, this spit of land looks like a castaway's hideout—thatched huts and a few palm trees rise from the sandy beach. The waters here are neon-blue, perfect for swimming or snorkeling.

Captain's Bay

Rent a four-wheel-drive and head to this remote beach on the northeastern end, where limestone cliffs edge the sand. The surf pounds the shore, making the water too rough for swimming, but you'll savor the isolation.

Scrub Island

Sailboat Racing

The island's national sport, and the islanders and visiting boaters alike participate in sailboat races held during Carnival and on other holidays.

Shoal Bay

Island Harbor

Crocus Hill

The Valley

The Quarter

Forest Bay

The Museum at Arawak

Situated in the Arawak Beach Resort, this small, privately operated museum has displays of Arawak artifacts, as well as replicas of everyday utensils once used by the natives.

The Valley

This small town is where you'll find the Roman Catholic church and Wallblake House. Built around 1796 by Will Blake, this plantation great house is the subject of legends. Now owned by the Catholic church, the structure can be toured by appointment. Built in 1966, the nearby St. Gerard's Catholic church has rock walls and stained glass windows.

ANGUILLA

Windsurfing and sailing are readily available at many Anguilla hotels.

Anguilla boasts some of the best beaches in the entire Caribbean, with sand as soft and white as talcum powder. **Rendezvous Bay**, one of the island's most spectacular strands, is two miles of pure sand dunes facing the rolling hills of St. Martin. Good for long, lonely walks, the beach is studded with pretty seashells and monstrous-shaped driftwood as well as coconuts that have dropped from the palm trees that shade the strand. **Shoal Bay**, on the western tip, boasts an expansive sweep and silvery glow. The sea is full of iridescent fish who beg for snorkelers. **Savannah Beach**, rife with palms, is where you go when you are looking for unadulterated privacy. **Captain's Bay**, tucked on the island's northeast edge, offers good treks past a field of wild frangipani; from here you get an excellent view of crashing waves among the coral reefs. A climb across the karst takes you to **Windward Point** on the easternmost tip. **Limestone** is good for a snooze or quiet reading time. **Crocus or Little Bay**, home to the boat races, is best for snorkeling; here you'll find lobster, turtles and huge shoals of fishes, armies of sergeant majors, butterflyfish, iridescent blue doctorfish, grunts, squirrelfish and *wrasses*. **Cove Bay's** white strands are terribly secluded except for fishing boats. Maunday's Bay Home is home to **Cap Juluca**, the luxurious resort, and sports some of the largest seagrape trees on the island. **Sandy Ground**, on Road Bay, is a must-see village of picturesque proportions, located between the big salt pond and the island's commercial and yacht harbor on Road Bay.

Underwater

Swimming through the carcasses of downed ships provides a delightful scuba conundrum: the wrecks are dead, yet teeming with life as the sea consumes their skeletal remains. Anguilla is a decidedly low-key dive destination, happily content to sink abandoned ships off its northern coast for the delight of visitors and fish alike. Seven of these artificial reefs have been put down over the past decade—four in 1990 alone during the island's offshore clean-up campaign—allowing Anguilla to proclaim itself the "wreck dive capital of the Caribbean." The most exciting wreck activity is somewhat less deliberate: a pair of Spanish galleons were recently discovered off **Junk's Hole Bay** for which excavation is just starting for bronze religious medallions (the site is unlikely to be open to the public until 1997). Because the remaining wrecks are more recent, they are a number of years away from true encrustation but, combined with an assortment of attractive nearby reefs, Anguilla is a pleasurable dive destination. The island's waters have not suffered from overuse, and the government recently created a Marine Parks system and instituted a mooring permit policy to minimize damage to reefs. An added attraction in March are the humpback whales that navigate the straight between Windward Point and Scrub Island. Snorkeling is excellent at a number of north coast locations and on the nearby reefs; check out Frenchman's Reef and the east side of Shoal Bay, both accessible from shore.

On Foot

Being slender in shape, and only modestly endowed with gentle limestone hills, coraline Anguilla would hardly seem to boast a wealth of hiking options. Scrubby **Crocus Hill** represents the island's high-point, a mere hiccup in the Eastern Caribbean at just 213 feet above sea level, which helps keep the island's focus firmly glued on its stunning beaches. However, a topographical map from the Land and Survey Department will display some of the tracks that cross Anguilla's interior, while several offshore islands can be reached by charter boats and provide additional exploration possibilities. Although there are no companies that specialize in touring the island on foot, the Anguilla Archeological and Historical Society conduct walks (typically on Friday afternoons) and can be reached through your hotel's receptionist. Keep in mind that the island's beaches and brushy interior are scrubby and dry; bring ample water and sunscreen for any excursions.

By Pedal

Anguilla is relatively flat and the main roads can easily be explored in a relaxing day or two. For a pleasant tour of the island's more remote parts, head north out of The Valley to Island Harbor on rolling hills, then south to **Sandy Hill Bay**, an excellent rest point for a swim in the quiet cove before heading back to The Valley. It's also possible to ride from Island Harbor out to **Windward Point** on mountain bikes on the foot trail mentioned above, but watch out for stickers and carry a patch kit if you plan to do much exploring off the main roads.

What Else to See

There's not much in the way of man-made attractions on Anguilla; most of your time will be spent on or in the water, happily lazing on the powdery soft sand or swimming, snorkeling or diving in the crystal-clear waters that make the island famous.

Crocus Hill, the island's highest point at a mere 213 feet above sea level, is the site of an old prison but is mainly worth visiting for sweeping views. At Road Bay, the ocean and a large salt pond meet with stunning results.

Island Harbour is a charming little fishing village peopled by Irish descendants, while Scilly Cay, two minutes off shore, is a great place to while away the day at its small beach bar and restaurant (great lobster). Look out for the hand-made conch shell sea wall.

The Fountain on Shoal Bay East, near La Fontana Restaurant and Fountain Beach Hotel at the western end of the beach, was an important Armerindian ceremonial site some 1600 years ago. Arawak petroglyphs (rock carvings) have been found there, but the area is presently closed to the public while the Anguilla Archaeological and Historical Society conducts scientific studies of the area. At presstime no opening date had been set; call ☎ *(809) 497-4164* to check the status.

St. Martin/St. Maarten, whose lights beckon invitingly just across the sea, is a great place to spend the day shopping, dining and testing your luck in the casinos that dot the Dutch side. Frequent ferry service makes getting back and forth a breeze.

City Celebrations

Festival ★★

Various locations, the Valley.

To celebrate Emancipation Day, or "August Monday" when the slaves were freed, Anguillans throw a week-long party each year that begins the first week of August. Festivities include boat races—the island's national sport—cultural events and general acts of merriment.

Historical Sites

Wallblake House ★★★

Crossroads, the Valley, ☎ *(809) 497-2405.*

This plantation house, circa 1787, can be toured only by appointment, but even if you just get to see the outside, it's worth a look. Great tales of intrigue, murder, a French invasion and dysfunctional family history surround the place, which is now owned by the Catholic Church. While you're here, check out the newer church next door with its open-air side walls. The best time to come is Saturday mornings in the winter, when local artisans display their works on the grounds.

Tours

Sandy Island

Off the northwest coast, near Sandy Ground, The Valley, ☎ *(809) 497-5643.*

This tiny island, which measures just 650 by 160 feet, is surrounded by a living reef with depths to 10 feet. Besides the obvious snorkeling and diving possibilities, you can enjoy all kinds of watersports, including deep-sea fishing, parasailing and glass-bottom boat rides. There's also a bar and restaurant. To get there, go to Sandy Ground at the top of the hour from 10 a.m. to 3 p.m., or call them and they'll pick you up at your hotel's beach. Fun, but keep in mind that Anguilla has such gorgeous beaches it's not really necessary to travel to one. The ferry ride costs $8; bring extra money to rent watersports equipment.

Fielding Tip:

Learn the language of land directions in Anguilla, inspired by the winds. East is "up." West is "down." And both north and south are "over."

Watersports are the dominant physical activity on Anguilla (unless you count turning over every half-hour for the perfect tan). Nearly all hotels have a good watersports center; if not, check out the two centers listed below. Snorkeling and diving are excellent with intact wrecks, reef systems and walls to be explored. Chocolat Catamaran Cruises ☎ *(809) 497-3394* offers ocean excursions, as does Wildcat Services ☎ *(809) 497-2665*, which also arranges fishing trips, horseback riding and historical tours. Boat racing is the national sport and occurs during virtually every holiday and festival. The island's easterly breezes average between 10 and 20 miles per hour and are best in August, when the majority of races take place. The competing sailboats are all wooden, hoist a jib and mainsail from a single spar and range in size from 15 to 28 feet. Tennis players will have no problem finding courts at the major hotels, but duffers are out of luck, as Anguilla has no golf course.

El Rancho Del Blues

Next to Anguilla Gases on the Blowing Point main road, the Valley, ☎ *(809) 497-6164.* Hop on a horse and take a beach or trail ride through gorgeous scenery. Beach rides depart daily at 9 a.m. and 2 p.m., while trail rides leave at 11 a.m. and 4 p.m. One-hour rides cost $25; two hours go for $45. One-hour private beach rides and full-moon beach rides are also available for $45. English and Western saddles are available, as are riding lessons.

Watersports

The Valley.

Anguilla has two watersports centers that offer diving excursions. Dive Shop Anguilla (formerly Tamariain Water Sports, ☎ *(809) 497-2020*) is a full-service PADI (Professional Association of Diving Instructors) dive facility offers dives to a variety of underwater sites, as well as a course that takes beginners on one open-water dive ($80). It also offers Sunfish sailboats for rent and host water-skiing excursions. Dive prices are $40 for a one-tank dive, $70 for two, and $50 for a night dive. Also offering dive trips is Anguillan Divers *(*☎ *(809)497-4750).*

Where to Stay

Fielding's Highest Rated Hotels in Anguilla

	Hotel	Price
★★★★★	Malliouhana Beach Hotel	$240–$1240
★★★★	Cap Juluca	$275–$2085
★★★★	Cinnamon Reef Beach Club	$150–$400
★★★★	La Sirena	$100–$280
★★★★	Sonesta Beach Resort	$205–$600
★★★	Arawak Beach Resort	$75–$100
★★★	Carimar Beach Club	$130–$630
★★★	Fountain Beach	$100–$365
★★★	Mariners, The	$115–$535
★★★	Paradise Cove	$310–$425

Fielding's Most Exclusive Hotels in Anguilla

	Hotel	Price
★★★★★	Malliouhana Beach Hotel	$240–$1240
★★★	Frangipani Beach Club	$250–$1050
★★★	Carimar Beach Club	$130–$630
★★★	Pineapple Beach Club	$260–$460
★★★	Coccoloba	$225–$425

Fielding's Best Value Hotels in Anguilla

	Hotel	Price
★★★	Lloyd's Guest House	$70–$94
★★★	Arawak Beach Resort	$75–$100
★★	Inter-Island Hotel	$35–$135
★★★★	La Sirena	$100–$280
★★★	Easy Corner Villas	$90–$295

ANGUILLA

Anguilla is almost as famous for its posh resorts as it is for its beaches. Expect to pay top dollar at these tony establishments—but know, at least, that you will get what you pay for. Service is professional, accommodations are splendidly decorated and every extra little amenity is usually on hand. The damage that resulted from hurricanes Luis and Marilyn in 1995 mean all properties have undergone extensive renovations, so everything is in great condition.

Anguilla is not generally associated with low-cost lodging, but there are a few choices for the budget traveler. Lloyd's Guest House is clean and sweet, while the Inter-Island Hotel, a simple guest house, also offers bargain rates. Note, however, that in both cases you'll sacrifice an on-beach location.

If you're not planning on renting a car, consider staying in Sandy Ground, Shoal Bay or Harbour Island, where restaurants and shops are within walking distance.

Hotels and Resorts

Paradise Cove, Anguilla's newest luxury property, located in the cove on the western end of the island, is sporting a new restaurant for breakfast and light meals, and an expanded children's playground, making the 14 fully furnished suites fully adaptable for families. La Sirena Hotel, overlooking Meads Bay, has added a fifth villa—three-bedrooms that can comfortably accommodate six adults or a large family. New athletic and entertainment facilities have been added to Cap Jaluca, and a 32-foot speedboat is available for excursions. A putting green on the southern shore of Maundays Bay Lagoon was installed as was an English-regulation croquet court.

Arawak Beach Resort   **$75–$100**   ★★★

P.O. Box 98, the Valley, Road Bay, ☎ *(800) 553-4939, (809) 497-4888. FAX (809) 497-4898.*
Single: $75–$100. Double: $75–$100.
Located on the site of an ancient Arawak Indian village, this newer resort consists of two-story villas furnished with Amerindian replicas. Lots of interesting touches here: a small museum exhibits artifacts found on the site; the courtyard is planted with traditional island crops like cotton and papaya; and the watersports include canoe rentals. Accommodations consist of standard guestrooms, junior suites with a kitchenette and split-level, one-bedroom suites complete with kitchen and two balconies. There's no air conditioning, but sea breezes usually do the job. No smoking throughout, and though you can bring your own, no liquor is served. 14 rooms.
Credit cards: A, MC, V.

Cap Jaluca   **$275–$2085**   ★★★★

Road Bay, ☎ *(800) 323-0139, (809) 497-6666. FAX (809) 497-6617.*
Single: $275–$2085. Double: $275–$2085.
It doesn't get much better than here at Cap Jaluca, the epitome of resort living at its swankest. Guestrooms, housed in whitewashed villas, are exquisitely decorated and boast giant walk-in closets, walnut louvered doors and windows and huge patios. They come in four categories, and some even include solariums, roof terraces

and private pools. Breakfast is served by two maids; when you return from dinner, you'll find they left flickering candles when they turned down the beds. The imaginatively landscaped grounds include scenic lagoons, two restaurants, three tennis courts with a resident pro, a fitness center, media room and the gorgeous beach. There's entertainment four nights a week. If you're dying to watch TV or a video, they'll install one for $20 per day, which seems a bit expensive considering the high rates. Still, the well-heeled guests here aren't worried about being nickled and dimed. This resort is more laid-back and casual than its chief competitor, Malliouhana. No kids under six. 91 rooms. Credit cards: A, MC, V.

Cinnamon Reef Beach Club $150–$400   ★ ★ ★ ★

Road Bay, ☎ *(800) 223-1108, (809) 497-2727. FAX (809) 497-3727.*
Single: $150–$400. Double: $150–$400.

Pleasantly informal is the atmosphere at this intimate 40-acre resort, long heralded for its unpretentious luxury. Accommodations are in whitewashed villas set on the beach or perched on a bluff; each has living and dining rooms, a raised bedroom, patio complete with hammock, and tiled sunken showers (no baths). For recreation, there's a huge pool (40 by 60 feet), three tennis courts and all kinds of complimentary watersports. Located on Anguilla's southern coast, this excellent resort's only downfall is its relatively small beach, though its calm waters make for great windsurfing. Rooms include a continental breakfast. 22 rooms. Credit cards: A, MC, V.

Coccoloba $225–$425   ★ ★ ★

Road Bay, ☎ *(800) 982-7729, (809) 497-6871. FAX (809) 497-6332.*
Single: $225–$425. Double: $225–$425.

A true tropical hideaway, chic Coccoloba is nestled on a rocky headland between two picture-perfect beaches. Most guest rooms are in cottages on a bluff above the beach, though seven units are housed in a beachside villa. All have sea views, but some are better than others. Each room is done in traditional West Indian decor, with bright Caribbean colors, marble baths and individual, though not secluded, patios. All watersports are free, and extras such as complimentary soft drinks on the beach and high tea daily keep you pampered. 51 rooms. Credit cards: A, MC, V.

Frangipani Beach Club $250–$1050   ★ ★ ★

Road Bay, ☎ *(800) 892-4564, (809) 497-6442. FAX (809) 497-6440.*
Single: $250–$1050. Double: $250–$1050.

This newer enclave of Spanish-style pink stucco and red-tile roof villas offers one- to three-bedroom suites on gorgeous Meads Bay Beach. All units have air conditioning, full kitchens, natural rattan furnishings and a patio or balcony; some boast Jacuzzis as well. The on-site restaurant is open for breakfast, lunch and dinner daily. Watersports cost extra. 21 rooms. Credit cards: A.

Malliouhana Beach Hotel $240–$1240   ★ ★ ★ ★ ★

Road Bay, ☎ *(800) 835-0796, (809) 497-6111. FAX (809) 497-6011.*
Single: $240–$810. Double: $240–$1240.

Every little detail is in place at this impeccable resort, set atop a hill overlooking two beaches. Just perusing the lovely Indian and Haitian artwork in the lobby is a treat in itself. Rooms are spacious and nicely decorated with high-quality rattan furniture,

Haitian art, marble baths with oversized tubs and patios or balconies. A new three-unit villa, called "Bougainvullea," contains a one-bedroom, two-bath suite with a private pool and two suites with private Jacuzzis. There are four tennis courts, three pools, complimentary watersports (you'll pay extra for windsurfing and water-skiing lessons) and an open-air exercise pavilion with lovely ocean views to keep you motivated. Mellow live music is offered each night during the winter (and three times a week in the summer), and parents can leave the little ones in free supervised programs. You'll pay $25 extra per day for a TV and VCR. But gorgeous as this spot is—and it is lovely—the staff can be a bit cool, and the overall atmosphere a bit snooty and reserved. 56 rooms.

Mariners, The   **$115–$535**   ★ ★ ★

Road Bay, ☎ *(800) 848-7938, (809) 497-2671. FAX (809) 497-2901.*
Single: $115–$190. Double: $115–$535.
A true West Indian-style resort, complete with gingerbread cottages and hand-crafted lattice. Accommodations have pitched ceilings, Haitian wicker furniture painted in pastels, and modest bathrooms. The nicer cottages boast living rooms and well-equipped kitchenettes. Be warned that not all units have air conditioning. This all-inclusive resort is situated at the far end of Anguilla's busiest beach, near a deepwater port. True couch potatoes can rent a TV and VCR for an added fee. Service is friendly but sometimes lacking. 25 rooms. Credit cards: A, D, MC, V.

Pineapple Beach Club   **$260–$460**   ★ ★ ★

Road Bay, ☎ *(800) 345-0356, (809) 497-6061. FAX (809) 497-6344.*
Single: $260–$360. Double: $350–$460.
A solid choice for those watching their pocketbooks, this cozy, all-inclusive resort is set on Anguilla's southernmost tip. Connected one-story bungalows set around a central courtyard open to a beautiful beach and have a distinctive West Indian style, with wide verandas, trellises and whimsical gingerbread trim. Rooms are spacious and nicely though sparsely done in mahogany furnishings, hand-crafted linens, ceiling fans and air conditioning. Formerly the Anguilla Great House, this pleasant spot offers complimentary watersports, great dining and lots of resident bunnies and turtles. There are many more luxurious resorts on the island, but this spot has its own very lovely charm and a wonderfully friendly staff. Highly recommended! 27 rooms. Credit cards: A, D, MC, V.

Rendezvous Bay Hotel   **$90–$240**   ★ ★

Road Bay, ☎ *(800) 274-4893, (809) 497-6549. FAX (809) 497-6026.*
Single: $90–$240. Double: $90–$240.
Set among 60 acres of coconut trees, this is the island's first resort, and though it draws a lot of repeat customers, it does show its age. Not a bad choice for the price, though, with the lovely beach making up for a lack of amenities—-no pool, for example. The original rooms are simple and lack air conditioning, while the newer villas have spacious one-bedroom suites and air; some also have kitchenettes. There are two lighted tennis courts, a game and TV room and, best of all, an elaborate electric train setup in the lounge. Decent value, and pleasantly informal. 47 rooms. Credit cards: D, MC, V.

Sonesta Beach Resort   **$205–$600**   ★★★★

Road Bay, ☎ *(800) 231-1945, (809) 497-6999. FAX (809) 497-6899.*
Single: $205–$475. Double: $255–$600.

This Moorish-influenced, pink and green resort is a rather incongruous sight on this laid-back island, but if you like pizazz, the Sonesta (formerly Casablanca) delivers. The $20-million, 200-acre resort boasts three miles of beach, two lit tennis courts, a 1200-square-foot pool, games room, library, three restaurants, gymnasium and such special touches as hand-carved and hand-painted mosaics created by Moroccan artisans. Beach wing rooms have the best views, but the garden rooms are bigger and have more luxurious baths. All are simply gorgeous with Moroccan rugs, lovely fabrics, stenciled accents on the walls and small marble baths. The rates include watersports (they have only non-motorized toys), breakfast, free tennis lessons from the pro who visits each week, and such pampering touches as fresh fruit four times each day on the beach. All-inclusive packages are also available. By far Anguilla's glitziest resort, and quite nice at that. No kids under 16. 100 rooms. Credit cards: A, MC, V.

Apartments and Condominiums

Independent-minded folks with time on their hands will enjoy the villa life in Anguilla, though there are drawbacks. Some staples might need to be bought in neighboring St. Martin/Sint Maarten. In general, prices will be much higher than at home. Check yearly for new listings since new properties are always being built. **Anguilla Connections** *(☎ [809] 497-4403)* specializes in villa rentals.

Carimar Beach Club   **$130–$630**   ★★★

Road Bay, ☎ *(800) 235-8667, (809) 497-6881. FAX (809) 497-6071.*
Single: $130–$630. Double: $250–$630.

These comfortable one-, two- and three-bedroom apartments are owned as condominiums and rented out when the owners aren't using them. The villas are Mediterranean style and nicely done with wicker and rattan furniture, TVs, full kitchens, large living rooms, dining areas and balconies or patios. Most offer only partial views of the magnificent beach. The tropical grounds include two tennis courts but no pool. There's no restaurant or bar on site, but the complex is within walking distance of Malliouhana and Coccoloba. 23 rooms. Credit cards: A, MC, V.

Cove Castles Villa Resort   **$350–$990**   ★★★

Road Bay, ☎ *(800) 348-4716, (809) 497-6801. FAX (809) 497-6051.*
Single: $350–$590. Double: $350–$990.

This ultra-modern apartment resort may take some getting used to at first, with its futuristic white structures a somewhat jarring site. Accommodations are in eight 2 bedroom beach houses and four 3 bedroom villas. All have two baths, cable TV, a well-stocked and very modern kitchen, living and dining rooms, skylights, nice furnishings and a covered beachfront veranda. There's a restaurant and bar on the premises, and unlike other apartment complexes, limited room service. The beach is fantastic. 12 rooms. Credit cards: A.

Easy Corner Villas   **$90–$295**   ★★★

Road Bay, ☎ *(800) 223-9815, (809) 497-6433. FAX (809) 497-6410.*

Single: $90–$295. Double: $90–$295.

Families are prevalent at this complex of one- to three-bedroom apartments with combination living and dining areas, full kitchens and a patio; only three are air-conditioned. A restaurant and coffee shop are located on-site, and daily maid service is available for an extra fee. Located on a bluff overlooking Road Bay, this simple spot represents good value for the price. 15 rooms. Credit cards: A, D, MC, V.

La Sirena   **$100–$280**   ★★★★

Road Bay, ☎ (800) 331-9358, (809) 497-6827. FAX (809) 497-6827.
Single: $100–$160. Double: $1200.

Accommodations at this pleasant property are in two- and three-bedroom apartments in Mediterranean-style white stucco buildings. Units are nicely done with rattan furnishings, ceiling fans and Caribbean pastels. There are two pools on-site, plus a formal restaurant and a casual poolside cafe. The beach is a two-minute walk. Not the most exciting place around, but good value for the rates. 24 rooms. Credit cards: A, MC, V.

Paradise Cove   **$310–$425**   ★★★

P.O. Box 135, The Cove, ☎ (800) 728-0784, (809) 497-3559. FAX (809) 497-2149.
Single: $310–$425. Double: $425.

An intimate and romantic hideaway nestled among palm trees and lush tropical gardens just a five-minute walk from beautiful Cove Beach. Centrally air-conditioned one- and two-bedroom units are quite spacious elegantly furnished and include fully equipped kitchens, telephones, private laundry facilities, huge bathrooms, cable TV, high-beamed ceilings and two large balconies. This is one of Anguilla's few locally owned properties, and it's a real winner, despite its slightly off the beach locale. The grounds include a barbecue area, a large but plain pool, two Jacuzzis, a restaurant that serves breakfast and lunch and a playground for the kids. Request an end unit for more privacy. Watersports await at nearby beaches. Very, very fine—it's especially neat that you can hire a private cook in the evenings for just $5 an hour (plus ingredients). Indulge! A seven-night package costs $1315-$2400 for a one-bedroom suite, $1840-$3205 for two bedrooms, and includes a rental car for the week. 14 rooms. Credit cards: A, MC, V.

Sea Grape Beach Club Villas   **$180–$450**   ★★

Road Bay, ☎ (800) 223-9815, (809) 497-6433. FAX (809) 497-6410.
Single: $180–$450. Double: $280–$450.

These modern two-bedroom condominiums are very nicely appointed; each has three bathrooms, ultra-large closets and private decks with sweeping ocean views. They're especially suited for those who like to spread out —- each unit encompasses some 2000 square feet. The grounds include a restaurant, bar, watersports (for a fee) and two tennis courts. 10 rooms. Credit cards: A, MC, V.

Shoal Bay Villas   **$147–$385**   ★★★

P.O. Box 81, North Coast, Road Bay, ☎ (800) 722-7045, (809) 497-2051. FAX (809) 497-3631.
Single: $147–$385. Double: $147–$385.

Contemporary villa-style condominiums located on the beach west of Island Harbour. The one- and two-bedroom units have kitchenettes and painted rattan furniture, but no air conditioning. The palm-studded beach is a tropical dream, and there's a restaurant and bar on-site with occasional live music. No children in the winter. 13 rooms. Credit cards: A, D, MC, V.

Inns

The lifestyle is breezier and more casual at Anguilla's handful of inns; management is often more attentive. Travelers young in spirit and weak on wallet should also check out the small properties in "Budget Bunks."

Ferryboat Inn $70–$225   ★ ★

Road Bay, ☎ (809) 497-6613. FAX (809) 497-6713.
Single: $70–$125. Double: $85–$225.
This family-owned and operated inn, near the ferry dock and beach, is a solid choice for those on a budget. Accommodations are comfortable and simple, consisting of one- and two-bedroom suites that are not air conditioned and a two-bedroom beach house that is; all have full kitchens. There's a bar and restaurant on-site, and the views at night of neighboring St. Martin are enchanting. 7 rooms. Credit cards: A, MC, V.

Fountain Beach $100–$365   ★ ★ ★

Road Bay, ☎ (800) 523-7505, (809) 497-3491. FAX (809) 497-3493.
Single: $100–$280. Double: $285–$365.
Set on a scrumptious beach along the rural north coast, this secluded resort appeals to those who like privacy. Accommodations are in oversized studios and one- and two-bedroom suites with Caribbean antique artwork, colorful rattan and wicker furniture, large marble baths and full kitchens. The grounds include two tennis courts and a pool. Decent digs for the rates. 10 rooms. Credit cards: A, D, MC, V.

Inter-Island Hotel $35–$135   ★ ★

Lower South Hill, Road Bay, ☎ (809) 497-6259. FAX (809) 497-5381.
Single: $35–$40. Double: $55–$135.
This small villa-style guest house, located near Sandy Ground, is a quarter-mile from the beach, but at these rates, who's complaining? Rooms are simple but very clean and comfortable with ceiling fans (no air conditioning) and tiny bathrooms; one- and two-bedroom suites are also available. Not much in the way of amenities, but an excellent choice for those who really can't afford Anguilla to begin with. 14 rooms. Credit cards: A, V.

Low Cost Lodging

You'll find best bargains on lodging anytime during low season (mid-April to December). During high season, the cheapest small hotel will bed two (no meals) for about $50, but you're risking seediness. In this very low-cost range, you'll find either cotlike beds and shared bathrooms in guest houses, or basic furnishings in no-atmosphere edifices. Don't even think about being near a beach.

Lloyd's Guest House $70–$94   ★ ★ ★

Crocus Hill, The Valley, ☎ (809) 497-2351. FAX (809) 497-3028.
Single: $70. Double: $94.
The only drawback to Lloyd's, which has been operational since 1959, is that the beach is a mile and a quarter away. You can walk it in five minutes or so, but it's

down a STEEP hill, so leave some energy for the return trip. Besides that, all is fine at this family-run guest house, where the rooms are small but sweet and very clean and accented with pretty fabrics, private baths and fans (no air conditioning). The rates include breakfast. 11 rooms.

Where to Eat

Fielding's Highest Rated Restaurants in Anguilla

Rating	Restaurant	Price
★★★★★	Pimms	$20–$35
★★★★	Hibernia	$20–$30
★★★★	Malliouhana Hotel Restaurant	$30–$40
★★★★	Palm Court	$20–$26
★★★★	Scilly Cay	
★★★	Barrel's Stay	$8–$30
★★★	Koal Keel	$20–$30
★★★	Mango's	$20–$35
★★★	Old House	$16–$20
★★★	Paradise Cafe	$10–$27

Fielding's Most Exclusive Restaurants in Anguilla

Rating	Restaurant	Price
★★★★	Malliouhana Hotel Restaurant	$30–$40
★★★	Mango's	$20–$35
★★★★★	Pimms	$20–$35
★★★★	Hibernia	$20–$30
★★★	Koal Keel	$20–$30

Fielding's Best Value Restaurants in Anguilla

Rating	Restaurant	Price
★★★★★	Pimms	$20–$35
★★★	Ferryboat Inn	$7–$26
★★★★	Palm Court	$20–$26
★★★	Old House	$16–$20
★★★★	Hibernia	$20–$30

ANGUILLA

Those with enough money for an Anguillian vacation demand the best, and they'll find it in the island's varied restaurants. Seafood is the mainstay, and you can count on fresh lobster, crayfish, red snapper, whelk and conch. Gorgeous Scilly Cay is known for its fresh lobster caught daily, while the Palm Court Restaurant in Cinnamon Reef Resort is renowned for its imaginatively prepared, creative dishes. You'll also find a good choice of restaurants offering gourmet French cuisine, Caribbean fare, even Italian and Asian. After dinner, check out Anguilla's new nightclub, Mirrors, on Upper South Hill (☎ *[809] 497-5522)*, or the Pump House (☎ *[809] 497-5154)* in Sandy Ground, an English-style pub in a former salt factory that's something of a mini-museum of Anguilla's salt industry.

Arlo's Place $ ★★★

South Hill, ☎ *(809) 497-6810.*
Italian cuisine. Closed: Sun.
This trattoria draws a local crowd hungry for authentic Italian cuisine such as homemade lasagna and fettuccini in a lobster tomato sauce, as well as tasty pizzas. Set right on the beach with great sunset views. Credit cards: MC, V.

Dunes, The $ ★★★

Near Pineapple Beach Club, Rendezvous Bay, ☎ *(809) 497-6699.*
International cuisine.
Lunch: 12:30-4 p.m., entrées $5–$10.
First of all, you'll need a four-wheel drive, or at least a sturdy rental car, to get to this unique spot on the beach. As they say, "follow the funky signs from the Pineapple Beach Club turnoff," and don't give up as you bump and grind down a dirt path that barely deserves to be called a road. It's worth it once you get here. The Dunes is owned and run by Bankie Banx, a talented reggae musician who is recently getting a lot of deserved recognition. Lunch is a casual affair—just the basics—but the setting on a wind-swept beach is fantastic. The best time to come, however, is the open-mike Friday and Sunday nights, when Bankie and friends let the music rip.

Barrel's Stay $$$ ★★★

Road Bay, Road Bay, ☎ *(809) 497-2831.*
French cuisine.
Lunch: 11 a.m.–3 p.m., entrées $8–$30.
Dinner: 6:30 p.m.–9:30 p.m., entrées $8–$30.
The name becomes obvious when you see this spot fashioned from old rum barrels and disassembled barrel stays. Tasty seafood and meat entrées dressed in creative sauces are served outside on a terrace. Some say the food is overpriced, but the French wines are reasonable. Credit cards: A, MC, V.

Ferryboat Inn $$$ ★★★

Cul de Sac Road, Road Bay, ☎ *(809) 497-6613.*
Latin American cuisine.
Lunch: Noon–2:30 p.m., entrées $7–$26.
Dinner: 7–10 p.m., entrées $7–$26.
Set on the beach near the Blowing Point Ferry Pier, this *très* romantic spot specializes in French/Caribbean dishes. Wonderful soups such as French onion and black

bean; lobster thermidor is the house favorite. The Ferryboat is especially inviting at night, with the flickering lights of St. Martin weaving an enchanting spell. Credit cards: A, MC, V.

Hibernia $$$ ★ ★ ★ ★

Island Harbour, Road Bay, ☎ *(809) 497-4290.*
Seafood cuisine.
Lunch: Noon–2 p.m., entrées $17–$30.
Dinner: 7–9 p.m., entrées $20–$30. Closed: Mon.
There are just 10 tables at this lovely spot, set in a West Indian-style cottage with a wide porch, on the island's northeast corner. Specialties include grilled and smoked seafood, creatively enhanced with fresh local ingredients. Hibernia whips up its own breads and ice cream daily. Closed September and October. Credit cards: A, MC, V.

Koal Keel $$$ ★ ★ ★

The Valley, Road Bay, ☎ *(809) 497-2930.*
Lunch: Noon–2:30 p.m., entrées $8–$28.
Dinner: 7–10:30 p.m., entrées $20–$30.
This lovely spot is situated in a beautifully restored plantation great house from the 18th century, with service as gracious as the surroundings. Especially fanciful is the bed, all dressed up in white lace, sitting smack in the middle of the courtyard. The cuisine is based on foods abundant in Anguilla: fresh fish, coconut, corn, pigeon peas, potatoes, mangoes, sugars, limes and native herbs and seasonings. Fresh breads and roast meats are prepared in a large rock oven, and the lobster crepes are to die for. The new wine cellar, located 17 feet below sea level, has a capacity for 25,000 bottles, so you're sure to find something tasty. The restaurant hosts daily wine tastings and tours of the grounds; after dinner, you can sample more than 30 rums in a complimentary tasting. A neat spot to try "EuroCaribe" cuisine. Reservations required. Credit cards: A, MC, V.

Lucy's Harbour View $$$ ★ ★ ★

South Hill, Road Bay, ☎ *(809) 497-6253.*
Latin American cuisine.
Lunch: 11:30 a.m.–3:30 p.m., entrées $8–$16.
Dinner: 7–10 p.m., entrées $15–$30. Closed: Sun.
Like the name implies, diners enjoy wonderful views from this casual cafe set high on a steep hill overlooking Sandy Ground. The menu focuses on fresh vegetables and lobster and fish dishes. Whole red snapper and pumpkin soup are house specialties. Credit cards: A, MC, V.

Malliouhana Hotel Restaurant $$$ ★ ★ ★ ★

Meads Bay, Road Bay, ☎ *(809) 497-6111.*
French cuisine.
Lunch: 12:30–3:30 p.m., entrées $11–$30.
Dinner: 7 p.m.–10:30 p.m., entrées $30–$40.
Set in an open-air pavilion on a rocky promontory overlooking the sea, the feel here is wonderfully elegant, with gracious service, fine china and crystal and gourmet goodies. Famed French chef Michel Rostang created the menu and occasionally whips up the dishes himself. It'd be easy to make an entire meal of the imaginative

hors d'oeuvres, but save room for the catch of the day. The wine cellar stocks some 25,000 bottles, most priced in the $25–$35 range. Credit cards: A, MC, V.

Mango's $$$ ★★★

Barnes Bay, Road Bay, ☎ *(809) 497-6491.*
American cuisine.
Dinner: 6:30– 9 p.m., entrées $20–$35. Closed: Tue.
Make reservations far in advance to get into this hot spot, which has two seatings for dinner, at 6:30 and 8:30. It uses the freshest ingredients, grill-cooks meat and fish, offers up some tasty vegetarian selections, makes its own bread, desserts and ice cream daily—and best of all, does it all with an absolute minimum of calories. You'd never know by the taste that you're actually eating healthful food! Credit cards: A, MC, V.

Old House $$$ ★★★

George Hill, Road Bay, ☎ *(809) 497-2228.*
Caribbean cuisine.
Lunch: Noon–5 p.m., entrées $5–$12.
Dinner: 6–11 p.m., entrées $16–$20.
Yes, this eatery really is situated in an old house, set on a hill near the airport. The decor is simple but the food's just fine. West Indian specialties include conch, local lamb, curry goat and Anguillan pot fish; the fruit pancakes keep the locals coming. It's nice to sit on the porch and watch the planes come and go. Also open for good, cheap breakfasts from 7-11:30 a.m. Credit cards: A, MC, V.

Palm Court $$$ ★★★★

Cinnamon Reef Resort, Road Bay, ☎ *(809) 497-2727.*
Latin American cuisine.
Lunch: Noon–2:30 p.m., entrées $12–$18.
Dinner: 7–9:30 p.m., entrées $20–$26.
Haitian furniture, colorful murals and huge picture windows overlooking the sea make this place special. The nouvelle Caribbean food is good, too, with items such as grouper encased in toasted pumpkin seeds or banana rum sauce. Lunch is more casual, with good salads, soups and sandwiches. Save room for the mango puffs in caramel sauce. Credit cards: A, MC, V.

Paradise Cafe $$$ ★★★

Shoal Bay West, Road Bay, ☎ *(809) 497-6010.*
Indian cuisine.
Lunch: Noon–2:30 p.m., entrées $8–$14.
Dinner: 7–9:30 p.m., entrées $10–$27.
Ocean breezes set many windchimes tinkling, a nice backdrop to tasty dishes with unique French and Asian influences. Try the West Indian bouillabaisse, individual pizzas or the catch of the day. Reservations are suggested; for better or worse, the rich and famous have discovered this spot. Closed in September. Credit cards: A, MC, V.

Pimms $$$ ★★★★★

Cap Juluca Hotel, Road Bay, ☎ *(809) 497-6666.*
French cuisine.
Dinner: 7–10 p.m., entrées $20–$35.
One of the finest restaurants in all the Caribbean, located in the wonderful resort of Cap Juluca. Candlelit tables overlook the gorgeous beach, and the continental-style

cuisine, spiced with West Indian accents, is fabulous. Try the local lobster or grouper. Dress up for this spot, and don't even think about getting in without reservations. Credit cards: A, MC, V.

Riviera Bar & Restaurant   **$$$**   ★ ★

Road Bay, Road Bay, ☎ *(809) 497-2833.*
French cuisine.
Lunch: 11 a.m.– 3 p.m., entrées $6–$16.
Dinner: 6– 9:30 p.m., entrées $20–$35.
This bistro on the beach compliments its French and Creole dishes with distinctive Asian accents—oysters sauteed in sake and soy sauce, for instance. There's occasional live music at this casual site, and the daily happy hour, 6–7 p.m., is happening. Credit cards: A, D, MC, V.

Roy's   **$$$**   ★ ★ ★

Crocus Bay, Road Bay, ☎ *(809) 497-2470.*
English cuisine.
Lunch: Noon–2 p.m., entrées $4–$16.
Dinner: 6–9 p.m., entrées $14–$30. Closed: Mon.
Two British expatriots set up this little slice of their home land, and they got it right, all the way down to the English beers (thankfully served cold) and dartboard. Dine al fresco on the veranda, with nice sea views, on fish and chips and Caribbean favorites such as barbecued chicken and lobster Creole. Credit cards: MC, V.

Scilly Cay   **$**   ★ ★ ★ ★

Just off the coast from Island Harbour, ☎ *(809) 497-5123.*
Closed: Mon.
Wonderful (but extremely expensive) fresh lobster, crayfish and marinated chicken are the reasons to hop the free ferry for the short ride over to this picture-perfect island. Live music varies—on Wednesdays, it's romantic ballads, Fridays steel pans and Sundays reggae. After lunch, you can stroll the gardens, snorkel (bring your own equipment) or just laze on one of the complimentary lounge chairs.

Where to Shop

Shops are almost as rare on Anguilla as rainfall; if you're really looking to hit the stores, head for St. Martin right across the water (a 20- to 30-minute ferry ride). Otherwise, you'll find some goods in the upscale shops at the major hotels. For fashions, try **Caribbean Fancy** (*George Hill,* ☎ *[809] 497-3133*) and the **Riviera** (*Sandy Ground,* ☎ *[809] 497-2833*), where they also have a good selection of wine.

Perhaps the best local wares to shop for are original artworks as the island is home to a small but thriving art colony. **Lucia Butler** (☎ *[808] 497-4259*) paints scenes of village life and wooden house plaques. **Marj Morani** (☎ *[809]*

497-4259) specializes in hand-thrown pottery and tiles and or **Anne Saunders** *(☎ [809] 497-4087)* offers her hand-crafted fabrics, murals, paintings and sculptures. **Devonish Art Gallery** *(George Hill, ☎ [809] 497-2949)* showcases many local artists, including Lynne Bernbaum, a watercolorist who depicts island life, and Courtney Devonish, a sculptor and potter who owns the studio.

Anguilla Directory

Arrival and Departure

American Airlines offers direct service from the United States to San Juan, Puerto Rico, where you can change to American Eagle for the one-hour hop to Anguilla. There are two American Eagle flights daily. You can also fly American or Continental to Dutch Sint Maarten's Juliana Airport, where connections to Anguilla can be found on WINAIR or LIAT. For about the same fee ($25 one way), Anguilla's own **Tyden Air** *(☎ [800] 842-0261 or [809] 497-2719)* makes the five-minute flight offering "Immediate Pickup" service that saves passengers baggage handling, all check-in procedures and waiting. During high season (mid-December to mid-April), the Sint Maarten/Anguilla fare on Tyden is raised to $45, due to the chaos at Juliana, but the return trip remains $25. You can also take a taxi from Juliana Airport to Marigot on the French side (about $10) and catch one of the Anguilla power boats ($10) departing every 30–40 minutes for the 15-minute ride. If returning by boat with a lot of luggage, ask the French immigration officials in Marigot to call you a cab; the taxi stand is a 10-minute walk away. Note that in the evening there are only two ferry rides.

The **Link Ferry** *(☎ [809] 497-2231)* offers the fastest ferry ride from Anguilla to St. Martin.

Upon leaving the island by air, all travelers are charged a $6 departure tax.

Business Hours

Stores open Monday–Saturday 8 a.m.–5 p.m. or 6 p.m. A few open on Sundays. Banks open 8 a.m.–3 p.m. Monday–Thursday and until 5 p.m. Friday.

Climate

Anguilla has one of the driest climates in the region—a bane to farmers, but a boon to tourists. As a result, vegetation is short and sparse, with few palm trees. With the lowest average annual rainfall in the Leeward Islands, Anguilla receives only 30-45 inches annually. Hurricane season is intense.

Current

Most outlets are 110 AC, as in the U.S.

Documents

Visitors must show ID with a photo, preferably a passport, and an ongoing ticket. Departure tax is $6 at the airport and $2 at the ferry port.

Getting Around

You'll need a car or open-air jeep called a mini-moke to visit more than one beach; hitchhiking is safe and accepted. Taxis are readily available at both Wallblake Airport and Blowing Point dock. You won't find any rental car agencies there; a taxi can deliver you there. Good local agencies are **Triple K** (representing Hertz), ☎ *(809) 497-2934*; **Maurice Connors** ☎ *(809) 497-6410*; and **Roy Rogers Rental,** ☎ *(809) 497-6290*, FAX *(809) 497-3345*. Note well that driving is on the left and you must obtain a local driver's license from your rental agency. If you're game to cycle, try **Boo's Cycle Rental**.

The island bus service begins from a roadside stop a few steps from the pier at Blowing Point.

Language

The official language is English spoken with a West Indian lilt.

Medical Emergencies

For serious problems, head for a hospital in Puerto Rico. The small hospital at Crocus Bay is usually overflowing with natives.

Money

Official currency is the Eastern Caribbean dollar (EC), usually marked by "$" sign in stores and restaurants. Before you shell out any dough, however, make sure the price is not referring to American dollars. Traveler's checks, personal checks (sometimes, with picture ID) and American dollars are also readily accepted.

Telephone

From North America to Anguilla, dial *809* (area code) + *497* (country code) + local number (4 digits). Faxes are widely used by hotels and other businesses. To save money when calling home from Anguilla, go to the Cable & Wireless office and buy a phone card. Before leaving home, check with your own telephone service to see how you can most cheaply call home using your own special card.

Time

Anguilla is on Atlantic standard time, one hour ahead of Eastern standard time in winter (that means 1 p.m. in New York, 2 p.m. in Anguilla). During the summer, it's the same time.

Tipping and Taxes

Service charges (10–15 percent) and an 8 percent government tax are usually included in hotel bills; 10 percent on all food and beverage tabs. Some establishments charge a fee for credit cards. Waiters and waitresses appreciate tips, but don't expect any. If a young boy carries your bag at the airport, one dollar per bag will put a smile on his face. More often, your taxi driver will tote them.

Tourist Information

Contact the **Anguilla Tourist Office** ☎ *(800) 553-4939*. Before you go, you can get an updated list of rates for accommodations and a map. Better maps are available in local stores.

ANGUILLA

When to Go

The Miller Genuine Draft Moonsplash Tour in January is a well-attended music festival. Anguilla Day is celebrated by a huge boat race on May 30. The Queen's Birthday is feted by celebrations in the month of June. The Anguilla National Summer Festival takes place on Aug. 4–12. The Christmas Fair at the Governor's Residence occurs in December. On holidays and during Carnival, the whole island turns out to bet on spectacular boat races. Carnival itself, in the month of August, is celebrated with early morning dancing, beachside barbecues and special pageants.

ANGUILLA HOTELS		RMS	RATES	PHONE	CR. CARDS
Road Bay					
★★★★★	Malliouhana Beach Hotel	56	$240–$1240	(800) 835-0796	
★★★★	Cap Juluca	91	$275–$2085	(800) 323-0139	A, MC, V
★★★★	Cinnamon Reef Beach Club	22	$150–$400	(800) 223-1108	A, MC, V
★★★★	La Sirena	24	$100–$280	(800) 331-9358	A, MC, V
★★★★	Sonesta Beach Resort	100	$205–$600	(800) 231-1945	A, MC, V
★★★	Arawak Beach Resort	14	$75–$100	(800) 553-4939	A, MC, V
★★★	Carimar Beach Club	23	$130–$630	(800) 235-8667	A, MC, V
★★★	Coccoloba	51	$225–$425	(800) 982-7729	A, MC, V
★★★	Cove Castles Villa Resort	12	$350–$990	(800) 348-4716	A
★★★	Easy Corner Villas	15	$90–$295	(800) 223-9815	A, D, MC, V
★★★	Fountain Beach	10	$100–$365	(800) 523-7505	A, D, MC, V
★★★	Frangipani Beach Club	21	$250–$1050	(800) 892-4564	A
★★★	Mariners, The	25	$115–$535	(800) 848-7938	A, D, MC, V
★★★	Pineapple Beach Club	27	$260–$460	(800) 345-0356	A, D, MC, V
★★★	Shoal Bay Villas	13	$147–$385	(800) 722-7045	A, D, MC, V
★★	Ferryboat Inn	7	$70–$225	(809) 497-6613	A, MC, V
★★	Inter-Island Hotel	14	$35–$135	(809) 497-6259	A, V
★★	Rendezvous Bay Hotel	47	$90–$240	(800) 274-4893	D, MC, V
★★	Sea Grape Beach Club Villas	10	$180–$450	(800) 223-9815	A, MC, V
The Cove					
★★★	Paradise Cove	14	$310–$425	(800) 728-0784	A, MC, V
The Valley					
★★★	Lloyd's Guest House	11	$70–$94	(809) 497-2351	

ANGUILLA RESTAURANTS   PHONE   ENTRÉE   CR. CARDS

Rendezvous Bay

	PHONE	ENTRÉE	CR. CARDS
★★★ Dunes, The	(809) 497-6699	$5–$10	

Road Bay

American

	PHONE	ENTRÉE	CR. CARDS
★★★ Mango's	(809) 497-6491	$20–$35	A, MC, V

Caribbean

	PHONE	ENTRÉE	CR. CARDS
★★★ Koal Keel	(809) 497-2930	$8–$30	A, MC, V
★★★ Old House	(809) 497-2228	$5–$20	A, MC, V

English

	PHONE	ENTRÉE	CR. CARDS
★★★ Roy's	(809) 497-2470	$4–$30	MC, V

French

	PHONE	ENTRÉE	CR. CARDS
★★★★★ Pimms	(809) 497-6666	$20–$35	A, MC, V
★★★★ Malliouhana Hotel Restaurant	(809) 497-6111	$11–$40	A, MC, V
★★★ Barrel's Stay	(809) 497-2831	$8–$30	A, MC, V
★★ Riviera Bar & Restaurant	(809) 497-2833	$6–$35	A, D, MC, V

Indian

	PHONE	ENTRÉE	CR. CARDS
★★★ Paradise Cafe	(809) 497-6010	$8–$27	A, MC, V

Latin American

	PHONE	ENTRÉE	CR. CARDS
★★★★ Palm Court	(809) 497-2727	$12–$26	A, MC, V
★★★ Ferryboat Inn	(809) 497-6613	$7–$26	A, MC, V
★★★ Lucy's Harbour View	(809) 497-6253	$8–$30	A, MC, V

Seafood

	PHONE	ENTRÉE	CR. CARDS
★★★★ Hibernia	(809) 497-4290	$17–$30	A, MC, V

Scilly Cay

Caribbean

	PHONE	ENTRÉE	CR. CARDS
★★★★ Scilly Cay	(809) 497-5123		

South Hill

Italian

	PHONE	ENTRÉE	CR. CARDS
★★★ Arlo's Place	(809) 497-6810		MC, V

ANGUILLA

ANTIGUA

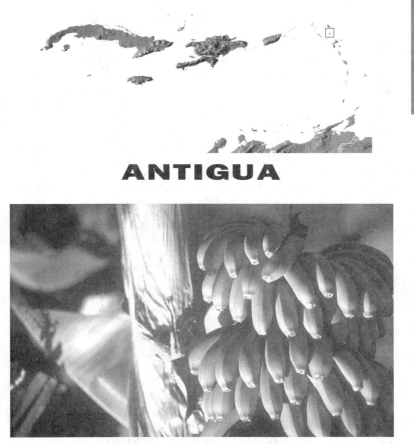

Farming on Antigua has shifted from sugarcane to fruits and vegetables.

With its trove of dazzling beaches, ideal and historic sailing anchorages, and a clutch of tony resorts, one thing is clear: tourism is big business in Antigua. It has been for years. When it became apparent in the 1960s that sugar production could no longer support the island, Antigua (pronounced An-tee-gah) began a very successful full-scale launch into tourism. The island has grown into one of the region's major destinations with about a half-million visitors annually, mostly from North America and England, though a growing number of Italians are also visiting in summer months. The island attracts a broad-based range of tourists, and though many of the resorts are clearly aimed at a clientele carrying a few Swiss bank accounts in their back pocket, there is plenty for the mid-range traveler. Those looking for a budget destination should be forewarned that although a few hotels and restaurants are less expensive, "hidden" charges add up quickly on this island. Still, the attractions of Antigua are not to be denied. The beaches are resplendent and the larger bays contain idyllic sailing anchorages. The island's rich naval and sugar history is on display in several areas, with Nelson's Dockyard and Betty's Hope being among the best historical sights in the region. Daytrips to neighboring Barbuda, Antigua's sibling, or to other nearby islands, are easy and rewarding. And the island seems positively dedicated to serious festivities: International yachting fans congregate in late April for Antigua Sailing Week—the premiere nautical event of the Caribbean—and color and music explode in late July/early August when Carnival comes to the streets of Antigua, filling the air with calypso competitions and the streets with fanciful costumes. Since flying is the easiest way to reach the Caribbean, it doesn't hurt that Antigua is one of the best connected to North America.

Antigua received the full brunt of Hurricane Luis' force, but the island rebuilt surprisingly quickly and, although a few hotels are still closed at press time, most visitors will see little if any of the storm's impact. The beaches have been combed and cleaned, and a few are actually bigger than they were before the hurricane.

Sprawling over about 108 square miles, Antigua is the largest and the most developed and heavily visited of the British Leewards. Antigua is well-positioned as a hub between a number of islands, with Guadeloupe to the south, Montserrat to the southwest, and St. Kitts-Nevis to the west. Together with Barbuda (28 miles to the north) and an uninhabited rocky islet named Redonda, the three islands form the independent nation of Antigua and Barbuda, within the Commonwealth of Nations. The capital is St. John's, which has a population of about 36,000 and is located at the mouth of one of the island's natural harbors. There are actually quite a few of these bays, inlets and coves scalloping the coastline, creating excellent sailing anchorages and numerous beaches. Antigua's interior is somewhat drier in appearance than the more mountainous islands to the south—the one truly verdant spot is the southwest portion of the island where Boggy Peak rises to 1319 feet, luring a few rain-producing clouds to its slopes. In the northeast, the terrain is flatter, with scrub and occasional cactus for vegetation. Otherwise, Antigua is generally remembered for its irregular coastline and the scenic harbors and coves of sand it creates.

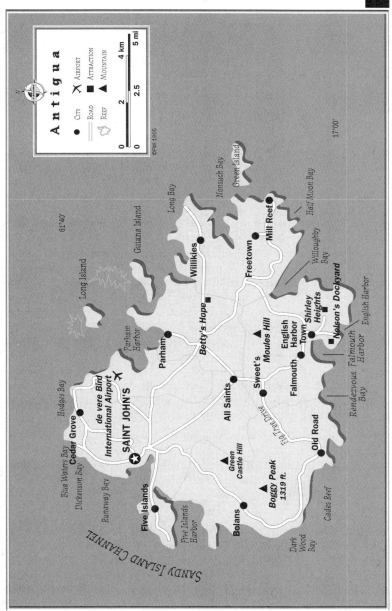

History

The Siboney Stone people were the first to graze the terrain of Antigua with settlements dating back to 2400 B.C. Arawaks lived on the islands between A.D. 35 and 1100. Columbus discovered the island on his second voyage in 1493, naming it Santa Maria de la Antigua. The absence of freshwater springs persuaded French and Spanish colonists to sail on, and by 1632, the English had successfully established colonization. Apart from a brief French invasion in 1666, the three islands of Antigua, Barbuda and Redonda have all remained British. The first large sugar estates were established in Antigua by Sir Christopher Codrington in 1674, who convinced the natives on Barbuda to raise provisions for the plantations (a village in Barbuda bears his name). As production increased forests were cleared for cultivation and African slaves were imported by the boatloads. (Today many Antiguans trace the lack of rainfall to this early forest devastation.) A vicious cycle of drought led eventually to barren lands, testimony of which can be seen in the ruined towers of sugarcane throughout the island. Abolition arrived in 1834, but the former slaves found they could barely subsist due to a lack of surplus farming and an economy that was based on agriculture and not manufacturing. Poor labor conditions and growing violence led to the organization of unions in 1939. A strong political Labor Party emerged seven years later, catapulting Antiguans into the 20th century. During World War II, Antigua was selected as a military base and American servicemen arrived in droves. Until 1959, Antigua was administered as part of the Leeward Islands, until attaining associated status with full self-internal government in 1967.

Since 1990 scandal and accusations of corruption have rocked the Antiguan government, including misuse of public funds and a series of arson attacks and murders investigated by Scotland Yard. In 1990 the governments of Antigua and Barbuda became embroiled in a scandal where they were accused of being involved in the sale of weapons to the Medellin cartel of drug traffickers in Colombia.

Today Antigua maintains strong links with the United States, having actively assisted in the U.S. military intervention in Grenada in 1983. Since 1982, both Antigua and Barbuda have intensified their programs of foreign relations and have agreed that the People's Republic of China could open an embassy. In 1990 Antigua opened relations with Russia and in April 1983 with the Ukraine. Today both islands are constitutional monarchies, with executive power invested in the British sovereign and exercised by the governor-general, who is appointed on the advice of the Antiguan prime minister.

Since the sugarcane industry fell off completely in 1972, tourism has monopolized the economy. In recent years, touristic activities have undergone a tremendous expansion, bringing the number of tourists who visit yearly to nearly half a million (half of which are cruise passengers).

People

Antigua's population is 64,000; 85 percent are of African descent, although there is also a small minority of English, Portuguese, Lebanese and Syrian inhabitants. Many islanders, particularly those working in the tourism sector, come cloaked with a British frostiness that is off-putting. If you can crack the facade of formality, a warm, generous character surfaces. Almost half of the population lives in St. John's, while the remainder are spread throughout the island, in 40 small towns and villages. Most Antiguans own some kind of property, even if it is just a small shack in the countryside. Because Antigua has an excellent harbor and relatively easy access to the outside world, its people are quite used to traveling and are well aware of current events.

For another glimpse into Antigua and its character, read Jamaica Kinkaid's devastating, bitter profile of the island, its people and the effect of tourism, *A Small Place* (1988).

Beaches

While the government's claim to possessing 365 beaches is laughably insupportable, you could indeed spend more than one vacation exploring the dozens ringing Antigua. Beginning in St. John's and working around the island clockwise, the first you'll encounter is Fort Bay, popular with locals and tourists alike, and recently developed with a bar, restaurant and performance stage—it remains busy well into the evening, and particularly when a cruise ship has docked. Just a little farther up the coast is Runaway Bay and Dickenson Bay, both of which have seen extensive resort growth over the past couple of decades. They're still attractive; head for Dickenson if you're in the mood for watersports and a lively beach scene, or to Runaway next door where crowds aren't quite as overwhelming. Hodges Bay is home to Jabber-

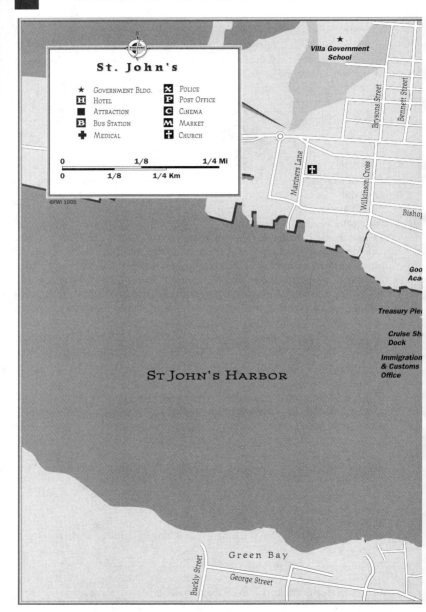

St. John's

★ GOVERNMENT BLDG.
H HOTEL
■ ATTRACTION
B BUS STATION
✚ MEDICAL

✖ POLICE
P POST OFFICE
C CINEMA
M MARKET
✚ CHURCH

0   1/8   1/4 Mi
0   1/8   1/4 Km

©FWI 1995

★ Villa Government School

Brysons Street
Bennett Street

Mariners Lane
Wilkinson Cross

Bishop

Goo Aca

Treasury Pie

Cruise Sh Dock

Immigration & Customs Office

St John's Harbor

Green Bay

Buckly Street
George Street

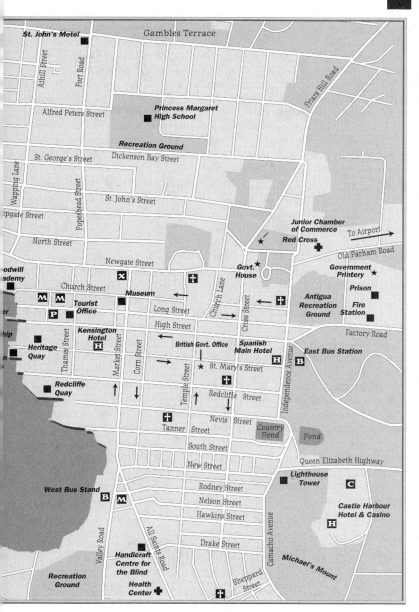

wock Beach, which has no facilities, but is a quiet spot with a reef that provides protection for swimmers and sights for snorkeling. There's little in the way of accessible sand along the coast between the airport and Indian Point, but at Long Bay, Hurricane Luis generously deposited tons of sand onto the shore to make one of the island's nicest beaches. Half Moon Bay takes the cake for sheer variety; most of it has been left natural, and there are waves for body surfing and quieter areas for swimming. The calm lagoon beach at the St. James Club comes with security guards and all the trappings of exclusivity, but as all Antigua beaches are open to the public, you may use it too. Several coves lie in the embrace of English and Falmouth Harbours, the best being quiet Pigeon Beach, just past the Falmouth Harbour Beach Apartments on the peninsula that divides the two harbors.

The coast that curls west and north away from English Harbour is a succession of one stunning and usually undeveloped beach after another, starting with secluded Rendezvous Bay, which is best reached by boat or on foot; the road to it begins in the village of Falmouth (you'll need to ask for directions). The foot of Fig Tree Drive is met by lovely, palm-lined Carlisle Bay, while just past the Curtain Bluff Hotel is Morris Bay, another long strand that is pleasant to walk and fine for swimming. A little farther is Crab Hill Bay, followed by one of the most spectacular, Dark Wood Beach, a Caribbean Shangri-La where a small beach bar and restaurant is located. Continuing north, you'll may pass lovely Fryes Beach without seeing the turnoff, but there's no missing Jolly Beach, a long strand with two mammoth resorts to provide watersports, bars, restaurants and plenty of people. By contrast, few make it out to ominously named Leper Colony Beach, reached by four-wheel-drive road out of the village of Jennings—it's a small cove with excellent snorkeling and protected by rocky headlands on each end. Heading out on the peninsula immediately west of St. John's, you'll pass Deep Bay, which has the monstrous Royal Antiguan Hotel as a signpost, then attractive Galley Bay, which is used by surfers January through March, and we finish our tour with Hawksbill, which is not one, but actually four beaches (plus another just before you enter the Hawksbill Resort). The beaches all face a landmark rock in the shape of a hawksbill turtle, but the last of the four, reached by a 10-minute trail past the resort, is the best—it's also known as the island's clothing-optional spot.

Similar in topography to nearby St. Martin, the coral reef surrounding Antigua and Barbuda—estimated to be upward of 1000 square miles in size—is part of a giant, sloping underwater platform. As such, there are no real wall dives, although the area below Shirley Heights does offer relatively sheer drop-offs exceeding 100 feet; most dive spots tend to be shallow in nature, typically bottoming out at 60 feet or so. The best sites line the south and west coasts, though the area just northeast of the airport is now being explored with some success. Underwater visibility is somewhat limited, averaging 70 to 80 feet due primarily to the healthy plankton growth, which thrives over the shallow reefs. Additionally, the government doesn't actively enforce the fishing ban within national parks, meaning that marine life can be skimpy, even at the island's best sites (such as Cades Reef). The island's massive, off-shore reef structure provides many underexplored areas; some of the charted sites lie several miles off the coastline, requiring long boat rides but, in the words of *Undercurrent Magazine*, these dives are "well worth it." Snorkelers can head to the remains of the *Andes*, in shallow water off Deep Bay in front of the Royal Antiguan Hotel; it's one of the few Caribbean wrecks that's easily accessible from shore (though not particularly interesting for divers).

Advanced divers head for 122-foot deep Sunken Rock.

On Foot

Antigua has heard the green-backed cry of the eco-tourism monster and is now attempting to mine its hillsides and coasts for trails and exploration pos-

ANTIGUA

sibilities. The island may be playing "catch-up" with the ecological advances made on other islands, but it's the thought that counts. Much of Antigua's interior, once covered in sugar cane, is dry and unappealing, which limits the hiking opportunities available. But the National Trust claims to be trying to identify trails, primarily in the southern region between Boggy Peak and English Harbor, and may have finally produced a hiking brochure by the time you visit.

By Pedal

After slowly developing a local following, visitors are now beginning to use bikes as a way to explore the country's many and varied beaches and as an alternative to the expensive local taxi service. Fig Tree Drive, a road leading through Antigua's greenest hills, is a beautiful ride of moderate difficulty; the loop leading south from St. John's to Swetes, over Fig Tree Hill, and back north via the vivid western coastline makes an excellent trip that passes one breathtakingly white cove after another (about 25 miles; allow the whole day for ample beach-sampling). The area around Five Islands Village is also popular for bicycling, but be wary of cars, particularly approaching and within busy St. John's. Mountain biking through the former cane fields should be fun, but carry a patch kit for the ever-present stickers you're guaranteed to encounter (and lucky to miss).

What Else to See

St. John's, the capital of Antigua, looks a bit tatty these days, though there are areas being developed for tourism and worthy of a stroll, particularly Redcliffe Quay, a picturesque district full of historical buildings, duty-free stores, souvenir shops and restaurants. Cruise ship passengers tend to crowd into Heritage Quay, off the harbor, where there is also a casino and satellite reception for a big screen TV. If you're looking for a cool interior to escape from the sun, dip into St. John's Cathedral, rebuilt several times due to earthquakes—no matter where you stand in town, you can see the twin towers. St. John's truly comes alive during the annual Carnival, a 10-day celebration that concludes the first Monday in August.

Outside St. John's, several places are worth driving to, but note that although there is always road work in progress, driving conditions overall are quite shoddy (locals bitterly note, however, that roads leading to the residence of the prime minister or his cronies are always in good shape). Start with the coastline south of Jolly Harbour, lined by one gorgeous beach after another—after passing through the town of Old Road, you'll head in Antigua's most verdant region, Fig Tree Drive, a rainforest with cow pastures and a variety of fruit trees (in Antigua, bananas are known as figs). Nelson's Dockyard in English Harbour is one of the region's most important historical sights—a secure port and hurricane hole that was used by Admiral Horatio Nelson as the regional facility for repairs to the British Royal Navy. Take the footpath that leads around the bay to Fort Berkeley for a great view you'll share with grazing goats. Nearby, the future King William IV spent his nights in Antigua at Clarence House when he served in the navy during the 1780s. Overlooking English Harbour, at Shirley Heights, are the ruins of 18th-century fortifications, with a million-dollar view over English and Falmouth harbors and extending to Montserrat and Guadeloupe in the distance. For a less historic, considerably more upbeat experience, visit Shirley Heights on Sunday afternoon, when steel bands play at the lookout point bar, the Battery—be prepared for loud music and a raucous atmosphere that draws hordes of locals, ex-pats and tourists alike.

There's a multimedia museum at Shirley Heights, the Dow's Hill Interpretation Center, which provides a Disney-ish explanation of the island's former slave economy. For a much more interesting, if decidedly more low-tech, account of the sugar plantation story, head to Betty's Hope, an award-winning historical site where a mill has been restored to working condition to help foster a better understanding into Antigua's history. The northeast coast of the island is quieter and flatter than the rest of Antigua; charming Parham is the island's oldest village, while Devil's Bridge is a natural bridge carved by the crashing Atlantic—it's not worth a substantial side trip.

City Celebrations

Carnival

What began some 20 years ago as a celebration to welcome Queen Elizabeth II has become a full-fledged annual festival with 11 days of art shows, parades and partying. The main event is "J'Ouvert," when hundreds of locals dance behind steel and brass bands. Held in late July and early August, you can pick up a full program once on the island.

Sailing Week   ★ ★ ★ ★

English Harbour, ☎ *(268) 462-8872.*
The Caribbean's premiere yachting event celebrates its 30th year in 1997. Some 200 boats from 25 countries pour into English Harbour for five races, and there's lots going on for landlubbers as well—food vendors, beach dancing and above all, lots of partying (and lots of cops to keep things from getting out of hand). For $30 you can dress up and attend Lord Nelson's Ball at the Admiral's Inn, but those in

ANTIGUA

the know say it's a bit too stuffy compared to the unabashed goings-on elsewhere. Held in late April.

Historical Sites

Betty's Hope   ★★★★★

Pares, ☎ *(268) 462-4930.*
Hours open: 10 a.m.–4 p.m.

Originally developed in the late 1600s and for many years one of the island's most prosperous sugar estates, Betty's Hope is now the site of a groundbreaking restoration project. Antiguans banded together after the plantation was designated as a historic landmark in 1990—the communal effort helped rebuild the mill with the old sugar crushing machinery and the site now boasts the only operational windmill in the Caribbean (the sails are stowed during hurricane season for safe keeping). The Betty's Hope Trust won the *Islands Magazine* Ecotourism Award in 1996. Future plans entail restoring the old boiling house and excavating the adjacent village—the first dig of a slave village ever in the Caribbean.

Nelson's Dockyard National Park   ★★★★★

Nelson's Dockyard, English Harbour, ☎ *(268) 460-1053.*
Hours open: 8 a.m.–6 p.m.

This pretty spot is the only Georgian-style naval dockyard left in the world. It has a rich history as home base for the British fleet during the Napoleonic Wars and was used by Admirals Nelson and Hood. The area includes colonial naval buildings, nice beaches, ancient archeological sites and lots of nature trails. Short dockyard tours, nature walks of varying length and boat cruises are offered daily. Check out the Admiral's House, a lovely inn and museum of colonial history, then have a drink at the popular bar. Children under 16 admitted to the park for free. General admission: $1.

St. John's Cathedral   ★★

Newgate Street and Church Lane, St. John's, ☎ *(809) 462-4686.*

This Anglican cathedral has a sorrowful history. Originally built of wood in 1683, it was replaced by a stone building in 1745, then destroyed by an earthquake in 1843. Replaced in 1847, it was once again heavily damaged by earthquake in 1973. Restoration continues as funds are available. The figures of St. John the Baptist and St. John the Divine were taken from a French ship in the early 19th century, and the iron railing entrance dates back to 1789.

Museums and Exhibits

Dow's Hill Interpretation Center   ★★

Shirley Heights, English Harbour.
Hours open: 9 a.m.–5 p.m.

The observation platforms at Shirley Heights yield stellar views of English and Falmouth Harbours, Antigua's southern coastline and, on a clear day, Guadeloupe and Montserrat—bring your camera. The museum's multimedia presentation of Antigua's six periods of history, from Amerindians to slavery to independence, is unusually polished, and perhaps the most upbeat "interpretation" of slavery you'll ever witness. $2 for kids under 16. General admission: $4.

Museum of Antigua and Barbuda ★★

Church and Market Street, St. John's, ☎ *(809) 462-1469.*
Hours open: 8 a.m.–4 p.m.

Mainly intended for the island's children but worth a look if you're in the neighborhood, this small museum spotlights Antigua's geological and political past. Some interesting exhibits include a life-size Arawak house, a wattle and daub house, models of sugar plantations and Arawak and pre-Columbian artifacts. There's also a decent giftshop selling local arts and crafts, books and historic artwork. Donation requested.

Tours

Jolly Roger

Redcliff Quay, ☎ *(809) 462-2064.*

This is the largest sailing ship in local waters—108 feet long—and a great way to spend the day. A "pirate" crew will have you walking the plank, dancing the limbo, eating, drinking and in general making merry as you sail the seas. General admission: $50.

Best View:

Even Antiguans still flock to the top of the Shirley Heights installations to view the fabulous sunsets. You can see the English and Falmouth harbors in the foreground and the hills and coast of Antigua in the distance. On a clear day you can see as far as Redonda, Montserrat and Guadeloupe.

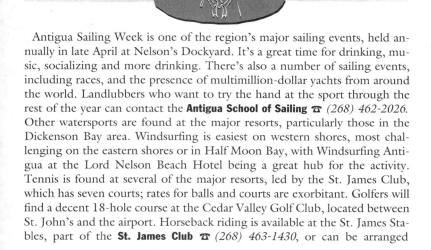

Sports

Antigua Sailing Week is one of the region's major sailing events, held annually in late April at Nelson's Dockyard. It's a great time for drinking, music, socializing and more drinking. There's also a number of sailing events, including races, and the presence of multimillion-dollar yachts from around the world. Landlubbers who want to try the hand at the sport through the rest of the year can contact the **Antigua School of Sailing** ☎ *(268) 462-2026.* Other watersports are found at the major resorts, particularly those in the Dickenson Bay area. Windsurfing is easiest on western shores, most challenging on the eastern shores or in Half Moon Bay, with Windsurfing Antigua at the Lord Nelson Beach Hotel being a great hub for the activity. Tennis is found at several of the major resorts, led by the St. James Club, which has seven courts; rates for balls and courts are exorbitant. Golfers will find a decent 18-hole course at the Cedar Valley Golf Club, located between St. John's and the airport. Horseback riding is available at the St. James Stables, part of the **St. James Club** ☎ *(268) 463-1430,* or can be arranged

ANTIGUA

through your hotel—the southeast countryside is rife with trails and a great half-day trek can be made to Monks Hill. **Tropikelly Trails** provides off-road 4 x 4 tours of the island with hiking for $55 per person ☎ *(268) 461-0383*.

Golf

Two locations.
Hours open: 8 a.m.–6 p.m.
The island has only two golf courses, so it won't be hard to make your choice. At **Half Moon Bay Hotel** ☎ *(268) 460-4300* there are nine holes (2410 yards, par 34), with more challenging conditions at **Cedar Valley Golf Club** ☎ *(268) 462-0161*. The 18-hole, par-70 course has some lovely views of the north coast. Green fees are $30 and cart rental is an additional $30.

Watersports

Long Bay Hotel, Long Bay, ☎ *(809) 463-2005.*
If it involves getting wet, they have it here at the Long Bay Hotel, where nonguests can rent equipment for scuba (experienced only), snorkeling, sailing, etc. They also offer snorkel trips (four minimum) to a few small islands, though conditions are great just off the beach, thanks to Long Bay's double reef. Also check out **Shorty's** *(☎ 462-6066)* where they have all kinds of watersports and glass-bottom excursions; and **Halcyon Cove Watersports** *(☎ 462-0256)*, where you can water ski. Both are at Dickenson Bay.

Windsurf Shop

Lord Nelson Beach Hotel, Dutchman's Bay, ☎ *(809) 462-3094.*
Here's your chance to try this ever-popular sport; Windsurf guarantees you'll be whisking around on your own after $50 and a two-hour lesson. (And in case you mess up, it has radio-assisted rescues.)

Where to Stay

Fielding's Highest Rated Hotels in Antigua

	Hotel	Price
★★★★★	Curtain Bluff	$425–$925
★★★★★	Jumby Bay	$550–$1200
★★★	Club Antigua	$95–$300
★★★	Copper and Lumber Store Hotel	$85–$325
★★★	Galley Bay	$260–$560
★★★	Hawksbill Beach Resort	$150–$400
★★★	Inn at English Harbour, The	$135–$390
★★★	Siboney Beach Club	$110–$290
★★★	St. James Club	$235–$595
★★★	Trade Winds Hotel	$194–$250

Fielding's Most Exclusive Hotels in Antigua

	Hotel	Price
★★★★★	Jumby Bay	$550–$1200
★★★	St. James Club	$235–$595
★★★	Pineapple Beach	$260–$470
★★★	Hawksbill Beach Resort	$150–$400
★★★	Inn at English Harbour, The	$135–$390

Fielding's Best Value Hotels in Antigua

	Hotel	Price
★★	Lord Nelson's Beach Hotel	$60–$115
★★	Admiral's Inn	$64–$132
★★	Antigua Beachcomber Hotel	$75–$135
★★	Rex Blue Heron Beach Hotel	$87–$128
★★	Hodges Bay Club Resort	$99–$147

Antigua offers an enormous array of resorts, all-inclusives and self-catering accommodations, though the government opted long ago to cater specifically to the up-market clientele, meaning less-expensive lodgings are few and far between. Construction is a constant reality, particularly post-hurricane, but conservation groups are taking the issue in hand to preserve the coastline. Most properties are close to St. John's, either along Runaway and Dickenson Bays just to the north, or out on the Five Islands peninsula that juts west of St. John's; another cluster of accommodations is found around English Harbour on the south coast of Antigua. A few hotels will close in September and/or October to spruce up for the winter season. If you arrive on Antigua without a reservation, the tourist office at the airport (next to baggage claim, before customs) will help you book a room.

Several small and large properties have not reopened following the devastation of Hurricane Luis. Runaway Beach Club, Blue Waters Beach Hotel and Half Moon Bay Hotel await reopening dates at press time.

Hotels and Resorts

All-inclusive resorts are an extensively developed option on Antigua. In addition to Sandals, part of the region's largest chain of all-inclusive resorts, there's Pineapple Beach, Club Antigua, Galley Bay and several others, some of which (like the Royal Antiguan), offer a choice of all-inclusive or regular European Plan. Mavens of luxury will be happily impressed with a pair of upscale resorts available: Jumby Bay is a private island two miles off the coast from Antigua's airport, and Curtain Bluff is dreamy vision perched on a bluff along the island's quiet southwest coast. A little lower on the price scale, secluded and inviting Hawksbill Beach Resort has added new club rooms.

Antigua Beachcomber Hotel   **$75–$135**   ★ ★

Winthrop Bay, St. John's, ☎ *(268) 462-3100. FAX (268) 462-4012.*
Single: $75–$135. Double: $95–$135.

A pleasant, quiet spot next to the boat dock for Jumby Bay, the Antigua Beachcomber is a locally owned operation with a small restaurant and bar on a small beach. Furnishings are basic, but clean—you'll pay extra for air conditioning (there are also six cottages that rent for $1200–$1300 per week). The isolated location is near the airport, but just far enough away to limit jet noise to takeoffs only. 28 rooms. Credit cards: MC, V.

Antigua Sugar Mill Inn   **$50–$100**   ★

Coolidge, St. John's, ☎ *(800) 223-6510, (268) 462-3044. FAX (268) 462-4790.*
Single: $50–$90. Double: $60–$100.

Because it is the closest hotel to the airport, this spot does a big business with overnight guests on their way to hither and yon. Rooms are simple but do have air conditioning, and there's a pool, restaurant, bar and historic stone sugar mill with an observation tower on-site. The beach is nearly a mile away, which helps explain the reasonable prices. 22 rooms. Credit cards: A, DC, D, MC, V.

Club Antigua   **$95–$300**   ★ ★ ★

Jolly Beach, St. John's, ☎ *(800) 777-1250, (268) 462-0061. FAX (268) 462-4900.*

Single: $95–$150. Double: $189–$300.

This all-inclusive resort, set on 40 acres with a half-mile beach, received a $2 million post-hurricane renovation. It hums with action and attracts mainly young people who don't mind the busy beach—lined with vendors hawking everything from jewelry to joints—and noisy nightlife. Lots to do, including four restaurants, six bars, a slot casino, happening disco, all watersports, eight tennis courts and, for the kids (and their parents), a supervised children's club. The cheapest rooms, called minimums, are just so and quite small; the other classes are larger and worth the extra bucks. Amenities: tennis, exercise room, family plan. 470 rooms. Credit cards: A, MC, V.

Curtain Bluff $425–$925 ★★★★★
Morris Bay, St. John's, ☎ (800) 672-5833, (268) 462-8400. FAX (268) 462-8409. Single: $425–$825. Double: $525–$925.

For over three decades Antigua's most famous and remarkable resort, Curtain Bluff lies on a spectacular bluff above a shimmering cove of sand. In addition to the dreamy setting, the hotel earned its reputation through lavish accommodations and excellent service. Extras like fresh flowers daily, bidets and plush robes accent the spotless rooms and suites. The best bets are the striking bluffside split-level suites, which offer up great views from two balconies. The all-inclusive rates include all watersports—even scuba—drinks, tennis, squash, fitness center, deep-sea fishing, putting green and fine meals (the wine cellar is stocked with roughly 25,000 bottles). The only thing missing is a pool, but the beach is lovely. This is one of the Caribbean's prettiest settings, but with jacket and tie required for gents at dinner (in high season), and a loyal, chummy clientele, the atmosphere can be a bit too refined for laid-back types. Amenities: tennis. 63 rooms. Credit cards: A.

Galley Bay $260–$560 ★★★
Five Islands, St. John's, ☎ (800) 345-0356, (268) 462-0302. FAX (268) 462-4551. Single: $260–$460. Double: $360–$560.

Battered by Hurricane Luis, this unique all-inclusive resort was doubled in size during the year-long renovation and was set to reopen November 1996. The resort is set on 40 lovely acres adjacent to a bird sanctuary near Five Islands Village. Accommodations are on the beach in Polynesian thatched huts or in modern cottages; all lack air conditioning but do have coffeemakers, robes and hair dryers. The best rooms are built around a salt pond and coconut grove; request these "Ganguin Cottage" units for the Tahitian experience. The beach is great and the hotel offers most watersports as well as tennis, a restaurant, bar and the very popular afternoon tea. This spot is popular with Europeans who aren't looking for much of a nightlife, though a new open-air movie theater plays movies at night—popcorn provided. Amenities: tennis, exercise room. 61 rooms. Credit cards: A, MC, V.

Hawksbill Beach Resort $150–$400 ★★★
Five Islands, St. John's, ☎ (800) 223-6510, (268) 462-0301. FAX (268) 462-1515. Single: $150–$300. Double: $226–$400.

Named after a turtle-shaped rock formation that juts out of the water, this lively spot is frequented by Europeans and young baby-boomer couples. The atmosphere is nicely informal, and restaurant prices are quite reasonable (an MAP set-up is available). Accommodations are in West Indian-style cottages near the main beach with nice lawns; all have tropical decor, pleasant furnishings and modern baths. There's also a Colonial-style Great House with three bedrooms and a kitchenette that rents for $1300–$1800 per night. The 37 acres include an old sugar mill that has been transformed into a boutique, tennis, watersports and not one but four beaches, one where you can shuck your bathing suit. Well run and quite pleasant. Amenities: tennis. 99 rooms. Credit cards: A, DC, MC, V.

Jumby Bay $550–$1200   ★★★★★

Jumby Bay Island, St. John's, ☎ *(800) 421-9016, (268) 462-6000. FAX (268) 462-6020.*
Single: $550–$1100. Double: $650–$1200.
Situated on its own 300-acre private island, this glorious Mediterranean-style all-inclusive resort attracts mature, affluent travelers who like everything just so. The former island home, some 230 years old, is now the main Great House with a lounge, library, games room and restaurant. The original accommodations are in semi-circular, cozy rondovals—two-unit cottages with separate sitting areas and lovely mahogany furnishings, though no phone, air conditioning or TV. Newer units are in the Pond Bay House, 26 rooms with a more spacious layout and glamorous showers. 12 lavish two- and three-bedroom villas are also available for $1325–$1650 per night. There are three beaches, one of which is frequented by nesting hawksbill turtles, and a pool—most watersports are included in the rates, as well as tennis, a fitness center and fine dining. Most guests get around the expansive grounds on bikes, and yachters pull in for dinner. One drawback: the resort lies under the flightpath for departing jets, but if you can live with the disruption three or four times each afternoon, the solitude will more than make up for it. Amenities: tennis, exercise room. 50 rooms. Credit cards: A, MC, V.

Pineapple Beach $260–$470   ★★★

Long Bay, St. John's, ☎ *(800) 345-0356, (268) 463-2006. FAX (268) 463-2452.*
Single: $260–$410. Double: $320–$470.
This 25-acre all-inclusive resort flanks a beautiful white sand beach on the remote eastern tip of the island. Pineapple is one of the nicest of the island's larger resorts, a good spot for those who want all-inclusive amenities without sacrificing an arm or leg at checkout time. Most accommodations front the ocean and are of average size with wicker furniture, local artwork, large balconies and Mexican tile floors; less-expensive rooms face the garden. This busy place teems with action throughout the day, with folks running from tennis to volleyball to croquet to windsurfing. Two restaurants (one by reservation—Friday is lobster night), several bars and a small casino stocked with one-armed bandits, round out the scene. Amenities: tennis, exercise room. 135 rooms. Credit cards: A, MC, V.

Rex Blue Heron Beach Hotel $87–$128   ★★

Johnson's Point Beach, St. John's, ☎ *(268) 462-8564. FAX (268) 462-8005.*
Single: $87–$128. Double: $87–$128.
This very basic and beach hotel appeals mainly to Europeans on a budget, and received a much-needed face-lift following the 1995 hurricane. The best units are right on the beach and have balconies; all are simply furnished with wood and for-

mica. Watersports are free, and there's a nice beach bar. Nothing quaint or especially charming here, and the location is miles from other tourist facilities. But if all you want is a quiet beach to crash on, it's a good budget option. 40 rooms. Credit cards: A, D, MC, V.

Rex Halcyon Cove   **$130–$380**   ★ ★

Dickenson Bay, St. John's, ☎ *(800) 255-5859, (268) 462-0256. FAX (268) 462-0271.*
Single: $130–$380. Double: $130–$380.
Lots of group tours from the U.S. and Europe congregate at this busy spot, made even more crowded by cruise passengers who spend the day at its excellent beach. The expansive complex includes several restaurants, four bars and a nightclub, a casino, and extensive watersports including scuba, water-skiing and glass-bottom boat rides. Of the six rooms types, standard units are barely adequate with simple furnishings and air conditioning; the beachside rooms are quite small but open right onto beach. Not bad if you want that resort experience, but you'll probably be happier in one of the higher room categories. 210 rooms. Credit cards: A, D, MC, V.

Royal Antiguan   **$120–$410**   ★ ★

Deep Bay, St. John's, ☎ *(800) 345-0356, (268) 462-3733. FAX (268) 462-3732.*
Single: $120–$360. Double: $150–$410.
Built in 1987 to the horror of many residents, this ugly high-rise is the island's most American-like resort and has yet to meet its full potential. It does a bang-up business, though, by offering modern conveniences such as direct-dial phones, TV and air conditioning—rooms are otherwise standard. There are also a dozen cottages with more-plush accommodations. Set on 150 acres, there's a lot to keep visitors occupied, including a full casino, enormous pool with swim-up bar, lots of tennis and watersports and a supervised children's program. An all-inclusive meal plan is also available. It's a few minutes' walk to the beach, which is frequented by local artists displaying their wares. Previously run by the Ramada chain, it recently became part of the Pineapple and Galley Bay operation. Amenities: tennis. 282 rooms. Credit cards: A, DC, MC, V.

Sandals Antigua   **$3280–$5140 per week**   ★ ★ ★

Dickenson Bay, St. John's, ☎ *(800) 726-3257, (268) 462-0267. FAX (268) 462-4135.*
Only heterosexual couples are allowed at this all-inclusive resort, set on a narrow, lively beach lined with palms and local vendors. Most accommodations are in motel-like units that are small but adequate; the 17 rooms in rondovals are better. There are five pools scattered through the property, four restaurants, tennis courts, a fitness center and more. There's tons going on here at all hours, and the staff will cheerfully badger you to participate—despite an ad campaign to the contrary, this is not the spot for discreet liaisons. Most of the couples are young, and many are honeymooning. One week rates range from $3280 to $5140 per couple; three nights is the minimum stay. The resort received a makeover following Hurricane Luis. Amenities: tennis, exercise room, Jacuzzi, houses, cottages or bungalows, balcony or patio. 189 rooms. Credit cards: A, MC, V.

St. James Club   **$235–$595**   ★ ★ ★

Mamora Bay, St. John's, ☎ *(800) 274-0008, (268) 460-5000. FAX (268) 460-3015.*

Single: $235–$595. Double: $235–$595.

Set on 100 lush acres a couple miles east of English Harbour, this very nice resort does not quite live up to its reputation as a playground for the rich and famous. Nevertheless, this is an amenity-heavy spot, with two pretty beaches, an attractive European-style casino, tony boutiques and a lively disco. Rooms are beautifully furnished, and the two-bedroom hillside villas are wonderful; an all-inclusive plan is also available. Guests can choose from watersports, horseback riding, working out in the gym, playing tennis or frolicking in three pools. Little true glamour perhaps, but lots of glitz anyway. Amenities: tennis, horseback riding, exercise room, Jacuzzi. 178 rooms. Credit cards: A, DC, MC, V.

Apartments and Condominiums

Antigua boasts of a number of self-catering complexes that work well for vacationers, particularly for families or for extended visits. If you plan to cook at home to save money, note that food staples are expensive and not always worth the time and trouble to uncover. Otherwise, options range from simply furnished studio apartments (some right on a beach), to glorious homes rented by the owner. Booking is usually done through the central office number.

Antigua Village　　　　　　　**$95–$245**　　　　　　★★

Dickenson Bay, St. John's, ☎ (800) 447-7462, (268) 462-2930. FAX (268) 462-0375.
Single: $95–$245. Double: $95–$245.

This rambling complex of two-story red-roof condominiums is located on a peninsula along a busy beach. Choose from spacious studios or one- and two-bedroom units, all with kitchenettes, bright tropical decor, air conditioning and daily maid service; only a few have TVs. Watersports are free, and there's a restaurant, bar and minimarket on-site. A reliable spot, but nothing too exciting. 100 rooms. Credit cards: D, MC, V.

Barrymore Beach Club　　　　　**$72–$240**　　　　　　★★

Runaway Bay, St. John's, ☎ (800) 542-2779, (268) 462-4101. FAX (268) 462-4140.
Single: $72–$240. Double: $72–$240.

This recently renovated beachfront complex consists of hotel rooms and one- and two-bedroom apartments with kitchenettes but no air conditioning. There are a number of restaurants within walking distance on nearby Dickenson Bay, but not much else to get excited about. The beach, however, is quite nice and reasonably quiet despite the proximity to a number of activities. 36 rooms. Credit cards: A, MC, V.

Dickenson Bay Cottages　　　　**$142–$199**　　　　　★★

Dickenson Bay, St. John's, ☎ (268) 462-4940. FAX (268) 462-4941.
Single: $142–$199. Double: $142–$199.

Attractive, well-kept apartments in a residential area overlooking the island's busiest beach. One-, two- and three-bedroom units, some quite spacious with full kitchens—all overlook a pleasant garden with a small pool. The beach is a 10-minute walk down the (steep) hill, and guests are welcome to use the facilities at the Rex Halcyon resort there, including the tennis courts. 12 rooms. Credit cards: A, DC, MC, V.

Falmouth Harbour Beach Apartments   **$68–$134**   ★

Falmouth Harbour, St. John's, ☎ (800) 223-5695, (268) 460-1027. FAX (268) 460-1534.

Single: $68–$98. Double: $88–$134.

A low-frills property with reasonable rates and a good location next door to English Harbour, this small apartment complex houses guests on or near a small beach. Rooms have ceiling fans, a full kitchen and little else. In addition to the sand the rooms overlook, another nice beach is a five-minute walk, limited watersports are nearby, as are a number of restaurants and a market. A good bet for the price. 28 rooms. Credit cards: MC, V.

Galleon Beach Club   **$130–$365**   ★

English Harbour, St. John's, ☎ (268) 460-1024. FAX (268) 460-1450.
Single: $130–$365. Double: $130–$365.

This is a time-share complex of cottages scattered about the beach or a steep hillside. Accommodations are in one-bedroom suites or two-bedroom cottages; all have rattan furnishings, living and dining areas and kitchenettes, but lack air conditioning, TVs and phones. There's a good Italian restaurant on the premises. Maintenance and housekeeping can be sloppy. 36 rooms. Credit cards: A, MC, V.

Hodges Bay Club Resort   **$99–$147**   ★ ★

Hodges Bay, St. John's, ☎ (268) 462-2300. FAX (268) 462-1962.
Single: $99–$115. Double: $124–$147.

Located in an exclusive residential neighborhood, this recently renovated complex has picturesque beachfront villas with one or two bedrooms, air conditioning, full kitchens and nice views off the balconies. The beach is excellent for snorkeling, and day trips are offered to Prickley Pear Island, one mile offshore. There's a bar and restaurant on-site, as well as a pool, two tennis courts and free watersports. Amenities: tennis. 26 rooms. Credit cards: A, MC, V.

Marina Bay Beach Resort   **$80–$200**   ★ ★

Runaway Bay, St. John's, ☎ (268) 462-3254. FAX (268) 462-2151.
Single: $80–$200. Double: $80–$200.

A basic, but pleasant spot, with spacious and bright studios and one- and two-bedroom villas. All have air conditioning, cable TV, full kitchens and Italian-tiled baths. Located on Corbinson Point, right between two of the island's best beaches with watersports available nearby. There's no restaurant on-site, but several within an easy walk. 27 rooms. Credit cards: A, DC, D, MC, V.

Siboney Beach Club   **$110–$290**   ★ ★ ★

Dickenson Bay, St. John's, ☎ (800) 533-0234, (268) 462-0806. FAX (268) 462-3356.
Single: $110–$270. Double: $130–$290.

This three-story all-suite property, enhanced by a cornucopia of palms and other greenery, is right on Dickenson Bay, a beautiful but busy beach. The 12 one-bedroom suites are nicely furnished with rattan, kitchenettes and ceiling fans; there's also a cozy treehouse studio peeking through the bamboo and palms (priced a few dollars less). A maid tidies things up and provides limited room service. An idyllic freshwater pool is in back, and a trademark British red phonebooth sits on the beach if you get homesick. There's a lovely restaurant and entertainment most nights at the bar; extensive watersports including excursions via catamaran or glass-bottom boat are available. The service is very friendly at this small, well-run spot. 12 rooms. Credit cards: A, DC, MC, V.

Trade Winds Hotel $194–$250 ★★★

Dickenson Bay, St. John's, ☎ *(268) 462-1223. FAX (268) 462-5007.*
Single: $194–$250. Double: $194–$250.
This all-suite hotel is located above Dickenson Bay with great ocean views. The beach is nearly a mile away, but the management will take you to and fro. There's a small pool on-site, as well as a restaurant and piano bar. Accommodations, in Spanish-style villas, are decent. Lots of Europeans like this spot. 49 rooms. Credit cards: A, DC, MC, V.

Yepton Beach Resort $125–$280 ★★

Five Islands Village, St. John's, ☎ *(800) 361-4621, (268) 462-2520. FAX (268) 462-3240.*
Single: $125–$280. Double: $125–$280.
This condominium resort is located outside St. John's Harbour and consists of Mediterranean-style white stucco buildings with nice views of the beach and lagoon. All units have air conditioning, and studios and suites include Murphy beds and kitchenettes; there are also one- and two-bedroom apartments. All line the excellent beach, where complimentary windsurfing and sunfish sailing await—a pool and golf driving range are also available. There's a restaurant and bar with live music three nights a week, with other eating choices within a short drive or moderate walk. All-inclusive plans are offered on request. Amenities: tennis, balcony or patio. 38 rooms. Credit cards: A, MC, V.

Inns

Inns on Antigua provide charming ambiance and down-home hospitality. The most authentically historic is the Admiral's Inn, set in an 18th-century building and overlooking Nelson's Dockyard. But the Copper and Lumber Store next door has plenty of bona-fide naval roots to deliver a history-tinged vacation. In either case, you might be sleeping in the vicinity of the billionaire yachties who occasionally tie up in English Harbour. A nice compromise that delivers both the rustic ambiance and a beach location is the Long Bay Hotel.

Admiral's Inn $64–$220 ★★

English Harbour, St. John's, ☎ *(800) 223-5695, (268) 460-1027. FAX (268) 460-1534.*
Single: $64–$98. Double: $78–$220.
Housed in a Georgian brick building dating back to 1788, this intimate inn has a nautical theme and is loaded with distinctive charm. Rooms are small with beam ceilings and antiques; some have air conditioning and patios. Each is unique in decor—the least expensive are in the attic, with room 6 the best of the mid-range rooms (minimal view), and rooms 1 and 4 the choice bets in the superior category (room 1 suffers a bit from foot traffic and bar noise). Four rooms in a one-story annex next door are pleasant, with room A the biggest and best-positioned. There's also a two-bedroom apartment with full kitchen, the "Joiner's Loft," that is priced

$130–$220 for two. Admiral's Inn is a tourist attraction in its own right, and can get crowded with folks coming through to take a look. Management transports guests to two nearby beaches. In addition to the on-site restaurant (decent pub food, lovely terrace setting for breakfast or lunch), other restaurants are a short stroll away. A great spot if you don't mind sacrificing resort amenities for quaint atmosphere in the lap of history—and a bargain at that. 13 rooms. Credit cards: A, MC, V.

Copper and Lumber Store Hotel   **$85–$325**   ★ ★ ★

English Harbour, St. John's, ☎ (800) 633-7411, (268) 460-1058. FAX (268) 460-1529.
Single: $85–$325. Double: $85–$325.
This charming inn is housed in a restored Georgian brick warehouse, dating back to 1782, which overlooks the marina at English Harbour. All named after Lord Nelson's ships, rooms are either studios or duplex suites, but the higher-priced rooms in each category have authentic or reproduction 18th-century furnishings, oil paintings and charts, canopy beds, brass chandeliers and hand-stenciled floors; all have kitchenettes. No air conditioning, but ceiling fans provide a breeze. There's no beach or pool—guests are whisked via ferry to nearby Galleon Beach. There is a restaurant and pub for dining, and other eateries are a short stroll away. A wonderful historic spot with the sound of clattering rigs against the masts of yachts for a soundtrack. One minor drawback: owing to its location next to Nelson's Dockyard, Copper and Lumber is a busy tourist attraction during the day. 14 rooms. Credit cards: A, MC, V.

Inn at English Harbour, The   **$135–$390**   ★ ★ ★

English Harbour, St. John's, ☎ (800) 223-6510, (268) 460-1014. FAX (268) 460-1603.
Single: $135–$390. Double: $135–$390.
Set on 10 acres of beach and hillside overlooking colorful Nelson's Dockyard, this small inn has rooms in cottage-style buildings on the beach or atop a breezy hill with views. All are nicely done with island-style rush rugs, wicker and modern furniture and ceiling fans. There are two restaurants and bars, and free watersports. The clientele is mostly English. 28 rooms. Credit cards: A, CB, DC, D, MC, V.

Long Bay Hotel   **$175–$400**   ★ ★

Long Bay, St. John's, ☎ (800) 291-2005, (268) 463-2005. FAX (268) 463-2439.
Single: $175–$300. Double: $255–$400.
This intimate resort, run by the Lafaurie family, is set far out on Antigua's northeast tip. The 20 guest rooms, situated in motel-style wings, are large but simple, and include breakfast and dinner. Six cottages are also available, with gabled ceilings, nice artwork and small but fully equipped kitchens—quite pleasant ($200–$400 per night without meals). For recreation, there's a tennis court, watersports (scuba costs extra), a library and a great beach. This is an authentic Caribbean retreat, not some corporation's idea of one—best exemplified by the newsletter that goes out to guests keeping everyone posted on the status of local birds, staff and island news. Lots of American families are attracted by the warm and friendly atmosphere. 26 rooms. Credit cards: A, MC, V.

Lord Nelson's Beach Hotel   **$60–$115**   ★★

Dutchman's Bay, St. John's, ☎ *(268) 462-3094. FAX (268) 462-0751.*
Single: $60–$90. Double: $70–$115.

This small and informal inn is the oldest on the island, built in 1954 by an American couple who run it today with their son-in-law. It has lots of lived-in beachcomber ambiance, but could use a renovation to bring it into the '90s. Rooms are simple but newer units have balconies, and there's a restaurant and bar on-site. There's a dive shop and other watersports, but this breezy spot is particularly loved by windsurfers—the staff of the on-site shop is eager to share the sport. There is no pool and the beach is adequate if unspectacular. Located on a rather isolated spot on the northeast coast near the airport, there's essentially nothing within walking distance, so you'll need a rental car. 17 rooms. Credit cards: A, MC, V.

Low Cost Lodging

Locating a budget room on Antigua is not impossible. A good source is the *Guide to Small Hotels and Guest Homes* provided by the tourist office. Of course, no money pays for no ambience; most low-cost lodgings are in modern, stucco buildings with only basic furnishings, and a beachside location is rare. As such, you'll probably need to throw your savings into renting a car.

Where to Eat

Fielding's Highest Rated Restaurants in Antigua

★★★★	Coconut Grove	$18–$43
★★★★	Le Bistro	$22–$34
★★★	Alberto's	$18–$27
★★★	Julian's	$18–$27
★★★	Le Cap Horn	$13–$20
★★★	Redcliffe Tavern	$10–$23

Fielding's Most Exclusive Restaurants in Antigua

★★★★	Coconut Grove	$18–$43
★★★★	Le Bistro	$22–$34
★★★	Alberto's	$18–$27
★★★	Julian's	$18–$27
★★★	Redcliffe Tavern	$10–$23

Fielding's Best Value Restaurants in Antigua

★★★	Redcliffe Tavern	$10–$23
★★★	Le Cap Horn	$13–$20
★★★★	Le Bistro	$22–$34
★★★	Julian's	$18–$27
★★★	Alberto's	$18–$27

Antigua has rarely suffered for lack of good restaurants, but additions are always cropping up. Unfortunately, the island lost its best, La Perrouche, to Hurricane Luis. The best scene on the island remains the Sunday barbecue at Shirley Heights Lookout, housed in a restored, 18th-century fort with memorable views of English Harbour and the southern coastline. In Dickenson

Bay, Warri Pier is a great setting for a sunset cocktail, while the island's most romantic spot may be beachside Coconut Grove. Elsewhere, prices for a top-class dinner aren't cheap; expect to fork over at least $100 for two in the best places. Spices, influenced by East Indian and Creole cooking, are liberally added and tend to run on the hot side. Look for local specialties such as banana and cinnamon pancakes with Antiguan rum syrup at breakfast, pepper-pot stew with fungi (a cornmeal dumpling), sea urchin flan, and lump crabmeat with avocado and lemon grass.

Admiral's Inn $$$ ★★★

Nelson's Dockyard, English Harbour, St. John's, ☎ *(268) 460-1027. Associated hotel: Admiral's Inn.*
American cuisine. Specialties: Pumpkin soup, red snapper.
Lunch: Noon–2:30 p.m., entrées $10–$25.
Dinner: 7–9:30 p.m., entrées $10–$25.

Like the Copper and Lumber Store Hotel alongside it, the Admiral's Inn is so long on atmosphere and history, the food doesn't have to be good to be worth a visit. But thankfully, that is not the case here, especially for a silky pumpkin soup and a fresh pan-fried snapper that draw raves. Some never get as far as the restaurant, preferring to stay in the dark bar or sit under the old trees outdoors, looking out at the convoys of ships in the harbor. Those so inclined can eat here three times a day, and breakfast, served daily from 7:30 to 10 a.m., is a terrific deal. Closed September. Reservations recommended. Credit cards: A, MC, V.

Alberto's $$$ ★★★

Willoughby Bay, St. John's, ☎ *(268) 460-3007.*
Italian cuisine.
Dinner: entrées $18–$27. Closed: Mon.

Locals rave about the Italian specialties served in Alberto's spacious gazebo that is wrapped in bougainvillea and features walls lined with Italian ceramics. The menu changes seasonally, but frequent offerings include osso buco, braised rabbit with polenta, farfalla with salmon, cream and vodka, and baked fish with a pinenut crust. For dessert, try the baked pears in marsala with creme fraiche. The loquacious and genial Alberto draws diners from English Harbour and St. James area to his rather isolated south coast location just outside Bethesda.

Big Banana Holding Co. $$$ ★★

Redcliffe Quay, St. John's, ☎ *(268) 462-2621.*
Italian cuisine. Specialties: Pizza, conch salad.
Lunch: Noon–4 p.m., entrées $6–$30.
Dinner: 4 p.m.–midnight, entrées $6–$30. Closed: Sun.

A lot of locals and tourists homesick for pizza flock here at all hours. The pies in question are rather pricey and not very exciting, but the location, in the interesting and trendy Redcliffe Quay shopping center, helps.

All in all it's considered very proper to sit under the whirring fans and just sip a cool tropical drink (these are bright, frothy and potent). Salads, seafood dishes and fruit plates are also available. Big Banana's best asset may be that its other, newly remodeled and expanded location at V.C. Bird Airport, is a truly welcome respite for those who are island-hopping via Antigua. Credit cards: A, DC, MC, V.

Calypso $$$ ★★
Redcliffe Street, St. John's, ☎ *(268) 462-1965.*
International cuisine. Specialties: Pumpkin soup, baked chicken with cornmeal.
Lunch: 10 a.m.–4 p.m., entrées $8–$25. Closed: Sun.
This open-air, lunch-only spot jumps weekdays, and is an accessible, friendly location to try West Indian specialties. These often include fresh seafood, sautéed or prepared in batter, washed down with local fruit juices. Homey stews and soups with pumpkin or okra satisfy; the less adventurous can chow down on burgers and sandwiches. Credit cards: A, DC, MC, V.

Chutneys $$ ★★
Fort Road, St. John's, ☎ *(268) 462-2977.*
Indian cuisine.
Dinner: entrées $10–$19. Closed: Mon.
One of the few East Indian restaurants in the West Indies with an authentic tandoori oven, Chutneys is the best spot on the island for curry, roti and other spice-enhanced dishes (you can request hot or mild for most dishes). The restaurants also has a "non-curry lovers menu" with steak, lobster and chicken kebabs. But most come for the specialties cooked in the clay Tandoori oven—the lamb tikka is succulent. Located on the outskirts of St. John's en route to the Dickenson Bay area; ideal for takeout. Credit cards: MC, V.

Coconut Grove $$$ ★★★★
Dickenson Bay, St. John's, ☎ *(268) 462-1538. Associated hotel: Siboney Beach Club.*
International cuisine. Specialties: Grilled local lobster, chilled gazpacho.
Lunch: 11:30 a.m.–3 p.m., entrées $9–$29.
Dinner: 6:30–10 p.m., entrées $18–$43.
A lovely beachfront spot surrounded by tall coconut palms swaying in the breeze, this eatery is a choice spot for privacy, moonlight and amore. The lobster is caught fresh daily and prepared grilled, in a sandwich (for lunch), thermador and other succulent ways. Chicken, hearty chops, creative pastas, tangy curry and salads are also on offer. The location, at the south end of Dickenson Bay and right on the water, is unbeatable—so are the daily drink specials, such as mango daiquiris. Reservations required. Credit cards: A, DC, MC, V.

Colombo's $$$ ★★
Galleon Beach, St. John's, ☎ *(268) 460-1452. Associated hotel: Galleon Beach Club.*
Italian cuisine. Specialties: Veal Scaloppine, carpaccio.
Lunch: 12:30-2:30 p.m., entrées $22–$32.
Dinner: 7–10 p.m., entrées $22–$32.
Only in the Caribbean can one eat spaghetti Bolognese or carpaccio in a thatched-roof hut and dance to a reggae band (Wednesday nights) on the beach. Though this was the first Italian eatery on Antigua, regulars note that the food has gone downhill yet the service is still amiable. There are daily specials and a variety of wines. Reservations required. Credit cards: A, DC, MC, V.

Copper and Lumber Store, The $$$ ★★

Nelson's Dockyard, St. John's, ☎ *(268) 460-1058. Associated hotel: Copper and Lumber Store.*
International cuisine. Specialties: West African groundnut soup, shepherd's pie.
Lunch: 11:30 a.m.–4:30 p.m., entrées $8–$25.
Dinner: 6–11 p.m., entrées $18–$30. Closed: Wed.
Old Antigua hands will be pleased with the new face given the 18th-century Copper and Lumber Store Hotel in Nelson's Dockyard. Others should come at least once to savor the Georgian atmosphere and nautical prints at the Wardroom, and eat adequate, if unspectacular food at rather high prices. But American-style or English lunches and cool drinks are within most everyone's reach at the hotel's pub, the Mainbrace, where fish and chips, shepherd's pie and draft beers are offered. Reservations recommended. Credit cards: A, MC, V.

Hemingway's $$$ ★★

St. Mary's Street, St. John's, ☎ *(268) 462-2763.*
International cuisine. Specialties: Lobster soup, tropical chicken with fruit salsa.
Lunch: 11:30 a.m.–4:30 p.m., entrées $7–$15.
Dinner: 4:30–11 p.m., entrées $9–$23. Closed: Sun.
Not very far from the sea Ernest Hemingway once wrote about is this 1829-era, gingerbread-trimmed tropical Victorian house with a restaurant on the second floor. There's a lot of activity on Heritage Quay below and people-watching opportunities on the porch, where frothy tropical drinks can be sipped. Nibble on lobster, salads, burgers and spicy chicken. Vegetarian specialties are also available and the pumpkin soup is tops. A nice, only-in-the-Caribbean treat, and a good value. Credit cards: A, MC, V.

Julian's $$$ ★★★

Church Street and Corn Alley, St. John's, ☎ *(268) 462-4766.*
Dinner: 7–10 p.m., entrées $18–$27. Closed: Mon.
A handsomely redecorated 18th-century Colonial house in the heart of St. John's is now home to this delightful eatery that provides both al fresco dining in a sheltered courtyard out back or in the lovingly appointed interior awash in white walls with green accents. Proprietor Julian Waterer does the cooking, preparing pan-seared veal sweetbreads, rich lamb casserole, escallops of fresh salmon and dangerous desserts, while Marie manages the friendly staff. Closed for lunch Sunday.

Le Bistro $$$ ★★★★

Hodges Bay, St. John's, ☎ *(268) 462-3881.*
French cuisine. Specialties: Red snapper baked in foil, seafood in puff pastry.
Dinner: 6:30–10:30 p.m., entrées $22–$34. Closed: Mon.
Le Bistro, on the island's north shore, caters to residents with expensive villas in the area, but anyone with a fancy for fine cuisine can repair here for classic French dishes prepared with care. Lobster (prepared six ways) and red snapper are always available, and made with cream, white wine and fresh herb sauces, or invest in the fine rack of lamb for two. Operated by the husband-and-wife team of Raffaele and Philippa Esposito since 1981, the dining room is inviting and plant-filled, and a great setting for crepes suzette or bananas flambe after all. Reservations required. Credit cards: A, MC, V.

Le Cap Horn $$$ ★★★

Falmouth Harbour, St. John's, ☎ *(268) 460-1194.*
French cuisine. Specialties: Seafood, pizzas, steak.
Lunch: Noon–6:30 p.m., entrées $10–$13.
Dinner: 6:30–11 p.m., entrées $13–$20.

A popular Argentinian and French restaurant in a verdant outdoor setting en route to Nelson's Dockyard. Snacks, wood-fired pizza or more substantial meat dishes are available for decent prices. Dine early or late on the greenery-embraced porch on daily specials for under $20. Reservations recommended. Credit cards: A, MC, V.

Lemon Tree $$$ ★★

Long and Church Streets, St. John's, ☎ *(268) 462-1969.*
International cuisine. Specialties: Cajun garlic shrimp, burritos.
Lunch: 10 a.m.–4 p.m., entrées $15–$25.
Dinner: 4–11 p.m., entrées $15–$25. Closed: Sun.

The atmosphere here is very South Seas, with a lot of wicker and wooden blinds, good for a cool-off drink or air-conditioned meal after a visit to the Museum of Antigua and Barbuda nearby. Graze Caribbean-style from a long menu of finger foods, Tex-Mex items and the usual lobster and chicken dishes, which vary in quality. Unfortunately, with a cruise crowd in attendance, service can be rushed, but it's good for music in the evening. Credit cards: A, DC, MC, V.

Lobster Pot $$$ ★★

Runaway Bay, St. John's, ☎ *(268) 462-2856. Associated hotel: Runaway Beach Club.*
Seafood cuisine. Specialties: Chicken in coconut milk and curry, fresh fish.
Lunch: entrées $7–$12.
Dinner: entrées $15–$25.

Even picky diners will find something to their liking at this airy eatery in Runaway Bay that does creative things with chicken and lobster at prices that won't leave you breathless. In spite of the titular item, the substantial menu runs the gamut from hearty breakfasts to leafy salads, sandwiches and fresh local fish and shellfish. Commune with nature at tables on the seaside veranda; come early for these or reserve a seat. Reservations recommended. Credit cards: DC, MC, V.

Miller's by the Sea $$$ ★★

Fort James Beach, St. John's, ☎ *(268) 462-9414.*
Specialties: Grilled seafood, steaks.
Lunch: 11 a.m.–5 p.m., entrées $8–$18.
Dinner: 5 p.m.–2 a.m., entrées $10–$25.

Formerly the happening spot of Dickenson Bay, in 1996 Tenniel Miller moved his booming restaurant and car rental business to the beach just northwest of St. John's, to near-overnight success. Food is pretty basic, with garlic or curried conch, grouper creole and grilled rock lobster being the prime offerings; steak, pork and lamb chops round out the selection. Miller's draws people for reasons other than the food: it's the only spot on this beach (frequented by cruise ship passengers and locals alike), the music is strong, and the food pours out of the kitchen later than any other on the island. The weekend scene is quite merry with live bands Fridays and Saturdays at 10 p.m. Features: late dining. Credit cards: MC, V.

Redcliffe Tavern   **$$$**   ★★★

Redcliffe Quay, St. John's, ☎ *(268) 461-4557.*
Italian cuisine. Specialties: Barbecued chicken, pasta, fresh local seafood.
Lunch: 11:30 a.m.–3 p.m., entrées $7–$20.
Dinner: 7–11 p.m., entrées $10–$23. Closed: Sun.

Begin or end a shopping tour at the charming Redcliffe Quay complex in St. John's harbor with lunch or dinner or a snack at the dependable Redcliffe Tavern. It's one of a handful of vintage structures that have been restored for commercial usage. Once an old warehouse, the Tavern sports island machinery from a pumping station for decor, and the waitstaff serves good burgers or barbecue or pastas and freshly caught lobster. Architecture buffs and Anglophiles should find the surroundings especially appealing. Credit cards: A, MC, V.

Shirley Heights Lookout   **$$$**   ★★

Shirley Heights, St. John's, ☎ *(268) 460-1785.*
Seafood cuisine. Specialties: Pumpkin soup, lobster with lime sauce.
Lunch: 9 a.m.–4 p.m., entrées $15–$26.
Dinner: 4–10 p.m., entrées $15–$26.

Something festive is always happening in this two-story pub/restaurant amidst the ruins of Fort Shirley—especially on Sunday, when there's dancing and live bands that play for free from mid-afternoon on (steel bands play on Thursday afternoons, but it hasn't quite yet become the same tradition). Barbecued meats at decent prices accompany the tunes, and the views behind the Lookout are superb. The rest of the week, eat in peace upstairs or downstairs for breakfast, lunch or dinner. The second-floor dining room is a very intimate trysting spot. Credit cards: AE, MC, V.

Warri Pier   **$$$**   ★★

Dickenson Bay, St. John's, ☎ *(268) 462-0256. Associated hotel: Rex Halcyon Cove.*
International cuisine. Specialties: Seafood linguine, marlin.
Lunch: Noon–6 p.m., entrées $7–$30.
Dinner: 6–10:30 p.m., entrées $12–$30.

Dine on marlin—"warri" is the local name—on a private pier belonging to the Rex Halcyon Cove Resort. This is a lovely setting poised above the sea like a great wooden bird on the northern edge of Dickinson Bay, about two miles from St. John's. It's an excellent perch from which to observe the setting sun, though the food doesn't live up to the staging. Light meals of chunky fruit salads or burgers and seafood soups are fine at lunch; dinner gets somewhat fancier with grilled lobster, steaks and the like and elaborate desserts. Features: outside dining. Reservations recommended. Credit cards: A, MC, V.

Where to Shop

The bulk of Antigua's shops are concentrated in St. John's at Redcliffe Quay and Heritage Quay, both within easy access of the main cruise ship dock. Go to Redcliffe for local shops and color, head for Heritage for duty-free international shopping. There are other good shops clustered on St. Mary's Street or High Street. Duty-free products are omnipresent, and there are also some special Antiguan crafts such as rum, silk-screened fabrics, native straw work and curios made from shells. Hot new clothing stores have also sprung up or expanded in the wake of Hurricane Luis. Check easy-to-wear cotton and cotton/lycra styles for men, women and children at Base (the flagship store for the Caribbean clothier). Also in Redcliffe is the chic Debra Moises boutique, which carries husband-and-wife-designed sensations in flowering gauze and one-of-a-kind hair accessories (carried by Bergdorf's and Sak's in Manhattan). Heritage houses Caribelle Batik, a store filled with one-of-a-kind batik clothing and art pieces made in St. Kitts with sea island cotton. Check out the Saturday fruit and vegetable market at the West Bus Station on Independence Avenue. There is usually a good selection of local handicrafts. For some strange reason, some Antigua shops close Thursday at noon.

Antigua Directory

Arrival and Departure

Antigua is well-connected to North America via several different carriers. American Airlines has both jet and commuter service out of its hub in San Juan, Puerto Rico daily. BWIA has almost-daily nonstop service from Miami and New York's JFK. Continental has several flights a week out of Newark. Within the Caribbean, Antigua serves as the hub for LIAT, with nonstop or direct flights to Anguilla, Barbados, Barbuda, Dominica, Grenada, Guadeloupe, Martinique, Montserrat, Nevis, St. Croix, St. Kitts, St. Lucia, Sint Maarten, St. Thomas, St. Vincent, San Juan and Tortola. V.C. Bird Airport, 4.5 miles east of St. John's, receives all air traffic.

The departure tax is $12.

Business Hours

Shops open Monday–Friday 8:30 a.m.–4 p.m. and Saturday 8 a.m.–noon or 3 p.m. Banks generally open Monday–Thursday 8 a.m.–2 and Friday 8 a.m.–4 p.m.

Climate

The Antiguan climate is probably the best in the Caribbean, with so little rainfall that water shortage sometimes becomes a problem. Any rainfall is usually restricted to brief heavy showers. Constant sea breezes and trade winds keep the air fresh and the temperatures hovering around 81 degrees F, except in the hot season (May-November), when temperatures can rise to 93 degrees F. The mean annual rainfall of 40 inches is slight for the region.

Documents

U.S. and Canadian citizens must show proof of citizenship (passport, birth certificate, or voter's registration) plus a photo ID, and an ongoing or return ticket.

Electricity

The majority of hotels use 110 volts, 60 cycles, same as the U.S. Some shaver outlets are 110-volt. Hotels generally have adapters.

Getting Around

Because there is no single, well-maintained primary route around the island, sightseeing on Antigua is time-consuming. If you want to rent a car, you must procure a local driver's license for the exorbitant sum of $20, available at the local police stations or through the car rental agency by showing your license from home. Be forewarned that Antiguan roads are infamous for gaping potholes, crumbling shoulders, poor signage and stray dogs; fortunately, outside St. John's, they are generally free of congestion. Antiguan drivers are about as courteous as French ones, so drive defensively... on the left! Several U.S.-based rental firms are represented on the island including Avis, Budget, Dollar and National, as well as a host of local outfits, many of which are represented at a bustling desk you'll pass immediately after leaving customs at the airport. Given the overall price and aggravation of renting a car for a day, you might be better off hiring a guide, and some of the best are taxi drivers. The main taxi stand is across from the market in St. John's and is open 24 hours. It's also possible to take the inexpensive local buses: In St. Johns, the West Bus Station on South Street (opposite the market) serves as the departure point for the west, south and English Harbour areas; the East Bus Station on Independence Avenue serves the north and east. The buses do not leave until they're jammed full—they connect St. John's with outlying residential or business areas, not necessarily the tourist sights such as Dickenson Bay or Shirley Heights (nor do they stop at the airport); check before boarding. To go to St. John's, head for one of the main roads leading to town and flag a bus down as it passes.

Daytrips to Barbuda can be arranged through Barbara Jappal at Caribrep for $125 per person, including airfare, lobster lunch and drinks, a visit to the bird sanctuary and beaches ☎ *(268) 462-3884.* Montserrat is also just a 15-minute flight away; Nevis and Guadeloupe are slightly farther. Carib Aviation also arranges charters for five to nine passengers, which can work out to be less expensive if you fill the plane; they work out of V.C. Bird Airport ☎ *(268) 462-3147.*

Language

English is the official language, though the special Antiguan lilt may make some words indistinguishable.

Medical Emergencies

Holberton Hospital, on the outskirts of St. John's, is a 220-bed hospital. Serious medical emergencies are usually flown off the island to Miami. Ask if your hotel has a doctor on call.

Money

The official currency is the Eastern Caribbean dollar, commonly referred to as "E.C." The exchange rate is pegged to the U.S. dollar, currently about $2.65 for one American dollar. You'll get the best exchange rate at banks, though most establishments will accept either currency. Make sure you note which currency is being used for your bill at restaurants or hotels, particularly smaller establishments.

Telephone

The new area code for Antigua and Barbuda is *(268)*. From the U.S., dial *1+(268)*, then the seven-digit local number.

Time

Atlantic standard time.

Tipping and Taxes

Most hotels and restaurants add a 10 percent service charge. When not included, tip 10–15 percent for waiters, $1 per room per day for maids, and 50 cents per bag for bellhops. Tip taxi drivers 10 percent.

Tourist Information

The government tourist office is located at Long and Thames Street in St. John's You can also find an information counter at the airport, in the baggage claim area (before customs). For more information ☎ *(268) 462-0480*, or call the New York office: ☎ *(212) 541-4117.*

When to Go

Antigua Sailing Week takes place in late April and draws sailors and spiffy yachts from all over the region for the last big blowout of the season. Carnival is held during the week before the first Monday and Tuesday in August. Independence Day is Nov. 1, and Christmas and Boxing Day are Dec. 25–26.

ANTIGUA HOTELS	RMS	RATES	PHONE	CR. CARDS
St. John's				
★★★★★ **Curtain Bluff**	63	$425–$925	(800) 672-5833	A
★★★★★ **Jumby Bay**	50	$550–$1200	(800) 421-9016	A, MC, V
★★★ **Club Antigua**	470	$95–$300	(800) 777-1250	A, MC, V
★★★ **Copper and Lumber Store Hotel**	14	$85–$325	(800) 633-7411	A, MC, V
★★★ **Galley Bay**	61	$260–$560	(800) 345-0356	A, MC, V
★★★ **Hawksbill Beach Resort**	99	$150–$400	(800) 223-6510	A, DC, MC, V
★★★ **Inn at English Harbour, The**	28	$135–$390	(800) 223-6510	A, CB, D, DC, MC, V
★★★ **Pineapple Beach**	135	$260–$470	(800) 345-0356	A, MC, V
★★★ **Sandals Antigua**	189	All-Inclusive	(800) 726-3257	A, MC, V

ANTIGUA

ANTIGUA HOTELS		RMS	RATES	PHONE	CR. CARDS
★★★	Siboney Beach Club	12	$110–$290	(800) 533-0234	A, DC, MC, V
★★★	St. James Club	178	$235–$595	(800) 274-0008	A, DC, MC, V
★★★	Trade Winds Hotel	49	$194–$250	(268) 462-1223	A, DC, MC, V
★★	Admiral's Inn	13	$64–$132	(800) 223-5695	A, MC, V
★★	Antigua Beachcomber Hotel	28	$75–$135	(268) 462-3100	MC, V
★★	Antigua Village	100	$95–$245	(800) 447-7462	D, MC, V
★★	Barrymore Beach Club	36	$72–$240	(800) 542-2779	A, MC, V
★★	Dickenson Bay Cottages	12	$142–$199	(268) 462-4940	A, DC, MC, V
★★	Hodges Bay Club Resort	26	$99–$147	(268) 462-2300	A, MC, V
★★	Long Bay Hotel	26	$175–$380	(800) 291-2005	A, MC, V
★★	Lord Nelson's Beach Hotel	17	$60–$115	(268) 462-3094	A, MC, V
★★	Marina Bay Beach Resort	27	$80–$200	(268) 462-3254	A, D, DC, MC, V
★★	Rex Blue Heron Beach Hotel	40	$87–$128	(268) 462-8564	A, D, MC, V
★★	Rex Halcyon Cove	210	$130–$380	(800) 255-5859	A, D, MC, V
★★	Royal Antiguan	282	$120–$410	(800) 345-0356	A, DC, MC, V
★★	Yepton Beach Resort	38	$125–$280	(800) 361-4621	A, MC, V
★	Antigua Sugar Mill Inn	22	$50–$100	(800) 223-6510	A, D, DC, MC, V
★	Falmouth Harbour Beach Apartments	28	$68–$134	(800) 223-5695	MC, V
★	Galleon Beach Club	36	$130–$365	(268) 460-1024	A, MC, V

ANTIGUA RESTAURANTS		PHONE	ENTRÉE	CR. CARDS
St. John's				
★★★	Julian's	(268) 462-4766	$18–$27	
★★	Miller's by the Sea	(268) 462-9414	$8–$25	MC, V
American				
★★	Admiral's Inn	(268) 460-1027	$10–$25	A, MC, V
French				
★★★★	Le Bistro	(268) 462-3881	$22–$34	A, MC, V
★★★	Le Cap Horn	(268) 460-1194	$10–$20	A, MC, V

ANTIGUA RESTAURANTS	PHONE	ENTRÉE	CR. CARDS
Indian			
★★ Chutneys	(268) 462-2977	$10–$19	MC, V
International			
★★★★ Coconut Grove	(268) 462-1538	$9–$43	A, DC, MC, V
★★ Calypso	(268) 462-1965	$8–$25	A, DC, MC, V
★★ Copper and Lumber Store, The	(268) 460-1058	$8–$30	A, MC, V
★★ Hemingway's	(268) 462-2763	$7–$23	A, MC, V
★★ Lemon Tree	(268) 462-1969	$15–$25	A, DC, MC, V
★★ Warri Pier	(268) 462-0256	$7–$30	A, MC, V
Italian			
★★★ Alberto's	(268) 460-3007	$18–$27	
★★★ Redcliffe Tavern	(268) 461-4557	$7–$23	A, MC, V
★★ Big Banana Holding Co.	(268) 462-2621	$6–$30	A, DC, MC, V
★★ Colombo's	(268) 460-1452	$22–$32	A, DC, MC, V
Seafood			
★★ Lobster Pot	(268) 462-2856	$7–$25	DC, MC, V
★★ Shirley Heights Lookout	(268) 460-1785	$15–$26	AE, MC, V

ARUBA

Windsurfing is Aruba's most popular sport.

Long one of the Caribbean's most popular destinations, Aruba is, appropriately enough, the "A" in the so-called ABC Islands (Bonaire and Curacao make up the trio) in the Netherlands Antilles—although Aruba is now considered a separate entity within the "Kingdom of the Netherlands." Some half-million tourists descend on the small island each year to hang out in its posh resorts, gamble in its 10 casinos, dine in 100 restaurants and shop for duty-free bargains in a seemingly endless array of stores.

Located just 15 miles off the coast of Venezuela, the small island is sated with luxury hotels lining the southwestern shore, near the capital city of Oranjestad. It is not a particularly pretty island; it's quite desertlike and the land is tough and scrubby, punctuated by cacti and the wind-sculpted Watpana (divi divi) trees. but that doesn't keep thousands of tourists from converging on the island each year, drawn by its unparalleled watersports and friendly, welcoming residents. the island has tourism down pat, with a sophisticated infrastructure evidenced in its large, modern airport that services many direct flights linking it to the United States and South America, a popular cruise port, excellent guest-pleasing hotels and resorts and a thriving nightlife. You won't find much in the way of historic sights and there's just a handful of museums and other man-made attractions, but obviously the island is doing something right. Watersports reign supreme, and there's hardly a better place to perfect your tan. Today's visitor will find it hard to believe that, back in 1499, it was officially declared an *isla inutil* (useless inland) upon its discovery by the Spanish.

Aruba is located in the southern Caribbean, 15 miles off the coast of Venezuela. It measures 19.6 miles long by six miles wide, for a total of 70 square miles. The island receives just 24 inches of rain each year, and the countryside is quite desertlike, marked by dramatic rock formations, cacti and windbent divi divi trees. Tiny bright red flowers called fioritas provide one of the few splashes of natural color—besides, of course, the ever-changing hues of the crystalline sea. The southwest coast, where most resorts are located, has seven miles of palm-fringed beaches of white sand, while the northeast coast is rugged, punctuated by coral cliffs and pounding surf. Because it is so close to the Equator, the median temperature for day to night and summer to winter varies by just 3.6 degrees. The scant rain that falls on Aruba occurs mainly in short spurts during the months of November and December. The island lies completely outside the hurricane belt.

Oranjestad, the capital city, is a real Dutch charmer with its gabled, pastel buildings. Shopping is popular along the pretty streets of Nassaustraat and Wilhelminastraat. But be sure to escape to the countryside to gaze at Aruba's unique, arid topography, so different from most other Caribbean destinations. Arubans have announced a $800 million plan to transform one-fourth of the island into a national park (adding to the existing Arikok National Park), develop the area of San Nicolas, the island's largest city, into a civic and cultural destination and rebuild roads, bike trails and water treatment plants.

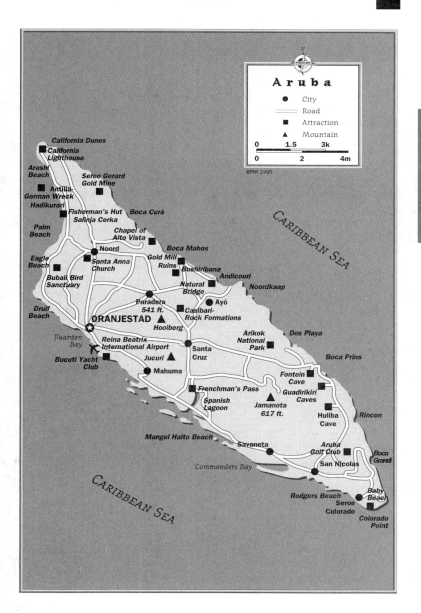

Aruba

- ● City
- ━━ Road
- ■ Attraction
- ▲ Mountain

0   1.5   3k
0   2   4m

©FWI 1995

CARIBBEAN SEA

California Dunes
California Lighthouse
Arashi Beach
Antilla German Wreck
Hadikurari
Sereo Gerard Gold Mine
Fisherman's Hut
Salinja Cerka
Boca Curá
Palm Beach
Chapel of Alto Vista
Noord
Boca Mahos
Eagle Beach
Santa Anna Church
Gold Mill Ruins
Bushiribana
Andicouri
Bubali Bird Sanctuary
Natural Bridge
Noordkaap
Druif Beach
Paradera 541 ft.
Ayó
Casibari Rock Formations
ORANJESTAD
Hooiberg
Arikok National Park
Dos Playa
Paarden Bay
Reina Beatrix International Airport
Santa Cruz
Boca Prins
Bucuti Yacht Club
Jucuri
Mahuma
Fontein Cave
Frenchman's Pass
Guadirikiri Caves
Spanish Lagoon
Jamanota 617 ft.
Huliba Cave
Rincon
Mangel Halto Beach
Sayaneta
Aruba Golf Club
Boca Grandi
Commanders Bay
San Nicolas
Rodgers Beach
Seroe Colorado
Baby Beach
Colorado Point

CARIBBEAN SEA

History

ARUBA

When Spanish explorers arrived in the 15th century, the Caiquetios, a tribe of Arawaks, may have already been living on Aruba for more than 4500 years, having migrated there from their ancestral homes in Venezuela. The Spanish exiled most of them in 1513, though more immigration occurred around 1640, when the Dutch permitted the Indian population to live a free—if difficult—life in Aruba. Though the last full-blooded natives died out in 1862, remains of their villages, workshops and cemeteries can be glimpsed throughout the Aruban countryside. Many place names still retain their Indian origins, such as Arashi, Daimari, Jamanota and perhaps the name Aruba itself, which some think is Arawak for "guide." Even the faces of modern Arubans—with their high cheekbones and tawny complexions—strongly reflect their native ancestry.

After being discovered by the Spanish explorer Alonso de Ojeda in 1499, Aruba was deemed useless along with its sister island Bonaire and Curaçao, and ignored for years. After the Spanish shipped off the resident male Indians to work the salt mines of Hispaniola, they began a limited colonization, turning the dusty mote into a large ranch and introducing horses, donkeys, sheep, dogs, goats, pigs, cats and chickens. In 1636, the Dutch took over and continued ranching. The English and the Spanish duked it out from 1792-1816, though the Dutch remained in control. Aloe cultivation and gold mining became important industries

In 1824 a lowly goat herder discovered the first gleaming nuggets of gold and started a tropical gold rush. Smelters were built and miners flooded the island. When the going got rough, major smelters shut down in 1914, but today there are those who still find nuggets. The real gold of Aruba became aloe vera, brought over from North America via Jamaica in the mid-19th century, a hardy succulent that adapted well to the climate. By 1900 Aruba had become the largest exporter of aloe vera, earning itself the nickname of Island of Aloe, for producing more than 90 percent of the world's supply. Today every Aruban home boasts its own small crop, using it as a natural laxative and wound-healer.

In 1924, oil refining arrived, ushering in an unprecedented era of prosperity. By 1985 the oil boom had gone bust, and the country's biggest employer Exxon went home, leaving the country its worst crisis, with 60 percent of the foreign exchange lost, 70 percent of the harbor space empty, and 40 percent of the population unemployed. In 1986, Aruba separated from its sister islands of the Netherlands Antilles (Curaçao, Bonaire, Sint Maarten, Saba and Statia), but still remained part of the Dutch Kingdom. This was a move favored by Arubans, but the time couldn't have been less favorable. It forced the island to totally depend on tourism. Government guarantees were given to the Hyatt, Sheraton and Holiday Inns—a plucky move that worked. Today tourism is Aruba's biggest industry, employing about half the population.

People

Expect to find some Dutch customs and windmills on Aruba.

Aruba is known for its welcoming, friendly people, and indeed, such warm hospitality is one of the prime reasons the island draws so many repeat visitors year after year. The island has some 81,500 residents who represent some 40 nationalities, mainly Dutch, South American, North American, European and Chinese. Native Arubans have a mix of Dutch, Spanish and Arawak Indian ancestry. While Dutch is the official language and Papiamento the local dialect (a lilting blend of Spanish, Dutch, Portuguese, Indian, English and French), most everyone speaks excellent English and Spanish. The education system is Dutch and high standards are the norm; fully 24 percent of the island's budget is devoted to education. English, Spanish, French and German are taught in the schools. Students who wish to pursue

ARUBA

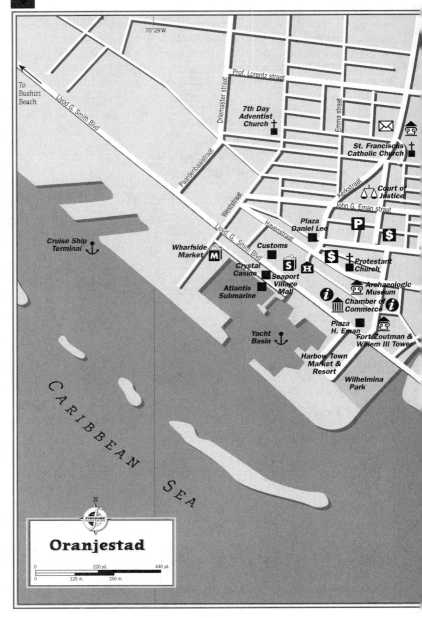

To
Bushiri
Beach

Lloyd G. Smith Blvd

70°29'W

Prof. Lorentz straat

Driemaster straat

Emma straat

**7th Day
Adventist
Church**

Paardenbaaistraat

Weststraat

Kerkstraat

**St. Franciscus
Catholic Church**

**Court of
Justice**

John G. Eman straat

**Plaza
Daniel Leo**

Havenstraat

P

$

Lloyd G. Smith Blvd

**Cruise Ship
Terminal**

**Wharfside
Market** **M**

Customs

**Crystal
Casino**

S

H

$

**Protestant
Church**

**Atlantis
Submarine**

**Seaport
Village
Mall**

**Archaeologic
Museum**

i

**Chamber of
Commerce**

i

**Yacht
Basin**

**Plaza
H. Eman**

**Fort Zoutman &
Willem III Tower**

**Harbow Town
Market &
Resort**

**Wilhelmina
Park**

C A R I B B E A N

S E A

N

FIELDING
WORLDWIDE

Oranjestad

0	220 yd.	440 yd.
0	125 m.	250 m.

ARUBA

12°32'N

De la Salle straat

A. van Leeuwenhoek straat

Numismatic
Museum

Hospitaal straat

Malanchi River

Nassaustraat

To
Santa
Cruz

Caya G.F. (Betico) Croes

Wilhelminastraat

Adriaf Laclé Blvd

Vondellaan

Ferguson straat

Beth Israel
Synagogue

Wilhelmina
Stadium

Methodist
Church

Stadion Weg

To Queen Beatrix
International
Airport

higher education attend Aruba's law school, teacher college or Hospitality Trades Training Center.

Aruba became a separate entity within the Kingdom of the Netherlands in 1986 (prior to that it was part of the Netherlands Antilles). The island has a democratic, Dutch form of government, with an appointed governor, parliament, council of ministers and elected prime minister. Arubans enjoy a high standard of living and live up to the line in their national anthem that proclaims, "The greatness of our people is their great cordiality."

Several yachts and catamarans offer cruises along Aruba's coast.

Of the three ABC Islands, Aruba has the most beautiful beaches. All are open to the public free of charge. Avoid swimming on the east side because the surf can get dangerously rough. **Palm Beach**, considered by some to be one of the 10 best beaches in the world, is the hub of Aruban beachlife—interpret that as *crowded*—but it is also excellent for swimming and other watersports. **Fishermen's Hut**, north of the hotel strip, is the favorite hangout of the windsurfing crowd. Here you'll see a lovely view of neon sailboats bobbing madly in the wind. **Rodger Beach** is notable for its lovely palm trees, and **Baby Lagoon** on the west is unusually calm. A truly wondrous wide stretch of strand, **Manchebo Beach** seems to magically inspire women to fling their tops off. Other good beaches are **Bachelor's Beach** and **Boca Grandi** in the east, which is good for windsurfing.

Underwater

Perpetually consigned to the impressive shadow cast by Bonaire and Curacao, Aruba will never attain premier status as a dive destination. There is a decent barrier reef extending between Oranjestad and the southern tip, but with all dive operators located a long boat ride away, visitors don't always hear about it. One does need to be wary of a brisk current, but there are lovely sites along this reef (two of them below) which are worthy of exploration. Shore diving is possible, but there is usually a maze of cuts and channels that must be negotiated in order to access the main reef; the current also allows for some drift dives, but these, too, can be difficult to locate. If you really want to experience the island's limited reef and wall diving, your best bet is to hook up with a dive shop that knows this area. What the island does offer is a bevy of wrecks, including one of the Caribbean's very finest, the *Antilla*, a WWII remnant which sits close enough to the surface to be explored by snorkelers. There's also a tug, a 200-foot freighter, a pair of rusting airplanes and, off the rugged northern tip, the remains of the *California*, which is notorious as the ship that didn't respond to the Titanic's S.O.S. signals. The best area for snorkeling is probably **DePalm Island**, a small resort served by a free ferry every half-hour.

On Foot

With an average annual rainfall of only about 20 inches, Aruba's interior is scraggly and desolate, with a series of low rolling hills that snuggle against the middle part of the northern coast. The island's highest elevation is **Yamanota Hill**, a rise of 617 feet near the center of Aruba. Its summit can be reached by car, and a series of trails trickle down the slopes, but hikers should be cautious in their explorations as a unique, venomous rattlesnake inhabits this rugged territory. **Arikok National Park** encompasses a triangle of land between San Fuego and Boca Prins (on the eastern coast); a group of short trails surround the park's focal point, **Mt. Arikok**, Aruba's second-highest summit. Also worth on-foot investigation is **California Point**, the island's northern tip, where sand dunes reach toward the sea and brown pelicans nest.

Wind-bent divi-divi (watpana) trees are a common sight on Aruba.

By Pedal

Offering an excellent escape from the pulse of resort activities concentrated on the leeward coast, most of Aruba's landscape is relatively flat and ideal for either road or mountain bike riding. The major consideration (as on Bonaire and Curacao) is the heat and sunlight, which can be ferocious; carry plenty of water and sunscreen. Using the roads closest to the shore, a circuit of the island is roughly 50 miles, though there are several ways to shorten the route if you desire; the south coast is entirely asphalt, while the north coast is composed of varying degrees of dirt roads. If you get lost, look to the divi divi trees to serve as a compass of sorts (winds keep them pointed southwest).

What Else to See

You won't find a slew of historical and man-made attractions on Aruba, but there are still some places well worth checking out. The **Natural Bridge**, located on the jagged northern coast, is the Caribbean's largest. The gaping coral bridge is a favorite stop for every tour bus on the island, so come early to avoid the crowds. The old indian caves known as Guadirikiri and Fontein have painted petroglyphs on the walls and ceilings, though some wags say they were actually painted for an Italian film years ago. San Nicolas, Aruba's oldest settlement and its largest city with a population of 25,000, is located on the southwestern tip. It's best known for the Exxon refinery that was attacked by German U-Boats in World War II. The refinery closed down in 1986 after 60 years in operation, and today San Nicolas is the target of an ambitious revitalization effort that will add a Caribbean Cultural Center, sports park, market square and waterfront park.

City Celebrations

Carnival

Various locales around Aruba, Oranjestad.

This yearly party starts two weeks before Lent (usually in February). Don't miss the Grand Parade, held on the Sunday before Lent. Other festivities include street dancing and the crowning of the Carnival Queen.

Jazz and Latin Music Festival ★★

Various venues, Oranjestad.

This yearly festival, begun in 1988 and run under the auspices of the Aruba Tourism Authority, is a local favorite. Held every June, it attracts some big names.

Historical Sites

Fort Zoutman ★★★

Off Lloyd G. Smith Boulevard, Oranjestad.

The fort, built in 1796, is the island's oldest building. The Willem III tower was added in 1868 and served as a lighthouse for decades. On the grounds is Museo Arubano, a historical museum in an 18th-century home that displays relics and artifacts found around Aruba.

Museums and Exhibits

Aruba Archeology Museum ★★

Zoutmanstraat 1, Oranjestad.

Artifacts from the precolonial period—including some skeletons 2000 years old— are on exhibit at this small museum. Its founder, Martin Bloom, conducts interesting island tours (see "Special Tours/Excursions").

De Man Shell Collection ★★★

18 Morgensten Street, Oranjestad.

The De Mans are proud owners of one of the world's largest private shell collections. Call ahead and if they're free, they'll let you check it out.

Numismatic Museum ★★★★

Irausquin Plein 2A, Oranjestad.

More than 3000 pieces of coins and currency from 400 countries from the private collection of J.M. Odor.

Tours

Atlantis Submarines   ★★

Seaport Village Marina, Oranjestad.
Hours open: 10 a.m.–3 p.m.

Not for the claustrophobic, but a great excursion for everyone else in a modern submarine that goes as deep as 150 feet below the sea to observe coral and fish along the Barcadera Reef. Trips depart every hour on the hour, and reservations are essential. The fee is $48 for adults, $34 under 16; children under 4 not permitted.

De Palm Tours   ★★★

L.G. Smith Boulevard 142, Oranjestad.

If it involves showing tourists around Aruba, they're happy to oblige at De Palm. On- and off-road excursions start at $49.95 and include lunch and snorkeling; three-hour treks for hikers cost $25; deep-sea fishing starts at $220; horseback rides are $30 for two hours. De Palm also does boat tours and snorkel excursions, with prices starting at $22.50.

Martin Booster Tracking   ★★★

Diamontbergweg 40, San Nicolas.

Martin Booster, an archeologist who founded the Archeology Museum, personally conducts these interesting tours that explore the island's pre-Columbian roots. Via jeep, he'll take you far into the interior and regale you with tales of Aruba past and present. The tour generally departs at 8:30 a.m. and goes until 3:30 p.m.; the $40 price includes lunch.

BEST VIEW:

Schooner Harbor is a great photo op for its colorfully docked sailboats and open market where fishermen and boatpeople hawk their wares in open-stall markets.

Aruba's remarkably clear and temperate waters are the island's chief attraction, and most visitors come for the plethora of excellent watersports that await. Scuba diving is excellent, with visibility often around 90 feet and some interesting wrecks to explore, including the German freighter *Antilla*, scuttled just off the beach of Malmok during World War II. This area and the waters east of Spanish Lagoon are the best for divers. For details on scuba, request the free "Discover Scuba in Aruba" brochure form the Tourist Board at ☎ *(800) TO-ARUBA*. Windsurfing conditions are ideal thanks to constant trade winds. Fisherman's Hut is a good spot for beginners, while those more advanced flock to the high waves of Boca Grandi and Manchebo

Bonaire

Windsurfing off Lac Bay, Bonaire

Beach, which has small, choppy waves. Each June, the island hosts the Aruba Hi-Winds Pro Am World Cup. The smooth sea of the south and west coasts is good for both water- and jet-skiing. A pair of golf courses awaits duffers, including the Tierra del Sol, the island's first championship links. Tennis courts can be found at virtually every major resort, or contact Aruba Racquet Club ☎ *(297) 8-60512* in Palm Beach, which boasts eight lighted courts, an exhibition center court, a fitness center and pool.

Aruba Golf Club

Golfweg 82, San Nicolas.
This desertlike course has nine holes and lots of sand traps and goats to keep things interesting. It is located on the island's southeastern part, and open only to members on weekends. Greens fees are $7.50 for nine holes, $10 if you want to go around twice. Hopefully, a long-awaited 18-hole championship course will open this year along the west end; inquire at your hotel.

Aruba Sail Cart

Bushire 23, Oranjestad.
Hours open: 10 a.m.–7 p.m.
Can't quite get the hang of windsurfing? This goofy sport is easy to learn instead. You'll be whisking about in no time on special carts equipped with a windsurf-type sail—fun! Costs about $15 for a half-hour.

Rancho El Paso

44 Washington, Oranjestad.
Here's the spot to come for trail rides on beautiful paso fino horses.

Red Sail Sports

Seaport Marketplace, Oranjestad.
The island's largest selection of watersport rentals, including scuba instructions and packages. One-tank dives start at $30.

Tierra del Sol Golf Course

Near the California Lighthouse, Northwest Coast.
Aruba finally has a championship golf course in the new Tierra del Sol, designed by the Robert Trent Jones II Group. The 18-hole, par-71 course totals 6,811 yards in length, with the highest tee at 98 feet above sea level. The links were built with an eye toward the environment; it was redesigned to leave the home of a rare island owl undisturbed, and irrigation system was installed without interfering with a bird sanctuary. Greens fees, which include cart rental and use of the driving range, are $115 in the winter and $65-$85 during summer months.

Where to Stay

Fielding's Highest Rated Hotels in Aruba

★★★★	Amsterdam Manor Beach	$90–$140
★★★★	Aruba Marriott Resort	$156–$450
★★★★	Aruba Sonesta Hotel	$115–$530
★★★★	Hyatt Regency Aruba	$205–$300
★★★	Americana Aruba Hotel	$175–$185
★★★	Aruba Palm Beach	$115–$255
★★★	Costa Linda Beach Resort	$270–$430
★★★	La Cabana Beach Resort	$95–$640
★★★	Playa Linda Beach Resort	$115–$605
★★★	Wyndham Aruba Beach Resort	$205–$375

Fielding's Most Exclusive Hotels in Aruba

★★★	La Cabana Beach Resort	$95–$640
★★★	Costa Linda Beach Resort	$270–$430
★★★★	Aruba Sonesta Hotel	$115–$530
★★★	Wyndham Aruba Beach Resort	$205–$375
★★	Bushiri Beach Hotel	$230–$330

Fielding's Best Value Hotels in Aruba

★★★★	Amsterdam Manor Beach	$90–$140
★★★	Americana Aruba Hotel	$175–$185
★★★	Aruba Palm Beach	$115–$255
★★★★	Hyatt Regency Aruba	$205–$300
★★	Best Western Manchebo	$100–$180

Most of Aruba's major properties are situated along J.E. Irausquin Boulevard on Palm Beach and L. G. Smith Boulevard just west of Oranjestad, two glorious beaches that make Aruba so popular with sun worshippers. As you would expect, prices in the resorts are quite high during wintertime; families looking to economize are best off in one of the island's many condominium units, though note that most are located in modern, somewhat sterile buildings. Many resorts have Las Vegas-style casinos attached, so finding things to do after dark is never a problem. Be sure to inquire about package deals, as active types who plan to golf and pursue watersports can often save big by paying for everything at once.

Gambling is a major attraction on Aruba and there are many casinos.

Hotels and Resorts

If you have a taste for the Vegas life, stay in one of Aruba's many top-class resorts that will serve your every need; between the health club, the casino, the lagoon-style pool and the full deck of restaurants, you'll never have to leave the premises. High-rises, of course, give you a better view of the sea; low-rises seem more intimate and are usually planted around fabulous gardens. Some hotels, such as the Sonesta, offer some of the best shopping malls on the island.

Americana Aruba Hotel　　　　　　**$175–$185**　　　　　★★★

J.E. Irausquin Boulevard 83, Oranjestad, ☎ *(800) 447-7642, (297) 8-64500. Single: $175–$185. Double: $175–$185.*

Situated directly on Palm Beach with its own full casino, this well-managed property consisting of twin high-rise towers is a busy spot, with lots going on and a social hostess to see that it stays that way. Most guests are from the U.S. and Canada. Accommodations are decent if not spectacular, with air conditioning, bamboo and wood furniture, cable TV and hair dryers; some overlook the "fantasy" swimming pool with waterfalls and spas. A great spot for kids with special supervised activities, though not exactly teeming with island flavor. 419 rooms. Credit cards: A, MC, V.

Aruba Beach Club   **$130–$290**   ★★

J.E. Irausquin Boulevard 51-53, Oranjestad, ☎ *(800) 445-8667, (297) 8-23000.*
Single: $130–$290. Double: $130–$290.

This time-share resort is on the sea at Druif Beach, and shares facilities with the Casa Del Mar Beach Resort, including three restaurants, three pools, three bars and four tennis courts. Accommodations are decent enough with air conditioning, cable TV, kitchens and balconies. The atmosphere is casual and lively. 131 rooms. Credit cards: A, DC, D, MC, V.

Aruba Marriott Resort   **$156–$450**   ★★★★

L.G. Smith Boulevard, Oranjestad, ☎ *(800) 223-6388.*
Single: $156–$450. Double: $156–$450.

Opened in May 1995, this new Marriott is a smashing full-service resort, with a magnificent free-form pool, huge casino, spiffy health spa, tennis and all the usual watersports. Lots of bars, restaurants and shopping on-site to keep visitors happy, though as with all these mega-resorts, genuine island atmosphere is scarce. 413 rooms.

Aruba Palm Beach   **$115–$255**   ★★★

J.E. Irausquin Boulevard 79, Oranjestad, ☎ *(800) 345-2782, (297) 8-63900.*
Single: $115–$255. Double: $115–$255.

This eight-story Moorish-style beachfront hotel is set amid exquisitely landscaped tropical grounds. Rooms are spacious and come with all the usual amenities, though their balconies are quite small, and not all have an ocean view. Walk-in closets are a nice touch. They offer all the expected recreational diversions, from tennis to watersports. A choice spot. 200 rooms. Credit cards: A, DC, D, MC, V.

Aruba Sonesta Hotel   **$115–$530**   ★★★★

L.G. Smith Boulevard 82, Oranjestad, ☎ *(800) 766-3782, (297) 8-36389.*
Single: $115–$530. Double: $115–$530.

No beach, but boats depart every 20 minutes to a private island seven minutes away where all sorts of watersports await. Located in the heart of Oranjestad in the Seaport Village complex, which offers some 85 shops and restaurants. After entering through an impressive atrium lobby, guests are brought to their very nice rooms, which have all the usual amenities plus minibars and tiny balconies. The children's program is free and highly rated, and the casino is huge and happening. A great spot, but only for those who don't mind being well off the beach. 299 rooms. Credit cards: A, DC, D, MC, V.

Best Western Bucuti   **$115–$235**   ★★

J.E. Irausquin Boulevard, Oranjestad, ☎ *(800) 528-1234, (297) 8-31100.*
Single: $115–$235. Double: $115–$235.

This casual low-rise has very nice accommodations with sitting areas, sofa beds, microwave ovens, refrigerators, TVs and pleasant furnishings. It shares facilities with the adjacent Best Western Manchebo Beach Resort, with all the usual watersports, tennis, pools and casino. The beach is large and wide, and Aruba's only sanctioned topless spot. 63 rooms. Credit cards: A, MC, V.

Best Western Manchebo   **$100–$180**   ★★

L.G. South Boulevard 55, Oranjestad, ☎ *(800) 528-1234, (297) 8-23444.*
Single: $100–$180. Double: $115–$180.

This sprawling low-rise, located on one of Aruba's best beaches, has guest rooms that are comfortable if unexciting; each has a refrigerator, which is always welcome. It's a sister property to the adjacent Best Western Bucuti, and between the two, guests are kept busy with all the typical resort amenities. Lots of Europeans like this spot. 71 rooms. Credit cards: A, DC, MC, V.

Best Western Talk of The Town   **$85–$215**   ★★

L.G. Smith Boulevard 2, Oranjestad, ☎ *(800) 528-1234, (297) 8-82380.*
Single: $85–$215. Double: $95–$215.

This low-rise motel near the airport has traditional guest rooms, some with microwaves and refrigerators, as well as apartments of one or two bedrooms and full kitchens. There's a good restaurant and two pools on-site; beach lovers are transported to a nicer beach than the one across a busy street. A good choice for budget travelers, as the service is quite caring. 63 rooms. Credit cards: A, DC, MC, V.

Bushiri Beach Hotel   **$230–$330**   ★★

L.G. Smith Boulevard 35, Oranjestad, ☎ *(800) 462-6868, (297) 8-25216.*
Single: $230–$330. Double: $230–$330.

Aruba's first all-inclusive resort is physically nondescript, but excellent service (this is a training school for budding hoteliers) makes up for the lack of atmosphere. There's tons to do—watersports, gambling classes, sight-seeing excursions, tennis, sailing—and lots of young people frequent this busy property. Rates are quite reasonable since everything is included—including all you can possibly drink, and then some. Parents can stash their kids in the supervised programs. 150 rooms. Credit cards: A, MC, V.

Divi Aruba Beach Resort   **$175–$370**   ★★★

J.E. Irausquin Boulevard 45, Oranjestad, ☎ *(800) 554-2008, (297) 8-23300.*
Single: $175–$370. Double: $175–$370.

Located on glorious Druif Beach, this popular low-rise is nicely casual and very friendly. Standard accommodations are in motel-like wings and feature tile floors, ceiling fans (as well as air), and small balconies. Concrete casitas offer more privacy. Other rooms front the ocean and have tiled patios and larger bathrooms, while the newer Divi Dos rooms include refrigerators and Jacuzzis. Lots of honeymooners at this spot, which comes highly recommended more for the excellent beach than for the property itself. 203 rooms. Credit cards: A, DC, MC, V.

Holiday Inn Aruba   **$121–$170**   ★★

J.E. Irausquin Boulevard 230, Oranjestad, ☎ *(800) 465-4329, (297) 8-63600.*
Single: $121–$170. Double: $121–$170.

It's a Holiday Inn, after all, so don't come looking for anything special. Rooms are acceptable but could really use a refurbishing; on the other hand, the outdoor gardens are quite nice. There's lots to keep you occupied, including watersports, six tennis courts, horseback riding, a large pool, health center and, of course, the ubiquitous casino. 600 rooms. Credit cards: A, DC, MC, V.

ARUBA

Hyatt Regency Aruba   **$205–$300**   ★★★★

J.E. Irausquin Boulevard 85, Oranjestad, ☎ *(800) 233-1234, (297) 8-61234.*
Single: $205–$300. Double: $205–$300.

Set on 12 acres fronting Palm Beach, this sprawling high-rise resort is known for its famous pool, a giant, multi-level swimming hole with waterslides, waterfalls and all sorts of bells and whistles. Rooms are all the same size (the view determines the price) with Southwestern decor, oversized baths and loads of amenities, though the balconies are disappointingly tiny. The grounds are lush and lovely with all the usual sporting diversions, a pretty lagoon dotted with black swans and lots of eateries. Grand, glorious and Aruba's best. 360 rooms. Credit cards: A, CB, DC, MC, V.

La Cabana Beach Resort   **$95–$640**   ★★★

J.E. Irausquin Boulevard 250, Oranjestad, ☎ *(800) 835-7193, (297) 8-79000.*
Single: $95–$640. Double: $95–$640.

All accommodations are suites at this beachfront resort located five minutes from Oranjestad. Choose from studios or apartments with up to three bedrooms; all have full kitchens, whirlpools, hair dryers and private balconies. Besides having the most rooms in Aruba, the hotel also boasts the biggest pool and biggest casino. One of the three pools has a 120-foot waterslide; another has a waterfall. The Club Cabana Nana ($80 per week) keeps kids out of the way. There's always something happening at this very fun and well-serviced resort. 803 rooms. Credit cards: A, DC, MC, V.

Tamarijn Aruba Resort   **$210–$200**   ★★

J.E. Irasquin Boulevard 41, Oranjestad, ☎ *(800) 554-2008, (297) 8-24150.*
Single: $210–$250. Double: $160–$200.

This all-inclusive resort is a sister property to the Aruba Divi Beach Resort, with golf carts whisking guests to and fro. The Dutch-style architecture consists of two-story townhouse-style units with the typical furnishings and amenities inside. The grounds include two tennis courts, restaurants and bars, watersports and mountain bikes. Guests can get free admittance and transport to the Alhambra Casino. Lots of honeymooners here. Note that the rates quoted are per night for at least seven days; if you're staying a shorter length of time, add $25 per person per stay. 236 rooms. Credit cards: A, CB, MC, V.

Wyndham Aruba Beach Resort   **$205–$375**   ★★★

J.E. Irausquin Boulevard 77, Oranjestad, ☎ *(800) 996-3426, (297) 8-64466.*
Single: $205–$375. Double: $205–$375.

After a brief stint by Hilton, Wyndham has taken over this former Concorde Hotel and $42 million later, has turned it into a decent and efficient operation. Accommodations are in a high-rise and nicely decorated with all the modern touches; all balconies have full ocean views. The grounds include a new watersports center, two pools (one for kids), very nice public spaces, a health club, two tennis courts and a full casino. Splurge on the VIP floors if your budget allows; the extra bucks buy a hair dryer, minibar and more space to move around. 444 rooms. Credit cards: A, DC, D, MC, V.

Apartments and Condominiums

Families and couples will find the best bargains in this section. Some complexes even throw in a rental car; if you don't plan on driving, make sure you are near an accessible bus route. Some of the most inexpensive deals can be found in the Malmok district.

Amsterdam Manor Beach   **$90–$140**   ★★★★

Oranjestad, ☎ (297) 8-31492. FAX (297) 8-71463.
Single: $90–$140. Double: $90–$140.
This complex is marked by its authentic Dutch style, with gabled roofs and inner courtyards, though it desperately needs some landscaping. Accommodations range from studios to two-bedroom apartments, all with pinewood furniture and full kitchens. The nice pool is set right on the road and lacks privacy. Eagle Beach is across the street, and guests can arrange watersports at various nearby properties. Not a top choice, but decent enough for the price. Lots of Europeans here. 72 rooms. Credit cards: A, DC, MC, V.

Caribbean Palm Village   **$85–$290**   ★★

Palm Beach Road, Oranjestad, ☎ (297) 8-62700. FAX (297) 8-62380.
Single: $85–$256. Double: $85–$290.
Located a mile from Palm Beach, this low-rise apartment complex is off the beach and away from shops and restaurants, so you'll be using the rental car that's included with the rates. Accommodations are in suites with two baths, living and dining areas and kitchens, and very nicely decorated. There's a decent Italian restaurant on-site, plus two pools and supervised programs for the kiddies. 170 rooms. Credit cards: A, DC, MC, V.

Casa del Mar Beach Resort   **$135–$400**   ★★

J.E. Irausquin Boulevard 53, Oranjestad, ☎ (297) 8-23000. FAX (297) 8-26557.
Single: $135–$400. Double: $135–$400.
This time-share resort has two-bedroom suites both on the beach and offshore, all with full kitchens. A social hostess keeps kids busy for parents who want some time alone. Facilities are shared with the Aruba Beach Club and include three restaurants, three bars, three pools, four tennis courts, watersports and a fitness center. 147 rooms. Credit cards: A, DC, D, MC, V.

Costa Linda Beach Resort   **$270–$430**   ★★★

J.E. Irausquin Boulevard 59, Oranjestad, ☎ (800) 346-7084, (297) 8-38000.
Single: $270–$430. Double: $270–$430.
This attractive beachfront resort consists of nicely appointed two- and three-bedroom suites with Roman tubs, full kitchens and two TVs. Two tennis courts, a large pool and three restaurants and bars with nightly entertainment round out the facilities. Supervised children's activities are offered during high season. 155 rooms. Credit cards: A, DC, MC, V.

Dutch Village   **$145–$415**   ★★

L.G. Smith Boulevard 39, Oranjestad, ☎ (800) 367-3484, (297) 8-32300.
Single: $145–$414. Double: $145–$415.
This stylish complex consists of time-share studios and apartments of one to three bedrooms, all with full kitchens. There's a pool, tennis and watersports on-site, but you'll have to cook in or go elsewhere for meals; several restaurants are within walk-

ing distance at the Aruba Divi and Tamrijn Aruba. 97 rooms. Credit cards: A, DC, MC, V.

Mill Resort $105–$550 ★★

J.E. Irausquin Boulevard 330, Oranjestad, ☎ *(297) 8-67700.*
Single: $105–$325. Double: $175–$550.

This condominium hotel is a five-minute walk from the beach; management will take you there if you're feeling lazy. The low-rise complex consists of studio and suites, most with full kitchens, Jacuzzis and patios; all are air-conditioned. No restaurant on-site, but the very good Old Mill is next door. The grounds include two pools, a kid's pool and two tennis courts. A good choice for families. 102 rooms. Credit cards: A, DC, D, MC, V.

Playa Linda Beach Resort $115–$605 ★★★

J.E. Irausquin Boulevard 87, Oranjestad, ☎ *(800) 346-7084, (297) 8-61000.*
Single: $115–$605. Double: $115–$605.

This time-share complex has a great location on a great beach. Accommodations are in studios and one- and two-bedroom apartments, tropically decorated and with modern kitchens and private verandas. There's an open-air restaurant, beach bar, snack bar, health club with masseuse on call and a neat swimming pool complete with falls and whirlpools. Each week Playa Linda throws a cocktail party for guests. 194 rooms. Credit cards: A, DC, MC, V.

Where to Eat

Fielding's Highest Rated Restaurants in Aruba

★★★★	Chez Mathilde	$19–$33
★★★★	Papiamento	$20–$33
★★★★	Valentino's	$16–$26
★★★	Die Olde Molen	$15–$30
★★★	La Dolce Vita	$11–$32
★★★	Mi Cushina	$12–$24
★★★	Old Cunucu House	$14–$27
★★★	Que Pasa?	$12–$26
★★★	Steamboat	$15–$15
★★★	Talk of the Town	$18–$20

Fielding's Most Exclusive Restaurants in Aruba

★★★★	Papiamento	$20–$33
★★★★	Chez Mathilde	$19–$33
★★★	Die Olde Molen	$15–$30
★★★	La Dolce Vita	$11–$32
★★★★	Valentino's	$16–$26

Fielding's Best Value Restaurants in Aruba

★★★	Steamboat	$15–$15
★★★	Charlie's Bar	$7–$22
★★★	Bali	$10–$20
★★★★	Valentino's	$16–$26
★★★	Mi Cushina	$12–$24

ARUBA

Arubans enjoy the people-to-people contact tourism has brought them.

Aruba may be small in size, but it boasts more than 100 restaurants offering just abut every type of cuisine imaginable. Be sure to try some authentic Aruban cuisine, found, among others, at Mi Cushina and Brisas del Mar, with dishes such as *sopi di yuana* (iguana soup, which tastes a lot like chicken soup), *pan bati* (griddle bread made with cornmeal) and *funchi* (cornmeal bread), *pastechi* (cheese or meat-filled turnovers) and *carbito stew* (a traditional seasoned goat meat dish). Those hankering for good old spaghetti and meatballs or cheeseburgers will have no problem in hotel coffeeshops.

Bali   **$$**   ★ ★ ★

Lloyd G. Smith Boulevard, #11, Oranjestad, ☎ *(297) 8-20680.*
Asian cuisine. Specialties: Indonesian Rijstaffel.
Lunch: Noon–3:30 p.m., prix fixe $10–$20.
Dinner: 6–11 p.m., prix fixe $10–$20.
Feast on almost 20 Indonesian specialties while bobbing gently on the sea in this intricately decorated houseboat in Schooner Harbour. In what could be Aruba's most exotic dining experience, servers present dishes of varying intensity (but nothing is overly spicy), including *nasi goreng* or *bami goreng*, rice and noodles with egg, peas, chicken or beef. Lighter meals are also served, including Western-style sandwiches. No lunch is served on Saturday. Reservations recommended. Credit cards: A, MC, V.

Boonoonoonoos   **$$$**   ★ ★

Wilhelminastraat 18A, Oranjestad, ☎ *(297) 8-31888.*
Latin American cuisine. Specialties: Ajaka (chicken in banana leaves), Jamaican jerk ribs.
Lunch: Noon–5 p.m., entrées $5–$13.
Dinner: 5:30–10:30 p.m., entrées $13–$33.

No, the eyes do not deceive, there really are four pairs of oo's in the name of this downtown restaurant, which means "extraordinary" in Jamaican patois. Located in a restored colonial home that's been brightly splashed with paint, cuisine covers the Caribbean in a large nutshell as conceived by Austrian chefs Kurt and Jacky Biermann. Signature dishes include Jamaican jerk ribs and a silky pumpkin cream soup; hungry diners will be more than satisfied with the Carib Combo platter, groaning with eight or nine dishes representing several Caribbean islands. The service is as good as the food. No lunch is served on Sunday. Reservations recommended. Credit cards: A, DC, MC, V.

Brisas del Mar $$$ ★★★

Savaneta 22A, Oranjestad, ☎ *(297) 8-47718.*
Seafood cuisine. Specialties: Broiled lobster, catch of the day.
Lunch: Noon–2:30 p.m., prix fixe $10–$30.
Dinner: 6:30–9:30 p.m., prix fixe $10–$30.
Bustling and jammed with locals, especially on music-filled weekends, Brisas del Mar is about 20 minutes away from downtown Oranjestad, but well worth the trek for spanking fresh seafood and some of the finest local dishes on the island. Reservations at this folksy beach shack are required because there are only 10 or so tables. A recurring special is a flavorful fish stew, loaded with whatever's fresh, in a tasty broth. Groups can order the Aruban special, a potpourri of lightly fried fish cakes, spiced minced shark, hot relishes, plenty of rice and corn pancakes. Reservations required. Credit cards: A, MC, V.

Buccaneer Restaurant $$ ★★

Gasparito 11-C, Oranjestad, ☎ *(297) 8-66172.*
Seafood cuisine.
Dinner: 5:30–10 p.m., entrées $7–$23. Closed: Sun.
Moderately priced seafood generally satisfies the crowds of diners who come back again and again to this aquarium-laden, cozy restaurant located just a short jog from the large hotel strip in Noord. I've heard some complaints, though, about overcooked fish, so buyer beware. If you don't want to eat, there's a popular bar, and plenty of swimming marine life at which to gaze. European-style meat dishes are also available for seafood-hating companions. No lunch is served on Mondays. Credit cards: A, DC, D, MC, V.

Chalet Suisse $$$ ★★

J.E. Irausquin Boulevard, Oranjestad,
International cuisine. Specialties: Dutch pea soup, veal in cream sauce.
Dinner: 6-10:30 p.m., entrées $15–$30. Closed: Sun.
For a change of pace, enjoy Old European specialties in a wood-panelled dining room that's a cool, comfortable spot protecting diners from the glare of the sun outside. Homey and rib-sticking dishes like Dutch split pea soup, veal and steak offer few surprises, but are exceptionally well prepared. Reservations recommended. Credit cards: A, DC, MC, V.

Charlie's Bar $$ ★★★

Main Street 56, Oranjestad, ☎ *(297) 8-45086.*
American cuisine. Specialties: Grilled shrimp, churrasco.

Lunch: Noon–4 p.m., entrées $7–$18.
Dinner: 4-9:30 p.m., entrées $7–$22. Closed: Sun.
You too can become a part of history by hanging a hankie or old tennis shoe to join
the hundreds of other artifacts on the ceiling of this 50-plus-year-old bar. It's
located in the once-thriving ghost town of San Nicolas, former headquarters of the
Standard Oil Company. Charlie's served as a watering hole for workers (no women
were allowed then) and it now overflows with tourists seeking a cold brew (or something stiffer) and a simple lunch or dinner of fresh seafood or steak. Overseeing all
this activity is Guus Dancker, who has manned the circular bar for more than 40
years. Credit cards: not accepted.

Chez Mathilde   **$$$**   ★★★★
Havenstraat 23, Oranjestad, ☎ (297) 8-34968.
French cuisine.
Lunch: 11:30 a.m.–2:30 p.m., entrées $16–$25.
Dinner: 6-11 p.m., entrées $19–$33.
Every Caribbean island must have a bastion of haute cuisine, and this elegant and
intimate beauty in a 19th-century town house is IT in Aruba. Dishes are prepared
in the classic French style by a Dutch chef, including thick and juicy lamb or veal
chops, pate, bouillabaisse, tournedos with peppercorns and lobster thermidor. The
romantic setting comes complete with candlelight, fine tableware and classical
music. No lunch is served on Sunday. Reservations required. Credit cards: A, DC, D,
MC, V.

Die Olde Molen   **$$$**   ★★★
J.E. Irausquin Boulevard, Oranjestad,
International cuisine.
Dinner: 6-10:30 p.m., entrées $15–$30. Closed: Sun.
Until the brisk winds that blow on the islands constantly threatened to ruin them,
this authentic Dutch windmill among the high-rise hotels in Palm Beach sported
real sails. Reassembled from an 1800s-era mill that was shipped over from the old
country, this tourist attraction is now a restaurant serving international food with
Aruban touches. Shrimp is often featured, prepared in a savory cheese sauce, as is
pepper steak and liqueured ice cream desserts. Worth a visit for the aesthetic value.
Credit cards: A, DC, MC, V.

La Dolce Vita   **$$$**   ★★★
Palm Beach 29, Oranjestad, ☎ (297) 8-65241.
Italian cuisine. Specialties: Veal, snapper.
Dinner: 6-11 p.m., entrées $11–$32. Closed: Wed.
Life is truly sweet here, especially for weary shoppers hoofing it down the fashion-
able Caya Betico Croes, where this well-known Italian restaurant is located. After
several hours perusing the almost duty-free jewelry and clothing shops, snag a table
(after reserving ahead) in this refurbished private home for veal and red snapper pre-
pared in different ways, or pastas and authentic Italian desserts and coffee drinks.
Reservations recommended. Credit cards: A, D, MC, V.

La Paloma   **$$$**   ★★
Noord 39, Oranjestad, ☎ (297) 8-62770.

Italian cuisine. Specialties: Conch stew with pan bati, caesar salad, red snapper.
Dinner: 6-11 p.m., entrées $13–$28. Closed: Tue.
A nice place to take the family for American-style Italian food, La Paloma is always full of patrons who like the huge menu chock-full of pasta with red sauces and huge steaks, the brisk service and old-fashioned decor (chianti bottles!). The restaurant is housed in a low-rise building in the Noord area. If you want peace and quiet, this place isn't it. The bar is a popular watering hole. Reservations recommended. Credit cards: A, MC, V.

Mi Cushina   **$$$**   ★ ★ ★

Noord Cura Cabai 24, Oranjestad, ☎ (297) 8-48335.
Latin American cuisine. Specialties: Bestia chiquito stoba, pan bati.
Lunch: Noon–2 p.m., entrées $12–$24.
Dinner: 6-10 p.m., entrées $12–$24. Closed: Tue.
There are a handful of charming small restaurants serving home-style Aruban cuisine, which is not readily available outside of the islands; one of the best is Mi Cushina, or owner Wijke Maduro's "kitchen" and family museum. Occasionally, Maduro serves iguana soup or goat stew, but usually there is fresh fish such as grouper or shark served lightly fried in cake form or minced with tangy sauce. A specialty is bestia chiquito stoba, or lamb stew in a Creole sauce. Entrées are reasonably priced because of the hearty portions, which include some of the best pan bati on the island. Reservations recommended. Credit cards: A, DC, MC, V.

Old Cunucu House   **$$$**   ★ ★ ★

Palm Beach 150, Oranjestad, ☎ (297) 8-61666.
International cuisine. Specialties: Pan fried conch, cornmeal, pan bati.
Dinner: 6-10 p.m., entrées $14–$27. Closed: Sun.
Experience the Aruba of bygone days in this 1920s-style dwelling with a restaurant whose name means "old country" house. Tasty seafood is featured, as well as New York steaks and a few Aruban specialties. The atmosphere here is very relaxed and informal, amid modern high-rise hotels that dwarf it. Even if you don't come to eat, there's a rustic bar with live and local entertainment on weekends. Reservations recommended. Credit cards: A, DC, MC, V.

Papiamento   **$$$**   ★ ★ ★ ★

Washington 61, Oranjestad, ☎ (297) 8-64544.
Latin American cuisine. Specialties: Meat or fish cooked on hot marble, clay pot seafood.
Dinner: 6-11 p.m., entrées $20–$33.
This is possibly one of Aruba's "don't miss" experiences if only for the exquisite surroundings. Dining here is like being invited to a gracious private home—which this is. Lenie and Eduardo Ellis design their own handwritten menus, garnish their Continental dishes with fresh garden herbs, and have decorated the various dining areas with distinctive plantings and antiques. You can dine by the pool or request a single honeymoon table. Perennial favorites are available on the ever-changing menu. Reservations required. Credit cards: A, MC, V.

Que Pasa?   **$$$**   ★ ★ ★

Schelpstraat Street 20, Oranjestad, ☎ (297) 8-33872.
International cuisine.

Dinner: 6 p.m.–2 a.m., entrées $12–$26.

Hang with the locals at this funky cafe/art gallery in an eclectic Dutch house. The imaginative menu features dishes from all over the world—especially good are the pasta specialties, fresh fish, homemade soups and interesting appetizers such as bitterballen and sate ajam.The portions are huge and the service friendly. The walls are adorned with colorful Haitian art; if one strikes your fancy, you can buy it on the spot. This fun spot is a real winner. Credit cards: MC, V.

Steamboat $$ ★★★

Lloyd G. Smith, Oranjestad, ☎ (297) 8-66700.
International cuisine. Specialties: Buffet brunch.
Lunch: Noon–5 p.m., entrées $7–$10.
Dinner: 5:30–11 p.m., prix fixe $15.

One of Aruba's best bargains is this buffet foodery in a shopping center near all the hotel action. Steamboat serves a large breakfast or brunch for under $8, and large sandwiches are available for lunch. Dinner is another all-you-can eat buffet that draws crowds (understandably) for $15 per person. Credit cards: A, MC, V.

Talk of the Town $$$ ★★★

L.G. Smith Boulevard 2, Oranjestad, ☎ (297) 8-23380. Associated hotel: Talk of the Town Resort.
American cuisine. Specialties: Prime rib, steaks.
Dinner: 5:30–11 p.m., entrées $18–$20. Closed: Mon.

This is an excellent stop for people with big appetites, with superb beefsteaks and prime rib feasts on Saturday nights for under $20. Located near the airport in a Best Western resort of the same name that resembles a Spanish hacienda, it's a surprisingly nice spot for quiet, intimate, candlelit dinners, and possibly the only restaurant in the Caribbean that's been awarded membership in the prestigious Chaine de Rotisseurs culinary society. Reservations recommended. Credit cards: A, DC, MC, V.

Valentino's $$$ ★★★★

Palm Beach Road, Oranjestad, ☎ (297) 8-64777. Associated hotel: Caribbean Palm Village.
Italian cuisine. Specialties: Mozzarella in carozza, penne del pastor.
Dinner: 6-11 p.m., entrées $16–$26. Closed: Sun.

Arubans like to come here to celebrate special occasions along with residents and guests at the chic Caribbean Palm Village Resort in Noord. The reason is delicious pastas—especially fettucini with salmon—intimate tables and gracious, friendly service. Before dining, patrons can unwind with drinks, then ascend to the second-story courtyard restaurant overlooking the pool and cooled by evening breezes. Reservations required. Credit cards: A, DC, MC, V.

ARUBA

Where to Shop

Aruba's duty-free status means great shopping, and the island has hundreds of stores offering everything from liquor to designer fashions. Most shops are open from 8 a.m. until 6 p.m., with a lunch hour from noon to 2 p.m. Stores in malls are shopping centers are open from 10:30 a.m. to 6 p.m. When cruise ships are in port, many stores open on Sunday and holidays. The capital city of Oranjestad is a shopper's haven, with many stores and boutiques lining the main streets. Savings of 20 to 30 percent on items such as electronics, crystal, china, perfumes, liquor, designer fashions and jewelry; you'll find brand-names such as Gucci, Cartier, Waterford, Baccarat and Tiffany's. For arts and crafts, try the street Art Gallery held the last Saturday of the month from May to October in downtown Oranjestad (between the Protestant Church and The Cellar), and The Watapana "One Cool Festival," held each Thursday from 6:30–8 p.m., again from May to October, at the parking lot in front of Parliament in Oranjestad.

Aruba Directory

Arrival and Departure

American Airlines flies nonstop to Aruba from New York's JFK Airport and Miami daily. The flight takes about 4.5 hours from NYC. ALM, United and Air Aruba fly nonstop from Miami to Aruba. If you book recommended accommodations and flights at the same time through American, you can receive substantial discounts. You can also save money by reserving your flight 14 days in advance, as well as flying Monday through Thursday. ALM also flies to Aruba six days a week from Miami. The Venezuela airline VIASA flies three times a week from Houston. Aruba's national carrier Air Aruba flies from Newark, Baltimore and Miami. Air Canada offers flights from Toronto or Montreal to either Miami or New York, and then transfer to American or ALM.

The departure tax is $10.

Business Hours

Shops open Monday–Saturday 8 a.m.–6 p.m. Alhambra Bazaar is open 5 p.m.–midnight. Banks open Monday–Friday 8 a.m.–noon and 1:30–4 p.m.

Climate

Dry and sunny, Aruba boasts average temperatures of 83 degrees F, though trade winds make the heat seem gentler. Mosquitoes get frisky in July and August, when it is less windy.

Documents

U.S. and Canadian citizens need to show some proof of citizenship—birth certificate, passport or voter's registration plus a photo ID; driver's license is not accepted. You must also show an ongoing or return ticket.

Electricity

Current runs at 110 volts, 60 cycles, as in the United States.

Getting Around

Taxis are plentiful, but the lack of meters requires firm negotiations with the driver before you take off. Drivers often know the city as well as private guides. Ask your hotel to recommend one. A dispatch office is also located at **Alhambra Bazaar and Casino** ☎ *(297) 8-21604*. You can also flag down taxis from the street. Rates are fixed (no meters) but you should confirm the price before you set off. All Aruban taxi drivers are specially trained guides; an hour's tour will run about $30.

Cars are easily rented on the island; you will need a valid U.S. or Canadian driver's license to rent a car; different agencies have various age requirements. You will save money if you rent from a local agency rather than from one of the well-known agencies. Among the best are **Hedwina Car Rental** ☎ *(297) 8-26442* and **Optima** ☎ *(297) 8-36263*. Avis, Budget and Hertz are all available at the airport.

Scooters are the best vehicle to toot around the island and are the most economical. You'll save money renting for two days or longer. **Ron's** ☎ *(297) 8-62090* and **George's** ☎ *(297) 8-25975* will deliver to the airport.

Inexpensive buses run hourly between the beach hotels and Oranjestad. The main terminal is located in South Zoutmanstraat, next to Fort Zoutman. A free Shopping Tour Bus departs hourly from 9:15 a.m.–3:15 p.m., starting at the Holiday Inn and making stops at all the major hotels on the way toward Oranjestad.

Language

Arubans are pleasantly multilingual. The official language is Dutch; also spoken are English, Spanish, Portuguese and the local dialect called Papiamento.

Medical Emergencies

Horacio Oduber Hospital ☎ *(297) 8-24300* is a modern facility near Eagle Beach, with an efficient staff. Ask your hotel about doctors and dentists on call.

Money

The official currency is the Aruban florin (also called the guilder), written as Af or Afl. American dollars are accepted at most establishments, but it might be cheaper to pay in florins.

Telephone

To call Aruba from the U.S., dial ☎ *011+297+8* followed by the five-digit number. Forget calling home from your hotel—surcharges can hike the price of an overseas call to exorbitant levels. Instead, head for SETAR, the local company, with several locations in Oranjestad and near the high-rise hotels in Palm Beach. From here, you can make phone calls using a card you purchase, and also send and receive faxes.

Time

Aruba is on Atlantic standard time, year round.

Tipping and Taxes

Aruban custom is to charge a 10–15 percent service charge and 5 percent government tax. The total of these two charges is usually written into the "tax" slot on credit cards. If you want to give more for service, feel free, but it is not expected. Hotels add 11 percent service charge.

Tourist Information

Aruba Tourism Authority, *A. Shuttestraat 2, Oranjestad, Aruba, N.A.* ☎ *011+297+82-3777*, FAX *83-4702*. From the U.S. call ☎ *(800) 862-7822*.

When to Go

New Year's is celebrated with an explosion of fireworks set off by the hotels and serenaded by strolling musicians and singers. Carnival is a blowout event, which starts two weeks before Lent, and culminates with a Grand Parade on the Sunday preceding Lent. National Anthem and Flag Day on March 18 is celebrated by displays of national dancing and folklore. A weekly Bonbini show in the courtyard of the Fort Zoutman museum on Tuesdays from 6:30–10:30 p.m. also presents island folklore, song, and dance. The International Theatre Festival is an annual event; contact the tourist board for exact dates.

ARUBA HOTELS	RMS	RATES	PHONE	CR. CARDS
Oranjestad				
★★★★ Amsterdam Manor Beach	72	$90–$140	(297) 8-31492	A, DC, MC, V
★★★★ Aruba Marriott Resort	413	$156–$450	(800) 223-6388	
★★★★ Aruba Sonesta Hotel	299	$115–$530	(800) 766-3782	A, D, DC, MC, V
★★★★ Hyatt Regency Aruba	360	$205–$300	(800) 233-1234	A, CB, DC, MC, V
★★★ Americana Aruba Hotel	419	$175–$185	(800) 447-7642	A, MC, V
★★★ Aruba Palm Beach	200	$115–$255	(800) 345-2782	A, D, DC, MC, V
★★★ Costa Linda Beach Resort	155	$270–$430	(800) 346-7084	A, DC, MC, V
★★★ Divi Aruba Beach Resort	203	$175–$370	(800) 554-2008	A, DC, MC, V
★★★ La Cabana Beach Resort	803	$95–$640	(800) 835-7193	A, DC, MC, V
★★★ Playa Linda Beach Resort	194	$115–$605	(800) 346-7084	A, DC, MC, V
★★★ Wyndham Aruba Beach Resort	444	$205–$375	(800) 996-3426	A, D, DC, MC, V
★★ Aruba Beach Club	131	$130–$290	(800) 445-8667	A, D, DC, MC, V

ARUBA HOTELS		RMS	RATES	PHONE	CR. CARDS
★★	Best Western Bucuti	63	$115–$235	(800) 528-1234	A, MC, V
★★	Best Western Manchebo	71	$100–$180	(800) 528-1234	A, DC, MC, V
★★	Best Western Talk of The Town	63	$85–$215	(800) 528-1234	A, DC, MC, V
★★	Bushiri Beach Hotel	150	$230–$330	(800) 462-6868	A, MC, V
★★	Caribbean Palm Village	170	$85–$290	(297) 8-62700	A, DC, MC, V
★★	Casa del Mar Beach Resort	147	$135–$400	(297) 8-23000	A, D, DC, MC, V
★★	Dutch Village	97	$145–$415	(800) 367-3484	A, DC, MC, V
★★	Holiday Inn Aruba	600	$121–$170	(800) 465-4329	A, DC, MC, V
★★	Mill Resort	102	$105–$550	(297) 8-67700	A, D, DC, MC, V
★★	Tamarijn Aruba Resort	236	$210–$200	(800) 554-2008	A, CB, MC, V

ARUBA RESTAURANTS		PHONE	ENTRÉE	CR. CARDS

Oranjestad

★★★	Que Pasa?	(297) 8-33872	$12–$26	MC, V

American

★★★	Charlie's Bar	(297) 8-45086	$7–$22	None
★★★	Talk of the Town	(297) 8-23380	$18–$20	A, DC, MC, V

Asian

★★★	Bali	(297) 8-20680	$10–$20	A, MC, V

French

★★★★	Chez Mathilde	(297) 8-34968	$16–$33	A, D, DC, MC, V

International

★★★	Die Olde Molen		$15–$30	A, DC, MC, V
★★★	Old Cunucu House	(297) 8-61666	$14–$27	A, DC, MC, V
★★★	Steamboat	(297) 8-66700	$7–$15	A, MC, V
★★	Chalet Suisse		$15–$30	A, DC, MC, V

Italian

★★★★	Valentino's	(297) 8-64777	$16–$26	A, DC, MC, V
★★★	La Dolce Vita	(297) 8-65241	$11–$32	A, D, MC, V
★★	La Paloma	(297) 8-62770	$13–$28	A, MC, V

ARUBA RESTAURANTS	PHONE	ENTRÉE	CR. CARDS
Latin American			
★★★★ Papiamento	(297) 8-64544	$20–$33	A, MC, V
★★★ Mi Cushina	(297) 8-48335	$12–$24	A, DC, MC, V
★★ Boonoonoonoos	(297) 8-31888	$5–$33	A, DC, MC, V
Seafood			
★★★ Brisas del Mar	(297) 8-47718	$10–$30	A, MC, V
★★ Buccaneer Restaurant	(297) 8-66172	$7–$23	A, D, DC, MC, V

ARUBA

BARBADOS

Barbados lives up to its island paradise reputation.

Barbados is the easternmost Caribbean island and part of the Lesser Antilles. Shaped a bit like a teardrop, it is known for its topographical diversity with a lovely coastline, vast fields of sugarcane, dramatic cliffs and an intriguing cave system. The island is one of the Caribbean's most sophisticated, though visitors will find the locals, known as Bajans, warm and welcoming.

Barbados offers all sorts of diversions for vacationers, making it a good choice for those who wish to do more than perfect their tan or frolic in the surf. Historic structures, botanical gardens, a handful of golf courses, duty-free shopping and a flourishing nightlife keep tourists occupied and happy. Though the island has been independent from Great Britain since 1966 (after 350 years as a colony), it retains a very British atmosphere reflected in the afternoon tea served at many resorts and a great passion for cricket and polo.

The island is believed to have gotten its name from Portuguese explorer Pedro a Campos in 1536, who called it *Los Barbados* ("the bearded ones") for the island's banyan trees that line the coast. Since the 1700s, it has been cultivating tourists; in fact, George Washington visited Barbados in 1751 with his tubercular brother Lawrence. (The island's pure air gave it the title "sanitarium of the West Indies" in the 19th century.) Today, Barbados does a large business with conventions, meetings and cruise ship passengers as well as those many who make the island their vacation destination. It has rated first among developing countries by the United Nations Development Reports in terms of living standards, and has one of the highest levels of literacy in the world. Bajans are justifiably proud of their island and share it with pleasure, rather than resentment, with visitors.

Because Barbados lies partially on the Atlantic and partly on the Caribbean, it enjoys an unusually diverse landscape and coastline, a plus when compared with many of the Caribbean's relatively flat and arid locales. The island measures 21 miles long by 14 miles wide; many of the hotels are on the western side, where the beaches are grand and the surf gentle (rougher waves are found along on the east coast). Included in the island's 166 square miles is a rainforest; a rugged, rocky coast; gentle rolling hills; and endless fields of sugarcane. Visitors would be remiss to not visit Harrison's Cave, a gorgeous cavern of crystallized limestone and subterranean pools. The climate is tropical year round, with temperatures averaging between 75 and 85 degrees Fahrenheit.

When the Portuguese explorer Pedro a Campos discovered Barbados in the 17th century, he found the island totally uninhabited. As the sailor took in the lush tropical surroundings, he spotted fig trees with clumps of bushy roots hanging from branches that resembled beards. From that came the name Barbados, which in Portuguese means "the bearded ones." Long before the first European contact, Arawak Indians were said to be living on the

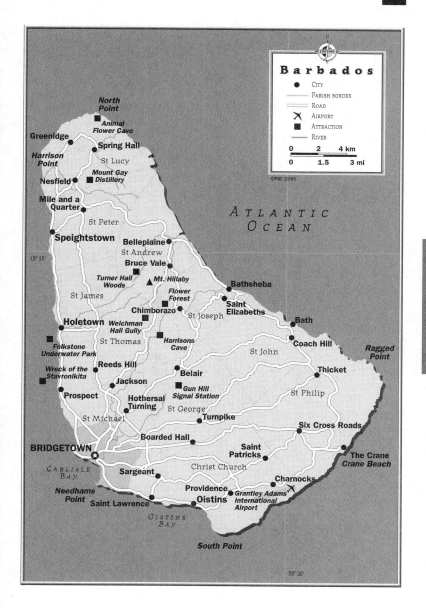

Barbados

- ● City
- Parish border
- Road
- ✕ Airport
- ■ Attraction
- River

| 0 | 2 | 4 km |
| 0 | 1.5 | 3 mi |

©FWI 1995

North Point

Animal Flower Cave

Greenidge

Spring Hall

Harrison Point

St Lucy

Nesfield

Mount Gay Distillery

Mile and a Quarter

St Peter

Speightstown

Belleplaine

St Andrew

Bruce Vale

13° 15'

Turner Hall Woods

Mt. Hillaby

Bathsheba

Flower Forest

Chimborazo

Saint Elizabeths

St Joseph

St James

Welchman Hall Gully

Bath

Holetown

St Thomas

Harrisons Cave

Coach Hill

Folkstone Underwater Park

Reeds Hill

St John

Ragged Point

Wreck of the Stavronikita

Belair

Thicket

Jackson

Gun Hill Signal Station

Prospect

Hothersal Turning

St George

St Philip

St Michael

Turnpike

Boarded Hall

Six Cross Roads

BRIDGETOWN

Saint Patricks

The Crane
Crane Beach

CARLISLE BAY

Sargeant

Christ Church

Charnocks

Needhams Point

Providence

Saint Lawrence

Oistins

Grantley Adams International Airport

OISTINS BAY

South Point

ATLANTIC OCEAN

59° 30'

BARBADOS

island, but they were long gone by the time of the first British expedition in 1625. Two years later, 80 British settlers under the leadership of Captain John Powell settled at Jamestown (later renamed Holetown). Soon, conditions proved highly favorable for tobacco, cotton and sugarcane production, and thousands of African and European slaves were shipped over to till the fields. A strong fortress system (26 forts along 21 miles of coast) kept the island from invasion, and Barbados became the only island in the Caribbean to be under uninterrupted British rule for more than three centuries. In 1937, economic problems caused by the fluctuating price of sugar led to demonstrations in Bridgetown, which resulted in the establishment of a British Royal Commonwealth to the West Indies—a gesture that proved instrumental in bringing about social and political reform, including universal adult suffrage in 1951. Fifteen years later, Barbados received its full sovereignty.

Today Barbados is a British Commonwealth nation with a parliamentary system of government headed by an appointed governor-general and an elected prime minister. British influence extends to the courts, laws, language and place names.

People

Barbados' population totals some 260,000 people, most descended from West Africa (slavery was abolished on the island in 1834) with a generous sprinkling of Great Brit descendants. Though 100 religions are represented on the island, the population is primarily Anglican. Despite independence 30 years ago (Barbados is officially a British Commonwealth nation), the Queen of Great Britain still serves as the Queen of Barbados, and government is a democratic parliamentary system headed by an appointed governor-general and an elected prime minister. Many locals retain a British accent. Children wear well-pressed school uniforms, everyone loves cricket and polo and afternoon tea is a common treat. The literacy rate is among the world's highest and people retain a fresh mix of Caribbean informality and British manners. Bajans are friendly and unassuming, patiently answering tourists' questions while throwing in a bit of sincere hospitality at the same time.

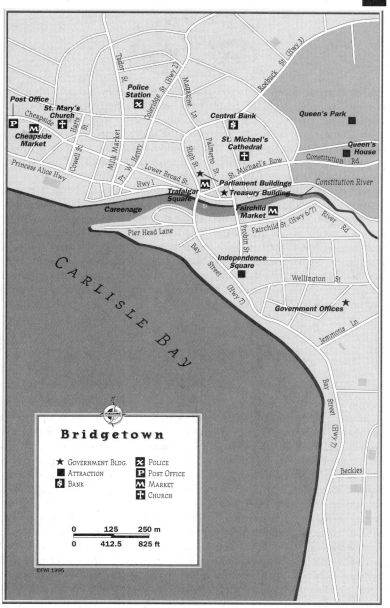

Beaches

All beaches in Barbados are open to the public, even those abutting the high-priced hotels; local law requires that access to the beaches be open, either through the road or through the hotel's entrance. A beautiful drive through sugarcane fields will take you to the rugged, surf-pounding beaches of the east coast (North Point, Cove Bay and Archer's Bay), but most people prefer the calmer western beaches called the **Gold Coast** (Paradise Beach, Paynes Bay and Sandy Lane Bay, Treasure Beach, Gibbs Bay, Heywoods Beach, Rockley and Bentson Beach). The water most everywhere stays a comfortable few degrees below body temperature. The most secluded and charming hotel beach is behind the **Coconut Creek Club**, in St. James. **Mulins Bay**, just south of Speightstown, is a particularly pleasant nonhotel beach with a good restaurant-bar and a free outdoor shower. Parking is in the lot across the road. The most dramatic beach is most likely **Batsheba**, on the rugged northeast side, where foamy waves pound the shores with huge salt sprays. Here you'll see lots of old Barbadian families taking their weekend and holiday escapes.

Underwater

Busy, industrious Barbados has long been preoccupied with maintaining its commercial needs, frequently at the expense of the marine life lying just off its shores. Pollution, dynamite fishing and anchors have each taken their toll on the reefs, so it should be no surprise that the best underwater attractions the island offers are of the unnatural kind: wrecks. There are rolling plains of coral along the west and south coasts, but divers expecting extensive formations or reasonable quantities of marine life inhabiting them will be in for a disappointment. Barbados' coral structures tend to lie flat, rather than producing the caves and caverns found on other islands. But, if you come for the wrecks, there are a number to hold your interest, including the huge *Stavronikita*, a freighter now developing a forest of black coral on its decks. Visitors who come to the island in fall may be able to dive the pristine and beautiful northern coast, which is otherwise fairly inaccessible due to rough water. Sharks are rare, islandwide, and this includes at misnamed Shark Reef. The inner fringe reef averages 40 to 60 feet deep and provides decent breeding ground, particularly along the southern coast, while some of the best diving lies right off **Bridgetown** in **Carlisle Bay**. Barbados has a recompression chamber available at St. Anne's Fort. Snorkelers can visit the *Pamir*, a 150-foot vessel resting in shallow waters (easily visible from the shoreline near Mullins Bay), while Holetown's **Folkestone Park** offers a popular underwater trail.

Walking is a beloved pastime for many locals. Indeed, the activity may remind visitors of country excursions in England: rolling green hills and breezy coastlines with scheduled, punctual walks. Thigh-challenging hikes are at a minimum; the island is one of the most densely populated countries in the world, its fields extensively cultivated and, owing to the limestone-based topography, the hillsides slope gently toward the muted summit of **Mount Hillaby** (1116 feet). Be sure to connect up with the local National Trust (☎ *[246] 426-2421*), which organizes free Sunday walks. These depart at 6 a.m. and 3:30 p.m. year-round, average three hours and provide visitors a chance to mingle with locals. The excursions are so well attended they break up the group into three speeds, from casual (termed "stop and stare," and guided with an educational p.o.v.) to breakneck. Several dedicated forest reserves (that charge admission) provide Barbados' most scenic natural environments, although solitude is probably best located on the broad east coast

Although its 800-plus miles of paved roads are busy with motor traffic, Barbados has a dedicated local cycling club and world-class riders. While many islands in the Eastern Caribbean are either limited in their road network or laced with killer hills, the Bajan countryside can be ridden for days with a variety of new challenges. One word of caution: the industrious area in and around Bridgetown and along the west coast is always choked with cars. Try taking Highway 6 out of Bridgetown, taking a right at Six Cross Roads and then left a couple miles later to Crane Bay; returning via Highway 7 (passing the airport) will provide a circuit of about 33 miles. A 55-mile tour of the island's perimeter on the main highway is geared toward seasoned cyclists. The area around Bathsheba provides beautiful coastal hills

BARBADOS

Barbados Off The Beaten Path

Animal Flower Cave

Located on the northern-most tip of Barbados, this cavern contains pools—some large enough to swim in—filled with colorful sea anemones. The views of the ocean from the cave can inspire stunning photographs.

North Point

St. Lucy

Mount Gay

Speightstown

St. Peter

Mullins Bay

St. Andrew

Turner's Hall Woods

St. Joseph

St. James

Cane Field

St. Thomas

St. Michael

Sugar Machinery

Situated in a modern sugar factory, the Sir Frank Huston Sugar Museum contains a collection of restored machinery gathered from Barbados sugar cane plantations. If you visit from February to June, you can also watch the modern "reaping" of sugar cane.

Cricket

The national sport of the island, cricket is played almost year-round at the Kensington Oval in Bridgetown. The domestic cricket season runs May to June, while international matches are held January through April.

The Wreck of the Berwyn

Sunk in Carlisle in 1919, this French tug is accessible to both divers and snorkelers. The hull provides shelter for parrot fish, angel fish, and sergeant majors, as well as corals, sponges and sea anemones.

Carlisle Bay

Morgan Lewis Windmill

Near Farley Hill Park, this 250-year-old cane-crushing mill is the largest remaining windmill in the Caribbean. Last operated in 1944, the mill occupies a hill-top that offers splendid panoramas.

Iron Gardens

Detour to Perry Gap to see Dr. Lance Bannister's "Iron Gardens," a collection of sculptures crafted out of old auto parts. Whimsical subjects include a horse and rider, as well as a "globe" of the Earth. (809) 426-1336.

Flower Forest

Explore 50 acres of flowers and tropical plants growing in what was once a sugar plantation. Take your time to inspect blossoms and foliage, or watch for wildlife.

Tent Bay

St. John

Harry Bayley Observatory

Built in 1963, this observatory is equipped with a 14-inch reflector telescope, and offers the public the chance to view night-time Caribbean skies every Friday evening from 8:30 to 11:30 p.m.

St. George

Grantley Adams International Airport

Oistins

Bridgetown

Mallalieu Motor Collection

Located near the Garrison, this small, privately owned collection of vintage cars includes a Vanden Plas Princess, a Wolseley, and a Lanchester. (809) 426 -4640.

BARBADOS

and quieter riding. Although major intersections are generally well-marked, it's easy to get lost on the maze of roads which navigate the interior; pick up an Ordnance Survey map that details the lattice of paved possibilities. Better yet, ride with Bajans who know their island's many twists and turns like the back of their hand. The Barbados Cycling Union holds rides and competitions nearly every weekend; contact Mario or Larry Williams at M.A. Williams for information.

Barbados' limestone foundation has created several caves of note. **Harrison's Cave** is the most famous, but visitors must experience the cave via a 20-minute electric tram ride that winds down into the cave's depths. There are stalactites and stalagmites dripping peacefully, and waterfalls leading to an underground lake. Spelunkers may be happier with nearby **Coles Cave** which, though well-explored, has not been turned into a ride and allows for a more personal experience. Bring a flashlight; ask for directions to Cole's at the Harrison gift shop. Finally, an underground experience of a different nature is provided at the **Animal Flower Cave** at the northern tip of Barbados. The caves are at sea level (and below) and the titular animals are sea anemones, referred to locally as animal flowers, which are found at water level throughout the caverns. Wear well-soled shoes as the rocks inside the cave are slippery.

With big swells landing on the east coast almost year-round, Barbados is one of the few legitimate surfing destinations in the Eastern Caribbean. The best action is found in **Bathsheba** (where the Barbados International Surfing Championship is held early November), although **South Point** and **Needham's Point** (just outside Bridgetown) are also good spots. Waves die down for the summer, with winter providing the best rides.

What Else to See

The capital city of Bridgetown is a major free port, which means shopping, and lots of it, along bustling Board Street, where prices are often 30 to 50 percent below those in the States in the tony, well-tended stores and boutiques. The city—and it is indeed one—is also home to several historic structures, including St. Michael's Cathedral, said to have been visited by George Washington. Dotted among Bridgetown's many modern buildings are Victorian Gothic structures and small colonial buildings with fanciful wrought-iron balconies. While in the city, be sure to check out the Barbados Museum, a former military prison turned into a fascinating look at island life in the 19th century.

More shopping can be found, at a much more relaxed pace, in Speightstown, on the west coast, which has a more colonial look and flavor than busy Bridgetown.

History buffs should make tracks for Gun Hill Signal Station, which also served as a military command post and a convalescent station. The views are extraordinary, and don't miss the huge lion statue carved from a single piece of rock in 1868 by an officer posted at Gun Hill. Another well-preserved signal station, Grenade Hall, is in St. Peter.

Besides its natural beauty, Barbados offers visitors a wealth of historical and botanical attractions. The most popular by far—and rightly so—is Harrison's Cave, an eerily beautiful cavern formed from crystallized limestone over the past hundreds of thousands of years. Though it was first discovered in 1796, it laid in sleepy solitude until 1970, when it was "rediscovered" by Ole Soresen. Visitors tour the cave via electric tram.

Other natural treasures include the Flower Forest, located among the hills of St. Joseph. Called Barbados' "Garden of Eden," its 50 acres of flowers and plants flourish wildly, and visitors are encouraged to touch and smell the fragrant blossoms. Other colorful sights await at Andromeda Gardens, where the Barbados National Trust has cultivated an excellent collection of indigenous and exotic tropical flowers and plants. The Trust also oversees Welchman Hall Gully, a mile-long gully of lovely trees, flowers and plants.

The Barbados Wildlife Reserve in St. Peter is a mahogany forest where a multitude of animals live in freedom—all, that is, except for a very large python. Visitors can catch up-close glimpses of the Barbados Green Monkey, otters, mongoose, porcupine and Brocket deer, among other creatures. There's also an information center, snack bar and aviary on the site.

Finally, Barbados is dotted with plantation houses well worth a look for anyone interested in antiques. Among the finest are Sam Lord's Castle (actually a mansion, and part of the Marriott resort of the same name), Francia Plantation House, a unique blend of Caribbean and European styles; and St. Nicholas Abbey, a Jacobean mansion form the late 1600s where you can view a home movie showing island life in 1935.

BEST VIEW:

Grenade Hall, a restored 19th century signal station, surrounded by a user-friendly tropical forest, offers the most spectacular panorama of the island.

Historical Sites

Francia Plantation ★★★

Highway X, St. George, ☎ *(246) 429-0474.*
Hours open: 10 a.m.–4 p.m.

This family house, still home to descendants of the original owner, provides an authentic look at old Barbados. Also worth checking out is the Sunbury Plantation Home in St. Philip (☎ *423-6270*), a 300-year-old home filled with fine antiques. General admission: $4.

Grenade Hall Signal Station

Farley Hill, St. Peter, ☎ *(246) 422-8826.*
Hours open: 10 a.m.–5 p.m.

In the early 1800s, six towering signal stations were erected around Barbados to relay intelligence information and other messages quickly around the island. Grenade Hall was the contact with Dover Fort to the West and Cotton Tower to the southeast. Restored by the Barbados Wildlife Reserve in 1992, the tower now houses detailed exhibits on the historical signaling system. Upstairs are wonderful panoramas in all directions and telescopes that give line of sight views to the other towers. Don't leave without exploring the surrounding forest, where a coral stone walkway winds languidly through trees and rock outcrops.

Gun Hill Signal Station ★★★★

Highway 4, St. George, ☎ *(246) 429-1358.*
Hours open: 9 a.m.–5 p.m.

This 1818 signal station was used by the British Army. Even if you're not into such things, the views from atop the highland are worth the trip. General admission: $4.

Morgan Lewis Sugar Windmill ★

Highway 2, St. Andrew, ☎ *(246) 426-2421.*
Hours open: 9 a.m.–5 p.m.

This historic spot provides a fine example of the windmills used to process sugarcane in the 17th-19th centuries. Nice views of the "Scotland District." General admission: $3.

Old Synagogue ★★★

Synagogue Lane, Bridgetown, ☎ *(246) 426-5792.*
Hours open: 9 a.m.–4 p.m.

Built by Jews from Brazil in 1654, the synagogue is the second-oldest in North America. It was partially destroyed by hurricane and rebuilt to its present state in 1833. The grounds include a cemetery, still used today, with graves of early Jewish settlers from as far back as the 1630s.

St. Nicholas Abbey ★★★

Cherry Tree Hill, St. Peter, ☎ *(246) 422-8725.*
Hours open: 10 a.m.–3:30 p.m.

This is Barbados' oldest structure, dating back to 1650, though it was actually an abbey only in the mind of a former owner, who dubbed it so in the 1800s. Two hundred acres of sugarcane surround the Jacobean-style great house of wood and stone. General admission: $3.

Museums and Exhibits

Barbados Museum ★★

St. Ann's Garrison, St. Michael, ☎ *(246) 427-0201.*
Hours open: 9 a.m.–5 p.m.

This unusually fine museum, housed in a former military prison, traces the island's history from prehistoric times to the present. Good exhibits on natural history, West Indian maps and arts and the slave trade. The grounds also include a decent gift shop and an excellent cafe. General admission: $5.

Parks and Gardens

Andromeda Gardens   ★★★

Bathsheba, St. Joseph, ☎ *(246) 433-9261.*
Hours open: 9 a.m.–5 p.m.
This unique spot encompasses eight acres of gardens set into oceanfront cliffs. The emphasis is on unusual plants from around the world, and they have those aplenty, plus hundreds of orchids, hibiscus and palm varieties—plus a babbling brook winding throughout. General admission: $5.

Barbados Wildlife Preserve

Farley Hill, St. Peter, ☎ *(246) 422-8826.*
Hours open: 10 a.m.–5 p.m.
Located in a pretty mahogany forest, this reserve is home to lots of animals that roam the grounds in freedom (though the large resident python is, happily for visitors, caged). The biggest attraction is the Barbados Green Monkey, a small long-tailed creature. You're also apt to spot mongoose, otters, Brocket deer, iguana, hyrax, tortoises and a number of bird species in the walk-in aviary. There's a Information and Education Center and snack bar on hand.

Farley Hill   ★★

Farley Hill, St. Peter.
Hours open: 8:30 a.m.–6 p.m.
Very rugged grounds and the ruins of a once-grand plantation house mark this picturesque national park. General admission: $2.

Flower Forest

Highway 2, St. Joseph, ☎ *(246) 433-8152.*
Hours open: 9 a.m.–5 p.m.
Set on an old sugar plantation in the scenic Scotland District, this park encompasses eight acres of flowering trees and shrubs. Great views of Mt. Hillaby, too. General admission: $6.

Welchman Hall Gully   ★★★

Highway 2, St. Thomas, ☎ *(246) 438-6671.*
Hours open: 9 a.m.–5 p.m.
A peaceful oasis owned by the Barbados National Trust, with acres of labeled trees and flowers, and possibly even a green monkey. The breadfruit trees are said to be descended from seeds brought by Captain Bly. General admission: $5.

Tours

Animal Flower Cave   ★★★

Highway 1B, North Point, ☎ *(246) 439-8797.*
Hours open: 9 a.m.–4 p.m.
The cavern takes its name from the small sea anemones that prettily open their tentacles, but don't expect to see too many nowadays. General admission: $2.

Atlantis Submarines Barbados   ★★

McGregor Street, Bridgetown, ☎ *(246) 436-8929.*
Hours open: 9 a.m.–6 p.m.

The perfect way to see the world below, without getting wet, is aboard an Atlantis submarine, which takes its passengers in air-conditioned comfort some 150 feet beneath the water's surface. The two-hour tour includes the sighting of a shipwreck. Recommended for everyone but the claustrophobic. General admission: $70.

Barbados Wildlife Preserve   ★★

Highway 1, St. Peter, ☎ *(246) 422-8826.*
Hours open: 10 a.m.–5 p.m.

This walk-through preserve, essentially a monkey sanctuary run by the Barbados Primate Research Center, features free-roaming land turtles, peacocks, parrots— even a kangaroo. It also has good exhibits on the island's natural history and an interesting walk-in aviary. General admission: $10.

Guided Tours

Bridgetown.

If you're itching to see Barbados but would rather leave the driving to someone else, contact one of these tour operators. Highland Outdoor Tours *(☎ [246] 438-8069)* totes tourists along in a tractor-drawn, open-air jitney, or horseback or foot. Secret Treasures Outdoor Expeditions *(☎ [246] 420-4488)* promises off-the-beaten-track leisurely treks along the East Coast to hidden beaches and coves. Margaret Leacock *(☎ [246] 425-0099)* offers customized tours, while VIP Tour Services *(☎ [246] 429-4617)* gives tailor-made tours in air-conditioned Mercedes Benz cars. Finally, Mystic Mountain Bike Tours *(☎ [441] 424-4370)* provides half- and full-day mountain bike trips.

Harrison's Cave   ★★

Highway 2, St. Thomas, ☎ *(246) 438-6640.*
Hours open: 9 a.m.–4 p.m.

This is the island's biggest tourist attraction, and rightfully so, as these limestone caverns are unique to the Caribbean. Better yet, it's all tastefully done with discreet lighting that preserves the feel of the place. Don a hard hat (more for drama than necessity) and ride an electric tram through the immense caverns, which come complete with waterfalls and streams. Reservations are recommended. General admission: $8.

Highland Outdoor Tours

Bridgetown, ☎ *(246) 438-8069.*

Experience the real Barbados—far from the glittery resorts and tony restaurants— with this new tour operator that specializes in adventure travel. Options include a 2.5-hour Horseback Trek to the island's east coast for a bareback ride in the surf and a Caribbean lunch on the beach ($100); the Scenic Safari Hike, a five-mile walk through the pristine Scotland district and lunch on the beach ($70); and the Plantation Tour, a two-hour jaunt on a tractor-driven open jitney through some of the Barbados' great plantations ($25). You can also tour the plantations via horseback ($50).

Jolly Roger Cruises ★★

Shallow Draft, Bridgetown, ☎ *(246) 436-2149.*

Lots of options for multihour cruises, including the *Bajan Queen*, a Mississippi riverboat replica that is the largest cruise ship of its kind and the only one offering sit-down dining. There are also two very fun pirate frigate replicas that offer snorkel trips and general merrymaking. Prices start at $52.50 and include transport from your hotel.

Where the Rum Comes From ★★

Pick up from your hotel, St. Peter.

The wonderful world of rum is the focus of this tour, held each Wednesday from noon–2:15 p.m. You'll tour Cockspur, manufacturers of Barbadian rum for more than 200 years, then sip the potable and groove to a steel band while supping on a buffet meal. General admission: $28.

Sports

Golf, tennis, horseback riding, watersports—Barbados has it all, and then some. Trekking is a popular pastime among both locals and tourists; contact the Barbados National Trust (☎ *[246] 426-2421)* to hook up on one of its free Sunday walks. The Railway Track, which covers some 37 miles along the east coast, makes for a particularly scenic stroll.

As on most Caribbean islands, watersports reign supreme; Barbados is especially good for windsurfers between November and May, when the trade winds make for perfect conditions along the south coast; Silver Sands is particularly challenging for intermediate to advanced surfers. (Contact the Barbados Windsurfing Club at ☎ *[246] 428-6001* for details.) Diving is popular and while there are no dramatic plunging walls, there is an extensive system of fringing, patch and bank reefs. Among the many interesting wrecks to explore is the Greek freighter *Stavronikita*, sunk intentionally in 1978 after gutted by fire. All doors and hatch covers have been removed to make virtually every part of the 356-foot-long ship accessible. Divers and snorkelers alike can inspect the *Berwyn*, a French tug sunk in 1919, that rests in just 20 feet of water. Those who want to experience the underwater world but not get wet can take a cruise in *Atlantic Submarine* or *Atlantis Seatrec*, a reef observation craft.

Dive Shop, The

Aquatic Gap, St. Michael, ☎ *(246) 426-9947.*
Hours open: 8:30 a.m.–4:30 p.m.

It offers great scuba excursions to colorful reefs and wrecks, with prices starting at $40 per one-tank dive. Beginners can take a resort course for $50, and deep-sea fishers can arrange a charter for $300 per boat per half-day.

Barbados Windsurfing Club

Silver Sands Hotel, Christ Church, ☎ (246) 428-6001.
Rent a windboard for $20 an hour, $40 per half day, or partake in a lesson to learn this challenging sport.

Fun Seekers, Inc.

78 Old Chancery Lane, Christ Church, ☎ (246) 435-9171.
You can rent motorbikes or bicycles here, or better yet, partake of a cruise aboard the 44-foot *Limbo Lady*. Lunch cruises cost $50 and include snorkeling; sunset sails are $40. They'll pick you up at your hotel if need be.

Caribbean International Riding

Auburn, St. Joseph, ☎ (246) 433-1453.
Hours open: 7:30 a.m.–6 p.m.
Trail rides on handsome horses range from a 75-minute jaunt ($28) to a three-hour tour of the historic Villa Nova Plantation, complete with lunch, for $88.

Heywoods Golf Course

St. Peter, ☎ (246) 422-4900.
Only guests of the Almond Beach Village can golf at this nine-hole, par-three course. Fees are $35, and if the mood suits you, you can go around twice without paying for the privilege.

Royal Westmoreland Golf Course

St. James, ☎ (246) 422-4653.
Situated just inland from the Colony Club, this St. James Beach Hotels-owned course covers 290 acres of well-manicured grounds. Robert Trent Jones Jr. designed the 18 holes, the back nine of which just opened in August 1995. (The first nine opened about six months earlier.) Greens fees, which include a cart and unlimited use of the driving range, range from $75 to $90 in the off season, $110-$145 in the winter. Guests at Coconut Creek, Tamarind Cove, Colony Club and Crystal Cove receive preferential access and start times.

Sandy Lane Golf Course

Sandy Lane Hotel, St. James, ☎ (246) 432-1311.
This is the island's best, an 18-hole championship course with a famed 7th hole that has an elevated tee and wonderful views. Greens fees are $120 for $18 holes, $90 for nine.

Where to Stay

Fielding's Highest Rated Hotels in Barbados

★★★★★	Glitter Bay	$200–$325
★★★★★	Royal Pavilion	$235–$330
★★★★★	Sandy Lane Hotel	$500–$955
★★★★	Barbados Hilton	$134–$285
★★★★	Cobblers Cove Hotel	$340–$850
★★★★	Coral Reef Club	$74–$250
★★★★	Marriott's Sam Lord's	$110–$225
★★★★	Sandals Barbados	$105–$335
★★★★	Sandpiper Inn	$110–$445
★★★	Island Inn	$135–$225

Fielding's Most Exclusive Hotels in Barbados

★★★★★	Sandy Lane Hotel	$500–$955
★★★★	Cobblers Cove Hotel	$340–$850
★★★	Tamarind Cove Hotel	$266–$466
★★★	Haywoods Wyndham	$185–$535
★★	Crystal Cove	$241–$442

Fielding's Best Value Hotels in Barbados

★★★	Ocean View Hotel	$34–$71
★★★	Woodville Beach Apartmens	$56–$110
★★	Sugar Cane Club	$40–$85
★★★★	Coral Reef Club	$74–$250
★★	Sea Foam Haciendas	$70–$93

Your budget is the only limit when choosing accommodations on Barbados. You can pay a small king's ransom at one of the tonier resorts such as Coconut Creek or Grand Barbados Beach, enjoy the hassle-free living on an all-inclusive resort, or tuck into a historic inn where friendly owners take you under their wing. There's even a hotel dedicated to windsurfers. The all-inclusive Almond Beach Village has undergone a $12-million face-lift, while the Sandridge Resort has added six waterfront suites, restyled rooms and a remodeled pool with a dramatic waterfall and coral stone deck.

Hotels and Resorts

Barbados' hotels are among the poshest in the Caribbean and resorts such as the Royal Pavilion and Sandy Lane compete with the world's best while Treasure Beach perhaps boasts the most repeat visitors. Like everything else in Barbados, many hotels have been renovated in recent years to gleaming effect. The **Coral Reef Club** and the **Sandpiper Inn** have gotten face-lifts. The Moorish-style **Tamarind Cove** has added suites, shops and a classy seafood restaurant. The first all-inclusive resort, once called Pineapple Beach Club, now the **Almond Beach Club**, features one of the best authentic Bajan restaurants, **Enid's**, as well as upgraded fitness facilities and an "All-inclusive Plus" program.

A new **Concorde** charter service package offers a two-hour flight from JFK Airport on a Concorde and an 8 day/7-night package in one of 15 luxury hotels. Prices range from $2800–$5500. For more information call ETM Travel Group at ☎ *(203) 454-0090*, or toll-free *(800) 992-7700*. This is a fine (and easy!) deal for honeymooners since most of the finer resort hotels also offer on-staff consultation for wedding arrangements.

Bridgetown

Barbados Hilton $134–$285   ★★★★

Needhams Point, Bridgetown, ☎ (800) 445-8667, (246) 426-0200.
Single: $134–$260. Double: $146–$285.
A good, safe choice—but don't expect a lot of Caribbean flavor at this hotel. Surrounded by nice beaches and near an oil refinery that sometimes produces pungent odors, this spot has all the modern conveniences you'd expect from a Hilton—plus lots of conventioneers running around in name tags. The pool is excellent but for unknown reasons closes at 6 p.m. There's a health club and tennis courts on site, as well as an old British Fort for exploring. Accommodations are fine and the service is professional. 184 rooms. Credit cards: MC, V.

Coconut Creek Club Hotel $216–$420   ★★★

St. James Street, Bridgetown, ☎ (800) 462-2566, (246) 432-0803.
Single: $216–$323. Double: $268–$420.
Set amid beautifully landscaped grounds, this very private resort attracts lots of European celebrities. Accommodations, in Spanish-style cottages, are small but very clean and chic, with tropical decor, air conditioning and walk-in closets. They sit on a low bluff overlooking two quite secluded beaches that almost disappear during high tide. Somehow, Coconut Creek manages to be both informal and sophisticated, and the service is outstanding. 53 rooms. Credit cards: A, MC, V.

Colony Club Hotel   **$272–$534**   ★ ★ ★
St. James Street, Bridgetown, ☎ *(800) 466-2526, (246) 422-2335.*
Single: $272–$455. Double: $322–$534.
A simple but gracious resort lining one of Barbados' best beaches, Colony Club
puts guests up in Mediterranean-style bungalows with private patios and the usual
amenities. TVs can be rented for those who can't go without. Watersports are complimentary, as is the shuttle that runs guests into town. A nice, quiet spot that
appeals mainly to travelers from England. 76 rooms. Credit cards: A, MC, V.

Crane Beach Hotel   **$105–$300**   ★ ★
Crane Beach, Bridgetown, ☎ *(800) 466-2526, (246) 423-6220.*
Single: $105–$300. Double: $105–$300.
Set on a remote area overlooking a gorgeous beach, the Crane has the feel of a private estate. Oceanview rooms are stocked with antiques (but no air conditioning);
some have kitchenettes. The picturesque Roman-style pool and a statue-punctuated
grassy courtyard add a nice touch of class. The grounds include four tennis courts
and a few restaurants. Novice swimmers beware: the surf here can be rough. 18
rooms. Credit cards: A, DC, MC, V.

Ginger Bay Beach Club   **$80–$205**   ★ ★
Crane, Bridgetown, ☎ *(800) 466-2526, (246) 423-5810.*
Single: $80–$205. Double: $80–$205.
Situated on a small bluff overlooking one of Barbados' best beaches, Ginger Bay is
a lovely property, but its remote location is not for everyone. All accommodations
are in spacious one-bedroom suites with kitchens, modern baths and canopied king
beds. They open onto private terraces complete with hammocks—a nice touch. The
beach is reached via a staircase though a cave. Except for a pool and tennis court,
there's not much happening here, but beach lovers are kept happy. 16 rooms. Credit
cards: A, DC, D, MC, V.

Grand Barbados Beach   **$125–$605**   ★ ★ ★
Aquatic Gap, Bridgetown, ☎ *(800) 466-2526, (246) 426-0890.*
Single: $125–$605. Double: $135–$605.
Set on Carlisle Bay, one mile from Bridgetown, this sophisticated hotel does big
business with leisure as well as business travelers, who like the full-service amenities
lacking at many other island resorts. Guest rooms are small but modern and come
equipped with the usual creature comforts, including air and satellite TV. The pool
is too small if everyone decides to partake, but the beach is nice and surprisingly
quiet given its near-city locale. All watersports are free, including sailing. The long
pier adds atmosphere. 133 rooms. Credit cards: A, DC, MC, V.

Marriott's Sam Lord's   **$110–$225**   ★ ★ ★ ★
Bridgetown, ☎ *(800) 228-9290, (246) 423-5918.*
Single: $110–$225. Double: $110–$225.
Marriott's Sam Lord's Castle takes its name from the 1820 great house built by
Samuel Hall Lord, known as the "Regency Rascal" for his penchant for tricking
ships to his jagged shore, then looting the smashed cargo. Today's resort is set
among 72 acres with formal gardens and all the resort amenities you'd expect from
a fine Marriott property. Accommodations are quite varied; choose a cottage if bud-

BARBADOS

get permits. All runs smoothly, but the overabundance of conventioneers can leave individual travelers feeling forgotten and overwhelmed. 234 rooms. Credit cards: A, DC, D, MC, V.

Sandals Barbados   **$105–$335**   ★★★★

Black Rock, Bridgetown, ☎ *(800) 726-3257, (246) 424-0888.*
Single: $105–$235. Double: $125–$335.
A complete overhaul has left Sandals looking shiny and spiffy. This all-inclusive resort, open only to heterosexual couples, provides all meals, drinks and recreational diversions in one price. The activity is there for the taking—those who would rather leave it may be happier at a less-organized resort. Everything you'd ever want to do is there for the asking, and guests work frantically to earn a tiny pair of sandals to show what good sports they are. Lots of honeymooners. 178 rooms. Credit cards: A, MC, V.

Christ Church

Benston Windsurfing Hotel   **$50–$70**   ★

Maxwell, Christ Church, ☎ *(246) 428-9095.*
Single: $50–$70. Double: $55–$70.
You know the windsurfing's gotta be good if an entire (albeit small) hotel is dedicated to it. Those staying at this basic property are devoted to the sport, and, as such, are generally young and lively. Accommodations are spacious but bare-bones; everyone's always out zipping along the surf, anyway. They'll teach you how to do it, but most who come here are already pretty darn good. 15 rooms. Credit cards: A, DC, D, MC, V.

Caribbee Beach Hotel   **$60–$105**   ★★

Hastings, Christ Church, ☎ *(800) 466-2526, (246) 436-6232.*
Single: $60–$90. Double: $65–$105.
There's no beach at this beach hotel, just the ocean slamming into a seawall. Oh well., the rates are low, though they probably should be even lower. Rooms are air-conditioned and furnished in basic motel style. The absence of both a beach and a pool make other budget properties a better choice. 55 rooms. Credit cards: A, DC, D, MC, V.

Divi Southwinds Resort   **$115–$245**   ★★

St. Lawrence Gap, Christ Church, ☎ *(800) 367-3484, (246) 428-8076.*
Single: $115–$245. Double: $115–$245.
Set on 20 acres, this resort partially lines the beach, though most of the complex is inland. Accommodations, in white stucco buildings, are mostly suites with full kitchens, living areas, air conditioning and attractive tropical furnishings. For fun, there are two tennis courts, two pools and a private beach. Lots of entertainment attracts a clientele of mostly young families. 160 rooms. Credit cards: A, DC, MC, V.

Southern Palms   **$69–$265**   ★★★

St. Lawrence Gap, Christ Church, ☎ *(800) 466-2526, (246) 428-7171.*
Single: $69–$265. Double: $94–$265.
Set on six acres surrounding an old plantation-style manor house, Southern Palms attracts a fun-loving set. The resort sprawls with a variety of buildings of different

influence, including Italian, Spanish and West Indian styles. Lots of organized activities keep guests busy, from miniature golf tournaments to steel band dances. All the usual watersports are free, and accommodations are pleasant. 92 rooms. Credit cards: A, DC, D, MC, V.

St. James

Crystal Cove   **$241–$442**   ★★

Fitt's Village, St. James, ☎ *(800) 223-6510, (246) 425-1440. FAX (246) 432-8290. Single: $241–$395. Double: $292–$442.*

Set on a sandy beach, this complex includes a mix of standard rooms and deluxe units with living areas, kitchens and separate bedrooms; all have motel-like furnishings, air conditioning and high ceilings. Typical resort recreational diversions are offered, including a pool with waterfall and "cave bar," swimming lagoons and tennis courts. Guests have guaranteed tee times at the Royal Westmoreland golf course. 88 rooms. Credit cards: A, DC, MC, V.

St. Peter

Almond Beach Club   **$259–$395**   ★★★

Vauxhall, St. Peter, ☎ *(246) 432-7840. Single: $259–$295. Double: $305–$395.*

This all-inclusive resort is refreshingly free of pressure to join in activities, but if you're game, there's a slew of stuff going on, from island tours to shopping trips to watersports. Half the accommodations are in one-bedroom suites with island decor. The grounds include three pools, tennis and squash, and lots of dining options. The beach is narrow and not great for swimming, but better ones are close by. 147 rooms. Credit cards: A, DC, MC, V.

Barbados Beach Village   **$100–$335**   ★★

Fitt's Village, St. Peter, ☎ *(800) 462-2426, (246) 425-1440. Single: $100–$335. Double: $110–$335.*

Set on a sandy beach, this complex includes a mix of standard rooms and deluxe units with living areas, kitchens and separate bedrooms; all have motel-like furnishings, air conditioning and high ceilings. Typical resort recreational diversions are offered, though maintenance and service can be shoddy. 88 rooms. Credit cards: A, DC, D, MC, V.

Buccaneer Bay Hotel   **$90–$330**   ★★★

Paynes Bay, St. Peter, ☎ *(246) 432-7981. Single: $90–$200. Double: $200–$330.*

Set on one of the best beaches on the west coast, this small hotel has large air-conditioned rooms with refrigerators, toasters and tea kettles, plus TV sets on request. The pool has a swim-up bar but other diversions, such as watersports, are lacking, though they can be arranged nearby. 29 rooms. Credit cards: A, MC, V.

Cobblers Cove Hotel   **$340–$850**   ★★★★

Road View, St. Peter, ☎ *(800) 223-6510, (246) 422-2291. FAX (246) 422-1460. Single: $340–$850. Double: $340–$850.*

Built on the site of a former British fort, this lovely and intimate all-suite hotel keeps guests pampered, earning its reputation as one of the island's finest resorts. Suites are nicely decorated and come with kitchenettes, a living area, balcony or patio and sitting room. New this year are two-bedroom deluxe units decorated in English style with marble floors and colorful fabrics. One has a roof-top terrace and whirlpool bath, with the other features a Jacuzzi and private plunge pool. The lush tropical grounds include a tennis court, pool, restaurant and nice beach. 40 rooms. Credit cards: MC.

Coral Reef Club   **$74–$250**   ★★★★

St. James Beach, St. Peter, ☎ *(800) 525-4800, (246) 422-2372.*
Single: $74–$134. Double: $117–$250.

Small cottages with spacious accommodations are scattered about the nicely landscaped grounds here at Coral Reef, one of Barbados' best bets. Flawlessly run by the O'Hara family—which does indeed give a damn—the grounds are lushly maintained and the beach is terrific, attracting a loyal following. All rooms come equipped with refrigerators, hair dryers, a small library of paperbacks and air conditioning. Most watersports are free, and tennis courts are a short stroll away. 71 rooms. Credit cards: A, MC, V.

Discovery Bay Hotel   **$120–$375**   ★★★

Holetown, St. Peter, ☎ *(800) 466-2526, (246) 432-1301.*
Single: $120–$375. Double: $170–$375.

This plantation-style hotel, set on four tropical acres, consists of two-story structures around an attractive courtyard. Accommodations are spacious and modern, though the air conditioning doesn't always keep up. There's also a three-bedroom villa for those who don't mind splurging. The grounds include watersports (most free), two tennis courts, a pool and a windsurfing school. The welcome drink you receive on arrival portends the excellent, friendly service. A good choice in the price range. 85 rooms. Credit cards: A, MC, V.

Glitter Bay   **$200–$325**   ★★★★★

Porter's, St. Peter, ☎ *(800) 283-8666, (246) 422-4111.*
Single: $200–$325. Double: $200–$325.

This refined beachfront resort, which sports an impressive Great House as its centerpiece, is top-drawer in every aspect. All accommodations are in suites set among beautifully landscaped grounds, and include air conditioning, marble baths, bidets, kitchenettes, living rooms and great views. The large free-form pool comes complete with waterfall, and the two tennis courts are in top condition. All watersports are complimentary, and guests can partake of the facilities at the Royal Pavilion next door. Luxury all the way! 81 rooms. Credit cards: A, DC, D, MC, V.

Haywoods Wyndham   **$185–$535**   ★★★

Highway 1, St. Peter, ☎ *(800) 822-4200, (246) 422-4900.*
Single: $185–$535. Double: $185–$535.

Located on the island's west coast on 32 tropically landscaped acres, Haywoods consists of seven buildings of various architectural influence. Reviews are mixed: some say it's grand, others say it's a legend only in its own mind. All agree that the service could use improvement, but that the wealth of recreational activities—free use of the nine-hole golf course, air-conditioned squash, three pools, five lighted

tennis courts, great beach—helps take out the sting. Judge for yourself. 288 rooms.
Credit cards: A, DC, MC, V.

King's Beach Hotel $105–$245 ★★

Road View, St. Peter, ☎ *(800) 466-2526, (246) 422-1690.*
Single: $105–$245. Double: $105–$245.
This Spanish-style beachfront hotel does a good business with families, with a playground and kid's club wooing the younger set. Guest rooms are air-conditioned and sport TVs and minibars as well as floor-to-ceiling windows affording great views. All the usual watersports, plus a pool and tennis court, round out the action. 57 rooms. Credit cards: A, D, MC, V.

Royal Pavilion $235–$330 ★★★★★

Porters, St. Peter, ☎ *(800) 283-8666, (246) 422-5555.*
Single: $235–$330. Double: $235–$330.
This elegant Mediterranean-style enclave is Barbados' best, with gorgeous grounds and excellent accommodations, all in junior suites with marble floors, lovely furnishings and lots of perks. Virtually all have ocean views. Use of the two lighted tennis courts and watersports is complimentary, as are afternoon tea and occasional evening cocktails. The beach is fine. Guests can use facilities at the neighboring Glitter Bay, which is a bit more informal. Those opting for the Royal Pavilion are indeed treated like royalty. Wonderful! 75 rooms. Credit cards: A, DC, D, MC, V.

Sandpiper Inn $110–$445 ★★★★

St. James Beach, St. Peter, ☎ *(800) 223-1108, (246) 422-2251.*
Single: $110–$141. Double: $285–$445.
There's a real island feel to this charming hotel, set right on the beach among coconut trees. Accommodations are in suites with kitchens, one or two bedrooms, air conditioning and nice local artwork. Two lighted tennis courts, a pool and free watersports (except skiing, which costs extra) round out the picture. 45 rooms.
Credit cards: A, MC, V.

Sandy Lane Hotel $500–$955 ★★★★★

St. Peter, ☎ *(800) 223-6800, (246) 432-1311.*
Single: $500–$955. Double: $500–$955.
Luxury doesn't come cheap here, but it's worth every hard-earned cent to retreat to Sandy Lane, one of the island's best choices. A recent refurbishment has put this place back on top, and all is impeccable. Accommodations are lovely with antique and local-style furnishings and lots of extras. There are all the usual watersports and complimentary golf on 18 holes. Lots of old money and Britains here, and while the service befits the rates, the atmosphere can be a tad snooty. Casual types will be happier (and spend lots less) elsewhere. 121 rooms. Credit cards: A, DC, MC, V.

Tamarind Cove Hotel $266–$466 ★★★

St. Peter, ☎ *(800) 466-2526, (246) 422-1726.*
Single: $266–$419. Double: $316–$466.
Classic Spanish architecture marks this romantic beachfront resort, which is nestled among coconut trees and coral sands. Guest rooms and suites are very nice; the newer suites have Roman tubs and bidets. Three pools, once complete with waterfall, enhance the grounds. All watersports are free, including sailing and skiing.

There's lots of nightlife here, including a Barbadian revue and boisterous barbecues. 116 rooms. Credit cards: A, MC, V.

Treasure Beach Hotel   **$155–$445**   ★★★

Paynes Bay, St. Peter, ☎ (800) 466-2526, (246) 432-1346.
Single: $155–$445. Double: $155–$445.

This small hotel is set on a nice coral beach, but its small grounds and tiny pool are definite drawbacks. Nevertheless, the hotel has a very loyal following and lots of repeat visitors. Accommodations are in suites (but lack kitchens) and are very nicely done with tropical art and furnishings; toasters and kettles are available on request. Request a unit on an upper floor for more privacy. 26 rooms. Credit cards: A, DC, MC, V.

Apartments and Condominiums

Noting the uneven supply and demand for Barbados accommodations, local businessmen have turned to building apartments and renovating private homes that suit many different lifestyles. Depending on your budget, you can choose to stay in a private home worthy of an exiled contessa or in a small, inexpensive apartment. A three-bedroom property on the west coast, on the beach but without sultanic amenities, could run $1500–$3000 a week in high season; $950–$2000 off season. Many homes come with built-in household help who often act quite proprietary. If you do your own cooking, stock the larder with provisions form **Eddie's and Jordan's**, supermarkets located in Speightstown. They offer nearly everything you're used to along with interesting local products such as a fiery hot yellow sauce, which makes a great gift to take home.

Christ Church

Casuarina Beach Club   **$80–$165**   ★★★

St. Lawrence Gap, Christ Church, ☎ (246) 428-3600.
Single: $80–$165. Double: $80–$165.

Set on seven acres of well-tended tropical palms and shrubs, this family-owned hotel has air-conditioned studios and apartments of one or two bedrooms, all with kitchenettes and spiffy accessories. Resort-style amenities include two tennis courts, squash, an Olympic-size pool, a few bars and a restaurant. Nice beach, too, but the choppy water isn't for everyone. The lovely gardens are reason enough to enjoy this very fine spot; another are the extremely reasonable prices. 129 rooms. Credit cards: A, D, MC, V.

Club Rockley Barbados   **$180–$535**   ★★

Worthing, Christ Church, ☎ (800) 462-2526, (246) 435-4880.
Single: $180–$535. Double: $180–$535.

This condominium resort consists of modest townhouses set along the fairway of a nine-hole golf course, in a predominantly residential neighborhood. Units come with one or two bedrooms, kitchens, air conditioning and uninspired decor. The grounds are extensive, with seven pools, five tennis courts, lawn games and two air-conditioned squash courts. A shuttle runs guests to a private beach club every half-hour when the usual water diversions are available, included in the all-inclusive package. 108 rooms. Credit cards: A, DC, D, MC, V.

Half Moon Beach Hotel   **$75–$215**   ★★

St. Lawrence Gap, Christ Church, ☎ (800) 466-2526, (246) 428-7131.

Single: $75–$215. Double: $90–$215.
Set on tropical Dover Beach, this small complex consists of one- and two-bedroom apartments with kitchens and modern furnishings. There's a pool and restaurant on-site, but not much else, though the friendly staff and reasonable rates make Half Moon worth a look if you're on a budget. 36 rooms. Credit cards: A, MC, V.

Sand Acres Beach Club   **$75–$125**   ★★
Maxwell Coast Road, Christ Church, ☎ *(800) 466-2526, (246) 428-7141.*
Single: $75–$125. Double: $75–$125.
Accommodations at this beachfront property are in studios or one-bedroom apartments with kitchens. The grounds include a simple restaurant, standard pool and a beach bar, as well as one tennis court and watersports for an additional fee. The beach is nice, but service can be harried. 37 rooms. Credit cards: A, MC, V.

Sandy Beach   **$100–$175**   ★★★
Worthing, Christ Church, ☎ *(800) 462-2526, (246) 435-8000.*
Single: $100–$175. Double: $100–$175.
This informal all-suite hotel offers units with one or two bedrooms; all have kitchens, satellite TV and air conditioning. There's a pool and restaurant on-site, and watersports can be had for an additional fee. The beach is small but pleasant. 89 rooms. Credit cards: A, DC, D, MC, V.

Sea Breeze Beach Hotel   **$45–$245**   ★★
Maxwell Coast Road, Christ Church, ☎ *(800) 822-7223, (246) 428-2825.*
Single: $45–$245. Double: $50–$245.
Located on two secluded beaches, this apartment complex has air-conditioned studios with kitchenettes and balconies overlooking gardens or the beach. There are also three 2 bedroom units for those who need the space. Two restaurants and a pool complete the scene. 60 rooms. Credit cards: A, DC, D, MC, V.

Sea Foam Haciendas   **$70–$93**   ★★
Worthing, Christ Church, ☎ *(800) 822-7223, (246) 435-7380. FAX (246) 435-7384.*
Single: $70–$93. Double: $70–$93.
Very comfortable two-bedroom apartments with kitchens, living/dining areas, air conditioning and full maid service at this Spanish-designed property. Many sport nice ocean views, and watersports are available. Full- or half-day cooks can be hired for a nominal charge, and if you request ahead, they'll stock your kitchen prior to arrival. No restaurant on site, but several nearby. 12 rooms. Credit cards: D, MC, V.

Woodville Beach Apartmens   **$56–$110**   ★★★
Hastings, Christ Church, ☎ *(800) 466-2526, (246) 435-9211.*
Single: $56–$110. Double: $56–$110.
Accommodations at this oceanfront complex range from studios to one- and two-bedroom units, each with full but tiny kitchens, though only some have air conditioning. They are rather basic, but clean and comfortable. The beach is quite rocky and recommended only for strong swimmers; better bathing is found at Rockley Beach, a five-minute walk. The family-run property has a pool on site, a small bar and restaurant and weekly parties where guests can mingle. There's lots to do within walking distance. 38 rooms. Credit cards: A, MC, V.

Yellow Bird Apartments   **$55–$105**   ★

St. Lawrence Bay, Christ Church, ☎ (246) 435-8444.
Single: $55–$105. Double: $65–$105.
Situated across the street from the bay and a small beach, this apartment complex offers air-conditioned studios with full kitchens and ocean-view balconies. There's a poolside bar and restaurant, but little else in the way of extras. 21 rooms. Credit cards: A, D, MC, V.

St. Peter

Asta Apartment Hotel   **$50–$235**   ★★

Palm Beach, St. Peter, ☎ (800) 466-2526, (246) 427-2541. FAX (246) 426-9566.
Single: $50–$235. Double: $50–$235.
Studios and apartments of one and two bedrooms offer guests the option of cooking in to save money. (There's also a restaurant on-site and several within walking distance when you tire of your own fare.) There's a pool on the grounds but little else, as reflected in the rates. One nice extra: the maid does the dishes. 60 rooms. Credit cards: A, MC, V.

Beachcomber Apartments   **$80–$300**   ★★

Paynes Bay, St. Peter, ☎ (246) 432-0489. FAX (246) 432-2824.
Single: $80–$195. Double: $155–$300.
Basic apartments are air-conditioned and come in studios or one- or two-bedroom configurations. Though they call themselves luxury apartments that may be stretching it. No pool or restaurant on-site, but the beach is nice and maid service is available. 9 rooms. Credit cards: MC, V.

Sandridge Beach Hotel   **$60–$195**   ★★

Roadview, St. Peter, ☎ (800) 466-2526, (246) 422-2361.
Single: $60–$195. Double: $70–$195.
This apartment hotel has studios and one-bedroom units with air conditioning, kitchenettes and TV rentals. There's a pool and restaurant, plus complimentary watersports, including free glass-bottom boat rides. A good choice for families. 52 rooms. Credit cards: A, MC, V.

Settler's Beach Hotel   **$555–$705**   ★★★

Holetown, St. Peter, ☎ (800) 466-2526, (246) 422-3052.
Single: $555–$705. Double: $555–$705.
Accommodations are in bi-level townhouses or cottages, each with large living/dining areas, kitchens, two bedrooms and spacious terraces; all are sunny and colorfully decorated. The lush grounds include a small pool, access to two tennis courts and a restaurant. Kids under 18 stay free, so expect to see lots of families. 22 rooms. Credit cards: A, MC, V.

Sugar Cane Club   **$40–$85**   ★★

Maynards, St. Peter, ☎ (246) 422-5046.
Single: $40–$85. Double: $40–$85.
Located in a remote region on a hilltop overlooking the Caribbean, the small hotel offers studios and apartments with modern touches such as air conditioning and color TV. There's a bar and restaurant on-site, as well as a pool, sauna and putting

green. Nothing too exciting, but at those rates, it doesn't have to be. 23 rooms. Credit cards: A, DC, D, MC, V.

Inns

The best inns in Barbados offer an intimate, relaxing escape from the bustle of top-class resorts and package deals. The most attractive are housed in buildings that date back to the 18th and 19th centuries. Furnishings are more often than not simple, but views, such as those from the **Kingsley Club**, sometimes rate as stupendous. **Sugar Cane Club** is best if you're seeking total peace and quiet.

Bridgetown

Island Inn   **$135–$225**   ★★★

Aquatic Gap, Bridgetown, ☎ *(800) 743-4276, (246) 436-6393.*
Single: $135–$175. Double: $185–$225.
This intimate all-inclusive resort, housed in an 1804 former rum store for the British Regiment, has lovely guest rooms for those who like modern luxury (all rooms are air-conditioned, for example) combined with historic charm. Accommodations are situated around a picturesque courtyard with gurgling fountains, and include Persian rugs, limestone brick walls and white rattan furniture. The all-inclusive rates three meals a day plus high tea, all liquor, occasional live entertainment and such extras as picnic baskets and a two-hour cruise. A good deal. 23 rooms. Credit cards: A, DC, D, MC, V.

Christ Church

Ocean View Hotel   **$34–$71**   ★★★

Hastings, Christ Church, ☎ *(246) 427-7871.*
Single: $34–$44. Double: $55–$71.
Don't be put off by the faded exterior along a busy street; the Ocean View's considerable charms lie within. This is Barbados' oldest hotel, dating back to 1898, and if you don't mind forgoing modern conveniences, a stay here will live on in your memory. Guest rooms are individually decorated with a decidedly funky slant, with lots of genuine antiques mixing with the merely old. Bunches of tropical flowers add to the ambience. This special spot is not for everyone, but well loved by those who appreciate its unique flair. 35 rooms. Credit cards: A, MC, V.

Seaview Hotel   **$95–$305**   ★★

Hastings Main Road, Christ Church, ☎ *(246) 426-1450.*
Single: $95–$305. Double: $95–$305.
Housed in a historic building from 1776, the Seaview is one of Barbados' oldest hotels. Rooms are air-conditioned and decorated in a faux-Georgian style that meshes nicely with the high ceilings and shuttered windows. The grounds include a small pool, tennis and squash. A bit overpriced for what you get. 25 rooms. Credit cards: A, MC, V.

St. Joseph

Atlantis Hotel   **$40–$60**

Bathsheba, St. Joseph, ☎ *(246) 433-9445*
Single: $40 Double: $60.

This 15 room inn offers some rooms with balconies overlooking gardens or the ocean. The seaside inn has been in business since 1882 and is famous for its West Indian buffet on Sundays.

Kingsley Club   **$79–$101**   ★ ★

Cattlewash, St. Joseph, ☎ *(246) 433-9422. FAX (246) 433-9226.*
Single: $79–$92. Double: $84–$101.

This remote and peaceful spot appeals to Barbadians and those who savor a true island experience. Rooms in the historic house are simple but clean, and the views are spectacular. The optional meal plan features West Indian and European cuisine. It's best not to attempt the very strong surf, although the beach, right across the street, is glorious. 7 rooms. Credit cards: A, MC, V.

Low Cost Lodging
Christ Church

Fairholme   **$35–$65**   ★

Maxwell, Christ Church, ☎ *(246) 428-9425.*
Single: $35–$65. Double: $35–$65.

A combination of hotel and apartment complex, the Fairholme consists of a converted plantation house that holds standard guest rooms and 20 Spanish-style studio apartments with air conditioning. There's a restaurant, bar and pool, but little else. Still, it's hard to beat the rates. 31 rooms. Credit cards: not accepted.

Where to Eat

Fielding's Highest Rated Restaurants in Barbados

★★★★	Bagatelle Great House	$30–$35
★★★★	Carambola	$20–$40
★★★★	David's Place	$14–$30
★★★★	Ile de France	$18–$38
★★★★	La Cage aux Folles	$25–$38
★★★★	Pisces	$15–$30
★★★★	Raffles Old Towne	$25–$35
★★★★	The Fathoms	$15–$29
★★★	Josef's	$25–$40
★★★	The Mews	$20–$30

Fielding's Most Exclusive Restaurants in Barbados

★★★	Josef's	$25–$40
★★★★	Bagatelle Great House	$30–$35
★★★	La Maison	$23–$40
★★★★	La Cage aux Folles	$25–$38
★★★	Reid's	$21–$40

Fielding's Best Value Restaurants in Barbados

★★★★	The Fathoms	$15–$29
★★★★	David's Place	$14–$30
★★	Carib Beach Bar	$6–$16
★★★	Koko's	$12–$22
★★★★	Pisces	$15–$30

BARBADOS

Wine bars and tapas are quite popular on this sophisticated island; head for the Waterfront Cafe, where Bajan-inspired tasty meals await. **Nico's Champagne & Wine Bar** *(St. James, [246] 432-6386)* and **39 Steps Wine Bar** *(Christ Church, [246] 427-0715)* are also well worth checking out. Those feeling adventurous should taste the treats that await at Baxter Road in Bridgetown, where vendors cook freshly caught fish outdoors on hot fires (Bagatelle Great House offers the same cuisine in a more refined—and pricey—atmosphere).

It's fun to browse a local supermarket with the inevitable huge variety of local spices and the many kinds of *mauby*, the local drink made from sugar and tree bark. You'll also find at least a dozen hot sauces concocted from mustard, garlic, scallions, scotch-bonnet peppers and spices—the perfect souvenir to bring the folks back home.

Bridgetown

Bagatelle Great House　　　　　　**$$$**　　　　　　★★★★

Highway 2A, Bridgetown, ☎ *(246) 421-6767.*
French cuisine.
Dinner: 7–9:30 p.m., entrées $30–$35. Closed: Sun.
Diners too timid to experience the vibrant street scene on the Baxter Road, an open-air market in the heart of Bridgetown where vendors cook fish on hot fires, come to Bagatelle Great House, which duplicates this method with whatever's fresh that day. The restaurant is located within the former residence of the first governor of Barbados, and this is probably one of the island's more elegant dining experiences, with stellar service—though the food is less distinguished than the surroundings. Guests can eat downstairs or on a small terrace one flight above. Reservations required. Credit cards: A, MC, V.

Brown Sugar　　　　　　**$$$**　　　　　　★★★

Aquatic Gap, Bridgetown, ☎ *(246) 426-7684.*
Latin American cuisine. Specialties: Flying fish, Creole orange chicken.
Lunch: Noon–2:30 p.m., prix fixe $14–$25.
Dinner: 6–9:45 p.m., entrées $10–$25.
One of the better values on the islands, and a lovely one to boot, is this lush, terraced, tropical-style restaurant located a few miles south of Bridgetown. Smart businesspeople and others in the know dine here at lunch on weekdays when a West Indian buffet is available for $14. There are various soups, salads and stews to choose from, including pepper pot. Other offerings include flying fish, jerk chicken and pork and luscious desserts. Dinner is more of a continental affair, with international touches added to local ingredients, like the popular Creole orange chicken. Reservations recommended. Credit cards: A, DC, MC, V.

Carib Beach Bar　　　　　　**$$**　　　　　　★★

Sandy Beach, Bridgetown,
International cuisine. Specialties: Fish fry, barbecue.
Lunch: 11:30 a.m.–3 p.m., entrées $6–$16.
Dinner: 3-10 p.m., entrées $6–$16.

One of a string of economical beach bars that pop up on several locations around the islands, Carib is right on the sand at Sandy Beach, offering fish sandwiches and fresh seafood in a comfortable upstairs restaurant, and potent rum punches in the lower-level bar. Better yet are the Wednesday night fish fries and Friday barbecue buffet, which both start at 7:30 p.m. and cost around $10 for a substantial amount of food. A happening place that stays open fairly late. The restaurant closes at 7:30 on Sundays. Credit cards: MC, V.

Chicken Barn, The   **$**   ★★
Highway 7, Bridgetown,
American cuisine. Specialties: Fried chicken.
Lunch: 10 a.m.–3:30 p.m., entrées $3–$11.
Dinner: 3:30–10:30 p.m., entrées $3–$11. Closed: Sun.
The Chicken Barn is a convenient quick lunch stop that serves fried chicken and decent burgers for a little over $1. In fact, the Barn is one of a group of inexpensive faster food establishments on Highway 7 not far from Sandy Beach in the town of Worthing, a great place for budget-minded travelers. You can also get salads and fish and chips for under $4. Credit cards: not accepted.

Josef's   **$$$**   ★★★
Waverly House, Bridgetown, ☎ (246) 435-6541.
International cuisine. Specialties: Toast skagen, dolphin meuniere.
Lunch: Noon–2:30 p.m., entrées $10–$13.
Dinner: 6:30–9:30 p.m., entrées $25–$40.
Although Austrian chef and restaurateur extraordinaire Josef Schwaiger sold his well-loved namesake restaurant to open two other fashionable spots, the flame has passed splendidly to Swedish chef Nils Ryman. Ryman has kept Josef's more stellar creations on the mostly seafood menu, including the sublime dolphin meuniere, but has added some fine dishes of his own, namely a *smorrebrod* of shrimp with dill mayonnaise. It might be difficult to snag a dinner reservation, but a weekday lunch is a viable option for a smoked fish or chef's salad. No lunch served on weekends. Reservations required. Credit cards: A, MC, V.

Waterfront Cafe   **$$$**   ★★
The Careenage, Bridgetown, ☎ (246) 431-0303.
International cuisine.
Lunch: 10 a.m.–2 p.m., entrées $8–$25.
Dinner: 2-10 p.m., entrées $8–$30. Closed: Sun.
The Waterfront Cafe is an inexpensive cool-off eatery on the Careenage, a small inlet for light craft. It serves Bajan-inspired quick meals such as pepper pot soup, a copious appetizer platter and flying fish interspersed with familiar burgers and English pub food. There's music every evening, usually jazz, and a relaxed bar scene. Seating is either outdoors facing the water or in the dining room. Reservations recommended. Credit cards: A, MC, V.

Christ Church

Da Luciano's   **$$$**   ★★
Staten, Christ Church, ☎ (246) 437-7544.
Italian cuisine.

Dinner: 6:30–10:30 p.m., entrées $19–$33.

A lot of care goes into the presentation and preparation of the Italian food served here in a handsome old home, Staten, a historical landmark near a white sand beach popular with locals. Starters include a mixed seafood platter and antipasto, and main courses and pastas are hearty and often infused with plenty of garlic. Reservations recommended. Credit cards: MC, V.

David's Place   **$$$**   ★★★★

St. Lawrence Main Road, Christ Church, ☎ (246) 435-6550.
Latin American cuisine. Specialties: Baxter Street fried chicken.
Lunch: 11 a.m.–3 p.m., entrées $9–$13.
Dinner: 6-10 p.m., entrées $14–$30.

Wear loose clothing to eat this delicious Bajan food in a pretty cottage beside St. Lawrence Bay, where every table has an ocean view. A spicy fried chicken named in honor of the Baxter Street food vendors is a specialty, as is pepperpot and pumpkin soup. Huge helpings of rice and peas, cheese bread, potatoes and vegetables come with all the entrées, but you can't stop there. Make room for fantastic desserts like coconut cream pie if you can—you won't regret it. Reservations recommended. Credit cards: A, MC, V.

Ile de France   **$$$**   ★★★★

Hastings, Christ Church, ☎ (246) 435-6869. Associated hotel: Windsor Arms Hotel.
French cuisine. Specialties: Foie gras.
Dinner: 6:30–10 p.m., entrées $18–$38. Closed: Mon.

An innovative French restaurant located on the lush grounds of one of Barbados' traditional hotels, the Windsor Arms, Ile de France brings Gallic intensity to its slower-paced, old-fashioned surroundings. Many classic dishes are represented, including a definitive foie gras and ballotine de canard (one of the owners is from Toulouse), escargots de Bourgogne, and crepes flambéed at tableside. The atmosphere is sublime and unobtrusive, with candlelight, subtle lighting and music. Reservations required. Credit cards: MC, V.

Pisces   **$$$**   ★★★★

St. Lawrence Gap, Christ Church, ☎ (246) 435-6564.
Seafood cuisine. Specialties: Red snapper caribe.
Dinner: 6–10 p.m., entrées $15–$30.

Flowers, greenery, an oceanfront table and an impeccable reputation for fresh seafood draws visitors to Pisces again and again. Red snapper caribe with tomatoes and shrimp is an ongoing special, although it may be difficult to choose an entrée from the long and varied menu that invariably includes the catch of the day served any style, with a butter sauce or with Jamaican jerk seasonings. There's a refreshing gazpacho and a few meat, chicken and vegetarian dishes. Reservations required. Credit cards: A, MC, V.

T.G.I. Boomers   **$$**   ★★

St. Lawrence Gap, Christ Church, ☎ (246) 428-8439.
International cuisine. Specialties: Flying fish.
Lunch: 11:30 a.m.–6 p.m., entrées $4–$11.
Dinner: 6–10 p.m., entrées $11–$17.

This very welcome (for variety and bargain prices) bar-restaurant near Rockley Beach serves three meals a day, including an all-American breakfast of bacon and eggs, french toast or an omelette (with coffee and juice) for $6.50. At lunch, burgers, deli and fish sandwiches and vegetarian dishes are offered for under $10. Dinner plates of steak or seafood are garnished with vegetables, rice or potatoes and soup or salad. It also serves the needs of party types and barhoppers with daiquiris and other blender drinks at the bar, which stays open until midnight. Credit cards: A, MC, V.

Witch Doctor   **$$$**   ★★
St. Lawrence Gap, Christ Church, ☎ *(246) 435-6581.*
Latin American cuisine. Specialties: Pumpkin soup.
Dinner: 6:15-9:45 p.m., entrées $13–$30.
You'll think you're on another island when dining at this wild jungle-themed dining room serving spicy, innovative and traditional island cuisine. If the decor doesn't get to you, the good food will satisfy, including creamy pumpkin soup, seafood cocktail marinated in lime and flying fish. Reservations recommended. Credit cards: A, MC, V.

St. Peter

Atlantis Hotel   **$$$**   ★★
Bathsheba, St. Peter, ☎ *(246) 433-9445. Associated hotel: Atlantis Hotel.*
Latin American cuisine. Specialties: Pepper pot stew, flying fish.
Lunch: Noon–3 p.m., prix fixe $12–$17.
Dinner: 7-9 p.m., prix fixe $15–$17.
You might go without a full meal for a week after the enormous Sunday brunch at the Atlantis Hotel, a traditional hostelry with a breathtaking sea vista. Although this dining room operated by owner Enid Maxwell serves set lunches and dinners at very reasonable prices, Sunday is when everyone (including tour groups) blows in for the $17 buffet. The tables groan with authentic "Bajan" specialties, including pepper pot stew (assorted meats in a rich broth, simmered for days), breadfruit, flying fish and rice and peas. If lines are overwhelming, try the Edgewater Hotel dining room nearby (☎ *433-9902).* Reservations required. Credit cards: A.

Carambola   **$$$**   ★★★★
Derricks, St. Peter, ☎ *(246) 432-0832.*
French cuisine.
Dinner: 6:30–9:30 p.m., entrées $20–$40. Closed: Sun.
This old favorite is still wowing a select group who ooh and aah over the spicy Thai-French cuisine (a unique combination) served in a cliffside dining room, with the sea lapping 10 feet below. Carambola is located in a converted old home north of Bridgetown in St. James Parish, where chef Paul Owens and owner Robin Walcott have prepared and planned such delights as green or red curry chicken or filet of dolphin with dijon mustard sauce. It's too bad that only dinner is served, because the view is spectacular. Reservations required. Credit cards: A, MC, V.

Koko's   **$$$**   ★★★
Prospect House, St. Peter, ☎ *(246) 424-4557.*
Latin American cuisine. Specialties: Pepper pot soup, seafood.
Dinner: 6:30–10 p.m., entrées $12–$22. Closed: Mon.

The chef here is a talented saucier, creating a symphony of flavors that accentuate the freshly caught shellfish and game garnishing the colorful plates. The beach setting is pretty, with tables set on the patio of a traditional Bajan house on the west coast of the island. The food is largely island-style, with pepper pot soup often on hand, as well as lightly fried shellfish cakes in a tangy citrus and mayonnaise sauce. Reservations recommended. Credit cards: MC, V.

La Cage aux Folles $$$ ★★★★

Summerland Great House, St. Peter, ☎ *(246) 424-2424.*
International cuisine. Specialties: Sesame prawn pate, orange peel chicken.
Dinner: 7-10:30 p.m., entrées $25–$38. Closed: Tue.
There aren't any showgirls with feathered plumes anywhere in sight at this eclectic Asian-Caribbean restaurant. The setting, in the Summerland Great House, a restored plantation, is entertainment enough. The food, luckily, plays a stellar role, with Chinese crispy duck, sesame prawn pate and orange peel chicken as predominant examples. There's a balcony for cocktails and a view of lush gardens, and an intimate antique-filled room for private parties within. Owners are experienced restaurateurs with establishments in London. Reservations required. Credit cards: MC, V.

La Maison $$$ ★★★

Balmore House, St. Peter, ☎ *(246) 432-1156.*
Seafood cuisine.
Dinner: 6:30–10 p.m., entrées $23–$40. Closed: Mon.
Comfortably positioned in yet another Great House on the St. James coast (will they ever run out of them?), La Maison has been wowing visitors and residents alike since it opened in the early 1990s with sophisticated, French-inspired seafood. Dining here is likened to a posh beach camp-out, with tables set out on the sand under a tent or indoors in a courtyard exposed to ocean breezes and views. The ever-changing menu may feature salmon with cream sauce, marinated flying fish and rich ice cream or chocolate desserts. Reservations required. Credit cards: MC, V.

Raffles Old Towne $$$ ★★★★

1st Street, St. Peter, ☎ *(246) 432-6557.*
International cuisine. Specialties: Curries.
Dinner: 7-10 p.m., entrées $25–$35.
Named after the Raffles Hotel in Singapore and inspired by British colonial exploits abroad, this highly regarded restaurant employs a big-game hunter theme in an intimate room close to the ocean in Holetown. Naturally, there are curries and chutneys, blackened fish and chicken, and a full-course dinner for $40. Raffles rates three "knives and forks" (the highest culinary honor) from the Barbados Tourism Authority. Reservations required. Credit cards: A, DC, MC, V.

Reid's $$$ ★★★

Derricks, St. Peter.
International cuisine. Specialties: Lobster.
Dinner: 7-10 p.m., entrées $21–$40. Closed: Mon.
Fresh fish, lobster and escargots in white wine and garlic are served to diners at this plantation building south of Holetown. Reservations should be made a few days in

advance to enjoy manicured garden views, gurgling fountains and a well-chosen wine list. Reservations required. Credit cards: A, MC, V.

The Fathoms $$$ ★★★★

Paynes Bay, St. Peter, ☎ *(246) 432-2568.*
International cuisine. Specialties: Lobster, octopus.
Lunch: 11 a.m.–3 p.m., entrées $6–$8.
Dinner: 6:30–10 p.m., entrées $15–$29.
Daring seafood dishes are the hallmark of this ocean-view, red-roofed spot on Paynes Bay, near Holetown. You can stick with a grilled lobster, stuffed crab or catch of the day, but octopus and sea eggs (white sea urchins' roe, prepared deviled or breaded) are sometimes on the menu. At night it's romantic with candlelight and crashing waves for sound effects; other times it's Bajan casual. Besides seafood, there are burgers, salads and pork crepes. With less than 25 tables in the dining area, make reservations well in advance. Reservations recommended. Credit cards: A, MC, V.

The Mews $$$ ★★★

Second Street, St. Peter, ☎ *(246) 432-1122.*
Seafood cuisine. Specialties: Fresh fish.
Dinner: 7-10 p.m., entrées $20–$30. Closed: Sun.
This is one of two new restaurants opened by award-winning chef Josef Schwaiger, who sold his popular Josef's in St. Lawrence Gap. It's already very successful among his many admirers and assorted fish fanciers (Josef's specialty) who like to dine in a trellised garden on paupiettes of snapper and a sublime lime mousse. Before or *après* dinner, walk across the street to Nico's Champagne and Wine Bar, ☎ *(246) 432-0832* for some bubbly or chablis by the glass. Reservations required. Credit cards: A, MC, V.

Where to Shop

Shopping is a high art form in the capital city of Bridgetown, where tony shops and boutiques line crowded Board Street. As a major duty-free port, you'll save as much as 30 to 50 percent on watches, crystal, gold, bone china, cameras, cashmere, tweeds and liquor. It would be a mistake, however, to confine your purchases to such items, as Barbados has a wealth of artisans and craftspeople who create unique mementoes from the island's resources of clay, wood, shells, weaving materials and fabrics. Craft fairs are held throughout the year in addition to the four major annual events: the Holetown Festival Street Market in February, the Oistins Fish Festival Street Market at Eastertime, the Crop Over Bridgetown Market in August and the Barbados Museum Annual Craft Fair in December.

Earthworks Pottery ☎ *(246) 425-0223* is a family-owned studio that produces decorative and functional ware, while Daphne's Sea Shell Studio ☎ *(246-*

432-6180), located in a 320-year-old plantation house, offers everything from hand-crafted mirrors to jewelry to Christmas ornaments. Pelican Village, located on Harbour Road just outside Bridgetown,. is a cluster of small shops, galleries and studios where local craftspeople sell their wares. Articrafts, which has two locations in Bridgetown (☎ *[246] 427-5767* or ☎ *[246] 431-0044*) also offers up Barbadian crafts, as well as the exquisite wallhangings and clay figurines by Roslyn. For an up-close and personal look at the craft of pottery, head for Chalky Mount, a village whose inhabitants have been potters for more than 300 years.

Barbados Directory

Arrival and Departure

American Airlines, Air Canada and BWIA are the principal carriers to Barbados, flying from New York, Toronto, Miami and San Juan to Grantley Adams Airport. Good connections can be made with other Caribbean islands, especially via British Airways, which has good deals between Antigua, St. Lucia, Barbados and Trinidad. It's best to buy ongoing tickets ahead of time as Barbados agents add a 20 percent service tax. Reserve months in advance for the Christmas season and during the Crop Over Festival in August. A departure tax, payable at the airport upon leaving, is U.S. $12.50.

Business Hours

Stores open weekdays 8 a.m.–4 p.m., Saturday 8 a.m.–1 p.m. Banks open Monday–Thursday 8 a.m.–3 p.m. and Friday 9 a.m.–5 p.m.

Climate

Constant northeast trade winds keep temperatures between 75-85 degrees F year-round. The wet season, from June to November, is more humid than at any other time; September and October are the rainiest months. Weather can change quickly—in a cross trip on the island from west to east, you can start out with sunny skies and end up in a raging storm. Rainfall varies from 50 inches on the coast to 75 inches in the higher interior.

Cruises

Cruise ships dock at the Deep Water Harbour's pier. Most folks on a limited time schedule head for Pelican Village to do some shopping. You can easily catch a taxi waiting at the dock. (The walk can get long and hot!) If you want to catch a smaller ship or sailboat to another island, hang around the port here and see who you can meet; ships are arriving all the time on their way to other islands.

Documents

U.S.and Canadian citizens need to show proof of citizenship (passport, birth certificate, or voter's registration card, along with a government-issued photo ID, such as a driver's license). Also required is an ongoing or return ticket.There is a departure tax of U.S. $12.50.

Electricity

The current is 100 volts, 50 cycles, as in the U.S., though the speed is somewhat slower. Hotels with 220 volts usually provide adapters.

Getting Around

From the airport it's a good hour's drive to the part of the west coast where many (but not all) of the best hotels and houses to let are located. You can rent a car at the airport, but only local agencies are available. Since the road from the airport is a bit hairy, visitors are better off taking a taxi to the hotel, and then renting a car from there. If you rent a car, you'll need your own license, plus a driver's permit issued at the airport by the police or your rental agency for a $5 fee. Take the insurance ($5 a day) if you're not sure you are already covered. Note that driving is on the left.

The most highly recommended car-rental agency is **National Car Rental**, Bush Hall, Main Road, St. Michael; ☎ *(246) 426-0603.* Cars will be delivered to a location anywhere on the island.

Also try **P&S Car Rentals** ☎ *(246) 424-2052* or *424-2907*, Pleasant View, Cave Hill, St. Michael; **Sunny Isle Motors**, ☎ *(246) 435-7979.*

In general, roads are well paved and locations well marked.

Taxi drivers are no longer naive on Barbados and know their way around know-nothing tourists. Ask your concierge or hotel management how much a particular trip should cost before you get in the taxi; otherwise you could get bilked.

Public buses are reliable and safe, but unbearably crowded at rush hours (8:30–9:30 a.m. and 3:30–6 p.m.). The route that runs down the south and west coast is an inexpensive way to see the island.

Guides

Although the more independent traveler prefers to rent his own car and toddle around on his own, hotels can arrange a personal guide for you if you want to see more of the island. Excellent service is offered by **Sally Shearn's VIP Tour Service** ☎ *(246) 429-4617.*

Language

English is the official language, spoken with a pronounced island lilt.

Medical Emergencies

Top-class hotels usually have a doctor on call. Queen Elizabeth Hospital, located on Martinsdale Road in Bridgetown, is the preeminent training hospital in the Caribbean.

Money

The official currency is the Barbados dollar, worth about 50 cents in American currency. Most stores will accept American dollars and traveler's checks. However, to get your best rate, it's better to exchange your American dollars for Bajan ones at a bank.

Telephone

Area code is *809.*

BARBADOS

Tipping and Taxes

Most hotels and restaurants add a 10 percent service charge. Feel free to tip extra if the service is especially fine.

Tourist Information

The tourist office is located in the Harbour Industrial Park near the Deep Water Harbour in Bridgetown. You'll also find information posts at the airport and at the cruise ship pier at the Deep Water Harbour. They are only open weekdays. From the U.S. call ☎ *(213) 380-2198.*

Water

Water is safe to drink in Barbados, pumped from an underground source in the island's coral reefs.

When to Go

Crop Over Festival in July and August is an islandwide celebration of Barbadian arts, food, music and dance, which harks back to the 19th century when the last of the year's sugarcane crop was feted. Three weeks of competitions, festivities, feasts and fairs celebrate the culture and history of the island. Kaddoment Day, a national holiday held on Aug. 1, is the culmination of the Crop Over Festival, with costumes, music, street dancing and fireworks. The Holetown Festival in February, commemorating the first settlement in 1627, is celebrated by a big street party, as is the Oistins Fish Festival at Easter. In November the National Independence Festival of Creative Arts (NIFCA) usually sponsors an annual month-long celebration of Barbadian talent competitions in art, music, song and dance. In July, the Sir Garfield Sobers International School's Cricket Tournament, named after a famous Barbadian cricketer, has become an international event, attracting worldwide participation.

Every Sunday year-round, traditional Sunday hikes are cosponsored by various charities, encouraging participants to walk at their own pace. Walks start at 6 a.m. and 3:30 p.m. Call the **Barbados National Trust** ☎ *(246) 428-5889.* On Sundays in January, **Barbados Horticultural Society's Open Garden Program** presents local gardeners displaying their gardens from 2–6 p.m. For more information, call ☎ *(246) 428-5889.* On Wednesday afternoons, January-April, **Barbados National Trust Open House Program** invites visitors to browse through the private homes of architectural and historical importance to the island.

The period between Christmas and Easter is the most popular time for tourists, though the British summer is busier than it used to be.

BARBADOS HOTELS	RMS	RATES	PHONE	CR. CARDS
Bridgetown				
★★★★ **Barbados Hilton**	184	$134–$285	(800) 445-8667	MC, V
★★★★ **Marriott's Sam Lord's**	234	$110–$225	(800) 228-9290	A, D, DC, MC, V

BARBADOS HOTELS		RMS	RATES	PHONE	CR. CARDS
★★★★	Sandals Barbados	178	$105–$335	(800) 726-3257	A, MC, V
★★★	Coconut Creek Club Hotel	53	$216–$420	(800) 462-2566	A, MC, V
★★★	Colony Club Hotel	76	$272–$534	(800) 466-2526	A, MC, V
★★★	Grand Barbados Beach	133	$125–$605	(800) 466-2526	A, DC, MC, V
★★★	Island Inn	23	$135–$225	(800) 743-4276	A, D, DC, MC, V
★★	Crane Beach Hotel	18	$105–$300	(800) 466-2526	A, DC, MC, V
★★	Ginger Bay Beach Club	16	$80–$205	(800) 466-2526	A, D, DC, MC, V

Christ Church

★★★	Casuarina Beach Club	129	$80–$165	(246) 428-3600	A, D, MC, V
★★★	Ocean View Hotel	35	$34–$71	(246) 427-7871	A, MC, V
★★★	Sandy Beach	89	$100–$175	(800) 462-2526	A, D, DC, MC, V
★★★	Southern Palms	92	$69–$265	(800) 466-2526	A, D, DC, MC, V
★★★	Woodville Beach Apartmens	38	$56–$110	(800) 466-2526	A, MC, V
★★	Caribbee Beach Hotel	55	$60–$105	(800) 466-2526	A, D, DC, MC, V
★★	Club Rockley Barbados	108	$180–$535	(800) 462-2526	A, D, DC, MC, V
★★	Divi Southwinds Resort	160	$115–$245	(800) 367-3484	A, DC, MC, V
★★	Half Moon Beach Hotel	36	$75–$215	(800) 466-2526	A, MC, V
★★	Sand Acres Beach Club	37	$75–$125	(800) 466-2526	A, MC, V
★★	Sea Breeze Beach Hotel	60	$45–$245	(800) 822-7223	A, D, DC, MC, V
★★	Sea Foam Haciendas	12	$70–$93	(800) 822-7223	D, MC, V
★★	Seaview Hotel	25	$95–$305	(246) 426-1450	A, MC, V
★	Benston Windsurfing Hotel	15	$50–$70	(246) 428-9095	A, D, DC, MC, V
★	Fairholme	31	$35–$65	(246) 428-9425	None
★	Yellow Bird Apartments	21	$55–$105	(246) 435-8444	A, D, MC, V

St. James

★★	Crystal Cove	88	$241–$442	(800) 223-6510	A, DC, MC, V

St. Joseph

★★	Kingsley Club	7	$79–$101	(246) 433-9422	A, MC, V

St. Peter

★★★★★	Glitter Bay	81	$200–$325	(800) 283-8666	A, D, DC, MC, V
★★★★★	Royal Pavilion	75	$235–$330	(800) 283-8666	A, D, DC, MC, V

BARBADOS

BARBADOS HOTELS		RMS	RATES	PHONE	CR. CARDS
★★★★★	Sandy Lane Hotel	121	$500–$955	(800) 223-6800	A, DC, MC, V
★★★★	Cobblers Cove Hotel	40	$340–$850	(800) 223-6510	MC
★★★★	Coral Reef Club	71	$74–$250	(800) 525-4800	A, MC, V
★★★★	Sandpiper Inn	45	$110–$445	(800) 223-1108	A, MC, V
★★★	Almond Beach Club	147	$259–$395	(246) 432-7840	A, DC, MC, V
★★★	Buccaneer Bay Hotel	29	$90–$330	(246) 432-7981	A, MC, V
★★★	Discovery Bay Hotel	85	$120–$375	(800) 466-2526	A, MC, V
★★★	Haywoods Wyndham	288	$185–$535	(800) 822-4200	A, DC, MC, V
★★★	Settler's Beach Hotel	22	$555–$705	(800) 466-2526	A, MC, V
★★★	Tamarind Cove Hotel	116	$266–$466	(800) 466-2526	A, MC, V
★★★	Treasure Beach Hotel	26	$155–$445	(800) 466-2526	A, DC, MC, V
★★	Asta Apartment Hotel	60	$50–$235	(800) 466-2526	A, MC, V
★★	Barbados Beach Village	88	$100–$335	(800) 462-2426	A, D, DC, MC, V
★★	Beachcomber Apartments	9	$80–$300	(246) 432-0489	MC, V
★★	King's Beach Hotel	57	$105–$245	(800) 466-2526	A, D, MC, V
★★	Sandridge Beach Hotel	52	$60–$195	(800) 466-2526	A, MC, V
★★	Sugar Cane Club	23	$40–$85	(246) 422-5046	A, D, DC, MC, V

BARBADOS RESTAURANTS		PHONE	ENTRÉE	CR. CARDS
Bridgetown				
American				
★★	Chicken Barn, The		$3–$11	None
French				
★★★★	Bagatelle Great House	(246) 421-6767	$30–$35	A, MC, V
International				
★★★	Josef's	(246) 435-6541	$10–$40	A, MC, V
★★	Carib Beach Bar		$6–$16	MC, V
★★	Waterfront Cafe	(246) 431-0303	$8–$30	A, MC, V
Latin American				
★★★	Brown Sugar	(246) 426-7684	$14–$25	A, DC, MC, V

BARBADOS

BARBADOS RESTAURANTS	PHONE	ENTRÉE	CR. CARDS

Christ Church

French

| ★★★★ Ile de France | (246) 435-6869 | $18–$38 | MC, V |

International

| ★★ T.G.I. Boomers | (246) 428-8439 | $4–$17 | A, MC, V |

Italian

| ★★ Da Luciano's | (246) 437-7544 | $19–$33 | MC, V |

Latin American

| ★★★★ David's Place | (246) 435-6550 | $9–$30 | A, MC, V |
| ★★ Witch Doctor | (246) 435-6581 | $13–$30 | A, MC, V |

Seafood

| ★★★★ Pisces | (246) 435-6564 | $15–$30 | A, MC, V |

St. Peter

French

| ★★★★ Carambola | (246) 432-0832 | $20–$40 | A, MC, V |

International

★★★★ La Cage aux Folles	(246) 424-2424	$25–$38	MC, V
★★★★ Raffles Old Towne	(246) 432-6557	$25–$35	A, DC, MC, V
★★★★ The Fathoms	(246) 432-2568	$6–$29	A, MC, V
★★★ Reid's		$21–$40	A, MC, V

Latin American

| ★★★ Koko's | (246) 424-4557 | $12–$22 | MC, V |
| ★★ Atlantis Hotel | (246) 433-9445 | $12–$17 | A |

Seafood

| ★★★ La Maison | (246) 432-1156 | $23–$40 | MC, V |
| ★★★ The Mews | (246) 432-1122 | $20–$30 | A, MC, V |

BARBADOS

BARBUDA

Barbuda is the perfect place to indulge in the "deserted island" experience.

Looking for a truly off-the-beaten-track experience? For an island that turns its desolate, barren landscape into an asset? Barbuda is one of the most unusual Caribbean backwaters, a curious anomaly whose charms almost defy description for its few visitors. Part of the twin-island nation of Antigua and Barbuda, the destination is almost as flat as a pancake and seemingly just as featureless, left to bake at the junction of the Caribbean and Atlantic. What makes this oversized coral atoll worth visiting are its stark isolation, a colony of magnificent frigate birds who proudly display a flashy mating ritual, and some of the most breathtaking beaches in the Caribbean, washed gently by luminous turquoise water. The limestone island is so rich with sand that, on and off through the years, its biggest business has been supplying sand for concrete and, or course, to supplement the beaches at more-deprived destinations. Adding further allure is a pair of ever-so-pricey resorts that draw a posh clientele dripping with money. One 1996 customer was Princess Diana, who took a winter sojourn at the K Club and so appreciated the escape from shutterbugs that she returned for another visit only a few months later. Another was William F. Buckley, who arrived by yacht and praised the island's loamy sands. But don't come here for star-gazing—exclusivity and privacy are very big on Barbuda.

Bird's-Eye View

Barbuda offers soft white sand, gorgeous sea views and a relaxed lifestyle.

Twenty-eight miles to the north of Antigua, coralline Barbuda is larger than its wafer-like appearance might otherwise indicate. The island encompasses about 62 square miles, and most of it rarely sees footprints or tire tracks. When you fly in, enjoy the view—it's the last elevated perspective you'll have during your visit. Barbuda receives little rain, and therefore vegetation is mostly limited to scrubby greenery that hugs the ground. There's almost no shade above ankle level. The only settlement on the island is Codrington, where almost all of Barbuda's 1200 residents live, and just west of town is a huge saltwater expanse, Codrington Lagoon, one mile wide and six miles from end to end. About a dozen palm trees offer an oasis along a sand bar that creates the lagoon's western edge. In the northern portion of the la-

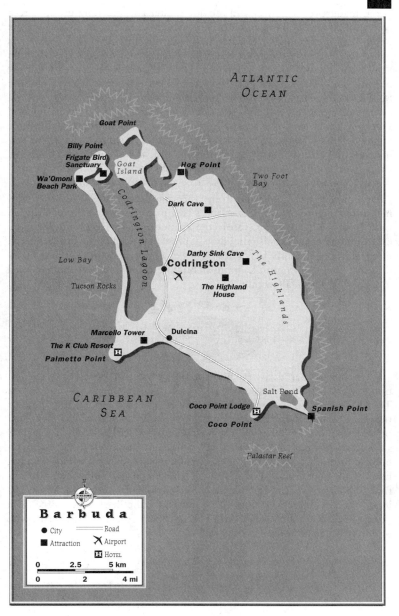

goon, mangroves take over and provide shelter and breeding grounds to a colony of about 2000 frigate birds. The main road on the island is called the River Road—presumably because it floods during heavy rains—and it is paved for three miles from Codrington south to the ruins of the Martello Tower and the waterfront, where a dilapidated dock is used, mostly for exporting sand. The eastern portion of the island provides whatever physical bulk Barbuda needs to keep it from drowning—the Highlands roll to an elevation of about 150 feet and conclude at the eastern edge of the island with Pigeon Cliff. Aside from a couple guest houses in Codrington, the three main accommodations are situated on the southern shore of Barbuda: Palmetto Hotel on the southwest tip of the island, and Coco Point Lodge and the K Club six miles to the southeast. Just past Coco Point is another promontory, Spanish Point, where the Atlantic and Caribbean collide.

Barbuda received a direct hit from Hurricane Luis in 1995, but the minimal infrastructure allowed the island's two main resorts to get in shape in time for the '95-'96 winter season (the Palmetto Beach Hotel suffered more extensive damage, but was rebuilding at press time). All of the beaches are in fine condition, and although a number of channels eroded through the isthmus that lines Codrington Lagoon, all but one at the southern end had filled in with sand within a few months.

People

The people of Barbuda were never subject to close supervision by plantation owners. Today, the island's 1200 residents are resilient, make-do types. They have to be to endure this hardscrabble existence. About 200 work for the three main hotels, though not all of them do so year-round. The next biggest employer is lobster catching and fishing, virtually all of which is shipped to Antigua and other islands. Some are employed by the sand exporting business, and the rest of the inhabitants get by with a little farming, hunting or other evanescent activities. There is some resentment toward Antigua's politicians, and an independence movement sprung to life in the '80s—the government responded by increasing the local police force from three to 25. The number has since been cut back to eight individuals, who undoubtedly have little to do.

Beaches

Barbuda's beaches are, in a word, resplendent. They crawl for miles on end, with sands that are plush and fine and, in one stretch, they have a pink sheen created by a thin layer of tiny shells washed up from the Caribbean. The two main resorts steer the focus to Coco Point, a finger of land that defines the east end of a single unbroken, nine-mile-long sweep of brilliant white sand that eventually reaches Palmetto Point. There is sometimes an undertow present around Palmetto, otherwise this is some of the most flawless sun-bathing territory in the Caribbean. The ribbon of sand doesn't end at Palmetto, however. It makes hard right to the north where it continues for another eight miles or so, soon forming the thin western edge of Codrington Lagoon. It is along this expanse that the sand shimmers with a rosy pink hue—a striking photo when set against baby blue skies and aquamarine seas. Midway up this slender isthmus is a sprout of palm trees around an abandoned beach house—this spot (perhaps the shadiest on the island) is sometimes referred to as Palm Beach. To the east of Coco Point is Gravenor Bay, a three-mile-long curl where the strip of beach is thinner, but the snorkeling is superb. One of the few spots on Barbuda where there is no beach is around the tip of Spanish Point, but just north, and facing the Atlantic, are a series of sand-dune-backed bays with idyllic coves of sand—Welch Bay, Pelican Bay, Castle Bay—that eventually lead to the bluffs that form The Highlands.

Underwater

Although several excellent reefs can be found in the waters off Barbuda, there is no professional dive facility at present—visitors are strongly advised to have tanks supplied and filled on Antigua, 28 miles away. Visibility is generally limited to 40-50 feet due to the rougher Atlantic weather conditions. There is a 20-mile-long barrier reef fronting the eastern coastline (too dangerous for snorkeling), while coral formations off Coco Point swarm with tropical fish and crustaceans. Snorkelers can charter a boat from fishermen to visit Tuson Rock, about three miles straight west of Codrington and a half-mile off the spit of sand that represents the western border of the lagoon; a few other good sites lie just north of here. All told, Barbuda is a challenging, isolated dive frontier for serious adventurers, and is best served by a live-aboard dive boat.

Palaster Reef

A Marine Park one mile off one of the Caribbean's choicest beaches, Palaster Reef houses at least 60 wrecks, including the 1000-ton *Payson Tucker* and several warships (look for cannons and anchors). The reef boasts voluminous quantities of fish and lobster, and divers are virtually assured of eyeing the nurse, lemon and gray-tipped sharks that frequent Barbuda's shallow depths.

Barbuda is one of the flattest of all Caribbean islands, peaking at a series of hills, termed The Highlands, rising to about 150 feet in elevation. As such, well-defined trails are basically nonexistent. Dry and unremarkable in appearance, greenery is limited to low-lying scrub with mangroves fringing the numerous salt-water ponds. But for travelers with a true bushwhacker's zeal, this 14- by 8-mile backwater has abundant exploration possibilities, most of it marginally charted. Beyond the magnificent frigate bird (see "Other Activities," below), additional wildlife, though sparse, includes fallow deer, guinea fowl and wild pigs and donkeys.

Five miles north of Codrington, at the end of The Highlands and inland from Two Foot Bay, is Dark Cave. Difficult to locate without a guide and impossible to explore without a flashlight, the entrance is near the north side of a scrubby sinkhole. An awkward descent though a narrow slot to a cavern leads to a passage involving a clamber under overhangs; the bottom of the cave is a huge chamber with deep pools containing blind shrimp. Easier to locate is Darby Sink Cave, a sinkhole approximately 300 feet in diameter which drops down 70 feet. The cave is two miles east of the ruins of the Highland House (the 18th-century estate of the Codrington family). The descent to the bat-guano floor is relatively easy and reveals stalagmites and a miniature tropical rain forest environment—the lushest spot of all on barren Barbuda.

Investigating Barbuda's backcountry—which is to say, seeing anything on foot—is serious business, by Caribbean standards, anyway. Once you leave the town of Codrington or venture far from the south coast beaches, you're on your own. There is essentially no shade on the island, making the sun a significant consideration; bring a hat, ample sunscreen and more water than you ever think you'll need. Give the wild donkeys wide berth; the males are quite protective of their mates. Lastly, although the details it provides on an island unscarred by pavement may be sparse, the maps available at the Codrington post office can be helpful. If you are a daytripper visiting Barbuda, you are best advised to hook up with the taxi drivers who greet each plane arrival, negotiating for a tour featuring some combination of caves, birdwatching and snorkeling. Oh, and sunning.

Tours

Frigate bird Sanctuary   ★ ★ ★ ★

Codrington Lagoon, Codrington Lagoon.
Reached only via small boat, this spot is one of only a few in the world where Fregata Magnificens, the magnificent frigate bird, brood their eggs in mangrove bushes. The impressive birds have eight-foot wingspans and soar to 2000 feet at speeds of up to 100 miles per hour. Mating season, August to November, is the best time to come, when the males puff up a huge bright red sack under their beaks; chicks hatch from December to March and remain in the nest for up to eight months. Also look out for pelicans, warblers, snipes, ibis, herons, kingfishers, tropical mockingbirds and cormorants. The site is visited by several local boatmen—try Foster Hopkins ☎ *(268) 460-0212*, who charges $10 per person (minimum of five) for the one-hour excursion from Codrington.

Beyond watersports and deep-sea fishing (arranged through K Club or Coco Point), there aren't many options on Barbuda. However, a scruffy nine-hole golf course is available for desperate duffers at the K Club.

Most of the island's highlights are seen with the assistance of your hotel or by arranging trips with locals. The nesting area for the magnificent frigate bird, reached by boat from Codrington, is the must-see. You can ask the same boatman to drop you off for a few hours at the "forest" of palms along the west side of the lagoon for a Robinson Crusoe escape.

Where to Stay

Fielding's Highest Rated Hotels in Barbuda

★★★★	Coco Point Lodge	$485–$1060
★★★★	K Club	$500–$2700

Fielding's Most Exclusive Hotels in Barbuda

★★★★	Coco Point Lodge	$485–$1060
★★★★	K Club	$500–$2700

Fielding's Best Value Hotels in Barbuda

★★★★	Coco Point Lodge	$485–$1060
★★	Palmetto Hotel	$252–$325
★★★★	K Club	$500–$2700

Barbuda offers frustratingly little selection when it comes to accommodations. There are two outrageously priced resorts on one end, and a smattering of very basic guest houses in Codrington. Fortunately, after a closure of more than a year following Hurricane Luis, the Palmetto Point Hotel plans to be open for the winter '96-'97 season with pleasant accommodations, though its rates are still pretty lofty for what you get.

There have seemingly been more abandoned hotel developments on Barbuda than there are properties that function today. Three deserted projects include the recently shuttered Sunset View Resort, next to Codrington's airstrip, the Dulcina Hotel, which was never completed, and a new property near Palmetto Point that was only a few weeks from opening when Hurricane Luis tore it apart in 1995. The future of these and other projects is anyone's guess, but a British firm is considering developing a 35-acre parcel near Spanish Point. Don't hold your breath—things move very slowly here.

Hotels and Resorts

Two infamous resorts dominate the scene here. The Coco Point Lodge opened in 1961 on a dazzling finger of sand protruding out into the aquamarine water. Built and managed to this day by William (Cody) Kelly and his family, for years, it was the only hotel on Barbuda and established a reputation as an ultra-exclusive, all-inclusive beach haven for East Coast establishment types. Sometime in the 1980s, the legend goes, a falling out between the Kelly family (that originally built and operates Coco Point to this day) and one of their best customers, Mariuccia Mandelli (of the Krizia Italian clothing line), lead to Mandelli pulling the ultimate one-upmanship by deciding to build her own resort, the $30 million, 241-acre K Club, just down the beach from Coco Point.

Today, the two are fortresses for the rich and famous, and although they share many qualities (beyond the same magnificent beach), they are still quite unique. Since its 1989 opening, K Club has had a succession of managers come and go, whereas Coco Point has had the same hands-on family operation for three-and-a-half decades. K Club is tastefully, fashionably chic, while Coco Point happily showcases a fashion sense straight out of the 60s. Princess Diana stays at K Club, William F. Buckley at Coco Point. Both properties are extravagantly priced.

Coco Point Lodge   **$485–$1060**   ★ ★ ★ ★

Coco Point, Codrington, ☎ *(212) 986-1416, (268) 462-3816. FAX (268) 464-8334. Single: $485–$960. Double: $585–$1060.*

This secluded resort, set on a spectacular, one-of-a-kind 164-acre peninsula at Barbuda's southern tip, is for those who really do want to get away from it all and don't need the bells and whistles of a traditional resort. Situated along one of the Caribbean's most glorious beaches, Coco Point accommodates guests in ranch-style villas that are comfortably though very simply furnished; the more expensive units share a common living area with one or two other rooms. The all-inclusive rates include most everything from soup to nuts (and drinks), as well as bonefishing, deep-sea fishing, water-skiing, tennis and more, but excursions to the frigate bird sanctuary or elsewhere by car are extra. There's little action at night—people come here to relax and socialize, not party. The very plain architecture is a turn-off to some, while others (including Andrew Harper's *Hideaway Report*) enthusiastically applaud the low-key ambience. Coco Point appeals to clubby establishment types—Wall Street bankers, lawyers, doctors and politicians—some of whom return year after year and are welcomed like family. Interlopers need not apply. The rate includes air transportation from Antigua to Coco's private airstrip. Amenities: tennis, houses, cottages or bungalows. 34 rooms.

K Club   **$500–$2700**   ★ ★ ★ ★

Coco Point, Codrington, ☎ *(800) 223-6800, (268) 460-0300. FAX (809) 460-0305. Single: $500–$1600. Double: $500–$2700.*

Most everything is perfect at this stylish enclave of 28 white cottages set on a spectacular beach. Accommodations are spacious and beautifully decorated by owner Krizia, the Milanese fashion designer, who oversaw every detail of the opulent development, down to the cotton lounging robes in each room. Units vary from a golf lodge (no air conditioning, but a mere $700 per night in winter), to two-bedroom beach villas; all suites have kitchens, although why K Club thinks a guest would want to tackle cooking here is strange (the all-inclusive rates include wonderful Italian meals). But, splendid as everything is, it's still vastly overpriced—beverages, fishing, water-skiing and golf at the struggling nine-hole course are not included. The resort draws Europeans and a select few from Hollywood who don't mind paying top, top dollar for a fabulous piece of sand, and true exclusivity. Know that service is not always up to par and management continues on a revolving-door basis. Air transport from Antigua via private plane is $150 round-trip, per person. No children under 12. Amenities: tennis, Jacuzzi, houses, cottages or bungalows. 39 rooms. Credit cards: A, DC, MC, V.

Palmetto Hotel   **$252–$325**   ★★★

Palmetto Point, Codrington, ☎ (268) 460-0440.
Single: $252–$325. Double: $252–$325.

Located amid scruffy sand dunes on the island's breezy southwestern tip, this small hotel offers a temperate alternative to Barbuda's two other, much pricier resorts. Guest rooms are air-conditioned and have separate living areas; the nine cottages offer more privacy. Swimming at the beach is a bit unreliable due to occasional currents, but a large pool is available. Tennis court and a few watersports round out the activities, and a restaurant keep guests sated (breakfast is included in rates). The Palmetto took a beating during Hurricane Luis, but rebuilding was underway at press time to get the property ready for the '96-'97 winter season. Amenities: balcony or patio. 35 rooms. Credit cards: A, D, MC, V.

Low Cost Lodging

There are a few options here, but expect little of the creature comforts you might have in a typical budget Caribbean property. The best choice for now is probably Nedd's Guest House, a five-room operation above a supermarket and two blocks from the airport in Codrington. Rates are $60 for a double, or $35 for a single, but some negotiating might be possible ☎ *(268) 460-0059.* Other guest houses are located in Codrington, but you may be best off contacting the Antigua and Barbuda Department of Tourism for their current recommendations ☎ *(268) 462-0480.* Remember, if you stay in town, you are several miles from the nearest beaches.

Where to Eat

Outside the three hotels, there are no sit-down restaurants on Barbuda. If you aren't staying at Palmetto Point, Coco Point or the K Club and want to eat at their restaurants for lunch or dinner, you'll need to phone ahead for reservations (K Club charges a walloping $100 per person for dinner, not including wine). In Codrington, there are a few snack stands that sell fried fish and lobster, and a bakery, but little else. The town also contains a few makeshift bars that are where fishermen and others congregate for gossip and drink. It is sometimes possible to arrange for a meal in a private home.

Barbuda and Codrington are not designed for shopping. There is a very small gift shop at Coco Point, and a duty-free Krizia Boutique for upmarket accessories at K Club, but otherwise, you'll need to leave your shopping ambitions at home, or tackle them on Antigua.

Barbuda Directory

Arrival and Departure

All scheduled flights into Barbuda originate in Antigua. The 15-minute flight is made twice daily by LIAT ☎ *(800) 468-0482 or (268) 462-0701* making daytrips from Antigua possible. Be aware that LIAT flights out of Barbuda leave as quickly as possible after loading passengers, which usually means flights depart as much as 15 minutes early. Carib Aviation also provides limited service to the island ☎ *(268) 462-3147*. The K Club has its own plane to bring in guests (for a fee), while Coco Point also has its own plane, and delivers guests to a private airstrip near the lodge (included in the nightly rates). Antigua is served from North America by American Airlines, BWIA and Continental. For additional information, see "Arrival and Departure" in "Antigua."

Business Hours

Shops open Monday–Friday 8:30 a.m.–4 p.m. and Saturday 8 a.m.–noon or 3 p.m. Banks generally open Monday–Thursday 8 a.m.–2 p.m. and Friday 8 a.m.–4 p.m.

Climate

Average temperatures hover around 75–85 degrees F. year-round.

Documents

U.S. and Canadian citizens need to present a valid passport (or original birth certificate and photo ID), plus an ongoing ticket. British citizens need to show a valid passport.

Electricity

Most of the island uses 220 volts, AC/60 cycles.

Getting Around

Most visitors hire a taxi for their island touring. Barbara Jappal at Caribrep sets up daytrips (daily except Sunday) to Barbuda from Antigua for $125 per person including airfare, lobster lunch and drinks, and a visit to the bird sanctuary and beaches ☎ *(268) 462-3884*. George (Prophet) Burton meets most planes and is a knowledgeable guide, but makes sure all arrangements and prices are very clearly understood; plan on about $75-100 for a day-long tour of the island ☎ *(268) 460-0103*. Car rental is a shaky prospect on Barbuda, and driving on the island's (mostly) dirt and sand roads is not for the timid. Burton Car Rental in Codrington has a few vehicles for hire, starting at about $50 per day for a small jeep ☎ *(268) 460-0078*. You'll need to purchase a Antigua/Barbuda driver's license for $20 (or EC$50); there is one tiny gas station in Codrington.

Language

The official language is English.

Medical Emergencies

There is a 10-bed hospital in Codrington. Anything remotely serious should be handled in Antigua or, better yet, Puerto Rico.

Money

Official currency is the Eastern Caribbean dollar, but most establishments welcome American dollars. Exchange houses are hard to find here; exchange before you come.

Telephone

The new area code for Antigua/Barbuda is *(268)*.

Tipping and Taxes

Most hotels add a 10 percent service charge; tip extra if the service is especially nice.

Tourist Information

The Antigua and Barbuda Department of Tourism is located in St. John's Box 363, Long and Thames Street, Antigua, W.I. ☎ *(268) 462-0480; FAX (268) 462-2483*. The country also maintains a U.S. office in New York ☎ *(212) 541-4717*.

Water

Officially, you can drink tapwater, but most visitors feel safer downing the bottled variety.

When to Go

See the calendar in the "When to Go" section of Antigua.

BARBUDA HOTELS	RMS	RATES	PHONE	CR. CARDS
Codrington				
★★★★ Coco Point Lodge	34	$485–$1060	(212) 986-1416	
★★★★ K Club	39	$500–$2700	(800) 223-6800	A, DC, MC, V
★★ Palmetto Hotel	35	$252–$325	(268) 460-0440	A, D, MC, V

BARBUDA

BONAIRE

Himer Hooker wreck dive site, Bonaire.

Long considered one of the Caribbean's prime diving destinations, Bonaire—the B in the ABC Dutch islands located off the coast of Venezuela—is starting to come on strong as an all-around resort island. The results are somewhat mixed—if you loved the island for its laid-back sleepiness, you'll be in for something of a shock when you get a gander at all the new hotels, restaurants and shops that have sprung up in the past few years. But not to fear: the island still is peaceful and relatively unspoiled, and though development continues, it remains primarily a nature lover's paradise. Though you can now gamble at two casinos, party in the one disco or shop for duty-free goods in the capital city of Kralendijk, it's mainly the natural beauty above and below the sea that keeps attracting tourists to Bonaire.

Besides unparalleled diving, Bonaire is known for Washington/Slagbaai National Park, a 13,500-acre wildlife sanctuary with some 300 kilometers for hikers, mountain bikers and horseback riders. Bird lovers flock to Gota Lake, a land-locked saltwater lake where a large share of the island's huge flamingo population hangs out. Keeping your eyes peeled for one of the elusive birds is de riguer on a Bonaire holiday.

Islanders are justifiably proud of their home, and a real effort has been underway in the past several years to keep it clean. Long before eco-tourism became the buzzword of the 1990s, Bonaire had the foresight to designate its surrounding waters as a protected marine park. On land, signs extolling all to *"Tene Boneiru Limpi"* ("Keep Bonaire Clean") remind both locals and tourists that litter has no place here. And while illegal drugs and petty crime (car rental theft in particular) are ongoing problems, the average tourist will find Bonaire nothing but lovely and charming, the perfect antidote to hectic, everyday life. A warning: Once you swim in these waters, you'll have a hard time accepting anything else.

Bird's-Eye View

Located 50 miles north of Venezuela and 86 miles from Aruba, Bonaire is the B in the ABC chain of islands in the Netherlands Antilles (Aruba and Curacao complete the trio). The island lies outside the hurricane belt and is very dry, with a desert-like landscape and climate. Rainfall averages just 12 inches each year, mostly occurring in December through March. The average temperature is a balmy 82 degrees Fahrenheit.

Bonaire, which sprawls over 112 square miles, is shaped something like a boomerang. It was formed from the tip of a 24-mile-long volcanic ridge poking out from the sea and is surrounded by the fringe reefs and exceptionally clear waters that make Bonaire so popular for divers. Since 1979, all waters around Bonaire have been designated a marine sanctuary, meaning it is illegal to spearfish, collect fish or coral or anchor on the reefs. The result is one of the richest reef systems in the West Indies and quite dramatic ones at that, with plunging walls, teeming schools of colorful fish and a fair amount of shipwrecks—including the notorious "Hooker," an 80-foot cargo ship busted for carrying 25,000 pounds of marijuana.

Above land, the crown jewel is Washington/Slagbaai National Park, which stretches out some 13,500 acres and acts as a sanctuary to iguanas, donkeys, goats and scores of exotic birds. The park's highlight is Boca Cocolishi, a black sand beach cradling a protected bay. The island is roughly divided into

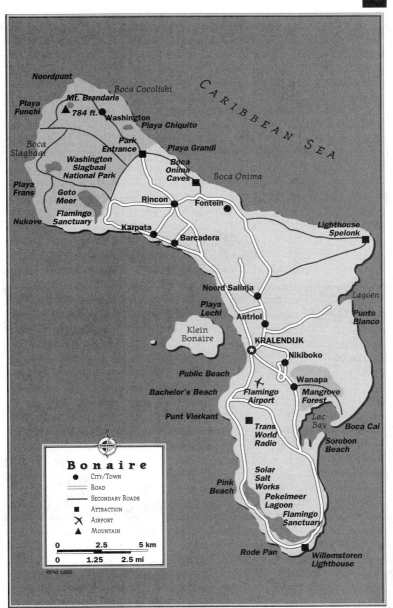

Noordpunt

Boca Cocolishi

Playa Funchi

Mt. Brandaris
▲ 784 ft.
Washington
Playa Chiquito

Park Entrance

Playa Grandi

Boca Slagbaai

Washington Slagbaai National Park

Boca Onima Caves

Boca Onima

Playa Frans

Goto Meer

Rincon

Fontein

Flamingo Sanctuary

Nukove

Karpata

Barcadera

Lighthouse Spelonk

C A R I B B E A N   S E A

Noord Salinja

Playa Lechi

Antriol

Lagoen

Punto Blanco

Klein Bonaire

KRALENDIJK

Nikiboko

Public Beach

Wanapa

Bachelor's Beach

Flamingo Airport

Mangrove Forest

Punt Vierkant

Lac Bay

Boca Cai

Trans World Radio

Sorobon Beach

Solar Salt Works

Pink Beach

Pekelmeer Lagoon

Flamingo Sanctuary

Rode Pan

Willemstoren Lighthouse

Bonaire

● CITY/TOWN

——— ROAD

——— SECONDARY ROADS

■ ATTRACTION

✕ AIRPORT

▲ MOUNTAIN

0	2.5	5 km
0	1.25	2.5 mi

©FWI 1996

thirds: the north end is hilly and green, the middle flatter and more arid, and the very flat south end punctuated by salt pans, mangrove swamps and sand dunes. It's here that it becomes obvious why Indians named the island "Banare," meaning low land.

The capital city of Kralendijk (population 2500) is small and neat, with Dutch influences apparent in the shops and restaurants that line the main drag, J.A. Abraham Boulevard (the name changes to Kaya Grandi in city center).

Klein ("Little") Bonaire, an uninhabited 1500-square-acre island, lies off the west coast about a half-mile offshore and is frequented by divers and snorkelers. Like its larger sister island, it is scrubby and arid.

Note that mosquitoes can be a real problem from October through December, so if you're visiting then, slather on the bug repellant.

Bonaire has one of the largest flamingo colonies in the world. The birds build their mud nests in the salt pans.

Ever since the Spanish explorer Amerigo Vespucci discovered Bonaire in 1499, entrepreneurs have been toying with how to exploit it. Failing to discover gold on the island, the Spanish turned to extracting salt from the seas, stripping the forests of hardwoods and dyewoods, and hunting wild goats

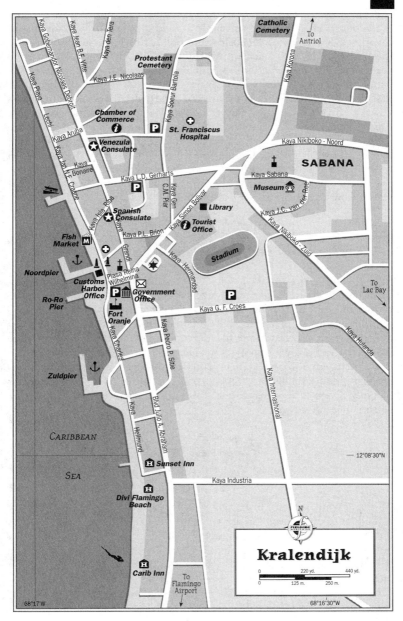

Kralendijk

0   220 yd.   440 yd.

0   125 m.   250 m.

and sheep. Neither the Dutch, who arrived in 1623, nor the British, who took control in the early 19th century, could discover any successful ventures. A U.S. merchant named Joseph Foulke, to whom the British leased the land in 1810, also failed to make good. When the Dutch returned six years later, they ventured into shipbuilding, brickmaking and stock raising with little success. In recent years, many of Bonaire's natives were forced to find work off-island in the oil refineries of Venezuela, Curaçao and Aruba. As news of Bonaire's natural wonders became disseminated by the emigration, tourists began to trickle onto the island: fishermen who gloried in the abundance of marine life and untouched coral reefs and bird-watchers who were astounded by the glorious flocks of pink flamingos at Goto Meer and Pekel Meer. But it wasn't until the first scuba divers arrived around 1962, when there were only two major hotels, that the island began to discover where its real treasures lay—right under water.

People

The population of Bonaire is around 11,000, mostly of mixed Arawak, European and African descent. They are a friendly and welcoming people who rely on tourism for their main livelihood, though salt mining, textiles and oil trans-shipment also contribute to the economy. While the official language is Dutch, most everyone speaks Papiamento, a mixture of Spanish, Dutch, Portuguese, English and French. Tourists, however, will usually have no problem finding English and Spanish speakers in the hotels, shops and restaurants. Dress is very casual but conservative; cover up your beachware when going into town.

Beaches

Brilliant white is the color of most beaches in Bonaire, but most are gritty and full of coral. Hence, they are not really suitable for long strolls. Beaches on the leeward coast tend to run narrow. All the major hotels are located on beaches (managements have tried to beef up the sand there) but some of the best ones are along the southern coast, such as the clothes-optional Sorobon or Boca Cai on Lac Bay, full of mangroves at the north end of the bay. At Playa Chiquito, the surf is treacherously strong (too dangerous for swimming), but the strand is good for sunbathing, though there are few places for shade. Pink Beach, south of Kraldendijk, is good for swimming but gritty for strolling. Snorkelers head for Playa Funchi, but the absence of facilities has left the beach in smelly disrepair. Lots of tour boats end up in Boca Slagbaai, where you can see flocks of flamingos dipping their long legs in the water. Stop there if you have just trekked through the National Park.

Underwater

Sometimes, dive operators can be a little uncooperative with journalists. Objectivity—particularly when comparing their island's sites and qualities with another—frequently flies headlong out the window. Other times, in asking opinions on the best dive sites available on a given island, outfits will list a few unfamiliar locations that, in fact, turn out to be sites only they can take you to because no one else knows/visits/cares about them. Speaking with Kitty at Bruce Bowker's Carib Inn on Bonaire, I was punished with a new style of reporter harassment. When asking what her three or four favorite dive spots on the island were, she sighed, and replied simply, "No, I'm not going to do that." She explained that Bonaire has many great dive sites and, although there are a few that are just a little better than the others, magazines keep writing about those few. "Divers come to the island and these spots are the only places they want to visit." With obvious frustration, she added, "we have to talk them into trying anything new."

The local dive operators can afford to be a little arrogant. Simply put, Bonaire offers one of the world's great dive locations, possibly the best in the Caribbean. The island is well outside the hurricane belt (which plagues most other Caribbean islands), allowing the coral reef wrapping the island to thrive and provide a dynamic playground for more than a thousand species of marine life. Although big creatures are few and far between, reef fish are in good supply and macro life is gloriously showcased (it's a perfect destination for photo enthusiasts). The angle of drop-offs rarely exceeds 60 degrees, so you won't find much in the way of walls. But the reef, which generally starts less than a hundred feet from shore along the island's leeward coast, is sublime. Rain averages 12 inches a year, visibility a reliable 60 to 80 feet, but sometimes reaches 100 feet or more. Currents are almost nonexistent—one diver referred to the whole leeward coast as "like a big lake"—but diving on the choppy windward side is rare (limited to occasional calm days in the fall). And, if you like shore diving, well, hop in the car and look for one of the painted yellow stones that mark the island's 30 or so "official" shore dive locations. Yes, you could park and dive for two weeks without visiting the same spot twice.

The reef is terrific, but Bonaire also has a leg up on the competition because it has long been a leader in marine conservation. In fact, what have become standards on the more progressive Caribbean islands—permanent mooring systems, bans on spearfishing, etc.—have been in effect here since the late '60s. Anchoring of any kind is illegal around the entire island, except for the harbor immediately in front of Kralendijk. In sum, because these practices have been in effect for decades here, the island is years ahead of most other Caribbean locales in terms of a genuinely protected undersea environment. When you arrive, you'll pay a $10 admission fee to the **Bonaire Marine Park**, which includes a one-hour orientation session by your dive shop. There are a few sites (Knife, Petrie's Pillar, Twixt and Valerie's Hill), that are currently off-limits to divers; these areas were overdived and local operators are giving them time to rejuvenate. For overachievers, there is a recompression chamber available at the island's San Francisco Hospital.

Scuba die-hards sometimes forget about snorkeling, but they shouldn't miss the shallow terraces which line shores. It's a whole 'nother world. Diver of not, you'll find outstanding snorkeling all along the west coast. **Klein Bonaire** is terrific, particularly Jerry's Jam (where the coral grows up to the surface) and Leonora's Reef. Other great sites on the main island are **Thousand Steps**, **Nukove**, **Playa Funchi** and **Windsock** (so named because it lies at the foot of Bonaire's airport runway). One other, albeit unpredictable, snorkeling possibility occurs for a few days each year (usually late summer or early fall) when krill swarm the placid Bonaire waters, followed by whale sharks and mantas which feed gleefully on the red crab larvae. While it's almost impossible to set a vacation to their schedule, in September 1995, the phenomena occupied local attention for an unprecedented 10-day stretch, as divers and swimmers donned snorkel and mask to swim with the big guys.

While Bonaire's interior isn't as colorful and diverse as its submarine display, the island's environmental awareness extends to the **Washington/Slagbaai National Park**, which occupies most of Bonaire's northern end. The 13,500-acre wildlife sanctuary is laced by dirt roads, and on-foot exploration is easy, as long as you're equipped with sun block and plenty of water. The area was once occupied by a plantation which produced aloe, charcoal and goats, and it was turned over to the government in the late '60s. After paying your $3 entry fee, you'll be handed a map detailing three tracks: the yellow route is a 22-mile circuit of the of the park, while the green route is a shorter, 15-mile track through the center (the two routes overlap at points). A dotted green track is actually a trail, which climbs to the top of **Brandaris Hill**, Bonaire's 784-foot high point; allow two hours round trip. Another area which deserves impromptu exploration is the solar salt pans that loom mysteriously on the horizon south of Kralendijk. You can spend a few minutes or a few hours here, depending on your curiosity. The nearby **Pekel Meer Lagoon** is a colorful, 135-acre flamingo sanctuary that serves as a home to as many as 10,000 greater flamingos.

Some Bonaire tours include the huts where salt mine slaves lived.

By Pedal

Bonaire features more than 200 miles of quiet dirt roads that create wonderful opportunities for mountain bike touring. One important consideration is the island's sun and heat, which can be oppressive. It's important to carry lots of water, and to liberally apply sunblock before any extended riding.

What Else to See

Though the main reason to come here is to spend as much time under water as possible, there are some land-based places to see on the island. The

BONAIRE

capital city of Kralendijk is laid-back and casual (though strolling around in swimwear is not appropriate). It comprises just a few blocks of colorful, Dutch Colonial low-rise buildings where you can shop and dine and is easily navigated by foot. (Though to really explore the island, you'll want to rent a car.) The Fish Market, located on the waterfront and surrounded by Romanesque stone aches, is great for people-watching, especially on Tuesdays, when the merchandise is freshest and most people come to shop for local produce and the catches of the day. Rincon, on the east coast, is the island's oldest village; nearby is Boca Onima, a 50-foot volcanic cliff with shallow caves where ancient petroglyphs can be viewed. Snorkelers, divers and kayakers frequent Klein Bonaire, a small uninhabited island with nice beaches but, alas, no shade.

Caves near Barcadera, Bonaire

Museums and Exhibits

Instituto Folklore Bonaire ★★★★
Ministry of Education, Bonaire.
If you happen to be in the neighborhood (don't bother otherwise), drop in for a look at local artifacts and musical instruments from the pre-Columbian days. The cramped and poor exhibits prevent this small museum from reaching its potential.

Parks and Gardens

Bonaire Marine Park ★
The entire coastline, Bonaire.
To keep its world-famous reefs intact, this government-run park, which includes the entire coastline of Bonaire and neighboring Klein Bonaire, has enacted strict rules for snorkelers and divers. You may not step on or collect the coral, and anchors are forbidden—patrolling marine police see that the rules are enforced. The undersea world includes some 80 species of colorful coral and 270 species of fish. The Visitors Center offers up brochures, slide shows and lectures. The $10 fee allows for one calendar year of diving.

Washington/Slagbaai National Park ★
Northwest Territory, Bonaire.
Hours open: 8 a.m.–5 p.m.
This 13,500-acre national park, dedicated to preserving the island's natural landscape, is well worth a visit. Opt for the short route (15 miles and marked with green arrows) or the longer version (22 miles and yellow arrows); if you're driving, a four-wheel-drive is essential for navigating the dirt roads. Once a plantation of divi-divi trees and aloe plants, the park has been a wildlife sanctuary since 1967, with additional acreage added in 1978. The roads take you past dramatic seascapes, freshwater lakes and low-land forest that is home to 130 species of birds (bring your binoculars) and a few mammals that include donkeys and goats. There's a small museum at the gatehouse; just past it colorful flamingos roost on a salt pond from October to January. Plan on at least a few hours in this special spot. General admission: $3.

Tours

Bonaire Sightseeing Tours ★★★
Bonaire.
If you prefer exploring Bonaire in the hands of professional guides, they'll take care of you. Excursions, via jeep or minivan, are offered to the northern coast, the low-lying south or Washington/Slagbaai National Park. Prices range from $12 to $45.

Cruises ★★
Various locales, Bonaire.
A few hours' excursion on the sea is always a wonderful way to unwind. A few companies offer such jaunts. The Bonaire Dream, a glass-bottom boat, lets you see underwater life without getting wet; catch it at the Harbour Village Marina. Sunset and snorkel cruises are offered by the **Woodwind** (☎ *[599] 7-607055*). Don't forget the sunscreen!

Getting wet is the order of the day here and the reason most tourists visit Bonaire. Because rainfall is so scarce, there is no freshwater run-off, so visibility is usually about 100 feet. Diving is hugely popular, with more than 80 sites to explore. The best reefs are found within the protected lee on the south coast, where the reefs have a narrow, sloping terrace. Thousand Steps is a popular walk-in dive site—there aren't nearly that many steps, though it will feel like it when you carry your tanks back up. Snorkelers enjoy the reefs off Klein Bonaire and Washington/Slagbaai Park. Bonaire is also a haven for fishers, with great bonefishing and angling for tarpon, permit and snook. Sea kayaking is relaxing along the leeward side and Klein Bonaire; on the windward side, paddle over to Lac Bay, a lagoon that is a nursery for fish life. Bonaire's steady trade winds make it ideal for windsurfing, popular all year round in Lac Bay and on the leeward side, where the winds are especially strong December through August. Finally, trekking or mountain biking through the national park is a lovely way to soak up the serene landscape, but be sure to bring plenty of water. For horseback riding, contact the Kunuku Warahama Riding Academy (☎ *[599] 7-7537*).

Boat Cruises

Bonaire.

The Bonaire Dream (☎ *[599] 7-4514*), the island's only glass-bottom boat, offers day and night trips through Bonaire Marine Park. **The Samar** (☎ *[599] 7-5433*) is an authentic, beautiful Siamese sailing junk offering everything from full moon sails to Thai dinners and snorkel trips. Finally, **Woodwind** (☎ *[599] 7-8285*) is a 37-foot trimaran with an open bar to make snorkel trips a little more jolly.

Deep-Sea Fishing

Various locales, Bonaire.

Piscatur Fishing (☎ *[599] 7-8774*) offers reef fish excursions aboard a 15-foot skiff for a full- or half-day. **Club Nautico** (☎ *[599] 7-5800*) offers fishing charters, as does the **Ocean Breeze** (☎ *[599] 7-5661*).

Guided Snorkeling

Most major hotels and resorts, Bonaire.

This new program, launched in conjunction with the government, hotel association, *Skin Diver* magazine and individual dive operators, is aimed at the many tourists who visit Bonaire but don't dive. Participants are taught all about snorkeling, with a half-hour slide presentation on underwater life and what to expect at each depth, full instructions and then the big moment: a guided snorkel to one of a dozen sites around the island. Though snorkelers are normally prohibited from touching or disturbing coral and marine life, the guide is able to handle the underwater treasures and share the experience with the group. Virtually every hotel and dive shop on the island participates in the program, which lasts about two hours and costs from $20 to $40 per person. You can even reserve a spot with your travel agent before reaching Bonaire.

Kayaking

Bonaire.

Kayaking though the calm waters that surround much of the island is as relaxing as it gets. Or explore Lac Bay, a peaceful lagoon punctuated by mangroves. **Jibe City Kayaking** *(☎ [599] 7-7363)* will set you up with half- or full-day rentals.

Scuba Diving

Various locations, Bonaire.

Bonaire's rich reefs make for excellent diving; in fact, it's considered one of the top three spots in the world for scuba. Many outfits offer lessons, equipment rentals and excursions. Best known is **Captain Don's Habitat Dive Center** *(Kaya Gobernador N. Deprot, ☎ [599] 7-8290)*, a PADI five-star training facility. Also check out: **Dive I and Dive II** *(Divi Flamingo Beach Resort, ☎ [599] 7-8285)*; **Bonaire Scuba Center** *(Black Durgon Inn, ☎ [599] 7-8978)*; **Sand Dollar Dive and Photo** *(Sand Dollar Condominiums, ☎ [599] 7-5252)*; **Neil Watson's Bonaire Undersea Adventures** *(Coral Regency Resort, ☎ [599] 7-5580)*; **Great Adventures Bonaire** *(Harbour Village Beach Resort, ☎ [599] 7-7500)*; and **Bruce Bowker's Carib Inn Dive Center** *(Carib Inn, ☎ [599] 7-8819)*. Personalized tours for twosomes are offered by **Dee Scarr's Touch the Sea** *(☎ [599] 7-8529)*.

Windsurfing Bonaire

Great Southern Travel & Adventures, Bonaire, ☎ (800) 748-8733.

This is a great spot for both beginners and experts. Lessons start at $20 an hour, and Windsurfing Bonaire will even pick you up at your hotel. Another spot to try is **Bonaire Windsurfing Place**, a new shop at Sorobon Beach, Lab Bay *(☎ [599] 7-5279)*.

Where to Stay

Fielding's Highest Rated Hotels in Bonaire

★★★★	Club Nautico Bonaire	$200–$450
★★★★	Harbour Village Beach Resort	$170–$400
★★★★	Plaza Resort Bonaire	$115–$220
★★★	Captain Don's Habitat	$150–$245
★★★	Coral Regency Resort	$150–$230
★★★	Divi Flamingo Resort	$85–$140
★★★	Port Bonaire Resort	$265–$385

Fielding's Most Exclusive Hotels in Bonaire

★★★	Port Bonaire Resort	$265–$385
★★★★	Harbour Village Beach Resort	$170–$400
★★★	Captain Don's Habitat	$150–$245
★★★★	Plaza Resort Bonaire	$115–$220
★★	Sunset Oceanfront Apartments	$60–$190

Fielding's Best Value Hotels in Bonaire

★★★	Divi Flamingo Resort	$85–$140
★★★★	Plaza Resort Bonaire	$115–$220
★★	Carib Inn	$64–$124
★★	Sunset Beach Hotel	$80–$140
★★	Buddy Dive Resort	$80–$165

Many of Bonaire's hotels and resorts cater to divers, and one, the Sorobon, is for nudists. Hotel development continues with three new hotels—the Plaza Resort, Port Bonaire and Club Nautico—added since late 1994. If you're looking to save money, consider staying in one of the many condominium and apartment complexes, but note that hotel prices are fairly decent anyway, and local food prices so high the savings from cooking it yourself may be negligible.

Hotels and Resorts

All hotels face the sea. All you need to do is choose whether you want to stay in town or in the countryside. Perhaps the liveliest hotel is **Captain Don's Habitat**, due to the wildcat personality of its owner, Don Stewart, who has been rumored to shoot a mosquito with a pistol. **Divi Flamingo Beach Hotel** has the best restaurants, the Chibi-Chibi and the Calabase Terrace, plus a casino that draws crowds. **Sorobon Beach Resort** is infamous for its clientele who like to take advantage of the nearby "clothes optional" beach.

Captain Don's Habitat   **$150–$245**   ★★★

Kralendijk, ☎ (800) 327-6709.
Single: $150–$245. Double: $150–$245.
The clientele at this casual spot is mostly scuba divers and the facilities cater to them well, with instruction, seven boats and an underwater photo shop. Landlubbers are kept happy, too, in two-bedroom cottages with kitchens or oceanfront rooms or villas. The beach is tiny, but the pool is nice, and kids are kept busy in supervised activities during high season. The atmosphere here is informal and fun, especially when Captain Don stops by to spin tall tales. 43 rooms. Credit cards: MC, V.

Divi Flamingo Resort   **$85–$140**   ★★★

J.A. Abraham Boulevard, Kralendijk, ☎ (800) 367-3484.
Single: $85–$140. Double: $85–$140.
Despite the need for at least a fresh coat of paint, the Divi remains a popular choice due to its friendly staff and lively atmosphere. The original buildings housed German prisoners of war during World War II, but from that dubious start the resort has grown into a pleasant and fun spot. Accommodations are merely adequate and desperately in need on a re-do, but the grounds are nice with tennis (including a resident pro), extensive dive facilities (with special programs for the handicapped), casino and lots of after-dark entertainment. 145 rooms. Credit cards: A, DC, MC, V.

Plaza Resort Bonaire   **$115–$220**   ★★★★

Kralendijk, ☎ (800) 766-6016, (599) 7-2500. FAX (599) 7-2517.
Single: $115–$220. Double: $115–$220.
Located right on the beach five minutes from Kralendijk and just opened in summer of 1995, the Plaza adds another resort to Bonaire, where the properties mainly cater to divers. Accommodations are in suites or one- and two-bedroom villas with fully equipped kitchens. Facilities include the requisite dive shop, other watersports, three restaurants and three bars, a mini-market and four tennis courts. It also sports the island's second—and largest—casino. 177 rooms. Credit cards: A, DC, MC, V.

Sunset Beach Hotel   **$80–$140**   ★★

Kaya Gobrenador Debrot 75, Kralendijk, ☎ (599) 7-8448. FAX (599) 7-8593.
Single: $80–$140. Double: $80–$140.
Located on one of the better beaches, the Sunset's accommodations are, unfortunately, set far inland, so ocean views are scarce. Rooms are quite plain, but do offer such extras as coffeemakers, refrigerators and air conditioning. The extensive

grounds, which could use more landscaping to reach their potential, include two tennis courts, a good dive center and a small pool. The friendly staff can't make up for the fact that this place is screaming for renovation. 145 rooms. Credit cards: A, DC, MC, V.

Apartments and Condominiums

One- and two-bedroom apartments are often chosen by visitors to Bonaire who want to save a little money, but you may empty your wallet anyway if you stock up on staples in Bonaire; the prices can be exorbitant. In most cases, you may need a car. For more information about housekeeping units, contact **Hugo Gerharts** (*Kralendijk, Bonaire, N.A.;* ☎ *(599) 7-8300)* or **Harbourstown Real Estate** *(Kaya Grandi 62, P.O. Box 311;* ☎ *(599) 7-5539, FAX (599) 7-5081).*

Buddy Dive Resort   **$80–$165**   ★ ★

Kaya Gobernador Debrot, Kralendijk, ☎ *(800) 359-0747.*
Single: $80–$165. Double: $80–$165.

Accommodations vary from small apartments with no air conditioning to newer and more spacious units with air conditioning and kitchens. Primarily serving divers, this no-frills complex provides clean towels daily, but maid service only once a week. There's a pool and bar, but no restaurant. A decent choice for those who don't mind fending for themselves and are seeking budget quarters. 30 rooms. Credit cards: A, DC, MC, V.

Club Nautico Bonaire   **$200–$450**   ★ ★ ★ ★

Waterfront Promenade, Kralendijk, ☎ *(800) 359-0747, (599) 7-5800.*
Single: $200–$450. Double: $200–$450.

This newer property, opened in the fall of 1994, offers colonial-style one-, two- and three-bedroom apartments on the oceanfront. Each unit is nicely appointed and comes with rattan furniture, full kitchens, air-conditioners in the bedrooms and living rooms. There's a PADI five-star dive shop on site, as well as a restaurant, bar, pool, private pier and marina. Inquire about money-saving dive packages. 40 rooms.

Coral Regency Resort   **$150–$230**   ★ ★ ★

Kaya Gobernador Debrot 90, Kralendijk, ☎ *(800) 327-8150. FAX (599) 7-5680.*
Single: $150–$210. Double: $150–$230.

This time-share resort (beware of hard sells) puts up guests in studios and one- and two-bedroom suites in two-story buildings arranged around a free-form pool. Units are attractive with large sitting areas, air and full kitchens. There's a recreation center and dive shop, as well as a bar and restaurant—but no beach to speak of. 28 rooms. Credit cards: A, DC, MC, V.

Harbour Village Beach Resort   **$170–$400**   ★ ★ ★ ★

Kaya Gobernador Debrot 71, Kralendijk, ☎ *(800) 424-0004, (599) 7-7500.*
Single: $170–$400. Double: $170–$400.

Catering to divers, this Iberian village-style complex offers both traditional rooms and condos with kitchens; all are spacious, nicely decorated and have air conditioning. The beach is wide by Bonaire standards, and the diving facilities are choice. There's also a spiffy new spa and fitness center offering pampering treatments, a pool and traditional watersports free of charge. The grounds are quite pretty and the digs luxurious; guest rooms were enlarged and renovated in 1995. 72 rooms. Credit cards: A, DC, MC, V.

Port Bonaire Resort $265–$385   ★ ★ ★

Kralendijk, ☎ (800) 766-6016, (599) 7-5639. FAX (599) 7-5639.
Single: $265–$385. Double: $265–$385.

This newer condo resort, opened in late 1994, is located directly across from the airport on the waterfront. Lodging is in one- and two-bedroom apartments, a penthouse and a two-bedroom beach house; all have fully equipped kitchens, cable TV, direct-dial phones, patios and other modern amenities. On-site facilities include a pool, private dock, playground, dive shop and coffee shop. The property is a sister to the new Plaza Resort Bonaire, and guests can use the facilities at both. 23 rooms.

Sand Dollar Condominium Resort $160–$350   ★ ★

Kaya Gobernador Debrot 79, Kralendijk, ☎ (800) 288-4773. FAX (599) 7-8760.
Single: $160–$350. Double: $160–$350.

Accommodations at this beachfront condominium complex, formerly called Sand Dollar Beach Club, include studios and apartments from one to three bedrooms, all with air conditioning, full kitchens and pleasant contemporary furnishings. Each is differently done as these units are individually owned. There's an excellent on-premise dive center, as well as two tennis courts, supervised children's programs during high season, a restaurant and a tiny beach strollable only during low tide. A nicely elegant spot. 73 rooms. Credit cards: A, MC, V.

Sorobon Beach Resort $110–$165   ★ ★

Kralendijk, ☎ (599) 7-8080. FAX (599) 7-5363.
Single: $110–$165. Double: $110–$165.

Bonaire's only "naturalist" resort means that clothes are optional- -and many guests take advantage of this fact. Accommodations are in cabinlike structures and consist of one-bedroom units with small kitchens and simple furnishings. The grounds include a small family-style restaurant, bar and private beach—the better to bare all on. The remote location also assures privacy, and a daily shuttle into town assures diversion. A nice, simple spot for the carefree set who don't mind forgoing air conditioning. 20 rooms. Credit cards: MC, V.

Sunset Oceanfront Apartments $60–$190   ★ ★

P.O. Box 333, Kralendijk, ☎ (599) 7-8291, (800) 344-4439.
Single: $60–$190. Double: $130–$190.

This small apartment complex is across the street from the ocean, but a half-mile from the beach. Accommodations are in one- and two-bedroom apartments that overlook the sea; each has a small kitchen, contemporary furnishings and air conditioning only in the bedrooms. There's a small pool on-site, but little else in the way of extras. Restaurants and a casino are within an easy walk. 12 rooms. Credit cards: A, DC, MC, V.

Inns

These are inns dedicated to serving the committed diver. Furnishings are usually very basic and require a no-nonsense attitude. **Sunset Inn** probably has the best location for walking to the city's restaurants and shops.

Carib Inn   **$64–$124**   ★★

J.A. Abraham Blvd., Kralendijk, ☎ *(599) 7-8819.*
Single: $64–$124. Double: $64–$124.

This intimate scuba resort, founded by American diver Bruce Bowker, attracts those who love the sport and are seeking simple lodgings without a lot of extras. Seven of the nine units have their own kitchen; all are air-conditioned and were recently redone. There's a pool but not much else; you'll have to cook in or walk to a nearby restaurant to be sated. Bowker runs a pleasant inn, with lots of repeat guests, so reserve early. The dive center is excellent. 9 rooms. Credit cards: A, MC, V.

Sunset Inn   **$60–$105**   ★

Kaya C.E.B. Hellmund 29, Kralendijk, ☎ *(599) 7-8291.*
Single: $60–$105. Double: $60–$105.

Located within walking distance of a few dive centers, the back-to-basics Sunset has air-conditioned rooms with kitchenettes and coffeemakers, though not much else. Its central location makes exploring Kralendijk on foot easy. 7 rooms. Credit cards: A, MC, V.

Low Cost Lodging

To save money in Bonaire, travel with several people and share the cost of an apartment or condominium. The tourist board can also supply names of private homes that will rent out individual rooms. Also, try to travel during low season (mid-April through mid-December), when rates are slashed.

BONAIRE

Where to Eat

Fielding's Highest Rated Restaurants in Bonaire

★★★	Chibi-Chibi	$15–$26
★★★	China Garden	$5–$24
★★★	Den Laman	$11–$22
★★★	Green Parrot	$10–$20
★★★	Mona Lisa	$15–$23
★★★	Raffles	$11–$25
★★★	Red Pelican	$20–$35
★★★	Richard's Waterfront	$13–$28
★★★	Toys Grand Cafe	$10–$23

Fielding's Most Exclusive Restaurants in Bonaire

★★★	Red Pelican	$20–$35
★★★	Richard's Waterfront	$13–$28
★★★	Chibi-Chibi	$15–$26
★★★	Mona Lisa	$15–$23
★★★	Raffles	$11–$25

Fielding's Best Value Restaurants in Bonaire

★★★	Green Parrot	$10–$20
★★★	China Garden	$5–$24
★★★	Toys Grand Cafe	$10–$23
★★★	Den Laman	$11–$22
★★★	Raffles	$11–$25

Food prices are high on the island because virtually everything besides fresh fish is imported. Among native specialties are wahoo, dolphin, conch, goat stew, red snapper, Dutch cheeses and fungi (a thick pudding made from cornmeal). Many hotels offer theme nights, including the popular Indonesian cuisine with rijstaffel, the traditional rice table. New restaurants worth checking out include Mi Poron, where the food is authentic Bonaireian and the atmosphere is that of a family museum; and Eddy's '50s, a rock-and-roll theme restaurant with very reasonable prices. Both are in Kralendijk. For nightlife, try your luck at the gaming hall at the Divi Flamingo Resort, billed as the world's first "barefoot" casino; or the new casino—the island's second and largest—at the Plaza Resort. Popular nightspots include Go Bananas, Fantasy Disco and Karel's Beach Bar.

Beefeater $$$ ★★

Kaya Grandi 12, Kralendijk.
American cuisine. Specialties: Steaks, scampi, homemade ice cream.
Dinner: 6:30–11:30 p.m., entrées $15–$25. Closed: Sun.
In the center of town is this restored, authentic Bonaireian town home, very intimate, serving rather dear beef and seafood dishes, as well as vegetarian cuisine. But the surroundings are lovely, with a courtyard view. It's nice to see how old Bonaire might have looked. Desserts are homemade and utilize local fruit. Reservations recommended. Credit cards: A, MC, V.

Chibi-Chibi $$$ ★★★

J.A. Abraham Boulevard, Kralendijk, ☎ *(599) 7-8285. Associated hotel: Divi Flamingo Beach Hotel.*
International cuisine. Specialties: Antillean onion soup, fettuccini flamingo.
Dinner: 6–10 p.m., entrées $15–$26.
Like the tropical bird that is its namesake, the Chibi-Chibi is positioned prettily on stilts, and for an experience like none other, the sea below is lit at night so diners can espy the vivid marine life below their tables. (Not surprisingly, you must reserve in advance.) Cuisine is familiar to American tastes, with fresh fish available, but local specialties are also on hand, including keshi yena, a whole Edam cheese stuffed with chicken and spices. Reservations recommended. Credit cards: A, DC, MC, V.

China Garden $$ ★★★

Kaya Grandi 47, Kralendijk, ☎ *(599) 7-8480.*
Chinese cuisine. Specialties: Goat Chinese-style, lobster in black bean sauce.
Lunch: 11:30 a.m.–2 p.m., entrées $5–$24.
Dinner: 4–10 p.m., entrées $5–$24. Closed: Tue.
Housed in a grand restored home downtown, this popular restaurant is possibly the best Chinese eatery from a handful of choices. In typical island hodgepodge style, the China Garden combines Cantonese specialties with local favorites such as goat, with a few American sandwiches thrown in. Everything is generously portioned, so you get what you pay for and then some. All sweet-and-sour and black-bean sauce dishes are recommended, and the seafood is fresh. Reservations recommended. Credit cards: A, MC, V.

Den Laman   **$$$**   ★★★

Kaya Gobernador, Kralendijk,
Seafood cuisine. Specialties: Red snapper Creole, conch flamingo, kingfish.
Dinner: 6–11 p.m., entrées $11–$22. Closed: Tue.
Seafood doesn't get much fresher or better prepared on the island than in this
indoor-outdoor restaurant. Red snapper lightly grilled or prepared Creole style is a
best bet and is usually available. Decor is piscatorial, with a huge aquarium provid-
ing a running conversation piece; it can be fun for kids. Closed September. Credit
cards: A, MC, V.

Green Parrot   **$$**   ★★★

Kaya Gobernador, Kralendijk, ☎ (599) 7-5454. Associated hotel: Sand Dollar Condominiums.
International cuisine. Specialties: Onion string appetizer, barbecue.
Lunch: 11:30 a.m.–3 p.m., entrées $5–$10.
Dinner: 4:30–10 p.m., entrées $10–$20.
Homesick Americans will like this jumping place, which has frothy and fruity margaritas, juicy burgers, barbecue and, familiar to habitues of the Tony Roma's chain,
an onion string loaf. The view is great at sunset since it is situated on a hotel pier
that is open to the breezes. It's a good place to grab a reasonably priced lunch when
coming from or going to the airport, which is only a few miles away. There is a buffet on Sunday with barbecued meats and lively entertainment. Reservations recommended. Credit cards: A, MC, V.

Mona Lisa   **$$$**   ★★★

Kaya Grandi 15, Kralendijk, ☎ (599) 7-8718.
International cuisine. Specialties: Pork tenderloin sate with peanut sauce, wahoo.
Lunch: Noon–2 p.m., entrées $12–$23.
Dinner: 6–10 p.m., entrées $15–$23. Closed: Sat., Sun.
Absorb some local color in this popular bar and restaurant, where the Dutch-born
chef personally oversees each table. The Mona Lisa's bar, decorated with a profu-
sion of hometown knick-knacks, is a riot of activity. Copious snacks are served there
until very late. The pretty restaurant wears a more demure face, with a diverse menu
of Indonesian, Dutch and French favorites. An ongoing special is pork sate (tender-
loin marinated with garlic, sesame oil, soy and other spices) served with peanut
sauce, but a popular French onion soup is always available. Reservations recom-
mended. Credit cards: A, MC, V.

Raffles   **$$$**   ★★★

Kaya C.E.B. Hellmund 5, Kralendijk, ☎ (599) 7-8617.
International cuisine. Specialties: Seafood platter Caribe, salmon cascade.
Dinner: 6:30–10 p.m., entrées $11–$25.
Bonaire has a number of old homesteads, but Raffles, with a red London phone
booth as its landmark and mascot, roosts in one of the oldest of the old. Patrons
have more than a hope for an intimate conversation in the indoor dining room,
along with Caribbean entrées, French-style desserts and soft jazz playing. There's
also a terrace for people watching. Pescado de mariscos, a Latin bouillabaisse, is usually available; also chicken and steaks. Make room for the mousse made with two
kinds of chocolate. Reservations recommended. Credit cards: A, MC, V.

Red Pelican   **$$$**   ★★★
Kaminda Sorobon 64, Kralendijk, ☎ (599) 7-8198. Associated hotel: Lac Bay Resort.
Seafood cuisine. Specialties: Seafood stew, marinated fish salad.
Lunch: Noon– 2 p.m., entrées $4–$6.
Dinner: 7–10 p.m., entrées $20–$35. Closed: Sun.
A sophisticated, intimate spot, the Red Pelican is very close to being the toniest restaurant on the isle, with a location a little ways off the tourist track, on the windward coast in Lac Bay. Decor is island-tropical and cuisine is international. Expect herring, stews and chicken dishes. Reservations recommended. Credit cards: A, MC, V.

Rendez-Vous Restaurant   **$$$**   ★★
3 Kaya L.D. Gerharts, Kralendijk, ☎ (599) 7-8454.
International cuisine. Specialties: Chicken apricot, keshi yena.
Dinner: 6–10:30 p.m., entrées $14–$26. Closed: Sun.
The livin' is easy at this midtown eatery which, like most on the island, has two dining areas—indoor and out. But wherever you sit, it's cozy, and a loaf of home-baked bread gets things off to a nice start. Local dishes are well represented, and keshi yena (Edam cheese stuffed with meat) is prepared picadillo style, with raisins. Otherwise, there's always good seafood, with a daily special, and vegetarians needn't feel slighted. Good fruit desserts, patisserie and espresso. Reservations recommended. Credit cards: A, MC, V.

Richard's Waterfront   **$$$**   ★★★
60 J.A. Abraham Boulevard, Kralendijk, ☎ (599) 7-5263.
Seafood cuisine. Specialties: Conch al Ajillo, grilled wahoo, seafood soup.
Dinner: 6:30–10:30 p.m., entrées $13–$28. Closed: Mon.
The food is usually stellar at this friendly waterfront charmer, especially when attentive owner Richard Beady, from Boston, is around to check on things. The daily special, on a blackboard, regularly features fresh fish of the day; wahoo is recommended. There won't be many surprises, such as extra hot pepper in the popular fish soup, which is a favored starter. Both conch and shrimp are often prepared with garlic-butter sauce. The bar is a favorite with locals and others, especially at sunset, for all the usual reasons. Reservations recommended. Credit cards: A, MC, V.

Toys Grand Cafe   **$$$**   ★★★
J.A. Abraham Boulevard, Kralendijk, ☎ (599) 7-6666.
International cuisine. Specialties: Snails in blue-cheese sauce, nasi goreng.
Lunch: 11:30 a.m.– 2 p.m., entrées $5–$15.
Dinner: 5–10 p.m., entrées $10–$23.
Someone with a touch of whimsy created this eclectic restaurant on the main drag in Kralendijk. The walls are covered with familiar figures from the cartoon and entertainment worlds. Not grand in cuisine, but in concept; it's mostly fun. Not really for kids (maybe grown-up ones), as the interesting and creative menu is peppered with Indonesian favorites, meats and shellfish with vivid sauces. At certain times of the day, a few meals are available at a substantial discount. Credit cards: not accepted. Credit cards: MC, V.

Zeezicht Restaurant   **$$$**   ★★
Kaya Corsow 10, Kralendijk, ☎ (599) 7-8434.
Seafood cuisine. Specialties: Ceviche, local snails in hot sauce, seafood soup.

Aruba

Cayman Islands

Lunch: 9 a.m.–4 p.m., entrées $5–$9.

Dinner: 4–11 p.m., entrées $9–$25.

See the zee (sea) at this waterfront eatery with a front porch at the water's edge. A good American breakfast is served from 9 a.m., and lunch is usually local fish and conch sandwiches, which are recommended. There are Indonesian specialties, including a mini-rijstaffel for those who can't handle the usual 16-dish feast. Whether eating inside or out, there is something for everyone here, food and ambience-wise. Service can be slow at peak times. Credit cards: A, MC, V.

Though you can find some bargains in the duty-free stores of Bonaire, the island is hardly the shopper's paradise of St. Thomas or Aruba. Most stores are located in the capital city of Kralendijk, whose narrow, picturesque streets offer up the typical T-shirt shops, boutiques and jewelry stores. Black-coral crafts are an island specialty. Harvesting is allowed only by authorized Bonaireians for sale in local shops; it's illegal to collect your own, so be sure to keep your receipt in case U.S. Customs gives you a hard time bringing the rare species back home. **Caribbean Arts & Crafts** *(38A Kaya Grandi,* ☎ *[599] 7-5051)* has black coral crafts, as well as Mexican onyx, wall tapestries and other local wares; the government-sponsored **Fundashon Arte Industri Bonairiano** (*next to the post office in Kralendijk on J.A. Abraham Blvd.*) is also a good source for coral jewelry and other crafts.

Bonaire Directory

Arrival and Departure

ALM offers nonstop flights to Bonaire from Atlanta (twice a week) and from Miami (once a week). **Air Aruba** also has a direct flight from Newark, New Jersey, three times a week (these flights first touch down in Aruba before flying onto Bonaire). **American Airlines** flies daily to Curaçao from Miami, allowing passengers to make immediate transfers to Bonaire, usually on ALM, which makes 4–5 daily nonstop flights to Bonaire from Curaçao. A plus for flying on American Airlines is that you can sometimes receive a discount if you book your hotel at the same time you make your flight reservation.

The departure tax is $10. There is also an inter-island departure tax of $5.65.

Business Hours

Stores open Monday–Saturday 8 a.m.–noon and 2–6 p.m. Banks open weekdays 8:30 a.m.–4 p.m.

Climate

Temperatures average 82 degrees F and vary only 6 degrees between summer and winter. Water temperatures range from 76–80 F. Bonaire gets less than 20 inches of rainfall per year. Bonaire is below the Hurricane Belt and is rarely bombarded by storms or heavy seas.

Documents

U.S. and Canadian citizens need show only proof of citizenship (passport, original or notarized birth certificate or voter's registration with photo ID), and an ongoing or return ticket.

Electricity

Current runs 127 volts, 50 cycles. American appliances will work slower; best to bring an adapter.

Getting Around

Expect to take a taxi from the airport to your hotel—about $10. Rates are established by the government, and most honest drivers will show the list of prices if you ask. Note that rates are higher (25 percent) after 8 p.m., and from 11–6 a.m. (50 percent).

Driving in Bonaire is on the right side of the road. Unless you are an experienced driver, tooting around Bonaire in a scooter or moped can be dangerous since roads are often strewn with rocks or full of holes. The best way to see the Washington National Park is in a Jeep, van or automobile. To rent a car, you will need to show a valid U.S., British or Canadian driver's license.

Budget, Avis and Dollar Rent a Car all have booths at the airport.

Language

Papiamento is the unofficial island language, Dutch the official. English is almost unilaterally spoken. Spanish is also well known.

Medical Emergencies

St. Francis Hospital in Kralendijk ☎ *8900* is run by well-trained doctors who studied in the Netherlands. Divers will be happy to know it comes equipped with a decompression chamber.

Money

Official currency is the Netherlands Antilles florin or guilder, written as NAf or Afl. Most establishments list prices in guilders, but will accept dollars (giving change in guilders). U.S. dollars and traveler's checks are accepted everywhere.

Telephone

From the U.S. dial 011 (international code), plus 5997 (country code), plus the 4-digit local number. Few lodgings have room phones, so most people head down to the Landsradio office in Kralendijk. The airport also has telephones.

Time

Bonaire is on Atlantic standard time.

Tipping and Taxes

Most hotels and restaurants add a 10–15 percent service charge. The government also requires hotels to add a $4.10-per-person daily room tax. Feel free to tip more for especially good service.

Tourist Information

The tourist office is located at *12 Kaya Libertador Simon Bolivar* in Kralendijk; ☎ *(599) 7-5322 or FAX (599) 7-8408*. For information in the U.S., contact the **Bonaire Tourist Office** at ☎ *(800) 826-6247 or FAX (212) 956-5913*.

Water

Tap water is safe to drink since it comes from distilled seawater.

When To Go

Carnival takes place in February. Coronation Day is April 30. St. John's Day is June 24. St. Peter's Day is celebrated in Rincon on June 28. Bonaire Day is Sept. 6. Annual Sailing Regatta are a series of races celebrated with a festive air in mid-October.

BONAIRE HOTELS		RMS	RATES	PHONE	CR. CARDS
Kralendijk					
★★★★	**Club Nautico Bonaire**	40	$200–$450	(800) 359-0747	
★★★★	**Harbour Village Beach Resort**	72	$170–$400	(800) 424-0004	A, DC, MC, V
★★★★	**Plaza Resort Bonaire**	177	$115–$220	(800) 766-6016	A, DC, MC, V
★★★	**Captain Don's Habitat**	43	$150–$245	(800) 327-6709	MC, V
★★★	**Coral Regency Resort**	28	$150–$230	(800) 327-8150	A, DC, MC, V
★★★	**Divi Flamingo Resort**	145	$85–$140	(800) 367-3484	A, DC, MC, V
★★★	**Port Bonaire Resort**	23	$265–$385	(800) 766-6016	
★★	**Buddy Dive Resort**	30	$80–$165	(800) 359-0747	A, DC, MC, V
★★	**Carib Inn**	9	$64–$124	(599) 7-8819	A, MC, V
★★	**Sand Dollar Condominium Resort**	73	$160–$350	(800) 288-4773	A, MC, V
★★	**Sorobon Beach Resort**	20	$110–$165	(599) 7-8080	MC, V
★★	**Sunset Beach Hotel**	145	$80–$140	(599) 7-8448	A, DC, MC, V
★★	**Sunset Oceanfront Apartments**	12	$60–$190	(800) 344-4439	A, DC, MC, V
★	**Sunset Inn**	7	$60–$105	(599) 7-8291	A, MC, V

BONAIRE

BONAIRE RESTAURANTS

Kralendijk

	Restaurant	PHONE	ENTRÉE	CR. CARDS
	American			
★★	Beefeater		$15–$25	A, MC, V
	Chinese			
★★★	China Garden	(599) 7-8480	$5–$24	A, MC, V
	International			
★★★	Chibi-Chibi	(599) 7-8285	$15–$26	A, DC, MC, V
★★★	Green Parrot	(599) 7-5454	$5–$20	A, MC, V
★★★	Mona Lisa	(599) 7-8718	$12–$23	A, MC, V
★★★	Raffles	(599) 7-8617	$11–$25	A, MC, V
★★★	Toys Grand Cafe	(599) 7-6666	$5–$23	MC, V
★★	Rendez-Vous Restaurant	(599) 7-8454	$14–$26	A, MC, V
	Seafood			
★★★	Den Laman		$11–$22	A, MC, V
★★★	Red Pelican	(599) 7-8198	$4–$35	A, MC, V
★★★	Richard's Waterfront	(599) 7-5263	$13–$28	A, MC, V
★★	Zeezicht Restaurant	(599) 7-8434	$5–$25	A, MC, V

BRITISH VIRGIN ISLANDS

Up close views of marine life await novice and experienced divers.

With countless pristine coves beneficently conspiring to create a sailor's paradise, the British Virgin Islands generously refer to themselves as Nature's Little Secrets. Until recently, the country has never sought nor desired mass tourism, preferring to let the discerning or curious traveler discover it over time—there are no direct flights from the continental United States to these islands (you'll probably fly through San Juan, or ferry over from St. Thomas). When compared against the frantic pace of St. Thomas in the U.S. Virgins next door, the BVIs are positively laid-back and friendly. Friendliness and charm, in fact, are particular sales points, and although the BVI government is cautiously expanding the tourism infrastructure, it's reassuring to note that they recognize that a chief lure for current and future visitors is the unspoiled nature of these idyllic outposts. Although there are a number of pricey resorts, high-rise accommodations are nowhere to be found on these islands. What nightlife there is typically focuses on the lively beach bars—on remote Jost Van Dyke, there's a bar for every 17 residents, though the island somehow still remains tranquil and unspoiled. In the U.S. Virgins, crime has become an everyday concern for both locals and tourists. On the other hand, in the BVIs, many of the smaller island properties don't bother with room keys.

During the day, the sailing ambience predominates, as it has for centuries. Norman Island is reputed to be the setting for Robert Louis Stevenson's *Treasure Island*, and stories of buried treasure in the holds of the many sunken galleons still percolate among the yachting set. Today, bare-boat charterers define much of the BVI character, most of them lured by the secluded bays and fine anchorages, not the least of which is Virgin Gorda's North Sound, a 150-acre hurricane hole, within rowing distance of several excellent restaurants and bars. There are fine beaches sprinkled throughout the chain, good diving and snorkeling along the Sir Francis Drake Channel, and delightful short hikes in Gorda Peak and Mount Sage National Parks. Don't overlook island-hopping during your visit—most of the islands are a short ferry- or charter-boat-ride away from Tortola, the easiest base from which to explore. Americans need a passport to visit the BVIs—even for a day-trip via ferry from the U.S. Virgins—but once you arrive, you'll be made to feel welcome in a fashion you might wish you could experience more of at home.

Bird's-Eye View

Lying 60 miles east of Puerto Rico and just a few miles northeast of St. John, more than 50 islands, crags and cays make up the complex referred to as the British Virgin Islands. Sixteen of the islands are inhabited, the most important being Tortola, where more than four-fifths of the 17,000-strong population lives, and where the archipelago's capital, Road Town, is positioned. The remaining 3500 or so residents are scattered among the other islands—principally on Virgin Gorda, with 170 living on Anegada and 150 on Jost Van Dyke.

From nearly any vantage point on Tortola, the sublime view is that of seemingly endless tropical islands stretching off into the horizon. The appearance of these islands—all but Anegada volcanic in origin—ranges from

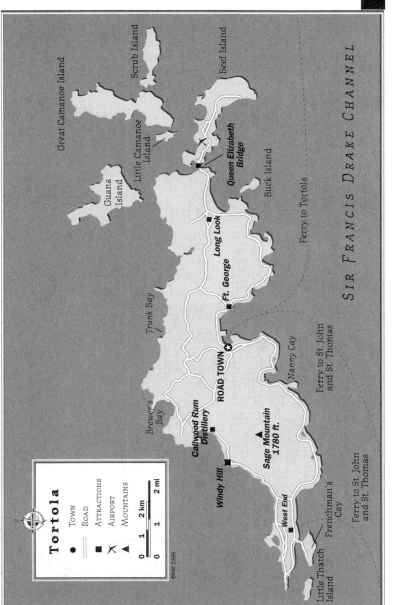

Tortola

TOWN ●
ROAD
ATTRACTIONS ■
AIRPORT ✈
MOUNTAINS ▲

0   1   2 km
0   1   2 mi

©PWI 1998

Great Camanoe Island

Scrub Island

Beef Island

Little Camanoe Island

Guana Island

Queen Elizabeth Bridge

Sir Francis Drake Channel

Buck Island

Long Look

Ft. George

Ferry to Tortola

Trunk Bay

Brewer's Bay

ROAD TOWN

Nanny Cay

Ferry to St. John and St. Thomas

Callwood Rum Distillery

Sage Mountain 1780 ft.

Windy Hill

West End

Frenchman's Cay

Ferry to St. John and St. Thomas

Little Thatch Island

sloping mountains cloaked with verdant green growth to scrub and cactus-covered hills layered with massive rounded boulders. Long stretches of palm-shaded beaches border much of Tortola's perimeter, while offshore, rough-hewn rock formations poke their heads out of the water to provide perches for seabirds. Tortola's highest point is 1780-foot Mount Sage, a peak enveloped by moist rainforest, even though the summit receives less than 100 inches of rain annually.

Devil's Bay, British Virgin Islands

Seven-mile-long Virgin Gorda has a similar crest, the 1370-foot Virgin Gorda Peak, and another claim to fame—the unforgettable Baths, a group of giant boulders strewn along the beach in Devil's Bay, at the island's southern tip. The rocks are a geological mystery, but remain a supremely photogenic location for swimming and snorkeling, except when cruise ships have called. The black sheep of the BVI family is 15-square-mile Anegada, a coralline outpost about 15 miles northwest of the other islands out in the Atlantic. Sometimes referred to as a drowned island, Anegada's highest point above sea level is 28 feet, and mariners have found the coral shelf that surrounds it treacherous—more than 300 ships are estimated to have been sent to their grave off the island's shores.

Cutting through the BVIs, and protected yearlong from the brunt of tradewinds is the Sir Francis Drake Channel, yielding one of the world's great sailing passages. On either side of the channel are a series of pristine anchorages, many of them next to uninhabited islands. Below the water, particularly on the south side of the Drake passage, are the archipelago's best dive sites, including the *RMS Rhone*, a magnificently encrusted (and preserved) steamer that went down in a hurricane in 1867—it is probably the Caribbean's most popular and treasured wreck.

History

The Virgin Islands were discovered by Christopher Columbus on his second voyage in 1493. Fascinated by the exquisite natural beauty of the islands, he named them *Las Once Mil Virgines* (the 11,000 Virgins) in honor of St. Ursula and her followers. The truth is, Columbus was the not the first human to set forth on the island. Prior to the European invasion, these islands had been populated by successive waves of Indian tribes migrating north from the Orinoco region of South America. Unfortunately, the arrival of the Europeans spelled the end of the native population; within a generation, there was not a trace of them. The occupation of the island by the Spanish and other Europeans followed a pattern similar to that of other Caribbean islands. For two centuries, control of the island was passed from one country to another while the islands remained mostly uninhabited. Many of those who balked at directly challenging the Spanish chose instead the path of piracy and pirateering, the most famous of whom were Sir John Hawkins, Henry Morgan, Jost Van Dyke and Edward Teach, better known as Blackbeard. These islands provided a secluded and safe anchorage for these brigands. Even today the legacy of piracy survives in the names of many islands and in the ever-persistent legends of buried treasure. Control of the Virgin

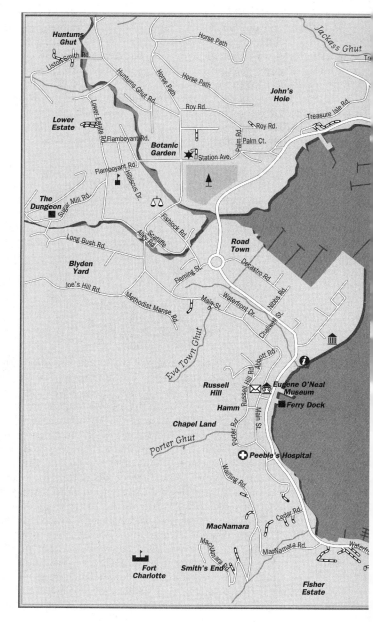

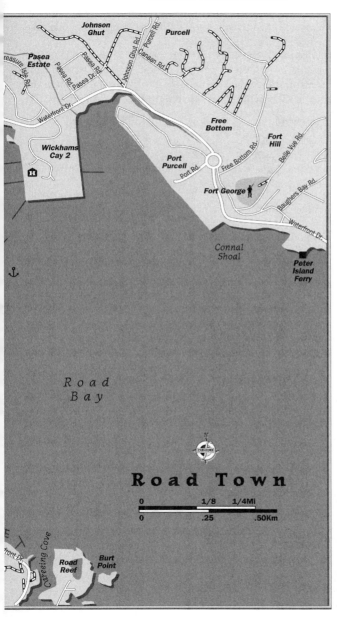

Islands finally equalized with the Danish taking control of the western islands, now known as the U.S. Virgin Islands, while the British controlled the eastern set—so-named the British Virgin Islands. In fact, Tortola (BVI) is separated from St. John (USV) by less than two miles. From the 1700s to the mid-1800s, a plantation economy supported these islands. The remnants of the sugar industry can still be seen in the ruins of sugar mills hidden in the bush. In 1967, the BVI became a self-governing member of the British Commonwealth.

People

Because of generous economic assistance received from Great Britain, islanders enjoy considerable enthusiasm for, and strong identification with, their mother country. As a group, the people have a reputation for being extraordinarily friendly and will naturally extend you greetings as you stroll down the street. In fact, an islander will be hurt if you don't return the salutation. At the same time, Gordians and Tortolans are said to be somewhat retiring and are not exactly prone to inviting travelers into their homes. Those who live in the interior mountains definitely tend to be shyer, but their lifestyle is also comparatively less pressured by touristic demands; these are older people in the hillside communities who still ride donkeys, make their own charcoal and harbor age-old superstitions about duppies or spirits. As tourism has blossomed due to the efforts of established black families as well as spunky outsiders, some of the island's women have become renowned for their cooking skills. Mrs. V. Thomas was decorated by the Queen of England for her guava jelly and mango chutney. As construction demands have risen, traditional island occupations such as stonemasonry and gardening, have begun returning, and sailors in the old school of sloops are finding another kind of work in more progressive boating.

Beaches

On Tortola, all the best beaches are located along the scalloped north shore, a number of them accessible only by boat (remember, this is a sailor's island). Starting at the west end of the island, Smuggler's Cove is often void of fellow bathers, and features good snorkeling along its length, while nearby Long Bay is a mile of perfect white sand that invites romantic sunset

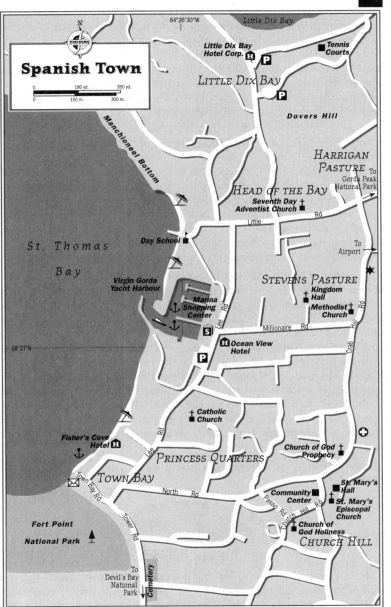

Spanish Town

180 yd. 350 yd.
150 m. 300 m.

64°26'30"W

Little Dix Bay

Little Dix Bay Hotel Corp.

Tennis Courts

LITTLE DIX BAY

Dovers Hill

Manchioneel Bottom

HARRIGAN PASTURE

To Gorda Peak National Park

HEAD OF THE BAY

Seventh Day Adventist Church

Little   Rd

St. Thomas

Bay

Day School

To Airport

STEVENS PASTURE

Virgin Gorda Yacht Harbour

Marina Shopping Center

Kingdom Hall

Methodist Church

Crab Hill Rd

Millionaire Rd

18°27'N

Lee Rd

Ocean View Hotel

Catholic Church

Fisher's Cove Hotel

Church of God Prophecy

PRINCESS QUARTERS

Lee Rd

St. Mary's Hall

St. Mary's Episcopal Church

Community Center

Town Bay

North   Rd

Passa Rd

Church Hill Rd

Church of God Holiness

Fort Point

National Park

CHURCH HILL

Town Bay Rd

Tower Rd

To Devil's Bay National Park

Cemetery

strolls. Surfers head for Apple Bay during the day, while at night, Bomba's Shack is the beach bar to end all. Cane Garden Bay is a popular anchorage for boaters, while its expansive curl of sand attracts visitors for the island's best collection of watersports activities. Another large cove, Brewers Bay, is ideal for snorkeling, while Elizabeth Beach has only recently become accessible by road; during the slower summer months, you may be the only one enjoying these quieter spots. Beef Island, which is connected to Tortola by bridge, has Long Bay and Trellis Bay, both nice pieces of real estate, but for the regular activity in and out of the airport.

As on Tortola, Virgin Gorda's best beaches are on the north side of the island, beginning with one of the most unique and picturesque swimming locations anywhere in the region, The Baths. Alas, the spot, scattered with massive boulders that create enchanting grottoes, is a hot ticket on cruise ship itineraries—visit before 9 a.m. or after 4 p.m. Next door is Spring Bay, a good place to duck over to when the crowds get thick at The Baths, and just beyond is glistening Trunk Bay, reached by a rough path through private lands from Spring Bay. Two other Gorda beauties are Savannah Bay and Mahoe Bay, with long, gentle curves of sand for sunning and swimming.

A number of excellent beaches are found off the two main BVIs. Perhaps the best for a day trip is Peter Island's idyllic Deadman's Bay, an isolated, palm-lined strand that has grown a beach bar and grill. Mountainous Jost Van Dyke has a beautiful sandy beach at White Bay, another at Great Harbour Bay, and lively bars at both. An uninhabited scrub-covered islet just off Jost Van Dyke, Sandy Cay, has a velvety swatch of radiant white sand, and little else. Prickly Pear Island (opposite the Bitter End Yacht Club), has a long shelf of sand, Vixen Point, which sometimes has a beach bar and watersports center when things are busy. And then there's flat Anegada, which could practically be considered a beach in itself. If you're making the trip to remote Anegada, head for Loblolly Bay—a few shelters are provided from the sun, the offshore reef is nice for snorkeling and a bar is positioned at each end.

In the British Virgin Islands, all beaches are public, including those on the private resort islands.

Underwater

The abundance of tiny islands that compose the British Virgins create a host of varied diving opportunities for all levels of experience. The islands offer little in the way of wall diving, but wrecks and reefs are plentiful, and visibility can top a crystalline 130 feet. Anegada is off limits to boat dives for the moment due to over-fishing (and shore diving is not easy); the snorkeling is fine. BVI's best is found mostly among the small, uninhabited islands southeast of Tortola including the spectacular 310-foot steamer, The Rhone, the Caribbean's most famous wreck, which sunk theatrically off the rocks of Salt Island in 1867 with most of its 300 passengers on board. Diving is more expensive here than in most of the Eastern Caribbean, but the British Virgins feature a nice concentration of worthy sites, even after one has taken in the must-see *Rhone.*

On Foot

Quiet and uncrowded, well-tended yet off-the-beaten track, the natural environments of the British Virgin Islands are a lot of things their U.S. counterparts aspire to, but only attain on protected St. John, which lies a scant mile off Tortola's southern coast. There are almost 60 islands in the BVIs, but almost all are uninhabited, which allows the option to travel to an island for a day of private exploration and contemplation. There are delightful, mostly short trails on the main islands (outlined below), while the outer destinations boast a wealth of unmarked possibilities.

By Pedal

In 1995, Christopher Ghiorse opened Last Stop Mountain Biking and a new island sport was born. Although a friend described it as "one big hill," Tortola is home to his shop. Tranquil Virgin Gorda offers the best riding and can easily be reached by ferry; the beautiful ride to the Baths is about as scenic as biking comes in the Caribbean, but time your ride to miss the midday onslaught of day-trippers and reschedule entirely if a cruise ship is docked nearby. Tortola can be circumnavigated in a half-day (40 miles, all paved); a shorter version of this trip leads west out of Road Town to Nanny Cay, West End and around Steel Point. More challenging is the sweaty ride up Sage Mountain. Local traffic is swift and requires caution on Tortola, but bikers are welcomed and respected, so far. Smaller Jost Van Dyke and Peter Island also can be toured using the local ferry service. Anegada features miles of flat sandy roads, and the Anegada Reef Hotel now has a small collection of bikes for rent.

What Else to See

The best sights in the British Virgin Islands are connected to the sun and sea—anything else should be left for a rainy or hazy day. Consider a frog-jumper's flight or a quick cruise to one of the neighboring islands (including St. John or St. Thomas, if so inclined). You can usually make it back the same day (check in advance), and a few of the private islands allow day-trippers for beach sunning and meals. Charter boats visit Cooper Island, which features a small dock, a lovely beach, and a beach bar for lunch or dinner; deserted Norman Island (see "On Foot" above) features lovely trails. The BVI Folk Museum in Road Town was closed for renovation at press time, but may reopen soon; it contains interesting relics from the wreck of the *RMS Rhone*.

City Celebrations

Virgin Gorda Tours Association   ★★★

Fischers Cove Beach Hotel, South Sound, ☎ (809) 495-5252.

Want to see the island but lack your own wheels? They'll shuttle you about, taking in all the high points, for $50. Two tours are offered daily; call for a schedule.

Parks and Gardens

J.R. O'Neal Botanical Gardens   ★★★

Station Avenue; Road Town, Road Town, ☎ (809) 494-4557.
Hours open: 8 a.m.–4 p.m.

Indigenous and exotic plants are beautifully showcased at this four-acre garden, which includes an herb garden and hothouses for orchids and ferns.

Gorda Peak National Park   ★★★★

North Sound Road, North Sound.

The "peak" in the name rises some 1370 feet, making it the island's highest point. This 265-acre preserve is home to indigenous and exotic plants and has been reforested with mahogany trees. Hike to the top, then catch your breath at the observation tower, though foliage obscures the view.

Mount Sage National Park   ★★★★

Ridge Road, West End.

Located on the peak of a volcanic mountain, this 92-acre national park protects the remains of a primeval rainforest—most, alas, was cut down over the years. A graveled path will take you to the top, some 1780 feet up, the highest elevation in the British and U.S. Virgin Islands. A nice day trip.

Tours

Travel Plan Tours   ★★★

Waterfront Plaza, Road Town, ☎ (809) 494-2872.

Island tours take about 2.5 hours and include all the hot spots. $50 per person.

When the sea is as inviting as it is in the BVIs, who needs other activities? Bare boat or crewed yacht charters are available from Moorings and a number of other outfits. It's probably the biggest local activity—navigation is not difficult and the weather is usually so clear you can't get lost, though the numerous inlets and rippled coastlines can give navigators a run for their money (note that bare-boaters aren't allowed around Anegada due to the dangerous reefs and prohibition against anchoring). If you're not an educated sailor, try a few classes at the Nick Trotter Sailing School at the Bitter End Yacht Club on Virgin Gorda (see "Where to Stay" in Virgin Gorda, below). Captain Dale provides deep-sea fishing trips from Virgin Gorda. Snorkeling is generally excellent throughout the BVIs. Several outfits provide snorkeling day trips aboard boats, and some of the dive operators will allow snorkelers to join them as they head off to some of the remote destinations; the *RMS Rhone* is close enough to the surface to be appreciated by snorkelers, and nearby Norman Island is an excellent spot. Windsurfing has become popular, and sea kayaking—sometimes between the U.S. and British islands with camping equipment stashed aboard—has developed quite a following (see "By Paddle" in "St. John").

Baths, The (Devil's Bay Nat'l Park) ★★★★★

Lee Road, North Sound.

Gigantic house-size boulders strewn about have formed saltwater grottoes and small pools great for snorkeling, and produced a geological mystery. The stones are granite, which is not usually found south of the Carolina's—are they the product of ancient volcanoes or were they carried south by glaciers during the ice age? No matter. The cave-like passages lead to seductive hidden pools and the snorkeling here is unique. A new step and ladder system and a protected swimming area are welcome additions to this must-see natural wonder. This is by far the island's most-visited spot, a big stop for cruise ship passengers, so come early in the morning or late in the afternoon to avoid the crowds.

Boardsailing B.V.I.

Trellis Bay or Nanny Cay, West End, ☎ *(809) 495-2447.*

Learn the popular sport of windsurfing for $20 for a one-hour lesson. Boards can be rented for $155 a week. On Virgin Gorda, the Nick Trotter Sailing School at the Bitter **End Yacht Club** *(800) 872-2392* or *(809) 494-2745* offers courses and rentals.

Boating

Road Town, ☎ *(809) 494-2331.*

At the Moorings Resort, you can rent all manner of sailing yachts, from bareboat (no crew) to the works, with a skipper, cook and crew. Try **Virgin Island Sailing**, also in Road Town, for charters. Call from the States: ☎ *(800) 535-7289.*

Deep-Sea Fishing

Various locations, Road Town.

Sport fishers can arrange a charter or join a scheduled excursion. **Captain Dale** *(*☎ *[809] 495-5225)* arranges trips out of Virgin Gorda.

Shadow's Ranch

Todman's Estate, Road Town, ☎ *(809) 494-2262.*

Hop aboard a horse and venture along the beach or through the countryside to Mount Sage National Park. Prices start at $25 per hour.

Tortola

Twelve miles long by three miles wide, Tortola is home to three-fourths of the residents of the BVI. It's a refreshingly unaffected combination of the young and new, a reflection of a refined and contemporary approach to West Indian culture. Years of British rule have given Tortola a well-educated and worldly population, one largely unaffected by tourism. Nevertheless, most of the hotels are located here, about a dozen around Road Town. There are a couple of places to stay near Wickam's Cay I and II, on the southeast shore, and on the northwest shore at Apple Bay. In general, the crime rate is low and many residents seldom lock their doors, but it's not suggested that tourists follow their habit.

Virgin Gorda

The most chic resorts of the BVI are located on Virgin Gorda, an eight-square-mile slab of scrub and cactus whose shape some say resembles a "fat virgin"—hence its name. Notwithstanding a brief gold rush in the 17th century, the idyllic island lay undiscovered until Laurence Rockefeller cruised the bay and decided to build his Little Dix Bay Hotel. Boats from Tortola regularly dock at the southern settlement of Spanish Town, where most of the 1500 islanders live. The best beaches lay south of Spanish Town, and in the extreme southeast you can find ruins of an old 19th-century copper mine. The road to the north of the island passes through Savannah Bay and Pond Bay before reaching Virgin Gorda's second town, Gun Creek. Below is North Sound, where two fine resorts are located.

The big attraction on Virgin Gorda is a spectacular series of massive granite boulders, the Baths, whose jumbled piles are backed by coconut palms. The stones, made of a granite that is not common to the Caribbean, are thought to have been carried there by glacial movement during the Ice Age. "Having nothing to do" is one of the major pastimes here, but if you say you're bored while staying at Little Dix Bay, they will scurry you off along the coast to a secluded beach, deposit you with drinking water, a picnic and an umbrella, and pick you up later.

Huge boulders form a natural swimming pool and underwater caves known as The Baths of Virgin Gorda.

Arrival

Most folks take the easy route and take a frog-jumper's flight with American Eagle or Sunair. Boats can also be chartered from Road Town, Tortola, or from St. Thomas in the USVI. Nothing seems to run on schedule here, which is okay, because there's no place to rush to.

Treks and Beaches

Virgin Gorda looks like two different islands north to south. The northern tip is mountainous, while the south is flat, with boulders blocking every curve. Everything above a thousand feet on Virgin Gorda is considered a national park. You'll find a self-guided trail at the 265-acre park at the forested peak near the island's center; it leads to an observation point. The lookout is the end of a paved road leading to Little Dix Bay resort. The first place most people head to are **The Baths**, where snorkeling in the limpid pools created by the pattern of the huge boulders is considered to be superb. (These days you may have to fight for space among the many cruise passengers who alight here; ask your hotel what their arrival schedule is.) Some hearty souls actually climb the island's tallest mount, the 1370-foot **Gorda Peak**; the trail boasts some unusual flora, including tropical orchids. Great treks can be made through **Devil's Bay National Park**; a 15-minute trail through a natural garden of native vegetation and massive boulders will take you to a fine secluded beach. Other beaches noted for their beauty include **Trunk Bay**, wide and sandy and reachable by boat or along a rough path from Spring Bay, a sandy beach north of Yacht Harbour. There is also **Mahoe Bay**, at Mango Bay Resort, with its gently curving beach and vivid blue water.

The greatest adventure in Virgin Gorda is to just get on a boat and explore the numerous other islands, such as **Necker**, **Mosquito**, **Jost Van Dyke** and **Anegada**. You'll usually find at least one resort on these islands, where you can have a fabulous lunch.

Sports

Beyond a tennis court at the Little Dix Bay resort, all other sports take advantage of the glorious seas. Most hotels will arrange diving, sailing expeditions, and deep-sea fishing; you can also find agencies at the Yacht Harbour or negotiate directly with crew members lolling about. At **Kilbrides Underwater Tours**, you can speed out to underwater caves, wrecks and coral forests in two 42-foot dive boats under the able direction of Bert Kilbride, considered a true pro in the area. Certification courses run about $60 and you can even get a video made of your dive. If you are interested in chartering a yacht, there are a couple of agencies beside the Little Dix Bay Resort. Both one-day trips and longer excursions can be arranged.

Jost Van Dyke

Jost Van Dyke (pronounced "yost") is that perfect island for Robinson Crusoe fans who want to get away from it all. No markets, no electricity, though there are some spiffy bars and restaurants where you can meet international yacht owners who cruise up in their multimillion-dollar schooners. **White Bay Beach** is most easily reached by boat and has a beautiful sandy beach, small hotel, and restaurant. **Sandy Cay**, an uninhabited islet off Jost Van Dyke, boasts a lovely white stretch of sand—and nothing else. Windsurfing and snorkeling are considered excellent. The BVI have established campgrounds on Jost Van Dyke—about 15 campsites, with a small restaurant, or snack bar and grocery. The camp is directly next to the ferry landing, a fortunate choice since the islands have no taxis or cars for hire. Bring your own bedding and cooking supplies; a few erected tents are available, but most are bare sites. Write ahead to reserve a space, because the idea has caught on with great popularity lately. Each campsite has its own prices.

For more information, write the **British Virgin Islands Tourist Board**, *1686 Union St. Ste 305, San Francisco, CA 94123* ☎ *(800) 835-8530.*

Anegada

Only 290 people live on Anegada, mostly in the community called The Settlement. They share this seven-mile curve of coral with some very large iguanas and about 16 flamingos that were released into the ponds in 1992. Hawksbill and green turtles nest along the northshore. The fishing here is excellent and enough vessels have crashed against the craggy coral reefs to make wreck diving a spectacular sport. Even snorkelers can find deep satisfaction exploring caverns and ledges just off the shore in the coral reefs, where they will see shoals of neon-colored fish, nurse sharks, rays, turtles, and barracudas. Lobloy Bay has a small beach bar and sun shelters. Over the years Anegadians have been the victims of several development schemes that have left them suspicious, not to mention poorer, but they remain friendly to the selected tourists who risk the small planes to arrive. Although there is no regular boat ferry, day trips to the island are available. (Note that only qualified crew are allowed to navigate the route to Anegada because of the dangerous reef system.)

Where to Stay

Fielding's Highest Rated Hotels in British Virgin Islands

★★★★★	Biras Creek Hotel	$275–$795
★★★★★	Guana Island	$445–$675
★★★★★	Little Dix Bay Hotel	$250–$650
★★★★★	Necker Island	
★★★★★	Peter Island Resort	$195–$565
★★★★	Drake's Anchorage	$223–$600
★★★	Bitter End Yacht Club	$220–$570
★★★	Long Bay Beach Hotel	$60–$270
★★★	Olde Yard Inn	$80–$195
★★★	Prospect Reef Resort	$88–$395

Fielding's Most Exclusive Hotels in British Virgin Islands

★★★★★	Guana Island	$445–$675
★★★★★	Little Dix Bay Hotel	$250–$650
★★★★	Drake's Anchorage	$223–$600
★★★★★	Peter Island Resort	$195–$565
★★	Virgin Gorda Villas	$575

Fielding's Best Value Hotels in British Virgin Islands

★★	Fort Burt Hotel	$60–$95
★★★	Olde Yard Inn	$80–$195
★★	Leverick Bay Resort	$89–$112
★★★	Treasure Isle Hotel	$80–$230
★★★	Long Bay Beach Hotel	$60–$270

Where to Stay—Tortola

Accommodations in the British Virgin Islands are the antithesis of the big-island resort; for the most part they are intimate and casual and reflect the style of the owner/management, frequently husband-and-wife teams. Although the islands are rarely overrun with tourists, even in peak season, travelers seeking maximum solitude will want to pick up a copy of *Intimate Inns and Villas*, a free pamphlet with color pictures covering a couple dozen small properties on the four main islands; it's available from the British Virgin Islands Tourist Board in New York ☎ *(800) 835-8530*.

Tortola accommodations tend to cater to moderate budgets and the yachting set and a number of the accommodations are situated in and around bustling Road Town. If you're seeking luxury, Tortola is the one BVI you'll want to steer away from, but if nightlife or a social scene is important, Tortola is as close as it comes in this chain. It also makes a convenient base from which to explore the other islands on day trips.

Hotels and Resorts

Tortola's lead property is Long Bay Beach Hotel, which also acts as the unofficial social hub of the island. It and several other hotels mix standard room accommodations with villas and condos; if the property you are considering mixes these room types, check to make sure the rate you're quoted includes maid service (which is sometimes a mandatory additional charge).

Long Bay Beach Hotel   **$60–$270**   ★ ★ ★

Long Bay, Road Town, ☎ *(800) 729-9599, (809) 495-4252. FAX (809) 495-4677. Single: $60–$250. Double: $120–$270.*

Situated on a 52-acre estate that slopes down to a powdery mile-long beach, Long Bay offers a variety of rooms with great summer rates for singles. Some units are located along a hillside (great views), others are right on the beach. All come equipped with air conditioning, ceiling fans, refrigerators, wet bars, hair dryers and phones, while the most expensive units also boast full kitchens, VCRs and huge decks. Active types are kept happy with the complimentary pitch-and-putt golf course, pool, and tennis courts. The restaurant, housed in an old sugar mill, offers fine gourmet fare and live music most nights. Villas also available, and dwellers can arrange to have a chef prepare a private dinner—nice! Credit cards accepted once on the island, but a check is required for your three-night room deposit. Amenities: tennis, houses, cottages or bungalows, balcony or patio. 83 rooms. Credit cards: A, D, MC, V.

Moorings-Mariner Inn   **$80–$230**   ★ ★

Road Town, ☎ *(800) 535-7289, (809) 494-2331. FAX (809) 494-2226. Single: $80–$155. Double: $95–$230.*

It's a yachting crowd here, dahling, but the hospitality is still warm, friendly and blessedly informal. Facing the busy marina and within walking distance of Road Town's shops and restaurants, this small hotel houses guests in lanai-style rooms with island decor and kitchenettes; there are also four suites available. Air conditioning was recently added to all rooms to supplement the sea breezes. Landlubbers are kept happy with a pool and tennis court, but may feel out of place among all the seafaring folk. A dive center, Underwater Safari, rounds out the scene. Amenities: tennis. 40 rooms. Credit cards: A, MC, V.

Prospect Reef Resort $88–$395   ★★★

Road Town, ☎ *(800) 356-8937, (809) 494-3311. FAX (809) 494-5595.*
Single: $88–$395. Double: $88–$395.

Set on lush oceanside grounds (but lacking a beach), the choices here range from standard guest rooms to studios to townhouses and villas (that sleep up to four), some with kitchenettes, some with air conditioning. Accommodations are uninspired, but there's lots going on, including six tennis courts, a pitch-and-putt golf course and a fitness center; three restaurants and three bars are on hand. Pools include one that is junior-Olympic sized and two sea enclosures for bobbing or snorkeling. A nice selection of children's activities, including an environmental program for 5- to 11-year-olds. Day sails are available at the small harbor, and an excellent dive shop is on property. Ten-minute walk to Road Town. Amenities: tennis, family plan. 130 rooms. Credit cards: A, MC, V.

Sebastian's on the Beach $75–$190   ★

Apple Bay, Road Town, ☎ *(800) 336-4870, (809) 495-4212. FAX (809) 495-4466.*
Single: $75–$180. Double: $85–$190.

Set on its own beach, this small hotel is split in two by a road; request a room on the beach side for obvious reasons, but ask that it not be one of the rear units, as they have no view. Just eight rooms have air conditioning; the rest make do with ceiling fans. The beach is fine for swimming, a good thing since there's no pool. There's a bar and restaurant, plus a fun weekly barbecue on Sunday. 26 rooms. Credit cards: A, D, MC, V.

Sugar Mill Hotel $135–$265   ★★★

Apple Bay, Road Town, ☎ *(800) 462-8834, (809) 495-4355. FAX (809) 495-4696.*
Single: $135–$250. Double: $150–$265.

The dining room is housed in a 360-year-old sugar mill and rum distillery, hence the name. All is quite nice at this lushly landscaped estate, with accommodations in simple cottages scattered about a hillside. Furnishings are basic but adequate; some have kitchens and most now have air conditioning. A two-bedroom villa is also available, complete with a full kitchen, large balcony and spacious stone terrace. There's a small pool for those who don't want to cross the street to get to the compact beach. The property is owned by an American couple who used to write about travel and food, so you know they know what they're doing. Great meals, and wonderful service to match. Just the spot for those who really want to get away from it all but don't want all the trappings of a full resort. Amenities: balcony or patio. 21 rooms. Credit cards: A, MC, V.

Treasure Isle Hotel $80–$230   ★★★

Road Town, ☎ *(800) 334-2435, (809) 494-2501. FAX (809) 494-2507.*
Single: $80–$230. Double: $95–$230.

All the air-conditioned rooms at this pretty resort overlook the harbor and marina, and include tropical art and pleasant rattan furniture. Situated on 15 acres of hillside, the grounds include a festive free-form pool and restaurant and the hotel provides complimentary transportation to one of the island's beaches daily. Management is friendly, and guests here are kept happy with lots of evening entertainment for the partying set. A full dive shop is across the street featuring a selection of water sports. 43 rooms. Credit cards: A, MC, V.

Village Cay Marina Hotel   **$77–$165**   ★ ★
Road Town, ☎ *(809) 494-2771.*
Single: $77–$138. Double: $99–$165.
This small hotel is located downtown in the Village Cay Marina Complex. Rooms are air-conditioned and have cathedral ceilings, Oriental rugs and cable TV; a laundry facility is available. There's a restaurant and bar on site, as well as a small pool and watersports. The clientele is largely composed of yachtsmen, and there's lots to do within walking distance. 19 rooms. Credit cards: A, MC, V.

Apartments and Condominiums

Yacht owners and vacationers prepared to settle in for a long stay take advantage of the many private homes rented by owners during high season. Apartments and condos also offer the opportunity for independent living, especially if you want to do your own cooking (bring staples from home since prices on Tortola run high). There are many brokers on the island; check with the **BVI Tourist Board** ☎ *(800) 835-8530* for an up-to-date list. Rates for a simple condo start as low as $500 per week and sometimes accommodate six or eight guests comfortably; winter rates start closer to $850 per week and soar heavenward from there. Luxury rentals are offered by **McLaughlin Anderson Villas** at ☎ *(800) 537-6246* or *(809) 776-0635.* For provisioning your villa with the best, head straight to Fort Wines Gourmet, where pates, Parisian chocolates, fine coffee and tea and, of course, wines from the U.S. and Europe are stocked; it's on Main Street in Road Town ☎ *(809) 494-3036.*

Fort Recovery Estates   **$125–$295**   ★ ★
Freshwater Pond, ☎ *(800) 367-8455, (809) 495-4354. FAX (809) 495-4036.*
Single: $125–$295. Double: $125–$295.
The stone tower is all that remains of this 17th-century Dutch fort, today a small enclave of attractive villas with TVs, full kitchens and air-conditioned bedrooms. Larger parties can rent a three- or four-bedroom, three-bathroom house ($378–$629 per night). Continental breakfast is included in the rates, and the small beach makes for good swimming and snorkeling, or unwind with a yoga class or massage. Daily maid service keeps things looking fresh. The grounds are nice and bright, with lots of colorful flowers scattered about. Amenities: balcony or patio. 17 rooms. Credit cards: A, MC, V.

Frenchman's Cay Resort   **$115–$210**   ★ ★
West End, West End, ☎ *(800) 235-4077, (809) 495-4844. FAX (809) 495-4056.*
Single: $115–$190. Double: $120–$210.
Set on Frenchman's Cay and connected via bridge to Tortola, this small luxury enclave of villas has nice views of the channel and neighboring islands. One- and

two-bedroom villas include a full kitchen, ceiling fans (no air conditioning), and island art. The small beach is good for snorkeling, but rocks make wading difficult. There's also a small pool, hammocks meant for snoozing, a tennis court and an open-air restaurant. A nice, quiet spot. 9 rooms. Credit cards: A, D, MC, V.

Nanny Cay Resort   **$60–$225**   ★ ★

Nanny Cay, Road Town, ☎ (800) 742-4276, (809) 494-2512. FAX (809) 494-0555.
Single: $60–$175. Double: $100–$225.

Set on a private 25-acre inlet on Sir Francis Drake Channel, Nanny Cay houses guests in studio apartments with kitchenettes, West Indian decor, ceiling fan and air conditioning. Lots of yachtsmen come here, lured by the 180-slip marina. Extras include two restaurants and bars, a pool and tennis. Service can be uneven. Amenities: tennis. 42 rooms. Credit cards: A, MC, V.

Rockview Holiday Homes   **$120–$850**

Throughout the West End, Road Town, ☎ (800) 621-1270, (809) 494-2550. FAX (809) 494-5866.
Double: $120–$850.

The villas managed by this agency are situated between Apple Bay and Smuggler's Bay, on the west end of Tortola. Accommodations range from one- to five-bedroom villas situated on a hillside amid lush tropical gardens or overlooking the beach, all with full kitchens. Some even have their own pool. Maid service is available, and you can hire a chef if you're not up for cooking. 30 units. Credit cards: A, D, MC, V.

Inns

Fort Burt Hotel   **$60–$95**   ★ ★

Road Town, ☎ (809) 494-2587. FAX (809) 494-2002.
Single: $60–$85. Double: $80–$95.

Set on a hillside and incorporating a 300-year-old Dutch-English fort, this small inn's guest rooms are dark, sparse and greatly in need of renovation. Still, the atmosphere is fun and friendly, with interesting tales of its long past. Great views of the harbor. The site includes a restaurant and small pool. 8 rooms. Credit cards: A, D, MC, V.

Low Cost Lodging

Budget accommodations are now available on Tortola, usually in a decent location that won't require you to rent a car. **Sea View**, a popular local restaurant, added rooms (with a view) to its property ☎ *(809) 494-2483*, while the **Cane Garden Bay Hotel** is a good place to meet local yacht owners ☎ *(809) 495-4639*. Fort Burt Hotel is located on the outskirts of **Road Town** ☎ *(809) 494-2587*. All three of these properties have rooms for under $100 a night during the winter season, but don't forget about apartments and condos—these offer savings by accommodating larger groups of people or through cooking you own meals. Camping is available at Brewer's Bay.

Where to Stay—Virgin Gorda

Notwithstanding a brief gold rush in the 17th century, this idyllic island lay undiscovered until Laurence Rockefeller cruised by in the 1950s and decided to build his Little Dix Bay Hotel. The island whose shape reminded Christopher Columbus of a "fat virgin"—hence the name—can be roughly divided into three sections. The central, heftiest land mass is lorded over by Virgin Gorda Peak, which is surrounded by a National Park and a few short trails. The flatter southwest wing of the island is the most populated and developed, and the location of the Little Dix Bay Hotel and several smaller inns. Boats and ferries from Tortola regularly dock here at Spanish Town (aka The Valley), while flights from Tortola and St. Thomas land at a small airstrip just beyond. A road connects Spanish Town to Virgin Gorda's second town, Gun Creek. Below it is a great sailing anchorage, North Sound, and beyond, the northeast wing where two fine resorts accessible only by boat are located amid the dollops of scalloped land leading to the Atlantic Ocean. A tiny island facing the Bitter End Yacht Club, Saba Rock, is home to a lively bar accessed by dinghy or brief swim. Beyond a number of fine pieces of sand, the biggest attraction on the island is The Baths, but don't miss Gorda Peak National Park (see "Beaches" and "What to See" above).

Hotels and Resorts

Little Dix Bay, built by Rockefeller and a sister property to Caneel Bay on St. John, remains the island's premiere lodging facility, though a renovation and new management at Biras Creek makes this smaller property on the other end of the island a very close second. For sailors and wannabes, the popular Bitter End Yacht Club is a one-of-a-kind resort for those who want to charter a boat but don't want to do the dishes.

Biras Creek Hotel $275–$795 ★★★★★

North Sound, ☎ (800) 223-1108, (809) 494-3555. FAX (809) 494-3557.
Single: $275–$720. Double: $350–$795.
Following a change of ownership and multi-million-dollar renovation in late 1995, Biras Creek is better than ever. Located on a 150-acre estate and accessible only by boat, all of the accommodations at this first-class tropical retreat are in suites with colorful decor and, best of all, open-walled private showers; there's also a two-bedroom villa for rent. The rooms now feature expanded terraces, air conditioning and phones, with tasteful new furnishings and fabrics. The beach is rather grassy, so most guests opt for sunning at the pool, which was retiled with Italian marble in 1995. Surrounded by water on three sides (the best swimming is at Deep Bay, a five-minute walk), Biras Creek is a true escape, and guests are appropriately pampered. The rates include all meals and most watersports (water skiing and diving costs extra). The restaurant is highly regarded, and the beach barbeques are themselves worth the trip. One of the Caribbean's great small resorts. Amenities: tennis. 33 rooms. Credit cards: A, MC, V.

Bitter End Yacht Club $220–$570 ★★★

North Sound, ☎ (800) 872-2392, (809) 494-2746. FAX (809) 494-4756.
Single: $220–$470. Double: $320–$570.
This lively all-inclusive yacht club and cottage colony houses guests in hillside or beachfront villas with tropical decor and wraparound porches draped with ham-

mocks. Visitors can also opt to stay in three Freedom-30 sailboats. The resort is accessible only by boat (transfer price included in week-long stays), so room keys are unnecessary. There's lots going on at all times; landlubbers seeking an island hideaway may be happier elsewhere. All kinds of watersports are for the taking, and the Nick Trotter Sailing School is highly touted as among the Caribbean's best (Course 101 is included in the daily rates). Water babies will be in heaven, though the food takes a drubbing from some guests. 94 rooms. Credit cards: A, MC, V.

Fischer's Cove Beach $90–$285 ★★

Spanish Town, The Valley, ☎ *(800) 621-1270, (809) 495-5252. FAX (809) 495-5820. Single: $90–$285. Double: $100–$285.*
This cottage enclave overlooks St. Thomas Bay, in Spanish Town. Accommodations are in eight stone cottages with one or two bedrooms and a kitchenette, or in a 12-room hotel building. The property includes two bars and a restaurant, but little else in the way of diversions. Great local food. 20 rooms. Credit cards: A, DC, D, MC, V.

Little Dix Bay Hotel $250–$650 ★★★★★

Little Dix Bay, ☎ *(800) 928-3000, (809) 495-5555. FAX (809) 495-5661. Single: $250–$650. Double: $250–$650.*
Built in 1964 by Laurence Rockefeller as a companion to St. John's Caneel Bay, Little Dix is one of the standard-bearers in Caribbean luxury resorts—a gem that curls around a half-mile of sparkling sand. The resort is now run (along with Caneel Bay) by Rosewood Hotels, which has worked to build a new following for this classic while maintaining its exclusive cache among the Ivy League set that made it famous. Set on a private bay in a 500-acre estate, Little Dix has formal gardens, seven tennis courts, and a fleet of boats to whisk you to the beach of your choice. The several styles of accommodations include wood-frame cottages on stilts, hexagonal hillside bungalows, or fieldstone-walled beach bungalows with peaked roofs sporting exposed beams; there are also four relatively new suites priced $450–$1100 per night. A late 1993 makeover added color and panache—the bamboo and wood decor embraces a southeast Asian aura; about half the units now have air conditioning. Telephones were also added (anathema to some long-timers) and refrigerators are now positioned in each room, but Rosewood wisely kept the TVs out. The resort's food is greatly improved under the eye of Executive Chef Benoit Pepin and nightly live entertainment is featured. There's no pool, but ample watersports are available. Little Dix still draws Old Money in the winter, while the summer season blossoms with honeymooners. Some consider the spot a tad pretentious, while the rest of those who can afford it are happy to sign up for the full-court treatment. Amenities: secluded garden atmosphere, tennis. 98 rooms. Credit cards: A, DC, MC, V.

Apartments and Condominiums

Self-catering cottages and villas are available; try Virgin Gorda Villa Rentals for houses with one to five bedrooms ☎ *(800) 848-7081* or *(809) 495-7421*, or Kakana Property Management for villas accommodating six persons ☎ *(809) 495-5201*. Otherwise, Guavaberry Spring Bay claims one of the island's best locations, a brief stroll from The Baths.

Guavaberry Spring Bay $90–$200 ★★

Spring Bay, The Valley, ☎ *(809) 495-5227. FAX (809) 495-5283.*

Single: $90–$142. Double: $140–$200.

A unique group of hexagonal or round cottages, perched on stilts less than a 10-minute walk from The Baths. The one or two bedroom units are simply furnished and feature a sitting room, modern bath and full kitchen—a commissary is on site. Great views of Sir Francis Drake's Passage and neighboring islands. The location a mile from The Valley (and any restaurants) means you'll want a car for mobility. This nice spot is enhanced by the friendly service. 18 rooms.

Leverick Bay Resort $89–$112   ★★

North Sound, ☎ (800) 848-7081, (809) 495-7421. FAX (809) 495-7367.
Single: $89–$112. Double: $89–$112.
A hillside villa complex with 16 standard guest rooms, with air conditioning, cable TV and balconies with ocean views; rates listed include daily maid service. The resort also features four two-bedroom condos ($1175–$1800 per week), and one- to five-bedroom villas with kitchens ($650–$6000 per week). There's an outdoor pool and 44-slip marina, as well as tennis, a dive shop, beauty salon and restaurant. The resort gets crowded with day-trippers when cruise ships are in port. 50 rooms.
Credit cards: A, MC, V.

Mango Bay Resort $85–$752   ★★

Mahoe Bay, The Valley, ☎ (800) 621-1270, (809) 495-5672. FAX (809) 495-4674.
Double: $85–$752.
Studios and villas from one to four bedrooms are provided at this small property overlooking the Sir Francis Drake Channel and one of Virgin Gorda's nicest slips of sand—Mahoe Bay. Units are clean and bright with tiled floors and pleasant porches, all with 50 yards of the water. A restaurant is on the property, or you can arrange for a cook (units have a full kitchen); nannies also available. No pool, but fine snorkeling offshore. Amenities: tennis, balcony or patio. 10 units. Credit cards: A, D, MC, V.

Virgin Gorda Villas $105–$575

P.O. Box 63, Virgin Gorda, ☎ (800) 621-1270, (809) 494-7421. FAX (847) 699-7583.
Double: $105–$575.
Virgin Gorda's largest villa rental agency features 60 individual properties ranging from one to five-bedrooms, with a number of beach- and hillside units in the area around The Baths, as well as North Sound and Mahoe Bay. Some of the villas have a pool or Jacuzzi, all provide maid service. 60 units. Credit cards: A, D, MC, V.

Inns

There's only one inn on the island, managed by the owner. The style is casual and comfortable, and you'll have close contact with other guests.

Olde Yard Inn $80–$195   ★★★

Spanish Town, The Valley, ☎ (800) 633-7411, (809) 495-5544. FAX (809) 495-5986.
Single: $80–$145. Double: $100–$195.
Situated in a garden setting overlooking Handsome Bay, this charming inn puts guests up in a two-story building (great views from the upper floors) with simple island furniture, tile floors and roomy baths. Four rooms are air-conditioned and a suite is also available (at a higher rate). Though the nearest beach is a half-mile, a reading and film library keeps visitors contented, and the staff happily accommo-

dates those with special interests, arranging day sails and the like. Recent additions include a pool, Jacuzzi, poolside bar and exercise room. The restaurant draws raves. Amenities: exercise room, Jacuzzi, balcony or patio. 13 rooms. Credit cards: A, MC, V.

Low Cost Lodging

Best bargains will be found outside the winter season. Try Bayview Vacation Apartments near The Valley ☎ *(809) 495-5329*, or also in The Valley is The Wheelhouse which has 12 rooms in a recently renovated property ☎ *(809) 495-5230*.

Where to Stay—Jost Van Dyke

Named after a Dutch pirate, three-square-mile Jost Van Dyke (pronounced "yost") still pursues a Robinson Crusoe atmosphere, though electricity finally came to the island in 1991 (it hasn't yet reached White Bay, where dinner is still served by candlelight). Most of Jost Van Dyke's 150 residents live in Great Harbour, a picturesque collection of wooden houses along a sandy beach, lined with palm trees and funky bars—the island is very popular among the yachting set and with tent-pitching landlubbers. Rastas happily trade in ganja and mushrooms at the island's numerous bars. White Bay, the island's nicest beach, previously could be reached only by boat, but a road was completed in March 1996; be sure to stop by the Soggy Dollar Bar, where the Painkiller was invented (the bar was named after the condition of payment after a swim in from a boat). A mile offshore is uninhabited Sandy Cay, with another spellbinding beach, and a path through the outcrop's interior.

Transportation to Jost Van Dyke is by water (there is no airstrip); a ferry serves the island from St. Thomas and St. John, or you can take a water taxi from Tortola. There is a sandy road around the island, and a couple of cars, but most people get around on foot or by boat. Eight island villas are rented by Sandy Ground Estates with rates starting at about $800 per week in the summer season ☎ *(809) 495-9466*. Budget accommodations are provided by **Abe's By the Sea in Little Harbour** ☎ *(809) 495-9329*, or **Rudy's Mariner Inn in Great Harbour** ☎ *(809) 495-9282*. Campsites are available on the island at two locations: the **White Bay Campground** is on a lovely beach with showers ☎ *(809) 495-9312*. **Tula's Campground** features a small snack bar and grocery store and is right next to the ferry landing; bare and tent sites are available ☎ *(809) 495-9566*. Call ahead to reserve a space for either of these campgrounds, particularly in the busy winter season.

Hotels and Resorts

Sandcastle   **$75–$195**   ★★

White Bay, ☎ *(809) 775-5262, (809) 690-1611. FAX (809) 775-5262.*
Single: $75–$160. Double: $95–$195.
This tiny resort consists of four octagonal cottages set among tropical gardens next to an idyllic beach. This place is not for everyone—there's no electricity and just limited hot water—but those who don't mind roughing it love the peace and seren-

ity. Dinner by candlelight is a romantic affair. A two-meal-a-day plan is available for $40 per person. You can arrive in your own boat, or the hotel will arrange for your pickup in Tortola in their private launch Amenities: secluded garden atmosphere. 4 rooms. Credit cards: MC, V.

Apartments and Condominiums

Sandy Ground Estates   ★★

Near Little Harbour, Great Harbour, ☎ *(809) 494-3391. FAX (809) 495-9379. Rack rate Per Week: $980–$1400.*

This isolated tropical retreat consists of eight houses amid 17 acres of private estate property above a beach from where you can dinghy over to small offshore islands. Each unit is different and individually designed with simple, casual furnishings and full kitchens. Arrange to have your refrigerator stocked prior to arrival. Rates are $980 to $1400 for a week; the larger houses sleep up at eight (at an additional charge). 8 rooms. Credit cards: MC, V.

Where to Stay—Anegada

With a population barely topping three digits, a flat and scrubby rather than mountainous interior, and positioned 15 miles from the nearest other BVI, Anegada proudly goes its own way in the archipelago. Most of the 170 residents live in The Settlement, a tranquil community positioned near the south shore of this 12-mile-long outpost—they share this curve of coral with some fierce-looking, endangered iguanas that grow up to five feet in length (they're rarely seen). A small colony of flamingos was donated by Bermuda in 1992 in hope of reintroducing the species to the BVIs—the species has not nested here since the 1950s, but in 1995 began hatching the first of the next generation.

The best beach is Loblolly Bay, where a small beach bar and sun shelters are found. The fishing here is excellent, and enough vessels have sunk on the craggy coral reefs to create some fine wreck dives; unfortunately, they're currently off limits since anchoring on Anegada's reefs is prohibited. Snorkelers can find deep satisfaction exploring caverns and ledges just off the shore in the coral reefs, where they may see shoals of neon-colored fish, rays, turtles and barracudas. Otherwise, on an island where a few dozen tourists is a crowd, activities are decidedly low-key in nature. Over the years, Anegadians have been the victim of several development schemes that have left them suspicious, not to mention poorer, but they remain friendly to the few travelers who make the trip. If you rent a jeep on the island (there are a couple), it's likely there won't be any rental agreement to sign. Although there is no regular boat ferry, day trips to the island are possible via Anegada's small airstrip.

The 16-room Anegada Reef Hotel, located five miles west of The Settlement and the airport, is the island's main tourist facility. However, Neptune's Treasure Guest House ☎ *(809) 495-9439* has some budget rooms, a couple of smaller guest houses can be found in town, and the Anegada Beach Campground provides rustic facilities ☎ *(809) 495-9466.*

Hotels and Resorts

Anegada Reef Hotel   **$130–$230**   ★★

Setting Point, Setting Point, ☎ (809) 495-8002. FAX (809) 495-9362.
Single: $130–$180. Double: $180–$230.

Located in a remote setting on unspoiled Anegada, this small hotel appeals to those who truly want to get away from it all. The air-conditioned, recently upgraded bungalow-style accommodations are simple, but tastefully decorated and comfortable, and the couple that runs the place goes out of their way to please. The hotel owns its own fishing boat for deep-sea or bonefishing excursions, but most guests stick to the bicycles, kayaks, snorkeling and hammocks. Lots of people come again and again, lured by the laid-back tranquility of this spot. Three meals a day are included with room rate. 16 rooms. Credit cards: MC, V.

Where to Eat

Fielding's Highest Rated Restaurants in British Virgin Islands

★★★★	Biras Creek	$40–$40
★★★★	Brandywine Bay	$20–$28
★★★★	Capriccio di Mare	$8–$15
★★★★	Skyworld	$23–$40
★★★★	Tradewinds Restaurant	$18–$36
★★★★	Upstairs, The	$16–$27
★★★	Mrs. Scatliffe's	$20–$27
★★★	Olde Yarde Inn	$18–$30
★★★	Pusser's Leverick Bay	$13–$24
★★★	Sugar Mill	$17–$26

Fielding's Most Exclusive Restaurants in British Virgin Islands

★★★★	Biras Creek	$40–$40
★★★★	Skyworld	$23–$40
★★★★	Tradewinds Restaurant	$18–$36
★★★	Apple, The	$15–$35
★★★	Olde Yarde Inn	$18–$30

Fielding's Best Value Restaurants in British Virgin Islands

★★★	Pirate's Pub & Grill	$5–$7
★★★★	Capriccio di Mare	$8–$15
★★★	Virgin Queen	$8–$16
★★★	Crab Hole, The	$10–$15
★★★★	Upstairs, The	$16–$27

BRITISH VIRGIN ISLANDS

Where to Eat—Tortola

With at least 65 restaurants currently in business—about one for every 200 residents—Tortola boasts one of the most Caribbean's most extensive food scenes. Credit the yachties, who obviously prefer jumping into the dinghy for the evening meal over assembling it at sea. From the inexpensive pepper- and chutney-laden rotis of Roti Palace in Road Town, to the romantic splurge proffered at the Florentine Brandywine's, there is a wide variety to choose from, with West Indian cuisine the front-and-center specialty. There's even a mini-chain, Pusser's, a popular trio of pub-style restaurants spread between the British Virgin's largest settlements. However, most BVI dining prices are extravagant and even the informal settings sometimes give New York tabs a run for their money. One place where the setting and view lives up to the bill is Skyworld, where a 360-degree view atop Ridge Road is sublime at sunset. A majority of restaurants are located in and around Road Town; this is also where the island's few bargains are found.

West Indian food is found throughout the British Virgins, but home-cooked meals have become increasingly popular on Tortola, led by the justifiably famous Mrs. Scatliffe, who serves guests out of her tin-roofed home at Carrot Bay—and may serenade you with gospel music for dessert (though we wonder about that rumor that Mr. Scatliffe is buried in the front yard). Other restaurants serving home-style native selections are The Apple, Oliver's and the North Shore Shell Museum. Reservations at these and other small eateries are essential, particularly during the busy winter season. The local drink is the Painkiller, made with Pusser's Rum (a BVI product), orange and pineapple juice and a splash of coconut creme. It's tasty, but more than one visitor has found the drink's name a double-edged sword.

Speaking of drinking, Bomba's Shack at Cappoons Bay near West End is a rum-soaked institution visited regularly by the region's best reggae bands. The monthly full moon parties at the plywood-and-nails beach hut draw callers from neighboring islands for raucous revelry 'til dawn.

Bing's Drop Inn Bar $$ ★★

Fat Hog's Bay, East End, ☎ (809) 495-2627.
Indian cuisine. Specialties: Conch fritters, fish stew.
Dinner: 7 p.m.–midnight, entrées $10–$20. Closed: Mon.
Do drop in to Bing's—and you'll probably make a local friend or two. Tasty home-style conch fritters and fish stew are specialties and more elaborate lobster, chicken and steak dishes are served as well. Come to dance and kibitz here after a meal elsewhere; it's a very unpressurized environment that stays open for snacks and drinks until midnight. Features: late dining. Reservations recommended. Credit cards: A, MC, V.

Brandywine Bay $$$ ★★★★

Blackburn Highway, Brandywine Bay, Road Town, ☎ (809) 495-2301.

Italian cuisine. Specialties: Homemade mozzarella, beef and lobster carpaccio, tiramisu.
Dinner: 6:30–9 p.m., entrées $20–$28. Closed: Sun.

For a special occasion, drive out a little east of Road Town to this hillside spot owned by Cele and David Pugliese for Florentine food that's widely praised. Whether it's local fish simply grilled with home-grown fresh herbs or an elaborately sauced roast duckling, everything is superb—the menu changes daily based on fresh ingredients. Dining is on the terrace outside the once-private home that overlooks the Sir Francis Drake Channel. Hostess Cele will personally describe each entrée on the menu while David prepares and arranges everything picture-perfectly (he's a former fashion photographer). Closed August-October. Reservations recommended. Credit cards: A, MC, V.

Capriccio di Mare   **$$**   ★★★★
Waterfront Drive, Road Town, Road Town, ☎ *(809) 494-5369.*
Italian cuisine. Specialties: Pastries, pasta and pizza, frozen granite.
Lunch: 8 a.m.–4 p.m., entrées $8–$15.
Dinner: 4–9 p.m., entrées $8–$15. Closed: Sun.

A welcome taste treat for seafood-dominated Tortola. A little sister operation to the popular Brandywine Bay, a bastion of cucina fiorentina, Capriccio di Mare is an informal Italian cafe—a place to sit and sip espresso or cappuccino and nibble pastries or sandwiches on foccacia bread. Pizzas with a choice of vegetable or meat toppings are also available, as well as pastas. Fresh pastries and cappuccino are delightful for breakfast at this sidewalk cafe. Credit cards: A, D, MC, V.

Fish Trap, The   **$$$**   ★★★
Columbus Centre; Road Town, Road Town, ☎ *(809) 494-3626.*
Seafood cuisine. Specialties: Prawns provencale, prime rib, teriyaki chicken.
Lunch: 11:30 a.m.– 3 p.m., entrées $8–$14.
Dinner: 6:30–11 p.m., entrées $14–$25. Closed: Sun.

An informal, open-air terrace restaurant in Wickham's Cay that always has some good-value meals happening, the Fishtrap features barbecues on Saturdays and Sundays, prime rib on Sundays and local fish, shellfish, teriyaki chicken and other hearty, honest food the rest of the week. Reservations required. Credit cards: A, MC, V.

Pusser's Pub and The Outpost   **$$$**   ★★
Waterfront Drive; Road Town, Road Town, ☎ *(809) 494-4199.*
International cuisine. Specialties: Beef Wellington, lobster club sandwich, mud pie.
Lunch: 11 a.m.–3 p.m., entrées $7–$9.
Dinner: 5–10 p.m., entrées $15–$25.

Enjoy varied international cuisine with the yachting set in this second link in the Pusser's (local rum) chain of eateries. The two-story establishment has a downstairs pub where the namesake libation can be quaffed, accompanied by sandwiches and snacks amid a boisterous atmosphere. Escape upstairs later to The Outpost for Beef Wellington prepared with choice cuts of beef tenderloin, mushroom duxelle and homemade pastry, served with Bearnaise sauce; a few Mexican selections and pitchers of sangria fill out the menu. Later, if you have room, down Pusser's famous mud pie, dessert-style or in a rum-Irish cream concoction. Reservations recommended. Credit cards: A, MC, V.

Skyworld $$$ ★★★★

Ridge Road; Leonards, Road Town, ☎ *(809) 494-3567.*
International cuisine.
Lunch: 10 a.m.–5:30 p.m., entrées $7–$13.
Dinner: 6:30–10 p.m., entrées $23–$40.

A perfect remembrance of a Tortola visit is dining or having a drink before sunset and watching a technicolor movie in the sky at this dining room perched some 1000 feet above sea level. You can partake from chef George Petcoff's *Gourmet*-praised international menu of veal with capers, beautifully grilled local fish, passion fruit sorbets or less elaborate conch fritters or french fries and onion rings. At lunch enjoy the view from a different perspective with a sandwich on home-baked bread while casting an eagle eye on neighboring islands in the distance. Closed in September. Reservations recommended. Credit cards: A, MC, V.

Spaghetti Junction $$$ ★★

Waterfront Drive; Road Town, Road Town, ☎ *(809) 494-4880.*
Italian cuisine. Specialties: Chilled roasted eggplant and plum tomatoes, veal scaloppine.
Dinner: 6–10 p.m., entrées $10–$21. Closed: Sun.

Boasting a chef who's cooked for not one but two American presidents, Spaghetti Junction is the Road Town spot for Italian, located upstairs in a small blue building. Favorites include fruiti di mari, penne arrabbiata, veal and chicken (Picatta or Marsala style), and eggplant Parmigiana and three other vegetarian dishes. The Caesar salad, served with sun-dried tomatoes, isn't bad, either. Formerly a bar that overlooked the water, it is now separated from the ocean by new roads and office buildings—all in the name of progress. Yachties and others like it for its infectious grooves. Daily chalkboard specials and desserts. Reservations recommended. Credit cards: not accepted. Credit cards: A, MC, V.

Upstairs, The $$$ ★★★★

One mile south of Road Town, Road Town, ☎ *(809) 494-2228. Associated hotel: Prospect Reef Hotel.*
International cuisine. Specialties: Filet mignon, roast duck.
Lunch: Noon–2 p.m., entrées $10–$16.
Dinner: 6–9 p.m., entrées $16–$27.

An intimate dining room with lovely views of the harbor, The Upstairs has received kudos from the likes of *Gourmet* magazine. The star of the Prospect Reef Resort, which is built on a coral reef, the restaurant offers simple but exceptionally well-prepared (and pricey) meals such as local lobster served grilled as an entrée or gratine as an appetizer. Service is attentive and gracious. Ask for a window table for stargazing. Reservations required. Credit cards: A, MC, V.

Virgin Queen $$ ★★★

Fleming Street; Road Town, Road Town, ☎ *(809) 494-2310.*
English cuisine. Specialties: Queen's pizza, shepherd's pie, bangers and mash.
Lunch: Noon–2 p.m., entrées $7–$12.
Dinner: 6–10 p.m., entrées $8–$16. Closed: Sun.

The Queen's pizza has been nominated for best in the islands, but it's also great finger food for sailors and other active types who like to quaff a few, throw darts at a board and shoot the breeze. There's a TV for background noise to go with the other fare offered—mostly English pub and West Indian food such as bangers and mash, saltfish and shepherd's pie.

Apple, The $$$ ★★★

Zion Hill Road; Little Apple Bay, West End, ☎ (809) 495-4437.
Indian cuisine. Specialties: Whelks in garlic butter, fish apple style, conch West Indian.
Dinner: 6:30–9:30 p.m., entrées $15–$35. Closed: Mon.

An enterprising and talented Tortolian, Liston Molyneux, has opened a restaurant in his home in Little Apple Bay, on Zion Hill, preparing local dishes such as uncommonly served *whelks* (a type of snail), and the more familiar conch. Lunches are varied and include curried chicken rotis (West Indian burritos), or crêpes. An interesting Sunday barbecue of West Indian treats is also offered from 7–9 p.m. Coconut chips and conch fritters are served at happy hour from 5 to 7 p.m. daily. Closed in September. Reservations recommended. Credit cards: A, MC, V.

Mrs. Scatliffe's $$$ ★★★

Carrot Bay, West End, ☎ (809) 495-4556.
Indian cuisine. Specialties: Pot roast, chicken or pork, spicy papaya soup.
Dinner: 7–9 p.m., entrées $20–$27.

Una Scatliffe, the former chef of the well-regarded Sugar Mill, a native Tortolian, operates this West-Indian restaurant on the deck of her home. It's a yellow-and-white, tin-roofed building across from the primary school in Carrot Bay. Diners come for the set meal of four courses, which are prepared with fruits and vegetables from her own garden. Popular starters are fresh fruit daiquiris, followed by soup, home-baked bread, chicken in a coconut shell or curried goat, and more of that fresh fruit in her imaginative ice cream desserts. Entertainment follows, usually a family sing-out with a live fungi band. Reservations essential. In light of all the acclaim, Scatliffe's daughter, Mona Donovan, has opened her own eatery and museum down the road, the North Shore Shell Museum.

Pusser's Landing $$$ ★★

Sopers Hole, Frenchmans Cay, West End, ☎ (809) 495-4554.
International cuisine. Specialties: Beef Wellington, guava chicken, nightly dessert specials.
Lunch: 11:30 a.m.–2:30 p.m., entrées $5–$9.
Dinner: 6:30–9:30 p.m., entrées $13–$25.

Diners can look out to the lights of St. Thomas from this waterfront restaurant in Tortola's West End, a fancier link in the Pusser's chain, serving black-bean soup, West Indian ribs, roasted half-chicken in guava sauce and the signature Pusser's dishes, Beef Wellington with Bearnaise sauce and mud pie for dessert. Special events include dancing under the stars to a live band on Saturdays and all-you-can-eat shrimp dinners on Tuesday nights for $17.95. The potent Pusser's Painkiller may cure what ails you, but don't quaff too many or you'll be back in pain in the morning. Credit cards: A, D, MC, V.

Sugar Mill $$$ ★★★

Apple Bay, West End, ☎ (809) 495-4355. Associated hotel: Sugar Mill Estate.
International cuisine.
Lunch: Noon–2 p.m., entrées $6–$12.
Dinner: 7–8:30 p.m., entrées $17–$26.

Bon Appetit columnists Jefferson and Jinx Morgan spent a lot of years cooking and writing about food and wine before they decided to buy a 300-year-old sugar mill in Apple Bay, converting it to a world-class inn and restaurant, decorated in Haitian paintings. The Morgans have wisely kept their menu small, allowing them to concentrate on the details of each dish, which might include a cold fruit soup and fresh fish in banana leaves with herbs from the Mill's own garden. A popular entrée is Cajun oysters with shrimp etouffee. Leave room for a scrumptious banana bread pudding with rum sauce when it's available. Reservations recommended. Credit cards: A, MC, V.

Where to Eat—Virgin Gorda

For such a tiny island, the cuisine on Virgin Gorda can run to the superb, especially at Little Dix Bay, where the hotel's distinctive Pavilion Restaurant offers stupendous views from the dining terrace for candlelight dinners of West Indian dishes presented with French flair, or afternoon teas complete with scones and clotted cream. At Biras Creek, the hotel dining is romantic, perched high on the hilltop, and the wine list is considered among the region's best. Pusser's Leverick Bay branch is the spot for Sunday brunch, served in a delightful pub at North Sound. If you're visiting the Baths, stop by Mad Dog, a bar set amongst the rocks that provides sandwiches until around sunset.

Bath and Turtle Pub, The $$$ ★★★

The Yacht Harbour, North Sound, ☎ *(809) 495-5239.*
African cuisine. Specialties: Fried shrimp in coconut batter, specialty pizzas.
Lunch: 11:30 a.m.–5 p.m., entrées $7–$15.
Dinner: 6:30–9:30 p.m., entrées $11–$30.
A convivial bar-tavern, The Bath and Turtle has two happy hours a day, one mid-morning, and another one before sundown. Drinks are usually fruity and tropical, accompanied by good pizzas (Mexican crabmeat, veggie and special of the day), a West Indian chicken sandwich with spicy local seasonings, filet mignon, lobster and burgers. The location is fine too, next to a shopping center and the local lending library. The Pub is open for breakfast from 8 a.m. and usually stays open until 9 p.m. Sunday brunch 8:30 a.m.–3 p.m. Reservations recommended. Credit cards: A, MC, V.

Biras Creek $$$ ★★★★

Biras Creek, North Sound, ☎ *(809) 494-3555. Associated hotel: Biras Creek Estate.*
International cuisine. Specialties: Half lobster any style, stilton with port.
Dinner: 7:30–9 p.m., prix fixe $40.
Dine in a stone "castle keep" with all-encompassing views of the Caribbean and Atlantic from the airy and luxurious main dining room of the tony Biras Creek Resort. The five-course, prix-fixe dinner menu changes each evening, but fresh half-lobster served grilled or poached with lemon or garlic butter is always available if requested by 4 p.m., for an extra $5. The well-chosen menus combine local specialties such as conch with spicy mango chutney or pumpkin soup with rum. For a

"veddy" English touch, stilton and port arrive shortly after dessert. Jacket requested. Reservations required. Credit cards: A, MC, V.

Pusser's Leverick Bay $$$ ★★★

Leverick Bay; North Sound, North Sound, ☎ *(809) 495-7369.*
American cuisine. Specialties: Filet of beef Wellington, mud pie.
Lunch: 11:30 a.m.–6 p.m., entrées $6–$10.
Dinner: 6–10 p.m., entrées $13–$24.

The Virgin Gorda branch of the popular Pusser's chain is located in a boisterously colored Victorian house, where familiar and tasty stateside favorites such as nachos with guacamole and jalapeno pepper and cheddar fries are served with drinks. The chain's filet of beef Wellington is a specialty, served with fresh mushrooms and encased in pastry. There's also lobster, and pasta with vegetables, and Friday brings all-you-can-eat Cajun shrimp. Desserts are huge and sweet, like mud pie with mocha ice cream and cookie crust, or the Mud Head, a chocolate and Pusser's rum concoction with gooey cream on top. Credit cards: A, MC, V.

Pirate's Pub & Grill $ ★★★

Saba Rock, Saba Rock, ☎ *(809) 495-9537.*
American cuisine. Specialties: Barbecue, sandwiches, dessert drinks.
Lunch: 10 a.m.–4 p.m., entrées $5–$7.
Dinner: 4–10 p.m., entrées $5–$7.

Located on Saba Rock, a minuscule outcrop within shouting distance of the Bitter End Yacht Club, Pirate's is one of the world's few bars most easily accessed by dinghy. It can get wild and woolly here some nights when the booze flows, but this informal pub is (relatively) kind to the pocketbook, serving a small menu of hefty sandwiches, ribs and chicken with all the trimmings for under $10, although a side order of potato salad at $2.50 is a tad much. Patrons are expected to drink their desserts here, downing such delights as raspberry pound cake and strawberry short cake blended at the bar. Entertainment is in the form of darts, or impromptu jam sessions with whomever washes up on the beach. Credit cards: A, MC, V.

Chez Michelle $$$ ★★★

The Valley, The Valley, ☎ *(809) 495-5510.*
International cuisine. Specialties: Lobster remy, pastas.
Dinner: 6:30–9:30 p.m., entrées $16–$28.

An intimate Gallic spot amidst the surf and turf, Chez Michelle provides cozy, candlelit surroundings in a West Indian house near the Yacht Harbour. The specialty is local lobster, flambeed in cognac and served with a delicately rich mushroom sauce. Fresh pastas made in-house are justifiably popular, as is the rack of lamb and roasted pork tenderloin. The Caesar salad with garlic walnuts is tasty. Reservations recommended. Credit cards: MC, V.

Crab Hole, The $$ ★★★

South Valley, The Valley, ☎ *(809) 495-5307.*
Latin American cuisine. Specialties: Calalloo soup, stewed goat, rotis.
Lunch: 11:30 a.m.– 6:30 p.m., entrées $6–$10.
Dinner: 6:30 p.m.–9:30 p.m., entrées $10–$15.

One of a growing handful of West Indian restaurants in Virgin Gorda, The Crab Hole draws locals who come to chow down on home-cooking, island style, be it callaloo (local spinach) soup, fish, spicy chicken curried rotis or plantains and rice and peas. There's lively entertainment as well on Friday and Saturday nights. Lobster (ordered in advance) is $25. Reservations recommended.

Olde Yarde Inn   **$$$**   ★ ★ ★

Handsome Bay, The Valley, ☎ *(809) 495-5544. Associated hotel: Olde Yarde Inn. International cuisine. Specialties: Seafood delight, fresh fish, grilled lamb chops. Dinner: 6:30–8:30 p.m., entrées $18–$30.*

The ambience is lovely at this garden restaurant in the Olde Yarde Inn, and the French-Continental food enhances the experience. Inn guests and others can dine here all day, starting with a breakfast menu that commences at 8 a.m. Lunch is served at the Slip and Dip Grill and includes burgers, fish and sandwiches. But the real draw is dinner, where classics such as escargot with garlic butter or Caesar salad for two can be paired with local fish of the day, or Caribbean lobster with lemon butter sauce. Soups and desserts are all homemade and change frequently. Sunday night barbecue. Reservations recommended. Credit cards: A, MC, V.

Where to Eat—Jost Van Dyke

Several of the BVI's more legendary beachside dining experiences can be found on Jost Van Dyke, not the least of which is the scene at Foxy's, a beach bar and grill that draws the yachting crowd in droves throughout the year. Against a steady reggae beat, the aforementioned Painkiller is served here in a plastic milk carton; the bar also sells its own rum—Foxy's Firewater. Foxy himself provides much of the music—impromptu ditties composed on the fly (be careful what you tell him—it's likely to wind up in a song.) Also worth checking into are Happy Laurry on the beach at Great Harbour (pig roast and barbecue on Friday evenings) and in Little Harbor, Sidney's Peace and Love where you keep your own bar tab, and Harris', where a "no-wait" lunch program is offered. On the other hand, on Jost Van Dyke, what's your hurry?

Abe's By the Sea   **$$$**   ★ ★

Little Harbour, Jost Van Dyke, ☎ *(809) 495-9329. Seafood cuisine. Specialties: Fresh lobster with lime and butter sauce, pig roast. Lunch: 11:30 a.m.–3 p.m., entrées $8–$25. Dinner: 7–9:30 p.m., entrées $12–$30.*

Abe's is a swinging place to try fresh fish, lobster and conch on a waterfront terrace in Jost Van Dyke's Little Harbour. Bright coral and fish nets decorate this popular hangout for yachtspeople and tourists who drop in morning, noon and night. An American breakfast with sausage, ham, bacon and eggs and juice is a good buy for $5. Lunches and dinners are substantial and served with rice and peas, coleslaw or green salad and corn on the cob; sandwiches are also available. There's a traditional pig roast Wednesdays. Reservations recommended. Credit cards: MC, V.

Club Paradise $$$ ★★

Great Harbour, Jost Van Dyke, ☎ *(809) 495-9267.*
Seafood cuisine. Specialties: Sauteed grouper, flying fish sandwich.
Lunch: 10:30 a.m.–4 p.m., entrées $4–$8.
Dinner: 6–9 p.m., entrées $15–$25.
There are many nice touches that make this simple open-air restaurant in Great Harbour a good place to alight. There's a delicious Barbados-style flying fish sandwich available for lunch for $5, served on home-baked bread. At dinner, patrons can pick a lobster from the tank. On Wednesdays there's a pig roast, and live entertainment is a regular feature. Cheeseburgers on that fresh bread, a whole cornish hen with honey-glazed carrots and garlic and sauteed grouper can also be enjoyed here on a regular basis. Bushwhackers are a specialty. Reservations recommended. Credit cards: A, MC, V.

Foxy's $$$ ★★

Great Harbour, Jost Van Dyke, ☎ *(809) 495-9258.*
American cuisine. Specialties: Filet mignon, rotis, painkiller punch.
Lunch: Noon–2:30 p.m., entrées $6–$9.
Dinner: 6:30–9 p.m., entrées $15–$30.
Don't expect luxury at this famous beach bar presided over by the magical Philicianno "Foxy" Callwood—only unabashed camaraderie and excellent grilled meat and seafood. An institution for close to 30 years, Foxy's Tamarind Bar draws an amazing yachting crowd for New Years' Eve, overwhelming Great Harbour with an overflow of boats and frenzied folks. The rest of the year it's calypso, reggae or soca (soul and calypso) music with burgers, rotis and killer rum punches. Lunch is served Monday–Friday only; the real closing time at Foxy's varies wildly. Credit cards: MC, V.

Sandcastle White Bay $$$ ★★

White Bay, Jost Van Dyke, ☎ *(809) 690-1611. Associated hotel: Sandcastle Hotel.*
International cuisine. Specialties: Boneless chicken breast, New York steak, fresh fish.
Lunch: 11 a.m.–4 p.m., prix fixe $5–$8.
Dinner: 7:30 p.m., prix fixe $30.
Arrive in your own boat or motor over by car from Great Harbour to dine simply and by candlelight (there's no electricity). Delightfully informal, yet the four-course prix fixe meal includes a basket of fresh bread, soup, a garden salad, an entrée (depending on what's fresh) and dessert—regular specials include duck a l'orange and stuffed grouper. Reservations have to made by 4 p.m. for dinner, with one seating nightly at 7:30; many patrons call from a VHF radio to relay their meal choices. The adjacent Soggy Dollar Bar concocts the original Painkiller. Reservations required. Credit cards: MC, V.

Where to Eat—Anegada

A small collection of restaurants is concentrated in The Settlement—though food is mostly limited to West Indian cooking, particularly lobster and conch. The Anegada Reef Hotel's restaurant is informal and pleasant, with a reliable menu served beachside, though food prices throughout the island edge well past "moderate." Big Bamboo's, amid the dunes of Loblolly Bay, might be the unlikeliest place for star-gazing, but both Princess Di and

Ted Kennedy are said to have stopped by while on sojourn at nearby Necker Island. The fresh lobster you dine on here and elsewhere is usually sitting out in the water when you order it; go for a snorkel while you're waiting for it to be brought in and cooked.

Anegada Reef Hotel $$$ ★★

Setting Point, Setting Point, ☎ (809) 495-8002. Associated hotel: Anegada Reef Hotel.
International cuisine. Specialties: Lobster.
Lunch: 8:30 a.m.– 4 p.m., entrées $7–$20.
Dinner: 4–9:30 p.m., entrées $17–$30.
Visions of lobster barbecuing on the beach at this low-key resort draw day-trippers to experience a very informal (if pricey) crustacean feast served on picnic tables. Sides usually include Caesar salad and garlic bread. Other entrée selections usually include steak, chicken, ribs, lamb and fish. To dine here, reserve by 4 p.m., and if you are flying in, the hotel will meet you with a private bus. Reservations required. Credit cards: MC, V.

Big Bamboo's $$$ ★★

Loblolly Bay, The Settlement, ☎ (809) 495-2019.
African cuisine. Specialties: Conch in pepper sauce, grilled lobster.
Lunch: Noon–6 p.m., entrées $12–$23.
Situated below the sea grape tress amid the sand dunes of Loblolly Bay, informal Big Bamboo's is just far enough off the beaten track that it pulls in the occasional celeb from nearby Necker Island, but you can eat there, too. The popular conch is topped with red and green sweet peppers, garlic and onions, but some call the lobster that owner Abrey Levons grills the best around. Or you can try the fresh catch, which might be triggerfish, snapper or grouper; there's also homemade brandy made from the sea grapes. Anegada native Levons opened his simple picnic-table restaurant in 1984, but he's about to start taking credit cards—a sure sign he's been found out. Lunch hours vary, but he'll stay open "as long as we're having a good laugh"; dinner by reservation only. Features: outside dining.

Resort Islands

Beyond the four main islands that seduce most visitors to the British Virgins are a series of privately owned resort islands—outposts with just one hostelry for accommodation. In all instances, the prices range from merely expensive to fabulously extravagant. They vary substantially in how they accommodate guests—Necker Island is a one-villa hinterland housing up to 24 guests for $11,000 per night (and up), while Peter Island possesses a 50-room resort that can be visited by Tortola day-trippers. It will take an extra effort to get to these resorts (private ferry, boat taxi or perhaps helicopter), but all you need do is ask the management to take care of arrangements when you make the reservation. What you get in return are resorts that take full advantage of the natural surroundings; you may not have a phone, TV or roads to remind you of civilization.

Guana Island

Where to Stay

Guana Island   **$445–$675**   ★★★★★

Guana Island, ☎ (800) 544-8262, (809) 494-2354. FAX (809) 495-2900.

Single: $445–$625. Double: $495–$675.

Situated on a pristine 850-acre island, this hideaway resort was formerly a sugarcane plantation and is now a nature sanctuary. Accommodations are in white stone cottages arranged along a hilltop with smashing views of neighboring islands. The rooms are simple but lovely and lack real-world distractions such as phones, televisions and air-conditioners. A secluded, one-bedroom cottage is located on North Beach and goes for $740–$995. Meals are served family style, and groups of 30 can rent the entire island—the perfect spot for a family reunion of jet-setters. Though there's great hiking, bird watching, tennis and watersports, Guana is not a high-amenity resort, nor does it dole out luxurious pampering. It's a tranquil and lovely retreat where evenings might be spent trading travel stories with fellow guests, or fussing over a game of Scrabble. Amenities: tennis. 15 rooms.

Mosquito Island

Privately owned by Drake's Anchorage resort, Mosquito Island has drop-dead views over North Sound to Virgin Gorda and Prickly Pear. The only way to get there is by boat. If you've got the dough, why not rent the whole island and let your friends come over? The beach at South Bay is extremely pleasant, dotted with huge boulders and quiet sandy coves.

Where to Stay

Drake's Anchorage　　　　　　　$223–$600　　　★★★★

Mosquito Island, ☎ (800) 624-6651, (809) 494-2254. FAX (617) 959-5147.
Single: $223–$600. Double: $316–$600.

Located on a private island just off Virgin Gorda, this resort has four beaches, with one just big enough for a snuggling couple. The recently redone accommodations are in three cottages lining a narrow beach and feature Haitian art, red-tile floors and modern baths; ceiling fans keep things cool. There are also two luxurious villas set off a bit. A popular restaurants draws the yachting set, and all the usual watersports are available. Life is laid-back at this peaceful and unpretentious spot that regularly snares eco-tourism awards. 12 rooms. Credit cards: A, MC, V.

Necker Island

Got $10,000 per day to spend on a Caribbean vacation? (Hey, meals included!) The hefty price tag at the incredible Necker Island includes everything, even the whole private island, which accommodates one group of up to 24 people at a time. Upon landing in St. Thomas, you're whisked away by helicopter to a tiny land mass—74 lush green acres covered with brilliantly red bougainvillea atop of which is a Bali-like tropical mansion that has brought ooh's and aah's to the lips of Princess Diana, Steven Spielberg, Oprah Winfrey, Robert Redford, etc. Created by British entrepreneur Richard Branson of Virgin Atlantic Airways and Virgin Records, the open-air house sports a living room with a 360-degree view of the sea. There are two guesthouses, besides the main 10-bedroom, eight-bathroom house, several freshwater pools, and a cheerful staff who can cook for you or assist you in cooking your own. In the main house, the 24-foot long dining table is bordered by 22 chairs, complete with beautiful settings, elegant placemats, gleaming silver, etc. Food is luscious, endless and irresistible, everything from nonstop desserts to the potpourri of freshly caught fish. Activities are endless, from tennis, snorkeling, water-skiing, swimming, banana boating, windsurfing, power boating and hiking, to just lazing about on the beach.

Where to Stay

Necker Island　　　　　　　　　　　　　★★★★★

Necker Island, ☎ (800) 557-4255, (809) 494-2757. FAX (212) 689-1598.
Rack rate Per Day: $1285–$10,900.

Got a wad of thousand dollar bills burning a hole in your pocket? Need room to spread out? Don't fret—simply join Steven Spielberg, Oprah Winfrey and other luminaries who have ponied up at least $10,000 per day to stash their duffle bags on Necker Island, a 74-acre paradise located three miles north of Virgin Gorda's North Sound. Among the guests who liked it enough to return for more are Princess Diana, Mel Gibson and, of course, the island's entrepreneurial owner Richard Branson (of Virgin Records and Virgin Atlantic Airways). Chilled Veuve Clicquot greets you on arrival, which might be by helicopter from St. Thomas (if you're staying seven nights or more). The hilltop mansion is draped in brilliant red bougainvillea and furnished in Balinese textures of elephant bamboo and plush batiks. This main villa has 10 of the 12 bedrooms, each with a private bath containing stone grottos for showers; the master bedroom has its own Jacuzzi. The living room sports a 360-degree view of the sea. A pair of cottages—Bali Hi and Bali Lo, each with their own private pool—were recently added for guests who want yet another degree of seclusion. Otherwise, Necker is a world unto itself. Activities are endless, and include tennis, snorkeling, water-skiing, swimming, banana boating, windsurfing and just lazing about on the beach. The professional staff of 22 includes a full-time chef (Scott Williams), and a boatman to whisk you off to neighboring islands. The year-round daily rates start at $11,000 and go all the way up to $15,000—based on the number of people in your group (the rooms accommodate 24), plus 2.5 percent service charge; rates include food and virtually all possible activities. Or, there's a nifty new development at Necker called Celebration Weeks, which are held four times per year. During these weeks you and your mate can share the island with 11 other couples, at an all-inclusive rate of $9000 for seven days.

ED: Normal price per day ranges from $11,000 to $15,000, depending on the number of guests (up to 24); the four Celebration Weeks each year drop the price to $1285 per day for two (7-day minimum). Don't refer to the rate as a Rack Rate; it's the only price available. Also, do not list this as an Apartment/Condo as it was last year. Amenities: tennis, exercise room, Jacuzzi, balcony or patio.

Peter Island

Where to Stay

Hotels and Resorts

Peter Island Resort $195–$565 ★★★★★

Peter Island, ☎ (800) 346-4451, (809) 495-2000. FAX (809) 495-2500.
Single: $195–$565. Double: $195–$565.
Located on its own private island south of Tortola, this smashing resort shuttles guests over by boat, or via helicopter ($550 one way). Everything is quite luxurious, and the beaches—five total—are to die for. Accommodations are beautifully done and include standard guest rooms and villas with two to four bedrooms (villa rates are $475–3950 per night). The resort takes up about half of the 1800-acre island, and the extensive grounds include a gorgeous free-form pool, four tennis courts (pro on hand during high season), a dive shop, a yachting marina and extensive trails for walking or mountain biking. The food is great and the service impeccable. Lovers can spend the day at their own private beach with a picnic lunch for a very reasonable price. Bravo! Amenities: tennis, exercise room, private spas. 50 rooms.
Credit cards: A, MC, V.

Where to Eat

Tradewinds Restaurant $$$ ★ ★ ★ ★

Peter Island, Peter Island, ☎ (809) 495-2000. Associated hotel: Peter Island Resort.
International cuisine. Specialties: Tortola seafood soup, crab-stuffed island chicken.
Dinner: 7–9 p.m., entrées $18–$36.

Glide onto the Peter Island ferry (after reservations are made, of course) for a short ride to this beautiful private island and its attached resort. The Tradewinds, the island's main dining room, is known for expensive but five-star gourmet dinners served year-round. A memorable meal might consist of an appetizer of grilled honey-glazed quail, followed by Caribbean pepperpot soup, caesar salad, lemon-poached shrimp with shrimp mousse, and strawberries Romanoff. Afterwards, dance with your partner under a star-lit sky. Reservations required. Credit cards: A, MC, V.

Where to Shop

The British Virgin Islands don't give American citizens the same duty-free break as do the U.S. Virgins, so you'll want to save serious shopping for a stopover in bustling St. Thomas on your way home. Additionally, there's not much to rave about here in terms of quality. In Road Town, the unofficial shopping hub is located on Main Street beginning with Sir Olva Georges Plaza. Pusser's Rum ("the Official Drink of the Royal British Navy") is one of the big island buys, available at the company store on Main Street. An aromatic excursion to the Sunny Caribee and Spice Company won't be time wasted, especially if you want to pick from the best selection of Caribbean spices and handicrafts on the island. Stop next door at Sunny Caribee Gallery, which features fine artwork by islanders as well as handpainted furniture and wood carvings. If you need to supplant your vacation wardrobe, there are several boutiques in the Abbot Building, including Sea Urchin and Kids in De Sun, which specializes in tropical attire for children.

On Virgin Gorda, boutiques at Little Dix Bay and the Bitter End resorts carry the proverbial casual wear and souvenir merchandise. Along the Yacht Harbour on Virgin Gorda you'll find another bevy of shops, including a few handicraft stores. Most of the work is imported from other islands, though you can find interesting buys on homemade preserves and spices. A local artist, Aragon, sells hand-painted shirts for $15 to $20 around the boat-dock at Trellis Bay near the Beef Island airport.

British Virgin Islands Directory

Arrival and Departure

There is no airport in the British Virgin Islands big enough to accommodate jets and, accordingly, there is no direct service between North America and the BVIs. All of the international flights enter the BVIs through the airport on Beef Island, which is connected to Tortola by bridge. American Eagle provides up to 10 flights per day out of San Juan, Puerto Rico. Sunaire provides daily service from St. Thomas and St. Croix. LIAT offers direct or nonstop service from Anguilla, Antigua, San Juan, St. Kitts, St. Maarten and St. Thomas. Air transport to Virgin Gorda is via Beef Island only (see "Getting Around" below for information on how to get to the other BVIs). Because government regulation forbids anyone to rent a car at the Beef Island airport, taxis are omnipresent when a plane arrives. Some hotels will arrange for a taxi to meet you. Another, frequently used option that can sometimes save a few dollars is to ferry over to the British Virgins from the U.S. Virgins. This option makes particular sense if a flight from North America to St. Thomas is significantly cheaper than a connection into Tortola (not uncommon).

Business Hours

Stores open Monday–Saturday 9 a.m.–5 p.m. Banks open Monday–Thursday 9 a.m.–2:30 p.m. and Friday 9 a.m.–2:30 p.m. and 4:30–6 p.m.

Climate

Little rain falls on this nearly-perfect temperate island, with temperatures hovering between 75 degrees F and 85 degrees F year-round. The constant trade winds keep the humidity low. Even during the rainy season, rain usually arrives in 10-minute bursts that stop as fast they start.

Cruises

BVI has become a ready port of call for many cruise liners. Many stop at Tortola and bring passengers aboard on small ships.

Documents

Customs officials prefer visitors bring passports, but will accept proof of citizenship (birth certificate or voter's registration car, plus driver's license or other photo identification). Travelers must also possess an ongoing or return ticket. Departure tax is $10.

Electricity

Current runs 110 volts, 60 cycles, as in the U.S.

Getting Around

Car rentals can be exorbitant during high season because the demand is so high. As such, it's best to reserve a car before you arrive. Rates seem to change daily based on availability, so reconfirm your quoted rate at least two days before your anticipated pickup. To rent a car, you must obtain a BVI driver's license by presenting your valid hometown license and shelling out $10. Though there are numerous local agencies with slightly lower prices, but it's easier to reserve a car with the American firms (and easier to rectify billing errors after-the-fact) based on Tortola: **Avis** ☎ *(800) 331-1212* or *(809) 494-3322*, **Budget** ☎ *(800) 527-0700* or *(809) 494-2639* and **National** ☎ *(800) 227-7368* or *(809) 494-3197*. On Virgin Gorda, try **Speedy's Car Rental** ☎ *(809) 495-5235*. On Anegada, the **Anegada Reef Hotel** has a small selection ☎ *(809) 495-8002*.

Transportation between islands is fairly comprehensive. From the Beef Island airport on Tortola, only two of the other BVIs are served by air. **Virgin Islands Airways** offers daily flights to Virgin Gorda ☎ *(809) 495-1972*, and **Gorda Aero Services** provides flights to Anegada on Monday, Wednesday and Friday ☎ *(809) 495-2271*. Otherwise, transportation between the islands is by ferry or water taxi.

At least four companies offer ferry service from Tortola to Virgin Gorda. **Speedy's Fantasy and Speedy's Delight** offer up to six trips daily out of Tortola ☎ *(809) 495-5240*. Smith's Ferry Services provides three to six trips daily out of Road Town with some service from West End, Tortola ☎ *(809) 495-4495*. **Virgin Gorda Ferry Service** provides one trip daily from Beef Island at 5:30 p.m. to The Valley, with a return trip to Beef Island leaving at 7:30 p.m. ☎ *(809) 495-5240*. **North Sound Express** operates three times daily between Beef Island and North Sound, Virgin Gorda ☎ *(809) 495-2271*. The large resorts on Virgin Gorda each have their own private ferry service, though prices may be higher than the public ferries.

The ferry to Jost Van Dyke leaves from West End, Tortola with four departures daily (three on Sunday); contact **Jost Van Dyke Ferry Service** ☎ *(809) 494-2997*. The resort on Peter Island operates its own private ferry out of Road Town; officially, by day it's only for guests of the resort, but it's available during the evening to non-resort guests who want to try the Peter Island Resort restaurant ☎ *(809) 494-2561*. There is no ferry service to Anegada; other islands, such as Ginger, Cooper, Norman and Salt, are reached by private water taxi.

Language

British English is spoken with a West Indian accent.

Medical Emergencies

The Peebles Hospital, Porter Road, Road Town; ☎ *(809) 494-3497* is a fully functioning facility with lab and X-ray machines. Hotels usually have a list of doctors on-call in Tortola.

Money

The American dollar is used exclusively.

Telephone

To reach BVI from the U.S., dial *809* (area code) + *49* (country code) + local number. Area code is *809*.

Time

Atlantic standard time throughout the year.

Tipping

Hotels customarily add a 10–15 percent service charge to the bill; feel free to tip more for special service. Waiters and taxi drivers both expect to be tipped 10–15 percent.

Tourist Information

The British Virgin Islands Tourist Board on Tortola is located in Road Town ☎ *(809) 494-3134*. In the United States an office in New York is set up for sending out brochures and providing tourist information ☎ *(800) 835-8530*. An additional office is based in San Francisco ☎ *(415) 775-0344*.

When to Go

The BVI Summer Festival in August is one of the island's biggest events, which includes two weeks of festivities, song, dance and parades. Also in August, fish enthusiasts can also attend the International Marlin Tournament at the Birch Creek resort. In November hop a ferry to Virgin Gorda's Bitter End Yacht Club when the Pro-Am Regatta sets sail. The annual Spring Regatta is a Caribbean-wide yacht race, featuring outdoor music and street fairs. For a schedule, call ☎ *(800) 835-8530* in the United States. Easter is celebrated by a three-day festival in Virgin Gorda.

BRITISH VIRGIN ISLANDS HOTELS		RMS	RATES	PHONE	CR. CARDS
Anegada					
Setting Point					
★★	**Anegada Reef Hotel**	16	$130–$230	(809) 495-8002	MC, V
Guana Island					
★★★★★	**Guana Island**	15	$445–$675	(800) 544-8262	
Jost Van Dyke					
Great Harbour					
★★	**Sandy Ground Estates**	8	All-Inclusive	(809) 494-3391	MC, V
White Bay					
★	**Sandcastle**	4	$75–$195	(809) 690-1611	MC, V
Mosquito Island					
★★★★	**Drake's Anchorage**	12	$223–$600	(800) 624-6651	A, MC, V
Necker Island					
★★★★★	**Necker Island**			(800) 557-4255	
Peter Island					
★★★★★	**Peter Island Resort**	50	$195–$565	(800) 346-4451	A, MC, V
Tortola					
★★	**Fort Recovery Estates**	17	$125–$295	(800) 367-8455	A, MC, V

BRITISH VIRGIN ISLANDS HOTELS		RMS	RATES	PHONE	CR. CARDS
Road Town					
★★★	Long Bay Beach Hotel	83	$60–$270	(800) 729-9599	A, D, MC, V
★★★	Prospect Reef Resort	130	$88–$395	(800) 356-8937	A, MC, V
★★★	Sugar Mill Hotel	21	$135–$265	(800) 462-8834	A, MC, V
★★★	Treasure Isle Hotel	43	$80–$230	(800) 334-2435	A, MC, V
★★	Fort Burt Hotel	8	$60–$95	(809) 494-2587	A, D, MC, V
★★	Moorings-Mariner Inn	40	$80–$230	(800) 535-7289	A, MC, V
★★	Nanny Cay Resort	42	$60–$225	(800) 742-4276	A, MC, V
★★	Rockview Holiday Homes	30	$120–$850	(800) 621-1270	A, D, MC, V
★★	Village Cay Marina Hotel	19	$77–$165	(809) 494-2771	A, MC, V
★	Sebastian's on the Beach	26	$75–$190	(800) 336-4870	A, D, MC, V
West End					
★★	Frenchman's Cay Resort	9	$115–$210	(800) 235-4077	A, D, MC, V
Virgin Gorda					
★★★★★	Little Dix Bay Hotel	98	$250–$650	(800) 928-3000	A, DC, MC, V
North Sound					
★★★★★	Biras Creek Hotel	33	$275–$795	(800) 223-1108	A, MC, V
★★★	Bitter End Yacht Club	94	$220–$570	(800) 872-2392	A, MC, V
★★	Leverick Bay Resort	50	$89–$112	(800) 848-7081	A, MC, V
The Valley					
★★★	Olde Yard Inn	13	$80–$195	(800) 633-7411	A, MC, V
★★	Fischer's Cove Beach	20	$90–$285	(800) 621-1270	A, D, DC, MC, V
★★	Guavaberry Spring Bay	18	$90–$200	(809) 495-5227	
★★	Mango Bay Resort	10	$85–$752	(800) 621-1270	A, D, MC, V
★★	Virgin Gorda Villas	60	$105–$575	(800) 621-1270	A, D, MC, V

BRITISH VIRGIN ISLANDS RESTAURANTS		PHONE	ENTRÉE	CR. CARDS
Anegada				
Setting Point				
International				
★★	Anegada Reef Hotel	(809) 495-8002	$7–$30	MC, V

BRITISH VIRGIN ISLANDS RESTAURANTS	PHONE	ENTRÉE	CR. CARDS

The Settlement

	African		
★★ Big Bamboo's	(809) 495-2019	$12–$23	

Jost Van Dyke

	American		
★★ Foxy's	(809) 495-9258	$6–$30	MC, V
	International		
★★ Sandcastle White Bay	(809) 690-1611	$5–$30	MC, V
	Seafood		
★★ Abe's By the Sea	(809) 495-9329	$8–$30	MC, V
★★ Club Paradise	(809) 495-9267	$4–$25	A, MC, V

Peter Island

	International		
★★★★ Tradewinds Restaurant	(809) 495-2000	$18–$36	A, MC, V

Tortola

East End

	Indian		
★★ Bing's Drop Inn Bar	(809) 495-2627	$10–$20	A, MC, V

Road Town

	English		
★★★ Virgin Queen	(809) 494-2310	$7–$16	
	International		
★★★★ Skyworld	(809) 494-3567	$7–$40	A, MC, V
★★★★ Upstairs, The	(809) 494-2228	$10–$27	A, MC, V
★★ Pusser's Pub and The Outpost	(809) 494-4199	$7–$25	A, MC, V
	Italian		
★★★★ Brandywine Bay	(809) 495-2301	$20–$28	A, MC, V
★★★★ Capriccio di Mare	(809) 494-5369	$8–$15	A, D, MC, V
★★ Spaghetti Junction	(809) 494-4880	$10–$21	A, MC, V
	Seafood		
★★★ Fish Trap, The	(809) 494-3626	$8–$25	A, MC, V

BRITISH VIRGIN ISLANDS

West End

	Indian		
★★★ Apple, The	(809) 495-4437	$15–$35	A, MC, V
★★★ Mrs. Scatliffe's	(809) 495-4556	$20–$27	
	International		
★★★ Sugar Mill	(809) 495-4355	$6–$26	A, MC, V
★★ Pusser's Landing	(809) 495-4554	$5–$25	A, D, MC, V

Virgin Gorda

North Sound

	African		
★★★ Bath and Turtle Pub, The	(809) 495-5239	$7–$30	A, MC, V
	American		
★★★ Pusser's Leverick Bay	(809) 495-7369	$6–$24	A, MC, V
	International		
★★★★ Biras Creek	(809) 494-3555	$40–$40	A, MC, V

Saba Rock

	American		
★★★ Pirate's Pub & Grill	(809) 495-9537	$5–$7	A, MC, V

The Valley

	International		
★★★ Chez Michelle	(809) 495-5510	$16–$28	MC, V
★★★ Olde Yarde Inn	(809) 495-5544	$18–$30	A, MC, V
	Latin American		
★★★ Crab Hole, The	(809) 495-5307	$6–$15	

CAYMAN ISLANDS

Divers in Sting Ray City, Cayman Islands

The trio of islands that makes up the Caymans has long been regarded world over as the spot for diving. Grand Cayman, the largest of the trio, has more than 130 dive sites, many less than a half-mile from shore, and visibility of 100 to 150 feet is common. Cayman Brac, a 20-minute flight away, is known for its spectacular drop-offs and fascinating coral gardens in both shallow and medium depths. And Little Cayman—where the drop off begins at 18 feet and plunges to 1000 feet, with visibility often reaching up to 200 feet—was voted the top Caribbean dive destination by the readers of *Rodale's Scuba Diving* magazine in 1996.

Obviously, diving and watersports are what it's all about on the Caymans. The British colony is not especially picturesque, and while you can score some deals in the shops, peruse a few museums and enjoy world-class accommodations, the whole idea of a Cayman sojourn is getting wet. Those not into watersports will be decidedly bored. Apparently that is not a problem for the island's tourist-based economy, as visitors outnumber residents each year by 10 to one. Finance also contributes to the healthy economic picture, with nearly 550 offshore banks located in Grand Cayman. (The 1993 Tom Cruise film, *The Firm*, falsely portrayed the Caymans as a money-laundering paradise.) The cost of living on the islands is high—some 20 percent higher than the United States—and Caymanians enjoy a robust, virtually crime-free lifestyle. Recognizing a good thing when it has one, the government is aggressively protecting its natural resources with far-sighted programs to keep pristine land free from development.

Located 480 miles south of Miami, the Caymans consist of three islands: Grand Cayman, Cayman Brac and Little Cayman. As the name suggests, Grand Cayman is the largest (but only relatively grand), coming in at just 22 miles long by eight miles wide. Despite the fact that half of its 76 square miles is swampland, Grand Cayman is by far the most populated and developed of the trio. The hub of tourism is West Bay Beach, a fantastic strand along the western shore. North Sound, a large bay to the west, is surrounded by a huge and colorful coral reef. There's good shopping and restaurants in the capital city of George Town, where cruise ships frequently dock.

Cayman Brac, 89 miles to the northeast (a 20-minute flight), is a 12-mile island of low-lying land that rises to a 140-foot bluff, from which the island takes its name (brac means "bluff" in Gaelic). Besides great diving all around the coastline—there's more than 50 designated sites—the island has several large caves and sinkholes that are a spelunker's joy. Protected woodlands are home to native cacti, thatch palms, rare orchids, frigate birds, peregrinate falcons, brown boobies and the rare Cayman Brac Parrot.

Little Cayman, sitting just seven miles away from Cayman Brac, totals just 12 square miles and about 50 residents. Diving reigns supreme at Bloody Bay Wall, whose 1,200 foot vertical plunge makes it one of the world's most spectacular spots There's a handful of small lodges catering to divers on the island but nightlife is nill; in fact, the entire island has just one pay phone. This is the place to come to really get away from it all, commune with nature and keep an eye peeled for the resident West Indian whistling birds, wild iguanas, egrets, herons and red-footed boobies.

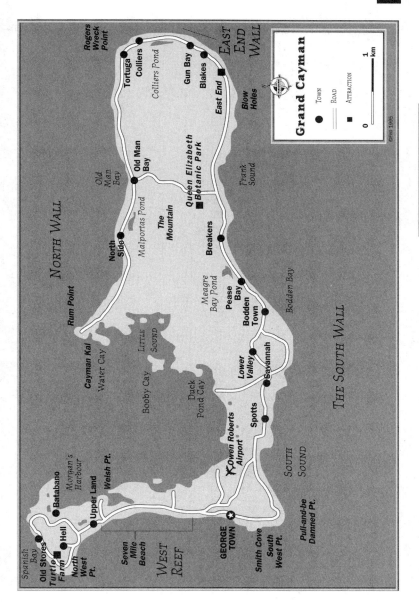

Grand Cayman

● TOWN
ROAD
■ ATTRACTION

0 ——— 1 km

GPWI 1995

CAYMAN ISLANDS

Rogers Wreck Point
Colliers
Tortuga
Colliers Pond
Gun Bay
Blakes
EAST END WALL
East End
Blow Holes

Old Man Bay
Old Man Bay
Queen Elizabeth Botanic Park ■
Frank Sound
Malportas Pond
The Mountain
Breakers
North Side
NORTH WALL
Rum Point
Meagre Bay Pond
Pease Bay
Bodden Town
Bodden Bay
Cayman Kai
Water Cay
LITTLE SOUND
Booby Cay
Duck Pond Cay
Lower Valley
Savannah
THE SOUTH WALL
Spotts
Owen Roberts Airport
SOUTH SOUND
Morgan's Harbour
Upper Land
Welsh Pt.
Batabano
Hell
Spanish Bay
Old Stores
Turtle Farm
North West Pt.
Seven Mile Beach
WEST REEF
GEORGE TOWN ✦
Smith Cove
South West Pt.
Pull-and-be Damned Pt.

Fielding   **GRAND CAYMAN DELIGHTS**

A Trio of Crown Jewels

Although best-known for the 544 offshore banks located in George Town, Grand Cayman holds treasures of another kind for those who enjoy history, diving, and bird-watching.

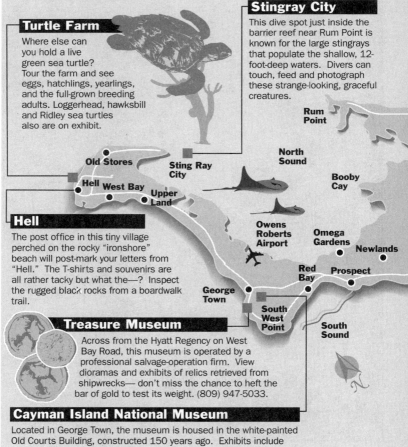

Turtle Farm

Where else can you hold a live green sea turtle? Tour the farm and see eggs, hatchlings, yearlings, and the full-grown breeding adults. Loggerhead, hawksbill and Ridley sea turtles also are on exhibit.

Stingray City

This dive spot just inside the barrier reef near Rum Point is known for the large stingrays that populate the shallow, 12-foot-deep waters. Divers can touch, feed and photograph these strange-looking, graceful creatures.

Rum Point

Old Stores

Sting Ray City

North Sound

Booby Cay

Hell   West Bay   Upper Land

Hell

The post office in this tiny village perched on the rocky "ironshore" beach will post-mark your letters from "Hell." The T-shirts and souvenirs are all rather tacky but what the—? Inspect the rugged black rocks from a boardwalk trail.

Owens Roberts Airport

Omega Gardens

Newlands

Red Bay

Prospect

George Town

South West Point

South Sound

Treasure Museum

Across from the Hyatt Regency on West Bay Road, this museum is operated by a professional salvage-operation firm. View dioramas and exhibits of relics retrieved from shipwrecks— don't miss the chance to heft the bar of gold to test its weight. (809) 947-5033.

Cayman Island National Museum

Located in George Town, the museum is housed in the white-painted Old Courts Building, constructed 150 years ago. Exhibits include displays of rare coins and a 14-foot catboat.

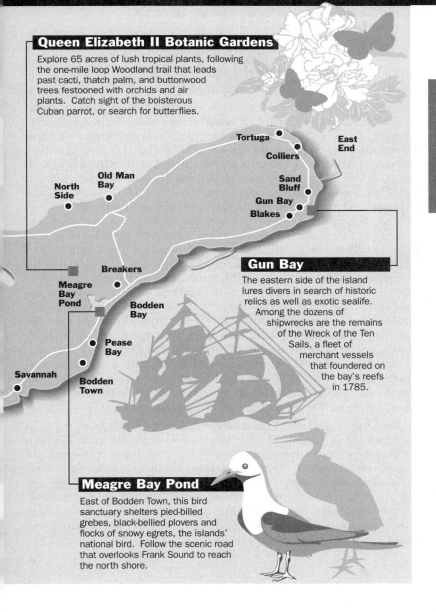

Queen Elizabeth II Botanic Gardens

Explore 65 acres of lush tropical plants, following the one-mile loop Woodland trail that leads past cacti, thatch palm, and buttonwood trees festooned with orchids and air plants. Catch sight of the boisterous Cuban parrot, or search for butterflies.

Tortuga

East End

Colliers

Old Man Bay

Sand Bluff

North Side

Gun Bay

Blakes

Breakers

Meagre Bay Pond

Bodden Bay

Pease Bay

Savannah

Bodden Town

Gun Bay

The eastern side of the island lures divers in search of historic relics as well as exotic sealife. Among the dozens of shipwrecks are the remains of the Wreck of the Ten Sails, a fleet of merchant vessels that foundered on the bay's reefs in 1785.

Meagre Bay Pond

East of Bodden Town, this bird sanctuary shelters pied-billed grebes, black-bellied plovers and flocks of snowy egrets, the islands' national bird. Follow the scenic road that overlooks Frank Sound to reach the north shore.

Just offshore Little Cayman is tiny Owen Island, whose welcoming sign ("Private Property—Visitors Welcome—Please Help Keep This Island Clean") pretty much sums up the Caymans all around.

History

Columbus discovered the Caymans in 1503 and dubbed them *Las Tortugas* for the enormous numbers of tortoises that would provide sustenance to English, Dutch and French sailors for centuries. (Las Tortugas somehow evolved into Los Caimanes, the Spanish name for a kind of tropical American crocodile). For a good 150 years after being sighted, the Caymans were almost entirely avoided. They were remote, perilous to approach by sea, and their interiors were inhospitable—swampy and mosquito-infested in Grand Cayman, and hard and scrubby on Little Cayman and Cayman Brac. Among the few creatures that thrived here were crocodiles, called *caymanas* in the language of the Carib Indians. For a time the critters shared the island with such buccaneers as Sir Henry Morgan and Edward Teach (the original Blackbeard) who hid out in the islands while preying on Spanish and French ships. (Cayman history abounds with stories of sunken treasure and derring-do.) The abundance of meaty sea turtles made the islands a convenient provisioning stop, but by most accounts, the first real settlers didn't arrive until 1655, when deserters from Oliver Cromwell's army abandoned their platoon in Jamaica as the English were taking it from the Spanish. In 1670, Spain ceded both Jamaica and the Caymans to Great Britain. A century later, Grand Cayman had 933 residents, most of whom were slaves. After emancipation by Britain in 1835, the island became home to many other freed slaves; their descendants gradually becoming part of the families of the island, paving the way for the harmony that still exists today.

Just 33 years ago Jamaica chose independence, but the Caymans stayed on a British Crown Colony. The first tourists started to arrive in the Caymans during the 1950s while the roads were still bad, the insects voluminous and the electrical supply iffy. Legislation creating tax-investment havens in 1966 favored offshore banking and trust companies whose executives began seeing vacation promise in the islands. A tourist board, established in 1966, began strictly supervising hotel inspections, which has succeeded in raising and maintaining a high standard of service. About half a million people visit the Cayman Islands each year.

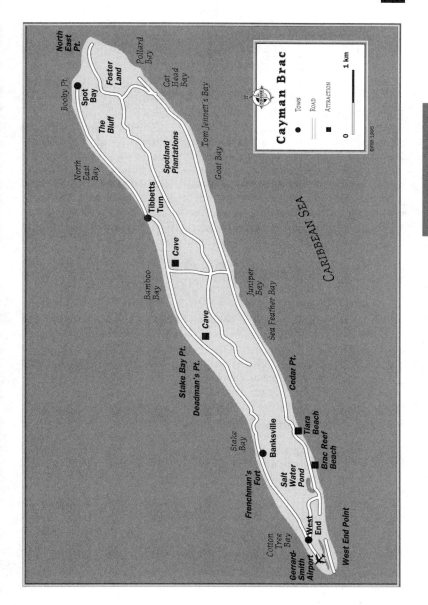

Cayman Brac

- ● TOWN
- ─── ROAD
- ■ ATTRACTION

0 1 km

©PW 1995

North East Pt.

Booby Pt.

Spot Bay

Pollard Bay

Foster Land

Cat Head Bay

The Bluff

Tom Jennett's Bay

North East Bay

Spotland Plantations

Goat Bay

Tibbetts Turn

Cave

Bamboo Bay

Juniper Bay

Cave

Sea Feather Bay

Stake Bay Pt.

Deadman's Pt.

CARIBBEAN SEA

Cedar Pt.

Stake Bay

Banksville

Tiara Beach

Frenchman's Fort

Salt Water Pond

Brac Reef Beach

Cotton Tree Bay

West End

Gerrard-Smith Airport

West End Point

People

The total population of the Caymans is 30,000 people, with the vast majority living on Grand Cayman—a quarter of them in the capital, George Town. About 1650 souls live on Cayman Brac and just 50 on Little Cayman. Caymanians enjoy a very high quality of living—highest in the Caribbean in fact—and there is little crime or racial tension. Locals—a mix of African and European descent who speak with a lilting brogue—are known for being exceptionally polite and helpful. Caymanians are well educated, with a literacy rate of more than 97 percent. The Caymans are a British colony with an appointed governor and elected Executive Council. Tourism contributes the most to the economy, though Grand Cayman also does a huge business in offshore banking. Though locals are quite well off compared to their Caribbean counterparts, life here is simple and nonmaterialistic.

Beaches

The beaches of the Caymans can be described in a few short words—powder-fine white strands with a handful of birds. **Seven Mile Beach** is considered one of the most fantastic beaches in the Caribbean, marked by a beautiful crescent shape and clear turquoise blue waters. Public buses operate hourly down the strand. North of the Holiday Inn, where most of the watersports facilities are based, is a public beach with small cabanas and tables and chairs. Most memorable sunsets can be seen from the beach at **Rum Point**, at the northeastern tip of North Sound, a sleepy little community of private homes and condos. **Little Cayman** is known for its long white beaches with nary a footprint to mar their beauty. For some reason, locals don't use the beaches much for sunbathing or swimming, so most of the strands are exquisitely private and not crowded.

Underwater

Make no doubt about it, diving is an industry in the Cayman Islands. Spurred on by magnificent underwater scenery, the islands have single-hand-

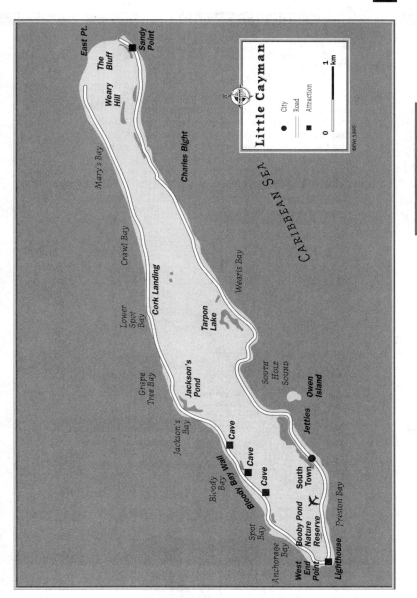

CAYMAN ISLANDS

Little Cayman

City
Road
Attraction

0   1
km

©PW 1995

CARIBBEAN SEA

East Pt.
The Bluff
Sandy Point
Weary Hill
Mary's Bay
Charles Bight
Crawl Bay
Cork Landing
Wearis Bay
Lower Spot Bay
Tarpon Lake
Grape Tree Bay
Jackson's Pond
SOUTH HOLE SOUND
Owen Island
Jackson's Bay
Cave
Jetties
Bloody Bay Wall
Cave
Cave
South Town
Preston Bay
Bloody Bay
Spot Bay
Booby Pond Nature Reserve
Anchorage Bay
West End Point
Lighthouse

CAYMAN ISLANDS

Fielding   **HIDDEN CAYMAN JEWELS**

Cayman Brac and Little Cayman

Less well-known, more pristine than Grand Cayman, The Brac is perfect for those who want to explore small, nameless caves that might hold pirate booty, or dive in near-virgin waters amid colorful fish. Little Cayman is where experienced divers head to explore steep drop-offs and virgin stands of coral. Much of the tiny island's south coast region is protected as bird sanctuaries and wilderness reserves.

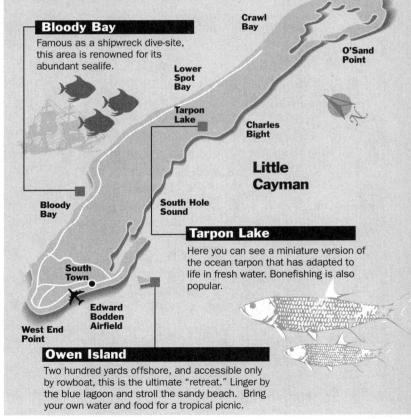

East Point

Bloody Bay

Famous as a shipwreck dive-site, this area is renowned for its abundant sealife.

Crawl Bay

O'Sand Point

Lower Spot Bay

Tarpon Lake

Charles Bight

Little Cayman

Bloody Bay

South Hole Sound

Tarpon Lake

Here you can see a miniature version of the ocean tarpon that has adapted to life in fresh water. Bonefishing is also popular.

South Town

West End Point

Edward Bodden Airfield

Owen Island

Two hundred yards offshore, and accessible only by rowboat, this is the ultimate "retreat." Linger by the blue lagoon and stroll the sandy beach. Bring your own water and food for a tropical picnic.

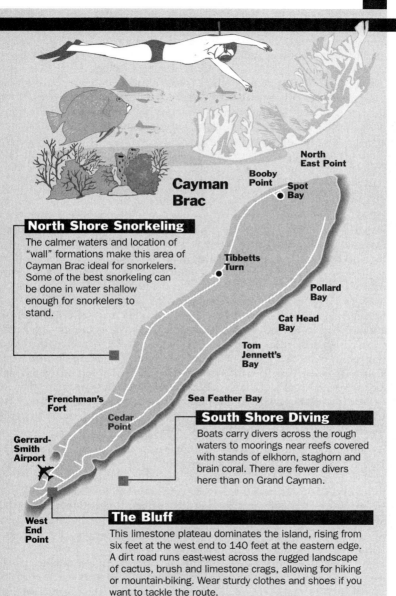

Cayman Brac

North East Point

Booby Point

Spot Bay

North Shore Snorkeling

The calmer waters and location of "wall" formations make this area of Cayman Brac ideal for snorkelers. Some of the best snorkeling can be done in water shallow enough for snorkelers to stand.

Tibbetts Turn

Pollard Bay

Cat Head Bay

Tom Jennett's Bay

Frenchman's Fort

Sea Feather Bay

Cedar Point

South Shore Diving

Boats carry divers across the rough waters to moorings near reefs covered with stands of elkhorn, staghorn and brain coral. There are fewer divers here than on Grand Cayman.

Gerrard-Smith Airport

West End Point

The Bluff

This limestone plateau dominates the island, rising from six feet at the west end to 140 feet at the eastern edge. A dirt road runs east-west across the rugged landscape of cactus, brush and limestone crags, allowing for hiking or mountain-biking. Wear sturdy clothes and shoes if you want to tackle the route.

edly captured the press, accolades and repeat business to secure a position as one of the two or three top dive destinations in the Caribbean. A series of immense walls, dropping to 6000 feet or more, line the islands and create ideal diving conditions. The downside is that dive operators are frequently accused of running a cattle show; as the number of shops on the island has increased over the last decade, competition has heated up and operators have begun using larger boats to increase their efficiency. Groups of 15 or 20 are the rule, but some operators will carry more, particularly when cruise ships dock. Some more-experienced divers, unaccustomed to crowded dive sites and stringent safety rules, disparagingly refer to the Caymans as "the Mc-Donald's of dive destinations." The good news is that the diving, from 119 permanent mooring sites off Grand Cayman alone, and with visibility some-times approaching 200 feet, is still among the world's best.

The structure of the Cayman Reef formation is relatively simple. Each of the islands represent the (possibly volcanic) summits of immense mountains which rise thousands of feet from the floor of the Caribbean Sea. Leading out from the shoreline, the first region is a very gentle sloping plane of sand, usually covered in turtle grass, which leads to a fringing reef of elkhorn or staghorn corals. The next section is a moderate incline of alternating chan-nels of patch reef and sand, referred to as a spur-and-groove system, which leads to a steeper drop-off. With the exception of Little Cayman's wall (which starts at only 20 or 30 feet), the sheer escarpment usually begins about 50 or 60 feet below the surface (diving on Cayman Brac and Little Cayman is discussed in more detail below). As a rule, depth approaches a staggering 6000 feet less than a mile off shore, continuing down on the south side of the islands to the Cayman Trench, 24,720 feet below the sur-face—the deepest part of the Caribbean. Divers are kept to a firm depth limit of 110 feet by shops who are members of the Cayman Islands Watersports Operator's Association (CIWOA), which regulates universal safety standards for the plethora of dive shops on the islands.

Four separate walls, named after the compass points, surround Grand Cay-man. The **West Reef** structure stretches along **Seven Mile Beach** and offers the best visibility and access, and some of the most famous dives. Since the ma-jority of dive operators and tourist accommodations are located along this beach, its sites are more heavily trafficked than most of the others on the is-land. The vast **North Sound** is the breeding ground for Grand Cayman, which in turn spills into the Caribbean at low tide, attracting bigger fish to the **North Wall** (on the flip side, the rich effluent can sometimes decrease visibili-ty, however); the diving here is exciting and somewhat more advanced, and summer months draw Caribbean reef and hammerhead sharks to the area for breeding. Sometimes referred to as "the last frontier," the rugged **East End Wall** has some of the island's most pristine, and least-visited dives—56, by

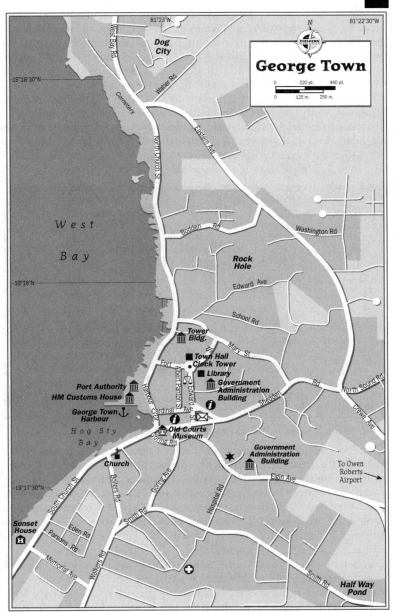

one count—featuring a great concentration of tunnels and caves. The main drawback is that the eastern reef is a solid two-hour boat ride from **West Bay** dive shops, but that's also its attraction. It's also worth noting that winds usually approach the island from the southeast, making the walls on the south and east sides somewhat more weather dependent. Several noteworthy wrecks lie at opposing ends of the island; the ***Ridgefield***, on the eastern tip, offers excellent snorkeling. It's possible to locate good snorkeling locations off almost any beach, but the south end of West Bay provides a number of sites close to shore. Snorkeling the channels which lead through reefs fringing North Sound, along Sand Cay and at Pedro Point is possible, but they should be approached with caution due to unpredictable currents (check around locally before visiting these areas).

The Cayman Islands provide many thrills for divers.

Beside the island's glorious walls, Grand Cayman's most famous site is well-nigh the single most-visited dive location in the Caribbean, perhaps anywhere: **Stingray City**. Even the most jaded divers continue to be seduced by this open-water petting zoo, sometimes referred to as "the world's greatest 12-foot dive." The site is an underwater sandbank that is frequented by a docile group of up to 100 southern Atlantic stingrays who have become accustomed to human interaction (though they are fed, they have yet to negotiate a cut of the huge financial dividend this attraction generates). Every dive shop on Grand Cayman visits Stingray City; most, but not all, tack on a $5 or $10 surcharge above their normal single tank price. They can afford to. The demand for this dive is tremendous and it's not unusual to see a hundred divers or more congregating on the rays at once. Although the interaction provided is not as swooning, you may also snorkel Stingray City, or another sight just east, named **Sandbar**, where the water is generally shoulder-level depth, allowing you to stand and feed the rays.

Cayman Brac—Underwater

Although many residents consider Brac the loveliest of the three Caymans topside, the island's dive sites—which would be rated excellent most anywhere else in the world—are always compared against the glories of Grand and Little Cayman. Yet Cayman Brac's wall, which starts at a depth of 50 to 60 feet, actually offers drama comparable to the better known Bloody Bay Wall. Tunnels and crevices abound throughout many sites, and fine diving is found on both sides of the island. Winter winds from the northwest can sometimes play havoc, but year-round visibility is roughly comparable to the 100+ foot average found on the sister islands. At popular **East Chute**, a small 1986 wreck sits placidly on the sand floor near the lip of the wall and has begun to develop soft corals and sponges on her hull. **Bert Brothers Boulders**, on the less-dived eastern tip of the island, is a spur-and-groove reef structure featuring beautiful swim-throughs and gorges. **Windsock Reef**, off the island's western tip, offers excellent snorkeling among forests of elkhorn and pillar coral, while the nearby barrier reef also provides good snorkeling possibilities.

Little Cayman—Underwater

From the air, an almost insignificant 11-mile strip of sand, Little Cayman anchors what is possibly the single most spectacular wall in the Caribbean. The top of the formation starts at only 20 or 25 feet below the surface on the northern coast of the island, then plunges to a pulse-quickening depth of more than 6000 feet, sometimes at a dead-vertical, or even inverse, angle. The three-mile stretch actually encompasses two areas that are slightly different near the crest; **Bloody Bay Wall**, to the west, is a sheer drop from 20 or 30 feet down, whereas the **Jackson Bay Wall** (on the east) is more typical of the spur-and-groove structure found on Grand Cayman. One unique aspect about Little Cayman is that virtually all sites along the cascading wall are accessible for beginners, weather and depth permitting. Although visibility averages 100 feet year-round, conditions are better from spring through fall, and can secure visibility approaching 200 feet in the placid summer months. Shore diving is possible from a number of points but, with very limited medical services no closer than Cayman Brac, local operators frown on it. The Bloody Bay Wall is also a spectacular setting for snorkelers, with coral heads rising to within 10 feet of the surface at some spots.

As if to literally portray the difference between Grand and Little Cayman diving, the noted animal show here is not a slew of southern stingrays, but a single, graceful manta named Molly who sports a 10-foot wingspan. Molly does not inhabit the Jackson Bay area year-round, but dive shops claim that she puts in an appearance about 95 percent of the time during their summer night dives. Molly is attracted by dive lights—which seduce a rich bounty of plankton for her to feed on—and she swoops, circles and plays with divers in appreciation. The local operators are very protective of Molly, who has been interacting with them since 1991, and she in turn has established a bond, even allowing them to sever nets and ropes she became entangled in on two separate occasions.

Three years ago, very few divers made it to Little Cayman, primarily due to transportation and accommodation considerations. However, airline service has increased and several new resorts have opened with a keen eye toward accommodating dive business. The government has stepped up the conservation effort at the island and limits each shop to a strict maximum of 14 weekly boat trips to the Jackson/Bloody Bay area, with no more than 20 divers on board each boat. So far, a backlash has not occurred, but the potential for disappointed visitors certainly exists. Still, with barely a hundred year-round residents on the substantially uninhabited island, this is a remote dive destination with an extraordinary payoff.

FIELDING'S CHOICE:

Stingray City, the world-famous dive site, in North Sound, is less than an hour's catamaran ride from the Hyatt Regency's dock. The surprise is that you can actually scuba and snorkel with a large family of sting rays, who, years ago, learned to bump a diver's mask so the diver would drop his bag of squid. Those who have done it have been scared out of their minds but have come back glowing.

On Foot

Cayman Islands Governor Michael Gore is an ardent bird-watcher, which has helped ensure protection for the island's 180 species. Some of the better known are the snowy egret, the bananaquit, many species of heron and, of course, the Cayman parrot. There are a series of mosquito control dikes on the peninsula at West Bay which are explored (repellent well in hand) by keen birders and there is a book, *Birds of the Cayman Islands*, available locally for die-hards. Trails on Grand Cayman are limited, but the Ordnance Survey map sold at the Land and Survey Department in George Town details the starts and stops of a number of possibilities. Among them are sporadic paths along the north shore, an area inhabited by the nearly extinct Cayman iguana. There is also an interpretive nature trail, just under a mile long, that tours wetlands, logwood swamp, air plant woodland and a cactus thicket; this trail is located in the **Queen Elizabeth Botanic Park** (admission $3 for adults). A newly restored 200-year-old footpath also explores the woodlands at the heart of Grand Cayman. The two-mile trail can only be done with a wildlife guide, **Albert Hines**, who offers a 2.5-hour tour Monday through Friday at 8:30 a.m. and 3 p.m., Saturdays at 8:30 a.m. only; the price of the excursion is $30 and profits are used to maintain the path *(reservations required:* ☎ *(809) 949-1996).*

Cayman Brac's 180-acre Brac Parrot Reserve is home to 500 rare parrots.

Cayman Brac—On Foot

Brac distinguishes itself among the Caymans by having the most interesting interior landscape. In particular, a limestone bluff (a "brac" in Gaelic) rises to an elevation of about 140 feet—the highest point in the Caymans—and provides the islands' best hike. The 180-acre **Brac Parrot Reserve** is located on the bluff and serves as home to about 500 of the rare birds, a unique subspecies of the Amazon parrot. Also located on the bluff is a series of caves, which are said to have once held pirate treasure. Most vehicular traffic is concentrated along the paved coastal roads, however, a dirt track follows the island's spine (between the north and south coasts) and provides secluded walking potential. Hikers should be on the alert for the maiden plum prevalent around the bluff, which can cause a skin rash if brushed against.

Little Cayman—On Foot

The smallest of the Caymans is a mostly undistinguished flat of sand accented by scrub and mangroves. Just past South Town is the 200-acre **Booby Pond Nature Reserve**, nesting grounds for roughly 3500 mating pairs of red-footed boobies; the island is also home to great blue herons, black-necked stilts and even some magnificent frigatebirds. The truly adventurous can head east along the island's coastline for solitude and exploration, or two simpler paths depart from the airport just outside town; one heads west to the lighthouse, while the other, referred to as **The Nature Trail**, crosses the island to the northwest and leads to **Spot Bay** (allow an hour round-trip for either of these walks).

With a maximum elevation of just 60 feet above sea level, riding on Grand Cayman can hardly be considered difficult, that is, unless you attempt the approximately 55-mile round-trip from George Town to **Rum Point** (and that's utilizing the north-south cut at Old Man Bay; the eastern coast scenery along the Queen's Highway is less appealing). This ride explores a good chunk of the island, including the lovely beaches at Rum Point, and is suitable for good cyclists who are equipped with sufficient water and stamina. Alternatively, you can also take the ferry which travels between the Hyatt and Rum Point; there's no charge for bikes and this reduces the riding to under 30 miles one way. Another area which is nice for cycling lies in the vicinity of Hell and the Turtle Farm; from George Town, a ride to the northern tip and back would come in under 10 miles.

No one in the know comes to the Caymans for its man-made or historic attractions—the islands' lure is their wonderfully translucent water and colorful reefs. Even so, a morning or afternoon spent exploring the capital city of George Town is pleasant and well worth the time. Though town center is dominated by modern office buildings, there are a few historic treasures, including the Grand Caymans National Museum, housed in an 1833 building formerly used as a jail, courthouse and even dance hall. Also worth checking out is the Treasure Museum on West Bay Road, near the Hyatt Regency, which has some good exhibits on shipwrecks and pirate folklore. At the north end of West Bay Beach, a formation of jagged rocks has the dubious name of Hell; stop at the nearby post office and your postcards back home will bear the postmark "Hell, Grand Cayman." On Cayman Brac, the chief on-land activities are birdwatching and spelunking among a half-dozen caves and sinkholes, while birdwatching is good on Little Cayman.

A turtle from the Cayman turtle farm

City Celebrations
Grand Cayman

Pirates' Week ★★

Various locations, Georgetown, ☎ *(809) 949-5078.*

To celebrate its history as a pirate haunt, this island-wide festival, held in late October, brings out the buccaneer in locals. There are costume parades, fishing tournaments, treasure hunts and the ever-popular kidnapping of the governor. Lots of ho-ho-hoing, and more than a few bottles of rum.

Historical Sites
Grand Cayman

Pedro St. James Historic Site

Savannah District, Georgetown.

This National Historic Site, the oldest existing structure on the Caymans, has undergone a three-year, $6.25-million major restoration. Formerly known as Pedro Castle, the building was constructed in 1780 as a great house, and, in 1831, was the meeting site of residents who formed the first democratically elected legislative assembly of the islands—which also held its first meeting here. It was destroyed by fire in 1877. Considered the birthplace of democracy of the Caymans, it is the islands' largest restoration project, with the original house accurately reconstructed, the addition of small Caymanian houses from the 19th century, a visitor center with a multimedia display, restaurant and botanical gardens.

Museums and Exhibits
Cayman Brac

Brac Museum   ★ ★ ★

Stake Bay.
Hours open: 9 a.m.–4 p.m.
This small museum exhibits local antiques and relics from shipwrecks.

Grand Cayman

Cayman Islands National Museum   ★ ★ ★

Harbour Drive, Georgetown, ☎ *(809) 949-8368.*
Hours open: 9 a.m.–5 p.m.
Housed in an 1833 West Indian building on the waterfront—which in previous incarnations was a jail, courthouse and dance hall—this museum exhibits more than 2000 items detailing the history of the islands and its peoples. Students and seniors $2.50. General admission: $5.

Treasure Museum   ★ ★ ★

West Bay Road, Georgetown, ☎ *(809) 947-5033.*
Hours open: 9 a.m.–5 p.m.
This small museum, located in front of the Hyatt Regency, specializes in recovered artifacts from shipwrecks, with lots of pieces from the Maravillas, a Spanish galleon that sank in 1656. Among the exhibits are a seven-pound gold bar, dioramas of the islands' seafaring history and an animated Blackbeard the Pirate, who regales visitors with long-ago tales that may or may not be true. General admission: $5.

Parks and Gardens
Grand Cayman

Queen Elizabeth II Botanic Park

Center island, Georgetown.
Hours open: 7:30 a.m.–5:30 p.m.
This new interpretive woodland trail is less than a mile long, but packs a lot in a relatively small space. The trail passes through more than a dozen Caymanian landscapes, from wetlands to cactus thicket, logwood swamp to woodland and mahogany trees. There's also an iguana habitat partially funded by the World Wildlife Fund that is home to the endangered native blue iguanas, a crocodile swamp with 300-year-old fossil bones and a pond housing small freshwater turtles found only in the Caymans. Birdwatchers may spot Grand Cayman parrots, Northern Flicker woodpeckers, Vitelline warblers, Zenaida doves and Bananaquits. The Botanic Park is the first of several ambitious projects to protect the Caymans' environment, and new additions include a visitor center, lake and Heritage Garden. General admission: $3.

Little Cayman

Booby Pond Nature Reserve

Little Cayman.

The National Trust for the Cayman Islands continues in its quest to protect its natural resources with improvements to this nature reserve, which consists of a saltwater pond and surrounding mangrove habitat that is a natural rookery. Some 3500 nesting pairs of red-footed boobies and 100 pairs of frigatebirds call the reserve home. A new visitor center, built to resemble a Cayman-style house, includes a reference library, observation deck with high-powered telescope and information center. This is the first tract of land on Little Cayman to become owned and protected by the National Trust, which is now working to acquire the remaining 67 acres of privately owned land that surrounds the area.

Tours
Grand Cayman

Atlantic Submarines Cayman ★★

Goring Avenue, Georgetown, ☎ *(809) 949-7700.*
Not for the claustrophobic but memorable for everyone else, this modern submarine seats 46 people in air-conditioned comfort. It travels along the Cayman Wall at depths of up to 90 feet, giving non-divers a taste of the fascinating underwater sights. Night dives are especially recommended. Prices range from $79-$90; half that for kids under 12 (children under 4 are not permitted). Atlantis also operates two research subs that go as deep as 800 feet and carry just two passengers at a time. This trip costs $275 per person; a highlight is the wreck of the cargo ship Kirk Pride.

Cayman Turtle Farm ★★★

West Bay, Georgetown, ☎ *(809) 949-3893.*
Hours open: 8:30 a.m.–5 p.m.
The island's most-visited tourist attraction houses more than 12,000 green turtles, from hatchlings to giant specimens weighing 600 pounds. It's the world's only green sea turtle farm, and while it supplies turtle meat to local restaurants, it also strives to replenish their numbers in the wild. You can taste turtle dishes at the cafe, but skip the gift shop, as U.S. citizens can't import anything made of these endangered critters. Children 6-10 are half price and under 6 are free. General admission: $5.

Sting Ray City ★★

North Sound.
Some two miles off the northwest tip and 12 feet down live several dozen stingrays that await handouts from divers and snorkelers. They are relatively tame, but beware of their stinger tails! One of the Caribbean's most popular dive sites.

Sports

"He Hath Founded It Upon the Seas" is the official motto of the Cayman Islands—but perhaps it should read in the seas, since that's the main reason so many tourists flock to this trio of islands each year. The Caribbean's first dive operation was established on Grand Cayman back in 1957 by Bob Soto; 40 years later, the three have more than 40 dive shops. Snorkeling is also hugely popular, with many good sites right off the beach and some shallow wrecks such as the Cali and Balboa, both off Grand Cayman. Both divers and snorkelers make tracks for Stingray City, where some two dozen "tame" Atlantic Southern Stingrays hang out, awaiting handouts from tourists and allowing themselves to be petted in return. Windsurfing is coming on strong here; it's best along the four miles of reef-protected shallows off East End where prevailing winds from November to March are a hefty 15-25 miles per hour. Deep-sea fishers search for blue marlin, yellowfin tuna, wahoo, dorado (dolphin) and barracuda year-round, and because the ocean floor drops off sharply as close as a quarter-mile offshore, you won't have to travel for hours to hook up. Light tackle and flyfishers angle for bonefish tarpon and permit, but note that fishing for these creatures is catch and release. Little Cayman is the best for such action year round. The annual Million Dollar Month International Fishing Tournament, held each year throughout the month of June, has a top prize of $250,000 for the first angler to break the Caymans' All-Tackle records for yellowfin tuna, wahoo and dolphin. Finally, those who don't want to get wet but do want to see what all the excitement is about can book a ride on the Atlantis Submarine, which drops to 150 feet, or the even more dramatic Research Submersibles sub, which carries just two passengers and descends to depths of up to 800 feet along a wall. If you're worried about claustrophobia, try a semi-submarine or glass-bottom-boat ride instead.

Grand Cayman

Deep-Sea Fishing

Various locations, Georgetown.

Several outfits offer charters and excursions for deep-sea, reef, bone and fly fishers: **Crosby Ebanks** (☎ *[809] 947-4049*), **Capt. Eugene's Watersports** (☎ *[809] 949-3099*); **Charter Boat Headquarters** (☎ *[809] 947-4340*), and **Island Girl** (☎ *[809] 947-3029*). Serious fishermen and women should plan to visit Grand Cayman in June, when the Million Dollar Month fishing tournament is held, featuring international competitors and cash prizes. For details, contact Box 878, West Wind Building, Grand Cayman.

Golf

Two locations, Georgetown.

The island's newest course is the Links at Safehaven (☎ *[809] 947-4155*), a par-71, 6519-yard championship course designed by Roy Case. Duffers can also tee off at Britannia, designed by Jack Nicklaus, which includes a nine-hole regulation course, an 18-hole executive course, and a Cayman course, in which special short-distance balls are used. Green fees are $25-$50; (☎ *809) 949-8020*.

Mastic Trail

Off Frank Sound Road, Georgetown, ☎ *(809) 949-1996.*

This newly restored 200-year-old footpath winds through a 2 million-year-old woodland in the heart of the island. Just reopened in 1995, the trail is located west of Frank Sound Road, a 45-minute drive east from George Town. The two-mile trail showcases the Mastic Reserve's scenic wonders, including a mangrove swamp, ancient woodland area and traditional farms. Birders should be on the lookout for the Grand Cayman parrot, Caribbean dove, West Indian woodpecker, Cuban bullfinch, smooth-billed Ani and Bananaquit. The new nonprofit reserve now numbers 200 acres, with the plan of adding 800 more acres as funds become available. Guided tours, which are not recommended to children under 6, the elderly and the infirm, last 2.5 hours and are limited to eight people, so reservations are essential. They are available Monday through Friday at 8:30 a.m. and 3 p.m. and on Saturdays at 8:30 a.m. General admission: $30.

Scuba Diving

Various locations, Cayman Islands.

Chances are excellent that your hotel will have its own dive center, or check out one of the following: Grand Cayman: **Dive Cayman BVI** *(☎ [809] 947-5133)*, **Parrot's Landing** *(☎ [800] 448-0428* or *[809] 949-7884)*, **Quabbin Dives** *(☎ [800] 238-6712* or *[809] 949-5597)*, **Sunset Divers** *(☎ [809] 949-7111)*, **Bob Soto's** *(☎ [809] 947-4631)*, **Don Foster's** *(☎ [809] 949-5679)* and **Red Sail Sports** *(☎ [809] 949-8745)*. Cayman Brac: **Divi Tiara** *(☎ [809] 948-1316)* and **Brac Aquatics** *(☎ [809] 858-7429)*. Little Cayman: **Southern Cross Club** *(☎ [809] 948-1099)*. Prices are generally about $40 for a single-tank dive; $55 for two tanks.

Windsurfing

Various locations, Georgetown.

Chances are good your hotel can set you up for windsurfing, but if it lacks facilities, try **Cayman Windsurf** *(☎ [809] 947-7492)* or **Sailboards Caribbean** *(☎ [809] 949-1068)*.

Where to Stay

Fielding's Highest Rated Hotels in Cayman Islands

★★★★	Beach Club Hotel	$125–$265
★★★★	Clarion Grand Pavilion	$155–$455
★★★★	Hyatt Regency Grand Cayman	$180–$500
★★★★	Little Cayman Beach	$230–$886
★★★★	Radisson Resort	$165–$390
★★★★	Spanish Bay Reef North Wall	$160–$218
★★★★	Treasure Island Resort	$160–$275
★★★★	West Indian Club	$130–$365
★★★	Caribbean Club	$160–$425
★★★	London House	$235–$750

Fielding's Most Exclusive Hotels in Cayman Islands

★★★★	Little Cayman Beach	$230–$886
★★★	London House	$235–$750
★★★	Conch Club	$300–$400
★	Brac Reef Cayman Beach Resort	$193–$458
★★★★	Clarion Grand Pavilion	$155–$455

Fielding's Best Value Hotels in Cayman Islands

★★	Sleep Inn	$90–$185
★★★	Island Hill Resort	$60–$80
★★★	Ambassadors Inn	$60–$80
★★	Seaview Hotel	$65–$105
★★★★	Spanish Bay Reef North Wall	$160–$218

Many of Grand Cayman's lodging choices are along Seven Mile Beach, a glorious strand that's considered one of the Caribbean's best. West Bay is also a good spot for a home away from home as it is within an easy walk to shops and restaurants. About half of the island's accommodations are found in condominium units for do-it-yourselfers; note, however, that food prices in the markets can be quite high. Late 1995 saw the opening of the new Westin Casuarina Resort, a $50 million property that helps fill the need for upscale lodging.

Hotels and Resorts

The big chain hotels, including **Holiday Inn**, **Radisson** and **Ramada**, give good service here and particularly lean toward providing package tours, some specifically for divers. The **Hyatt Regency**, luxurious and lushly landscaped, is known for being the hub of lively social activities, especially at night. (Hyatt's private villas come with their own pool, Jacuzzi and cabaña.) The **Spanish Bay Reef**, the first all-inclusive property on Grand Cayman, rates as the island's most secluded—a true dive hotel. **Pirates Point Resort** is run by a Cordon-Bleu educated-chef. The Beach Club Colony should be avoided if you don't care for your personal beach space to be invaded by loads of cruise passengers.

Cayman Brac

Brac Reef Cayman Beach Resort $193–$458 ★

West End Point, West End Point, ☎ *(800) 327-3835, (809) 948-7323. FAX (813) 323-8827.*

Single: $193–$379. Double: $386–$458.

Divers like this casual hotel and its all-inclusive package rates that include all drinks, transportation from the airport and three buffet meals daily. Dive packages are available at additional cost. The rooms are basic but at least air cooled, and recent renovations have added decks or patios as well as new carpeting and wallpaper. There's a pool and tennis court to keep nondivers occupied. 40 rooms. Credit cards: A, MC, V.

Divi Tiara Beach Resort $95–$200 ★★

West End Point, West End Point, ☎ *(800) 948-1553, (809) 948-7553. FAX (809) 948-1316.*

Single: $95–$185. Double: $100–$200.

Set on a fine beach, this pleasant hotel appeals to those who want to avoid crowds. Rooms are typical but do offer air conditioning and were recently redone; a few have Jacuzzis to boot. There's a pool and tennis court, and most meals are served buffet-style. Good service. The dive center is excellent. 58 rooms. Credit cards: A, D, MC, V.

Grand Cayman

Beach Club Hotel $125–$265 ★★★★

Seven Mile Beach, Georgetown, ☎ *(800) 223-6510, (809) 949-8100. FAX (809) 947-5167.*

Single: $125–$240. Double: $125–$265.

Dating back to the 1960s (making it one of the island's oldest resorts), the Beach Club resembles a colonial plantation villa. Accommodations are strung along the beach and include standard and unexciting guest rooms and villas. Watersports cost extra, and there's a great dive shop on-site. Lots of cruise passengers converge here when their ship is in port, so don't expect tranquility. 41 rooms. Credit cards: A, DC, MC, V.

Clarion Grand Pavilion $155–$455   ★★★★

West Bay Road, Georgetown, ☎ (809) 947-5656.
Single: $155–$455. Double: $155–$455.
This spot was reopened in February 1994 by new Cayman owners after extensive refurbishing. Accommodations are tasteful and well-appointed, and all have central air and such extras as coffeemakers, minibars, a trouser press (do you really need creases in the Caribbean?) and hair dryers. The pool is found in a lovely garden courtyard complete with lush foliage and a cascading waterfall. Other facilities include a fitness center, tennis courts, a 24-hour business center and nearby watersports. Parents can stash the kids in supervised programs year-round. 90 rooms. Credit cards: A, DC, D, MC, V.

Holiday Inn Grand Cayman $238–$832   ★★★

Seven Mile Beach, Georgetown, ☎ (800) 465-4329, (809) 947-4444. FAX (809) 947-4213.
Single: $238–$298. Double: $238–$832.
Lots of action at this busy and pleasant hotel. Guest rooms are air-conditioned and nicely done, though only some boast views. There's a full dive shop, twice-weekly barbecues by the great pool and all sorts of watersports for rent (though prices are a tad high). One of the hotel's best assets is its picturesque location on Seven Mile Beach. It's not too close to the cruise ship port, so guests are not overrun with day-trippers. Not a lot of island flavor—this is, after all, a Holiday Inn—but the lodgings are dependable and the two restaurants, two bars and a comedy club keep the doldrums away. Current renovations are spiffing up all guest rooms and adding an exercise room and Jacuzzi. 212 rooms. Credit cards: A, DC, MC, V.

Hyatt Regency Grand Cayman $180–$500   ★★★★

Seven Mile Beach, Georgetown, ☎ (800) 233-1234, (809) 949-1234. FAX (809) 949-1234.
Single: $180–$400. Double: $225–$500.
This is a world-class resort all the way, and definitely Grand Cayman's finest resort. Accommodations are in British Colonial-style buildings surrounding a central courtyard, and are simply fabulous, with expensive furnishings, original art, air conditioning (of course) and Italian marble baths. Landscaping is lush, and guests can choose from four pools, four tennis courts, a dive shop, all watersports and 18 holes of golf designed by Jack Nicklaus. Lots of bars and lounges, including one seen in *The Firm*. Elegant! 236 rooms. Credit cards: A, MC, V.

Radisson Resort $165–$390   ★★★★

Seven Mile Beach, Georgetown, ☎ (800) 333-3333, (809) 949-0088. FAX (809) 949-0288.
Single: $165–$240. Double: $165–$390.
Set on a scenic spread of beach, the Radisson is a five-story hotel with comfortable and contemporary guest rooms. A very nice deck houses a pool, bar and Jacuzzi set among potted plants. All the usual watersports, plus a dive shop and health club,

keep guests busy, and the disco hops once the sun goes down. A truly pleasant spot, with lots of elegant touches. 315 rooms. Credit cards: A, DC, MC, V.

Sleep Inn $90–$185 ★★

Seven Mile Beach, Georgetown, ☎ *(800) 627-5337, (809) 949-9111. FAX (809) 949-6699.*
Single: $90–$185. Double: $997.
This modern hotel, set right on the beach, has air-conditioned guest rooms with all the typical amenities. Eight suites have kitchenettes. The grounds are basic, with just a pool and Jacuzzi for recreation, but watersports can be found nearby. 116 rooms. Credit cards: A, CB, DC, D, MC, V.

Spanish Bay Reef North Wall $160–$218 ★★★★

West Bay Road, Georgetown, ☎ *(800) 223-6510, (809) 949-3765. FAX (809) 949-1842.*
Single: $160–$218. Double: $160–$218.
Situated on a private coral reef on the island's isolated northwest tip, this all-inclusive resort houses guests in air-conditioned rooms with Caribbean decor. Popular with divers, it offers good facilities for scuba, as well as other watersports and the typical resort pool. The rates include all meals and activities. The atmosphere is nicely casual, but service is not always up to par. 50 rooms. Credit cards: A, DC, D, MC, V.

Sunset House $90–$190 ★★

South of GeorgeTown, Georgetown, ☎ *(800) 854-4767, (809) 949-7111. FAX (809) 949-7101.*
Single: $90–$185. Double: $95–$190.
Great diving and snorkeling right offshore, but there's no beach to speak of at this casual hotel that dates back to the late 1950s. Accommodations are in standard guest rooms and two efficiencies; all are nicely done and air-cooled. Two pools help make up for the lack of beach, and there's a full-service dive shop, with a fleet of six boats, on-site. A really nice spot. 59 rooms. Credit cards: A, D, MC, V.

Treasure Island Resort $160–$275 ★★★★

Seven Mile Beach, Georgetown, ☎ *(800) 327-8777, (809) 949-7777. FAX (809) 949-8489.*
Single: $160–$195. Double: $160–$275.
One of the island's largest resorts, this former Ramada fronts the beach and situates its guest rooms around a courtyard with two pools, a Jacuzzi and a gurgling waterfall. Accommodations are larger than usual and nicely done with minibars and sitting areas. There's live music in the nightclub six nights a week, and by day lots to keep busy with, including two tennis courts, a dive shop and all watersports. A good choice for those who like a lot of action. 280 rooms. Credit cards: A, MC, V.

Westin Casuarina Resort $185–$375 ★★

Seven Mile Beach, Grand Cayman, ☎ *(800) 228-3000, (809) 945-3800.*
Single: $185–$375. Double: $185–$375.
The new $50-million Westin is the largest resort in the Cayman Islands. The eight-acre beachfront property was originally conceived as a Marriott. Facilities include a dive shop, tennis courts, two freshwater pools, two whirlpools, a swim-up bar and fitness center. The spacious guestrooms are done up in Caribbean style and feature

oversized bathrooms with hair dryers and French doors opening onto balconies. The Links at Save Haven are close by for duffers. 343 rooms. Credit cards: A, MC, V.

Little Cayman

Little Cayman Beach   **$230–$886**   ★ ★ ★ ★

Blossom Village, Crawl Bay, ☎ (800) 327-3835, (809) 948-1033. FAX (809) 948-1040.
Single: $230–$443. Double: $460–$886.
This newer resort, opened in 1993, has a nice sandy beach off a reef-protected bay. Air-conditioned guest rooms are a cut above the competition on the island and attractively furnished. Guests keep busy diving (they have an excellent shop), hanging out by the pool, riding bikes, or playing pickup volleyball games. The bar and restaurant are good and popular with locals. Guests can choose from a variety of packages that include all meals and diving. 40 rooms. Credit cards: A, MC, V.

Southern Cross Club   **$125–$285**   ★ ★

Crawl Bay, ☎ (800) 899-2582, (809) 948-3255.
Single: $125–$185. Double: $215–$285.
This 1950s cottage resort sits on a pretty beach. Rooms are basic and rely on ceiling fans to keep things cool. The rates include three family-style meals a day and watersports. Most who come are into deep-sea fishing, with the hotel arranging excursions. The bar attracts lots of tale-swapping fishermen and women. 10 rooms. Credit cards: not accepted.

Apartments and Condominiums

Lots of visitors who come to the Caymans come for rough and rugged adventure underwater, so they're used to taking care of themselves. More and more self-catering accommodations are appearing every year. The downside is that if you plan to cook for yourself, food costs are extremely high; this year at least the markets seemed to be getting better stocked. Amid the action on Seven Mile Beach, a short walk from restaurants and a supermarket, are **Pan Cayman** in the Caribbean Club; here you'll find a better beach and a lot more peace and quiet. Golfers congregate in the **Britannia Villas**, which is part of the Hyatt complex, at the golf course. The **Indies Suites** are a good bargain for travelers who spend most of their time underwater and shut their eyes the minute their head hits the pillow (one plus is the free breakfast).

Grand Cayman

Beachcomber Condos   **$190–$395**   ★

Seven Mile Beach, Georgetown, ☎ (800) 327-8777, (809) 947-4470. FAX (809) 947-5019.
Single: $190–$395. Double: $190–$395.
This condo complex has two-bedroom, two-bath units with air conditioning, fully equipped kitchens and a balcony or patio with ocean views. Several units have dens that can convert into a third bedroom if needed. There's a pool on-site, and maid service is available, but you'll have to dine elsewhere. 19 rooms. Credit cards: MC, V.

Caribbean Club   **$160–$425**   ★ ★ ★

Seven Mile Beach, P.O. Box 30499, Georgetown, ☎ (800) 327-8777, (809) 947-4099. FAX (809) 947-4443.

Single: $160–$280. Double: $160–$425.

This colony of villas includes one- and two-bedroom units (only six are actually on the beach) in a secluded atmosphere. The pink cottages are air-conditioned and include large living/dining areas, full kitchens and attractive, comfortable decor. The restaurant is popular with visitors as well as locals. There's a tennis court, but no pool. No kids under 11 during the winter season. 18 rooms. Credit cards: A, MC, V.

Cayman Kai Resort   **$140–$220**   ★★

North Side, East of Rum Plantation, Georgetown, ☎ *(800) 223-5427, (809) 947-9055. FAX (809) 947-9102.*
Single: $140–$215. Double: $150–$220.

Situated in a 20-acre grove along the secluded north shore beach, this secluded resort houses guests in one- and two-bedroom lodges and villas, all with kitchens but only some with air conditioning. The beach is not great for swimming, but the snorkeling is great. The property caters primarily to divers, but is a bit more formal than the island's other dive resorts. A restaurant, bar and three tennis courts keep nondivers occupied. 20 rooms. Credit cards: A, MC, V.

Christopher Columbus Apts   **$190–$390**   ★★

Seven Mile Beach, Georgetown, ☎ *(809) 947-4354. FAX (809) 947-5062.*
Single: $190–$390. Double: $190–$390.

Popular with families, this condominium resort offers individually decorated two-bedroom, two-bath units with air conditioning, small but complete kitchens and light, tropical furnishings. As expected, the penthouse units are by far the nicest (and most expensive). No restaurant or bar, so guests congregate at the pool, tennis courts and sandy beach. 28 rooms. Credit cards: A, MC, V.

Colonial Club   **$230–$500**   ★

West Bay Road, West Side, Georgetown, ☎ *(809) 947-4660. FAX (809) 947-4839.*
Single: $230–$455. Double: $255–$500.

Built in the Bermudian style with a pink and white exterior, this condo complex has comfortable two- and three-bedroom units with central air, complete kitchens and maid service. Located on an especially nice stretch of beach, extras include a pool and lighted tennis court. No restaurant on-site, so you'll have to cook in or venture out. 15 rooms. Credit cards: A, MC, V.

Discovery Point Club   **$145–$315**   ★★

Seven Mile Road, Georgetown, ☎ *(809) 947-4724. FAX (809) 947-5051.*
Single: $145–$285. Double: $145–$315.

Located on Seven Mile Beach, this well-appointed resort offers one- and two-bedroom condos with all the modern conveniences, including air and full kitchens. There are also studios sans cooking facilities. A pretty pool and two tennis courts are on-site, but no restaurant or bar. 45 rooms. Credit cards: A, MC, V.

George Town Villas   **$165–$420**   ★

Seven Mile Beach, Georgetown, ☎ *(809) 949-5172. FAX (809) 947-0256.*
Single: $165–$405. Double: $165–$420.

A condominium community with two-bedroom units that come equipped with two baths, full kitchens, air conditioning, living and dining areas and washer/dryers.

There's a pool and tennis court, and shopping and restaurants are nearby. 54 rooms. Credit cards: A, MC, V.

Grand Bay Club $120–$310   ★ ★ ★

Seven Mile Beach, Georgetown, ☎ *(809) 947-4728. FAX (809) 947-5681.*
Single: $120–$195. Double: $120–$310.

All units at this modern complex are suites, ranging from studios that lack kitchens to one- and two-bedroom units with cooking facilities. Maids keep things tidy. The site includes a large pool, Jacuzzi and tennis. No restaurant, but there are many within a walk. 21 rooms. Credit cards: A, MC, V.

Grapetree/Cocoplum Condos $135–$280   ★ ★

Georgetown ☎ *(800) 635-4824, (809) 949-5640.*
Single: $135–$280. Double: $135–$280.

Situated in a secluded area of Seven Mile Beach—though the beach here is not the greatest—this condo complex includes one- to three-bedroom units with all the usual amenities, as well as daily maid service. Watersports are available nearby, and the grounds include a tennis court and two pools. No restaurant, though. 50 rooms. Credit cards: A, MC, V.

Harbour Heights $190–$295   ★ ★ ★

Seven Mile Beach, Georgetown, ☎ *(800) 327-8777, (809) 947-4295. FAX (809) 947-4522.*
Single: $190–$280. Double: $190–$295.

This three-story condominium overlooks the pool and seafront along Seven Mile Beach. Two-bedroom suites are attractive, with living/dining areas, complete kitchens, air conditioning and balconies. The grounds are nicely landscaped, and the beach is good for swimmers. Restaurants are nearby. 46 rooms. Credit cards: not accepted. Credit cards: A, MC, V.

Indies Suites $160–$305   ★ ★ ★

West Bay Road, Georgetown, ☎ *(800) 654-3130, (809) 947-5025. FAX (809) 947-5024.*
Single: $160–$305. Double: $160–$305.

This very comfortable and attractive hotel houses guests in nicely furnished one- and two-bedroom suites with full-size kitchens, satellite TV, telephones and a private balcony or patio. Kids under 12 stay free with their parents. Facilities include a large pool and Jacuzzi and a dive shop. There's no restaurant, but guests can grab snacks at the pool bar, and the daily complimentary continental breakfast is a nice touch. The beach is across the street, a liability when so many similar properties lie directly on the sand. Nevertheless, this is a good choice. 40 rooms. Credit cards: A, MC, V.

Island Pine Villas $110–$225   ★

Seven Mile Beach, Georgetown, ☎ *(800) 223-9815, (809) 949-6586. FAX (809) 949-0428.*
Single: $110–$220. Double: $110–$225.

This two-story condo complex is within walking distance of shops and restaurants. Units are quite comfortable, with one or two bedrooms, air conditioning, kitchenettes and patios or balconies. No pool or restaurant, but a good value nonetheless. 40 rooms. Credit cards: A, DC, D, MC, V.

Lacovia Condominiums **$200–$285** ★★★

Seven Mile Beach, Georgetown, ☎ *(800) 223-9815, (809) 949-7599. FAX (809) 949-0172.*
Single: $200–$285. Double: $200–$285.
Stylish and tasteful, this condo complex surrounds a free-form pool and clubhouse with sauna and games. Units have one to three bedrooms with separate living/dining areas, full kitchens and Spanish-style balconies; most also boast oversized tubs. Maids tidy up daily. The grounds include nice landscaping, and there's a tennis court for working up a sweat. 45 rooms. Credit cards: A.

London House **$235–$750** ★★★

West Bay Beach, Georgetown, ☎ *(800) 423-4095, (809) 947-4060. FAX (809) 947-4087.*
Single: $235–$290. Double: $235–$750.
This mission-style complex has well-maintained accommodations and a pool, watersports and maid service to round out the picture. Units have one or two bedrooms and kitchenettes. Ceiling fans supplement the air conditioning. The beach is nice and quiet, happily not frequented by cruise ship passengers. 21 rooms. Credit cards: A, MC, V.

Morrit's Tortuga Club **$145–$440** ★★★

East End, Georgetown, ☎ *(800) 447-0309, (809) 947-7449. FAX (809) 947-7669.*
Single: $145–$380. Double: $130–$440.
This plantation-style condo complex is situated on eight beachfront acres near some of Grand Cayman's best diving sites. Three-story buildings house comfortable one- and two-bedroom units with full kitchens. Built on the site of the former Tortuga Club, today's resort is a far cry from that hideaway spot, but it remains popular with divers. In addition to a pool, there's a decent restaurant and both windsurfing and diving schools. 85 rooms. Credit cards: A, D, MC, V.

Pan-Cayman House **$150–$370** ★★★

Seven Mile Beach, Georgetown, ☎ *(800) 248-5115, (809) 947-4002. FAX (809) 947-4002.*
Single: $150–$370. Double: $150–$370.
A popular apartment complex with 10 units ranging from two to three bedrooms, all with two baths, air conditioning, full kitchens and maid service. Great views from the private balconies or patios. 10 rooms. Credit cards: MC, V.

Plantana **$180–$425** ★★

Seven Mile Beach, Georgetown, ☎ *(809) 947-4430. FAX (809) 947-5076.*
Single: $180–$425. Double: $180–$425.
One- and two-bedroom condominiums are arranged on three floors, with the ones higher up offering the best views. All are individually decorated and have full kitchens and screened balconies or patios; most also have washer/dryers. A pool supplements the sea for splashing about. One of the nicer condo complexes on the island. 49 rooms. Credit cards: A, MC, V.

Plantation Village Resort **$145–$405** ★

Seven Mile Beach, Georgetown, ☎ *(800) 822-8903, (809) 949-4199. FAX (809) 949-0646.*

Single: $145–$405. Double: $145–$405.

Set on four acres of Seven Mile Beach, this condo complex has individually decorated two- and three-bedroom units with two baths, complete kitchens, central air and screened lanais. Maids pick up daily. There are two pools, a Jacuzzi, a tennis court and a playground for the kids. Lots of families here. 70 rooms. Credit cards: A, MC, V.

Silver Sands $200–$235 ★★

West Bay Road, Seven Mile Beach, Georgetown, ☎ (800) 327-8777, (809) 949-3343. FAX (809) 949-1223.
Single: $200–$235. Double: $200–$235.

Set amid tropical gardens, this casual complex has air-conditioned two-bedroom units with all the modern amenities. There's a nice resort feel to this place with its extra-large pool, gazebo, two tennis courts and nearby watersports. 42 rooms. Credit cards: A, MC, V.

Tarquynn Manor $143–$395 ★★

Seven Mile Beach, Georgetown, ☎ (800) 223-9815, (809) 947-5060. FAX (809) 947-5060.
Single: $143–$395. Double: $230–$395.

At least one bedroom in these two- or three-bedroom units fronts the beach. The modern units have air conditioning, kitchens and patios or balconies. A concierge handles special requests. There's an outdoor pool and games room to keep kids occupied. 20 rooms. Credit cards: MC, V.

Victoria House $165–$395 ★★

Seven Mile Beach, Georgetown, ☎ (800) 327-8777, (809) 947-4233. FAX (809) 947-5320.
Single: $165–$380. Double: $175–$395.

These Caribbean-style apartments front the ocean and are far from the madding tourist crowds. Units are air-conditioned and come in a variety of configurations, from studios to penthouses. All are comfortable with tropical styling and have full kitchens. There's no pool on-site, but watersports are available nearby, and there is one tennis court. Sea turtles frequent the quiet beach in the mornings. 26 rooms. Credit cards: A, MC, V.

Villas Pappagallo $160–$284 ★★

Seven Mile Beach, Georgetown, ☎ (800) 232-1034, (809) 949-8098. FAX (809) 947-7054.
Single: $160–$284. Double: $180–$284.

Located on a private, secluded beach on the northwest shore, this complex consists of Mediterranean-style villas, all with air conditioning, kitchenettes and balconies. Lots to do here, including two tennis courts, a pool and noshing at the Italian restaurant. You'll have to travel a half-mile for watersports. 40 rooms. Credit cards: A, MC, V.

Villas of the Galleon $200–$430 ★★

West Bay Beach, Georgetown, ☎ (809) 947-4433.
Single: $200–$430. Double: $200–$430.

Facing a private beach, this condo complex offers units with one or two bedrooms, all with air conditioning, modern kitchen, small baths and balconies; maids tidy up daily but take Sundays off. Most folks here are staying for a long time. Request an upper floor unit for the best sea views. 75 rooms. Credit cards: A, MC, V.

West Indian Club   **$130–$365**   ★★★★
West Bay Beach, Georgetown, ☎ *(809) 947-5255.*
Single: $130–$365. Double: $130–$365.
These two-story beachfront apartments are situated near the center of famed Seven Mile Beach. The well-appointed one- and two-bedroom units have full kitchens, terraces and air conditioning only in the bedrooms. A maid keeps things looking fresh, and you can hire a cook for a custom-made meal. 6 rooms. Credit cards: A, MC, V.

Little Cayman

Conch Club   **$300–$400**   ★★
Blossom Village, Little Cayman, ☎ *(813) 323-8727. FAX (813) 323-8827.*
Single: $300–$400. Double: $300–$400.
This new luxury townhouses are rented out when the owners are off-island. Accommodations consist of two- and three-bedroom oceanfront units, each with a patio downstairs and a balcony up above, fully equipped kitchen and spacious living and dining areas. There's a dock, pool and Jacuzzi on site, and meals can be taken at the nearby Bird of Paradise restaurant at the Little Cayman Beach Resort, which also has a full-service dive shop. Credit cards: A, MC, V.

Inns

These are basically scuba-devoted inns, low on luxury, but high on congeniality. Seaview hotels attracts a very young crowd.

Grand Cayman

Island Hill Resort   **$60–$80**   ★★★
Church Street, West Bay, Grand Cayman, ☎ *(809) 949-4242. FAX (809) 949-3347.*
Single: $60–$80. Double: $60–$80.
Discover the real Caymans at this friendly, intimate inn near Seven Mile Beach. The large guest rooms are air-conditioned and come with welcome extras such as hammocks and portable ice chests to take to the beach. Locals hang at the open-air bar, and there's live reggae music each Wednesday, Friday and Saturday night. The food's good, too. 10 rooms.

Seaview Hotel   **$65–$105**   ★★
Near GeorgeTown, Georgetown, ☎ *(809) 949-8804. FAX (809) 949-8507.*
Single: $65–$105. Double: $65–$105.
Opened in 1952, this is the oldest operating hotel on the island. Rooms are air-conditioned and have private baths. Guests can splash in the outdoor pool or head for the beach, where a dive center and watersports are offered. The piano lounge is a pleasant spot by night. 15 rooms. Credit cards: A, D, MC, V.

Little Cayman

Pirates Point Resort   **$185–$150**   ★
Pirates Point, Crawl Bay, ☎ *(809) 948-1010. FAX (809) 948-1011.*
Single: $185–$200. Double: $135–$150.

Most accommodations at this pleasant inn are in air-conditioned rooms with private baths; there are also four cottages overlooking the sea. The best reason to come, however, is mealtime: owner Gladys Howard is a graduate of Paris' Cordon Bleu, and judging from the food, she passed with flying colors. The rates include meals, and dive packages are also available. A friendly, peaceful spot. No kids under five. 10 rooms. Credit cards: MC, V.

Sam McCoy's Lodge $105–$185   ★★

Crawl Bay, ☎ *(800) 626-0496, (809) 948-4526.*

Single: $105–$185. Double: $105–$185.

Only some rooms at this very informal spot have their own bath. The food's great, though, with casual meals taken with Sam, his family and fellow guests. The rates include three squares a day and transportation to and from the airport. 6 rooms. Credit cards: not accepted.

Low Cost Lodging

One way to save money in the Caymans is to cram a lot of people into a multi-bedroom apartment. But individuals can find single rooms for rent in guest houses (don't hesitate to ask the tourist board). The nightclub keeps things hopping at **Windjammer Hotel**, where rooms are also air-conditioned and come with kitchenettes. Diving is the main topic of conversation at these lodgings, especially at the **Ambassadors Inn**, which attracts the diehards.

Grand Cayman

Ambassadors Inn $60–$80   ★★★

South Church Street, Georgetown, ☎ *(800) 648-7748, (809) 949-7577. FAX (809) 949-7050.*

Single: $60–$70. Double: $70–$80.

Located a mile from George Town and some 200 yards and across the street from the beach, this casual spot appeals to divers on a budget. Rooms are basic but do offer air conditioning and private baths. There's a pool on site. 18 rooms. Credit cards: A, MC, V.

Windjammer Hotel $100–$155   ★

West Bay Road, Georgetown, ☎ *(809) 947-4608. FAX (809) 947-4391.*

Single: $100–$155. Double: $100–$155.

Located at the Cayman Falls Shopping Plaza, across from Seven Mile Beach, this small hotel offers air-conditioned rooms with kitchenettes. There are two restaurants, a bar and a nightclub, and this place does a good after-dark trade. 12 rooms. Credit cards: A, MC, V.

Where to Eat

★★★★★	Fielding's Highest Rated Restaurants in Cayman Islands	
★★★★★	Hemingway's	$17–$23
★★★★★	Lantana's	$20–$34
★★★★★	Ottmar's Restaurant	$12–$25
★★★	Crow's Nest	$12–$19

	Fielding's Most Exclusive Restaurants in Cayman Islands	
★★★★★	Lantana's	$20–$34
★★★★★	Hemingway's	$17–$23
★★★★★	Ottmar's Restaurant	$12–$25
★★★	Crow's Nest	$12–$19

	Fielding's Best Value Restaurants in Cayman Islands	
★★★★★	Ottmar's Restaurant	$12–$25
★★★★★	Hemingway's	$17–$23
★★★	Crow's Nest	$12–$19
★★★★★	Lantana's	$20–$34
★★	Hog Sty Bay Cafe	$12–$19

Not surprisingly, seafood is a staple in a Cayman diet; nearly everything else is imported and, as a result, food prices can be quite high—though portions are generally generous. Turtle is a local specialty—they are specially bred to be eaten—and lobster is especially good from August through January. Hemingway's, at the Hyatt Regency, is considered the best place for seafood and turtle steak, while Benjamin's Roof, off West Bay Road, is known for the blackened alligator tail that lures those who must try everything at least once. If you're hankering for good old American food, try the Hog Sty Bay Cafe, a casual American-English style pub. Restaurants are limited on Cayman Brac and Little Cayman—it's the diving that attracts tourists, not the cuisine.

Cayman Brac

Edd's Place   **$$$**   ★ ★

West End, West End Point, ☎ (809) 948-1208.
Asian cuisine.
Lunch: 7 a.m.–4 p.m., entrées $6–$15.
Dinner: 4–11 p.m., entrées $10–$25.

A nice change from resort cookery on Cayman Brac is this restaurant and bar that's open early for breakfast and later on serves Chinese food and local favorites. If you phone the management, they'll arrange to pick you up, as there is no bus service, and taxis are expensive. Reservations recommended. Credit cards: MC, V.

Grand Cayman

Almond Tree, The   **$$$**   ★ ★

North Church Street, Georgetown, ☎ (809) 949-2893.
Seafood cuisine. Specialties: Callaloo, conch, turtle steak.
Dinner: 5:30–10 p.m., entrées $14–$22. Closed: Tue.

An informal and reliable restaurant located just north of George Town, the Almond Tree is a good place to try turtle steak, which is unavailable stateside. More sensitive diners will find all types of seafood, including conch, lobster, filets and a popular all-you-can-eat main course extravaganza for under $15 on Wednesdays and Fridays. It's lit up dramatically at night with tiki torches. Reservations recommended. Credit cards: A, MC, V.

Benjamin's Roof   **$$$**   ★

Coconut Place, Georgetown, ☎ (809) 947-4080.
International cuisine. Specialties: Lobster bisque, Cajun shrimp.
Dinner: 3–10 p.m., entrées $12–$30.

Greenery abounds in this cool spot in the Coconut Place retail center with a bar dispensing strong libations, a pianist in the corner and spicy blackened-Cajun style fish and seafood, with barbecued ribs, lamb and pastas to round out the menu. Desserts are also notable for their richness. Reservations required. Credit cards: A, MC, V.

Corita's Copper Kettle II   **$$**   ★ ★

Eastern Avenue, Georgetown, ☎ (809) 949-5475.
Latin American cuisine. Specialties: Conch, callaloo.
Lunch: entrées $10–$15.

Busy office workers grab a Jamaican-style breakfast and come back for lunch at this spic-and-span diner located in George Town. Simple, island-style fare includes conch and lobster burgers and local spinach soup. Hot peppers are sprinkled liberally here and there, so beware. Credit cards: A, MC, V.

Cracked Conch   **$$$**   ★ ★

Selkirk's Street Plaza, Georgetown, ☎ (809) 947-5217.
Seafood cuisine. Specialties: Cracked conch, conch fritters, key lime pie.
Lunch: 11:30 a.m.–3 p.m., entrées $6–$15.
Dinner: 6–10 p.m., entrées $10–$25.

Not a place for intimate conversation, the noisy Cracked Conch serves lots of seafood in dim, rather stark surroundings. But the food, especially conch, served lightly fried, is smashing. Burgers, soups and other fast meals are also available, and all meals are prepared for take-out. Reservations recommended. Credit cards: A, MC, V.

Crow's Nest $$$ ★★★

South Sound, Georgetown, ☎ *(809) 949-9366.*
Latin American cuisine. Specialties: Lobster, conch.
Lunch: 11:30 a.m.–2 p.m., entrées $5–$8.
Dinner: 5:30–10 p.m., entrées $12–$19.
Romance is in the air at this exquisite little eatery on the south point of the island, where diners eat with the ocean waves lapping behind them. Wonderful for a star-filled evening meal or view lunch, the Crow's Nest offers tasty, usually spicy dishes including chicken with hot pepper sauce, coconut fried shrimp and key lime pie. It's hard to believe that George Town is only four miles away. Reservations required. Credit cards: A, MC, V.

Garden Loggia Cafe $$$ ★★

West Bay Road, Georgetown, ☎ *(809) 949-1234. Associated hotel: Hyatt Regency.*
International cuisine. Specialties: Roast suckling pig, lobster.
Lunch: entrées $9–$16.
Dinner: entrées $16–$34.
This top-rated indoor-outdoor cafe facing an elegant expanse of greenery is noted for Sunday buffets replete with champagne and roast suckling pig, and a Friday night all-you-can-eat seafood spread. Otherwise, the bill of fare usually includes jerk chicken and seafood. Reservations required. Credit cards: A, MC, V.

Grand Old House $$$ ★★

Petra Plantation, Georgetown, ☎ *(809) 949-9333.*
International cuisine. Specialties: Grouper.
Lunch: 11:45 a.m.–2:30 p.m., entrées $13–$32.
Dinner: 6–10:30 p.m., entrées $20–$34. Closed: Sun.
This lovely gingerbread house in George Town is owned by jolly, red-cheeked TV celebrity Chef Tell Erhardt, who also labors in the kitchen. Cuisine is savory and often deep-fried, but good for a splurge. Erhardt uses herbs, curries and sauces liberally, but with a sure hand, as befits the island's number-one caterer. German specialties are also offered from time to time, reflecting the chef's heritage. Expect spaetzle and sauerkraut interspersed with local delicacies. Closed May through October. Reservations required. Credit cards: A, MC, V.

Hemingway's $$$ ★★★★★

West Bay Road, Georgetown, ☎ *(809) 949-1234. Associated hotel: Hyatt Regency.*
International cuisine. Specialties: Jerk chicken, lobster.
Lunch: 11:30 a.m.–2:30 p.m., entrées $17–$23.
Dinner: 6–10 p.m., entrées $17–$23.
Spectacular Seven Mile Beach looms blue in front of diners supping at this, the Hyatt Regency Grand Cayman's luxury dining room. The chefs here create nouvelle Caribbean dishes utilizing local fish, turtle steak and chicken, accompanied by lightly zingy herb and citrus sauces. Cocktails are creative and service is attentive. Reservations required. Credit cards: A, MC, V.

Hog Sty Bay Cafe   **$$$**   ★★

North Church Street, Georgetown, ☎ *(809) 949-6163.*
English cuisine.
Lunch: 11:30 a.m.–5:30 p.m., entrées $5–$12.
Dinner: 6–10 p.m., entrées $12–$19.
A good, casual American-English style pub, the Hog Sty Bay Cafe in George Town
Harbor is a relaxing perch for burgers and sandwiches or fish and chips. It's hard to
miss the brightly painted bungalow that hums inside with a crowd of regulars who
also like to come for the swoony sunset views and happy hour drinks. Breakfast is
also served, with all the usual offerings plus Mexican-style eggs for added zing. Res-
ervations required. Credit cards: A, MC, V.

Lantana's   **$$$**   ★★★★★

West Bay Road, Georgetown, ☎ *(809) 947-5595. Associated hotel: The Caribbean
Club.*
Mexican cuisine. Specialties: Conch fritters with ancho chile mayonnaise.
Dinner: 5:30–10 p.m., entrées $20–$34.
Lantana's is one of the island's most prestigious dining establishments, due to its
creative New Mexican-style food. Most dishes are prepared with flair by an Austrian
chef, Alfred Schrock, who understands how well West Indian culinary treats blend
with desert hot sauces and condiments. Witness his lightly fried conch fritters with
ancho chile mayonnaise and Santa Fe cilantro pesto pasta with seafood. A Viennese
tarte tatin is scrumptious. Surroundings recall Santa Fe's Coyote Cafe. Reservations
required. Credit cards: A, D, MC, V.

Lobster Pot   **$$$**   ★★

North Church Street, Georgetown, ☎ *(809) 949-2736.*
Seafood cuisine. Specialties: Lobster, turtle soup.
Lunch: 11:30 a.m.–2:30 p.m., entrées $10–$25.
Dinner: 5–10 p.m., entrées $15–$28. Closed: Sun.
When the Hog Sty Bay Cafe is busy, this upper-level pub facing West Bay fits the
bill. The Lobster Pot manages an intimate atmosphere despite its popularity and the
tendency of servers to rush diners through their meals. Nevertheless, the food is
good, encompassing lobster, salads and frozen tropical drinks. There's a dart board,
natch, for diversion. Reservations required. Credit cards: A, D, MC, V.

Ottmar's Restaurant   **$$$**   ★★★★★

West Bay Road, Georgetown,
International cuisine. Specialties: Fresh fish, rijstaffel.
Dinner: 6-10 p.m., entrées $12–$25. Closed: Sun.
Another excellent dining room run by an Austrian expatriate, Ottmar's in the Clar-
ion Grand Hotel proffers classical-French bouillabaisse and then turns around and
offers a Dutch-Javanese rijstaffel (a spicy feast of 16 courses surrounded by steamed
rice). The room is elegant and spacious, and conversations are carried on unheard
by diners at neighboring tables. Reservations required. Credit cards: A, MC, V.

Ristorante Pappagallo   **$$$**   ★★

Palmetto Drive, Georgetown, ☎ *(809) 949-1119.*
Italian cuisine.
Dinner: 6–10:30 p.m., entrées $14–$25.

Northern Italian cuisine is served in a series of thatched-roof huts facing a lagoon, surrounded by palm trees and wooden bridges. Despite the overwhelming atmosphere and chattering macaws in cages for background music, the food is reasonably good, with veal and seafood predominating. Even if you don't come to eat, it's a good spot for a cocktail. Reservations required. Credit cards: A, MC, V.

The Wharf   **$$$**   ★★

West Bay Road, Georgetown, ☎ (809) 949-2231.
Latin American cuisine. Specialties: Seafood.
Lunch: Noon–2:30 p.m., entrées $21–$30.
Dinner: 6–10 p.m., entrées $21–$30.
The ultimate West Indian dining experience is a seafood supper on a huge deck overlooking the waterfront at the Wharf, which is justly famous for its sublime conch chowder and great service. Chef Tony Egger likes to pair fresh local seafare with Caribbean touches, including a seafood medley baked with a papaya sauce. Harp players rove from table to table, taking requests, and calypso bands play in the attached popular bar. Come at 9 p.m. to see them feed giant tarpon off the rear dock. Reservations recommended. Credit cards: D, MC, V.

Verandah Restaurant, The   **$$$**   ★

West Bay Road, Georgetown, ☎ (809) 947-4444. Associated hotel: Holiday Inn Grand Cayman.
American cuisine. Specialties: Breakfast buffet.
Lunch: 6 a.m.–4 p.m., entrées $6–$15.
Dinner: 6–9 p.m., entrées $18–$32.
The only reason this restaurant in the Holiday Inn is mentioned is because it serves up a bountiful all-you-can-eat breakfast for $10, a great buy in bargain-starved Grand Cayman. This morning feast could easily get you through the rest of the day. Reservations recommended. Credit cards: A, MC, V.

Little Cayman

Pirate's Point Resort   **$$$**   ★★

Crawl Bay, ☎ (809) 948-4210. Associated hotel: Pirate's Point Resort.
International cuisine.
Lunch: entrées $25–$35.
Dinner: entrées $25–$35.
Owner Gladys Howard, trained at Paris' Cordon Bleu, whips up wonderful seafood dishes supplemented by lots of local fruits and vegetables. You can try to recreate some of her dishes back home by buying one of her cookbooks. Reservations required. Credit cards: not accepted.

Shopping is not the reason to visit the Caymans, though George Town has a decent selection of boutiques and stores with duty- and sales-tax-free items such as Irish linen, French perfumes, china, crystal, silver and British woolens. Do not buy any products made of turtle, as you will not be able to get them past customs in the United States. For jewelry head to the **Jewelry Centre** *(George Street, ☎ [809] 949-0070)*, where they have the island's biggest selection. For crafts, try **Viking Gallery** *(South Church Street, George Town, ☎ [809] 949-4090)*, the nearby **Caymandicraft** *(☎ [809] 949-2405)* and **Heritage Crafts Shop** *(☎ [809] 949-7093)*, near the harbour in George Town. Jewelry made from black coral is popular but controversial, as the species is rare, though you can legally bring it back home. Stamp and rare coin collectors should check out **Artifacts Ltd.** *(Harbour Drive, George Town ☎ [809] 949-2442)*, which boasts an excellent collection, as well as antiques prints and maps.

Cayman Islands Directory

Arrival and Departure

Grand Cayman is serviced by **Cayman Airways** ☎ *(800) 422-9626)* from Miami, Tampa, Atlanta and Houston; by **American Airlines** ☎ *(800) 433-7300* from Miami and Raleigh-Durham, by **USAir** ☎ *(800) 428-4322* from Baltimore-Washington, and by **Northwest Airlines** ☎ *(800) 447-4747* from Detroit, Minneapolis and Memphis via Miami. Cayman Airways is also the only airline that services Little Cayman and Cayman Brac.

A taxi from the airport to central Seven Mile Beach is $8–$12, Seven Mile Beach to George Town is about $8, taxi rates are set by law.

Business Hours

Shops open Monday–Saturday 9 a.m.–5 p.m. Banks open Monday–Thursday 9 a.m.–2:30 p.m. and on Friday 9 a.m.–1 p.m. and 2:30–4:30 p.m.

Climate

With an average temperature of 79 degrees, the Caymans are pleasant year-round. High season runs from mid-December to mid-April, but July and August, when waters are clearest, are the prime times for diving.

Documents

U.S. and Canadian citizens may show either a valid passport or proof of citizenship (voter registration or birth certificate with photo ID) and an ongoing or return ticket.

Electricity

The current runs 110 volt, 60-cycles, as in the United States.

Getting Around

Taxis are omnipresent whenever a plane arrives, and rates are officially fixed. Since the islands are small and flat, bicycling and walking are pleasant alternatives to walking. Autos, are nevertheless, easy to rent. Major U.S. firms are here as well as local ones, such as **Just Jeeps** ☎ *(809) 949-7263*. Motorcycles and motorscooters are for hire at **Soto's** ☎ *(809) 947-4652*.

Driving is on the left side of the street.

Language

English is the main tongue, though the accent is a highly musical mélange of Irish, Welsh, Scottish and West Indian lilts.

Medical Emergencies

George Town Hospital ☎ *949-8600* is the only facility on Grand Cayman, located on Hospital Road. Cayman Brac has an 18-bed facility called **Faith Hospital** ☎ *948-2243*.

Money

The official currency is the Cayman Islands dollar, unique to the islands. Most tourist establishments accept U.S. dollars and credit cards. Local banks will cash traveler's checks. Keep track which dollars (American or Cayman) are being quoted on menus, etc. If quoted in Cayman dollars, the price will look a lot cheaper than it actually is.

Telephone

Area code is *809*. International calls can be made 24 hours a day. Local calls now use 7 digits (as opposed to 5 digits in the past).

Time

Eastern standard time all year long, with no change during the northern shift to daylight savings.

Tipping and Taxes

Service charges are not standardized among hotel establishments and can range from 5 percent at condos to 15 percent at top hotels. Always check your bill before adding your own tips. Taxi drivers generally don't expect tips unless you've exhausted them with huge trunks. Bellboys expect 50 cents per bag.

Tourist Information

The **Cayman Islands Department of Tourism** is located in the Harbour Centre in George Town ☎ *(809) 49-0623*. Tourist information booths can also be found at the pier and at the airport. In the U.S. call ☎ *(213) 738-1968* or *(212) 682-5582*.

Tours

Half-day guided sightseeing tours (Turtle Farm, Hell, Governor's Residence, George Town) average $30 per person a half-day; a tour to the caves and blowhole sites on the eastern end is $45 per person; full-day tours including lunch and stops at all island sites average $65 per person. None include swimstops. An all-day snorkel trip with lunch averages $50 per person; a one-tank offshore dive is $30–$35, with all equipment, $35–$40. **Evco Tours** ☎ *(809) 949-2118* offers six-hour tours around the island, as does **Greyline** ☎ *(809) 949-2791* and **Reids** ☎ *(809) 949-6311*.

When to Go

Pirates Week Festival in October is celebrated with parades, songs, contests and games; even businessmen arrive at the office dressed in costume. Million Dollar Month brings anglers from all over the world to compete in one of the world's biggest big-fish contests. Batabano, the weekend before Easter, is the island's cultural carnival weekend. Queen Elizabeth's birthday in mid-June is celebrated with a full-dress uniform parade, marching band and 21-gun salute.

CAYMAN ISLANDS HOTELS		RMS	RATES	PHONE	CR. CARDS
Cayman Brac					
West End Point					
★★	Divi Tiara Beach Resort	58	$95–$200	(800) 948-1553	A, D, MC, V
★	Brac Reef Cayman Beach Resort	40	$193–$458	(800) 327-3835	A, MC, V
Grand Cayman					
Georgetown					
★★★★	Beach Club Hotel	41	$125–$265	(800) 223-6510	A, DC, MC, V
★★★★	Clarion Grand Pavilion	90	$155–$455	(809) 947-5656	A, D, DC, MC, V
★★★★	Hyatt Regency Grand Cayman	236	$180–$500	(800) 233-1234	A, MC, V
★★★★	Radisson Resort	315	$165–$390	(800) 333-3333	A, DC, MC, V
★★★★	Spanish Bay Reef North Wall	50	$160–$218	(800) 223-6510	A, D, DC, MC, V
★★★★	Treasure Island Resort	280	$160–$275	(800) 327-8777	A, MC, V
★★★★	West Indian Club	6	$130–$365	(809) 947-5255	A, MC, V
★★★	Ambassadors Inn	18	$60–$80	(800) 648-7748	A, MC, V
★★★	Caribbean Club	18	$160–$425	(800) 327-8777	A, MC, V
★★★	Grand Bay Club	21	$120–$310	(809) 947-4728	A, MC, V
★★★	Holiday Inn Grand Cayman	212	$238–$832	(800) 465-4329	A, DC, MC, V
★★★	Indies Suites	40	$160–$305	(800) 654-3130	A, MC, V
★★★	Island Hill Resort	10	$60–$80	(809) 949-4242	
★★★	Lacovia Condominiums	45	$200–$285	(800) 223-9815	A
★★★	London House	21	$235–$750	(800) 423-4095	A, MC, V
★★★	Morrit's Tortuga Club	85	$145–$440	(800) 447-0309	A, D, MC, V
★★★	Pan-Cayman House	10	$150–$370	(800) 248-5115	MC, V
★★	Cayman Kai Resort	20	$140–$220	(800) 223-5427	A, MC, V
★★	Christopher Columbus Apts	28	$190–$390	(809) 947-4354	A, MC, V
★★	Discovery Point Club	45	$145–$315	(809) 947-4724	A, MC, V
★★	Grapetree/Cocoplum Condos	50	$135–$280	(800) 635-4824	A, MC, V
★★	Harbour Heights	46	$190–$295	(800) 327-8777	A, MC, V

CAYMAN ISLANDS HOTELS		RMS	RATES	PHONE	CR. CARDS
★★	Plantana	49	$180–$425	(809) 947-4430	A, MC, V
★★	Seaview Hotel	15	$65–$105	(809) 949-8804	A, D, MC, V
★★	Silver Sands	42	$200–$235	(800) 327-8777	A, MC, V
★★	Sleep Inn	116	$90–$185	(800) 627-5337	A, CB, D, DC, MC, V
★★	Sunset House	59	$90–$190	(800) 854-4767	A, D, MC, V
★★	Tarquynn Manor	20	$143–$395	(800) 223-9815	MC, V
★★	Victoria House	26	$165–$395	(800) 327-8777	A, MC, V
★★	Villas Pappagallo	40	$160–$284	(800) 232-1034	A, MC, V
★★	Villas of the Galleon	75	$200–$430	(809) 947-4433	A, MC, V
★★	Westin Casuarina Resort	343	$185–$375	(800) 228-3000	A, MC, V
★	Beachcomber Condos	19	$190–$395	(800) 327-8777	MC, V
★	Colonial Club	15	$230–$500	(809) 947-4660	A, MC, V
★	George Town Villas	54	$165–$420	(809) 949-5172	A, MC, V
★	Island Pine Villas	40	$110–$225	(800) 223-9815	A, D, DC, MC, V
★	Plantation Village Resort	70	$145–$405	(800) 822-8903	A, MC, V
★	Windjammer Hotel	12	$100–$155	(809) 947-4608	A, MC, V

Little Cayman

Crawl Bay

★★★★	Little Cayman Beach	40	$230–$886	(800) 327-3835	A, MC, V
★★★	Conch Club		$300–$400	(813) 323-8727	A, MC, V
★★	Sam McCoy's Lodge	6	$105–$185	(800) 626-0496	None
★★	Southern Cross Club	10	$125–$285	(800) 899-2582	None
★	Pirates Point Resort	10	$185–$150	(809) 948-1010	MC, V

CAYMAN ISLANDS RESTAURANTS		PHONE	ENTRÉE	CR. CARDS

Cayman Brac

West End Point

Asian				
★★	Edd's Place	(809) 948-1208	$6–$25	MC, V

CAYMAN ISLANDS

CAYMAN ISLANDS RESTAURANTS	PHONE	ENTRÉE	CR. CARDS

Grand Cayman

Georgetown

	American			
★ Verandah Restaurant, The	(809) 947-4444	$6–$32	A, MC, V

	English			
★★ Hog Sty Bay Cafe	(809) 949-6163	$5–$19	A, MC, V

	International			
★★★★★ Hemingway's	(809) 949-1234	$17–$23	A, MC, V
★★★★★ Ottmar's Restaurant		$12–$25	A, MC, V
★★ Garden Loggia Cafe	(809) 949-1234	$9–$34	A, MC, V
★★ Grand Old House	(809) 949-9333	$13–$34	A, MC, V
★ Benjamin's Roof	(809) 947-4080	$12–$30	A, MC, V

	Italian			
★★ Ristorante Pappagallo	(809) 949-1119	$14–$25	A, MC, V

	Latin American			
★★★ Crow's Nest	(809) 949-9366	$5–$19	A, MC, V
★★ Corita's Copper Kettle II	(809) 949-5475	$10–$15	A, MC, V
★★ The Wharf	(809) 949-2231	$21–$30	D, MC, V

	Mexican			
★★★★★ Lantana's	(809) 947-5595	$20–$34	A, D, MC, V

	Seafood			
★★ Almond Tree, The	(809) 949-2893	$14–$22	A, MC, V
★★ Cracked Conch	(809) 947-5217	$6–$25	A, MC, V
★★ Lobster Pot	(809) 949-2736	$10–$28	A, D, MC, V

Little Cayman

Crawl Bay

	International			
★★ Pirate's Point Resort	(809) 948-4210	$25–$35	None

Cascade Aux Ecrevisses, Guadeloupe

Grenada

CURAÇAO

Curaçao offers great beaches, diving, excellent restaurants, shops and casinos.

The C in the ABC Dutch islands known as the Netherlands Antilles, Curaçao (pronounced CURE-a-sow) lies between the A (Aruba, 42 miles to the west) and B (Bonaire, 30 miles to the east). Like its siblings, it is a hilly island that is quite dry and desertlike, with little chance of rain to ruin your vacation. The island is large—174 square miles—and heavily populated for Caribbean, with more than 170,000 residents. While it is not necessarily blessed with splendid natural treasures (it's rather stark and arid), its whimsical Dutch-inspired architecture, especially in the charming capital city of Willemstad, makes it a real gem. In fact, Curaçao is considered the most architecturally important island in the entire Caribbean.

As is true with its siblings in the ABC trio, the diving here is superb, and while Curaçao may lack the instant name recognition of Aruba or Bonaire, the underwater world here is just as fantastic—a fact not unknown to the many Europeans who come year after year, primarily to dive.

Willemstad is a picture storybook come to life with its rows and rows of immaculate townhouses trimmed with dormers, gables and cupolas. Everything is painted in bright pastels; legend has it that 200 years ago, Curaçao's first governor got migraine headaches from the sun glaring off the white houses, so decreed that color off limit for facades.

Curaçao is an excellent destination for couples that consist of one avid diver and one who isn't. There's plenty to see and do outside the water, and thanks to the proliferation of casinos scattered about, a more vibrant nightlife than on many diving-oriented islands. What Curaçao does lack, however, are truly glorious beaches; while there are places to wiggle your toes in the sand and work on a tan, you won't find the long, crescent stretches typical of the Caribbean. No one seems to mind, as Curaçao is constantly expanding its tourism facilities, and the tourists keep on coming back for more.

Bird's-Eye View

Curaçao lies 35 miles off the coast of Venezuela and is one of five islands that compose the Netherlands Antilles. It is one of the Caribbean's southernmost islands, located 1,710 miles from New York (a four-hour flight) and is of volcanic origin. It's quite dry and arid, with annual rainfall of just 23 inches. The average temperature is 82 degrees Fahrenheit, and the low humidity and constant trade winds, which average 15 miles per hour, help keep things quite comfortable. Curaçao is completely outside the hurricane belt.

Willemstad, the capital city (and also capital of the Netherlands Antilles), is one of the world's busiest ports and a real charmer with its Dutch-influenced architecture, bright pastel facades and cosmopolitan shopping. Built around two old forts, it is split in two by the Santa Ana Bay.

On the north shore, near the airport, the limestone Hato Caves are a major tourist attraction. These living caverns are a treat, with guided tours taking gawking visitors into large chambers and past still pools and a waterfall. Recent improvements, including new pathways and improved lighting and cooling systems, made them even better to visit.

The rest of the countryside (known as *cunucu*) is quite stark, reminiscent of the southwest deserts of the United States; vegetation is generally confined to cacti and shrubbery. The best beaches are along the west coast, but be-

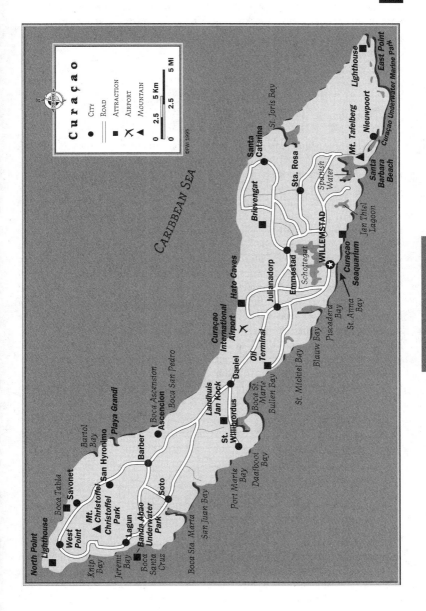

ware of the small green apples that grow on manchineel trees; they are poisonous and contact with the skin causes a painful blistering.

Off the east coast is the small uninhabited island of Klein Curaçao, an excellent spot for sun bathing, scuba diving and snorkeling.

History

Long before Alonso de Ojeda set foot on the island in 1499, Arawak tribes—from the clan of the Caquetios called Curaçaos—were inhabiting the island. After Ojeda marked his claim, a Spanish settlement followed in 1527. A hundred years later, the Spanish unceremoniously left the island, leaving it in the hands of Holland, which deemed it a possession of the Dutch West Indies Company. The island's natural harbors and strategic location in the Caribbean inspired predatory interest among the French and British, who continually tried to send the Dutch packing, with little success. In 1642, a young Dutchman named Peter Stuyvesant became governor of the island, a mere three years before he took over governorship of the Dutch colony of New Amsterdam, today known as New York. During Dutch rule, the island was divided up into plantations. Not all were devoted to agriculture; some of the estates were utilized for salt mining. In 1863 emancipation freed the slaves. The island made waves on the international scene until oil was discovered in Venezuela, and the Royal Dutch Shell Company, impressed with Curaçao's fine harbor potential, erected the world's largest oil refinery there. The industry lasted well into this century, attracting laborers from many nations who have created the melting pot that makes up Curaçao's population today.

Today Curaçao is part of the kingdom of the Netherlands. The other Dutch territories—Bonaire, Saba, St. Eustatius and St. Martin—are administered through Willemstad, the capital of the Netherlands Antilles.

People

More than 170,00 people—known as Curacaoans—live on the island, most around the capital city of Willemstad. The people represent more than 55 nationalities, but are mostly of African or mixed African and European descent. The official language is Dutch, but most people actually speak Papiamento, a blend of Portuguese, Dutch, African, English, French and

Arawak Indian. In fact, a law is pending to make Papiamento the official language, along with Dutch and English. In 1987, the first school opened to specifically teach Papiamento, and some hotels offer classes for guests. English speakers are common, and tourists should have no problem communicating.

Curacao's government is based on the parliamentary system, with elections held each four years. The island is governed by an executive council and a legislative council. Curacao is known for its religious tolerance and has churches representing faiths from Judaism to Mormonism to Jehovah's Witnesses, though some 80 percent of the population is Roman Catholic.

Besides tourism, oil refining and international banking contribute to the island's economy. Curacaoans are a warm and hospitable lot who welcome visitors with true sincerity.

Beaches

Good beaches are hard to come by in Curaçao. The northwestern coast should be avoided by swimmers since it is too rough, though the west has some calm bays good for swimming and snorkeling. Many of the beaches are private and charge a fee, but in return you get changing facilities, clean stretches and snack bars. Public beaches are notoriously unkempt. Avoid the beach near Willemstad (at the Avila Beach Hotel); it's artificial, gritty and too dense for good snorkeling. **Santa Barbara**, located at the mouth of Spanish Water Bay, is popular with locals and has full services. The Curaçao Yacht Club is close by. On the northwest side, **Boca St. Martha**, where the Coral Cliff Resort is located, exudes a certain peacefulness and the bay is gorgeous. **Knip**, farther up the coast, rates as one of the best on the island, with its large, sandy stretch; on weekends it can get crowded and noisy with music. **Playa Forti**, on the western tip, has dark sand and is good for swimming.

Klein Curaçao, a small, uninhabited island off East Point, makes a nifty day excursion; many charter boats and dive operators offer packages with lunch included.

Underwater

The independent spirit will be well-served on Curaçao, where shore diving from rugged cliffs is a chief attraction. The island is encircled by a fringing

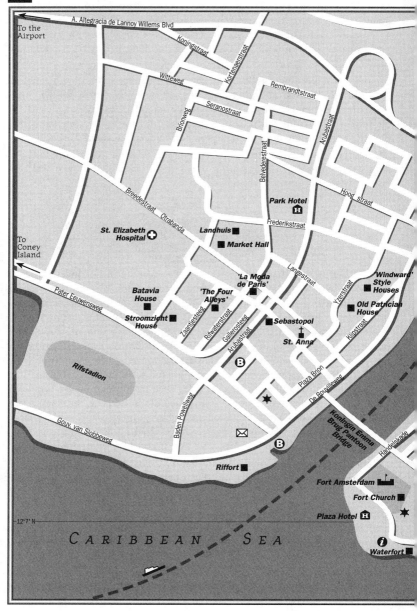

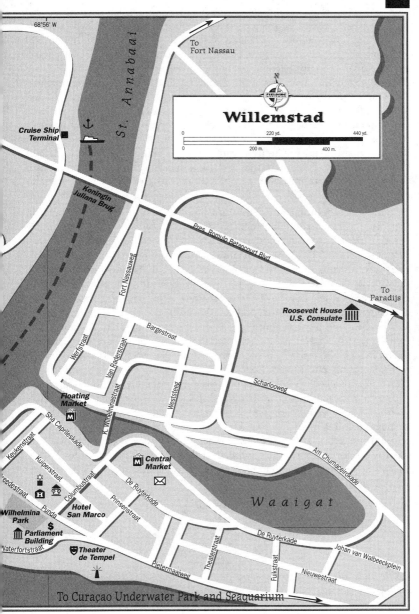

68°56' W

To
Fort Nassau

Willemstad

N

0   220 yd.   440 yd.
0   200 m.   400 m.

St. Annabaai

Cruise Ship
Terminal

Koningin
Juliana Brug

Pres. Romulo Betancourt Blvd

To
Paradijs

Roosevelt House
U.S. Consulate

Fort Nassauweg

Bargestraat

Weststeeg

Scharlooweg

Wardstraat

Van Raderstraat

K. Wilhelminastraat

Floating
Market

Sha Caprileskade

Am Chumaceirokade

Keukenstraat

Kuiperstraat

Central
Market

Columbusstraat

Freedestraat

Punda

De Ruyterstraat

Prinsenstraat

Waaigat

Hotel
San Marco

Theaterstraat

De Ruyterkade

Johan van Walbeeckplein

Wilhelmina
Park

Parliament
Building

Waterfortstraat

Theater
de Tempel

Fuikstraat

Nieuwestraat

Pietermaaiweg

To Curaçao Underwater Park and Seaquarium

reef, which features several dozen excellent sites along its southern (leeward) side; there are over 40 permanent mooring buoys established. Typically, the shallow reef drops gently to 50 feet followed by a second slope 200 to 300 feet from shore; the terrain in between is frequently undulating and surreal. Because diving did not become established here until the 1980s, the reefs are in good shape and new sites await discovery. Local marine biologists claim that Curaçao actually possesses a greater diversity of hard and soft corals and sponge life than the reefs of famed Bonaire. However, heavily populated Curaçao has depleted much of the fish life existing on the reefs. Otherwise, while not always as convenient or accessible as the diving available on its sibling to the east, many of Curaçao's sites are genuinely comparable to the best dives on Bonaire. The main drawback in comparing the two destinations is that Curaçao is a more developed island, and little of its coastline remains untouched.

Curaçao's underwater attractions are just beginning to generate press in the United States, though American divers are still substantially outnumbered by their European counterparts, who have been coming here for years. The newly created **Banda Abao Underwater Park** is home to some of Curaçao's most adventurous diving and occupies much of the island's northern half; the **Central Underwater Park** lies north of Willemstad. The island's original marine reserve, the **Curaçao Underwater Park**, situated along the 12.5-mile shoreline east from the Princess Beach Hotel to the tip of the island, offers good diving and a snorkeling trail (in front of the Jan Thiel Lagoon). The south coast, from Newport east to the lighthouse, is private property and diving must be accessed by boat; at press time a plan to develop this coastline was generating considerable controversy. A locally available *Guide to the Curaçao Underwater Park* by Jeffrey Sybesma and Tom van't Hos, provides additional information about dive sites, and the *Complete Guide to Landside Diving and Snorkeling Locations in Curaçao* by Jeffrey Sybesma and Suzanne Koelega, features maps and road directions to shore sites. Among a number of good snorkeling areas are **Playa Lagoon**, a beach tucked between two outsized rocks formations, and the **Jan Thiel Reef**, located just outside the bay and snorkeling trail. A decompression tank is available at the island's St. Elizabeth Hospital.

On Foot

Although most of Curaçao's arid interior is composed of rocky hills or flat scrublands, as one heads northwest on the island's two main roads, a bumpier topography of chalky mountains and relatively greener valleys emerges.

The terrain, including a flat-topped mesa, will remind some visitors of the rugged beauty found in the American Southwest. **Mount Christoffel National Park** occupies 4500 acres, much of Curaçao's northern tip, and is home to four tracks, each color-coded for easy identification, including a path that ascends 1238-foot Christoffel itself, the highest point on the island. The remaining three tracks are named after the three plantations which once tenanted this land—Savonet, Zevenbergen and Zorgvlied—and are usually driven, although each is suitable for (exposed) on-foot exploration. They crawl through a varied and interesting landscape, between century plants (which bloom only once every hundred years), wind-shaped divi divi trees, and fields of oversize cactus; keen eyes will also spot the several species of orchids growing on the hillsides. There are roughly 150 species of birds, as well as the tiny, indigenous Curaçao deer, a subspecies of the more common white-tailed deer. Two small slitherers inhabit the park, whipsnakes and silver snakes, but neither are poisonous. The park administration office can provide you with detailed maps, or you can purchase the in-depth *Excursion Guide to the Christoffel Park*, by Peer Reijns. Christoffel's summit is an ideal location to enjoy the sunrise or sunset, but the park is open only between 8 a.m.–5 p.m. (6 a.m.–3 p.m. on Sundays). There are, however, occasional guided walks at dawn or dusk; additional information may be obtained by calling the park at ☎ *(599) 9-640363.*

FIELDING'S CHOICE:

With more than 150–200 deer on the island, Christoffel National Park now offers a deer-watching program. Sessions are held in the afternoon 4-6:30 p.m., with small groups led by guides (maximum of eight people) on a 10-minute walk to the observation tower for a presentation and to await the deer. Call for reservations. Located on the highest point of the island, the park also offers unusual walking trails that take you past fascinating flora, Indian caves and wildlife. A museum on the grounds features an exhibit on the geology of the island.

What Else to See

Willemstad, the capital city, is a little slice of Denmark right in the southern Caribbean. A walk around the pristine city makes it quickly obvious why Curaçao is a favorite port for cruise ships. Split in two by Santa Ana Bay, the city has two districts: Punta and, on the other side, Otrabanda (literally "the other side"). Otrabanda is mostly residential, while Punta is for tourists, with a good variety of shops and restaurants. To get from one side to the other, you can catch the free ferry, take a cab over Juliana Bridge or walk across the Queen Emma Pontoon Bridge, a 700-foot floating bridge that swings open up to 30 times a day to allow ships to pass through. Known as "the swinging old lady," it was designed by American consul Leonard B. Smith in 1888, who made a fortune charging tolls. Today, it's free.

Willemstad, capital of Curaçao, features Dutch-inspired architecture.

Just a few minutes' walk from the Queen Emma, on the Punda side, is the Floating Market, where you'll easily use up an entire roll of film capturing the colorful sights. Each day schooners from Venezuela, Columbia and other West Indian islands tie up alongside the canal to see fresh fish, fruits, produce and spices. If you can bear to get up early on your vacation, come at 6:30 a.m. as owners set up shop under colorful canopies. The action takes place most of the day if you'd rather sleep in.

Another must-see site in Willemstad is the Mikve Israel Emmanuel Synagogue, built in 1732 and the oldest continually operating synagogue in the Western Hemisphere. (The congregation actually dates to 1651 and was started by 12 Jewish families from Amsterdam.) Adjacent to the synagogue is the restored 18th-century house of the original rabbi, which now houses the Jewish Cultural Historical Museum.

If you prefer to leave the driving to someone else, hop aboard the new trolley that tours the city in an hour and a quarter. The open-sided cars make two tours each week (Mondays at 11 a.m. and Wednesdays at 4 p.m.)

There's plenty to see and do outside city limits. Sea Aquarium is home to some 400 varieties of exotic fish and vegetation indigenous to the area, including sharks, giant turtles, moray ells and a five-foot-long jewfish named Herbie. Near the airport, the Hato Caves are gorgeous limestone formations that can be toured daily.

History buffs revel in Curaçao's many vintage structures, including Landhuis Jan Kock, which dates to 1650 and is said to be haunted; and Landhuis Habaai, a 17th-century plantation house in Ortabanda. The island also boasts several historic forts constructed on the hills around Willemstad to protect its deepwater harbor.

Finally, Christoffel National Park, located at the island's western end, encompasses 4,500 acres consisting of three former plantations and 20 miles of driving trails to view divi divi trees, pear cactus and resident iguanas, donkeys and deer.

BEST VIEW:

A spectacular view of the sunset is available at Fort Nassau, on one of the highest hills in the city.

Historical Sites

Landhuis Brievengat ★★★

Brievengat, Willemstad.
This restored 18th-century plantation house has 18-inch-thick walls, watchtowers (where long-ago lovers met), and antiques of the era. The last Sunday of each month sees crafts demonstrations and folkloric shows, and there's live music on Wednesdays and Fridays. Located about 10 minutes out of Willemstad. General admission: $2.

Museums and Exhibits

Curaçao Museum ★★★

Van Leeuwenhoekstraat, Willemstad.
Housed in a former military quarantine hospital for those with yellow fever, this 1853 building displays art and Indian artifacts of historical significance. There's also a garden with specimens of all the plants and trees of Curaçao, and the small Children's Museum of Science, where kids are asked to please touch. General admission: $2.

Curaçao Seaquarium ★

Bapur Kibra, Willemstad.
More than 400 species of fish and marine life—in fact, EVERY species native to the area—is on display at this excellent aquarium. You can touch some of the creatures and take a glass-bottom boat ride—the truly daring can enjoy the "Animal Encounters" in which divers and snorkelers feed sharks by hand through a thick (let's hope so) mesh fence. You can also swim with sting rays, angelfish and grouper—or just watch the fun from a 46-foot-deep underwater observatory. General admission: $6.

Jewish Cultural Historical Museum ★★★

Kuiperstraat, Willemstad.

Located in two buildings constructed in 1728, this fine museum exhibits ceremonial and cultural objects from the 17th and 18th centuries used by one of the oldest Jewish communities in this hemisphere. General admission: $2.

Octagon House   ★★★★

Penstraat, Willemstad.

This small museum houses antiques and personal items of Venezuelan liberator Simon Bolivar.

Parks and Gardens

Christoffel National Park   ★★

Savonet, West Point.
Hours open: 8 a.m.–4 p.m.

This 4500-acre nature preserve is located on the island's highest point, crowned by 1230-foot-high St. Christoffelberg, the highest point in all the Dutch Leewards. Well worth a visit, but come early to avoid the overwhelming late-afternoon heat. The park includes 20 miles of one-way roads, hiking trails, a small museum, rare orchids, cacti, divi-divi trees, palms, lots of birds and wild goats, Curaçao deer and donkeys. General admission: $5.

Curacao Underwater Marine Park   ★

Princess Hotel, East Point.

A wonderful spot for divers and snorkelers, this 12.5-mile unspoiled reef is a protected national park. Sights include two well-preserved shipwrecks and an 875-foot underwater nature trail. On a clear day, you can see almost forever—or up to 150 feet, anyway.

Tours

Curaçao Liqueur Distillery   ★★★★

Salinja, Willemstad.

The orange-flavored liquor chobolobo is produced here in a 17th-century *landhuis* (land house). Witness the process and sample the results. While in the area, head over to the Amstel Brewery, where beer is made from distilled seawater. Tours are conducted only on Tuesdays and Thursdays at 10 a.m., after which you can drink all you want for free (designate a driver!). ☎ *612944* for information.

Hato Caves   ★★

F.D. Rooseveltweg, Willemstad.
Hours open: 10 a.m.–5 p.m.

Just recently opened to the public, these limestone caves are imbedded with fossil coral formations. An hour-long guided tour takes you into several caverns and past Indian petroglyphs, active stalagmites and stalactites, and underwater pools. Neat! General admission: $4.

Old City Tours   ★★★

De Ruyterkade 53, Willemstad.

Interesting walking tours of Willemstad and its wonderful architecture are sometimes led by owner Anko van der Woude, a local expert on the island's history. The two- to three-tour trek costs $15. Old City also conducts harbor tours on a small fishing bark. Prices range from $10–$17.

Trolley Tour

Fort Anderson, Willemstad.

This new tour takes visitors on open-sided cars throughout the best of Willemstad. The tour starts at historic Fort Amsterdam, continues along the waterfront Handelskade, visits the Floating Market, tours the district of Scharloo, stops at Mikve Emanuel Synagogue and explores other sites. The trolley tour takes place only on Mondays at 11 a.m. and Wednesdays at 4 p.m. The cost is $15 per person, $10 for children 2–12.

Scuba diving is hugely popular all around Curaçao, and the government-protected Curaçao Underwater Marine Park ensures it will stay that way. The park, which includes nearly a third of the island's southern waters, has more than 12 miles of protected reefs and shores, and on a good day, visibility is as high as 150 feet. (Expect a normal range of 60 to 80 feet—still quite decent.) Thanks to the constant trade winds that breeze over the island, Curaçao is also big with windsurfers, with year-round winds of 13 to 25 knots. The Curaçao Open International Pro-Am Windsurfing Championship, which attracts serious competitors from around the world, is held each year on the southeast coast between Jan Thiel and Princess beaches. If you're new to the sport, try the calmer and more protected waters at Spanish Water lagoon. Those winds are also the delight of sailors, and you'll have no problem finding places to rent a hobie-cat or sunfish. Deep-sea fishing for sailfish, marlin, tuna and wahoo is good; each March, the island hosts an international blue marlin tournament. Duffers are limited to the "greens" at the nine-hole Curaçao Gold & Squash Club—though those greens are actually made of tightly packed sand. Once on island, inquire as to the status of a new 18-hole golf course, part of the Curasol Resort complex, which is due to open sometime in 1997.

Cruises

Various locations, Willemstad.

Take to the high seas aboard a variety of crafts. **Tabor Tours** (☎ *376637*) offers sunset cruises with wine and munchies, snorkel trips to Point Marine, and excursions aboard the Seaworld Explorer, a "semi-submarine" that cruises five feet below the water's surface. The 120-foot *Insulinde* (☎ *601340*), a rigged sail logger, offers sunset and afternoon sails. Finally, **Sail Curaçao** (☎ *676003*) has day and evening sails and snorkel trips. Bon voyage!

Curaçao Golf & Squash Club

Wilhelminalaan, Emmastad.

Tourists and other nonmembers can golf on this nine-hole course only from 8 a.m.–noon Fridays through Wednesdays, and Thursdays from 10 a.m. to dusk. Greens fees are $15.

Watersports

Various locations, Willemstad.

Lots of outfits offer all kinds of watersports; chances are good your hotel also has facilities. Try one of the following: **Coral Cliff Diving** *(☎ 642822)* for dive and snorkel excursions and one-week courses on scuba, sailing and windsurfing; **Underwater Curaçao** *(☎ 618131)*, a PADI-accredited dive shop; **Seascape Dive and Watersports** *(☎ 625000)* for snorkel and scuba trips and lessons, deep-sea fishing, water-skiing and glass-bottom boat rides; **Peter Hughes Diving** *(☎ 367888)* for diving, snorkeling and deep-sea fishing; and **Curaçao High Wind Center** *(☎ 614944)* at the Princess Beach Hotel for windsurfing lessons and rentals.

Where to Stay

Fielding's Highest Rated Hotels in Curaçao

★★★★★	Avila Beach Hotel	$85–$198
★★★★★	Lions Dive Hotel & Marina	$105–$145
★★★★	Curacao Caribbean Hotel	$140–$210
★★★★	Holland Hotel	$70–$130
★★★★	Princess Beach Resort	$95–$225
★★★★	Sonesta Beach Hotel	$160–$335
★★★★	Van der Valk Plaza Hotel	$105–$210
★★★	Habitat Curacao	$382–$817
★★★	Ortabanda Hotel & Casino	$105–$105

Fielding's Most Exclusive Hotels in Curaçao

★★★	Habitat Curacao	$382–$817
★★★★	Curacao Caribbean Hotel	$140–$210
★★★★	Van der Valk Plaza Hotel	$105–$210
★★	Holiday Beach Hotel	$110–$163
★★	Las Palmas Hotel	$93–$140

Fielding's Best Value Hotels in Curaçao

★★★★★	Lions Dive Hotel & Marina	$105–$145
★★★★	Holland Hotel	$70–$130
★★★★★	Avila Beach Hotel	$85–$198
★★★	Ortabanda Hotel & Casino	$105–$105
★★★★	Van der Valk Plaza Hotel	$105–$210

CURAÇAO

Many of Curaçao's major hotels have casinos and the accompanying night-life. If that's not your style, consider a small family-run inn. Most hotels are in or near Willemstad and lack beaches. Curaçao's newest additions are the Buona Sera Inn, located in the historic Pietermaai section of Willemstad, and Habitat Curaçao, a new dive hotel at Rif St. Marie, west of the capital. Unlike many other Caribbean islands, the pickings are rather slim for self-catering holidays at apartments or condominiums, though Tropic Resorts Marketing (*[599] 9-372328*) can probably set you up in style. Note that most properties charge a 12 percent service charge (so extra tipping is not necessary) and a government tax of 7 percent, usually above and beyond the quoted room rate.

Hotels and Resorts

Resorts in Curaçao run from the intimate, cliff-hugging kind (**Coral Cliff Resort**) to the deluxe beachfront extravaganza (**Curaçao Caribbean Hotel & Casino**), where there's no lack of nighttime entertainment. Serious divers tend to head for the **Lions Dive Hotel & Marina**. One of the best locations is the **Van der Calk Plaza Hotel & Casino**, which is tucked into an ancient fort at the mouth of Willemstad's harbor. Nearby the ancient arches have been renovated into a charming enclave of shops.

Avila Beach Hotel   **$85–$198**   ★ ★ ★ ★ ★

Netherlands, Penstraat 130-134, Willemstad, ☎ (599) 9-614377. FAX (599) 9-614493. Single: $85–$188. Double: $90–$198.

History buffs revel in this hotel, which was the former Governor's Mansion dating back to 1780; a modern extension was added in 1991, and a new cluster of 25 rooms opened in December 1996. This is Willemstad's only beachfront hotel and the spot where the royal family of Holland stays when in town. Rooms in the original mansion come in two categories: moderate, which are small and simple; and preferred, which are more spacious. All are individually decorated and rather charming, but note that the water is only sun heated, which means cold showers at night. Those seeking more luxurious digs—and dependable hot water—should book the newer sections, which have modern amenities and 18 spacious one- and two-bedroom apartments, some with kitchenette. All units are air conditioned and have cable TV and phones. The two small cove beachs are private and quite pretty, while the three European-style restaurants are grand. There's also one tennis court lit for night play. A lovely spot. 85 rooms. Credit cards: A, DC, MC, V.

Coral Cliff Hotel   **$68–$122**   ★

Santa Marta Bay, Willemstad, ☎ (599) 9-641610. FAX (599) 9-641781. Single: $68–$122. Double: $68–$122.

Lots of Europeans stay at this beachfront enclave of bungalows situated on a bluff overlooking Spain Main. Guest rooms are quite spartan and could use an overhaul, but the rates are reasonable and the beach is gorgeous. There's lots to do here, including tennis, watersports, a slot casino and miniature golf. A daily shuttle transports guests to the restaurants and shopping of Willemstad, some 25 minutes away. 35 rooms. Credit cards: A, DC, MC, V.

Curaçao Caribbean Hotel   **$140–$210**   ★★★★

John F. Kennedy Boulevard, Willemstad, ☎ *(599) 9-625000. FAX (599) 9-625846.*
Single: $140. Double: $150–$210.
Located at the site of historic Fort Piscadera, just outside of Willemstad, this five-story hotel overlooks a tiny beach. Guest rooms are adequate but cry out for renovation; even the nicest rooms, on the top Executive Floor have seen better days. Nonetheless, there's a lot happening here, with organized parties, theme nights and dance lessons. A free bus takes you into town. Facilities include a dive shop, two tennis courts, pool and casino. 200 rooms. Credit cards: A, DC, MC, V.

Habitat Curaçao   **$382–$817**   ★★★

Coral Estates, Rif St. Marie, ☎ *(800) 327-6709, (599) 9-607263. FAX (305) 371-2337.*
Single: $382–$817. Double: $382–$817.
Before you gasp too loudly at the quoted prices, note they are for four-night packages that include accommodations, daily buffet breakfast, airport transfers, two-tank boat dive daily, unlimited shore diving and all sorts of other goodies. This new dive property, just opened in late 1996, is located west of Willemstad and is a sister to the well-established Captain Don's Habitat. Guests are accommodated in junior suites or two-bedroom cottages, all with fully equipped kitchenettes and a patio or balcony. Facilities include a bar and restaurant, PADI five-star dive shop, convenience store and private beach. Seven-night and honeymoon packages are also available. 56 rooms.

Holiday Beach Hotel   **$110–$163**   ★★

Nether Angelus, Willemstad, ☎ *(599) 9-625400. FAX (599) 9-624973.*
Single: $110–$163. Double: $110–$163.
Though it's located on one of the island's better beaches and has a large, happening casino, this former Holiday Inn still brings to mind, well, a Holiday Inn. Still, this is a good middle-market property for those seeking all the amenities without sacrificing a year's salary. Recently renovated guest rooms are decent but only a few have ocean views. There's lots to do here: two recently resurfaced lighted tennis courts, watersports and scuba, supervised children's activities, a lively beach bar, organized tours and a large pool. 200 rooms. Credit cards: A, DC, D, MC, V.

Holland Hotel   **$70–$130**   ★★★★

Roosevelt Weg, FDR weg 524, Willemstad, ☎ *(599) 9-688044. FAX (599) 9-688114.*
Single: $70. Double: $80–$130.
The air-conditioned guest rooms are basic but comfortable at this small hotel near the airport. Though it's not on the beach, Holland does offer scuba packages, and has a pool and small casino to keep guests busy. 40 rooms. Credit cards: A, DC, MC, V.

Las Palmas Hotel   **$93–$140**   ★★

Willemstad, ☎ *(599) 9-625200.*
Single: $93–$140. Double: $93–$140.
Located two miles out of Willemstad on a hillside near a private beach, this sprawling complex—its full name is Las Palmas Hotel Villas Casino Beach Club—is a decent choice for those watching the purse strings. Accommodations are in air-conditioned guest rooms and two-bedroom villas with kitchens. All the expected recre-

ational facilities, from watersports to pool to tennis to casino. 184 rooms. Credit cards: A, DC, MC, V.

Lions Dive Hotel & Marina $105–$145   ★★★★★

Bapor Kibra Street, Willemstad, ☎ *(599) 9-618100. FAX (599) 9-618200.*
Single: $105–$145. Double: $105–$145.
Located next to Willemstad's Seaquarium on the island's largest beach, this spot specializes in the scuba diving trade. Their PADI dive center is superb, and offers everything from resort courses to excursions to sunset sails. There's also an excellent fitness center with all the latest equipment for whipping that body into shape. The air-conditioned guest rooms are standard but fine. Guests get to visit the aquarium for free; the shuttle that runs back and forth to town is also complimentary. 72 rooms. Credit cards: A, DC, MC, V.

Ortabanda Hotel & Casino $105–$105   ★★★

Hoek Breedesstraat, Willemstad, ☎ *(599) 9-627400. FAX (599) 9-627299.*
Single: $105. Double: $105.
Located in the heart of Willemstad's business and shopping district next to Queen Emma Bridge, some air-conditioned guest rooms have great harbor views. There's a restaurant and casino on site, but little else in the way of extras. Reasonable rates make this a good value. 45 rooms. Credit cards: A, DC, D, MC, V.

Porto Paseo Hotel $95–$125   ★★

De Rouvilleweg 47 Street, Willemstad, ☎ *(599) 9-627878. FAX (599) 9-627969.*
Single: $95. Double: $95–$125.
A peaceful oasis right in city center, this newer (1993) hotel has basic but comfortable air-conditioned rooms that were recently renovated, with the addition of refrigerators and coffeemakers. The ubiquitous pool, casino and restaurant cater to recreational needs, and the gardens are splendid. A good in-town choice. 44 rooms. Credit cards: A, DC, MC, V.

Princess Beach Resort $95–$225   ★★★★

Dr. Martin Luther King Boulevard, Willemstad, ☎ *(800) 327-3286, (599) 9-367888.*
FAX (599) 9-617205.
Single: $95–$225. Double: $95–$225.
Despite the name, this hotel is a Holiday Inn Crowne Plaza property, and is not affiliated with the cruise line. Located directly in front of Curaçao's Underwater Park on a lovely but small beach, the hotel offers spacious guest rooms with all the modern comforts. The grounds are nicely landscaped and include two restaurants, four bars, a happening casino, pool and tennis court and all watersports. This lively spot leaves visitors satisfied. 341 rooms. Credit cards: A, DC, D, MC, V.

Sonesta Beach Hotel $160–$335   ★★★★

Willemstad, ☎ *(800) 766-3782, (599) 9-368800.*
Single: $160–$335. Double: $160–$335.
Set on the beach and built in Dutch Colonial style, this newer (1992) resort receives raves for its luxurious appointments, beautiful landscaping and attractive guest rooms, all with a patio or balcony and at least a partial ocean view. Parents like the fact that two of their kids (up to age 12) can stay with them free, and that complimentary activities keep the little ones busy. Lots of nice artwork scattered about—a

CURAÇAO

Sonesta trademark—and gracious service help make this place tops. Health club, full casino, pool, tennis and watersports as well. 248 rooms. Credit cards: A, DC, MC, V.

Van der Valk Plaza Hotel   **$105–$210**   ★ ★ ★ ★
Plaza Piar, Willemstad, ☎ *(599) 9-612500. FAX (599) 9-618347.*
Single: $105–$180. Double: $105–$210.
Its 12-story tower sticks out like a sore thumb in quaint Willemstad, and the nearest beach is a 15-minute drive away. But nice harbor views make this hotel, built in the walls of a 17th-century fort, a pleasant choice. The central city location attracts lots of working travelers who are catered to with secretarial and business services. Rooms are merely adequate, but the great views of passing ships make a lot forgivable. There's a full casino and pool on site. 350 rooms. Credit cards: A, MC, V.

Apartments and Condominiums

Options range from the elegant at **La Belle Alliance** and **Las Palmas** to uninspiring apartment buildings that have basic kitchenettes.

Inns

One of the most atmospheric of all Curaçao's accommodations is the **Landhuis Hotel**. If you can get one of its few charming bedrooms, you'll feel as if you've been transported back 100 years ☎ *(599) 9-648-400*. **Porta Paseo** is more run-of-the-mill, though the restaurant attracts a lot of movement.

Low Cost Lodging

Best bet is to arrive in town and ask around for rooms in private homes. The tourist office can direct you to possibilities. In the off-season, Coral Cliff Resort's rooms drop down to 450, and a free shuttle bus will take you to Willemstad. Cheap rooms with kitchen privileges are also available, though they take a young, adventurous constitution to enjoy them.

Trupial Inn Hotel   **$80–$95**   ★ ★
5, Groot Davelaarweg, Willemstad.
Single: $80–$95. Double: $80–$95.
This bungalow-style motel is located in a residential neighborhood and has no beach, though a free shuttle will take you to the sea. Rooms are basic but comfortable and have air conditioning; there are also eight suites with kitchenettes. There's a restaurant, pool and tennis court, with additional eateries and shops within walking distance. 74 rooms. Credit cards: A, DC, MC, V.

Where to Eat

Fielding's Highest Rated Restaurants in Curaçao

★★★★★	De Taveerne	$18–$32
★★★★★	L'Alouette	$30–$40
★★★★	Bistro Le Clochard	$20–$30
★★★★	Fort Nassau	$20–$28
★★★★	Rijstaffel Restaurant	$13–$20
★★★★	Seaview	$15–$30
★★★	Belle Terrace	$14–$24
★★★	Golden Star	$8–$26
★★★	La Pergola	$30–$35
★★★	Wine Cellar	$20–$35

Fielding's Most Exclusive Restaurants in Curaçao

★★★★★	L'Alouette	$30–$40
★★★	La Pergola	$30–$35
★★★	Wine Cellar	$20–$35
★★★	Pirates	$15–$35
★★★★★	De Taveerne	$18–$32

Fielding's Best Value Restaurants in Curaçao

★★★★	Rijstaffel Restaurant	$13–$20
★★★★★	De Taveerne	$18–$32
★★	Cactus Club	$7–$15
★★★	Golden Star	$8–$26
★★★★	Seaview	$15–$30

CURAÇAO

The fact that Curaçao is populated by so many diverse nationalities is reflected in its foods, a wonderful mix of Creole, Chinese, South American, Dutch, French Indian and Indonesian cuisine. Restaurants can be pricey, but in this case, you do get what you pay for, as service and preparation are usually superb. The antique-filled De Taveerne is about as romantic as it gets; Belle Terrace, housed in a 200-year-old mansion right on the beach, also gets high marks for mood and setting. For Dutch fare, try 'T Kokkeltje; for the rijstaffel Indonesian buffet that's popular in these parts, try the restaurant of the same name, located in Salina. Curaçao's numerous casinos and handful of discos keep night owls happy; be sure to try Curaçao liqueur, an orange-flavored drink that turned 100 in 1996 and is also available in run raisin, chocolate and coffee flavors.

Belle Terrace   **$$$**   ★★★

Penstraat 130, Willemstad, ☎ (599) 961-4377. Associated hotel: Avila Beach Hotel.
Scandinavian cuisine. Specialties: Danish smorgasbord, keshi yena, barracuda.
Lunch: Noon–3 p.m., entrées $10–$15.
Dinner: 7–10 p.m., entrées $14–$24.
Eating out in Willemstad is very often a historic experience—one day it's breakfast high above the sea (never far away here) on a hilltop in a converted 18th-century fort, or, in the case of the Belle Terrace, right on the beach (albeit a rocky one) in a 200-year-old mansion, the former home of the island's governor. Sometimes the cuisine, which includes a smorgasbord at lunch, featuring salmon and other fish smoked on the premises, can be less than stellar, but with a setting like this, who cares? Breads and ice creams are homemade. Reservations required. Credit cards: A, DC, MC, V.

Bistro Le Clochard   **$$$**   ★★★★

Rif Fort, Willemstad, ☎ (599) 962-5666.
French cuisine. Specialties: Bouillabaisse, raclette, fondue.
Lunch: Noon–2 p.m., entrées $20–$30.
Dinner: 6:30–11 p.m., entrées $20–$30. Closed: Sun.
Dine in this traditional French/Swiss bistro, one of a number of restaurants built in the vaults of what is left of the old (early 19th century) Rif Fort near the harbor. As with many Willemstad restaurants, you may dine indoors or on the open-air Harborside Terrace. Various fondues reflect the tastes of the owner's wife (who is Swiss), and they include raclette with potatoes, pickles and onions, and bourguignone. There's also fresh fish, veal and lobster. The outdoor terrace is only open for dinner, and there's no lunch served on weekends. Reservations required. Credit cards: A, DC, MC, V.

Cactus Club   **$$**   ★★

6 van Staverenweg, Willemstad, ☎ (599) 937-1600.
American cuisine. Specialties: Fajitas, buffalo wings, cajun snapper.
Lunch: 11:30 a.m.–3 p.m., entrées $4–$15.
Dinner: 5–11:30 p.m., entrées $7–$15.
A transplanted, stateside-style after-work restaurant and bar, the Cactus Club doles out tasty burgers, shakes, nachos, pastas and fajitas to homesick Americans and

locals who love the place, which is always full. Decor is Southwest-desert, but it's nice and cool inside. Credit cards: DC, MC, V.

De Taveerne $$$ ★★★★★

Landhuis Groot Davelaar, Willemstad, ☎ (599) 937-0669.
French cuisine. Specialties: Salmon carpaccio, chateaubriand stroganoff for two.
Lunch: Noon–2 p.m., entrées $18–$32.
Dinner: 7–11 p.m., entrées $18–$32. Closed: Sun.

The owners of this innovative and highly regarded French restaurant in the Salina residential area have renovated a traditional old octagonal country mansion—the Landhuis Groot Davelaar, built in the early 18th century by a South American revolutionary—into an antique-filled mini-museum. Once the main house of a cattle-producing estate, it is one of many scattered throughout the arid countryside. Prime beef shows up on its tables in the form of platter-size steaks and chateaubriand for two. Closed for lunch on Saturdays. Reservations required. Credit cards: A, DC, MC, V.

Fort Nassau $$$ ★★★★

Fort Nassau, Willemstad, ☎ (599) 961-3086.
International cuisine. Specialties: Smoked salmon, shrimp with red linguine in a spicy sauce.
Lunch: Noon–3 p.m., entrées $20–$28.
Dinner: 7–10 p.m., entrées $20–$28.

If you never dine anywhere else in Curaçao, don't miss Fort Nassau, which sings with history even though some dishes may be over-ambitious and miss the mark at times. Perched like an eagle's nest above Willemstad and overlooking Santa Anna Bay, diners can see forever from here. Used as a fort by the Dutch in the late 18th century and by Americans in World War II, it became a restaurant in the 1950s. Cuisine runs the gamut from Asian to Italian, utilizing fresh fish, pasta and game in combination with local tropical fruits. No lunch served on weekends. Reservations recommended. Credit cards: A, DC, MC, V.

Fort Waakzaamheid Bistro $$$ ★★

Seru di Domi, Willemstad, ☎ (599) 962-3633.
Seafood cuisine. Specialties: Veal curry, barbecued steaks.
Dinner: 5–11 p.m., entrées $17–$26. Closed: Tue.

An alternative to the often-crowded Fort Nassau, which gets inundated with cruise-ship passengers, this hilltop aerie in the Otrabanda was held captive many moons ago by the notorious Captain Bligh, probably in part because he was spellbound by the view. There is no need to dress up for this American-style tavern and bar, which is open for dinner only. There is a fresh fish and salad special daily, as well as barbecued steaks, scampi and veal curry. Credit cards: A, MC, V.

Golden Star $$$ ★★★

Socratesstraat 2, Willemstad, ☎ (599) 965-4795.
Latin American cuisine. Specialties: Carni stoba, stoba de Carco, grilled conch.
Lunch: 11 a.m.–6 p.m., entrées $8–$26.
Dinner: 4 p.m.–1 a.m., entrées $8–$26.

Go local in this deliberately tacky restaurant dive, which has the best authentic Antillean food in town. There may be no better place for carni stoba (meat stew), conch served lightly grilled or with vegetables, goat and criollo shrimp, accompanied with plenty of starchy and filling (and good) rice, fried bananas and funchi (cornmeal pancakes). Beer, especially locally brewed Amstel, is the preferred beverage with this food. Golden Star is open until 1 a.m. Credit cards: A, DC, MC, V.

L'Alouette   **$$$**   ★★★★★
Orionweig 12, Willemstad, ☎ *(599) 961-8222.*
International cuisine. Specialties: Cheese flan, seafood sausage.
Lunch: Noon–2:30 p.m., entrées $18–$30.
Dinner: 6–9 p.m., entrées $30–$40. Closed: Sun.
Amid beautiful, sleek surroundings, you can eat creative French cuisine and still keep your weight down at this sophisticated eatery specializing in the best ingredients available, embellished with light and springlike herbs and spices. Chef Maria Eugenia Saban pays close attention to detail in this restored house in a residential area on the east side of the harbor. Specials that never change are her cheese flan duet with mushroom and basil sauces. Cuisine may be light, but portions are substantial and worth the high tariff. Reservations required. Credit cards: A, DC, MC, V.

La Pergola   **$$$**   ★★★
Waterfort Arches, Willemstad, ☎ *(599) 961-3482.*
Italian cuisine. Specialties: Smoked salmon with olive oil and cloves, grouper siciliana.
Lunch: Noon–2 p.m., entrées $25–$35.
Dinner: 6:30–10:30 p.m., entrées $30–$35. Closed: Sun.
A seaside Italian eatery in the trendy Waterfort Arches shopping center, La Pergola serves pizzas, fresh fish and desserts with a light hand—no heavy tomato or gloppy cream sauces here. Take your seat on the lovely terrace facing wrap-around windows and watch the wavy action below, and feast on the likes of grouper Sicilian-style with a puttanesca sauce and conclude with an airy, angelic Zuppa Inglese. Closed for Sunday lunch. Reservations recommended. Credit cards: A, DC, D, MC, V.

Pirates   **$$$**   ★★★
Piscadera Bay, Willemstad, ☎ *(599) 962-5000.*
Associated hotel: Curaçao Caribbean Hotel.
Latin American cuisine. Specialties: Paella, red snapper almendrado, ceviche.
Lunch: entrées $15–$35.
Dinner: entrées $15–$35.
In addition to an Indonesian restaurant, La Garuda, and bountiful buffets served on the Pisca Terrace bar facing a spectacular swimming pool, this newcomer to the Curaçao Caribbean Hotel and Casino's dining scene might assure that its guests needn't leave this minicity-within-a-city resort on Piscadera Bay. Famous for theme-night parties, the hotel's latest successful scheme is Pirates, specializing in tasty Latin-style seafood, including paella and ceviche, served by a charming waitstaff in nautical garb. Reservations recommended. Credit cards: A, DC, MC, V.

Playa Forti   **$$**   ★★
Westpunt, Willemstad, ☎ *(599) 964-0273.*
Latin American cuisine. Specialties: Cabrito, fish soup, keshi yena.
Lunch: entrées $5–$16.
Dinner: entrées $6–$16.
If you find yourself in the northwest point of the island, dine at this clifftop retreat overlooking Playa Forti beach. It's a hangout for tasty criollo food, and a good place

to try keshi yena, an island specialty of meats cooked with Creole sauce and covered with Edam or Gouda cheese. Other specialties to try are cabrito or goat stew, and funchi, or local cornbread. Sunsets are gorgeous here as well. Meals are served from 10 a.m. to 6 p.m. Credit cards: A, MC, V.

Rijstaffel Restaurant $$$ ★ ★ ★ ★

Mercuriusstraat 13, Willemstad, ☎ *(599) 961-2999.*
Asian cuisine. Specialties: Rijstaffel, bami goreng, jumbo shrimp in garlic sauce.
Lunch: Noon–2 p.m., prix fixe $9–$17.
Dinner: 6–9:30 p.m., prix fixe $13–$20.
A carry-over of Dutch colonial days, rijstaffel is a banquet of up to 25 spicy and savory Indonesian-Javanese dishes surrounded by a mound of steaming rice. A delightful change from the usual steaks and surf and turf awaits at this restaurant in the Salina area, known for its nightlife. To eat here, get a group together and book a table several days ahead for a 16-to-25 dish feast that includes bami goreng (fried noodles, shrimp, meat and vegetables) and krupuk (gigantic shrimp chips). Vegetarian and a la carte dishes are also available. Reservations recommended. Credit cards: A, DC, MC, V.

Seaview $$$ ★ ★ ★ ★

Waterfort Arches, Willemstad, ☎ *(599) 961-6688.*
Seafood cuisine. Specialties: Salpicon de mariscos, pepper filet.
Lunch: Noon–2 p.m., entrées $15–$30.
Dinner: 6–10 p.m., entrées $15–$30. Closed: Sun.
An amiable surfside spot located right in the heart of the Waterfort Arches, one of Willemstad's many converted old army posts and now a busy retail, nightlife and culinary bazaar, Seaview offers up spectacular ocean and sunset vistas from a breezy terrace or air-conditioned dining room. Its forte, naturally, is fresh-from-the-briny fish and shellfish, as well as prime meats, fresh vegetables and international dishes. Reservations recommended. Credit cards: A.

'T Kokkeltje $$$ ★ ★

F.D. Rooseveltweg 524, Willemstad.
International cuisine. Specialties: Split-pea soup, herring, Caribbean chicken.
Lunch: entrées $12–$27.
Dinner: entrées $12–$27.
Sample Dutch fare by the pool at the Hotel Holland located on the highway to the airport. The hard-to-pronounce name means cockles and this cozy restaurant serves marinated mussels when available. Other specialties to savor are split-pea soup, pickled herring and salads. There is also a dimly lit dining room for those who prefer it. Food is served from 7 a.m. to 10:30 p.m. Credit cards: A, MC, V.

Wine Cellar $$$ ★ ★ ★

Concordiastraat, Willemstad, ☎ *(599) 961-2178.*
International cuisine. Specialties: Roast goose, lobster salad, red snapper.
Lunch: Noon–2 p.m., entrées $20–$35.
Dinner: 5–11 p.m., entrées $20–$35. Closed: Mon.
Connoisseurs of fine wines repair here to master sommelier and rotisseur Nico Cornelisse's lair, a traditional, small (about eight tables) and comfortable Dutch home near the cathedral in downtown Willemstad. The voluminous wine list consists of

vintages from the Alsace region of France, as well as Germany and Italy. To complement these refined labels are some hearty dishes to warm the blood, including filet of beef with goat cheese sauce, venison and roast goose. More delicate appetites will appreciate light seafood salads and red snapper. Service is attentive and personable. Reservations required. Credit cards: A, MC, V.

Unlike the other two islands that make up the ABCs, Curaçao is great for shoppers, with trendy boutiques and upscale shops in picturesque Willemstad, where two of the main shopping streets are pedestrian malls. Because it has no duty or sales tax, good deals can be found on imported cameras, china, crystal, electronics, linens, jewelry and perfume. As always, if you plan on doing some serious dropping of cash, check the prices back home first to see if you're really saving enough to justify the hassle of transporting your purchases and obtaining refunds or repairs if necessary. For name-brand imports, check out **Penha & Sons** *(Heerenstraat 1,* ☎ *[599] 9-612266)*, housed in a 1708 building; **Little Switzerland** *(Breedesstraat 44, Punda,* ☎ *[599] 9-612111)*, and **Boolchand's** *(Heerenstraat,* ☎ *[599] 9-616233)*. For handicrafts by local artisans, check out **Fundason Obra di Man** *(Bargenstraat 57,* ☎ *[599] 9-612413)*. If you're interested in unique pieces of jewelry made from rare black coral, try the boutique in the Princess Beach Hotel, appropriated named **Black Coral** *(*☎ *[599] 9-614944)*.Though stores usually close for a lunch hour and on Sundays, they stay open during those times when cruise ships are in port.

Curaçao Directory

Arrival and Departure

American Airlines provides daily nonstop flights to Curaçao from Miami. American also offers flights to Aruba from New York, Miami, and San Juan, Puerto Rico, where you can make an easy transfer to Curaçao. American also offers discounts if their agent makes your hotel reservation at the same time as your air passage. **ALM**, the national carrier of Curaçao, also flies 13 times a week from Miami to Curaçao (three nonstop) and four times a week from Atlanta. **Air Aruba** also flies seven times a week to Aruba from Newark; easy transfers can be made to Curaçao.

Business Hours

Shops open Monday–Saturday 8 a.m.–noon and 2–6 p.m. Banks open Monday–Friday 8:30 a.m.–noon and 1:30–4:30 p.m.

Climate

Like Bonaire and Aruba, its neighbors, Curaçao is to the south of the Hurricane Belt, making storms an extremely unusual occurrence. The island is constantly refreshed by trade winds blowing from 10–20 miles per hour and the temperature stays constant all year round, seldom fluctuating out of the mid-80s. Summer can be a few degrees hotter and winter a little cooler. Light, casual clothing is the rule. Hotels and casinos are air-conditioned so you may wish to bring fancier clothes, or a sweater.

Documents

U.S. and Canadian citizens need to show proof of citizenship (passport, birth certificate, or voter's registration) plus a photo ID, and an ongoing or return ticket beyond the Netherlands Antilles.

Electricity

Current is 110–130 volts AC, 50 cycles. Outlets are American-style. Converters are not necessarily needed for American appliances, but hotels have supplies.

Getting Around

Inquire whether your hotel has a free shuttle service to the shopping district of Willemstad. If not, yellow city buses stop at Wilhelmina Plein, near the shopping center, and travel to most parts of the city. Buses stop when you hail them.

Taxi rates are regulated by the government. Don't tip a driver unless he carries your luggage. Charges after 11 p.m. go up by 25 percent. You'll find lots of taxis waiting for passengers on the Otrabanda side of the floating bridge. If you want to make a tour by taxi, expect to pay about $20 per hour (up to four passengers allowed).

Rental cars are represented by **Avis** toll-free ☎ *(800) 31-2112*, **Budget** toll free ☎ *(800) 527-0700* and **Hertz** toll-free ☎ *(800) 654-3001*. Check your credit card to see if you can obtain insurance just by charging. To save money, reserve the car from the States before you arrive. Do note that all driving is on the right.

Language

The native language is Papiamento, the official language Dutch, but most everybody speaks some form of English, as well as Spanish.

Medical Emergencies

The 550-bed St. Elizabeth Hospital is the main facility of the island.

Money

Official currency is guilder (Netherlands Antilles florin), noted as NAf. U.S. dollars and credit cards are accepted unilaterally.

Telephone

Country code is *5999*. From the States, dial *011* (international access code), *5999* (country code) + local number. If you are calling from another Caribbean island, check to see if the same code applies. Within Curaçao itself, use only the six-digit number.

Time

Atlantic standard time all year long.

Tipping and Taxes

Ten percent service charge is added to restaurant bills, but waiters appreciate an extra five percent.

Tourist Information

The **Curaçao Tourist Board** has offices in *Willemstad at the Waterfront Arches* ☎ *613397, closed weekends, and 19 Pietermaai* ☎ *661600.* At all offices you can obtain brochures, maps and have questions answered by English-speaking staff. An office is also at the airport ☎ *668678* (open daily till last flight arrives). In the U.S. call ☎ *(800) 270-3350.*

Water

Tap water, distilled seawater, is safe to drink.

When to Go

Carnival takes place in January, an unrestrained revel complete with costumes, parades and street parties. Best time is the weekend right before Ash Wednesday. The International Sailing Regatta is held in March.

CURAÇAO HOTELS		RMS	RATES	PHONE	CR. CARDS
Rif St. Marie					
★★★	**Habitat Curacao**	56	$382–$817	(800) 327-6709	
Willemstad					
★★★★★	**Avila Beach Hotel**	85	$85–$198	(599) 9-614377	A, DC, MC, V
★★★★★	**Lions Dive Hotel & Marina**	72	$105–$145	(599) 9-618100	A, DC, MC, V
★★★★	**Curacao Caribbean Hotel**	200	$140–$210	(599) 9-625000	A, DC, MC, V
★★★★	**Holland Hotel**	40	$70–$130	(599) 9-688044	A, DC, MC, V
★★★★	**Princess Beach Resort**	341	$95–$225	(800) 327-3286	A, D, DC, MC, V
★★★★	**Sonesta Beach Hotel**	248	$160–$335	(800) 766-3782	A, DC, MC, V
★★★★	**Van der Valk Plaza Hotel**	350	$105–$210	(599) 9-612500	A, MC, V
★★★	**Ortabanda Hotel & Casino**	45	$105–$105	(599) 9-627400	A, D, DC, MC, V
★★	**Holiday Beach Hotel**	200	$110–$163	(599) 9-625400	A, D, DC, MC, V
★★	**Las Palmas Hotel**	184	$93–$140	(599) 9-625200	A, DC, MC, V
★★	**Porto Paseo Hotel**	44	$95–$125	(599) 9-627878	A, DC, MC, V
★★	**Trupial Inn Hotel**	74	$80–$95		A, DC, MC, V
★	**Coral Cliff Hotel**	35	$68–$122	(599) 9-641610	A, DC, MC, V

CURAÇAO

CURAÇAO RESTAURANTS	PHONE	ENTRÉE	CR. CARDS
Willemstad			
American			
★★ Cactus Club	(599) 937-1600	$4–$15	DC, MC, V
Asian			
★★★★ Rijstaffel Restaurant	(599) 961-2999	$9–$20	A, DC, MC, V
French			
★★★★★ De Taveerne	(599) 937-0669	$18–$32	A, DC, MC, V
★★★★ Bistro Le Clochard	(599) 962-5666	$20–$30	A, DC, MC, V
International			
★★★★ Fort Nassau	(599) 961-3086	$20–$28	A, DC, MC, V
★★★★★ L'Alouette	(599) 961-8222	$18–$40	A, DC, MC, V
★★★ Wine Cellar	(599) 961-2178	$20–$35	A, MC, V
★★ 'T Kokkeltje		$12–$27	A, MC, V
Italian			
★★★ La Pergola	(599) 961-3482	$25–$35	A, D, DC, MC, V
Latin American			
★★★ Golden Star	(599) 965-4795	$8–$26	A, DC, MC, V
★★★ Pirates	(599) 962-5000	$15–$35	A, DC, MC, V
★★ Playa Forti	(599) 964-0273	$5–$16	A, MC, V
Scandinavian			
★★★ Belle Terrace	(599) 961-4377	$10–$24	A, DC, MC, V
Seafood			
★★★★ Seaview	(599) 961-6688	$15–$30	A
★★ Fort Waakzaamheid Bistro	(599) 962-3633	$17–$26	A, MC, V

CURAÇAO

DOMINICA

Bananas, coconuts, grapefruit, limes and passionfruit are important to Dominica's economy.

Quite fairly labeling itself the "Nature Island of the Caribbean," Dominica has changed little since Columbus set foot on its shore some 500 years ago. Although the 290-square-mile island has grown up a little since 1493, there are still no McDonald's, no casinos, no duty-free stores and precious little nightlife. It might be the one Caribbean island that Columbus might recognize today. Blame Dominica's backwoods quality on the absence of white sand beaches, a "setback" that helped create a silver lining many other islands are now emulating: eco-tourism. For what Dominica does have is one of the world's last ocean rainforests, a flooded and boiling fumarole said to be the second-largest anywhere, a lake covered with purple hyacinths, and so many species of trees that one of them is actually called "no-name." Here is an earth of striking, lava-formed landscapes, of forests dense with bromeliads and lianas, chataigniers and goumiers, of terrain so dazzlingly accented with heliconia and anthurium blossoms you could easily believe you're in the Garden of Eden. The island receives so much rain—250 inches a year—that literally hundreds of rivers cascade from the steep mountain slopes. It may be the only Caribbean island that exports its water, and there is so much mist from the morning and afternoon showers that rainbows are as predictable as the sun. "Liquid sunshine" is practically a commodity here—evanescent drizzles of mist that waft onto the mountain slopes with generous blades of sunlight cutting through the thick air.

A vacation to Dominica is, quite simply, a different one than is offered on any other Caribbean isle. The Dominica experience isn't about beaches (though there are a number of gray-sand coves ringing the island), nor is it about sunshine (though sunlight makes regular appearances between showers on most days). Instead, Dominica is about fighting your way up muddy mountain paths, boiling your body in hot sulfur springs, and tracking the flight of the rare, endangered sisserou parrot, a bird whose numbers are counted in the dozens. Divers can exploit a real surf-and-turf vacation by plunging into the dazzling depths one day, then tackling an equally daunting land excursion the next. In sum, Dominica is not for the faint-hearted, and those who are in shape will be rewarded the most. Although a long-planned, 87-room Aman luxury resort is now set for a late 1997 debut, and hydro-electric, marina and other eco-threatening projects have been called into question, the government wants to continue its pursuit of eco-dollars. If they can keep the tourism infrastructure small and manageable, Dominica will continue to reward visitors with a one-of-a-kind Caribbean experience.

Bird's-Eye View

Not to be confused with the much larger Dominican Republic, the Commonwealth of Dominica sprawls over a mountainous, 29- by 16-mile territory, lying between Guadeloupe to the north and Martinique to the south. Like the two French islands, Dominica is part of the Caribbean's chain of active volcanoes, with a jagged terrain born from the violence of past eruptions. The northern half of the island is dominated by a single peak, Morne Diablotins, which rises to 4747 feet—its slopes are uninhabited except along the shoreline. This is also the location of the vast Northern Forest Reserve, and the habitat of the island's two indigenous and endangered parrots: the brown and green sisserou (or imperial), the largest and perhaps rarest Ama-

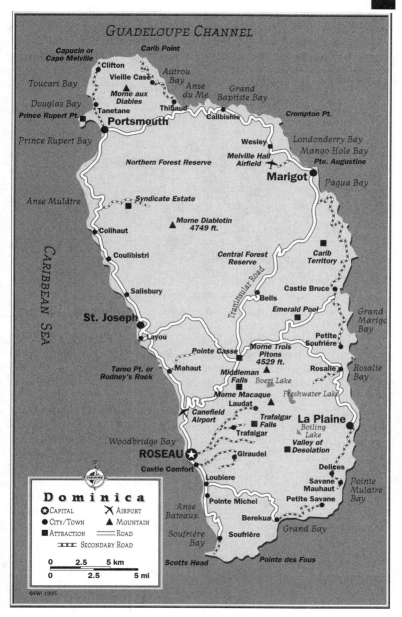

DOMINICA

GUADELOUPE CHANNEL

Capucin or Cape Melville
Carib Point
Clifton
Vielle Case
Autrou Bay
Anse du Me
Grand Baptiste Bay
Toucari Bay
Morne aux Diables
Thibaud
Douglas Bay
Tanetane
Calibishie
Crompton Pt.
Prince Rupert Pt.
Portsmouth
Prince Rupert Bay
Wesley
Londonderry Bay
Mango Hole Bay
Melville Hall Airfield
Pte. Augustine
Northern Forest Reserve
Marigot
Pagua Bay
Anse Muldtre
Syndicate Estate
Colihaut
Morne Diablotin 4749 ft.
Carib Territory
Coulibistri
Central Forest Reserve
Salisbury
Castle Bruce
Bells
Emerald Pool
Grand Marigot Bay
St. Joseph
Layou
Pointe Casse
Petite Soufriére
Tarou Pt. or Rodney's Rock
Mahaut
Morne Trois Pitons 4529 ft.
Rosalie
Rosalie Bay
Middleman Falls
Boeri Lake
Morne Macaque
Freshwater Lake
Laudat
Canefield Airport
Trafalgar Falls
La Plaine
Trafalgar
Boiling Lake
Valley of Desolation
ROSEAU
Giraudel
Delices
Castle Comfort
Savane Mauhaut
Pointe Mulatre Bay
Loubiere
Woodbridge Bay
Pointe Michel
Petite Savane
Anse Bateaux
Berekua
Soufriére Bay
Soufriére
Grand Bay
Scotts Head
Pointe des Fous

CARIBBEAN SEA

Transinsular Road

Dominica

- ⊕ CAPITAL
- ✕ AIRPORT
- ● CITY/TOWN
- ▲ MOUNTAIN
- ■ ATTRACTION
- ═══ ROAD
- ⅢⅢ SECONDARY ROAD

0   2.5   5 km
0   2.5   5 mi

©FWI 1995

DOMINICA

zon species in the world; and the jaco (or rednecked), a more colorful bird whose population numbers in the hundreds. The second-largest town on the island, Plymouth, lies in a large bay near the northwest tip.

Dominica's small Emerald Pool waterfall attracts hordes of tourists.

The center portion of the island is less mountainous, with its small Central Forest Reserve and plantations of lime and banana, but rising above Pont Casse, a crossroads near the middle of the island, is steep Morne Trois Pitons, the island's second-highest point at 4403 feet. The deeply indented valleys and soaring peaks south of here allow primal rainforests to grow unfettered, and waterfalls to tumble into ravines. On the slopes of Morne Nicholls is the Boiling Lake, a rain-choked volcanic crater that bubbles with temperatures ranging from simmering to torrid—next to the crater is the Valley of Desolation, a basin filled with vivid geothermal activity. The area is protected as part of the 16,000-acre Morne Trois Pitons National Park. Roseau is the prototypical West Indian port, as many of them appeared a few decades ago—it is slightly unkempt, but it rings of the authentic bustle of island trade rather than of chasing the beat of Dominica's relatively few tourists. About a third of the 82,000 residents live in and around Roseau, the rest reside in smallish communities that dot the coastline on both the Caribbean and wilder Atlantic coasts.

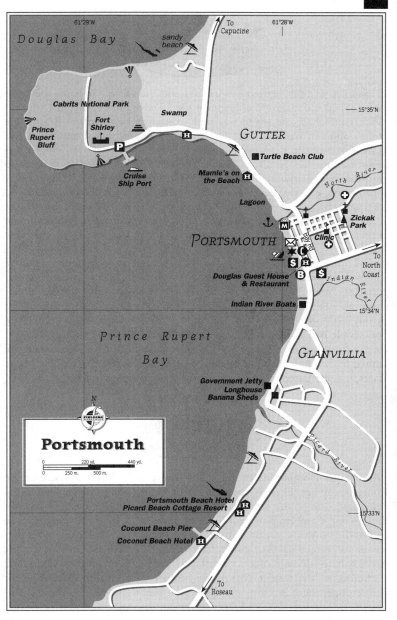

61°29'W

61°28'W

To
Capucine

Douglas Bay

sandy
beach

Cabrits National Park

Swamp

— 15°35'N

Fort
Shirley

GUTTER

Prince
Rupert
Bluff

P

■Turtle Beach Club

H

Cruise
Ship Port

Mamie's on
the Beach   H

North River

Lagoon

⚓

PORTSMOUTH   M

Zickak
Park

Bay Rd

Clinic

To
North
Coast

S   H

Douglas Guest House
& Restaurant   B

S

Indian River

Indian River Boats ■

— 15°34'N

Prince   Rupert

Bay

GLANVILLIA

Government Jetty ■
Longhouse
Banana Sheds ■

N

Picard River

Portsmouth

| 0 | 220 yd. | 440 yd. |

| 0 | 250 m. | 500 m. |

Portsmouth Beach Hotel
Picard Beach Cottage Resort   H
H

— 15°33'N

Coconut Beach Pier
Coconut Beach Hotel   H

To
Roseau

History

Dominica was first settled by Arawaks and then Carib Indians, the latter who dubbed the island "Tall Is Her Body." During the 17th and 18th centuries, control for the island was hotly contested between the British, the French and the native tribes. The British finally prevailed and Dominica formed part of the Leeward Islands federation until 1939. In 1940 it was transferred to the Windward Islands and remained attached to that group until the federal arrangement was ended in December 1959. Under a new constitution, effective from January 1960, Dominica achieved a separate status with its own administrator and an enlarged legislative council. In 1967, it became one of the West Indies Associated States, gaining full autonomy in internal affairs with the United Kingdom retaining responsibility for defense and foreign relations. Following a decision in 1975 by the Associated States to seek independence separately, Dominica became an independent republic within the Commonwealth on Nov. 3, 1978. A program instigated in August 1991, granting Dominican citizenship to foreigners in return for a minimum of U.S. $35,000 in the country, caused considerable controversy, but by July 1992, the amount had been reduced and a quota set. By mid-1993, 466 people had taken advantage of the program, however, mostly Taiwanese. In foreign policy, Dominica has close links both with France and the United States. As a member of the Organization of the Eastern Caribbean States, it contributed assistance to the U.S. intervention in Grenada.

People

Almost all Dominicans profess Christianity and about 80 percent are Roman Catholics. There is a community of about 3000 Carib Indians on the east coast, one of the last two in existence (the other is on St. Vincent), though few if any are pure-blooded and none speak the Carib language. In part of the northeast, an English dialect known as cocoy is spoken by the descendants of freed slaves originally from Antigua. The French influence is felt strongly here—Dominica was part of the French empire for many years, and a number of the tourist arrivals are visitors from nearby Martinique or Guadeloupe; there is a thriving Alliance Francaise outlet. Tourism is a secondary economic pursuit and farming remains the principal industry, heavily dependent on the banana, which is vulnerable to weather conditions. The island has historically been one of the region's poorest, but conditions are improving. The amiable population is almost 98 percent black, and has not been hardened to outsiders in the way that residents of more heavily trammeled islands have been. As such, what hotels and restaurants may lack in efficiency and amenities is made up by friendly, generous nature. Novelist Jean Rhys was born here, and wrote about Dominica memorably in Wide Sargasso Sea (made into a panting 1992 movie shot in Jamaica), while contemporary author Lennox Honeychurch has documented the island's history in Our Island Culture and other books.

Dominica has only a few beaches of note, and many will happily point to the rivers as the best place for swimming. The west coast has some decent strands, particularly the long cove just south of Portsmouth at the Picard Estate. Farther south at Mero, just south of Salisbury, the sand is black but well kept at the Castaways Beach Hotel. The best beach near Roseau is at Scott's Head, a 20-minute drive south of the capital to lovely Soufriere Bay. Light sand beaches can be found on the north coast, such as Woodford Hill (near the Melville Hall airport) and Hampstead but currents are tricky all along the Atlantic coast. The sand is a beautiful golden color at Point Baptiste.

Diving on Dominica was an insider's secret only a few years ago, but the island has quietly emerged as one of the four or five best dive locations in the Eastern Caribbean. The terrain under water looks much like the mountains above: walls drop for hundreds of feet but are still manageable for beginning-to-intermediate divers. Visibility, despite frequent rain run-off, averages a respectable 75 feet; sediment is quickly carried to plunging depths (the mountain soil actually contributes to the underwater scene far more than it detracts by supplying nutrients to the reef's many filter feeders). Most of the diving is concentrated in Soufriere Bay, a submerged volcanic crater a mile wide, that drops to nearly a thousand feet in its center; pinnacles are scattered liberally along the sheer lip and invertebrate life is superbly displayed. There is also good diving in Douglas Bay just north of Portsmouth, and in

Castle Comfort, the rocky cove immediately south of Roseau. Snorkelers will enjoy the inside of Scott's Head and should not miss the singular sparkle of Champagne.

Waterfalls tumbling past wild orchids, slender ridges leading to mist-blown peaks, and three crater lakes—cool or boiling, take your pick. If there's a better adventure destination in the Caribbean than Dominica, step forward now. The government has guarded precious wild assets with remarkable foresight for an island of such fragile economic resources. In 1996 the government was investigating the novel policy of instituting a fee to visit some of the island's special sights. Time will tell if such a surcharge is supported by tourists, or if the moneys generated will in turn be spent wisely maintaining the island's considerable National Park and Forest Reserve areas. But why wait and see? Your visit to the verdant forests and volcanic innards of this out-of-the-way destination will be nothing less than memorable.

Guides are available for all excursions, but are not absolutely necessary for experienced hikers tackling the Freshwater and Boeri lakes or Trafalgar Falls trails listed below. Visitors do become lost, however, and the trek to the Boiling Lake, in particular, should not be attempted without a guide. Dominica's regular and heavy rainfall works against trails in two ways: paths become washed out or engulfed with mud, and the forest never stops growing, enveloping the trails in green with lightning speed. Guides almost always carry a machete and can frequently be seen maintaining trails even when they're not leading hikes.

Insider Tip:

Dress right for trekking: sturdy shoes with good ankle supports and loose-fitting, lightweight clothes. Take your own water supply and make sure you use sunscreen, even if there seems to be no light filtering through the treetops.

By Pedal

Biking on Dominica is not for the faint-hearted. Yet those who are up to its steep and winding roads will discover numerous possibilities. One demanding all-day trip laced with spectacular views of Morne Trois Pitons through the mists totals about 25 miles and heads north out of Roseau to take in the western coastline, turning inland at Layou River. Where the main road splits a couple of miles later, take the right branch, which climbs steadily toward Pont Casse before heading down the precipitate main artery into Roseau. The route around the island's perimeter is strictly for Tour de France types: 55 dizzying, thigh-busting miles.

What Else to See

In Roseau, all the sights are within walking distance of each other. Many of the attractive older buildings are standing, even after the devastation of 1979's Hurricane David, though newer structures increasingly dominate the scene. Dawbiney Market Plaza is chock-full of art exhibits, handicrafts and local fruits and vegetable stands—the big market day is Saturday morning. On the outskirts of town, heading toward Trafalgar Falls, is the 40-acre Botanical Gardens, which houses an orchid collection and also a breeding program for the endangered sisserou and jaco parrots. Several roads out of Roseau snake high into the mountains, leading to the trailheads that access the lush Morne Trois Pitons National Park (see "On Foot"). The easiest trail is the 15-minute hike to Trafalgar Falls—stop by Papillote Wilderness Retreat on the way back to your car for lunch or a sip of their fine rum punch. The road south from Roseau passes through the quaint village of Soufriere on the way to Scotts Head, a promontory jutting into the Caribbean. Views of Martinique can be excellent, and snorkeling in Soufriere Bay, a submerged volcanic crater, is excellent.

The main road circuiting the island is in pretty good shape, and a rental car is the best way to tour the major sights, but even though there's only one traffic light on the island, be sure to allow a full day. The west coast of Dominica is spectacular, a succession of tiny fishing villages perched at the mouths of steep river valleys. The island's second largest town is Portsmouth, which isn't anything special, but it lies next the Indian River, where it is possible to take a one-hour cruise by paddle up the peaceful, mangrove-fringed river (about $8 per person). Just north of Portsmouth is Cabrits National Park, a double-peaked peninsula that defines the north edge of Prince Rupert Bay, lovely natural harbor watched over by Morne Diablotins. Cabrits contains the ruins of Fort Shirley, a British fort dating back to the mid-1700s. Heading east out of Portsmouth, one passes coconut plantations and several scenic beaches en route to the village of Calibishie, and Almond Beach Restaurant, a good lunch stop; farther down the coast is another good rest stop, Floral Gardens in Concord. This is Carib Indian Territory. You can drive through the 3700-acre reservation (established in 1903), but a guide will provide a better appreciation of the area. Continuing toward Pont Casse (a rotary near the center of the island), you'll soon reach a turnoff for Emerald Pool, where a 50-foot waterfall plunges into a basin surrounded by dense forest. The trail is short, and the falls are nice, but avoid the spot if a cruise ship tour has invaded.

Roseau, Dominica's capital, has made Old Market Plaza a pedestrian area.

Parks and Gardens

Cabrits National Park   ★★★★

   Portsmouth, ☎ *(809) 448-2401.*

   Located on the northwestern coast, this gorgeous peninsula encompasses 1313 acres of tropical forests, swampland, beaches, coral reefs and various ruins. The most notable structure is Fort Shirley, a 1770 military complex which has been undergoing restoration and it includes a small museum. Good for birding.

Morne Trois Pitons National Park   ★★★★★

   South-central region, Roseau, ☎ *(809) 448-2733.*

The 25-square-mile slice of nature, named after Dominica's second-highest peak, is a primordial rainforest high in the mountains above Roseau. Most of the park is reached on foot only, and guides are a good idea. The highlight is the Boiling Lake, a bubbling mass of muddy water that's seen only by the hardy—it takes six to seven strenuous hours to hike there and back. The Valley of Desolation you pass through to get to the Boiling Lake is another area of geothermal activity. Short trails include one to Freshwater and Boeri Lakes, which were once one body of water until a younger volcano, Morne Micotrin, sprouted and split them in two. Another trail goes to the thundering Middleham Falls; see "On Foot" for more hiking information.

Tours

Guided Tours ★ ★ ★ ★

Various locations, Roseau.

A number of outfits will take you on driving tours around Dominica, from the city sights of Roseau to the rainforest, Trafalgar Falls to Portmouth: **Wilderness Adventure Tours** ☎ *(809) 448-2198*, **Rainbow Rover Tours** ☎ *(809) 448-8650*, **Dominica Tours** ☎ *(809) 448-2638*, **Emerald Safaris** ☎ *(809) 448-4545*, **Mally's Tour Service** ☎ *(809) 448-3114*, and **Sun Link Tours** ☎ *(809) 448-2552*, which also offers sea excursions. Prices are generally in the $30–$50 range for half- or full-day driving tours. **Anchorage Dive Center** offers whale watching trips along the Dominica coast for $50–$65 ☎ *(809) 448-2638*. There are a number of good hiking guides on the island: **Ken's Hinterland Adventure Tours** is a good bet ☎ *(809) 448-4850*. Other hiking guides for Morne Trois Pitons National Park typically hang out in the villages of Laudat and Trafalgar, and the Papillote Wilderness Retreat is a good source of guide information ☎ *(809) 448-2287*. The going rate for a guide to the Boiling Lake is $100–$120 for up to four people; Middleham Falls $75–$80.

BEST VIEW:

Stop for a pick-me-up drink at the Picard Beach Cottages and enjoy a spectacular view of Prince Rupert's Bay.

Sports

Hiking and diving predominate in Dominica. Tennis can be played at two hotels: Reigate Hall in Roseau and Castaways Beach in Mero. A squash court is found at the Anchorage Hotel in Castle Comfort. Game fishing is provided by **Dominica Tours** in Castle Comfort ☎ *(809) 448-2638*

Sailing, windsurfing and deep-sea fishing are popular pastimes in Dominica.

Scuba Diving

Various locations, Roseau.

If your hotel can't help you arrange a diving excursion, try one of these: **Castaways Hotel Dive Center** (☎ *(809) 449-6244*), **Dominica Dive Resorts** (☎ *(809) 448-2638*), and **Nature Island Dive** (☎ *(809) 449-8181*). All offer classes and dive trips. Prices are generally about $65 for a two-tank dive, $90 for a resort course. They also rent equipment to snorkelers.

Where to Stay

Fielding's Highest Rated Hotels in Dominica	
★★★★ Fort Young Hotel	$95–$135
★★★ Evergreen Hotel	$72–$113
★★★ Garraway Hotel	$95–$185
★★★ Lauro Club	$73–$140
★★★ Papillotte Wilderness Retreat	$60–$75

Fielding's Most Exclusive Hotels in Dominica	
★★★ Garraway Hotel	$95–$185
★★★★ Fort Young Hotel	$95–$135
★★★ Lauro Club	$73–$140
★ Reigate Waterfront Hotel	$42–$150
★★ Layou River Hotel	$70–$120

Fielding's Best Value Hotels in Dominica	
★★★ Papillotte Wilderness Retreat	$60–$75
★★★★ Fort Young Hotel	$95–$135
★★★ Evergreen Hotel	$72–$113
★★ Springfield Plantation	$45–$90
★★★ Lauro Club	$73–$140

Those in need of serious pampering best head elsewhere, as Dominica is not the spot for luxury resorts—for now. A high-amenity Layou Valley hotel is under construction for a late 1997 opening that may dramatically change the clientele that has been visiting Dominica so far. Otherwise, the low price of accommodations here may surprise you, particularly if you're used to the inflated ones on other Caribbean islands. All of the hotels are small (the largest has 35 rooms), most are locally owned, and there is an extensive selection of properties with rooms under $75 per night. Most properties are clustered around Roseau—a few are on the coast near Layou or around Plymouth. Other spots around the island tend to be family-run guests houses in remote areas.

Hotels and Resorts

Fort Young Hotel, on the site of the erstwhile fort at the edge of Roseau, gets high marks for historical value and civilized service. It's probably the best on the island, though Garraway Hotel lays on the modern conveniences. The closest thing to a beach resort is provided at Castaways Beach Hotel.

Portsmouth

Portsmouth Beach Hotel　　　　　　**$35–$145**　　　　　　★

Picard; Bagatelle, Portsmouth, ☎ (809) 445-5142. FAX (809) 445-5599.
Single: $35–$145. Double: $45–$145.
Located near Cabrits National Park and on the beach, this casual spot has simple, motel-like rooms that rely on ceiling fans to keep things cool. There are also eight cottages that offer more room to spread out. There's a pool and watersports, and a dive center is nearby. Weekly entertainment is a plus. 104 rooms. Credit cards: A, D, MC, V.

Roseau

Anchorage Hotel　　　　　　**$52–$110**　　　　　　★★

Castle Comfort, Roseau, ☎ (800) 223-6510, (809) 448-2638. FAX (809) 448-5680.
Single: $52–$80. Double: $68–$110.
Located about a mile south of Roseau, this casual hotel appeals mainly to divers. Accommodations are basic, and the older rooms need refurbishment, so be sure to book one of the newer units. There's a pool, good restaurant, dive center and watersports, which cost extra. Though it's located on the water, there is no beach to speak of, but this spot remains popular for its friendly, family-run service. 32 rooms. Credit cards: A, DC, D, MC, V.

Castle Comfort Lodge　　　　　　**$85–$130**　　　　　　★★

Castle Comfort Street;, Roseau, ☎ (800) 544-7631, (809) 448-2188. FAX (809) 448-6088.
Single: $85. Double: $125–$130.
Located on the waterfront immediately south of Roseau but three miles from the nearest beach, this small lodge attracts primarily divers. The rooms are basic but at least air-conditioned. The owners arrange dive trips and nature walks. There's a restaurant, but little else in the way of amenities. 11 rooms. Credit cards: A, MC, V.

Evergreen Hotel　　　　　　**$72–$113**　　　　　　★★★

Castle Comfort, Roseau, ☎ (809) 448-3288. FAX (809) 448-6800.
Single: $72–$82. Double: $98–$113.
Plenty of island character at this small, family-run hotel just south of Roseau. The converted two-story house is complimented by a lovely, lush garden that separates the property from a rocky beach. Accommodations are comfortable and bright and have air conditioning; the newer units are better, though the original rooms have

more character. There's a pool and restaurant, and they'll help arrange watersports. 16 rooms. Credit cards: A, D, MC, V.

Fort Young Hotel   **$95–$135**   ★★★★

Victoria Street, Roseau, ☎ (800) 223-6510, (809) 448-5000. FAX (809) 448-5006. Single: $95–$115. Double: $115–$135.

Built within the ruins of old Fort Young, which dates back to the 1720s, this is Dominica's best property, though it draws mainly business travelers. Nicely accented with antique art, rooms are air-conditioned and look out over the harbor. The three suites are beautifully done, filled with antiques, and well worth the extra splurge. The pool is decent, too. A great in-town spot. 33 rooms. Credit cards: A, MC, V.

Garraway Hotel   **$95–$185**   ★★★

Bay Front, Roseau, ☎ (809) 449-8800. FAX (809) 449-8807. Single: $95–$185. Double: $110–$185.

The newest hotel on the island, Garraway is a four-story building with great views extending to Scotts Head at the southern tip of the island. Rooms are modern and plush, with air-conditioning, king-size beds, rattan furnishings and floral print fabrics. Geared somewhat more to business travelers, but the Garraway family lives next door and keeps the atmosphere cordial. 31 rooms. Credit cards: A, MC, V.

Reigate Hall Hotel   **$50–$180**   ★★

Reigate Street, Roseau, ☎ (809) 448-4031. FAX (809) 448-4034. Single: $50–$150. Double: $67–$180.

Set high on a hill overlooking Roseau, this once-stylish hotel is adorned with lots of antiques and artwork, but is in need of a spruce-up. Accommodations offer air conditioning, heavy wood furnishings, antique four-poster beds and balconies. The dining room chandelier hangs from the ceiling via a heavy chain. The beach is 2.5 miles away; a gym, sauna, pool and tennis court keep guest occupied. Amenities: tennis, exercise room, balcony or patio. 15 rooms. Credit cards: A, MC, V.

Reigate Waterfront Hotel   **$42–$150**   ★

Castle Comfort, Roseau, ☎ (809) 448-3111. FAX (809) 448-4034. Single: $42–$150. Double: $57–$150.

Located a mile south of Roseau and overlooking the sea, this motel-like property offers basic rooms that let you sleep in air-conditioned comfort. There's a pool, and diving and watersports can be arranged. Other than a weekly barbecue, not much happens here. 25 rooms. Credit cards: A, MC, V.

Salisbury

Castaways Beach Hotel   **$72–$96**   ★★

Mero, Salisbury, ☎ (800) 322-2223, (809) 449-6244. FAX (809) 449-6246. Single: $72. Double: $96.

Situated on the edge of a rainforest along a gray-sand beach, the Castaways is Dominica's major beach resort. Accommodations are in a two-story wing running along the beach; only a few have air conditioning, but all are pleasant and comfortable. Recreational pursuits include a full dive shop, tennis and watersports. A nice property and the sunsets are memorable, but if you're looking for a truly wonderful

beach resort, pick another island. MAP plan available. Amenities: tennis. 26 rooms.
Credit cards: A, MC, V.

Layou River Hotel   **$70–$120**   ★★

Clark Hill Estate; Layou, Salisbury, ☎ (800) 776-7256, (809) 449-6281. FAX (809) 449-6713.
Single: $70–$120. Double: $82–$120.

Set besides a beautiful river that is cold but swimmable, this modern hotel houses guests in standard air-conditioned rooms. Futuristic structures house a restaurant (the Sunday buffet is popular) and a small boutique. There's two pools for cooling off, and a free shuttle transports guests to the beach, about five minutes away. A neat spot for families. 35 rooms. Credit cards: A, D, MC, V.

Apartments and Condominiums

Dominica has a handful of self-catering places for rent, but don't expect to find modern shopping facilities or anywhere near the variety you're used to at home. If you want to stay some place long-term, come to the island and snoop around to find exactly what you want. Prices are sometimes negotiable, depending on the length of your stay. Those interested in a villa should consider Pointe Baptiste, a house and cottage (rented separately) set near a beach at the north coast village of Calibishi ☎ (809) 445-7322.

Portsmouth

Coconut Beach Hotel   **$55–$150**   ★

Picard Beach, Portsmouth, ☎ (809) 445-5393. FAX (809) 445-5693.
Single: $55–$150. Double: $65–$150.

Located on one of the island's better beaches, this is an enclave of cottages and apartments that lack air conditioning but include kitchenettes; furnishings are simple and basic. There's also a restaurant on site if you're not up to cooking. Activities include watersports, river tours and hiking; there's no pool. Populated mainly with European tourists. 22 rooms. Credit cards: A, D, MC, V.

Picard Beach Cottages   **$50–$140**   ★★

Prince Rupert Bay, Portsmouth, ☎ (800) 223-6510, (809) 445-5142. FAX (809) 445-5599.
Single: $50–$120. Double: $60–$140.

Set on the northwest coast on a former coconut plantation at the foot of Morne Diablotin, the island's highest mountain, the eight cottages here are designed in 18th-century Dominican-style architecture. Each has a kitchenette and veranda; ceiling fans help cool things off. There's a bar and restaurant, and guests can use the pool at the Portsmouth Beach Hotel (which is now used for medical students) next door. 8 rooms. Credit cards: A, D, MC, V.

Salisbury

Lauro Club   **$73–$140**   ★★★

Salisbury ☎ (809) 449-6602. FAX (809) 449-6603.
Single: $73–$135. Double: $105–$140.

Situated on a cliff and bordered by two nearby beaches, this rustic villa complex offers separate living rooms and kitchens on a large veranda—but no air conditioning. A long staircase takes you to the beach; if you're feeling lazy, just hang by the pool. The restaurant is a nice spot to escape kitchen duties; a tennis court rounds out the facilities. You'll want to rent a car as this spot is rather remote. Amenities: tennis. 10 rooms. Credit cards: A, DC, MC, V.

Inns

Papillote Wilderness Retreat is a unique mountain hostelry nestled against a steep hillside brimming with orchid-laced waterfalls. For nature-lovers it's paradise, and Papillote has helped to shape much of the hotel "industry" Dominica has. However, of the properties listed below, note that each is remote and unless you plan on hanging out at the hotel each day, you'll need a car to get around.

Roseau

Papillotte Wilderness Retreat   **$60–$75**   ★ ★ ★

Trafalgar Falls Road, Roseau, ☎ (809) 448-2287. FAX (809) 448-2285.
Single: $60–$75. Double: $70–$75.
This small family-owned inn is set right in the cool rainforest, 1000 feet above sea level and some 20 minutes from Roseau. The location, in a lush valley amid mineral pools, gardens and waterfalls, can't be beat. Standard rooms are simple and basic and are without air conditioning; there's also a two-bedroom, two-bath cottage with a kitchen. Meals are served outdoors with lots of fresh fruits and vegetables— the food is delicious (the hotel's meal plan is a good idea). Come prepared for some rain—this is, after all, the rainforest, but if you don't mind that, this is a very special escape far removed from city life. Amenities: secluded garden atmosphere. 10 rooms. Credit cards: A, D, MC, V.

Springfield Plantation   **$45–$90**   ★ ★

Springfield, Roseau, ☎ (809) 449-1401. FAX (809) 449-2160.
Single: $45–$70. Double: $65–$90.
This mountain inn dates back to 1940. Accommodations are beautifully done with antique four-poster beds complete with mosquito netting, huge wooden armoires and other antiques. There are also several cottages available for monthly rental. There's a protected river pool for splashing about, nature trails for hiking and safari tours for exploring. Nature lovers love it here, but those into a resort atmosphere will be happier at a more commercial establishment. 12 rooms.

Salisbury

Layou Valley Inn   **$55–$90**   ★

Layou Valley, Salisbury, ☎ (809) 449-6203. FAX (809) 448-5212.
Single: $55–$90. Double: $66–$90.
Perfect for nature lovers, this appealing country inn is situated in the foothills of Morne Trios Pitos, seven miles from the beach. Overlooking a primordial forest with great views, the inn has comfortable rooms with private baths but no air. A good jumping-off spot for hiking and rafting, and the French cuisine is tasty, but you're a long ways from "civilization." 8 rooms. Credit cards: A, DC, MC, V.

Low Cost Lodging

Inexpensive guest houses are abundant, though the quality varies considerably. You may be best off beginning your vacation with one of the spots listed above, then switching to a lower priced guest house after you've had a chance to personally inspect it. The island's National Development Corporation publishes a free accommodations directory with prices that may help you select the place you want ☎ *(809) 448-2351*. One historic Roseau spot, Vena's, was the childhood home of novelist Jean Rhys—rooms are just $25 a night, but somewhat gloomy ☎ *(809) 448-3286*. Another is the Cherry Lodge, a rustic six-room hotel downtown that oozes with character for $35 a night ☎ *(809) 448-2366*. A number of other guest houses are situated in the mountains and valleys well away from Roseau.

Roseau

Continental Inn   **$30–$50**   ★

37 Queen Mary Street, Roseau, ☎ *(809) 448-2214. FAX (809) 448-7702. Single: $30–$35. Double: $45–$50.*

This small hotel in the heart of Roseau has air-conditioned rooms, but only some have a private bath. The restaurant serves Creole dishes. Mainly used by business travelers. 11 rooms. Credit cards: A, MC, V.

Where to Eat

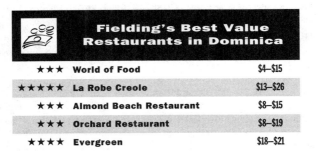

Fielding's Highest Rated Restaurants in Dominica

★★★★★	La Robe Creole	$13–$26
★★★★	Evergreen	$18–$21
★★★★	Guiyave	
★★★	Almond Beach Restaurant	$8–$15
★★★	Balisier	$18–$26
★★★	De Bouille	$14–$30
★★★	Floral Gardens	$14–$25
★★★	Orchard Restaurant	$8–$19
★★★	Papillotte Wilderness Retreat	$20–$20
★★★	World of Food	$4–$15

Fielding's Most Exclusive Restaurants in Dominica

★★★	De Bouille	$14–$30
★★★	Balisier	$18–$26
★★★★★	La Robe Creole	$13–$26
★★★	Floral Gardens	$14–$25
★★★★	Evergreen	$18–$21

Fielding's Best Value Restaurants in Dominica

★★★	World of Food	$4–$15
★★★★★	La Robe Creole	$13–$26
★★★	Almond Beach Restaurant	$8–$15
★★★	Orchard Restaurant	$8–$19
★★★★	Evergreen	$18–$21

DOMINICA

Although the island is sandwiched between Martinique and Guadeloupe, French-style cooking has not invaded Dominica. Flavors tend to lean toward English (meaning basic and/or bland), and the quantity of budget-minded travelers hasn't pushed the quality upscale. The major exception by all accounts is La Robe Creole, where rich soups, stuffed crab backs, and local delicacies tempt diners. Many visitors dine at their hotel more often than not, particularly those staying outside Roseau. A few hotel restaurants are pretty good, particularly Papillote Wilderness Retreat, where souk, a local river shrimp, is a tasty treat in season. "In season" is an important concept on Dominica because mountain chicken (the legs of frogs that burrow in the woods), land crabs and freshwater crayfish are to be obtained September through February only; restaurants serving them out of that period should not be supported.

Bagatelle

Almond Beach Restaurant $$ ★★★

Calibishi, Bagatelle, ☎ *(809) 445-7783.*
Latin American cuisine. Specialties: Callaloo, chicken palau.
Lunch: Noon–2 p.m., entrées $8–$15.
Dinner: 6–8 p.m., entrées $8–$15. Closed: Sun.
A convenient village restaurant on the north coast, Almond Beach is a cool spot to stop for refreshing and exotic fruit and spice beverages made with anise or ginger. The view of the sea is just ahead, and meals include a savory chicken and rice dish, lobster or *callaloo* (dasheen) soup. A great lunch spot if you're hitting the north coast beaches. Credit cards: D, MC, V.

Castaways Beach Hotel $$ ★★

Mero, Bagatelle, ☎ *(809) 449-6244. Associated hotel: Castaways Beach Hotel.*
Latin American cuisine.
Lunch: Noon–2 p.m., entrées $12–$18.
Dinner: 7–9 p.m., entrées $12–$18.
Dine informally by the ocean at this hotel restaurant popular for good breakfasts, tropical rum punches and the ubiquitous national dish of crapaud, or frog legs. Sometimes there is crab and conch, and although most of the food is freshly prepared, it varies in quality. Credit cards: MC, V.

Coconut Beach $$$ ★★

Picard Beach, Bagatelle, ☎ *(809) 445-5393. Associated hotel: Coconut Beach Hotel.*
Seafood cuisine.
Lunch: Noon–2:30 p.m., entrées $10–$15.
Dinner: 6:30–10:30 p.m., entrées $10–$25.
A casual sandwich and seafood foodery right on the beach located south of Portsmouth, the Coconut Beach serves as a yacht and boat stop as well as a watering hole for day-trippers passing through the island's second-largest town. It's also a good place to try rotis, or flatbread rolled around curried meat or vegetables. Credit cards: A, DC, MC, V.

De Bouille $$$ ★★★

Victoria Street, Bagatelle, ☎ (809) 448-5000. Associated hotel: Fort Young Hotel.
International cuisine. Specialties: Pumpkin soup, lobster.
Lunch: Noon–2:30 p.m., entrées $5–$14.
Dinner: 7–10 p.m., entrées $14–$30.
A baronial and stately restaurant serving a varied cuisine, De Bouille is ensconced in an old fort, now one of Roseau's best hotels. Diners can feel history in the stone walls, which add plenty of atmosphere to go along with the pumpkin soup, seafood and steaks served here. A good place to spot local movers and shakers. Reservations required. Credit cards: A, MC, V.

Floral Gardens $$$ ★★★

Concord Valley, Bagatelle, ☎ (809) 445-7636. Associated hotel: Floral Gardens Guest House.
Latin American cuisine.
Lunch: 11 a.m.–3 p.m., entrées $14–$25.
Dinner: 7 p.m.–midnight, entrées $14–$25.
The name of this restaurant near the Carib Territory couldn't be more apt—the grounds are surrounded by amazingly fertile plants and flowers. Owned by a former prime minister and his wife, Floral Gardens serves Creole and international specialties in a room overlooking the Pagua River. Tour groups often stop here for refreshments, so service can be slow. Credit cards: A, DC, D, MC, V.

Guiyave $$ ★★★★

15 Cork Street, Bagatelle, ☎ (809) 448-2930.
Latin American cuisine. Specialties: Goat water, rotis.
Lunch: 8 a.m.–5 p.m., entrées $8–$19. Closed: Sun.
This informal eatery in a wood-frame house is a popular breakfast and lunch spot serving ham and eggs, French toast, and sandwiches during the week. Saturday's home-cooked creole food is a tradition, and that may involve goat water (a spicy meat stew), blood pudding, calalloo, pumpkin soup, and rotis. Guiyave is also THE local juice bar, squeezing out whatever's fresh that day, including tamarind, mango, or soursop, a tangy citrus fruit. Credit cards: A, MC, V.

La Robe Creole $$$ ★★★★★

3 Victoria Street, Bagatelle, ☎ (809) 448-2896.
Latin American cuisine. Specialties: Mountain chicken and river crayfish (in season), calalloo.
Lunch: 11 a.m.–3:30 p.m., entrées $7–$26.
Dinner: 3:30–9:30 p.m., entrées $13–$26. Closed: Sun.
Long regarded as Dominica's best restaurant, the 22-year-old la Robe Creole, named after the native madras costume, serves a sublime vegetarian callaloo soup with coconut, and a fine creole octopus. There's also pizza and chicken brought up from the Mouse Hole, and tropical fruit and coconut pies—the rum punch is one of the best around. Patrons are prominent Dominicans who come to see and be seen in air-conditioned luxury, but as sometimes happens on this relaxed isle, service can be very slow. Reservations required. Credit cards: D, MC, V.

Le Flambeau $$ ★★

Prince Rupert Bay, Bagatelle, ☎ (809) 445-5131. Associated hotel: Picard Beach Resort.

International cuisine. Specialties: Creole pork chops, homemade ice cream.
Lunch: 7 a.m.–4 p.m., entrées $4–$6.
Dinner: 4–11 p.m., entrées $9–$13.

A pleasing change from exotic Creole specialties, Le Flambeau, located on the sand at the Picard Beach Cottage Resort, flips omelettes, pancakes and French toast to an appreciative crowd at breakfast. The rest of the day and well into the evening, pork chops and vegetarian specialties are available, and the fresh fruit ice creams are delightful. Credit cards: A, DC, MC, V.

Orchard Restaurant   **$$**   ★ ★ ★

31 King George V Street, Bagatelle, ☎ (809) 448-3051.
Latin American cuisine. Specialties: Callaloo, conch.
Lunch: 8 a.m.–3 p.m., entrées $8–$19.
Dinner: 3–10 p.m., entrées $8–$19. Closed: Sun.

Hearty, complete meals for under $20 draw patrons to this informal downtown eatery, which also has a popular bar. Entrées such as conch (called lambi here) are served with trimmings, which in this case involve rice, relishes, salads and whatever the chef has on hand. Those wishing to eat lighter can order a la carte sandwiches and soups, or get food to go. No dinner is served on Saturdays. Reservations required. Credit cards: A, MC, V.

Papillotte Wilderness Retreat   **$$$**   ★ ★ ★

Trafalgar Falls Road, Bagatelle, ☎ (809) 448-2287. Associated hotel: Papillote Wilderness Retreat.
Latin American cuisine. Specialties: Flying fish, callaloo soup.
Lunch: 11 a.m.–3 p.m., entrées $8–$19.
Dinner: 7:30 p.m., prix fixe $20.

Paradise awaits in this garden of eden near Trafalgar Falls, a haven for nature lovers; amateur botanists will be in seventh heaven. The Retreat's restaurant is now open to nonguests for dinner, and some selections from the small menu, like river shrimp and flying fish, are rarely available elsewhere. Under the eye of den mom Anne Grey-Jean Baptiste, the menu leans to healthy and fresh selections using much of the produce grown locally—there's a barbecue on Wednesday nights. A gushing hot springs pool invites daytrippers for a dip before or after meals. The coconut rum punch produced here is awesome. Reservations recommended. Credit cards: A, MC, V.

Reigate Hall   **$$$**   ★ ★

Mountain Road, Bagatelle, ☎ (809) 448-4031. Associated hotel: Reigate Hall Hotel.
French cuisine. Specialties: Mountain Chicken.
Lunch: 12:30–2:30 p.m., entrées $7–$12.
Dinner: 7–10 p.m., entrées $15–$28.

High up on King's Hill below Trafalgar Falls is the Reigate Hall Hotel, a refurbished plantation home with an attached restaurant serving French and Creole specialties. Not unlike eating in a castle, guests enjoy coq au vin, scampi or mountain chicken in champagne sauce. The atmosphere is more formal than at most Dominica restaurants, though the waitstaff can be less than alert on occasion. Reservations required. Credit cards: A, MC, V.

The Mouse Hole   **$**   ★ ★

3 Victoria Street, Bagatelle, ☎ (809) 448-2896.

Latin American cuisine. Specialties: Rotis, pastries.
Lunch: 10 a.m.–2:30 p.m., entrées $6–$10.
Dinner: 2:30–9:30 p.m., entrées $6–$10. Closed: Sun.
The cutely monikered Mouse Hole serves as the takeout/short order adjunct to its big sister, La Robe Creole, which holds court upstairs. There is a counter for sit-down service, but most patrons order rotis of curried chicken, sandwiches, pastries and small meals to go. Credit cards: A, MC, V.

World of Food   **$$**   ★★★
48 Cork Street, Bagatelle, ☎ *(809) 448-3286. Associated hotel: Vena's Guest House.*
Latin American cuisine. Specialties: Fresh fish, lambi (conch).
Lunch: Noon–3 p.m., entrées $4–$15.
Dinner: 6–10:30 p.m., entrées $4–$15.
Literary lions will delight in the fact that this restaurant is located at the site of author Jean Rhys' birthplace. Owner Vena McDougal has turned it into a patio restaurant that brims with office workers at cocktail hour. Diners can sit under a spreading mango tree and partake of local fish cakes, souse (black pudding) or reasonably priced sandwiches and soups.

Roseau

Balisier   **$$$**   ★★★
Bay Street, Roseau, ☎ *(809) 449-8800. Associated hotel: Garraway Hotel.*
International cuisine. Specialties: Chicken garraway.
Lunch: Noon–2:30 p.m., entrées $17–$25.
Dinner: 6:30–10 p.m., entrées $18–$26.
Located in a modern, newish hotel on the oceanfront in Roseau, the Balisier is a view restaurant on the first floor, serving competently prepared local fish, curries and a specialty, Chicken Garraway, a moist breast rolled around a local banana and exotic spices. Pumpkin, cabbage and callaloo soups are popular, as is the lobster newburg. Pies are home-baked and tasty. Reservations recommended. Credit cards: A, MC, V.

Callaloo Restaurant   **$$**   ★★
66 King George V Street, Roseau, ☎ *(809) 448-3386.*
Latin American cuisine. Specialties: Curried conch, callaloo.
Lunch: 11:30 a.m.– 2:30 p.m., entrées $6–$14.
Dinner: 6:30–10 p.m., entrées $6–$14.
Chefs at Callaloo present home-style cooking on a terrace overlooking downtown Roseau. Like its namesake, the hearty soup made from the omnipresent dasheen (a spinach-like green) is made from scratch daily. There are daily specials, which often include conch prepared in a number of different ways, and crayfish or mountain chicken (when in season).

Evergreen   **$$$**   ★★★★
Castle Comfort, Roseau, ☎ *(809) 448-3288. Associated hotel: Evergreen Hotel.*
International cuisine. Specialties: Frogs' legs, crab.
Lunch: 1–2:30 p.m., prix fixe $17–$21.
Dinner: 7–9 p.m., prix fixe $18–$21.
One of the island's most convivial spots, the Evergreen Hotel's dining room is open to nonguests for a prix-fixe five-course meal with a choice of soup and salad, entrées

DOMINICA

of chicken, frogs' legs (in season) and lamb, side dishes, relishes and homemade desserts. The owners, the Winston family, run a very tight ship, with excellent service all around. Reservations recommended. Credit cards: A, MC, V.

Local arts and crafts will take some effort to uncover, but since most are found in Roseau, you can usually locate them on foot. Look for the locally produced after shave and body lotion, Bay Rum, while Macoucherie is the local drinking rum. Tropicrafts on Turkey Lane sells sturdy, hand-woven grass mats, pottery, and baskets and hats produced by Carib Indians (another outlet is on Bay Street in Plymouth). Cotton House Batiks on Kings Lane designs batik clothing, napkins and wall hangings, while Artwear Gallery on King George V Street sells handpainted T-shirts and other garments. A small business complex on Great Marlborough Street has additional shops selling local goods. In Laudat, Papillote Wilderness Retreat has a nice gift store selling other local arts and crafts.

Dominica Directory

Arrival and Departure

Dominica cannot be reached directly from the United States, but American Eagle began serving the island daily from San Juan, Puerto Rico in December 1996, allowing connecting service from a number of North American departure points. Otherwise, the predominant carrier for the island is LIAT, which offers nonstop or direct service from Anguilla, Antigua, Guadeloupe, Martinique, St. Lucia and St. Maarten, with connecting service available from most other islands served by LIAT. A Dominica-based outfit, **Cardinal Airlines** provides service from Antigua, Barbados and Sint Maarten ☎ *(809) 449-0322*, and **Air Guadeloupe** provides connections from Martinique and Guadeloupe ☎ *(809) 448-2181*. There are two airports on the island: The larger airstrip is Melville Hall, used by American Eagle and LIAT, but it is located on the northeast coast, a one-hour drive from Roseau and most island hotels. For most visitors, Canefield Airport, about three miles north of Roseau, is the more convenient entry point, but it is served only by smaller aircraft (including most of LIAT flights). Scheduled ferry service connects Dominica with Martinique and Guadeloupe: **Caribbean Express** ☎ *(809) 448-2181* and Madikera ☎ *(809) 448-6977*.

The departure tax is $8.

Business Hours

Stores open weekdays 8 a.m.–1 p.m. and 2–4 p.m. and Saturday 8 a.m.–1 p.m. Banks open Monday–Thursday 8 a.m.–3 p.m. and Friday 8 a.m.–5 p.m.

Climate

Climate is tropical, though tempered by the sea winds that sometimes reach hurricane force, especially from July-September. Average temperature is 80 degrees F., with little seasonal variation. Rainfall is heavy especially in the mountainous areas, where the annual average is 250 inches compared with 70 inches along the coast.

Documents

Visitors will need a passport or proof of citizenship in conjunction with a photo ID as well as a return or ongoing ticket.

Electricity

The current is 220 volts/50 cycles, which means you must have a transformer with the proper plug adapters. Rechargeable strobes and lights should be charged on the stabilized lines most dive operators have available for his purpose.

Getting Around

Taxis and buses are plentiful, but renting a car may be your best way to explore the island. Although most main roads are in good shape, roads are narrow, twisting and steep. There are a number of rental outfits on the island, including two American-based firms, Avis and Budget. Driving is on the left. If you are flying in to Melville Hall Airport, the shared taxi to Roseau will be about $16 per person; to Portsmouth, about $12. From Canefield Airport, a taxi to Roseau is $8 (up to four passengers); to Papillote, $18; to Portsmouth, $43.

Language

English is the official language, but a local French patois, or Creole is widely spoken.

Medical Emergencies

There are two main hospitals at Roseau and Portsmouth, with 242 and 50 beds, respectively. Serious emergencies require airlift to San Juan, Puerto Rico.

Money

The official currency is the Eastern Caribbean dollar, which is pegged to American currency at about $2.65 to one U.S. dollar. However, U.S. dollars are accepted virtually everywhere.

Telephone

The area code is *809*. To call Dominica from the United States, dial *011* (international code)+*809* (country Code)+*44* (local access) +five-digit number. If you want to save money, head for the Cable & Wireless (West Indies) Ltd. company where you can make international calls, send faxes, telexes, teletypes and telegrams. You can also purchase phone cards here which can be used in pay phones. You can make both local and international calls from pay phones.

(Avoid making long-distance calls from your room —if your room indeed
even has a phone—as hotel surcharges and operator assistance can raise the bill
even higher than the room rate.)

Time

Atlantic standard time, one hour later than New York.

Tipping and Taxes

Hotels collect a five percent government tax; restaurants collect a three percent sales tax. A 10 percent service charge is added to your bill by most hotels
and restaurants. If you feel inclined to leave more for service, do so.

Tourist Information

For more information write to the **Dominica Division of Tourism** *(Box 293,
Roseau, Dominica, WI; ☎ (809) 448-2186, FAX (809) 448-5840).* Mail
from the States takes about two weeks to arrive.

When to Go

Carnival takes place the Monday and Tuesday preceding Ash Wednesday.
Labor Day is May 1. Independence Day is Nov. 3.

DOMINICA HOTELS	RMS	RATES	PHONE	CR. CARDS
Portsmouth				
★★ **Picard Beach Cottages**	8	$50–$140	(800) 223-6510	A, D, MC, V
★ **Coconut Beach Hotel**	22	$55–$150	(809) 445-5393	A, D, MC, V
★ **Portsmouth Beach Hotel**	104	$35–$145	(809) 445-5142	A, D, MC, V
Roseau				
★★★★ **Fort Young Hotel**	33	$95–$135	(800) 223-6510	A, MC, V
★★★ **Evergreen Hotel**	16	$72–$113	(809) 448-3288	A, D, MC, V
★★★ **Garraway Hotel**	31	$95–$185	(809) 449-8800	A, MC, V
★★★ **Papillotte Wilderness Retreat**	10	$60–$75	(809) 448-2287	A, D, MC, V
★★ **Anchorage Hotel**	32	$52–$110	(800) 223-6510	A, D, DC, MC, V
★★ **Castle Comfort Lodge**	11	$85–$130	(800) 544-7631	A, MC, V
★★ **Reigate Hall Hotel**	15	$50–$180	(809) 448-4031	A, MC, V
★★ **Springfield Plantation**	12	$45–$90	(809) 449-1401	
★ **Continental Inn**	11	$30–$50	(809) 448-2214	A, MC, V
★ **Reigate Waterfront Hotel**	25	$42–$150	(809) 448-3111	A, MC, V
Salisbury				
★★★ **Lauro Club**	10	$73–$140	(809) 449-6602	A, DC, MC, V
★★ **Castaways Beach Hotel**	26	$72–$96	(800) 322-2223	A, MC, V

DOMINICA

DOMINICA HOTELS	RMS	RATES	PHONE	CR. CARDS
★★ Layou River Hotel	35	$70–$120	(800) 776-7256	A, D, MC, V
★ Layou Valley Inn	8	$55–$90	(809) 449-6203	A, DC, MC, V

DOMINICA RESTAURANTS	PHONE	ENTRÉE	CR. CARDS

Bagatelle

French

	PHONE	ENTRÉE	CR. CARDS
★★ Reigate Hall	(809) 448-4031	$7–$28	A, MC, V

International

	PHONE	ENTRÉE	CR. CARDS
★★★ De Bouille	(809) 448-5000	$5–$30	A, MC, V
★★ Le Flambeau	(809) 445-5131	$4–$13	A, DC, MC, V

Latin American

	PHONE	ENTRÉE	CR. CARDS
★★★★★ La Robe Creole	(809) 448-2896	$7–$26	D, MC, V
★★★★ Guiyave	(809) 448-2930	$8–$19	A, MC, V
★★★ Almond Beach Restaurant	(809) 445-7783	$8–$15	D, MC, V
★★★ Floral Gardens	(809) 445-7636	$14–$25	A, D, DC, MC, V
★★★ Orchard Restaurant	(809) 448-3051	$8–$19	A, MC, V
★★★ Papillotte Wilderness Retreat	(809) 448-2287	$8–$20	A, MC, V
★★★ World of Food	(809) 448-3286	$4–$15	
★★ Castaways Beach Hotel	(809) 449-6244	$12–$18	MC, V
★★ The Mouse Hole	(809) 448-2896	$6–$10	A, MC, V

Seafood

	PHONE	ENTRÉE	CR. CARDS
★★ Coconut Beach	(809) 445-5393	$10–$25	A, DC, MC, V

Roseau

International

	PHONE	ENTRÉE	CR. CARDS
★★★★ Evergreen	(809) 448-3288	$17–$21	A, MC, V
★★★ Balisier	(809) 449-8800	$17–$26	A, MC, V

Latin American

	PHONE	ENTRÉE	CR. CARDS
★★ Callaloo Restaurant	(809) 448-3386	$6–$14	

DOMINICA

DOMINICA

DOMINICAN REPUBLIC

The best place to tee off in Santo Domingo is the course at Casa de Campo.

The Dominican Republic isn't for everyone. Poverty is rampant, crime high in the city of Santo Domingo, power blackouts common. But that's just the black lining around this silver cloud of the Caribbean, which brims with history, lush scenery, vibrant people, pulsating nightlife and glorious beaches—all at a fraction of the cost of a typical Caribbean holiday.

The Dominican Republic is the Western Hemisphere's oldest European settlement, the spot where Christopher Columbus first landed upon journeying to the New World. The capital city of Santo Domingo dates back to 1496 and was established by Columbus' brother, after a few disastrous attempts by the more famous sibling at earlier colonization. Though it has had a particularly bloody history, with many revolutions, coups and tyrannical leaders, the nation has been fairly stable since the 1970s, and Americans are warmly welcomed—though tourists should exercise more than the usual cautions associated with most of the Caribbean.

Tourism didn't start to come on strong here until after the 1961 assassination of Generalissimo Rafael Leónidas Trujillo, the ruthless dictator who ruled the nation for more than 30 years. But by the mid-1970s, interest in the country as a vacation destination was strong, and today's Dominican Republic attracts some 2 million tourists each year.

The Dominican Republic boasts literally thousands of beaches, soaring mountain ranges, fertile valleys, dense jungles and the Caribbean's lowest inland spot—a million-year-old lake the size of Manhattan. It's no wonder the island attracts so many outdoors types who revel in the ample opportunities for diving, trekking, deep-sea fishing and boating. At the other extreme, swank resorts lure those who like spending their holiday being pampered and sun-kissed.

Bird's-Eye View

Sprawling over two-thirds of the island of Hispaniola (Haiti comprises the rest), the Dominican Republic is located some 800 miles south of Florida and lies between Cuba and Puerto Rico. On the north is the Atlantic Ocean, to the south the Caribbean Sea. The island is much larger than most of its Caribbean counterparts, totaling 48,422 square kilometers, and quite geographically diverse. Besides its literally thousands of miles of unspoiled beaches, it has tropical rainforests, dense jungles, mangrove swamps and the Caribbean's highest mountains. National parks comprise more than 10 percent of the island's territory, and more than 5,600 species of flora have been identified. Mountain ranges run down the backbone of the country, including Pico Duarte at 10,400 feet, the highest mountain in the Caribbean. At the other extreme, the Dominican Republic also lays claim to the Caribbean's lowest point, a large salt-water lake called Lago Enriquillo. whose 125 square miles is home to endangered crocodiles, rhinoceros. variegated shell turtles and pink flamingos.

The opening scene of the film *Jurassic Park,* which shows DNA being extracted from an insect trapped in amber, was shot in the Dominican Republic, with good reason, as it is a prime source of the ancient substance. You'll find many samples of the translucent substance in jewelry stores.

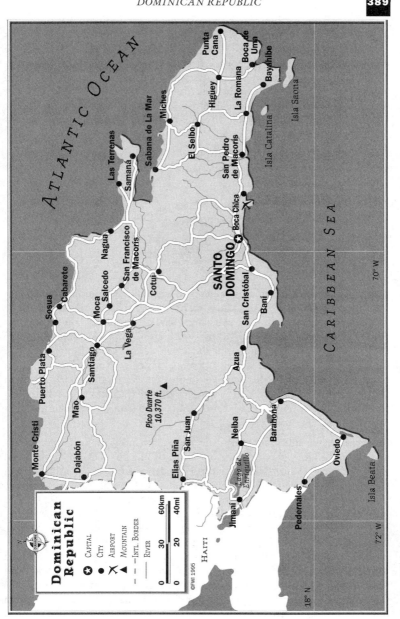

The city of Santo Domingo, home to some two million souls, is the oldest capital in the New World, and history buffs will go crazy inspecting all its treasures in the Zona Colonial (Colonial Zone).Along the north coast, the highway runs closely along the path laid out by Christopher Columbus, winding through fishing villages, cattle farms and sugar plantations. Puerto Plata, where many of the tony resorts hug the coast, is a particular charmer with its gingerbread structures. Tourists also flock to Punta Cana on the far eastern end and the 7000-acre resort community of La Romana, east of Santo Domingo.

The average temperature island-wide is 77 degrees Fahrenheit, with August the warmest month and January the coolest, though the difference is only about 10 degrees or so.

History

One could say that the Dominican Republic is really a family affair. The great Christopher Columbus dropped anchor in the Dominican Republic on his first voyage in 1492; four years later, his brother Bartolomeo founded the colony of Santo Domingo; 13 years after that, Christopher's son became the colony's governor, serving as viceroy when the Dominican Republic, then the colony of Santo Domingo, was the provisioning port and jump-off place for some of Spain's greatest expeditions to the New World. The list of explorers who sailed from this port is as impressive as a Hollywood A-list: Juan Ponce de Léon to Puerto Rico, Velasquez to Cuba, Cortés to Mexico. Even Sir Francis Drake put his mark on the port, attacking it, ransacking it, and then setting fire to it in 1586.

Over the next 300 years, the island changed hands among France, Spain and Cuba, and for a time it was even self-ruled in a phase called "Ephemeral Independence." Since winning its independence from Spain in 1821 and from Haiti in 1844, the Dominican Republic has been plagued by recurrent domestic conflicts and foreign intervention; between 1916 and 1924 it was occupied by U.S. forces. In 1930 the country entered into a 30-year dictatorship led by General Rafael Leónidas Trujillo Molina, who ruled personally until 1947 and indirectly thereafter until his assassination in 1961. His death gave rise to renewed political turmoil, and an election in December 1962 led to the inauguration of Juan Bosch Gaviño, a left-of-center democrat, as president in February 1963. In the same year, Bosch was overthrown by a military coup; subsequently the military installed a civilian triumvirate that ruled until April 1965, when civil war erupted. Military forces intervened on April

28, 1965, and imposed a truce while arrangements were made to establish a provisional government and prepare for elections. For the next 12 years the country was run by a moderate, Dr. Joaquin Balaguer, who returned after one term for another two consecutive ones. Presently there are at least 10 political parties representing diverse ideological viewpoints, including the Social Christian Reformed Party of 80-year-old Dr. Balaguer to the Dominican Revolutionary Party, a left-democratic grouping, to the right-wing Quisqueyan Democratic Party, the Dominican Communist Party (a traditionally pro-Moscow party), and the Dominican Popular Movement, which is pro-Peking.

People

The population of the Dominican Republic is a hefty 9 million. Spanish is the official language, but at the major tourist areas you'll find English, French and even German speakers as well. Dominicans are polite and very friendly and have a great passion for music and dancing, particularly the merengue. Islanders are informally broken into four categories: *blanco* (white), *indio claro* (mixed white and black), *indio oscuro* (black, but not 100 percent so) and *negro* (100 percent black). The island's chaotic history and sometimes-corrupt political structure leads to occasional violent strikes and demonstrations—if you are visiting during such a time, resist the temptation to join the fray and stay far away from any unrest. Because the country has so much poverty, crime is prevalent, and tourists should use more than even the usual caution—never leave cameras unattended at the beach, for instance, and hold tight to your purse when walking about. Some 80 percent of Dominicans are Roman Catholic, with a small minority of Jewish and Protestant communities. Despite their often hard lives, locals are a wonderfully friendly bunch—virtually everyone smiles and is quite outgoing. Americans will be surprised to find that many Dominicans know a lot about the United States—be prepared for impromptu conversations and lots of questions.

Beaches

A whopping 1000 miles of beaches await visitors, who often have a hard time just deciding which beach to pick for the day. Unfortunately, the beach closest to the city—**Boca Chica** (about 21 miles from the capital)—is also the

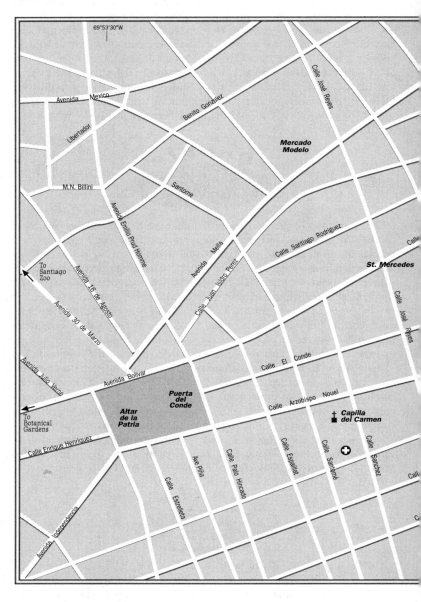

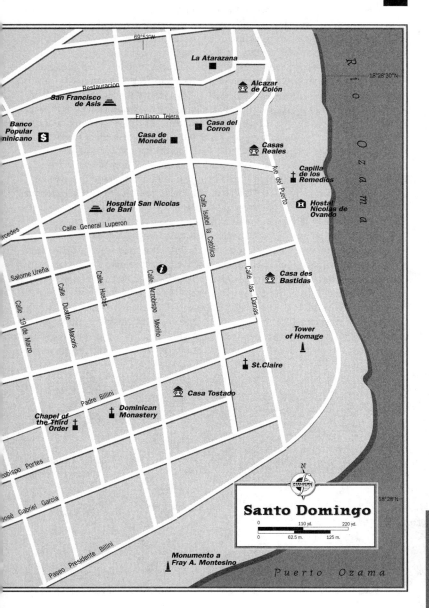

La Atarazana

Alcazar
de Colón

Restauracion

San Francisco
de Asís

Emiliano Tejera

Casa del
Corron

Banco
Popular
Dominicano

Casa de
Moneda

Casas
Reales

Capilla
de los
Remedios

Ave. del Puerto

Hostal
Nicolas de
Ovando

Hospital San Nicolas
de Bari

Calle Isabel la Católica

Calle General Luperon

Mercedes

Salome Ureña

Calle Duarte

Calle Hostos

Calle Arzobispo Merino

Casa des
Bastidas

Calle las Damas

Calle 19 de Marzo

Tower
of Homage

St. Claire

Padre Billini

Casa Tostado

Chapel of
the Third
Order

Dominican
Monastery

Arzobispo. Portes

José Gabriel Garcia

N

FIELDING
EXCLUSIVE

Santo Domingo

| 0 | 110 yd. | 220 yd. |
| 0 | 62.5 m. | 125 m. |

18°28'N

Monumento a
Fray A. Montesino

Paseo Presidente Billini

Puerto Ozama

69°53'W

16°28'30"N

R
i
o

O
z
a
m
a

most crowded, a veritable zoo on the weekends as locals and tourists alike invade the vanilla-white strands. In the past five years the fine white sands have gone from nearly deserted to a clutter of pizza huts, plastic beach tables and lounge chairs, and rental cottages full of screaming babies. The one thing that has remained protected here are the coral reefs, which serve to keep dangerous marine life from getting too close. As such, feel free to walk out in to the sea. Twenty minutes east of Boca Chica is **Juan Dolio**, with its powdery white beach. Here you'll find the Villas del Mar Hotel and the Punta Garza Beach Club. Other excellent beaches are the thumbprint-sized **Minitas** beach and lagoon, and the palm-fringed **Bayahibe**, only accessible by boat. This area, called **La Romana**, also houses the Casa de Campo Resort, which means it is usually crowded. The island's pride and joy is **Punta Cana**, a 20-mile sprawl (though it seems longer for its beauty), lined with shady trees and coconut palms. Here is located **Club Med**, the **Melia Punta Cara** and the **Bavaro Beach Resort**. Primitive is the only description for **Las Terrenas**, tucked into the north coast of the Samaná peninsula. You'll be hard-pressed to find anything here other than tall palms, sea, mountains and sand. **Sosuá** could be pleasant since the waves are gentle and the sand white and soft, but the scene is marred by camping tents and hawkers selling cheap trinkets. The beach of the future is **Puerto Plata**, on the north Amber Coast, where there are excellent reefs for snorkeling and the horizon hasn't yet been marred by too much civilization. Windsurfers and water-skiers particularly love the conditions, and many fishing expeditions take off from here. Windsurfing conditions on **Cabarete Beach** are excellent; between June and October wind speeds at 20–25 knots and 3- to 15-foot waves attract some of the best windsurfers in the Caribbean.

The Dominican Republic is known for its beautiful beaches.

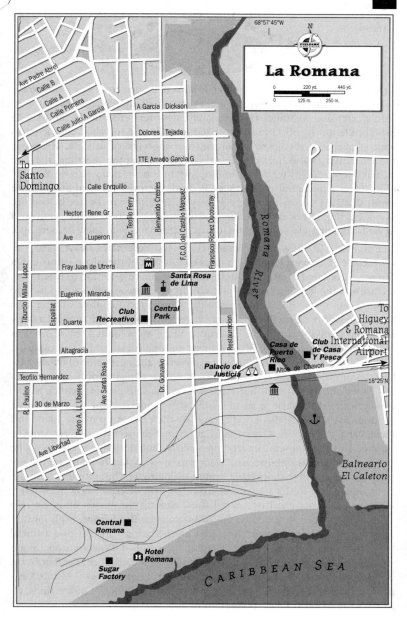

La Romana

68°57'45"W

N

0   220 yd.   440 yd.
0   125 m.   250 m.

Ave Padre Abrel
Calle B
Calle A
Calle Primera
Calle Julio A Garcia

A Garcia Dickson

Dolores Tejada

TTE Amado Garcia G

To
Santo
Domingo

Calle Enriquillo

Hector Rene Gr

Ave Luperon

Dr. Teofilo Ferry

Bienvenido Creales

F.C.O. del Castillo Marquez

Francisco Richez Ducoudray

Fray Juan de Utrera

Santa Rosa
de Lima

Eugenio Miranda

Tiburcio Millan Lopez

Espaillat

Duarte

Club
Recreativo

Central
Park

Altagracia

Teofilo Hernandez

R. Paulino

30 de Marzo

Pedro A. L. Uberes

Ave Santa Rosa

Dr. Gonzalvo

Restauracion

Ave Libertad

Romana River

To
Higuey
& Romana
International
Airport

Casa de
Puerto
Rico

Club
de Casa
Y Pesca

Altos de Chavon

Palacio de
Justicia

18°25'N

Balneario
El Caleton

Central
Romana

Hotel
Romana

Sugar
Factory

CARIBBEAN SEA

Underwater

Diving in the Dominican Republic is an activity undergoing a slow evolution. There have always been a number of good diving possibilities off the island's extensive coastline. Unfortunately, with few exceptions, the island's fish population is substantially depleted, even in the so-called marine parks which have been set up to counteract the shortage of fish life. Extensive spear fishing has also hurt the reefs themselves along the coastline; they are battered and trashed within swimming distance from many shores. Reportedly, most of the coral off **Barahona** is dead; even the reefs ringing remote **Monte Cristi** are said to be largely destroyed. Artificial wrecks (see below) are slowly helping to boost the marine creatures, but the entire island, sadly, will never be the first-class dive destination it might have been a few decades ago.

Perhaps the island's best diving lies off the **Pedernales Coast**, near the southern border with Haiti, but access to this part of the island is through a distant, forbidding frontier, requiring a sort of mini-expedition to reach. The seclusion is the key to its beauty and serious dive visitors will want to inquire about a multi-day trip. A number of the Dominican Republic's better sites are located off the **Boca Chica Lagoon**, where two small islands within **La Caleta Marine Park**, provide some diversion. Visibility is limited, by Caribbean standards, to an average of 50 to 60 feet, though it can hit 75 feet on good days. There is a wall (15 to 100 feet) and reef on the north side of **Catalina Island**, an outpost just off the coast from Romana—"real Caribbean-style diving," says one local diver—but plans for a cruise ship pier may wreck havoc. Farther east, at **Bayahibe**, a small fishing village approaching tourism with a cautious eye, there is also good diving. At the eastern tip of the island, off **Punta Cana**, the Atlantic Ocean and Caribbean Sea meet; there is reported to be nice reefs and several interesting wrecks, but dive shops appear to be based only out of the all-inclusive resorts for now. At **Las Terrenas**, on the Samana Peninsula, dive shops have started springing up, but visibility here can be hampered by freshwater runoff from the lush forests. Those who enjoy wrecks can be occupied by several sites. Among the major finds are two 17th-century Spanish galleons, the *Tolosa* and the *Guadeloupe*, both located near the entrance to Samana Bay. La Caleta Marine Park has two artificial reefs for diving; the wreck of the 140-foot steel-hulled *Hickory* sits on a slope which drops to 60 feet, while the wooden 90-foot patrol boat *Capitan Alcina* is wedged in a canyon, 126 feet down. The north coast reefs off Monte Cristi, near the Haitian border, are a graveyard for a number of pirate ships, although the wooden hulls are long gone.

Outside the major resorts, Dominican dive shops have mixed reputations and tend to change hands with alarming frequency. Although most of the Dominican Republic's visitors are European, the outfit listed below caters to Americans. It's also possible to contact the major coastal resorts and arrange a day or two of diving with them. There is a recompression chamber located in Santo Domingo.

Supporting one of the most diverse eco-systems in the Caribbean basin, the Dominican Republic is an explorer's paradise. Cresting at a majestic 10,370 feet, **Pico Duarte** represents the highest point in the Caribbean basin, high enough to attract a delicate mantle of snow a few times each winter. Physically, the island's major summits—almost a dozen rising higher than 8000 feet—do not look anything like the craggy Sierras or Rockies, but actually more resemble the gentle terrain found in the Adirondacks of New York. The country features 5500 species of flowering plants and ferns. The **Armando Bermudez National Park**, which encompasses most of the island's highest points, is a prime destination for visitors inclined toward outdoor activities.

FIELDING'S CHOICE:

From January to late February, whales can be seen at the mouth of the Samaná Bay. There are no organized excursions, but local boatmen will arrange trips, though permission must be obtained from the Naval Station in advance. From late December to early March, 3000 migrating humpback whales come to mate in Silver Bank, a marine sanctuary located 50 miles off the coast, directly north of Cabrera. Occasional expeditions by scientists are taken to the site, which run about 7–12 hours. To join an expedition, contact the National Parks Office in Santo Domingo.

BEST VIEW:

The panoramic sweep of the island, seen from the top of the Pico Duarte mountain, is spectacular. At almost 11,000 feet, it's a climb only the truly fit should attempt. It's best to go with a guide. Beginning in late fall 1994, Eco-turisa, in partnership with Occidental Hotels, began offering five-day packages, blankets, flashlights, guides, mules and meals. Part of the climb is covered on muleback, the rest on foot. During December and January, frost glazes the tropical landscape and intensifies the grandeur of the view.

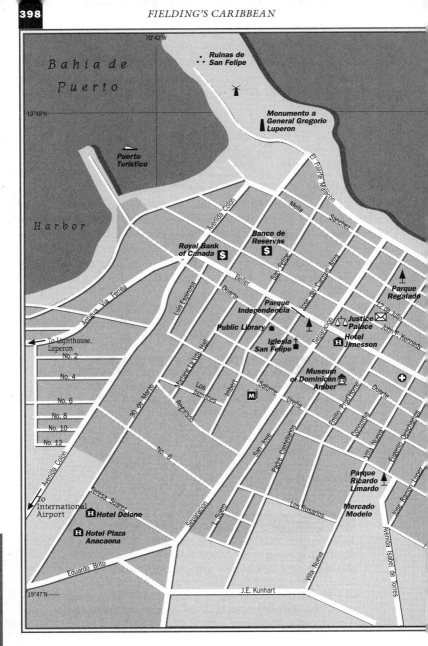

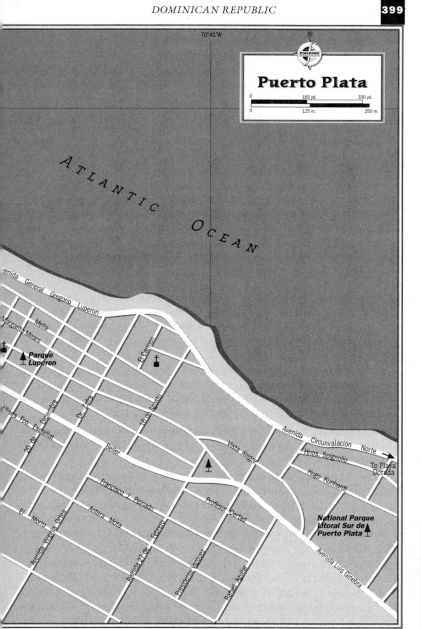

70°41'W

N

Puerto Plata

| 0 | 165 yd. | 330 yd. |
| 0 | 125 m. | 250 m. |

ATLANTIC

OCEAN

enida General Gregorio Luperon

Melta

Margarita Mears

El Carmen

**Parque
Luperon**

Ulises Fco. Espaillat

Duarte

Dr. Zafra

16 de Agosto

20 de

Beller

Vista Alegre

Avenida Circunvalacion Norte

Hnos. Spignolio

Hugo Kunhardt

To Playa
Dorada

Francisco J. Peinado

Profesor Certad

El Morro

Antera Mota

27 de Febrero

Presidente Vasquez

Rafael Aguilar

**National Parque
litoral Sur de
Puerto Plata**

Avenida Virginia Ortea

Avenida 27 de

Avenida Luis Ginebra

By Pedal

The Dominican Republic is an old-fashioned country in many ways, but is slowly building a network of cyclists. Many locals still wonder why anyone would want to bike through their country on a vacation, but will receive you openly. One of the best areas to ride is in the **Bermudez National Park**, which features virtually no paved access, but offers a surfeit of single track roads and donkey trails through the dense forests.

What Else to See

Santo Domingo's Zona Colonial (Colonial Zone), which sprawls over 12 blocks, is a must. The narrow cobbled streets, jammed with cars, locals and tourists alike, wind past buildings that look just as they did when first erected nearly 500 years ago, and an ongoing restoration program assures they will stay historically accurate. It's odd and exciting to walk down the same streets traveled by such legendary explorers as Ponce de Leon, Cortés and Sir Frances Drake.

The wide boulevard that runs along the oceanfront is officially called Avenida George Washington, though locals call it The Malecon. This is the place to be during the annual carnival, when a frantic mass of merengue dancers will have even the most inhibited tourist swinging along.

Along the north coast is the world's richest deposits of amber and a fast-growing tourist region called Playa Dorada. The area's Fort of San Felipe heralds back to 1540.

The city of Sousa, also in the north, was built in 1939 as a model community by European Jewish refugees fleeing the impending Holocaust. (Dominicans are justifiably proud of the fact that they welcomed Jewish refugees with open arms during World War II.) Pedro Clisante, its main street, has a humble synagogue and a newer museum that chronicles the settlement.

Traveling east from Santo Domingo, you'll encounter Les Tres Ojos de Agua (the Three Eyes of Water), a huge open cave that contains three translucent, spring-fed lagoons. This luscious area, called the Coata Sur, is home to the luxurious resort of Casa de Campo, and, further east, Altos de Chavon, which houses an exact reproduction of a 15th-century Spanish village, a good spot to pick up locally crafted works of art.

It's well worth renting a car to visit the Dominican Republic's central region, where verdant valleys, towering mountains and fields of tobacco and sugarcane conjure up images not usually associated with the Caribbean. The town of Santiago is considered the birthplace of merengue music and is a good place to learn of the island's centuries-old traditions.

Finally, you won't want to miss Lago Enriquillo, the lowest inland point in all the Caribbean. This 125-square-mile lake, which sits some 130 feet below sea level, has brackish waters and an island that's usually off-limits to all but scientists. Access to this ecologically sensitive area is limited, so join one of the occasionally offered photo safaris for a glimpse of the world's largest surviving population of American Crocodiles and endangered Rhinoceros Iguana and variegated-shell turtles. Birders may add pink flamingoes, herons, ibis, parrots and spoonbills to their lists.

Historical Sites

Alcazar de Colon ★★★

Calle Las Damas, Santo Domingo, ☎ *(809) 687-5361.*
Hours open: 9 a.m.–5 p.m.
Situated on the bluffs of the Ozama River, this is the castle of Don Diego Colon, Christopher Columbus' son, who was the colony's governor in 1509. Built in 1514 and reconstructed, after decades of neglect, in 1957, the 22-room house has 40-inch-thick limestone walls and 22 rooms filled with antiques from the 16th century. General admission: $1.

Capilla de los Remedios ★★★★

Calle Las Damas, Santo Domingo.
Hours open: 9 a.m.–6 p.m.
The Chapel of Our Lady of Remedies was built in the 17th century in the Castilian-Romanesque style. Sunday masses begin at 6 a.m.

Cathedral Santa Maria la Menor ★★★

Calle Arzobispo Merino, Santo Domingo.
Hours open: 9 a.m.–4 p.m.
This is the first cathedral built in the Americas, begun in 1514 and completed three decades later. The Spanish Renaissance-style building has a gold coral limestone facade and houses an impressive art collection and a high altar of beaten silver. Sunday masses begin at 6 a.m.

El Faro a Colon ★★★★

Av Espana, Santo Domingo.
Hours open: 9 a.m.–4 p.m.
The Columbus Memorial Lighthouse was completed in 1992 to celebrate the 500th anniversary of his "discovery" of the Dominican Republic. The impressive pyramid cross-shaped monument houses six museums on the explorer and the early days of the New World. It also reportedly contains the remains of Columbus. Several institutions around the world make similar claims. At night, the monument projects a huge cross on the clouds above that can be seen as far away as Puerto Rico.

Fort San Felipe ★★★

Puerto Plata.

This, the oldest fort in the New World, dates back to 1564. You can explore its small rooms and eight-inch-thick walls and be glad you weren't a prisoner here during Trujillo's rule. Lots of sidewalk vendors lend a tawdry air. General admission: $1.

National Pantheon ★★★

Calle Las Damas, Santo Domingo.
Hours open: 10 a.m.–5 p.m.
This Spanish-American colonial-style building dates back to 1714 and was once a Jesuit monastery. A mural of Trujillo's assassination is on the ceiling above the altar, and the ashes of martyrs who tried to oust him in 1959 are preserved here.

Santa Barbara Church ★★★★

Av Mella, Santo Domingo.
Hours open: 8 a.m.–midnight.
This combination church and fortress, unique to the city, was built in 1562 and is worth a gander if you're in the neighborhood. Sunday masses begin at 6 a.m.

Torre del Homenaje ★★★

Paseo Presidente Belini, Santo Domingo.
Hours open: 8 a.m.–7 p.m.
The Tower of Homage in Fort Ozama was built in 1503, and was the place where condemned prisoners awaited execution. General admission: $1.

Museums and Exhibits

Museo de la Familia Dominicana ★★★★

Calle Padre Bellini, Santo Domingo, ☎ *(809) 689-5057.*
See how the other (richer) half lived during the 19th century at this Museum of the Dominian Family. General admission: $1.

Museo de las Casas Reales ★★★

Calle Las Damas, Santo Domingo, ☎ *(809) 682-4202.*
Hours open: 9 a.m.–5 p.m.
Two 16th-century palaces house the Museum of the Royal Houses, which spotlights Dominican history from 1492-1821. Exhibits include antiques and artwork, Indian artifacts, relics from two galleons sunk in 1724, pre-Columbian artwork, and replicas of Columbus' ships. General admission: $1.

Museum of Dominican Amber ★★★

Calle Duante 61, Puerto Plata, ☎ *(809) 586-2848.*
Hours open: 9 a.m.–5 p.m.
A beautiful mansion houses exhibits on amber, the country's national stone, which is found only in the Dominican Republic, Germany and the former Soviet Union. You can buy amber pieces and jewelry at the giftshop. Guided tours are conducted in English daily. General admission: $1.

Plaza de la Cultura ★★

Av Maximo Gomez, Santo Domingo.

This large, modern complex includes a theater, the national library and museums of Dominican man, natural history and modern art—each well worth a look. Guided tours of the complex are offered in English on Tuesday and Saturday afternoons at 2:30 p.m.

Parks and Gardens

Jardin Botanico Nacional   ★ ★ ★

Arroyo Hondo, Santo Domingo.
Hours open: 10 a.m.–6 p.m.
This is the largest botanical garden in the entire Caribbean, with 445 acres of orchids, Japanese plants and trees, colorful flowers and 200 varieties of palms. You can tour it via foot, boat, train or horse-drawn carriage.

Los Haitises National Park   ★ ★

Samana, Santo Domingo.
A natural rainforest, pristine and primitive, with mangrove swamps, lakes and caves with Indian petroglyphs.

Tours

Acuario Nacional   ★ ★ ★

Av de las Americas, Santo Domingo.
Hours open: 10 a.m.–6 p.m.
This is the Caribbean's largest aquarium, with lots of tropical fishes and dolphins swimming about. General admission: $1.

Parque Zoologico Nacional   ★ ★ ★

Av Maximo Gomez, Santo Domingo, ☎ *(809) 562-2080.*
Hours open: 10 a.m.–6 p.m.
Lions and tigers and bears roam in relative freedom at this 320-acre national zoo. There's also an aquatic bird lake, a pond teeming with crocodiles, a snake pit and a large aviary. General admission: $2.

Sports

The country has a national passion for baseball; in fact, Dominican Republicans outnumber all other Latin American nations with the most players on North American Major League teams. Most U.S ballclubs have academies or camps in the Dominican Republic, with games played at Quisqueya Stadium in Santo Domingo and other stadiums in Santiago, San Pedro de Macoris and La Romana. The professional season runs from October to the end of January; if you're on island then, inquire at your hotel about a schedule. Other spectator sports include professional basketball from June though late August, and boxing, both at Palacio de los Deportes. There's also horse and dog racing, and, unfortunately, the cruel "sport" of cock fighting.

All the typical watersports associated with the Caribbean can be partaken in the DR; your hotel can usually arrange all equipment rentals right on site. If your hotel lacks a watersports center, you're usually welcome at a large resort, for a fee of course. Scuba diving and snorkeling are good, as if wishing in the deep sea for marlin and wahoo. Tennis players will have no problem finding courts at virtually every hotel and resort. Windsurfing is good year round, but especially from June to October at Cabarete Beach, with wind speeds of 20-25 knots and three- to 15-foot waves.

Canodromo el Coco

Av Monumental, Santo Domingo, ☎ *(809) 560-6968.*
Greyhounds race at this track about 15 minutes from Santo Domingo. Post times are Monday, Wednesday and Friday at 7:30 p.m. and Sunday at 4 p.m.

Golf

Various locations, Santo Domingo.
The best place to tee off is at one of the courses at Casa de Campo in La Romana; ☎ *(809) 523-3333* for details. Over at Puerto Plata, the Robert Trent Jones, Jr.- designed links are also good; ☎ *(809) 320-4340.* Santo Domingo's only course is private, but if you're staying at one of the better hotels, they can arrange to get you in on weekdays.

Hipodromo Perla Antillana

Av San Cristobel, Santo Domingo, ☎ *(809) 565-2353.*
You can wager on a horse year-round at this racetrack. Post times are Tuesday, Thursday and Saturday at 3 p.m.

Watersports

Various locations, Santo Domingo.
Your hotel will probably offer all you need in the way of aqua activity. If not, try one of these: Deep-sea fishing: **Andres Boca Chica Club** *(Boca Chica,* ☎ *(809) 685-4950),* and **Casa de Campo** *(La Romana,* ☎ *(809) 682-2111).* Scuba diving: **Mundo Submarino** *(Santo Domingo,* ☎ *(809) 566-0344).* Boat rentals: **Heavens** *(Playa Dorada,* ☎ *(809) 568-5250),* and **Casa de Campo** *(La Romana,* ☎ *(809) 682-2111).* Windsurfing: **CaribBIC Windsurfing Center** *(Caberete Beach,* ☎ *(809) 635-1155).*

Where to Stay

★★★★★	Fielding's Highest Rated Hotels in Dominican Republic	
★★★★★	Club Mediterranee	$110–$230
★★★★★	Hotel Gran Bahia	$105–$155
★★★★★	Hotel Santo Domingo	$150–$150
★★★★★	Hotel V Centenario Global	$215–$285
★★★★★	Jaragua	$80–$125
★★★★	Bavaro Beach Resort	$80–$220
★★★★	Casa de Campo	$180–$240
★★★★	El Embajador Hotel	$105–$115
★★★★	Renaissance Capella Beach Resort	$120–$160
★★★★	Sand Castle Beach Resort	$80–$125

	Fielding's Most Exclusive Hotels in Dominican Republic	
★★	Boca Chica Resort	$150–$390
★★★★★	Hotel V Centenario Global	$215–$285
★★	Paradise Beach Club	$110–$330
★★	Decameron Super Club	$100–$300
★★★★	Hotel Rio Taino	$80–$305

	Fielding's Best Value Hotels in Dominican Republic	
★★★★	Hotel Cayacoa Beach	$105
★★★★★	Jaragua	$80–$125
★★	Hotel Sousa	$35–$65
★★★★	Sand Castle Beach Resort	$80–$125
★★★★★	Hotel Gran Bahia	$105–$155

The Dominican Republic has more rooms than any other destination in the Caribbean, with some 6000 units scattered around the island. Luxury resorts, virtually all situated on fine, sprawling beaches, are centered around Punta Cana on the east coast, Puerto Plata on the far north coast, and Playa Juan Dolloa, Boca Chica and La Romana on the south coast. Those into a vibrant city life and lots of history should consider a stay in the capital city of Santo Domingo, which has several fine European-style hotels. One drawback to a Dominican vacation: Few restaurants are usually within walking distance from the large hotels, so you're better off signing up for a full meal plan at your property. On the other hand, hotel restaurants are generally quite good As you flip through the following list accommodations, you'll notice that room rates are extremely reasonable, making the Dominican Republic one of the Caribbean's best travel bargains.

Hotels and Resorts

The trend among resorts today is toward the all-inclusive program. Always check your contract to make sure what your particular program includes, but most include all meals and sports activities. The hotels in Santo Domingo, at least 30 minutes by car from any acceptable beach for swimming, often provide excellent views of the sea. (In contrast, hotels in Playa Dorado that are not situated on a beach offer a shuttle bus service that takes you to a suitable strand.) Among the top hotels in Santo Domingo are the **Ramada Renaissance Jaragua** resort, with its splashy Vegas-type casino, luxurious bedrooms and bathrooms that belong on a Hollywood set. **Gran Hotel Lina** is known island-wide for its excellent restaurant and the nearby casino, which can be happening if you pick the right day (depends on the traffic). **Hotel Santo Domingo** retains both the elegance and the tropical feel of the island, and its views of the sea from many of the rooms are stellar.

Puerto Plata

Bayside Hill Resort   **$180–$350**   ★ ★

Costambar, Puerto Plata, ☎ (800) 877-3648, (809) 523-3333. FAX (809) 523-8548. Single: $180–$185. Double: $180–$350.

Leave the kids at home—only adults are welcome at this resort set on a hill, with nice views of the Caribbean. All watersports are available, and there are also two pools, a gym, tennis and a handfull of bars and restaurants. 150 rooms. Credit cards: A, MC, V.

Boca Chica Resort   **$150–$390**   ★ ★

Juan Bautista Vicini, Puerto Plata, ☎ (809) 523-4522. FAX (809) 523-4438. Single: $150. Double: $240–$390.

Located near but not on the beach, this property offers decent accommodations and resort amenities such as watersports and tennis. The all-inclusive rates cover all activities, meals and drinks. 273 rooms. Credit cards: A, MC, V.

Caribbean Village Club   **$120–$330**   ★ ★

Playa Dorada, Puerto Plata, ☎ (809) 320-1111. Single: $120. Double: $190–$330.

What is it with swim-up bars? Does anyone really use them? In any event, you'll find another one at this all-inclusive resort with accommodations in two-story buildings in a landscaped garden setting. The health club is excellent, and there are 18 holes of golf and seven tennis courts for the active set. Guests can choose from three restaurants, and there's nightly entertainment. The beach is a good 10-minute walk, or you can catch the free shuttle. 336 rooms. Credit cards: A, MC, V.

Club Mediterranee $110–$230 ★★★★★

Alta Gracia, Puerto Plata, ☎ *(800) 258-2633, (809) 687-2606.*
Single: $110–$230. Double: $110–$230.
This all-inclusive vacation village appeals to singles and fun lovers who spend beads in lieu of cash. Accommodations are in bungalows clustered above the beach; nothing fancy, but the idea is to spend lots of time out and about among your fellow guests. There's tons going on at all hours—tennis, watersports, circus workshops—and the disco is lively. Nice, if you like Club Meds. Note that the company charges a one-time $30 initiation fee plus a $50 per year membership fee, on top of the rates. 339 rooms. Credit cards: A, V.

Flamengo Beach Resort $110–$150 ★★

Playa Dorada, Puerto Plata, ☎ *(809) 320-5084. FAX (809) 320-6319.*
Single: $110. Double: $110–$150.
Spanish-style in appearance, this resort is on a nice stretch of beach and has lushly landscaped grounds and a pretty lagoon. Accommodations, scattered about the property, are spacious and nicely decorated. All the standard resort diversions, including a pool, two tennis courts, watersports and nightly entertainment. Not bad. 310 rooms. Credit cards: A, DC, MC.

Heavens $65–$150 ★★

Playa Dorada, Puerto Plata, ☎ *(809) 586-5250. FAX (809) 320-4733.*
Single: $65–$120. Double: $75–$150.
This all-inclusive resort has a casual environment and tons of activities to keep guests busy. Rooms are pleasant and all have air conditioning, but the ones closest to the disco—which hops—can be noisy. You can choose to eat at a few restaurants, and for an added fee, dine at a steak house. 150 rooms. Credit cards: A, MC, V.

Hotel Confresi $100–$120 ★

Puerto Plata, ☎ *(809) 586-2898. FAX (809) 658-6806.*
Single: $100–$120. Double: $100–$120.
Situated on a rocky promontory over the Caribbean Sea, this all-inclusive resort appeals to those who crave a casual getaway. Rooms are air-conditioned, though you probably won't be spending much time in them, as the rates include tennis, watersports, scuba and the gym. There are also two pools, and for nightlife, live shows and a disco. 200 rooms. Credit cards: A, MC, V.

Hotel Rio Taino $80–$305 ★★★★

Playa de Arena Gorda, Puerto Plata, ☎ *(809) 221-2290. FAX (809) 685-9537.*
Single: $80–$305. Double: $115–$305.
Sitting right on a lovely beach, this newer (1991) hotel has pretty tropical gardens surrounding Dominican-style white two-story bungalows; inside are pleasant, air-conditioned rooms. The usual pool, tennis courts and watersports are on hand;

those looking to dance head to the disco at sister property Riu Naiboa next door. If you're torn between the two, choose this one—it's nicer all around. 360 rooms. Credit cards: A, DC, MC, V.

Hotel Rui Naiboa   **$101–$277**   ★★★★

Playa de Arena Gorda, Puerto Plata, ☎ *(809) 221-7515. FAX (809) 658-6806.*
Single: $101–$277. Double: $101–$277.
It's a five-minute walk to the beach—no big deal, but all the other hotels in the area are right on the sand. This newer (1992) property has pretty guest rooms done up in pink and gray. The lagoon-style pool has a sandy area for those who don't feel like hoofing it to the real thing. There's also tennis and a disco, and lots of activities for children, making this primarily a family resort. 372 rooms. Credit cards: A, DC, MC, V.

Hotel Sousa   **$35–$65**   ★★

El Batey, Puerto Plata, ☎ *(809) 571-2683. FAX (809) 571-2180.*
Single: $35–$50. Double: $50–$65.
Set five minutes from the beach in a suburban neighborhood, this budget, three-story hotel has basic but clean rooms that rely on ceiling fans to keep things cool. Three apartments offer kitchenettes. There's a pool and restaurant, but not much else in the way of extras. Good value for the money, though. 39 rooms. Credit cards: A, MC, V.

Jack Tar Village   **$90–$160**   ★★★

Playa Dorada, Puerto Plata, ☎ *(800) 999-9182, (809) 586-3800. FAX (809) 809-4161.*
Single: $90–$110. Double: $150–$160.
Situated on extensive grounds, this all-inclusive resort offers accommodations in Mediterranean-style villas with one to three bedrooms. Rates include all meals and most activities, but you'll pay extra for golf. Those into organized activity love this place; you get points for joining the fun, then redeem them for prizes at the end. Corny perhaps, but no one's complaining. All the usual amenities: tennis, pool, watersports, horseback riding and 18 holes of golf. 283 rooms. Credit cards: A, DC, MC, V.

La Esplanada   **$90–$225**   ★★

Pedro Clisante Street, Puerto Plata, ☎ *(809) 571-3333. FAX (809) 571-3922.*
Single: $90. Double: $150–$225.
Located 10 minutes from downtown Sousa, as well as the beach, this newer (1991) resort has light and airy air-conditioned guest rooms, some with minibar and balcony. There are also 12 apartments for those who like to spread out. The grounds include a few restaurants and bars, a pool and two tennis courts. Decent. 210 rooms. Credit cards: A, DC, MC, V.

Melia Bavaro Resort   **$90–$225**   ★★★★

Playas de Bavaro, Puerto Plata, ☎ *(800) 336-3542, (809) 221-2311. FAX (809) 686-5427.*
Single: $90–$200. Double: $150–$225.
This newer (1992) resort houses guests in split-level suites with high-quality furnishings and impressive touches or bungalows with kitchenettes and platform beds. Fountains and ponds dotted throughout the grounds lend a nice touch. A shuttle takes guests back and forth to the beach, where there is also a large free-form pool

with that inescapable swim-up bar. Tennis, horseback riding and watersports keep the doldrums away. 776 rooms. Credit cards: A, DC, MC, V.

Paradise Beach Club $110–$330 ★★

Playa Dorada, Puerto Plata, ☎ *(800) 752-9236, (809) 586-3663. FAX (809) 320-4858. Single: $110–$150. Double: $220–$330.*

Another of the area's many all-inclusive resorts, Paradise is stylish, with pretty architecture lending an elegant touch. Accommodations run the gamut from standard rooms to two-bedroom suites on two levels; all are pleasant and comfortable. Guests can dine in five restaurants and toss some back in another five bars. The lushly landscaped grounds include a cute artificial river, large pool, two tennis courts, watersports and a disco. Nice. 436 rooms. Credit cards: A, MC, V.

Playa Dorada Hotel $95–$155 ★★

Playa Dorada, Puerto Plata, ☎ *(800) 423-6902. Single: $95–$155. Double: $95–$155.*

This contemporary beach resort, located two minutes out of Puerto Plata, has nice accommodations, most with balconies. Like many of the other properties in the area, the pool has a swim-up bar, and there are three tennis courts for working up a sweat. Watersports and 18 holes of golf complete the scene. 254 rooms. Credit cards: MC, V.

Puerto Plata Beach Resort $130–$210 ★★★

Malecon Avenue, Puerto Plata, ☎ *(809) 586-4243. FAX (809) 568-4377. Single: $130–$175. Double: $210.*

Victorian-style in design, all accommodations are in suites with limited kitchenettes. All the typical resort amenities, including a pool, three tennis courts, sauna and watersports. The tiny beach is across the road and not especially good for swimming, but the restaurants and casino are nice. Generally a good choice. 216 rooms. Credit cards: A, DC, MC, V.

Punta Cana Beach Resort $105–$200 ★★★

Punta Cana, Puerto Plata, ☎ *(809) 686-0084. FAX (809) 687-8745. Single: $105–$195. Double: $160–$200.*

Located on a long, sandy beach, this well-run resort has nicely landscaped grounds. Accommodations are in studios, suites and villas, all with air conditioning, kitchenettes and balconies. The grounds include five restaurants, eight bars, a pool, four tennis courts, watersports, horseback riding and, for kids, supervised activities. Guests are mainly from Europe. 340 rooms. Credit cards: A, DC, MC, V.

Victoria Resort $100–$120 ★★★★

Playa Dorada, Puerto Plata, ☎ *(809) 586-1200. FAX (809) 320-4862. Single: $100–$120. Double: $100–$120.*

Surrounded by a golf course on two sides, this family-run hotel has nice country and mountain views. The large guest rooms are well furnished. The beach is a bit of a stroll; if you're feeling lazy they'll shuttle you there, or you can hang by the pool. All watersports, tennis and even horseback riding is complimentary. Peaceful and elegant. 120 rooms. Credit cards: A, MC, V.

Villas Doradas Beach   **$115–$270**   ★ ★ ★

Playa Dorada, Puerto Plata, ☎ *(809) 320-3000. FAX (809) 320-4790.*
Single: $115–$185. Double: $180–$270.

Situated in a lush tropical setting, all accommodations at this resort have kitchen-ettes. A short walk leads to the private beach, which provides plenty of shade and has 24-hour security, a nice touch. Eighteen holes of golf, three tennis courts, horseback riding and organized tours keep folks active. An inviting spot. 207 rooms. Credit cards: A, MC, V.

Santo Domingo

Bavaro Beach Resort   **$80–$220**   ★ ★ ★ ★

Playa Bavaro, Santo Domingo, ☎ *(800) 858-0606.*
Single: $80–$220. Double: $105–$220.

Located on its own private beach, this sprawling resort consists of several low-rise properties. Accommodations vary from standard guest rooms to apartments; all are air-conditioned and pleasant. The facilities are varied and ample, with nine restau-rants, 16 bars, a disco, live entertainment, 18 holes of golf, six tennis courts, horse-back riding, watersports and organized tours. Supervised programs keep kids out of harm's way. Tight security, too. A fun and very busy complex. 1295 rooms. Credit cards: A, MC, V.

Casa de Campo   **$180–$240**   ★ ★ ★ ★

La Romana Street, Santo Domingo, ☎ *(800) 773-6437, (809) 523-3333. FAX (809) 523-8541.*
Single: $180–$240. Double: $180–$240.

A true mega-resort, set on 7000 acres, this is the country's best resort—in fact, it's one of the best in the entire Caribbean. The resort is essentially its own town—you can even fly directly into their own airstrip—with 16 bars and restaurants, seven pools, 13 tennis courts, 36 holes of golf, beaches, etc., etc. Guests get around on electric carts. Despite its sheer size, they do everything right here. The accommoda-tions, designed by Oscar de la Renta, are in two-story villas with plush furnishings and kitchenettes. You'll hate to leave. 750 rooms. Credit cards: A, MC, V.

Decameron Super Club   **$100–$300**   ★ ★

Juan Dolio Beach, Santo Domingo, ☎ *(809) 526-2009. FAX (809) 526-1430.*
Single: $100–$200. Double: $200–$300.

The name makes it sound like a restaurant, but in fact this is an all-inclusive resort with one- and two-bedroom suites. There's lots happening, from horseback riding to disco dancing to tennis to bike rides to the casino, and this place appeals mostly to a young crowd. Those with refined tastes will be put off by the gaudy decor, and the service is nothing to brag about. 292 rooms. Credit cards: A, MC, V.

Dominican Fiesta Hotel   **$100–$200**   ★ ★ ★ ★

Avna Anacaona, Santo Domingo, ☎ *(809) 562-8222. FAX (809) 562-8938.*
Single: $100–$200. Double: $110–$200.

Located opposite Paseo de los Indios Park, this full-service resort and convention hotel has nice guest rooms with original artwork, refrigerators and balconies. The extensive grounds include a huge pool with swim-up bar, eight tennis courts, bas-ketball, volleyball, a gym and casino. A great spot for those seeking all the bells and whistles of a large resort, as long as they don't mind sharing the facilities with a bunch of name tag-wearing business travelers. 337 rooms. Credit cards: A, DC, MC, V.

El Embajador Hotel   **$105–$115**   ★★★★
Ave Sarasota 65, Santo Domingo, ☎ *(800) 457-0067, (809) 221-2131. FAX (809) 532-9444.*
Single: $105–$115. Double: $105–$115.
One of the island's original resorts, dating back to 1956, this hotel was built as dictator Rafael Trujillo's showplace. Guest rooms are oversized and done in French provincial style; each has a large balcony with sea or city views but could use an overhaul. There are all kinds of things to keep you busy here: Olympic-size pool, four tennis courts, wonderful restaurants (especially the Chinese one), casino, even a Turkish bath. 300 rooms. Credit cards: A, DC, MC, V.

El Portillo Beach Club   **$95–$145**   ★
Las Terrenas Beach, Santo Domingo, ☎ *(809) 688-5715.*
Single: $95. Double: $145.
Set on a lovely beach, this all-inclusive resort houses guests in cottages or standard hotel rooms. A pool, two tennis courts, watersports and horseback riding supply recreation at this fairly isolated property. Nice, if you don't mind being far from other attractions. 159 rooms. Credit cards: A, MC, V.

Gran Hotel Lina   **$105–$135**   ★★★
Maximo Gomez Avenue, Santo Domingo, ☎ *(800) 942-2461, (809) 563-5000. FAX (809) 686-5521.*
Single: $105–$110. Double: $110–$135.
This Spanish-style high-rise is stylish, though guest rooms are disappointingly basic and only some have terraces. The public spaces are grand, though, with lots of colorful modern art and elegant touches. The gym is well-equipped, and there's a large pool, boutiques, a casino and several restaurants and bars. Frequented by both tourists and business travelers. 217 rooms. Credit cards: A, DC, MC, V.

Hotel Cayacoa Beach   **$105–$155**   ★★★★
Samana Bay, Santo Domingo, ☎ *(800) 421-5192, (809) 538-3131.*
Single: $105. Double: $155.
Surrounded by a park and near the National Park of the Haitises, this all-inclusive resort has attractive, air-conditioned accommodations. All the typical recreational pursuits, including tennis and watersports. All meals are served in a single restaurant; two bars provide a little more variety. 70 rooms. Credit cards: A, DC, MC, V.

Hotel Cayo Levantado   **$125–$200**   ★
Cayo Vigia, Santo Domingo, ☎ *(800) 423-6902, (809) 538-3426.*
Single: $125. Double: $200.
This all-inclusive hotel reopened in 1993 after extensive renovations. The grounds are lush and green, with wonderful beaches—one that remains secluded and one that is popular with locals and vendors. Accommodations are in standard guest rooms or cabanas of two or three bedrooms; all have air conditioning and bright artwork. No pool, but ample watersports on the beach. 37 rooms. Credit cards: A, MC, V.

Hotel Gran Bahia   **$105–$155**   ★★★★★
Samana Bay, Santo Domingo.

Single: $105–$120. Double: $130–$155.

Set on a bluff near a mountainside rain forest, this Victorian-style hotel appeals to lovers of all ages. Wonderful views abound everywhere. Guest rooms are spacious and comfortably done. The rocky shore below has sandy inlets for sunbathing, and there's also a pool. A good spot for whalewatching. 96 rooms. Credit cards: MC, V.

Hotel Hispaniola $80–$125   ★★

Avenida Independencia, Santo Domingo, ☎ *(800) 877-3643, (809) 221-1511. FAX (809) 535-4050.*
Single: $80–$90. Double: $90–$125.

Located in the heart of the city and certainly one of its better bargains, this older (1956) hotel has nicely appointed guest rooms with hand-crafted pine furniture, large walk-in closets and tiled balconies. There's a restaurant, bar, elegant casino and disco on-site, and guests can use the tennis courts at sister property Hotel Santo Domingo. The rates make this one worth a look. 165 rooms. Credit cards: A, MC, V.

Hotel Santo Domingo $150–$150   ★★★★★

Av Independencia, Santo Domingo, ☎ *(809) 221-1511. FAX (809) 535-4050.*
Single: $150. Double: $150.

This elegant resort is appreciated especially by business travelers—the true jet set can land right on their helipad and then check in. Accommodations are beautifully done with handsome furnishings, large modern baths, and good views. Three tennis courts and a pool offer recreational diversion. Located some 15 minutes from downtown, tourists may be happier in the historic district, but either way, this place is a winner. 220 rooms. Credit cards: A, DC, MC, V.

Hotel V Centenario Global $215–$285   ★★★★★

Avenue George Washington, Santo Domingo, ☎ *(800) 221-0000, (809) 221-0000. FAX (809) 221-2020.*
Single: $215–$270. Double: $230–$285.

This Inter-Continental high-rise, opened in 1992, has spacious guestrooms with marble accents, original art and minibars; only the suites, alas, have balconies. Facilities include four restaurants, four bars, a casino, pool, tennis, squash, racquetball and a health club. Locals like the cellar tapas bar; you will too. 200 rooms. Credit cards: A, DC, MC, V.

Jaragua $80–$125   ★★★★★

367 George Washington Avenue, Santo Domingo, ☎ *(800) 327-0200, (809) 221-2222. FAX (809) 535-4050.*
Single: $80–$125. Double: $90–$125.

This elaborate resort complex, situated on 14 garden acres facing the Caribbean, is a Ramada Renaissance property. The glittering resort includes a large and happening casino, a large pool, four tennis courts and very nice guest rooms with all kinds of amenities, such as three phones. Six restaurants and five bars give you lots of evening options, and the upscale spa and health club will help you burn it back off. Resort lovers need look no further. 310 rooms. Credit cards: A, MC, V.

Metro Hotel & Marina $75–$115   ★★

Juan Dolio Beach, Santo Domingo, ☎ *(809) 526-2811. FAX (809) 526-1808.*
Single: $75–$115. Double: $75–$115.

Situated on a nice, palm-studded beach, this modern hotel houses guests in adequate, if unexciting, standard rooms. Two restaurants and two bars keep people sated, and the activities range from watersports to a lively disco. There's also two pools and a pair of tennis courts. 180 rooms. Credit cards: A, DC, MC, V.

Naco Hotel and Casino   **$40–$80**   ★

Av Tiradentes 22, Santo Domingo, ☎ *(809) 562-3100. FAX (809) 544-0957.*
Single: $40–$80. Double: $45–$80.

Near a large shopping mall in a mixed commercial and residential area, this budget property is 10 minutes from downtown. Rooms are clean and comfortable and come with kitchenettes. Reflecting the rates, the casino draws mainly low-rollers. The pool, set in a pleasant garden, is small. Nothing too exciting, but rates are extremely reasonable. 107 rooms. Credit cards: A, DC, MC, V.

Punta Goleta Beach Resort   **$85–$100**   ★★

Punta Goleta, Santo Domingo, ☎ *(809) 571-0700. FAX (809) 571-0707.*
Single: $85–$90. Double: $85–$100.

Set on 100 acres across the street from a beach known for good windsurfing, this resort has large rooms with air conditioning and Victorian-style balconies. All the typical amenities, including a pool and tennis, at this all-inclusive resort, as well as three restaurants and four bars to keep things interesting. 130 rooms. Credit cards: A, DC, MC, V.

Renaissance Capella Beach Resort   **$120–$160**   ★★★★

Villas del Mar Beach, Santo Domingo, ☎ *(800) 228-9898, (809) 562-4010.*
Single: $120–$160. Double: $120–$160.

This new beachfront resort, opened in spring 1994, offers all the luxury amenities resort guests expect, including an excellent health club. Spread out over several buildings in eclectic architectural styles, the grounds include three restaurants, a picturesque beach, two free-from pools, a watersports center and a disco. Guest rooms are nicely done; those opting to spend extra for the "Renaissance Club" units get VIP treatment, special amenities and complimentary continental breakfast. Oceanview penthouse suites feature Jacuzzis and wraparound decks. The 17-acre site is lushly landscaped; city center is 45 minutes away. 283 rooms. Credit cards: A, DC, MC, V.

Sand Castle Beach Resort   **$80–$125**   ★★★★

Puerto Chiquito, Santo Domingo, ☎ *(809) 571-2420.*
Single: $80–$120. Double: $85–$125.

Set on a bluff between the ocean and a saltwater pond, this isolated spot offers dramatic views and prettily furnished rooms; 80 suites offer up kitchenettes and very large baths as well. Everything is really nicely done here, with lots of marble, stained glass and finished stone. The beach below, reached via a stairway, is decent. Five restaurants, another five bars, two tennis courts and two pools keep folks busy. 240 rooms. Credit cards: A, DC, MC, V.

Sheraton Santo Domingo   **$110–$130**   ★★★★

Av George Washington, Santo Domingo, ☎ *(800) 325-3535, (809) 221-6666. FAX (809) 687-8150.*
Single: $110–$130. Double: $120–$130.

This high-rise, overlooking the sea, offers stylish rooms with the typical extras. A casino, two restaurants, disco and a few bars provide nightlife. By day, there's a large pool and two tennis courts. Nice, but not terribly noteworthy. 258 rooms. Credit cards: A, DC, MC, V.

Talanquera   **$70–$130**   ★★

Juan Dolio Beach, Santo Domingo, ☎ *(809) 541-1166.*
Single: $70–$130. Double: $70–$130.
The well-landscaped grounds here lead to a nice beach, where all the usual watersports take place. There are also three pools and atypical activities such as shooting and archery. Accommodations run the gamut from standard rooms to junior suites in cabanas; only some have balconies. Four bars and a disco keep things interesting once the sun goes down. 250 rooms. Credit cards: A, MC, V.

Tropics Club   **$115–$165**   ★★

Juan Dolio Beach, Santo Domingo, ☎ *(809) 529-8531.*
Single: $115–$165. Double: $145–$165.
This small resort offers all-inclusive packages, but lacks many of the facilities you'll find at its larger competitors. Rooms are air-conditioned, and those wishing to cook in can rent a suite with kitchen. There's the standard handful of restaurants and bars, but you'll have to indulge in watersports and gambling next door at the Decameron Super Club. 77 rooms. Credit cards: A.

Yaroa Hotel   **$45–$55**   ★

El Batey, Santo Domingo, ☎ *(809) 571-2651. FAX (809) 571-2651.*
Single: $45–$55. Double: $45–$55.
Located on a quiet street five minutes from the beach, the comfortable hotel is in a U shape surrounding a small pool. Guest rooms are nicely appointed, with air conditioning and screened balconies. Pleasant. 24 rooms. Credit cards: A, MC, V.

Apartments and Condominiums

In general, few of the self-catering units available in the Dominican Republic are anything to write home about, except for the luxury villas at Casa de Campo. If you don't speak good English, you will have a real adventure trying to communicate your needs to the management. Boca Chica and Juan Dolio boast more modern apartments; kitchens are usually fully furnished. For units in the cityscape, contact **ARAH** (*194 Avenida 27 de Febrero, Santo Domingo, R.D.* Another source is the **Villa, Condo and Apartment Rental Service**, *Box 30076, Pedro Henriques Urena 37, Santo Domingo, R.D.,* ☎ *(809) 686-0608.*

Puerto Plata

Dorado Naco Suite Resort   **$80–$145**   ★★★★

Playa Dorada, Puerto Plata, ☎ *(800) 322-2388, (809) 586-2019.*
Single: $80–$145. Double: $80–$145.
All accommodations are in one- and two-bedroom suites with full kitchens and balconies at this Spanish Caribbean-style hotel. The beach is a short stroll away. There's live entertainment nightly around the pool and two restaurants and three bars for after-dark diversions. Kids are kept occupied in supervised programs year-

round. Guests can also use the facilities at the adjacent Playa Naco. 150 rooms. Credit cards: A, DC, MC, V.

Plaza Nico Hotel   **$85–$85**   ★

Plaza Nico Mall, Puerto Plata, ☎ *(809) 541-6226. FAX (809) 541-7251.*
Single: $85. Double: $85.

Every room at this 12-story twin tower is a suite with kitchenette. Handy, but could use a redo. There's a disco, fitness center and cafe on-site, as well as lots of shopping and eating options in the adjacent shopping center, but this spot doesn't offer much of a resort feel for tourists. Decent for business travelers, though. 220 rooms. Credit cards: A, CB, DC, MC, V.

Low Cost Lodging

In a country where hotel rates start low (comparatively for the Caribbean), the cheapest rooms are not going to be impressive, or even acceptable according to some Western standards of cleanliness. However, deals can be found, especially among hotels geared to Dominican businessmen and Dominican tourists, which are always lower than the European and American-owned hotels and resorts. Figure out beforehand if you are really saving any money, since you will no doubt have to rent a car to get around. Also be careful you have not stumbled upon a front for a brothel or pay-by-the-hour-room rate.

Puerto Plata

Hotel Montemar   **$45–$120**   ★★

Av Hermanas Mirabel, Puerto Plata, ☎ *(809) 586-2800. FAX (809) 586-2009.*
Single: $45. Double: $90–$120.

This is the nation's hotel-training school, so you can be assured of perky, attentive service. Guest rooms are decent but lack balconies. There's no beach at this in-town spot, but guests can use the one at sister property Villas Doradas in Playa Dorada. Two tennis courts and a pool help make up for the off-sea location. Good value. 95 rooms. Credit cards: A, MC, V.

Santo Domingo

Continental Hotel   **$60–$65**   ★★

Maximo Gomex 16, Santo Domingo, ☎ *(809) 689-1151. FAX (809) 687-8397.*
Single: $60–$65. Double: $65.

Located opposite the Palace of Fine Arts, this modern hotel is a block from the beach. Guest rooms are adequate; don't bother upgrading to a "deluxe" unless you really want that refrigerator. There's a disco, restaurant and small pool, but not much else to justify the rates. You can do better elsewhere in the same price range. 100 rooms. Credit cards: A, DC, MC, V.

El Napolitano   **$50–$75**   ★

51 George Washington Avenue, Santo Domingo, ☎ *(809) 687-1131. FAX (809) 387-6814.*
Single: $50. Double: $55–$75.

It's bare bones here, but the rates appeal to those on a tight budget. Rooms are air-conditioned and have sea views. There's a pool and restaurant, but not much else, though plenty to do within an easy walk. This hotel does big business with Dominicans, and the atmosphere can be lively. 73 rooms. Credit cards: A, DC, MC, V.

Hostal Nicolas de Ovando   **$45–$75**   ★

53 Calle las Damas, Santo Domingo.
Single: $45–$75. Double: $45–$75.

Originally the palace of the first Spanish governor, dating from the 16th century, this hotel has old-fashioned, Spanish-style guest rooms with antique or reproduction furniture but little else of note. One courtyard houses a pool; the other three have patios and fountains. A restaurant and two bars round out the facilities. History buffs will like it here, but it has a way to go to reach its true potential. 107 rooms. Credit cards: A, DC, MC, V.

San Geronimo Hotel   **$35–$40**   ★

1067 Av Independencia, Santo Domingo, ☎ (809) 533-1000.
Single: $35. Double: $40.

Located near the sea and five minutes from downtown, this budget choice has small, air-conditioned rooms, some with kitchenettes. There's a restaurant, two bars, a pool and the inescapable casino. 72 rooms. Credit cards: A, DC, MC, V.

Where to Eat

Fielding's Highest Rated Restaurants in Dominican Republic

★★★★★	Casa del Rio	$18–$26
★★★★★	Lina Restaurant	$15–$30
★★★★	Chopin	
★★★★	De Armando	$10–$22
★★★★	La Bahia	$12–$20
★★★★	Restaurant Montparnasse	$11–$20
★★★	El Alcazar	$10–$25
★★★	El Conuco	$8–$15
★★★	Pez Dorado	$18–$30

Fielding's Most Exclusive Restaurants in Dominican Republic

★★★	Pez Dorado	$18–$30
★★★★★	Lina Restaurant	$15–$30
★★★★★	Casa del Rio	$18–$26
★★★	El Alcazar	$10–$25
★★★★	De Armando	$10–$22

Fielding's Best Value Restaurants in Dominican Republic

★★★★	Restaurant Montparnasse	$11–$20
★★★★	La Bahia	$12–$20
★★★	El Conuco	$8–$15
★★★★	De Armando	$10–$22
★★★★★	Casa del Rio	$18–$26

Though restaurants generally open around 6 p.m. for dinner, you'll find that most locals don't venture out until 9 or 10 p.m.—and they make a real occasion of their evening out. Though tourists can get away with casual clothing just about anywhere, you may want to dress up for dinner, as locals do. Some local dishes to try include *bollito de yucca* (a tiny hors d'oeuvre made of ground yucca root and cheese), *sancocho* (a thick stew of at least five different meats), *platanos* (plantains), *chicharrones* (fried pork rinds), *galletas* (flat, biscuit crackers) and *tortilla de jamon* (spicy ham omelette). Save room for desert, maybe a *majarete* (cornmeal custard) or a simple *añejo* (dark aged rum over ice). Don't despair if your palate is conservative—you'll be able to find American-style fixings in most of the hotel coffee shops.

While meals are generally quite reasonably priced, note that all wine is imported, so tends to be pricey.

After dinner, join the many locals who stroll along Santo Domingo's Malecon. Check out **Las Palmas** in the Hotel Santo Domingo *(Av. Independencia, ☎ 809-535-1511)* for dancing to local merengue bands; the younger crowd flocks to **Alexanders** *(Av. Pasteur 23, ☎ 809-685-9728)*. The island's many casinos, which open at 3 p.m. and don't close till 4 a.m. provide the chance to test lady luck; note that you must be at least 18 to enter and jackets are required for men.

Puerto Plata

Chopin   **$**   ★★★★

Playas de Bavaro, Puerto Plata, ☎ *(809) 221-2311. Associated hotel: Melia Bavaro.*
This wonderfully romantic open-air restaurant at the equally romantic Melia Bavaro resort is reached via a short stroll through the rainforest. The restaurant offers a different buffet each night; Tuesday, for example, features Italian fare. Other nights you may find smoked salmon, paella or Spanish ham. After dinner, you're serenaded by a quartet from the Symphony Orchestra of Belgrade playing classical tunes. Lovely! Hotel guests on the meal plan pay $5, while the fee for non-guests is $25. Reservations recommended. Credit cards: A, DC, MC, V.

De Armando   **$$$**   ★★★★

Avenida Antera Mota 23, Puerto Plata, ☎ *(809) 586-3418.*
International cuisine. Specialties: Fresh fish, lamb in wine sauce.
Lunch: 11 a.m.–3 p.m., entrées $10–$22.
Dinner: 3–11 p.m., entrées $10–$22.
The pride of North Coast dining is this top-rated restaurant in a Victorian building, where guests are served international cuisine serenaded by a guitar and string trio. Specialties have included fresh sea bass prepared with shellfish or mushroom sauces, lamb marinated in red wine, steaks and lobster. The menu also features Dominican specialties such as lentils and rice and green plantains. Reservations recommended. Credit cards: A, DC, MC, V.

Roma II   **$$**   ★★

Calle Beller, Puerto Plata, ☎ *(809) 586-3904.*

International cuisine. Specialties: Pizza, octopus.
Lunch: 11 a.m.–2 p.m., entrées $6–$15.
Dinner: 2 p.m.–midnight, entrées $6–$15.

This plain but comfortably air-conditioned bistro with charming service serves an excellent array of pizzas, plain or fancy—cheese or perhaps shrimp, made on dough baked fresh daily. More challenging appetites might go for the octopus, a specialty here, served with a vinaigrette sauce, or with fresh tomatoes, or on pasta. Steaks and filets are also on the menu. Credit cards: A, MC, V.

Santo Domingo

Cafe del Sol **$** ★ ★

Altos de Chavon Village, Santo Domingo, ☎ (809) 523-3333.
Italian cuisine.
Lunch: 11 a.m.–4: p.m., entrées $8–$10.
Dinner: 6–11 p.m., entrées $8–$10.

This pretty roof-top cafe in the artists' colony of Altos de Chavon is a perfect stop for a light repast of pizza or salad. Credit cards: A, MC, V.

Caribae **$$$** ★ ★

Camino Libre 70, Santo Domingo.
International cuisine.
Dinner: entrées $20–$30.

Pick your own lobster or shrimp from myriad tanks in this unpretentious little restaurant in the gorgeous beach resort town of Sosua. The crustaceans you choose are all raised at the restaurant's private shrimp farm nearby. For accompaniment, a plate of organic vegetables from the same farm round out a healthy meal. Credit cards: MC, V.

Casa del Rio **$$$** ★ ★ ★ ★ ★

Altos de Chavon Village, Santo Domingo, ☎ (809) 523-3333.
French cuisine.
Lunch: 11 a.m.–4 p.m., entrées $14.
Dinner: 6:30–11 p.m., entrées $18–$26.

Possibly the most expensive restaurant in the Dominican Republic (and the chicest), Casa del Rio is just the place for resort dwellers at the nearby Casa de Campo to go for a night on the town, but many fans have no compunction about driving the 100 miles from Santo Domingo to eat here. Any why not—it's hard to resist dining in a tower room glowing with candlelight, overlooking the Chavon River. French chef Philippe Mongereau likes a challenge, and constantly experiments with Asian and Caribbean spices to dress up shellfish, meats and poultry. Reservations required. Credit cards: A, MC, V.

Che Bandoneon **$$$** ★ ★

El Conde, Santo Domingo, ☎ (809) 687-0023.
Latin American cuisine. Specialties: Argentinian churrasco.
Dinner: 6 p.m.–midnight, entrées $15–$30.

Tango to this Argentinian charmer that nests in a restored home in the Old City area of Santo Domingo. Specialties include huge, choice cuts of ranch-style beef fillets or steaks. Seating is indoors or out on a pretty terrace, serenaded by troubadours playing the bandoneon (Argentinian accordion) for you. Desserts are rich and very French. Reservations recommended. Credit cards: MC, V.

El Alcazar $$$ ★★★

Avenida Independencia, Santo Domingo, ☎ *(809) 221-1511. Associated hotel: Hotel Santo Domingo.*
International cuisine.
Lunch: Noon–3 p.m., prix fixe $9.
Dinner: 6–11 p.m., entrées $10–$25.

The noonday lunch buffet at the El Alcazar is an exotic and very reasonable dining adventure, with a bevy of international dishes and succulent seafood items available daily. World-renowned couturier (and local hero) Oscar de la Renta designed the interiors of the chic hotel-restaurant on a grand North African theme, with gorgeous fabrics, shells and mirrors for accents. Reservations recommended. Credit cards: A, DC, MC, V.

El Conuco $$ ★★★

Calle Casimiro de Moya, Santo Domingo, ☎ *(809) 686-0129.*
Latin American cuisine. Specialties: Sancocho, chicharrones de pollo.
Lunch: 11 a.m.–4 p.m., entrées $8–$15.
Dinner: 6–11 p.m., entrées $8–$15.

This comically hokey but fun restaurant is situated in an ersatz thatched-roof house, where hanging artifacts from former diners provide a running commentary along with the hearty country cooking (conuco). Fill up on rice and kidney beans, stews, cod and crunchy fried chicken bits while hammy waiters turn into musicians and/or dancers at the drop of a sombrero. Reservations recommended. Credit cards: MC, V.

Fonda La Aterazana $$ ★★

Calle Aterazana 5, Santo Domingo, ☎ *(809) 689-2900.*
Latin American cuisine. Specialties: Chicharrones de pollo.
Lunch: 10 a.m.–4 p.m., entrées $5–$20.
Dinner: 4 p.m.–1 a.m., entrées $5–$20. Closed: Sun.

Feel like a Spanish grandee in this whitewashed-stone building in the Aterazana section of the Colonial Zone, sharing seafood or crunchy fried Dominican chicken strips (more delicious than it sounds) with someone special. This bright and festive spot is often jumping with musical groups and dancers performing to a merengue beat. Credit cards: A, DC, MC, V.

Jade Garden $$$ ★★

Avenida Sarasota 65, Santo Domingo, ☎ *(809) 221-2131. Associated hotel: Hotel Embajador.*
Chinese cuisine. Specialties: Peking chicken and duck.
Lunch: Noon–3 p.m., entrées $12–$22.
Dinner: 7:30–11:30 p.m., entrées $12–$30.

Considered one of the best Chinese restaurants in town, Jade Garden boasts Hong Kong-trained chefs who prepare Peking duck or chicken in a beautifully decorated room in the imposing Hotel Embajador. Reservations recommended. Credit cards: A, DC, MC, V.

La Bahia $$$ ★★★★

Avenida George Washington, Santo Domingo, ☎ *(809) 682-4022.*
Seafood cuisine. Specialties: Kingfish in coconut sauce, conch.
Lunch: 9 a.m.–2:30 p.m., entrées $10–$18.

Dinner: 2:30–11:30 p.m., entrées $12–$20.

Completely unpretentious and a very popular local hangout, La Bahia sits quietly on Santo Domingo's wide seafront and park, surrounded by towering luxury hotels and convivial cafes. It's very difficult to choose from a huge variety of luscious sea creatures served here, but you can't go wrong with a fish and shellfish soup loaded with shrimp and lobster, or kingfish with a tropical coconut sauce. The prices are so reasonable for what you're served, it's almost beyond belief. Credit cards: A, MC, V.

Lago Grill $$ ★★
Casa de Campo, Santo Domingo, ☎ *(809) 523-3333. Associated hotel: Casa de Campo Resort.*
American cuisine.
Lunch: Noon–4 p.m., entrées $5–$15.
Terrific breakfasts and lunches are served at this view spot on the golf course of the Casa de Campo resort. Happily for the many top stateside executives who stay here, they (and you) can have cooked-to-order eggs and omelets any style or an array of freshly squeezed juices from an exotic fruit bar. Dominican and Caribbean entrées, delicious burgers and sandwiches, and a copious salad bar are top choices for lunch.
Credit cards: A, DC, MC, V.

Lina Restaurant $$$ ★★★★★
Avenida Maximo Gomez, Santo Domingo, ☎ *(809) 685-5000. Associated hotel: Gran Hotel Lina.*
Spanish cuisine. Specialties: Zarzuela de mariscos, paella.
Lunch: 11 a.m.–4:30 p.m., entrées $15–$24.
Dinner: 6 p.m.–midnight, entrées $15–$30.
Before the Dominican Republic became a popular tourist destination, Chef Lina Aguado was already a legend; after serving as personal chef to long-reigning president Rafael Trujillo, she opened a small eatery which grew like Topsy into a hotel/restaurant that bears her name. Today, others with equal skill and passion have inherited the great cucinera's recipes for paella valenciana or cazuela de mariscos with Pernod, and interpret them with aplomb. Reservations required. Credit cards: A, DC, MC, V.

Meson de la Cava $$$ ★★
Avenida Mirador del Sur, Santo Domingo, ☎ *(809) 533-2818.*
International cuisine.
Lunch: 11 a.m.–3:30 p.m., entrées $25–$30.
Dinner: 6 p.m.–midnight, entrées $25–$40.
In order to eat here, diners must descend to a cavern way below ground (some 50 feet), reached via a scary staircase. What's down under is some rollicking entertainment from a live band (contemporary and merengue) and simply prepared, unsurprising, but delicious food. Some people might find this sort of thing silly, but kudos must be given to whomever thought up this clever idea, which seems to be working. Reserve way in advance, and dress fashionably. Reservations required. Credit cards: A, DC, MC, V.

Neptuno's Club $$$ ★★
Boca Chica Beach, Santo Domingo, ☎ *(809) 523-4703.*
Seafood cuisine.

Lunch: 9 a.m.–2 p.m., entrées $10–$20.
Dinner: 2–10 p.m., entrées $10–$25. Closed: Mon.

Calm and warm waters and a short (about 45 minute) drive from the capital make Boca Chica Beach, where this little hut is located, popular with day-trippers. Neptuno's has a good reputation for fish stews and sautéed kingfish, although international meals are served as well. Reservations recommended. Credit cards: MC, V.

Pez Dorado   **$$$**   ★★★

43 Calle el Sol, Santo Domingo, ☎ (809) 582-2518.
Chinese cuisine. Specialties: Chinese seafood.
Lunch: 11 a.m.–3 p.m., entrées $18–$30.
Dinner: 6-11:30 p.m., entrées $18–$30.

If you find yourself visiting the historical city of Santiago de los Caballeros, about two hours away from Santo Domingo, this restaurant serving seafood Chinese-style in a posh, comfortable room is one of the best dining choices in town. Perhaps afterward, you can wend your way to a local dance club—after all, this is the birthplace of the merengue. Reservations recommended. Credit cards: MC, V.

Reina de Espana   **$$**   ★★

Avenida Cervantes 103, Santo Domingo, ☎ (809) 685-2588.
Spanish cuisine.
Lunch: Noon–4 p.m., entrées $8–$20.
Dinner: 4-11 p.m., entrées $8–$20.

In a city where Spanish food is treated with respect, Reina de Espana, located in a restored home not far from the sea, manages to present more than just the average paella or seafood stew for discriminating diners. The menu traverses each region of Spain, with roast quail or suckling pig prepared as specials from time to time. But the old favorites such as gazpacho are all represented and rarely disappoint. Reservations required. Credit cards: A, MC, V.

Restaurant Montparnasse   **$$$**   ★★★★

Avenida Lope de Vega 24, Santo Domingo, ☎ (809) 562-4141.
Latin American cuisine.
Lunch: Noon–2 p.m., entrées $5–$18.
Dinner: 2 p.m.–midnight, entrées $11–$20.

Prominent local folk like to eat here, especially for lunch, making this creative Franco-Caribbean bistro a good place to observe them. But those not inclined to eavesdropping or voyeurism will still enjoy the unusual combinations of native vegetables such as pumpkin and plantain puréed into creamy bisques or a vichyssoise. Decadent desserts such as chocolate soufflé are served all day and night—in true Dominican fashion, the place stays open late. Reservations recommended. Credit cards: A, DC, MC, V.

Vesuvio I   **$$**   ★★

Avenida G. Washington, Santo Domingo, ☎ (809) 221-3333.
Italian cuisine.
Lunch: 11 a.m.–2 p.m., entrées $8–$18.
Dinner: 2 p.m.–midnight, entrées $8–$20.

The Bonarelli family from Naples has been running this boisterous family restaurant on the Malecon since the 1950s. As they are not content to rest on past laurels, every visit brings a new specialty or improvements on old favorites. The voluminous menu features seafood and plenty of it, including crayfish with garlic, although veal scaloppine with fresh herbs is worth noting. Decor is contemporary, with plenty of colorful marine life painted on the walls. Credit cards: A, DC, MC, V.

Because exchange rates between the U.S. dollar and Dominican Peso are usually extremely favorable, the DR can be a real bargain. Among the best souvenirs are cigars (best purchased at the end of a tour of a cigar factory near Santiago); pieces of translucent amber with a leaf or insect embedded inside (think *Jurassic Park*); rum, fashions by native son Oscar de la Renta; and wood carvings. Note, however, that while legal, it's best not to purchase items made from mahogany, as this only encourages the destruction of the rainforest. Haiti-influenced local artwork is also popular, but usually is of poor quality compared with the far-superior work put out by Haitians.

Bargaining is standard practice throughout the country and it's all a big game, so join in the fun and hold out for a good price, which will often be less than half of what you were first quoted. While street vendors who work the stalls at El Mercado Modelo (Santo Domingo's huge covered market) expect you to haggle, they also are slow to give up—you will have to be firm in your refusals if you decide against the item after all.

Besides El Mercado, the main shopping areas in Santo Domingo are in La Atarazana and along Calle El Conde and Calle Duarte in the Colonial Zone.

Dominican Republic Directory

Arrival and Departure

Travelers to the Dominican Republic use two major international airports: Las Américas International Airport, about 20 miles outside Santo Domingo, and La Unión International Airport, about 25 miles east of Puérto Plata on the north coast. (Both airports have been undergoing extensive renovation; a major fire in the old terminal at Las Américas has caused congestion in a new terminal that was meant to solve the problem.) **American Airlines** offers the most flights to the island, with nonstops from New York to Santo Domingo. **American**, **Continental** and **Dominica** also fly nonstop from New York to Puerto Plata. Continental Airlines offers connecting service to both Santo Domingo and Puerto Plata from San Juan, Puerto Rico; and **American Eagle** has two flights a day from San Juan to La Romana.

For inter-island service, ALM flies from Santo Domingo to St. Maarten and Curaçao. There is also limited domestic service available from La Herrera Airport in Santo Domingo to smaller airfields in La Romana, Samana and Santiago.

Be cautious in both airports with regard to your luggage and personal valuables. Luggage theft is a common occurrence, and the general confusion can often lead to "lost" luggage. Try to carry your own luggage as you will be royally hassled for service by porters. The island is famous for *buscones*, who offer you assistance and then disappear with your belongings. If you have arranged for transport by your hotel, the representative should be awaiting you in the immigration hall.

Business Hours

Stores open weekdays 8 a.m.–12:30 p.m. and 2:30–5 p.m., and Saturday 8 a.m.–noon. Banks open weekdays 8:30 a.m.–4:30 p.m.

Climate

The climate is subtropical; with an average annual temperature of 80 degrees in Santo Domingo, temperatures are generally between 66 and 88 degrees F. The west and southwest of the country are arid. Hispaniola lis in the path of tropical cyclones.

Documents

In order to purchase a $10 tourist card, good for 90 days, visitors must present a valid passport or other proof of citizenship (birth certificate, voter's registration card, with an official photo ID such as driver's license). Cards may be purchased upon arrival, or through the consulate.

Electricity

Current is 100 volts, 60 cycles, as in the United States.

Getting Around

Taxis are available at the airports, and the 25-minute ride into Santo Domingo averages about U.S.$20. There is no bus service, but fellow travelers are usually open to sharing a taxi.

Buses in Santo Domingo are called *públicos*, small blue-and-white or blue-and-red cars that run regular routes, stopping to let passengers on and off. The fare is two pesos. There are also *conchos* or *coléctivos* (privately owned buses) whose drivers tool around the major thoroughfares, leaning out the window and trying to seduce passengers onboard. (For this inconvenience you get to pay a peso less.) Privately owned air-conditioned buses make regular runs to Santiago, Puerto Plata and other destinations. Avoid night travel because the country is rife with potholes. Reservations can be made by calling **Metro Buses** *(Av. Winston Churchill;* ☎ *[809] 586-6063* in Puerto Plata).

Cars can be rented in the airports and at many hotels. The top names are **Budget** ☎ *(809) 562-6812*; and **Hertz** ☎ *(809) 688-2277*. Driving is on the right side of the street, but drivers here are maniacs, often driving down the middle of the road and passing dangerously whenever they feel like it. They are nice enough, however, to flash their light-on when they know the highway patrol is lurking about—the 50 mph (80 kph) limit is strictly enforced. (Police have been known to stop drivers on the pretext of some violation and insinuate the need for a bribe. If you must drive around the unilluminated mountain roads at night, drive with utmost caution since many cars do not have headlights or taillights, cows stand in the middle of the road, and bicycles are rarely well lit. Gas stations are few and far between.

Motorbikes, called *motoconchos*, are a popular and inexpensive way to tool around the island, especially in such places as Puerto Plata, Sasúa and Jarabacoa. Bikes can be flagged down in road and town.

Language

The official language is Spanish, so do as much as you can to bone up on Spanish before you go. Officially, nearly everyone involved in tourism speaks English, but it is sometimes a quizzical version and many people have trouble understanding English. Waitresses in coffee shops may simply drop their jaws when you speak to them in English. In the outlying areas, it is absolutely necessary to speak Spanish. Bring along a phrase book and keep it handy in your purse.

Medical Emergencies

The island has numerous hospitals and clinics; that is not say that you should pursue any medical attention with enthusiasm. The biggest and most revered is **José Maria Cabral y Baez**; ☎ *(809) 583-4311* on Central, near the church in the town of Santiago. You'll find a number of American medical students working here since the national medical school uses the facilities. Hospitals in Santiago tend to be crowded and harassed. Hospital Marion in Santo Domingo is known for its cardiovascular center. Bring your Spanish phrase book, particularly if you get stuck in a hospital for any length of time. Do your best to fly home to the States. Remember to bring any medications you need from home, with a copy of the prescription and a letter from your doctor that you have been medically directed to take them.

Money

Official currency is the Dominican peso. Most hotels and shops welcome American dollars as well as major credit cards and traveler's checks. Try to spend your pesos rather than having to exchange them back into dollars before you leave.

Telephone

The country code is *809*. To call the Dominican Republic from the United States, dial *011* (international access), the country code *(809)* and the local number. Connections from the U.S. are generally made with ease and are clear. Calling from the Dominican Republic can become a headache—fast. There is a direct-dial system, but you should feel extraordinarily blessed to have it work right. Try dialing 1, then the area code, followed by the number.

Time

Atlantic standard time year-round.

Tipping

Hotels and restaurants add a whopping 21 percent government tax (which includes a 10 percent service charge) to all bills. It is customary to leave a dollar per day for the maid; if you balk, just imagine her income status in such a poor country. In restaurants and nightclubs, an extra 5–10 percent above the service charge included on the bill will be greatly appreciated by the waiters and waitresses. Taxi drivers expect a 10 percent tip; tip more if you arrive alive. Skycaps and hotel porters expect at least five pesos per bag.

Tourist Information

The **Dominican Tourist Information Center** is located at the corner of *Avs. México an d30 de Marzo;* ☎ *(809) 221-4660* or *00-752-1151.* There are also information booths in Santiago (City Hall Av. Duarte; ☎ *(809) 582-5885* and in Puerto Plata Av. Hermanas Mirabel ☎ *(809) 586-3676.* You can also find a booth at the airport open daily. In the U.S. call ☎ *(212) 768-2481.*

When to Go

Merengue Week explodes in late July, the island's biggest rum-filled festival dedicated to the national dance. Carnival is held on Feb. 27.

DOMINCAN REPUBLIC HOTELS		RMS	RATES	PHONE	CR. CARDS
Puerto Plata					
★★★★★	**Club Mediterranee**	339	$110–$230	(800) 258-2633	A, V
★★★★	**Dorado Naco Suite Resort**	150	$80–$145	(800) 322-2388	A, DC, MC, V
★★★★	**Hotel Rio Taino**	360	$80–$305	(809) 221-2290	A, DC, MC, V
★★★★	**Hotel Rui Naiboa**	372	$101–$277	(809) 221-7515	A, DC, MC, V
★★★★	**Melia Bavaro Resort**	776	$90–$225	(800) 336-3542	A, DC, MC, V
★★★★	**Victoria Resort**	120	$100–$120	(809) 586-1200	A, MC, V
★★★	**Jack Tar Village**	283	$90–$160	(800) 999-9182	A, DC, MC, V
★★★	**Puerto Plata Beach Resort**	216	$130–$210	(809) 586-4243	A, DC, MC, V
★★★	**Punta Cana Beach Resort**	340	$105–$200	(809) 686-0084	A, DC, MC, V
★★★	**Villas Doradas Beach**	207	$115–$270	(809) 320-3000	A, MC, V
★★	**Bayside Hill Resort**	150	$180–$350	(800) 877-3648	A, MC, V
★★	**Boca Chica Resort**	273	$150–$390	(809) 523-4522	A, MC, V
★★	**Caribbean Village Club**	336	$120–$330	(809) 320-1111	A, MC, V
★★	**Flamengo Beach Resort**	310	$110–$150	(809) 320-5084	A, DC, MC
★★	**Heavens**	150	$65–$150	(809) 586-5250	A, MC, V
★★	**Hotel Montemar**	95	$45–$120	(809) 586-2800	A, MC, V

DOMINCAN REPUBLIC HOTELS	RMS	RATES	PHONE	CR. CARDS
★★ Hotel Sousa	39	$35–$65	(809) 571-2683	A, MC, V
★★ La Esplanada	210	$90–$225	(809) 571-3333	A, DC, MC, V
★★ Paradise Beach Club	436	$110–$330	(800) 752-9236	A, MC, V
★★ Playa Dorada Hotel	254	$95–$155	(800) 423-6902	MC, V
★ Hotel Confresi	200	$100–$120	(809) 586-2898	A, MC, V
★ Plaza Nico Hotel	220	$85–$85	(809) 541-6226	A, CB, DC, MC, V

Santo Domingo

	RMS	RATES	PHONE	CR. CARDS
★★★★★ Hotel Gran Bahia	96	$105–$155		MC, V
★★★★★ Hotel Santo Domingo	220	$150–$150	(809) 221-1511	A, DC, MC, V
★★★★★ Hotel V Centenario Global	200	$215–$285	(800) 221-0000	A, DC, MC, V
★★★★★ Jaragua	310	$80–$125	(800) 327-0200	A, MC, V
★★★★ Bavaro Beach Resort	1295	$80–$220	(800) 858-0606	A, MC, V
★★★★ Casa de Campo	750	$180–$240	(800) 773-6437	A, MC, V
★★★★ Dominican Fiesta Hotel	337	$100–$200	(809) 562-8222	A, DC, MC, V
★★★★ El Embajador Hotel	300	$105–$115	(800) 457-0067	A, DC, MC, V
★★★★ Hotel Cayacoa Beach	70	$105–$105	(800) 421-5192	A, DC, MC, V
★★★★ Renaissance Capella Beach Resort	283	$120–$160	(800) 228-9898	A, DC, MC, V
★★★★ Sand Castle Beach Resort	240	$80–$125	(809) 571-2420	A, DC, MC, V
★★★★ Sheraton Santo Domingo	258	$110–$130	(800) 325-3535	A, DC, MC, V
★★★ Gran Hotel Lina	217	$105–$135	(800) 942-2461	A, DC, MC, V
★★ Continental Hotel	100	$60–$65	(809) 689-1151	A, DC, MC, V
★★ Decameron Super Club	292	$100–$300	(809) 526-2009	A, MC, V
★★ Hotel Hispaniola	165	$80–$125	(800) 877-3643	A, MC, V
★★ Metro Hotel & Marina	180	$75–$115	(809) 526-2811	A, DC, MC, V
★★ Punta Goleta Beach Resort	130	$85–$100	(809) 571-0700	A, DC, MC, V
★★ Talanquera	250	$70–$130	(809) 541-1166	A, MC, V
★★ Tropics Club	77	$115–$165	(809) 529-8531	A
★ El Napolitano	73	$50–$75	(809) 687-1131	A, DC, MC, V
★ El Portillo Beach Club	159	$95–$145	(809) 688-5715	A, MC, V
★ Hostal Nicolas de Ovando	107	$45–$75		A, DC, MC, V

DOMINCAN REPUBLIC HOTELS	RMS	RATES	PHONE	CR. CARDS
★ Hotel Cayo Levantado	37	$125–$200	(800) 423-6902	A, MC, V
★ Naco Hotel and Casino	107	$40–$80	(809) 562-3100	A, DC, MC, V
★ San Geronimo Hotel	72	$35–$40	(809) 533-1000	A, DC, MC, V
★ Yaroa Hotel	24	$45–$55	(809) 571-2651	A, MC, V

DOMINICAN REPUBLIC RESTAURANTS	PHONE	ENTRÉE	CR. CARDS
Puerto Plata			
Continental			
★★★★ Chopin	(809) 221-2311		A, DC, MC, V
International			
★★★★ De Armando	(809) 586-3418	$10–$22	A, DC, MC, V
★★ Roma II	(809) 586-3904	$6–$15	A, MC, V
Santo Domingo			
American			
★★ Lago Grill	(809) 523-3333	$5–$15	A, DC, MC, V
Chinese			
★★★ Pez Dorado	(809) 582-2518	$18–$30	MC, V
★★ Jade Garden	(809) 221-2131	$12–$30	A, DC, MC, V
French			
★★★★★ Casa del Rio	(809) 523-3333	$14–$26	A, MC, V
International			
★★★ El Alcazar	(809) 221-1511	$9–$25	A, DC, MC, V
★★ Caribae		$20–$30	MC, V
★★ Meson de la Cava	(809) 533-2818	$25–$40	A, DC, MC, V
Italian			
★★ Cafe del Sol	(809) 523-3333	$8–$10	A, MC, V
★★ Vesuvio I	(809) 221-3333	$8–$20	A, DC, MC, V
Latin American			
★★★★ Restaurant Montparnasse	(809) 562-4141	$5–$20	A, DC, MC, V
★★★ El Conuco	(809) 686-0129	$8–$15	MC, V

DOMINICAN REPUBLIC RESTAURANTS	PHONE	ENTRÉE	CR. CARDS
★★ Che Bandoneon	(809) 687-0023	$15–$30	MC, V
★★ Fonda La Aterazana	(809) 689-2900	$5–$20	A, DC, MC, V
Seafood			
★★★★ La Bahia	(809) 682-4022	$10–$20	A, MC, V
★★ Neptuno's Club	(809) 523-4703	$10–$25	MC, V
Spanish			
★★★★★ Lina Restaurant	(809) 685-5000	$15–$30	A, DC, MC, V
★★ Reina de Espana	(809) 685-2588	$8–$20	A, MC, V

GRENADA

Horseback riding is fun for adults and children on Grenada's beaches.

Grenada isn't called the Spice Island for nothing. Walk along the Carenage, the capital's lovely waterfront, and you'll see dozens of turbaned black ladies selling their fragrant cloves, allspice, cinnamon, turmeric and nutmeg with a merry song and a spiel. Stroll onto the estate of Morne Fendue and your feet trample the discarded nutmeg shells recycled as driveway gravel, stirring their sweet scent into the air. Aroma, it seems, takes on a seductive, almost musical quality on this sweet island, though admittedly color plays an equally important role in defining Grenada—from the lush green of its dense forests, to the pearly bright sand of Grand Anse, to the neatly ironed burgundy dresses of schoolgirls in Sauteurs, to the artist's palette that greets buyers at the weekly market. The island's rich panoply of natural wonders complete a delightful package that American tourists are now discovering 14 years after U.S. troops quelled the Marxist-based coup. Things are quiet now on the local political front and, although the Reagan-initiated intervention undoubtedly (and unnecessarily) scares some potential visitors away, it also works in the island's favor, keeping tourist development to a reasonable scale. From rum shop to fishing village to market square, Grenada preserves the Caribbean the way it was. The island showcases the way the region operated long before the American cultural invasion of Big Macs and Coke began to take over the daily life of other islands. But Americans are welcomed with unusually warm smiles and islanders generally refer to the military intervention only in positive terms today.

In addition to supplying roughly one-third of the world's nutmeg, 120-square-mile Grenada also grows bananas, sugar cane, cocoa, breadfruit and most of the other fruits and vegetables it consumes. The independent, three-island nation also includes Carriacou and Petit Martinique, part of the necklace of Grenadines that stretch between Grenada and St. Vincent, as well as a few mostly uninhabited islets. Carriacou makes a fine day trip, or it can be visited as part of a trip along the exquisite sailing passage through the Grenadines. But Grenada itself is hardly short on sights and activities to fill a vacation. Beyond the 45 or so beaches, travelers can hike rain forest trails riddled with cascading rivers, seek out some of the more than 450 flowering plant species and 150 varieties of birds, or dive into the depths to reach the Bianca C, a luxury liner that went down in 1961 and is called "The Titanic of the Caribbean." For refreshment, there's dining in plantation homes and in roadside restaurants, where delicious callaloo soup can be sampled a hundred different ways, and for adventure, you can spend a few hours lost in the ramparts and tunnels of forts that the British and French built during their 100-year-old custody battle.

Bird's-Eye View

Sixty miles southwest of St. Vincent, 90 miles north of Trinidad, Grenada (pronounced Gre-nay-da) lies at the southern end of the Windward Islands, and is one of the smallest nations in the Western Hemisphere. The oval-shaped island is 12 miles wide at its center, 21 miles in length, and volcanic in origin, with extinct Mt. St. Catherine rising to 2757 feet. The nation also includes Carriacou and Petit St. Martinique, as well as a quantity of uninhabited islands winding north toward the Grenadines, bringing the total land mass to 133 square miles (there's also an island-to-be in the form of an undersea volcano, intriguingly named Kick 'em Jenny, that's slowly building its

Ronde Island

Caille Island

London Bridge

12° 15'

Grenada

● CITY/TOWN
── ROAD
✕ AIRPORT
■ ATTRACTION
▲ MOUNTAIN
── RIVER

| 0 | | 3 | | 6 km |
| 0 | | 2 | | 4 mi |

©FWI 1995

C A R I B B E A N
S E A

Green Island

Sandy
Island

Sauteurs

Victoria

Tivoli

Gouyave

Mt. St. Catherine
▲ *2757 ft.*

Grand Roy

Grenville

*Concord
Falls*
■

Mt. Qua Qua
▲ *2373 ft.*

*Grand Etang
Lake*

The Seven Sisters
■

Mt. Sinai
▲ *2306 ft.*

ST. GEORGE'S
★

Grand Anse Bay

Saint David's

*La Sagasse
Nature Center*
■

G R E N A D A

*Wreck of
the Bianca*
■

**L'Anse
aux Epines**
●

*Glover
Island*

Calvigny Island

A T L A N T I C
O C E A N

12° 00'

Hog Island

61° 45'

way to the surface between Grenada and Carriacou). Inhabited by mona monkeys and armadillos, the interior of Grenada is mountainous and lush, and the fertile volcanic soil inspires vegetation so thick that the island looks as if it were upholstered in deep green velvet. You'll spot residents carrying machetes, as though the path they cleared yesterday is once again overgrown with green tangles today. It's difficult to imagine a prettier Caribbean town than Grenada's capital, St. George's, with its pedestrian walkway, the Carenage, that hugs the horseshoe-shaped, postcard-perfect harbor. Several lofty lookouts—Fort George with cannons aimed seaward, Fort Frederick and Cemetery Hill—present splendid views of the town clambering up the slopes from the waterfront. Although a number of restaurants are located here, the majority of the island's hotels are concentrated to the south of St. George's—primarily in the sweep of two-mile-long Grand Anse Beach, and on a south-facing peninsula, Lance aux Epines.

In Grand Anse, no development may be taller than a coconut palm.

History

Grenada was discovered by Columbus on his third voyage in 1498. The French built Grenada's first settlement, first appeasing and then battling the native Carib Indians, the last of whom leaped to their death from Morne de Sauteurs, a rock promontory in the island's north coast, in 1651. Over the next century, Grenada was a battlefield between the French and British until

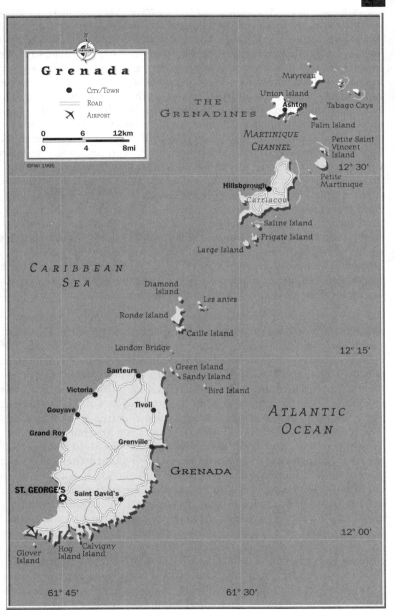

Grenada

- ● CITY/TOWN
- ═ ROAD
- ✈ AIRPORT

| 0 | 6 | 12km |
| 0 | 4 | 8mi |

©FWI 1995

Mayreau

Union Island

Ashton

Tabago Cays

THE
GRENADINES

Palm Island

MARTINIQUE
CHANNEL

Petite Saint
Vincent
Island

12° 30'

Petite
Martinique

Hillsborough

Carriacou

Saline Island

Frigate Island

Large Island

CARIBBEAN
SEA

Diamond
Island

Les antes

Ronde Island

Caille Island

London Bridge

12° 15'

Green Island

Sandy Island

Sauteurs

Bird Island

Victoria

Tivoli

ATLANTIC
OCEAN

Gouyave

Grand Roy

Grenville

ST. GEORGE'S

Saint David's

GRENADA

12° 00'

Glover
Island

Hog
Island

Calvigny
Island

61° 45'

61° 30'

the island was declared British under the Treaty of Versailles in 1783. Soon after, the island experienced the first rebellion led by a French plantocrat, Julien Fedon, resulting in the murder of 51 British colonists. (Fedon, who was never captured, remains a legend today in Grenada.) In 1838, the Emancipation Act freed Grenada's African slaves, forcing plantation owners to import indentured laborers from India, Malta and Madera. The descendants of this cultural stew live on today in the multiethnic cuisine, the French-African lilt to the language, and the British and French village names. Until 1958, the island remained a British colony, when it joined the abortive Federation of the West Indies. In 1967 it became a member of the West Indies Associated States, with Britain retaining responsibility. Many Grenadians were opposed to self-rule under Eric Gairy, the first prime minister, who was often compared to Haiti's Papa Doc Duvalier. Nevertheless, Gairy became a champion of the poor overnight, though he gained an irreverent reputation for some strange actions—for example, marching a steel band through an opponent's meeting and lecturing the U.N. about UFOs. In the early '70s, Maurice Bishop, a charismatic lawyer, just back from his studies in England, earned popular support as a human-rights activist when his New Jewel Movement convicted Gairy of 27 crimes in a mock trial that called for his resignation. Bishop, along with other members of his party, was mercilessly beaten by Gairy's police and thrown into jail for the night.

Such was the climate when Grenada (and its two dependencies, Carriacou and Petite Martinique) gained its independence from the British Commonwealth on Feb. 7, 1974. That very day management of the Holiday Inn pulled out, leaving an entire independence banquet in the hands of one pastry chef. By the late '70s, Gairy's economy was a shambles and his support diminished, even among the poor. On March 13, 1979, Bishop staged the first modern coup in the English-speaking Caribbean while Gairy was off-island. The economy improved early in his tenure and countries around the world accepted Bishop and the new Jewel Movement as a governing force. Still, free elections were never held. Bishop fostered ties with Cuba and the Eastern Bloc countries, and as his friend Fidel Castro granted Grenada aid and labor to build a larger airport at Port Salines in the south, U.S. ties began to unravel. In 1983 Bishop was ousted by a more Marxist/Leninist member of his own party, Bernard Coard, who placed Bishop under house arrest and imprisoned some of his followers. At a rally to support the release of Bishop, members of the People's Revolutionary Army fired into the throng; today no one is sure how many men, women and children were killed. The U.S. government, using the subsequent brutal execution of Bishop as pretext, landed 7000 troops on Oct. 26, 1983, on the shores of Grenada, accompanied by the military forces of other neighboring islands—ostensibly to protect democracy and defend the lives of some 1000 Americans residing there, mostly

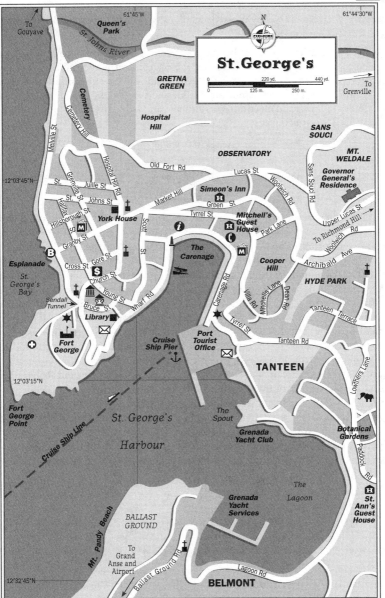

medical students at St. George's University. The American troops were welcomed with open arms by most Grenadians who called the mission not an invasion, but an "intervention."

The aftermath of what has been considered a bad dream by Grenadians has been a stars-and stripes p.r. blitz—new bridges, a retrained police force, and a renewed sense of democracy. The Americans put the finishing touches on the airport, and in 1990 American Airlines began its daily run. Today Grenada holds democratic elections every five years, with five major political parties vying for votes.

People

Like other, recently created Caribbean countries freed from colonial ties, Grenadians are politically aware and fascinated by foreigners. Warm and witty, islanders are insatiably curious, often quizzing tourists on Clintonomics or the latest about Michael Jackson. The three-island population is about 91,000 (of which 86,000 live on Grenada), many of whom live off the land or sea. Grenada is a youthful country and more than half of the population is under 30 years of age, though unfortunately, unemployment is a substantial problem to be reckoned with. Agriculture still employs a considerable number of people, but the government is increasingly committed to tourism as a long-term solution to economic woes, and in 1996 announced a $75 million commitment to upgrade and expand the current infrastructure. Grenadians are very pro-American, and still grateful to the United States and Ronald Reagan for the military intervention of 1983. They receive visitors with open arms, though like many in the region, they prefer to be asked before you snap their picture, particularly at the (very photogenic) market square in St. George's. An innovative "People to People" program invites visitors to experience Grenada through the eyes of a local for a few hours, whether at church, during a game of golf, or over a meal. Call **New Trends Tours** ☎ *(809) 444-1236.*

Beaches

Grenada has a number of fine beaches, though some are accessible only by boat and, as with most of the islands in the part of the Caribbean, the Atlantic side comes equipped with an undertow that can make swimming tricky.

The most famous and popular is Grand Anse, a two-mile stretch that begins just south of St. George's and is a center for watersports, beach peddlers and hair-braiders. When cruise ships dock, day-trippers tend to gather at the western end (where most of the accommodations are clustered), otherwise there's almost always room to spread out on this excellent beach. The best of the rest are also on the southwest end of the island. Just west of Grand Anse is Morne Rouge, a quiet cove with a small snack bar. A little farther is tranquil Pink Gin Beach, at LaSource, while the Rex Grenadian overlooks Tamarind Beach. East of the Point Salines Airport is Lance aux Epines, a peninsula with several coves lining Prickly Bay. Along the deeply scalloped southern shore are a number of other beaches, most reached by boat or four-wheel-drive vehicle. A more-accessible cove is La Sagesse, where a gray-sand beach is backed by cow pastures and a nature preserve. One other popular beach, Levera, is at the northern tip of the Grenada and overlooking several islets at the point where the Atlantic and Caribbean meet; Bathway Beach just south of here is also nice. Carriacou's best beaches are Sandy Island, reached by five-minute boat ride, l'Anse la Roche at the foot of High North Peak, and Tyrrel Bay on the southwest coast.

Diving is a low-key, comfortable pursuit in Grenada, free of much of the hustle and crowding prevalent at better-established locations. Part of this can simply be attributed to the newness of the sport here. In the rush to attract visitors and develop a tourism infrastructure in the years following the excitement of 1983, it took awhile to recognize that the island boasted attractive dive sights. Most are located at **Moliniere Point**, a 10- to 15-minute boat ride north from the Grand Anse area, where the dive shops are based. The *Bianca C*, easily the Caribbean's largest wreck, is a very dramatic dive which will thrill sunken ship enthusiasts. Farther afield, the pristine area off Carriacou should not be overlooked. Snorkelers looking for shore dives should check out the cliffs at the south end of **Grand Anse** or nearby **Point Salines**; boat trips will take snorkelers to Moliniere or to Boss Reef off Grand Anse Bay.

GRENADA

On Foot

For a bantam destination, the rumpled topography of Grenada provides splendid hiking opportunities, making the island one of the best walking destinations in the Eastern Caribbean. As you trek through Grenada's gentle range of mountains amid wafts of the local nutmeg and cloves, the term "spice island" will float through your senses. A number fruits and vegetables are also grown here, and contribute to this lovely island's interior appeal. Though some may tell you they are three separate hikes, the truly ambitious can combine **Mount Qua Qua**, **Fedon's Camp** and **Concord Falls**, which are relatively close to each other, for a vivid all-day trek. Less grandiose ambitions can be sated in the coves and hills surrounding **La Sagesse Nature Center**; the pleasant owners will eagerly point you toward several lovely trails, particularly if you stay for lunch. Several of the island's bigger hikes invite a guide's familiarity for uncomplicated navigation. But it's worth noting that escorts are available for anything harder than getting out of your car, which means you are in the awkward position of evaluating your physical stamina and Caribbean route-finding abilities—always carry the *Ordnance Survey* map—vs. the leadership and amiable banter of a knowledgeable tour guide. If in doubt, spring for the local help; but it helps to know that, although tracks divide, cross and converge with maddening frequency, it's hard to get lost for long on this cozy island.

Concord Falls

Although the lower falls are approached by road, few visitors take the obvious trail to the second drop, which is reached after about 30 minutes of stream fordings. The plunge is only about 40 feet, but this is an idyllic location for a swimming hole and it provides a quick respite from touring. Guides will make themselves well known, but really aren't necessary if you are reasonably sure-footed.

Fedon's Camp

This is the outpost used by rebel Julian Fedon, a French plantation owner who staged an insurrection against the British in 1795, killing the island's governor and 47 others. The hike starts at the Concord Falls trailhead, and continues past the second falls along a steep valley that gradually levels as it enters the forest reserve. This section can be hard to follow in places, but you'll eventually arrive at a shallow cave that served as Fedon's hideout and is now a historical landmark. Allow six-to-eight hours for the round-trip from Concord to Fedon and back. Or, continue on to nearby Mount Qua Qua and descend to Grand Etang; beginning the one-way trek from Grand Etang allows you to start at a higher elevation and (mostly) descend to Concord Falls.

Grand Etang Circuit

Grenada's volcanic crater lake is photographed from the nearby road by many, but this relatively easy path around the water is worthy for its eclectic mix of wildlife. A small pond before you reach the lake is home to freshwater lobster and crayfish; mona monkeys (imported from Africa by slave traders) hover in the stands of bamboo, cattle egrets and blue herons troll the etang, while orchids dangle from many of the trees. A lovely hour-and-a-half walk.

Morne La Baye Trail

A short interpretive trail ascends the small hill that lies just behind the visitor center overlooking Grand Etang. Marouba trees tower above, orange heliconias color the path and the endemic grand etang fern blankets the ground. The self-guided walk takes about 20 minutes.

Mount St. Catherine

Grenada's highest point (2757 feet) is a moderately difficult hike with a number of routing possibilities. The easiest takes off from the road that dead-ends at the tiny town of Mount Hope, four miles northwest of Grenville. From the end of the road, you are less than one steep mile from the summit, although you'll need to ask specific directions from one of the townspeople. Another, longer trail can be attempted from the other side, from the village of Mount Nelson (above Victoria); this route is probably more interesting, but even less maintained, and requires a solid half-day. If in doubt, hire a guide, the standard method of ascent.

Mount Sinai

This 2306-foot peak is approached not from the Grand Etang area (which the summit overlooks), but from the tiny village of Petit Etang nestled amid banana fields; the trailhead is reached by a side-road which climbs into the hills from the town of Providence. The path is faint and ill-maintained, but heads generally northwest toward the top where it steepens, then yields splendid views of the south coast. Allow two hours round-trip.

Mount Qua Qua

From Grand Etang, the marked trail to the summit of 2373-foot Mount Qua Qua ascends a slippery, sometimes narrow ridge of red clay. As you rise above the lake, the foliage evolves into elfin woodland (smaller trees sculpted by the wind), the angle increasing as you approach the top. The summit offers excellent views on clear days, but hikers should be prepared for rain, which can top 150 inches annually. Allow one-and-a-half hours to the top, slightly less for the return.

The Seven Sisters

Perhaps Grenada's nicest adventure, and the trek for which guides are most regularly hired, the Seven Sisters is series of waterfalls that tumble into lush pools a mile northeast of Grand Etang. The hike can be done several ways, but ideally your guide should take you to the top of the falls (if you're up for it) and on to the Park Center above Grand Etang. Allow a half-day and bring a swimsuit.

Fielding **GRENADA**

Heavenly Hikes through Grenada

Volcanic crater lakes, rain forests, dramatic mountains, and soaring sea-side cliffs—the diverse topography of Grenada is a walker's paradise. Hire a guide to lead you on the more strenuous treks.

Petite Martinique

Windward

Camp Fedon

This challenging, five-hour (one-way) walk over an ancient Carib Indian path begins at the top of Concord Falls. The trail passes giant mahogany trees, teak trees and huge ferns and leads to a cave once used as a hide-out by Grenadian rebel Julian Fedon in 1795.

Hillsborough

Carriacou

St. Mark Bay

Mt. Granby

Concord Falls

The first stage of the falls lies close to the highway and is popular with swimmers. A footpath across slippery rocks leads to the second-stage falls, a moderately strenuous 45-minute hike (faster coming back). The third stage, Fountainbleu Falls, is a challenging hike that requires three hours for a round trip if you start from the second-stage falls.

Annandale Falls

The most accessible falls on Grenada, Annandale Falls can be reached via a set of cement steps. Enjoy a picnic or a swim beneath the falls. Nearby, an herb and spice garden provides an up-close look at the island's main crops.

Moliniére Pt.

St Ge

Bay Gardens

Winding paths of crushed nutmeg shells lead strollers through more than three acres planted with 3000 tropical species. Situated on the site of an old sugar mill, Bay Gardens also features fish ponds and a turtle aquarium.

Pt. Saline

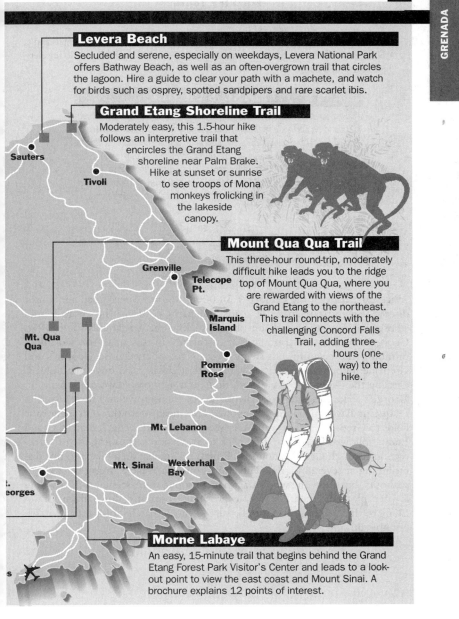

Levera Beach

Secluded and serene, especially on weekdays, Levera National Park offers Bathway Beach, as well as an often-overgrown trail that circles the lagoon. Hire a guide to clear your path with a machete, and watch for birds such as osprey, spotted sandpipers and rare scarlet ibis.

Grand Etang Shoreline Trail

Moderately easy, this 1.5-hour hike follows an interpretive trail that encircles the Grand Etang shoreline near Palm Brake. Hike at sunset or sunrise to see troops of Mona monkeys frolicking in the lakeside canopy.

Sauters

Tivoli

Mount Qua Qua Trail

This three-hour round-trip, moderately difficult hike leads you to the ridge top of Mount Qua Qua, where you are rewarded with views of the Grand Etang to the northeast. This trail connects with the challenging Concord Falls Trail, adding three-hours (one-way) to the hike.

Grenville

Telecope Pt.

Marquis Island

Mt. Qua Qua

Pomme Rose

Mt. Lebanon

Mt. Sinai **Westerhall Bay**

t. eorges

Morne Labaye

An easy, 15-minute trail that begins behind the Grand Etang Forest Park Visitor's Center and leads to a look-out point to view the east coast and Mount Sinai. A brochure explains 12 points of interest.

GRENADA

Trekking Tours

Henry's Safari Tours

St. George's; ☎ *(809) 444-5313.*

The very pleasant Denis Henry manages a group of guides who handle the island's hikes as well as driving tours. The trek to the Seven Sisters is $70 for a solo traveler, $45 each for a pair.

FIELDING'S CHOICE:

Prepare yourself first for dodging chickens, bikes and pedestrians, but rent a car and go north along the coastline, turning inward at Halifax Harbour toward the central mountain range, leading to Grand Etang Lake, a 36-acre volcanic crater whose glassy waters shimmer in the shadow of 2373-foot Mount Qua Qua. Add to that a boisterous hike around the lake or a heroic trek along a five-hour trail from Concord Falls deep in the central mountains, where the Concord River plummets down a series of rocky ravines.

By Pedal

Pick up a copy of the detailed 1:50,000 *Ordnance Survey* map and you'll discover an intricate maze of roads and paths covering the entire island. Those looking for a casual spin should stick to the gentle hills south of St. George's, but stay alert; traffic is at its thickest in this area. Also worthy of caution is the beautiful but steep, twisting road between St. George's and Grenville; minibus drivers assault this as though they can drive blindfolded. Circling the island by bicycle is a serious, but memorable workout: from St. George's, take the main coastal road north to Gouyave and turn inland at Duquesne Bay, which leads to Sauteur. Then head south through sugar cane fields to Grenville, where you'll veer west and ascend the lush road to Grand Etang, followed by a sharp drop back to St. George's (heading the other direction through Grand Etang is well-nigh impossible on a bike without dismounting at several points). The entire route will take a strong rider about six hours, but allow the whole day to incorporate sight-seeing. If off-roading is your pleasure, there are ample possibilities leading down from Grand Etang to the eastern shores, but be sure to carry a patch kit for the inevitable bramble bushes.

What Else to See

St. George's, Grenada

Grenada is full of natural wonders, but begin your tour by strolling through the narrow streets and cobbled alleys of St. George's, the impossibly picturesque capital. There are centuries-old churches to explore and you can even walk through Fort George, where Maurice Bishop et al were assassinated in 1983, precipitating the American intervention (today it houses the police headquarters). Stop by the National Museum, once a French garrison, where an antique rum still, wildlife specimens and even personal effects of Josephine Bonaparte—including the marble tub she used as a child—are kept. The best day to drink in St. George's market square is on Saturday, when the plaza bustles with the brightest aromas and colors of the Caribbean as vendors set out the fruits, vegetables and spices. For a few dollars, you can come home laden with baskets of cocoa balls (to make cocoa tea), sorrel, tannia, yams, limes, mangoes and luscious papayas.

Outside St. George's stick to the sensory theme by heading up the Caribbean coast to the Douglaldston Spice Plantation outside the town of Gouyave, where you can explore the secrets of nutmeg cultivation. Afterward, a dollar will get you into the Nutmeg Processing Plant, where the nuts and mace are separated and graded by hand, then loaded into huge burlap bags for shipping. A trip through the lush Grand Etang Forest Reserve is a must (see "On Foot" for hiking possibilities). The east coast of Grenada is riddled with winding roads, inviting you to get lost on your way to Grenville, the island's second-largest town, and also home to a Saturday morning market, and another spice-processing facility. Farther north, a small side road takes you to the Rive Antoine Rum Distillery, one of the last factories of any kind in the Western Hemisphere powered by water wheel. The men who work the machinery will provide a brief, impromptu tour, though the rum they produce is true firewater.

Historical Sites

Fort George   ★★★

Church Street, St. George's.

Built by the French in 1705 on a promontory to guard the entrance to the harbor, this old fort has lots of small rooms and four-inch-thick walls. But it is most famous for its more recent history—it is the site where Maurice Bishop et al were killed, precipitating the American intervention of Grenada in 1983. The fort is now in use as part of the police barracks; the nondescript basketball court is where the assassinations took place.

Museums and Exhibits

Grenada National Museum   ★★★

Monckton Street, St. George's, ☎ *(809) 440-3725.*

Hours open: 9 a.m.–4:30 p.m.

Set in the foundations of an old French army barracks and prison dating back to 1704, this small museum has some interesting exhibits on the island's natural and historical past. Don't miss Josephine Bonaparte's marble bathtub! General admission: $1.

Parks and Gardens

Annandale Falls   ★★★★★

Main Interior Road, ☎ *(809) 440-2452.*

Hours open: 8 a.m.–4 p.m.

Bring a picnic and your swimsuit (changing rooms are available) to this pretty spot, where water from Mount Qua Qua cascades down some 50 feet into a pool perfect for dips. There's a good gift shop on site with handicrafts and species native to the island.

Grand Etang National Park   ★★★★★

Main Interior Road, St. George's, ☎ *(809) 442-7425.*

Hours open: 8:30 a.m.–4 p.m.

This rainforest and bird sanctuary, located in the island's interior between St. George's and Grenville, has lots of gorgeous, unspoiled scenery. Several trails wind throughout for easy to difficult treks (see "On Foot"). Don't miss Grand Etang Lake, whose 13 acres of cobalt blue waters are nestled in the crater of an extinct volcano—the shoreline is canvassed by mona monkeys. General admission: $1.

Tours

Nutmeg Processing Plant   ★ ★

Gouyave.

You'll never again take this little spice for granted after a half-hour tour of the processing plant. Nutmeg is Grenada's largest export and smells sweet, too. General admission: $1.

FIELDING'S CHOICE:

The Tower was a fabulous plantation house built in 1917 by a Grenadian lawyer to please his bride. Today, the owners, Paul Slinger and his wife, Victoria, open their historic home to visitors for a $10 tour every Thursday. The Tower is full of antiques, including Hogarth prints collected by Paul's grandfather (who commanded the West Indian regiment in World War I). Situated on nine acres of land, the property is a veritable plantation of tropical fruits, samples of which are served during your tour along with a fruit punch.

Sailing is the premier sport on Grenada, particularly the classic trip through the Grenadines to the north, with conditions sometimes referred to as the best in the world. Seagoing travelers always come back with great tales of derring-do, hidden coves, and the occasional near-disaster. Numerous charter operations can arrange programs of any length or for any vessel (rates are about 30 percent lower in the off-season). The Carriacou Regatta, held the first weekend in August, attracts seamen from all over the world who thrive on the ferocious competition. Hobie cats, sailfish, sunfish and other small boats can be rented on Grand Anse for short excursions. Sometimes the easiest thing to do for escape is to hop on a fishing boat early one morning to nearby Hog Island or Calivigny Island, just east of Lanse aux Epines. **Sportfishing** is excellent November through May; a few operators offer four-hour or longer charters. Several hotels have tennis courts, including Calabash, Coral Cove, LaSource, Secret Harbour, Spice Island Inn and the Grenada Renaissance. Golf can be found at the nine-hole Grenada Golf and Country Club.

Grenada Golf Club

Grand Anse, ☎ *(809) 444-4128.*

Not the greatest golf in the world, but since it's the only one on the island, it'll do. The nine-hole course has some nice views. Greens fees are a reasonable $20 and club rentals are available.

Watersports

Various locations, St. George's.

Your hotel will probably offer watersports for free or a nominal fee, or check out one of these outfits. Boating: **Seabreeze Yacht Charters** ☎ *(809) 444-4924*, and **The Moorings** ☎ *(809) 444-4548*. Cruises: **Best of Grenada** ☎ *(809) 440-2198*. Deep-sea fishing: **Dive Grenada** ☎ *(809) 444-4371*, and the **Best of Grenada** ☎ *(809) 440-2198*. A major fishing tournament is held each January.

FIELDING'S CHOICE:

Every other Saturday a bunch of Grenadians known as the Hash House Harriers get together, split into teams, and set off on chases through glorious countryside on trails that always end up at Rudolf's, a bar next to the Carenage in St. George's. It's a great way to meet and mingle with those Grenadians not in good enough shape for the triathlon.

Where to Stay

Fielding's Highest Rated Hotels in Grenada

★★★★★	Calabash Hotel	$170–$495
★★★★★	La Source	$250–$590
★★★★★	Spice Island Inn	$270–$475
★★★★	Rex Grenadian	$115–$360
★★★★	Secret Harbour Hotel	$100–$225
★★★	Blue Horizons Cottages	$100–$165
★★★	Coyaba Beach Resort	$75–$165
★★★	Grenada Renaissance Hotel	$120–$170
★★★	Silver Beach Resort	$80–$95
★★★	Twelve Degrees North	$130–$285

Fielding's Most Exclusive Hotels in Grenada

★★★★★	La Source	$250–$590
★★★★★	Calabash Hotel	$170–$495
★★★	Twelve Degrees North	$130–$285
★★★	Grenada Renaissance Hotel	$120–$170
★★★	Blue Horizons Cottages	$100–$165

Fielding's Best Value Hotels in Grenada

★★★	Silver Beach Resort	$80–$95
★★	No Problem Apartments	$55–$85
★★★	Coyaba Beach Resort	$75–$165
★★★★	Secret Harbour Hotel	$100–$225
★★	True Blue Inn	$65–$110

More than 85 percent of Grenada's hotels are owned by Grenadians; their stake in tourism accounts for the pride they show in personal touches that make their guests feel special. In 1996, a new initiative to substantially increase the number of rooms available on all three islands was announced by the government—hopefully construction will remain relatively low-key and new hotels will continue to mingle well with the verdant setting that has brought so many of the island's visitors back for another more. Many of the islands accommodations are found along Grand Anse Beach. These are not high-rise hotels, but generally small, intimate inns and guest houses (by law, no hotel in Grenada can be more than three stories). Other properties are scattered around the southern tip of the island. The variety of accommodations on Grenada, from budget guest houses to luxury properties and everything in between, is excellent, providing rooms for virtually any type of Caribbean traveler. The Grenada Hotel Association produces an accommodations directory listing all properties on the three islands; they also act as a booking service for hotels and can be reached toll-free from the United States, ☎ *(800) 322-1753.* See "Carriacou" and "Petit Martinique" below for accommodations on those islands.

Hotels and Resorts

The past decade has brought a surfeit of hotels and renovations to Grenada. The newest additions to the island are LaSource, an all-inclusive 100-room resort with a spa and a nine-hole, nonregulation golf course, and the Rex Grenadian, the island's largest hotel on a three-acre lagoon. Both hotels benefit from their own white sandy beaches. The Spice Island Inn sits astride Grand Anse and remains a Caribbean classic, and benefited from a $2 million renovation that added suites with private pools.

Hillsborough

Cassada Bay Resort $80–$125 ★★

Belmont, Hillsborough, ☎ *(809) 443-7494.*
Single: $80–$95. Double: $95–$125.
Accommodations are in simple cabins with ceiling fans set on a hillside sloping down to the beach. Wonderful views and lots of watersports, plus free ferry rides to neighboring islands. Good bird-watching possibilities. 16 rooms. Credit cards: A, MC, V.

Silver Beach Resort $80–$95 ★★★

Hillsborough, ☎ *(809) 443-7337. FAX (809) 443-7165.*
Single: $80–$90. Double: $85–$95.
Set on a quiet beach, this family-run hotel has comfortable rooms with ceiling fans; eight cottages offer more room to spread out and full kitchens. Activities include fishing and boating to nearby islands, and all the usual watersports, including good scuba. 16 rooms. Credit cards: A, DC, MC, V.

St. George's

Calabash Hotel $170–$495 ★★★★★

L'Anse aux Epines, St. George's, ☎ *(800) 528-5835, (809) 444-4334. FAX (809) 444-5050.*

Single: $170–$465. Double: $205–$495.

Set among coconut groves and gardens on an eight-acre estate, all accommodations are suites housed in stone and wood cottages at this very fine resort. Some have private pools, others kitchens, others Jacuzzis and all are bright and cheery. There are three bars and a restaurant, watersports and tennis, frequent live entertainment and wonderful, attentive service. A great choice. 28 rooms. Credit cards: A, MC, V.

Coyaba Beach Resort   **$75–$165**   ★ ★ ★

Grand Anse, St. George's, ☎ (809) 444-4129. FAX (809) 444-4808.
Single: $75–$115. Double: $95–$165.
Set on the site of an ancient Arawak Indian village, this family-run resort puts guests up in tropically decorated rooms with bright island artwork. The pool has a swim-up bar, perfect for cooling off after a set or two on the tennis court. The restaurant and cafe are open-air. The beach is a short stroll from the rooms. 40 rooms. Credit cards: A, DC, D, MC, V.

Flamboyant Hotel   **$70–$220**   ★ ★

Grand Anse Beach, St. George's, ☎ (800) 223-9815, (809) 444-4247. FAX (809) 444-1234.
Single: $70–$215. Double: $85–$220.
Set on a hillside that slopes gently to the beach, this complex offers standard guest rooms and 23 suites with kitchenettes, most with sweeping views. The good location makes this a relative bargain, and the friendly staff keeps guests happy. There's a restaurant, pool and free snorkel equipment. 39 rooms. Credit cards: A, DC, D, MC, V.

Grenada Renaissance Hotel   **$120–$170**   ★ ★ ★

Grand Anse Beach, St. George's, ☎ (800) 228-9898, (809) 444-4371. FAX (809) 444-4800.
Single: $120–$170. Double: $120–$170.
This handsome complex has a nice location—-right on the beach and across from a good shopping complex—-but lacks island flavor. Accommodations are comfortable but on the small side, and the motel-like furnishings are generic. On the plus side, the hotel offers a complete range of amenities, from watersports to tennis courts to yacht charters, and attracts families with its supervised children's programs (on holidays). A lively night scene, too. 186 rooms. Credit cards: A, DC, D, MC, V.

Hibiscus Hotel   **$60–$125**   ★

Grand Anse, St. George's, ☎ (809) 444-4233. FAX (809) 444-2873.
Single: $60–$125. Double: $80–$125.
This small hotel is 300 yards from Grand Anse Beach. Accommodations are in air-conditioned duplex cottages with patios. There's a restaurant and pool on site. 10 rooms. Credit cards: A, D, MC, V.

Horse Shoe Beach Hotel   **$70–$155**   ★ ★

L'Anne Aux Epines, St. George's, ☎ (809) 444-4244. FAX (809) 444-4844.
Single: $70–$130. Double: $80–$155.
Set on a hillside overlooking the bay, this hotel puts up guests in cottages with air conditioning, period furnishings and patios; some also have four-poster beds. Each two units share a kitchen. The six suites in the main building are the best choice.

Nicely landscaped grounds hold a pool and beach, with watersports nearby. 22 rooms. Credit cards: A, D, MC, V.

La Source $250–$590 ★★★★★

Pink Gin Beach, St. George's, ☎ (800) 544-2883, (809) 444-2556. FAX (809) 444-2561.
Single: $250–$345. Double: $420–$590.

Opened in late 1993, this all-inclusive resort is situated on two beaches on Grenada's southwest tip. The price is steep, but includes all meals, drinks, watersports and—-best of all—-pampering treatments in the excellent spa. Accommodations are simply gorgeous, with Persian rugs, mahogany furniture, four-poster beds and Asian artwork. When you're not being spoiled in the spa, you can play tennis or nine holes of golf, swim in the two-level pool or enjoy a good array of watersports. Simply fabulous. 100 rooms. Credit cards: A, MC, V.

Rex Grenadian $115–$360 ★★★★

Magazine Beach, St. George's, ☎ (800) 255-5859, (809) 444-3333. FAX (809) 444-1111.
Single: $115–$360. Double: $115–$360.

New in December 1993, this large property offers all the bells and whistles resort lovers expect. Set on 12 acres that open onto two beaches, the hotel houses guests in nicely done standard rooms; you'll pay a bit extra for air conditioning and a bigger bathroom. A couple of neat restaurants give guests dining choices, and the typical watersports, fitness center and tennis prevail. There's even a man-made lake stretching over two acres. Nice, but expect a lot of business groups. 212 rooms. Credit cards: A, MC, V.

Secret Harbour Hotel $100–$225 ★★★★

L'Anse aux Epines, St. George's, ☎ (800) 334-2435, (809) 444-4548. FAX (813) 530-9747.
Single: $100–$213. Double: $100–$225.

Overlooking Mount Hartman Bay on Grenada's southernmost tip, this elegant property consists of Mediterranean-style villas in which each unit is a suite. They're nicely decorated with four-poster beds, local art, trouser presses, large balconies and baths with Roman tubs. The grounds are lovely and the views breathtaking. The small beach offers all the usual watersports. Special packages allow guests to spend a few nights aboard one of their many yachts. Nice! 20 rooms. Credit cards: A, MC, V.

Siesta Hotel $55–$140 ★★

Grand Anse, St. George's, ☎ (809) 444-4645. FAX (809) 444-4647.
Single: $55–$110. Double: $60–$140.

Located slightly inland from the beach, this small hotel has air-conditioned rooms with comfortable furnishings; some have kitchens. There's a restaurant and pool, but not much else in the way of extras. 37 rooms. Credit cards: A, D, MC, V.

Spice Island Inn $270–$475 ★★★★★

Grand Anse Beach, St. George's, ☎ (809) 444-4258. FAX (809) 444-4807.
Single: $270–$425. Double: $320–$475.

Set on eight tropical acres on a gorgeous stretch of Grand Anse Beach, all accommodations at this very fine resort are in suites. Some have whirlpools (and even private dip pools), and all are simply but comfortably furnished with huge, pampering bathrooms. The grounds are nicely done with lots of flowers, and there's a gym and tennis court for the active set. Others are happy just lounging on the picturesque beach. Great food and service, too. Simply charming. 56 rooms. Credit cards: A, DC, D, MC, V.

Apartments and Condominiums

Grenadians are leaders in the Caribbean self-catering business. Don't be shy about bringing provisions from home, though the variety of fresh tropical fruits and vegetables available here is almost unsurpassed. The best views are to be had at Cinnamon Hill, which overlooks Grand Anse, but Twelve Degrees North also has excellent sea views.

St. George's

Blue Horizons Cottages   **$100–$165**   ★★★

Grand Anse, St. George's, ☎ (809) 444-4592. FAX (809) 444-2815.
Single: $100–$155. Double: $110–$165.
Set on a terraced hillside some 300 yards from Grand Anse Beach, accommodations are in one-bedroom cottages and duplex suites, each air-conditioned and sporting kitchens. There's a restaurant and two bars on hand, as well as a pool and Jacuzzi. Watersports take place at nearby sister property, the Spice Island Inn. Good value. 32 rooms. Credit cards: A, DC, D, MC, V.

Cinnamon Hill Hotel   **$85–$153**   ★★

Grand Anse Beach, St. George's, ☎ (809) 444-4301. FAX (809) 444-2874.
Single: $85–$130. Double: $114–$153.
This Spanish-style hotel village consists of several buildings scattered over a hillside overlooking Grand Anse Beach; it's steep going so those with mobility problems should look elsewhere. Accommodations are in one- and two-bedroom apartments with kitchens and balconies. There's a restaurant and pool on-site, with all water-sports available on the public beach. 20 rooms. Credit cards: A, D, MC, V.

Coral Cove Cottages   **$65–$120**   ★

Coral Cove Beach, St. George's, ☎ (809) 444-4422. FAX (809) 444-4718.
Single: $65–$120. Double: $65–$120.
Situated on a peaceful cove with nice views six miles from St. George's, this complex offers Spanish-style apartments and cottages with kitchenettes and terraces. There's a tennis court and small pool, but no dining facilities. 11 rooms. Credit cards: D, MC, V.

Gem Holiday Beach Resort   **$55–$140**   ★

Morne Rouge Bay, St. George's, ☎ (800) 223-9815, (809) 444-1189.
Single: $55–$120. Double: $65–$140.
Located on the beach some six miles from St. George's, this apartment hotel houses guests in one- and two-bedroom units that are air-conditioned and have full kitchens. There's a restaurant and bar if you'd rather leave the cooking to someone else, and a lively disco. You'll probably want a rental car to get around. 23 rooms. Credit cards: A, DC, D, MC, V.

Holiday Haven   **$60–$145**   ★

L'Anse aux Epines, St. George's, ☎ (809) 440-2606.
Single: $60–$145. Double: $65–$145.

This basic complex offers one- to three-bedroom apartments with full kitchens and verandas; most have two bathrooms. Maids keep everything looking spiffy. Nothing extra in the way of facilities, so you'll have to venture out. 3 cottages. 12 rooms.

La Sagesse Nature Center   **$40–$90**   ★

St. David's, St. George's, ☎ *(809) 444-6458. FAX (809) 444-6458.*
Single: $40–$75. Double: $65–$90.
Located in a remote setting 10 miles from the airport, this small, family-run operation has six apartments in a guest house with full kitchens and ceiling fans to keep things cool. The surrounding grounds are really pretty, with lots of hiking and bird-watching opportunities. Really appealing for nature lovers. 6 rooms. Credit cards: A, MC, V.

Maffiken Apartments   **$60–$85**   ★

Grand Anse, St. George's, ☎ *(809) 444-4255. FAX (809) 444-2832.*
Single: $60–$70. Double: $70–$85.
Set on a hillside overlooking Grand Anse Beach a short stroll away, this small stucco hotel houses one- and two-bedroom apartments with air conditioning, kitchenettes and maid service. No recreational facilities, but restaurants and shopping are nearby. 12 rooms. Credit cards: A, MC, V.

No Problem Apartments   **$55–$85**   ★★

True Blue, St. George's, ☎ *(809) 444-4634. FAX (809) 444-2803.*
Single: $55–$75. Double: $65–$85.
Located near the airport on the outskirts of town, this Mediterranean-style complex has air-conditioned suites with full kitchens. A free shuttle takes you to town and Grand Anse Beach, so you won't need a rental car as with most other apartment hotels. There's a restaurant and pool, and a fleet of bicycles for the asking. Decent. 20 rooms. Credit cards: A, D, MC, V.

South Winds Holiday   **$40–$80**   ★

Grand Anse, St. George's, ☎ *(809) 444-4310. FAX (800) 233-9815.*
Single: $40–$80. Double: $40–$80.
Grand Anse Beach is about 500 yards from this complex of cottages and apartments, all with kitchens and most with air conditioning. Popular with families, there's maid service, but little else in the way of extras. Good rates for the location, though. 19 rooms. Credit cards: A, DC, D, MC, V.

True Blue Inn   **$65–$110**   ★★

St. George's, ☎ *(800) 742-4276, (809) 444-2000. FAX (809) 444-1247.*
Single: $65–$95. Double: $75–$110.
Accommodations at this south coast property are in one-bedroom apartments and two-bedroom cottages, all with air conditioning and full kitchens. There's maid service, a sailing school for both adults and children, a pool and bicycles for tooling about. A nice, friendly atmosphere. 7 rooms. Credit cards: A, DC, D, MC, V.

Twelve Degrees North   **$130–$285**   ★★★

St. George's, ☎ *(800) 322-1753, (809) 444-4580.*
Single: $130–$285. Double: $130–$285.
Located on the southeast coast and facing the sea, this small property has one- and two-bedroom apartments with kitchens and—what a plus!—a housekeeper who

cooks, cleans and even does laundry. No air conditioning, but ceiling fans do the job nicely. The grounds include a lot for an apartment complex, with a pool, tennis court, private beach and watersports. No kids under 12. 8 rooms. Credit cards: not accepted.

Villamar Holiday Resort   **$42–$62**   ★

L'Anse aux Epines, St. George's, ☎ *(809) 444-1614. FAX (809) 444-1341.*
Single: $42–$52. Double: $52–$62.
Located in a remote spot two minutes from Grand Anse Beach, this complex has one- and two-bedroom suites with air conditioning, kitchens and private balconies. There's a bar, restaurant and pool, and they'll help arrange watersports and golf. 20 rooms. Credit cards: A, MC, V.

Wave Crest Holiday Apts.   **$75–$95**   ★

Grand Anse, St. George's, ☎ *(809) 444-4116.*
Single: $75–$95. Double: $75–$95.
Grand Anse Beach is a five-minute walk from this small property, where you can choose from standard guest rooms and one- and two-bedroom apartments with air conditioning, verandas and kitchens. There's a bar, but not much else. 20 rooms. Credit cards: A, D, MC, V.

Inns

Grenada's inns are run and owned by devoted families who make their unique personalities known in every detail. The Hibiscus Hotel gives the feeling of a tiny village with its five small cottages situated near a common pool. True Blue Inn is commendable for its modern kitchen facilities in the one-bedroom apartments and cottages, and the attractive seaside restaurant (see "Apartments and Condominiums").

Hillsborough

Caribbee Inn   **$95–$135**   ★★

Prospect, Hillsborough, ☎ *(809) 443-8142.*
Single: $95–$135. Double: $95–$135.
All accommodations are in cottages on a hillside, with the beach a short stroll away. Ceiling fans keep things cool. Tasty dinners are served from a price-fixed menu. Great views of neighboring islands at this pleasant spot. 10 rooms. Credit cards: A.

Caribbee Inn   **$95–$135**   ★★

Prospect, Hillsborough, ☎ *(809) 443-8142.*
Single: $95–$135. Double: $95–$135.
All accommodations are in cottages on a hillside, with the beach a short stroll away. Ceiling fans keep things cool. Tasty dinners are served from a price-fixed menu. Great views of neighboring islands at this pleasant spot. 10 rooms. Credit cards: A.

Low Cost Lodging

Grenada is stocked with inexpensive guest houses in and around St. George's. The quality of accommodations varies considerably, but a clean, decent double for under $40 or $50 a night is definitely possible. Try **Mamma's Lodge**, affiliated with Mamma's Restaurant and within walking distance of both St. George's and Grand Anse ☎ *(809) 440-1623*. Peace and quiet relaxation is the business at **Morne Fendue**, the rustic private home of a native Grenadian that is still full of her family antiques ☎ *(809) 442-9330.*

Where to Eat

GRENADA

Fielding's Highest Rated Restaurants in Grenada

★★★★★	Morne Fendue	
★★★★	Canboulay	$10–$30
★★★★	Coconut's Beach	$13–$26
★★★★	La Belle Creole	$10–$21
★★★★	Nutmeg, The	$9–$20
★★★	La Sagesse	$5–$18
★★★	La Source	$45

Fielding's Most Exclusive Restaurants in Grenada

★★★★	Canboulay	$10–$30
★★★	La Source	$45
★★★★	Coconut's Beach	$13–$26
★★★★	La Belle Creole	$10–$21
★★★★	Nutmeg, The	$9–$20

Fielding's Best Value Restaurants in Grenada

★★★★	Nutmeg, The	$9–$20
★★★	La Sagesse	$5–$18
★★★★	La Belle Creole	$10–$21
★★★★	Coconut's Beach	$13–$26
★★★★	Canboulay	$10–$30

Few West Indians have mastered the art of adapting local fruits, vegetables, seafood and spices to Continental-style recipes as well as Grenadians have. The restaurant scene, which traditionally centered around the island's hotels, now includes newcomers that have added not only spice but variety to island cuisine. The national dish, "oil down," concocted with breadfruit and salt pork wrapped in dasheen leaves and steamed in coconut milk, is delicious. Don't miss tasting callaloo soup (made with the spinach-like leaves of the dasheen), christophene au gratin, pepperpot stew, and nutmeg ice cream. All options are possible, however, when you dine at famous (or infamous?) Mamma's, where possum and armadillo are but a few of the native dishes prepared for you during an elaborate, 20-or-so-course feast. Canboulay is arguably the island's best dining experience, overlooking Grand Anse, while Morne Fendue is an island institution hosted by a woman who cooked five Thanksgiving turkeys and 40 pumpkin pies for U.S. troops in 1983. A good bakery and coffee shop is located in Le Marquis Complex, in the Grand Anse district.

Bird's Nest $$ ★

Grand Anse, St. George's, ☎ (809) 444-4264.
Chinese cuisine.
Lunch: 9:30 a.m.–3 p.m., entrées $3–$25.
Dinner: 3–11 p.m., entrées $3–$25.
A no-surprises, pleasant Chinese restaurant that also serves good sandwiches for lunch, Bird's Nest roosts opposite the supermarket in Grand Anse. Specialties include sweet and sour chicken or fish, served with tasty fried rice, or you may splurge on lobster. Take-out is available. The restaurant is open on Sunday for dinner only, from 4 p.m. to 11 p.m. Reservations recommended. Credit cards: A, D, MC, V.

Canboulay $$$ ★★★★

Morne Rouge, St. George's, ☎ (809) 444-4401.
International cuisine.
Lunch: 11:30 a.m.– 2:30 p.m., entrées $7–$20.
Dinner: 6:30–10 p.m, entrées $10–$30. Closed: Sun.
For a grand night out in exotic surroundings, most visitors choose this festive, relatively new restaurant with a view of the lights of the capital across the bay. The decor and the tropical cuisine reflect the heritage of Trinidad-born owners Erik and Gina-lee Johnson, where spices, heady scents and Carnival are a way of life. Though they tell people the food is free, they just charge for the stellar view, the Johnsons really shine in the kitchen, particularly with shrimp prepared in interesting ways, including an Indonesian peanut and fruit satay. Desserts are memorable, especially a chocolate-orange mousse and a custard-filled coconut cake called Oh Goood! Reservations recommended. Credit cards: A, MC, V.

Coconut's Beach $$$ ★★★★

Grand Anse, St. George's, ☎ (809) 444-4644.
French cuisine. Specialties: Lobster, conch.
Lunch: 10 a.m.–6 p.m., entrées $6–$13.
Dinner: 7–10 p.m., entrées $13–$26. Closed: Tue.
As the name implies, guests can eat with their feet in the sand of Grand Anse in high style under palm-frond shelters, or in the dining room of a spiffy, native house with an open kitchen where the chefs deftly saute the catch of the day in gleaming cookware. French flair takes over with lobster in various butter sauces or lambi (conch)

GRENADA

curry; other mouth-watering choices are ribs, chicken or steak. A good lunch menu of crepes, salads or sandwiches offers most dishes for under $10. Reservations recommended. Credit cards: MC, V.

Cot Bam   **$$$**   ★

Grand Anse, St. George's, ☎ *(809) 444-2050.*
Lunch: 9 a.m.–2 p.m., entrées $6–$30.
Dinner: 2–11 p.m., entrées $6–$30.
Savory, quick meals and a cold brew draw guests to this convivial tin-roofed bar and grill after a hard day at the beach. Since it's within strolling distance of all hotels on Grand Anse, why settle for room service? Snacks and plate meals include West Indian rotis, salads, shrimp and chips, etc. Live entertainment takes over in the evenings, particularly on weekends. Credit cards: A, D, MC, V.

Delicious Landing   **$$**   ★★

The Carenage, St. George's, ☎ *(809) 440-9747.*
Seafood cuisine.
Lunch: 10:30 a.m.–2 p.m., entrées $4–$9.
Dinner: 6:30–11:30 p.m., entrées $10–$19. Closed: Sun.
Although many eating establishments on this island boast enviable views, Delicious Landing may have the best one of all, situated right on the water's edge at St. George's Harbor. Decently prepared seafood and fish is featured, as well as local specialties such as conch stew, barbecue chicken, oil down and lobster pando, all at reasonable prices. The sea vistas, breezes and excellent tropical drinks (try a cinnamon daiquiri) are a good reason to linger. Credit cards: MC, V.

La Belle Creole   **$$$**   ★★★★

Grand Anse, St. George's, ☎ *(809) 444-4316. Associated hotel: Blue Horizons.*
Seafood cuisine. Specialties: Callaloo quiche.
Lunch: 12:30–2:30 p.m., entrées $5–$13.
Dinner: 7–9 p.m., entrées $10–$21.
Some of the most creative West Indian food is served in this airy terrace restaurant on the grounds of the Blue Horizons Cottages. For many years "Mamma" Audrey Hopkin earned a deserved reputation as the best Creole home chef in town, and now her sons have carried the torch with admirable results. Real men (and women) eat quiche here, which is an unusual combo of *callaloo* (dasheen leaf) and lobster or shrimp; there's also a veal creole, crab and a tasty fish mousse. Desserts are equally imaginative—try the unique farine pudding. An ever-changing fixed-price dinner of up to five courses, including dessert, is available nightly for $35–$40. The service is as good as the food, and the atmosphere is perfect for lovers. Reservations required.
Credit cards: A, DC, D, MC, V.

La Sagesse   **$$**   ★★★

Eastern Main Road, St. George's, ☎ *(809) 444-6458. Associated hotel: La Sagesse Nature Center.*
American cuisine.
Lunch: 11 a.m.–3:30 p.m., entrées $5–$18.
Dinner: 6:30–9 p.m., entrées $5–$18.
This charming restaurant by the sea is part of the La Sagesse Nature Center, formerly the home of a cousin of Queen Elizabeth, now a rustic guest house and

banana plantation. Fittingly, patrons can get a nice organic vegetarian platter or blended tropical fruit drinks. Other dishes include seafood, pastas, sandwiches and burgers (red meat is otherwise scarce)—all very fresh and nicely prepared. The calm waters here are about 25 minutes away from St. George's. Credit cards: A, MC, V.

La Source $$$ ★★★

Pink Gin Beach, St. Georges, ☎ *(809) 444-2556.*
Dinner: 7:30–9:30 p.m., prix fixe $45.
Chef Richard Lovett gives new meaning to spa entrées at this tasty restaurant at the all-inclusive La Source. Thanks to wonderful entrées such as vegetable cutlets coated with parmesan cheese and crab-stuffed chicken, you can pig out without an ounce of guilt. There's even a selection of low-fat desserts. Items like braised shank of lamb are also featured for those not watching their waistline. The prix-fixe dinner includes drinks and wine, appetizer, entrée and dessert. Reservations required. Credit cards: A, MC, V.

Mamma's $$$ ★★

Lagoon Road, St. George's, ☎ *(809) 440-1459.*
Specialties: Oil down, exotic small game.
Dinner: 7:30–11 p.m., prix fixe $19.
Yes, eating here is like Sunday dinner at Mamma's—if she was West Indian. But no one has to wait until the end of the week to dine here; Mamma's daughter Cleo and other family members set out a groaning buffet of some 20-plus local dishes in a friendly, boardinghouse atmosphere every day of the week. The menu features the overwhelming bounty of this verdant isle, including the pear-shaped christophene vegetable stuffed with crab, oil down (breadfruit, meats, callaloo in coconut milk), curries and even stewed armadillo and iguana. It's not really a fine culinary experience, but still plenty of fun. Reservations required.

Morne Fendue $$$ ★★★

St. Patrick's, near Sateurs, St. George's, ☎ *(809) 442-9330.*
Specialties: Pepper pot, callaloo soup.
Lunch: 12:30–3 p.m., prix fixe $17. Closed: Sun.
Lunch at this history-laden plantation home under owner Betty Mascoll, who has been holding court here for many years (and is well into her 80s), is an island institution. So come while you can, and reserve a place at this traditional West Indian buffet, making friends with the repeat visitors and a faithful staff that prepares peas and rice, stewed chicken and island vegetables every afternoon except Sundays and holidays. Mrs. Mascoll says the original pepper pot was "killed off by the communists in '83," but the current version has been brewing since January 1984. The house itself, built of native stone and decorated with family keepsakes, is a national treasure. Reservations required. Credit cards: not accepted.

Nutmeg, The $$ ★★★

The Carenage, St. George's, ☎ *(809) 440-2539.*
Specialties: Nutmeg ice cream, conch.
Lunch: 9 a.m.– 4 p.m., entrées $5–$15.
Dinner: 4–11 p.m., entrées $9–$20.

This well-known and widely visited restaurant with a view of seagoing vessels in St. George's Harbor features its heady namesake spice in a few specialties, including a nutmeg ice cream and fine rum punch. Otherwise, for a few dollars, sample local dishes such as callaloo soup, roti, curried lambi or fish sandwiches and fries, washed down with Carib beer. The scenery is great, and the restaurant is popular with local yachties and cruise ship passengers alike. Credit cards: A, D, MC, V.

Portofino $$ ★★

The Carenage, St. George's, ☎ *(809) 440-3986.*
Italian cuisine. Specialties: Pizza, Pastas.
Lunch: 11 a.m.–3 p.m., entrées $6–$22.
Dinner: 3–11 p.m., entrées $6–$22.
A comforting plate of pasta plus a harbor view make this upper-level Italian charmer an unbeatable draw. Jazz often plays in the background, putting everyone in a relaxed mood. It's also a good place for the kids, who can choose from a wide variety of their favorite food: pizza. A variety of pasta, lobster and veal dishes are also available. Open Sundays for dinner only, from 6 p.m. Reservations recommended. Credit cards: A, MC, V.

Red Crab, The $$$ ★

L'Anse aux Epines, St. George's, ☎ *(809) 444-4424.*
International cuisine. Specialties: Steak.
Lunch: 11 a.m.–2 p.m., entrées $10–$31.
Dinner: 6–11 p.m., entrées $10–$31. Closed: Sun.
This place should have been named the Plush Cow, because although it serves seafood, old-timers roll in here for the beefsteaks, which are the best on the island. Curried lambi and shrimp crêpes under the pines are also reliable. It's located in the posh southern point of the island near the Calabash, one of Grenada's original tourist developments. Travelers staying in the Grand Anse area can get here by car in five minutes. Reservations recommended. Credit cards: A, D, MC, V.

Rudolf's $$ ★

The Carenage, St. George's, ☎ *(809) 440-2241.*
International cuisine. Specialties: Conch, steaks.
Lunch: 10 a.m.–3 p.m., entrées $8–$19.
Dinner: 3 p.m.–midnight, entrées $8–$19. Closed: Sun.
Although it's got a humming bar scene with yacht-owners, Rudolf's features a large selection of seafood and steak dishes for those who want to eat here. It also helps that this pub-style eatery with a harbor view has some of the best prices in town—many dishes are under $10. There are daily specials, usually lobster or conch (highly recommended), as well as sandwiches, salads and fish and chips. Stick with these and other traditional favorites and you'll have a decent meal.

Where to Shop

Shopping isn't duty-free on Grenada, but bargains do exist. Special buys to bring home are spice baskets or coconut shells full of native-grown nutmeg, cinnamon, cloves, coriander and others—perfect for Christmas gifts or spicing the eggnog. At the Grand Anse Shopping Center (closest to the hotels) there are spice vendors who stroll up and down the streets barking their prices (don't be shy about bargaining). Imported china can be found at prices 60 percent cheaper than in the States. You can find other shopping centers on the Esplanade side of Fort George, and on Melville Street, facing the harbor. Grenada shops open and close with their own schedules, but usually cater their hours to cruise ship arrivals. The best time to visit market square on Granby Street is on Saturday mornings.

Carriacou

Thirteen-square-mile Carriacou (pronounced Carry-a-coo) is the largest of the Grenadines, the chain of tiny islands that pepper the channel between Grenada and St. Vincent. Unlike the other Grenadines, this postage-stamp paradise (and Petit Martinique, discussed below) is politically connected to Grenada, though the occasional call for secession can rise up now and again as Carriacou carves out its own unique identity. But many overlook the island, including the U.S. marines that landed on Grenada on Oct. 25, 1983—it is said they weren't aware of Carriacou and didn't reach the smaller island until Nov. 1, when they were greeted, not by Cuban soldiers, but islanders who had been patiently awaiting their arrival with soft drinks and beer.

The seat of government is Hillsborough, where a portion of the island's population of 5000 lives. Carriacou is drier than Grenada, and somewhat less mountainous, with coconut palms and almond trees lining the beaches. The economy here, as elsewhere in the Grenadines, centers around boatbuilding—the sturdy boats are still constructed by hand. Monday is a big day on Carriacou, when the local market sputters to life with fruits and vegetables brought in from Grenada and nearby Union Island, and mail from the twice-weekly mail boat is distributed. Shops in town have charmingly direct signage: the Variety Store, the Industrious Store, the Novelty Store. There's a tiny museum, the Carriacou Historical Society, with a collection of Amerindian and European artifacts. One of the region's best artists lives here—Canute Calliste, whose paintings are exhibited at his house and gallery in

L'Estere. A unique local tradition called Big Drum, a vibrant dance linked to African tribal roots, is performed at weddings, boat launches and house warmings. An old-fashioned Carnival is celebrated the week prior to Ash Wednesday in February, but the island's big event is the Carriacou Regatta, a four-day bash that lures sailors and fine yachts from around the region.

Carriacou is so far untouched by big developments, though cruise ships have begun to call on the island and there's talk of developing more accommodations than the few currently available. For now, it's a refreshingly laid-back destination, and a jumping-off point for exploring the Grenadines by mail boat. Located 23 miles north of Grenada, you can reach Carriacou by plane from Grenada (20 minutes), Union Island or St. Vincent, or boat from Grenada (three-and-a-half hours). See "Arrival and Departure" below for more information.

Where to Stay

Lodging is humble on Carriacou, but not without grace. The Caribbee Inn is perhaps the best choice—a simple but very special island inn. There are at least a dozen informal guest houses and apartment complexes available; for rates and more information, obtain the **Grenada Accommodations Directory** from the **Board of Tourism** ☎ *(800) 927-9554.* Restaurants are simple, but Gramma's Place on Main Street is the island's unofficial meeting place and serves breakfast and snacks.

Petite Martinique

A tiny burp in the sea two-and-a-half miles east of Carriacou and the third member of Grenada's troika, 486-acre Petit Martinique is inhabited by about 600 people who live at the base of a 745-foot volcanic cone. The island economy (reputedly one of the wealthiest per-capita in the West Indies) is similar to Carriacou's—fishing and boat building—but there's virtually no tourism. It has never quite eclipsed its age-old reputation as a pirate's den. You'll need to hop on a mail boat or hire a local boat in Carriacou to reach Petit Martinique (there is no airport). A spare, five-room guest house, the **Sea Side View Holiday Cottages**, is available for $35 a night for a double; its owners will help arrange transfer from Carriacou ☎ *(809) 443-9210.*

Grenada Directory

Arrival and Departure

The opening of Point Salines Airport in 1984, exactly one year after the arrival of American troops, has made flying to Grenada much easier—you can thank Fidel Castro for initiating the airport's construction (with Soviet support) a few years earlier. American Airlines offers daily jet service to Grenada from its

Caribbean hub in San Juan, Puerto Rico, with connecting service available from a number of North American cities. At press time, BWIA had discontinued its direct service to the island from New York's JFK, but still had limited service to Grenada from Miami. LIAT provides non-stop or direct service to Grenada from Antigua, Barbados, St. Lucia, Sint Maarten, St. Vincent, Tobago, Trinidad and Union Island. Connecting service to a number of other islands is available via LIAT.

Carriacou is reached via daily LIAT service out of Grenada or St. Vincent, or via **Airlines of Carriacou** ☎ *(809) 444-1475*. One may also use the inter-island boats that ply the Grenadines. The northbound boat heads to Carriacou on Wednesday and Saturday mornings, southbound on Monday and Wednesday mornings; the 3.5-hour crossing is about $10. Confirm exact departure times and days with the Tourist Office. Other boats continue the route north from Carriacou to Union Island, Bequia and St. Vincent. There is no scheduled boat service to Petit Martinique (nor an airport); you'll need to hire a boat in Carriacou.

The departure tax is $13.

Business Hours

Shops are generally open Monday through Friday from 8 a.m. to noon, and 1 to 4 p.m., and Saturdays from 8 a.m. to noon. Many stores in St. George's will open on Sunday if a cruise ship is docked. Banking hours are 8 a.m. to 1:30 or 2 p.m. Monday through Friday, as well as 2:30 to 5 p.m. on Fridays.

Climate

June through November is the rainy season, December through May is dry. Showers tend to be frequent, but brief during the summer and fall, with the total annual rainfall averaging 78 inches. The temperature hovers around 80 degrees with cooling trade winds reliable year-round.

Documents

U.S. citizens must present a valid passport or proof of citizenship (birth certificate or voter's registration card), plus a photo ID) and an ongoing or return ticket. All visitors pay a departure tax of $14.

Electricity

The current is 220 volts, 50 cycles, AC.

Getting Around

Driving is on the left, but somewhat risky for the constant flow of goats and pedestrians out onto roadways, and the twisting and winding roads are poorly-maintained in some areas of the island. A true dearth of appropriate signage can make sight-seeing a challenge, though if you carry a good road map, you won't get lost for long. There are three American-based car rental outfits represented on the island: **Avis**, **Budget** and **Dollar**. Local firms include **Y&R Rentals** ☎ *(809) 444-4984* and **C. Thomas and Sons** ☎ *(809) 444-4384*. On Carriacou, contact **Barba Gabriel** ☎ *(809) 443-7574*. You will need to obtain a local driver's license for $12, usually available from the car rental agencies.

Taxis are easily obtained at the airport, at the Carenage, and at most major hotels. Rates for frequently driven routes are fixed, but confirm the cost of a particular destination. The price from the airport to St. George's is $12; from St. George's to Grand Anse, $7, etc. Outside the southern area rates are $1.60 per mile for the first 10 miles, $1.35 per mile thereafter. The hourly rate to hire a taxi is $15.

Many visitors use the frequent and cheap local bus service. Traditional, wooden-seat buses originate in the market square of St. George's and can be used to reach almost any point on the island. A newer arrival to the island is minibuses, vans that carry up to 20 passengers along short-haul routes. You can use these from the market square to most nearby points, including Grand Anse.

Language

Since Grenada was formerly under the British throne, natives speak English with a beautiful lilt. A local dialect mixes French with African slang.

Medical Emergencies

The General Hospital in St. George's has limited facilities; you might find better advice at the Grenada School of Medicine, a privately owned, U.S.-managed school of medicine in **True Blue** ☎ *(809) 444-4271*. Serious emergencies may warrant airlift to San Juan, Puerto Rico.

Money

The official currency is the Eastern Caribbean dollar, commonly referred to as "E.C." The exchange rate is tied to the U.S. dollar, and currently trades at $2.65 for one American dollar. Prices are usually quoted in E.C., but you should always ask to make sure. Traveler's checks and credit cards are widely accepted. If you plan to pay by cash, you will usually receive a slightly better exchange rate by converting your money to E.C. at a bank.

Telephone

Area code is *809*. To save money, head for the Grenada Telecommunications, Ltd., in St. George or use a special phone card on other telephones. Cellular phone service can be purchased through **Boatphone** ☎ *(800) 567-8336*.

Time

Atlantic standard time, which is one hour earlier than New York time half of the year, the same for the rest of the year.

Tipping

Expect a 10 percent service charge; no need to tip help further. At eateries not connected to your hotel, leave a 10–15 percent tip. Only tip a taxi driver if he carries your bags.

Tourist Information

Grenada Board of Tourism is located at The Carenage, St. George's ☎ *(809) 440-2001* and will answer questions, offer brochures and maps. Stop here if you are traveling on to other Grenadine islands. **Grenada Hotel Association Ross Point Inn, Lagoon Road, St. George's** ☎ *(809) 444-1353*. In the United States call ☎ *(800) 927-9554*.

When to Go

Don't miss Grenada's Carnival in early August, a four-day-to-night blowout of calypso songs and steel bands, and the traditional "jump-up" parades. Carriacou comes alive in early August for its annual Regatta. Also check out the ninth annual International Triathlon, usually held in January. Competitors come from as far away as Australia and Norway and it takes place along and near Grand Anse Beach.

GRENADA HOTELS		RMS	RATES	PHONE	CR. CARDS
Carriacou					
Hillsborough					
★★★	Silver Beach Resort	16	$80–$95	(809) 443-7337	A, DC, MC, V
★★	Caribbee Inn	10	$95–$135	(809) 443-8142	A
★★	Cassada Bay Resort	16	$80–$125	(809) 443-7494	A, MC, V
Grenada					
St. George's					
★★★★★	Calabash Hotel	28	$170–$495	(800) 528-5835	A, MC, V
★★★★★	La Source	100	$250–$590	(800) 544-2883	A, MC, V
★★★★★	Spice Island Inn	56	$270–$475	(809) 444-4258	A, D, DC, MC, V
★★★★	Rex Grenadian	212	$115–$360	(800) 255-5859	A, MC, V
★★★★	Secret Harbour Hotel	20	$100–$225	(800) 334-2435	A, MC, V
★★★	Blue Horizons Cottages	32	$100–$165	(809) 444-4592	A, D, DC, MC, V
★★★	Coyaba Beach Resort	40	$75–$165	(809) 444-4129	A, D, DC, MC, V
★★★	Grenada Renaissance Hotel	186	$120–$170	(800) 228-9898	A, D, DC, MC, V
★★★	Twelve Degrees North	8	$130–$285	(800) 322-1753	None
★★	Cinnamon Hill Hotel	20	$85–$153	(809) 444-4301	A, D, MC, V
★★	Flamboyant Hotel	39	$70–$220	(800) 223-9815	A, D, DC, MC, V
★★	Horse Shoe Beach Hotel	22	$70–$155	(809) 444-4244	A, D, MC, V
★★	No Problem Apartments	20	$55–$85	(809) 444-4634	A, D, MC, V
★★	Siesta Hotel	37	$55–$140	(809) 444-4645	A, D, MC, V
★★	True Blue Inn	7	$65–$110	(800) 742-4276	A, D, DC, MC, V
★	Coral Cove Cottages	11	$65–$120	(809) 444-4422	D, MC, V
★	Gem Holiday Beach Resort	23	$55–$140	(800) 223-9815	A, D, DC, MC, V
★	Hibiscus Hotel	10	$60–$125	(809) 444-4233	A, D, MC, V

GRENADA

GRENADA HOTELS		RMS	RATES	PHONE	CR. CARDS
★	Holiday Haven	12	$60–$145	(809) 440-2606	
★	La Sagesse Nature Center	6	$40–$90	(809) 444-6458	A, MC, V
★	Maffiken Apartments	12	$60–$85	(809) 444-4255	A, MC, V
★	South Winds Holiday	19	$40–$80	(809) 444-4310	A, D, DC, MC, V
★	Villamar Holiday Resort	20	$42–$62	(809) 444-1614	A, MC, V
★	Wave Crest Holiday Apts.	20	$75–$95	(809) 444-4116	A, D, MC, V

GRENADA RESTAURANTS		PHONE	ENTRÉE	CR. CARDS
St. George's				
★★★★★	Morne Fendue	(809) 442-9330	$17–$17	None
★★★★	Nutmeg, The	(809) 440-2539	$5–$20	A, D, MC, V
★★	Mamma's	(809) 440-1459	$19–$19	
★	Cot Bam	(809) 444-2050	$6–$30	A, D, MC, V
American				
★★★	La Sagesse	(809) 444-6458	$5–$18	A, MC, V
Chinese				
★	Bird's Nest	(809) 444-4264	$3–$25	A, D, MC, V
Continental				
★★★	La Source	(809) 444-2556	$45	A, MC, V
French				
★★★★	Coconut's Beach	(809) 444-4644	$6–$26	MC, V
International				
★★★★	Canboulay	(809) 444-4401	$7–$30	A, MC, V
★	Red Crab, The	(809) 444-4424	$10–$31	A, D, MC, V
★	Rudolf's	(809) 440-2241	$8–$19	
Italian				
★★	Portofino	(809) 440-3986	$6–$22	A, MC, V
Seafood				
★★★★	La Belle Creole	(809) 444-4316	$5–$21	A, D, DC, MC, V
★★	Delicious Landing	(809) 440-9747	$4–$19	MC, V

GUADELOUPE

Guadeloupe's Ste.-Anne offers white sand beaches and crystal-clear water.

Looking for something completely different from the typical Caribbean holiday? Guadeloupe may be just the ticket. This large French island has the typical wonderful beaches and plush resorts, but also a thriving rainforest, verdant mountains (including a not-quite-dormant volcano), a decidedly non-touristy large city and more eco-adventures than many other islands combined. It also boasts three satellite islands, Marie-Galante, Les Saintes, and La Desirade, that offer visitors the chance to experience the Caribbean in a laid-back, natural state that's hard to find in these days of mega-resorts and all-inclusives. In fact, because Guadeloupe's economy depends more on sugarcane than tourism, you'll find a refreshing change of pace on this French-owned—but not particularly influenced—island.

Diving is big here, but don't come to be certified if you're a wimp—the courses are considered some of the toughest anywhere. Cycling is another craze—and it helps to be a little crazy to try it on this hilly terrain and among drivers who act as if the roads are their personal driveways.

Guadeloupe is composed of two large islands, Basse-Terre to the west and Grande-Terre to the east, separated by a seawater channel, the Riviere Salee, and connected via the Pont de la Gabare bridge. Basse-Terre is the more scenic and houses the island's crown jewel: the 74,100-acre Parc National de la Guadeloupe, which includes a vibrant rainforest, a zoo, a botanical garden, picture-perfect waterfalls and Les Mammells—twin peaks that resemble, and indeed were named for, female breasts.

Though the park takes up most of Basse-Terre, the island is also home to the city of Basse-Terre, Guadeloupe's capital, which lives in the shadow of 48,000-foot La Soufriere. The volcano hasn't erupted since the 16th century, though still sputters and smokes often enough to keep locals on their toes.

Grande-Terre is flatter and not as scenic, though it does hold Guadeloupe's principle city, Pointe-a-Pitre. It's here you'll find the majority of tourist accommodations, the best beaches and two small casinos.

French is the official language, and Creole is also widely spoken—tourists who don't parle vous will find it tough going. Be sure to buy a phrase book before arriving on the island, as they are surprisingly difficult to find once here, even in Point-a-Pitre. While most hotels are staffed with at least a few English speakers, most locals have only a limited English vocabulary. Nearly two-thirds of the 330,000 tourists who visit each year are from Europe, particularly France.

Bird's-Eye View

Located some 1845 miles from New York and part of an archipelago that also includes St. Barthelemy and St. Martin, Guadeloupe sits in the Caribbean Sea between the Tropic of Cancer and the Equator. Guadeloupe proper resembles a butterfly and consists of two islands, Basse-Terre (330 square miles) to the west and Grande-Terre (230 square miles) to the east. The two are connected by drawbridge. Though they are so close together, these siblings barely resemble one another. Triangular-shaped Grande-Terre has the undulating fields of sugarcane, historic windmills and the best beaches, and also the most tourist facilities. Basse-Terre is a nature lover's dream, dominated to the north by the National Park, which encompasses some 74,100

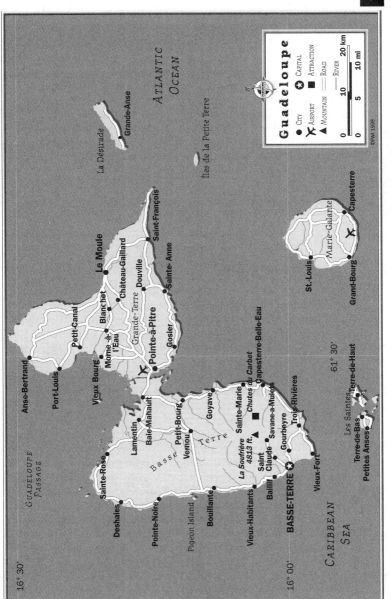

Guadeloupe

- CITY
- ✪ CAPITAL
- ✈ AIRPORT
- ▲ MOUNTAIN
- ■ ATTRACTION
- ROAD
- RIVER

0   10   20 km
0   5   10 mi

©FWI 1998

ATLANTIC OCEAN

Grande-Anse

La Désirade

Îles de la Petite Terre

Saint-François

Le Moule

Château-Gaillard

Douville

Sainte-Anne

Blanchet

Petit-Canal

Grande-Terre

Pointe-à-Pitre

Gosier

Morne-à-l'Eau

Vieux Bourg

Port-Louis

Anse-Bertrand

Capesterre

Marie-Galante

St-Louis

Grand-Bourg

Baie-Mahault

Lamentin

Petit-Bourg

Goyave

Sainte-Marie

Capesterre-Belle-Eau

Trois-Rivières

Chutes du Carbet

Savane-à-Mulets

Sainte-Rose

Vernou

La Soufrière
4813 ft.

Saint Claude

Gourbeyre

Terre-de-Haut

Deshaies

Pointe-Noire

Bouillante

Pigeon Island

Vieux-Habitants

Baillif

Vieux-Fort

BASSE-TERRE

Les Saintes

Terre-de-Bas

Petites Anses

Basse Terre

GUADELOUPE PASSAGE

CARIBBEAN SEA

16° 30'

16° 00'

61° 30'

acres and includes more than 180 miles of trails that pass waterfalls, hot springs, sulfurous waters, craters and banana fields. To the south is the island's highest peak, La Soufriere, a 4800-foot volcano.

Iles des Saintes, six miles south of Guadeloupe, consists of nine tiny islands (just five square miles total) that make up their own archipelago. Just 3100 people live here, most on Terre-de-Haute, a charming spot of land with an arid and breezy climate. Marie-Galante, 25 miles south of Guadeloupe, encompasses 62 square miles and has some 16,000 inhabitants. This quiet spot is given over mainly to sugarcane and rum production and has several historic plantations intact—complete with working windmills. La Desirade, located six miles east of the mainland, is a nine-square-mile spit of land with 1700 residents. Formerly a leper colony and then home to "undesirables" from the mainland, today the island, noted for its rugged landscape, is primarily a fishing village with less than 20 rooms for tourists. These satellite islands are connected to Guadeloupe by ferry and plane.

Christopher Columbus stumbled upon Guadeloupe during his 1493 excursions, dubbing it Santa Maria de Guadeloupe de Estremadura in honor of a Spanish monastery with which he had close ties. Some 143 years later, the French landed, peopling the island with settlers who had to work in indentured conditions for three years to pay off their sea passage from France. Unfortunately, many proved to be unskilled and unacquainted with tropical farming, and the island soon fell into disrepair while nearby Martinique continued to prosper. The French Revolution inspired the settlers to revolt; they eventually declared themselves independent and even solicited the help of the British enemy. In response, the French government sent more than a thousand soldiers to whip the settlers into shape, expelling the British and executing more than 4000 Guadeloupian rebels on guillotines set up in the main squares. Under the Napoleonic reign, slavery was reinstated. In 1810 the British successfully reinvaded the island, handing it over to Louis XVIII during the Restoration, and returning when Napoleon came to power; the Brits finally surrendered the island for the last time when the French emperor was exiled to St. Helena in 1815. Since then, Guadeloupe has retained its distinct French flavor combined with a spicy West Indian allure. In September 1989, Hurricane Hugo struck the islands, causing widespread devastation and leaving about 12,000 people homeless. But by the mid-1990s the banana industry and the tourist industry had recovered and the majority are looking forward to prosperous years.

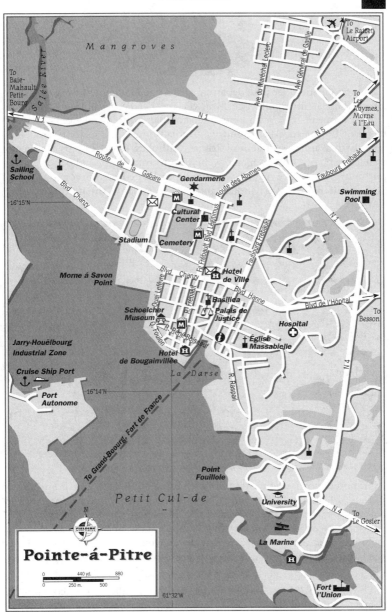

M a n g r o v e s

Salée River

To
Baie-
Mahault
Petit-
Bourg

N 1

N 1

To
Les
Abymes,
Morne
á l'Eau

Ave du Maréchal Leclerc

Ave Général de Gaulle

To
Le Raizet
Airport

N 5

Faubourg Frebault

N 1

Route de la Gabare

Route des Abymes

⚓
**Sailing
School**

Blvd Chanzy

16°15'N

Gendarmerie

✉

M

**Cultural
Center**

M

Stadium

Cemetery

Fd Frébault Blvd Légitimus

Faubourg Frébault

**Swimming
Pool**

**Morne á Savon
Point**

Blvd Chanzy

Blvd Chanzy

R. Frébault

H
**Hotel
de Ville**

Basilica

**Schoelcher
Museum**

Quai Lefèvre

M

R. Richepiolsseur

R. Toulon

**Palais de
Justice**

Blvd Hanne

Blvd de l'Hôpital

To
Besson

Hospital ✚

**Jarry-Houëlbourg
Industrial Zone**

ℹ

H

**Hotel
de Bougainvillée**

✝ **Église
Massabielle**

R. Raspail

N 4

Cruise Ship Port
⚓

La Darse

**Port
Autonome**

16°14'N

To Grand-Bourg: Fort de France

Petit Cul-de-

**Point
Fouillole**

University

N 4

To
Le Gosier

La Marina

H

N
Pointe-á-Pitre

0	440 yd.	880
0	250 m.	500

61°32'W

**Fort
l'Union**

People

Though Guadeloupe is a "departement" owned by France, besides the language there is little influence from the mother land—although shops do close, European-style, for a long lunch complete with fine wine. Locals are a blend of European, African and East Indian origin; the majority are Christians, with a large contingent of Roman Catholics. A love of music is a major characteristic of Guadeloupans, so be sure to tune in the radio at every opportunity, as you'll be regaled with the supercharged rhythms of zonk, a beat born in the French West Indies (and quite popular in the mother country, too).

Bananas are the largest export for Guadeloupe.

The population is about 408,000, with some 26,000 living in Point-a-Pitre and just 14,000 on Basse-Terre. Many are employed in agriculture; sugarcane and bananas are the primary crops, though the island also exports melons (introduced in 1984) and yams. Though most Guadeloupans are black, the population on Les Saintes is virtually all white; since the climate prohibited sugarcane production, no slaves were ever brought there.

Locals are a generally superstitious lot. *Quimboiseurs*, described as "half witch-doctor, half bone-setter" are frequently consulted to concoct potions or cast a spell.

Though few people outside the hotels speak English, they all seem to think they do—if you ask "parlez-vous anglais?" the answer will invariably be "a little"—though that's usually the extent of the English! Carry your trusty phrase book everywhere; locals are patient and friendly with those who made at least a little effort to speak their language.

Beaches

Most of Guadeloupe's beaches are lovely white strand open to the public at no extra charge. Hotels sometimes charge minimal fees for nonguests to utilize the resources of their changing facilities, including beach chairs and towels. Some of the best beaches, with long white stretches, are to be found in Grande-Terre. Gray volcanic sand characterizes the beaches in the southern tip of Basse-Terre; the color is gloriously golden as you move toward the northwest coast. Beaches on the windward (Atlantic side) are simply too rough for swimming; divers who use the water should be exceptionally skilled in maneuvering strong currents. Beaches are generally accessible by roads, paved and otherwise. The exception is Islet du Gosier, which is a blip off the shore of Gosier that welcomes nude bathers. It's a great place to plop yourself for a daylong picnic, and arrangements for watersports can be made through the Creole Beach hotel in Gosier.

Caravelle Beach probably wins the award for the most stunning in Guadeloupe—tropical beauty with an immense strand. The sand is exceedingly powdery. Reefs surrounding the beach make excellent conditions for snorkeling. **Club Med** makes use of one end of the beach, but the **Hotel La Toubana** in the hills above has snorkeling equipment for rent. Le Meridien Hotel also sports a fine beach at Raisin-Clairs, where equipment for water sports can be hired. Most popular with the weekend crowd—best to go during the week if you want seclusion—is **Anse de la Gourde**; you will find a restaurant and snack bar there. Lots of nude bathers head for **Tarare**, a private strand just before the tip of Pointe des Châteaux. Another popular nude beach is **Place Crawen**, Les'Saintes' placid half-mile strand on Terre-de-Haut. Changing facilities are available a five-minute walk away at **Bois Joli Hotel**. A lovely "feet in the water" restaurant can be found on **La Grande Anse**, just outside of Dashaies, on the northwest coast of Basse-Terre. the Creole cuisine is excellent here at the **Karacoli Restaurant**. Along the western shore, you'll find lots of beaches in miniature, including the gray sands of **Pigeon Beach** and the blackish ones farther south. **Petit-Anse**, on Marie-Galante, is a beautiful large beach with gleaming gold sand that fills up fast on the weekends.

Underwater

When Jacques Cousteau names a destination one of the top 10 dive spots in the world, you can expect that a sizable industry will spring up around it. In reality, Cousteau placed **Pigeon Island** on his top ten list some years ago, when many areas of the undersea world were still waiting to be explored, so the designation is of a qualified nature today. Still, the locally named **Reserve du Commandant Cousteau** at Pigeon Island is a marvelous dive location, and at least one Guadeloupe operator paves the way for American visitors to experience its lush depths. Beginners will find a number of easier sites surrounding Pigeon, although one must remember that French dive tables and apparatus are different from those used by most American-run operations. Visibility off Pigeon often exceeds 100 feet, although showers will carry mountain silt down to the reefs surrounding Basse-Terre; usually this settles in a matter of hours. Unfortunately, crowded boats are a common complaint from many visitors at this busy location, and avid divers should also try to explore other portions of the expansive west coast, sometimes referred to as "the Kingdom of Sponges." It's worth noting that, unlike most other Caribbean islands, Guadeloupe dive shops price their dives based on the distance traveled from shore, creating a diverse price structure. The **Iles des Saintes** also offer pristine diving, centered around the island's reef plateau, which offers relatively shallow depths. In addition to the western face of Pigeon Island, snorkeling is good in the coral garden below the bluffs just north of the harbor at **Deshaies**, off the **Ilet du Gosier** (the tiny island with a lighthouse facing Gosier), at **Anse a la Barque** (small cove six miles north of Basse Terre), and in the reefs surrounding **Ilet a Fajou** (north of the Riviere Salee).

On Foot

Guadeloupe is second only to Martinique for maintaining the best and most extensive trail system in the Caribbean. From easy walks approaching tall waterfalls to a fierce traverse of the island's volcanic spine, there is no shortage of trails to keep active travelers engaged. The island's geologic focus, Soufriere in the vast **Parc National**, is one of the region's more recently troubled summits—a series of eruptions in 1976–1977 were exciting enough to occasion the evacuation of Basse-Terre—and, ironically, it's probably the most-visited. Almost every day, dozens of hikers gamely ascend the moderate path to its moonlike crown, the highest in the Eastern Caribbean. Because island trails are so well-maintained, guides are generally unnecessary. A guidebook containing routes within the Parc National is available from the **Organization des Guides de Montagne** in Basse-Terre *(☎ (590) 814-579);* they also conduct guided walks in English.

A winter home to French racers, Guadeloupe is well-established as one of the Caribbean's leading cycling destinations. Bringing your own bike from home is a reasonable option (repair shops are sprinkled island-wide), while rental outfits can be found in Pointe-a-Pitre and most major towns. Guadeloupe boasts a well-maintained road system covering more than 1200 miles. Navigating the island's busier roads can be a challenge in itself. In particular, use caution on the fast N4 that plows east from Pointe-a-Pitre along the developed southern coastline of **Grande-Terre** (it quiets down east of St. Francois) and on the busy N1, which is the main route between Pointe-a-Pitre and the capital of **Basse-Terre**. Otherwise, Guadeloupe's eastern wing offers some of the Caribbean's most pleasant riding, over rolling hills and through green sugarcane fields. Head north from any of the south-coast resort areas for a delightful tour of the French countryside, Caribbean-style. The seven-mile stretch from **St. Francois** to **Pointe des Chateaux** is lovely and easy. On Guadeloupe's other wing, exacting rides rule the day. Basse-Terre's mountainous interior frequently extends right to its busy coastline, providing little relief for riders but plenty of challenges for the fit. The beautiful **Route de la Traversee** is a real thigh-buster, while the hilly coastline north of **Pigeon Island** accesses quieter beaches and villages that happily proffer *croissant* and *cafe au lait* for early morning cyclists. The islands of **Terre-de-Haut** and **Marie-Galante,** both considerably easier (or smaller, anyway) to conquer than Guadeloupe, offer mountain bike rentals at some scooter and motorcycle outlets.

The city of Point-a-Pitre, on Grand-Terre, is one of the Caribbean's busiest, and though it's doubtful you'll want to spend your entire vacation here, it's worth a visit of at least a few hours. Though some French colonial structures still remain, the city is basically modern and quite hectic, with 100,000 residents all seemingly trying to negotiate the same narrow streets and sidewalks at the same time. The Tourist Office, at Place de la Victire, is a good place to pick up maps and brochures on the area's attractions. Lots of nearby local vendors sell everything from kitchenware to underwear, and unlike on some other islands, they'll let you stop and browse without being obnoxiously persistent about making a sale. The same is true at the local Marketplace, located between the streets of St. John Perse, Freebault, Schoelchen and Peynier, where women in brightly colored madras sell fresh fruits and vegetables. The busy ferry port bustles with activity as locals and tourists jostle to buy tickets and catch the boats that travel to and from Marie-Galante, Les Saintes and La Desirade. For some strange reason, all the competing ferries leave for the exact same destinations at the exact same time.

Basse-Terre, the other wing of Guadeloupe's "butterfly," is a must for any visitor. You could easily spend days just exploring the National Park, which includes such sites as the Cascade aux Ecrevisses, a lovely waterfall and pond; and the Parc Zoologique et Botaninque, a zoo and botanical garden whose restaurant offers great panoramas from its 1500-foot-high perch. Farther north, you can tour a working sugar factory called Compagnie Fermiere de Gross Montagne, or learn probably more than you need to know about the rum-making process at the Musée du Rhum.

A day trip, via plane or ferry, to Marie-Galante or Les Saintes, is highly recommended. The former island is quite picturesque and laid-back with its lush rolling hills, excellent beaches, fields of undulating sugarcane and vintage windmills. The main town of Grand-Bourg, near the ferry depot, makes for a nice, quiet stroll under flowering flamboyant trees; that lovely old church you'll spot dominating the dead end of Rue de l'Eglise (Church Street) is well worth a peek inside to see its high wooden ceiling, stained glass windows, elaborate murals and old wooden pews. Other sites to visit on the island include Distillerie Poisson, a rum distillery that produces Pere Labat and is open for tours each morning; Chateau Murat, which houses interesting exhibits on the island's sugar industry as well as an arts and traditions museum; and, for natural beauty, Capesterre, a historic village with nearby "galeries": large cliffs the sea has formed into a covered walkway.

Tourist facilities on Les Saintes are limited to the island of Terre de Haut, where the ferry drops passengers off in a village so picturesque you'll swear you're on a Hollywood movie set. But it's all real here on this tiny isle that time has seemingly forgot. Attractions are basically limited to Fort Napoleon, an early 19th-century fort that offers excellent exhibits on sea battles from the 1700s, huge model ships and other historic gems. Look closely in the surrounding cacti garden and chances are good you'll spot at least one or two giant iguanas. The views from up here are astounding.

Archeological Park, Basse-Terre, Guadeloupe

Historical Sites
Basse-Terre

Parc Archeologique des Roches ★★★

Trois-Rivieres.
Hours open: 9 a.m.–5 p.m.

At this peaceful spot near the wharf, displays interpret the rock engravings by Carib Indians that date back to A.D. 300.

Museums and Exhibits
Basse-Terre

Musee du Rhum

Bellevue, Sainte-Rose, Basse-Terre.
Hours open: 9 a.m.–5 p.m.
The Rum Museum showcases three centuries in the making of the quaff, which is produced with sugarcane. After a guided tour, you get to taste the potable, and, of course, buy some to take home. But perhaps the best reason to come here is to check out "la Galerie des Plus Beaux Insectes du Monde," where you can marvel at more than 5000 (safely dead) critters—from beautiful butterflies to spine-tingling spiders, roaches and other huge creepy-crawlies. Those interested in the rum-making process should also check out the Domaine de Severin in Sainte-Rose *(northern Basse-Terre, ☎ (590) 28-91-86).* This distillery still functions with a paddle wheel; a guided tour takes you though each step of production. It's open daily from 8 a.m.–1 p.m. and from 2-6 p.m., and from 9 a.m.–noon on Sundays.

Pointe-a-Pitre

Edgar Clerc Archaeological Museum　　　　　　　★★★

La Rosete, Moule.
This small museum displays artifacts from the Carib and Arawak Indians found on the islands of the Eastern Caribbean. Closed Wednesday afternoons and Tuesdays.

Musee Schoelcher　　　　　　　★★★★

24 Rue Peynier, Pointe-a-Pitre.
Displays highlight the personal papers and belongings of Victor Schoelcher, who, in the 19th century, worked to abolish slavery in the French West Indies.

Musee St. John Perse　　　　　　　★★★★

Achille Rene-Boisneuf Rue, Pointe-a-Pitre.
Hours open: 9 a.m.–5 p.m.
This museum in a restored colonial house contains the works of St. John Perse, a local boy made good who won the Nobel Prize in Literature in 1960.

Parks and Gardens
Basse-Terre

Floral Park

Cabout, Petit-Bourg, Basse-Terre.
Hours open: 9 a.m.–5 p.m.
Le Domaine de Valombreuse is the official name of this Eden-like spot on the east coast of Basse-Terre. Numerous shady valleys house 300 species and 200 sub-species of flowers and a slew of exotic birds. The Park Restaurant is open daily for lunch, and there's a playground on site for little tykes. Admission is $5 for kids under 12. General admission: $8.

Parc Naturel de la Guadeloupe　　　　　　　★

Route de la Traversee, Basse-Terre.

Covering 74,000 acres with 200 miles of trails, this national park has something for everyone: waterfalls, thick vegetation, nature walks and the centerpiece, La Soufriere, a smoldering volcano that last erupted in 1975. Stop by the Maison de la Foret for a look at the park's history (only, alas, in French) and a booklet on hiking trails. Wear rain gear, as this area gets some 250 inches per year. If you're interested in a guided hike tailored to your level, contact the **Organisation des Guides de Montagne de Caraibe** at ☎ *80-05-79.*

Zoological and Botanical Park

> *Route de la Traversee, Bouillante, Basse-Terre.*
> *Hours open: 9 a.m.–4:30 p.m.*

Located high in the hills of Basse-Terre, this reserve is home to myriad trees, bushes, and creepers that lots of little critters including mongoose, iguana, land turtle, and raccoon (called ti-raccoon here) call home. Great views abound at Le Ti-Raccoon restaurant (open daily for lunch except Mondays), which serves up authentic Creole cuisine. Admission for children is $3. General admission: $5.

Tours

Pointe-a-Pitre

Aquarium de la Guadeloupe ★★

> *Place Creole, Marina Bas-du-Fort.*
> *Hours open: 9 a.m.–7 p.m.*

This is the Caribbean's largest aquarium and considered to be France's third-most important. Good exhibits feature everything from tiny fishes to giant sharks. While in the area, check out the 18th-century Fort Fleur d'Epee, complete with dungeons and spectacular views. General admission: $7.

Watersports reign supreme on Guadeloupe, with the most popular sites at Pigeon Island off the west coast, called one of the world's 10 best diving sites by none other than Jacques Cousteau. Several diving centers offer everything from equipment to excursions at Malendure Beach, which faces the island. Novices can get certified on Guadeloupe and be assured of a good education; the courses here are considered some of the toughest anywhere. Snorkeling is especially good at St. Francois reef and Ilet du Gosier, as well as Pigeon Island. Deep-sea fishers hunt for barracuda and kingfish from January to May, and tuna, dolphin and bonito from December to March. Strong currents and good winds make yachting popular; *Boating Magazine* calls Bas du Fort's Port de Plaisance marina one of the finest in the Western Hemisphere.

Golfers are limited to the island's sole course, the 18-hole Golf de St. Francois, designed by Robert Trent Jones Sr. Tennis courts are plentiful at the major hotels and resorts. Cycling is a major passion with locals, and each August the island hosts the Tour de la Guadeloupe, a 10-day race that draws international competitors. Finally, for spectators, there is occasional horseracing at the St. Jacques Hippodrome at Anse Bertrand (☎ *[590] 22-11-08)* and the dubious "sport" of cockfighting from November through April.

Pointe-a-Pitre

Golf Municipal Saint-Francois

St.-Francois.
The island's only golf course features 18 holes designed by Robert Trent Jones and an English-speaking pro. Greens fees for the par-71 course are $45.

Holywind

Pointe de la Verdure, Gosier.
Feeling daring? Fly along the coastline in an Ultra Leger Motorise, a lightweight seaplane.

Watersports

Various locations, Pointe-a-Pitre.
Your hotel probably has enough watersports to keep you happy. If not, check out one of the following. Scuba diving: **Chez Guy et Christian** *(☎ (590) 98-82-43)*, **Aqua-Fari** *(☎ (590) 84-26-26)*, and **Nauticase** *(☎ (590) 84-22-22)*. On Isle des Saintes, **Centre Nautique des Saintes** *(☎ (590) 99-54-25)*. Windsurfing: **Callinago** *(☎ (590) 84-25-25)* and **UCPA Hotel Club** *(☎ (590) 88-64-80)*. Deep-sea fishing: **Caraibe Peche** *(☎ 90-97-51)*, **La Rocher de Malendere** *(☎ (590) 98-70-84)*, **Evasion Exotic** *(☎ (590) 90-94-17)*, and **Fishing Club Antilles** *(☎ (590) 86-73-77)*. Boat rentals: **Soleil et Voile** *(☎ (590) 90-81-81)*, **Vacances Yachting Antilles** *(☎ (590) 90-82-95)*, and **Locaraibes** *(☎ (590) 90-82-80)*.

Where to Stay

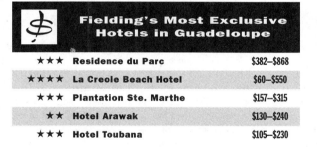

Fielding's Highest Rated Hotels in Guadeloupe

★★★★★	Le Meridien St. Francois	$199–$285
★★★★★	Le Meridien la Cocoteraie	$160–$680
★★★★	Auberge de la Vieille Tour	$118–$231
★★★★	Auberge les Petits Saints	$65–$130
★★★★	Fleur d'Epee Novotel	$123–$213
★★★★	Hotel Hamak Beach	$175–$255
★★★★	PLM Azur Marissol Hotel	$94–$185
★★★★	Villa Creole Hotel	$71–$115
★★★★	Village Creole	$0–$168
★★★★	Village de Menard	$60–$100

Fielding's Most Exclusive Hotels in Guadeloupe

★★★	Residence du Parc	$382–$868
★★★★	La Creole Beach Hotel	$60–$550
★★★	Plantation Ste. Marthe	$157–$315
★★	Hotel Arawak	$130–$240
★★★	Hotel Toubana	$105–$230

Fielding's Best Value Hotels in Guadeloupe

★★★	Auberge de l'Arbre a Pain	$40–$50
★★★★	Village de Menard	$60–$100
★★★★	Village Creole	$168
★★★★	Villa Creole Hotel	$71–$115
★★★	Relais Grand Soufriere	$49–$93

GUADELOUPE

Guadeloupe and its offshore islands offer more than 5,000 rooms, most located on sandy beaches and in the 100- to 200-room range. Choices range from the sprawling and excellent Club Med Caravelle to tiny boutique-style inns. Gosier is the hub of tourism but its beaches are not the best; the resorts around Sainte-Anne and Saint-Francois have better strands. To reap great savings and get a real feel for the island, consider lodging with a family; the Office of Tourism in Basse-Terre *(Maison du Port, 97100 Basse-Terre; ☎ [590] 81-24-83)* can help with arrangements. For villa rentals, contact AVMT (Association des Villas et Meubles de Tourisme de la Region Guadeloupe) at *12, Faubourg Alexandre Issac, B.P. 1297, 97186 Point-a-Pitre; ☎ [590] 82-02-62.* Camping is available in tents or bungalows at two locations: Les Sables d'Or *(Deshaines, ☎ [590] 28-44-60)* and La Traversee *(Point-Noire, ☎ [590] 98-21-23).*

Hotels and Resorts

It's hard to believe, but on Guadeloupe room service is hard to obtain, even in the finest hotels. **Club Med** remains a winner on Guadeloupe, the all-inclusive regime attracting a lot of French and Americans.

Basse-Terre

Sucrerie du Comte   **$50–$100**   ★★★

Sainte Rose, Basse-Terre, ☎ (590) 28-60-17. FAX (590) 28-65-63.
Single: $50–$100. Double: $50–$100.
Built on the grounds of an old sugarcane factory, this peaceful spot opened in 1994. Many ruins of the factory remain, including an 18th-century aqueduct and a large processing plant that was ruined in a 1966 hurricane. Guestrooms are very small and simple, furnished with twin or queen beds, tile floors, and telephones. Each has air conditioning, ceiling fans, and a small, shower-only bath. The grounds include a small but pretty pool, one tennis court, a fabulous restaurant, and a wonderfully atmospheric bar where you'll find the only TV on site. The beach is a five-minute walk through grounds dotted with papaya, orange, mango and other fruit trees. Recommended for nature lovers as opposed to resort seekers. 50 rooms. Credit cards: MC.

Villa Creole Hotel   **$71–$115**   ★★★★

Petionville, Basse-Terre, ☎ (509) 45-62-41.
Single: $71–$115. Double: $83–$115.
Set high on the hills and surrounded by a forest, this comfortable, family-run hotel has a loyal following. The spacious guest rooms are air-conditioned and accented with Haitian furniture. There's a free-form pool in a nicely landscaped garden and lots of interesting local art in the public areas. Two tennis courts await the strenuous set. A nice property with lots of island flavor. 72 rooms. Credit cards: A, MC, V.

Gosier

Canella Beach Residence   **$87–$230**   ★★★★

Pointe de la Verdure, Gosier, ☎ (590) 90-44-00.
Single: $87–$230. Double: $109–$230.

Set in the heart of Gosier's hotel scene, this hotel has small but adequate air-conditioned guest rooms and suites. All have a simple kitchenette on the terrace with cheap cooking utensils and dishware. The beach consists of gray sand, the no-see-ums are everywhere, and the ocean is downright dirty—so look elsewhere if you're intent on a tropical paradise. On the plus side, there's all the usual resort diversions at this busy property and lots within an easy walk, including one of Guadeloupe's few casinos. Parents can stash the kids in supervised programs during high season. The staff is friendly and eager to practice their English—a definite plus on this French-speaking island. 146 rooms. Credit cards: A, DC, MC, V.

Grande-Terre

Cottage Hotel $112–$220 ★★

Le Moule, Grande-Terre, ☎ *(590) 23-78-38. FAX (590) 23-78-39.*
Single: $112–$194. Double: $142–$220.
Just opened in early 1995, this friendly property accommodates guests in a pretty building in yellow and blues with fanciful gingerbread trim. Lodgings are in nicely done duplexes with high ceilings, two sofa beds in the living room, one and a half baths, a kitchenette on the balcony, and a small loft bedroom. Excellent for families, each unit has a TV, telephone and air conditioning. The balconies overlook a parking lot and the sea; it's just a minute or two stroll to the beach. Guests can use the pool, restaurants and watersports facilities at the adjacent Tropical Club Hotel. 24 rooms. Credit cards: A, MC, V.

Domaine de l'Anse des Rochers $80–$220 ★★

Sainte-Francois, Grande-Terre, ☎ *(590) 93-90-00. FAX (590) 93-91-00.*
Single: $80–$220. Double: $80–$220.
An immaculate collection of pastel-colored Creole buildings trimmed with white gingerbread is the core of this upscale resort near Sainte-Francois. Guests are accommodated in nicely decorated rooms or in 34 villas on the hillside. Each room is air-conditioned and has a furnished terrace, modern bath, radio, refrigerator and direct-dial telephone. The expansive grounds include several restaurants, the largest natural lagoon pool in the Caribbean, a gorgeous swimming pool, tennis and two reef-protected beaches. There's also a disco on site and various theme evenings each week. 356 rooms. Credit cards: MC, V.

Plantation Ste. Marthe $157–$315 ★★★

Sainte-Francois, Grande-Terre, ☎ *(800) 333-1970, (590) 88-72-46. FAX (590) 88-72-47.*
Single: $157–$315. Double: $181–$315.
Sitting high on a hill with sweeping views and surrounded by 15 acres of fields and gardens, this great choice puts up guests in Louisiana-style buildings housing very nice guest rooms and duplexes, all with air conditioning and extras such as room service, minibars, and hair dryers. Shuttles transport beach lovers to the sand. There's a pool and fitness center on site, while 18 holes of golf are nearby. The hotel's French Creole restaurant is highly regarded. Very pleasant, if you don't mind the off-beach location. 120 rooms. Credit cards: MC, V.

Tropical Club Hotel   **$92–$192**   ★★★

Le Moule, Grande-Terre, ☎ *(590) 23-78-38. FAX (590) 23-78-39.*
Single: $92–$168. Double: $114–$192.

Built up against an untamed cliff lush with yucca trees, this family-friendly hotel has rooms with a queen bed and, ion a small alcove, bunk beds for the little tykes. The pretty blonde furnishings are enhanced by gaily colored fabrics. Other features include a kitchenette on the terrace, air conditioning and ceiling fans, TV, telephones and small shower-only baths. Request a unit on the second or third floor for the best sea views. The grounds include a nice pool area, a fitness room, several restaurants, a watersports center with diving facilities, a beach bar and a long, reef-protected beach great for windsurfing. The rates include breakfast and a free diving or windsurf lesson; an extra $224 per person per week buys dinner nightly. This is one of the few hotels favored by Hurricane Hugo's devastation—prior to the storm, the beach was so full of coconut trees it has hard to get a decent tan! 84 rooms. Credit cards: A, MC, V.

Pointe-a-Pitre

Auberge de la Vieille Tour   **$118–$231**   ★★★★

Point a Pitre, Pointe-a-Pitre, ☎ *(800) 221-4542, (590) 84-23-23. FAX (590) 8-43343.*
Single: $118–$208. Double: $128–$231.

Set on a 15-acre estate overlooking the Caribbean Sea, this posh property includes the tower of an 18th-century sugar mill. Accommodations are nicely done with expensive furnishings and lots of amenities; request one of the newer ones, added a few years ago and situated in townhouses. There's two tennis courts and a pool, with watersports available nearby. The resort just reopened in spring 1996 following a six-month refurbishing that enlarged the beach and redesigned the lobby, restaurants and bar. 136 rooms. Credit cards: A, MC, V.

Callinago Hotel & Village   **$102–$216**   ★

Pointe de la Verdure, Pointe-a-Pitre, ☎ *(590) 84-25-25. FAX (590) 84-24-90.*
Single: $102–$166. Double: $121–$216.

This complex comprises a 40-room hotel on a hill and a 115-unit apartment building on the beach. All units are fairly nice with European baths; the apartments have kitchens, too. There are two restaurants, a pool and watersports, with a casino adjacent. We've received complaints about indifferent service and poor in-room amenities—such as a lack of hangers and tiny bars of soap. 110 rooms. Credit cards: A, DC, MC, V.

Club Med Caravelle   ★★★★

Pointe-a-Pitre, ☎ *(800) 258-2633, (590) 88-21-00.*

Encompassing 45 acres with a wonderful mile-long private beach, this Club Med appeals mainly to tourists from France, so much so that many activities are held in French. (A good chance to learn the language, and they have labs to help you do just that.) The all-inclusive rates cover just about everything. All the resort amenities are here, from tennis to watersports to a lively night scene—but while nice, this is not one of the better Club Meds. 310 rooms. Credit cards: A.

Ecotel Guadeloupe　　　　　　**$60–$130**　　　　　★★

Montauban, Pointe-a-Pitre, ☎ *(590) 90-60-00. FAX (590) 90-60-60.*
Single: $60–$95. Double: $85–$130.
Located less than half a mile from the beach and a mile from Gosier Village, this motel-like operation is a hotel school, so you can count on professional, enthusiastic service. Rooms are comfortable and air-conditioned, but nothing too exciting. There are two restaurant and a pool, but not much else. A good bargain though, with a mostly European clientele. 44 rooms. Credit cards: A, DC, MC, V.

Fleur d'Epee Novotel　　　　　　**$123–$213**　　　　★★★★

Pointe-a-Pitre, ☎ *(800) 221-4542, (590) 90-40-00. FAX (590) 90-99-07.*
Single: $123–$182. Double: $142–$213.
Set on a peninsula near a fine sandy beach, this Y-shaped hotel is informal and friendly, attracting laid-back types who enjoy a range of activities from watersports to tennis to bridge. Guest rooms are air-conditioned and most have sea views from the balconies. Supervised programs keep kids busy while their parents laze at the pool or beach. Lots of young Europeans like this spot. 190 rooms. Credit cards: A, DC, MC, V.

Hotel Arawak　　　　　　**$130–$240**　　　　★★

Pointe de la Verdure, Pointe-a-Pitre, ☎ *(590) 84-24-24. FAX (590) 84-38-45.*
Single: $130–$200. Double: $150–$240.
Catering to a mostly European and Canadian clientele, this 10-story complex has bright and comfortable guest rooms, most with a nice ocean view and balcony. Three tennis courts, a pool, casino, watersports and a fitness center keep guests busy. The top-floor suites are enormous and worth the splurge. The beach is lively and topless. 154 rooms. Credit cards: A, DC, MC, V.

Hotel Hamak Beach　　　　　　**$175–$255**　　　★★★★

Pointe-a-Pitre, ☎ *(590) 88-59-59.*
Single: $175–$225. Double: $205–$255.
Set on 200 secluded acres bordering a reef-protected lagoon, this lushly landscaped property is elegant and exclusive. Accommodations are in air-conditioned bungalows with one or two bedrooms, kitchenettes and outdoor showers. There's an 18-hole golf course across the street, and tennis, air-charter tours (they have their own landing strip) and three small private beaches on site. Excellent service and a well-heeled atmosphere make this one of Guadeloupe's finest resorts. 56 rooms. Credit cards: A, CB, MC.

Kaliko Beach Club　　　　　　**$80–$99**　　　　★

La Gonave Bay, Pointe-a-Pitre, ☎ *(590) 22-80-40.*
Single: $80. Double: $99.
Situated on 15 acres in the Arcahaie beach area, this complex houses guests in circular stone bungalows nicely furnished and air-conditioned. The beach is quite nice and affords all the usual watersports, plus a good diving center. There's also a pool and tennis on two courts. 40 rooms. Credit cards: A, MC, V.

La Creole Beach Hotel　　　　　　**$60–$550**　　　★★★★

Point de la Verdure, Pointe-a-Pitre, ☎ *(590) 90-46-46. FAX (590) 90-46-00.*
Single: $60–$550. Double: $151–$550.

Located on a 10-acre estate on Pointe de la Verdure Beach, this resort offers large and modern air-conditioned guest rooms. Entertainment nightly under the stars is a nice touch. The wide beach offers up all watersports, including free scuba lessons, and there are also a pool, two tennis courts, and a gym. The casino is nearby. 321 rooms. Credit cards: A, DC, MC, V.

Le Meridien St. Francois   **$199–$285**   ★★★★★

Pointe-a-Pitre, ☎ *(800) 543-4300, (590) 88-51-00. FAX (590) 88-40-71.*
Single: $199–$285. Double: $199–$285.

Located on the southern shore of Grand Terre, this contemporary resort sits on 150 acres fronting one of the best beaches in the country. The European-style resort is self-contained, with lots going on in the protected lagoon and on the tennis courts, in the marina and on the archery range. Guest rooms are on the plain side, but have comfortable tropical furnishings and English-language stations on the TV. A casino and the municipal golf course are nearby. *Très chic,* and one of the few resorts where North Americans won't feel out of place. 265 rooms. Credit cards: A, DC, MC, V.

Le Meridien la Cocoteraie   **$160–$680**   ★★★★★

Avenue de L'Europe, Pointe-a-Pitre, ☎ *(590) 88-79-81. FAX (590) 88-78-33.*
Single: $160–$335. Double: $335–$680.

Mostly well-heeled Europeans visit this resort, where every room is a nicely furnished suite. The beach is quite small and there are two tennis courts and a restaurant. All other facilities are found next door, at the Meridien St. Francois, including a marina and watersports. Elegant, but English speakers may feel out of place (and out of touch). 50 rooms. Credit cards: A, MC, V.

PLM Azur Marissol Hotel   **$94–$185**   ★★★★

Pointe-a-Pitre, ☎ *(590) 90-84-44. FAX (590) 90-83-32.*
Single: $94–$139. Double: $111–$185.

Facing the bay of Point-a-Pitre, this resort complex shares its fine beach with the Fleur d'Epee Novotel. Accommodations range from standard guest rooms to bungalows, all air-conditioned and sporting balconies. Pampering treatments await in the spa. A few restaurants, large pool and watersports provide other diversions. There's also tennis on site and a marina nearby. Like many of its competitors, this one attracts mostly young and casual Europeans. 200 rooms. Credit cards: A, DC, MC, V.

Sainte-Anne

Hotel Toubana   **$105–$230**   ★★★

Fonds Thezan, Sainte-Anne, ☎ *(590) 88-25-78. FAX (590) 88-38-90.*
Single: $105–$170. Double: $130–$230.

Set on a hill overlooking the south shore of Grande Terre, this charming complex boasts magnificent views of the raging sea. Guests stay in air-conditioned bungalows with kitchenettes and private gardens. The grounds include a pool, tennis court, bar and restaurant. The beach is a short stroll down a very steep hill, where watersports await. Not bad. 32 rooms. Credit cards: A, DC, MC, V.

Mini Beach Hotel   **$70–$150**

Plage de Sainte-Anne, Sainte-Anne, ☎ *(590) 88-21-13. FAX (590) 88-19-29.*
Single: $70–$150. Double: $70–$150.

This small spot is set right on Sainte-Anne's pretty beach. Accommodations are in air-conditioned guest rooms with colonial-style decor. There are also three bungalows for those desiring more room. The on-site restaurant serves up tasty Creole and French fare daily except Wednesdays, and breakfast is included in the room rate. Watersports are nearby. 9 rooms. Credit cards: MC, V.

Apartments and Condominiums

Since eating out is an art in Guadeloupe, cooking on the island in your own facilities may seem superfluous or beside the point. However, it's nice to know you can whip up your own breakfast, and maybe picnic lunch, then apply the savings to fabulous dinners. Many French ex-pats rent out their fashionable villas and apartments during high season, however, some of the digs don't even have hot running water. Do your best to find out all facts before shacking up with a rental; some clients have been shocked at the results. Most rental operators don't speak English, so your French should be superb, particularly to verify any "small print" on your contract. Rentals can be arranged for one week (usually the minimum) to longer stays. Some beautiful seaside homes are among the prize of the lot. Specify your exact needs (location, sea view, distance to the beach, proximity to shopping, restaurants, etc.).

Grande-Terre

Residence du Parc   **$382–$868**   ★★★

Le Moule, Grande-Terre, ☎ *(590) 23-78-50. FAX (590) 23-78-39.*
Single: $382–$868. Double: $382–$868.
Self-caterers will find all they need at this complex of studios and one- and two-bedroom apartments adjacent to the Tropical Club Hotel. Bedrooms are on the small side and plainly furnished, but pleasant enough. Each unit has ceiling fans (but no air conditioning), complete kitchens on large balconies overlooking the sea, pretty fabrics, shower-only baths, and less-than-desirable plastic dining tables and chairs. Maid service is optional. Guests can use all the facilities at the Tropical Club, including a pool, watersports center and several restaurants. Note that the price quoted above is per week. Credit cards: A, MC, V.

Sainte-Anne

Relais du Moulin   **$105–$156**   ★

Chateaubrun, Sainte-Anne, ☎ *(590) 88-23-96. FAX (590) 88-03-92.*
Single: $105–$129. Double: $128–$156.
Located on an old sugar plantation amid tropical gardens, this complex is somewhat isolated, set in the remote, though scenic, countryside. Accommodations are in air-conditioned bungalows with kitchenettes and patios complete with hammocks. Tennis, archery and a swimming pool await. The beach is not too far a walk. Great views reward those who climb the beautifully preserved windmill. 40 rooms. Credit cards: A, DC, MC, V.

Inns

Inns on Guadeloupe are often defined as a lodging with fewer than 50 rooms. Such accommodations are handled through a local association of hotels called **Relais Créoles**. Membership in the association does not ensure quality, so make sure you acquire as much information as possible. The best inns, like **Relais de Grand Soufriere**, combine the elegance of high ceilings and mansionlike elegance with the tropical breeziness. The smaller the hotel, the more necessary it is to speak French well; although hosts can be congenial, don't expect too much in the way of room service. **Auberge du Grand Large** boasts excellent creole food for both lunch and dinner.

Basse-Terre

L'Auberge de Distillerie   **$105–$125**   ★ ★ ★

> *Route de Versailles, Basse-Terre,* ☎ *(590) 94-25-91. FAX (590) 9-41191.*
> *Single: $105–$125. Double: $105–$125.*
> This French-style country inn in a residential area near the national park appeals to nature lovers. Guest rooms are simple but comfortable with air conditioning and television sets. The Creole restaurant and bar are popular with locals. There's also a pool on site. You may feel left out if *vous ne parlez pas francais.* 15 rooms. Credit cards: A, DC, MC, V.

Relais Grand Soufriere   **$49–$93**   ★ ★ ★

> *St. Claude, Basse-Terre,.*
> *Single: $49–$76. Double: $49–$93.*
> This historic inn dates back to 1859 and reopened in 1986 after extensive renovations. The lovely hillside grounds include a pool. Accommodations are in a mansion, once a private residence, and are elegant and quite comfortable. 21 rooms. Credit cards: A, DC, MC, V.

Pointe-a-Pitre

Auberge du Grand Large   **$100–$105**   ★ ★

> *Route de la Plage, Pointe-a-Pitre,* ☎ *(590) 88-20-06.*
> *Single: $100–$105. Double: $100–$105.*
> Located on Ste. Anne Beach, a nice stretch frequented by locals, this casual spot places guests in air-conditioned bungalows. Besides a bar and Creole restaurant, there's not much in the way of extras, but the rates are reasonable. 10 rooms. Credit cards: A, MC, V.

Low Cost Lodging

Considerable discounts can be arranged from mid-April to November, when the season moves into low status. Rates may vary with current fluctuations. **Relais Bleus de Raizet** is a motel whose chief virtue is that it is a 10-minute ride from the airport. Rooms are minuscule and the air conditioning could keep you up all night, but it's cheap.

Where to Eat

Fielding's Highest Rated Restaurants in Guadeloupe

★★★★★	Auberge de la Vielle Tour	$23–$39
★★★★★	La Canne A Sucre	$18–$32
★★★★★	La Plantation	$14–$54
★★★★★	Le Chateau de Feuilles	$18–$29
★★★★	La Rocher de Malendure	$8–$18
★★★	Chez Clara	$9–$27
★★★	Chez Paul de Matouba	$12–$18
★★★	Chez Violetta	$11–$25
★★★	Le Poisson d'Or	$14–$27
★★★	Nilce's Bar	

Fielding's Most Exclusive Restaurants in Guadeloupe

★★★★★	La Plantation	$14–$54
★★★	Le Restaurant	$25–$40
★★★★★	Auberge de la Vielle Tour	$23–$39
★★★	La Louisiane	$22–$30
★★★★★	La Canne A Sucre	$18–$32

Fielding's Best Value Restaurants in Guadeloupe

★★★★	La Rocher de Malendure	$8–$18
★★★★★	Le Chateau de Feuilles	$18–$29
★★★★★	La Canne A Sucre	$18–$32
★★★	Chez Paul de Matouba	$12–$18
★★★	Chez Violetta	$11–$25

Fresh seafood is a staple in the Guadeloupean diet, and you'll find it at most restaurants around the island. Other specialties to look for include smoked fish, shellfish, stuffed land crabs, seasoned pork sausage, curry dishes, stewed conch and luscious salads with goat cheese. Dishes typically have a Creole flair with a touch of African influence. Be sure to save room for a "digestive" called *petit punch* (called "ti punch" by locals)—a luscious blend of local rum, lime juice and sugar.

The island's two casinos are located at Gosier and Saint-Francois and open at 9 p.m. Discos can be found throughout Gosier, Saint-Francois and Pointa-Pitre. Nightlife is quite limited on the outer islands of Marie-Galante, La Desirade and Les Saintes; at the latter, head for the great live music and camaraderie at Nilce's Bar.

Basse-Terre

Chez Clara　　　　$$$　　　　★★★

Ste. Rose, Basse-Terre, ☎ (590) 28-72-99.
Latin American cuisine.
Lunch: Noon–2:30 p.m., entrées $9–$27.
Dinner: 7–10 p.m., entrées $9–$27. Closed: Wed.

Like the jazz she once danced to, native chef Clara Lesueur's culinary improvisations are realized by years of perfecting basic techniques. Guests that patronize Clara's chez on Ste. Rose's seafront are fans of long-standing, guaranteeing a bit of a wait, but the refreshing rum drinks at the bar help ease the pain. Go easy on the cocktails so you can enjoy the Creole specials of lambi with lime and peppers, crayfish and crab backs. No dinner is served Sundays. Reservations recommended. Credit cards: MC, V.

Chez Paul de Matouba　　　　$$　　　　★★★

Riviere Rouge, Basse-Terre, ☎ (590) 80-29-20.
International cuisine.
Dinner: entrées $12–$18. Closed: Mon.

Enjoy a refreshing country lunch in this Creole restaurant in Matouba, formerly a Hindu settlement, in the mountains above Basse-Terre. The ambience here is similar to a fishing lodge, where diners enjoy a veritable marketplace of local greens and fresh seafood while a river runs outside. Specialties include *accras* (codfish fritters) with an incendiary sauce, or grilled *ouassous* (crayfish). Fixed-price meals under $20 are available. Credit cards: MC, V.

La Rocher de Malendure　　　　$$　　　　★★★★

Malendure Beach, Basse-Terre, ☎ (590) 98-70-84.
French cuisine.
Dinner: entrées $8–$18. Closed: Sun.

The vista from this upscale eatery perched on a bluff above Malendure Beach is Pigeon Island, a top diving locale and underwater reserve. If you can keep your eyes from the scenery, you'll be drawn to the delectable Creole treats on the fixed-price lunch that runs under $20—accras, barbecued chicken, crayfish in sauce and a bev-

San San Bay, Jamaica

Baie Longue Beach, Jamaica

erage. Dinners are served Fridays and Saturdays only. Reservations recommended.
Credit cards: DC, MC, V.

Pointe-a-Pitre

Auberge de la Vielle Tour   **$$$**   ★★★★★

Montauban, Pointe-a-Pitre, ☎ *(590) 84-23-23.*
Associated hotel: Pullman Vielle Tour Hotel.
French cuisine.
Dinner: 7–10 p.m., entrées $23–$39.

Possibly the finest cuisine in Gosier can be found in the main dining room of the Pullman Auberge de la Vielle Tour. The view alone, of the Ilet du Gosier and its lighthouse in the distance, is worth the high tariff. Tables facing the wrap-around windows are, naturally, the most sought-after, so request one way in advance. A la carte offerings include red snapper or catch of the day served with exotic fruit butters, or lamb loin roasted with herbs. A prix-fixe menu ($45) is also available. Reservations recommended. Credit cards: A, DC, MC, V.

Chez Violetta   **$$$**   ★★★

Perinette Gosier, Pointe-a-Pitre, ☎ *(590) 84-10-34.*
French cuisine.
Lunch: Noon–3:30 p.m., entrées $11–$25.
Dinner: 7:30–11 p.m., entrées $11–$25.

One of the best-known tourist establishments in the islands is this restaurant serving traditional Creole specials in a room resplendent with baroque trappings. This mecca for delicacies such as *accra* (cod fritters) and *lambi* (conch) is still going strong, even after the death of its creator, Violetta Chaville. Service is by women in traditional dress. This is an excellent visual and culinary experience for first-time visitors. Credit cards: A, DC, MC, V.

Folie Plage   **$$$**   ★★

Anse Laborde, Pointe-a-Pitre, ☎ *(590) 22-11-17. Associated hotel: Chez Prudence.*
French cuisine.
Lunch: Noon–3 p.m., entrées $14–$18.
Dinner: 7–10 p.m., entrées $14–$18.

Local families flock to this restaurant/guesthouse in Anse Laborde on the north coast of Grand-Terre, especially on weekends, for a combination of beach-combing and grilled fish, court bouillon and chicken curry. If you're so inclined, rent a simple room from Madame Marcelin for under $50. Reservations recommended. Credit cards: A, DC, V.

La Canne A Sucre   **$$$**   ★★★★★

Quai No. 1, Pointe-a-Pitre, ☎ *(590) 82-10-19.*
French cuisine.
Lunch: Noon–2:30 p.m., entrées $18–$32.
Dinner: 7:30–10 p.m., entrées $18–$32. Closed: Sun.

This fine restaurant in Pointe-a-Pitre's port of Centre Saint-John Perse has a seagull's eye view of arriving ships, with a location on the quay. Patrons have a choice of dining in a ground floor brasserie on grilled lamb and mixed seafood platters, or upstairs in a tony, rose-hued chamber. Chef Gerard Virginius is fond of enhancing the finest seafood and poultry available locally with soursop and starfruit-infused vinegars and wine sauces. Reservations recommended. Credit cards: A, MC, V.

La Louisiane $$$ ★★★

Quartier Ste. Marthe, Pointe-a-Pitre, ☎ (590) 88-44-34.
French cuisine.
Lunch: Noon–2 p.m., entrées $22–$30.
Dinner: 7-10 p.m., entrées $22–$30. Closed: Mon.

Located a few miles from the chic resort of St. Francois in Sainte Marthe, this bloom-filled hillside house has an established reputation for creative French-Antillean cuisine. Dinner for two can get pricey, but the experience is worth the splurge—specialties include shark prepared in a saffron sauce and pate of sea urchin roe. Credit cards: MC, V.

La Plantation $$$ ★★★★★

Galerie Commerciale, Pointe-a-Pitre, ☎ (590) 90-84-83.
French cuisine.
Lunch: Noon–2:30 p.m., entrées $14–$54.
Dinner: 7-10:30 p.m., entrées $14–$54. Closed: Sun.

Guadeloupe's largest marina also boasts this well-known four-star establishment housed in two rosy, intimate dining rooms. La Plantation presents French classic cuisine with an emphasis on natural ingredients. Crayfish is a specialty, prepared in myriad ways—sometimes in a salad with foie gras, an unusual combination that works. Reservations required. Credit cards: A, DC, MC, V.

Le Chateau de Feuilles $$$ ★★★★★

Campeche, Pointe-a-Pitre, ☎ (590) 22-30-30.
French cuisine.
Lunch: 11 a.m.–3 p.m., entrées $18–$29.
Dinner: entrées $18–$29. Closed: Mon.

If you pass the remains of a crumbling old sugar mill in off-the-beaten-path Anse Bertrand, you're close to your goal—a four-star culinary landmark in an unlikely location—of a farm owned by chef-hosts Jean-Pierre and Martine Dubost. The atmosphere is like a house party, with a pool to swim in after lunch and a breathtaking choice of 20 flavors of rum, including a sophisticated Baskin-Robbins for adults. If you had a hard time finding the restaurant, don't indulge too much or you may never make it home. Dinner is served on Fridays and Saturdays, for a minimum of 10 people. Reservations required. Credit cards: MC, V.

Le Poisson d'Or $$$ ★★★

Rue Sadi-Carnot 2, Pointe-a-Pitre, ☎ (590) 22-88-63.
Latin American cuisine.
Lunch: 9:30 a.m.–4:30 p.m., entrées $14–$27.
Dinner: 6–9 p.m., entrées $14–$27.

The pride of the quiet fishing town of St. Louis is this cozy spot serving Creole specialties and seafood in a homey atmosphere. Specials change frequently, but usually feature crab farcis with spicy stuffing and homemade ice cream. Reservations required. Credit cards: MC, V.

Le Restaurant   **$$$**   ★ ★ ★

Chateaubrun, Pointe-a-Pitre, ☎ *(590) 88-23-96. Associated hotel: Relais du Moulin.*
French cuisine.
Lunch: 12:30–2:30 p.m., entrées $25–$40.
Dinner: 7:30–9:30 p.m., entrées $25–$40.
Le Restaurant at the tropical village-style Le Relais du Moulin serves the usual Anti-llean-French dishes with some flair in an elegant dining room facing the resort's pool. Fixed price meals for $40 and a la carte offerings include grilled langoustes with herbs, blaff (fresh seafood in a spicy infusion) and lobster. After dinner, stroll the grounds; an old mill (moulin) dating back to the inn's plantation days makes a picturesque photo opportunity. Reservations recommended. Credit cards: A, DC, MC, V.

Les Oiseaux   **$$$**   ★ ★ ★

Anse des Rochers, Pointe-a-Pitre.
French cuisine.
Lunch: Noon–3 p.m., entrées $14–$29.
Dinner: 5–10:30 p.m., entrées $14–$29. Closed: Mon.
It's easy to imagine that you're in the south of France while dining on the terrace of this stone structure facing the sea, located a few miles south of St. Francois. The tal-ented chef is a whiz with seafood, attesting to the popularity of his *cassoulet de fruits de mer,* and a cheeseless fondue of various fish and shellfish cooked with aro-matic oils. Reservations required. Credit cards: V.

Sucrerie du Comte   **$$$**   ★ ★

Comte de Loheac, Sainte-Rose, Pointe-a-Pitre, ☎ *(590) 28-60-17.*
Lunch: Noon–3 p.m., entrées $13–$35.
Dinner: 7–9:30 p.m., entrées $13–$35.
This pretty open-air restaurant, built of Brazilian woods and volcanic rock, is on the site of a former sugarcane factory and a small hotel that bears the same name. It's open all day for salads and sandwiches and offers such evening specialties as Tahitian fish with coconut milk, fish stew, mahi in parchment paper, and fresh fruit crepes. A good wine list accompanies the tasty dishes, many accented with local spices. On Sundays, the menu features traditional Creole dishes. Credit cards: MC.

Victoria   **$$$**   ★ ★ ★

Cottage and Troical Club hotels, Le Moule, Pointe-a-Pitre, ☎ *(590) 23-78-38.*
French cuisine.
Dinner: 7–10 p.m., entrées $10–$37.
Ceiling fans, coral-colored walls and rattan furniture with blue seat cushions is the pleasing decor at this pretty open-air cafe across from the beach at la Moule. Choose from imaginative meat, chicken and fish dishes with traditional heavy creams; the goat cheese salad is to die for. Besides the tasty food and fine wine list, a big plus is the fact they speak fluent English here—a rare find on Guadeloupe. Also open for breakfast from 7–9:30 a.m. daily; lunch hours can vary, so call first. Credit cards: MC, V.

The market at Pointe-a-Pitre is a bonanza of straw hats.

Shopping is not high on the list of things that makes Guadeloupe worth a visit, though you'll have no problem finding ways to spend your French francs. The Juan Perse Cruise Terminal in Point-a-Pitre is a nicely done mall with some two dozen shops catering to upscale shoppers. Other shopping areas in the city are the streets of rue Frébault, rue Schoelcher and rue de

Nozieres. In Bas-du-Fort, check out the Mammoth Shopping Center and the Marina. Duty-free goods can be found at Raizet Airport.

Some stores offer a 20 percent discount on purchases paid with traveler's checks or major credit cards—it's always worth asking. Bargains are generally limited to items form the mother land of France, including perfumes, fashions, china, crystal and scarves. For rum—always a popular souvenir—try the **Musée du Rhum** or **Distillerie Severin**, both in Sainte-Rose. Haitian handicrafts and artworks can be found at **Artisans Caraibes in Saint-Francois** *(Avenuede l'Europe,* ☎ *[590] 90-87-28);* for local handiworks such as wood carvings, intricate lace and brightly costumed dolls, try **L'Imagerie Creole** in Bas-du-Fort *(*☎ *[590] 90-87-28)* and **Mariposa** in Saint-Francois *(13, Galerie du Port).* **Domaine de Valombreuse** *(Petit-Bourg,* ☎ *[590] 95-50-50)* ships tropical flowers and gift packages all over the world. Shops are generally open from 9 a.m. to 1 p.m. and 3–6 p.m. weekdays, as well as on Saturday mornings.

Iles des Saintes

The sailing school at Petite Anse, Terre-de-Haut, offers half or full day windsurfing courses.

Terre-de-Haut is the largest island in an archipelago of eight islands called Les Saintes, off the south coast of Guadeloupe. The 35-minute ferry ride to reach there from Trois-Rivieres or 60-minute ride from Pointe-a-Pitre can be torturous due to choppy waves; take motion sickness pills if you are susceptible. Terre-de-Haut has but 1500 residents on its five-square-mile terrain; its largest city is Bourg with seerla boutiques, restaurants and gingerbread houses hugging the hillsides. Daring explorers can scope out secluded coves; there's even a nude beach at Anse Crawen, which has been compared to Rio de Janeiro for its beauty. A third of the island's economy is dedicated to tourism, so expect locals to be generous and friendly. Among the most important sites (there really aren't that many) is **Fort Napoléon**, leftover from the days when the English warred with the native population, and a nearby museum that houses a modern collection of paintings.

The real reason to come to Terre-de-Haut is to revel in its tranquil, laid-back charms. The quaint European-style village is a treat with its pastel wooden buildings (resist peeking in—many are private residences), friendly locals (who speak little English but are patient as tourists butcher their native French), decent restaurants, and limited shopping (note that virtually all stores close from noon to 2 or 3—or even 4 p.m.—for siesta). Don't miss the old Catholic Church at town center with its marble floor and high wooden ceiling; for five francs (about $1), you can light a candle in memory of a loved one. Then stroll up the street to **Chicken George's**, a local character who makes unforgettable (unless you drink too many) local punches. Also be on the lookout for **Kaz an Nou** ☎ *(590) 99-52-29*, where artisans make traditional wooden creole facades, the perfect souvenir to take home. While most of the island's beaches are not the greatest, the water is wonderfully clear and inviting. Be sure to check out Grande-Anse Beach on the Atlantic side, a lovely, lonely stretch you'll probably have all to yourself. The tide is much too strong for safe swimming (and signs forbid it), but it's the perfect spot for a picnic lunch.

The entire island has only about 30 cars; tourists get around on foot (easily done, though the trek up to Fort Napoléon is quite steep) or rent a motor scooter. You can arrange this just as you get off the ferry; expect to pay about $30 per day, including gas and insurance. You may plan to come just for the day, but just in case, pack an overnight bag. **Les Saintes** is magical, especially in the evening as the children play in the ferry square, locals emerge sleepily from their afternoon siestas, and atmospheric cafes prepare creole dinners; you'll be hard-pressed to bid *au revoir* to this enchanted isle.

What to See

Historical Sites

Fort Napoleon ★★★

Bourg, Les Saintes.
Hours open: 9 a.m.–12:30 p.m.
This old French fort, wherein you can survey barracks and prison cells, is quite well preserved and a nice place to while away a few hours. All signage is in French, but you can buy an English brochure for $5—a bit of a rip off after the $4 admission fee. Still, it's a nice spot, with many interesting exhibits inside—huge model ships, massive oil paintings depicting sea battles, and, oddly enough, a modern art museum—

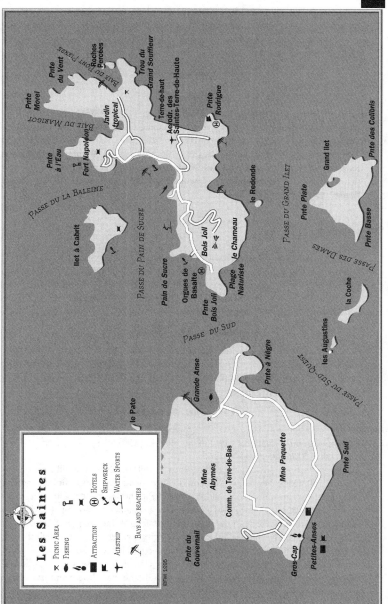

Les Saintes

- ⚓ Picnic Area
- 🎣 Fishing
- ⚑ Attraction
- ✈ Airstrip
- Ⓗ Hotels
- ✕ Shipwreck
- ⚓ Water Sports
- ⚓ Bays and beaches

©SPdN 1995

Pnte du Vent
Roches Percées
Trou du Grand Souffleur
Baie du Pont Pierre
Pnte Morel
Terre-de-haut
Jardin tropical
Aérodr. des Saintes-Terre-de-Haute
Pnte Rodrigue
Baie du Marigot
Pnte à l'Eau
Fort Napoléon
Grand Ilet
Pnte des Colibris
Passe du la Baleine
Ilet à Cabrit
Passe du Pain de Sucre
Pnte Plate
Passe du Grand Ilet
Pnte Basse
le Redonde
Pain de Sucre
Bois Joli
le Chameau
Passe des Dames
Orgues de Basalte
Plage Naturiste
Pnte Bois Joli
la Coche
Passe du Sud
les Augustins
le Pate
Passe du Sud-Ouest
Grande Anse
Pnte à Negre
Pnte Sud
Mne Abymes
Comm. de Terre-de-Bas
Mne Paquette
Pnte du Gouvernail
Gros-Cap
Petites-Anses

and breathtaking views and lovely botanical gardens outside. Look closely among the many varieties of cacti and you're sure to spot an iguana or two. Wear sturdy shoes as the ground is uneven, and bring lots of water if you plan to hike up the steep very road to the fort. General admission: $4.

Sports/Recreation

Watersports in Les Saintes

Les Saintes.

Les Saintes may not have the most beautiful beaches in the Caribbean, but its crystal-clear waters beckon to be explored. For sailing excursions, try **Paradoxe Croisieres** (☎ *[590] 88-41-73)* and **Atlantis** (☎ *[590] 99-50-56)*. For general watersports and diving, try **UPCA** (☎ *[590] 99-54-94)*, **Diving Nautique des Saintes** (☎ *[590] 99-54-25)*, **Land Maidonneuvre Guy** (☎ *[590] 99-53-13)*. For pedal boat and canoe rentals, call **Lognos Paul** (☎ *[590] 99-54-08)* and **Deher Daniel** (☎ *[590] 99-52-42)*.

Tours

Guided Tours in Les Saintes

Les Saintes.

Terre-de-Haut is easily explored by foot or motor scooter—you can't rent a car. If you'd rather leave the navigating to someone else, try one of these operators, who provide island tours in small busses: **Procida** (☎ *[590] 99-55-13)*, **Emilien Pineau** (☎ *[590] 99-51-42)*, **Rose Rosette** (☎ *[590] 99-50-61)*, **Sigiscar** (☎ *[590] 99-53-08)*, and **Ch. Henri Vincent** (☎ *[590] 99-51-79)*.

Where to Stay

Hotels are small here, with the general atmosphere of a West Indian inn. Service is congenial, and at times so familiar you'll feel as if you are renting from your own family. Now is the time to visit the island before it succumbs to more commercial enterprises.

Hotels and Resorts

| **Auberge les Petits Saints** | $65–$130 | ★★★★ |

La Savane, Terre-de-Haut, ☎ (590) 99-50-99. FAX (590) 99-54-51.
Single: $65–$120. Double: $74–$130.

Lovely views from this elegant and eccentric hotel, perched on a hill about a 15-minute walk from the village. You could easily spend your entire holiday poking through the whimsically crammed lobby, a glorious hodge-podge of antiques from around the world, including my favorite: a huge ornamental birdcage (more like a mansion) from Asia. Many of the items are for sale, so bring your checkbook! Four guest rooms share bathing facilities but have private toilets across the hall; the rest have connected private baths. All rooms are air-conditioned and individually decorated with antiques and interesting artwork; the overall look is simple, yet clean and pleasant. My favorite is room 12, which is outside the main house and has a large stone wall, queen bed and large balcony. The grounds include an excellent seafood restaurant, a small but pretty pool, and a sauna. This unique spot is a real winner, provided you don't mind the steep walks into town and the beach. 10 rooms. Credit cards: MC, V.

Hotel Bois Joli   **$98–$192**   ★★★

Terre-de-Haut, ☎ *(590) 99-52-53. FAX (590) 99-55-05.*
Single: $98–$139. Double: $130–$192.

Set in a pretty location with great views, this decent hotel is the island's oldest, dating back to the 1960s. Guest rooms are simply furnished, and only some have air conditioning and private baths. The new bungalows are a better bet; each comes with white wooden furniture, twin beds in the master bedroom, bunk beds in the second bedroom, modern baths, refrigerators and a large patio overlooking the sea. There's a nice restaurant and bar on site as well. With its cute bridge adding a touch of atmosphere, the pool is quite pleasant. Watersports await on the beach for an extra charge. This is one of Les Sainte's few full-service hotels, but its remote location—two miles from the village—is a definite drawback. You'll need to rent scooters to get around. 40 rooms. Credit cards: MC, V.

Apartments and Condominiums

Village Creole   **$80–$168**   ★★★★

Pointe Coquelet, Terre-de-Haut, ☎ *(590) 99-53-83. FAX (590) 99-55-55.*
Double: $80–$168.

This charming spot perched on the Caribbean Sea, far below Fort Napoleon, offers oceanfront or garden duplexes just perfect for self-catering holidays. Each duplex is nicely decorated with a large living and dining area, a full bathroom, a complete and modern kitchen with high-quality cooking and dishware, and a patio on the first floor. Up the pine spiral staircase you'll find two bedrooms and another full bath; both have French-style hand-held showers. Bedrooms are air-conditioned while the common areas rely on sea breezes to keep things cool. The rates include maid service and transportation from the ferry or airport. The beach and lovely village of Terre-de-Haut with its myriad restaurants are a short stroll away. French-born owner Ghyslain Laps is the consummate host, making sure his guests are kept happy and pampered. He's also a whiz at languages, speaking enough English, German, Swedish and Italian to keep the lines of communication humming. Like all hotels on Les Saites, rates rise sharply during the Christmas and Carnival seasons (mid-February to mid-March); expect to pay from $228 to $288 then. Very highly recommended. 22 rooms. Credit cards: CB, MC, V.

Where to Eat

La Saladerie   **$$**   ★★

Anse Marie, Terre de Haute, ☎ *(590) 99-50-92.*
International cuisine.
Lunch: Noon–2 p.m., entrées $7–$19.
Dinner: 7–9 p.m., entrées $7–$19. Closed: Tue.

As the name implies, guests can get a good green salad as well as seafood lightly grilled with fresh vegetables on the side at this lovely little oasis filled with plants and good music from owner Edward's eclectic CD collection. Prices are very reasonable for the great sea views, the high quality of the food, and the very gracious service.

Save room for the luscious deserts, especially the fresh fruit sorbets. Highly recommended! Credit cards: MC, V.

Le Amandiers $$ ★★

Place de la Mairie, Terre de Haute, ☎ *(590) 99-50-06.*
Latin American cuisine.
Lunch: 11 a.m.–2:30 p.m., entrées $12–$16.
Dinner: 7–11 p.m., entrées $12–$16.
This casual bistro is a superb base from which to wile away the hours in the quaint Norman-flavored town of Bourg de Saintes, with its location right on the central square. A set-price lunch of local vegetables, salads, cod fritters and dessert is a bargain at $10. At dinner, sea-fresh selections such as conch and crayfish keep visitors coming back for more. Reservations recommended. Credit cards: A, MC, V.

Le Jardin Creole $ ★★

Place du Debarcadere (the ferry pier), Terre de Haute, ☎ *(590) 99-55-08.*
Seafood cuisine.
Lunch: 9 a.m.–2 p.m., entrées $4–$14.
Dinner: 7–10 p.m., entrées $4–$14.
This casual spot is perfect for grabbing a quick bite before or after the ferry—or anytime, for that matter. Inside is rather plain, but outside, on the patio, patrons have a bird's-eye view of the goings-on below in the square; it's especially charming at night, when the children come out to play (and happily ignore the restaurant owner's pleas of "*silence, si vous plait!*") The menu offers up a large selection of crepes, steaks, mussels and smoked fish; I particularly liked the hardy fish pie with its golden, flaky crust. An added bonus: the owner speaks excellent English. Credit cards: DC, MC, V.

Nilce's Bar $ ★★★

Place du Debarcadere (ferry pier), Terre de Haute, ☎ *(590) 99-56-80.*
This place debuted in June 1995 to instant success—I was there just three days after the grand opening, and it was mobbed! With good reason, too. Nilce, a beautiful Brazilian-born singer married to the owner of Village Creole (see "Hotels"), wows the crowd as she and an incredibly talented keyboardist belt out tunes from 6 p.m. nightly. The atmosphere is unmistakingly French—even the furniture came from an old French bistro—and depending on the crowd, there'll be local musicians jamming, abandoned dancing, and a hell of a good time for all. Set in an old house, the cafe serves American and French breakfasts and a tapas menu for lunch and dinner. Look for the old white building with fresh green trim and prepare for an evening of new friends and general merriment.

La Désirade

La Désirade, five miles east of Guadeloupe, was coveted by Columbus when he spotted the island on Nov. 3, 1493. The name he chose, which means "desired land," showed his true feelings about the exotic nature of the terrain. Ironically, the island became a leper colony for several years. Today it is a perfect place to escape with a picnic to one of the more beautiful beaches of **Souffleur** and **Baie Mahault**. Presently, the island is nearly pristine. In the main village of Grand Anse, there is a charming old church to visit and a hotel called **La Guitone**, where you can get a fine fish meal.

Marie-Galante

At 60 square miles, Marie-Galante is the largest of Guadeloupe's islands. The Caribs retreated here when they were driven from the mainland by the French; centuries later it's become a favorite haven for tourists, both local and foreign, who find the beach at Petit-Anse particularly charming. The island is the epitome of laid-back, though back in the 1800s it had a thriving sugar plantation industry. Ruins of sugar mills can be found all over the island. To get here, take the ferry from Pointe-a-Pitre, which drops you off at Grand Bourg, its largest city with a population of 8000, or one of the numerous short flights offered from Pointe-a-Pitre.

What to See
Museums and Exhibits

Chateau Murat

Near Grand-Bourg, Marie-Galante.

After being destroyed by an earthquake in 1843, this 18th-century sugar plantation has been faithfully restored to its former glory. The mill is constructed of hand-hewn stone and houses the Ecomusee, an arts and traditions museum on island life. The adjoining botanical garden produces many of the medicinal herbs used on Marie-Galante.

Rhum Magaalda

Domaine de Bellevue, Capesterre, Marie-Galante.

This rum factory, located on the Bellevue property, dates back to 1821 and was completely rebuilt after being felled by a hurricane in 1928. The hospitable elderly owners welcome the public for impromptu tours—"just drop by and knock"—but come with a French phrase book, as they don't speak much English. Also bring lots of insect repellant-this place is charming, but crawling with mosquitoes.

Sports/Recreation

Guided Tours of Marie-Galante

Marie-Galante.

The island is best explored by rental car, which costs about $50 per day. If you'd rather leave the driving to someone else, call one of the following: **Bavarday Philippe** (☎ *[590] 97-81-97)*, **Jernival Roseline** (☎ *[590] 97-73-14)*, **Glovert Gino** (☎ *[590] 97-34-18)* **Moysan Eugene** (☎ *[590] 97-31-05)*, **Leveille Etiene** (☎ *[590] 97-72-97)*, **El Rancho** (☎ *[590] 97-81-60)* or **Goram Frederic** (☎ *[590] 97-09-89)*.

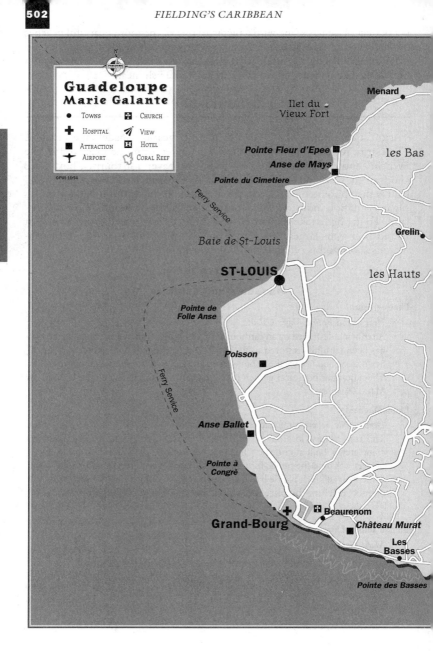

Guadeloupe
Marie Galante

● TOWNS	✚ CHURCH
✚ HOSPITAL	◢ VIEW
■ ATTRACTION	H HOTEL
✈ AIRPORT	CORAL REEF

©FWI 1894

Menard

Îlet du
Vieux Fort

Pointe Fleur d'Epee
Anse de Mays

les Bas

Pointe du Cimetiere

Grelin

Ferry Service

Baie de St-Louis

ST-LOUIS

les Hauts

Pointe de
Folle Anse

Poisson

Ferry Service

Anse Ballet

Pointe à
Congrê

Beaurenom

✚

Grand-Bourg

Château Murat

Les
Basses

Pointe des Basses

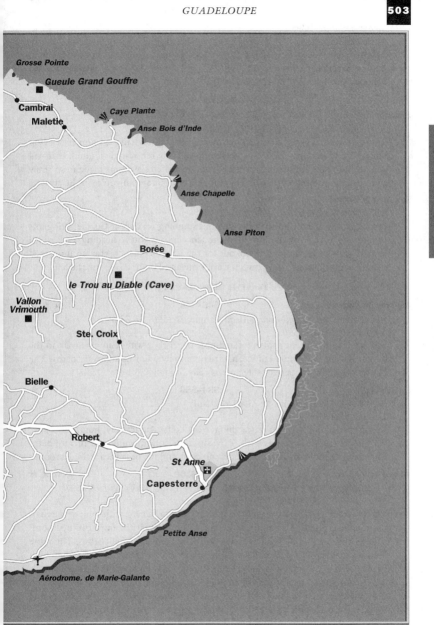

Grosse Pointe

Gueule Grand Gouffre

Cambrai

Maletie

Caye Plante

Anse Bois d'Inde

Anse Chapelle

Anse Piton

Borée

le Trou au Diable (Cave)

Vallon Vrimouth

Ste. Croix

Bielle

Robert

St Anne

Capesterre

Petite Anse

Aérodrome. de Marie-Galante

GUADELOUPE

Watersports on Marie-Galante

Marie-Galante.

Take advantage of Marie-Galante's lovely beaches and inviting sea. For windsurfing, try **Fun Evasion** *(Capesterre,* ☎ *[590] 97-35-21)*; for diving, call **Maison Poullet Section Murat** *(Grand-Bourg,* ☎ *[590] 97-75-24).*

Tours

Bezard

Between Etang-Noir and Grand Case, Marie-Galante.

This spot was still under construction when I passed though in the summer of 1995, but it should be open for 1996. It features a newly renovated windmill that will demonstrate how sugar cane is crushed, and recreated slave huts made from straw and goelette wood that will house boutiques. Worth a stop if you're in the area.

Sea Arch at Gueule

The islands's northern tip, Marie-Galante.

It's well worth the scenic drive to reach this stunning sea arch at Gueule. Bring lots of film and beware of climbing past the fenceline. If you're heading back south toward Capesterre, be on the lookout for the island's oldest house, an unmarked shack made from cane. It's between Caye Plate and Pointe Pisiou, on the left.

Where to Stay

Auberge de l'Arbre a Pain   **$40–$50**   ★★★

Rue Jeanne d'Arc, Grand-Bourg, Marie-Galante, ☎ *(590) 97-73-69.*
Single: $40. Double: $50.

This small and pleasant spot is located near the harbor within an easy walk to the beach. Rooms are simple but clean, air-conditioned, and have private baths. The Creole restaurant is open for three meals daily. 7 rooms.

Le Salut   **$34–$50**   ★

Saint-Louis, Marie-Galante, ☎ *(590) 97-02-67.*
Double: $34–$50.

Recommended only if you're watching every dollar (or actually, franc), this low-frills hotel has basic rooms with or without air conditioning and private bath. There's a bar and restaurant on site, but no pool, and the beach is a walk. 15 rooms.

Village de Menard   **$60–$100**   ★★★★

Menard, Saint-Louis, Marie-Galante, ☎ *(590) 97-77-02. FAX (590) 97-76-89.*
Single: $60–$100. Double: $60–$100.

This peaceful spot is located on the site of an old rum factory, with some stone ruins dotting the grounds. Accommodations are in bungalows with one or two bedrooms (the second one has bunk beds and a twin) and complete kitchenettes. The more deluxe units are well worth the small bump in price and feature tile floors, high beamed ceilings, telephones and TV. In all units, air conditioning is available only in the bedrooms. Save for an inviting pool, there's nothing on site and not much in the immediate area, so you'll definitely want to rent a car. The beach is a 15-minute walk. A new package is a great deal: $200 per person per day (at a minimum of seven nights) includes round trip air from Pointe-A-Pitre to Marie-Galante, accommodations, bicycles, three meals a day (via coupons at area restaurants) and a car. Add $120 per day for each additional person. 5 rooms. Credit cards: MC, V.

Where to Eat

Auberge de la Roche d'Or   **$$$**   ★★

Capesterre, Marie-Galante, ☎ *(590) 97-37-42.*
Dinner: 7:30–9:30 p.m., entrées $20–$30.
This inviting spot offers up pleasing specialties such as conch pannes, breadfruit gratin, and iced pineapple flambé. You'll also find red snapper, local river shrimp and other treats from la mer. Closed each May and Wednesday and Sunday for dinner year-round.

L'Auberge L'Arbre a Pain   **$$$**   ★★

Rue Jeanne d'Arc, Marie-Galante, ☎ *(590) 97-73-69. Associated hotel: L'Auberge L'Arbre a Pain.*
International cuisine.
Lunch: entrées $10–$30.
Dinner: entrées $10–$30. Closed: Sun.
It may help if you have a working knowledge of French in order to stay or eat at this small (seven room) inn located in Grand-Bourg, the civic center of Marie-Galante. But most visitors to this rural outpost are drawn to the simple country ways and lack of development that make this destination choice. Guests who fly down for the day can enjoy unique seafood dishes here, like octopus, or a more familiar grilled conch or seafood platter. There's also a five-course meal for $30. Reservations recommended. Credit cards: V.

La Braise Marine   **$$$**   ★★

Face Plage de la Ferriere, Capesterre, Marie-Galante, ☎ *(590) 97-42-57.*
Lunch: 11:30 a.m.–3:30 p.m., entrées $8–$30.
Dinner: 7–11 p.m., entrées $8–$30. Closed: Thurs.
The menu changes daily at this casual eatery right across the street from one of Marie-Galante's most beautiful beaches. Expect to see sea urchin fritters, grilled fish, and Creole blood sausages. If *ouassou* is offered, grab it. This large prawn-like delicacy, unique to the rivers of Guadeloupe and its islands, tastes like lobster and is just fabulous!

Guadeloupe Directory

Arrival and Departure

American Airlines makes year-round flights to Guadeloupe from more than 100 cities direct to San Juan, with nonstop connections to Guadeloupe via **American Eagle**. **Minerve Airlines**, a French charter carrier, has flights Friday-Sunday from New York during December-March peak season. **Air Canada** flies nonstop from Paris and Fort-de-France and has direct service from Miami, San Juan and Port-au-Prince. **Air Guadeloupe** flies daily from St. Martin and St. Maarten, St. Barts, Marie-Galante, La Desirade and Les Saintes. **LIAT** flies from St. Croix, Antigua and St. Maarten.

All flights arrive at La Raizet International Airport, 2.5 miles from Pointe-a-Pitre. It's easy to hire a cab, from the many lined up at the airport. Cars can be rented at the airport.

Business Hours

Stores open weekdays 9 a.m.–1 p.m. and 3–6 p.m. Banks open weekdays 8 a.m.–noon and 2–4 p.m. Some shops and banks are also open Saturday mornings.

Climate

The climate is tropical with an average temperature of 79 degrees F. The more humid and wet season runs between June and November.

Documents

If you're only staying up to three weeks, you need show only a current or expired passport (five years old or less) or proof of citizenship (voter's registration, birth certificate and official photo ID), as well as an ongoing or return ticket. Longer stays require a valid passport.

Electricity

Current is 220 volts, AC, 50 cycles. Adapters for U.S. appliances are needed.

Getting Around

Taxis are plentiful and fares are set by the government. Between 9 p.m. and 7 a.m., fares increase 40 percent. You will have to be able to speak French to hire radio cabs.

Buses throughout the island run from 5:30 a.m.–7:30 p.m., and connect the island's major towns to Pointe-a-Pitre. Conditions are modern. Bus stops are included along the road and in shelters marked arrêtbus, but buses will often stop if you flag them down. Fares are inexpensive but the schedules are not reliable and they are often too crowded for comfort. Avoid riding them before and after school.

Since biking is a major sport here, you won't feel alone if you rent one. Bike rentals average about $10 a day, somewhat more for mountain bikes. Vespas are also good vehicles to rent, costing about $40 a day, plus a $200 deposit or a major credit card.

Cars are easy to rent on Guadeloupe. You may use your own driver's license up to 20 days; after that you need to obtain an international driver's permit. Roads are excellent here (more than 1225 miles), though the hairpins on Basse-Terre will take some careful negotiating. Natives drive well but fast, so be aware of passers. Stick with the top names such as Hertz, Budget and Avis, in case there is trouble with your bill once you return home. In general, rentals here, about $60 a day, are a bit higher than on other islands. Check with your travel agent to see if prearranged rentals will save you money.

For some reason known only to Guadeloupeons (and even they're not too sure why), the three ferries that service Marie-Galante, Les Saintes and La Desirade all offer virtually the same schedule. It's quite an amusing sight as they all pull into Point-a-Pitre at the exact same time and vie for passengers. Each leaves Pointe-a-Pitre at about 8 a.m. and departs for the return at about 4 p.m.

Depending on the weather, the ferry ride can be quite rough, so take motion-sickness pills if you don't have great sea legs. Other times, it can be a smooth and exhilarating ride, especially if you sit on top in the open air. Call for information. **ATE** ☎ *(590) 95-13-43*, **Brudey Freres** ☎ *(590) 90-04-48* and **Princess Caroline** ☎ *(590) 99-53-79*.

Language

The official language is French. The African-influenced Creole is spoken by nearly everyone. Only some people speak English, so bring a French phrase book.

Medical Emergencies

There are five hospitals and 23 clinics in Guadeloupe. Your hotel or the tourist office can assist you in finding an English-speaking physician.

Money

The official currency is the French franc. The best exchange rate is to be found at banks or bureau de change; to convert francs back to dollars, you must go to a bank. For some reason, paying for purchases with dollar-denomination traveler's checks or credit cards may get you the best exchange rate.

Telephone

The area code is *590*. To phone from Guadeloupe, buy a "telecarte," a plastic credit card sold at post offices and other outlets marked "Teleporte en Vente Ici." Use these cards on phones marked "Telecom." Operator-assisted calls and those made from your hotel room are much more expensive.

Time

Guadeloupe is one hour later than Eastern standard time.

Tipping

Restaurants and bars are required by law to add a 15 percent service charge. Most taxi drivers don't expect tips, especially if they own their own cars. Room maids should be tipped $1–$2, bellboys 50 cents–$1 a bag.

Tourist Information

Brochures, maps and advice can be found at the Office Départemental du Tourisme de la Guadeloupe located near the waterfront in *Pointe-á-Pitre at 5 Pl. de la Banque*; ☎ *(590) 82-09-30*. The office is open Monday–Saturday. In the U.S. call ☎ *(213) 658-7462*.

When to Go

Between December and May. June–November is the humid and wet season.

GUADELOUPE HOTELS	RMS	RATES	PHONE	CR. CARDS
Basse-Terre				
Basse-Terre				
★★★★ **Villa Creole Hotel**	72	$71–$115	(590) 45-62-41	A, MC, V
★★★ **L'Auberge de Distillerie**	15	$105–$125	(590) 94-25-91	A, DC, MC, V

GUADELOUPE

GUADELOUPE HOTELS	RMS	RATES	PHONE	CR. CARDS
★★★ Relais Grand Soufriere	21	$49–$93		A, DC, MC, V
★★★ Sucrerie du Comte	50	$50–$100	(590) 28-60-17	MC

Grande-Terre

Gosier

★★★★ Canella Beach Residence	146	$87–$230	(590) 90-44-00	A, DC, MC, V

Grande-Terre

★★★ Plantation Ste. Marthe	120	$157–$315	(800) 333-1970	MC, V
★★★ Residence du Parc		$382–$868	(590) 23-78-50	A, MC, V
★★★ Tropical Club Hotel	84	$92–$192	(590) 23-78-38	A, MC, V
★★ Cottage Hotel	24	$112–$220	(590) 23-78-38	A, MC, V
★★ Domaine de l'Anse des Rochers	356	$80–$220	(590) 93-90-00	MC, V

Pointe-a-Pitre

★★★★★ Le Meridien St. Francois	265	$199–$285	(800) 543-4300	A, DC, MC, V
★★★★★ Le Meridien la Cocoteraie	50	$160–$680	(590) 88-79-81	A, MC, V
★★★★ Auberge de la Vieille Tour	136	$118–$231	(800) 221-4542	A, MC, V
★★★★ Club Med Caravelle	310	All-Inclusive	(800) 258-2633	A
★★★★ Fleur d'Epee Novotel	190	$123–$213	(800) 221-4542	A, DC, MC, V
★★★★ Hotel Hamak Beach	56	$175–$255	(590) 88-59-59	A, CB, MC
★★★★ La Creole Beach Hotel	321	$60–$550	(590) 90-46-46	A, DC, MC, V
★★★★ PLM Azur Marissol Hotel	200	$94–$185	(590) 90-84-44	A, DC, MC, V
★★ Auberge du Grand Large	10	$100–$105	(590) 88-20-06	A, MC, V
★★ Ecotel Guadeloupe	44	$60–$130	(590) 90-60-00	A, DC, MC, V
★★ Hotel Arawak	154	$130–$240	(590) 84-24-24	A, DC, MC, V
★ Callinago Hotel & Village	110	$102–$216	(590) 84-25-25	A, DC, MC, V
★ Kaliko Beach Club	40	$80–$99	(590) 22-80-40	A, MC, V

Sainte-Anne

★★★ Hotel Toubana	32	$105–$230	(590) 88-25-78	A, DC, MC, V
★★ Mini Beach Hotel	9	$70–$150	(590) 88-21-13	MC, V
★ Relais du Moulin	40	$105–$156	(590) 88-23-96	A, DC, MC, V

GUADELOUPE

GUADELOUPE HOTELS		RMS	RATES	PHONE	CR. CARDS
Lles des Saintes					

Terre-de-Haut

★★★★	Auberge les Petits Saints	10	$65–$130	(590) 99-50-99	MC, V
★★★★	Village Creole	22	$80–$168	(590) 99-53-83	CB, MC, V
★★★	Hotel Bois Joli	40	$98–$192	(590) 99-52-53	MC, V

Marie-Galante

★★★★	Village de Menard	5	$60–$100	(590) 97-77-02	MC, V
★★★	Auberge de l'Arbre a Pain	7	$40–$50	(590) 97-73-69	
★	Le Salut	15	$34–$50	(590) 97-02-67	

GUADELOUPE RESTAURANTS		PHONE	ENTRÉE	CR. CARDS
Basse-Terre				

Basse-Terre

French				
★★★★	La Rocher de Malendure	(590) 98-70-84	$8–$18	DC, MC, V

International				
★★★	Chez Paul de Matouba	(590) 80-29-20	$12–$18	MC, V

Latin American				
★★★	Chez Clara	(590) 28-72-99	$9–$27	MC, V

Grande-Terre

Pointe-a-Pitre

★★	Sucrerie du Comte	(590) 28-60-17	$13–$35	MC

French				
★★★★★	Auberge de la Vielle Tour	(590) 84-23-23	$23–$39	A, DC, MC, V
★★★★★	La Canne A Sucre	(590) 82-10-19	$18–$32	A, MC, V
★★★★★	La Plantation	(590) 90-84-83	$14–$54	A, DC, MC, V
★★★★★	Le Chateau de Feuilles	(590) 22-30-30	$18–$29	MC, V
★★★	Chez Violetta	(590) 84-10-34	$11–$25	A, DC, MC, V
★★★	La Louisiane	(590) 88-44-34	$22–$30	MC, V
★★★	Le Restaurant	(590) 88-23-96	$25–$40	A, DC, MC, V
★★★	Les Oiseaux		$14–$29	V

GUADELOUPE

GUADELOUPE RESTAURANTS	PHONE	ENTRÉE	CR. CARDS
★★★ **Victoria**	(590) 23-78-38	$10–$37	MC, V
★★ **Folie Plage**	(590) 22-11-17	$14–$18	A, DC, V
Latin American			
★★★ **Le Poisson d'Or**	(590) 22-88-63	$14–$27	MC, V

Lies des Saintes

Terre de Haute

★★★ **Nilce's Bar**	(590) 99-56-80		
International			
★★ **La Saladerie**	(590) 99-50-92	$7–$19	MC, V
Latin American			
★★ **Le Amandiers**	(590) 99-50-06	$12–$16	A, MC, V
Seafood			
★★ **Le Jardin Creole**	(590) 99-55-08	$4–$14	DC, MC, V

Marie-Galante

Creole			
★★ **Auberge de la Roche d'Or**	(590) 97-37-42	$20–$30	
★★ **La Braise Marine**	(590) 97-42-57	$8–$30	
International			
★★ **L'Auberge L'Arbre a Pain**	(590) 97-73-69	$10–$30	V

JAMAICA

Jamaica is famous for its magnificent waterfalls.

Certainly one of the most popular Caribbean islands, Jamaica is also the Caribbean's third largest, totaling some 4411 square miles that encompass picture-postcard beaches, dramatic coastlines, towering mountains, lush valleys, plunging waterfalls and 120—count 'em—rivers. While the pleasures on some small islands are confined to beaches and watersports, Jamaica offers visitors just about anything they could possibly want—all to the thriving, ever-present reggae beat.

Besides the well-known tourist areas of Montego Bay and Ocho Rios, Jamaica offers the vibrant city life of Kingston, the historic mountain village of Mandeville, the laid-back charm of Port Antonio and the flower-child enclave of Negril, which is fast becoming one of the nation's biggest draws.

Choose "Mo Bay" if you'd like all the modern resort amenities, restaurants, watersports, golf courses and great beaches—but note that the area has become so touristy it has an almost generic feel. Life's a bit more laid-back in Ocho Rios, home of fine accommodations, historic plantations and the famous, 600-foot-high Dunn's River Falls. With its high crime rate, Kingston is not for everyone, but those seeking more than the typical island escape can revel in its myriad cultural attractions and vibrant nightlife. Mandeville is a mountain-lover's delight complete with historic buildings, mineral baths, bird-watching tours and the island's oldest golf course. Port Antonio, called the most exquisite port on earth, is an interesting mix of well-heeled resorts and an unassuming village that belies the fact that this is a place frequented by the rich and famous. Unfortunately, the word is out on funky Negril, long considered Jamaica's best-kept secret. Long a haven for hippie-types and Rastafarians, the village has come on strong as a tourist destination, though it still oozes with laid-back charm.

The island has more than 16,000 guestrooms, enabling tourists to book exactly what they want. The popular concept of all-inclusives resorts was born here and, as it rapidly spreads throughout the Caribbean like whitecaps on a windy day, Jamaica continues to refine the concept to ever-higher levels, with all-inclusives catering to couples, singles and families. You'll also find five-star resorts, affordable, low-frills hotels, hedonistic spa-resorts and small country inns.

Bird's-Eye View

Jamaica is the Caribbean's third-largest island (after Cuba and Puerto Rico), totaling 4411 square miles. It is located 1551 miles from New York. a nearly four-hour flight. The island is 146 miles long, with widths varying from 22 to 51 miles, and quite mountainous; almost half of the island lies 1000 feet above sea level. The highest point is Blue Mountain Peak, with rises up 7402 feet. Jamaica's other notable feature is its wealth of rivers—120 in all, which is quite unusual for the Caribbean. Floating downstream on bamboo rafts is a lovely way to spend a day; at night, some routes are romantically lit with tiki torches. If that's not your style, choose from 150 miles of beach where you can laze away the day.

The average temperature is 82 degrees Fahrenheit, and average rainfall is 78 inches, mostly occurring from October through November and May through June. Don't despair if you're coming during the rainy season, though—usually the rain falls in big, quick, bursts, then the clouds move

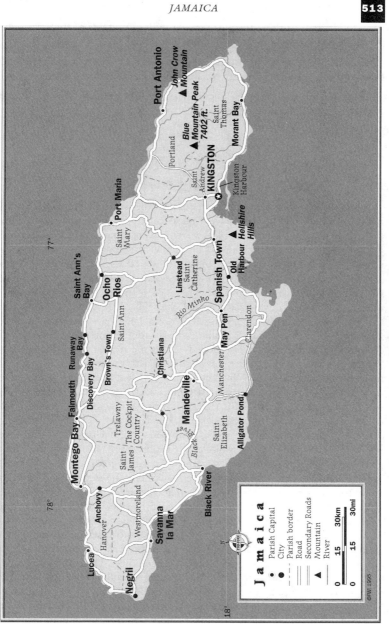

Port Antonio

John Crow Mountain ▲

Mountain Peak ▲

Blue ▲ Mountain Peak 7402 ft.

Saint Thomas

Morant Bay

Portland

Saint Andrew

KINGSTON ✪

Kingston Harbour

Port Maria

Saint Mary

▲ Hellshire Hills

Old Harbour

Spanish Town

Saint Ann's Bay

Ocho Rios

Linstead

Saint Catherine

Saint Ann

Rio Minho

May Pen

Runaway Bay

Brown's Town

Discovery Bay

Falmouth

Christiana

Clarendon

Montego Bay

Trelawny

The Cockpit Country

Mandeville

Manchester

Saint James

Saint Elizabeth

Alligator Pond

Anchovy

Black River

Black River

Hanover

Westmoreland

Savanna la Mar

Lucea

Negril

77°

78°

18°

Jamaica

● Parish Capital
● City
– · – Parish border
═══ Road
═══ Secondary Roads
▲ Mountain
—— River

0   15   30km
0   15   30mi

N

©PW 1995

away to let the sun shine through. In the high mountains of the east, temperatures can drop as low as 40 degrees Fahrenheit.

Much of the island is limestone, and there are a variety of underground caves and offshore reefs that are the delight of divers and snorkelers.

Kingston, the capital city, has more than 700,000 residents, making it one of the Caribbean's largest cities.

History

Columbus first glimpsed the north coast of the island in May 1494, landing in Montego Bay before he went back to Cuba. When he returned nine years later, stormy weather crippled two of his ships and he was forced to anchor at St. Ann's Bay, where he and his men were shipwrecked until the governor of Hispaniola retrieved them. In 1510, a permanent Spanish settlement was finally established under the orders of Don Diego, the son of Columbus, who was then governor of the West Indies, based in Santo Domingo. A new capital was erected in 1935 at Villa de la Vega (the Town on the Plain), now known as Spanish Town. In 1655, Britain, under Oliver Cromwell, challenged Spain's claim on the island, ultimately triumphing and establishing a head base at Port Royal, across the harbor from what is now Kingston. (The Spaniards fled to Windsor Cave, the home even today of many of their descendants.) The new headquarters at Port Royal became the hub of some of the most nefarious activities on the high seas, under the direction of the buccaneer Henry Morgan, whose sacking of the Spanish colony in Panama clinched England's claim to Jamaica. A massive earthquake in 1692 actually shook half the town—like Sodom and Gomorrah—into the sea. The multi-ethnic, though black-based, population of Jamaica began to grow over the next centuries as sugarcane farming took root, and the need for imported labor in the form of black slaves became imperative. After Jamaica's slave population rose to 300,000 at the end of the 18th century, the ratio of blacks to whites was a staggering 15 to one. Included in the mix were "free coloureds," the offspring of white men and slave women, and Maroons, descendants of free slaves. (For more information about the Maroons, see below under "People.") Slave revolts became a common occurrence in Jamaica, the largest, bloodiest conflict led by "Daddy" Sam Sharpe, a Baptist preacher whose oratory and convictions led the way to the abolishment of slavery in Jamaica in 1838. Emancipation, however, led directly to the fall of the sugarcane industry since there was a decided lack of labor. The condition of the freed blacks was further worsened by drought and unsteady economic conditions, leading to another revolt in 1865, which resulted in the murder of a government official. As a result, the island was designated a British Crown Colony in 1866, which it remained until 1944, when full adult suffrage was granted.

A British colony from 1655–1962, Jamaica developed a two-party system before World War II. A considerable measure of self-government was introduced in 1944, but full independence was delayed by attempts to set up a wider federation embracing all or most of the Caribbean Commonwealth territories. Jamaica joined the now-defunct West Indies Federation in 1958, but withdrew in 1961 because of disagreements over taxation, voting rights, and location of the federal capital. Sir Alexander Bustaments, one of the original founders of the two-party system, became the nation's first prime minister at independence in 1962. Under the 1962 constitution, the Queen is the titular head of state. Her representative, a governor general, is advised in areas bearing on the royal perogative, by a six-member privy council. Jamaica is divided into 13 parishes and the Kingston and St. Andrew Corporation, a special administrative entity encompassing the principal urban areas.

People

The country's motto, "Out of Many, One People," is certainly appropriate for Jamaica. The population of 2.4 million is a racial mix of African, European, Afro-European, East Indian, Afro-East Indian, Chinese and Afro-Chinese. A visible minority follows the religion Rastafarianism, characterized by dreadlocks and a great love of marijuana, locally called *ganga*. Rastas believe the late Emperor Haile Selassie was a divine being who believed God would lead the blacks from oppression to the Promised Land. Though they can look scary with their ratty, unwashed hair, often tucked into huge knit caps, Rastas are actually a nonviolent, peace-loving people. But, as with all Jamaicans (indeed, all peoples everywhere) it is considered very rude to take a photo without first asking permission—and if it is refused, accept politely. Other religions include Protestant (the majority belong to the Church of Jamaica, formerly the Church of England), Roman Catholic, Judaism, Seventh Day Adventists, Pentecostals, even Muslims, Hindus and Quakers.

Another interesting minority lives in the rugged Cockpit country. The Maroons are descendants of escaped slaves who eluded capture for some 100 years, and their modern leaders are believed to have spiritual powers. Chances are you won't encounter any Maroons—they live hidden inside the hills in villages barely reached by road. If you do try to find them, use caution; some tourists report being forced to pay a "road tax" by Maroons bearing machetes.

Jamaicans are a cheerful, outgoing group with a great sense of humor and a fierce national pride. The reply to any statement or query will invariably be "no problem, mon," and it's not sarcasm, but a truly held belief that things will work out. You'll also hear a lot of "*irie*" (EYE-ree), which means "everything's okay." English is the official language, spoken in a charming musical lilt, and many also speak Patios, a blend of English and African.

For a great change to really know Jamaica, sign up for the Meet the People program, in which you'll be matched with a volunteer Jamaican family with similar interests. Arrange this far in advance by calling the Jamaica Tourist Board at ☎ *(800) 233-4582.*

Jamaicans love their music, particularly reggae, made popular throughout the world by Bob Marley, something of a national hero. You'll hear it everywhere, and one of the nicest pleasures of a Jamaican sojourn is simply listening to the radio.

INSIDER TIP

Note: Illegal under Jamaican law, the "herb" locally called ganja (marijuana) is known to be a major source of income in the highlands. Officials, however, claim that ganja does not grow anywhere in the residential areas, adding that if it grows "anywhere," it is in the wilderness.

Beaches

The best way to acquaint yourself with the beaches of Jamaica—before even buying a ticket—is to rent a video of the first James Bond film, *Dr. No*—it's practically a travel promotional for the island's most beautiful strands. Then look for more specific information under the individual areas—Kingston, Montego Bay, Port Antonio—below.

Underwater

Although the deep Cayman Trench lies off Jamaica's north coast, one unfortunate trade-off on a densely populated Caribbean island is that every shoreline is a potential fishing area. As such, divers will find most of Jamaica's touristy north coast overfished and barren, despite having attractive reef architecture and well-developed sponge life. The island's main exception is **Negril**, situated on the smallish west coast, and more protected from the wind and currents that sometimes play havoc with the rest of the island. Negril's 10-mile reef parallels the beach and encircles nearby Booby Cay, and features more than 40 known dive sites at all levels of ability. **Montego Bay** is the location of Jamaica's first marine park, but virtually all sites close to shore are well-trammeled and contain few fish. The **Falmouth/Runaway Bay** area represents probably the best of the north coast diving; fish life is a little better developed, and the reef structure features good wall and canyon diving. The name Ocho Rios translates to eight rivers, each of which come pouring down from the mountains and can create less-than-stellar underwater visibility after wet weather. Otherwise, north coast diving visibility averages 60 to 100 feet, with occasional summer days soaring to 150 feet.

The true dive frontier of Jamaica lies on the largely unvisited south coast, where offshore cays, wrecks and walls, await more extensive exploration. One of the Caribbean's most unusual underwater locations is a veritable sunken Pompeii lying in Kingston Harbor, **Port Royal**. The current (aboveground) fishing village of the same name bears little resemblance to its former self: a pirate lair that was once referred to as "the wickedest city in Christendom," and which succumbed to a devastating earthquake in 1692 by sinking, literally, into the bay. Old Port Royal has since been frozen in time over the ensuing 300 years, collecting silt and rust from the harbor; unfortunately, the government has closed the site to sport diving while it contemplates how best to salvage the site. There are other locations to enjoy, including **Wreck Reef**, a shallow bank of coral off the Hellshire Hills which has proven a disastrous magnet for many ships. Visibility off Kingston is limited by harbor traffic and turbulent waters, but averages 50 to 70 feet. A fledgling operation has recently sprung up at tiny **Alligator Pond**, and offers diving along the southern offshore reefs with some success.

A local saying has it that "you can walk anywhere in Jamaica." Maybe so, but hiking in Jamaica is no small adventure. The 14- or 27-mile trek to the 7402-foot summit of the **Blue Mountains** takes the better part of two days. Nighttime temperatures can drop to freezing in this magnificent mountain range, the second-highest in the Caribbean. Several areas of the country are rarely traveled, and at least one range, the **John Crow Mountains** above Port Antonio, have been uncharted since a major British expedition explored in

1819. Shorter trails are few and far between, although there are plenty of goat paths and unmarked foot trails that will appeal to intrepid walkers. In sum, the wilds of Jamaica are truly spectacular, but are best ventured through in the company of a qualified guide.

The island features a great diversity of flowering plants—about 3000—and among the species, 827 are found only on Jamaica. Jamaica boasts more than 550 types of fern, most of which are found in lovely **Fern Gully** near Ocho Rios. Jamaica's wildlife is also a chief asset in the island's first tentative steps toward developing eco-tourism. An endemic lizard, the Jamaican iguana, was thought to be extinct for several decades, but a family made an appearance in 1990 in the **Hellshire Hills** southwest of Kingston, an uninhabited area that local conservationists are now trying to protect. The Jamaican boa grows to eight feet and also lives in these gentle hills of dry scrub and cactus. Several species of snake on the island; none are poisonous. A very rare native butterfly, *Papillio homerus*—one of the world's largest—can sometimes be spotted in the foothills of the John Crow Mountains. Several places outside the rugged Blue Mountains invite birdwatching: the Kingston foothills and nearby Clydesdale National Park (near Hardwar Gap), Marshall's Pen (a nature reserve three miles outside Mandeville), the Black River area, the mangrove swamps of Falmouth Lagoon, and on the trails surrounding the Rockland Bird Sanctuary, west of Montego Bay. A 1990 book, *Birds of Jamaica: A Photographic Field Guide* by Audrey Downer and Robert Sutton, can be located in some stores and will aid in identifying the island's many species.

In addition to the popular Blue Mountain Peak hike, a classic 25-mile trading route between Kingston and Port Antonio, the **Vinegar Hill Trail**, is available for those excited by a true, jungle backpacking adventure (allow two-to-three days). Another ambitious hike is one which traverses the mysterious **Cockpit Country**, from the village of Cockpit to Windsor Caves (nine miles each way); the muggy area can only be visited on foot, but reveals a strange landscape of limestone karst formations and a reclusive community of ex-slaves, the Maroons. Both of these rewarding treks should be undertaken only with a guide. A simpler excursion for those wanting to experience the Blue Mountains without the commitment of an overnight adventure are the paths which climb above Jack's Hill to Peter's Rock (two hours) and nearby points. **Catherine's Peak** (5060 feet) can be attained via a short military track out of Newcastle; this and other nearby trails are maintained by the forestry department, which has an office in Hollywell. An area that may eventually develop into a hiking destination is the **Montego Bay River Valley**, a surprising respite from the pace and intensity of Montego Bay, but trails are not yet marked or mapped, leaving this a somewhat spunky option without a guide. Although the vast majority of Jamaicans are friendly and helpful, and are proud to show off their verdant backcountry, it's worth noting that some in-nocent-looking paths may wind up in the middle of an otherwise secluded *ganja* field. Those who till these fields are understandably protective of their illegal crop; these are not places to hang out should you stumble onto one. When hiking below 3000 feet and near cow pastures, you'll need to be pre-pared for ticks, particularly during February and March; in swampy areas, mosquitoes are generally combated with repellent. The topographical map is the best resource for heading off the beaten track, and is available at the Land and Survey department in Kingston on Charles Street; unfortunately, black-and-white reproductions are all that are available at this writing.

Blue Mountain Peak

One of the Caribbean's premiere treks ascends the lush, stream-carved slopes of the Blue Mountains, which represent the majestic eastern spine of the island between Kingston and Port Antonio. Although there are several summits in the range, the main crest (Blue Mountain Peak), is a lofty goal and requires most of two days to accomplish, one night spent halfway up in a hostel. The 27-mile trail (a shorter option is explained below) begins in the town of Mavis Bank, elevation 2500 feet, where a coffee plantation processes the famed Blue Mountain coffee grown on the slopes above you. From here, the track drops into a valley, crosses two rivers and then ascends an exposed hillside to village of Penlyne Castle (elevation 3900 feet), and continues for a mile through fields of banana, coffee and vegetable gardens. Typically, this seven-mile section of the hike is done in the afternoon, reaching accommodations before dusk (Either Whitfield Hall Hostel, a rustic plantation house, or Wildflower Lodge, a newer facility with views; both have showers avail-able, but no electricity or meal service, $12.50 per person at either location). The next morning, you'll climb Jacob's Ladder, the steepest part of the trek, and then ascend a series of switchbacks through tree ferns and elfin forest that lead to the summit, 7502 feet above sea level. The summit is usually shrouded in clouds and can actually be quite chilly; you'll need to come prepared with a windbreaker, sweater and long pants, particularly in the winter months. If you are lucky to have reached the summit on a cloudless day, you'll see Kingston and Port Antonio, and possibly Cuba, 90 miles to the north. One popular plan is to depart the hostel about 2 a.m. and reach the summit just prior to sunrise, which is the most likely time for clear skies; you'll need to carry a flashlight, even if traveling under the light of a full moon. A shorter option is available by driving a four-wheel vehicle on a difficult road to Penlyne Castle, reducing the trek to 13 miles round-trip. Although the trail is long and requires some stamina, it is well-marked and not technically difficult; a guide is a good idea if you are new to hiking in the region, but not necessary for those comfortable in a rugged rainforest environment.

Trekking Shops

Sense Adventures

Jack's Hill; ☎ *(809) 927-2097.*

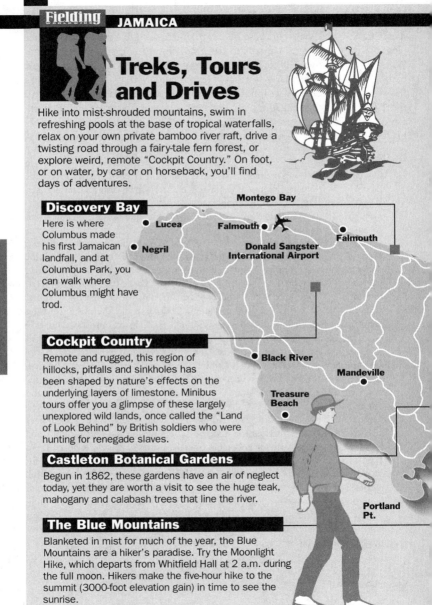

Fielding JAMAICA

Treks, Tours and Drives

Hike into mist-shrouded mountains, swim in refreshing pools at the base of tropical waterfalls, relax on your own private bamboo river raft, drive a twisting road through a fairy-tale fern forest, or explore weird, remote "Cockpit Country." On foot, or on water, by car or on horseback, you'll find days of adventures.

Discovery Bay

Here is where Columbus made his first Jamaican landfall, and at Columbus Park, you can walk where Columbus might have trod.

Cockpit Country

Remote and rugged, this region of hillocks, pitfalls and sinkholes has been shaped by nature's effects on the underlying layers of limestone. Minibus tours offer you a glimpse of these largely unexplored wild lands, once called the "Land of Look Behind" by British soldiers who were hunting for renegade slaves.

Castleton Botanical Gardens

Begun in 1862, these gardens have an air of neglect today, yet they are worth a visit to see the huge teak, mahogany and calabash trees that line the river.

The Blue Mountains

Blanketed in mist for much of the year, the Blue Mountains are a hiker's paradise. Try the Moonlight Hike, which departs from Whitfield Hall at 2 a.m. during the full moon. Hikers make the five-hour hike to the summit (3000-foot elevation gain) in time to see the sunrise.

Dunn's River Falls

Fed by the Ocho Rios, these 600-foot falls spill down stone "steps" into the Caribbean. The boulders provide slippery footing for a popular hike where swimsuit-clad tourists, arms linked in a human chain, scramble up the rocks.

Fern Gully Auto Road

Jamaica is home to 500 species of fern, and you'll see dozens of varieties on this three-mile stretch of road. The ferns, trees and bamboo clusters are so large they form an overhead canopy.

Ocho Rios

Known as the "Garden of Jamaica," this region is home to the Fern Gully, Dunn's River Falls and other sites. Spend time at the Shaw Park Botanical Gardens, a lovely landscaped retreat, or ramble through the Prospect Plantation, a 1100-acre plantation that features tours by jitney or horseback.

Rio Grande Rafting

Don't leave Jamaica without taking a ride on the long, slim bamboo rafts that ply an eight-mile stretch of the Rio Grande River from Berrydale to Rafter's Rest near St. Margaret Bay. Enjoy lunch on your raft while the rafter poles you along for a three-hour tour.

Blue Hole

Six miles east of Port Antonio, this crater-like lagoon has depths that range from 185 to 282 feet. Fed by freshwater springs, the lagoon is a popular swimming hole, and has the reputation for enhancing virility.

Ocho Rios

Boston Bay

Kingston

Spanish Town

St. Margaret's Bay

Blue Mountains

Holland Bay

Norman Manley International Airport

Golden Grove

President of the Jamaican Alternative Tourism, Camping and Hiking Association, Peter Bentley oversees this guide company that specializes in two-day treks to Blue Mountain Peak, $125 per person including ground transportation to the Penlyne Castle hostels (or $75 per person if hiking from Mavis Bank). Other itineraries include day-trips in the Newcastle area, iguana tours, raft and canoe trips and "clothes optional recreation." Bentley's operation is based out of the Maya Lodge overlooking Kingston.

Perhaps wisely intimidated by the bristling pace of minibus (and other) drivers, cyclists have yet to find their niche in Jamaica. As overwhelming as vehicular traffic can be, it's heavily concentrated along the north coast drag, between Negril and Ocho Rios, and in the vicinity of Kingston. Surprisingly, visiting riders tell us that even north coast drivers are actually respectful of cyclists, providing they spot you as they careen around those hairpin turns. Although there aren't many east-west alternates to this well-traveled corridor, heading into the hills along some of the dirt or so-called "inoperable" roads will transport you to the real Jamaica, the one which exists outside the purview of most tourists. Distances can be deceiving on this big island—plot your general route in advance, carry a good road map and don't be shy about requesting directions from villagers (you'll be at least as curious a sight to them as vice versa). If you're determined to tour the north coast, consider the beautiful stretch between Port Maria (20 miles east of Ocho Rios) and Port Antonio. This magnificent, 40-mile ride (one way) visits breezy bays, cool forests and rolling coastline, with friendly locals vastly outnumbering tourists en route to east coast resorts (the ill-maintained road past Port Antonio around the eastern tip of the island is known for bad drivers). Out of Montego Bay, one attractive 40-mile loop heads east out of town on route B15 (not the coastal road) up the lush Montego River Valley to Wakefield. From here, rough, potholed roads head south toward Maroon Town, skirting the northwest side of the Cockpit Country, and then descend back into Montego Bay using the other side of the valley you came up. Both of these rides, and virtually any others heading off the busy road between Negril and Ocho Rios, are best-suited for mountain bikes. A circuit of the entire island is roughly 435 miles, though there are a number of possibilities to shorten or extend that figure; plan to maintain a flexible itinerary and allow at least 10 days. For those bringing their own bikes onto the island, there are repair shops in Montego Bay, Ocho Rios and Kingston. It may be overstating the obvious, but always wear a helmet, and do not ride after dark; Jamaican traffic accidents result in hundreds of deaths annually.

Bike Tours and Rental Shops

Blue Mountain Tours

Ocho Rios; ☎ *(809) 974-7075.*
Six-hour, 18-mile guided rides in the Blue Mountains, $78; includes transportation, brunch and lunch and 18-speed mountain bike.

Montego Bike Rentals

Walter Fletcher Beach, Montego Bay; ☎ *(809) 952-4984.*
Rents Diamond Back and other mountain bikes; $10 per day, weekly rentals, $65. 15 bikes on hand.

Though its 120 rivers occasionally muddy up the ocean, Jamaica's water is generally clean and clear and makes for great diving and snorkeling. Visibility does suffer, however, after heavy rains The large influx of tourists can mean few fish at overly popular spots such as Montego Bay's underwater park. Diving is especially good off the shores of Negril and along the south coast.

Hiking is popular in this mountainous country; if you're among the adventurous who attempt to scale 7402-foot Blue Mountain Peak, plan on at least two days to reach the summit. Backpackers may also want to tackle the Vinegar Hill Trail, a 25-mile trading route between Kingston and Port Antonio.

For more sedate pleasures, Jamaica boasts 11 golf courses, tennis at most of the major resorts, and excellent horseback riding at **Chukka Cove** in Ocho Rios (☎ *[809] 972-2506*), among other places. Deep-sea fishing for yellowfin tuna, sailfish, blue marlin and bonito can be arranged through your hotel or a number of independent operators. Reputable operators of recreational activities are licensed through the tourist board; stick with the identifying decal to be assured of professional service.

Where to Stay

Fielding's Highest Rated Hotels in Jamaica

★★★★★	Grand Lido	$350–$290
★★★★★	Half Moon Beach Club	$255–$805
★★★★★	Round Hill Hotel & Villas	$160–$420
★★★★★	Sans Souci Lido	$465–$945
★★★★★	Trident Villas & Hotel	$255–$755
★★★★	Breezes Runaway Bay	$240–$439
★★★★	Jamaica Inn	$200–$475
★★★★	Negril Tree House	$85–$275
★★★★	Plantation Inn	$300–$999
★★★★	Tryall Resort	$235–$465

Fielding's Most Exclusive Hotels in Jamaica

★★★★★	Sans Souci Lido	$465–$945
★★★★★	Trident Villas & Hotel	$255–$755
★★★★	Boscobel Beach Hotel	$415–$995
★★★★	Ciboney Ocho Rios	$175–$690
★★★★	Tryall Resort	$235–$465

Fielding's Best Value Hotels in Jamaica

★★★	Natania's Guest House	$50–$60
★★★	H.E.A.R.T. Country Club	$55–$75
★★★	Rock Cliff Resort	$55–$100
★★★	Hibiscus Lodge	$65–$93
★★	Coral Cliff Hotel	$54–$64

Jamaica has a wealth of accommodations to suit every taste. The island invented the popular concept of the all-inclusive resort, where one price pays for a room, all meals, drinks, most watersports, nightly entertainment and lots of activities. These all-inclusives aren't for everyone, as the rooms are generally on the basic side and guests can sometimes feel practically forced into participating in corny group activities. Another downside is that the all-inclusives are practically walled fortresses with heavy security (true for virtually all the resorts on the island), so if you don't venture off the grounds you'll never get a feel for the real Jamaica. But there is a lot to be said for the relaxation that comes from having every whim catered to under one roof, so to speak, and knowing exactly what your vacation will cost beforehand.

If an all-inclusive is not for you, consider one of Jamaica's many fine resorts, which sit right on the beach and offer plush amenities. Those on a budget should consider a housekeeping unit; although the price of groceries on the island is high, you'll still save money over the cost eating all meals out.

The tourism infrastructure is so well-developed that there are many housing options in Jamaica. Many hotels are dedicated on-the-property dive services, from villas (Villa Draybar at Ocho Rios) to smaller dive resorts such as Fisherman's Inn in Falmouth to small hotels such as Seaworld's Cariblue (Montego Bay) and Rock Cliff (Negril), the larger all-inclusive resorts. The all-inclusive has become one of Jamaica's most popular resort options—in fact, winter occupancies have risen back to the 80–90 percent range because of their popularity. One prepaid fee covers everything from food to alcohol to water- and land-sports and some island excursions. Resorts can be luxurious with long beaches, superb dining, sports facilities and entertainment, such as Hedonism in Negril (though it is a dedicated singles resort). Others are geared for couples or families, while still others have an open policy. The focus of activities at these all-inclusive resorts vary. Some, including Swept Away in Negril or Jamaica, Jamaica in Runaway Bay, are very sports- and health-oriented. While some resorts have dedicated dive operations, others will offer only a single tank per day. Do research and contact the resort to ask questions before you go. Many a misunderstanding that might have been diverted with some careful questioning has resulted in near-disaster vacations. (For more information, see "Where to Stay" under the individual sections.)

Where to Eat

Fielding's Highest Rated Restaurants in Jamaica

★★★★★	Evita's	$7–$19
★★★★★	Reading Reef Club	$10–$24
★★★★★	Temple Hall	$25–$25
★★★★★	Trident Hotel Restaurant	$50
★★★★	Almond Tree	$12–$26
★★★★	Blue Mountain Inn	$12–$24
★★★★	Norma's at the Wharfhouse	$26–$34
★★★★	Sugar Mill	$14–$31
★★★	De Montevin Lodge	$11–$18
★★★	Pork Pit	$2–$9

Fielding's Most Exclusive Restaurants in Jamaica

★★★★★	Trident Hotel Restaurant	$50
★★★★	Norma's at the Wharfhouse	$26–$34
★★★★★	Temple Hall	$25–$25
★★★★	Sugar Mill	$14–$31
★★★★	Almond Tree	$12–$26

Fielding's Best Value Restaurants in Jamaica

★★★	Pork Pit	$2–$9
★★	Hot Pot, The	$3–$4
★★	Chicken Lavish	$3–$5
★★★★★	Evita's	$7–$19
★★★★★	Reading Reef Club	$10–$24

With its sophisticated tourist infrastructure, rest assured Jamaica has suburb restaurants island-wide to suit any palate. Jamaica's harmonious mix of many races and religions translates into an impressive international cuisine Rastafarian restaurants, which don't serve alcohol or meat (both taboo in the religion) are great for tasty vegetarian fare; specialties include Rasta Pasta, which features the Rasta colors of red (tomatoes), green (bell peppers) and gold (*ackee*), all served over pasta. Other typical Rasta ingredients include *choco* (a pear-shaped squash), pumpkin, yams and *callallo*, a spinach-like vegetable. You'll also see johnnycakes and *bammies* (Ameridian cassava bread) on the menu.

Jerked cooking—barbecuing over spiced wood such as green pimento or allspice—is extremely popular throughout the island, and you'll see many a roadside stand offering jerked chicken and pork.

Other Jamaican specialties include some that are reportedly aphrodisiacs, including *cowfoot soup* (a spicy stew of cow feet and vegetables) and *mannish water* (goat meat and vegetable soup flavored with white rum and hot peppers). If you're not brave enough for either, stick to bun (a dark fruitcake served with cheese), *matrimony* (orange and star apple pulp in cream), Solomon gundy (spiced pickled herring) and rundown (mackerel or codfish boiled in coconut milk and served with ashed onions and peppers). The national dish is saltfish and *ackee*, gently spiced.

The motto "Out of many, one people" goes as much for politics as it does for cuisine in Jamaica—for the influences that have gone into the *dutchie*, or cast-iron cooking pot, to create Jamaican menus, are many—the barbecuing techniques of the Arawaks, the African meat-preserving techniques in the country's best known dish, jerk pork; Spanish marinades meet New World vegetables in twice-cooked *escovitch* fish. British **cornish pastries**, which are meat-and-potato-filled pastries, have become Jamaican spicy beef patties. And the spices of Asia and the Levant come together in dishes such as curried goat. Today nouvelle cuisine is also dressing up traditional ingredients in trendy resort restaurants along the North Coast. Rastafarianism—Jamaica's contribution to 20th-century religion—has created a cuisine all its own, one that places the accent on nature's bounty. Rastas don't drink alcohol or eat meat, but their vegetarian cooking is delicious, including hearty vegetable stews with ingredients such as *callallo* (a spinach-like vegetable), *chocho* (a pear-shaped squash), pumpkin and yams. Johnnycakes—flat, dense, unleavened breads—were a slave adaptation of British breads, while *bammie* was the Amerindian cassava bread that Columbus wrote about in his journals. One of the foundations of Jamaican cooking is "poor folk's food," such as codfish, stew peas and roast breadfruit. It takes some experience to learn to like boiled green bananas as a breakfast dish.

JAMAICA

Other Jamaican delicacies include: *bun* (a dark fruitcake served with cheese usually at Easter time); *cowfoot soup* (spicy soup of cow trotters and vegetables, claimed by Jamaican men to be an aphrodisiac); *dunkanoo* (a dessert of grated corn, flavored with sugar, cinnamon, ginger, and coconut milk, and steamed in a banana leaf); *pepper rum* (a mixture of fiery Scotch bonnet chiles and dark rum, used as a seasoning); *matrimony* (a dessert that blends orange segments with star apple pulp in cream); *mannish water* (a heavy goatmeat and vegetable soup, flavored with white rum and hot peppers; *rundown* (mackerel or codfish boiled in coconut milk and eaten with ashed onions and peppers); *Solomon gundy* (pungent spiced pickled herring); and *stamp-and-go* (batter-fried saltfish fritters, usually eaten as a finger snack).

In Kingston, Sunday brunch is special at Devon House, a restored historic home dear to many Jamaicans for its food and ice cream. Seated on the wide veranda of mansions such as The Coffee Terrace, with whirling fans overhead, you can indulge in fluffy yellow *ackee*, a Jamaican-grown tree vegetable, whose custardy flesh tastes and looks somewhat like scrambled eggs. This mixture of the savory *ackee* and salt fish harks back to the days of slavery when feeding the slaves was a major concern for plantation owners. **Jerked cooking** is a method of barbecue using well-seasoned meat, said to have originated with the Maroons, the fierce, escaped slaves who retreated to the mountains of Cockpit Country and kept the British at bay for more than a century. They would roast pork over hot coals in earthen pits that were covered with branches of green pimento or allspice wood. The smoking wood is what provides the unique seasoning. At Boston Beach today, pit men such as Vasco "Kojak" Allen at Front Line #1, are famous for their grill-work, which includes jerked pork, the classic dish, as well as jerked chicken, sausage, and fish.

In Ocho Rios, the **Ciboney Beach Resort** has some of the best options for dining: head for Orchid's, for pork chops filled with bread and chutney, or the alfresco **Casa Nina**, for ackee and callallo. The **Ciboney Grill and Market Place** is designed like a Jamaican outdoor market with colorful food stalls.

In Montego Bay, the restaurant at the four-bedroom hostelry called **Norma's** at the Warehouse is a treasurehouse of delicacies, from smoked marlin with papaya salsa to roast loin pork with prunes. Desserts run the course between plantain turnover with brandied whipped cream or a vine-ripened papaya, with a drizzle of island grown ortanique (cross between an orange and a tangerine). Less fancy digs on the North Coast include the **Rite Stuff Café** and Caterers in Montego Bay's Westgate Plaza, where you can dig into curried goat, stew bee, or a steaming bowl of pumpkin soup. Meat patties, flaky turnovers stuffed with a savory chopped meat and herb mixture, are a favorite snack on this island of nibblers.

Kingston

For many tourists, Kingston on first sight is everything they don't want in a Caribbean isle—grimy, traffic-clogged, polluted, noisy, crime-ridden and irrespressibly raucous, but it represents, nevertheless, the soul and spirit of most native islanders whose eyes wax over when they remember their childhood memories. This is where the ethnic melting pot first produced the crossbreeding that makes up the present heady spice called Jamaican society. What Kingston truly is today is Bob Marley turf, the undisputed (albeit deceased) king of reggae whose 1974 song "Lively Up Yourself" became the cry of the masses. Today you can't go anywhere in Kingston without making homage to his name; indeed, some travelers come to Kingston *only* for that. His dreadlocked statue stands in the middle of the square across from the National Arena and his records can be found in every store on the island. The **Bob Marley Museum**, ensconced into a 19th-century home on Hope Road, is a visual testimony to his life, struggles and musical influence.

To see the full variety of sights in Kingston, you will probably need to rent a car, or hire a taxi for the day. At the top of the itinerary should be the **Devon House**, a restored 19th-century mansion that first belonged to one of the Caribbean's first black millionaires, George Steibel. The **National Gallery of Jamaica** is a fine place to appreciate the island's art, from 17th-century portraits to impressionist paintings and sculptures. **Hope Botanical Gardens** is a lovely pace to stroll and enjoy the exotic flora of the island; Sundays are crowded but give you a chance to see Jamaican families in action. Across the harbor is **Port Royal**, or what is left of Port Royal, once the island's premier city in the 17th century when buccaneers ruled the waves. Henry Morgan, the British pirate, called the city his home, before it toppled, in 1692, into the harbor by an earthquake and subsequent tidal wave. There's still quite a lot left to see, including the cockeyed **Giddy House**, which has been tilting off-center since a 1907 earthquake, as well as **St. Peter's Church**, **Fort Charles** and the old **Naval Hospital**. At **Morgan's Harbor** marina you'll find a few restaurants, bar and small hotel.

West of Kingston is **Spanish Town**, Jamaica's old capital, with a few historical sites still standing. On the south coast, **Madeville** represents a quieter, calmer Jamaica. Bird-watchers will enjoy **Marshal's Pen**, an 18th-century greathouse set on a 300-acre wildlife sanctuary. Two of the best places to see the sunset are **Yardley Chase** and **South St. Elizabeth**. For touring the area as an ecologist, contact **South Coast Safaris** (on the Black Rover); ☎ *(809) 965-2513* for a 1.5-hour excursion covering 10 miles round-trip where you can photograph a variety of birds, crocodiles and other wildlife. Special fishing tours can also be arranged.

Beaches in Kingston

Gunboat Beach is one of the most popular beaches around Kingston. A rare black sand beach is found at **Fort Clarence**, tucked into the Hellshire Hills southwest of the city. There you'll find changing facilities and live entertainment. Locals think nothing of driving the 30-odd miles for the special surroundings at **Lyssons Beach** at Morant Bay, whose golden sands gleam in the sun.

A delightful excursion is to hire a boat at the Morgan's Harbor Marina at Port Royal to cruise to **Lime Cay**, an island just beyond Kingston Harbor. Here is an ideal place to picnic, swim and sunbathe.

City Celebrations

Reggae Sunsplash   ★

Jam World, Kingston.
The annual week-long party of all parties takes place each summer, usually in July. Lots of top-name reggae bands and groovin' folks. Book your hotel way in advance or you'll never get in.

Historical Sites

Devon House   ★★

26 Hope Road, Kingston, ☎ *(809) 929-7029.*
Hours open: 10 a.m.–5 p.m.
This 1881 mansion is filled with period furnishings but the best reason to come is for the excellent crafts shops on the grounds. There are two restaurants and a great ice cream shop. General admission: $2.

Museums and Exhibits

Bob Marley Museum   ★★★

56 Hope Road, Kingston, ☎ *(809) 927-9152.*
Hours open: 9:30 a.m.–4:30 p.m.
The national hero's clapboard house was his home and recording studio for many years. Reggae fans will appreciate the collection of Marley memorabilia and consider this a five-star attraction. Those not into Marley's brand of music can pass. General admission: $3.

Institute of Jamaica   ★★★

12 East Street, Kingston, ☎ *(809) 922-0620.*
Hours open: 8:30 a.m.–5 p.m.
This museum has excellent exhibits on the island's history, with some impressive old charts and almanacs. It also houses the National Library.

National Gallery ★★

12 Ocean Boulevard, Kingston, ☎ *(809) 922-1561.*

This waterfront gallery displays paintings, sculpture and other works of art by Jamaica's most famous artist, Kapo. Other artists' works include Edna Manley, Alvin Marriott, Isaac Belisari and Augustine Brunias.

Parks and Gardens

Royal Botanical Gardens ★★★

Hope Road, Kingston, ☎ *(809) 927-1257.*

A peaceful refuge from city life, these gardens encompass 50 acres. Most plants and trees are marked for identification.

Theater

Little Theatre ★★★

4 Tom Redcam Road, Kingston, ☎ *(809) 926-6129.*

This theater presents a variety of dramas, musical and special performances. Each December 26-April they produce the LTM Pantomime, a variety show with song, dance and stories.

Theme/Amusement Parks

Anancy Family Fun ★★★

Negril, Kingston, ☎ *(809) 957-4100.*

This newer attraction consists of three acres of miniature golf, a fishing pond, go-carts and a nature trail. Geared toward kids.

Tours

Cruises

Various locations, Kingston.

Lots of choices for cruising the ocean blue. Montego Bay: *Paco Rabanne (*☎ *[809] 951-5020),* the *Mary-Ann (*☎ *[809] 953-2231),* the *Calico (*☎ *[809] 952-5860),* and the *Rhapsody (*☎ *[809] 979-0104).* Port Antonio: *Lady Jamaica (*☎ *[809] 993-3318).* Ocho Rios: Heave-Ho Charters *(*☎ *[809] 974-5367)* and *Red Stripe (*☎ *[809] 974-2446).* Negril: Aqua Nova Water Sports *(*☎ *[809] 957-4323)* and the *Lollypop (*☎ *[809] 952-4121).* Excursions range from snorkel trips to catamaran sails to booze cruises with live bands.

Port Royal ★★

Near Kingston ☎ *(809) 924-8706.*
Hours open: 9 a.m.–5 p.m.

Now it's more touristy than anything, but this port used to be known as the "wickedest city in the world" because of its buccaneering past and frequent visits by Blackbeard. That all changed in 1692, when it was destroyed by an earthquake. There's lots to see in the complex, including St. Peter's Church, which dates back to 1725; the Archaeological and Historical Museum; a small maritime museum housed in the former British navel headquarters; Fort Charles, which dates back to 1656 and is the port's only remaining fort; and the Giddy House, permanently tilted after an earthquake.

Kingston

Restorations and Ruins

Jamaica's historical heritage lives on in its myriad architectural styles—Spanish-, English-, and French-colonial buildings are scattered across the island. From mysterious castles to graciously appointed plantation great halls, Jamaica offers a wealth of architectural sights.

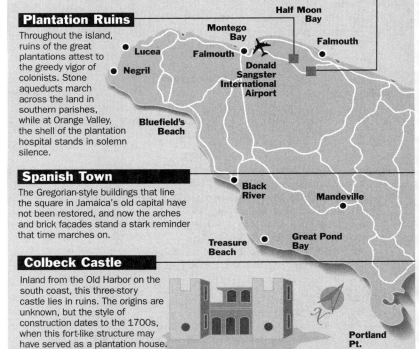

Plantation Ruins

Throughout the island, ruins of the great plantations attest to the greedy vigor of colonists. Stone aqueducts march across the land in southern parishes, while at Orange Valley, the shell of the plantation hospital stands in solemn silence.

Half Moon Bay

Montego Bay

Falmouth

Lucea   **Falmouth**

Negril

Donald Sangster International Airport

Bluefield's Beach

Spanish Town

The Gregorian-style buildings that line the square in Jamaica's old capital have not been restored, and now the arches and brick facades stand a stark reminder that time marches on.

Black River

Mandeville

Treasure Beach   **Great Pond Bay**

Colbeck Castle

Inland from the Old Harbor on the south coast, this three-story castle lies in ruins. The origins are unknown, but the style of construction dates to the 1700s, when this fort-like structure may have served as a plantation house.

Portland Pt.

Vale Royal

Home to the prime minister, this building was constructed in the 1700s as a plantation house. The lookout tower enabled residents to watch the ships entering the harbor.

Kingston

Rose Hall Great House

Considered one of the grandest restored plantation great houses, Rose Hall is steeped in grisly legend—its second mistress, Annie Palmer, allegedly murdered three husbands and one lover on the premises.

Devon House (Kingston)

This 19th-century great house has been restored and furnished with period antiques. The stables have been converted to rather touristy craft and souvenir shops.

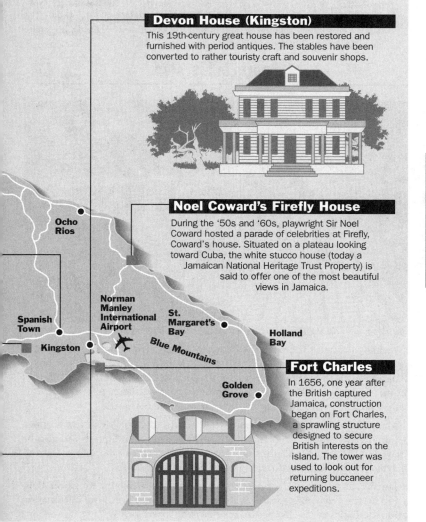

Noel Coward's Firefly House

During the '50s and '60s, playwright Sir Noel Coward hosted a parade of celebrities at Firefly, Coward's house. Situated on a plateau looking toward Cuba, the white stucco house (today a Jamaican National Heritage Trust Property) is said to offer one of the most beautiful views in Jamaica.

Ocho Rios

Spanish Town

Norman Manley International Airport

St. Margaret's Bay

Holland Bay

Kingston

Blue Mountains

Golden Grove

Fort Charles

In 1656, one year after the British captured Jamaica, construction began on Fort Charles, a sprawling structure designed to secure British interests on the island. The tower was used to look out for returning buccaneer expeditions.

Kingston

River Rafting   ★★

Various locations, Kingston.

Jamaica's many rivers make for great float trips, usually in a bamboo raft that holds just two and is piloted by a character who spins tales of local lore. Several outfits offer trips that last an hour or so and cost about $40 per couple. In the Montego Bay area, try **Martha Brae's Rafting Village** (☎ *[809] 952-0889)* or **Mountain Valley Rafting** (☎ *[809] 952-0527)*. Near Port Antonio, try the **Rio Grande** (☎ *[809] 993-2778)*. In Ocho Rios, call **Calypso Rafting** (☎ *[809] 974-2527)*. "An Evening on the Great River" is a touristy but fun boat ride down the river lined with torch-lights, followed by dinner and a folkloric show.

Sports in Kingston

Bamboo rafts on the Rio Grande River take tourists past magnificent scenery.

Yachting is one of the major activities in Kingston since there are so many attractive offshore islets in the area. A well-attended regatta is sponsored in August by the Morgans Harbor Hotel. If you belong to a yacht club at home, inquire whether you have privileges to participate. Ask at the Morgans Harbour Hotel regarding cruises around the harbor.

Many resorts have **tennis courts**. Public courts are available at the Ligunea Club across the road from the hotels in New Kingston. Squash can also be played at the Ligunea Club. Eighteen-hole **golf courses** can be found at the Caymanas Golf Club and the Constant Spring Golf Club.

Jamaica has a passion for **polo**. In the Kingston area, the Kingston Polo Club on the Caymanas Estates holds regular matches. For more information about activities at Chukka Cove, see "North Coast" below.

Golf

Various locations, Kingston.

Jamaica has lots of golf courses. The best by far are the links at **Tryall**, a PGA tour-approved, par-71 course that is considered one of the world's best. Call ☎ *(809) 952-5110.* Also in the Montego Bay area are the **Half Moon Golf Club**, ☎ *(809) 953-2280,* a spacious, par-72 course designed by Robert Trent Jones; **Ironshore Golf and Country Club**, ☎ *(809) 953-2800),* par 72 and known for its many blind holes; and **Wyndham Rose Hall Country Club**, ☎ *(809) 953-2650,* a par-72 course on the historic Rose Hall estate with an imaginative layout. In Kingston, try **Caymanas Golf Club**, ☎ *(809) 926-8144,* a par 72 known for its very challenging 12th hole; and **Constant Springs**, ☎ *(809) 924-1610,* a par-70 course.

Horseback Riding

Various locations, Kingston.

Several operations offer horseback riding. Ocho Rios: **Chukka Cove Farm** ☎ *(809) 972-2506,* $20 per hour; and **Prospect Plantation**, ☎ *(809) 974-2373,* $18 per hour. Montego Bay: **Rocky Point Stables**, ☎ *(809) 953-2212,* where 1.5-hour rides start at $38. Negril: **Horseman Riding Sables**, ☎ *(809) 957-4474,* $25 for two hours.

Watersports

Various locations, Kingston.

Most hotels offer a variety of watersports, or check out one of the following operations. For scuba and snorkel, try **Fisherman's Inn in Falmouth,** ☎ *(809) 247-0475.* Runaway Bay: **Jamaqua Watersports**, ☎ *(809) 973-4845,* and **Sun Divers Jamaica**, ☎ *(809) 973-2346.* Negril: **Negril Scuba Centre**, ☎ *(809) 957-4425* and **Sun Divers Jamaica**, ☎ *(809) 957-4069.* Ocho Rios: **Sea and Dive Jamaica**, ☎ *(809) 947-5762.* Montego Bay: **Seaworld**, ☎ *(809) 953-2180* and **Sandals Beach Watersports**, ☎ *(809) 949-0104.* Port Antonio: **Lady Godiva**, ☎ *(809) 993-3281* and **Aqua Action**, ☎ *(809) 993-3318.* In addition to the above, **Resort Divers**, ☎ *(809) 974-0577* has six locations around the island. For deep-sea fishing, check out **Seaworld Resorts**, ☎ *(809) 993-3086* and **Sans Souci**, ☎ *(809) 974-2353.*

Where to Stay

Hotels and Resorts

Courtleigh House & Hotel $79–$195 ★ ★

31 Trafalgar Road, Kingston, ☎ (800) 526-2400, (809) 926-8174. FAX (809) 926-7801.

Single: $79–$195. Double: $83–$195.

This traditional garden-style property accommodates guests in large hotel rooms and suites and apartments with one-to-three bedrooms and kitchens. There are two pools, a few restaurants and a very popular disco on-site. Friendly service, but this spot could really use a renovation. Still, this is good value for the rates. 80 rooms. Credit cards: A, MC.

Kingston

Four Seasons Hotel $75–$135 ★

18 Ruthven Road, Kingston, ☎ *(800) 526-2422, (809) 929-7655. FAX (809) 929-5964.*

Single: $75–$135. Double: $75–$135.

Obviously (if you noticed the rates) not affiliated with the luxury hotel chain of the same name, this small hotel in New Kingston is housed in an old mansion. Guestrooms are simple but adequate, and come with air conditioning and satellite TV. Forty additional units opened in late 1996. There's a restaurant and bar on the premises, as well as a pool and gym. 79 rooms. Credit cards: A, CB, DC, MC, V.

Jamaica Pegasus Hotel $180–$564 ★★★★

81 Knutsford Boulevard, Kingston, ☎ *(809) 926-3690. FAX (809) 929-5850.*

Single: $180–$564. Double: $185–$564.

Located in New Kingston, three miles north of downtown, this high-rise hotel offers a sophisticated atmosphere that attracts lots of business travelers and conventioneers. Guestrooms are nice, with extras like coffeemakers and large balconies. There's a large pool, two tennis courts, and a jogging track, and guests can work out at a nearby fitness club. The top five floors of the 17-story building, the Executive Club, have added amenities. An excellent choice for the business traveler, though tourists may feel out of place. 350 rooms. Credit cards: A, DC, MC, V.

Medallion Hall Hotel $79–$83 ★★

53 Hope Road, Kingston, ☎ *(809) 927-5721.*

Single: $79–$83. Double: $79–$83.

This small hotel, a former private residence, has an inn-like feel. Accommodations are simple but pleasant with traditional decor and dark woods. There's a small restaurant and bar, but nothing else in the way of diversions; you'll have to venture out for excitement. Good value, though. 16 rooms. Credit cards: A, DC, MC, V.

Morgan's Harbour Hotel $98–$255 ★★★

Port Royal, Kingston, ☎ *(809) 924-8464.*

Single: $98–$255. Double: $216–$255.

Downtown Kingston is 20 minutes away from this colonial-style hotel. Completely rebuilt after devastating Hurricane Gilbert, it houses guests in extra-nice rooms with luxurious furnishings, good artwork, and wet bars. The pleasantly landscaped grounds include a saltwater pool, a marina that attracts lots of yachters, a disco and watersports. Perfect for those who need to be near Kingston but want the resort feel of a waterfront property. 45 rooms. Credit cards: A, MC, V.

Terra Nova Hotel $120–$150 ★★★

17 Waterloo Road, Kingston, ☎ *(809) 926-2211. FAX (809) 929-4933.*

Single: $120–$150. Double: $120–$150.

Set on five acres near a commercial area, this motel-style property has an excellent restaurant, and recently redone, but rather drab, guestrooms. Still, this is a popular spot for business travelers not looking to spend an arm or leg on a room. Resort amenities are in short supply, save for the pool, oddly set out front in full view of passersby. 33 rooms. Credit cards: A, DC, MC, V.

Wyndham Kingston **$165–$505** ★★★

77 Knutsford Boulevard, Kingston, ☎ *(800) 322-4200, (809) 926-5511. FAX (809) 929-7439.*
Single: $165–$505. Double: $165–$505.
Situated in the business center on 7.5 acres, this towering hotel was recently redone, with good results. Primarily appealing to business travelers and conventioneers, it offers modern accommodations in the 16-story tower or older and funkier cabana units. There are two tennis courts, a pool and a fully equipped health club, as well as several bars and restaurants. Quite decent, but the Pegasus remains superior. 384 rooms. Credit cards: A, DC, MC, V.

Apartments and Condominiums
Strawberry Hill **$175–$450** ★★

Irish Town, ☎ *(800) 688-7678, (809) 944-8400. FAX (809) 944-8408.*
Single: $175–$450. Double: $175–$450.
Located 50 minutes from Kingston airport, this new resort is comprised of villas designed in the style of 19th-century Jamaican architecture, with carved fretwork in the doorways, antique island furniture and wrap-around wooden verandas. Set halfway up the Blue Mountains at an altitude of 3,100 feet, the resort pampers guests with its plush studio, one-, two-, and three-bedroom accommodations, which include four-poster beds, mosquito netting, ceiling fans, terra cotta baths and, in the larger units, modern kitchens. There's a bar and restaurant on site, and the rates include airport transfers. No pool, unfortunately, but this place does the job for those who prefer privacy and communing with nature. 12 rooms.

Low Cost Lodging
Indies Hotel **$35–$62** ★

5 Holborn Road, Kingston, ☎ *(809) 926-2952. FAX (809) 926-2879.*
Single: $35–$58. Double: $58–$62.
This small guesthouse offers incredible rates, but not much else besides a popular restaurant. 15 rooms. Credit cards: A, MC, V.

Where to Eat

Blue Mountain Inn **$$$** ★★★★

Gordon Town Road, Kingston, ☎ *(809) 927-1700.*
International cuisine.
Dinner: 7–9 p.m., entrées $12–$24.
One of Jamaica's most elegant dining experiences, this restaurant is set in an old coffee plantation house overlooking the Mamee River, located about half an hour from Kingston. It's a good excuse for women to air out a little black dress and men a jacket (ties are not required) while sampling continental cuisine that's impeccably prepared and served by a gracious staff. Steak and lobster thermidor and flambeed desserts are some of the old fashioned but delicious choices frequently on the menu. Reservations required. Credit cards: A, DC, MC, V.

Chelsea Jerk Centre **$** ★

9 Chelsea Avenue, Kingston, ☎ *(809) 926-6322.*

Latin American cuisine. Specialties: Jerk chicken and pork.
Lunch: Noon–3:30 p.m., entrées $3–$5.
Dinner: 3:30–10 p.m., entrées $3–$5.

No, this isn't a self-improvement workshop for nerds on Chelsea Avenue—the Jerk Centre proffers blazingly hot barbecued chicken or pork that's been marinating for hours in a medley of incendiary spices that are a closely-guarded secret. Most dishes here are under $5 and come with sides of rice and peas (white rice with red beans). A half-chicken or pork slab can be packaged to go. Credit cards: not accepted. Credit cards: A, MC, V.

Devon House Restaurants $$ ★★

Devon House, Kingston, ☎ *(809) 929-6602.*
Latin American cuisine.
Lunch: 10 a.m.–4 p.m., entrées $6–$16.
Dinner: 4 p.m.–midnight, entrées $6–$16. Closed: Sun.

This former colonial mansion turned restaurant/coffee house/craft emporium is one of Kingston's most visited tourist sites. An incredible Jamaican breakfast is served on the breezy Coffee Terrace every day except Sunday. Diners saunter to a long table topped with red-checked country cloths for a buffet of beautifully carved fresh fruit, ackee and saltfish, cod fish balls and breads. Blue Mountain coffee and exotic juices are included. If you have room, pop into the adjoining I-Scream for a frozen concoction of soursop or mango. Reservations recommended. Credit cards: A, MC, V.

El Dorado Room $$ ★

17 Waterloo Road, Kingston, ☎ *(809) 926-9334. Associated hotel: Terra Nova Hotel.*
International cuisine.
Lunch: Noon–2:30 p.m., entrées $7–$20.
Dinner: 7:30–11 p.m., entrées $7–$20.

The main dining room of the Terra Nova Hotel, a boutique style hostelry, provides a gracious ambience for local residents taking a breather from the vibrant Kingston restaurant scene. Picture windows look out onto the spacious grounds of the former private estate built in the early 20s. Seafood shines here, whether it's freshly-caught grilled lobster or red snapper in ginger sauce. Reservations recommended. Credit cards: A, DC, MC, V.

Gap Cafe, The $$$ ★★

Hardwar Gap, Kingston, ☎ *(809) 923-7055.*
International cuisine.
Lunch: entrées $12–$15.
Dinner: entrées $17–$22.

A visit to the Gap Cafe is a journey to another Jamaica—one where a fireplace may be glowing all year round, understandable at a height of 4200 feet. Gloria Palomino welcomes guests to sip Blue Mountain coffee and savor some of the best pastries on the island, served all day and at high tea on Sundays. Native guavas are used in the cheesecake, as well as soursop and passion fruit for the cakes and mousses. The Cafe, once an old fixer-upper, is now a cozy, flower-filled charmer decked out in tones of maroon and blue. There's a gift shop on the premises. Reservations recommended. Credit cards: A, MC, V.

Hot Pot, The   **$**   ★★

2 Altamont Terrace, Kingston, ☎ *(809) 929-3906.*
Latin American cuisine. Specialties: Fricassee chicken, saltfish and ackee.
Lunch: 8 a.m.–4 p.m., entrées $3–$4.
Dinner: 4–10 p.m., entrées $3–$4.
A dandy place to try Jamaican specialties is this informal joint behind the Wyndham Hotel. The decor isn't much, but the authentic dishes are cheap and filling. The Hot Pot serves three meals a day, including the legendary saltfish and ackee (a vegetable brought over by Captain Bligh of Bounty fame) for breakfast. Credit cards: V.

Indies Pub and Grill   **$**   ★

8 Holborn Road, Kingston, ☎ *(809) 926-5050.*
Latin American cuisine.
Lunch: entrées $4–$12.
Dinner: entrées $4–$12.
This is the Jamaican version of a local pub - roosting companionably in a New Kingston neighborhood. The fare is nothing fancy: just burgers, fish and chips or pizza, but sometimes there's nothing better than rubbing elbows with office workers on a comfortable alfresco terrace. The Indies is a popular late night spot as well—it serves food and drink until 1:30 a.m. on weekends and until midnight the rest of the week. Credit cards: A, MC, V.

Ivor Guest House   **$$$**   ★

Jack's Hill, Kingston, ☎ *(809) 977-0033. Associated hotel: Ivor Guest House.*
International cuisine.
Lunch: entrées $18–$22.
Dinner: entrées $22–$30.
This cozy guest house/dining room on a hill high above Kingston boasts a million dollar view (at 2000 feet) and the chef prepares reasonably-priced lunches and dinners with a Jamaican flair. The terrace of this small colonial inn is a popular spot for high tea and cocktails on the open terrace. On a clear night, the lights of the city in the distance make strong men (and women) swoon. Reservations required. Credit cards: A, MC, V.

Minnie's Ethiopian   **$$**   ★

176 Old Hope Road, Kingston, ☎ *(809) 927-9207.*
Latin American cuisine. Specialties: Gungo-Pea Stew, Festival Bread, Juices.
Lunch: entrées $10–$20.
Dinner: entrées $10–$20.
After a pilgrimage to reggae icon Bob Marley's Museum and Tuff Gong Recording Studio nearby, fans can repair to his former chef's eating establishment for some Rasta Ital food (mostly vegetarian, utilizing local bounty) prepared by Chef Minnie. The full name of this round wooden restaurant is Minnie's Ethiopian Herbal Health Food, and after a few freshly-squeezed juices and her signature *gungo* (pigeon pea stew, you'll feel truly cleansed. Reservations recommended. Credit cards: not accepted.

Norma's at the Wharfhouse   **$$$**   ★★★★

Reading Road, Kingston, ☎ *(809) 979-2745. Associated hotel: The Wharfhouse.*
Latin American cuisine.
Lunch: Noon–2:30 p.m., entrées $26–$34.

Kingston

Dinner: 7:30–10:30 p.m., entrées $26–$34. Closed: Mon., Tue., Wed.

The finest restaurant on the island may be this historical dockside beauty created by Norma Shirley, Jamaica's most famous chef. Dine with influential Jamaicans and visiting celebrities while watching the action at a table set on the wharf at this 300-year-old warehouse, or in an antique-filled salon. Shirley, who owned a restaurant in New York, utilizes the rich bounty of the region to spectacular effect; the menu, which changes daily, often includes succulent smoked marlin with papaya or grilled deviled crab backs. The elegantly-dressed plates are a treat. Reservations recommended. Credit cards: MC, V.

Port Royal   **$$$**   ★★

81 Knutsford Boulevard, Kingston, ☎ *(809) 926-3690. Associated hotel: Jamaica Pegasus Hotel.*

International cuisine.

Lunch: 12:30–3 p.m., prix fixe $16.

Dinner: 7-11 p.m., entrées $16–$26. Closed: Sun.

As hotel dining rooms go, Port Royal (formerly called Le Pavilion) just might be the most popular downtown meeting spot. Sophisticated city dwellers flock here for high tea on weekdays, while others like the seafood buffets on Fridays and the reasonably priced three-course lunches with a variety of Caribbean and Continental meat and fish concoctions. No lunch is served on Saturday. Reservations recommended. Credit cards: A, DC, MC, V.

Temple Hall   **$$$**   ★★★★★

Temple Hall Estate, Kingston, ☎ *(809) 942-2340.*

Latin American cuisine. Specialties: Fettucine Boston jerk.

Dinner: 6:30–11:30 p.m., entrées $25.

Of the handful of gracious plantation homes on the outskirts of Kingston, The Restaurant at Temple Hall Estate is probably on most gourmet lists of "don't miss" experiences. For the most part the vast property is self-sustaining, growing most of the herbs and vegetables and raising the livestock used as ingredients in the scrumptious meals. Guests are provided with complimentary transportation by the owners, who like to put on a light show at night by illuminating the long driveway with torches. Reservations required. Reservations required. Credit cards: A, DC, MC.

Montego Bay

Known to locals as Mo' Bay, Montego Bay is the primary port of entry by air for Jamaica. It's here, along the shoreline, where Jamaican tourism was born. Once a sleepy town, Montego Bay has burgeoned into the apotheosis of what some tourists feel is the Caribbean nightmare, but for others it's a town that epitomizes the bustling, sweaty, crowded charm of a Third World port. Downtown is a joggerhead of traffic, markets, people and vendors —if you want to stay in the middle of all that, you'll be able to find some small (but noisy, count on it) hotels. The Montego Bay experience starts even on arrival at the Donald Sangster International Airport, where you'll jostle your way past crowds, walk long hot distances to your luggage, and nearly kill your fellow travelers to get a porter's attention. In order to minimize the discomfort, arrange for your hotel to pick you up (many all-inclusives include airport transfer in the package). There's nothing like seeing a sign with your name on it and a helpful assistant when you are hot, tired and cranky after an international flight. (For more taxi information, see the directory under "Getting Around" at the end of the chapter.)

Beaches in Montego Bay

Cornwall Beach is a man-made phenomenon to provide tourists with an alternative to the postage-stamp patch called Doctor's Cave Beach—once the hub of Montego Bay's social scene during its heyday in the'60s. The scene is still happening at Cornwall, but with so many locals and tourists, that if you're the kind of person who likes to see the color of the sand beneath your feet, stay away. These days Doctor's Cave itself is just too reminiscent of Florida to get our vote for exotica. The five-mile stretch of vanilla-colored sand still has its charm, though its overexposure in the press has brought every loud obnoxious tourist out of the woodwork. On the plus side, the changing facilities can be useful and you can grab a quick bite to eat from vendors or small cafes. **Walter Fletch Beach**, on the bay near the center of town, is very good for swimming, since it is well protected from the strong winds.

What Else to See

Historical Sites

Greenwood Great House　　　　　　　　　　　　　　　★ ★
　　Highway A1, Montego Bay.

Hours open: 9 a.m.–6 p.m.

One of Jamaica's greatest great houses, this one belonged to the Barrett family, of which Elizabeth Barrett Browning is a descendant. The early 19th-century mansion is filled with antiques, unusual musical instruments, rare books, custom-made china, and portraits of the family. General admission: $8.

Rose Hall Great House ★★

Rose Hall Highway, Montego Bay, ☎ (809) 953-2323.
Hours open: 9 a.m.–6 p.m.

Not as architecturally impressive as Greenwood, this great house from the 1700s plays the leading role in tales of murder and intrigue. It seems that mistress Annie Palmer seduced slaves and then killed them, as well as murdering three husbands. Her story has been fictionalized in several books, which you'll find in the giftshop. There's also a neat pub in the basement. General admission: $10.

Parks and Gardens

Columbus Park Museum ★★

Queens Highway, Discovery Bay, ☎ (809) 973-2135.
Hours open: 9 a.m.–5 p.m.

This outdoor park, studded with pimento trees, has some interesting and eclectic exhibits. There are 18th-century cannons, a stone cross, a large mural of Columbus' landing in 1494, and displays on the history of sugar cane. Stop by if you're in the area, but don't bother making a special trip.

Rocklands Wildlife Station ★★★

Anchovy, St. James, ☎ (809) 952-2009.
Hours open: 2–5 p.m.

This privately owned reserve is a must for birders (the rest can probably live without it). Doves, finches and other feathered creatures eat right off your hands. General admission: $4.

Tours

Appelton Estate Express ★★

Appelton Estate Station, Montego Bay, ☎ (809) 952-3692.

All aboard the Appelton Express, an air-conditioned diesel railcar that chugs some 40 miles into the mountains. Along the way you'll pass Jamaican villages, coffee and fruit plantations, and wonderful scenery. You'll also tour a rum factory and get to taste the goods. The fee includes transportation from your hotel, continental breakfast, buffet lunch, and an open bar. The train departs at 8:50 a.m. on Monday, Thursday and Friday, and returns about 5 p.m. General admission: $70.

JUTA Tour Company ★★

Claude Clarke Avenue, Montego Bay, ☎ (809) 952-0813.

This well-established tour company has offices all over Jamaica. They'll take you river rafting, on sea cruises, through great houses, and into Kingston.

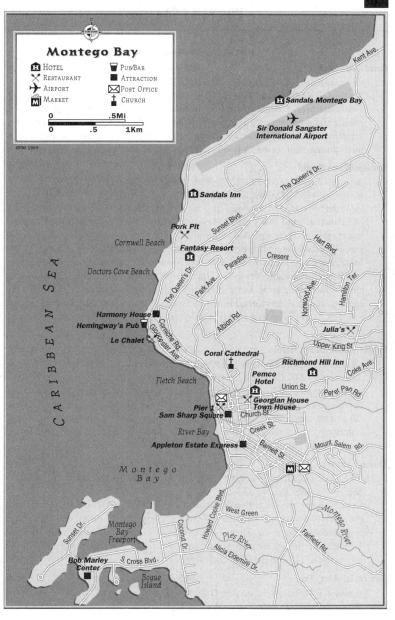

Montego Bay

Montego Bay

🏨 HOTEL   🍺 PUB/BAR
✕ RESTAURANT   ■ ATTRACTION
✈ AIRPORT   ✉ POST OFFICE
🏪 MARKET   † CHURCH

0   .5Mi
0   .5   1Km

©RWI 1995

🏨 Sandals Montego Bay

✈
Sir Donald Sangster International Airport

The Queen's Dr.

Kent Ave.

🏨 **Sandals Inn**

Pork Pit ✕

Sunset Blvd.

Hart Blvd.

Cornwell Beach

Fantasy Resort 🏨

Cresent

Doctors Cove Beach

Paradise

Park Ave.

The Queen's Dr.

Norwood Ave.

Hamilton Ter.

Harmony House ■
Hemingway's Pub 🍺

Corniche Rd.

Gloucester Ave.

Albion Rd.

Julia's ✕

Le Chalet ✕

Upper King St.

Coral Cathedral †

Richmond Hill Inn 🏨

Coke Ave.

Pemco Hotel 🏨

Fletch Beach

Union St.

Peter Pan Rd.

✉ Pier 1 🍺
Sam Sharp Square ■

Georgian House Town House ✕

Church St.

River Bay

Creek St.

Appleton Estate Express ■

Barnett St.

Mount Salem Rd.

🏪 ✉

Montego Bay

Howard Cooke Blvd.

West Green

Montego River

CARIBBEAN SEA

Sunset Dr.

Montego Bay Freeport

Coconut Dr.

Pies River

Fairfield Rd.

Bob Marley Center ■

S. Cross Blvd.

Alicia Eldemire Dr.

Bogue Island

Where to Stay

Hotels and Resorts

Coral Cliff Hotel   **$54–$64**   ★★

Gloucester Avenue, Montego Bay, *(809) 952-4130.*
Single: $54–$63. Double: $58–$64.

This older hotel consists of a former mansion and a newer addition, perched on a hillside about five minutes from Doctor's Cave Beach. Rooms are pleasant and comfortable, but lack extras like TV. There's a bar and restaurant, pool, and entertainment during high season. A good budget hotel. 32 rooms. Credit cards: A, MC.

Coyaba Beach Resort   **$85–$326**   ★★★

Montego Bay, ☎ *(800) 237-3237, (809) 953-9150. FAX (809) 953-2244.*
Single: $85–$306. Double: $105–$326.

"Coyaba" is the Arawak word for "a kind of heaven where time is passed feasting and dancing," and that's the kind of atmosphere they strive to offer at this plush resort (though there's no disco, so you're left to your own devices for the dancing part). Guestrooms are luxurious with central air conditioning, ceiling fans, TVs and french doors leading to oversized private balconies. The deluxe ocean view rooms— which fetch the highest rate—are quite large and have four-poster beds, dining alcoves and sitting areas. On-site facilities include two restaurants and a bar, a private beach with watersports, a fitness room and a tennis court. Rates include airport transfers, a welcome basket, day tennis, watersports and daily afternoon tea. 50 rooms.

Doctor's Cave Beach Hotel   **$85–$135**   ★★★

Gloucester Avenue, Montego Bay, ☎ *(800) 223-6510, (809) 952-4355.*
Single: $85–$135. Double: $105–$135.

Set on four acres of tropical gardens in the heart of the resort district, this informal hotel is across the street from Doctor's Cave Beach. Guestrooms, decorated in rattan and air-conditioned, are comfortable. Facilities include a pool, two restaurants, watersports across the street and a small gym. The atmosphere is lively, with lots of special events like crab races and rum parties. 90 rooms. Credit cards: A, MC, V.

Fantasy Resort   **$55–$85**   ★★

2 Kent Avenue, Montego Bay, ☎ *(800) 237-3421, (809) 952-4150.*
Single: $55–$85. Double: $55–$85.

Located across the street from Doctor's Cave Beach, this highrise property is only the fantasy of someone with low self-esteem. Everything is quite dated here and in real need of renovation. There's tennis on two courts, a fitness center, pool and Jacuzzi. Guestrooms are small but do have nice ocean views. Decent value, but not too exciting. 119 rooms. Credit cards: A, MC.

Gloucestershire, The   **$60–$80**   ★★

Gloucester Avenue, Montego Bay, ☎ *(800) 423-4095, (809) 952-4420.*
Single: $60–$80. Double: $60–$80.

Doctor's Cave Beach is across the street from this modern hotel. Guestrooms are adequate with cable TV and air conditioning. Besides the Jacuzzi, there's not much in the way of resort amenities. 88 rooms. Credit cards: A, MC.

Half Moon Beach Club $255–$805 ★★★★★

Rose Hall, Montego Bay, ☎ *(800) 626-0592, (809) 953-2211.*
Single: $255–$505. Double: $305–$805.

Located on 400 acres with its own one-mile private beach, this resort is simply outstanding in every way. Accommodations are in standard rooms, cottages, and villas. All are luxurious, with tropical furnishings, antique reproductions, sitting areas, and patios or balconies with sea views. One-bedroom suites have full kitchens and spacious living areas, while the villas offer lots of space on two levels. There are two main swimming pools, plus 17 other pools shared among the villas, an equestrian center, 13 tennis courts, four squash courts, all kinds of watersports, and a children's center. There is also 18 holes of golf on a Robert Trent Jones–designed course. Aerobics classes are available in the fitness center, as well as sauna and massage for working out the kinks. Eating choices are varied and fine. This is one of Jamaica's best resorts, well worth the high rates. 213 rooms. Credit cards: A, MC.

Holiday Inn Montego Bay $160–$205 ★★

Rosehall, Montego Bay, ☎ *(800) 465-4329, (809) 953-2485.*
Single: $160–$205. Double: $160–$205.

Located on a private beach and part of the historic Rosehall Sugar Plantation Estate, this large resort complex lives up to the dependable, if unexciting, Holiday Inn name. Accommodations are acceptable but many lack water views. There's lots going on, from organized activities and entertainment (crab races, anyone?) to a large pool, health club, four tennis courts, watersports and supervised activities for the kids. Good security keeps non-guests at bay. Decent, and a recent $13-million renovation has kept things looking nice. 516 rooms. Credit cards: A, MC, V.

Jack Tar Village $155–$205 ★★

Gloucester Avenue, Montego Bay, ☎ *(800) 999-9182, (809) 952-4340.*
Single: $155–$205. Double: $134–$205.

Located a mile from downtown Montego Bay, this all-inclusive resort is perched right on the beach, albeit, a narrow one. Guestrooms are comfortable and modern. The rates include all meals, drinks and activities, and there's lots to do, including four tennis courts, volleyball, watersports, and nightly entertainment. (You'll pay extra for scuba and jet skiing.) Those who book far in advance are rewarded with lower rates. 128 rooms. Credit cards: A, MC.

Montego Bay Racquet Club $50–$155 ★★

Sewell Avenue, Montego Bay, ☎ *(809) 952-0200.*
Single: $50–$155. Double: $55–$155.

Located in the Red Hills area overlooking the harbor, three minutes from Doctor's Cave Beach (they'll shuttle you over for free), this informal resort lures tennis lovers with excellent facilities, including seven courts and two pros on hand to offer tips. Choose from simple and not especially pleasing villas or traditional guestrooms, which are a bit nicer. Besides the restaurant and pool, not much happens here other than tennis, tennis and tennis. Unless you're into that racquet, stay elsewhere. 51 rooms. Credit cards: A, MC, V.

Reading Reef Club   **$65–$370**   ★★★

Bogue Lagoon, Montego Bay, ☎ *(800) 223-6510, (809) 952-5909.*
Single: $65–$370. Double: $80–$370.
Located some 15 minutes west of Montego Bay, this small resort sets on 2.5 acres with its own small beach. Air-conditioned accommodations include rooms and suites. There's a few restaurants, a pool, and watersports, and, best of all, a lack of hustlers on the beach. A nice, quiet spot. 26 rooms. Credit cards: A, MC.

Round Hill Hotel & Villas   **$160–$420**   ★★★★★

Highway A1, Montego Bay, ☎ *(800) 972-2159, (809) 952-5150. FAX (809) 952-2505.*
Single: $160–$360. Double: $220–$420.
Set on a lush green peninsula with a private beach eight miles from Montego Bay, this exclusive resort encompasses nearly 100 acres. Accommodations are in the main building (most rooms have twin beds) or luxurious villas, some with their own private pools and all with the pampering of a maid, gardener and cook. Lots of rich and famous types stay here; keep your gawking to a minimum, please. Activities include five tennis courts, morning exercise classes, a pool, watersports, and glass-bottom boat rides. Tres chic—if you can afford it. Inquire about meal plans and all-inclusive rates. 110 rooms. Credit cards: A, MC, V.

Royal Court Hotel   **$45–$85**   ★

Sewell Avenue, Montego Bay, ☎ *(809) 952-4531.*
Single: $45–$100. Double: $55–$85.
Located on a hillside with nice views, this simple hotel is a half-mile from the beach (they'll shuttle you there). Rooms are nicely done, and some sport kitchenettes. Two restaurants, a pool and disco complete the scene. Decent for the rates. 25 rooms. Credit cards: A, MC.

Sandals Inn   **$290–$348**   ★★★

Kent Avenue, Montego Bay, ☎ *(800) 726-3257, (809) 952-4140.*
Single: $290–$348. Double: $290–$348.
Open only to heterosexual couples, this small, all-inclusive resort is hampered by its location across from, not on, the beach. Guestrooms are colonial-themed and large, but the sea is only visible from the more expensive units. There's lots to keep busy couples happy, including a pool, tennis, a gym and watersports. Guests can hop a free shuttle to the area's other two larger Sandals. This is the most inexpensive one of the trio. 52 rooms. Credit cards: A, MC.

Sandals Montego Bay   **$2375–$2835 per week**   ★★★★

Kent Avenue, Montego Bay, ☎ *(800) 726-3257, (809) 952-5510.*
$2375–$2835 per couple per week.
The largest of the area's three Sandals couples-only resorts, this one sits right on its own private beach. Guestrooms are quite nice, but avoid the few over the dining room if you can help it. The all-inclusive rates cover all meals, drinks, entertainment and facilities. Diversions include two pools, two tennis courts, a gym, all watersports, exercise classes, and several Jacuzzis. Dining options range from Jamaican to

Asian to Continental. Decent, but the noise from the nearby airport can be a drag. 243 rooms. Credit cards: A, MC.

Sandals Royal Caribbean   **$2465–$2920 per week**   ★★★★

Kent Avenue, Montego Bay, ☎ *(800) 726-3257, (809) 953-2231.*
$2465–$2920 per couple per week.

The most expensive of the three Sandals in the area, this couples-only (heterosexual please) resort operates on an all-inclusive plan. Many guestrooms open right onto the beach. All the bells and whistles associated with the chain are here, including four restaurants and four bars, three pools, three tennis courts, a good health club, all watersports, and lots of organized activities and entertainment. Those wanting to tan sans suits have their own private island. A bit more sophisticated than its siblings. 190 rooms. Credit cards: A, MC.

Sea Garden Beach Hotel   **$297–$357**   ★★

Kent Avenue, Montego Bay, ☎ *(800) 545-9001, (809) 952-4780.*
Single: $297–$357. Double: $297–$357.

Located across the street from the beach, this all-inclusive resort suffers from some airport noise. Guestrooms are dated and could use spiffing up. The rates include all meals, drinks and activities, including tennis, volleyball and watersports. There's nightly entertainment and a disco. Service is not the greatest, and Sandals remains a superior choice. 104 rooms. Credit cards: A, MC.

Seawind Beach Resort   **$75–$120**   ★★★

Montego Freeport, Montego Bay, ☎ *(800) 526-2422, (809) 979-8070.*
Single: $75–$120. Double: $90–$120.

Situated on a private 100-acre peninsula, this complex includes two 10-story towers and two-story wings. The towers house most of the guestrooms and are local landmarks with their colorful bands. There are also studios and one-bedroom apartments with kitchen facilities. Lots going on at this lively spot, including four tennis courts, two pools, watersports and horseback riding. Several restaurants and five bars, including a popular disco. The locale, near the busy port, is a bit removed from the action. 468 rooms. Credit cards: A, D, MC, V.

Tryall Resort   **$235–$465**   ★★★★

Sandy Bay, Montego Bay, ☎ *(800) 742-0498, (809) 965-5660.*
Single: $235–$415. Double: $285–$465.

Set on 2200 acres of a former sugar plantation estate some 30 minutes out of Montego Bay, this deluxe resort has a true country club feel. Guestrooms are located in the 1834 Great House and are beautifully done; luxurious villas with maid and cook service are also available. The resort's centerpiece is the 18-hole PGA championship golf course, but there are also nine tennis courts, a pool, a private beach, and all watersports. Lovely and grand. 52 rooms. Credit cards: A, MC, V.

Wexford, The   **$85–$130**   ★★

Gloucester Avenue, Montego Bay, ☎ *(800) 237-3421, (809) 952-3679.*
Single: $85–$120. Double: $95–$130.

This small hotel is across the street from Doctor's Cave Beach, and it's a bit of a walk to the sand. Accommodations are simple but adequate, and one-bedroom

Montego Bay

apartments with kitchenettes are available. The pool is small and uninspired. You can do better at comparable rates elsewhere. 61 rooms. Credit cards: A, MC.

Winged Victory   **$95–$230**   ★★

5 Queens Drive, Montego Bay, ☎ (800) 223-9815, (809) 952-3891.
Single: $95–$230. Double: $95–$230.

Situated on a hill overlooking the bay, five minutes from Doctor's Cave Beach, this is a peaceful, off-the-beaten-track spot. Guestrooms are comfortable and most face the ocean. There's a small pool, and the restaurant is good. 27 rooms. Credit cards: A, MC.

Wyndham Rose Hall Resort   **$165–$705**   ★★★

Rose Hall, Montego Bay, ☎ (809) 631-4200, (809) 953-2650.
Single: $165–$705. Double: $165–$705.

Set on 400 acres fronting a beach, this stylish property has large guestrooms accented by nice artwork and quality furnishings. Guests can choose from 18 holes of golf, six tennis courts with a pro on hand, a fitness center, three interconnected swimming pools and all watersports. Lots in the way of dining options, too. Parents can stash the little ones in the supervised Kid's Klub, and there are also lots of organized activities for adults. Very nice, but lacks a true Jamaican feel. 500 rooms. Credit cards: A, MC, V.

Apartments and Condominiums

Seacastles   **$75–$155**   ★★★

Rose Hall, Montego Bay, ☎ (800) 526-2422, (809) 953-3259.
Single: $75–$155. Double: $75–$155.

Located on a 14-acre estate, this modern complex has one- to three-bedroom apartments, all with nice tropical furnishings and kitchenettes. Combining the convenience of apartment living with the amenities of a hotel, the staff offers turndown service and limited room service. There's a pool, two tennis courts, a playground for the kids, watersports, and a private, though small, beach. Nice, especially for families who don't mind the somewhat remote location. 198 rooms. Credit cards: A, MC, V.

Inns

Breezes Montego Bay   **$415–$1380**   ★★

Doctor's Cave Beach, Montego Bay, ☎ (800) 859-7873, (809) 940-1150.

This brand-new property, part of the SuperClubs chain, just opened in the fall of 1995. The $13-million resort sits on Doctor's Cave Beach and has two restaurants, a beach grill, disco, piano bar, and watersports. There's also nightly entertainment, theme nights and a pool. Open to couples and singles aged 16 and over. Rates for three nights (minimum stay) are single: $415–740, double: $830–$1380. Rates include all meals, drinks and activities. 124 rooms. Credit cards: A, MC, V.

Richmond Hill Inn   **$78–$112**   ★★

Union Street, Montego Bay, ☎ (809) 952-3859.
Single: $78. Double: $112.

Set high on a hill with stunning views, the main building of this casual inn dates from the 1700s. Guestrooms are simple but comfortable, and a few suites with kitchenettes are available for those who prefer to cook in. A pool and game room offer daytime diversions; the piano bar and open-air restaurant help fill evening hours. Not the greatest, especially since lots of tour groups troop through to check out the view. The beach is a 10-minute drive. 20 rooms. Credit cards: A, MC.

Toby Inn   **$45–$80**   ★★

1 Kent Avenue, Montego Bay, ☎ (809) 952-4370.
Single: $45–$55. Double: $70–$80.
Located in a few acres of tropical gardens one block from Doctor's Cave Beach, this relatively peaceful inn houses guests in simple but attractive rooms that lack telephones and TV. There are two pools, one with a waterfall, a restaurant, and two bars, one built to resemble a treehouse. Shopping, restaurants and nightlife are within an easy walk. Excellent value. 60 rooms. Credit cards: A, MC.

Low Cost Lodging

Belvedere Beach Hotel   **$50–$80**   ★

33 Gloucester Avenue, Montego Bay, ☎ (809) 952-0593.
Single: $50–$75. Double: $55–$80.
This small hotel is across the street from Walter Fletcher Beach and within walking distance of city center. There's a pool, restaurant and bar, but not much else. It gets noisy here. Not especially recommended. 27 rooms. Credit cards: A, CB, MC, V.

Blue Harbour Hotel   **$35–$105**   ★★

Sewell Avenue, Montego Bay, ☎ (809) 952-5445.
Single: $35–$105. Double: $47–$105.
Set on a hill on the site of an old Spanish fort, this small hotel has adequate accommodations for the rates. Besides the pool, there's not much here to keep visitors occupied. 24 rooms. Credit cards: A, MC, V.

Buccaneer Beach Hotel   **$83–$175**   ★

7 Kent Avenue, Montego Bay, ☎ (809) 952-6489.
Single: $83–$175. Double: $83–$175.
Located near the airport and across the street from a public beach, this budget choice offers bland but functional rooms. Appealing mainly to college students hell-bent on having a good time, during spring break, it is best avoided by anyone over 25. Typical hotel amenities include a restaurant, bar, nightclub and pool. 72 rooms. Credit cards: A, MC.

Where to Eat

Georgian House   **$$$**   ★

2 Orange Street, Montego Bay, ☎ (809) 952-3353.
International cuisine. Specialties: Pan-barbecued shrimp, coconut pie.
Lunch: Noon–2:30 p.m., entrées $22–$32.
Dinner: 6–10:30 p.m., entrées $22–$32.
This restaurant's private van will pick you up from your hotel to dine in an 18th century townhouse and art gallery. Once there, you can eat outdoors on the patio if you prefer a more casual atmosphere—in any case feel free to dress resort-casual. Specialties are from the sea; usually shrimp or spiny lobster, barbecued, or sauteed with vegetables, or in a wine sauce. Steaks and filets are also marvelous, the coconut pie

is luscious, and the wine list is well-chosen. Reservations recommended. Credit cards: A, DC, MC, V.

Julia's $$$ ★

Bogue Hill, Montego Bay, ☎ *(809) 952-0632.*
International cuisine.
Dinner: 6–10:30 p.m., prix fixe $35.

It's highly advisable to take this mountaintop restaurant's offer of a private van to pick you up at your door. Negotiating the steep road that leads to this estate above Mo' Bay (800 feet or thereabouts) can be hazardous. Once ensconced in your seat, relax and enjoy a four-course dinner served by an attentive staff, while the lights of the bay and the city glow below. The mostly-Italian entrées of veal (usually parmesan), chicken, or fish will include a salad, pasta, dessert and choice of beverage. Reservations required. Credit cards: A, DC, MC, V.

Pier I $$$ ★

Howard Cooke Boulevard, Montego Bay, ☎ *(809) 952-2452.*
Seafood cuisine.
Lunch: 11 a.m.–4 p.m., entrées $16–$25.
Dinner: 4 p.m.–midnight, entrées $16–$25.

The cocktails and punches are fruity and potent, and the burgers are juicy; but even if kibble was served, the view from the waterfront bar would still be stellar. There's a tony dining room within where you can dine on well-prepared seafood and hearty soups, chicken and steaks. Credit cards: A, MC, V.

Pork Pit $ ★★★

Gloucester Avenue, corner, Montego Bay, ☎ *(809) 952-1046.*
Latin American cuisine.
Lunch: 11 a.m.–4:30 p.m., entrées $2–$9.
Dinner: 4:30–11:30 p.m., entrées $2–$9.

Eat fiery jerk pork, chicken or spare ribs picnic-style on benches or tables open to the sea breeze. Common accompaniments include local cornbread (called festival bread) and Red Stripe beer. Location is close to Cornwall Beach and the airport. Credit cards: not accepted.

Reading Reef Club $$$ ★★★★★

Bogue Lagoon, Montego Bay, ☎ *(809) 952-5909. Associated hotel: Reading Reef Club.*
Italian cuisine.
Lunch: Noon–3 p.m., entrées $10–$24.
Dinner: 7–10 p.m., entrées $10–$24.

Located in a discreet, small (21-room) hotel situated halfway between Montego Bay and the Round Hill Resort, this Caribbean-influenced Italian restaurant reflects the tastes of the hotel's owner, JoAnne Rowe, a New York-born expatriate. Dishes include a strange combination of pasta served with ginger that works quite well, judging by its popularity. Crayfish, seafood and steaks are other standards paired with local produce. Reservations required. Credit cards: A, DC, MC, V.

Sugar Mill $$$ ★★★★

Rose Hall, Montego Bay, ☎ *(809) 953-2228. Associated hotel: Half Moon Club.*
International cuisine. Specialties: Bouillabaise, smoked marlin.

Montego Bay

Lunch: Noon–2:30 p.m., entrées $14–$31.
Dinner: 7–10 p.m., entrées $14–$31.

Swiss chef Hans Schenck creates Jamaican-continental specialties at this restaurant in a historical house with a terrace that overlooks the ocean and the golf course of the Half Moon Club. Marlin, a specialty catch of the area, is often smoked and served with pasta; bouillabaisse is spiced with local pepper and citrus sauces. Even if you're just passing through, come for a look at the remains of the old sugar plantation that have been incorporated into the grounds of this soigné resort. Reservations required. Credit cards: A, MC, V.

Town House   **$$$**   ★ ★

16 Church Street, Montego Bay, ☎ (809) 952-2660.
Latin American cuisine. Specialties: Red snapper baked in parchment.
Lunch: 11:30 a.m.–2:30 p.m., entrées $13–$30.
Dinner: 6–10 p.m., entrées $13–$30.

This grand, 300-year-old Georgian building is a fun place to eat, especially in the art-filled, brick-walled cellar room, which is a novel change from the favored practice of dining alfresco. But that can also be achieved here on an outdoor terrace. Specialties include a signature fresh red snapper baked in parchment with a cheese and seafood sauce. Reservations recommended. Credit cards: A, DC, MC, V.

Montego Bay

Negril

Negril became known to the world at large in the early '70s, when it was a mecca for hippies, escapists, artists and visionaries who spent most of the day bonged out on the local weed. Located on the extreme northwestern point of the island, the town has grown from a sleepy bohemian enclave to one of Jamaica's finest resort areas—some of the best allinclusives are situated right on the beach here. There are also campsites at the **Negril Lighthouse Park** and at **Roots Bamboo** (both off West End). The seven-mile stretch of pure-white, powder-fine beach dotted with sea grape and coconut palms has inspired many a fantasy, and numerous fashion shoots have been conducted here. For some unexplained reason, the sunsets at Negril are extraordinarily spectacular, bursts of neon color across the horizon. Although there's little sight-seeing available, most visitors are just happy to relax and soak up the atmosphere. For the active, there are numerous watersports, superb scuba diving (see below), and fine snorkeling.

If you get to Negril, you must make an extra excursion to **Booby Cay**, a small island across from Rutland Point that attracts an inordinate number of nude bathers. Also spectacular is the sunset cruise on the *Sunsplash*, a 155-foot catamaran that can be booked through Sandals Negril. After you pass through town and head west to Negril Point, the resorts tend to be smaller and more quaint. The beach gives way to high limestone cliffs. At **Xtabi**, the sea caves cut into the cliffs to create a romantic setting that is ideal for sunset viewing. Everyone heads for **Rick's Cafe**—a terrific place to watch divers jump off from the cliff below and a perfect place to celebrate the glorious sunset, but if you don't like crowds, you won't love Rick's. If you're a night prowler, you'll find some of the biggest reggae stars in Jamaica performing throughout Negril until the wee hours. Recently, Negril, through the efforts of the Coral Reef Preservation Society, has instituted an active mooring and education program. At present, 35 separate moorings virtually eliminate the need for anchoring.

Beaches in Negril

Negril Beach is seven long miles of heaven—everyone's idea of Eden. Unfortunately, much of it is fenced off today, especially the nude area. Fortunately, some resorts have had the foresight to build their properties overlooking the nude areas. The famous (infamous) singles-only club **Hedonism II** is located on this beach. If you saw the movie *Exit to Eden* and fantasized about being at a resort like *that*, you will probably love Hedonism II.

Negril

Divers enjoy the beautiful cliffs and caves at the west end of Negril.

Sports in Negril

Negril Hills Golf Club

Negril, ☎ *(809) 957-4638.*

This brand-new golf club opened in late 1995. It is designed by Roy Case and Robert Simons and has 18 championship holes. The site also includes a club house and pro shop.

Where to Stay

Hotels and Resorts

Chuckles $75–$260 ★★

Negril Square, Negril, ☎ *(809) 957-4277.*
Single: $75–$260. Double: $90–$260.

Located on a hill above the commercial center, this Mediterranean-style resort is peaceful and quiet. Guestrooms are nicely done and very clean; two-bedroom villas have kitchens. On-site facilities include two tennis courts, a large pool, volleyball and a disco. The public beach is down the hill. 78 rooms. Credit cards: A, MC.

Drumville Cove Resort $40–$100 ★★

West End, Negril, ☎ *(800) 423-4095, (809) 957-4369.*
Single: $40–$100. Double: $45–$100.

Set on the side of a cliff overlooking the sea, this complex is 2.5 miles from town. Accommodations are in cottages, some with kitchenettes. Enjoy nightly entertainment, a weekly barbecue, restaurant and bar. 20 rooms. Credit cards: A, MC, V.

Foote Prints on the Sands $85–$145 ★★★

Norman Manley Boulevard, Negril, ☎ *(809) 957-4300.*
Single: $85–$145. Double: $85–$145.

This family-run hotel sits right on Seven Mile Beach. Guestrooms are nice and comfortable, and a few have whirlpool tubs. Four kitchenette suites are also available, as well as two-bedroom units. There's no TV in the rooms, though you can watch the tube in the lounge. No pool, but lots of watersports, and a beach barbecue twice a week. 33 rooms. Credit cards: A, MC.

Grand Lido $350–$290 ★★★★★

Norman Manley Boulevard, Negril, ☎ *(800) 423-4095, (809) 957-4010.*
Single: $350–$390. Double: $250–$290.

Very glamorous and elegant, this all-inclusive resort is open only to adults, though it's a lot less of a meat market than its neighbor, Hedonism II. Set on 22 acres, the Mediterranean-style property wows guests with a dramatic entrance, personalized check-in, and the *M.Y. Zein*, a yacht given by Aristotle Onassis as a wedding gift to Princess Grace and Prince Rainier. Accommodations are in wings that run parallel to the beach, all with sea views. They are beautifully done with tasteful decor, large baths, sitting areas, and such niceties as stereos. While away the hours with our restaurants, six bars, two pools, four tennis courts, a full health club, cruises aboard the yacht, a beauty salon, and on and on and on. The large beach is divided in two for those who wear suits and those who don't. Service, of course, is superb. Part of the SuperClubs group, this resort is designed for those who like to splurge and be in the company of equally monied people. 200 rooms. Credit cards: A, MC.

Hedonism II   **$205–$376**   ★★★

Norman Manley Boulevard, Negril, ☎ *(800) 423-4095, (809) 957-4200.*
Single: $205–$260. Double: $305–$376.
This all-inclusive resort, open only to those over 18, is aptly named, as it is dedicated to the pursuit of pleasure—and partying. Lots of singles are mixed in with the couples, and depending on the clientele, the resort can be a bit of a meat market. Set on 22 acres at the northern end of Seven Mile Beach, the resort houses guests in comfortable though uninspired rooms; the whole point is to be out frolicking, anyway. Rates include all meals, drinks (drinking is a big pastime), and activities, and tips are forbidden. Amenities include two restaurants, five bars, a pool and two Jacuzzis, six tennis courts, all watersports, a gym, and nightly entertainment in the disco. The beach is divided for "prudes" and "nudes." Not for the conservative by any stretch, but lively and fun for young partyers. 280 rooms. Credit cards: A, MC.

Negril Beach Club Hotel   **$77–$185**   ★★

Negril Main Road, Negril, ☎ *(800) 526-2422, (809) 957-4220.*
Single: $77–$185. Double: $65–$185.
Very, very casual and informal, this complex includes traditional rooms, studios, and one-bedroom suites with kitchens. Amenities include a small pool, health club and two tennis courts, but most activity centers around the beach, where watersports await and most bathers are topless. 85 rooms. Credit cards: A, MC.

Negril Cabins   **$110–$190**   ★★

Bloody Bay, Negril, ☎ *(800) 382-3444, (809) 957-4350.*
Single: $110–$162. Double: $130–$190.
Set on 10 acres in a forest across from Bloody Bay beach, this complex of log cabins on stilts offers rustic accommodations—the basic units have two bedrooms and tree-level balconies. If you want air conditioning and satellite TV, book a superior room for about $20 more per night. Other than two restaurants and occasional live entertainment, there's not much else in the way of amenities, though families like the supervised children's program and the fact that kids under 16 stay free. A nice alternative to the cookie-cutter beach hotels. 50 rooms. Credit cards: A, MC.

Negril Inn   **$115–$145**   ★★

Negril Beach, Negril, ☎ *(800) 634-7456, (809) 957-4209.*
Single: $115–$145. Double: $115–$145.
A nice alternative to the larger and livelier all-inclusives, this small resort offers everything for one price in a more peaceful setting. Guestrooms are simple but pleasant. Most meals are served buffet-style, and there are two bars and nightly entertainment for dessert. Recreational facilities include two tennis courts, bicycles, horseshoes, a pool and gym. No kids under 16. 46 rooms. Credit cards: A, MC.

Negril Tree House   **$85–$275**   ★★★★

Norman Manley Boulevard, Negril, ☎ *(800) 423-4095, (809) 957-4288.*
Single: $85–$275. Double: $85–$275.

Negril

Set right on Seven Mile Beach, this unusual spot accommodates guests in two-story octagonal "tree house" cottages and oceanfront villas. They are generally nicely done with rattan furniture, but some could use repairs. Ask for a room on the second floor; they have better views and more atmosphere. Twelve suites offer one or two bedrooms, full kitchens and wide verandas. Enjoy the pool, watersports, a handful of bars and restaurants where locals hang out, a Monday night beach party and twice-weekly island picnics. Very nice, if you don't mind rustic. The elevated bar and restaurant, perched in a mango tree, attract lots of locals. 70 rooms. Credit cards: A, MC.

Paradise View $75–$135   ★★

Norman Manley Boulevard, Negril, ☎ *(809) 957-4375.*
Single: $75–$95. Double: $100–$135.
Modest in most ways, this hotel's real asset is its location on a gorgeous beach. Guestrooms are comfortable but on the small side. Watersports are offered on the beach, but there is no pool. 17 rooms. Credit cards: A, MC.

Poinciana Beach Hotel $249–$294   ★★★

Norman Manley Boulevard, Negril, ☎ *(800) 468-6728, (809) 957-4100.*
Single: $249–$499. Double: $165–$294.
Set on six tropical acres fronting Seven Mile Beach, this resort went all-inclusive in late 1994, making it Negril's only one-price property. Guests are housed in a varied mix of standard rooms, studios, and one- and two-bedroom apartments in villas. All are nicely done, with Murphy beds in the studios and kitchens, as well as cooks in the apartments. All kinds of watersports await, including PADI certification for divers. Amenities include two tennis courts, miniature golf, a weight room, rental bikes, two pools and a disco. Good for the active set. 130 rooms. Credit cards: A, MC.

Sandals Negril $2890–$3995   ★★★★

Rutland Point, Negril, ☎ *(800) 726-3257, (809) 957-4216.*
Another of the chain's couples-only resorts, this operation is set on a narrow beach, with a boat shuttling guests to a small island where they can tan in the buff. Rooms are comfortable, but only the more expensive units have balconies and sea views. All kinds of activities (plus meals and drinks) are covered in the rate, including three tennis courts, watersports, a gym, two pools, and the usual resort diversions. A few bars and a disco provide nighttime fun. Appeals mainly to the young and in love. Most find it a bit more subdued than Hedonism II. Rates are $2890 to $3995 per couple per week. Partying couples may be happier at Hedonism II, which is cheaper. 199 rooms. Credit cards: A, MC.

Swept Away Resort $2770–$3785   ★★★★

Long Bay, Negril, ☎ *(800) 545-7937, (809) 957-4040.*
Yet another all-inclusive resort open only to couples, this special spot puts an emphasis on sports and fitness. Accommodations are in two-story villas near the beach and are beautifully decorated with large verandas. The centerpiece is the fitness center, an excellent facility with a gym, lap pool, 10 tennis courts, as well as courts for squash and racquetball. Save time for all the usual watersports plus be sure to enjoy a few laps in the lagoon-style pool. Alcoholic drinks are available, but the

emphasis is on juice and veggie bars. Dedicated partyers look elsewhere! $2770 to $3785 per couple per week. 134 rooms. Credit cards: A, MC, V.

T-Water Beach Hotel $125–$155 ★★
Norman Manley Boulevard, Negril, ☎ *(800) 654-1592, (809) 957-4270.*
Single: $125–$155. Double: $125–$155.
Set on Seven Mile Beach, this resort accommodates guests in a varied mix of traditional rooms, studios with kitchens, and suites. Popular with families (kids under 12 stay free), it offers a pool, watersports, and constant volleyball games. Not too exciting, but the rates are relatively reasonable. 70 rooms. Credit cards: A, MC.

Apartments and Condominiums

Beachcomber Club $100–$325 ★★★
Norman Manley Boulevard, Negril, ☎ *(800) 423-4095, (809) 957-4171.*
Single: $100–$150. Double: $100–$325.
Set right on Seven Mile Beach, this Georgian-style condominium complex has standard rooms, studios and one- and two-bedroom units with attractive furnishings, large verandas and full kitchens. Some also sport four-poster beds. Hotel-like touches include room service and nightly turndowns. Amenities include an Italian restaurant, bar, tennis, watersports, a pool, and supervised programs for children year-round. Wedding packages are available. 46 rooms. Credit cards: A, MC.

Crystal Waters Villas $85–$110 ★★
Negril ☎ *(800) 443-3020, (809) 957-4889.*
Single: $85–$110. Double: $85–$110.
Located right on the beach, this complex offers villas with full kitchens, porches, one to three bedrooms, and the services of a personal maid and cook. No restaurant on-site, but many are nearby. Reasonable rates. 10 rooms. Credit cards: A, MC.

Point Village $100–$155 ★★★
Rutland Point, Negril, ☎ *(809) 957-4351.*
Single: $100–$145. Double: $115–$155.
Set on Rutland Point on the northern coastline among lush foliage, this village-style resort has tropically decorated studios and suites with kitchens and one to three bedrooms. A house band entertains six nights a week, and there are also occasional theme parties, as well as a few bars for nighttime recreation. By day, you can enjoy the pool, private beach with watersports, and tennis. Parents can stash the kids in supervised programs. 130 rooms. Credit cards: A, MC.

Xtabi Club Resort $50–$145 ★★★
West End, Negril, ☎ *(809) 957-4336.*
Single: $50–$145. Double: $50–$145.
Perfect for nature lovers as well as just plain lovers, this resort houses guests in octagonal cottages set on rugged cliffs or across the road in a garden setting. All are simply furnished and have small kitchens and enclosed outdoor showers, but no air conditioning. The grounds are lovely and natural, with dense foliage, sea caves and nice views—the sunsets are especially dramatic. Spiral stairs lead down though a cave to a tiny beach, where great snorkeling awaits; there's also is a pool for cooling off. Lots of nude sunbathers here. 26 rooms. Credit cards: A, MC.

Negril

Inns

Charela Inn   **$80–$170**   ★ ★ ★

Norman Manley Boulevard, Negril, ☎ (800) 423-4095, (809) 957-4648. FAX (809) 957-4414.

Single: $80–$150. Double: $96–$170.

This small Spanish hacienda-style inn has lush inner gardens and is set right on Seven Mile Beach. Guestrooms have plenty of character with four-poster beds and balconies. Request one on the upper floor for the best views. Amenities include a pool and free watersports, and a decent restaurant serving French and Jamaican cuisine. Rooms have no TV, but you can get your fix in the lounge area. Live shows each Thursday and Saturday nights. Peaceful and friendly. 39 rooms. Credit cards: MC, V.

Natania's Guest House   **$50–$60**   ★ ★ ★

Little Culloden (near Whitehouse), Westmorland, ☎ (800) 330-2332, (809) 963-5342. FAX (809) 963-5342.

Single: $50–$60. Double: $50–$60.

Natania's is located on Jamaica's south coast, 37 miles from Montego Bay. This unassuming little inn is on 2.5 acres of private, waterfront tropical gardens, with a beach, swimming pool, bar and restaurant on site. Each pleasant room has a private bath and ceiling fans. The lounge has satellite TV for those who need their daily fix of CNN. Friendly and charming. 8 rooms.

Low Cost Lodging

Hotel Samsara   **$40–$115**   ★ ★

Light House Road, Negril, ☎ (809) 957-4395.

Single: $40–$115. Double: $40–$115.

Perched on low cliffs overlooking the sea, this small hotel has no beach, but a waterslide will dunk you right into the ocean, if you so desire. Accommodations are in spacious cottages, decorated with a minimal of fuss. Only some are air-conditioned. Relaxed and informal, the place hops during the Monday night reggae concerts. There's also a pool and tennis court. 50 rooms. Credit cards: A, MC.

Negril Gardens   **$105–$140**   ★ ★

Norman Manley Boulevard, Negril, ☎ (800) 423-4095, (809) 957-4408.

Single: $105–$140. Double: $105–$140.

Located on Seven Mile Beach, this two-story hotel puts up guests on the beach or across the road near the pool. Entertainment is offered four nights a week, and by day, you can enjoy a pool, tennis and watersports on the public beach. Informal and friendly. 54 rooms. Credit cards: A, MC.

Rock Cliff Resort   **$55–$100**   ★ ★ ★

Light House Road, Negril, ☎ (809) 957-4331.

Single: $55–$100. Double: $55–$100.

This complex of two-story colonial-style buildings appeals mainly to divers—many come for its excellent PADI center. There's no beach, but a free shuttle will take you to one. Guestrooms are modestly decorated but of good size. Amenities include a pool, volleyball, basketball, and two restaurants. Unless you're into diving, you'll probably be happier at a beach property. 33 rooms. Credit cards: A, MC.

Where to Eat

Cafe au Lait   **$$$**   ★★
Lighthouse Road, Negril, ☎ *(809) 957-4471. Associated hotel: Mirage Resort.*
French cuisine.
Lunch: Noon–3 p.m., entrées $9–$29.
Dinner: 5–10 p.m., entrées $9–$29.
Located in a cottage resort on the West End, this authentic bistro (for Jamaica) fea-
tures island-influenced, light French meals, including pizza and crepes (some made
with callaloo), French bread, local seafood and French wines. A pleasant spot if you
are passing through the area. Credit cards: MC, V.

Chicken Lavish   **$**   ★★
West End Road, Negril, ☎ *(809) 957-4410.*
Latin American cuisine.
Lunch: 9 a.m.–4 p.m., entrées $3–$5.
Dinner: 4–10 p.m., entrées $3–$5.
Super informal, super cheap, and super delicious—with a juicy name like that what
else can you expect? Once a local hangout jealously guarded by those in the know,
the word is out about this unpretentious little spot on the that is beach renowned
for its toothsome fried chicken and curried goat. Credit cards: MC, V.

Cosmo's   **$**   ★★
Norman Manley Boulevard, Negril, ☎ *(809) 957-4330.*
Seafood cuisine. Specialties: Curried Conch.
Lunch: 11 a.m.–4 p.m., entrées $5–$12.
Dinner: 4–10 p.m., entrées $5–$12.
Seafood is pretty much IT here, but what seafood! Owner-character Cosmo Brown
specializes in conch, either stewed, curried or served in a generous vat of soup. Since
this chewy gastropod isn't as commonly found in Jamaica, this is a good spot to try
it. Otherwise, a grilled or baked escovitch (well-marinated in spices) whole fish is a
popular choice. Cosmo's is situated in an informal, thatched-roof hut on a sparsely-
populated East End beach. Credit cards: MC, V.

Hungry Lion   **$$$**   ★★
West End Road, Negril.
Latin American cuisine.
Lunch: entrées $18–$30.
Dinner: entrées $18–$30.
The setting at this small and popular restaurant is as verdant and colorful as the Ras-
tafarian Ital cuisine served here. Ital, which is based on local vegetarian ingredients,
often features foods that display the Rasta colors of green, red and gold. At the
Hungry Lion, if you dine outside by a fountain, you'll be surrounded by a green-
house of flowering plants. Inside, the dining room is a lively canvas of sophisticated
tie-dye hues. A plate consisting of a marinated whole fish comes dressed with a
hibiscus flower. It's that kind of place. Credit cards: MC, V.

Paradise Yard   **$$**   ★★
Gas Station Road, Negril, ☎ *(809) 957-4006.*

Negril

Latin American cuisine. Specialties: Rasta Pasta.
Lunch: 8 a.m.–4 p.m., entrées $6–$15.
Dinner: 4–10 p.m., entrées $6–$15.

Life is fine at this relaxing open-air restaurant with a tin roof situated on the road to the port city of Savannah-del-Mar. You can get here early for a full-on Jamaican breakfast of saltfish and ackee, juicy local fruits and *bammies* (cassava bread). At lunch and dinner, ackee appears again in the Rasta Pasta. The golden vegetable tastes like scrambled eggs and also is teamed with a thick tomato sauce and green peppers over fettuccine. Other choices include curried goat, pumpkin soup and enchiladas. This is a very authentic experience. Credit cards: not accepted.

Rick's Cafe   **$$$**   ★

West End Road, Negril, ☎ *(809) 957-4335.*
Seafood cuisine. Specialties: Grilled Lobster, Fresh-Fruit Daiquiris.
Lunch: Noon–4 p.m., entrées $11–$28.
Dinner: 4–10 p.m., entrées $11–$28.

This famous (circa 1974) bar-restaurant-hangout is a scene and a place to be seen. One of the many draws here is a concept inspired by the La Quebrada divers in Acapulco—locals and visitors plunge some 25 feet into the sea from the cliffs at Rick's before emerging (it's hoped) for a papaya daiquiri. A tamer ritual takes place just before sunset when crowds of tanned and buffed young people pack the rock-encrusted, palm-fronded terrace for fun and frolic and the day's last glimpse of Old Sol. You can also come here for lunch or brunch, but for that you can go anywhere. Credit cards: not accepted.

Tan-ya's   **$$$**   ★

Norman Manley Boulevard, Negril, ☎ *(809) 957-4041. Associated hotel: Seasplash Resort.*
Latin American cuisine.
Lunch: 11 a.m.–3 p.m., entrées $5–$8.
Dinner: 6:30–10 p.m., entrées $8–$25.

This oceanside restaurant at the quietly elegant Seasplash Resort is where guests and others go to dress up (just a little) for French-inspired seafood. The chef has a creative way with lobster. Reservations recommended. Credit cards: A, MC, V.

North Coast

About 30 miles east from Montego Bay, **Falmouth** gives you the feeling of being a fairly quiet area while still maintaining proximity to the cities of Mo' Bay and Ocho Rios. This small, 18th-century port town takes about a half-hour to explore on foot. There are a number of historical buildings that are interesting to see, such as the courthouse, a reconstruction of the 19th-century building, the customs office, the William Knubb Memorial Church, at George and King Street, and the 1796 parish church. Nearby is the **Good Hope** great house (leaving town, turn south), the 18th-century estate of John Thorpe, one of the richest Jamaican planters. The restoration of the main house and several outbuildings is exquisite, and it now stands as a fine hotel. Save time for a magnificent horseback ride through the countryside, over the estate's 6000 acres. Make your reservations in advance; ☎ *(809) 954-3289.* Near here, you will find the turnoff to **Rafter's Village**, where you can take a bamboo raft down the Martha Brae River (for information about river rafting and other river treks, see the section "On Foot" above). Two miles east of Falmouth is the **Caribatik factory**, which is the artwork of a fine Jamaican artist, Muriel Chandler. At **Glistening Waters Marina**, east of Caribatik, you'll discover Oyster Bay, which glows with bioluminescence caused by microorganisms in the water.

Where to Stay

Hotels and Resorts

| **Ambiance Jamaica** | **$70–$138** | ★★ |

Runaway Bay, ☎ *(800) 523-6504, (809) 973-4606.*
Single: $70–$138. Double: $138.

Set on a small private beach, this casual hotel offers adequate accommodations and services. There's a pool, gym and two restaurants, but not much else to write home about. In 1995, the hotel began offering reasonably priced all-inclusive packages; call for details. 80 rooms. Credit cards: A, MC.

| **Breezes Runaway Bay** | **$240–$439** | ★★★★ |

Runaway Bay, ☎ *(800) 859-7873, (809) 973-2436. FAX (809) 973-2352.*
Single: $240–$319. Double: $330–$439.

Encompassing 214 acres opening onto a wide, sandy beach, this all-inclusive resort (formerly Jamaica) near Ocho Rios does just about everything right. Not only do the rates include all meals, drinks and activities, they even throw in free cigarettes. Accommodations are basically bare-bones, but everyone's too busy with organized activities to notice. There's an excellent golf course, plus four tennis courts, classes in Jamaican handicrafts, all watersports, horseback riding, as well as a full healthclub with aerobics classes. The disco hops and the snorkeling offshore is great. Kids under 14 stay free. All visits are a three-night minimum. 238 rooms. Credit cards: A, MC.

Caribbean Isle Hotel   **$55–$65**   ★

Runaway Bay, ☎ *(809) 973-2364.*
Single: $55–$60. Double: $60–$65.
This small, casual hotel offers budget accommodations and not much else, though there is a pool. The beach comes and goes, depending on the tides. 24 rooms. Credit cards: A, MC.

Club Caribbean   **$125–$295**   ★★

Runaway Bay, ☎ *(800) 647-2740, (809) 973-4702.*
Single: $125–$395. Double: $215–$295.
This resort offers all-inclusive resort amenities with self-serve accommodations. Guests are put up in octagonal cottages with ceiling fans (no air conditioning) and kitchenettes. There's lots happening in the activities department, with organized crab races, volleyball games and the like. Other amenities include watersports, two tennis courts, a swim-up bar in the pool, and a disco. Just about everything but lunch is included in the rates. 128 rooms. Credit cards: A, MC, V.

Eaton Hall Beach Hotel   **$135–$299**   ★★★

Runaway Bay, ☎ *(809) 973-3503.*
Single: $135–$299. Double: $185–$299.
This former 18th-century Georgian-style slave station is an all-inclusive resort that caters to a predominantly young crowd. Guests stay in standard rooms, suites, or villas with kitchenettes; all comfortable, but showing their age. No beach to speak of, but there are two pools, as well as tennis, watersports, glass-bottom boat rides, and organized activities. 52 rooms. Credit cards: A, CB, MC, V.

H.E.A.R.T. Country Club   **$55–$75**   ★★★

Runaway Bay, ☎ *(809) 973-2671.*
Single: $55. Double: $75.
This plantation-style country club is staffed by people learning the hotel business (the name stands for Human Employment and Resource Training), so you can count on enthusiastic service. Set on a hillside with nice views, guestrooms are nice and bright. There's a decent restaurant and pool, golf next door, and they'll shuttle you to a small private beach. Really good for the rates. 20 rooms. Credit cards: A, MC.

Apartments and Condominiums

Franklyn D. Resort   **$286–$298**   ★★★★

Runaway Bay, ☎ *(800) 654-1337, (809) 973-3067. FAX (809) 973-3071.*
Single: $286–$348. Double: $236–$298.
This Georgian-style, all-inclusive resort is especially suited to families. Accommodations are in suites with one to three bedrooms, kitchens, and a "Girl Friday" to cook clean and look after the kids by day (there's an extra charge for night-time babysitting). There's only one television set per unit, and air conditioners only in the bedrooms. Kids under 16 stay free, so you'll see a lot of them here; romantic couples will probably be happier elsewhere. The beach is small but quite nice, and there are two pools (one for kids), tennis, exercise room, and tons of organized activities for

both kids and their parents. The rates include everything from soup to nuts, and even cigarettes. Inquire about weekly rates. 76 rooms. Credit cards: A, MC.

Portside Villas & Condos $85–$280 ★★

Highway A-1, Runaway Bay, ☎ *(809) 973-2007.*
Single: $85–$280. Double: $85–$280.

Located 20 minutes outside of Ocho Rios at Discovery Bay, this complex has studios and suites of one to three bedrooms, all with kitchens and cooks for an extra fee. The beach is small, but there are also two pools. Amenities include nonmotorized watersports. You're on your own for meals. 15 rooms. Credit cards: A, MC.

Ocho Rios

Over the past 15 years, Ocho Rios has become one of the busiest, if most elite, tourism sites in Jamaica. Cruise ships dock nearly daily and a number of fine resorts are located here. Five outstanding beaches, excellent restaurants, abundant nightlife and lots of sports make the area ideal for those who want to escape the Third World chaos of Kingston and Montego Bay. The town has fiercely hung onto its charm despite the massive development. The most exciting natural phenomenon near here is **Dunn's River Falls**, the internationally renowned stair-stepped falls that rush under the road and reappear to join the sea on the white beach to the left. Even if you don't throw yourself to the wetness in a fun tour of the falls, you must come to see its dramatic descent over the mountainside. Other natural attractions include the Shaw Park Botanical Garden, where you can wile away a few hours studying the exotic tropical plants of the island.

If you're feeling athletic, a terrific horseback riding jaunt can be arranged at the **Prospect Plantation**, which will take you through trails of citrus groves and coffee trees, and down by the banks of the White River. Jitney tours of the estate are free of charge. Rafting tours on the nearby White River are also available (see the section under "Treks.") Out on Annotto Bay, you'll find the 250-acre **Crystal Springs**, a natural garden replete with hundreds of birds, tropical orchids, fierce waterfalls, rivers and a restaurant.

Beaches in Ocho Rios

Ocho Rios beach is giving Mo' Bay a run for its money these days in terms of traffic. Mallard's attracts the most crowds, somewhat due to the presence of the Jamaica Grande hotel, which caters to the convention crowd. Turtle Beach is the adjacent strand, which has a very good reputation for swimming.

What Else to See

Historical Sites

Firefly ★★★

Grants Pen, St. Mary.
Hours open: 9 a.m.–5 p.m.
This is the home of Sir Noel Coward, who spent the last 25 years of his life in Jamaica. Donated to the Jamaican government upon his death in 1973, the mansion remains unchanged since Coward, an actor and author, lived there. Guided

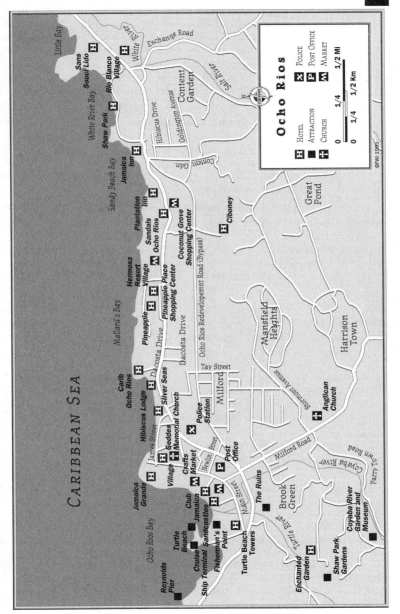

Ocho Rios

HOTEL, POLICE, POST OFFICE, MARKET, ATTRACTION, CHURCH

1/2 MI, 1/4, 1/2 Km, 1/4

©FW 1995

CARIBBEAN SEA

Little Bay
White River
Exchange Road
Sans Souci Lido
Rio Blanco Village
White River Bay
Salt River
Content Garden
Shaw Park
Hibiscus Drive
Goldington Avenue
Sandy Beach Bay
Jamaica Inn
Content Gdn.
Great Pond
Plantation Inn
Sandals Ocho Rios
Coconut Grove Shopping Center
Ciboney
Hermosa Resort Village
Pineapple Place Shopping Center
Ocho Rios Redevelopment Road (Bypass)
Mallard's Bay
Pineapple
Dacosta Drive
Dacosta Drive
Mansfield Heights
Harrison Town
Carib Ocho Rios
Tay Street
Milford
Silver Seas
Stormont Avenue
Hibiscus Lodge
James Street
Geddes Memorial Church
Police Station
Anglican Church
Village
Crafts Market
Newlin Street
Post Office
Ocho Rios Bay
Jamaica Grande
Milford Road
The Ruins
Coyaba River
Parry Town Road
Reynolds Pier
Turtle Beach
Club Jamaica
Sandcastles
Main Street
Brook Green
Cruise Ship Terminal
Fisherman's Point
Turtle River
Coyaba River Garden and Museum
Turtle Beach Towers
Enchanted Garden
Shaw Park Gardens

Ocho Rios

tours take you through the house to gawk at his bedroom, closets filled with clothes, antique furnishings, and paintings by the man himself. His grave is also on the site, as well as a cafe and gift shop. Continue your literary tour at **Goldeneye** (☎ *[809] 974-5833*), located on the outskirts of Oracabessa, 20 miles east of Ocho Rios. This 15-acre beachfront estate was the winter home of Ian Fleming, creator of the James Bond books. He penned 14 of the popular novels here; five set in Jamaica. The house is much more modest than Firefly, but the grounds are gorgeous. General admission: $10.

Museums and Exhibits

Harmony Hall   ★★★

Highway A3, Tower Isle, ☎ *(809) 460-4120.*
Hours open: 10 a.m.–6 p.m.
This late 19th-century great house is now a gallery displaying high-quality paintings and arts and crafts by Jamaican artists.

Parks and Gardens

Coyaba River Garden and Museum   ★★★

Shaw Park, Ocho Rios, ☎ *(809) 974-6235.*
This former plantation is now a private estate with lovely gardens, waterfalls, a river and fish ponds. The small museum displays relics from pre-Columbian days. Coyaba is the Arawak word for paradise and this spot is certainly a small slice of it. General admission: $5.

Tours

Dunn's River Falls   ★★

Highway A3, Ocho Rios, ☎ *(809) 974-2857.*
Hours open: 9 a.m.–5 p.m.
These much-photographed falls cascade down some 600 feet into the sea. The best way to experience them is to hire a guide and make a human chain that climbs right up the slippery rocks. Wear sneakers, and don't forget to tip your guide. You can stop along the way to dip in pools and be massaged by the tumbling water. There's a path on dry land for the less daring. General admission: $3.

Prospect Plantation   ★★★

Highway A3, St. Ann, ☎ *(809) 974-2058.*
Located just east of Ocho Rios, this working plantation can be toured via jitney. Among the highlights are sweeping views, gorgeous scenery, and lots of trees planted by famous folks, including Noel Coward and Charlie Chaplin. General admission: $10.

Where to Stay

Hotels and Resorts

Boscobel Beach Hotel   **$415–$995**   ★★★★

Ocho Rios, ☎ *(800) 423-4095, (809) 975-3330.*
Double: $415–$995.

Set on the beach, this all-inclusive resort, part of the SuperClubs group, caters to families. Accommodations range from spacious guestrooms to suites, all nicely done. Some with sunken tubs. The grounds include a large playground, two theaters showing films, a disco and two pools, one in the adults-only section. Four tennis courts, watersports and a healthclub round out the action. Kids are kept busy with supervised programs, and for additional fee, will be minded by their own private nanny. Great for families (and superior to the Franklyn D. Resort for those with more than one kid). Those without kids should look elsewhere. 228 rooms. Credit cards: A, MC.

Braco Village Resort   **$270–$280**   ★ ★ ★

Rio Bueno, Ocho Rios, ☎ *(800) 654-1337, (809) 973-4882. FAX (809) 954-0020. Single: $270–$360. Double: $190–$280.*

Opened in spring 1995, this new all-inclusive village is located 38 miles east of Montego Bay and 30 miles west of Ocho Rios. The village reflects Jamaica's various architectural styles, from Georgian to gingerbread. The centerpiece is the Town Square, which features several restaurants, bars, and artists in residence creating and exhibiting their work. The idea is to make the village as authentically Jamaican as possible, while still spoiling guests with the amenities of a resort. Recreational facilities include an Olympic-size pool, a nine-hole golf course, four tennis courts, a soccer field, 85 acres of jogging and hiking trails, a fitness center, and all watersports, including scuba and kayaking. Each guestroom has a unique feature such as a gazebo, balcony, or love seat. The 2000-foot beach has a clothing-optional section. 180 rooms.

Ciboney Ocho Rios   **$175–$690**   ★ ★ ★ ★

Main Street, Ocho Rios, ☎ *(800) 777-7800, (809) 974-1036. Single: $175–$345. Double: $350–$690.*

Set just outside of town on 45 hillside acres, this all-inclusive resort is impressive and stylish. Most accommodations are in villas with full kitchens, semi-private pools, and personal attendants. You can work out and be pampered in the European-style spa, play golf on six courts, swim in two pools, and partake in all watersports. Very nice. 300 rooms. Credit cards: A, MC.

Club Jamaica Beach Resort   **$180–$235**   ★ ★

Main Street, Ocho Rios, ☎ *(800) 423-4095, (809) 974-6642. Single: $180–$235. Double: $115–$235.*

Located on Turtle Beach near the crafts market, the all-inclusive property has comfortable guestrooms. As with other all-inclusives, there's lots to do, including themed buffets at poolside, nightly entertainment, a disco, and organized activities. No kids under 12. 95 rooms. Credit cards: A, MC, V.

Couples Jamaica   **$365–$520**   ★ ★ ★ ★

Autoroute 3, Ocho Rios, ☎ *(800) 423-4095, (809) 975-4271. Double: $365–$520.*

Like the name applies, this all-inclusive resort is open to couples only—the resort logo is two lions copulating, in case you don't get the message. Guestrooms are modern and comfortable, with king-sized beds, cable TV and CD players (pack your own discs). The bathrooms sometimes run out of hot water. The beach is small but great and there's always something happening, from nightly entertainment to five tennis courts with pros and free lessons to all watersports—there's even a wind-surfing school. Guests can dine at any of the three restaurants, all of which have live entertainment at mealtime. There's also ferry service to the small nude island just off the coast, plus sunset sails, scuba lessons, and optional day trips. If you get carried away by romance, the resort staff can marry you for free. You'll be making like lions in no time. 172 rooms. Credit cards: A, MC.

Enchanted Garden $150–$215   ★ ★ ★

Main Road, Ocho Rios, ☎ *(800) 554-2008, (809) 974-1400. FAX (809) 974-5823. Single: $150–$240. Double: $125–$215.*

It really is rather enchanting at this all-inclusive resort set in the foothills and sur-rounded by jungle greenery on the former estate of one-time Jamaica's Prime Min-ister, Edward Seaga. The many gardens and waterfalls lend a truly exotic feel. Accommodations range from standard rooms to villas with kitchens and one to three bedrooms, all nicely done. You can swim in the pool or in natural ponds with waterfalls. Dining is quite varied, with lots of ethnic choices as well as spa cuisine. Two tennis courts, a fully equipped health spa that specializes in aromatherapy, and an aviary are also on site. The staff can take you to the beach or into town for free. 113 rooms. Credit cards: A, MC, V.

Jamaica Grande $135–$195   ★ ★ ★ ★

Ocho Rios, ☎ *(800) 228-9898, (809) 974-2201. Single: $135–$195. Double: $135–$195.*

Ocho Rios' largest hotel is a modern high-rise known for its fantasy pool, a large and fanciful body of water with grottos, waterfalls, a swinging bridge, and a swim-up bar. Accommodations are found in two towers and the rooms are generally nicely done. Facilities include a fitness center, four tennis courts, all watersports, activities for children, and a large and happening disco. Nightly entertainment and lots of theme parties rev up your evenings. Nice, but the sheer size can be a bit over-whelming, and there's not much in the way of authentic Jamaican style. 720 rooms. Credit cards: A, CB, MC, V.

Jamaica Inn $200–$475   ★ ★ ★ ★

Ocho Rios, ☎ *(809) 974-2516. FAX (809) 974-2449. Single: $200–$475. Double: $250–$475.*

Located in a tropical setting on a private beach, this intimate resort requires guests to dress up in the evening—the better to dance to the small orchestra that plays nightly. Most accommodations are in junior or full suites all recently upgraded and decorated with antiques, local artwork and large lanais. There's an exercise room, pool and watersports, and guests can play tennis for free at a nearby resort. No kids under 14 are allowed at this very affluent and rather conservative property, called one of the Caribbean's top places to stay by both *Travel & Leisure* and *Condo Nast Traveler* magazines. If you're looking for riotous action, look elsewhere. Both full and modified American meal plans are offered. 45 rooms. Credit cards: A, MC.

Plantation Inn   **$300–$999**   ★ ★ ★

Ocho Rios, ☎ *(800) 423-4095, (809) 974-5601.*
Double: $300–$999.

Located on a lush hillside, this colonial-style hotel has a country club atmosphere that draws a predominantly conservative (and rich) crowd. Rooms are quite nicely done with pampering amenities. The grounds include two beaches reached via a steep walk down the hill, two tennis courts, a small pool, watersports, a gym and massage services. Not as nice as its neighbor, the Jamaica Inn, but a bit more casual, though you're still required to dress up at night. 78 rooms. Credit cards: A, MC, V.

Sandals Dunn's River   **$2295–$4200**   ★ ★ ★ ★

Main Street, Ocho Rios, ☎ *(800) 726-3257, (809) 972-1610.*

Set on 10 tropical acres fronting a beach, this couples-only resort is among the chain's best. Guestrooms come in a variety of configurations and are generally pleasant and comfortable. There's lots happening at all hours: 18 holes of golf (included in the rates), four restaurants and seven bars, frequent live entertainment, a huge pool and another smaller one, four tennis courts, a gym, all watersports, a free trip to Dunn's River Falls, and your package includes a 20-minute massage. A bit more sophisticated than its siblings. $2295 to $4200 per couple per week. 256 rooms. Credit cards: A, MC.

Sandals Ocho Rios   **$355–$455**   ★ ★ ★ ★

Main Street, Ocho Rios, ☎ *(800) 726-3257, (809) 974-5691.*
Double: $355–$455.

Set among lush beachfront gardens, this couples-only resort boasts immaculate grounds and excellent service. The all-inclusive rates cover all meals, drinks and activities, including nightly entertainment, all watersports, a gym with exercise classes, two tennis courts and nearby golf on 18 holes. Accommodations are nice and open onto furnished balconies, most with sea views. Dining is varied with three restaurants; afterwards, there are four bars and a disco in which to unwind. Very professional and well run. 237 rooms. Credit cards: A, MC.

Sans Souci Lido   **$465–$945**   ★ ★ ★ ★ ★

Ocho Rios, ☎ *(800) 203-7450, (809) 974-2353.*
Single: $465–$945. Double: $465–$945.

This elegant all-inclusive resort, part of the SuperClubs group, is tops in any book. It is best known for its rejuvenating Charlie's Spa, where guests are pampered and treated like royalty. Accommodations are quite smashing and range from standard rooms to suites with one or two bedrooms, some with Jacuzzis and kitchens. The hotel is set on a lush, steep hillside overlooking the sea—the small beach is reached via elevator or steep walkways. There are three tennis courts, two outdoor pools, mineral baths, and watersports. The Terrace restaurant is a lovely outdoor spot where you dine to the light of candles and stars; afterwards, there's live entertainment with local cabaret artists and cultural shows. Really special. 111 rooms. Credit cards: A, MC, V.

Shaw Park Beach Hotel   **$165–$436**   ★ ★ ★

Cutlass Bay, Ocho Rios, ☎ *(800) 243-9420, (809) 974-2552.*
Single: $165–$436. Double: $179–$436.

Ocho Rios

Set on a private though narrow beach, this Georgian-style resort has adequate but quite simple guestrooms; the two-bedroom suites with kitchens are much nicer, but also much pricier. Standard recreational activities include two tennis courts, a pool, watersports, and exercise classes. Nights are kept busy with three bars, a lively disco and organized entertainment. Decent, but aging in a not particularly graceful fashion. 118 rooms. Credit cards: A, MC, V.

Apartments and Condominiums

Comfort Suites   **$105–$205**   ★★★

17 DeCosta Drive, Ocho Rios, ☎ (800) 423-4095, (809) 974-7084.
Single: $105–$180. Double: $125–$205.

This downtown hotel accommodates guests in suites with kitchenettes and patios. Amenities include a pool, tennis and year-round supervised kids' programs, as well as maid service and a restaurant. Beaches are found within walking distance. 137 rooms. Credit cards: A, CB, MC, V.

Sea Palms   **$145–$145**   ★★★

61 Main Street, Ocho Rios, ☎ (800) 423-4095, (809) 974-4400.
Single: $145. Double: $145.

A casual complex of apartments with a pool, but no other facilities. Units are comfortable and range from one to three bedrooms, all with patios or balconies and kitchens. 45 rooms. Credit cards: A, MC.

Inns

Hibiscus Lodge   **$65–$93**   ★★★

Main Street, Ocho Rios, ☎ (800) 526-2422, (809) 974-2676.
Single: $65–$93. Double: $65–$93.

Situated in a quiet topical garden fronting the sea, this intimate, Jamaican-style inn has no beach, but there is a pool for cooling off. Guestrooms are spacious and comfortable, but only a few have air conditioning. There's tennis and a well-regarded restaurant on site, as well as a bar built into the cliffs. Lots of atmosphere here. 26 rooms. Credit cards: A, CB, MC, V.

Apartments and Condos

Fisherman's Point   **$95–$135**   ★★

Turtle Beach, Ocho Rios, ☎ (800) 423-4095, (809) 974-5317.
Single: $95–$103. Double: $125–$135.

This complex on Turtle Beach has one-, two-, and three-bedroom apartments with kitchenettes and maid and cook services. Head to the bar and restaurant if you can't face your own cooking. The modest grounds include a pool. The Ocean Village Shopping Centre is within walking distance. 64 rooms. Credit cards: A, MC.

Turtle Beach Towers   **$87–$225**   ★★

Ocean Village, Ocho Rios, ☎ (809) 974-2801.
Single: $87–$225. Double: $93–$225.

These modern high-rises are on the beach, next to the Ocean Village Shopping Centre. Units are nicely done and run the gamut from studios to apartments with one to three bedrooms. Most have balconies and all have maid service. The grounds include a coffee shop, pool, two tennis courts, and watersports. 218 rooms. Credit cards: A, MC.

Where to Eat

Almond Tree   **$$$**   ★★★★

87 Main Street, Ocho Rios, ☎ *(809) 974-2813. Associated hotel: Hibiscus Lodge.*
Latin American cuisine. Specialties: Roast suckling pig, pumpkin soup.
Lunch: Noon–2:30 p.m., entrées $12–$26.
Dinner: 6–9:30 p.m., entrées $12–$26.
If you can stop swinging in the unique chairs suspended from the ceiling in the bar of this small inn on a cliff overlooking the sea, you'll find the food in the restaurant to be quite good. The Almond Tree has a real tree growing through its roof, a diverse clientele (famous rock stars have been known to swing in) and roast suckling pig on the menu. Soups are divine, especially the pumpkin. Drop in at the piano bar on the hotel grounds for some good tunes to accompany after-dinner drinks in a more subdued atmosphere. Reservations recommended. Credit cards: A, DC, MC, V.

Evita's   **$$**   ★★★★★

Eden Bower Road, Ocho Rios, ☎ *(809) 974-2333.*
Italian cuisine. Specialties: Homemade pasta.
Lunch: 11 a.m.–4 p.m., entrées $7–$19.
Dinner: 4–11 p.m., entrées $7–$19.
Don't cry for Evita—in this instance, restaurateur Eva Myers—who has no trouble drawing in pasta lovers and others to this 1860s-era gingerbread house perched over Ocho Rios Bay. Many guests prefer eating on the terrace as the sun sets over the deep blue Caribbean waters. Some of the seemingly endless parade of pastas include a lasagne Rastafari with bell peppers, tomatoes and ackee—the Rastafarian (and Italian) colors. Fresh and delicious fish, especially red snapper, steaks and ribs are also available. Reservations recommended. Credit cards: A, MC, V.

Parkway Restaurant   **$$$**   ★★

60 Da Costa Drive, Ocho Rios, ☎ *(809) 974-2667.*
Latin American cuisine.
Lunch: 7:30 a.m.–4 p.m., entrées $6–$25.
Dinner: 4–11 p.m., entrées $6–$25.
This tropical diner-roadhouse in downtown Ocho Rios serves very reasonably priced and tasty Jamaican specialties to simple folk as well as prime movers and shakers. You can join them too, while watching local programming from the ever-present TV. Spicy Jamaican chicken or curries and banana cake or pie are popular choices. Credit cards: A, MC, V.

Ruins Restaurant   **$$$**   ★

Da Costa Drive, Ocho Rios, ☎ *(809) 974-2442.*
Chinese cuisine.
Lunch: Noon–2:30 p.m., entrées $12–$33.
Dinner: 6–9:30 p.m., entrées $12–$33.
The cuisine is mostly American-Chinese (chop suey, chow mein, etc.), but the scene is the thing at this refreshing alfresco restaurant named after the ruins of an old

sugar mill that once occupied the site. Expect a lot of fellow revelers marveling at the surrounding waterfalls and pools that are softly lit at night. Dress is casual, and there is a cocktail lounge in an adjoining building. Specialties include shellfish and lobster; but you can also order a steak. No lunch is served on Sunday. Reservations required. Credit cards: A, DC, MC, V.

Port Antonio

Port Antonio is a miniature island port built around two **picturesque harbors** that could have served well as a Hollywood set. Indeed, Port Antonio *was* nearly a Hollywood set, at least the winter stomping ground, for such luminaries as Ginger Rogers, Bette Davis, Clara Bow, as well as such financial magnates as J.P. Morgan and William Randolph Hearst, who in the '20s, '30s, and '40s were drawn to the tropical exoticism and serene beauty of the bay. Port Antonio's biggest fan was actor Errol Flynn, who often could be seen prowling the bars at night. Strange architectural fantasies took shape in this town: the dream castle of architect Earl Levy, complete with turrets, over the shoreline east of the Trident Hotel, and the sprawling concrete mansion built by a Connecticut tycoon, now in crumbling remains. Nature lovers won't want to miss the 282-foot deep lagoon called **Blue Hole** off Route 44, or **Somerset Falls**, in the gorge of the Daniel River, above Hope Bay (you can't find a more romantic trip than the gondola ride under the falls). Hiking up to the **Blue Mountains** is spectacular and offers a terrific vista (for more information, see under "Treks"). At Machioneal, only the hardiest climbers will make it to the top of **Reach Falls** (no wonder the name!), but the effort is worth it since the falls are considered to be the most beautiful in Jamaica. Nonsuch Cave is a few miles to the southeast where there are fossils and hieroglypic signs of the Arawak tribes. There is no public transportation available to these sites so you will have to take a taxi and ask the driver to wait (about $10 round trip). The entrance fee is $5.

Beaches in Port Antonio

The best beaches in Port Antonio are **Boston Bay** and **San San Beach**. A delicacy of the area is the eye-watering, peppery jerk pork, which will drive you to down a beer as quickly as possible. Just follow your nose to the smoke-spewing shacks, where local chefs cook right on the beach. **Cave Beach** is a notable place to plop east of the town. **Navy Island** is located in the harbor and boasts two nude beaches—take the jetty on West Street near Musgrave Market. The island, once owned by Errol Flynn, has a memorial gallery to his life and career, where you can view movie stills and screenings of his old films. Snorkeling is available for a small fee, but the currents are strong and the fish are few. A complete wedding ceremony can be conducted in the chapel, for more information contact ☎ *(809) 993-2667.*

Parks and Gardens

Athenry Gardens and Cave of Nu

Portland, Port Antonio, ☎ *(809) 993-3740.*
Hours open: 9 a.m.–5:30 p.m.
The Nonsuch Cave dates back some 1.5 million years give or take a century or two, and can be toured to see its stalagmites and stalactites. Back on ground level, take in the great views at the pretty flowering gardens. Port Antonio is about 20 minutes away. General admission: $5.

Crystal Springs ★★★

Highway A2, Port Antonio, ☎ *(809) 993-2609.*
This former sugar plantation is a privately owned estate that covers 158 acres. A peaceful spot to while away the hours, it has more than 15,000 orchids and lots of hummingbirds and other feathered friends. Bring binoculars. General admission: $1.

Where to Stay

Hotels and Resorts

Bonnie View Plantation $49–$83   ★★

Port Antonio, Port Antonio, ☎ *(800) 448-5398, (809) 993-2752.*
Single: $49–$63. Double: $71–$83.
Sweeping views entice guests from this small hotel perched atop a hill and set on a farm. Guestrooms are quite simple, fitting in with the bargain rates. You'll find a pool, restaurant and bar, but not much else in the way of extras. The staff can shuttle you down to the beach. 20 rooms. Credit cards: A, MC, V.

Dragon Bay $80–$110   ★★

Port Antonio, Port Antonio, ☎ *(800) 423-4095, (809) 993-8514. FAX (809) 993-3284.*
Single: $80–$110. Double: $80–$110.
Set on 55 acres with its own private cove, this villa-style resort is adjacent to Blue Lagoon. Accommodations are pleasant and run the gamut from single rooms to three-bedroom villas. One villa even has its own pool. Two restaurants and bars, weekly reggae concerts, a pair of pools and tennis courts, fitness center, and all the usual resort amenities. A bit off the beaten track, so you'll want a rental car. 86 rooms. Credit cards: A, MC.

Fern Hill Club $215–$385   ★★★

Port Antonio, Port Antonio, ☎ *(800) 263-4354, (809) 993-3222.*
Double: $215–$385.

Set on a hillside and encompassing 40 acres, this is an all-inclusive resort with wonderful views and a predominantly Canadian clientele. Accommodations vary from standard guestrooms to villas with kitchens; none are air-conditioned. The grounds include four pools, a restaurant and two bars, tennis, and an exercise room. The beach is down a steep hill; a shuttle bus will take you there if you're not up to the hike. This place is a favorite with honeymooners. 36 rooms. Credit cards: A, MC.

Hotel Mocking Bird Hill $95–$140 ★★

Near Frenchman's Cove, Port Antonio, ☎ *(809) 993-3370. FAX (809) 993-7133. Single: $95–$140. Double: $95–$140.*

This small hotel accommodates guests in traditional Caribbean-style villas on seven acres of lushly landscaped land some 15 minutes from the center of Port Antonio. The spacious units have double or twin beds and a balcony or patio, most with sea views. Facilities include a restaurant serving Jamaican cuisine and a bar with spectacular views. New is an on-site art gallery featuring the works of co-owner Barbara Walker and other local artists. Credit cards: MC, V.

Jamaica Palace Hotel $115–$285 ★★★

Port Antonio, ☎ *(800) 423-4095, (809) 993-2020. Single: $115–$285. Double: $115–$285.*

Set on five well-manicured acres, this colonial-style mansion draws mainly European guests. The elegant guestrooms are decorated with antiques, Oriental rugs, and marble floors. There's no beach nearby, but you can dip in the 114-foot pool, which is shaped like Jamaica. Elegant and refined, but a bit too out of the way for some folks. 80 rooms. Credit cards: A, MC.

Navy Island Resort/Marina $75–$185 ★★

Port Antonio Harbour, Port Antonio, ☎ *(809) 993-2667. Single: $75–$185. Double: $135–$185.*

Comprising 64 acres on a 17th-century British naval station, this secluded resort once served as Errol Flynn's personal hideaway. As the name implies, it is located on its own small island a quarter-mile off the coast. Accommodations are in oceanfront villas with sun decks and kitchens, but no rooms have air conditioning. One of the three beaches is clothes optional. Other amenities include a pool, tennis and watersports. 21 rooms. Credit cards: A, MC.

Trident Villas & Hotel $255–$755 ★★★★★

Port Antonio, ☎ *(800) 237-3237, (809) 993-2705. Single: $255–$480. Double: $305–$755.*

This is one of Jamaica's most luxurious resorts, set on 14 lush acres fronting the sea, two miles east of town. Guestrooms and villa suites are exquisitely furnished with antiques, plush fabrics, and ocean views. Only some are air-conditioned, but constant breezes keep everything cool. The lovely grounds include a small private beach, flowering gardens, pretty walkways, and two pools. Dinner is a formal affair that includes white-glove service; you'll have to dress up for the occasion. Service, of course, is outstanding. 28 rooms. Credit cards: A, MC.

Port Antonio

Apartments and Condominiums

Goblin Hill Villas   **$1760–$2135**   ★★★

Port Antonio, ☎ *(800) 423-4095, (809) 925-8108.*

Situated on 12 tropical acres of a hill above San San Beach, this complex has Georgian-style villas perfect for families. All are very nicely done, with locally made furniture and artwork, kitchens, and air-conditioned bedrooms. Each comes with a maid and cook. There are two lighted tennis courts, the beach down the hill, a pool and watersports. There's also a bar and restaurant, but besides occasional entertainment, not much of a nightlife. Rates range from $1760 to $2135 per couple weekly. Room rates include a rental car. 28 rooms. Credit cards: A, MC.

Where to Eat

De Montevin Lodge   **$$**   ★★★

21 Fort George Street, Port Antonio, ☎ *(809) 993-2604. Associated hotel: De Montevin Lodge.*
Latin American cuisine.
Lunch: 12:30–2 p.m., prix fixe $11–$18.
Dinner: 7–9 p.m., prix fixe $11–$18.

Errol Flynn's chef used to rule the kitchen at this veddy British Victorian-style inn on Titchfield Hill, but the food served here now is unadulterated Jamaican, prepared home-style; the number of courses that arrive depends on what you paid - the cheaper menus are just a tad over $10. Dishes include pumpkin soup, fricassee chicken, dessert and coffee. Reservations recommended. Credit cards: not accepted.

Front Line, The   **$**   ★★

Boston Bay, Port Antonio.
Latin American cuisine.
Lunch: entrées $5–$8.
Dinner: entrées $5–$8.

After leaving the chic resorts of Port Antonio (a town bereft of inexpensive eateries) travelers eagerly stop at Boston Bay beach for a soak and the best jerk barbecue on the islands. Of course, nothing is fancy, just a series of roadside stands vying for your attention—but the best one may be The Front Line, with the grills presided over by colorful pit men. Marinated chicken, pork or sausage swathed with a top-secret sauce (lots of hot pepper and cayenne) is perfect with Red Stripe beer or rum. Credit cards: not accepted.

Trident Hotel Restaurant   **$$$**   ★★★★★

Route A4, Port Antonio, ☎ *(809) 993-2602. Associated hotel: Trident Villas & Hotel.*
International cuisine.
Lunch: Noon–2:30 p.m., entrées $25–$35.
Dinner: 8–10 p.m., prix fixe $50.

Even if you aren't staying at this bastion of subdued luxury, it's a memorable experience to dine in the high-ceilinged restaurant of this 14-acre hotel. Here five-course dinners are served on the terrace or in the main dining room by white-gloved waiters; the only sounds you hear are gentle murmurings from fellow guests and the softly-whirring ceiling fans above. Reservations required. Credit cards: A, MC, V.

Port Antonio

South Coast

The south coast is Jamaica's ecological haven—the place where Jamaicans long to visit when they go on holiday. Here you'll find some truly "undiscovered" beaches, though you'll have to do a bit of driving to get to them. The South Coast is also known as the best place for **deep-sea fishing**, and boat trips sail out from Belmont to the offshore banks and reefs. The bay is so calm here that **snorkeling** is often an exciting experience. Southeast of Bluefield are simply some of the most pristine, unspoiled strands in all Jamaica, but unfortunately, a new Sandals resort is moving in soon. Transport from Montego Bay is easily arranged. If you take the A2 road past Scotts Cove, proceed to the town of **Black River**, one of the oldest on the island, once a thriving port during the 18th-century for logwood dyes. Along the coast are some handsome colonial mansions presently being restored. The longest river in Jamaica, the Black River is perfect for **canoe** and **rafting** trips. If you stay on A2 instead of turning off at Black River, proceed past Middle Quarters to the left turn that takes you to the **Y.S. Falls**, a glorious unspoiled area in the middle of a plantation—be prepared for a 15-minute hike from where you park your car. (For more information on Black River and Y.S. Falls excursions, see above under "Treks").

Mandeville is a lovely, peaceful upland town with what locals feel is the best climate on the island. For some reason, there are no slums among the population of 50,000—its present prosperity is due to the production of bauxite/alumina. The village green is reminiscent of New England, with its Georgian courthouse and parish church. Visit on Mondays, Wednesdays and Fridays, if you want to see the market in full swing. Horseback riding, tennis, and golf on an 18-hole course are available. The Seventh Day Adventists run the Westici Health Foods store and also a vegetarian restaurant behind the church in the center of town. A craft center is located on Manchester Road.

Bluefield Beach, near Savanna-la-Mer south of Negril, is the easiest to find. Farther out, another gem is **Crane Beach** at Black River. Most secluded is **Treasure Beach** (a strand that truly lives up to its name), 20 miles along the coast beyond Crane. To the east of Treasure Beach is **Lovers Leap**, which has a gorgeous view. Legend has it that a plantation owner's daughter and her love, a slave, leaped from the cliff to their death.

South Coast

Museums and Exhibits

Arawak Museum   ★★★

White Marl, Spanish Town, ☎ *(809) 922-0620.*
Hours open: 10 a.m.–5 p.m.
Located on the site of a large Arawak settlement, this small museum houses relics
and artifacts from that era.

Jamaica People's Museum   ★★★

Constitution Square, Spanish Town, ☎ *(809) 922- 620.*
Hours open: 9 a.m.–5 p.m.
This museum of native craft and technology has displays of farm implements. Tour
a sugar mill, see an old fire engine and a hearse, as well as vintage prints, models and
maps.

Tours

Milk River Mineral Baths   ★★★

Milk River, Clarendon, ☎ *(809) 924-9544.*
Arthritis acting up? Rheumatism got you down? Liver ailing? Come for a half-hour
soak in what is reportedly the world's most radioactive mineral waters, said to help
all those conditions—and more. The baths are private and tepid at 90 degrees. General admission: $2.

Somerset Falls   ★★★

Highway A4, Hope Bay, ☎ *(809) 926-2950.*
Hours open: 9 a.m.–5 p.m.
Ride in a gondola to these scenic falls, located in a deep grove and surrounded by
tropical rainforest. Wear your swimsuit so you can take a dip in the refreshing pools.
General admission: $2.

Where to Stay

Astra Country Inn   **$60–$115**   ★★

62 Ward Avenue, South Coast, ☎ *(809) 962-3265.*
Single: $60–$115. Double: $60–$115.
Set high up, some 2000 feet above sea level in the mid-island hills, this informal
hotel is in a former home. Guestrooms are comfortable though not air- conditioned. You'll find a pool and sauna on site, as well as horseback riding. Great for
birders and nature lovers. 22 rooms. Credit cards: A, MC.

Mandeville Hotel   **$60–$200**   ★

4 Hotel Street, South Coast, ☎ *(809) 962-2460.*
Single: $60–$200. Double: $60–$200.

This mountain hotel has traditional guestrooms, some with air conditioning, as well as apartments with kitchen facilities. Amenities include two restaurants, three bars, a disco, and, for recreation, a pool and horseback riding. Guests can golf at the nearby Manchester Club. 60 rooms. Credit cards: A, MC.

Duty-free shopping makes Jamaica a great place for bargain hunters and is especially good in Kingston. If you plan to do some serious shopping on luxury items, check prices before you leave the States. You will generally find good buys on Swiss watches, electronic equipment, gold jewelry, European crystal, china, French perfumes, British woolens, liquor and cigarettes. Carry identification to get duty-free prices. Local goods that make great souvenirs include Blue Mountain Coffee, Tia Maria (coffee liqueur), Jamaican rum and handmade Macanudo cigars.

Craft markets are common, and a good place to pick up fine wooden carvings (amazingly cheap), straw work, colorful silk-screened resort wear and silk batiks sold by the yard. Be warned: Merchants at the craft markets are sometimes overly aggressive.

It would be a sin to leave the island without purchasing at least one reggae tape. The best place to shop is **Randy's Record Mart** *(17 N. Parade, Kingston,* ☎ *(809) 922-4859)*, where you'll find everything from classic Bob Marley to the latest releases from local up-and-coming bands.

While touring around the island, you will be constantly harangued by people hawking everything from T-shirts to *ganga*. These dealers can be obnoxiously persistent, so don't be afraid to utter a firm "NO!," then keep walking.

Jamaica Directory

Arrival and Departure

American Airlines and **Air Jamaica** both fly nonstop from New York; **Air Jamaica** also flies nonstop from Miami and has service from Atlanta, Baltimore, Orlando and Philadelphia. **BWIA** flies from San Juan. **Continental** flies in daily from Newark. **Northwest Airlines** flies in daily from Minneapolis and Tampa and **Aeroflot** flies in from Havana. **Air Canada** offers service from Toronto and Montreal in conjunction with **Air Jamaica**, and both **British Airways** and **Air Jamaica** fly to London.

Donald Sangester International Airport in Montego Bay is the best place to arrive if you are headed for Montego Bay, Round Hill-Tryall, Ocho Rios,

South Coast

Runaway Bay and Negril. If you are staying in Port Antonio or Kingston, the capital, it's best to land at Norman Manley Airport in Kingston. **Trans-Jamaican Airlines** ☎ *(809) 923-8680* offers a shuttle service.

In general, there is no public transportation to and from the airports. Taxi rates are not fixed, but sample fares to popular destinations are usually posted in public places. Negotiate beforehand. All-inclusive resorts provide free transfers from the airport, as do many small hotels when you have booked a package. Sometimes a hotel will throw it in for free if you ask in advance. If transfers are included in your package, you will normally be given a voucher with the name of the operator, and a company representative will meet you at the airport. If not, it's a good idea to ask your travel agent to reserve space in advance. **JUTA** (Jamaica Union of Travellers Association) offers taxis that hold up to five people and (total price $80) run from the nearest airports to hotels in Negril, Ocho Rios and Port Antonio. Runs to Montego Bay and Kingston, which are much closer, are much cheaper. If you are heading beyond Montego Bay (and you have time to spare), you'll save lots of money if you book one of Tropical Tours' air-conditioned minibuses at their desk just outside the luggage area of **Sangster Airport** ☎ *(809) 953-1111.* Tropical Tours runs to Ocho Rios and Negril and charge a per-person fare. Unfortunately, you won't be able to leave until the bus is at least half full.

Business Hours

Stores open weekdays 9 a.m.–5 p.m. and Saturday 9 a.m.–6 p.m. Banks open weekdays 9 a.m.–5 p.m.

Climate

Jamaica has a tropical climate with considerable variation. High temperatures on the coast are usually mitigated by sea breezes, while upland areas enjoy cooler and less humid conditions. Jamaica lies in the hurricane zone, so always check weather reports before you come (even before you book). Rainfall falls plentifully throughout Jamaica; the heaviest season is in May and from August–November. In Kingston temperatures range from 6 degrees Fahrenheit in January to 81 degrees Fahrenheit in July.

Documents

U.S. citizens need either a passport or other proof of citizenship (birth certificate, voter's registration) and a photo ID. All others need a passport. Departure tax is U.S. $5.

Electricity

Current is not consistent throughout the island. Some hotels feature 110, some 220. Adapters and converters for those who need them are supplied by hotels. Ask at your hotel.

Getting Around

Taxis are best taken for short trips. At the airport you can always find a JUTA taxi and coach, as well as at most resorts. If you're planning an out-of-the-way excursion, particularly for dinner, arrange for the driver to pick you up afterwards and negotiate a round-trip fare. Most taxis are unmetered; if you seem to be having trouble with the driver, enlist the help of your hotel's concierge or doorman, though you can never be sure if they are in cahoots with each other. When in doubt, ask to see the rate sheet, which all cabs are supposed to carry. After midnight, a 25 percent surcharge is added, though that is often negotiable, particularly if you have arranged for a round-trip deal or if your destination is especially far away.

Buses prove to be a cheap way to toot around the Kingston and Montego Bay areas; they run often but they are often unbearably overcrowded, hot and dirty. (Moreover, a tourist on a crowded local bus is often a sitting duck for crime; if you are wearing your camera and an "I Love Jamaica" T-shirt, you might as well just hand over your valuables before being asked for them.) Kingston bus fares range from $3 JDS to $7.50 JDS (about 15 cents to 35 cents in American currency) at press time. The fee depends on the distance traveled. You can tour the island on a bus, but here you will have to share aisle space with the local riffraff—meaning chickens on their way to getting their heads chopped off at market. Minibus jitneys also travel around the island, but they are unscheduled and you may have to flag them down in the street—not a reliable way to get somewhere on time. As a result, most people cave in and rent cars or hire a cab.

Car rentals are a good idea on Jamaica since the roads are well-paved and your own car will allow you to conduct your sightseeing at your own pace. You must be able, however, to handle that "British thing" of driving on the left—which takes getting used to—so be careful the first few days. The moment you "space out," a common occurrence on long trips or in new lands, you may find yourself veering to the right, which will be disastrous in the face of on-coming traffic. If you're driving with a companion, let them be a front-seat driver for a while and spot for you.

About a dozen agencies on the island offer rentals; among the best are **Avis** ☎ *(809) 926-1560*; **Budget** ☎ *(809) 952-1943*; and **National** ☎ *(809) 924-8344*. In Ocho Rios you'll find **Sunshine Car Rental** ☎ *(809) 974-2980*. In Port Antonio try **Eastern Car Rental** ☎ *(809) 993-3624*. Major international chains accept bookings through stateside toll-free *(800)* numbers. Always ask for a written confirmation (a fax will do) and be sure you bring it along. There have been numerous cases of lost reservations, and supply often runs low, despite the presence of 2800 rental cars on the island. Also remember to add the cost of gas to your expenses and a 10 percent government tax. Valid U.S. and Canadian licenses are acceptable, but many agencies have a 25-and-over age limit (ask before you book). Beware of Jamaican drivers who suddenly and unexpectedly turn macho and wipe the road with the tar of their tires. In such cases, it is always best to yield. **Vacation Network**, an agency in Chicago ☎ *(800) 423-4095* offers a special "Fly-Drive Jamaica/The Great Escape Package," which combines a rental car with air transportation and overnight accommodations. Vouchers that come with the package allow you to use them

South Coast

at 45 participating small hotels and inns; the package comes with a guidebook geared for drivers as well as road maps.

Language

The official language is English. The unique Jamaican dialect, used by natives, is English with African and native words and a British inflection and tropical rhythm.

Medical Emergencies

The most efficient and advanced medical facilities are in Kingston, where you will find the country's largest hospital.

Money

The official currency is the Jamaican dollar, which has proven to be quite unstable in relation to the American dollar. American dollars are accepted in most establishments, but exchange rates will vary (also make sure when you are quoted a price, that you know which "dollar" is being used). All airports have exchange houses; best rates are found at banks. Major credit cards are accepted by most hotels and many restaurants, as are traveler's checks. When changing money, be sure you keep the receipt so you can change the money back before you leave.

Security

Crime in Jamaica is lower per capita than in most large U.S. cities, but the city of Kingston is rife with incidents. Downtown Kingston is particularly bad, and you should never walk the streets after dark. Don't even think about going to West Kingston, even in a car with the doors locked. Don't ever leave money, wallets, purses or valuables such as cameras unattended at the beach. Police foot patrols are present in all the major tourist areas, so head directly for one if you sense trouble. Also avoid standing in the middle of a street to hail a taxi; it's best to head for a shopping center or ask your hotel to arrange one ahead of time.

Telephone

The area code is *809*. Direct telephone, telegraph, telefax and telex services are all available.

Time

Eastern Standard Time throughout the year.

Tipping

Most Jamaican hotels and restaurants add a service charge of 10 percent; always check first to see if it's included. If not, tip waiters 10–15 percent, depending on the service. Hotel maids should receive about $1–2 per person per day. Airport porters and hotel bellhops should be tipped 50 cents per bag (but not less than a $1). It's not necessary to tip taxi drivers, although 10 percent of the fare is usually appreciated.

Tourist Information

The main office of the Jamaica Tourist Board is in Kingston; contact *Tourism Centre Building, New Kingston, Box 360, Kingston 5;* ☎ *(809) 929-9200.*

JTB desks are located at both Montego Bay and Kingston airports and in all resort areas. In the U.S. ☎ *(213) 384-1123.*

When to Go

Carnival is a recent addition to Jamaica, held oddly at Easter time. The annual reggae festival called Sun Splash is usually held in the middle of August in Montego Bay at the Bob Marley Centre. The Independence celebrations, also held for a week in August, are colorful blowout bashes (beginning usually on Independence Day, August 1). In October, the annual International Marlin Tournament at Port Antonio attracts fishermen from all over the world and includes festivals other than fishing. Contact the Tourist Board for a twice-yearly calendar of events covering a wide spectrum of sports and arts festivals.

JAMAICA HOTELS	RMS	RATES	PHONE	CR. CARDS
Kingston				
★★★★ Jamaica Pegasus Hotel	350	$180–$564	(809) 926-3690	A, DC, MC, V
★★★ Morgan's Harbour Hotel	45	$98–$255	(809) 924-8464	A, MC, V
★★★ Terra Nova Hotel	33	$120–$150	(809) 926-2211	A, DC, MC, V
★★★ Wyndham Kingston	384	$165–$505	(800) 322-4200	A, DC, MC, V
★★ Courtleigh House & Hotel	80	$79–$195	(800) 526-2400	A, MC
★★ Medallion Hall Hotel	16	$79–$83	(809) 927-5721	A, DC, MC, V
★★ Strawberry Hill	12	$175–$450	(800) 688-7678	
★ Four Seasons Hotel	79	$75–$135	(800) 526-2422	A, CB, DC, MC, V
★ Indies Hotel	15	$35–$62	(809) 926-2952	A, MC, V
Montego Bay				
★★★★★ Half Moon Beach Club	213	$255–$805	(800) 626-0592	A, MC
★★★★★ Round Hill Hotel & Villas	110	$160–$420	(800) 972-2159	A, MC, V
★★★★ Sandals Montego Bay	243	All-Inclusive	(800) 726-3257	A, MC
★★★★ Sandals Royal Caribbean	190	All-Inclusive	(800) 726-3257	A, MC
★★★★ Tryall Resort	52	$235–$465	(800) 742-0498	A, MC, V
★★★ Coyaba Beach Resort	50	$85–$326	(800) 237-3237	
★★★ Doctor's Cave Beach Hotel	90	$85–$135	(800) 223-6510	A, MC, V
★★★ Reading Reef Club	26	$65–$370	(800) 223-6510	A, MC
★★★ Sandals Inn	52	$290–$348	(800) 726-3257	A, MC
★★★ Seacastles	198	$75–$155	(800) 526-2422	A, MC, V
★★★ Seawind Beach Resort	468	$75–$120	(800) 526-2422	A, D, MC, V

South Coast

South Coast

JAMAICA HOTELS		RMS	RATES	PHONE	CR. CARDS
★★★	Wyndham Rose Hall Resort	500	$165–$705	(809) 631-4200	A, MC, V
★★	Blue Harbour Hotel	24	$35–$105	(809) 952-5445	A, MC, V
★★	Breezes Montego Bay	124	All-Inclusive	(800) 859-7873	A, MC, V
★★	Coral Cliff Hotel	32	$54–$64	(809) 952-4130	A, MC
★★	Fantasy Resort	119	$55–$85	(800) 237-3421	A, MC
★★	Gloucestershire, The	88	$60–$80	(800) 423-4095	A, MC
★★	Holiday Inn Montego Bay	516	$160–$205	(800) 465-4329	A, MC, V
★★	Jack Tar Village	128	$155–$205	(800) 999-9182	A, MC
★★	Montego Bay Racquet Club	51	$50–$155	(809) 952-0200	A, MC, V
★★	Richmond Hill Inn	20	$78–$112	(809) 952-3859	A, MC
★★	Sea Garden Beach Hotel	104	$297–$357	(800) 545-9001	A, MC
★★	Toby Inn	60	$45–$80	(809) 952-4370	A, MC
★★	Wexford, The	61	$85–$130	(800) 237-3421	A, MC
★★	Winged Victory	27	$95–$230	(800) 223-9815	A, MC
★	Belvedere Beach Hotel	27	$50–$80	(809) 952-0593	A, CB, MC, V
★	Buccaneer Beach Hotel	72	$83–$175	(809) 952-6489	A, MC
★	Royal Court Hotel	25	$45–$85	(809) 952-4531	A, MC

Negril

★★★★★	Grand Lido	200	$350–$290	(800) 423-4095	A, MC
★★★★	Negril Tree House	70	$85–$275	(800) 423-4095	A, MC
★★★★	Sandals Negril	199	All-Inclusive	(800) 726-3257	A, MC
★★★★	Swept Away Resort	134	All-Inclusive	(800) 545-7937	A, MC, V
★★★	Beachcomber Club	46	$100–$325	(800) 423-4095	A, MC
★★★	Charela Inn	39	$80–$170	(800) 423-4095	MC, V
★★★	Foote Prints on the Sands	33	$85–$145	(809) 957-4300	A, MC
★★★	Hedonism II	280	$205–$376	(800) 423-4095	A, MC
★★★	Poinciana Beach Hotel	130	$249–$294	(800) 468-6728	A, MC
★★★	Point Village	130	$100–$155	(809) 957-4351	A, MC
★★★	Rock Cliff Resort	33	$55–$100	(809) 957-4331	A, MC
★★★	Xtabi Club Resort	26	$50–$145	(809) 957-4336	A, MC
★★	Chuckles	78	$75–$260	(809) 957-4277	A, MC

JAMAICA HOTELS		RMS	RATES	PHONE	CR. CARDS
★★	Crystal Waters Villas	10	$85–$110	(800) 443-3020	A, MC
★★	Drumville Cove Resort	20	$40–$100	(800) 423-4095	A, MC, V
★★	Hotel Samsara	50	$40–$115	(809) 957-4395	A, MC
★★	Negril Beach Club Hotel	85	$77–$185	(800) 526-2422	A, MC
★★	Negril Cabins	50	$110–$190	(800) 382-3444	A, MC
★★	Negril Gardens	54	$105–$140	(800) 423-4095	A, MC
★★	Negril Inn	46	$115–$145	(800) 634-7456	A, MC
★★	Paradise View	17	$75–$135	(809) 957-4375	A, MC
★★	T-Water Beach Hotel	70	$125–$155	(800) 654-1592	A, MC

Ocho Rios

★★★★★	Sans Souci Lido	111	$465–$945	(800) 203-7450	A, MC, V
★★★★	Boscobel Beach Hotel	228	$415–$995	(800) 423-4095	A, MC
★★★★	Ciboney Ocho Rios	300	$175–$690	(800) 777-7800	A, MC
★★★★	Couples Jamaica	172	$365–$520	(800) 423-4095	A, MC
★★★★	Jamaica Grande	720	$135–$195	(800) 228-9898	A, CB, MC, V
★★★★	Jamaica Inn	45	$200–$475	(809) 974-2516	A, MC
★★★★	Plantation Inn	78	$300–$999	(800) 423-4095	A, MC, V
★★★★	Sandals Dunn's River	256		(800) 726-3257	A, MC
★★★★	Sandals Ocho Rios	237	$355–$455	(800) 726-3257	A, MC
★★★	Braco Village Resort	180	$270–$280	(800) 654-1337	
★★★	Comfort Suites	137	$105–$205	(800) 423-4095	A, CB, MC, V
★★★	Enchanted Garden	113	$150–$215	(800) 554-2008	A, MC, V
★★★	Hibiscus Lodge	26	$65–$93	(800) 526-2422	A, CB, MC, V
★★★	Sea Palms	45	$145–$145	(80) 423-4095	A, MC
★★★	Shaw Park Beach Hotel	118	$165–$436	(800) 243-9420	A, MC, V
★★	Club Jamaica Beach Resort	95	$180–$235	(800) 423-4095	A, MC, V
★★	Fisherman's Point	64	$95–$135	(800) 423-4095	A, MC
★★	Turtle Beach Towers	218	$87–$225	(809) 974-2801	A, MC

Port Antonio

★★★★★	Trident Villas & Hotel	28	$255–$755	(800) 237-3237	A, MC
★★★	Fern Hill Club	36	$215–$385	(800) 263-4354	A, MC

South Coast

JAMAICA HOTELS	RMS	RATES	PHONE	CR. CARDS
★★★ Goblin Hill Villas	28		(800) 423-4095	A, MC
★★★ Jamaica Palace Hotel	80	$115–$285	(800) 423-4095	A, MC
★★ Bonnie View Plantation	20	$49–$83	(800) 448-5398	A, MC, V
★★ Dragon Bay	86	$80–$110	(800) 423-4095	A, MC
★★ Hotel Mocking Bird Hill		$95–$140	(809) 993-3370	MC, V
★★ Navy Island Resort/ Marina	21	$75–$185	(809) 993-2667	A, MC

Runaway Bay

	RMS	RATES	PHONE	CR. CARDS
★★★★ Breezes Runaway Bay	238	$240–$439	(800) 859-7873	A, MC
★★★★ Franklyn D. Resort	76	$286–$298	(800) 654-1337	A, MC
★★★ Eaton Hall Beach Hotel	52	$135–$299	(809) 973-3503	A, CB, MC, V
★★★ H.E.A.R.T. Country Club	20	$55–$75	(809) 973-2671	A, MC
★★ Ambiance Jamaica	80	$70–$138	(800) 523-6504	A, MC
★★ Club Caribbean	128	$125–$295	(800) 647-2740	A, MC, V
★★ Portside Villas & Condos	15	$85–$280	(809) 973-2007	A, MC
★ Caribbean Isle Hotel	24	$55–$65	(809) 973-2364	A, MC

South Coast

	RMS	RATES	PHONE	CR. CARDS
★★ Astra Country Inn	22	$60–$115	(809) 962-3265	A, MC
★ Mandeville Hotel	60	$60–$200	(809) 962-2460	A, MC

Westmorland

	RMS	RATES	PHONE	CR. CARDS
★★★ Natania's Guest House	8	$50–$60	(800) 330-2332	

JAMAICA RESTAURANTS	PHONE	ENTRÉE	CR. CARDS
Kingston			
International			
★★★★ Blue Mountain Inn	(809) 927-1700	$12–$24	A, DC, MC, V
★★ Gap Cafe, The	(809) 923-7055	$12–$22	A, MC, V
★★ Port Royal	(809) 926-3690	$16–$26	A, DC, MC, V
★ El Dorado Room	(809) 926-9334	$7–$20	A, DC, MC, V
★ Ivor Guest House	(809) 977-33	$18–$30	A, MC, V
Latin American			
★★★★★ Temple Hall	(809) 942-2340	$25–$25	A, DC, MC

South Coast

View of Pitons-du-Carbet from Balata Gardens, Martinque

Maison de la France, Martinique

JAMAICA RESTAURANTS	PHONE	ENTRÉE	CR. CARDS
★★★★ Norma's at the Wharfhouse	(809) 979-2745	$26–$34	MC, V
★★ Devon House Restaurants	(809) 929-6602	$6–$16	A, MC, V
★★ Hot Pot, The	(809) 929-3906	$3–$4	V
★ Chelsea Jerk Centre	(809) 926-6322	$3–$5	A, MC, V
★ Indies Pub and Grill	(809) 926-5050	$4–$12	A, MC, V
★ Minnie's Ethiopian	(809) 927-9207	$10–$20	None

Montego Bay

International

	PHONE	ENTRÉE	CR. CARDS
★★★★ Sugar Mill	(809) 953-2228	$14–$31	A, MC, V
★ Georgian House	(809) 952-3353	$22–$32	A, DC, MC, V
★ Julia's	(809) 952-632	$35–$35	A, DC, MC, V

Italian

	PHONE	ENTRÉE	CR. CARDS
★★★★★ Reading Reef Club	(809) 952-5909	$10–$24	A, DC, MC, V

Latin American

	PHONE	ENTRÉE	CR. CARDS
★★★ Pork Pit	(809) 952-1046	$2–$9	None
★★ Town House	(809) 952-2660	$13–$30	A, DC, MC, V

Seafood

	PHONE	ENTRÉE	CR. CARDS
★ Pier I	(809) 952-2452	$16–$25	A, MC, V

Negril

French

	PHONE	ENTRÉE	CR. CARDS
★★ Cafe au Lait	(809) 957-4471	$9–$29	MC, V

Latin American

	PHONE	ENTRÉE	CR. CARDS
★★ Chicken Lavish	(809) 957-4410	$3–$5	MC, V
★★ Hungry Lion		$18–$30	MC, V
★★ Paradise Yard	(809) 957-4006	$6–$15	None
★ Tan-ya's	(809) 957-4041	$5–$25	A, MC, V

Seafood

	PHONE	ENTRÉE	CR. CARDS
★★ Cosmo's	(809) 957-4330	$5–$12	MC, V
★ Rick's Cafe	(809) 957-4335	$11–$28	None

Ocho Rios

Chinese

	PHONE	ENTRÉE	CR. CARDS
★ Ruins Restaurant	(809) 974-2442	$12–$33	A, DC, MC, V

South Coast

JAMAICA RESTAURANTS	PHONE	ENTRÉE	CR. CARDS
Italian			
★★★★★ **Evita's**	(809) 974-2333	$7–$19	A, MC, V
Latin American			
★★★★ **Almond Tree**	(809) 974-2813	$12–$26	A, DC, MC, V
★★ **Parkway Restaurant**	(809) 974-2667	$6–$25	A, MC, V

Port Antonio

	PHONE	ENTRÉE	CR. CARDS
International			
★★★★★ **Trident Hotel Restaurant**	(809) 993-2602	$25–$50	A, MC, V
Latin American			
★★★ **De Montevin Lodge**	(809) 993-2604	$11–$18	None
★★ **Front Line, The**		$5–$8	None

South Coast

MARTINIQUE

Mt. Pelee towers above St. Pierre village in northern Martinique.

Martinique is a little bit of foie gras in the middle of the Caribbean. From the cuisine to the chic style of the women, to the lilt of the language, Martinique exudes the charm of its mother country—France. But add to that a decidedly West Indian cachet and shopping values that would make a Parisian's jaw drop open, and you have a tiny island nation waiting to be loved. Rising from beaches to rain forest to the heights of a volcanic mountain that wiped out an entire city in 1902, Martinique is rife with opportunities to dive, trek, sail, surf, parasail and about any other sport imaginable—from mountain biking to deep-sea fishing in some of the clearest waters in the Caribbean. The island has stayed ecologically pure enough to still boast good sightings of many birds in the mangroves, including the yellow-breasted sandbird, a symbol of the island. Best of all, tourism is just beginning to snap at the heels of this nearly forgotten island and locals are still green enough—business-wise—to have escaped becoming jaded. Of course, on an island such as this one, there will always be a few cases of French snoots, but try to ignore them and concentrate on the natural beauties.

Fifty miles long and 22 miles wide, Martinique covers 425 square miles. Of its neighboring islands, Dominica lies to the north and St. Lucia to the south; Miami is 1470 miles away. San Juan, Puerto Rico is only 425 miles away. Martinique comes from volcanic origins, and today the 4575-ft. Mount Pelé in the Parc Naturel Regional de la Martinique is the only active volcano, situated in the northwest island. Most of the island is mountainous. In the center of the island lie the Pitons de Carbet and the Montagne du Vauclin is in the south. The capital city of Fort-de-France, built like an amphitheater around the yacht-filled harbor, is backed by luxurious mountains and is one of the most picturesque settings in the Caribbean. The north of the island is covered by an enormous rainforest; banana and pineapples are cultivated there, while sugarcane dominates the rest of the island. Black sandy coves are found throughout the south and along the rugged coast open to the Atlantic, white and gray sands characterize the beaches facing the Caribbean and in the south. Salines Beach, on the southernmost tip of the island, looks as if it is straight out of a beautiful postcard. On the east coast, the peninsula of Caravelle, the oldest volcanic formation of the island, stretches into the rough Atlantic, boasting a mangrove swamp lined with a coral reef. Along the Caravelle coastline are a large number of picturesque coves and bays. The capital, Fort-de-France, is situated on the Baie des Fla-mandes on the western coast, while the burgeoning town of Lamentin is slightly more inland. The new ultramodern International Fort-de-France La-mentin Airport has been a boon for the local tourist industry. Located adja-cent to the old terminal at Lamentin, it is 10 minutes away from Fort-de-France. Martinique's climate is mild averaging 79F. Breezes known as the "alizes" blow in from the east and northeast, constantly cooling the air.

MARTINIQUE

MARTINIQUE PASSAGE

61° W

ATLANTIC OCEAN

Grand' Rivière

Basse-Pointe

Les Gorges de la Falaise

Montagne Pelée 4467 ft. ▲

Marigot

Le Prêcheur

Le Morne Rouge

Caravelle Peninsula

Saint-Pierre

Canal de Beauregard

Gros-Morne

La Trinité

Baie du Galion

Le Carbet

Piton du Carbet 3890 ft. ▲

Saint Joseph

Le Robert

Havre du Robert

Bellefontaine

Le Lamentin

FORT-DE-FRANCE ✪

Le François

BAIE DE FORT-DE-FRANCE

Le Lamentin Airport ✈

Ducos

Le Saint-Esprit

Montagne du Vauclin 1954 ft. ▲

Les Trois-Îlets

Rivière-Salée

Le Vauclin

14° 30'N

Grand Anse

Les Anses-d'Arlets

Le Diamant

Ste. Luce

Rivière-Pilote

Le Marin

CARIBBEAN SEA

Ste. Anne

SAINT LUCIA CHANNEL

Martinique

▲ MOUNTAIN   ROAD
● CITY   — TRAIL
✕ AIRPORT   — RIVER

0   5   10 km
0   2.5   5 mi

©FWI 1995

MARTINIQUE

History

Columbus was stunned when he chanced upon Martinique—historians can't decide whether it was 1493 or 1502—but phrases like "the most fertile, the softest...the most charming place in the world" leave no doubt regarding his true feelings. Carib Indians were the resident locals on Martinique when Columbus happened by. Martinica was the name Columbus bestowed on the volcanic island, in honor of St. Martin. The Caribs called it *madinina*, meaning "island of flowers." The Caribs proved too hostile for the Spaniards who moved on to other shores, but they continued to fight the French who settled on the island in 1635. Twenty-five years later the French signed a treaty with the Caribs who agreed to stay on the Atlantic side of the island; nevertheless, they were soon exterminated. The next 200 years was a struggle between the Brits and the French. In 1762 the Brits took control, only to pass it over in exchange for Canada, Senegal, the Grenadines, St. Vincent and Tobago. France remained with Guadeloupe and Martinique because they were knee-deep in the sugarcane. The English took over again between 1794–1802, at the request of plantation owners who needed assistance in the face of growing dissent among slaves. Slavery was abolished in 1848 by the French but not before a major slave rebellion occurred in 1879, encouraged by the French Revolution. Eventually, a new wave of immigrant workers from India began to change the dominant color of skin in the island's population. Martinique finally became a French Department in 1946 and a region in 1974.

People

There are about 385,000 people in Martinique, about half of which are living in the capital of Fort-de-France. A racially mixed batch of Africans, East Indians, Caucasians and others, they are all considered citizens of France, and governed by a Prefect, appointed by the French Government. Unemployment is quite high, about a third of the people have no jobs. About a quarter of those employed are in tourism. To get a good glimpse of social life, hang out in the Savane, a 12-acre park of lawn, shade trees, footpaths and benches where families relax and children play, and old men play serious games of dominoes. Locals are called Martiniquaises.

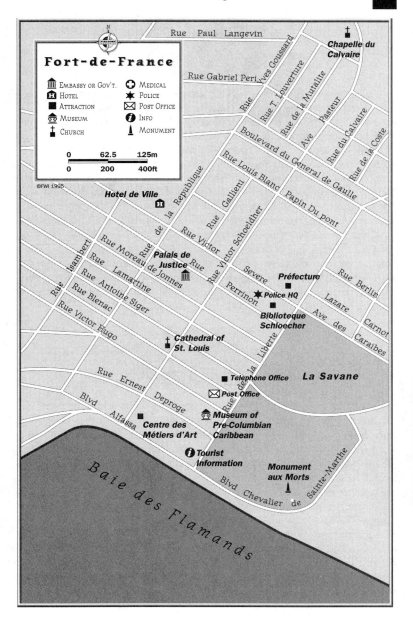

Fort-de-France

Legend:
- 🏛 EMBASSY OR GOV'T.
- 🏨 HOTEL
- ■ ATTRACTION
- 🏛 MUSEUM
- ✝ CHURCH
- ✚ MEDICAL
- ★ POLICE
- ✉ POST OFFICE
- ℹ INFO
- ⚲ MONUMENT

| 0 | 62.5 | 125m |
| 0 | 200 | 400ft |

©FWI 1995

Rue Paul Langevin
Chapelle du Calvaire
Rue Yves Goussard
Rue Gabriel Peri
Rue T. Louverture
Rue de la Mutalile
Ave. Pasteur
Rue du Calvaire
Boulevard du General de Gaulle
Rue de la Coste
Hotel de Ville
Rue de la Republique
Rue Louis Blanc
Rue Gallieni
Papin Du pont
Rue Victor
Rue Moreau de Jonnes
Palais de Justice
Rue Victor Schoeldher
Rue Isambert
Rue Lamartine
Rue Severe
Préfecture
Rue Berlin
Rue Antoine Siger
Perrinon
Police HQ
Lazare
Rue Blenac
Biblioteque Schloecher
Ave. des Caraibes
Carnot
Rue Victor Hugo
Cathedral of St. Louis
Rue de la Liberte
Telephone Office
La Savane
Rue Ernest Deproge
Post Office
Blvd Alfassa
Centre des Métiers d'Art
Museum of Pre-Columbian Caribbean
Tourist Information
Monument aux Morts
Blvd Chevalier de Sainte-Marthe
Baie des Flamands

Beaches

You can find a magnificent beach at **Grand Anse** in South Martinique. It is less visited by tourists than the beaches at Pointe du Bout, although it can get more crowded on weekends. Nearby is the petite pretty village of **Anse d'Arlets**. **Diamant Beach**, just south of Ande d'Arlets, is a paradisiacal stretch of 2.5 miles along the south coast dominated by the **Diamond Rock**, a famous volcanic rock that stands about a mile out to sea where the English stationed cannons in the 18th century (British ships still passing it salute her Majesty's "Ship Diamond Rock"). The beach is nearly deserted and fringed with coconut palms and almond trees. It is not advised for swimming since the currents are strong. From the town of Le Marin south, you'll find long white sand beaches fringed with palms trees and calm, clear seas. **Ste. Anne**, where the Club Med is, has its own fine beach, adjacent to the public one, where you can see a terrific view of the southwest coast. There are many places for shade on Ste. Anne under trees that sometimes overhang into the sea. There are lots of bars and restaurants here. There's a family beach on the road heading east from Marin called Cap Chevalier.

Underwater

Walls and caves, reefs and wrecks, Martinique offers a little of everything for divers. Sites are situated along the western coast, north and south of Fort-de-France, with the scalloped coastline between Pointe du Bout and Le Diamant noteworthy for its abundance of smaller reef fish and colorful coral life, particularly Cap Salomon and nearby Les Anses d'Arlets. Because the island is so densely populated, many of the reefs are overfished and some of the coral is damaged. However, the bay off St. Pierre provides one of the Caribbean's most unusual wreck sites, a veritable graveyard created by the eruption of Mt. Pelee in 1902. There are over a dozen dive companies on Martinique, and most of them provide the French "baptism" dive for first-timers, priced only slightly more than a single-tank dive; many resorts also provide underwater initiation in a hotel pool at no charge. Two-tank boat trips are not generally offered in the French West Indies; it is *de rigueur* to share a casual meal between dives. A medical certificate must be produced before diving, and although PADI and NAUI instructors can be found, it's helpful to be familiar with the French dive standards before heading out on a boat.

On Foot

Showcasing a variety of trails through a surprisingly diverse selection of landscapes and climate regions, Martinique is truly a hiker's paradise. All of this coexists in relatively close proximity to the island's fast-paced and cosmopolitan lifestyle, creating a breathtaking juxtaposition, even by Caribbean standards, where contrasting environments are the spice of life. The island's population and tourist center is heavily concentrated in and around Fort-de-France, leaving Martinique's outlying forests well-visited, but comparatively unscathed by development. Hikers must beware the rare fer de lance, a poisonous snake found predominantly in the drier areas to the south (see "On Foot" introductory chapter). An excellent trail guidebook, *Guide des Sentiers Pedestres a la Martinique,* (in French) is available in local bookstores, and the tourist maps of the island mark many of the major trails.

By Pedal

The unofficial national sport of the French West Indies, cycling is officially celebrated with the annual "Tour de la Martinique," which takes place mid-July. You'll find a number of locals on bikes on weekends, while the **Parc Naturel Regional de la Martinique** has worked with local biking organizations to identify mountain trails and routes of interest (*☎ 596) 64-42-59).* A beautiful route for less advanced riders circumnavigates the island's tiny southernmost tip on dirt and secondary roads; the tour visits the Petrified Forest and lovely Grande Anse des Salines. The bigger peninsula bordered by Trois-Ilets and Le Diamant offers slightly more difficult riding, while heading into the mountains of Martinique's northern half will present clear challenges and inspiring riding. Also appealing is the coastal road between Fort-de-France and St. Pierre.

What Else to See

Paul Gauguin Museum, Martinique

The capital of Martinique, **Fort-de-France**, is one of the most charming cities in the Caribbean to see on foot. Among the first sites to check out is the city's architectural pride and joy, the **Bibliotheque Schoelcher**, or Schoelcher Library, a Romanesque Byzantine treasure constructed a century ago for the Paris Exposition of 1889, then dismantled and shipped to Martinique piece by piece. It sits close to **La Savane**, the city's central park, full of exotic flora; it's a lovely place to stroll and eavesdrop on locals. La Savan's gardens boast two impressive statues: one of Pierre Belain d'Esnambue, the French nobleman who claimed the island for France in 1635; the other of Marie Josephe Rose Tascher de la Pagerie, who was born in Trois Ilets across the bay and made history as Napoleon's Empress Josephine. Narrow streets with beautiful balconies overhanging sidewalks filled with shops and restaurants lead you to another must-see: the **Cathedral of Saint-Louis**. Nearby is the Palais de Justice with its statue of Victor Schoelcher. The Musée Departemental de la Martinique presents archaeological finds from prehistoric Martinique. The **Jardin de Balata** (Balata gardens) is a tropical botanical park around a restored Creole house. It's a lovely place for browsing and relaxing. By the Riviere Madame (Madame River) you'll find the bustling fish markets. If you want a guided tour, you can find excellent ones offered by **Azimut** ☎ *(596) 60-16-59.*

Time should also be carved out on your itinerary for travels outside the city of Martinique.

North along the coast, you'll discover **St. Pierre**, considered the "Paris of the West Indies" until 1902 when Mount Pelé Volcano erupted and flowed lava Pompeii-style all over it. You can see the full extent of the tragedy in the exhibits of the museum there. To get there with style, take the little train called **Cyparis Express**, which presents one-hour tours during the week and half-hour tours on the weekend *(40F for adults, 20F for children).*The drive from Fort-de-France is less than an hour, but make time to stop at such atmospheric fishing villages as **Case-Pilote** and **Bellefontaine**, as well as **Carbet**, where Columbus landed in 1502; Gauguin lived and painted there in 1887. A museum featuring his work is found in Carbet.

In the north, a dazzling route through the rain forest, called **La Trace**, is lush with banana and pineapple plantations, avocado groves, cane fields and lovely inns such as **Leyritz** and **Habitation Lagrange**. Le Précheur, the last village along the northern Caribbean coast, is known for hot springs of volcanic origin as well as the **Tomb of the Carib Indians**. Ajoupa Bouillon is an enchanting flower-lined town with a nature trail called **Les Ombrages**.

Rum is king on Martinique and most visitors enjoy sampling the island-brewed wares at distilleries. The St. James Distillery at Sainte-Marie in the north operates the **Musée du Rhum**. Nearby is a straw-weaving center called **Horne des Esses**. The **Fonds Saint Jacques**, a historically important 17th-century sugar estate in the north, attracts visitors with its museum, Musée du Pere Labat. A modern museum devoted to sugar and rum, called **Maison de la Canne**, is just outside Trois Ilets. Also near Trois Ilets is Joséphone Bonaparte's birthplace, **La Pagerie**, which has a museum chock full of her mementos.

MARTINIQUE

St. Louis Cathedral, Fort-de-France, Martinique

Martinique is often known as the "Isle of Flowers" and there are numerous floral gardens that are lovely to visit. **Morne Rouge**, a pretty town with a cool climate, is the site of **MacIntosh Plantation**, a renowned cultivator of Martinique's best known flower, the anthurium. Near La Pagerie is **Parc des Floralies**, a peaceful and pretty botanical park. One of the most beautiful is the **Jardin de Balata** on the Route de La Trace in the suburbs north of the capital. A short drive from here is the Sacré Coeur de Balata, a replica of the well-known basilica that dominates Montmarte in Paris. Other attractions south of Martinique include the H.M.S. *Diamond Rock*, a kind of Rock of Gibralter Caribbean-style rising 600 feet from the sea as used by the British in 1804 as a sloop of war. Anyone not venturing into the depths of the sea with a dive tank should really take a ride on the thrilling **Aquascope**, a semi-submersible craft that makes about an hour tour. One is located at the Marina Pointe du Bout ☎ (596) 68-36-09 and the other at Le Marin ☎ (596) 74-87-41).

Martinique has two **gambling casinos**. Located in the **Meridien** and the **La Bateliere** hotels, they are open nightly from 9 p.m. to 3 a.m. Both feature American and French roulette and blackjack. Proof of identity in the form of a passport, driver's license or other photo ID is required. The legal gambling age is 18. Dress is casual and an entrance fee of 70F is charged. There is no entrance fee to play the slot machines, which are located just outside the casinos.

There are about a dozen good nightspots in Fort-de-France featuring Latin music or jazz, a few piano bars and late night discos in the larger hotels. The legal drinking age is 18. Any town celebrating a *fete patronale* will feature street dancing where you are welcome to participate.

Museums and Exhibits

Maison de la Canne   ★ ★ ★

Trois-Ilets, Fort-de-France.
Hours open: 9 a.m.–5:30 p.m.
You've probably always taken sugar for granted, but won't anymore after touring this museum dedicated to the history and production of sugarcane. Signage is in both French and English. Really quite interesting

Musee Departemental de la Martinique   ★ ★ ★

9 Rue de la Liberte, Fort-de-France.
Decent exhibits on the history of slavery, clothing and furniture from the colonial period and artifacts from the pre-Columbian eras of the Arawak and the Carib indians.

Musee Paul Gauguin   ★ ★ ★

Anse-Turin, Le Carbet.
Hours open: 10 a.m.–5 p.m.
Famed artist Paul Gauguin lived in Martinique in 1887. This museum pays homage to that period, with reproductions of works he created while here, letters and other

memorabilia pertaining to his life. The museum also displays the works of other noted artists and changing displays by local artists.

Musee Vulcanologique ★★★★

St. Pierre, Fort-de-France.
Hours open: 9 a.m.–5 p.m.

American Frank Perrot established this museum in 1932, an homage to St. Pierre, the island's oldest city and a bustling one at that, until a devastating eruption of volcano Mt. Pelee on May 8, 1902. The entire town was buried in minutes and some 30,000 residents perished, all except for a prisoner whose underground cell saved him. (He later joined Barnum and Bailey's circus as a sideshow oddity.) Residents had been warned of the imminent danger but city fathers played it down because of an upcoming election. St. Pierre today is a modest village, but you can get a feel for its former glory days at the museum, which exhibits photographs and documents from the period.

Musee de Poupees Vegetables ★★★

Leyritz Plantation, Basse-Pointe.
Hours open: 7 a.m.–5:30 p.m.

Certainly the only one of its kind in Martinique (or possibly the world for that matter), this small museum displays sculptures made entirely of leaves and plants, designed to look like famous women in French history. It is located at the scenic Leyritz Plantation, which is detailed in the lodging section.

Musee du Rhum ★★★

Ste. Matie, Fort-de-France.
Hours open: 9 a.m.–6 p.m.

The St. James Distillery owns this monument to rum, located on a sugar plantation in an old creole house. After a guided tour showing the history and production of rum, you can taste-test the product yourself.

Musee le la Pagerie ★★★★

Trois-Ilets, Fort-de-France.
Hours open: 9 a.m.–5 p.m.

Located on the grounds of the birthplace of Josephine, Napoleon's wife and empress of France from 1804–1809, this museum is housed in a stone building that was formerly the kitchen (the rest of the estate was destroyed by hurricane). Memorabilia of her life, her childhood bed, and a passionate love letter by Napoleon are among the interesting exhibits.

Parks and Gardens

Jardin de Balata ★★★

Rte de Balata, Balata.
Hours open: 9 a.m.–5 p.m.

This tropical park, located on a hillside some 1475 feet above sea level, has stunning views and more than a thousand varieties of trees, flowers and plants. A lovely spot to while away the afternoon exploring winding walkways, lily pond, and breathtaking overlooks.

Tours

Zoo du Carbet ★★★

Le Coin, Le Carbet, ☎ *(596) 78-00-64*
Hours open: 9 a.m.–6 p.m.
Admission: 20F adults; 10F children.

This recently renovated park showcases animals from the Amazon, Caribbean and Africa. Nearby, the Valley of Butterflies at Carbet's Botanical Garden is situated among the ruins of Martinique's earliest 17th century settlements. The refreshment parlor on the grounds, Le Poids du Roy, is a pleasant rest stop.

Sailing, scuba, snorkeling, golf, deep-sea fishing, windsurfing, horseback riding, squash, tennis, cycling and motorbiking, hiking —the list of sports on Martinique is endless and depends only on your skill, passion and time. Consider touring the island by bike. For more information contact the **Parc Naturel Régional**; ☎ *(596) 60-25-72*, which has designed highly unusual itineraries. You can even rent your own plane (have a license from back home in order to get the French equivalent at the Lamentin Airport). Then contact local plane owners through the **Aero Club de la Martinique** ☎ *(596) 55-01-84.* As for sailing, an enormous combination of excursions can be made to neighboring islands, among them Antigua, Dominica, Barbados, St. Lucia, St. Vincent and the Grenadines, and Mystique among others. Look for the comprehensive bilingual yachting manual "Guide Trois Rivieres: A Cruising Guide to Martinique" available in local bookstores, about $35 or from *Edition Trois Riviere, B.P. 566, 97242 Fort-de-France* ☎ *(596) 75-07-07.* Spectator sports on the island are weird but exciting if you have a taste for blood: mongoose and snake fights, and cockfights seem to be national pastimes and can be seen December to the beginning of August at Pitt Ducos, **Quartier Brac** ☎ *(596) 56-05-60* and **Pitt Marceny**. Horse racing can be found at the Carere racetrack in Lamentin ☎ *(596) 51-25-09.*

Golf

Trois-Ilets, near Pointe du Bont.

Martinique's only course, the Golf de Imperatrice Josephine, was designed by Robert Trent Jones. The 18-hole, par-71 course covers 150 acres and is quite scenic. The grounds include a pro shop (with an English-speaking pro), restaurant and three tennis courts. Greens fees are about $45; guests in some hotels receive a discount, so be sure to ask.

Horseback Riding

Various locations, Martinique.

MARTINIQUE

Several outfits offer trail rides: **La Cavale** *(☎ [596] 76-22-94)*, **Ranch Jack** *(☎ [596] 68-37-67)*, **Black Horse Ranch** *(☎ [596] 68-37-80)*, and **Ranch Val d'Or** *(☎ [596] 76-70-58)*.

Watersports

Various locations, Fort-de-France.

Most hotels offer watersports. If not, try one of following. Scuba diving: **Bathy's Club** *(Pointe du Bont, ☎ [596] 66-00-00)*, **Sud Diamant Rock** *(Le Diamant, ☎ [596] 76-42-42)* **Cressmal** *(Fort-de-France, ☎ [596] 61-34-36)*, **Planete Bleue** *(Trois-Ilets, ☎ [596] 66-08-79)*, Oxygene Bleu *(Lamentin, ☎ [596] 50-25-78)*, and **Tropic Alizes** *(Le Bateliere, ☎ [596] 61-49-49)*. Boating and sailing: **Soleil et Voile** *(Pointe du Bont, ☎ [596] 66-09-14)*, **Captains Shop** *(Pointe du Bont, ☎ [596] 66-06-77)*, **Ship Shop** *(Fort-de-France, ☎ [596] 71-43-40)*, **Carib Charter** *(Schoelcher, ☎ [596] 73-08-80)*, **Caraibes Nautique** *(Trois-Ilets ☎ [596] 66-06-06)*, and **Cercle Nautique** *(Schoelcher, ☎ [596] 61-15-21)*. Snorkeling: **Aquarium** *(Fort-de-France, ☎ [596] 61-49-49)*.

Where to Stay

Fielding's Highest Rated Hotels in Martinique

★★★★★	**Bakoua-Sofitel Hotel**	$116–$529
★★★★	**Habitation Lagrange**	$275–$385
★★★★	**Leyritz Plantation**	$87–$167
★★★★	**Meridien Martinique**	$253–$779
★★★	**Diamant Novotel**	$105–$371
★★★	**Fregate Bleue Inn**	$100–$225
★★★	**La Bateliere Hotel**	$135–$400
★★★	**St. Aubin Hotel**	$93–$142

Fielding's Most Exclusive Hotels in Martinique

★★★★	**Meridien Martinique**	$253–$779
★★★★★	**Bakoua-Sofitel Hotel**	$116–$529
★★★	**La Bateliere Hotel**	$135–$400
★★★★	**Habitation Lagrange**	$275–$385
★★	**Carayou Novotel Hotel**	$115–$375

Fielding's Best Value Hotels in Martinique

★★	**Martinique Cottages**	$60–$75
★	**Balisier**	$62–$93
★★	**Victoria Hotel**	$88–$101
★★★	**St. Aubin Hotel**	$93–$142
★★	**Rivage Hotel**	$75–$100

MARTINIQUE

Accommodations on Martinique run from the 300-room resort to the inn with 10 rooms. You can choose between resorts happily ensconced on the seashore to guesthouses run by congenial families, part of the "Relais Creoles" organization. Prices range from expensive to modest. All of the larger hotels have sports facilities, a choice of restaurants and evening entertainment. All beachfront hotels offer a full watersports program. Some hotels have kitchenette studios.

Bakoua-Sofitel Hotel, Martinique

Hotels and Resorts

Bakoua Sofitel Hotel, perched on a hillside, is the leading resort, retaining a distinct local feel in the historical plantation-style surroundings. **La Bateliere Hotel**, with its recent renovations, comes in a close second for style, service and location.

Alamandas   **$110–$166**   ★★

Anse Mitan, ☎ *(596) 66-03-18, FAX (596) 66-07-01.*
Single: $110. Double: $166.
Located right in the heart of the tourist region and within walking distance to the beach, this small hotel accommodates guests in studios, some with kitchens. There's not much here in the way of diversions, but you'll find watersports, shopping and restaurants nearby. Credit cards: MC.

Anchorage Hotel   **$135**   ★★

Domaine de Belford, ☎ *(596) 76-92-32.*
Single: $135. Double: $135.
This village-style resort is perched on a hillside overlooking the sea. Accommodations are in country French-style buildings, each with its own check-in and swimming pool. Rooms are very nicely done with good-quality furnishings, high ceilings and comfortable appointments. All have kitchenettes either inside or on the balcony. The beach at Salines is a 10-minute drive. Credit cards: A, MC.

Bakoua-Sofitel Hotel   **$116–$529**   ★★★★★

Pointe du Bout, ☎ *(800) 221-4542, (596) 66-02-02, FAX (596) 66-00-41.*

Single: $116–$336. Double: $150–$529.

Located in a garden setting on a bluff above a private beach, this deluxe hotel is one of Martinique's best. Accommodations are on the hillside or the beach; all quite nice but on the small side. There are two lighted tennis courts, a lovely pool, all watersports and a nearby golf course. The service is among the island's best, and most of the French staff speaks at least some English. The beach is fine. Worth the splurge. Credit cards: A, CB, MC, V.

Balisier   **$62–$83**   ★

21 Victor Hugo Street, ☎ *(596) 71-46-54, FAX (596) 71-46-54.*
Single: $62–$78 Double: $78–$83.
Set in the heart of Fort-de-France, this budget property offers small and simple rooms. There are also three apartments with kitchenettes. There are no dining or recreation facilities on-site, but many within walking distance. Credit cards: A, MC.

Carayou Novotel Hotel   **$115–$375**   ★★

Pointe de Bout, ☎ *(800) 221-4542, (596) 66-04-04, FAX (596) 66-00-41.*
Single: $115–$260. Double: $140–$375.
Located on Fort-de-France Bay, this hotel caters mainly to groups. Accommodations are quite nice, with large, modern baths that include bidets. All units have a balcony. The small beach is found in a sheltered cove. There's also a large pool, two tennis courts, archery, a driving range and watersports. The disco is popular during high season. Credit cards: A, DC, V.

Diamant les Bains Hotel   **$78–$124**   ★★

Diamant, ☎ *(596) 76-40-14, FAX (596) 76-27-00.*
Single: $78–$98. Double: $103–$124.
Set on a sandy beach overlooking Diamond Rock, this small family-run property accommodates guests in the main house or in small, rustic bungalows with refrigerators. There's a pool and restaurant on-site, with watersports nearby. Service is cheerful and caring. Credit cards: MC, V.

Diamant Novotel   **$105–$371**   ★★★

Le Diamant, ☎ *(800) 221-4542, (596) 76-42-42, FAX (596) 76-25-99.*
Single: $105-$256. Double: $128-$371.
Bordered by white sand beaches near a fishing village, this hotel houses guests in comfortable rooms in three-story buildings. Most rooms have nice views of the sea. There's a pool, table tennis, a floating barge on which to sun, two tennis courts and supervised programs for children. A handful of bars and restaurants complete the scene. Popular with families. Credit cards: A, MC, V.

La Bateliere Hotel   **$135–$400**   ★★★

Schoelcher, ☎ *(596) 61-49-49, FAX (596) 61-70-57.*
Single: $135–$400. Double: $135–$400.
Located on 6.5 acres on a bluff overlooking the sea, this five-story hotel opened as a Hilton. Guest rooms are spacious, with all the modern amenities. For recreation, there are eight lighted tennis courts and a pro, all watersports, a pool, excursions in a cabin cruiser, and a fine, sandy beach. Several restaurants, a disco, and the island's first casino. Dependable service. Credit cards: A, MC, V.

MARTINIQUE

La Dunette   **$55–$120**   ★

Ste. Anne, ☎ *(596) 76-73-90, FAX (596) 76-76-05.*
Single: $55-$80. Double: $80-$120.

Located in a fishing village, this three-story hotel offers simple rooms, some with balconies. Besides the bar and dining room, there is little in the way of extras. Credit cards: MC, V.

La Pagerie—Mercure Inn   **$79–$182**   ★★

Pointe du Bout, ☎ *(800) 221-4542, (596) 66-05-30, FAX (596) 66-00-99.*
Single: $79–$139. Double: $94–$182.

This informal hotel faces the marina across the bay from Fort-de-France. Guest rooms are spacious with bidets in the bathrooms; some have kitchenettes while others have only refrigerators. Located in a high-density hotel area, there is a pool but little else on-site. Guests can use the facilities at the nearby Carayou Novotel, where they have restaurants, tennis and watersports. Credit cards: A, MC, V.

L'Imperatrice Village   **$78–$123**   ★★

Anse Mitan, ☎ *(596) 66-08-09, FAX (596) 72-66-30.*
Single: $78–$103. Double: $98–$123.

Set on tropical grounds across the bay from Fort-de-France, this resort houses guests in standard rooms, studios, and bungalows with kitchens. All are on the modest side, but pleasant enough. A bit off the beaten path, so you'll want to rent a car. On-site features include a restaurant and bar, pool and games like billiards and ping-pong. Credit cards: A, MC.

Meridien Martinique   **$253–$779**   ★★★★

Point du Bont, ☎ *(800) 543-4300, (596) 66-00-00, FAX (596) 66-00-74.*
Single: $253–$779. Double: $305–$779.

Located across the harbor from Fort-de-France, this seven-story property shows its age, and attracts mainly convention groups. Rooms are small but comfortable. There's lots to do at this busy resort, including complimentary watersports, a pool, health club, two tennis courts and a 100-slip marina. The man-made beach is small and gets crowded. There's also a casino and nightly entertainment during high season. A ferry transports passengers to Fort-de-France. Decent for its wide range of facilities, but best suited to the group market. Credit cards: A, CB, V.

Squash Hotel   **$81–$136**   ★★

3 Blvd. de la MArne, ☎ *(596) 63-00-01, FAX (596) 63-00-74.*
Single: $81–$106. Double: $96–$136.

Located in a residential neighborhood close to the center of town, this modern hotel is frequented by business travelers. Accommodations are clean, comfortable and tastefully decorated. There's live entertainment in the bar twice weekly. The well-equipped health club includes an exercise room, sauna, Jacuzzi and Turkish bath. There's also a pool and three squash courts. The beach is nearby.

Apartments and Condominiums

The **Villa Rental Service** of the Martinique Tourist Office ☎ *(596) 63-79-60* can arrange vacation home rentals. Among the choices are apartments, studios, or villas. Most of the properties are located in the southern sector, near good beaches. Rentals can be arranged for the week or month.

Les Ilets de l'Impératrice are two tiny islands off Le François on the windward coast, each with a 19th-century vacation house, beach, watersports, full-time maid and cook. Ilet Thierry's house has six double bedrooms; Ilet Oscar's has five. All-inclusive rates (airport pickup, lodging, food and drink, and sports, etc.) runs $200 per person per day year round. Contact Jean-Louis de Lucy ☎ *(596) 65-82-30*, FAX *(596) 63-18-22.*

Martinique Cottages   **$60–$75**   ★★
Lamentin, ☎ *(596) 50-16-08, FAX (596) 50-26-83.*
Single: $60. Double: $75.
Located in a residential area 15 minutes from Fort-de-France, this small operation is popular, especially with business travelers. Accommodations are in bungalows nestled among the trees. Each is nicely done with small kitchens and verandas. The beach is 15 minutes away; if that's too far, you can relax by the free-form pool. There's also a restaurant and bar. This family-owned spot is peaceful and pleasant. Credit cards: A, CB, D, DC, MC, V.

Residence Grand Large   **$98-$161**   ★★
Ste. Luce, ☎ *62-54-42, FAX (596) 62-54-32.*
Single: $98 Double: $98-$161
Off on its own on the south shore of Ste. Luce, a fishing village, this small complex offers fully furnished studios with kitchens and ocean views. There's nothing onsite, so you'll need a car to get around. The rates are quite reasonable. Credit cards: A, CD, D, MC, V.

Rivage Hotel   **$75–$100**   ★★
Anse Mitan, ☎ *(596) 66-00-53, FAX (596) 66-06-56.*
Single: $75. Double: $75-$100.
This small, family-run operation is near the beach. All rooms have a kitchenette and balcony; if you want a TV, you'll pay extra. There's a bar and pool, and lots of diversions within walking distance. Credit cards: MC, V.

Inns
For those seeking a more intimate island experience, an inn may be the best choice. The **Fregate Bleue Inn** and **Manor de Beauregard** are two of the charming inns with breakfast included in the price.

Fregate Bleue Inn   **$100–$225**   ★★★
Le Francois, ☎ *(800) 633-7411, (596) 54-54-66, FAX (596) 54-78-48.*
Single: $100-$2000 Double: $120–$225
Set on a hillside overlooking the sea, this gingerbread-trimmed inn is positively charming. All accommodations are in spacious studios with kitchenettes, armoires, antiques and four-poster beds. Breakfast is complimentary each morning, but you'll have to cook in or venture off-site for other meals. There's a pool for those too relaxed to walk three minutes to the beach. Very elegant and gracious, this lovely inn is best suited to those not seeking a lot of action. Credit cards: A, MC.

Habitation Lagrange   **$275–$385**   ★★★★
Marigot, ☎ *(800) 633-7411, (596) 53-60-60, FAX (596) 53-50-58.*

Single: $275–$385. Double: $275–$385.

This 18th-century creole mansion was refurbished and opened as an inn in 1991. Some guest rooms are in the great house, the former headquarters of a sugar and rum factory. Others are found in new two-story buildings. All are elegantly decorated with canopy beds, antique furnishings, VCRs and minibars, plus modern comforts like air conditioning. For recreation, there's a putting green, pool and tennis courts, plus exploring the ruins of the former plant. Charming and romantic. Credit cards: A, MC.

| **Leyritz Plantation** | **$87–$167** | ★★★★ |

Basse-Point, ☎ *(596) 78-53-92, FAX (596) 78-92-44.*
Single: $87–$121. Double: $117–$167.

This inn is another charmer, though its remote location isn't for everyone. Set on the grounds of a 230-acre banana plantation, it accommodates guests in a converted 18th-century great house and in the former guardhouse and slave quarters, as well as in bamboo and stone cottages. All are air conditioned, antique filled, have four-poster beds and loads of charm. The most atmospheric rooms are in the main house with its high ceilings, dormer windows, and thick walls. The beach is a full half-hour away, but there's a pool on-site. There's also a tennis court, and you can spend hours exploring the former plant. A major drawback are the hordes of tourists on organized tours. Nonetheless, this picturesque spot is hard to leave. Credit cards: A, MC.

| **Manor de Beauregard** | **$93-$223** | ★★★ |

Sainte Anne, ☎ *76-73-40, FAX (596) 76-93-24*
Single: $93 Double: $120-$223

This manor house features 11 rooms with views of Sainte Anne. The friendly owners include breakfast in the price. Public rooms are elegantly furnished in mahogany and marble. Those who prefer a more intimate atmosphere will love the ambience.

| **St. Aubin Hotel** | **$93–$142** | ★★★ |

Trinite, ☎ *(596) 69-34-77, FAX (596) 69-41-14*
Single: $93. Double: $120-$142.

This colonial-style inn, a former private residence, sits on a hillside with nice views of the surrounding area. An old-fashioned porch wraps around the building on two floors; you'll spend a lot of time on it reading or just taking in the view. Each room is individually decorated with modern amenities. The grounds include a pool and good dining room serving French and creole fare. You'll definitely need a car to explore beyond this remote spot. Credit cards: A, MC, V.

Low Cost Lodging

Martinique has more than 200 **Gites de France** ☎ *(596) 73-67-92*, which are apartments, studios and guest rooms in private homes. **Logis Vacances Antilles** ☎ *(596) 63-12-91* also offers rooms in private homes, as well as holiday studios and houses. Camping can be done almost anywhere—in the mountains, forest, and on many beaches, although indiscriminate camping is not permitted. **Tropicamp** at Gros Raisins Plage, Ste. Luce ☎ *(596) 62-49-66* is one of several companies with full services, including hot showers. Other comfortable camps with showers and toilets are **Nid Tropical** at Anse-a-l'Ane near

Trois Ilets ☎ *(596) 68-31-30*; one at **Vauclin** on the southeast Atlantic coast ☎ *(596) 74-45-88*; an another at **Pointe Marin** near the public beach of Ste. Anne ☎ *(596) 76-72-79*. A nominal fee is charged for facilities. For details, contact the **Office National des Dorês**, 3.5 km, route de Mouette, Fort-de-France; ☎ *(596) 71-34-50*.

The trend these days is to rent a camping car, which allows you opportunity to discover many of the treasures along Martinique's 300-mile roadway. One recommended camping-car operation is **West Indies Tours**, whose campers are outfitted with beds for four, refrigerator, shower, sink, 430-gallon water tank, dining table, stove and radio/cassette player. Contact **Michel Yula, West Indies Tours, Le François**; ☎ *(596) 54-50-71*; or **Wind Martinique, Anse Mitan**; ☎ *(596) 66-02-22*.

It's also possible to rent rooms in private houses, apartments, and houses in all price ranges with weekly or monthly rates. To rent a gîte as they as called, contact **Gîtes de France**, *Martinique, Maison du Tourisme Vert, 9 BD du Général-de-Gaulle, BP 1122, 97248 Fort-De-France*; ☎ *(596) 73-67-92*.

Auberge de l'Anse Mitan   **$83–$98**   ★

Anse Mitan, ☎ *(596) 66-01-12, FAX (596) 66-01-05.*
Single: $83-$98 Double: $83–$98.
This casual French-style inn is within walking distance of the beach in Anse Mitan. Accommodations include standard rooms in the three-story main building and six studios with kitchenettes. All are air-conditioned and have private baths and telephones. There's a bar and restaurant serving French and creole fare, but little else in the way of extras. Friendly and cheerful service at this family-run establishment.
Credit cards: A, DC, MC, V.

Victoria Hotel   **$88–$101**   ★ ★

Rte de Didier, ☎ *(596) 60-56-78, FAX (596) 60-00-24.*
Single: $88–$101. Double: $88–$101
Located on a hillside in a residential neighborhood with nice views, this colonial-style hotel offers good value for its reasonable rates, and attracts mainly business travelers. Accommodations are in comfortable rooms, some with TVs and others with kitchenettes. There's a French restaurant and a pool on site. Credit cards: MC, V.

Where to Eat

Fielding's Highest Rated Restaurants in Martinique

★★★★	La Fontane	$30–$50
★★★★	Leyritz Plantation	$27–$50
★★★	Athanor	$11–$30
★★★	Aux Filets Bleus	$13–$30
★★★	Chez Mally Edjam	$11–$29
★★★	La Mouina	$15–$30
★★★	La Villa Creole	$14–$18
★★★	Le Colibri	$18–$27
★★★	Le Coq Hardi	$18–$36
★★★	Le Poisson d'Or	$25–$30

Fielding's Most Exclusive Restaurants in Martinique

★★★★	La Fontane	$30–$50
★★★★	Leyritz Plantation	$27–$50
★★★	Le Poisson d'Or	$25–$30
★★★	Le Coq Hardi	$18–$36
★★★	Le Colibri	$18–$27

Fielding's Budget Restaurants in Martinique

★★★	Le Second Souffle	$8–$12
★★	La Dunette	$6–$20
★★★	La Villa Creole	$14–$18
★★	Le Cantonnais	$14–$20
★★	Diamant Les Bains	$16–$20

MARTINIQUE

Perhaps it's the irrepressible French dedication to cuisine, but chefs in Martinique seem to take special care with their menus, overseeing both the preparation and the service. Throughout the island you will generally find one of two cuisines: traditional French or island Creole; many restaurants combine the two on their menus. Fresh seafood dishes are omnipresent, among the tastiest are *chatrou* (octopus), *langouste* (small clawless lobster), *lambi* (conch), and *cribiches* (large river shrimp). Red snapper is served in a variety of ways. *Coquille de lambi* (minced conch in creamy sauce served in a shell) is an island must; the *blaff de poisson* (steamed fish in local spices) is excellent at Le Mareyeur. Another island specialty, *pâté en pot*, is a thick creole soup made with mutton. A good afternoon drink to cool you off is *les planteurs*— a planter's punch in a sweet fruit juice base. Heart islanders tend to chug down *décollage*—aged herbal rum with a fruit juice chaser. Most restaurants have excellent selections of French wines. Prices per person for a three-course meal without wine range from $30–$45 and up. The French & English booklet *Ti Gourmet*, available from the Tourist Office, will give out more information about where and what to eat.

Fort-de-France

Diamant Les Bains   **$$$**   ★★

Le Diamant, 97223, Le Diamant.
Latin American cuisine. Specialties: Blaff, Coconut Flan.
Lunch: entrees $16–$20.
Dinner: entrees $16–$20.
Good local fare is served in a motel-like hostelry in Le Diamant, a cozy beach town whose claim to fame is the imposing Diamond Rock, majestically rising from the deep to an almost 600-foot height. The beach it fronts is nothing special, but it's a nice spot to dine on blaff fish (cooked with thyme, peppers, clove and other spices), boudin and coconut flan.

La Fontane   **$$$**   ★★★★

Km. 4 Rue de Balata, ☎ (596) 64-65-89.
French cuisine.
Lunch: entrees $30–$50.
Dinner: entrees $30–$50.
A highly-regarded French-creole restaurant, La Fontane is located in a restored gingerbread house surrounded by fruit trees. The service is formal, the interior is antique-filled and tasteful, with exotic carpets on the floors. Dishes have included crayfish salad with fruit, lamb and mango and red-snapper with a citrus sauce.

La Mouina   **$$$**   ★★★

route de Redoute ☎ (596) 79-34-57.
French cuisine. Specialties: Crab Farcis.
Lunch: Noon–4 p.m., entrees $15–$30.
Dinner: 7:30–9:30 p.m., entrees $15–$30.
This is suburbia Fort-de-France style—fine dining in a typical upper-class home in Redoute, high above the capital below. Guests are made welcome in a dining salon

MARTINIQUE

on a balcony with a garden view. The smart set likes to make La Mouina a regular stop for luncheons of stuffed crab backs, tournedos and crayfish. Dinners are served by candlelight.

La Villa Creole   **$$$**   ★★★

Anse Mitan 97229, Anse Mitan.
Latin American cuisine.
Lunch: Noon–2 p.m., entrees $14–$18.
Dinner: 7–10 p.m., entrees $14–$18.

A friendly and warm atmosphere permeates this gingerbread house with tables set on a seaside terrace in Anse Mitan, a beach resort famed for low-key, moderately priced hotels. There are several prixe-fixe meals to choose from, from plain to fancy, but all feature a bevy of side dishes, vegetables and dessert. The owner sometimes gives impromptu song and dance performances.

Le Cantonnais   **$$$**   ★★

La Marina.
Chinese cuisine.
Dinner: 6:30–11 p.m., prix fixe $14–$20.

Guests staying at the large resort hotels near the marina in Pointe du Bout can take a break from French-creole cuisine at this Chinese foodery serving a voluminous menu of unusual dishes including broiled shark's fin and bird's nest soup. Vegetarians also have a choice of several meatless entrees.

Le Colibri   **$$$**   ★★★

allee du Colibri, Morne des Esses.
Latin American cuisine. Specialties: Colombo, Tourte aux Lambis, Flan au Coco.
Lunch: Noon–3 p.m., entrees $18–$27.
Dinner: 7–11 p.m., entrees $18–$27.

A family-run operation, Le Colibri (The Hummingbird), located in the northwestern side of the island, could be named for the friendly bustling about hither and tither of Mme Paladino and her daughters, who are busy serving scrumptious creole meals to weekenders from Fort-de-France. These denizens often fill the veranda of the house for conch pie, crayfish stew and a dreamy coconut flan. Come early to nab these choice seats or you'll be seated inside facing the open kitchen (not so bad an idea).

Le Coq Hardi   **$$$**   ★★★

Rue Martin Luther King, ☎ (596) 63-66-83.
International cuisine. Specialties: Tournedos Rossini, Prime Rib.
Lunch: Noon–2 p.m., entrees $18–$36.
Dinner: 7–11 p.m., entrees $18–$36.

Red meat is god here, prepared *au bleu* (very rare) which is the French way. Master charcutier Alphonse Sintive regularly imports the choice cuts of T-Bone, filet mignon and entrecote from France. After you choose your own steak, it's cooked over an open wood fire. An old-fashioned tournedos rossini is prepared with foie gras and truffles, and is a favorite here. If you still have room after the huge portions served, there's still a wide selection of scrumptious desserts and sorbets.

Le Poisson d'Or   **$$$**   ★★★

On the road from Anse Mitan to Pointe du Bout, (596) 66-01-80.
Latin American cuisine.
Lunch: Noon–2:30 p.m., prix fixe $25–$30.
Dinner: 7–10 p.m., prix fixe $25–$30.

This is a casual roadside seafood eatery set between the beach cities of Anse Mitan and Pointe du Bout. Tropical greenery and a bamboo ceiling make you feel like you're dining on an isle in the South Seas. A fixed-price meal for $25 is a good buy for an array of creole specialties including a conch appetizer and an elegant dessert.

Le Second Souffle   **$$**   ★★★

27 Rue Blenac, ☎ (596) 63-44-11.
Latin American cuisine.
Lunch: Noon–3 p.m., entrees $8–$12.
Dinner: 7:30–10 p.m., entrees $8–$12.

A treat for the body and soul is a cleansing visit to this pleasant vegetarian restaurant after a tour of the Byzantine Saint Louis Cathedral nearby. Le Second Souffle (is there a first?) dishes up a salad of seasonal fruits with honey sauce, or a meatless plat du jour, which may include a christophene or callaloo souffle.

Leyritz Plantation   **$$$**   ★★★★

Basse Pointe 97218, Leyritz, ☎ (596) 78-53-92.
Latin American cuisine.
Lunch: 12:30–2 p.m., entrees $27–$40.
Dinner: 7:30–9 p.m., entrees $36–$50.

Dining at one of Martinique's prime tourist attractions sounds like a recipe for disaster, but surprisingly, the Creole cuisine remains first rate. Guests also get a lot of food for their francs, especially a set luncheon of stuffed crab, blood pudding, an entree (sometimes conch), rice and vegetables and dessert. The million-dollar setting amidst an 18th century sugar plantation is a fond postcard memory. Although lunch is the preferred time, come for dinner when the tour bus pandemonium becomes practically nonexistent.

Basse Pointe

Athanor   **$$$**   ★★★

Rue de Bord de Mer, Ste. Anne, ☎ (596) 76-72-93.
French cuisine. Specialties: Grilled Lobster.
Dinner: 7–10 p.m., entrees $11–$30.

This informal eatery located one block from the beach in Ste. Anne prepares tasty pizzas, salads and other casual meals from a large menu. Diners can choose a few fancier items including the specialty, grilled lobster, which is delicious. There's a choice of seating in a pretty garden behind the restaurant or in a greenery-draped dining room indoors.

Aux Filets Bleus   **$$$**   ★★★

Point Marin, Ste. Anne, ☎ (596) 76-73-42.
Latin American cuisine. Specialties: Delices de la Mer, Turtle Soup, Court Bouillon.
Lunch: 12:30–2:30 p.m., entrees $13–$30.
Dinner: 7:30–9:30 p.m., entrees $13–$30.

A restaurant of many contrasts—although Aux Filets Bleus charges haute cuisine prices, the place is so casual you can come here in a beach cover-up after a swim in the briny which is in full view of the tables. Also, dishes are mostly hearty West Indian dishes like *chatrous* (octopus) with red beans and rice, hardly justifying the stiff tab. Still, what you're served is usually very good, and the ambience is friendly and intimate.

Chez Mally Edjam $$$ ★★★

Route de la Cote, ☎ *(596) 78-51-18.*
French cuisine. Specialties: Fruit Confitures, Colombo de Porc.
Dinner: entrees $11–$29.

It's a very pleasant drive to get to this home-style restaurant run by stellar cuisiniere Mally Edjam and her family. The surrounding landscape en route is dotted with pineapple plantations, and trees hung heavily with boughs of green bananas. That's just a prelude to the symphony of flavors on the fixed-price lunches served here, which may include *pork colombo* (local curry), conch and fabulous desserts. Don't miss the homemade preserves made from local fruits. Dinners may be arranged by appointment.

La Dunette $$ ★★

Sainte Anne, 97227, Ste. Anne, ☎ *(596) 76-73-90.*
Seafood cuisine.
Lunch: entrees $6–$20.
Dinner: entrees $6–$20.

La Dunette is like a lot of pleasant seaside restaurants on the island that serves seafood specialties. Dine inside or out in a tropical garden facing the sea on poached sea urchins, curries or grilled fish. Connected to a pleasant, intimate hotel where you might consider staying if you're in the area, which is noted for gorgeous beaches and fine weather.

Yva Chez Vava $$$ ★★

Boulevard de Gaulle, Grand Riviere, ☎ *(596) 55-72-55.*
French cuisine.
Dinner: entrees $18–$27.

This chez on the northern tip of the island is the domain of local legend Vava and her daughter Yva, who now continues the tradition of cooking family-style creole meals in their own residence near a river. As Grand Riviere is a fishing village, seafood appears prominently on the menu. Specialties include *accras* (cod fritters), *chicken colombo* and *z'habitants* (crayfish prepared Martinique style). After lunch, you might want to visit the fish market where your food originated, or stroll on the black sand beach.

MARTINIQUE

Where to Shop

Martinique is the best place for bargains on French imports from perfume to clothes and crystal.

"Go French" is the password when trying to decode what to buy in Martinique, a place where you can find the best bargains among French imports—perfumes, cosmetics, clothes, china, and crystal—at prices 25-40 percent lower than in the U.S. If you pay in traveler's checks, you'll receive an additional 20 percent discount. You will never find these prices in France. Don't miss picking up a few bottles of Martinique-brewed rum. Craft buys range from folk-styled appliqué wall hangings to the Martiniquais doll dressed in the national costume, which can be seen in nearly every store and in every size imaginable. Paintings and sculptures by native-born Martiniquais or artists who have moved to the islands can be found at galleries in Fort-de-France and at some hotels. A conical bakoua straw hat does nicely as a sunstopper. Madras, long popular in traditional folk costumes, is available in shops on every street for $6-$12 a meter. If you're interested in the bright gold Creole jewelry that seems to be around many women's necks, ears and wrists, you will be joining a long-standing cultural tradition. The special "convict's chain" called *chaîne forçat*, and the *tremblants*, gold brooches with special adornment, can be found in several stores, where you should be able to judge authenticity by the price. Among the most reputable are **Cadet**

Daniel, **Bijouterie Onyx** and **Emile Mothie's** workshop in Trenelle. (The latter is for serious fans who want to observe his work.) For delicious French delicacies, wines, foie gras and chocolates, head for **Boutique Michel Montignac**. Gourmet chefs will find a plethora of exotic spices in many of the open air markets. To pick up the latest in island music, try **Hit Parade** on Rue Lamartine. Boutiques like *La Chamade* on rue Victor Hugo in Fort de France carry Cote d'Azur designers and fashions from Paris.Other shops on or near rue Victor Hugo are *Georgia*, *Kookai*, *Alain Moanoukian* and *Ah!Nana*. Others, like *Mounia* on rue Perrignon, carry top names such as Claude Montana, Dorothee Bis and Yves St. Laurent. Young Martinique designers are also now presenting their own collections in shops like *Anacaona*, featuring designs by Paul-Herve Elisabeth.

Martinique Directory

Arrival and Departure

Direct flights are available from New York/JFK every Saturday on North **American Airlines** ☎ *(212) 333-8680*. You can also catch one of many regular flights American Airlines offers to San Juan (via many gateways in the U.S.) and a Sunday flight on Air France from Miami. Interisland connections to Martinique, from St. Martin, Antigua, Dominica, St. Lucia, Barbados, St. Vincent, Mustique and Union Island can be made on **Air Martinique** ☎ *(596) 60-00-23*. **LIAT** flies to and from neighboring islands ☎ *(596) 51-10-00*. From Guadeloupe, you can catch frequent daily flights on Réseau Aérien Francais des Caraibes, a French Caribbean airline consortium that includes **Air Martinique**, **Air Guadeloupe** and **Air France** ☎ *(596) 55-33-00*.

Martinique can also be reached from other islands by the ultra-modern catamaran Emeraude Express. Contact **Caribbean Express** ☎ *(596) 63-12-11*, FAX *(596) 63-34-47*.

Many cruise ships pull into Martinique as a port of call. Some dock at the attractive Passenger Terminal located at the harbor port a few minutes' drive from the center of the city; others anchor in Fort-de-France Bay and transfer passengers by tender, a 10-minute ride.

There is no departure tax charged for visitors, except charter flights.

Business Hours

Stores open weekdays 8:30 a.m.–6 p.m. and Saturday 8:30 a.m.–1 p.m. Banks have varied hours but are generally open weekdays 7:30–noon and 2:30–4 p.m.

Climate

Martinique's temperatures stay temperate all year long, hovering around 79 degrees F, with only a five degree difference between seasons. The air is cooled by constant wind currents (east and northeast); trade winds are called *les alizés*.

Documents

For stays up to three weeks, U.S. and Canadian citizens traveling as tourists must show proof of citizenship in the form of a valid passport, or a passport that expired no more than five years ago, or other proof in the form of a birth certificate or voter's registration card with a government-authorized photo ID. For stays of more than three weeks, or for nontourist visas, a valid passport is necessary. Resident aliens of the U.S. and Canada and other foreign nationals other than those in the Common Market must have a valid passport and visa. All passengers must show an ongoing or return ticket.

Electricity

Current is 220 AC, 50 cycles. American and Canadian appliances require a French plug, converter and transformers.

Getting Around

Taxi stands are located at the airport, in downtown Fort-de-France, and at major hotels. Rates rise 60 percent between 8 p.m. and 6 a.m. Eighty percent of the taxis are Mercedes Benz. There are also collective taxis (eight-passenger limousines bearing the sign TC).

Car rentals are available at Lamentin Airport, though hours are dependent on international flights. A valid driver's license is required, the minimum age is 21. Other agencies can be found in Fort-de-France. Among the best are **Avis**, *4 rue Ernest Deproge* ☎ *(596) 70-11-60*; **Budget**, *12 rue Félix Eboué, Fort-de-France* ☎ *(596) 63-69-00*; and **Hertz**, *24 rue Ernest Deproge, Fort-de-France* ☎ *(596) 60-64-54*.

Ferries, called vedettes, link Fort-de-France with Pointe du Bout daily from early morning until after midnight, and with Anse Mitan, Anse-a-l'Ane, Grand Anse d'Arlet from early morning till late afternoon. All ferries leave and arrive at Quai d'Esnambuc.

Language

The languages of the isle are French and Creole. You'll find English spoken in most hotels, restaurants and tourist facilities, but you'll be happy if you remember to bring along a French phase book and pocket dictionary.

Medical Emergencies

There are 20 hospitals and clinics on the island, many well equipped; the best is **La Meynard** ☎ *(596) 55-20-00*. Ask the Tourist Office to assist you in securing an English-speaking physician.

Money

The official currency is the French franc, but U.S. and Canadian dollars are accepted almost everywhere. The rate of exchange, approximately five francs to the dollar, can change due to currency fluctuation. Fort-de-France banks include: **Credit Martiniquais** ☎ *(596)59-93-00*, open 7:30 a.m.- noon and 2:05 p.m.-4:45 p.m., closed Wednesday afternoons.; **Banque Nationale de Paris** ☎ *(596)63-82-57*, open 7:15 a.m.-2:30 p.m. weekdays; and **Banque des Antilles Francaises**, ☎ *(596)73-93-44*, open 7:30 a.m.-12:30 p.m. and 2:15-4:15 p.m., Monday-Friday. Banks close on Saturdays and on the afternoons preceding holidays. A money exchange service, **Change Caraibes** ☎ *(596)51-57-91* operates Monday-Friday, 8 a.m.-7 p.m.; Saturday 8 a.m.-2:30 p.m., located in the Arrivals Building at the airport and on rue Ernest Deproge ☎ *(596)60-28-40* in Fort-de France.

Telephone

The area code is *596*. To direct-dial from the U.S., dial ☎ *011-596*, plus the local Martinique number for station to station, or *01-596* plus local number for person to person. The best way to make international calls in Martinique is to purchase a "Telecarte" (a one-minute call to the U.S. is about $2.10. These credit cards can be purchased at all post offices and other outlets marked "Télécarte en vente Ici."; the booths you use them in are marked "Télécom." To use the assistance of an operator or to make a call from a hotel room will raise the price enormously.

Time

Martinique is one hour later than New York (Eastern Standard Time). Time is related on the 24-hour schedule; i.e., 1 p.m. is 13:00 hours.

Tipping and Taxes

Some hotels add a 10 percent service charge and/or 5 percent government tax to the bill. Check your bill carefully and avoid adding on an extra service charge. If there is no charge added, a 10–15 percent charge would be appreciated by waiters and waitresses.

Tourist Information

The **Martinique Tourist Office** ☎ *(596) 63-79-60* is located in handsome quarters on the Boulevard Alfassa, which borders on the waterfront in Fort-de-France. Hours are Monday-Friday 7:30 a.m.–12:30 p.m. and 2:30–5:30 p.m., and Saturday 8 a.m.–noon. Pick up complimentary maps, magazines and information bulletins; the English-speaking staff is quite helpful. A tourist office information desk at Lamentin Airport is open daily until the last flight comes in. In the U.S. ☎ *(800) 391-4909*. *Internet Address*: http://www.nyo.com/martinique. E-mail: Martinique@nyo.com

When to Go

Carnival begins on Jan. 7 for five days, a total-island experience with parties and parades. Ash Wednesday is a blowout affair on March 1, with jammed streets, flowing rum, wild dancing and a funeral cortege at La Savane, Fort-de-France. The Aqua Festival du Robert on April 15–22 is a sea extravaganza in this Atlantic coastal town with yawl races, regattas, and concerts. Jazz a la Plantation on June 2, for two weeks at Basse Pointe, is a New Orleans-meets-French Antilles affair, with concert jams, street bands, Creole nights, and jazz lectures and workshops. Images Caraibes, on June 2 for two weeks, is the 5th Caribbean Film Festival in Fort-de-France. Tour de la Martinique is July 7–16, a week-long bicycle race throughout the island. The tenth Tour des Yoles Rondes on July 30–Aug. 6, is a race of rawls used by Martinique fishermen. The Semi-Marathon, on Nov. 19, is a large race contest. Christmas Eve is celebrated with a midnight mass followed by a sumptuous supper, called Le

Réveillon. New Year's Eve is another huge bash celebrated at hotels and restaurants.

MARTINIQUE HOTELS		RMS	RATES	PHONE	CR. CARDS
Fort-de-France					
★★★★★	Bakoua-Sofitel Hotel	138	$116–$529	(800) 221-4542	A, CB, MC, V
★★★★	Habitation Lagrange	17	$275–$385	(800) 633-7411	A, MC
★★★★	Leyritz Plantation	70	$87–$167	(596) 78-53-92	A, MC
★★★★	Meridien Martinique	295	$253–$779	(800) 543-4300	A, CB, V
★★★	Diamant Novotel	181	$105–$371	(800) 221-4542	A, MC, V
★★★	Fregate Bleue Inn	7	$100–$225	(800) 633-7411	A, MC
★★★	La Bateliere Hotel	199	$135–$400	(596) 61-49-49	A, MC, V
★★★	Manor de Beauregard	11	$93–$223	(596) 76-73-40	MC, V
★★★	Martinique Cottages	8	$60–$75	(596) 50-16-08	A, CB, D, DC, MC, V
★★★	St. Aubin Hotel	15	$93–$142	(596) 69-34-77	A, MC, V
★★	Alamandas	30	$110–$166	(596) 66-03-18	MC
★★	Anchorage Hotel	187	$135	(596) 76-92-32	A, MC
★★	Carayou Novotel Hotel	197	$115–$375	(800) 221-4542	A, DC, V
★★	Diamant les Bains Hotel	26	$78–$124	(596) 76-40-14	MC, V
★★	La Pagerie—Mercure Inn	98	$79–$182	(800) 221-4542	A, MC, V
★★	L'Imperatrice Village	59	$78–$123	(596) 66-08-09	A, MC
★★	Residence Grand Large	18	$98–$161	(596) 62-54-42	A, CB, D, MC, V
★★	Rivage Hotel	20	$75–$100	(596) 66-00-53	MC, V
★★	Squash Hotel	108	$81–$136	(596) 63-00-01	A, MC, V
★★	Victoria Hotel	32	$88–$101	(596) 60-56-78	MC, V
★	Auberge de l'Anse Mitan	20	$83–$98	(596) 66-01-12	A, DC, MC, V
★	Balisier	27	$62–$83	(596) 71-46-54	A, MC
★	La Dunette	18	$55–$120	(596) 76-73-90	MC, V

MARTINIQUE RESTAURANTS	PHONE	ENTREE	CR. CARDS

Basse Pointe

French			
★★★ Athanor	(596) 76-72-93	$11–$30	MC, V
★★★ Chez Mally Edjam	(596) 78-51-18	$11–$29	A, MC, V
★★ Yva Chez Vava	(596) 55-72-55	$18–$27	None

Latin American			
★★★ Aux Filets Bleus	(596) 76-73-42	$13–$30	MC, V

Seafood			
★★ La Dunette	(596) 76-73-90	$6–$20	MC, V

Fort-de-France

Chinese			
★★ Le Cantonnais		$14–$20	

French			
★★★★ La Fontane	(596) 64-65-89	$30–$50	A
★★★ La Mouina	(596) 79-34-57	$15–$30	MC, V

International			
★★★ Le Coq Hardi	(596) 63-66-83	$18–$36	A, MC, V

Latin American			
★★★★ Leyritz Plantation	(596) 78-53-92	$27–$50	MC, V
★★★ La Villa Creole		$14–$18	
★★★ Le Colibri		$18–$27	
★★★ Le Poisson d'Or	(596) 66-01-80	$25–$30	
★★★ Le Second Souffle	(596) 63-44-11	$8–$12	MC, V
★★ Diamant Les Bains		$16–$20	

MARTINIQUE

MONTSERRAT

Montserrat boasts three mountain ranges and lush green terrain.

One of the most charming and undiscovered communities of the Caribbean, Montserrat, the Emerald Isle, has long benefited from a fertile blanket of volcanic soil that is perfect for growing bountiful fresh produce. The island's mountainous interior invites hikers who explore its peaks and *ghauts* (ravines), and mountain bikers who toil gamely through the forests of paradise. Although tourist arrivals have been on the upswing in the early 1990s, the island is in no imminent danger of becoming oversaturated and the local tourist board can honestly call Montserrat, "the way the Caribbean used to be." The slogan now has another meaning. In July 1995, a fissure opened up in English Crater beneath volcanic Chances Peak and spewed ash over the surprised residents of Plymouth, the island's quaint capital. The ashfall was the first sign of real volcanic activity on Montserrat in more than six decades, and the event was dramatic enough to send vulcanologists from the United States and England scurrying to the tiny outpost for evaluation and monitoring. Over the following year, the situation evolved repeatedly but, at press time, Plymouth and the southern third of the island had been evacuated due to the growth of a lava dome which is now taller than Chances Peak and glows red at night. The volcano produces regular ash eruptions that soar as high as 40,000 feet into the air. The pyroclastic flows have reached the sea, adding new acreage to the island.

What sounds like a vacation fit for Dante has yet to deter a few intrepid souls who are making the trek to Montserrat to visit the site of a living, breathing volcano. The northern half of the island is considered safe enough for residents to live and, in the words of one geologist, "If we think it's safe enough for them, it's safe enough for tourists." The few visitors who arrive will find a delightful backwater whose cozy dimensions invite thorough exploration, and a populace that appreciates the attention from outsiders. Hopefully, by the time you read this, the volcanic activity will have settled down, and residents will be putting the turmoil behind them. Geologists are understandably wary about laying out a long-term prognosis—the year-old activity could stop as we go to press, or it may continue for months or years. Although it was initially a worry, the likelihood of an explosive eruption similar to what decimated Martinique in 1902 has become less of a concern. However, before planning your trip, call Montserrat's U.S. information line for the latest information ☎ *(516) 425-0900.*

The British Crown Colony of Montserrat is 39 square miles in size, and lies some 27 miles southwest of Antigua. The island is compact—only 11 miles long by seven across at its widest point—but large enough to encompass a diverse natural environment. The lower coastal elevations tend to be covered in woodlands, while the northern reaches are much drier, with scrubby bushes and the occasional cactus dotting the rocky hillsides. A prominent saddle in the middle of the island is home to a small rain forest and the slopes above, called "the bread basket," are where, until the recent volcanic activity, most of Montserrat's rich bounty of produce has been grown. The island has three distinct mountain ranges: the lowest is Silver Hill which dominates the mostly unpopulated northern tip; the middle section of the island rises to verdant Katy Hill, which is surrounded by smaller mountains and valleys. The southern portion of the island is governed by steep Chances Peak, rising 3002 feet

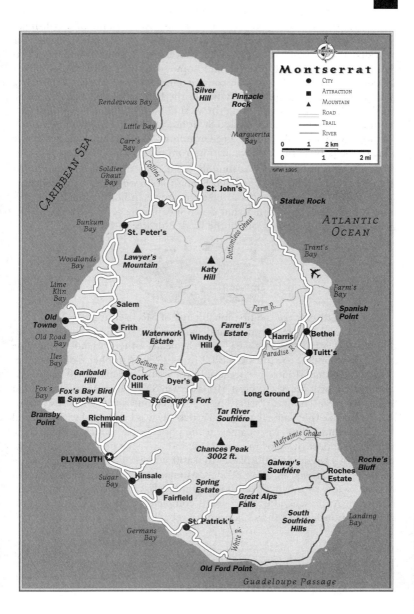

Montserrat

- ● CITY
- ■ ATTRACTION
- ▲ MOUNTAIN
- ROAD
- TRAIL
- RIVER

0   1   2 km
0   1   2 mi

©FWI 1995

Rendezvous Bay

▲ **Silver Hill**

Pinnacle Rock

Little Bay

Marguerita Bay

Carr's Bay

Collins R.

CARIBBEAN SEA

Soldier Ghaut Bay

● **St. John's**

Statue Rock

Bunkum Bay

● **St. Peter's**

Bottomless Ghaut

ATLANTIC OCEAN

Woodlands Bay

▲ **Lawyer's Mountain**

▲ **Katy Hill**

Trant's Bay

Lime Klin Bay

✈

Farm's Bay

● **Salem**

Farm R.

Spanish Point

● **Old Towne**

● **Frith**

Waterwork Estate

Farrell's Estate

● **Windy Hill**

● **Harris**

● **Bethel**

Old Road Bay

Paradise R.

● **Tuitt's**

Iles Bay

Belham R.

Garibaldi Hill

● **Cork Hill**

● **Dyer's**

● **Long Ground**

Fox's Bay

■ **Fox's Bay Bird Sanctuary**

■ **St. George's Fort**

Bransby Point

● **Richmond Hill**

Tar River Soufrière ■

Meftaimie Ghaut

▲ **Chances Peak 3002 ft.**

Roche's Bluff

✦ **PLYMOUTH**

Galway's Soufriére ■

Roches Estate

Sugar Bay

● **Kinsale**

Spring Estate

Great Alps Falls

South Soufriére Hills

Landing Bay

● **Fairfield**

● **St. Patrick's**

Germans Bay

White R.

Old Ford Point

Guadeloupe Passage

majestically into the clouds. Sometimes referred to as the erupting volcano itself, the peak is actually the highest, most-western point of a half-mile-wide, horseshoe-shaped crater rim that is open on its east side. Chances has provided an important barrier from the volcanic activity for residents of Plymouth, the capital of Montserrat, and home to about a third of the island's 11,000 population (though the town is currently relocated). Although a small number of residents usually live in the lush saddle beneath Chances' northern slope, most reside along the west coast of the island, north of Plymouth, and between Cork Hill and St. John. Only a few residents remain in the now-evacuated village of Long Ground or Tar River, which lies at the edge of the pyroclastic flows emanating from the volcano to date.

The current "unsafe area" is roughly defined by drawing a line between Bransby Point on the west coast and Spanish Point on the east. All residents south of this line have been relocated to the north end of the island, and Plymouth businesses have either shut down indefinitely or moved north. The government is functioning out of the Cork Hill area.

History

Ciboney Indians were the first inhabitants of Montserrat some 1500 years ago, later replaced by Arawaks and cannibalistic Caribs, the latter who dubbed the island "Alliouagana," which means either "island of the aloe plant" or "island of the prickly bush." In 1493, Christopher Columbus bestowed the name Montserrat because of the island's resemblance to the luscious terrain near the Montserrat Monastery in Spain. Irish roots were laid in 1623, when Sir Thomas Warner, in St. Kitts, commanded rebellious Catholics to colonize the island. Today St. Patrick's Day is celebrated with glee and you'll still find lots of Irish names in the phonebook. After the slave trade began to support the growing sugarcane industry, the ratio between blacks and whites soared—10,000 blacks to 1300 whites in 1678. Emancipation for the slaves arrived in 1834. Today, Montserrat remains a British Crown Colony, with a resident governor appointed by and representing Queen Elizabeth. At present, the island seems completely at peace with its protectorate relationship and shows no signs of rebelling,

People

Most of the towns and place names, and even many of the names of residents on Montserrat are of Irish origin, dating back to the mid-1600s, when there were a thousand Irish families living here. Today, only a handful of full-blooded Irishmen still live here. Most of the remaining are those of West African descent, whose ancestors were imported as plantation slaves from the 1660s to 1834. With a population barely topping 11,000, expect everyone on Montserrat to know each other, and if you stay more than a few days, they'll get to know you—the people are unhesitatingly friendly. In recent years, numerous Americans, Canadians and Britons, nicknamed "snowbirds," have bought retirement homes here. Consequently, much of the cultural life today in Montserrat, including the fine museum, is run by ex-pats who have improved the quality of service, though a bit of contact with the native locals has been lost in the process. At the same time, perhaps because of the island's genuine physical beauty, locals tend to feel an intense connection to their land, and it's not surprising they have discovered numerous healing properties from native plants. Superstitions and beliefs in other-worldly things still run high, and some native born carry not only their birth name but a "jumby" name—a magical name that helps protect them from spirits. *Obeah*, a voodoo-type religion with African roots, has been outlawed on the island, but expect to find a few secret devotees amid the more Catholic masses.

Beaches

Montserrat is known for its black volcanic beaches, which in reality tend to mean sand that is dark golden brown or silvery gray. The best are on the west coast, and the sands become lighter as one proceeds north, climaxed by lovely and secluded Rendezvous Bay—accessible only by boat or via a 30-minute trail over a rocky bluff. As one heads south from Rendezvous, two nearby beaches, Little Bay and Carr's Bay, are quite pleasant, and are popular as the sites of local parties and events. A pair of tiny and little visited coves, Bunkum Bay and Woodlands Bay, are nestled against the cliffs below Woodlands and provide decent swimming. Old Road Bay is perhaps the island's most popular spot, situated at the foot of both the Vue Point Hotel and the golf course, though many locals are content to use the mile-long sprawl of black sand that stretches north from Plymouth.

Volcano Warning!

Mother Nature knows how to keep tiny Montserrat on the map. The devastation from 1989's Hurricane Hugo that wiped out much of the island's greenery and many homes was all but forgotten when a fissure opened up on the slopes of volcanic Chances Peak in July 1995 and spewed ash and smoke over surprised Plymouth residents. The ashfall the first sign of real volcanic activity on the island in more than six decades, it was dramatic enough to send vulcanologists from the United States and England scurrying to the tiny outpost for evaluation and monitoring. At press time, Plymouth and the southern half of the island has been evacuated and tourist arrivals have slowed to a standstill. Hopefully, the volcanic activity will have settled down by the time you read this and the island's residents will be successfully putting the turmoil behind them. Before planning your trip, call Montserrat's toll-free information line for the latest information: ☎ *(800) 646-2002.*

Underwater

Virgin reefs featuring excellent soft coral growth and the relaxed charm of an undiscovered island characterize the fledgling activity of diving on Montserrat. Most sites are spread along the length of the western coastline. Visibility approaches 100 feet on good days, particularly on the southern coast, and shore dives are possible from several bays. There's a 200-foot pirate ship that went down off the east coast in 1889 and is still partially intact while it awaits excavation and preservation by the local National Trust. Snorkeling is feasible at Woodlands Bay and Old Road, and strong swimmers should investigate the long reef between Little Bay and Rendezvous Bay. At press time, the impact of volcanic ash on dive sites was unknown, but is most likely to have affected locations on the southern half of the island. Two dive shops were in operation for most of 1995, but shut down when tourist arrivals slowed. When the volcanic activity lessens, these shops should reopen or a new operator will provide services.

On Foot

Montserrat's small dimensions offer many hiking options, though some of the best hikes lie in what is currently called the "unsafe area" and the island's longest hike, from Galways Soufriere to Roches Estate and Long Ground, is no longer possible due to pyroclastic flows. A lattice of goat trails and old footpaths between the crumbling plantations appear on the detailed 1:25,000 map available from the tourists office. The underexplored northern tip of the island behind and southeast of Rendezvous Bay makes for splendid adventuring through a hot, near-desert environment. A shorter excursion can be undertaken out to Bransby Point, a bird sanctuary along the shore. If the volcano's rumblings have settled down, there is a steep trail to the summit of Chances Peak out of Plymouth, and shorter hikes that visit the beautiful Great Alps Falls or steaming Galways Soufriere on the southern slopes. Check ahead of time with local authorities before attempting either of these.

By Pedal

Montserrat boasts more than 100 miles of paved roads and a determined bike rental outfit with a staff that is familiar with many of the old cart trails, making the island ideal for cyclists seeking a relaxed, offbeat riding destination. A November "fat tire festival" has found its way onto regional biking calendars. The winding, 28-mile road circumnavigating the island is an excellent half-day excursion, but requires healthy thighs for the numerous short, steep switchbacks; the parched area between Little Bay and the airport features dramatic scenery and little traffic. Off-roading possibilities are endless, but carry a patch kit for the ever-present stickers.

What Else to See

Led by **Chances Peak** and the smoldering **volcano**, the most compelling sights on Montserrat are the natural ones, and you'll want to schedule most of your vacation time around them. History buffs will want to stop by the **Montserrat Museum**, ensconced in an old sugar mill at Richmond Hill. Some artifacts date back to the original native inhabitants, as far back as pre-Columbian history. Above Belham Valley, **Waterwork Estate** is a 250-year-old plantation under restoration; ancestors of the original owners provide a two-hour tour for $20 ☎ *(809) 491-2389*. If residents are allowed into **Plymouth** during your visit, stop by to see some of the charming old buildings of various styles and sizes. The grounds of the Victorian Government House, topped with a shamrock, may be toured on some weekdays—it's located on the green hills above the Plymouth community of Wapping. If the volcanic activity permits, you may be able to visit the Great Alps Falls or Galways Soufriere, but do so with a guide and only if the local authorities have established them as safe to tour.

City Celebrations

Pilgrimage ★★★★

Plymouth, ☎ (809) 491-8288.

This annual celebration takes place each August and runs over 10 days. Talk about something for everyone: Festivities include traditional street jump ups, African dance shows, fashion exhibitions, beach parties, barbecues, large markets, cultural concerts, bike races and tours, special hikes, and cricket and domino tournaments with competitors from neighboring islands. The island also goes wild each St. Patrick's Day, which is not as incongruous as it first seems. The first European settlers on Montserrat were Irish, and on St. Patrick's Day, March 17, 1768, Montserrat slaves staged a revolt and marched on the Government House. Today, St. Patty-related week-long events include a masquerade, jump-ups, street theater, Irish music and the Freedom Run Slave Fest.

Historical Sites

Galways Estate ★★★

Above St. Patrick's.

A thriving sugar plantation for some 250 years, this estate dates back to the 1700s. It's now in ruins, but has been selected for renovation by the Smithsonian Institute under the auspices of the Montserrat National Trust. You can inspect the impressive sugar mill, great house, windmill tower and other structures. Check with local authorities before heading up—it's high on the slopes of Chances Peak and was considered part of the unsafe area for most of 1996.

Museums and Exhibits

Montserrat Museum ★★★

Richmond Hill, Plymouth, ☎ (809) 491-5443.

Located in an old sugar mill, the country's national museum tells its history from pre-Columbian times to the present. On display are old photographs, maps, natural history exhibits and ancient artifacts. Donations are welcome.

Tours

Fox's Bay Bird Sanctuary ★★★

Bransby Point, Richmond Estate.

This mangrove swamp and bog encompasses 15 acres and is home to lots of feathered friends, including egrets and cuckoos. The nature trail leads to the beach.

BEST VIEW:

Panoramic seascapes are compelling from the top of the 18th-century Fort St. George, 1184 feet above sea level. It's a 15-minute drive from Plymouth.

Located in Belham Valley, the Montserrat Golf Club's 11-hole course is beloved by local duffers, and keeps most visitors happy. Three tennis courts are available, at the Vue Point and Montserrat Springs hotels. Day sails to tiny Redonda, an uninhabited island 16 miles away between Montserrat and Nevis, can be arranged, as well as other boat trips. Horseback riding can be mapped out at Sanford Farms for riders of all expertise and ages—over the beach, through the countryside, or on all-day picnic excursions.

Montserrat Golf club
Old Town, Belham Valley.
This very hilly (and therefore rather challenging) course encompasses 100 acres. It has just 11 holes, but by playing seven twice, you get a full 18. There's a bar and clubhouse in a converted cotton gin. Greens fees are about $23 and club rentals are available.

Watersports
Various locations, Plymouth.
Try these outfits for watersports: Vue Point Hotel ☎ *(809) 491-5210* for general equipment, Danny Water Sports ☎ *(809) 491-5645* for windsurfing and other equipment, and Captain Martin ☎ *(809) 491-5738* for sailing and snorkeling.

Where to Stay

Fielding's Highest Rated Hotels in Montserrat

★★★★	Vue Pointe Hotel	$90–$160
★★★	Montserrat Springs Hotel	$85–$165

Fielding's Most Exclusive Hotels in Montserrat

★★★★	Vue Pointe Hotel	$90–$160
★★	Providence Estate House	$50–$92
★	Lime Court Apartments	$30–$50

Fielding's Best Value Hotels in Montserrat

★	Marie's Guest House	$35–$35
★★	Providence Estate House	$50–$92
★	Lime Court Apartments	$30–$50
★★★	Vue Pointe Hotel	$90–$160
★★★	Montserrat Springs Hotel	$85–$165

The lodging options on Montserrat could fit in the palm of your hand—perhaps even more so if the volcano renders Plymouth rooms unavailable. Take your pick from two resort hotels or consider a villa rental. Count on trade winds to keep you cool, not air conditioning.

Hotels and Resorts

There are two pleasant resort hotels, though Montserrat Springs Hotel lies at the edge of the "unsafe area" and may or may not be functioning when you plan your trip—however, the Montserrat Springs recently underwent a nice renovation that has gone unappreciated due to the volcano. The hotel lies as the spot of natural hot springs that lie on the beach just outside Plymouth. Otherwise, the venerable Vue Pointe has been the island's leading choice for two generations (the third is in training) of operation by the Osborne family. The Vue Pointe is the scene of a popular West Indian barbecue on Wednesday nights that attracts everyone around, including islanders, ex-pats and visitors.

Montserrat Springs Hotel   **$85–$165**   ★★★

Richmond Hill, Plymouth, ☎ *(809) 491-2481. FAX (809) 491-4070.*
Single: $85–$145. Double: $115–$165.
Set on a hillside with pretty views extending to Plymouth and the sea, this hotel has its own hot mineral springs, and guests can while away the hours soaking in a hot or cold whirlpool. Guest rooms, located in villas, are generally spacious and nicely done—the property received a lovely makeover in early 1996. There are also six suites with full kitchens. The steeply sloping grounds include a restaurant, two bars, a huge pool, two tennis courts, and the beach, where watersports await. Amenities: Jacuzzi. 46 rooms. Credit cards: A, D, MC, V.

Vue Pointe Hotel   **$90–$160**   ★★★★

Old Towne, Plymouth, ☎ *(800) 235-0709, (809) 491-5210. FAX (809) 491-4813.*
Single: $90–$150. Double: $100–$160.
Situated on a secluded hill above the beach, four miles from Plymouth, this well-run family-owned property is Montserrat's best bet. Accommodations are housed in stucco apartment buildings or hexagonal villas, all decorated with Danish teak and rattan furnishings, twin beds and sitting areas. No air conditioning, but breezes help keep things cool. The grounds, which slope down to a black sand beach, include a pool, two tennis courts, a dining room and two bars. Service is excellent. 40 rooms.
Credit cards: A, D, MC, V.

Apartments and Condominiums

During the early 90s, a number of Americans, Canadians and Britons built retirement homes on Montserrat, contributing to a mini-building boom of condos and villas. If you stay in a house around the Vue Point, you'll be close to center of government and business during the relocation. But many opt for homes further up the coast, though a car is an essential for getting around. The three largest of the villa-rental companies are the Neville Bradshaw Agency ☎ *(809) 491-5270,* Montserrat Enterprises ☎ *(809) 491-2431,* and West Indies Real Estate ☎ *(809) 491-8668.*

Belham Valley Hotel   **$40–$75**   ★

Old Towne, Plymouth, ☎ *(809) 491-5553. FAX (809) 491-5283.*
Single: $40–$75. Double: $40–$75.
This small complex sits on a hill overlooking Belham Valley (hence the name) and its river, near the Montserrat Golf Course. The complex includes one studio apartment, one two-bedroom apartment and a studio cottage, all with fully equipped kitchens and stereos, but no air conditioning. The restaurant is highly regarded, but there's nothing else on-site. The beach is less than away 10 minutes on foot. Rates are $255 to $480 per week. 5 rooms. Credit cards: A, MC.

Low Cost Lodging

A beautifully restored plantation home, the Providence Estate House, can be yours for well under a hundred dollars a night. It's located high in the hills and well away from volcanic activity (you'll need a car). Check with Susan Goldin of Island Bikes to see if her cliffside guesthouse in Woodlands is available ☎ *(809) 491-5552.* Another budget possibility is rustic Moose's Guest House, located at a small pier south of Plymouth in Kinsale ☎ *(809) 491-3146.* However, Moose's, the Lime Court Apartments and Marie's

Guest House are located in what is considered the "unsafe area" at press time, and may not be open during your visit.

Lime Court Apartments $30–$50   ★

Plymouth ☎ (809) 491-5069.
Single: $30–$50. Double: $30–$50.
Located in the center of town, this small apartment building sells out fast due to its very reasonable rates. Units range from studios to two-bedroom apartments, all with full kitchenettes and maid service. The penthouse unit is by far the best and well worth the few extra dollars. There's nothing on-site in the way of recreation or dining, but it's located in the heart of Plymouth, so lots is within walking distance. 8 rooms. Credit cards: A, MC, V.

Marie's Guest House $35–$35   ★

Plymouth ☎ (809) 419-2745.
Single: $35. Double: $35.
This small inn in a garden setting outside Plymouth offers simple but comfortable non-air-conditioned rooms at a price that's hard to beat. Guests share the kitchen, while each room has its own bath. Well-run and pleasant. 4 rooms. Credit cards: not accepted.

Providence Estate House $50–$92   ★ ★

St. Peter's, Plymouth, ☎ (809) 491-6476. FAX (809) 491-8476.
Single: $50–$70. Double: $70–$92.
Located about 20 minutes from Plymouth in a country setting, this lovely guest-house has hosted the likes of Paul McCartney and Stevie Wonder. The old plantation home has been beautifully restored and has just two rooms for guests, both on the ground floor and each very nicely decorated. Wonderful views from the pool deck. There's a communal kitchenette, or you can arrange for the owners to make you dinner. You'll definitely want a car. 2 rooms. Credit cards: not accepted. Credit cards: MC, V.

Where to Eat

Fielding's Highest Rated Restaurants in Montserrat

★★★★	Belham Valley Restaurant	$14–$23
★★★★	Ziggy's	$15–$26
★★★	Blue Dolphin	$9–$20
★★★	Emerald Cafe	$4–$20
★★★	Montserrat Springs Hotel	$11–$19
★★★	Mrs. Morgan's	$4–$5
★★★	Vue Pointe Restaurant	$13–$23

Fielding's Most Exclusive Restaurants in Montserrat

★★★★	Ziggy's	$15–$26
★★★★	Belham Valley Restaurant	$14–$23
★★★	Vue Pointe Restaurant	$13–$23
★★★	Montserrat Springs Hotel	$11–$19
★★★	Blue Dolphin	$9–$20

Fielding's Best Value Restaurants in Montserrat

★★★	Mrs. Morgan's	$4–$5
★★★	Emerald Cafe	$4–$20
★★★★	Belham Valley Restaurant	$14–$23
★★★	Montserrat Springs Hotel	$11–$19
★★★	Blue Dolphin	$9–$20

An enormous variety of vegetables grows on Montserrat with gusto, including cucumbers, breadfruit, tomatoes, pumpkin, cabbage and the less-familiar West Indian squash, *christophene*. The two national dishes are *goat water*, a goat stew with scallions and thyme of Irish origin, and *mountain chicken*, which is actually gigantic frogs legs cooked in a variety of ways. The Blue Dolphin and Emerald Cafe are located in Plymouth, and may or may not be open at the time of your visit. Two spots in Kinsale we hope will reopen soon are Niggy's Bistro, an Italian establishment with a bar operated out of a boat, and Ida's, where tasty and cheap food is served outside on the pier below Moose's Guest House.

Belham Valley Restaurant   **$$$**   ★★★★

Old Towne, Plymouth, ☎ (809) 491-5553. Associated hotel: Belham Valley Hotel.
International cuisine. Specialties: Conch fritters, Seafood Delight.
Lunch: Noon–2 p.m., entrées $14–$23.
Dinner: 6:30–11 p.m., entrées $14–$23.

This hotel dining room in a posh residential section of the island draws everyone in sooner or later for the serene views from the outdoor terrace and the chef's creative ways with fine local ingredients. The Seafood Delight, a trio of piscatorial pleasures (often including lobster) is blanketed with an herbed Vermouth sauce. The moderately priced dinners often include a salad and fresh vegetables. When available, try the mango mousse or coconut cheesecake. Lunch is a viable option during the week in high season. Reservations recommended. Credit cards: A, MC, V.

Blue Dolphin   **$$**   ★★★

Plymouth, ☎ (809) 491-3263.
International cuisine. Specialties: Mountain chicken.
Lunch: Noon–2 p.m., entrées $9–$20.
Dinner: 6 p.m.–midnight, entrées $9–$20. Closed: Sun.

The interior of this West Indian restaurant in the Plymouth hills is nothing to brag about, but the mountain chicken (frog's legs) is the best in town, often prepared with a garlic sauce. Vegetarians won't feel slighted either, since a wide variety of fresh greens and starches are available, including peas and rice and pumpkin soup. Reservations required. Credit cards: not accepted.

Emerald Cafe   **$$**   ★★★

Wapping Road; Plymouth, ☎ (809) 491-3821.
International cuisine.
Lunch: 8 a.m.–4 p.m., entrées $4–$20.
Dinner: 4 p.m.–midnight, entrées $4–$20.

There's something for everyone at this indoor-outdoor eatery located in Plymouth—burgers, crepes and West Indian blue plate specials. That often means mountain chicken, or fresh seafood served with rice and local vegetables. If you don't rate a table on the terrace under umbrellas, join a companionable group inside. This is also a good spot for a drink. Reservations recommended. Credit cards: not accepted.

Golden Apple   **$**   ★★

Cork Hill, Plymouth, ☎ (809) 491-2187.
Latin American cuisine. Specialties: Goat Water.
Lunch: entrées $5–$10.
Dinner: entrées $5–$10. Closed: Sun.

This spacious local eatery is one of a growing number of weekend-only goat water pit stops. The bizarrely-named national dish of Montserrat is a heady brew of goat meat cooked until tender, in a broth of cloves, spices, and vegetables. Portions served are pretty hefty. Chicken and rice, conch and fish dishes are also available. Credit cards: not accepted.

Montserrat Springs Hotel $$ ★★★

Richmond Hill, Plymouth, ☎ (809) 491-2481. Associated hotel: Montserrat Springs Hotel.
Latin American cuisine.
Lunch: 8 a.m.–3 p.m., entrées $4–$7.
Dinner: 3–11 p.m., entrées $11–$19.
The vista from the poolside restaurant of this upscale hotel is spectacular, encompassing Chance's Peak and the Caribbean Sea. The best bet is the Sunday barbecue served from noon to 3 p.m.—for under $25, you get grilled chicken, fish or meat, served with island veggies, a plethora of salads, and a choice of two homemade desserts. The regular menu aims for spa-inspired selections, but the restaurant has undergone several chef changes since the volcano started acting up. Reservations recommended. Credit cards: A, D, MC, V.

Mrs. Morgan's $ ★★★

St. John's, Plymouth, ☎ (809) 491-5419.
Latin American cuisine. Specialties: Goat Water.
Dinner: entrées $4–$5. Closed: Mon.–Thur., Sun.
Visitors and residents return time and time again for Mrs. Morgan's homemade goat water stew served only on Friday and Saturday. The humble hut, which serves as a bar the rest of the week, is located between the airport and Carr's Bay, a tiny fishing port. At these prices, a few bowls (bet you can eat only one) could feed a crowd. Call ahead to see what else she's preparing—it's a very informal operation. Usually open from 11:30 a.m. until the food runs out. Credit cards: not accepted.

Village Place $$ ★★

Salem, Plymouth, ☎ (809) 491-5202.
American cuisine.
Dinner: 6 p.m.–midnight, entrées $5–$16. Closed: Tue.
This bar and restaurant (with an emphasis on bar) used to be the hangout of Jagger, Clapton and other visiting British rock greats when George Martin's Air Studios was up and running during the pre-Hurricane Hugo era. The Place is still popular with locals and other scene-makers who like the loud party atmosphere, the rum drinks and owner Andy Lawrence's thyme-marinated fried chicken. Since there's not much nightlife on this peaceful island, the Place, which stays open until at least midnight, should keep night owls pacified. Credit cards: not accepted.

Vue Pointe Restaurant $$$ ★★★

Old Road, Plymouth, ☎ (809) 491-5211. Associated hotel: Vue Pointe Hotel.
Latin American cuisine.
Lunch: 12:30–2 p.m., entrées $13–$23.
Dinner: 7–9:30 p.m., entrées $13–$23.

Few people can resist the charms of this place—welcoming proprietors, a jumping Wednesday evening barbecue, lovely views of a black sand beach below, and simple, but tasty cuisine. You can visit it for a simple lunch of seasonal fruit salads or sandwiches, a fixed-price ($25) dinner of mountain chicken and all the trimmings, or the aforementioned barbecue. If you opt for barbecue, arrive early; it's popular local social event. Reservations recommended. Credit cards: A, MC, V.

Ziggy's   **$$$**   ★★★★

Belham Valley, Plymouth, ☎ *(809) 491-8282.*
Dinner: 6–9 p.m., entrées $15–$26.

John and Marcia Punter moved and expanded their popular restaurant into the happening Belham Valley area. Making the most of local produce, the Punters' simple, handsome dining room is filled to capacity most evenings, though they have no plans to change their one-seating-per-evening policy. The menu changes daily, but the lobster quadrille and Jamaican jerk tenderloin are favorites. Don't miss one semi-regular dessert offering: the famous chocolate sludge. Credit cards: MC, V.

Montserrat has a surprising number of crafts for a tiny island, though most shops operate out of volcano-beleaguered Plymouth. Hand-woven tapestries make excellent gifts, available from Montserrat Tapestries. A number of island craftsmen work with wood, carving fabulous furniture—chairs, beds, and tables that can be custom ordered (inquire first about shipping charges). Fine leather jewelry made by local artists can be found at Carol's Corner at the Vue Point Hotel, as well as the Montserrat cookbook, *Goatwater*.

Montserrat Directory

Arrival and Departure

There is no direct service from North America to Montserrat's tiny **W. H. Bramble Airport**. **LIAT** makes several round-trips daily from Antigua, 18 minutes away. Antigua is served from North America by **American Airlines**, **BWIA** and **Continental**. Connecting flights to Montserrat from most other Caribbean islands are available via Antigua on **LIAT**. The departure tax is $8.

Business Hours

Stores open Monday–Saturday 8 a.m.–5 p.m. Banks open Monday–Thursday 8 a.m.–3 p.m. and Friday 3–5 p.m.

Climate

Temperate and tropical, temperatures average 73.5 degrees Fahrenheit to 86.5 degrees Fahrenheit, with very little variation from season to season. Humidity is blissfully low. Rain is most frequent in April and May, and July–September.

Documents

U.S. and Canadian visitors need to show proof of citizenship (passport, birth certificate with photo ID) for stays up to six months. Those who do not show an ongoing or return ticket may be required to deposit a sum of money equivalent to that needed for repatriation.

Electricity

Current runs 220–230 volts AC, 60 cycles, so you will need an electrical transformer and an adapter.

Getting Around

Taxi drivers are omnipresent whenever a flight arrives. Expect to pay about $11 from the airport to the town of Plymouth. Buses, another easy way to travel, cost about $1–$2 one day.

Car rental agencies are only local outfits. Toyotas, Jeeps and Daihatsus are available at the reliable **Pauline's Car Rentals**, on Church Road *P.O. Box 171, Plymouth* ☎ *(809) 491-2345*. Cars can be delivered to the airport or your hotel. Cards are accepted. To rent a car, you need to show a valid driver's license and pay $12. Ask the police officers at the Immigration Department at the airport for assistance.

Language

Most everyone speaks English, though the lilt resembles a strong Irish brogue.

Medical Emergencies

Glendon Hospital in Plymouth ☎ *(809) 491-2552* has 68 beds and can provide adequate care for short-term cases. Serious emergencies should be flown to larger islands. Ask your hotel to suggest a doctor on call.

Money

The official currency is the Eastern Caribbean dollar. Some of the best exchange rates can be found at the Royal Bank of Canada.

Telephone

The area code is *809*. Local numbers are four digits.

For international calls, skip calling from your room and head for the **Cable and Wireless, Ltd.** on *Houston Street*, ☎ *2112*, open Monday–Thursday, 7:30 a.m.–6 p.m.; Friday, 7:30 a.m.–10 p.m.; and Saturday 7:30 a.m.–6 p.m. You'll find a new digital telephone system, faxes, telegraph, telex and data facilities. Phone cards (purchased there) and credit cards, toll-free service, and cellular phones can be used.

Time

Atlantic Standard Time, one hour later than New York City.

Tipping and Taxes

Expect a 10 percent service charge to be added to all bills. Tipping a taxi driver will make him (or her) happy, but there is no expectation.

MONTSERRAT

Tourist Information

The permanent home of the **Montserrat Tourist Board** is on Church Road in Plymouth at the Government Headquarters building. They are currently relocated in Salem ☎ *(809) 491-2230*. **Medhurst and Associates**, the island's U.S. representative, will field inquiries about visiting Montserrat, including providing up-to-date information about the status of the volcanic eruption ☎ *(516) 425-0900*.

MONTSERRAT HOTELS	RMS	RATES	PHONE	CR. CARDS
Plymouth				
★★★★ **Vue Pointe Hotel**	40	$90–$160	(800) 235-0709	A, D, MC, V
★★★ **Montserrat Springs Hotel**	46	$85–$165	(809) 491-2481	A, D, MC, V
★★ **Providence Estate House**	2	$50–$92	(809) 491-6476	MC, V
★ **Belham Valley Hotel**	5	$40–$75	(809) 491-5553	A, MC
★ **Lime Court Apartments**	8	$30–$50	(809) 491-5069	A, MC, V
★ **Marie's Guest House**	4	$35–$35	(809) 419-2745	None

MONTSERRAT RESTAURANTS	PHONE	ENTRÉE	CR. CARDS
Plymouth			
★★★★ **Ziggy's**	(809) 491-8282	$15–$26	MC, V
American			
★★ **Village Place**	(809) 491-5202	$5–$16	None
International			
★★★★ **Belham Valley Restaurant**	(809) 491-5553	$14–$23	A, MC, V
★★★ **Blue Dolphin**	(809) 491-3263	$9–$20	None
★★★ **Emerald Cafe**	(809) 491-3821	$4–$20	None
Latin American			
★★★ **Montserrat Springs Hotel**	(809) 491-2481	$4–$19	A, D, MC, V
★★★ **Mrs. Morgan's**	(809) 491-5419	$4–$5	None
★★★ **Vue Pointe Restaurant**	(809) 491-5211	$13–$23	A, MC, V
★★ **Golden Apple**	(809) 491-2187	$5–$10	None

NEVIS

Colorful costumes on Nevis

Nevis offers a taste of the old Caribbean. Sister to St. Kitts, Nevis is the quiet child, shunning the hustle of Kittian casinos for the leisure of quiet drinks on the verandas of 200-year-old inns. A ribbon of sand encircles much of this round island, and a volcanic summit protrudes straight up into the clouds, but the character of Nevis is defined by the genteel plantation inns, five in all, that recall an earlier, slower-paced era. With the exception of the recent opening of the Four Seasons Resort on Pinney's Beach, which contains more rooms than all other properties combined, nothing aggressive is being done about tourism. This makes the island a good hang-out for celebrities—Oprah Winfrey, Wayne Gretsky, Janet Jackson and Gerald R. Ford are among recent visitors. What they find on Nevis are genuinely hospitable people—about 9000 of them—willing to share the quiet charm and history of their tiny island. There's a Nevisian independence movement afoot. Its roots are said to lie in politics and the island's status as an off-shore tax haven, but a bigger reason may simply be that the strong local economy is seeing too much of its revenue head across the channel to St. Kitts. But don't hold your breath for overnight or dramatic changes. No one seems to move any faster than a ceiling fan in Nevis, and the dreams you might have, after a lavish gourmet dinner in a history-filled plantation home, will be about the luscious array of tropical fruits that will grace your breakfast buffet in the morning. Despite the laid-back nature of the island, however, locals have not remained lax in regard to ecology. For that reason, the hundred or so cruise liners that stopped in Charlestown last year did little to upset the island's ideal ecological balance. Hurricane Hugo damaged Nevis badly in 1989, and Marilyn grazed it in 1995, but the island quickly recovered from each. Nevis is as deep green and lush as ever, beckoning well-healed travelers for a slice of the Caribbean at its most natural.

Separated from St. Kitts by a two-mile channel, the Narrows, Nevis is a little, 39-square-mile gumdrop-shaped island about six or seven miles across with a classic volcanic cone named Nevis Peak rising out of its center. At 3232 feet, this high point is usually shrouded in clouds and mist, which inspired Columbus to name the island "Las Nieves." Two smaller rises, Round Hill in the north and Saddle Hill in the south, create a watershed between the east and west sides of the island. The northern half of Nevis is drier and covered in scrub in the lower elevations, but the southern portion has an exuberant rampage of trees, creepers and giant ferns that appear the moment you head east out of the sleepy capital of Charlestown. This portion of Nevis is where the round-island road climbs to 800 feet above sea level before descending to the undeveloped east coast, and it is also the most-inhabited part of the island, with small enclaves nestled on the hillside. A number of huge plantations lie in this region of Nevis Peak's flanks. The plantations include gardens lovingly cultivated by islanders. Above 1300 feet, evergreen tropical forest blankets the increasingly steep slopes of Nevis Peak, while its summit holds dense, mossy jungle with clutches of orchids peaking through the vines. Throughout the higher elevations, the gregarious vervet monkey is the chief inhabitant—in fact, the combined simian population of St. Kitts/ Nevis outnumbers humans almost three to one. Charlestown, home to about 1200 Nevisians, is a laconic sprawl of pastel walls, tin roofs and shady

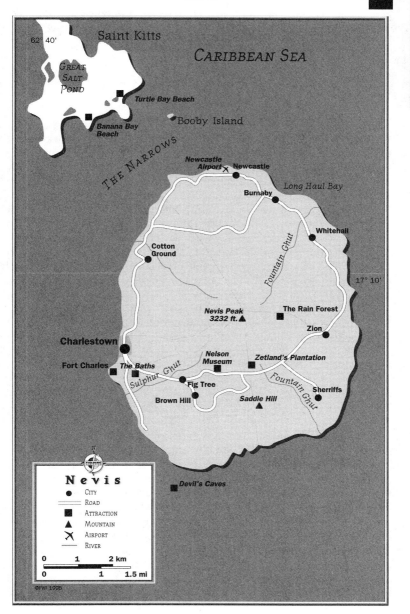

Saint Kitts

CARIBBEAN SEA

62° 40'

GREAT SALT POND

Turtle Bay Beach

Banana Bay Beach

Booby Island

THE NARROWS

Newcastle Airport Newcastle

Burnaby

Long Haul Bay

Whitehall

Cotton Ground

Fountain Ghut

17° 10'

Nevis Peak 3232 ft. ▲

The Rain Forest

Zion

Charlestown

Nelson Museum

Zetland's Plantation

Fort Charles The Baths

Sulphur Ghut

Fig Tree

Fountain Ghut

Sherriffs

Brown Hill

Saddle Hill

Devil's Caves

N e v i s

● CITY
ROAD
■ ATTRACTION
▲ MOUNTAIN
✕ AIRPORT
RIVER

| 0 | 1 | 2 km |

| 0 | 1 | 1.5 mi |

©FWI 1995

gardens, and remains one of the best preserved towns in the West Indies. As on St. Kitts, regulations prohibit any building taller than a palm tree.

Nevis has had a long history for such a small island. After spotting an island and naming it St.Christopher (later nicknamed St. Kitts) for his patron saint, Columbus spied a cloud-covered conic island rising out of the water during his second voyage, dubbing it "Nuestra Señora de las Nieves," or "Our lady of the Snows," since it reminded him of the snow-capped Pyrenees. British troops arrived in 1623, first joining forces with the French to conquer the Spanish and decimate the resident Carib Indian tribes, then later duking it out with the Gallic forces for the next 150 years. The British used St. Kitts as a base to colonize Nevis, Antigua, Barbuda, Tortola and Montserrat, while the French dominated Martinique, St. Martin, Guadeloupe, St. Barts, La Désirade and Les Saintes. The Treaty of Versailles in 1783 ceded the islands to Britain. Known as the "Queen of the Carribbees" in the late 18th century for its thriving sugar trade, Nevis later saw its fortunes decline with the abolition of slavery in 1834. Almost 150 years later in 1983, Nevis, with St. Kitts, became the Caribbean's newest independent country, with the establishment of the federation of St. Kitts-Nevis.

Perhaps a key reason the Four Seasons chose Nevis for its first Caribbean resort is due to the caliber the islanders employed by the hotel firm—about 700 island employees. On the surface, Nevisians are as laid-back and friendly as in most of the region, but the island also claims the highest literacy rate in the Western Hemisphere—98 percent of Nevisians read and write with ease. To savvy insiders, the island is a prime candidate for a posh resort, and yet the rhythm of life is gentle and noninvasive, much quieter than on St. Kitts. Many local people are still imbued with age-old superstitions; door frames are painted blue to keep "jumby" spirits out in accordance with ancient *obeah* voodoo customs. Many people still use herbal cures and some retain their respect for the mystical powers of the big, fat native toads called *crappos.* Social interaction has both written and unwritten rules. Of the former, note that the use of profanity in public is prohibited by law, and it is an offense to splash water on pedestrians while driving. This small community also embraces customs long gone from most parts of "civilized" society: because most Nevisians are related in some way, conversations typically begin with a caring inquiry into the health or well-being of one another. And when there is a death on the island, it is not uncommon for hundreds to pay their respect at multi-hour church service that can tie up road traffic for hundreds of yards.

Nelson Spring on Nevis is one of the beautiful lagoons author James Michener visited while researching his novel **Caribbean.**

Nevis isn't typically thought of as a beach destination, and yet it has several luxuriant strips of velvety sand curling around its waist—the best are on the west and north coasts, facing St. Kitts. The most famous is **Pinney's Beach**, a four-mile shore that starts at the edge of Charlestown and winds north, passing the Four Seasons on its languid course to the ruin of Ashby Fort and the site of the former colony, Jamestown. Although the sand is gray rather than pearly white, it is fine and plush, and bordered by whispering surf on one side and rows of coconut trees on the other; extensive watersports activities are proffered by the Four Seasons, along with bars and beachside restaurants. Continuing north, Mosquito Bay is home to **Oualie Beach**, one of the island's few coves—a quiet spot ideal for swimming, snorkeling, windsurfing and more. Just before reaching the airport is an infrequently visited outpost below **Round Hill**, and just past Newcastle is **Nisbet Plantation**, where a fine white shoreline provides good swimming and snorkeling lies on the nearby reef.

Until recently, only one dive operator has been available, thus with no competition, prices are high. Consequently, the waters off Nevis have yet to become a high-profile destination for divers. However, a diverse selection of interesting sites are available, including a unique ride through long-dormant underwater lava tubes. The relative paucity of dive business means that Nevis' reefs are in better shape than a number of other islands; visibility averages 80 to 100 feet. The channel between St. Kitts and Nevis, **The Narrows**, contains many of the best dives, including **Nag's Head** (see "Underwater" in "St. Kitts"); these sites are shared by the operators on both islands. **Redonda Reef** off the remote southern coast offers a little-visited wilderness where hammerheads and whales sometimes tarry (calm seas are required for diving). Many visiting divers inquire about the mysterious settlement of **Jamestown**, rumored to lie underwater off the island's west coast. One story goes that the village submerged dramatically as a result of a cataclysmic earthquake, while others say a tidal wave or hurricane washed it out to sea. There are those who claim to have explored the actual site but, if so, it lies under a thick blanket of sand today. Consumed in myth and folklore, the reality may be simply that the village was abandoned and/or overgrown by marshland. No one knows the whole truth, and historical records are conveniently contradictory, but local fishermen say that one can hear the church bells ringing as you near the ruins of Jamestown. Experienced snorkelers should head for **Longhaul Bay**, southeast of Newcastle, where a protected inner reef is hidden just past the last jetty southeast of the main reef; novices will enjoy the shallows around the jetty. Snorkeling also is reported to be good at the north end of **Oualie Beach** near the rocks, and around the reefs off **Nisbet Plantation**.

On Foot

Life on Nevis is wrapped, literally, around the island's classically shaped volcanic cone. For adventurous visitors, hiking the steep slopes of **Nevis Peak** is the main trek on the island, completed by relatively few intrepid outsiders, which leaves the trail overgrown and difficult to follow in some sections. However, walking is really a way of life for islanders. Nevis is small enough and vehicular traffic light enough that many locals continue to use foot travel between the small villages. Join them in their informal method of transportation, even along the 20-mile main road circling the island, for an inviting glimpse into a slower Caribbean life-style.

By Pedal

Nevis' perimeter road is ideal for pleasant, casual riding, although those seeking to conquer the entire 20-mile circuit should be advised that steep hills, climbing to over 800 feet above sea level, lie in the several-mile section east of Charlestown. This paved road is quietest between Zion and the airport, where you'll find a series of tiny villages that haven't yet benefited from the economic impact of the Four Seasons. Interesting off-road possibilities also exist on the unsettled western coast south of Charlestown. If you want to spend more than a couple days riding, consider taking a bike on the ferry over to St. Kitts, which offers other extensive possibilities. (See "By Pedal" in "St. Kitts").

St. John's Fig Tree Church in Nevis contains interesting memorials to Admiral Nelson and his wife, Fanny Nisbet.

The history of Nevis is found behind the shutters and porches of its great **plantation houses**, five of them now playing host to fine hotels. A taste of the leisure elegance of Colonial times can still be experienced at any of them, all of which provide brochures that detail tidbits about their individual pasts. **Charlestown**, the island's capital, is a tropical rainbow of pastel storefronts, tin roofs and palm shaded gardens—good for strolling and lingering. Many visitors will be surprised to discover that Nevis was once the home of a thriving Jewish community, and their restored **cemetery** lies just behind Charlestown. A **mikvah**, or ritual bath, was discovered in 1992, and excavation continues to determine if the adjacent foundation ruins are what remains of the earliest known synagogue in the Caribbean (potentially dating back to 1650). Just south of town, the crumbling **Bath Hotel** sits above mineral hot springs where, until recently, guests could soak in the rejuvenating waters. The hotel itself has been closed for over a century and currently houses the Nevis police force, but there is hope of restoring it.

Continuing around the island in a clockwise direction, the **St. Thomas Anglican Church** dates to 1643 making the oldest church in Nevis, and possibly the oldest still-standing in the British Leewards. Nearby is the community of **Cotton Ground** and **Nelson Spring**, where Captain Nelson obtained fresh water for his troops in the 1780s, and just past the spring is the ruin of **Ashby Fort**, one of the oldest on the island. Along the shore here is the site of **Jamestown**, a community that was protected by the fort, but is said to have perished in an earthquake or tidal wave around 1680. Just before reaching the Newcastle Airport and off the road is the **Cottle Church**, the first church in the Caribbean where slaves were allowed to worship with their master—in this case John Cottle, owner of the 980-acre Round Hill Estate. Just past Newcastle is the **St. James Anglican Church**, built in the late 1600s, and one of only three churches in the region that contains a black crucifix. After passing what's left of the **Eden Brown Estate** (see below), you'll begin a climb onto a prominent shoulder of Nevis Peak, passing four plantation homes that have been turned into inns. Any of the four make an excellent stop for lunch, an afternoon tea, or leisurely stroll. On the way down into Charlestown, keep an eye out for **St. John's Fig Tree Anglican Church**, where Admiral Nelson and Fanny Nisbet's marriage certificate is on display.

Historical Sites

Eden Brown Estate ★★

Near Huggins Bay, Charlestown.

This government-owned estate house was built in 1740. It is said to be haunted by the ghost of Julia Huggins, who was all set to get married in 1822. But the night before the wedding, the groom and best man got drunk, argued and ended up killing each other in a duel. Poor Julia became a recluse and is said to still hang around the house. The estate also includes stone ruins from other buildings on the plantation.

Museums and Exhibits

Museum of Nevis History ★★★

Low Street; Charlestown.
Hours open: 8 a.m.–4 p.m.

This Georgian-style house on the waterfront is actually a replica of Alexander Hamilton's childhood home, which was built in 1680 and destroyed by hurricane in the 19th century. Hamilton was born on Nevis in 1755—the ruins of his birthplace are immediately behind the museum. Hamilton later emigrated to the fledgling United States, where he was appointed by George Washington as the first secretary of the U.S. Treasury. He died in a duel with Aaron Burr. The building contains memorabilia of his life, as well as photographs and exhibits on the island's history. The Nevis House of Assembly is on the second floor. General admission: $2.

Nelson Museum, The ★★★

Bath Road, Charlestown, ☎ *(809) 469-0408.*
Hours open: 8 a.m.–4:30 p.m.

This small museum commemorates the life of Lord Nelson, who met and married local girl Frances Nisbet at the Montpelier Estate in 1787. Reproductions of paintings, engravings, costumes and more recalls the bravery of England's great naval hero. General admission: $2.

NEVIS

Water-skiing, windsurfing, sport fishing, golf, tennis and horseback riding are all prime activities on Nevis, and if your hotel can't arrange it there are several agencies that will. A number of **watersports** are concentrated at the Four Seasons, but Oualie Beach also has its share, with **windsurfing** leading the bill. **Sport fishing** takes advantage of a good supply of wahoo, tuna, kingfish and dorado, and seasoned skippers will guide you to the best waters. The 18-hole Four Seasons **golf course** is spectacular, with narrow difficult fairways that snake up the slopes of Nevis Peak; it's one of the two or three best courses in the Caribbean. Several hotels have **tennis courts**, though the Four Seasons' (predictably) leads the pack, with 10 beautifully-maintained hard surface and clay courts and managed by Peter Burwash International. The latest craze on Nevis is **horse racing**, which are sponsored by the Nevis Turf and Jockey Club at a ramshackle track near White Bay. The races are generally held on holidays, such as Easter Monday, Whit Monday, Boxing Day, the first Sunday of August, and Independence Day. Admission is $4.

Four Seasons Golf Course

Four Seasons Resort; Pinney's Beach, Pinney's Beach, ☎ *(809) 469-1111.*

Designed by Robert Trent Jones, Jr., this is one of the Caribbean's most scenic and challenging courses. It encompasses 18 holes with tremendous views up the slopes of 3232-foot Nevis Peak and down to palm fringed shoreline—concentrating on your game is a tad difficult. The 15th hole, a 660-yard par five, is a whopper. Greens fees are $95 for 18 holes if you are staying at the hotel otherwise you'll pay $110. Celebrate the 19th hole at one of this posh resort's watering holes.

Horseback Riding

Various locations.

You can hop on a horse and ride into the sunset at one of three outfits: Nisbet Plantation ☎ *(809) 469-9325* ($45 for two hours), Nevis Equestrian Centre in Cole Hill ☎ *(809) 469-2638*, and Garner Estate's ☎ *(809) 469-5528* ($35 for two hours).

Watersports

Various locations.

A number of companies offer aqua activity. For general watersports equipment and boating, try **Newcastle Bay Marina** ☎ *(809) 469-9373* or **Captain Julian Rigby** at Oualie Beach ☎ *(809) 469-9735*. For deep-sea fishing, contact **The Lady James** ☎ *(809) 469-1989* or **Jans Travel Agency** ☎ *(809) 469-5578*. Windsurfing can be arranged through **Winston Cooke** ☎ *(809) 469-9615*.

Where to Stay

Fielding's Highest Rated Hotels in Nevis

★★★★★	Four Seasons Resort Nevis	$250–$625
★★★★	Montpelier Plantation Inn	$150–$330
★★★★	Nisbet Plantation	$191–$475
★★★	Golden Rock Estate	$100–$230
★★★	Hermitage, The	$85–$335
★★★	Mount Nevis Hotel and Beach Club	$130–$485
★★★	Old Manor Estate and Hotel	$125–$225

Fielding's Most Exclusive Hotels in Nevis

★★★★★	Four Seasons Resort Nevis	$250–$625
★★★	Mount Nevis Hotel and Beach Club	$130–$485
★★★	Hermitage, The	$85–$335
★★	Oualie Beach Hotel	$100–$255
★★★	Golden Rock Estate	$100–$230

Fielding's Best Value Hotels in Nevis

★★★	Golden Rock Estate	$100–$230
★★★	Old Manor Estate and Hotel	$125–$225
★★★★	Montpelier Plantation Inn	$150–$330
★	Meadville Cottages	$40–$80
★★	Croney's Old Manor Hotel	$85–$175

The long-defunct Bath Hotel, with its soothing hot springs, still draws more visitors than any other attraction on Nevis.

Until the 1991 opening of the 350-acre Four Seasons Nevis, the island was known primarily for its intimate old plantation inns, five of which flourish today. They are rich in history and color, though they aren't the spot for visitors who crave tremendous luxury and air conditioning. For this, look no further than the Four Seasons, a 196-room resort plopped down smack in the middle of the island's best beach. The debut of this hotel has changed the character of the island dramatically, but all shared in the pride when the hotel snared the top slot in a *Conde Nast Traveler* reader survey of the world's best hotels in late 1995.

All properties add a 10 percent service charge and seven percent government tax.

Hotels and Resorts

The Four Seasons Nevis dominates the scene in most every way. In addition to a four-mile stretch of beach, the resort offers superb tennis and golf facilities and will arrange almost any other island activity you can think of.

Four Seasons Resort Nevis   **$250–$625**   ★ ★ ★ ★ ★

Pinney's Beach, ☎ *(800) 332-3442, (809) 469-1111. FAX (809) 469-1112.*
Single: $250–$625. Double: $250–$625.

You can always count on a Four Seasons property for the utmost in style and luxury, and this resort is no exception—in 1995 it was voted as the number one hotel in the world by readers of *Conde Nast Traveler*. Scattered over 350 acres opening right onto Pinney's Beach, the low-rise buildings house two restaurants, three bars, a well-equipped health club, and air-conditioned guestrooms. Accommodations are lovely, with high-quality furnishings, Persian rugs, large baths, robes, and fresh plants and flowers. The choices range from standard guestrooms to three different types of one- two- and three-bedroom suites ($425–3450 per night). A series of villas and estate homes with two, three or four bedrooms are sprinkled on the slopes of Nevis Peak, some come with private pools. These luxurious digs, which cost $700–$3,800 per night with a minimum five-night rental, are situated around the acclaimed championship golf course. The grounds also include 10 tennis courts, a large pool, and several restaurants. All watersports can be found on the very fine beach. Parents can relax after putting their kids in varied supervised programs. Simply fantastic in every aspect, but note that the atmosphere here is rather formal; you'll have to dress for dinner. Inquire about the myriad golf, tennis and honeymoon packages. Amenities: tennis, health club, exercise room, balcony or patio, family plan. 196 rooms. Credit cards: A, MC, V.

Mount Nevis Hotel and Beach Club $130–$485   ★ ★ ★

Shaws Road, Newcastle, ☎ (800) 756-3847, (809) 469-9373. FAX (809) 469-9375.
Single: $130–$270. Double: $130–$485.
Located on the drier northern slopes of Mt. Nevis, this newer, family-run property includes air-conditioned guestrooms with VCRs (videos are loaned to guests) and private patios with great views of St. Kitts. Studio units also have full kitchens, as do the two-bedroom suites. Facilities include a good, expensive restaurant, as well as a bar, pool, and a beach club with watersports and a dive operation a mile away (free shuttle). A bit lonely in the off season. Five minutes from the Nevis airport. Amenities: balcony or patio. 32 rooms. Credit cards: A, MC, V.

Oualie Beach Hotel $100–$255   ★ ★

Oualie Beach; Mosquito Bay, ☎ (800) 682-5431, (809) 469-9735. FAX (809) 469-9176.
Single: $100–$215. Double: $140–$255.
Located right on the beach, this small, family-run property accommodates guests in charming gingerbread-style duplex cottages that are pleasant and comfortable. Only some have air conditioning and kitchens, but all sport screened verandas with nice views of St. Kitts. There's a dive shop on-site that handles most watersports, including windsurfing. This is one of the few Nevis hotels without a pool, but the beach is fine, and a few yards wider following 1995's hurricanes. Amenities: balcony or patio. 22 rooms. Credit cards: A, D, MC, V.

Apartments and Condominiums

The focus on Nevis is on plantation-style inns, but Hurricane Cove is a good choice if cooking at home is on your agenda. Villa rentals are available from the Four Seasons Nevis ($700 per night and up) ☎ *(809) 469-1111*, while Oualie Reality has a few less-pricey options ☎ *(809) 469-9817*. Super Foods, a well-stocked grocery store that caters to the ex-pat and villa community, is located in Charlestown on Main Street. Nevis Bakery, on Happy Hill Drive in Charlestown, sells fresh breads, buns, pastries and cakes.

Hurricane Cove Bungalows $95–$265   ★ ★

Mosquito Bay, ☎ (809) 469-9462. FAX (809) 469-9462.
Single: $95–$225. Double: $95–$265.

NEVIS

Set on a steep hill with glorious views, this small complex consists of one- to three-bedroom bungalows with ceiling fans, complete kitchens and covered porches. There's a shared splash pool on-site, but most of the units have their own small pool. The beach is at the foot of the hill. Rustic, but one of Nevis' better buys. 10 rooms. Credit cards: A, MC.

Inns

Plantation inns are a particular specialty on Nevis and, until the Four Seasons opened, they were the island's main calling card. For many visitors who enjoy a few basic luxury perks amid rustic atmosphere, the inns are still a top choice. One, the Montpelier Plantation Inn, provided enough of a chic retreat to keep Princess Diana happy a few years ago. Four of the five inns are located on the southern slopes of Nevis Peak, around 800 feet above sea level, which allows them to get away without air conditioning. The nearest beach is a 10-minute drive from each of these four, though all have a pool for relaxing. Nisbet Plantation, on the other hand, has a manicured lawn with rows of palms that extend from the great house past the cottage accommodations to a nice curl of sand—it's located on the north end of the island, a short drive from the picayune Nevis airport. Note that all of the plantations have a quantity of stairs to navigate and do not work well for those who are physically challenged.

Golden Rock Estate   **$100–$230**   ★ ★ ★

St. George Gingerland Parish, ☎ *(809) 469-3346. FAX (809) 469-2113.*
Single: $100–$180. Double: $120–$230.

This 18th-century sugar estate, set high up in the hills, encompasses some 100 acres. Run by the great-great-great granddaughter of the man who built the main house in 1815, it practically oozes charm. Accommodations are in a converted sugar mill or in cottages, all filled with antiques, island art, canopied king beds, and fitted with large verandas and ceiling fans in lieu of air conditioning. The prize is a suite located inside the converted old stone windmill—perfect for honeymooners or a family of four. The estate is surrounded by lush rain forest, with a good hiking trail starting at the property. The grounds include a spring-fed pool, tropical gardens, a tennis court, and free transportation to two beaches or into town. Amenities: tennis. 15 rooms. Credit cards: A, MC, V.

Hermitage, The   **$85–$335**   ★ ★ ★

St. John Fig Tree Parish, ☎ *(809) 469-3477. FAX (809) 469-2481.*
Single: $85–$270. Double: $120–$335.

Set on a 250-year-old plantation up in the hills, this charming property accommodates guests in colorful, restored cottages that are nicely done with Oriental rugs, pitched ceilings, canopied four-poster or twin beds, large verandas with hammocks and antiques. Some also have full kitchens. A gorgeous two-bedroom house set on two private acres with its own pool, oversized baths, full kitchen and antique canopy beds is also available for $600 nightly. The terraced grounds include stables for horseback riding, a small pool, tennis and a plantation-style restaurant in an antique-filled room. A meal plan is available for $50 per day and includes a full American breakfast, afternoon tea and four-course dinner. Amenities: tennis. 14 rooms. Credit cards: A, D, MC, V.

Montpelier Plantation Inn   **$150–$330**   ★★★★

St. John Fig Tree Parish, ☎ *(800) 243-9420, (809) 469-3462. FAX (809) 469-2932. Single: $150–$225. Double: $180–$330.*

Set on a shoulder of Nevis Peak high above the sea, this former sugar plantation encompasses 100 lovingly landscaped acres, including an organic garden and orchard that supplies ingredients for much of the excellent food. Accommodations are roomy in cottages; all have large, private patios. Ceiling fans keep things cool. A two-bedroom suite goes for $230–330. There's a brilliant blue pool (the largest on the island) and tennis court on-site, and the staff will shuttle you to the beach, about 10 minutes away, where you can play with their speedboat. Rates include breakfast, and afternoon tea is served daily poolside on request. The fine restaurant is acclaimed for its English Mediterranean-fusion cuisine. Children under eight not allowed during the winter. Amenities: tennis. 17 rooms. Credit cards: MC, V.

Nisbet Plantation   **$191–$475**   ★★★★

Newcastle Bay, Newcastle, ☎ *(800) 742-6008, (809) 469-9325. FAX (809) 469-9864. Single: $191–$356. Double: $255–$475.*

This well-run property combines the charm of an 18th-century coconut plantation with the amenities of a resort. Set on 30 acres fronting a mile-long beach, one of the island's best, this is the former home of Frances Nisbet, who married Lord Nelson. Accommodations are in air-conditioned cottages, all individually decorated and nicely done with screened-in porches. Amenities include two restaurants, two bars, a tennis court, a large pool, a small library, croquet and watersports. Complimentary laundry service and evening turndown are nice perks. The management will help arrange horseback riding and hiking for the active set. Rates include breakfast and dinner in Nisbet's fine Great House dining room, and afternoon tea. Very posh. 38 rooms. Credit cards: A, MC, V.

Old Manor Estate and Hotel   **$125–$225**   ★★★

St. George Gingerland Parish, ☎ *(800) 892-7093, (809) 469-3445. FAX (809) 469-3388. Single: $125–$225. Double: $125–$225.*

Perched high in the hills, this converted plantation house dates back to 1832. Many of the Georgian-styled buildings are made from lava rock. Guestrooms are nicely done and spacious, with marble floors, high ceilings, canopied beds or twins with mosquito netting, verandas and ceiling fans instead air conditioning. A 1996 renovation under the property's new manager/owners provides a much-needed sprucing up with new furnishings and linens, and a fresh paint job to replace the old dark brown. Facilities include a bar, excellent restaurant and a pool that has views of t Nevis Peak. They'll shuttle you back and forth to the beach. 17 rooms. Credit cards: A, MC, V.

Low Cost Lodging

Nevis is one of the Caribbean's more expensive destinations, and low-priced bunks are few and far between. The Mead family makes the Meadville Guest House the friendliest option. **Paradise Guest House** outside Cotton Ground is another possibility ☎ *(809) 469-0394,* while the spartan **Sea Spawn Guest House** will do in a pinch ☎ *(809) 469-5239.* **Pinney's Beach Hotel** was formerly a budget option, but their location (at the end of Pinney's Beach, a half-mile from the Four Seasons) has gone to their head and the edging-toward-moderate rates are unreasonable for its well-worn rooms ☎ *(809) 469-5207.*

Meadville Cottages   **$40–$80**   ★

Meadville Lane; Charlestown, ☎ (809) 469-5235.
Single: $40–$50. Double: $60–$80.

Located 10 minutes from Pinney's Beach on the outskirts of Charlestown, this small complex consists of modest cottages with one or two bedrooms, living/dining rooms, kitchenettes, and verandas. Maid service is available, but that's it for extras. Mountain bike rentals available on-site. 10 rooms. Credit cards: MC, V.

Where to Eat

Fielding's Highest Rated Restaurants in Nevis

★★★★	Cooperage	$13–$21
★★★★	Miss June's	$65–$75
★★★	Cla-Cha-Del	$9–$15

Fielding's Most Exclusive Restaurants in Nevis

★★★★	Miss June's	$65–$75
★★★★	Cooperage	$13–$21
★★★	Cla-Cha-Del	$9–$15

Fielding's Best Value Restaurants in Nevis

★★★	Cla-Cha-Del	$9–$15
★★★★	Cooperage	$13–$21
★★	Eddy's	$9–$12
★★	Unella's	$5–$21
★★	Muriel's Cuisine	$12–$18

Driven by the island's up-market accommodations, and due to the fact that there is little in the way of an agricultural economy, dining on Nevis is expensive. The best restaurants are located in the plantation inns and at the Four Seasons, but in every case, plan on spending at least $50 per person for dinner. Although dress is casual (long pants for men), the atmosphere in each of these establishments is such that romantic dinners are embellished by hauling out your best resort duds. Many visitors make a nightly ritual of stopping at each of these spots over the course of a four- or five-night visit; the Nisbet Plantation also proffers a fine afternoon tea. But don't miss a trip to one of the island's smaller eateries for local fare. Here, such Nevisian delicacies as jerk chicken, curried goat, salt-fish casserole, johnnycakes, breadfruit salad and piles of steamed squash and rice 'n' peas may be heaped onto your plate. There's also the infamous Miss June's, who provides a long meal rich in traditional West Indian fare, but which is thought to be over-priced and over-rated by some. A popular beach bar, Tequila Sheila's, lies at the water's edge in Cades Bay and serves brunch on Sunday.

Callaloo $$$ ★★

Main Street; Charlestown, ☎ (809) 469-5389.
Latin American cuisine.
Specialties: Grilled kingfish, burgers, French pastries, broasted chicken.
Lunch: 10 a.m.–4 p.m., entrées $5–$7.
Dinner: 4–10 p.m., entrées $15–$22. Closed: Sun.
This unprepossessing place on Main Street in Charlestown is the place to come for everything from tasty charbroiled burgers to grilled lobster ($22). West Indian specialties also abound, and you have a choice of seating either squeezed in at little tables on a sidewalk patio or in an air-conditioned dining room. Callaloo offers a wide variety of dishes from pizza to pastries. Bring your own wine or beer. Credit cards: A, MC, V.

Cla-Cha-Del $$ ★★★

Cade's Bay; Cotton Ground, Charlestown, ☎ (809) 469-1841.
African cuisine. Specialties: Goat water, conch, lobster, mutton.
Lunch: entrées $5–$9.
Dinner: 9–11 p.m., entrées $9–$15. Closed: Thur.
Cade's Bay, on the north end of Pinney's Beach, is home to the Pinney family's eatery, Cla-Cha-Del. Named after siblings Claudina, Charlie and Delroy, this West Indian dining spot showcases the family's ties to the local fishing industry. Try parrotfish, conch or lobster, or drop in on a weekend for goat water, a stew with Irish origins. Burgers, soups and sandwiches are also available. Reservations recommended. Credit cards: A, MC, V.

Cooperage $$$ ★★★★

Old Manor Estate, Charlestown, ☎ (809) 469-3445.
Associated hotel: Old Manor Hotel.
International cuisine. Specialties: Provimi veal, jerk pork or chicken, filet mignon.
Dinner: 6:30–9:30 p.m., entrées $13–$21.
The historical setting and solidly good food make a meal here well worth your reservation. Located in a restored, 17th-century plantation inn, the stone-walled dining room once reverberated with the sounds of coopers making barrels for the sugar mill. For under $20 you can have filet mignon or veal scallopini. The green-pepper soup is delicious. Reservations recommended. Credit cards: A, MC, V.

Courtyard, The $$$ ★★

Main Street, Charlestown, ☎ (809) 469-5685.
International cuisine. Specialties: Pumpkin bread, lamb curry.
Lunch: 8 a.m.–3 p.m., entrées $4–$10.
Dinner: 5–11 p.m., entrées $12–$20. Closed: Sun.
This popular downtown spot is known for fresh-from-the-oven pumpkin and ginger-infused sweets. Ferry passengers who alight near here come for the hearty breakfasts; others might drop in for lunch or dinner when the menu is either burg-

ers, salads, curries or seafood specials. Dine indoors or in the tree-shaded garden restaurant known as the Courtyard Cafe. Credit cards: A, MC, V.

Eddy's $$ ★ ★

Main Street, Charlestown, ☎ *(809) 469-5958.*
Latin American cuisine. Specialties: Flying fish, conch fritters.
Lunch: Noon–3 p.m., entrées $2–$7.
Dinner: 7:30–9:30 p.m., entrées $9–$12. Closed: Thur., Sun.
Ever had a flying fish sandwich? Don't let it get away from you at this informal, second-story patio restaurant that's an ideal vantage point for tourist-watching. Inside the warmly decorated old wood townhouse, the crowd tends to be dominated by repeat visitors and permanent residents. Eddy's has a jumpin' bar with potent drinks and a well-attended Wednesday happy hour. Credit cards: A, MC, V.

Miss June's $$$ ★ ★ ★ ★

Jones Bay, Charlestown, ☎ *(809) 469-5330.*
Latin American cuisine. Specialties: All-inclusive West Indian buffet.
Dinner: 7:30 p.m., prix fixe $65–$75.
Trinidadian Miss June Mestier serves a bountiful buffet groaning with delectable dishes (some 26 in all) several evenings a week, at one seating only, and strictly by reservation. Promptly at 7:30 p.m., guests assemble for a cocktail hour. Dinner begins at 8:30 p.m. with soup and fish, and then everyone is let loose at the buffet tables. After dinner, everyone adjourns to a parlor for aperitifs and anecdotes. Inquire about serving times when you make your reservation; visitors staying at the Four Seasons pay $75 to dine here, everyone else is charged $65. Reservations required. Credit cards: MC, V.

Muriel's Cuisine $$ ★ ★

Upper Happy Hill Drive; Charlestown, ☎ *(809) 469-5920.*
Latin American cuisine. Specialties: Curries, seafood rotis, johnnycakes.
Lunch: 8:30 a.m.–4 p.m., entrées $5–$7.
Dinner: 4–10 p.m., entrées $12–$18. Closed: Sun.
Miss Muriel's establishment is fast becoming a choice spot to dine in Charlestown, especially for her substantial West Indian buffet lunches served on Wednesdays ($8). This talented lady can't offer a sea view, but the food is rib-stickin', especially the curries (chicken, goat, sometimes seafood) served with local vegetables, which may include *christophene* (chayote), plantain and rice and peas. Breakfast is served Monday through Saturday, and features salt fish and eggs with bacon, ham or cheese. Reservations recommended. Credit cards: A, MC, V.

Unella's $$ ★ ★

The Waterfront, Charlestown, ☎ *(809) 469-5574.*
Latin American cuisine.
Lunch: 9 a.m.–noon, entrées $4–$10.
Dinner: Noon–8 p.m., entrées $5–$21.
If Eddy's nearby gets too crowded, give Unella's a try—it also has a second-floor patio, a more subdued atmosphere and luscious fresh lobster. Other fare includes scampi or conch, and Caribbean-style plate meals, although most of it is unexceptional. Credit cards: D, MC, V.

Shopping on Nevis pursues simple pleasures as a rule, but several spots are worth a stop. **Island Hopper** carries the full line of Caribelle Batik fashions. Swimsuits and cotton handmade dresses can be picked up at **Amanda's Fashions**. **Knick Knacks** has artwork and souvenirs and is located just behind the Bank of Nevis on Main Street. An excellent array of souvenirs, crafts, guava jelly, gooseberry or soursop jam, banana chutney and fruit wines are available at **Nevis Handicraft Co-Op**. Stamp collectors should know that Nevis and St. Kitts are known throughout the world for their issued stamps, and the **Nevis Philatelic Bureau** issues stamps. The commemorative stamps of September 19, 1993, which celebrate the 10th anniversary of the federation's independence, are considered instant collectibles. All of these stores are located in Charlestown, and the local market is held on Saturdays.

The **Eva Wilkin Gallery**, located in a sugar mill at the **Clay Ghaut Estate** (opposite the Old Manor Hotel) commemorates the work of a now-deceased elderly lady artist whose evocative pastels and watercolors of Nevis life were beloved by islanders. Today the gallery, which also sells postcards and other contemporary Nevis art, is run by a Canadian couple and is open to the public. Photo needs and one-hour processing can be served at **Rawlins Photo Color Lab and Studio** in Fig Tree or Pemberton's on Main Street in Charlestown.

Nevis Directory

Arrival and Departure

Although a small air strip is located on Nevis in **Newcastle**, no airline service connects this island (or St. Kitts) to North America, though there is talk of extending the puny runway to allow for larger planes. For now, most air service to Nevis is via St. Kitts and several options are available. **American Eagle** flies into St. Kitts three to five times daily from their hub in San Juan. **LIAT** serves St. Kitts from a number of Caribbean islands, but they also fly directly into the Nevis Airport with nonstop flights from both St. Kitts and Antigua. Nevis is also served by two local airlines: **Air St. Kitts-Nevis** ☎ *(809) 465-8571* and **Nevis Express** ☎ *(809) 469-3346.*

Guests of the Four Seasons typically fly into St. Kitts, where they are met at the airport by a van and transferred to a private ferry out of Basseterre for a 30-minute trip to the resort's beachside dock (non-guests may use this ferry for a $45 round-trip fee on a space-available basis). Public ferry service, aboard the

Caribe Queen or the *Spirit of Mount Nevis*, makes the 45-minute crossing between Charlestown and Basseterre one to three times daily for $4 one way ☎ *(809) 469-9373.*

Business Hours

Shops open Monday–Saturday 8 a.m.–noon and 1–4 p.m. Most close earlier on Thursday. Banks open Monday–Thursday 8 a.m.–3 p.m. and Friday 8 a.m.–5 p.m.

Climate

As on St. Kitts, average temperatures hover between 78 and 85 degrees Fahrenheit, during the day; nighttime temperatures can drop to 68 degrees Fahrenheit. Trade winds keep it breezy, though the humidity can rise to uncomfortable levels during the summer. Downpours are quick but heavy between mid-June through mid-November, which is considered the rainy season.

Documents

U.S. citizens need to present proof of citizenship (passport, voter's registration card or birth certificate), along with a return or ongoing ticket. There is a departure tax of $10.

Electricity

The current is 230 volts, though some hotels have 110 volts. Bring a transformer and adapter just in case.

Getting Around

Taxis are available in both Charlestown and at the Newcastle Airport. From the airport to the Four Seasons, figure $12; to the plantation inns west of Charlestown, it will be $15–17. From Charlestown to the Four Seasons, the price is $6; to the plantation inns, $11–12; to Nisbet Plantation, $14. Three- to four-hour island tours are common; try **All Seasons Streamline Tours** which has comfortable, air conditioned vans ☎ *(809) 469-1138.* **Minibus** service around the island is fairly reliable and cheap—about $1 to almost anywhere—although there's less service on Thursday and Sunday. All routes originate in Charlestown; one usually heads north and around to Newcastle, the other heads west and up to Newcastle, but service is largely dependent on the needs of local riders, not sightseers. Rental cars start at $35 per day, or $65 if the Four Seasons arranges it for you. You'll need to shell out $12 for a Nevis drivers license, and don't forget to drive on the left. Daytrips to St. Kitts are possible either via air or ferry; see "Arrival and Departure" above.

Language

English is the official language, spoken with a rhythmic lilt. Natives also speak a local patois.

Medical Emergencies

Alexandra Hospital in Charlestown ☎ *(809) 469-5473)* operates a 24-hour emergency room service.

Money

Currency on both islands is the Eastern Caribbean dollar. In a pinch, shop-keepers and businesses will accept American and Canadian currency, but they have a hard time exchanging it.

Telephone

The area code is *809*, for both St. Kitts and Nevis. Telegrams can be sent from the **Cable & Wireless office** on Main Street in Charlestown ☎ *(809) 469-5000*. You can also make international telephone calls from this office, which will save you a lot of money. Do what you can to avoid making any international calls from your hotel room (if, indeed, your room even has a phone) since hotel surcharges will make the final bill outrageously expensive. The Cable & Wireless office is open from Monday–Friday 8 a.m.–6 p.m., and on Saturday from 8 a.m.–noon. The office is closed on Sunday and on public holidays.

Time

Atlantic Standard Time, which is one hour later than New York time, except during Daylight Saving Time, when it is the same.

Tipping and Taxes

Expect your hotel to add a 10 percent service charge. Check restaurant bills before adding your own 10–15 percent service tip. If a taxi driver hasn't added the tip himself, do so (10–15 percent).

Tourist Information

The **Nevis Tourist Office** is located on Main Street in Charlestown ☎ *(809) 469-1042*. You can pick up brochures and maps, and they can assist with budget accommodations. It's open Monday through Saturday. A St. Kitts/Nevis tourism office is also operated in New York ☎ *(212) 535-1234*.

When to Go

December is the month of Carnival, celebrated with blowout parties, costumed parades, and general merrymaking for days. Alexander Hamilton's Birthday is celebrated on Jan. 11. St. Kitts Horticultural Society holds an annual show usually in the last week of May featuring the work of local gardeners and nurserymen. The St. Kitts and Nevis Regatta of windsurfing and sunfish, an 11-mile race from Frigate Bay, is usually held in June. Culturama, a popular and festive event, celebrates the island's history, folklore and arts with presentations, talent shows, beauty pageants, calypso contests and West Indian delicacies.

NEVIS HOTELS	RMS	RATES	PHONE	CR. CARDS
Charlestown				
★★★★★ **Four Seasons Resort Nevis**	196	$250–$625	(800) 332-3442	A, MC, V
★★★★ **Montpelier Plantation Inn**	17	$150–$330	(800) 243-9420	MC, V
★★★ **Hermitage, The**	14	$85–$335	(809) 469-3477	A, D, MC, V

NEVIS HOTELS		RMS	RATES	PHONE	CR. CARDS
★★	Hurricane Cove Bungalows	10	$95–$265	(809) 469-9462	A, MC
★★	Oualie Beach Hotel	22	$100–$255	(800) 682-5431	A, D, MC, V
★	Meadville Cottages	10	$40–$80	(809) 469-5235	MC, V

Gingerland

★★★	Golden Rock Estate	15	$100–$230	(809) 469-3346	A, MC, V
★★★	Old Manor Estate and Hotel	17	$125–$225	(800) 892-7093	A, MC, V
★★	Croney's Old Manor Hotel	17	$85–$175	(809) 469-3445	A, D, MC, V

Newcastle

★★★★	Nisbet Plantation	38	$191–$475	(800) 742-6008	A, MC, V
★★★	Mount Nevis Hotel and Beach Club	32	$130–$485	(800) 756-3847	A, MC, V

NEVIS RESTAURANTS		PHONE	ENTRÉE	CR. CARDS
Charlestown				
African				
★★★	Cla-Cha-Del	(809) 469-1841	$5–$15	A, MC, V
International				
★★★★	Cooperage	(809) 469-3445	$13–$21	A, MC, V
★★	Courtyard, The	(809) 469-5685	$4–$20	A, MC, V
Latin American				
★★★★	Miss June's	(809) 469-5330	$65–$75	MC, V
★★	Callaloo	(809) 469-5389	$5–$22	A, MC, V
★★	Eddy's	(809) 469-5958	$2–$12	A, MC, V
★★	Muriel's Cuisine	(809) 469-5920	$5–$18	A, MC, V
★★	Unella's	(809) 469-5574	$4–$21	D, MC, V

PUERTO RICO

Watersports of all kinds are available at Sun Bay.

One of the Caribbean's largest islands, Puerto Rico is also one of the most popular, and it's easy to see why. The U.S. Commonwealth offers just about anything a tourist could want, from sleepy villages to sophisticated cosmopolitan cities to tony beach resorts; a rich culture; thriving nightlife and casino gambling; well-preserved historic buildings and a wealth of cultural museums. Americans looking to escape everyday life may feel Puerto Rico is too close to home, but in fact, the island is a unique world onto itself.

Word continues to get out: Hotel registrations in 1995 jumped 14.1 percent over the previous year, according to the Puerto Rico Tourism Company, and at presstime, registrations were going just as strong in 1996. The U.S. market is the island's largest, but Puerto Rico also is popular with visitors from other Caribbean islands and Europe. Part of the reason Puerto Rico does so well is due to its accessibility. Many carriers that service the Caribbean use San Juan's Luis Munoz Marin International Airport as a hub; if you're not into the hassle of laying over and changing planes, there's no reason not to just stay put in Puerto Rico. The island's well-developed tourism infrastructure makes vacations a breeze, whether you're seeking the newest, plushest accommodations or the charming country inns, called *paradors*, that dot the countryside. With an average temperature of 82 degrees and more than 200 miles of coastline, as well as numerous satellite islands, Puerto Rico draws sun lovers, watersports enthusiasts, history buffs and partyers who find something special in every corner of the island.

Perhaps the only drawback to Puerto Rico its large size means you'll be hard-pressed to see all its treasures, unless you have both several weeks to spare and energy to burn. So plan carefully when booking a Puerto Rican sojourn to find the region that fits you best. Wherever you end up, do be sure to venture out on the island (*"es la isla"* in local parlance) to experience some of the richness that is Puerto Rico.

Located in the Greater Antilles some 1045 miles from New York, Puerto Rico is surrounded by the Atlantic Ocean to the north and the Caribbean Sea to the south. The island measures 110 by 35 miles (about the size of Connecticut) and has a variety of ecosystems, including more than 200 miles of coastline, old volcanic mountains, a sprawling cave system and 20 designated forest reserves, including the famed 28,000-acre El Yunque rainforest near San Juan.

San Juan, the capital city whose metropolitan area stretches out some 300 square miles, draws the lion's share of tourists who flock to the excellent beach resorts in Condado and Isla Verde and the beautifully preserved historic section called Old San Juan.

The north coast, known as karst country, is named for its limestone, and region is pocked with hills, holes and one of the world's largest river cave systems, called Rio Camuy. Visitors can visit part of the 300-acre network at two huge sinkholes, Tres Pueblos and Cueva Clara de Empalme.

The city of Ponce, called the "pearl of the south," is a charming coastal city fronting the Caribbean Sea. Noted for its distinctive architecture that dates from the mid-1800s to the 1930s, Ponce has restored more than 600 of its

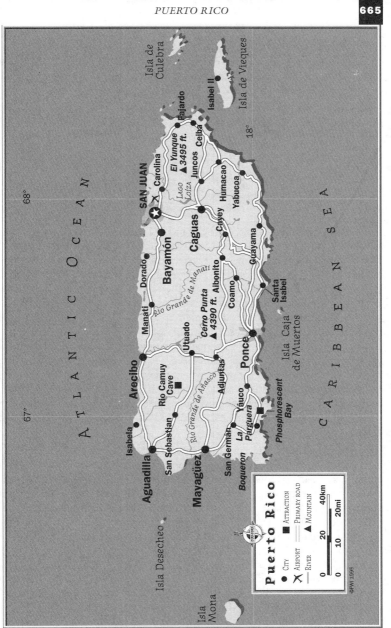

Puerto Rico

CITY •
ATTRACTION ■
AIRPORT ✕
PRIMARY ROAD
MOUNTAIN ▲
RIVER

0   20   40km
0   10   20mi

©FWI 1998

1000 historic buildings, and is a good spot for history buffs with its variety of museums and vintage sites.

Because of its agriculturally intense past, less than one percent of the island today is virgin forest. Coffee and bananas are grown in the mountains, while coastal farmers produce sugar cane and pineapples.

Two of Puerto Rico's nearby islands are inhabited: Culebra, located halfway between the mainland and St. Thomas; and Vieques, six miles east of Fajardo. Tourist facilities on both are decidedly casual.

History

In 1493, Columbus arrived on the island of Puerto Rico in the company of one Ponce de León, who named the island for his patron saint, San Juan. The island, however, already had a name—*Borinquen*—a Taino Indian nomenclature and one that is still lovingly used today by native Puerto Ricans. Caparra, inland and across the bay, was the first choice for a capital in 1508. With the permission of supreme cacique Agueybana, Juan Ponce de León (the island's first governor) and his men first scouted the island of San Juan Bautista. Eventually de León set off on his journey to discover eternal youth and never actually resided in the handsome home, Casa Blanca, that had been built for him. Thirteen years later, settlers decamped for the drier, windier islet fronting the Atlantic, where they permanently settled. During early years of colonization, the city repelled the British, French and Dutch corsairs. La Fortaleza, now the governor's mansion, and El Morro and San Cristóbal forts were built during those times with the specific aim of keeping marauders at bay.

By the early 1800s, the era of Caribbean piracy was finally brought to a halt. At the same time, Spain threw open her doors to immigration; subsequent increase in economic prosperity coupled with new aesthetic influences from abroad were soon reflected in the island's architectural styles. It was during this period that Old San Juan developed the colonial/neoclassic look that predominates today—all within the urban grid pattern envisioned by the original Spanish planners. In 1897 the island gained independence from Spanish rule in 1897. On July 25, 1898, however, Spanish troops landed in Guánica, in the middle of the Spanish-American War, and disturbed whatever modicum of peace had been achieved. The Treaty of Paris of 1899 handed the island over to the U.S. In 1917, Puerto Ricans were granted American citizenship; in 1952, the island achieved unique status by becoming the only member of the commonwealth to receive its own constitution and govern-

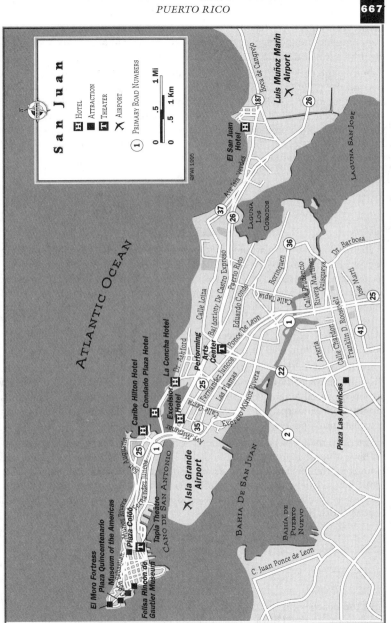

San Juan

- 🏨 Hotel
- ■ Attraction
- 🎭 Theater
- ✈ Airport
- ① Primary Road Numbers

0 .5 1 Mi
0 .5 1 Km

©PW 1995

ATLANTIC OCEAN

Luis Muñoz Marín Airport

El San Juan Hotel

Ave Isla Verde

Laguna San Jose

Laguna Los Corozos

Boca de Cangrejo

Dr. Barbosa

Borinquen

Calle Prudencio Rivera Martinez

Chusqueya

Jose Marti

Calle Loiza

Baldorioty De Castro Expreso

Puerto Rico

Eduardo Conde

Ponce De Leon

Calle Tapia

Caribe Hilton Hotel

Condado Plaza Hotel

La Concha Hotel

Performing Arts Center

Dr. Ashford

Excelsior Hotel

Las Palmas

Fernandez Juncos

Calle Juan

Expreso Muñoz Rivera

Artería

Calle Chardon

Franklin D. Roosevelt

Plaza Las Américas

Isla Grande Airport

Ave Muñoz

Caño De San Antonio

Bahia De San Juan

Bahía De Puerto Nuevo

C. Juan Ponce de Leon

El Moro Fortress

Plaza Quincentenario

Museum of the Americas

Muñoz Rivera

San Sebastian

Plaza Colón

Tapia Theatre

Fernandez Juncos

Felisa Rincon de Gautier Museum

Agustin

ment. Although there have been several movements geared toward achieving complete independence, the 1993 vote to remain a U.S. possession has ensured a long-standing and stable future with the mother country.

During the early 20th century, a burgeoning population brought growth beyond the Old City gates and soon after, the destruction of substantial sections of its massive walls. Today, Old San Juan boasts only 5000 residents. No longer the financial hub, it still pulls 5000 workers to offices and government buildings, eateries and shops. A seven-block enclave that boasts a large number of art studios, florists, doctor's offices, and galleries is considered one of the more desirable spots to live in on the island.

People

The total island population is 3.56 million, with some one million living in the San Juan metropolitan area. Puerto Rico is the Caribbean's most industrially developed island, and annual income is the highest in Latin America. Education is good, and more than a third of high school students go on to higher learning. Besides tourism, which represents just six percent of the gross national product, Puerto Rico is a major producer and exporter of manufactured goods, pharmaceutical and high-tech equipment. Some 83 percent of the rum sold in the United States comes from the territory.

Freedom of faith is guaranteed by the Commonwealth Constitution, though the majority of islanders are Roman Catholic. Spanish and English are both official languages; the former is predominant, but since English is taught from kindergarten to high school in public schools, communication is usually not a problem, especially around San Juan.

American media has a huge influence on Puerto Ricans, who, paradoxically, have a fierce national pride, and, for many, a longing for independence from the United States. Islanders are generally a friendly lot, but note that crime around the cities can be high, so use the typical precautions and discretion in displaying cash, cameras and valuable jewelry. Avoid deserted beaches both day and night.

Beaches

All the beaches on the island are public with one exception—the artificial beach at the Caribe Hilton in San Juan. Many hotels are situated right on the beach; if they aren't, they are but a short walk away. Hotels that do not enjoy such proximity usually provide a shuttle to the beach free of charge. **Luquillo Beach** is probably the best beach on the island for swimming. The waters are calm, and the coral reefs protect the pristine lagoon from the stronger waves of the Atlantic. Picnic tables are available as well as camp facilities. Also suitable for swimming is **Seven Seas**, a long strand with compacted sand. Trailers may be parked nearby and campers can pitch tents. Watersports of all kinds can be arranged at **Sun Bay**, a sugar-white beach on Vieques. Vessels for sailing also can be rented. One of the most famous beaches is **Condado Beach**, along Ashford Avenue in San Juan. It's a beauty-watcher's delight, especially for those who want to see the latest trend in swimwear and the prettiest island girls. Within walking distance are the long beaches of **Rincón**, **Cabo Rojo** and **Paguera**. Surfers claim that the best waves are along the Atlantic coastline from Borinquén Point south to Rincón. The surf is best from October through April. In summer, La Concha and Aviones have the best curls. All these beaches have board rentals nearby.

The best beaches near San Juan, are at Isla Verde in front of the major hotels.

Underwater

Many knowledgeable divers regard the Puerto Rico as little more than a hub for changing planes en route to Bonaire. The undersea reality is quite different. Some of the Caribbean's best and least exploited diving can be found in Puerto Rico. Why isn't it more famous? One reason may be that San Juan and the island's biggest resort area lie on the long northern coast, which offers none of Puerto Rico's prime diving. You have to venture away from the tourist mecca—to **Fajardo**, tiny **Parguera**, or the offshore islands—

PUERTO RICO

Puerto Rico's Best Bets

You can spend several days exploring the island's sights. Visit the only tropical rain forest in the U.S. National Park System, venture through a sublime series of caves and sinkholes, or take in the cultural highlights of the City of Ponce.

Río Camuy Cave Park

One of the world's largest cave networks, the Río Camuy system boasts the world's second-largest underground river. Reserve ahead to take a tram into the cave system, then explore the caverns on foot. Weekdays are less crowded.

Ponce

Puerto Rico's second city, Ponce is known as the "Pearl of the South." Founded in 1692, this intellectual and cultural center is home to the Ponce Art Museum. Don't miss the Victorian-style fire station.

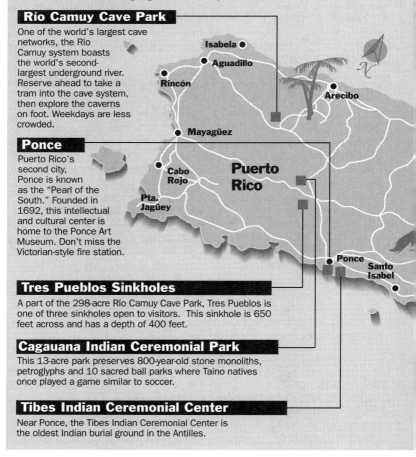

Tres Pueblos Sinkholes

A part of the 298-acre Río Camuy Cave Park, Tres Pueblos is one of three sinkholes open to visitors. This sinkhole is 650 feet across and has a depth of 400 feet.

Cagauana Indian Ceremonial Park

This 13-acre park preserves 800-year-old stone monoliths, petroglyphs and 10 sacred ball parks where Taino natives once played a game similar to soccer.

Tibes Indian Ceremonial Center

Near Ponce, the Tibes Indian Ceremonial Center is the oldest Indian burial ground in the Antilles.

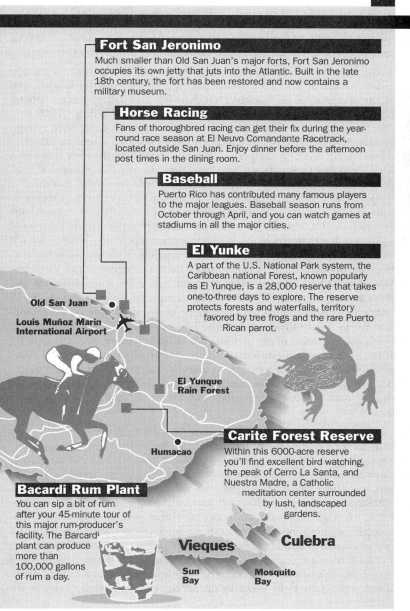

Fort San Jeronimo

Much smaller than Old San Juan's major forts, Fort San Jeronimo occupies its own jetty that juts into the Atlantic. Built in the late 18th century, the fort has been restored and now contains a military museum.

Horse Racing

Fans of thoroughbred racing can get their fix during the year-round race season at El Neuvo Comandante Racetrack, located outside San Juan. Enjoy dinner before the afternoon post times in the dining room.

Baseball

Puerto Rico has contributed many famous players to the major leagues. Baseball season runs from October through April, and you can watch games at stadiums in all the major cities.

El Yunke

A part of the U.S. National Park system, the Caribbean national Forest, known popularly as El Yunque, is a 28,000 reserve that takes one-to-three days to explore. The reserve protects forests and waterfalls, territory favored by tree frogs and the rare Puerto Rican parrot.

PUERTO RICO

Old San Juan

Louis Muñoz Marin International Airport

El Yunque Rain Forest

Carite Forest Reserve

Within this 6000-acre reserve you'll find excellent bird watching, the peak of Cerro La Santa, and Nuestra Madre, a Catholic meditation center surrounded by lush, landscaped gardens.

Humacao

Bacardi Rum Plant

You can sip a bit of rum after your 45-minute tour of this major rum-producer's facility. The Barcardi plant can produce more than 100,000 gallons of rum a day.

Vieques

Culebra

Sun Bay

Mosquito Bay

to experience the most succulent reefs and walls. Additionally, as happens on some other regional islands with a substantial variety of top-side activities, diving frequently takes a back-seat to a diversified vacation. So, to whet your appetite, pack up the car for a front-row tour of Puerto Rico's coastline.

When combined with **Culebra**, the east coast offers the island's greatest concentration of dive sites. Mini-walls, spur-and-groove formations, and plenty of marine life are available, but there is a wide variety of reef topographies to sample; at **Red Hog**, for instance, the abrupt wall drops 1000 feet. Day trips from San Juan are possible (it's less than an hour drive to Fajardo or Humacao) while offshore Culebra, in particular, has several outstanding dives. Diving on the sprawling south coast is found on the stretch between Ponce and tiny **La Parguera** where hotels are low-key and swamps of mangrove replace beaches, deterring a number of would-be visitors. But the dive shops overlooking the patch reefs of La Parguera will proudly stack their precipitate wall—which is 22 miles long and plunges 3000 feet—against any other in the Caribbean. Throw in a stunning phosphorescent bay (you'll swim, not dive) and you have a sparkling marine experience. Circling around to Puerto Rico's choppy west coast, there are lightly visited patch reef sites between Boqueron and Aguadilla, and attractive underwater caves near **Isabela**. But the best is found around two offshore destinations, **Desecheo** and **Mona Islands**, which yield a spectacular glimpse of what Caribbean diving might have been like a few decades ago, before overfishing and coral destruction began to take their toll. These two islands (and Culebra) illustrate one local problem: many of the best sites are an hour or more away from a dock. If you want convenient diving, stick to the reefs off **Humacao** or quiet La Parguera, where great sites are closer to shore. Visibility varies more than wildly, but averages 75 feet or more, and can extend to 150 feet on really good days; the east coast sites can be impacted by freshwater runoff more than the other areas.

Long ignored, environmental concerns have finally become a front burner issue for local divers. The government has not instituted a permanent mooring system, which means a number of reefs in heavily traveled cruising locations are anchor-damaged; the busy Fajardo area is one abused spot. The dive operations will apparently have to undertake this project on their own. Although there are more than two dozen dive shops on the island, the three listed below are the standouts. Some of the other operations are not environmentally oriented and others have shown inconsistent ownership. Watch for this to change in coming years as dedicated divers focus more attention on Puerto Rico as a legitimate underwater destination. Dive style is friendly and casual, and it's not uncommon to be diving with the actual owners of the shops, which tend to be generally smaller outfits than typically found in the Caribbean.

On Foot

It speaks well of Puerto Rico and its visitors that **El Yunque National Forest** is probably the single most popular day trip outside San Juan, drawing upward of 1 million visitors annually. Thirteen trails of varying length cover 23 miles of the park's verdant terrain, though it may surprise you to discover that most of these paths are paved. In theory, this helps prevent erosion (the summits receive up to 240 inches of rain a year), but the pavement may also be a slight concession to taming the wilds for city dwellers and tourists. With the exception of the longer **El Toro** and **El Yunque** trails, most of these hikes will take no more than an hour or two. The 28,000-acre El Yunque preserve covers four different types of forest, and is home to 240 species of tropical trees, flowers and wildlife, including 20 varieties of orchids and 50 types of ferns. A quarter-sized tree frog, the *coqui*, exists only on Puerto Rico and has become a local mascot, while the island's extremely rare Puerto Rican parrot—only a couple dozen left by the mid-'70s—is making a gradual comeback in the El Yunque forests.

Trails are not limited to those found in El Yunque; it's worth investigating some of the 19 other existing forest preserves sprinkled around the island. The bat-filled **Rio Camuy Cave** features the third-largest subterranean river in the world. **Pinones Forest**, just east of San Juan, contains the island's biggest thicket of mangroves, and several other preserves line the island's scenic **Panoramic Route**. There are a few snake species on the island, but none are poisonous; one, the Puerto Rican boa constrictor is large enough to be intimidating—as long as seven feet—but it's considered harmless to humans.

By Pedal

Puerto Ricans are devoted to touring their island. They also adore driving and positively love their cars. Bicycles are regrettably few and far between. This isn't to say that cyclists aren't welcome on the island's roads. One visiting rider noted that, although locals drive everywhere and quickly, they respected his right-of-way, perhaps only out of curiosity. The intricate network of paved roads provides stirring cycling challenges, from coastal highways to meandering mountain byways. One obvious route is to circumnavigate the island's perimeter—almost 300 miles, plus side-trips—which would make for an excellent one-week biking vacation, but don't discount the island's lush interior, which is more interesting than many parts of the developed coastline. One area that invites exploration by mountain bike is **El Yunque National Forest**. Route 191 used to connect the north and south entrances of the park for cars, but a huge landslides closed the road and there are currently no plans to reopen it; tooling through this lightly traveled section of the park on a mountain bike would be quite enjoyable (the landslide area can be traversed on a path). This ride can be done as a moderate day trip out of San Juan. Another attractive area for off-roading is the **Bosque de Susua**, a forest reserve located between Mayagüez and Ponce; the entire southwest offers excellent riding, but carry a patch kit for thorns. A pair of associations covering both mountain and road bikers exist on the island, and we may see cycling activities develop in coming years. Bike rentals are available from Encantos Ecotours in San Juan (see "One Foot" above); their staff is an excellent resource for visitors interested in adventurous excursions.

What Else to See

Puerto Rico is so diverse that renting a car and getting out into the countryside is highly recommended. Two hours west of San Juan is the town of **Arecibo**, which dates to 1556, and the **Arecibo Observatory**, the world's largest radar/radio telescope. Operated by Cornell University and the National Science Foundation, the facility monitors radio emissions from outer space. SETI, the Search for Extraterrestrial Intelligence, is based here as well, but don't expect the people working there to share any secrets. The center is open for self-guilded tours Tuesday through Friday from 2–3 p.m. and on Sundays from 1–4 p.m. Call ☎ *(787) 787-2612* for information.

On the island's southwest corner, the quaint town of **San German** retains much of its original Spanish architecture. The town's **Porta Coeli Church**, built in 1606, is the oldest church still intact under the U.S. flag.

Just 45 minutes from San Juan is **Las Cabezas de San Juan Nature Reserve** ☎ *(787) 722-5834)*, just opened in 1991. Its 316 acres house a 19th-century working **lighthouse**, called El Faro, and seven different ecological systems, including forest, mangroves, beaches, lagoons and offshore coral reefs.

Those interested in the long-gone Taino Indian way of life can check out two well-preserved ceremonial sites. **Tibes Indian Ceremonial Park**, near Ponce, has seven ceremonial ball courts, two dance grounds and a recreated Taino Indian village, as well as a museum displaying artifacts from the era. **Caguana Indian Ceremonial Ball Park**, in Utuado, was built by the Taino Indians some 800 years ago, and includes 10 ball courts and stone monoliths, some etched with petroglyphs.

The **LeLoLai VIP Program** offers discounted sightseeing tours and savings at participating shops, restaurants and sports operators, as well as free performances showcasing Puerto Rico's Indian, Spanish and African heritage. For information, call ☎ *(787) 723-3135* or *(787) 723-3136* during business hours on weekdays.

Puerto Rico's free tourist publication, *Que Pasa*, has many good ideas for sightseeing and tours.

Historical Sites

Capilla de Cristo ★ ★ ★

Calle del Cristo, Old San Juan, ☎ *(787) 721-2400.*
The Christ Chapel was built in 1753 after a horse rider's life was supposedly spared after a tragic accident. (Supposedly, because historical records say the youth did, indeed, die.) In any event, the small silver altar is dedicated to the Christ of Miracles.

Casa de los Contrafuertes ★ ★

Calle San Sebastian 101, Old San Juan, ☎ *(787) 724-5477.*
Hours open: 9 a.m.–4:30 p.m.
Called the House of Buttresses (for obvious reasons once you see it), this is believed to be the oldest residence left in Old San Juan, dating back to the early 18th century. Inside are two museums, one devoted to graphic arts, the other displaying a 19th-century pharmacy.

Cathedral de San Juan ★ ★ ★

Calle del Cristo 151, Old San Juan, ☎ *(787) 722- 861.*
Hours open: 8:30 a.m.–4:30 p.m.
The San Juan Cathedral was built in 1540, destroyed by hurricane in 1529, looted in 1598, and damaged by another hurricane in 1615. Today it holds the remains of Ponce de Leon and the relic of San Pio, a Roman martyr. Sunday masses begin at 9 a.m.

Convento de los Dominicos ★ ★ ★

Plaza de San Jose, Old San Juan, ☎ *(787) 724-5949.*
This was Puerto Rico's first convent, started in 1523. It was home to Dominican friars until 1838, when it became a barracks for the United States Army. Today, it is headquarters for the Institute of Puerto Rican Culture. Inside you'll find the old chapel, art exhibits and a fine gift shop.

Fort San Cristobel ★ ★

Calle Norzagaray, Old San Juan, ☎ *(787) 729-6960.*
Hours open: 9 a.m.–5 p.m.
This massive fort dates back to 1634. Its walls rise 150 feet above sea level, and it covers 27 acres. Now run under the auspices of the National Park Service, the site includes a replica of 18th-century Spanish troop barracks. Free tours are given daily from 10 a.m.–4 p.m. General admission: free

Fort San Jeronimo   ★★★

Next to the Caribe Hilton, Cordado Bay, ☎ *(787) 724-5949.*

This tiny fort was attacked by the British in 1797, 11 years after it was built. Now run by the Institute of Puerto Rican Culture, it houses a small military museum.

Fuerte San Felipe del Morro   ★★

Calle Norzagaray, Old San Juan, ☎ *(787) 729-6960.*
Hours open: 9 a.m.–5 p.m.

This fort, commonly known as El Morro, guards the entrance to San Juan Bay. The Spaniards started construction in 1540, but it wasn't until 1787 that the fort was deemed complete. Now run under the auspices of the National Park Service, the six-level fort can be explored via guided tours (from 10 a.m. to 4 p.m.) or on your own. This impressive fort contains dungeons, lookouts, barracks and vaults, as well as a small museum on its history. General admission: free

Governor Mansion

Recito Oeste Street, Old San Juan, ☎ *(787) 721-2400.*
Hours open: 9 a.m.–4 p.m.

Puerto Rico boasts a lot of "oldest in the Western Hemisphere"—here's the oldest executive mansion in continuous use. It started as a fortress in 1553 and is the office and residence of Puerto Rico's governor. Now a U.S. National Historic Site, the mansion can be toured in the mornings, with tours of the gardens running all day.

Hacienda Buena Vista

Route 10, Barrio Magueyes, ☎ *(787) 722-5822.*
Hours open: 8:30 a.m.–5 p.m.

The rich aroma of fresh coffee hangs in the air at this historic spot, a working coffee plantation from 1833 to the 1950s. The grounds include a museum housed in the former manor estate, rooms furnished in authentic period pieces from the 1850s, mills, water wheels, and original machinery in all action. The machinery is considered especially significant because few such iron items from the era remain, as most were converted for use in the two world wars. Tours are conducted Friday through Sunday at 8:30 and 10:30 a.m.; 1:30 and 3:30 p.m. Reservations are required.

Inglesia de San Jose   ★★★

Plaza de San Jose, Old San Juan, ☎ *(787) 725-7501.*
Hours open: 8:30 a.m.–4 p.m.

The San Jose Church is the second-oldest in the Western Hemisphere, dating back to 1532. It was originally a Dominican chapel and was the family church of Ponce de Leon's descendants, many of whom are buried here. Among the highlights are a crucifix that belonged to the explorer, oil paintings by Jose Campeche and Francisco Oller, and ornate processional floats. Sunday mass is at 12:15.

Museums and Exhibits

Casa Blanca   ★★★

Calle San Sebastian 1, San Juan, ☎ *(787) 724-4102.*

The land on which the "White House" sits was given to explorer Ponce de Leon by the Spanish Crown. He died before the house was built in 1521, but his descendants lived there for some 250 years. In 1779, it was taken over by the Spanish military, then used later by the United States as a residence for military commanders. Today the mansion is restored to its former glory and is a National Historic Monument. It houses two museums, one on the Taino Indians (believed to be Puerto Rico's first inhabitants) and one on the house's history, with emphasis on life in the 16th and 18th centuries. Casa Blanca is the oldest continuously occupied residence in the Western Hemisphere.

La Casa del Libro ★★★

Calle del Cristo, Old San Juan, ☎ (787) 723-0354.
Hours open: 11 a.m.–4:30 p.m.
Exhibits on printing and bookmaking are displayed at this 19th-century house. Noteworthy are pages from the Gutenberg Bible, a decree signed by Ferdinand and Isabella concerning Columbus' second voyage, and other pre-16th century documents and manuscripts.

Museo de Arte y Historia ★★★

Calle Norzagaray, Old San Juan, ☎ (787) 724-1875.
This center for Puerto Rican arts and crafts displays works by local artists. It was a marketplace in the 1850s in a previous incarnation. Audio-visual shows in English on the city's history are shown daily at 11 a.m. and 1:15 p.m.

Museo de Pablo Casals ★★★

Calle San Sebastian 101, Old San Juan, ☎ (787) 723-9185.
Hours open: 9:30 a.m.–5:30 p.m.
The famed Spanish cellist spent his last years in Puerto Rico, leaving behind a collection of memorabilia from his long and distinguished career. The 18th-century house displays his cello, manuscripts and photos from his life, as well as videotaped performances, shown on request. General admission: $1.

Theater

Centro de Ballas Artes ★★

De Diego and Ponce de Leon avs, San Juan, ☎ (787) 721-0000.
This fine arts center is the largest in the Caribbean. Call the box office or inquire at your hotel about events—from operas to plays—while you're in town

Teatro Tapia ★★

Avenue Ponce de Leon, San Juan, ☎ (787) 722-0407.
Dating back to 1832, this is one of the Western Hemisphere's oldest theaters. It is named after Puerto Rican playwright Alejandro Tapia y Rivera. Check with the box office for a schedule for upcoming plays and cultural events.

Tours

Bacardi Rum Plant ★★★

Poute 888, Catano, ☎ (787) 788-1500.
Located across the bay from San Juan (a short hop ferry), this plant offers 45-minute tours at 9 and 10:30 a.m.; noon and 4 p.m. You'll see the distillery and bottling plant, and get to judge the results yourself.

Caribbean National Forest ★★★★★

Near Luquillo Beach, Puerto Rico, ☎ (787) 887-2875.

Known simply as El Yunque, this pristine spot encompasses 28,000 acres of virgin rainforest, with some 240 species of tropical trees, flowers and wildlife. It is home to rare creatures like the Puerto Rican boa, which grows to seven feet, as well as the colorful Puerto Rican parrot, and 26 other species found nowhere else. There are more than 20 kinds of orchids, 50 varieties of ferns, and millions of tiny tree frogs, who serenade visitors with their tiny croaks. Stop at the Sierra Palm Visitor Center on Route 191 to peruse the interesting exhibits and pick up a map. Numerous trails traverse the park, leading to waterfalls, natural pools and the peak of El Toro.

Rio Camuy Cave Park ★★★

Route 129, Arecibo, ☎ *(787) 898-3100.*

Hours open: 8 a.m.–4 p.m.

Located in northwest Puerto Rico, 2.5 hours from San Juan, is one of the world's largest cave networks. Sixteen entrances have been found and seven miles of passages explored so far. A tram takes you to the cave, where you get out and walk through, passing sinkholes, one of the world's largest underground rivers, and giant stalagmites and stalactites. The Taino Indians, believed to be Puerto Rico's first inhabitants, also explored the cave. Reservations are essential, as this place is understandably popular. General admission: $10.

With more than 200 miles of coastline, rest assured that Puerto Rico has all the watersports you could desire—including surfing, something many Caribbean islands, with their calm seas, lack. The Puerto Rico Water Sport Federation sets standards for member-operators who offer diving, snorkeling, sailing, deep-sea fishing, windsurfing and other aquatic activities; stick with a member-company to be assured of good service.

Deep-sea fishing for white and blue martin, allison tuna, mackerel, tarpon, sailfish and wahoo is excellent year-round. Some 30 world records have been broken in some of the island's many deep-sea fishing tournaments held each year. Lake fishers can try for largemouth bass, peacock bass, sunfish, catfish and tilapia. For details, contact the Department of Natural Resources at ☎ *(787) 722-5938.*

The best beaches for catching a wave, especially October through April, are along the Atlantic coastline from **Rincón** north to **Borinquen Point**. In the summer, try **Casa de Pesca** in Arecibo and **La Concha** in San Juan. All good surfing beaches have surf shops nearby for lessons and equipment rentals.

For spectator sports, check out **thoroughbred races** at 2:30 p.m. each Sunday, Wednesday, Friday and holiday at **El Comandante** at Canovanas ☎ *(787) 724-6060).* The professional baseball season runs from October through

April, with games held at stadiums in San Juan, Ponce, Caguas, Santurce, Mayagüez and Arecibo. For a schedule, contact Professional Baseball of Puerto Rico at ☎ *(787) 765-6285*. The dubious "sport" of **cockfighting** takes place from November through August in Isla Verde at the Coliseo Gallistico.

Duffers have nine **golf courses** from which to choose, while more than 100 **tennis courts** dot the island. If your hotel doesn't have one, you can rent one of 17 courts at San Juan Central Park ☎ *(787) 722-1646*, or Club Riomar in Rio Grande ☎ *(787) 887-3964*, which has 13 clay courts.

Boating and Cruising

Various locations, Puerto Rico.

Lots of firms will take you out on the high seas for a simple sail or snorkel trip. Most charge about $45 per person. Try: **Fondo de Cristal**, ☎ *(787) 889-5891*; **Island Safari**, ☎ *(787) 728-6606*; **Spread Eagle**, ☎ *(787) 863-1905*; **Erin Go Braugh**, ☎ *(787) 860-4401*; **East Wind Catamaran**, ☎ *(787) 863-2821*; **Captain Jack Becker**, ☎ *(787) 860-0861*; and **Land and Sea Excursions**, ☎ *(787) 382-4877*.

Golf

Various locations, Puerto Rico.

Unlike most of the Caribbean islands, which have just one or two golf courses (if any), Puerto Rico has a wealth of greens. All are 18-hole courses unless otherwise noted. Rio Grande: **Bahia Beach Plantation**, ☎ *(787) 256-5600;* **Berwind Country Club**, ☎ *(787) 876-3056;* **Club Riomar**, ☎ *(787) 887-3964*. Fajardo: **Conquistador Resort** ☎ *(787) 863-1000*. Dorado: **Dorado del Mar Country Club**, *nine holes*, ☎ *(787) 796-2030;* **Hyatts Dorado and Cerromar**, *38 holes*, ☎ *(787) 796-1234*. Humacao: **Palmas del Mar Resort**, ☎ *(787) 852-6000)*. Aguadilla: **Punta Borinquen**, ☎ *(787) 890-2987*. Check at your hotel or call Luiz Ortiz, ☎ *(787) 786-3859*, for access to courses in metropolitan San Juan.

Horseback Riding

Various locations, Puerto Rico.

Just hop on a horse and ride off into the sunset (or along the beach or through the rainforest) at **Hacienda Carabali**, ☎ *(787) 889-5820*, or **Palmas del Mar's Equestrian Center**, ☎ *(787) 852-6000*.

Watersports

Various locations, Puerto Rico.

If your hotel doesn't offer watersports, try one of these. For general watersport equipment rentals, **Carib Aquatic Adventures in Miramar**, ☎ *(787) 724-1882*, does everything from boat rentals to deep-sea fishing excursions. For scuba diving, call: **Adventure by the Sea**, *Cerro Gordo*, ☎ *(787) 251-4923;* **Caribbean Divers**, ☎ *(787) 722-7393;* **Caribbean School of Aquatics**, *Condado*, ☎ *(787) 728-6606;* **Coral Head Divers**, *Humacao*, ☎ *(787) 850-7208;* Dorado Marine Center, ☎ *(787) 796-4645;* and **Mundo Submarino**, *Isla Verde*, ☎ *(787) 791-5764*. For deep-sea fishing, try: **Benitez**, *San Juan*, ☎ *(787) 723-2292;* **Makaira Hunter**, *Miramar*, ☎ *(787) 397-8028;* **Southern Witch**, *Miramar*, ☎ *(787) 731-9252;* **Western Tourist Services**, ☎ *(787) 834-4008*.

Where to Stay

Fielding's Highest Rated Hotels in Puerto Rico

★★★★★	El Conquistador Resort	$170–$420
★★★★★	El San Juan Hotel/Casino	$250–$995
★★★★★	Horned Dorset Primavera	$150–$440
★★★★★	Hyatt Dorado Beach	$160–$490
★★★★★	Hyatt Regency Cerromar	$165–$420
★★★★★	Sands Hotel & Casino	$290–$305
★★★★	Caribe Hilton & Casino	$200–$1200
★★★★	Condado Plaza Hotel	$195–$355
★★★★	Palmas del Mar Humacao	$145–$715
★★★★	Radisson Ambassador Plaza	$170–$320

Fielding's Most Exclusive Hotels in Puerto Rico

★★★★	Caribe Hilton & Casino	$200–$1200
★★★★	Palmas del Mar Humacao	$145–$715
★★★★★	Hyatt Dorado Beach	$160–$490
★★★★★	Horned Dorset Primavera	$150–$440
★★★★★	Hyatt Regency Cerromar	$165–$420

Fielding's Best Value Hotels in Puerto Rico

★★★	Villa Esperanza	$65–$101
★★	Parador Banos de Coamo	$55–$65
★★	Sea Gate Guest House	$40–$85
★★	Parador Vistamar	$60–$75
★★	Harbour View Villas	$50–$95

You'll find it all in Puerto Rico, from huge, self-contained resorts to house-keeping units to government-sponsored *paradores puertorriqueños*, which are country inns that are generally situated in historic buildings or particularly scenic sites. These family-run lodgings are usually quite affordable. To book one, call ☎ *(800) 443-0266.*

One of our favorites in the San Juan area is the El San Juan Hotel & Casino, which has a heavenly lobby just perfect for whiling away the hours. In fact, this is a great place to kill time if you find yourself with a long layover at the airport on your way to another destination; it's just a five-minute taxi ride away from the terminal. The casino is quite upscale, but be careful not to spend all your vacation money killing time until your flight!

The ever-growing island has several hotels that just opened in 1996, including the Westin Rio Mar Beach Resort & Country Club and the Wyndham Old San Juan Hotel & Casino. For details, see the following individual listings. The venerable El Convento Hotel reopened in late November 1996, after a year-long renovation nad has been restored to its original glory.

In San Juan and Condado Area

Running around the Atlantic between Ocean Park and Miramar, the Condado area, now returning to its glitzy rep of years gone by and is now one of the main areas for hotels and resorts. The **Condado Plaza Hotel & Casino** is practically a planet unto itself, with a full range of eateries, casinos, Vegas-type shows, its own shopping mall and top American furnishings. One of the closest to the airport is **El San Juan Hotel & Casino**, also a luxury property of top proportions, features an enormous pool that inspires a lot of social climbing. A good moderate option is **Carib Inn**, near the airport, but a mere short walk to the beach. In Isla Verde, east of San Juan/ Santurce, is the U.S.-run **TraveLodge**, with comfortably large beds, modernized bathrooms and an acceptable pool.

Hotels and Resorts

Best Western Pierre   **$97–$145**   ★ ★ ★

105 de Diego Avenue, San Juan, ☎ *(800) 528-1234, (787) 721-1200. FAX (787) 721-3118.*
Single: $97–$135. Double: $107–$145.
Located in the heart of the Santurce business district, four blocks from Condado, this Best Western appeals to business travelers on a budget. Facilities are limited to a restaurant, bar, and pool. 184 rooms. Credit cards: A, CB, DC, D, MC, V.

Carib Inn Tennis Club   **$105–$320**   ★ ★

Isla Verde, San Juan, ☎ *(800) 548-8217, (787) 791-3535. FAX (787) 791-0104.*
Single: $105–$120. Double: $110–$320.
Located near the airport and a few minutes from the beach, this resort caters to tennis players, with eight courts, a ball machine, and video playback. Oddly enough, guests must pay extra to use the courts, and even more still for night play, which gives the feeling of being nickeled and dimed. The tennis theme continues with a pool shaped like a racquet. Accommodations are adequate but cry out for renova-

tion. There are a few restaurants and bars on-site, and the salsa bands on Friday and Saturday nights are popular. 225 rooms. Credit cards: A, CB, DC, D, MC, V.

Caribe Hilton & Casino $200–$1200   ★★★★

Fort San Jeronimo, San Juan, ☎ *(800) 468-8585, (787) 721-0303.*
FAX (787) 724-6992.
Single: $200–$755. Double: $225–$1200.

This behemoth does a huge business with meetings and conventions, so you'll be sharing facilities with lots of folks wearing name tags. Nevertheless, this is a smashing resort, with lots going on all the time. Amenities include a putting green, six tennis courts, a health club with air-conditioned racquetball and squash courts, supervised programs for kids, six restaurants, and several bars, one with live entertainment. Snorkel and scuba equipment can be obtained on the small beach. Guestrooms are housed in two towers, one 10 stories, the other 20. All are quite decent, and most have ocean views. Business travelers are catered to on three executive levels. Fort San Jeronimo, which dates back to the 16th century, is footsteps away. The $40 million that Hilton poured into the resort a few years back really shows, but individual travelers may be happier at a smaller property, away from conventioneers. 670 rooms. Credit cards: A, CB, D, MC, V.

Condado Beach Trio $140–$195   ★★★

Ashford Avenue, San Juan, ☎ *(800) 468-2775, (787) 721-6090.*
Single: $140–$195. Double: $140–$195.

This government-owned complex consists of two hotels and the El Centro Convention Center, recently all greatly renovated with great results. The Spanish Colonial-style Hotel Condado Beach dates back to 1919. Guestrooms are elegant and tastefully done with nice furnishings and original art. The grounds include a few restaurants and bars, a casino and a pool. The nearby La Concha Hotel is oriented more toward families, with facilities like two tennis courts and a pool. Guestrooms there are not as nice as at Condado Beach, but they are cheaper. La Concha offers a disco, two restaurants, and live entertainment in one of the two bars. The upscale disco is shaped like a conch shell. Guests can use the facilities at both hotels; Condado Beach has better service. The "beach" in the title is quite narrow. Lots of conventioneers meet and stay at this complex. 481 rooms. Credit cards: A, CB, DC, D, MC, V.

Condado Plaza Hotel $195–$355   ★★★★

999 Ashford Avenue, San Juan, ☎ *(800) 468-8588, (787) 721-1000.*
FAX (787) 722-4613.
Single: $195–$335. Double: $225–$355.

This full-service resort has a small beach, but most guests hang out at one of the five pools. The five-acre property was renovated in 1993, with good results. Accommodations are housed in two towers and are quite nice, though only some have sea views. Those shelling out extra for a Plaza Club room enjoy added amenities and the use of a lounge. The grounds include two tennis courts, a fitness center, air-conditioned squash and racquetball courts, a business center, and Puerto Rico's largest casino. Food and drink can be found at the several eateries and bars, plus you can check out the hoppin' disco. 575 rooms. Credit cards: A, CB, D, MC, V.

Curacao

San Juan Cathedral, Puerto Rico

El Canario by the Lagoon   **$65–$110**   ★ ★

4 Calle Clemenceau, San Juan, ☎ *(800) 533-2649, (787) 722-5058.*
FAX (787) 723-8590.
Single: $65–$110. Double: $65–$110.

Located in the heart of Condado, this small European-style hotel is just a block from the beach. Rooms are basic but comfortable, with air conditioning and cable TV. The complimentary continental breakfast includes fresh fruits and pastries. Other than a tour desk, there are few facilities on-site, but many are within walking distance. Not bad for the rates. 40 rooms. Credit cards: A, D, MC, V.

El Canario by the Sea   **$60–$99**   ★

4 Condado Avenue, San Juan, ☎ *(800) 533-2649, (787) 722-8640.*
FAX (787) 725-4921.
Single: $60–$99. Double: $60–$99.

Located just off the beach, this small hotel is family-run. Rooms are modest but comfortable, air-conditioned and have cable TV. Each morning, a complimentary continental breakfast is served in the courtyard. You'll find a bar and tour desk, but little else in the way of extras. Good value, though. 25 rooms. Credit cards: A, DC, MC, V.

El Convento Hotel   **$195–$380**   ★ ★

100 Cristo Street, Old San Juan, ☎ *(800) 468-2779, (787) 723-9020.*
FAX (787) 721-2877.
Single: $195–$380. Double: $195–$380.

Once a Carmelite convent, the El Convento reopened in November 1996 after an extensive, year-long renovation. The building, listed in the National Historic Registry, dates back 350 years; construction was authorized in 1636 by Spain's King Philip IV and it was designed and built by the Spanish Army. The hotel retains its authentic 17th-century Spanish style and is filled with original, hand-crafted vintage furnishings. Facilities include a pool, Jacuzzi, fitness center, business center, bar, small casino and garden terrace for breakfasts. Guestrooms are equipped with extras like a fax machine, VCR, robes, refrigerator and hair dryer. 57 rooms.

El San Juan Hotel/Casino   **$250–$995**   ★ ★ ★ ★ ★

Isla Verde Avenue, San Juan, ☎ *(800) 468-2818, (787) 791-1000.*
FAX (787) 263-0178.
Single: $250–$430. Double: $305–$995.

Opulence dominates at this well-known resort, one of the Caribbean's best and certainly among the most lavish. Accommodations are luxurious, with VCRs, stereos, TVs in the bathroom, minibars and modern art. Some rooms have lanais and sitting areas, while others have sunken baths, whirlpools, or private garden spas. Facilities are quite extensive, and the service is excellent. The grounds include seven restaurants ranging from the formal Dar Tiffany to casual snackbars, eight bars, a disco, a casino, and three lighted tennis courts. There's also a Chinese restaurant housed in a pavilion from the 1964 New York World's Fair. Other amenities include all watersports such as diving and waterskiing, a modern health club, and a pool for the kiddies. Staying here is an experience you won't soon forget. 390 rooms. Credit cards: A, CB, MC, V.

PUERTO RICO

Grande Hotel El Convento $85–$200 ★★

55 Condado Avenue, Cristo Street, San Juan, ☎ (800) 468-2779, (787) 721-0810. FAX (787) 725-7895.

Single: $85–$175. Double: $95–$200.

This high-rise hotel consists of two linked towers. Accommodations range from standard guestrooms to suites with kitchenettes. The modest grounds include a casino, two restaurants, a bar and two pools, one for kids. Decent for the rates, but nothing special. 150 rooms. Credit cards: A, CB, DC, D, MC, V.

Holiday Inn Crowne Plaza $185–$390 ★★★

Highway 187, San Juan, ☎ (800) 468-4578, (787) 253-2929. FAX (787) 253-0079.

Single: $185. Double: $205–$390.

Located on Isla Verde Beach, close to the airport, this high-rise is just a few years old. Accommodations are modern and comfortable, and most have sea views off the balcony. Facilities include a pretty casino, business center, gym, a pool, and two restaurants and three bars. All quite acceptable, but this hotel is so generic you'd hardly know you're in the Caribbean, and airport noise, particularly from low-flying jets, can be obnoxious. 254 rooms. Credit cards: A, CB, DC, D, MC, V.

Hotel Portal Del Condado $95–$125 ★★

76 Condado Avenue, San Juan, ☎ (787) 721-9010. FAX (787) 724-3714.

Single: $95. Double: $115–$125.

Located in Condado within walking distance of the beach, this modest hotel offers clean and comfortable rooms for reasonable rates. There's no pool, but guests can work on their tans on a rooftop deck. 48 rooms. Credit cards: A, CB, DC, D, MC, V.

Hyatt Dorado Beach $160–$490

Dorado, San Juan, ☎ (800) 233-1234, (787) 796-1234.

Single: $160–$490. Double: $160–$490.

Located on a 1000-acre estate shared with its sister property, the Hyatt Regency Cerromar, this deluxe operation aims to please—and succeeds. Superior to its sibling, it has extensive facilities, all of the highest quality. The plush accommodations are in 14 two-story buildings. Large guestrooms feature rattan furnishings, balconies or terraces, minibars, and marble baths. Cottages with two- or three-bedrooms that line the fairway. Recreational options are the best on the island, with two 18-hole golf courses designed by Robert Trent Jones, a club house, two pools (one Olympic sized), a health club with aerobics classes, eight tennis courts, a windsurfing school and a private beach with watersports. Dining options range from formal restaurants to the casual beach bar to theme night dinners; the food is high-priced, but if you can afford the rates, you probably can afford the meals, too. A shuttle bus takes you to the casino and other facilities at the Hyatt Regency Cerromar. If you're torn between the two, keep in mind that the Dorado has nicer rooms, a better beach and appeals to an older crowd, while the Cerromar has a better pool and a younger clientele (including children). 298 rooms. Credit cards: A, CB, D, MC, V.

Hyatt Regency Cerromar $165–$420 ★★★★★

Dorado, San Juan, ☎ (800) 233-1234, (787) 796-1234.

Single: $165–$420. Double: $165–$420.

Sister property to the above-mentioned Hyatt Dorado and sharing its 1000 acres, this plush resort centers around a seven-story Y-shaped hotel. Decorated in an island theme, guestrooms have minibars, spacious baths and balconies. The hotel boasts of having the world's largest pool, which comes in at 1776 feet, complete with whirlpools, a Jacuzzi grotto, a swim-up bar, 14 waterfalls, five separate swimming areas and an impressive water slide. There's also an Olympic-size pool for the more sedate crowd. Amenities include a health club, 14 tennis courts, a fine beach, supervised children's activities, all watersports, bicycle and jogging trails, and 36 holes of golf on Robert Trent Jones-designed courses. Guests can choose from four restaurants—one serving sushi, a rarity in Puerto Rico—or hop the shuttle to try the food at the Hyatt Dorado. For nightlife, try the casino disco, or several bars. Excellent all the way, though expect to see a fair amount of business travelers and families. 504 rooms. Credit cards: A, CB, D, MC, V.

Radisson Ambassador Plaza $170–$320 ★★★★

1369 Ashford Avenue, San Juan, ☎ *(800) 333-3333, (787) 721-7300. FAX (787) 723-6151.*
Single: $170–$310. Double: $180–$320.
Set in the heart of the Condado district, this glitzy hotel consists of an older hotel and an all-suite tower. Accommodations vary, but all are pleasant, though only some have ocean views. As expected, the suites offer the plushest digs and are well-suited to business travelers. Facilities include a rooftop swimming pool, business services center, health club, supervised children's programs, casino, and several restaurants and bars, one with entertainment nightly. This place has come a long way from its Howard Johnson roots. 233 rooms. Credit cards: A, CB, D, MC, V.

Radisson Normandie $160–$240 ★★★

Munoz Rivera Avenue, San Juan, ☎ *(800) 333-3333, (787) 729-2929. FAX (787) 729-3083.*
Single: $160–$200. Double: $240.
Housed in a landmark art deco building that dates back to 1940, this hotel is located on the outskirts of Old San Juan. The hotel is shaped like a ship, and the staff wears nautical garb. Guestrooms are spacious and nicely decorated with art deco touches. Rooms on the Concierge Level enjoy extra amenities. Facilities include a few bars and restaurants and a pool. There's also a small beach. 177 rooms. Credit cards: A, CB, DC, D, MC, V.

Ramada Hotel Condado $130–$300 ★★

1045 Ashford Avenue, San Juan, ☎ *(800) 468-2040, (787) 723-8000. FAX (787) 722-8230.*
Single: $130–$160. Double: $160–$300.
Located adjacent to the San Juan Convention Center and on the beach, this highrise offers adequate yet uninspired guestrooms and public areas. Facilities are limited to a bar, restaurant and pool. You can do better at these rates. 96 rooms. Credit cards: A, DC, D, MC, V.

Regency Hotel $140–$225 ★★

1005 Ashford Avenue, San Juan, ☎ *(800) 468-2823, (787) 721-0505. FAX (787) 722-2909.*

Single: $140–$225. Double: $140–$225.

This modest operation offers spacious guestrooms, studios with kitchenettes, and suites with full kitchens. All have balconies but not necessarily ocean views. Facilities are limited to a restaurant, pool and Jacuzzi. The beach is reached through an underground parking garage, an odd arrangement. Continental breakfast is included in the rates. While nothing to write home about, this hotel offers comfortable housing at a decent price. 127 rooms. Credit cards: A, CB, D, MC, V.

San Juan Travelodge $125–$175   ★★

1313 Isla Verde Avenue, San Juan, ☎ (800) 428-2028, (787) 728-1300. FAX (787) 268-0637.
Single: $125. Double: $140–$175.

Located near the airport, this budget choice offers acceptable rooms, some with balconies. You'll find a restaurant, deli and lounge on-site, as well as limited room service and a pool. 88 rooms. Credit cards: A, CB, D, MC, V.

Sands Hotel & Casino $290–$305   ★★★★★

Isla Verde Road, San Juan, ☎ (787) 791-6100. FAX (787) 791-8525.
Single: $290. Double: $305.

Situated on five acres fronting three miles of sandy beach, this luxurious property is next door to the splashier El San Juan. Accommodations are generally plush with extras like minibars and floor-to-ceiling windows. All rooms have balconies but not all have an ocean view. The extensive grounds include five restaurants, three lounges, a huge casino, daily activities, and a large free-form pool with a waterfall and swim-up bar. Nice, but the El San Juan is better, and the rates are comparable. 410 rooms. Credit cards: A, CB, DC, D, MC, V.

Wyndham Old San Juan Hotel $200–$330   ★★★

100 Brumbaugh Street, San Juan, ☎ (800) 996-3426, (787) 721-5100. FAX (787) 721-1111.
Single: $200–$330. Double: $200–$330.

Just opened in December1996, this new hotel is located on the waterfront of Old San Juan, directly opposite the cruise ship terminals. Facilities at the nine-story property include a fine dining restaurant, two lounges, a roof-top, open-air swimming pool, a health center and a large casino. Business travelers are catered to with a business center and the seventh-floor concierge level with extra amenities. Guestrooms are plush with two-line telephones with dataport access, coffeemakers, hair dryers and satellite TV. 240 rooms.

Apartments and Condominiums

Local Puerto Ricans with luxury apartments or villas often rent their homes during high season, especially those located near the Hyatt Dorado Beach resort. Condominiums in high-rise buildings are also popular for tourist rentals; even rooms in hotels that have kitchenettes can be rented. Among the latter are ESJ Towers, the Regency, and the Excelsior. Shopping is easy because supermarkets tend to boast traditional mainland products along with more Latin-flavored spices, vegetables and fruits.

Inns

Puerto Rico is famous for its network of charming country inns called *paradores puertorriqueños*. Established in 1973, the network offers superb accommodations and the ideal location for exploring the island's diverse attractions. Several privately owned and operated guest houses also serve as quiet and quaint accommodations far from the maddening crowds. What makes the *paradores* so special is they are each situated in a historic place or site of unusual scenic beauty. Prices range from $38–$96 per night, double occupancy, and *paradores* are located from mountains to sea. Most have swimming pools and all offer the island's tantalizing cuisine. Many are even within driving distance from San Juan. Perhaps one of the most special sites is that of the **Parador Baõs de Coamo**, situated on the site of America's oldest thermal springs, once believed to be Ponce de Leon's "fountain of youth." Even FDR took advantage of the medicinal waters, praised by the Indians for more than three centuries. Just a half-hour away is Ponce, the island's second largest city and home to the Caribbean's most extensive art museum.

Casa San Jose   **$205–$315**   ★★★

159 San Jose Street, Old San Juan, San Juan, ☎ (800) 223-6510, (787) 723-1212. FAX (787) 723-7620.
Single: $205–$225. Double: $245–$315.
Set in Old San Juan, this charmer is housed in a converted 17th-century mansion. Each room and suite in the four-story Spanish Colonial house is decorated differently, and all are lovely, furnished with antiques, Persian rugs, Roman tubs, exquisite artworks, and ceiling fans. Suites have one or two bedrooms and even more opulent trappings. The rates include continental breakfast, afternoon tea and evening cocktails. The interior courtyard is accented by a fountain; its pleasant trickling can be heard in every room. Marvelous! 10 rooms. Credit cards: A, DC, MC, V.

El Canario Inn   **$60–$100**   ★★

1317 Ashford Avenue, Condado, San Juan, ☎ (800) 533-2649, (787) 722-3861. FAX (787) 722-0391.
Single: $60–$100. Double: $60–$100.
This modest inn is located a block from the beach. Rooms are air-conditioned and also have ceiling fans and private baths; decor is comfortable with wicker and rattan furnishings. The staff will feed you breakfast for free, and there's a communal kitchen for self-caterers, as well as lots of eateries within walking distance. The very reasonable rates make this a real bargain. 25 rooms. Credit cards: A, CB, DC, D, MC, V.

Parador Hacienda Gripinas   **$64–$107**   ★★

6a Ocean Drive, San Juan, ☎ (800) 443-0266, (787) 721-2884. FAX (787) 889-4520.
Single: $64–$74. Double: $64–$107.
Located on a 20-acre plantation that in the 18th-century produced coffee, this small country inn in the mountains is loaded with character. Guestrooms are simple but attractive; most have ceiling fans in lieu of air conditioning. There's little in the way of recreational facilities save a pool and basketball court—a downside is that this area gets a lot of rain. The dining room serves up three tasty squares a day; Sunday brunch is especially popular. Not for those seeking a partying holiday, but perfect for relaxing and enjoying the scenery. 11 rooms. Credit cards: MC, V.

Low Cost Lodging

During low season, mid-April through December, expect to find the most expensive hotels dropping their rates down to a moderate range. Other hotels give special packages for low season. It doesn't hurt to bargain a little, just do it tactfully. The Puerto Rico Tourism Company currently recognizes 35 camping areas throughout the island, from El Yunque National Forest to Luquillo Beach and many of the public beaches around the island. Camping facilities in Puerto Rico come with a broad definition, including cottages, pup tents, huts, lean-tos and even trailer homes. Fees range from $5–$12. Don't always count on finding hot water or toilets. Be prepared to go rustic, if necessary.

Arcade Inn $40–$90   ★

8 Taft Street, San Juan, ☎ (787) 728-7524.
Single: $40–$90. Double: $50–$90.

This guesthouse is within walking distance to the beach. Rooms are modest but air-conditioned and have private baths; a few efficiencies are also available. There's a bar on the premises, but you'll have to venture out for meals. That's easily done, as there is much within an easy walk. 19 rooms. Credit cards: A, MC.

Atlantic Beach Hotel $60–$140   ★★

1 Calle Vendig, San Juan, ☎ (787) 721-6900. FAX (787) 721-6917.
Single: $60–$110. Double: $75–$140.

This modest hotel caters mostly to gays, though anyone is welcome, except for children, so check your homophobia at the door. Rooms are spartan but comfortable and air-conditioned; not all have private baths, so be sure to request one if that's important to you. The beach is footsteps away. There's no pool but the Jacuzzi offers pleasant soaking. The restaurant serves only breakfast and lunch, with lots of dinner options within walking distance. A complimentary continental breakfast is served daily on the new roof-top sundeck. 37 rooms. Credit cards: A, D, MC, V.

Green Isle Inn $43–$73   ★

Villamar Street, San Juan, ☎ (800) 677-8860, (787) 726-4330. FAX (787) 268-2415.
Single: $43–$73. Double: $43–$73.

This small hotel has basic air-conditioned rooms, many with kitchenettes. There's a bar and restaurant, and two pools. Limited room service is available. The beach is an easy walk. 44 rooms. Credit cards: A, MC, V.

International Airport $80–$90   ★★

Isla Verde, San Juan, ☎ (787) 791-1700. FAX (787) 291-4050.
Single: $80. Double: $90.

Located right in the airport, on the third floor of the terminal building, this budget choice is adequate, but unless you're between flights, there's really no reason to stay here. More atmospheric lodging can be found at similar rates. 57 rooms. Credit cards: A, CB, MC, V.

Where to Eat

Fielding's Highest Rated Restaurants in Puerto Rico

★★★★★	Horned Dorset Primavera	$45–$45
★★★★★	La Compostela	$15–$29
★★★★★	Ramiro's	$22–$33
★★★★	Amadeus	$8–$16
★★★★	La Chaumiere	$22–$37
★★★	Ajilli-Mojili	$15–$25
★★★	El Ancla	$3–$28
★★★	La Casona de Serafin	$21–$31
★★★	La Mallorquina	$14–$30
★★★	Parador Villa Parguera	$5–$20

Fielding's Most Exclusive Restaurants in Puerto Rico

★★★★★	Horned Dorset Primavera	$45–$45
★★★★	La Chaumiere	$22–$37
★★★★★	Ramiro's	$22–$33
★★★	La Casona de Serafin	$21–$31
★★★	Back Street Hong Kong	$15–$32

Fielding's Best Value Restaurants in Puerto Rico

★★★	La Bombonera	$5–$8
★★★★	Amadeus	$8–$16
★★★	Parador Villa Parguera	$5–$20
★★★★★	La Compostela	$15–$29
★★★★★	Ramiro's	$22–$33

Puerto Rican cuisine is a rich blend of Spanish, African and Taino Indian cooking. *Cocina criolla*, or creole cuisine, began with the Tainos, the island's indigenous people who cultivated *yuca* (yucca), *yautia* (*taniers*) and yams. They also made *casabe*, a flat bread still made today. Spaniards introduced wheat, chick peas, eggplant, cilantro, coconut, onions, garlic and rum, while African slaves brought pigeon peas, okra, plantains, and many coconut dishes.

Favorite appetizers include fritters, especially *tostones* (fried green plantains), *empanadillas* (deep-fried flour turnovers filled with cheese, ground meat or shredded chicken), and *rellenos de papa* (deep-fried stuffed mashed potato balls). Common side dishes are *arroz blanco* (white rice boiled in water and oil), tomato and coriander sauce and beans stewed in *sofrito* (a puree of onions, peppers, cilantro, garlic and salt pork). You can also try *mofongo*, fried green plantains mashed with salt, garlic and salt pork rinds and rolled into a ball; or *amarillos*, long, thin slices of yellow plantains sautéed in butter or olive oil.

Puerto Rico's national soup is *asopao*, a gumbo-like concoction of chicken and rice. Roast sucking pig, another national dish, is traditionally served on holidays. Fresh seafood, always in great abundance, is mostly prepared in a *sofrito*-based sauce or marinated in *escabeche*, a combination of olive oil, white vinegar and spices. The island's national dessert, flan, is a condensed milk and vanilla custard with optional ingredients such as coconut milk, masked pumpkin, breadfruit or cream cheese. And be sure to try Puerto Rican rum, considered by many to be the best in the world.

San Juan

Ajilli-Mojili $$$ ★★★

Calle Clemenceau, San Juan.
Latin American cuisine. Specialties: Mofongo.
Lunch: entrées $15–$25.
Dinner: entrées $15–$25.

This is probably one of the most popular eateries for *tipico* Puerto Rican food. A specialty is *mofongo*, fried plantain stuffed with seafood, beef or chicken (here it's usually shrimp), a dish you probably won't find outside of these isles. Although it's located in a Condado hotel, many local families make this a regular gathering spot, so the ambience is cheerful and festive. Reservations recommended. Credit cards: A, MC, V.

Al Dente $$ ★★

Calle Recinto Sur, San Juan, ☎ *(787) 723-7303.*
Italian cuisine. Specialties: Fresh pasta.
Lunch: Noon–4 p.m., entrées $10–$15.
Dinner: 4–10 p.m., entrées $10–$15. Closed: Sun.

This restaurant is a touch of old Palermo in Old San Juan. Located in a historical building in the heart of the colonial city, the dining room features fresh pasta, chicken and fish in light sauces, made with fresh herbs and spices. The atmosphere is as unstuffy as the food. Reservations recommended. Credit cards: A, MC, V.

Amadeus $$ ★ ★ ★ ★

Calle San Sebastian, San Juan, ☎ *(787) 722-8635.*
Latin American cuisine.
Lunch: Noon–5 p.m., entrées $8–$16.
Dinner: 5 p.m.–midnight, entrées $8–$16. Closed: Mon.

A name like Amadeus connotes glittering candelabra, spinets and powdered wigs. Contrary to that idea, this restaurant and cafe is as modern as can be—the clever chef adds a dash of French flair to native fare, with dishes such as the combination of caviar and sour cream with green plantain. A version of cassoulet is made here with *chorizo* and black beans. Some people could make a whole meal from a plate of some very creative appetizers that a group of four or more can share; a sort of Puerto Rican dim sum. Call in advance to reserve space in the back room. Reservations recommended. Credit cards: A, MC, V.

Anchor's Inn $$$ ★ ★

Route 987, Km. 2.7, San Juan, ☎ *(787) 863-7200.*
Latin American cuisine.
Lunch: 11 a.m.–4 p.m., entrées $8–$15.
Dinner: 4–11 p.m., entrées $15–$20.

This unpretentious spot by the sea offers a scrumptious plate of *paella* and an equally appealing vista of the Fajardo harbor. It's an ideal stopping point for people driving around the island, with a location near one of Puerto Rico's prime boating and watersports areas. If you tire of the nine restaurants at the posh El Conquistador resort nearby, give this place a try; it stays open late. Reservations recommended. Credit cards: A, MC, V.

Back Street Hong Kong $$$ ★ ★ ★

Avenida de Isla Verde, San Juan, ☎ *(787) 791-1000. Associated hotel: El San Juan Hotel/Casino.*
Chinese cuisine.
Dinner: 6 p.m.–midnight, entrées $15–$32.

This isn't your typical greasy spoon chop-suey, in fact, people like to dress up a bit to eat the savory Chinese food in a restaurant that recreates a Hong Kong back alley. The eclectic dining room was transported piecemeal from a Seattle World's Fair exhibition; it also contains a tropical aquarium that delights young children. Reservations recommended. Credit cards: A, MC, V.

Butterfly People $ ★ ★

152 Calle Fortaleza, San Juan, ☎ *(787) 723-2432.*
International cuisine.
Lunch: 10 a.m.–6 p.m., entrées $5–$9. Closed: Sun.

Notice to lepidopterists—you will be dazzled at this restaurant and gallery that sells butterflies under glass from one of the most extensive private collections in the world. While the prices for these winged beauties range from moderate to stratospheric, the mostly-Puerto Rican dishes here are fairly reasonable. You can also have a soup (gazpacho is good), or salad served in a plant-filled patio. Credit cards: A, DC, MC, V.

El Patio de Sam $$$ ★★★

102 Calle San Sebastian, San Juan, ☎ *(787) 723-1149.*
International cuisine.
Lunch: entrées $9–$25.
Dinner: entrées $9–$25.
This popular place is remarkable for serving the juiciest burgers in town in the oldest building in town. Of course, there's a well-balanced menu of lobster tail, soups, desserts and tropical fruit libations. The late-night crowd likes to party here; it stays open till the wee hours on weekends. Credit cards: A, DC, MC, V.

La Bombonera $ ★★★

Calle San Francisco, San Juan, ☎ *(787) 722-0658.*
Latin American cuisine.
Lunch: 7:30 a.m.–5 p.m., entrées $5–$8.
Dinner: 5 p.m.–8:30 p.m., entrées $5–$8.
Like its name says, this old-fashioned eatery proffers a plethora of bonbons both sweet and savory. You can have a plate of *calamares en su tinta* (squid in its own ink served with rice), while your youngster sips hot chocolate. This place serves as the corner malt shop and tryst spot for locals who have been flocking to it since 1902. It's great for breakfast, very crowded at lunch, and ideal for tea and snacks. Take-out available. Reservations recommended. Credit cards: A, MC, V.

La Casona de Serafin $$$ ★★★

Highway 102, Km. 9, San Juan, ☎ *(787) 851-0066.*
Latin American cuisine. Specialties: Lobster.
Lunch: entrées $10–$20.
Dinner: entrées $21–$31.
Some people think the best seafood in Puerto Rico is served in this area of Joyuda Beach. Certainly the atmosphere at La Casona is great for eating peel-it-yourself shrimp or its specialty, lobster. Steaks and Puerto Rican dishes are also available, and there's a full bar and lounge. This restaurant is popular with local families who flock here on weekends, when the sleepy town wakes up to a noisy string of craft shops and oyster bars along the beach. Reservations recommended. Credit cards: A, MC, V.

La Chaumiere $$$ ★★★★

367 Tetuan Street, San Juan, ☎ *(787) 722-3330.*
French cuisine.
Dinner: 6 p.m.–midnight, entrées $22–$37. Closed: Sun.
This restaurant serves classic French cuisine to a faithful clientele in surroundings that transport guests to the Gallic countryside. It's the kind of place where you can order rarely found specialties like floating island (merengues in a sauce of creme anglaise) or oysters Rockefeller. Perfect for a pre-show supper; the restaurant is located behind the famous Tapia Theater. Reservations recommended. Credit cards: A, DC, MC, V.

La Compostela $$$ ★★★★★

Avenida Condado, San Juan, ☎ *(787) 724-6088.*

Spanish cuisine.
Lunch: Noon–3 p.m., entrées $15–$29.
Dinner: 6:30–10:30 p.m., entrées $15–$29. Closed: Sun.

Many repeat visitors recommend this Spanish restaurant with a French touch in a commercial suburb of San Juan. The owner has spent time laboring in the kitchens in both countries; he blends the styles effortlessly. The wine cellar is amazing—close to 10,000 bottles! Reservations recommended. Credit cards: A, DC, MC, V.

La Mallorquina   **$$$**   ★★★

Calle San Justo 207, San Juan, ☎ *(787) 722-3261.*
Latin American cuisine.
Lunch: 11:30 a.m.–3 p.m., entrées $14–$30.
Dinner: 4–10 p.m., entrées $14–$30. Closed: Sun.

This restaurant may be a bit of a tourist trap, but it's still worth visiting for the house special *asopao*, the Puerto Rican version of risotto, served with a choice of seafood or chicken. One of the oldest restaurants in town, La Mallorquina was founded in 1848. Service is gracious and attentive. Credit cards: A, DC, MC, V.

Parador Villa Parguera   **$$**   ★★★

Route 307, San Juan, ☎ *(787) 899-7777. Associated hotel: Parador Villa Parguera.*
Latin American cuisine. Specialties: Red snapper stuffed with seafood.
Lunch: 7:30 a.m.–4 p.m., entrées $5–$20.
Dinner: 4–9:30 p.m., entrées $5–$20.

Simply prepared but very fresh seafood is a specialty at this seaside inn (one of the island's touted *paradores*) surrounded by coconut palms on Phosphorescent Bay, on the West Coast. The Parador is an excellent base for viewing the local phenomenon—on moonlit nights, the bay is "lit" by thousands of tiny organisms called dinoflagellates. Come during the week, as hordes of families crowd the area on weekends. Reservations recommended. Credit cards: A, CB, DC, D, MC, V.

Ramiro's   **$$$**   ★★★★★

Avenida Magdalena 1106, San Juan, ☎ *(787) 721-9049.*
Spanish cuisine. Specialties: Lamb, homemade desserts.
Lunch: Noon–3 p.m., entrées $24–$33.
Dinner: 6:30–10:30 p.m., prix fixe $22–$33. Closed: Mon.

Patrons dress up to dine at this plush salon of *cocina fantastica*; owner Jesus Ramiro may be the island's most creative chef. Although he uses local produce and ingredients, his technique is distinctly French, especially in the elaborate constructions of his sinful desserts. Lamb is one of his favorite meats, on the menu you will find it in ravioli or paired with buffalo or venison in a spicy sauce, or a perfectly roasted rack. Reservations recommended. Credit cards: A, DC, MC, V.

The Chart House   **$$$**   ★★

1214 Ashford Avenue, San Juan, ☎ *(787) 728-0110.*
American cuisine. Specialties: Prime rib, mud pie.
Dinner: 6–11 p.m., entrées $16–$25.

If the food here seems familiar to mainland guests, it is. The Chart House is a local link in the California-based steak-and-lobster chain, but what a link! The setting is in a historic turn-of-the-century homestead, which belonged to the Rauschenplat family. The property is surrounded by well-tended gardens and a treehouse. The all-

American food is very popular with locals as well. Reservations required. Credit cards: A, DC, MC, V.

Where to Shop

Though Puerto Rico is not a free port, good deals can be found on items such as china, jewelry, and crystal because shopkeepers are quite competitive—be sure to shop around before making a major purchase, and remember, you won't have to pay duty upon entering the U.S. mainland. The island has lots of U.S.-style malls with ubiquitous chain stores; the largest (in the entire Caribbean, in fact) is the upscale 200-store Plaza las Americas, located south of San Juan in the Hato Rey district, just off the Las Americas Expressway.

Locally made crafts are always a good buy, especially the small, hand-craved figurines of saints called *santos*. Carnival masks made from *papier-maché* (in Ponce) or coconut husks (in Loirz, near San Juan) also make good mementos, as do hand-rolled cigars, needlework, ceramics, rum, and paintings by local artisans. Good crafts shops include **Ole**, *San Juan,* ☎ *(787) 724-2445,* and **Puerto Rican arts & Crafts**, *Old San Juan,* ☎ *(787) 725-5596.*

The Northwest Coast

Dorado

Dorado, about 20 miles from San Juan off Route 693, is the closest town to the Hyatt Regency Cerromar Beach and the Hyatt Dorado Beach hotels. (If you're cruising the area, these are two fine resorts to plunk yourself down for a lunch or a drink.) The town has remained stuck in time despite the construction of the hotels. A few distracting hours can be whiled away at the shopping center and the handful of arts and crafts stores on the main streets. If you are staying at the resorts, a limousine will be sent to pick you up at San Juan's International Airport, about a 45-minute drive. The hotels also use a small airstrip a few minutes away from their front doors.

There are numerous mountain treks that can be taken in this area, especially through the **Parque de las Cavernas del Rio Camuy**, a 268-acre reserve featuring caves with an amazing array of stalactites and stalagmites. (For more information, see the section called "Treks" above.) The **Arecibo Observatory** also makes a fascinating excursion. (For more information see "What Else to See on the Island," above.) Excursions from Dorado can easily be made to see the historic center of Old San Juan (45 minutes by car), as well as day trips down the southern coast at La Parguera and Cabo Rojo.

Where to Stay

The **Hyatt Dorado** is a no-holds-barred resort set on lushly landscaped grounds that caters to families as well as conventioneers. That might mean you forsake a bit of honeymoon-type privacy for the all-inclusive touch that makes some vacationers feel at home and others overwhelmed. The **Hyatt Regency Cerromar Beach** is a bit less tropical, ensconced in a tall high-rise, with an absolutely spectacular pool that includes a waterfall, hydro-massage and other diversions.

Hotels and Resorts

Days Inn   **$80–$140**   ★★

Route 1, Northwest Coast, ☎ *(800) 325-2525, (787) 841-1000. FAX (787) 841-2560. Single: $80. Double: $90–$140.*

Located near the Intra-American University, this budget choice offers typical Days Inn accommodations and facilities. Rooms are on the basic side, but provide modern conveniences like TV and air conditioning. The amenities include a pool, Jacuzzi, restaurant, nightclub and a game room. 121 rooms. Credit cards: A, CB, DC, D, MC, V.

Parador El Guajataca   **$77–$95**   ★★

Route 2, Quebradjlas, Northwest Coast, ☎ *(800) 964-3065, (787) 895-3070. FAX (787) 895-3589.*

Single: $77–$83. Double: $83–$95.

Set on a bluff overlooking the beach, this small hotel offers many resort amenities at an unbeatable price. Accommodations are comfortable and modern. Guests can enjoy the nice beach, play tennis on two courts, or swim in the Olympic-size pool. The restaurant serves creole cuisine, and there's entertainment in the bar on weekends. 38 rooms. Credit cards: A, CB, DC, D, MC.

Inns

Puerto Rico is famous for its network of charming country inns called *paradores puetorriqueños*, which offer superb accommodations and the ideal location for exploring the island's diverse attractions. Several privately owned and operated guest houses also serve as quiet and quaint accommodations far from the madding crowds. What makes the *paradores* so special is they are each situated in a historic place or site of unusual scenic beauty. Prices range from $38–$96 per night, double occupancy, and *paradores* are located from mountains to sea. Most have swimming pools and all offer the island's tantalizing cuisine. Many are even within driving distance from San Juan.

Parador Vistamar $60–$75 ★★

Highway 113, Northwest Coast, ☎ *(800) 443-0266, (787) 895-2065. FAX (787) 895-2294.*

Single: $60–$75. Double: $60–$75.

Fine views of the sea from this hilltop inn, which offers air-conditioned rooms that are comfortable but on the plain side. You'll find a large pool, Jacuzzi, tennis court, and game room, as well as a few dining outlets and three bars, one with music and dancing on the weekends. 55 rooms. Credit cards: A, CB, D, MC, V.

Low Cost Lodging

Ask the Tourist Board about the possibility of renting rooms in the houses of local families. Do note that you may not find standards of cleanliness at the level to which you are accustomed.

Where to Eat

The best international cuisine is found at the two Hyatt resorts, where you can be assured of cleanliness and safety. True Puerto Rican delicacies, with a Spanish twist, can be found at **Los Naborias**. You will probably run into a strong local family scene at **La Famillia**, a warm, inviting, if simple place, particularly lively on Sundays.

East and Southeast Coast

Fajardo and Humacao

Full of small-town spirit, the seaport of Fajardo lies but five miles south of Las Cabezas on Route 3. The lifestyle is slower-paced than in San Juan, and you can take morning and afternoon ferries to Culebra and Vieques. Treks can be made to the **Caribbean National Forest**, of which El Yunque Mountain is a part (see "Treks" above) and Losquillo Beach. Special expeditions can be arranged through **Las Cabezas Nature Reserve** (see "Trek" above) which could last all day, especially if you are interested in bird-watching. Native sloops set sail for **Iacos** where you will find fine snorkeling and swimming conditions. Deep-sea fishing and other watersports can be arranged at the **Puerto del Rey Marina**. The region has a fine 18-hole golf course and myriads of opportunities for scuba (see "Dive Sites" above.) Also see "Sports" above for more information.

This part of the island can be reached by rental car or taxis (expensive from the international airport), by small planes that land at the airport of Palmas del Mar, near Humacao; or by ferry boat (the cheapest at $2.50).

Where to Stay

Two hotels/resorts command the region with their enormous facilities. The patron saint of resorts, **El Conquistador**, has an amazing 16 restaurants and lounges—if you want to avoid the conventioneer crush, you should probably stay elsewhere. **Candelero**, near the beach at Palmas in the south, is more intimate, and less demanding socially, with activities geared for the athletic, including fine horseback riding, golf, tennis and artistic performances. You also will find several Puerto Rican *paradores*, intimate inns that reflect the congeniality of the owner/host, as well as numerous cheaper guest houses.

Hotels and Resorts

El Conquistador Resort   **$170–$420**   ★★★★★
Las Crobas, East and Southeast Coast, ☎ *(800) 468-8365, (787) 863-1000.*
FAX (787) 253-4387.
Single: $170–$420. Double: $170–$420.
This is the mega-resort of mega-resorts, a huge enclave perched atop a cliff, overlooking the Caribbean on one side and the Atlantic on the other. The complex consists of five hotels, each a self-contained unit. Guestrooms are quite spiffy, with three phones, two TVs, VCRs, stereos, and refrigerators. Other room choices include 88 suites and 176 *casitas* with more room and special amenities. The resort's 500 acres include a casino, six pools, eight tennis courts, pro shops, a health spa, 16

restaurants and bars, and watersports. There's also an 18-hole golf course, with another one on the drawing board. It's easy to see that the owners plucked down a cool $250 million to create this resort, which just opened in 1993. Among the gee-whiz attractions is an extensive art collection, a private island where you can spend the day, a 55-slip marina, and tons of shops. Despite its sheer size, service is efficient and cheerful. 926 rooms. Credit cards: A, CB, D, MC, V.

Palmas del Mar Humacao $145–$715   ★★★★

Palmas del Mar, East and Southeast Coast, ☎ *(800) 468-3331, (787) 852-6000. FAX (787) 852-6320.*
Single: $145–$715. Double: $145–$715.
This resort community, still under development in some sections, encompasses 2750 acres and fronts three miles of beach. Guests have a number of lodging options. The 100-room Candelero Hotel has spacious rooms with high ceilings and tropical decor, and offers the most affordable accommodations. The Palmas Inn has 23 suites with large living rooms, combination baths with bidets, and opulent furnishings. You can also book a two- or three-bedroom villa complete with kitchen. The grounds include an equestrian center (Warning: we have received complaints about both the condition of the horses and the facility), casino, marina, watersports, seven pools, 20 tennis courts (six lighted), 18 holes of golf, a fitness center with exercise classes, and supervised children's programs year-round. Dining outlets include a formal French restaurant, a casual Oriental eatery, and lots more. There's nightly entertainment at the Candelero. A free shuttle takes you to and from the action. Inquire about golf and tennis packages that can save you bucks. Note: Readers have alerted us to the fact that the villas are less than desirable and that overall, service is indifferent at best. 298 rooms. Credit cards: A, MC, V.

Westin Rio Mar Beach Resort $205–$475   ★★★

Luquillo & Rio Grande, ☎ *(800) 474-6627, (787) 888-6000. FAX (787) 888-6600.*
Single: $205–$475. Double: $205–$475.
Just opened in the summer of 1996, this resort marks Westin's first foray into the Caribbean. The property is situated on 481 acres of land in the municipalities of Luquillo and Rio Grande on a one-mile beach on the island's northeast coast. Guestrooms come in six categories, all feature private balconies or patios, cable TV and minibars. The concierge level added amenities on the seventh floor. Facilities include 12 restaurants and lounges, a casino, 36 holes of golf, a 35,000-square-foot clubhouse, 13 tennis courts and a tennis clubhouse, a fitness center and spa, business center, and watersports. 600 rooms. Credit cards: A, CB, DC, MC, V.

Apartments and Condominiums

Accommodations with fully equipped kitchens are available in any range of luxury, from the bareback simple near the seashore to the more luxurious privately owned condos rented in the owner's absence, usually during high season.

Inns

Paradores, or small inns, are for the more adventurous-minded who like to take chances on quality and ambiance. The best are true gems, and usually come complete with a very congenial host.

Parador La Familia   **$50–$70**   ★

Route 987, East and Southeast Coast, ☎ *(800) 443-0266, (787) 869-5345.*
Single: $50–$61. Double: $61–$70.
Located near Las Cabezas de San Juan Nature Preserve, this guesthouse is three
miles from town; you'll definitely want a car for mobility. Rooms are basic but air-
conditioned and comfortable. You'll find a good restaurant and pool on the premises. 28 rooms. Credit cards: A, D, MC, V.

Parador Martorell   **$50–$85**   ★

Ocean Drive 6-A, East and Southeast Coast, ☎ *(800) 443-0266, (787) 889-2710.*
Single: $50–$85. Double: $70–$85.
This small family-run inn is located in Puerto Rico's northeast section. Rooms are
small but comfortable; three share a bath and rely on ceiling fans to keep cool. The
other seven have private baths and air conditioning, well worth the small bump in
rates. A restaurant and pool are located on-site, and the beach is just two minutes
away. 10 rooms. Credit cards: A, MC.

Where to Eat

The best cuisine is found at the resorts; with so many facilities at **El Conquistador**, you may never have to leave the premises (that's their goal). Snacks
can be found beachside (a cheap way to get through lunch on your way to a
more expensive dinner). The best Italian food (if the most expensive) is at
the **Azzuro** at the Palamas Mar Marriott hotel.

East and Southeast Coast

The South Coast

Ponce

Located about 70 miles south and west of San Juan, Ponce is Puerto Rico's second-largest city. Ponce dates back to 1692 when Ponce de Léon's great-grandson founded the small community. Today, a high-speed road connects Ponce and San Juan, which takes only about 90 minutes to traverse; you can also reach the area by plane from San Juan's International Airport. The historical buildings, such as the stunning Cathedral of Our Lady of Guadeloupe, are masterpieces of construction, as are some 1000 colonial houses that have been designated national historic sites in a 40-by-80-block area. Nineteenth-century gas lamps illuminate the marble-edged streets with a pink glow; at night the stroll is extremely romantic. A fine collection of Latin American artists and international masters can be found in the **Museu de Arte de Ponce**, a light, airy place to stroll and relax out of the sun. Particularly fine are the works by Rubens and Rodin as well as many pre-Raphaelite paintings and sculptures. Anyone interested in sugarcane production and plantations will find an interesting exhibit at the **Castillo Serralles**, a restored 19th-century mansion, which has been refurbished to its 1930s furnishings. On Route 10, you'll discover the **Hacienda Buena Vista**, a restored coffee plantation which is open to visitors. (For more information, see under "What Else to See on the Island" above.)

Trekkers should head straightaway to the **Toro State Forest**, a 7000-acre preserve with waterfalls, the island's tallest peak, and an observation tour. (For more information, see under "Treks" above).

BEST VIEW:

A terrific perspective of the surrounding countryside and town of Ponce can be seen from the 100-foot-tall El Vigia, an observatory tower, next to Castillo Serrallés.

What Else to See

Historical Sites

Hacienda Buena Vista ★★★

> Route 10, Ponce, ☎ *(787) 848-7020.*
> From 1833 to the 1950s, this thriving plantation produced corn, citrus fruits and coffee. Today, under the auspices of Puerto Rico's Conservation Trust, it is a reconstructed farm that illustrates life during the late 19th century. Reservations are required for 1.5-hour tours, which are conducted Friday through Sunday; call ☎ *(787) 722-5882.* The grounds include the estate house, former slave quarters, a 60-foot water slide, and working corn and coffee mills. General admission: $5.

Tibes Indian Ceremonial Center ★★★

Route 503, Ponce, ☎ *(787) 840-2255.*
Hours open: 9 a.m.–4:30 p.m.
This is the oldest cemetery in the Antilles, with some 200 skeletons unearthed from A.D. 300 and ballcourts and dance grounds from A.D. 700. The site also includes a recreated Taino village and a museum. General admission: $2.

Museums and Exhibits

El Museo Castillo Serralles ★★★

El Virgia 17, Ponce, ☎ *(787) 259-1774.*
Hours open: 10 a.m.–5 p.m.
This Spanish-Revival mansion, Ponce's largest building, dates back to the 1930s. It is the former home of the Serralles family, producers of Don Q rum. Today it is a museum exhibiting elegant furnishings, the history of the local rum industry and a cafe. The lavishly landscaped grounds are a treat, and the views are breathtaking. General admission: $3.

Museo de Arte de Ponce ★★

Ave. las Americas 25, Ponce, ☎ *(787) 848-0505.*
Designed by Edward Durell Stone, this fanciful museum exhibits traditional and modern art from the Americas and Europe, as well as contemporary works by Puerto Ricans. General admission: $3.

Ponce History Museum ★★★

Calle Isabel, Ponce, ☎ *(787) 844-7071.*
Hours open: 10 a.m.–5 p.m.
The name says it all: the history of Ponce detailed in two wooden houses dating back to the turn of the century. Closed Tuesday. General admission: $3.

Parks and Gardens

Cabezas de San Juan Nature Reserve ★★★

Route 987, Fajardo, ☎ *(787) 722-5882.*
Located on a peninsula, this nature reserve encompasses 316 acres of dry land and 124 acres of lagoons. It contains all of Puerto Rico's ecosystems except for the rainforest. A two-hour guided tour (reservations essential) will take you through a half-mile-long coral reef, mangrove swamps, beaches, a dry forest, and beds of turtle grass (*thalassia*). A highlight is El Faro, a lighthouse built in 1880 and still used by the U.S. Coast Guard. The small nature center in the lighthouse, which is a designated National Historic Place, has touch tanks, aquariums, and an observation deck. Bilingual tours are at 9:30, 10, 10:30 a.m.; the one at 2 p.m. is in English only. Well worth a visit. General admission: $5.

Where to Stay

On the south shore of Ponce, the Hilton is making waves among southern resorts, but it's high-rise modernity takes a bit away from the tropical feel. It does have, however, an extensive watersports program and can make arrangements for treks and other local excursions. Other hotels in the middle of town give you easy access to the historic part of the city, especially at night when Ponce is most atmospheric.

Hotels and Resorts

Copamarina Beach Resort $135–$155   ★★★

Road No. 333, Cana Groda, Guanica, ☎ (800) 981-4676, (787) 821-0505.
FAX (787) 821-0070.
Single: $135–$155. Double: $135–$155.

This resort, which dates to the late 1950s, just added 50 rooms and a second swimming pool in 1996. Located 20 minutes south of Ponce, it includes a mile-long beach tennis courts, two cafes—also renovated in '96—a dive shop, and the offshore "Gilligan's Island," a mangrove cay perfect for picnics or snorkeling. Inquire about dive packages. Nearby is Guanica Dry Forest, the largest region of tropical dry coastal forest in the world. 120 rooms.

Melia Hotel $70–$90   ★★

2 Cristina Street, South Coast, ☎ (800) 742-4276, (787) 842-0260.
FAX (787) 841-3602.
Single: $70–$80. Double: $75–$90.

This hotel in the historic district is pretty historic itself, as it dates back to 1914. The Spanish-colonial building includes interesting touches such as antiques and old chandeliers. Guestrooms are small and the furnishings are not antiques, just old. There's a decent restaurant on-site, but no other extras. Not a top choice by any means, but those who like historic hotels will be satisfied. Light sleeps should request a room in the back, as street noise can be loud. Note that this hotel is not affiliated with the upscale Melia chain. 77 rooms. Credit cards: A, MC, V.

Parador Boquemar $65–$70   ★

Route 101, Cabo Rojo, South Coast, ☎ (800) 443-0266, (787) 851-2158.
FAX (787) 851-7600.
Single: $65–$70. Double: $65–$70.

This three-story hotel is near the beach. All the guestrooms, which are quite basic, have air conditioning, but some share baths. There's a restaurant and bar on-site, as well as a pool. 63 rooms. Credit cards: A, CB, DC, MC, V.

Parador Villa Parguera $80–$90   ★

Route 304, Lajas, South Coast, ☎ (800) 443-0266, (787) 899-3975.
FAX (787) 899-6040.
Single: $80–$90. Double: $80–$90.

Located near the beach on the southwestern shore, this *parador* offers rooms in an older guest house and in more modern wings, all with air conditioning, private baths, and balconies or patios. A restaurant and nightclub are located on the premises. The pool is filled with saltwater. 63 rooms. Credit cards: A, CB, DC, D, MC, V.

Ponce Hilton and Casino $170–$375   ★★★

P.R. 14 Avenue, Santiado de los Caballeros, South Coast, ☎ (800) 445-8667, (787) 259-7676. FAX (787) 259-7674.
Single: $170–$190. Double: $190–$375.

By far the area's nicest hotel, this Hilton sits on 80 acres of beachfront. Accommodations are stylish, with high-quality furniture, minibars, bidets, and balconies or patios. Nice public spaces and lots of recreational facilities, including a large lagoon-style pool, Jacuzzi, four tennis courts, gym, game room, and watersports on the private beach. Amenities include five restaurants, several watering holes and a casino. This well-run property does a lot of business with the meetings and convention markets. 153 rooms. Credit cards: A, CB, DC, D, MC, V.

Ponce Holiday Inn   **$97–$145**   ★★

Highway 2, South Coast, ☎ *(800) 465-4329, (787) 844-1200. FAX (787) 841-8683. Single: $97–$120. Double: $99–$145.*

Perched on a hillside one mile from the ocean, this commercial hotel has wonderful views of the surrounding area. Guestrooms are comfortable and pleasant; all have balconies with nice views. For an extra charge, you can request a refrigerator. There's nightly entertainment in the lounge, as well as a disco, game room, pool and restaurant. You can count on the reliability that comes with a Holiday Inn, but you won't be writing home about it. Good especially for business travelers. 119 rooms. Credit cards: A, CB, DC, D, MC, V.

Inns

Some of the nicest paradores, or government-sponsored inns, are located in this area; the **Parador Baõs de Coamo** is famous for its hot springs, and its most celebrated guest, Franklin Delano Roosevelt, who came here to be healed. Many locals flock to the spring even today—the waters are reputed to cure many illnesses. Find a map of the panoramic route of this area; many of the *paradores* make good stops for atmospheric lunch or dinner.

Parador Baños de Coamo   **$55–$65**   ★★

Route 546, South Coast, ☎ *(787) 825-2239. FAX (787) 825-4739. Single: $55. Double: $65.*

Situated on the south coast on plains at the base of the mountains, this guest house dates back to 1847 and was once visited by Franklin Roosevelt. Guests can soak in natural hot springs that are said to be the most radioactive in the world—a dubious claim to fame. Guestrooms are large and comfortable, though minimally furnished. Besides the hot springs, you'll enjoy swimming pool and a tennis court. 48 rooms. Credit cards: A, CB, DC, D, MC, V.

Parador Posada Porlamar   **$45–$90**   ★

La Parguera Road, South Coast, ☎ *(800) 443-0266, (787) 899-4015. FAX (787) 899-6082. Single: $45. Double: $60–$90.*

This modest inn is located in the heart of this picturesque fishing village. Rooms are simple but comfortable and air-conditioned; all have private baths. There's no restaurant on-site, but guests have free use of a common kitchen, or they can walk to nearby eateries. No pool, either. 18 rooms. Credit cards: A, MC, V.

Where to Eat

The Hilton has fine dining facilities, and you can always be assured of safe cooking techniques. Seafood is a specialty along the south coast. As you head west, along Route 2, you'll run across several possibilities.

El Ancla $$$ ★★★

9 Hostos Avenue, South Coast, ☎ *(787) 840-2450.*
Seafood cuisine.
Lunch: 11 a.m.–4 p.m., entrées $3–$28.
Dinner: 4 p.m.–midnight, entrées $3–$28.
This established family-owned restaurant is perched over the water in Ponce Beach.
Long been popular with Poncenos and visitors, the welcome is always warm. That's
probably what sets it apart from other restaurants serving seafood, which is the spe-
cialty of this eatery. Enjoy red snapper stuffed with lobster and shrimp served on a
plate heaped with plenty of starchy side dishes. Credit cards: A, DC, MC, V.

Lupita's Mexican $$$ ★★

Calle Isabel 60, South Coast, ☎ *(787) 848-8808.*
Mexican cuisine.
Lunch: 11 a.m.–4 p.m., entrées $7–$26.
Dinner: 4–11 p.m., entrées $7–$26.
The better-than-average Mexican fare served here is blended with local specialties—
lobster is grilled and served with green plantain, but you can also have tacos and
nachos. Mariachis provide entertainment several times a week. Lupita's is located in
a historic building near Plaza las Delicias, Ponce's main square, and stays open until
2 a.m. on Saturdays and until midnight on Sundays. Reservations required. Credit
cards: A, DC, MC, V.

The South Coast

The West Coast

Mayagüez

Mayagüez is the island's third-largest town, located about 10 miles from Rincón on Route 2. Baroque and Victorian buildings make this pretty, bustling port even more charming. Mayagüez is the launching pad for treks into the western and southwestern interior; routes into the mountains lead to some spectacular climbs (see "Treks") and can be easily reached by car. Long a center of fine needlepoint, intrepid shoppers can still find some wonderful samples of fine island artistry in some of the older shops downtown. The island's only zoo is located behind the University of Puerto Rico's campus. The city itself is centered around the impressive Spanish-style **Plaza Colón**, a tribute to Christopher Columbus, whose statue stands in the middle of the square. The **Cathédrale de la Virgen de la Candelaria** is also a fine structure, dating back four centuries.

About 50 miles off the coast west of Mayagüez, stands Mona Island, a rugged, uninhabited island whose only residents are large colonies of seabirds and enormous iguanas. The stunning cliffs make excellent photo ops; years ago it was said the cliffs held the booty of pirates who combed these waters. Rustic adventurers can find perfect places for camping overlooking the sea. Permission to visit must be granted by the tourist office. Twenty miles south of Mayagüez is **Boqueón Beach**, a stunning mile-long beach that boasts *balneario* facilities and excellent low prices for lodging. The small cottages are owned by the government and must be applied for four months in advance through the **Recreation and Sports Department**, *Box 2923, San Juan, PR 00903;* ☎ *(787) 722-1551.* Avoid weekends when local families with noisy teenagers carrying boom boxes disrupt the peacefulness of the area. Excellent seafood restaurants can be found a bit farther north at **Joyuda Beach**. Along Route 301 can be found the **Cabo Rojo Wildlife Refuge** (see "Treks"). If you would like a guide, check at the visitor's desk, where you can also get maps and individual assistance. At the southwesternmost top of the island, the best place to watch sunsets is at the **Cabo Rojo Lighthouse** at El Faro. The lighthouse is not open to the public, but the promontory overlooking red cliffs and ocean make for a spectacular lookout.

What Else to See

Puerto Rico Zoological Gardens   ★★★

Route 108, Mayagüez, ☎ *(787) 834-8110.*
Hours open: 9 a.m.–5 p.m.
Check out the birds and beasts—500 in all—at this tropical zoo spread over 45 acres. General admission: $1.

Where to Stay

Hotels and Resorts

Holiday Inn Mayagüez   **$120–$240**   ★★

2701 Highway 2, West Coast, ☎ *(800) 465-4329, (787) 833-1100. FAX (787) 833-1300.*

Single: $120–$130. Double: $130–$240.

The beach is eight miles away from this typical Holiday Inn. Guestrooms fit the standard HI formula, which means clean, comfortable, air-conditioned, and on the bland side. One nice touch is a signal alert system for the hearing impaired. The hotel has a restaurant, lounge with live music, gym, sauna, and pool. Not exactly bursting with local flavor, but a safe choice. 152 rooms. Credit cards: A, D, MC.

Horned Dorset Primavera   **$150–$440**   ★★★★★

Route 429, West Coast, ☎ *(787) 823-4030. FAX (787) 823-5580.*

Single: $150–$245. Double: $325–$440.

The name may be odd, but everything else is nearly perfect at this small and exclusive enclave. Guests are housed in plush suites with Persian rugs, armoires, four-poster beds, sitting areas, furnished balconies, and large baths. Few facilities are found on-site, as the idea is to rest, relax and be pampered by the excellent staff. You'll find a pool and library, but that's about it. The grounds are exquisitely landscaped and open onto the sea, but there's really no beach to speak of. Dinner is a memorable affair with six courses nightly. No kids under 12 permitted. 30 rooms. Credit cards: A, MC, V.

Mayagüez Hilton   **$135–$180**   ★★

Route 104, West Coast, ☎ *(800) 445-8667, (787) 831-7575. FAX (787) 834-3475.*

Single: $135–$170. Double: $155–$180.

Set on 20 landscaped acres overlooking the harbor, this Hilton has a country club feel. Rooms are very comfortable and nicely furnished with all the amenities expected from Hilton. The grounds include a casino, nightclub, Olympic-size pool, three tennis courts, and a putting green. Children's activities are scheduled during high season. Very nice, but as the beach is 20 minutes away, this hotel caters mainly to a business clientele. 141 rooms. Credit cards: A, MC.

Inns

The *paradores* system offers several choices on the west coast, but be warned that there is no real standard of quality and there may be big differences in service and surroundings. **Parador Hacienda Gripinas** is perhaps one of the most natural, replete with the sounds of nature. The **Parador Villa Antonio** tends to caters to the older; younger travelers might enjoy the **Parador Perichi** more. Businessmen tend to tuck in at the **El Sol**.

Parador Oasis   **$107–$107**   ★★

72 Luna Street, West Coast, ☎ *(800) 223-9815, (787) 892-1175. FAX (787) 892-1175.*

Single: $107. Double: $107.

This Spanish-style mansion dates back to 1896and is located three blocks from the Inter-American University. Rooms are in the mansion (the least desirable ones, in fact) and a newer annex; all are air-conditioned and most are comfortable, though on the basic side. Facilities include a pool in a pretty courtyard, gym, sauna, restaurant, and bar. 53 rooms. Credit cards: A, CB, D, MC, V.

Where to Eat

Horned Dorset Primavera $$$ ★ ★ ★ ★ ★

Route 429, Km. 3, West Coast, ☎ *(787) 823-4030. Associated hotel: Horned Dorset Primavera.*
Seafood cuisine.
Lunch: Noon– 2:30 p.m., entrées $15–$25.
Dinner: 7–9 p.m., prix fixe $45.

This plush, white-washed hotel/restaurant stands quite alone in its glory in a frontier location catering to surfers and day-trippers. That isn't to say the area isn't sublimely beautiful; it is. Many visitors make a special trip to eat here; it's quiet, it's right on the beach and the $40 fixed-price, six-course dinner is served with great ceremony. Although named after a breed of English sheep, seafood is this restaurant's specialty. Location is six miles northwest of Mayagüez. Lunch hours vary, call for information. Reservations recommended. Credit cards: A, MC, V.

San Germán

About 25 miles beyond the Cabo Rojo Lighthouse is San Germán, the island's second-oldest city.

It takes about three hours to drive from San Juan, and one hour from Mayagüez. The colonial atmosphere still pervades, despite the presence of a new highway; small-town customs still linger. A stroll around the town should reveal fine architecture including shops with gingerbread trim and turrets. The **Porta Coeli** Cathedral is considered to be the New World's oldest, dating back to 1606. Today the old church houses a fine museum with impressive sacred and secular art that dates back even a hundred years earlier than the building itself. The restoration of the former monastery and church is a model of perfection, and the cathedral is considered one of the island's finest possessions.

The West Coast

Puerto Rico's Islands

Culebra

Culebra is one of several islands located off the east coast between Puerto Rico and the U.S. Virgin Islands, and it is a haven rich in natural resources but not yet developed for tourism. The five-mile-long island of Culebra is actually an archipelago of one main island and 20 surrounding cays. Most of the cays are part of the Culebra National Wildlife Refuge, which offers fine opportunities for bird-watching. More than 86 bird species are represented, including several nearly extinct ones. Four endangered sea turtles—green, loggerhead, hawksbill and leatherback—are also protected. From April to July, the ecological organization Earthwatch sends teams of volunteers to the island for scientific studies, particularly along the beaches of Resaca and Brava.

Local families run watersports businesses here, and boats can be chartered for a day-sailing around the islands. Windsurfing and limited deep-sea fishing can also be arranged from Dewey, the island's sole community. There are also excellent snorkeling sites here, especially at Punta Molines and Punta del Soldado.

To get to Culebra, you have two options. Ferryboats sail from Fajardo, which takes about one hour (the fee is extremely cheap). Getting to Fajardo, though, will tax your wallet, as taxi drivers charge exorbitant amounts for the ride. A small plane can be taken from Isla Grande airport aboard Flamenco Airways (though other local airlines also fly). The landing on the tiny strip can cause fibrillation, so it's best just to shut your eyes and keep breathing.

Where to Stay

Accommodations in this region run toward the simple, unpretentious and cheap.

Hotels and Resorts

Club Seabourne   **$95–$105**   ★★

Culebra Island, ☎ *(787) 742-3169. FAX (787) 742-3176.*
Single: $95–$105. Double: $95–$105.
Overlooking Fullodosa Bay, this small complex consists of air-conditioned rooms, villas and cottages, with refrigerators in the larger accommodations. One large cottage has two bedrooms and a full kitchen. Morning coffee and juice is on the house. The grounds include a pool, bar and restaurant that is closed on Mondays. 10 rooms. Credit cards: A, MC, V.

Apartments and Condominiums

Several options are available for self-catering, the best being the **Culebra Island Villas**, situated near enough to sea to make sports activities a cinch. Six people can pile into one of two houses that make up the **Harbor View Villas**, a perfect option for a small group of friends or a family who want to do their own thing.

| **Harbour View Villas** | **$50–$95** | ★★ |

Culebra Island, off the coast of Fajardo, ☎ *(787) 742-3855.*
Single: $50–$75. Double: $75–$95.

This small enclave of villas is on the island of Culebra, reached via a 10-minute ferry ride from Fajardo. The town and beach are a quarter-mile stroll. All units are air-conditioned, have kitchens for do-it-yourselfers, and sleep up to six. French doors open onto large balconies overlooking the town and the Vieques Sound. You'll want a car to get around, as there's not much on-site. 8 rooms. Credit cards: MC, V.

Low Cost Lodging

You get what you pay for, and anything cheap in this region tends to run toward the dilapidated and unclean. An exception is the **Coral Island Guest House,** which is mostly used by divers.

Vieques

Vieques is larger and a bit more cosmopolitan than Culebra, though the difference may be negligible. The port, **Isabel Segunda**, holds the distinction of having the last fort built by the Spaniards in the New World. Indian settlements date back to 200 B.C. Two-thirds of the present land of Vieques is used by the U.S. Navy, some for military maneuvers, and some for the grazing of livestock. Some of the greatest primitive, unspoiled beaches are located on Navy land, which you can enter when there are no military maneuvers taking place. A fine beach is Sun Bay, which has bathing facilities and camping grounds. From Esperanza, you can make a nightly visit on a boat to the nearby bioluminescent bay, which is more spectacular than the better-known Phosphorescent Bay near La Parguera. With three protected sites called "hurricane holes," diving options can be arranged, along with other watersports, including windsurfing, at **Vieques Divers** at Esperanza. Certification courses are also available. There are also opportunities for horseback riding.

As a shopping hub, Isabel Segunda is best described as lethargic until tourists arrive on the ferry. Taxis and rental cars (Suzuki are best), available though local agencies, are the way to get around the island. To get to the island, you can either take a small plane from San Juan's Isla Grande airport, or a ferry boat from Fajardo—a two-hour sojourn. (As mentioned above, getting to Fajardo is the difficulty here, since taxi rides from San Juan and its airports can be enormously expensive.)

Where to Stay

Don't expect any fancy resort here; most accommodations run the gamut from simple to simpler. The most atmospheric is **La Casa del Frances**, a restored Victorian house that gives off the ambience of a country inn.

Hotels and Resorts

Villa Esperanza $65–$101   ★★★

Calle Flamboyan, Vieques.
Single: $65–$101. Double: $65–$101.
Most rooms at this beachfront hotel have air conditioning, but five do not, so be sure to ask. Located on the site of a former sugar mill, this hotel offers basic rooms in a villa complex. The grounds include a good deal of recreation for the rates, with a pool, two tennis courts, watersports, volleyball, and nine holes of miniature golf. Visit the restaurant or the two bars. 25 rooms. Credit cards: A, MC.

Inns

La Casa del Frances $96–$175   ★★★

P.O. Box 458, Vieques, ☎ *(787) 741-3751.*
Doubles: $96–$175.
This sprawling Victorian mansion on a hill above Esperanza oozes with ambience.

Sea Gate Guest House $40–$85   ★★

Vieques Island, Vieques, ☎ *(787) 741-4661.*
Single: $40–$85. Double: $45–$85.
This small property is up on a hill overlooking the harbor town of Isabel Segunda and the sea beyond. Most rooms are efficiencies with kitchenettes. There's a very small pool on the premises, or the friendly owners will take you to the beach and arrange watersports. 17 rooms. Credit cards: not accepted.

Where to Eat

Fresh seafood is the way to go on this island. Anything else is probably shipped in. The best local cooking can be found at **Cerromar** in Puerto Real; you can tell it's good because most of the locals congregate there and you can enjoy watching how they interact. A plate of land crabs at the **Cayo Blanco** in Isabella Segunda is considered a must-do. In Esperanza, most of the local traffic ends up at the casual, laid-back **La Central Café**—ask anybody where it is.

Puerto Rico Directory

Arrival and Departure

There are three airports in Puerto Rico, all undergoing extensive and expensive renovation. The **Luis Muñoz Marin** in San Juan is the major hub for international travel. Since 1988 **American Airlines** has spent $260 million tripling the size of its San Juan hub, including the reservation center. The Mercedita Airport is located in Ponce, and the Rafael Hernandez is in Aguadilla. Major airlines including **American**, **Delta**, **TWA**, **Tower**, **United** and **USAir** fly into San

Juan from most major U.S. cities. **Carnival Airlines** operates service to Aguadilla and Ponce from New York and Newark. American has made San Juan its hub for all flights from Puerto Rico to other Caribbean destinations, the U.S., Europe and Latin America. American Airlines also operates nonstop service from Miami and New York's JFK to Aguadilla and from Miami to Ponce. International carriers include **British Airways**, **Iberia** and **Lufthansa**. **Continental Airlines** will begin nonstop service to San Juan. Starting December 15, the airline will offer three flights a day from Newark, NJ. Packages start at $468 per person for four days including air fare and hotel accommodations.

The airport departure tax is included in the price of the airline ticket.

Business Hours

Shops open 9 a.m.–6 p.m. Banks open weekdays 8:30 a.m.–2:30 p.m. and Saturday 9:45 a.m.–noon.

Climate

Coastal weather in Puerto Rico is warm and sunny year-round. During the summer, temperatures average in the mid 80s Fahrenheit; during the winter, they hover in the low 70s to the low 80s. The rainiest months are May to December, generally heavier on the north than the south coast. Temperatures in the mountains tend to be 5–10 degrees cooler.

Documents

Since Puerto Rico is a commonwealth of the United States, no passports are required for U.S. citizens. Visitors do need a valid driver's license to rent a car. If you are a citizen of any other country, a visa is required. Vaccinations are not necessary. U.S. citizens do not need to clear customs or immigration (other citizens do). On departure, luggage must be inspected by the U.S. Agriculture Department, as law prohibits the taking of certain fruits and plants in the U.S. Dogs and cats may be brought to Puerto Rico from the U.S. with two documents: a health certificate dated not more than 10 days prior to departure showing that the animal is certified disease-free by an official or registered veterinarian, and a certificate of rabies vaccination, dated not more than 30 days prior to departure, authenticated by the proper authorities.

Electricity

Current runs A.C. 60 cycles, 100 volts, single phase or 220 volts, three phase.

Getting Around

Taxis, buses and rental cars are available at the airport and major hotels. All taxicabs are metered, but they may be rented unmetered for an hourly rate. There's an additional charge of 50 cents for every suitcase. *Publicos* (public cars) run on frequent schedules to all island towns (usually during daytime hours) and depart from main squares. They run on fixed rates. The *Ruta Panoramica* is a scenic road meandering across the island that offers stunning vistas.

San Juan is the largest home-based cruise port in the world. Twenty-eight vessels use San Juan as their home port and each year new cruise ships either originate or call at the port.

Ferries shuttle passengers to and from Culebra and Vieques at reasonable rates. Car transport is also available. San Juan's harbor can also be crossed by the Catana ferry (50 cents) to the Bacardi Rum plant's free tours.

Language

Spanish and English are both official languages of Puerto Rico. Many speak English—and many people don't, especially older people in outlying rural areas. In San Juan however, English is taught from kindergarten to high school as part of the school curriculum.

Medical Emergencies

Officially, the medical community of Puerto Rico meets the same standards as those required on the U.S. mainland. Most physicians on the island are based in San Juan with almost all medical specializations represented. San Juan has 14 hospitals, most districts have at least one. Ask your hotel to recommend a physician on call.

Money

The official currency is the U.S. dollar and credit cards are widely accepted by hotels, restaurants and shops. Several foreign exchange offices are available in San Juan and at the airport.

Telephone

The area code is *787*. Postage stamps are equivalent to those in the U.S. as are mail costs. You can dial direct to the mainland.

Time

Atlantic Standard Time, year-round, which is one hour earlier than New York. During Daylight Saving Time, it is the same.

Tipping and Taxes

All hotels include a six percent government tax on the bill. Gratuities on restaurant bills are not included, but a usual 15 percent tip is expected.

Tourist Information

For more information about the island, contact the **Puerto Rico Tourism Company**, *La Princesa Building, Old San Juan, PR 00901;* ☎ *(787) 721-2400.* There are offices in New York, Los Angeles, Coral Gables, London, Madrid, Mexico City, Milan, Paris, Stockholm, Toronto and Weisbaden, Germany. In the U.S. ☎ *(213) 874-5991.*

When to Go

January–May the Puerto Rico Symphony Orchestra conducts its season with performances through May. January 6 is traditional gift-giving day in Puerto Rico, celebrated by island-wide festivals with music, dance, parades, puppet shows and caroling troubadours. January 1–19 is the International Folklore Festival, featuring dance groups from around the world. February (usually 3rd weekend) is the Coffee Harvest Festival. Carnival usually happens the second week in February. The Sugar Harvest Festival takes place in May. The Festival Casals takes place in early June, honoring the late cellist. San Juan Bautista Day is June 23, celebrating the island's patron saint, as sanjuaneros walk backward into the sea three times at midnight for good luck. The Albonito Flower Festival takes place in July. The Barranquitas Artisans Fair is held July 16–18, the island's oldest crafts fair with 130 local artisans. The 42nd International Billfish Tournament takes place in September. The Inter-American Festival of the Arts takes place in September. The National Plantain Festival occurs in late October. The baseball season begins in October. The Festival of Typical Dishes lasts from November-December. Old San Juan's White Christmas Festival takes place December-January. Island-wide Christmas festivities with life-size nativity scenes are held December–January. The Bacardi Arts Festival featuring more than 200 craftsmen is in December. Lighting of the Town of Bethlehem occurs for three days in mid-December.

In general, spring is always a good time to visit San Juan. Old San Juan is less crowded with cruise ship day trippers than during the winter, hotels rates begin to drop, and many hotels offer inexpensive summer packages to lure visitors during the slowest months. Puerto Rico doesn't have extreme seasonal changes so you may see that quintessential Christmas flower, the poinsettia blooming and mangoes ripening in the same gardens. San Juan shuts down for much of Holy Week, but there are Easter celebrations. An annual sunrise Easter service is usually held at **El Morro**. For more information call Rev. Martha McCracken ☎ *(787) 722-5372.*

PUERTO RICO HOTELS		RMS	RATES	PHONE	CR. CARDS
Fajardo					
★★	Club Seabourne	10	$95–$105	(809) 742-3169	A, MC, V
★★	Harbour View Villas	8	$50–$95	(809) 742-3855	MC, V
San Juan					
★★★★★	El San Juan Hotel/Casino	390	$250–$995	(800) 468-2818	A, CB, MC, V
★★★★★	Hyatt Dorado Beach	298	$160–$490	(800) 233-1234	A, CB, D, MC, V
★★★★★	Hyatt Regency Cerromar	504	$165–$420	(800) 233-1234	A, CB, D, MC, V
★★★★★	Sands Hotel & Casino	410	$290–$305	(809) 791-6100	A, CB, D, DC, MC, V
★★★★	Caribe Hilton & Casino	670	$200–$1200	(800) 468-8585	A, CB, D, MC, V
★★★★	Condado Plaza Hotel	575	$195–$355	(800) 468-8588	A, CB, D, MC, V
★★★★	Radisson Ambassador Plaza	233	$170–$320	(800) 333-3333	A, CB, D, MC, V
★★★	Best Western Pierre	184	$97–$145	(800) 528-1234	A, CB, D, DC, MC, V
★★★	Casa San Jose	10	$205–$315	(800) 223-6510	A, DC, MC, V
★★★	Condado Beach Trio	481	$140–$195	(800) 468-2775	A, CB, D, DC, MC, V

PUERTO RICO HOTELS		RMS	RATES	PHONE	CR. CARDS
★★★	Copamarina Beach Resort	120	$135–$155	(800) 981-4676	
★★★	Holiday Inn Crowne Plaza	254	$185–$390	(800) 468-4578	A, CB, D, DC, MC, V
★★★	Radisson Normandie	177	$160–$240	(800) 333-3333	A, CB, D, DC, MC, V
★★★	Westin Rio Mar Beach Resort	600	$205–$475	(800) 474-6627	A, CB, DC, MC, V
★★★	Wyndham Old San Juan Hotel	240	$200–$330	(800) 996-3426	
★★	Atlantic Beach Hotel	37	$60–$140	(809) 721-6900	A, D, MC, V
★★	Carib Inn Tennis Club	225	$105–$320	(800) 548-8217	A, CB, D, DC, MC, V
★★	El Canario Inn	25	$60–$100	(800) 533-2649	A, CB, D, DC, MC, V
★★	El Canario by the Lagoon	40	$65–$110	(800) 533-2649	A, D, MC, V
★★	El Convento Hotel	57	$195–$380	(800) 468-2779	
★★	Grande Hotel El Convento	150	$85–$200	(800) 468-2779	A, CB, D, DC, MC, V
★★	Hotel Portal Del Condado	48	$95–$125	(809) 721-9010	A, CB, D, DC, MC, V
★★	International Airport	57	$80–$90	(809) 791-1700	A, CB, MC, V
★★	Parador Hacienda Gripinas	11	$64–$107	(800) 443-0266	MC, V
★★	Ramada Hotel Condado	96	$130–$300	(800) 468-2040	A, D, DC, MC, V
★★	Regency Hotel	127	$140–$225	(800) 468-2823	A, CB, D, MC, V
★★	San Juan Travelodge	88	$125–$175	(800) 428-2028	A, CB, D, MC, V
★	Arcade Inn	19	$40–$90	(809) 728-7524	A, MC
★	El Canario by the Sea	25	$60–$99	(800) 533-2649	A, DC, MC, V
★	Green Isle Inn	44	$43–$73	(800) 677-8860	A, MC, V

South Coast

		RMS	RATES	PHONE	CR. CARDS
★★★★★	El Conquistador Resort	926	$170–$420	(800) 468-8365	A, CB, D, MC, V
★★★★	Palmas del Mar Humacao	298	$145–$715	(800) 468-3331	A, MC, V
★★★	Ponce Hilton and Casino	153	$170–$375	(800) 445-8667	A, CB, D, DC, MC, V
★★	Melia Hotel	77	$70–$90	(800) 742-4276	A, MC, V
★★	Parador Banos de Coamo	48	$55–$65	(809) 825-2239	A, CB, D, DC, MC, V

PUERTO RICO HOTELS	RMS	RATES	PHONE	CR. CARDS
★★ Ponce Holiday Inn	119	$97–$145	(800) 465-4329	A, CB, D, DC, MC, V
★ Parador Boquemar	63	$65–$70	(800) 443-0266	A, CB, DC, MC, V
★ Parador La Familia	28	$50–$70	(800) 443-0266	A, D, MC, V
★ Parador Martorell	10	$50–$85	(800) 443-0266	A, MC
★ Parador Posada Porlamar	18	$45–$90	(800) 443-0266	A, MC, V
★ Parador Villa Parguera	63	$80–$90	(800) 443-0266	A, CB, D, DC, MC, V

West Coast

	RMS	RATES	PHONE	CR. CARDS
★★★★★ Horned Dorset Primavera	30	$150–$440	(809) 823-4030	A, MC, V
★★★ Mayagüez Hilton	141	$135–$180	(800) 445-8667	A, MC
★★ Days Inn	121	$80–$140	(800) 325-2525	A, CB, D, DC, MC, V
★★ Holiday Inn Mayagüez	152	$120–$240	(800) 465-4329	A, D, MC
★★ Parador El Guajataca	38	$77–$95	(800) 964-3065	A, CB, D, DC, MC
★★ Parador Oasis	53	$107–$107	(800) 223-9815	A, CB, D, MC, V
★★ Parador Vistamar	55	$60–$75	(800) 443-0266	A, CB, D, MC, V

Vieques

	RMS	RATES	PHONE	CR. CARDS
★★★ Villa Esperanza	25	$65–$101		A, MC
★★ Sea Gate Guest House	17	$40–$85	(809) 741-4661	None

PUERTO RICO RESTAURANTS	PHONE	ENTRÉE	CR. CARDS

San Juan

American			
★★ The Chart House	(809) 728-0110	$16–$25	A, DC, MC, V
Chinese			
★★★ Back Street Hong Kong	(809) 791-1000	$15–$32	A, MC, V
French			
★★★★ La Chaumiere	(809) 722-3330	$22–$37	A, DC, MC, V
International			
★★★ El Patio de Sam	(809) 723-1149	$9–$25	A, DC, MC, V
★★ Butterfly People	(809) 723-2432	$5–$9	A, DC, MC, V

PUERTO RICO RESTAURANTS	PHONE	ENTRÉE	CR. CARDS
Italian			
★★ **Al Dente**	(809) 723-7303	$10–$15	A, MC, V
Latin American			
★★★★ **Amadeus**	(809) 722-8635	$8–$16	A, MC, V
★★★ **Ajilli-Mojili**		$15–$25	A, MC, V
★★★ **La Bombonera**	(809) 722-0658	$5–$8	A, MC, V
★★★ **La Casona de Serafin**	(809) 851-0066	$10–$31	A, MC, V
★★★ **La Mallorquina**	(809) 722-3261	$14–$30	A, DC, MC, V
★★★ **Parador Villa Parguera**	(809) 899-7777	$5–$20	A, CB, D, DC, MC, V
★★ **Anchor's Inn**	(809) 863-7200	$8–$20	A, MC, V
Spanish			
★★★★★ **La Compostela**	(809) 724-6088	$15–$29	A, DC, MC, V
★★★★★ **Ramiro's**	(809) 721-9049	$24–$33	A, DC, MC, V

South Coast

	PHONE	ENTRÉE	CR. CARDS
Mexican			
★★ **Lupita's Mexican**	(809) 848-8808	$7–$26	A, DC, MC, V
Seafood			
★★★ **El Ancla**	(809) 840-2450	$3–$28	A, DC, MC, V

West Coast

	PHONE	ENTRÉE	CR. CARDS
Seafood			
★★★★★ **Horned Dorset Primavera**	(809) 823-4030	$15–$45	A, MC, V

SABA

SABA

Saba is lush with tropical vegetation and has 26 dive sites.

An island many have never even heard of, much less are sure of how to pronounce (it's SAY-bah), tiny Saba is called the "unspoiled queen" of the Caribbean, and the description fits. The island totals just five square miles and has only 1200 citizens. You won't find much in the way of shopping, and even less nightlife, but if you're really yearning to leave the nine-to-five world behind and experience something completely different, take a close look at Saba.

Located 28 miles south of Saint Martin/Saint Maarten, Saba is literally an extinct volcano that juts up from the sea. There are no beaches on the island, so it's best suited to hikers—everything is a climb—and divers. Saba boasts just four small villages—Hell's Gate, Windwardside, St. Johns and the Bottom—each clinging precariously to the mountainside. Save a few shops and restaurants, their attractions are few—Saba is not the place to come if you have trouble amusing yourself.

The diving here is excellent, with lava tunnels, hot springs and sheer walls that plunge down some 1000 feet. Among the coral gardens and teeming fish life, you'll also spot dramatic submerged "sea-mounts," pinnacles rising from the ocean floor that thrive with coral and sea life. The Saba Marine Park was established in 1987 and encompasses all the waters around the island to a depth of 200 feet, keeping the area pristine. As park literature points out, the Marine Park "was not set up in an attempt to help repair a damaged environment. It is a timely effort to safeguard the quality of an extraordinary resource." The park also includes a four-person recompression chamber, pretty impressive for such a small island.

The above-water terrain beckons hikers with its rocky cliffs and carved steps that rise all the way to the top of the appropriately named Mount Scenery, 2864 feet above sea level, where a dense rainforest awaits exploration.

Less than 25,000 tourists come yearly, a fraction of the amount that jams onto St. Thomas or St. Martin, and most of these are day-trippers. That lack of a sophisticated tourist base is a large part of Saba's charm.

Most of the houses on Saba are painted white with red roofs and green shutters.

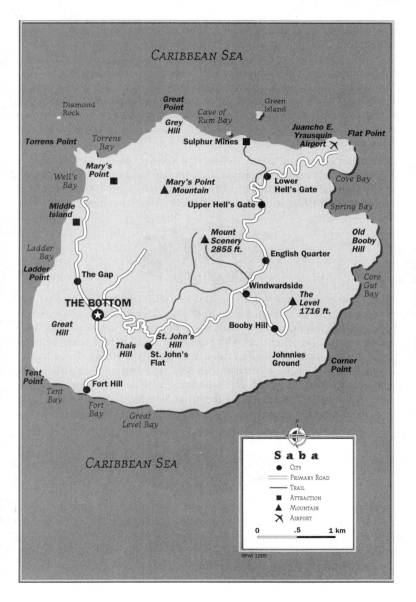

CARIBBEAN SEA

Diamond
Rock

**Great
Point**

Cave of
Rum Bay

Green
Island

**Grey
Hill**

**Juancho E.
Yrausquin
Airport**

Flat Point

Torrens Point

*Torrens
Bay*

Sulphur Mines

**Mary's
Point**

*Well's
Bay*

**Mary's Point
▲ Mountain**

**Lower
Hell's Gate**

Cove Bay

**Middle
Island**

Upper Hell's Gate

Spring Bay

*Ladder
Bay*

**Mount
▲ Scenery
2855 ft.**

**Old
Booby
Hill**

**Ladder
Point**

The Gap

English Quarter

*Core
Gut
Bay*

THE BOTTOM
☆

Windwardside

**The
▲ Level
1716 ft.**

**Great
Hill**

Booby Hill

**Thais
Hill**

**St. John's
Hill**

**St. John's
Flat**

**Johnnies
Ground**

**Corner
Point**

**Tent
Point**

*Tent
Bay*

Fort Hill

*Fort
Bay*

*Great
Level Bay*

CARIBBEAN SEA

N

S a b a

● CITY
═══ PRIMARY ROAD
─── TRAIL
■ ATTRACTION
▲ MOUNTAIN
✕ AIRPORT

0   .5   1 km

©RWI 1995

SABA

A five-square-mile island in the northeastern Caribbean, Saba is part of the three islands (St. Maarten and St. Eustatius are the other two) that form the Windward Islands of the Dutch Caribbean. Daytime temperatures average 80 degrees Fahrenheit, and steady breezes help keep mosquitoes at bay. Of the four villages, the capital is the Bottom, which is actually located halfway up the mountain. Windwardside, a lovely little town of red roofs and white clapboard walls, is the base of most tourist facilities. The rainforest atop 2864-foot Mount Scenery thrives with tree ferns, banana trees, elephant ear philodendrons, wild orchids and palm and mahogany trees. Birders can look out for some 60 species; other wildlife is limited to the occasional lizard or iguana. Annual rainfall is just 42 inches.

The island's one road, build in 1943, is somewhat of a modern-day marvel, as previous engineers had deemed such construction impossible on Saba's rugged, vertical terrain. Saba did not get an airport until 1963 and a deep-water pier until 1972, so tourism is relatively new to the island.

History

Columbus sighted the volcanic island in 1493, but it took another 129 years for some unlucky Englishman to shipwreck against the rocky coast. In 1665, the English privateer Thomas Morgan captured the island and threw out the original Dutch settlers. Morgan's men stayed behind when he left, a fact that some locals use to claim their ancestors were pirates. Some historians purport that Saba's original British settlers were actually Scottish refugees or exiles from the British civil wars in the 17th century. Until a pier was constructed in 1972, ships had to anchor in Fort Bay, where wooden long-boats would transfer people and products to shore in a very wet ride.

People

With just 1200 souls calling Saba home, everyone knows everyone and all seem to get along quite well. About half the population is black, descended from slaves who toiled on small farms and toted things up and down the mountain. The whites are descendants of Dutch, Scottish and English settlers. An interesting piece of trivia: Nearly half the island's residents—regardless of race—have the surname Hassell. Everyone speaks English, though the official language is Dutch.

Those not involved with tourism make their living farming, fishing, seafaring or working at the Medical School, which opened in 1993. As you can imagine, islanders lead a casual lifestyle and visitors can get away with shorts and a tee shirt nearly everywhere, but keep in mind that bathing suits are not appropriate in the villages.

Saba is an autonomous part of the Kingdom of the Netherlands and is self-governing. Crime is virtually unheard of—as the tourist board says, it's "limited to excessive partying or minor traffic violations."

Saba has only one fat sandy beach, accessible only by a hilly walk or a drive guaranteed to cause fibrillation. If you want to swim, it's best done in a hotel pool—Queens Gardens, Captain's Quarters, Willard's of Saba, Juliana's, Scout's Place (small) and Cranston's Antique Inn.

It's no longer news that tiny Saba has emerged as one of the Caribbean's top dive locations. Part of the popularity is its unique underwater layout, which mirrors the above-water topography: sheer. Additionally, the island was one of the first in the Caribbean—close on the heels of eco-sensitive Bonaire—to aggressively protect its marine environment through the use of permanent mooring buoys; the **Saba Marine Park** is currently the only self-supporting underwater reserve in the world. The increasing awareness of Saba's undersea paradise has ballooned the number of divers but, although the island is minute and dives are concentrated into a small area, you'll never feel crowded and the diving is still pristine. Saba remains a somewhat exotic destination, even by Caribbean standards, and the total number of divers visiting the island in 1994 was a mere 5165 (averaging five dives apiece).

The diving is centered off the island's west coast. Black sand covers the sea floor, keeping silt to a minimum and visibility sterling (approaching 125 feet in winter), while dramatic walls and substantial fish and coral life contribute to the vivid underwater environment. With the bottom dropping to more than 1000 feet as close as a half-mile from shore, the diving is serious. It's also a little more expensive here, but above-water costs tend to balance out the difference; there is also a $2-per-dive fee to help support the Marine Park (you'll save money by booking a dive package). Almost all of the island's 27 primary dive sites are within 10 minutes of the boat dock at Fort Bay, and permanent mooring buoys protect the reefs below. In winter, a north swell will sometimes make snorkeling a little rocky, but a dynamic underwater trail featuring an alley through the rocks is available at **Torren's Point**; a moderate swim will take snorkelers from **Well's Bay** to the Torren's trail. Weather permitting, **Cove Bay**, near the airport, can also be a good location for snorkeling from shore. Saba has the only recompression chamber in this section of the Caribbean.

Divers find coral gardens and fascinating sea life around Saba.

On Foot

Visitors are tempted to call Saba quaint—that is, until they climb the stair steps leading up **Mount Scenery**, the island's 2855-foot summit. On second thought, any hiker who spends a few moments observing Saba's sheer outline from an approaching plane or a neighboring island should know what they're getting into: the vacation equivalent of a stairmaster. Trails are discussed not in terms of mileage, but in number of steps (1064 to the top of Mount Scenery, the trailhead sign announces). Nonetheless, this is a walker's island, with a detailed lattice of paths snaking between the villages and peaks. Prior to 1943 when Saba's first (and only) road went into use, transportation was strictly on donkey or foot. But with the import of cars and construction of the airport in 1963, the trails fell into disrepair. In recent years, the tracks have found new fans among the more active tourists drawn to the island and the government now promotes hiking eagerly. A guide is not necessary for anyone reasonably fit, but the verdant valleys offer a diverse ecosystem and trekkers will appreciate the assistance of a knowledgeable guide. Some trails cross private property; stay on the established paths. Stop by the tourist office to pick up a pamphlet outlining island hikes or the walking tour of Windwardside, one of the most charming villages in the region.

What Else to See

As previously noted, no one comes to Saba to take in the sights; besides natural beauty, there are virtually none. The **Saba Museum** is well worth a gander, especially on the first Sunday of each month, when croquet matches draw lots of locals, all clad in white (tourists should do the same). If you're interested in vintage structures, head for the Bottom, where you'll spot the **Wesleyan Holiness Church**, which dates to 1919. Day trips via ferry to nearby St. Barts and St. Maarten are good for shopping and touristy attractions.

Museums and Exhibits

Saba Museum   ★★★

Behind the Captain's Quarters, Windwardside.
This small museum is found in the 19th-century home of a sea captain. It exhibits antiques from that era and pre-Columbian artifacts found around the island. Croquet matches are held the first Sunday of each month, a good chance to meet and greet the locals. Wear all white for that outing. General admission: $1.

Tours

Mount Scenery   ★★★★

Mt. Scenery.
Pack a picnic lunch, catch your breath, then head up the 1064 steps that lead up 2855 feet to the top of Mount Scenery. Along the way you'll pass through gorgeous scenery, six ecosystems, all kinds of interesting flora and fauna (signs tell you what's what), and, the higher you climb, cooler temperatures. The summit has a mahogany grove and incredible views.

Sports

Watersports and hiking are just about the only sporting activities to be had on Saba, though there is one tennis court in the Bottom at Sunny Valley Youth Centre, where visitors are welcome. Willard's of Saba also has one count, though it's reserved for guests.

Saba has three dive shops, all offering instruction, resort courses, certification programs, rentals and excursions: **Saba Deep Diving Center**, *Fort Bay*, ☎ *(599) 4-63347*, **Sea Saba Dive Center**, *Windwardside*, ☎ *(599) 4-62246*, and **Wilson's Dive Shop**, *Fort Bay,* ☎ *(599) 4-62541*. Expect to pay about $45 for a single-tank dive and $60 for a night-dive. There is also a $2 per-dive fee for use of the Marine Park. The park boasts a four-person decompression chamber, impressive for such a small island.

Snorkeling is good around the island, especially along the Edward S. Arnold Snorkel Trail in the Marine Park. The trail encompasses tunnels, caves, alleys and a wall; a waterproof guide with descriptions of 11 sites you'll pass is available at dive shops and at the Marine Park office in Fort Bay

Trekkers can scale 2864-foot Mount Scenery on several trails with varied difficulty levels. Perhaps the easiest (relatively speaking) is scaling the 1064 steps to the top.

Watersports

Various locations, The Bottom.

Scuba diving is very good in Saba, which is dedicated to preserving its underwater treasures. The Saba Marine Park circles the entire island and has various zoned sections, including five re-creating dive sites, where you'll see towering pinnacles, colorful coral and sponges, and tons of sea creatures. The Harbor Office ☎ *(599) 4-63295* in Fort Bay provides literature and offers occasional slide shows. The Marine Park also includes Saba's only harbor and its only beach, a tiny stretch of sand only existing in the late spring and summer, submerged by the tides in winter. The park charges $2 per person per dive, in addition to the fees charged by dive centers.

Where to Stay

	Fielding's Highest Rated Hotel in Saba	
★★★	Captain's Quarters	$85–$130

	Fielding's Most Exclusive Hotels in Saba	
★★★	Captain's Quarters	$85–$130
★	Scout's Place	$40–$105

	Fielding's Best Value Hotels in Saba	
★★★	Captain's Quarters	$85–$130
★★	Juliana's	$65–$130
★	Cranston's Antique Inn	$40–$75
★	Scout's Place	$40–$105

Saba's handful of lodging choices virtually all resemble charming inns. All offer money-saving dive packages, so be sure to inquire if that's the purpose of your Saba vacation. The new Queen's Garden Resort, set in lush gardens overlooking The Bottom, has 12 luxury apartments with all the latest amenities, adding an upscale touch to this decidedly casual island. Divers may want to look into booking through **Dive Saba Travel**, ☎ *(800) 883-SABA or* ☎ *(713) 467-8835*, which offers personalized dive charters and hotel-dive packages.

Hotels and Resorts

Juliana's	$65–$130	★★

Windwardside, The Bottom, ☎ *(599) 4-62389. FAX (599) 4-62389.*
Single: $65. Double: $80–$130.

Guests can choose from a variety of accommodations at this small property. There are standard guestrooms, an apartment with a kitchenette, and a nearly 90-year-old cottage with two bedrooms, a kitchen and a porch. All are quite decent, and the daily fresh flowers are a nice touch. The rec room has a TV, VCR, games and books for whiling away the hours. You also find a pool and restaurant. 10 rooms. Credit cards: A, MC, V.

Apartments and Condominiums

Cottage rentals are a steal—$200–$300 per week—compared to prices on other islands in the Caribbean. The charming, small, wooden Saban variety will make you feel all tucked in and cozy. The tourist office will have more complete listings.

Inns

Captain's Quarters   **$85–$130**   ★★★

Windwardside, The Bottom, ☎ *(599) 4-62377. FAX (599) 4-62377.*
Single: $85–$100. Double: $100–$130.
This charming inn is Saba's best bet—not that there are a lot of choices, but this place would get high marks anywhere. Set high on a hill with spectacular ocean views, this inn centers around an old wooden home, built by a sea captain in 1832. Four rooms are in this house, the rest in a newer wing. All are spacious and bright and have private baths; some also boast antique four-poster beds. The grounds are nicely landscaped with citrus trees and tropical blooms. The site includes a library, swimming pool and a very good restaurant. Divine! 10 rooms. Credit cards: A, D, MC.

Cranston's Antique Inn   **$40–$75**   ★

The Bottom, The Bottom, ☎ *(599) 4-63203. FAX (599) 4-63469.*
Single: $40–$60. Double: $63–$75.
This former government guest house dates back to 1830. Only one room has a private bath, but all have antiques and four-poster beds. Some of the decor borders on the tacky and the whole place could use a re-do. There's a pool and decent dining room on the premises, and the open-air bar is a locals' favorite. Ladder Bay is within walking distance. 6 rooms. Credit cards: A.

Scout's Place   **$40–$105**   ★

Windwardside, The Bottom, ☎ *(599) 4-62388. FAX (599) 4-62388.*
Single: $40–$105. Double: $60–$105.
Great views from this casual inn, located some 1300 feet above the sea. Unless you're really into roughing it (or saving some bucks), reserve one of the newer rooms, which have private baths and hot water. (The original rooms have neither.) There's also an apartment with kitchenette that sleeps five. Known locally for its very good food, this spot also has a small pool and a bar. 15 rooms. Credit cards: A, MC.

Low Cost Lodging

Rooms in private homes might be secured if you come in person and ask about. Cottages listed above, especially packed with several people, can be quite reasonable.

Where to Eat

	Fielding's Best Value Restaurants in Saba	
★★	**Tea House**	$2–$7
★★	**Tropics Cafe**	$4–$10
★★	**Guido's**	$4–$10
★★	**Corner Deli**	$4–$10
★★	**Saba Chinese Restaurant**	$13–$19

Don't plan on finding gourmet food on Saba; dining is generally as low-key as the rest of the island. **Brigadoon** is probably your best bet for upscale dining. **Scout's Place** is a favorite with locals and visitors who come for the good American and local dishes such as fresh seafood and stewed mutton. **Lollipop**'s specializes in local cuisine such as goat meat, spicy fishcakes and stuffed land crab. Be sure to try Saba spice—a powerful spiced rum drink that really packs a punch.

Brigadoon $$$ ★★

Windwardside, The Bottom, ☎ *(599) 4-62380.*
International cuisine. Specialties: Saba fish pot, lobster, peanut chicken.
Dinner: Entrées $14–$17.
One of the newer eating establishments on the island, Brigadoon is developing a reputation for innovative seafood cuisine. Grilled fish with tomato sauce or a spicy local bouillabaisse are standouts. Plenty of chicken and beef dishes are available, all served with fresh vegetables. Lighter fare is also featured. Reservations recommended. Credit cards: A, DC, MC, V.

Captain's Quarters $$$ ★★

Windwardside, The Bottom, ☎ *(590) 4-62201. Associated hotel: Captain's Quarters.*
International cuisine. Specialties: Grouper, lobster bisque.
Lunch: Noon–2 p.m., entrées $13–$22.
Dinner: 6:30–9 p.m., entrées $13–$22.
Guests dine comfortably in this pretty outdoor terrace restaurant on the grounds of the historical Captain's Quarters hotel. Greenery and fruit trees provide shade. If you're staying here it's a nice spot for breakfast, but most non-guests come for lunch or hearty dinners. The menu changes often, but the chef is known for her way with lobster. Credit cards: MC, V.

Corner Deli $ ★★

Windwardside, The Bottom.
American cuisine.
Dinner: 2–6 p.m., entrées $4–$10. Closed: Sun.

Homesick New Yorkers and others can pick up a thick sandwich on homemade bread at this deli-market owned by a seasoned restaurateur. Specialty coffees, pastries, and desserts can be sampled here or packaged for takeout. Stop by for picnic fixings on the way to Mount Scenery. Credit cards: A, MC, V.

Guido's   **$**   ★★

Windwardside, The Bottom.
Italian cuisine. Specialties: Pizza.
Dinner: Entrées $4–$10.

Yes, there is nightlife on Saba, contrary to the rumors. It's here at Guido's, which masquerades as a burger and pizza joint during the week and dons a few sequins as Mountain High Club and Disco on Saturday evenings. The food is okay, but it's better for pool or darts and informal socializing. Credit cards: A, MC, V.

Lollipop's   **$$$**   ★★

The Bottom, ☎ *(599) 4-63330.*
Seafood cuisine. Specialties: Stuffed crab.
Lunch: Entrées $10–$15.
Dinner: prix fixe $26.

Lollipop, or Carmen Hassell (everyone in town is either a Hassell or a Johnson) offers free pickup to and from her outdoor eatery—and you're in good hands, because she moonlights as a cab driver. Located in the suburb of St. John's, above The Bottom, the dining area is on a patio with a view, and the food is basically West Indian—curries, fish cakes, seafood, and goat. Reservations recommended. Credit cards: not accepted.

Saba Chinese Restaurant   **$$$**   ★★

Windwardside, The Bottom, ☎ *(599) 4-62268.*
Chinese cuisine. Specialties: Conch chop suey, lobster cantonese.
Lunch: 11 a.m.–4 p.m., Entrées $13–$19.
Dinner: 4 p.m.–midnight, Entrées $13–$19. Closed: Mon.

This Chinese restaurant on the north side of Windwardside offers rather pricey Cantonese and Indonesian dishes. It seems to satisfy a lot of locals, who patronize it often. There's a wide variety of choices, including an old favorite, sweet and sour pork, and a more unusual conch chop suey. Credit cards: not accepted.

Scout's Place   **$$$**   ★★

Windwardside, The Bottom, ☎ *(599) 4-62295. Associated hotel: Scout's Place.*
International cuisine. Specialties: Curried goat.
Lunch: 12:30–2 p.m., prix fixe $12.
Dinner: 7:30–10 p.m., prix fixe $17–$25.

Scout's is the creation of Ohioan Scout Thirlkield, who also turned the Captain's Quarters into a hotel-restaurant. He is still around, but has passed the mantle onto chef Dianna Medero. The outdoor restaurant, attached to the hotel of the same name, is a beloved local hangout. The fixed-price menu features fresh seafood, and a delicious curried goat often appears. You'll find a bar plus a snack shop in front provide short-order meals, snacks and ice cream. Reservations required. Credit cards: MC, V.

Tea House $ ★★

 Windwardside, The Bottom,
 American cuisine. Specialties: Pastries.
 Dinner: 9:30–6 p.m., entrées $2–$7. Closed: Sun.
 After picking up some tips and brochures at the tourist office, stop at the Tea House
 right behind it for homemade, old-fashioned pastry treats like sticky cinnamon and
 raisin buns. Or choose from a selection of soft drinks, coffees, teas and sandwiches.
 Credit cards: not accepted.

Tropics Cafe $ ★★

 Windwardside, The Bottom, ☎ *(599) 4-63203. Associated hotel: Juliana's Apartments.*
 American cuisine.
 Dinner: Entrées $4–$10. Closed: Sun.
 The Tropics is a no-frills eatery attached to Juliana's Apartments, located near Captain's Quarters. It's good to know about for the decently priced breakfasts, burgers
 and sandwiches for under $10. Get them to pack up a picnic basket for you. Credit
 cards: MC, V.

Don't expect great bargains or streets lined with duty-free shops, but there
are a few things to look out for: Saba lace and Saba Spice. Delicate Saba lace
has been made on the island for the past 125 years, and it's quite beautiful.
You can buy hand-crafted tea towels, napkins, collars and tablecloths at the
Community Center in Hell's Gate each weekday, and also from the homes of
artisans; just look for the signs. Saba Spice is a heady quaff made of 151-
proof cask rum, brown sugar, cinnamon and other spices. The village of
Windwardside has a number of art galleries, mainly featuring locally created
watercolors and paintings.

Saba Directory

Arrival and Departure

 Because the runway is short, large planes cannot fly to Saba, nor can any plane
 land or take off in bad weather. **Winair** ☎ *(599) 4-62255*, the only scheduled
 airline, makes up to five daily 20-seater flights from St. Maarten, 20 minutes
 away ($62 round trip). One or two flights are made from Eustatius. Flights
 with a stopover in St. Barts can be arranged ahead of time. Saba can sometimes
 be reached by boat; contact the **Great Bay Marina** in Sint Maarten ☎ *(599)
 4-22167*. Cruise ships can call at a deep-water pier at Fort Bay.
 The airport departure tax is U.S. $2 to the Netherland Antilles, U.S. $5 elsewhere.

Business Hours

Stores generally open 8 a.m.–5 p.m. Bank (there's only one) open weekdays 8:30 a.m.–12:30 p.m.

Climate

Temperatures average about 85 degrees Fahrenheit, but can dip as low as 65 degrees F on a cool night.

Documents

U.S. and Canadian citizens need to show a current passport or one that expired less than five years ago, or other proof of citizenship (birth certificate or voter's registration plus a photo ID), as well as an ongoing or return ticket.

Electricity

The current is 100 volts, 60 cycles, the same as in the U.S.

Getting Around

Numerous **taxis** are awaiting flights when they arrive, and drivers are usually the best guides on the island. Don't hesitate to ask one for a half-day tour or to stay with you the whole day until your flight leaves. If you want to join a group and save money, **minibuses** at the airport usually will make a 1.5 hour tour. There are numerous agencies that will rent cars.

Language

The official language is English, though public signs are written in Dutch. English is the spoken language.

Medical Emergencies

Try not to get sick in Saba. Emergencies are flown to Sint Maarten; the clinic at The Bottom is limited in facilities. In cases of extreme illness, a chartered flight (one hour) should be arranged to San Juan, Puerto Rico. Saba has a decompression chamber, located at the Marine Park Hyperbaric Facility in Fort Bay ☎ *(599) 4-63205.*

Money

The official currency is the Netherlands Antilles *florin*, also called the *guilder* and abbreviated NAf. U.S. dollars are accepted by most businesses.

Telephone

The country code is *599-4.* If you are calling from another Caribbean country, the code might differ, so check with the operator. From the U.S. dial direct *011* (international access code)-*5994*-local number.

Time

Atlantic Standard Time, one hour ahead of eastern standard time, and the same as Eastern Daylight Saving Time.

Tipping and Taxes

Most hotels, restaurants and bars add a 10–15 percent service charge; if they don't that's what you should leave. No porters at the airport to carry your bags, but taxi drivers expect $1 or $2 as tip.

SABA

Tourist Information

The **Saba Tourist Bureau** is located in Windwardside, in the renovated Lambert Hassell Building ☎ *(599) 4-62231*, FAX *(599) 4-62350*. It's open only Monday–Friday. In the U.S. ☎ *(407) 394-8580, 1-800-722-2394*.

When to Go

The Queen's birthday on April 30 celebrates the life of Beatrix of Holland with festive fireworks, parades and sports competitions. The Saba Summer Festival takes place in late July (10 days) with much merry-making, music (steel bands), dancing and games. Saba Days in December is a festival featuring maypole dancing, spearfishing and other games.

SABA HOTELS	RMS	RATES	PHONE	CR. CARDS
The Bottom				
★★★ **Captain's Quarters**	10	$85–$130	(599) 4-62377	A, D, MC
★★ **Juliana's**	10	$65–$130	(599) 4-62389	A, MC, V
★ **Cranston's Antique Inn**	6	$40–$75	(599) 4-63203	A
★ **Scout's Place**	15	$40–$105	(599) 4-62388	A, MC

SABA RESTAURANTS	PHONE	ENTRÉE	CR. CARDS
The Bottom			
American			
★★ **Corner Deli**		$4–$10	A, MC, V
★★ **Tea House**		$2–$7	None
★★ **Tropics Cafe**	(599) 4-63203	$4–$10	MC, V
Chinese			
★★ **Saba Chinese Restaurant**	(599) 4-62268	$13–$19	None
International			
★★ **Brigadoon**	(599) 4-62380	$14–$17	A, DC, MC, V
★★ **Captain's Quarters**	599-4-62201	$13–$22	MC, V
★★ **Scout's Place**	(599) 4-62295	$12–$25	MC, V
Italian			
★★ **Guido's**		$4–$10	A, MC, V
Seafood			
★★ **Lollipop's**	(599) 4-63330	$10–$26	None

SABA

ST. BARTHÉLÉMY

Gustavia Harbor, St. Bart's

The Caribbean connoisseur who visits one island after another knows that each is a little different, with commonalities between the culture and people. St. Barthélémy, however, is truly a destination unto itself. With a small population that is almost exclusively white and affluent, cuisine that leans to the

French rather than creole, and a thumb-your-nose attitude toward cruiseship passengers, St. Barts looks, tastes and feels unlike any other island in the region. From the moment you touch down at the hilariously abrupt airstrip, the island subtly begins to work its charms on you, but only if you have a ready wallet, and are willing to embrace the island's chic lifestyle, and attitude with full fervor. Thumbprint-sized St. Barts is simply the antithesis of ramshackle outpost, and the luxurious dining and accommodations are the most expensive in the region. Even though you'll discover gorgeous scenery, pristine beaches and a charming harbor, the island remains a place to snooze, to cruise, and to be seen. In high season, particularly the week following Christmas, St. Barts makes L.A. look limp as celebrities descend. But beyond the hoity-toity glitter is a very special sophistication marked by delightful contrasts. The couple who casually spends three or four hundred dollars a night on their hotel room will happily tool around the island by day in a rattling rental car long past its prime. And while fine food is greatly respected, dressing up at dinner will only make you stick out like a wannabe—the one thing to which you must absolutely not succumb.

As the word began to creep out in the 1980s that St. Barts was the *in* spot, the last decade has seen considerable development on the tiny isle. Fortunately, recent hotel building has been kept relatively small by Caribbean standards, though the newer properties have continued to skew toward the high-end clientele the island prides itself on pleasing. This has made St. Barts a hot day-trip from nearby Sint Maarten/St. Martin for those who cannot afford the four-star luxe living for more than a few hours, and an even hotter destination for cruise ships, which locals strongly feel threatens their special (read: exclusive) lifestyle. Sint Maarten/St. Martin represents a woeful example of an island that became a victim of its success, and it remains firmly within eyesight for St. Barts' long-time residents. The cruise ship backlash that has intensified over the last couple of years—Gustavia shopowners are known to shut down in protest when a big ship comes in—is such that St. Barts will be forced soon to make a few hard choices regarding tourism and its infrastructure. Despite a hurricane that wiped out most tourism for the fall of 1995, St. Barts still enjoyed a record number of arrivals—over a quarter-million visitors for the year (including day-trippers and cruise ship passengers). Yes, the island's been discovered. But the good news is that St. Barts is more accessible than ever for the rest of us.

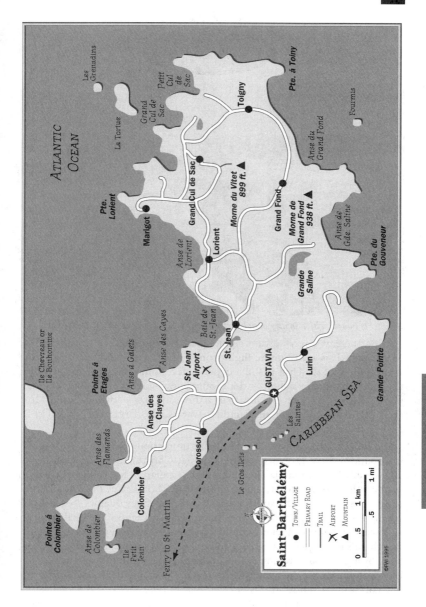

St. Barts boasts white sandy beaches surrounded by lush, volcanic hillsides.

St. Barthélémy covers a scant eight square miles—less than half the size of Manhattan. It is a 10-minute flight from Sint Maarten, and 125 miles from Guadeloupe, of which it is still a dependency. Somewhat arid and scrubby, the island has a tropical air and a mountainous appearance, yet its highest point—Morne du Vitet—is less than a thousand feet above sea level. More than 20 islands dot the surrounding waters, the largest of which is Ile Fourchue off the northeast tip.

The official 1990 census counted a full-time population of 5043, though it's bound to have grown since then, and at Christmas, a number closer to 18,000 inhabit the island. The bulk of the population lives along the length of the ruffled north coast, where most of the hotels are, or in the harbor town of Gustavia on the south coast. Gustavia defines quaint—a storybook setting for a fairytale seasoned with million-dollar yachts. The eerily romantic streets are a mix of French, colonial creole and Swedish styles, and so pristine there's nary a piece of garbage to be spotted. Just over the hill is St. Jean, lined by a gorgeous stretch of sand and peppered by a number of well-established hostelries. At the western terminus of this bay is the island's airport—one end of the landing strip is St. Jean Beach, the other end is a heart-stopping mountain pass. Camera-laden visitors hang out at this absurd photo op,

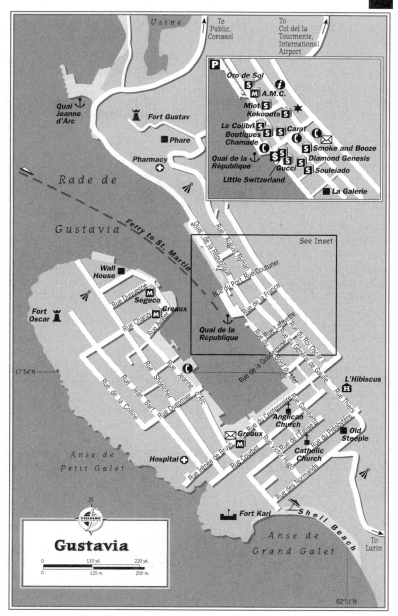

U s i n e

To Public, Corossol

To Col del la Tourmente, International Airport

P

Oro de Sol
S
M *A.M.C.*

Miot **S**
Kokonuts **S**

Le Colibri **S** **S** Carat
Boutiques **S**
Chamade
Quai de la **S** **S** Smoke and Booze
République **S** **S** Diamond Genesis
S Gucci **S** Souleiado

Little Switzerland
La Galerie

Quai Jeanne d'Arc

Fort Gustav

Phare

Pharmacy

Rade de

Gustavia

Ferry to St. Martin

Quai de la République

Rue August Nyman

Rue du Port Rue Couturier

Rue de la France

See Inset

Quai de la République

Wall House

Segeco **M**

M Greaux

Fort Oscar

Rue Duquesne
Rue Charry
Rue Aviat
Rue Shoecher
Rue Jeanne d'Arc
Rue Dugomier
Rue Jean Bart
Rue de la Colline

17°54'N

Rue Lafayette
Rue du Roi Oscar II
Rue du Général de Gaulle
Rue de la Guadeloupe
Rue Bord du Mer

L'Hibiscus

Rue Thiers

Rue du Centennaire
Rue Gambetta
Rue de l'Église
Rue du Presbytère

Anglican Church

Greaux
M

Rue Irénée de Brun
Rue Courbet
Rue Victor Hugo

Hospital

Catholic Church

Old Steeple

Anse de Petit Galet

N

FIELDING

Gustavia

0   110 yd.   220 yd.
0   125 m.   250 m.

Fort Karl

Rue des Normands

Shell Beach

Anse de Grand Galet

To Lurin

62°51'W

ST. BARTHÉLÉMY

the Col de la Tourmente, and giddily snap away as planes drop down to the runway, clearing the pass at an altitude seemingly close enough for a buzz cut.

In September 1995, Hurricane Luis took a swipe at St. Barts, leaving several hotels and restaurants in shambles. The French government responded quickly and efficiently, and the island was reasonably in shape for the 1995–'96 winter season. With the exception of a few beaches that have not yet fully recovered, and several permanent hotel and restaurant closures, the island is back to business as usual.

History

Some people believe Columbus discovered St. Barts, naming it after his brother, but the island didn't appear on any map until 1523, when a speck of dirt was labeled San Bartoleme by a Spanish cartographer. After being summarily ignored by both Carib Indians and European pirates, St. Barts was finally explored in 1637, eight years after St. Kitts was colonized, though some of the first Norman and British settlers were scalped by Carib Indians. Over time, the island became a secret hiding place for pirates, while the culture itself became tenaciously French. When Louis XVI traded the flagging island to the Swedes for some warehouses in Goteborg, the island magically flourished with new management (Thomas Jefferson himself declared the port free of all duties). By 1847, the island had been ravaged by hurricanes, trade competition, fires and piracy, leaving Gustavia, the capital, dirt poor—a fact that convinced the Swedes in 1878 to dump the island back in the lap of the French. Not until 1946 did the French government declare St. Barts a commune in the department of Guadeloupe. In 1947, aviator/hotelier Rémy de Haenen landed the first airplane here on the short, grassy pasture of St. Jean. With the construction of the airport and the island's first runway for STOL (short-takeoff-and-landing) planes, the floodgates of tourism were opened, with most visitors flocking to St. Jean, on the central point of the island.

People

The first thing one notices is the near-absence of any black islanders. The topography of St. Barthélémy is so rocky it was deemed unsuitable for growing sugarcane, so most slave ships simply passed the island by. However, during the early-19th century, about 1400 slaves from Africa were used primarily for domestic work and for loading and unloading at the harbor. After emancipation, most of the black population left St. Barts, leaving the islanders to their hard lifestyle. St. Barts also has the unique characteristic of having been the only Caribbean island governed by Sweden—a few reminders of Swedish presence can be seen in the form of architecture, a Swedish cemetery (in Public), and in the name Gustavia. Today, the most traditional sect of the population are the fiercely independent grandmothers (or *grand-meres*)—tough old ladies, and thoroughly Caucasian. West Indian by birth and French by heritage, these women single-handedly raised their huge families in the absence of husbands who frequently had to leave the island to make ends meet. Yes, at one time in the 20th century, everyone on St. Barts was relatively poor. Today, with the influx of well over 1000 ex-pats (most of them French) and thousands of high-class international tourists, the old traditions are slowly dying out. The middle-aged generation is caught in transition while their children are looking solidly into a modernized future.

Anyone anticipating political struggles or racial tension simply won't find them on St. Barts. Instead, an uncommon feeling of unity exists among the locals, though the businessmen who sponsored the building boom of the last decade are observed with some disdain by the two or three thousand residents who have lived here since the 1960s. Crime is almost unheard of, and most everyone is gainfully employed, from fishermen, to builders, to shopkeepers, to hoteliers and restaurateurs—even the dogs are well-fed. As such, many visitors hitchhike around to see the island, which is also a great way to meet the locals (it is not acceptable behavior to pass up hitchhikers). French is the official language, and a quaint Norman dialect works its way into casual conversation. Much of the population speaks some English (more than on Martinique or Guadeloupe), and language problems are rare at hotels, restaurants or shops. Nonetheless, it's worth bringing a French-English dictionary to ease awkward moments. A note on spelling: the proper French abbreviation of the island's name is St. Barts, but most Americans have dropped the "h" if only as a reminder as to how to pronounce the name.

Beaches

St. Barthélémy has what might be the finest collection of beaches per square mile of any Caribbean island. The official count is 14, though more can be tallied by the dedicated eye. A few of the coves took a beating from Hurricane Luis in 1995—in most cases this simply meant the beaches were a few yards less in depth, though a couple, including famed **Colombier** (see "On Foot" below) have some exposed coral at water's edge for the moment. All beaches are public and free.

The most developed beach is **St. Jean**, with several hotels, a number of restaurants, plentiful watersports and Eden Rock splitting the cove in two. While all of this activity is anathema to those seeking true solitude, it creates a lively social scene throughout the day. **Anse des Flamands** is more quiet—white sand fringed by lantana palms and a residential area where the cluck of chickens provides a charming soundtrack. On the other end of the north coast, a series of striking coves lies between lush **Marigot** and **Petit Cul-de-Sac**. The rugged coastline on the southern slope of Morne du Vitet is the least developed part of St. Barts, with two rugged, little-visited beaches, **Toiny** and **Grand Fond**, but both can be rough for swimming. Nudism is prohibited on St. Barts, though topless is common. There is, of course, an official, unofficial nude beach, **Grande Saline**, a ravishing and undeveloped cove reached via a short path through the brush. It's well-known by now, meaning there's more people with clothes than without—as you enter the beach, hip/gay is to the right, conservative swings to the left. Perhaps the loveliest of all is **Anse du Gouverneur**, reached by a steep road from Lurin and backed by sea grapes over plush sand dunes. Just south of Gustavia is one more beauty, **Shell Beach**, with calm seas and ideal sunset views—it's a five-minute walk from the town harbor.

Underwater

Shallow reefs abound at this tony outpost, which makes snorkeling delightful and diving easy, bottoming out at about 80 feet. The best diving is on the southwest coast and around the tiny islets decorating St. Barthélemy's outlying waters, most of it no more than 10 or 15 minutes from the dock at Gustavia. Nearby **Ile Fourchue** is one such possibility, and **Les Petits Saints**, the three rock outcrops just outside the Gustavia harbor, features pompano and occasional dolphins. **Marigot Bay** offers excellent snorkeling, and a narrow reef stretches into the channel toward the rock offshore, **La Tortue ou l'Ecaille**; winter currents can make this area unsafe, however. The north end of **Anse de Colombier's** beautiful sands yield coral growth over the rocks, which are sprinkled with colorful reef fish and, in calm waters, one can snorkel the rocks past the south end, at **Ile de la Pointe**. **Shell Beach**, **La Petite Anse** and **St. Jean Bay** (northwest of Eden Rock) are other snorkeling possibilities.

On Foot

Physically, St. Barthélémy looks a little more impressive than it actually is. The island is tiny—just eight square miles—but appears larger due to the spunky hills that rise to a pair of 900-foot peaks on the island's eastern side. The preferred method of visitor transport is the ubiquitous Mini-Moke, but you needn't be hostage to these sputtering upstarts. See St. Barts' compact interior of pastures and charming villages and its scalloped coastline on foot and you'll be experiencing island over attitude. A few beaches hide in coves that are difficult to reach on wheels, while an early morning stroll through Gustavia rewards with bold coffee, fresh croissants and a glimmer of the village that once was—St. Barts before it was overtaken by the chic set. Another fine area for walking is along the southern coastline between Grand Fond and Toiny—although a road exists, it's little traveled and yields the most rugged and undeveloped portion of the island. Similarly, a road climbs the slopes of Morne du Vitet (to within a couple hundred feet of the summit); leave your car at the Hostellerie des Trois Forces for a delightful stroll yielding superlative views of the north and east coasts. Boats can be taken to nearby Ile Fourchue, a half-sunk crater that rises to 340 feet off St. Barts' northwest tip and offers intriguing exploration on foot among cactus and brush across a rocky desert landscape.

By Pedal

St. Barts' is a pretty island, and bicycles should be an ideal way to experience it. Goat paths bisect the thorny countryside, providing ample exploration possibilities. Although **Rent Some Fun** once offered mountain bikes, their customers found St. Barthélémy too hot and hilly for enjoyable riding; bicycles are no longer available. Further, residents have collectively thumbed their noses at visiting cyclists, letting them know that, on no uncertain terms, cyclists are not welcome on St. Barts. And these people call themselves French! No laws are in effect, yet, but with this kind of attitude, do you really want to lug your wheels on and off tiny planes to tool around in this environment?

St. Barthélémy is blissfully free of tourist traps and boring museums. Anything worth finding will probably be your own special discovery. To find the last threads of traditional life, head for **Corossol**, a tiny fishing village at the bottom of a deep valley just northwest of Gustavia. Its population of about 300 is somewhat secluded from the modern St. Barts—the older women still weave handicrafts with *lantana* (palm straw) and wear dresses that recall their French provincial origins. Drive to the mountain-top hamlet of **Colombier**; just a little further up the road and you'll arrive at one of the island's best views, encompassing Sint Maarten/St. Martin, Saba and Sint Eustatius. Another fine view can be obtained by driving up the steep slopes of **Morne du Vitet** above the community of Vitet—how many beaches can you count from here? No one who comes to the island should miss stopping at the **Col de la Tourmente**, the ridgetop intersection above the head of the landing strip where airplanes drop precipitously over your head during their final approach. Lastly, the dinner prices are sky-high, but so is the view, which makes a stop at the **Carl Gustaf Hotel** for at least a sunset cocktail mandatory—the glittering sight of Gustavia from here is worth a million bucks. Or more.

There are several island tours available, but your money is far better spent on a rental car for a day or two. St. Barts' charms are not the kind that can be pointed out from a passing car, and the island is small enough that it can easily be explored by outsiders.

Museums and Exhibits

Inter-Oceans Museum

Corossol.

A remarkable collection of some 7000 shells—said to be the second largest in the world—has been assembled by Ingenu Magras, who has never traveled off the island. General admission: $4.

Musee de St. Barthélémy   ★ ★ ★

Le Pointe; Gustavia.

This winsome little museum tells the island's history through costumes, antiques, photos and artwork, including portraits and documents relating to the island's Swedish period. Also featuring exhibits on St. Bart's vegetation and sea creatures, the museum is located near the Wall House on the far side of the harbor. General admission: $2.

Sports

Waterskiing is permitted only in Colombier Bay.

Boating is more than a passion on St. Barthélémy—it's a way of life, and sailors are often judged socially by the make of their boat. The location of St. Barts, midway between Antigua and the Virgin Islands and next to Sint Maarten—all regional sailing centers—provide sailors with a wide variety of destinations. The island can handle upwards of 500 yachts at anchor— Gustavia has docking facilities and moorings for at least 40 vessels at one time. Other prime locations nearby include Corossol and Public, though other deeply carved bays around the island also provide a number of fine anchorages. Annual **yachting events** include the St. Barts Regatta, celebrated just before Lent, the St. Barts Cup, held in April, and the three-day International Regatta in May.

Deep-sea fishing enthusiasts will want to head for Gustavia, where boat charters with gear can be hired. Snorkeling equipment can be rented at **Marine Service** or purchased at **Loulou's Marine**, both in Gustavia, though a number of hotels will loan their own set to guests. **Windsurfing** has become a big sport on the island, with the bigger bays along the north coast providing ideal locations. **Surfing** can be good at Lorient and Grand Fond, while experts can dare the churn of Washing Machine next door. **Waterskiing** is provided by Stephan Jouany through **Marine Service**, and **parasailing** through Wind Wave Power ☎ *(590) 27-62-73*.

On land, **tennis** is the most accessible sporting activity, with courts provided at a number of hotels, and at the Flamboyant Tennis Club. Pro Yves Lacoste provides tennis lessons at a court in Toiny ☎ *(590) 27-68-06*. The Hotel St. Barts Isle de France has an air-conditioned **squash court**.

Horseback Riding

Ranch des Flamands, Anse des Flamands.
Laure Nicolas is the person to see at Ranch des Flamands for trail rides and other excursions. Two-hour excursions are offered daily for both beginners and experienced riders—one departs at 9 a.m., the other at 3 p.m. Cost: $35.

Watersports

Various locations, Gustavia.
Marine Service ☎ *(590) 27-70-34* offers the island's most complete watersports center, with PADI-certified scuba diving, deep-sea fishing, snorkel excursions, and boat rides in the Aquascope from which you espy colorful coral, sea creatures, and a submerged yacht wreck. For windsurfing instruction and rentals, try **St. Barts Wind School** ☎ *(590) 27-71-22*, and **Wind Wave Power** ☎ *(590) 27-62-73*. For deep-sea fishing or sailing trips, call **Ocean Must** ☎ *(590) 27-62-25* and Marine Service. For scuba, see "Underwater" above.

Where to Stay

Fielding's Highest Rated Hotels in St. Barthélémy

★★★★★	Castelets	$100–$700
★★★★★	Guanahani	$230–$965
★★★★	Carl Gustaf	$410–$1250
★★★★	Christopher Hotel	$225–$500
★★★★	Hotel St. Barth Isle de France	$300–$780
★★★★	Hotel le Toiny	$510–$1350
★★★★	Le Toiny	$490–$820
★★★	Eden Rock	$240–$600
★★★	Emeraude Plage Hotel	$130–$560
★★★	Francois Plantation	$216–$450

Fielding's Most Exclusive Hotels in St. Barthélémy

★★★	Taiwana Hotel	$955–$999
★★★★	Carl Gustaf	$410–$1250
★★★★★	Guanahani	$230–$965
★★★★	Hotel St. Barth Isle de France	$300–$780
★★★	Eden Rock	$240–$600

Fielding's Best Value Hotels in St. Barthélémy

★★★	Hotel Baie des Flamands	$95–$135
★★	Le P'tit Morne	$95–$145
★★	Hostellerie Trois Forces	$75–$170
★★	Marigot Bay Club	$75–$180
★★★	Les Jardins de St. Jean	$60–$355

Don't arrive on St. Barthélémy without your gold card. The island has a deserved reputation as the region's most expensive, and the squeeze begins here. Simply put, you will get more hotel for your money on any other island in the Caribbean. What you won't get, of course, is St. Barts' unique mix of sophistication and charm—an intangible essence exported only in the form of satisfied visitors who always seem to come back for another fix.

Though the choices are extensive, when it comes to hotels, small is big on St. Barts. There are no mega-resorts, all-inclusives, high-rises or properties with extensive meeting facilities. With one exception, the Guanahani, all the hotels are under 50 rooms and several of the best have barely a dozen. Except for the Christopher, none of the hotels are connected to chains. These are intimate hostelries where you'll get to know the manager rather than a security guard. Privacy is zealously guarded and several hotels vaunt completely private plunge pools with magnificent views, all but a few steps from your bed.

All of this comes with a price, of course. If you're on a budget, we can mention a few options (see "Low Cost Lodging"), but the best advice for penny-pinchers is to avoid the winter season entirely when prices everywhere rocket into the stratosphere. And, one bit of good news: most hotels quote rooms prices with tax and service charge included, minimizing the check-out surprises (verify this when booking your room). If money's no object and a winter sojourn is paramount, book your room well in advance, particularly during the last week of December, when accommodations are typically locked up months beforehand (a few properties even hike their rates above the usual high season prices for that one week). Also note that a larger than usual percentage of hotels on this island close for a few weeks during the slow, late summer/early fall period. If air conditioning is important to you, ask in advance, because many properties depend on ceiling fans and trade winds.

Hurricane Luis closed several properties either for the short term or indefinitely. The biggest loss was famed mountain-top retreat Castelets, for which a re-building plan has not been determined. The Baie des Flamands is closed indefinitely, while the snobby Taiwana was under construction at press time, although a re-opening date was not forthcoming. All other properties listed below are fully operational now, or will be by December 1996.

Hotels and Resorts

The Guanahani is the island's biggest hotel, though with 80 units spread over 17 acres, you probably won't feel crowded or hemmed in. Two very exclusive hotels, the Carl Gustaf and Le Toiny, provide rooms with their own private plunge pools, while a few properties like Francois Plantation and Hostellerie des Trois Forces are perched high in the hills and require a car for the trip to the nearest sand. But most of St. Barts' extensive roster of possibilities lie in or near the embrace of its fabled beaches, and there are several favorites. **Baie de St. John** is the most famous stretch, with the recently re-opened **Eden Rock** positioned on a throne at the center—a number of other properties are on or close to this beach, which keeps it bustling. **Anse des Flamands** is the sybarite's choice along with the elegant, plantation-themed **Hotel St. Barth Isle de France**.

Baie des Anges Hotel $145–$320 ★★
Baie des Flamands, Gustavia, ☎ *(800) 755-9313, (590) 27-63-61.*
FAX (590) 27-83-44.
Single: $145–$320. Double: $185–$320.
Located on a picturesque beach, this small hotel has air-conditioned rooms with private bath and terrace, as well as bungalows with kitchenettes. A complete post-hurricane makeover spruced up the rooms and added a Creole restaurant. No pool or other facilities, but the hotel boasts one of the island's best beaches, Flamands, is right out your door. 9 rooms. Credit cards: A, CB, MC, V.

Carl Gustaf $410–$1250 ★★★★
Gustavia, ☎ *(800) 948-7823, (590) 27-82-83. FAX (590) 27-82-37.*
Single: $410–$970. Double: $410–$1250.
Named in honor of the king of Sweden, this all-suite hotel is situated on a hillside overlooking Gustavia harbor. Guests are housed in cottages of one or two bedrooms with wooden sundecks and very private plunge pools. The units are quite stylishly done, with high ceilings, marble floors, luxurious furnishings, fax machines, stereos, VCRs, and fully equipped kitchens—the view of Gustavia is stupendous, but be sure to request one of the upper-level rooms. Two-bedroom suites have bunk beds for kids. The honeymoon suite sits above the rest (sans private pool) but has lower rates. Facilities include a gourmet French restaurant, two bars, a fitness center, and a private cabin-cruiser for sea and fishing excursions; the restaurant-side pool is for true exhibitionists. It's a five minute walk down the (steep) hill into town or to Shell Beach. Outside the actual rooms, the hotel feels a little tight—primarily in the interest of providing guests ultimate seclusion on their decks. The prices are high, but you're paying for a unique, perhaps unequalled combination of privacy, view and location at this sophisticated French-style resort. Amenities: exercise room. 14 rooms. Credit cards: A, MC, V.

Castelets $100–$700 ★★★★★
Mount Lurin, Gustavia, ☎ *(590) 27-61-73.*
Single: $100–$700. Double: $100–$700.
This exclusive villa resort is perched high on a mountain, with stunning views. Formerly called the Sapore Di Mare, it is now back to its original owner. Two rooms are available in the main house, the rest are in two-bedroom duplex villas furnished with fine antiques, very luxurious accoutrements, spacious living rooms, terraces and kitchens. The atmosphere is sophisticated and discreet, attracting many celebrities. The grounds include a small pool and excellent French restaurant. You'll want a car to get around; the beach is five minutes' driving time. 10 rooms. Credit cards: not accepted.

Christopher Hotel $225–$500 ★★★★
Pointe Milou, Gustavia, ☎ *(800) 763-4835, (590) 27-63-63. FAX (590) 27-92-92.*
Single: $225–$500. Double: $225–$500.

Sleek, French colonial in design, this is St. Barts' only chain hotel, opening in 1993 to great consternation. But the 40 rooms are stylish and quite comfortable, with high-quality mahogany furnishings, mini-bars, and great views from the terrace or balcony; the showers are in an outdoor patio. The beach is a 10-minute drive, so most guests hang by the fine pool—the island's largest. The hotel also offers a full-service health spa, two restaurants, three bars, and a concierge to arrange off-premises activities. Service at this Sofitel-managed hotel is reliable. Amenities: health club. 40 rooms. Credit cards: A, MC, V.

Eden Rock $240–$600   ★ ★ ★

Baie de St. Jean, Gustavia, ☎ (800) 932-3222, (590) 27-72-94. FAX (590) 27-88-37.
Single: $240–$600. Double: $240–$600.

The Eden Rock Hotel was the first on St. Barts, built by the first pilot to fly to the island, Rémy de Haenen, an entrepreneur who spent some years as local mayor and made his hotel a swank social hub. After several years of decline while newer, tonier properties were built, the Eden Rock was purchased, refurbished and re-imagined by a British couple, Jane and David Matthews, who opened its doors in 1996 to fresh acclaim. The romantic rooms on the rock are filled with antiques and four poster beds—each room is unique, and a couple are cramped, but all have charm. Three new one-bedroom suites have been built on the beach, along with a pool—a few more beach rooms will be built. The original restaurant, helmed by Didier Guyot, is top dollar, while a new restaurant on the beach should be a big draw. Perched on a striking promontory in the middle of St. Jean Bay, the location is unmatched, with views extending up and down the beach to the picayune airport and the slap of crashing waves for an endless soundtrack. A true one-of-a-kind hotel. Amenities: balcony or patio. 10 rooms. Credit cards: A, MC, V.

El Sereno Beach Hotel $200–$580   ★ ★ ★

Grand Cul de Sac, Gustavia, ☎ (800) 932-3222, (590) 27-64-80. FAX (590) 27-75-47.
Single: $200–$580. Double: $200–$580.

Located on the beach twenty minutes from Gustavia, this growing operation consists of a hotel and gingerbread-trimmed villas, each housing three one-bedroom suites with full kitchens and lots of room—some accommodations are right on the beach. The 18 charming standard rooms are not as expansive, but are comfortable enough and fringed by banana and hibiscus. You'll enjoy the sexy pool on the premises, as well an acclaimed restaurant, two bars and lush gardens. A windsurfing school is on site, as well as a glass-walled gym that attracts dedicated body builders. Amenities: exercise room. 41 rooms. Credit cards: A, MC, V.

Filao Beach Hotel $200–$640   ★ ★ ★

St. Jean, Gustavia, ☎ (800) 932-3222, (590) 27-64-84. FAX (590) 27-62-24.
Single: $200–$640. Double: $200–$640.

Located in the heart of the action on St. Jean Beach, this is a well-run operation, convenient to activities, many restaurants, and the airport. Guest rooms are pleasant, recently refurbished, and located in air-conditioned bungalows with all the modern comforts. Rooms are quite private, but most don't have ocean views (and some of the garden rooms suffer from traffic noise). Amenities include a large pool, windsurfing and snorkeling, and a good bar and restaurant. The prime location makes Filao a great place to take in the full St. Barts experience. This property is a member of the Relais and Chateaux hotel group. Amenities: houses, cottages or bungalows. 30 rooms. Credit cards: A, CB, DC, D, MC, V.

Francois Plantation $216–$450 ★ ★ ★

Colombier, Gustavia, ☎ (590) 27-78-82. FAX (590) 27-61-26.
Single: $216–$450. Double: $240–$450.
Positioned on a hilltop overlooking Baie des Flamands amid tropical gardens, this elegant spot consists of 12 charming bungalows. All are very nicely done, with mahogany furniture, four-poster beds, minibars, air conditioning, TVs, and terraces with views of the ocean or gardens. The views everywhere are simply astounding, especially from the pool terrace, which sits atop Le P'tit Morne. The restaurant and its wine cellar, run by owner Francois Beret, is one of the best on the island, but ask about the garden and his eyes sparkle with pride—it bursts with jasmine, impatiens, hibiscus, bougainvillea and more, creating the lushest, most fragrant spot on St. Barts. The beach is a five-minute drive. Rates include full breakfast. Amenities: secluded garden atmosphere. 12 rooms. Credit cards: A, MC, V.

Grand Cul de Sac Hotel $110–$335 ★ ★

Grand Cul de Sac, Gustavia, ☎ (590) 27-60-7. FAX (590) 27-75-57.
Single: $110–$185. Double: $195–$335.
Half the rooms at this bungalow complex have beach views and kitchenettes, while the other half have mountain views and refrigerators. All are air-conditioned and basic but comfortable. There's a bar and restaurant on the premises, as well as a salt-water pool and gym. Guests can play tennis at sister property St. Barth's Beach Hotel and Tennis Club. 36 rooms. Credit cards: A, MC.

Guanahani $230–$965 ★ ★ ★ ★ ★

Grand Cul de Sac, Gustavia, ☎ (800) 223-6800, (590) 27-66-60. FAX (590) 27-70-70.
Single: $230–$965. Double: $230–$965.
Located on seven beachfront acres at Cul de Sac, this romantic spot is especially popular with couples, who enjoy its intimate atmosphere, and the seclusion offered by the spacious grounds. Accommodations, in gingerbread-trimmed cottages, are deluxe, swathed in rich, contrasting hues of green, blues, pinks and yellows. The higher-priced studios and one-bedroom suites have full kitchens, as well as whirl-pools in the studios and plunge pools for the suites (some have more privacy than others). The grounds include two restaurants, two tennis courts, two pools, and watersports at not one but two beaches—Anse Marechal and Anse du Grand Cul de Sac on either side of the promontory. On an island of small hotels, Guanahani is by far St. Barts' largest property, yet it remains low-key, friendly and very, very chic. 80 rooms. Credit cards: A, MC, V.

Hostellerie Trois Forces $75–$170 ★ ★

Vitet, Gustavia, ☎ (590) 27-61-25. FAX (590) 27-81-38.
Single: $75–$150. Double: $75–$170.
When someone asks "What's your sign?" here it's not just the old come-on—each cottage is individually decorated and designed to compliment the astrological sign

after which it's named. Located up in the mountains above Vitet, this peaceful retreat is run by the island's leading astrologer, who also happens to be a quite decent chef. The gingerbread-trimmed cottages are tiny but nicely done with hand-made wooden furnishings and large terraces. Only four are air-conditioned, and none have phones or TV. There's a pool on-site, and this is probably the only hotel in the Caribbean where you can take yoga lessons, have your tarot cards read, and get your chart done. A very pleasant retreat. 8 rooms. Credit cards: A, MC.

Hotel Baie des Flamands   **$95–$135**   ★★★

Anse de Flamands, Gustavia, ☎ *(590) 27-64-85.*
Single: $95–$105. Double: $105–$135.

Set on a half-mile stretch of beach, one of the island's best, this small motel-like property is fairly isolated, so you'll want a rental car to get around. Accommodations are clean and basic, with the more expensive rooms offering a kitchenette on the patio. The other rooms come with a refrigerator. Amenities include a very fine French restaurant, bar and a saltwater pool. Good service at this family-run operation. 24 rooms. Credit cards: A, MC.

Hotel St. Barth Isle de France   **$300–$780**   ★★★★

Anse des Flamands, Gustavia, ☎ *(800) 628-8929, (590) 27-61-81.*
FAX (590) 27-86-83.
Single: $300–$780. Double: $300–$780.

Set along one of the island's best coves of sand, this newer luxury property houses guests in boardwalk-connected garden cottages or in a plantation-style house that sits above the beach. The chic, marble-floored guest rooms are spacious and furnished with mahogany antiques, locally made pieces, expensive linens, huge bathrooms (some with whirlpool tubs), refrigerators, and patios or balconies. The nine beach-front rooms have undeniably spectacular views, but are quite expensive—the peaceful garden bungalows are a two-minute walk to the sand and a better value. Facilities include an air-conditioned squash court, tennis court, a pool, and a fitness center. Ultra-tasteful, yet the warm management by director Evelyn Weber (formerly of La Samanna) will make you feel right at home. Though the resort lost both its restaurant and swimming pool (superfluous on a beach this grand) to Hurricane Luis, both were scheduled to be rebuilt in time for the winter 1996–'97 season. Amenities: balcony or patio. 28 rooms. Credit cards: A, MC, V.

Hotel le Toiny   **$510–$1350**   ★★★★

Anse de Toiny, Gustavia, ☎ *(800) 298-6469, (590) 27-88-88. FAX (590) 27-89-30.*
Single: $510–$820. Double: $510–$1350.

Set on a remote hillside on the southeastern coast, this newer hotel is set in a grove of cacti and *gaiac* trees. Accommodations are lovely, consisting of one-, two- and three-bedroom suites in individual cottages all fitted with quality furnishing and linens, four-poster beds, full kitchens, and TVs with VCRs—plus a 10-by-20-foot pool for each. With St. Eustatius, St. Kitts and Nevis off in the distance, spectacular views abound, and each villa is cleverly positioned to ensure maximum privacy. Dine at the open-air French restaurant, or take a dip in the large communal pool as well. The beach is a 10-minute walk, and hiking awaits on the undeveloped Pointe a Toiny, but you'll need a car to do any other exploring. Elegant and secluded.

Amenities: exercise room, houses, cottages or bungalows. 12 rooms. Credit cards: A, DC, MC, V.

La Banane   **$150–$480**   ★ ★ ★

Quartier Lorient, Gustavia, ☎ (800) 932-3222, (590) 27-68-25. FAX (590) 27-68-44. Single: $150–$480. Double: $150–$480.

Located two miles from Gustavia, this small complex consists of nine inviting bungalows, each individually decorated. All are quite nice, filled with antiques, local artwork, TVs with VCRs, private terraces, and ceiling fans in lieu of air conditioners. The lovely showers are decorated with Mexican tiles. The atmosphere is that of an oasis, with lush gardens surrounding the place, laced by pink and green wooden boardwalks. The restaurant is open only in the evenings, and a famed cabaret show takes place nightly. There's a pool on the premises and the beach is within walking distance. Nice. Amenities: secluded garden atmosphere. 9 rooms. Credit cards: A, MC, V.

Le Toiny   **$490–$820**   ★ ★ ★ ★

Anse Toiny, Gustavia, ☎ (800) 932-3222, (590) 27-88-88. FAX (590) 27-89-30. Single: $490–$820. Double: $490–$820.

A member of the prestigious Relais and Chateaux association, Le Toiny is the epitome of St. Barts luxury living. 12 ultra-secluded villas are carefully sprinkled on a rugged hillside on the remote southeastern coast in a grove of gaiac trees. The interiors are lovely, with antique furnishings, four poster beds, full kitchens and TVs with VCRs—the deluxe bathrooms are stocked with fine linens and toiletries. The coup de grace is a private plunge pool (about 10 by 20 feet) that overlooks the ocean. A superb open-air restaurant, Le Gaiac, sits in the main building overlooking a larger communal pool (24-hour room service is available). The beach is a ten minute walk, you'll need a car for exploring. However, this elegant and refined property is so peaceful and unique, you'll have to be dragged out at the end of your stay. Amenities: exercise room, balcony or patio. 12 rooms. Credit cards: A, MC, V.

Le Tom Beach   **$150–$610**   ★ ★ ★

St. Jean, Gustavia, ☎ (800) 322-2223, (590) 27-53-13. FAX (590) 27-53-15. Single: $150–$610. Double: $150–$610.

Creatively tucked into what seemed like the last whisper of beachfront property available in St. Jean, Le Tom is a complete and successful makeover of the original Tom Beach Hotel, and it maintains the original's intimacy and charm. Rooms have tile floors, patios or verandas and four-poster beds. There's a small pool with a arching footbridge plus an excellent restaurant. An underground garage (the first ever on the island) helps make the most of the prime location. 12 rooms. Credit cards: A, MC, V.

Manapany Cottages   **$150–$950**   ★ ★ ★

Anse des Cayes, Gustavia, ☎ (800) 932-3222, (590) 27-66-55. FAX (590) 27-75-28. Single: $150–$950. Double: $195–$950.

Set in a small cove on the north shore, this property consists of a complex of cottages along a hillside or the beach. Accommodations vary from standard guestrooms to suites with one or two bedrooms and full kitchens. All are fine, but not as luxurious as the rates suggest—some of the hillside cottages are a little tight. The site includes two restaurants, an exercise room, a lovely pool and tennis court. The beach is pretty but tiny, and constantly windy. This operation is quite chic and once attracted a fair share of celebrities, but Manapany may be overshadowed by some of the other luxury properties that have been built since. Amenities: houses, cottages or bungalows. 52 rooms. Credit cards: A, MC.

Sea Horse Hotel   **$80–$295**   ★★

Marigot Bay, Gustavia, ☎ *(800) 742-4276, (590) 27-75-36. FAX (590) 27-85-33.*
Single: $80–$235. Double: $90–$295.
The delightful Sea Horse provides great value in a pleasant setting, a few hundred feet from the beach at Marigot Bay. Two types of rooms, a regular or junior suite are positioned on a hillside alongside the pool. Interiors are tastefully appointed with kitchenettes, air conditioning and tiled terraces. There's also a two-bedroom villa perfect for families. A number of savvy Americans have discovered the relaxed Sea Horse—its young manager, Loic Lecouteller, makes them feel most welcome. 11 rooms. Credit cards: A, MC, V.

St. Barth's Beach Hotel   **$155–$280**   ★★

Grand Cul de Sac, Gustavia, ☎ *(590) 27-60-70. FAX (590) 27-75-57.*
Single: $155–$280. Double: $155–$280.
This two-story hotel is right on a nice beach, but is in need of a polish—rooms are strictly modern and functional, though they have lovely ocean views and a good breeze. All have air conditioning and minibars, and eight have kitchenettes. Other facilities include a saltwater pool, gym and a windsurfing school; the restaurant, Le Rivage, is well-respected. You'll want a rental car, as this spot is fairly isolated (car rental is available on site). Amenities: tennis. 44 rooms. Credit cards: A, MC.

Taiwana Hotel   **$955–$999**   ★★★

Anse des Flamands, Gustavia, ☎ *(590) 27-65-01. FAX (590) 27 68 82.*
Single: $955–$999. Double: $955–$999.
Located on a secluded beach, this incredibly expensive spot houses its well-heeled guests in beautifully furnished, large suites loaded with antiques, modern furniture, hand-painted tiles and enormous bathrooms, many with whirlpools. There are two pools (one for kids), tennis, and a restaurant. Watersports are available on the beach. The service can be sullen—not exactly what one has in mind when forking over $1000 for a night's stay. Unless you're turned on by paying exorbitant prices, try someplace else. 9 rooms. Credit cards: not accepted.

Tropical Hotel   **$110–$350**   ★★★

Baie de St. Jean, Gustavia, ☎ *(800) 932-3222, (590) 27-64-87. FAX (590) 27-81-74.*
Single: $110–$350. Double: $145–$350.
Set a few hundred yards from the beach on a hill overlooking St. Jean Bay, this small creole-style hotel centers around a gingerbread-trimmed building that houses the reception area, a lounge and bar. Guestrooms are all-white and airy, with comfortable trappings and furnished patios overlooking the ocean or lush gardens. You'll find a restaurant and pool on-site. Pleasant. 20 rooms. Credit cards: A, MC.

Village St. Jean Hotel   **$89–$460**   ★★★

St. Jean, Gustavia, ☎ *(800) 322-2223, (590) 27-61-39. FAX (590) 27-77-96.*

Single: $89–$460. Double: $89–$460.

Set on a hillside close to the beach, this respected property consists of 21 cottages with one or two bedrooms. Each is simply furnished but pleasant enough, with full kitchens and private terraces. Half were refurbished handsomely in 1995 with halogen lights, soft Marseille bedspreads and blue-tiled bathrooms. There are also four standard hotel rooms with twin beds and small refrigerators that go for $150 a night at peak season. A restaurant, pool and Jacuzzi are on the premises, with lots to see and do within walking distance. This friendly, family-run operation is a good buy. Amenities: secluded garden atmosphere, Jacuzzi, houses, cottages or bungalows. 25 rooms. Credit cards: A, MC, V.

Apartments and Condominiums

Self-catering in St. Barts can hardly be termed "roughing it." Prices on villas, usually with fully equipped kitchens and many with private pool, can be extravagant, but the surroundings and convenience are often worth it. The villa leader is **Sibarth**, a real estate agency in Gustavia run by Brook and Roger Lacour. She is a former U.S. citizen who vacationed on the island years ago, fell in love, and married into the St. Barts life. Sibarth rents out 200 island properties that range from modest and quaint (starting at about $900 in the low season, $1200 in the winter), to luxurious abodes at Pointe Milou with three or four bedrooms, a pool, spellbinding views and Hollywood pedigree. All offer a chance to experience the island at its most uncomplicated. Sibarth can be contacted directly on-island ☎ *(590) 27-62-38*, or through its U.S. representative, WIMCO ☎ *(800) 932-3222*. Request a copy of Sibarth's comprehensive, 108-page Vendome Guide in English. In addition to color photos of most Sibarth rentals, the guide contains information on the island hotels WIMCO represents, as well as restaurants, watersports and other activities. Two other companies also provide villa rentals: **French Caribbean International** handles about 80 properties ☎ *(800) 322-2223* or *(805) 967-9850*, while **St. Barth Properties**, represents about 60 villas on the island. ☎ *(590) 27-50-18* or *(800) 421-3396*.

Emeraude Plage Hotel   **$130–$560**   ★★★

Baie St. Jean, Gustavia, ☎ *(590) 27-64-78. FAX (590) 27-83-08.*
Single: $130–$560. Double: $130–$560.

Situated right on St. Jean Beach, this popular spot does a lot of repeat business, so book early. Accommodations are in simple yet comfortable bungalows with all the modern conveniences, plus kitchenettes on the patios. Three units have two bedrooms, and there's a beachside villa with two bedrooms, two baths and great views. All is kept in tip-top shape by the very friendly staff. There's little in the way of extras, but no one seems to mind. Guests get a discount on watersports at the nearby concession. Amenities: houses, cottages or bungalows. 31 rooms. Credit cards: MC, V.

Le P'tit Morne   **$95–$145**   ★★

Colombier, Gustavia, ☎ *(590) 27-62-64. FAX (590) 27-84-63.*
Single: $95–$145. Double: $95–$145.

Set high in the hills far from the madding crowds, the rates at this family-run apartment complex are quite reasonable. Spare but spacious units are air-conditioned studios with cable TV, minibars, fully equipped kitchens and decks. The premises include a pool and snack bar, which serves breakfast only. The beach is a five-minute drive down a twisting road. 12 rooms. Credit cards: A, MC.

Les Islets Fleuris　　　　　　　$72–$230　　　★★

Lorient, Gustavia, ☎ *(800) 223-9815, (590) 27-64-22. FAX (590) 27-69-72.*
Single: $72–$207. Double: $80–$230.

This small complex has seven cottages set on the hillside. All are studios with full kitchens and large terraces that rely on ceiling fans for comfort. There's a pool on-site, with restaurants nearby; the beach is a five-minute drive. 7 rooms. Credit cards: A, V.

Les Jardins de St. Jean　　　　$60–$355　　　★★★

St. Jean, Gustavia, ☎ *(800) 755-9313, (590) 27-70-19. FAX (590) 27-84-40.*
Single: $60–$255. Double: $88–$355.

This condominium hotel is located on a hillside, a few hundred yards from the beach. Accommodations are in a cluster of two-story bungalows and run the gamut from studios to units with one or two bedrooms. All have full kitchens, private terraces and air conditioning. TV and radio are available for an extra charge. There's a large pool is located on the premises and much more is within walking distance. Amenities: balcony or patio. 22 rooms. Credit cards: A, DC, MC, V.

Marigot Bay Club　　　　　　　$75–$180　　　★★

Marigot Bay, Gustavia, ☎ *(590) 27-75-45. FAX (590) 27-90-04.*
Single: $75–$150. Double: $90–$180.

This small apartment hotel offers clean and basic units at a fair price. Set on a hillside overlooking the Atlantic, units are simply furnished and include full kitchens, private terraces, TVs and living rooms. Maids keep things tidy. There's a terrific lobster restaurant on-site, but not much else. The beach is a short walk. 6 rooms. Credit cards: A, MC, V.

White Sand Beach Cottages　　　$125–$200　　★★

Baie de Flamands, Gustavia, ☎ *(590) 27-82-08. FAX (590) 27 70 69.*
Single: $125–$200. Double: $125–$200.

This casual spot has four cottages with wood decks on fabulous Flamands Beach. The accommodations are simple yet pleasant, with kitchenettes and air conditioning. No facilities on-site, but a couple restaurants are within walking distance. 4 rooms. Credit cards: A, MC.

Yuana Hotel　　　　　　　　　　$165–$360　　★★★

Quartier du Roy, Gustavia, ☎ *(800) 932-3222, (590) 27-80-84. FAX (590) 27-78-45.*
Single: $165–$360. Double: $165–$360.

Set in a lush garden, this hillside hotel has great views but a somewhat awkward location. Guests are put up in spacious studios with full kitchenettes, TVs with VCRs, and comfortable furnishings. The restaurant serves breakfast only; you'll have to cook or rent a car for other meals. There's a small, shady pool for cooling off. 12 rooms. Credit cards: A, MC.

Low Cost Lodging

Affordable accommodations on St. Barts? Say it isn't so! Truly budget lodging is not really found on this most-expensive of Caribbean isles, but there are a few lower priced options. In addition to the listings below, seriously consider making your trip during low season, when a few delights like the Sea Horse and Hostellerie des Trois Forces dip below the triple-digit mark. Beyond the listings below, a few other budget possibilities include **Les Igloos** on Pointe Milou ☎ *(590) 27-56-14*, the **Manoir de St. Barth** in Lorient ☎ *(590) 27-79-27*, and the harborside Sunset Hotel in Gustavia ☎ *(590) 27-77-21*.

The cost-conscious visitor to St. Barts should be forewarned that the daily food bill for two can easily outpace your accommodation tab. Unless you're planning on a Cheeseburger in Paradise for breakfast, lunch and dinner daily, be sure to allot a good portion of your budget for food. Finally, though shopping on the island is not inexpensive, make-do types can get by admirably on the fine French cheese, pâte and other items stocked at the **AMC Supermarket** in Gustavia. This opens up one more option, particularly for families—a villa rental. Sibarth has a charming group of rustic one-bedroom bungalows with full kitchens where you can step right onto St. Jean beach for $1045 a week in low season. Two-bedroom properties start at about $1400 per week during the summer (see "Apartments and Condominiums" above).

Paradise doesn't come cheap, but it's a little more attainable than the pages of *Conde Nast Traveler* might lead you to think.

La Presqui'ile   **$40–$100**   ★

Gustavia Harbor, Gustavia, ☎ *(590) 27-64-60. FAX (590) 27-72-30.*
Single: $40–$60. Double: $60–$100.
Built in 1963, La Presqui'ile was the second hotel on St. Barts, and somehow remains a great bargain for those expecting no more than the very basics. The bathroom is shared and decor is spartan, but this harborside property will leave a few francs in your pocket for dinner. No pool, but Shell Beach is a 10-minute walk. 10 rooms.

Normandie   **$56–$84**   ★

Lorient, Gustavia, ☎ *(590) 27-61-66. FAX (590) 27 98 83.*
Single: $56–$84. Double: $56–$84.
This basic, family-run place offers some of St. Barth's cheapest accommodations. The rooms are decent for the rates—obviously quite basic, but clean and comfortable. Only two (the most expensive) have air conditioners; the rest rely on ceiling fans. There's a small pool but nothing else, so you'll want a car. 8 rooms. Credit cards: not accepted.

Where to Eat

Fielding's Highest Rated Restaurants in St. Barthélémy

★★★★★	Le Toque Lyonnaise	$43–$61
★★★★	Au Port	$19–$28
★★★★	Ballahou	$27–$45
★★★★	Eddy's	$18–$24
★★★★	Francois Plantation	$16–$50
★★★★	La Fregate	$10–$19
★★★★	Le Gaiac	$22–$31
★★★★	Le Sapotillier	$47–$47
★★★★	Maya's	$27–$35
★★★	Wall House	$19–$39

Fielding's Most Exclusive Restaurants in St. Barthélémy

★★★★★	Le Toque Lyonnaise	$43–$61
★★★★	Le Sapotillier	$47–$47
★★★★	Le Gaiac	$22–$31
★★★	Wall House	$19–$39
★★★★	Ballahou	$27–$45

Fielding's Best Value Restaurants in St. Barthélémy

★★★★	La Fregate	$10–$19
★★★★	Eddy's	$18–$24
★★★	Vietnam	$14–$18
★★★	Ines' Ghetto	$15–$17
★★★	La Mandala	$11–$25

Dining in the Caribbean doesn't come much better than on St. Barts. It has to be good to suit persnickety jetsetters who arrive with expectations of gastronomique cuisine on par with what might be found in France. Indeed, unlike on Martinique and Guadeloupe, menus on St. Barts usually steer to the French, often using the spoils of the sea, such as lobster and redfish, though you can find some West Indian restaurants, as well as a smattering of Asian and Italian. Still, French is king here, and is celebrated in high style in April when the one-week Festival Gastronomique rolls into town and showcases the best of French food and wine.

Current favorites include the shoreside **Maya's**, which continues to be the hippest celebrity hangout, in large part due to its lack of pretense; the atmosphere is relaxed and the exotic cuisine—from French to creole to Vietnamese—is superb. Equally noteworthy is **Eddy's**, a newer addition to the Stakelborough family that sets the fine food against a backdrop of teak and bamboo mementos from Bali, a favorite destination for the affable owner. An estimable wine cellar containing rare and precious vintages tempts diners at **Francois Plantation**, where young chef Philippe Ruiz works magic in the kitchen—the desserts are memorable. The island's best view is proffered by the tres cher Carl Gustaf, though you'll enjoy it even more at lunch or for a sunset cocktail, when Gustavia's panoply of color is fleshed out by the sun.

At the average St. Barts restaurant, expect lunch for two to run $50 to $75, and the dinner check to top $100; these prices don't include a bottle of fancy wine. However, when wallets get low there are a few options. First, seek out the many spots that offer fixed-price menus—the lower price has little relationship to the quality of your meal. A dinner with dessert at one of these restaurants will run $25–35 per person (plus drinks). Next, pick up a copy of *Ti Gourmet*, a free illustrated guide to many island establishments—flash your copy at any of the several dozen restaurants listed in its pages and you will receive a complimentary cocktail. And don't forego a trip to one of the many island rotisseries for tasty and relatively cheap fast food.

Among the more affordable restaurants on the island are the reliable **Le Repaire** and **Wall House** on the outer end of the harbor in Gustavia. In the heart of Gustavia is **Paradisio** for the island's best Italian and **Vietnam** for splendid Asian. A romantic splurge is safely indulged at the moderately-priced and scenic **Marigot Bay Club**. Less expensive still, amid simpler surroundings are **Brasserie Creole** for West Indian at St. Jean Bay, colorful **Chez Ginette** in Anse des Cayes which caters to poets with Ginette's infamous **Punch Coco**, **Chez JoJo** for burgers and fried chicken in Lorient, **Chez Pompi** for modest meals in Grand Cul de Sac, while American food is celebrated at **Santa Fe**, high on the hill above Gustavia. **Le Select** is the island's most famous and down-home bar (a Red Stripe is $2), but its adjoining garden and snack stand—**Cheeseburger in Paradise**—sells the titular item for about $6. Several other low-priced eateries in Gustavia compete for the burger-and-sandwich business: **Chez Joe Cafe** and **Bar de L'Oubli** are two contenders. Finally, if the wealth of choices begins to seem overwhelming, stop by the real estate office Sibarth, where menus from many restaurants are available for browsing.

There are a few post-hurricane developments of note. The esteemed **Castelets** awaits rebuilding, while **La Fregate** and **Le Pelican** are closed indefinitely. **El Sereno's La Toque** was recently replaced with a gym. **Eddy's Ghetto** was sold in 1996 and now operates under the name **Ines' Ghetto**—the menu's the same, and you still have to ask for directions since there is no sign out front. The new owners of the **Eden Rock** hired chef Gilles Malfroid, formerly of Vincent Adam, to man their restaurant—the initial word is very good.

Au Port   **$$$**   ★★★★

Rue Sadi-Carnot; Gustavia ☎ (590) 27-62-36.
French cuisine.
Dinner: 6:30–10 p.m., entrées $19–$28.

Guests navigate a steep staircase to get to the second-floor dining room of this charming old house above the port of Gustavia. Cuisine is a fanciful blend of traditional French and creole—witness the popular *colombo* (creole curry) of prawns or lamb served with seasoned rice. A three-course creole menu is an excellent value at $36 and might include lamb curry or conch and lobster sausage. There are several foie gras items—it's made on the premises. Reservations recommended. Credit cards: A, V.

Ballahou   **$$$**   ★★★★

Anse des Cayes, Gustavia, ☎ (590) 27-66-55. Associated hotel: Hotel Manapany.
French cuisine.
Lunch: 12:30–4 p.m., entrées $15–$30.
Dinner: 7:30–9:30 p.m., entrées $27–$45.

There's a lot of understandable ballyhoo (and hip-hooray) about this gorgeous restaurant in the sleek Hotel Manapany—architecturally, it seems to blend as one with the rim of the swimming pool. Specialties usually include seafood, but chef Jerome Le Dore's menu changes often. Guests of the hotel and others dine here by candlelight only five months out of the year; it's closed in the warmer months. Manapany's Italian restaurant, Ouanalao, serves lunch and dinner all year round; try the gazpacho and risotto with prawns. Reservations required. Credit cards: A, DC, MC, V.

Castelets   **$$$**   ★★★

Morne Lurin, Gustavia, ☎ (590) 27-6173. Associated hotel: Castelets.
French cuisine.
Dinner: 7–9 p.m., entrées $25–$35. Closed: Tue.

This long-established hotel went through a brief Italian phase as Sapore de Mare. Manager Genevieve Jouany returned and brought everything back to normal, including the chic dining salon presided over by two under-30s chefs (aren't they all?). These young wizards eschew heavy cream sauces in favor of fresh herbs and virgin olive oils. They also exhibit a propensity for wild morel and boletus mush-

rooms that show up frequently in pasta and seafood dishes. Reservations required.
Credit cards: A, MC, V.

Eddy's $$$ ★★★★

Rue du Centenaire; Gustavia ☎ *(590) 27-54-17.*
International cuisine.
Dinner: 7–10 p.m., entrées $18–$24.
Following the long-running success of Eddy's Ghetto, Eddy Stakelborough (son of
island institution, Marius, the founder of Le Select), opened a slightly more upscale
and eclectic version of his French-meets-West Indian establishment. The appealing
decor is Balinese teak and bamboo, while the menu includes creole curry, a shrimp
in Thai-style green curry, and pork tenderloin breaded in fresh coconut and topped
with pineapple sauce. Fish dishes are prepared grilled, fried or in parchment. Like
the Ghetto (which now operates under the name Ines), Eddy's has no sign—it's
across the street from Le Sapotillier. Drop by in person to reserve a table. Credit cards:
A, MC, V.

Francois Plantation $$$ ★★★★

Colombier, Gustavia, ☎ *(590) 27-78-82. Associated hotel: Francois Plantation.*
French cuisine.
Dinner: 6:30–10 p.m., entrées $16–$50. Closed: Sun.
No one doubts the serene beauty of this place—for exotic plantings, greenery and
an interior boasting highly polished woods, and the food, under the watchful eye of
owner Francois Beret, lives up to the setting with a new chef, 25-year-old Philippe
Ruiz, at the helm. Lighter versions of traditional French favorites take a front seat,
with delicate, unusual spices accenting innovative dishes such as lobster taboule,
roasted tournedos of ostrich, and home-smoked salmon in a mille-feuilles pastry.
Desserts are outstanding, and the island's best cellar produces a wine list some 180
vintages strong. Reservations required. Credit cards: A, MC, V.

Hostellerie des Trois Forces $$$ ★★★

Vitet, Gustavia, ☎ *(590) 27-61-25. Associated hotel: Hostellerie Trois Forces.*
French cuisine.
Lunch: Noon–3 p.m., entrées $10–$50.
Dinner: 7–9:45 p.m., entrées $10–$50.
Tarot readings and fine food commingle nicely at this surprisingly unpretentious
holistic, New Age resort-restaurant in the small town of Vitet, high in the hills
above Marigot. Chef and chief astrologer Hubert Delemotte serves creole/French
meals with a nod to organic and vegetarian diners, although the focus is on grilled
meats and fish—produced from a wood-burning fireplace. A three-course, prix-fixe
dinner offering nightly. Ambience is low-key and pleasant, and Delamotte's rum
drinks have a loyal following. Closed for lunch on Sunday. Reservations required.
Credit cards: A, MC, V.

Ines' Ghetto $$$ ★★★

Rue du General de Gaulle; Gustavia, ☎ *(590) 27-53-20.*
French cuisine.
Dinner: 7–10 p.m., entrées $15–$17. Closed: Sun.

Formerly infamous as Eddy's Ghetto, when locals go "slumming" they still go to Ines' for simple grills, salads, ribs, beef ragouts, pumpkin soup, *entrecote* and island music. The yacht crowd often dominates the wicker- and plant-filled restaurant the moment it opens at 7 p.m., if the locals haven't gotten there first. The place fills the need for light meals and provides a casual ambience not found in some of the island's pricier establishments. You'll need to ask for directions since there's no sign (it's close to the Sibarth office), but this is one spot everyone can point you to.

L'Entrepont $$$ ★★★

La Pointe; Gustavia, ☎ *(590) 27-90-60.*
Italian cuisine.
Dinner: entrées $25–$33.
Located in a newly fashionable area on the west side of Gustavia's harbor, this Italian restaurant owned by a Neapolitan family is renowned for unusual pizzas. Guests eat well in a garden setting under coconut trees that's open to the breezes. Other choices include beef carpaccio, pastas and veal. The location goes under the name Chez Francine at lunch. Reservations recommended. Credit cards: A, MC, V.

L'Escale $$$ ★★★

La Pointe, Gustavia, ☎ *(590) 27-81-06.*
Italian cuisine.
Dinner: 7 p.m.–midnight, entrées $12–$29. Closed: Tue.
This mostly Italian trattoria on the west side of the harbor has many faithful followers who clamor for the variety of *tagliatelle*, ravioli, lasagna and grilled meats and seafood. But most come for the delicious pizzas, priced $12–17. Lately L'Escale has been facing some competition from other eateries in the area serving similar cuisine, although it swings at night, especially in the hip bar. Reservations required. Credit cards: MC, V.

L'Iguane $$$ ★★★

Carre d'Or mall; Gustavia, ☎ *(590) 27-88-46.*
Lunch: 8 a.m.–5 p.m., entrées $6–$15.
Dinner: 5 p.m.–midnight, entrées $15–$20.
A nice spot in a newer shopping area, L'Iguane serves ice cream, inexpensive crab and pasta salads and foccacia sandwiches. But at night, a sushi menu is rolled and served until midnight (daily except Monday). A plate for one averages $15-20, while combination platters run $30–70.

La Fregate $$ ★★★★

Flamandes Beach, Gustavia, ☎ *(590) 27-6651. Associated hotel: Baie des Flamandes.*
French cuisine.
Lunch: Noon–3 p.m., entrées $10–$19.
Dinner: 7–9 p.m., entrées $10–$19. Closed: Mon.
Aim for an outside patio table at this excellent restaurant—if you can. The word is out about the incredible edibles emerging from Jean-Pierre Crouzet's kitchen in a somewhat tacky beachfront motel in Baie des Flamandes. Island regulars know him from his past successes at Gustavia's La Sapotillier, where he was chef de cuisine. Here he continues to unleash a plethora of dishes utilizing the freshest local ingredients possible with a tried and true technique—although he is not yet 30, he has

already worked his way through quite a few three-star establishments in France. Reservations required. Credit cards: A, MC, V.

La Langouste $$$ ★★★

Rue Bord-de-la-Mer, Gustavia, ☎ *(590) 27-69-47.*
Latin American cuisine. Specialties: Langouste.
Lunch: Noon–2 p.m., entrées $23–$42.
Dinner: 7–10 p.m., entrées $23–$42.
The island's national crustacean (a clawless lobster) is the star at this pleasant creole/French eatery owned by Annie Ange, a member of a St. Barts landowning family (St. Barth Beach Hotel). The delectable seafood is dependably fresh, and other finny offerings include stuffed crabs and *accra de morue* (cod fritters). It's located is a traditional Swedish-style dwelling near several public offices. Reservations required. Credit cards: MC, V.

La Mandala $$$ ★★★

Rue Thiers; Gustavia, ☎ *(590) 27-96-96.*
Dinner: 5–11 p.m., entrées $11–$25.
New this year, La Mandala is the swank creation of Boubou (stepson of Roger Vadim) and his partner Christophe, who have converted the former Hibiscus Hotel into a outdoor restaurant perched on a deck with a fabulous Gustavia view. The menu has a multicultural flair (like the eclectic decor), with an emphasis on tapas— appetizer plates priced $7–10. Entrées include beef, chicken, salmon and pasta dishes and there's a sitting table in the rear for small parties. The $34 prix fixe menu is a good value, and the view is almost as good as from the nearby, much pricier Carl Gustaf. Features: Sunday brunch. Credit cards: A, MC, V.

Le Gaiac $$$ ★★★★

Anse de Toiny, Gustavia, ☎ *(590) 27-88-88. Associated hotel: Le Toiny.*
French cuisine.
Lunch: entrées $12–$28.
Dinner: entrées $22–$31.
This small, very in spot at Le Toiny, a resort on a hilltop above a windswept beach, has quickly developed a new following after bringing in 28-year-old cuisinier Chef Maxime des Champs. The intimate, 30-seat outdoor restaurant (book far in advance) features a menu that artfully marries traditional Provencal French with West Indian cuisine. Specialties include yellowtail snapper with curried lentils and squash, a gateau of roast boneless pigeon layered with red cabbage, sweet potato and herbs, and a light monkfish stew with spring vegetables and bacon. Poolside lunch (very popular on Sunday) offers chilled soups, sandwiches pasta and grilled seafood. The name Gaiac comes from the rare trees that dot the property. Reservations required. Credit cards: A, MC, V.

Le Paradisio $$$ ★★★

Rue de Roi; Gustavia, ☎ *(590) 27-80-78.*
French cuisine.
Lunch: prix fixe $20.
Dinner: entrées $15–$30.

French-inspired Italian food is served at this very popular restaurant in a traditional, historic building in Gustavia. Formerly the site of La Citronelle, the jolly exterior features gingerbread trim, white shutters, tangerine and white railings and a tropical mural. Guests can dine on several different daily pasta offerings in air-conditioned insularity or on a breeze-cooled patio. The menu also features lobster in saffron oil and beef filets, and the variety of carpaccios—beef, lamb, salmon, red snapper and tuna—are well-liked. The fixed price lunch is a particularly good value. Reservations recommended. Credit cards: MC, V.

Le Pelican $$$ ★★

Plage de St. Jean, Gustavia, ☎ *(590) 27-6464.*
Latin American cuisine.
Lunch: 11:30 a.m.–3 p.m., entrées $20–$40.
Dinner: 6:30–1 p.m., entrées $20–$40.

This pleasant restaurant located a few steps from St. Barth's most popular beach satisfies on many counts. At lunch it's perfect for casual meals and ocean- and people-watching from a vast, covered terrace. Later, for dinner, the large dining rooms are awash in candlelight while sounds of piano music grace the background. Cuisine is a melange of creole and French favorites. Closed for dinner on Sundays. Reservations recommended. Credit cards: A, V.

Le Sapotillier $$$ ★★★★

Rue Sadi-Carnot; Gustavia, ☎ *(590) 27-60-28.*
French cuisine. Specialties: Couscous with shrimp creole, fish mousse.
Dinner: from 6:30 p.m., prix fixe $47. Closed: Sun.

Some fine chefs have emerged with an appreciative following from the kitchens of this memorable restaurant in a traditional old stone structure in Gustavia, including Le Fregate's Jean-Pierre Crouzette. La Sapotillier's reputation is still stellar, with classic French cuisine served with finesse in a small, dark dining room or alfresco under the branches of a vast sapodilla tree. Specialties include lasagna of escargots in a garlic sauce, foie gras of duck with juniper berry sauce, and veal stew with roquefort and vegetables. The many fish dishes are prepared with a Provencal flair. Reservations required. Credit cards: MC, V.

Le Select $ ★★

Rue de la France; Gustavia, ☎ *(590) 27-86-87.*
International cuisine. Specialties: Burgers.
Lunch: 10 a.m.–4 p.m., entrées $5–$10.
Dinner: 4–11 p.m., entrées $5–$10. Closed: Sun.

This old favorite (circa 1950) provides a safe haven for ordinary folk seeking refuge from the high prices and sometimes over-stuffed, precious atmosphere of some island dining establishments. Besides serving what is probably the best cheeseburger in town at an adjoining snack stand, the scruffy, poster-festooned old warehouse is great for loud reggae, *zouk*, or *soca* music—Jimmy Buffett schedules impromptu concerts here regularly. Newcomers can't possibly miss Le Select—it sits at a prime location in the middle of town; at night you hear it before you see it. Credit cards: not accepted.

ST. BARTHÉLEMY

Le Tamarin   **$$$**   ★ ★ ★

Plage de Saline, Gustavia, ☎ *(590) 27-72-12.*
Lunch: 11 a.m.–5 p.m., entrées $22–$34.
Located a half-mile inland from Grand Saline, perhaps the island's best beach, Le
Tamarin is the sole restaurant in the area, with a steady stream of sunbathers seeking
nourishment for clientele. The crab, avocado and grapefruit salad is a winner for a
lighter meal ($16), or go for the grilled tenderloin embellished with a roquefort or
green peppercorn sauce. Desserts are delicious, and owner Cat Cent keeps the
atmosphere hip under an ancient tamarind tree. In season, Le Tamarin is open for
dinner on weekends. Credit cards: A, MC, V.

Le Toque Lyonnaise   **$$$**   ★ ★ ★ ★ ★

Grand Cul-de-Sac, Gustavia, ☎ *(590) 27-6480.*
Associated hotel: El Sereno Beach Hotel.
French cuisine. Specialties: Grilled lobster with vanilla bean.
Dinner: 7–10 p.m., prix fixe $43–$61.
It's hard not to have a good meal here—chefs are from Lyon, which is the gourmet
capital of France. This modern, oceanfront eatery, located a few miles out of Gustavia, boasts chefs who have trained with Paul Bocuse. Grilled seafood is the specialty,
and the wine list is extensive and well-chosen. Closed June through October. Reservations recommended. Credit cards: A, DC, MC, V.

Marigot Bay Club   **$$$**   ★ ★ ★

Marigot Bay, Gustavia, ☎ *(590) 27-75-45.*
French cuisine.
Lunch: entrées $11–$26.
Dinner: entrées $20–$28.
Two giant grilled langoustines appear on your plate here like creatures from Mars—
yet they were freshly caught only this morning. Marigot Bay Club is an intimate res-
taurant offering romance without pretense on a bayside deck in the small village of
Marigot. Grilled fish, filet mignon and duck are offered, but lobster is the specialty,
available tucked in ravioli, as a pastry-wrapped stew, with a creole sauce or in a
creamy mushroom and gruyere sauce. Specialties rarely change, which is how most
people who eat here like it. Closed for lunch on Monday. Reservations required.
Credit cards: A, MC, V.

Maya's   **$$$**   ★ ★ ★ ★

Public, Gustavia, ☎ *(590) 27-73-61.*
Latin American cuisine.
Dinner: 6–11 p.m., entrées $27–$35. Closed: Sun.
Maya from Martinique serves savory creole cuisine with some spicy touches to an
always appreciative (and expansive) crowd; it's one of the more popular eateries on
the island. Fresh seafood and grilled lobster are the focus, but a spicy callallo soup
is unlike any other in the islands. Situated on a waterfront location in Public (west
of Gustavia) the restaurant offers tables on a plant-filled patio. The menu changes
frequently, but one thing stays the same—the table-hopping coterie of stars who
keep the atmosphere lively night after night. Closed June through October. Reservations required. Credit cards: A, MC, V.

ST. BARTHÉLÉMY

Santa Fe $$ ★★

Lurin, Gustavia, ☎ (590) 27-61-04.
American cuisine. Specialties: Burgers, steaks.
Lunch: Noon–2 p.m., entrées $10–$21.
Dinner: 5–10 p.m., entrées $10–$21. Closed: Mon.

Attracting more than its share of local characters, the food served at Santa Fe is basically burgers (excellent), steak, and barbecue at American prices (reasonable). It's also a hangout for Anglais-speakers and sports fans of any stripe who come to watch their favorite teams play on an "epic screen" television, especially on Sundays. Located just a few miles east of Gustavia, it seems worlds away in atmosphere and in its isolation on a lofty hilltop. There's no ocean view, but plenty of local ambiance.

Vietnam $$$ ★★★

Rue du Roi Oscar II; Gustavia ☎ (590) 27-81-37.
Lunch: prix fixe $12.
Dinner: entrées $14–$18.

Thai, Chinese and Vietnamese dishes are featured on the menu of this inexpensive spot. Seating is in an air-conditioned dining room, or out on a lovely outdoor covered patio overlooking the bustle of Gustavia. The $12 fixed-price lunch has to be one of the best deals on the island, while glazed duck, spring rolls and stuffed shrimp are dinner highlights. Angelique and Tuyen are the charming owners. Closed for lunch on Sundays.

Vincent Adam $$$ ★★★

St. Jean, Gustavia, ☎ (590) 27-93-22.
French cuisine.
Dinner: prix fixe $38–$48. Closed: Tue.

On an island where fabulous eateries come and go, Vincent Adam prevails by proffering a seemingly infinite variety of three-course, prix-fixe dinners for $38; a lobster menu is also available for $48. The wide selection includes filet mignon, lobster tabouli, or filet of pork with a coconut sauce, capped off with creme brulee or other heavenly desserts. The setting is also paradisiacal, high on a hillside with garden and lagoon views; there's art on the walls as well as on the plates. Also known as Adam. Reservations recommended. Credit cards: A, V.

Wall House $$$ ★★★

Gustavia Harbor, Gustavia, ☎ (590) 27-71-83.
French cuisine.
Dinner: 6:30–10 p.m., entrées $19–$39.

Almost every table in this whitewashed restaurant in the harbor has a lovely view; the wide picture windows in the dining room offer a quayside panorama of swaying palms, small craft, azure waters, and a row of red tile-roofed, gingerbread-trimmed buildings. Diners can also sit outside to be closer to the action. The regular menu is fine, of you may choose from three, three-course fixed-price menus: the $30 and $38 groupings include mahi mahi in a mint cream, or fillet of lamb in marjoram. A $56 lobster menu features grilled lobster along with a lobster appetizer. Reservations recommended. Credit cards: A, MC, V.

ST. BARTHÉLÉMY

Duty-free reigns supreme in St. Barts. If you're in the market for fine perfumes, china, crystal and liquor, you can find some of the best bargains in the Caribbean. In recent years, several haute couture boutiques have opened on the island, including Stephane & Bernard, Hermes, Gucci, Polo and Cartier. Some French perfumes, like Chanel, are cheaper here than in Paris. Most name brand shops are located in Gustavia, though a few are scattered through the St. Jean area, and at La Savane Commercial Center, across the street from the airport. Yacht owners and wannabes tend to congregate at Loulou's Marine in Gustavia, where everything you ever needed for a cruise is available—from clothes to rigs, with the canvas tote bags stamped with the store logo a particular favorite.

Beyond the duty-free products, a few local items are unique to St. Barts and have established an international reputation. Skin lotions and tanning oils made from local plants are created by Belou's P including beautifully bottled fragrant oils, each named for a different beach—you'll find them at 'Ti Marche, the open air market in Gustavia. Another line of beauty lotions and suntan products is Ligne de St. Barth, sold in Lorient by Herve Brin. M'Bolo produces delicious rum punch from vanilla, coconut, prune, apricot and other fruits—they are hand-bottled, make lovely gifts, and can be found along with other items at a store in Gustavia's Carre d'Or shopping arcade. St. Barts Pottery, located just past the Gustavia post office, handles stoneware and terra cotta by Jennifer May, along with a few baskets, paintings and jewelry (open daily, but closed during the summer). To find one of the last vestiges of traditional life, go to the once-isolated fishing village of Corossol, where you can still see older St. Bartian women weaving delicate handicrafts from lantana palm. Magazine spreads to the contrary, the woven, nun-style bonnets called *caleches* or *quichenottes* ("kiss me not") are rarely if ever seen on their heads anymore (the women are notoriously camera-shy). Other local crafts sold in Gustavia include sandals and shell jewelry, as well as paintings and lithographs by island artists. One of the most admired local painters is impressionist Denis Hermenge.

St. Barthélémy Directory

Arrival and Departure

There are no direct flights from North America to St. Barthélémy's tiny airstrip. The principal gateway is Sint Maarten's Juliana Airport which is served by **American Airlines** nonstop from New York's JFK, Miami and San Juan, Puerto Rico; by USAir out of Baltimore; and by **Continental** from Newark. For additional service to Sint Maarten see "Arrival and Departure" in "Sint Maarten."

The 10-minute flight from Sint Maarten to St. Barts is handled by **Windward Island Airways** ☎ *(590) 27-61-01* and **Air St. Barthélémy** ☎ *(590) 27-71-90*, both of which operate 19-seat STOL (Short Takeoff and Landing) aircraft. These small airlines purport to follow a schedule, but the reality is that they tend to leave when their plane fills up—fortunately departures are relatively frequent, particularly during the afternoon when most of the jets land on Sint Maarten. Have patience when you arrive in Sint Maarten; you'll get to St. Barts eventually as long as there's light out (the runway shuts down at dusk). Round-trip fare is about $95. Also from within the Caribbean, **Air St. Barthélémy** and **Air Guadeloupe** ☎ *(590) 27-61-90* each provide service out of San Juan, Guadeloupe and Espérance Airport (on French St. Martin). Air St. Thomas ☎ *(590) 27-71-76* provides flights from San Juan and St. Thomas.

It is also possible to get to St. Barts by boat. The *White Octopus*, a 75-foot catamaran, makes the 90-minute crossing from Sint Maarten on Tuesdays and Thursdays. The cat leaves Philipsburg at 9 a.m. and departs Gustavia for the return trip at 4 p.m., allowing just enough time for lunch and a round of shopping. The trip is $25 each way, plus $5 tax (open bar included) ☎ *(599) 5-23170*. Several ferry services are also available: **Gustavia Express** plies the route to St. Barts from both Philipsburg and Marigot (on French St. Martin) ☎ *(590) 27-77-24; Voyageur I* makes the trip from Marigot to Gustavia ☎ *(590) 87-99-03*; and *Bateau Dakar* serves both St. Martin and Guadeloupe ☎ *(590) 27-70-05.*

There is an airport departure tax of about $6.

Business Hours

Shops are open weekdays 8:30 a.m.–noon and 2–5 p.m. (some until 7 p.m.) and Saturday 8:30 a.m.–noon. Banks open weekdays 8 a.m.–noon and 2–3:30 p.m.

Climate

St. Barts has an ideal dry climate and an average temperature of 72–86 degrees Fahrenheit.

Documents

For stays of up to three weeks, U.S. and Canadian citizens traveling as tourists must have proof of citizenship in the form of a valid passport or that has expired not more than five years ago, or a birth certificate (original or copy) or voter's registration accompanied by a government authorized ID with photo. For stays over three weeks, or for nontourist visits, a valid passport is necessary. Resident aliens of the U.S. and Canada, and visitors from countries other than those in the Common Market (E.E.C.) and Japan, must have a valid passport and visa. A return or onward ticket is also required of all visitors.

Electricity

Current runs at 220 AC, 60 cycles. American-made appliances require French plug converters and transformers.

Getting Around

Car rentals are easy to secure on the island, but it is best to ask your hotel to reserve one for you in advance, especially during the winter season. Roads are hilly, steep, narrow and winding, and drivers must know how to use a stick shift; your best options are VW Beetles, little open Gurgels, and Mini-Mokes. You'll save money if you rent by the week —daily rates go as high as $60 a day, which includes unlimited mileage, collision damage insurance (first $500 deductible) and free delivery. Gas costs about $3.25 a gallon. None of the two gas stations (near the airport and in Lorient) is open on Sunday. St. Barts' first all-night automatic gas station recently opened near the airport, requiring magnetically sensitized cards on sale at the station.

Some reliable agencies are: **Avis** at the airport ☎ *(590) 27-71-43*; **Budget** airport and town ☎ *(590) 27-67-43*; **Hertz** at the airport ☎ *(590) 27-71-14* or *(590) 27-60-21*. A few hotels have their own fleet of rentals, and may ask you to book through them because of limited parking.

Taxis stations (two) are located at the airport and one in Gustavia on rue de la République. To call a **taxi**, dial ☎ *(590) 27-66-31* on a local phone. For night taxis, call **Jean-Paul Janin** ☎ *(590) 27-61-86*, **Raymond Gréaux** ☎ *(590) 27-66-32*, or **Mathilde Laplace** ☎ *(590) 27-60-59*.

Motorbikes, mopeds, and scooters are easy to rent, but you must wear a helmet, required by law. You must also have a motorbike or driver's license. Rentals can be found at: **Denis Dufau's Rent Some Fun** ☎ *(590) 27-70-59*, which also carries 18-speed mountain bikes or **Frédéric Supligeau** ☎ *(590) 27-67-89*.

For information on ferries to Sint Maarten, St. Martin or Guadeloupe, see "Arrival and Departure" above.

You can also arrive on St. Barts by ferryboats from St. Martin, such as the *St. Barth Express III*, which leaves at 7:30 a.m. and returns from Marina Porte La Royale in Mariot at 3:30 p.m. and Bobby's Marina in Philipsburg at 4:15 p.m., arriving in Gustavia 45 minutes later. To reserve, ☎ *(590) 27-77-24*, FAX ☎ *(590) 27-7723*. Two other ferryboats are the *Dauphin II* and the *Bateau Dakar*.

Private boat charters can be arranged through Sibarth in Gustavia ☎ *(590) 27-62-38* or its American affiliate WIMGO, Newport RI ☎ *(800) 932-3222* or *(410) 849-8012*.

Language

French is the official language, spoken with a quaint Norman dialect. Most people speak English, but do plan to expecting an attitude to match that of the French employees at many hotels.

Medical Emergencies

Gustavia has a **hospital** ☎ *(590) 27-60-35*, eight resident doctors, three dentists, one gynecologist, and specialists in opthalmology, dermatology, etc. There are pharmacies at **La Savane Commercial Center** ☎ *(590) 27-66-61* and in Gustavia ☎ *(590) 27-61-82*.

Money

The official currency is the French franc. The exchange rate (August 1996) was approximately five francs to one American dollar, the figure used to calculate all hotel and restaurant prices listed in this book. The rate is subject to change due to currency fluctuations. Dollars are accepted almost everywhere, and prices in some hotels and restaurants are quoted in dollars. Credit cards are more readily accepted on the island than in the past, but a few notable restaurants still do not take plastic.

Telephone

The area code for St. Barts is *590*. To call from the U.S. dial *011* (international access code), then *590* plus the local number in St. Barts. To call St. Barts from Dutch St. Maarten, dial 6 plus St. Barts's local six-digit number. To call St. Barts from other F.W.I (Martinique, Guadeloupe, and French St. Martin), you can dial direct.

Public phones require the use of "Telecartes" that look like credit cards and can be easily purchased at the Gustavia, St. Jean and Lorient post offices and at the gas station near the airport. Both local and international calls can be made from these phones using the card.

Time

St. Barts is one hour ahead of Eastern Standard Time. When it is nine o'clock in St. Barts, it is eight o'clock in New York. During daylight saving time, there is no time difference.

Tipping and Taxes

Most hotels include tax and service in their quoted room rates; others add 5–15 percent to the bill.

Tourist Information

The Tourist Board, called the *Office de Tourisme*, is located in attractive quarters on the Quai Général de Gaulle, across from the Capitainerie in Gustavia, open Monday–Friday 8:30 a.m.–6 p.m., and Saturday 8:30 a.m.–noon. From May to November, hours are a bit shorter. When writing to the **St. Barts Tourist Office**, use the address: *B.P. 113, Gustavia, 97098 Cedex, St. Barthélémy, F.W.I.*

For what's happening weekly, pick up a current issue of *St. Barth Magazine*, distributed throughout the island. There's also an English language program at noon on Mondays and Thursdays called "This Week in St. Barts."

When to Go

Three Kings Day on January 8 is celebrated with special Epiphany cakes served at festivals. The 11th Anniversary of the St. Barts Music Festival is held January 8–22, with jazz, chamber music and guests from the Metropolitan Opera. Carnival is celebrated February 24, with a school parade, Mardi Gras pageant and parade, and the burning of Vaval, King of Carnival, at Shell Beach. The award-winning cookbook author and instructor Steven Raichlen presents a one-week class on Caribbean cuisine at Hotel Yuana. The Festival of Gustavia is celebrated on August 20, with dragnet fishing contests, dances and parties. The Festival of St. Barthélémy is a feast day of the island's patron saint, celebrated with the pealing of church bells, a regatta, public ball, fireworks and the blessing of boats. The Fête du Vent on August 26–27 is honored with dragnet fishing contests, dances, fireworks and a lottery in the village of Lorient. The Swedish Marathon Race is held in December 6. The Réveillon de la Saint Sylvestre, on New Year's Eve, is a grand gala at the island's hotels and restaurants.

ST. BARTHÉLÉMY HOTELS	RMS	RATES	PHONE	CR. CARDS
Gustavia				
★★★★★ Castelets	10	$100–$700	(590) 27-61-73	None
★★★★★ Guanahani	80	$230–$965	(800) 223-6800	A, MC, V
★★★★ Carl Gustaf	14	$410–$1250	(800) 948-7823	A, MC, V
★★★★ Christopher Hotel	40	$225–$500	(800) 763-4835	A, MC, V
★★★★ Hotel St. Barth Isle de France	28	$300–$780	(800) 628-8929	A, MC, V
★★★★ Hotel le Toiny	12	$510–$1350	(800) 298-6469	A, DC, MC, V
★★★★ Le Toiny	12	$490–$820	(800) 932-3222	A, MC, V
★★★ Eden Rock	10	$240–$600	(800) 932-3222	A, MC, V
★★★ El Sereno Beach Hotel	41	$200–$580	(800) 932-3222	A, MC, V
★★★ Emeraude Plage Hotel	31	$130–$560	(590) 27-64-78	MC, V
★★★ Filao Beach Hotel	30	$200–$640	(800) 932-3222	A, CB, D, DC, MC, V
★★★ Francois Plantation	12	$216–$450	(590) 27-78-82	A, MC, V
★★★ Hotel Baie des Flamands	24	$95–$135	(590) 27-64-85	A, MC
★★★ La Banane	9	$150–$480	(800) 932-3222	A, MC, V
★★★ Le Tom Beach	12	$150–$610	(800) 322-2223	A, MC, V
★★★ Les Jardins de St. Jean	22	$60–$355	(800) 755-9313	A, DC, MC, V
★★★ Manapany Cottages	52	$150–$950	(800) 932-3222	A, MC
★★★ Taiwana Hotel	9	$955–$999	(590) 27-65-01	None
★★★ Tropical Hotel	20	$110–$350	(800) 932-3222	A, MC

ST. BARTHÉLÉMY

ST. BARTHÉLÉMY HOTELS	RMS	RATES	PHONE	CR. CARDS
★★★ Village St. Jean Hotel	25	$89–$460	(800) 322-2223	A, MC, V
★★★ Yuana Hotel	12	$165–$360	(800) 932-3222	A, MC
★★ Baie des Anges Hotel	9	$145–$320	(800) 755-9313	A, CB, MC, V
★★ Grand Cul de Sac Hotel	36	$110–$335	(590) 27-60-7	A, MC
★★ Hostellerie Trois Forces	8	$75–$170	(590) 27-61-25	A, MC
★★ Le P'tit Morne	12	$95–$145	(590) 27-62-64	A, MC
★★ Les Islets Fleuris	7	$72–$230	(800) 223-9815	A, V
★★ Marigot Bay Club	6	$75–$180	(590) 27-75-45	A, MC, V
★★ Sea Horse Hotel	11	$80–$295	(800) 742-4276	A, MC, V
★★ St. Barth's Beach Hotel	44	$155–$280	(590) 27-60-70	A, MC
★★ White Sand Beach Cottages	4	$125–$200	(590) 27-82-08	A, MC
★ La Presqui'ile	10	$40–$100	(590) 27-64-60	
★ Normandie	8	$56–$84	(590) 27-61-66	None

ST. BARTHÉLÉMY RESTAURANTS	PHONE	ENTRÉE	CR. CARDS
Gustavia			
★★★★ Eddy's	(590) 27-54-17	$18–$24	A, MC, V
★★★ L'Iguane	(590) 27-88-46	$6–$20	
★★★ La Mandala	(590) 27-96-96	$11–$25	A, MC, V
★★★ Le Tamarin	(590) 27-72-12	$22–$34	A, MC, V
★★★ Vietnam	(590) 27-81-37	$12–$18	
American			
★★ Santa Fe	(590) 27-61-04	$10–$21	
French			
★★★★★ Le Toque Lyonnaise	(590) 27-6480	$43–$61	A, DC, MC, V
★★★★ Au Port	(590) 27-62-36	$19–$28	A, V
★★★★ Ballahou	(590) 27-66-55	$15–$45	A, DC, MC, V
★★★★ Francois Plantation	(590) 27-78-82	$16–$50	A, MC, V
★★★★ La Fregate	(590) 27-6651	$10–$19	A, MC, V
★★★★ Le Gaiac	(590) 27-88-88	$12–$31	A, MC, V

ST. BARTHÉLÉMY

ST. BARTHÉLÉMY RESTAURANTS	PHONE	ENTRÉE	CR. CARDS
★★★★ Le Sapotillier	(590) 27-60-28	$47–$47	MC, V
★★★ Castelets	(590) 27-61-73	$25–$35	A, MC, V
★★★ Hostellerie des Trois Forces	(590) 27-61-25	$10–$50	A, MC, V
★★★ Ines' Ghetto	(590) 27-53-20	$15–$17	
★★★ Le Paradisio	(590) 27-80-78	$20–$30	MC, V
★★★ Marigot Bay Club	(590) 27-75-45	$11–$28	A, MC, V
★★★ Wall House	(590) 27-71-83	$19–$39	A, MC, V
★★★ Vincent Adam	(590) 27-93-22	$38–$48	A, V
International			
★★ Le Select	(590) 27-86-87	$5–$10	None
Italian			
★★★ L'Entrepont	(590) 27-90-60	$25–$33	A, MC, V
★★★ L'Escale	(590) 27-81-06	$12–$29	MC, V
Latin American			
★★★★ Maya's	(590) 27-73-61	$27–$35	A, MC, V
★★★ La Langouste	(590) 27-69-47	$23–$42	MC, V
★★ Le Pelican	(590) 27-6464	$20–$40	A, V

ST. BARTHÉLÉMY

ST. BARTHÉLÉMY

ST. CROIX

Straw hats of every style entice shoppers at the market in Christiansted.

The U.S. Virgin Islands are often referred to as three sisters, with St. Thomas the older and more sophisticated sibling and rustic St. John the pretty baby over which everyone dotes. That leaves St. Croix as the middle child—often overlooked, often misunderstood. The fact is, St. Croix combines the best of its sisters, with the good shopping and varied accommodations of St. Thomas, and the wide-open spaces and rural feel of St. John.

More than its siblings, the island shows many signs of its Dutch heritage, especially in its two towns, Christiansted and Frederiksted. Here the narrow streets are lined with historic buildings painted in colorful pastels and adorned with wooden shutters. The largest of the three U.S. Virgins, St. Croix covers 82 square miles, and besides the usual enclave of shops and hotels, you'll see rolling hills, undulating sugarcane fields, cattle grazing in emerald-green pastures, gorgeous beaches, desert plains and even a rainforest. Life here is more laid-back than on busy St. Thomas, and there's much more to do and see than on St. John.

By the time you read this, St. Croix may have something new: casino gambling. Virgin Islanders have passed a referendum that will allow up to six casinos around the island, some self-standing, others in new or existing hotels. At presstime, the local government was actively courting casino companies to invest in the island. Eventually, St. Thomas will add casinos as well.

One of the best reasons to visit St. Croix lies just offshore—Buck Island Reef National Monument. The only underwater national monument in the United States, this uninhabited island makes for great hiking and picnicking, but the real reason to come is to snorkel among its coral gardens and rich sea life.

Severely devastated by Hurricane Hugo in 1989, St. Croix was happily just grazed by 1995's Hurricane's Marilyn and Luis—each packed a huge wallop on St. Thomas and St. John. Visitors to the island today will be hard-pressed to find evidence of Hugo's wrath—a true tribute to the pride and perseverance of Crucians, as locals are called.

Bird's-Eye View

At 82 square miles, St. Croix is the largest of the U.S Virgin Islands. It lies in the Caribbean Sea some 1700 miles south of New York. The island is separated from St. Thomas and St. John by 32 miles and a 12,000-foot oceanic trench. The topography is quite varied; the west end is lusher, higher and more forested, while the eastern side is rocky and dry. In between lie rolling hills and sweeping pastures dotted with grazing cattle and sugarcane fields. The annual average temperature is 80 degrees Fahrenheit, with constant trade winds to help cool things down. Average annual rainfall is 40 inches.

The island's largest town is Christiansted, a pretty waterfront enclave of narrow streets, pastel-colored buildings from the 18th century, T-shirt shops, tonier boutiques and open-air restaurants. On the other side of the island lies Fredericksted, which dates to 1751. The architecture here is more Victorian than Danish, and this is the spot where cruise ships disgorge hundreds of bargain-hunting passengers.

Located one and half miles off the northeastern coast is Buck Island, a true treasure that is the United State's only underwater national monument. Though the famed underwater trail has yet to fully recover from the damage

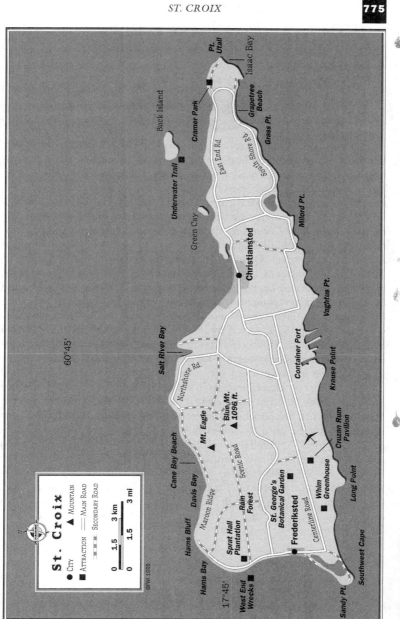

St. Croix

● City   ▲ Mountain
■ Attraction   ═══ Main Road
▄▄▄ Secondary Road

0   1.5   3 km
0   1.5   3 mi

60°45'

17°45'

Pt. Utall
Isaac Bay
Cramer Park
Grapetree Beach
Grass Pt.
Buck Island
East End Rd.
South Shore Rd.
Underwater Trail
Green Cay
Milord Pt.
Christiansted
Vaghtus Pt.
Salt River Bay
Container Port
Krause Point
Northshore Rd.
Cane Bay Beach
Mt. Eagle ▲
Blue Mt.
▲ 1096 ft.
Scenic Road
Cruzan Rum
Pavilion
Long Point
Hams Bluff
Davis Bay
Maroon Ridge
Ram
Forest
St. George's
Botanical Garden
Whim
Greenhouse
Centerline Road
Hams Bay
Sprat Hall
Plantation
Frederiksted
Southwest Cape
Sandy Pt.
West End
Wrecks

of 1989's Hurricane Hugo, the area is still splendid for snorkelers, and the short boat ride from Christiansted is quite pleasant. It's a must for any visit to St. Croix.

History

Columbus and his crew first came ashore at St. Croix's Salt River in 1493, but native Caribs did their best to fight them off. In haste he named the island Santa Cruz (Holy Cross) and sailed on to lay claim to St. John and St. Thomas. Eventually he renamed the entire group—including the British Virgin Islands at the time—for the legendary 11,000 virgin followers of St. Ursula. Today, we know that he wildly exaggerated the number of islands in the area. Soon after Columbus' departure, British, Dutch and French colonists began to establish farms on St. Croix, and in 1653, the island was awarded the crusaders' Order of St. John, better known as the Knights of Malta. France took control a few years later, and for the next 50 or so years, possession alternated between the French and the Spanish. As St. John and St. Thomas became acquired by the Danish West India Company and Guinea Company, St. Croix remained in the background. In 1773 the Danes also purchased St. Croix, attracted by its already burgeoning slave population and sugarcane fields. Planters and pirates mingled together during this golden age; some secluded coves are still said to harbor buried treasure. As the sugar beet was introduced to Europe, and the uprisings of slaves threatened the status quo, commercial interest in the island began to flag. Over the past 250 years, seven different conquerors took control of the island, though the Danish influence has remained the most lasting. During World War I, the Danes, sensing the sugarcane industry had all but dissolved, looked for buyers, finding the U.S. which was seeking a Caribbean base from which it could protect the Panama Canal. Eventually a great deal was struck between the two powers—$25 million dollars for three islands. The opening of the Carambola Beach Resort and Golf Club attracted a new wave of visitors to St. Croix starting in 1986. Though St. Croix was hard hit by Hurricane Hugo in 1989, islanders were not daunted and threw themselves body and soul into renovating the tourist facilities.

People

St. Croix's population is about 60,000; the majority are descendants of African slaves who toiled on the many sugar plantations that dotted the island. Those born on St. Croix are called Crucians. Everyone speaks English—the official language—with a local lilt referred to a Cruzan; Spanish is also widely spoken. Crime is relatively low but tourists should never wander along the beach alone at night, and use common sense in the cities once the sun goes down.

Music you're apt to hear while out at night includes calypso, reggae, steel pan bands and scratch bands, whose instruments are made of washboards, gourds and the like. During Carnival and at hotel theme parties, you're likely to see a Mocko Jumbie, an "elevated spirit" on 10 to 20-foot stilts dressed in bright colors.

Beaches

Buck Island offers guided tours of underwater snorkeling trails.

All beaches on St. Croix are public and free of charge, but if you go to a beach that is maintained by the resident hotel, you may have to pay a small fee for facilities. Lying 1.5 miles off northeast St. Croix, **Buck Island**, an 850-

acre national monument, has some of the best beaches in the St. Croix area, reachable by boat from Christiansted; the six-mile trip takes 45 minutes to an hour. Some concessionaires that offer sail or motorboat tours also include a picnic lunch and an overland hike to the island's 400-foot summit with terrific views. Turtles also lay their eggs there. **Cane Bay** also has a stunning beach on the island's north side. Other fine beaches can be found at **Protestant Cay**, **Davis Bay**, **Cramer Park** on the east shore, and **Frederiksted Beach** to the north of town. The latter two have changing facilities and showers. Surfing is best on the north coast, and you'll find great shells on the northwest coast, from **Northside Beach** to **Ham's Bay**, as well as on **Sprat Hall Beach**.

Underwater

St. Croix offers a splendid, immense wall, a trench that stretches the island's northern coast from Christiansted west past Maroon Ridge and rivals similar attractions off Cozumel and the Caymans. The wall alone makes St. Croix the best dive destination in the U.S. Virgins. In particular, two areas along the northern coast, **Cane Bay** and **Salt River Canyon**, are among the best locations in the Eastern Caribbean; the first is a prime access to the sheer wall (and accessible from shore), the latter is an unusual formation in a sprawling undersea valley. The original **Frederiksted Pier**, famed for its profusion of sea horses and other macro life, is no more. In a controversial decision, it was torn down and replaced by another facility which is better able to accommodate shipping needs. Fortunately, sea life, including the delightful horses, is slowly regenerating on the new pilings and in a few years it may almost mirror the old site. Although a decent site showcasing four wrecks has been created off Butler Bay, if you're a sunken ship devotee, you'll want to head for St. Thomas or the British Virgins. St. Croix's visibility averages 75 feet year-round but can approach 100 feet in the summer. First-time snorkelers have been delighted for years by the underwater trail at **Buck Island**, just north of St. Croix's eastern tip, but the never-ending crowds can be a bit overwhelming. Additionally, Buck Island's conditions vary, causing jaded snorkelers to shrug off the site if visibility is poor or if fish are percolating elsewhere. Other good snorkeling sites are **Cane Bay**, **Green Cay** (a short swim off Chenay Bay), and Grapetree Beach (on the south coast near eastern tip).

On Foot

It doesn't have St. Thomas' cosmopolitan infrastructure nor St. John's well-established National Park system. Neither fish nor fowl, St. Croix appears to be pondering a more environmentally conscious use of its interior. But its recently anointed **Salt River Bay National Park** lacks the funds to develop a trail system, and there is, so far, little organization of the paths and dirt roads which lead through the rainforest and hills surrounding **Blue Mountain** (the island's highest, 1096 feet). Interestingly, from afar, the island's fledgling environmental movement seems to be an outgrowth of community concerns, particularly the island's beautification program (originating from Hurricane Hugo) and a new recycling program (due to a landfill approaching capacity). It would appear that the island will soon be diversifying its forest management to include eco-tourism.

By Pedal

Easily the best cycling destination in the Virgins, St. Croix is less hilly and more spread out than its neighbors and features at least two inviting possibilities that visit the island's most scenic areas. The first starts one-and-a-half miles north of Frederiksted and uses Creque Dam Road—the easiest climb into St. Croix's rainforest—to access the main ridge (average elevation 700 feet), which snakes toward Salt River Bay. The other route is about 25 miles and takes in the rolling hills east of Christiansted: follow the East End Road along the north coast out to **Point Udall**, returning via the South Shore Road; the **Seven Hills** rising between these two roads offer excellent off-road and single-track potential and are frequented by the island's local riders. Those wanting easier pastures should stick to the area between Christiansted and Salt River Bay or to the fields along the southern coast (west of the airport), although both areas are subject to heavy vehicular traffic.

ST. CROIX

Plantation ruins, St. Croix

St. Croix's two large towns are Christiansted and Frederiksted; most cruise ships dock at the latter. Christiansted, on the north coast, is the more interesting of the two. The town is a real charmer with its bright, shutter-accented buildings; even the trash cans are whimsically painted. A walking tour should include a visit to Fort Christiansvaern, built by the Danes in the 1700s; and a stop at the Steeple Building, another 18th century Danish structure with good exhibits on the island's past.

Frederiksted, on the island's western end, also has an impressive fort (Fort Frederik) and an excellent aquarium. The town's shady streets are home to lovely Victorian houses and 19th-century churches.

You won't want to miss a drive along Mahogany Road, which winds through the island's rainforest, home of wild lilies, yellow cedar trees, wild parakeets and mountain doves. At St. Croix Leap, located amidst the forest, craftspeople build fine furniture from mahogany. It's an interesting spot to stop and take a look.

Other don't misses include St. George's Village and the Whim Greathouse, both impressive with their lovely gardens and vintage structures.

City Celebrations
Frederiksted

Crucian Christmas Fiesta　　　　　　　　　　　　　　★ ★

Various locations, Frederiksted.
This annual two-week festival celebrates the Christmas season with arts and crafts exhibits, food fairs, parades (one for children, the other for adults), the selection of Miss St. Croix, and the coronation of the festival's Prince and Princess. Most events take place in Christiansted and Frederiksted. Each town has a Festival Village complete with amusement rides and nightly entertainment.

Historical Sites
Christiansted

Fort Christiansvaern　　　　　　　　　　　　　　★ ★

Downtown, Christiansted, ☎ (809) 773-1460.
Hours open: 8 a.m.–5 p.m.
This fort was built by the Danes in 1738 and rebuilt after hurricane damage in 1772. Its five rooms are decorated as they were in the 1840s. The admission charge (free for those under 16) includes entry to the Steeple Building. The fort's newest attraction is the St. Croix Police Museum, just opened in 1994. Created by Lt. Elton Lewis a 20-year veteran of the St. Croix Police Department, the idea behind the museum is to "promote high morale" and esprit de corps among police officers.

Exhibits include weapons, photos, artifacts, and an old police motorcycle from St. Croix's past. General admission: $2.

Steeple Building   ★★

Downtown, Christiansted, ☎ *(809) 773-1460.*

Built by the Danish in 1754, this was their first Lutheran church, called the Church of Lord God of Sabaoth. Deconsecrated in 1831, it served as everything from a bakery to a school, and is now under the auspices of the U.S. National Park Service. Interesting exhibits tell the island's history, with emphasis on Native Americans and African Americans. The entry fee includes admission to Fort Christiansvaern. General admission: $2.

Frederiksted

Fort Frederik   ★★★

Emancipation Park, Frederiksted, ☎ *(809) 772-2021.*
Hours open: 8:30 a.m.–4:30 p.m.

This fort dates back to 1760, and is now an art gallery and museum. It is best known as the site where on July 3, 1848, Governor General Peter Von Scholten freed the Danish West Indies slaves.

Museums and Exhibits
Christiansted

Aquarium   ★★

Caravelle Arcade, Christiansted, ☎ *(809) 772-1345.*
Hours open: 11 a.m.–4 p.m.

Opened in 1990 by marine biologist Lonnie Kaczmarsky, this aquarium displays some 40 species of marine animals and more than 100 species of invertebrates. What makes it really unique is its "recycling" of sea life—after doing a stint in the tanks, creatures are released back to the open seas. Kaczmarsky is passionate on preserving the ocean environment; this a good place to pick up hints before diving and snorkeling on how to minimize your impact. General admission: $3.

Frederiksted

Estate Whim Plantation Museum   ★★

Centerline Road, Frederiksted, ☎ *(809) 772-0598.*
Hours open: 10 a.m.–4 p.m.

This partially restored sugar plantation gives a good look at what life was like in St. Croix in the 1800s. The handsome great house, built of lime, stone and coral and boasting walls three feet thick, is beautifully restored and filled with antiques. The grounds also include the cookhouse where you can feast on Johnny cakes ($1 each and well worth it, but the old woman who cooks them is a real crab and forbids pictures, and charges another dollar for the recipe), a woodworking shop, a windmill, and an apothecary. The giftshop is excellent; even if you're not interested in seeing the plantation, it's worth a trip just to peruse the interesting wares for sale. $1 for children. General admission: $5.

Parks and Gardens
Christiansted

St. George Village Botanical Gardens ★

St. George Estate, Kingshill, ☎ *(809) 772-3874.*
Hours open: 9 a.m.–5 p.m.
Built among the ruins of a 19th-century sugarcane plantation workers' village, this little slice of paradise is not to be missed. The 17 acres were the site of an Arawak settlement dating to A.D. 100. Stop by the Great Hall to pick up a brochure for a self-guided walking tour, then feast your senses on the lovely gardens, which include 850 species of trees and plants. Each ecosystem of St. Croix is represented, from rainforest to desert. The grounds also include restored buildings from the plantation era, including workers' cottages, storehouses and a blacksmith shop. Warning: Don't buy the Aqua Venus bottled water in the giftshop. It's literally impossible to open! $1.00 for kids. General admission: $5.

Tours
Buck Island

Buck Island Reef National Monument ★

Buck Island.
No trip to St. Croix is complete without a trip this national monument island, located three miles northeast of the mainland. It's a volcanic rock comprising some 300 acres with hiking trails, an observation tower, picnic tables and lovely beaches. The real attraction, however, is its surrounding 550 acres of underwater coral gardens, home to more than 250 species of fish. This is a true snorkelers' paradise, with an underwater trail and visibility of more than 100 feet. Several operators will take you there and set you up with snorkel equipment: **Big Beard's Adventure Tours** (☎ *[809] 773-4482*), **Diva** (☎ *[809] 778-3161*), **Llewellyn's Charter** (☎ *[809] 773-9027*), **Teroro II** (☎ *[809] 773-3161*), and **Mile Mark Water Sports** (☎ *[809] 773-2628*). Not to be missed!

Frederiksted

Cruzan Rum Factory ★★★

West Airport Road, Frederiksted, ☎ *(809) 772-0799.*
Tours of the rum distillery and bottling plant are offered Monday-Friday from 9:00-11:30 a.m. and 1:00-4:15 p.m. Check out the colorful mural in the tasting room, which depicts an old sugar plantation of the 1840s. You get to sample the product at the conclusion, but unless you're really interested and have never seen a rum factory before, skip this brief and relatively expensive tour (most such factories let you tour for free). One amusing sight: the mango tree, where workers write their names on the ripening fruit to keep the tourists from picking it. General admission: $3.

Estate Mount Washington Plantation ★★★

West coast, Frederiksted, ☎ *(809) 772-1026.*
Take a self-guided walking tour through the excavated ruins of a sugar plantation.

Guided Tours ★★★

Various locations, Frederiksted.

ST. CROIX

If you choose to leave the driving to someone else, these companies are happy to oblige with guided tours of St. Croix's highlights. Be sure to check in advance if admission charges to attractions are included in the rates. Eagle Tours (☎ [809] 778-3313), **St. Croix Safari Tours** (☎ [809] 773-6700), and **Travellers Tours** (☎ [809] 778-1636). Take-a-Hike offers walking tours and hikes; call ☎ (809) 778-6997. For a birds-eye view of the island, call **St. Croix Aviation** (☎ [809] 778-0090), which offers sightseeing flights.

Salt River Bay National Historical Park ★★

Route 80 near Route 75, Frederiksted.

These 912 tropical acres were added to the national park system under the Bush Administration. The park remains in a pristine condition and is home to many threatened and endangered plant and animal species. It is the largest remaining mangrove forest in the Virgin Islands and a great spot for birdwatching. The site includes an old earthen fort, an Indian ceremonial ball court, and burial grounds. This is also the only documented site on U.S. soil on which Christopher Columbus landed. His ill-fated "discovery" in 1493 led to a skirmish with Carib Indians, with fatalities on both sides.

Watersports and golf are the major attractions for a sports enthusiast on St. Croix. Snorkeling is especially divine at Buck Island, the national monument that lies just offshore the mainland. Any number of boat companies can take you there and supply equipment, but be sure to pack a lunch and drinks, as there are no facilities on the isle. Divers should be on the lookout for the colony of seahorses that congregate around the pier at Frederiksted, and the ancient black coral forest at Salt River Dropoff.

Christiansted

Golf

Various locations, Christiansted.

Duffers have three choices on St. Croix. **Carambol Golf Club** (☎ [809] 778-5638) is a gorgeous, par-72 course designed by Robert Trent Jones. Located in St. Croix's northwest part, golfing on scenic 18 holes costs $50 per person per day (you can go around as many as you want), plus $18 mandatory cart rental for 18 holes. Near Christiansted, the **Buccaneer** course is a challenging 18 holes. Greens fees are about $25. Call ☎ (809) 773-2100. **The Reef Club at Tegue Bay** (☎ [809] 773-8844) is a nine-hole course. Greens fees are $8 for nine holes, $12 for 18.

Frederiksted

Paul and Jill's Equestrian Stables

Sprat Hall, near Frederiksted, ☎ *(809) 772-2880.*

ST. CROIX

Well-regarded for their high-quality horses, this stable takes folks out for two-hour trail rides through the rainforest and past Danish ruins. Jill's family has lived on St. Croix for some 200 years. Two-hour rides are about $50, and reservations are essential. Closed Sundays.

Watersports

Various locations, Frederiksted.

For scuba diving, try: **Dive Experience** (☎ *[809] 773-3307*), **Virgin Island Divers** (☎ *[809] 773-6045*), **Anchor Dive Center** (☎ *[809] 778-1522*), **Blue Dolphin Divers** (☎ *[809] 773-8634*), **Cruzan Divers** (☎ *[809] 772-3701*), **Cane Bay Dive Shop** (☎ *[809] 773-9913*), and **Dive St. Croix** (☎ *[809] 773-3434*). For deep-sea fishing: **St. Croix Marin** (☎ *[809] 773-7165*), **Captain Pete's Sportfishing** (☎ *[809] 773-1123*), and **Cruzan Divers** (☎ *[809] 772-3701*). For cruises and boating, try **Mile Mark Chaters** (☎ *[809] 773-2628*), **Sundance** (☎ *[809] 778-9650*), **Llwewellyn's Charter** (☎ *[809] 773-9027*), **Bilinda Charters** (☎ *[809] 773-1641*), and **Junie Bomba's** (☎ *[809] 772-2482*). For windsurfing: **Lisa Neuburger Windsurfing Center** (☎ *[809] 778-8312*) and **Minstral School** (☎ *[809] 773-4810*).

Where to Stay

Fielding's Highest Rated Hotels in St. Croix

★★★★★	Buccaneer Hotel	$210–$341
★★★★★	Westin Carambola Beach Resort	$235–$330
★★★★	Villa Madeleine	$300–$425
★★★	Cane Bay Reef Club	$85–$165
★★★	Club St. Croix	$120–$225
★★★	Cormorant Beach Club	$120–$230
★★★	Cormorant Cove	$105–$230
★★★	Hilty House Inn	$70–$110
★★★	Horizons	$1400–$5000
★★★	Hotel on the Cay	$95–$198

Fielding's Most Exclusive Hotels in St. Croix

★★★	Horizons	$1400–$5000
★★★★	Villa Madeleine	$300–$425
★★★★★	Buccaneer Hotel	$210–$341
★★	Sugar Beach Condominiums	$110–$250
★★★	Cormorant Beach Club	$120–$230

Fielding's Best Value Hotels in St. Croix

★★★	Hilty House Inn	$70–$110
★★★	King Christian Hotel	$80–$135
★★★	St. Croix by the Sea	$90–$145
★★★	Cane Bay Reef Club	$85–$165
★	Cactus Inn	$39–$45

Accommodations on St. Croix are as varied as its topography. Christianst-ed has a number of small, quaint hotels, but they all lack a beach, so if it's im-portant to you to get a killer tan, look elsewhere around the island (though the **Hotel on the Cay** does have a tiny strand of sand). **The Buccaneer** and the **Westin Carombola** both offer all a resort lover dreams of, including excellent beaches. **Villa Madeleine**, perched high on a hill, has decent-sized private pools with each accommodation. **Tamarind Reef** is a laid-back charmer. If you're interested in renting a private home or villa, contact **The Collection** *(609) 751-2413 or FAX (609) 751-2414).*

Hotels and Resorts

The premier property on most anybody's list (not to mention the most expensive) is the **Buccaneer**, which sprawls down a hillside. It simply boasts the best facilities on the island—with three beaches, 18-hole golf course, jogging trail, spa, shops and a full water-sports program. In any property on the beach, ask for rooms above the first floor, so you will feel safe leaving the window open to the breeze at night.Christiansted

Christiansted

Anchor Inn   **$80–$145**   ★★

58 King Street, Christiansted, ☎ *(800) 524-2030, (809) 773-4000.*
FAX (809) 773-4408.
Single: $80–$125. Double: $90–$145.

This small hotel is set in a quiet courtyard on the waterfront in the heart of Chris-tiansted's National Historic District. Rooms have colorful rattan furnishings, cable TV, refrigerators, air conditioning and telephones; some have porches as well. The on-site restaurant features American and West Indian fare. Other facilities include a lounge, pool and tour desk. There's lots to see and do within walking distance. 30 rooms. Credit cards: MC, V.

Buccaneer Hotel   **$210–$341**   ★★★★★

Gallows Bay, Christiansted, ☎ *(800) 223-1108, (809) 773-2100.*
Single: $210–$341. Double: $210–$341.

Set on a landscaped peninsula and encompassing 240 acres with three beaches, this deluxe property is located two miles east of Christiansted. A former sugar plantation has been transformed into a well-polished resort that the same family has run since its inception in 1946. Accommodations vary widely, through all are comfortable and include refrigerators and patios or balconies. The best rooms are right on the beach, and there are also beautifully decorated suites, rooms atop the hillside, and one-bedroom, two-bath cottages, also on the hill. Guests are kept busy with lots of recreational facilities, including an 18-hole championship golf course, eight tennis courts, two pools, a health club with sauna, and a shopping arcade. There are lots of organized activities and watersports. Four restaurants, four bars and nightly enter-tainment round out the action. Resort lovers are kept happy. 150 rooms. Credit cards: A, CB, D, MC, V.

Club Comanche   **$35–$126**   ★

1 Strand Street, Christiansted, ☎ *(800) 524-2066, (809) 773-0210.*
FAX 809 773 0210.

Single: $35–$126. Double: $45–$126.

This hotel dates back to 1948 and it shows—not necessarily because of historical charm, but because it would really benefit from an overhaul. Guest rooms are small and simple; most have TV sets. The premises include two good restaurants and a pool. There's nothing special about this budget choice except the fine food, but the rates are quite reasonable. 42 rooms. Credit cards: A, MC.

Cormorant Beach Club   **$120–$230**   ★★★

4126 La Grande Princesse, Christiansted, ☎ (800) 548-4460, (809) 778-8920.
FAX (809) 778-9218.
Single: $120–$200. Double: $140–$230.

Located three miles west of Christiansted on the north shore, this intimate resort makes for a great getaway. Guest rooms are in three-story beachfront villas, tastefully decorated with rattan furniture, bright fabrics, island artwork, and luxurious touches like bathrobes and fresh flowers. The grounds include a large free-form pool, two tennis courts, croquet, and a library. Guests can choose from several plans that include meals and drinks. The beach is excellent, and this spot gets high marks for service. No kids under five during the winter. 38 rooms. Credit cards: A, MC, V.

Hibiscus Beach Hotel   **$120–$240**   ★★★

4131 La Grande Princesse, Christiansted, ☎ (800) 442-0121, (809) 773-4042.
FAX (809) 773-7668.
Single: $120–$240. Double: $120–$240.

Located three miles outside of Christiansted, this small hotel opened in 1992. Accommodations are in two-story buildings that line the palm-studded beach. All have ocean views off the balcony or patio, and are on the plain side, though comfortable. The baths are on the small side. There's a pretty pool on-site, as well as a beachfront restaurant and lounge. The beach is excellent and this property's best feature. Snorkel equipment is included in the rates, and other watersports (which cost extra) are found nearby. Nice and small, with the feel of a resort but not the cost of one. Inquire about special golf, dive and all-inclusive packages. 37 rooms. Credit cards: A, D, MC, V.

Hotel Caravelle   **$79–$255**   ★★

44A Queen Cross Street, Christiansted, ☎ (800) 524-0410, (809) 773-0687.
FAX (809) 778-7004.
Single: $79–$255. Double: $89–$255.

This waterfront hotel is in Christiansted's downtown historic district, overlooking the bay. Guestrooms are comfortable and pleasant, with modern furnishings and colorful fabrics. There's a pool on-site and watersports nearby. The waterfront restaurant and bar are lively and popular with boaters. A good in-town choice, and the rates are reasonable. 43 rooms. Credit cards: A, CB, D, MC, V.

Hotel on the Cay   **$95–$198**   ★★★

Protestant Cay, Christiansted, ☎ (800) 524-2035, (809) 773-2035.
FAX (809) 773-7046.
Single: $95–$188. Double: $95–$198.

Located on a small cay in Christiansted Harbor, a two-minute ferry ride from the mainland, this imaginatively landscaped hotel offers great seclusion, though boat service to Christiansted is frequent. Guest rooms are comfortable and pleasing, with extras like coffeemakers, VCRs, and private terraces with water views. The grounds are dotted with waterfalls, canals, and bridges, lending a welcome tropical feel. Recreational options include a pool, tennis court and watersports on the small beach. Nice, if you don't mind the isolated location. 55 rooms. Credit cards: A, MC, V.

King Christian Hotel   **$80–$135**   ★★★
59 King's Wharf, Christiansted, ☎ *(800) 524-2012, (809) 773-2285. FAX 809 773 9411.*
Single: $80–$125. Double: $100–$135.
Located in the heart of town overlooking Christiansted Harbor, this hotel opened in 1940, though the building it is housed in is some 200 years old. Guest rooms are spacious and air-conditioned; the best ones have large furnished balconies with harbor views. Those counting every penny can stay in one of the 15 budget rooms which have no views but are clean and comfortable. There's a restaurant and coffeeshop on the premises, as well as a pool and dive center. Boats to Buck Island leave right from their dock. A great in-town choice. 39 rooms. Credit cards: A, CB, D, MC, V.

St. Croix by the Sea   **$90–$145**   ★★★
St. John's Estate, Christiansted, ☎ *(800) 524-5006, (809) 778-8600.*
Single: $90–$145. Double: $90–$145.
This family-run resort is located three miles west of Christiansted. Guestrooms are contemporary and comfortable enough, but not particularly special. The grounds include a large saltwater pool, (the site of scuba lessons), four tennis courts, two restaurants and a bar. A European plan is available for an extra $10 per person per day. 65 rooms. Credit cards: A, MC, V.

Tamarind Reef Hotel   **$145–$180**   ★★★
5001 Tamarind Reef, Christiansted, ☎ *(800) 619-0014, (809) 773-4455. FAX (809) 773-3989.*
Single: $145–$180. Double: $145–$180.
Located three miles west of Christiansted, this small hotel is laid-back and friendly, thanks in no small part to the hospitable owners, Dick and Marcy Pelton. Guestrooms either have a patio or balcony and all come equipped with ceiling fan, air conditioners, TV, radio, refrigerators, coffeemakers, hairdryers and bathrobes. The downstairs units have full kitchens; the accommodations on the second floor are larger, but lack the cooking facilities. On-site amenities include a large pool, watersports, a snackbar, two small beaches and the Green Cay Marina, which has slips for 144 boats, a dive shop and a gourmet restaurant. Very nice. 46 rooms. Credit cards: A, MC, V.

Westin Carambola Beach Resort   **$235–$330**   ★★★★★
Kings Hill, Christiansted, ☎ *(800) 333-3333, (809) 778-3800. FAX (809) 778-1682.*
Single: $235–$330. Double: $235–$330.
Situated on 26 acres on the north shore of Davis Bay, this property reopened in the summer of 1993 after renovations and joining the Westin hotel family. Guestrooms (which any other property would rightfully call suites) are found in villa-style, red-roofed buildings surrounded by lush landscaping. All are quite extraordinary, with sitting areas, coffeemakers, minibars, enormous bathrooms and lovely English

country furnishings. Best of all are the large screened porches—the perfect spot to while away the hours far from mosquitoes' harm. The only drawback is that many rooms are not right on the beach, though it's only a quick stroll to the sand. Request a second-floor unit, which offers better views, higher ceilings and more privacy. Facilities include 18 holes of golf, a pool, four tennis courts, three restaurants, two bars and watersports, including a dive shop. Very fine, and the beach is divine. 151 rooms. Credit cards: A, D, MC, V.

Frederiksted

On the Beach Resort   **$50–$180**   ★★

127 Smithfield, Frederiksted, ☎ (800) 524-2018, (809) 772-1205.
FAX (809) 772-1757.
Single: $50–$180. Double: $50–$180.
No kids under 14 at this small hotel (formerly called the King Frederik), which caters to a mostly gay and lesbian clientele. Accommodations are spacious and tropically furnished; most have kitchens but only some have balconies. Six new villas have one or two bedrooms and complete kitchens. The premises include a good beach for snorkeling, two pools, a Jacuzzi, a bar and a bistro. You'll want a car to get around, though downtown Frederiksted can be walked to in about 10 minutes. Rates include continental breakfast and maid service (except on Sundays). 20 rooms. Credit cards: A, CB, D, MC, V.

Sprat Hall Plantation   **$95–$220**   ★★

Route 63N, Frederiksted, ☎ (809) 772-0305.
Single: $95–$215. Double: $110–$220.
This family-run hotel is structured around the island's oldest great house, which dates back to 1670. Located just north of Frederiksted, accommodations range from non-smoking, antique-filled rooms in the great house to air-conditioned contemporary seaview units, some with TV. There are also several one-bedroom cottages with kitchenettes for rent. The grounds are lush and inviting, and dinner is a somewhat formal affair. No kids under 16 in the great house rooms. You'll be needing a car. 16 rooms.

Apartments and Condominiums

Self-catering is easy, and most properties—from private homes to condos—are available with maid service. Supermarkets are modern and well-stocked, and fresh local fruits and vegetables can be bought at market. You will probably need to count the cost of a car rental into most choices.

Christiansted

Cane Bay Reef Club   **$85–$165**   ★★★

1407 Kingshill Street, Christiansted, ☎ (800) 253-8534, (809) 778-2966.
FAX (809) 778-2966.
Single: $85–$165. Double: $85–$165.
Located about 20 minutes from both Christiansted and Frederiksted, this property was rebuilt after Hurricane Hugo's extensive damage. All units are one-bedroom apartments with modern kitchens, tiled balconies and ceiling fans. The best choices are the two condominium units—the only ones that are air-conditioned—which are

much more nicely furnished. There's a restaurant, bar, and saltwater pool on-site; the beach is a three-minute walk. You'll definitely want a rental car, as this place is fairly remote. 9 rooms. Credit cards: A, MC.

Caribbean View All-Suites $80–$120   ★

66 La Grande Princesse, Christiansted, ☎ *(809) 773-3335. FAX (809) 773-1596. Single: $80–$120. Double: $80–$120.*

Located a half-mile from the sea and 10 minutes from downtown Christiansted, this complex consists of two-story apartment buildings. Each has four one-bedroom units with VCRs, kitchens, terraces and maid service. Facilities are limited to a pool and shuffleboard court; you'll need a car to get around. Decent for the rates. 18 rooms. Credit cards: A, CB, D, MC, V.

Chenay Bay Beach Resort $125–$210   ★ ★

Estate Green Cay, Christiansted, ☎ *(800) 548-4457, (809) 773-2918. FAX (809) 773-2918. Single: $125–$180. Double: $125–$210.*

This cottage colony is located on 30 acres three miles from Christiansted. The West Indian-style cottages are scattered about well-landscaped grounds; all have kitchenettes and patios, and most are air-conditioned. The grounds, surrounded by a 14-acre wildlife preserve, include a pool, two tennis courts, watersports (snorkeling and kayaking are free), the beach, and a casual restaurant and bar. Nice and relaxing, but you'll want a car to get around. 50 rooms. Credit cards: A, MC.

Club St. Croix $120–$225   ★ ★ ★

3280 Golden Rock, Christiansted, ☎ *(800) 635-1533, (809) 773-4800. FAX (809) 778-4009. Single: $120–$225. Double: $120–$225.*

This friendly beachfront condominium resort is one mile out of Christiansted. Accommodations include well-furnished studios, a penthouse, and one- and two-bedroom apartments, all with full kitchens, cable TV, private balconies, ceiling fans and air conditioning. A nearby oil refinery sometimes taints the air if the wind comes from the east. Recreational choices are good for a condo operation, with three tennis courts, a large pool, Jacuzzi, limited watersports, a catamaran for cruising the high seas and a bar and restaurant. Inquire about special packages. 54 rooms. Credit cards: A, CB, D, MC, V.

Colony Cove $130–$185   ★ ★

3221A Golden Rock, Christiansted, ☎ *(800) 524-2025, (809) 773-1965. FAX (809) 778-4009. Single: $130–$185. Double: $130–$185.*

Set on the beach two miles from Christiansted, this condominium complex offers two-bedroom, two-bath units with full kitchens, laundry facilities, private balconies and ocean views. Each is individually owned and decorated, but all can be counted on for clean, comfortable living. The premises includes a restaurant, two tennis courts, a business center and a pool. Watersports await on the wide beach. 60 rooms. Credit cards: A, D, MC.

Cormorant Cove   **$105–$230**   ★ ★ ★

4126 La Grande Princesse, Christiansted, ☎ (800) 548-4460, (809) 778-8920.
FAX (809) 778-9218.
Single: $105–$230. Double: $105–$230.

Set right on the beach near its sister property, the Cormorant Beach Club, this condo complex has 16 units of one to three bedrooms. All are luxuriously furnished, air-conditioned, and have fully equipped kitchens, private terraces, maid service, washers and dryers and Jacuzzis. The grounds include a large pool and two tennis courts. Guests can use all the facilities at the Cormorant Beach Club, so it works out as the best of both: apartment living and hotel amenities. 38 rooms. Credit cards: A, MC, V.

Gentle Winds Resort   **$230–$305**   ★ ★

9003 Gentle Winds, Christiansted, ☎ (809) 773-3400. FAX 809 778 3400.
Single: $230–$305. Double: $230–$305.

Set on the beach some eight miles northwest of Christiansted, this contemporary condo complex offers two- and three-bedroom units. All are air-conditioned, have two or three baths, full kitchens, VCRs, telephones, and nice sea views. There's a pool, two tennis courts, games room, and a beach bar, but you're on your own for meals. Guests can get reduced rates at the Carambola Beach Golf Course, eight miles away. Ideal for families. 66 rooms. Credit cards: not accepted.

Horizons   **$1400–$5000**   ★ ★ ★

Kings Hill, Christiansted, ☎ (609) 751-2413. FAX (609) 751-2414.
Double: $1400–$5000.

Horizons combines the privacy and luxury of a private villa along with full resort amenities. Located on the grounds of the Carambola Beach Hotel, the house has four master bedrooms each with its own bath and air conditioner, a gourmet kitchen, a 40-foot great room with stereo, cable TV, VCR and a video library, a full-sized pool, expansive sundecks and a whirlpool bath. The fee, which is for seven nights, includes maid service and transfers to and from the airport. Guests can use the services at Carambola and get discounted greens fees at its golf course.

Schooner Bay Resort   **$110–$150**   ★ ★

5002 Gallows Bay, Christiansted, ☎ (800) 524-2025, (809) 773-9150.
FAX (809) 778-4009.
Single: $110–$150. Double: $110–$150.

You can walk to downtown Christiansted from this three-story condominium resort, which overlooks the harbor. Two- and three-bedroom units are plush, with full kitchens, nice decor, living and dining areas, VCRs, radios, telephones, washer/dryers, and private balconies. The three-bedroom condos have an upstairs and downstairs. There's a pool, Jacuzzi, and tennis court on-site, but you'll have to look elsewhere for meals. 62 rooms. Credit cards: A, D, MC.

Sugar Beach Condominiums   **$110–$250**   ★ ★

3245 Estate Golden Riock, Christiansted, ☎ (800) 524-2049, (809) 773-5345.
FAX (809) 773-1359.
Single: $110–$250. Double: $110–$250.

Situated on a reef-protected beach beside a historic sugar mill in a residential neighborhood two miles out of Christiansted, this condo complex has studios and apartments with one to three bedrooms. All have full kitchens, seaview balconies, and modern, comfortable appointments. You'll pay extra for maid service. There are two tennis courts, a pool, and the private beach, but no restaurant. 46 rooms. Credit cards: A, MC, V.

Villa Madeleine	**$300–$425**	★ ★ ★ ★

19A Teague Bay, Christiansted, ☎ *(800) 548-4461, (809) 778-7377. FAX (809) 773-7518.*
Single: $300–$425. Double: $300–$425.

This deluxe operation is set on a hill between two beaches, some 15 minutes from Christiansted, with sweeping views of Buck Island and Duggins Reef. Accommodations are in one- and two-bedroom villas beautifully done and including sitting rooms, modern, full modern kitchens, four-poster beds and chaise lounges in the bedrooms, two full baths, and—best of all—decent-sized private pools. Really luxurious! The on-site restaurant draws raves for its gorgeous decor and smashing food, and there's also a bar, billiards room and tennis court. This is one of St. Croix's best properties, and all is quite sophisticated and elegant. The only drawback is the distance to the beach—you'll have to drive. 43 rooms. Credit cards: A, MC.

Waves at Cane Bay	**$85–$195**	★ ★

Kingshill, Christiansted, ☎ *(800) 545-0603, (809) 778-1805. FAX (809) 778-4945.*
Single: $85–$195. Double: $85–$195.

Located on the north shore a short walk from Cane Bay Beach, this operation offers large studios with kitchens, screened porches, ceiling fans and TVs. Only some are air-conditioned, but all are quite comfortable. Maids tidy up six days a week. The pool is a natural sea-fed grotto and the snorkeling is great off the small beach. There's a bar but no restaurant, and you'll definitely need a car, as this spot is somewhat remote. 12 rooms. Credit cards: A, D, MC.

Frederiksted

Cottages by the Sea	**$70–$110**	★

127A Smithfield, Frederiksted, ☎ *(800) 323-7252, (809) 772-0495. FAX 809 772 0495.*
Single: $70–$110. Double: $70–$110.

Located on the western end of the island just outside of Frederiksted, this basic complex is right on the beach. The 20 wood and fieldstone cottages are simply furnished and have kitchenettes, patios, and air conditioning. Maids tidy things up daily. Three large patios are situated on the beach for sunning and barbecueing. No children under eight at this agreeable spot. 20 rooms. Credit cards: A, D, MC.

Inns

Most of the inns on St.Croix are located in historic buildings in Christiansted, rife with Danish colonial architecture. A few are situated on the shores. All exude the personality of the owners, who tend to be extremely personable.

Christiansted

Anchor Inn of St. Croix $80–$150 ★★

58 King Street, Christiansted, ☎ (800) 524-2030, (809) 773-4000. FAX 809 773 4408.
Single: $80–$130. Double: $95–$150.

This friendly little spot is located in downtown Christiansted in a courtyard at the harbor's edge. Due to motel-like furnishings and tinted windows that keep the sun out, rooms are on the drab side. There's a pool, restaurant, coffeeshop, and bar on-site, as well as extensive watersports—everything from scuba to deep-sea fishing. Popular despite its uninspired accommodations. 31 rooms. Credit cards: A, CB, D, MC, V.

Hilty House Inn $70–$110 ★★★

2 Hermon Hill, Christiansted, ☎ (809) 773-2594. FAX 809 773 2594.
Single: $70–$85. Double: $95–$110.

This bed and breakfast was built on the ruins of an 18th-century rum distillery, 1.5 miles from the beach. The great room, open to guests, totals 1000 square feet and is quite gorgeous, with an old-fashioned fireplace and lovely tile work. Guest rooms are individually decorated and have private baths, but no air conditioning. There are also two one-bedroom cottages with kitchenettes. TV can be watched in the library, and there's a large pool on-site. The rates for standard guest rooms include continental breakfast. 6 rooms.

Pink Fancy Hotel $65–$120 ★★

27 Prince Street, Christiansted, ☎ (800) 524-2045, (809) 773-8460.
FAX (809) 773-6448.
Single: $65–$75. Double: $90–$120.

It is indeed pink (the shutters, anyway) and it is indeed somewhat fancy at this popular inn, which comprises four buildings, the oldest dating to 1780. Located downtown within walking distance of Christiansted's shops and restaurants, this intimate inn is loaded with charm. Guest rooms are immaculate, and each boasts West Indian decor, air conditioning, and a kitchenette. The grounds are lush with lots of plants, and include a nice pool and hammocks for lazy afternoons; like other in-town hotels, there is no beach. The rates include continental breakfast and free drinks during the daily happy hour. 13 rooms. Credit cards: A, MC.

Low Cost Lodging

Since lodging is based on the scale of the American dollar, not much is to be found in the category of cheap, unless you can bear very small rooms and basic furnishings. Make sure the property is close enough to a beach or stores/restaurants if you can't afford to rent a car. **Danish Manor** takes advantage of its location in the center of Christiansted, although you'll need to take a bus to the beach.

Christiansted

Cactus Inn $39–$45 ★

48 King Street, Christiansted, ☎ (809) 692-9331.
Single: $39. Double: $45.

As the rates suggest, you won't find much in the way of amenities here. But if you're seeking a decent, no-frills room with air conditioning, cable TV, and private bath, they'll do right by you.

Danish Manor Hotel   **$49–$95**   ★

2 Company Street, Christiansted, ☎ *(800) 524-2069, (809) 773-1377.*
FAX (809) 773-1913.
Single: $49–$85. Double: $59–$95.

This downtown inn consists of an old West Indian-style manor house and a newer addition. The motel-style guestrooms are small and simply furnished, but do have private baths, air conditioners, refrigerators and cable television. There's a pool, Italian restaurant, and bar on the premises. Good value for the rates, and lots (including the beach) within walking distance. 35 rooms. Credit cards: A, MC, V.

Frederiksted

Frederiksted Hotel   **$80–$110**   ★ ★

20 Strand Street, Frederiksted, ☎ *(800) 524-2025, (809) 772-0500.*
FAX (809) 772-0500.
Single: $80–$100. Double: $90–$110.

This small hotel overlooks the harbor at the edge of town. The air-conditioned guest rooms are comfortable enough, but lack phones and are somewhat dark. Ask for a seaview room, by far the best accommodations. There's a pool and pool bar, the site of entertainment on the weekends. The restaurant serves breakfast only. A free shuttle transports guests to the beach and nearby tennis courts. 40 rooms. Credit cards: A, MC, V.

Where to Eat

Fielding's Highest Rated Restaurants in St. Croix

★★★★★	Cafe Madeleine	$18–$26
★★★★	Kendrick's	$14–$26
★★★	Blue Moon	$10–$20
★★★	Harvey's	$8–$20
★★★	Le St. Tropez	$10–$25
★★★	Mahogany	$26–$36
★★★	Top Hat	$14–$28

Fielding's Most Exclusive Restaurants in St. Croix

★★★	Mahogany	$26–$36
★★★★★	Cafe Madeleine	$18–$26
★★★	Top Hat	$14–$28
★★★★	Kendrick's	$14–$26
★★★	Le St. Tropez	$10–$25

Fielding's Best Value Restaurants in St. Croix

★★★★★	Cafe Madeleine	$18–$26
★★★	Harvey's	$8–$20
★★★★	Kendrick's	$14–$26
★★★	Blue Moon	$10–$20
★★★	Le St. Tropez	$10–$25

Most eateries are centered in Christiansted; Frederiksted has a smaller, but still decent, selection. Local favorite foods include saltfish, lobster, fungi, red beans and rice, plantains, stewed mutton, curried chicken, conch fritters and johnny cakes.

Christiansted

Antoine's   **$$$**   ★ ★

58A King Street, Christiansted, ☎ (809) 773-0263. Associated hotel: Anchor Inn.
International cuisine. Specialties: Omelets, goulash, wienerschnitzel, lobster.
Lunch: 11 a.m.–2:30 p.m., entrées $14–$32.
Dinner: 6:30–9:30 p.m., entrées $14–$32.
Many visitors get their wakeup javas at this second-floor charmer in the Anchor Inn.
The breakfast menu boasts at least a dozen omelets loaded with interesting combi-
nations. But that's not all that's here—bartenders proffer tropical concoctions and
a huge selection of beer to a lively crowd. At dinner, hearty and tasty German and
Middle-European food appears on the generous plates—despite the restaurant's
French name. From the terrace, there's a great view of seagoing vessels on the wharf
below. Reservations required. Credit cards: A, MC, V.

Banana Bay Club   **$$$**   ★ ★

44A Queen Cross St., Christiansted, ☎ (809) 778-9110.
Associated hotel: Caravelle Hotel.
Seafood cuisine.
Lunch: 7 a.m.–4 p.m., entrées $15–$25.
Dinner: 4–11 p.m., entrées $15–$25.
Sit surrounded by 18th-century buildings and 20th-century businessfolk who
gather for gossip and low-key deal-making in this open-air eatery known for fresh
seafood, burgers and steaks. The Banana Bay Club is located in the Caravelle Hotel,
one of downtown's lodging bargains. You don't have to pay high prices for unsurprising, well-prepared food and a great view of the Christiansted harbor. Reservations recommended. Credit cards: A, MC, V.

Cafe Madeleine   **$$$**   ★ ★ ★ ★ ★

Estate Teague Bay, Christiansted, ☎ (809) 773-8141.
Italian cuisine.
Dinner: 6–10 p.m., entrées $18–$26. Closed: Mon.
The crowning glory of the Villa Madeleine, the romantic haven on the east coast of
the island, this restaurant recalls a posh plantation house of bygone days. It's all
dolled up in butter-yellow paint, and the patio bursts with bright blooms. The pri-
marily Italian-continental cuisine is some of the finest on the island, with specialties
like lamb served with rosemary and garlic in a Barolo wine glaze and open ravioli
with fresh lobster in a sauterne sauce. On Sundays, brunch is served from 11 a.m.–
2 p.m. for $16. Reservations recommended. Credit cards: A, DC, MC, V.

Chart House   **$$$**   ★ ★

59 King's Wharf, Christiansted, ☎ (809) 773-7718.
American cuisine. Specialties: Prime rib, mud pie.
Dinner: 6–10 p.m., entrées $14–$26.
Most stateside visitors are familiar with this chain restaurant based in California.
Christiansted's version does not disappoint—the waitstaff is perky, the prime rib is
cut the way you like it, the copious salad bar is one of the best on the island, and it's
constantly mobbed. There's no outdoor dining, but the decor is nautical and it's so
close to the water that it really doesn't matter, especially when you're lucky to get a
seat with a harbor view. Reservations recommended. Credit cards: A, DC, MC, V.

Comanche $$ ★★

1 Strand Street, Christiansted, ☎ *(809) 773-2665. Associated hotel: Club Comanche.*
International cuisine.
Lunch: 11:30 a.m.–2:30 p.m., entrées $9–$21.
Dinner: 6–9 p.m., entrées $9–$21.

A pianist tickles the ivories nightly at this intimate and consistently reliable terrace restaurant in the Comanche Inn. Decor is south-seas style, with wicker chairs and fans, and the cuisine runs the gamut from Chinese specialties to conch chowder. Serving three meals a day, the Comanche is also known for a filling West Indian lunch. Reservations recommended. Credit cards: A, MC, V.

Dino's $$$ ★★

4-C Hospital Street, Christiansted, ☎ *(809) 778-8005.*
Mediterranean cuisine. Specialties: Fresh pasta.
Dinner: entrées $14–$20.

After a tour of the nearby 17th-century Fort Christiansvaern, repair to this historical house serving thoroughly modern Italian fare. Chef Dwight deLude makes his pasta fresh every day, and he likes to experiment; sometimes there's ravioli made with sweet potatoes or other interesting vegetables. Sauces are always intensely flavored and made with fresh garden herbs. Reservations recommended. Credit cards: not accepted.

Harvey's $$ ★★★

11 Company Street, Christiansted, ☎ *(809) 773-3433.*
Latin American cuisine.
Lunch: entrées $8–$20.
Dinner: entrées $8–$20. Closed: Sun.

Motherly Sarah Harvey is the chef-owner of this small West Indian dinner house and local hangout. Timid diners won't remain so for long, because Harvey likes to visit at every table, and since there's no real menu, she'll discuss what's cookin' for the evening. Sometimes there's goat water or local seafood in butter sauce, and a mountain of island-grown veggies and starches. The decor could be described best as thrift-shop modern: plastic tableware and folding chairs. Reservations recommended. Credit cards: not accepted.

Kendrick's $$$ ★★★★

52 King Street, Christiansted, ☎ *(809) 773-9199.*
International cuisine.
Dinner: 6–10 p.m., entrées $14–$26. Closed: Sun.

Dine among the antiques in yet another restored old Danish home that's one of the island's toniest (and priciest) eating establishments. The nattily attired and well-trained wait staff keeps wineglasses full and dishes cleared deftly between courses. Chef David prepares island-inspired French cuisine and his specialties often include a luscious pork loin with a roasted pecan crust or rack of lamb marinated with crushed herbs and served with roasted garlic and thyme sauce. There are three dining rooms, and you'll be equally well-treated no matter which one you end up in. Reservations recommended. Credit cards: A, MC, V.

Mahogany $$$ ★★★

Kings Hill, Christiansted, ☎ *(809) 778-3800. Associated hotel: Westin Carombola.*
Seafood cuisine.
Dinner: 6–10 p.m., entrées $26–$36.

This gourmet outlet at the Westin Carombola is open only on Tuesday, Thursday and Saturday. The formal dining room has a high, high beamed ceiling and pretty furniture for a gracious atmosphere. The menu, new in 1995, features such delicacies as French snails sauteed in garlic, shallots and pernod and wrapped in chicken tenderloins; pan-seared mahi mahi encrusted with hazelnuts; and West Indian shrimp filled with backfin lump crabmeat and fine herbs. There's also beef and lamb dishes for carnivores. Men are requested to don collared shirts and slacks. Reservations recommended. Credit cards: A, MC, V.

Mango Grove $ ★

King and Queen Cross streets, Christiansted, ☎ *(809) 773-0200.*
American cuisine.
Lunch: from 11 a.m., entrées $5–$8.
Dinner: to late, entrées $5–$8. Closed: Sun.

I couldn't resist checking this place out after spotting their sign out front: "Hostess is getting a pedicure. Please seat yourself." That about sums up the casual atmosphere at this cool little spot in a nicely shaded courtyard. Munch on typical salads, burgers or sandwiches and quaff a cool beer at this friendly spot—and be sure to compliment the hostess on her perfect feet. Credit cards: A.

Picnic in Paradise $$ ★★

Cane Bay, Christiansted, ☎ *(809) 778-1212.*
Italian cuisine.
Dinner: entrées $10–$20.

It's worth a drive up the north coast to dine at this lovely indoor-outdoor restaurant in a protected coral cove near Cane Bay. Whether on the deck or in a breeze-filled dining room, meals are generally well-prepared and often include conch fritters, filet mignon and other West Indian-Continental specialties. If not quite paradise, it comes pretty close, if only for an hour. Reservations recommended. Credit cards: A, MC, V.

Saman $$$ ★★

Kings Hill, Christiansted, ☎ *(809) 778-3800. Associated hotel: Westin Carombola.*
American cuisine.
Dinner: 6–10 p.m., entrées $15–$20.

The best reason to come to this restaurant at the Westin Carombola is to sit outside, enjoy the sea breeze, and groove to the excellent live jazz every Tuesday evening (other nights see steel, calypso and island bands). The menu offers up seafood, steaks, chicken and pasta dishes; the Caesar salad with char-grilled shrimp, salmon or chicken is especially good. Wednesday nights are given over to a seafood buffet ($29), while Friday is a pirate theme night with limbo dancers and other entertainment (also $29). Credit cards: A, MC, V.

Tivoli Gardens $$$ ★★

39 Strand, Christiansted, ☎ *(809) 773-6782.*

International cuisine.
Lunch: 11:15 a.m.–2:30 p.m., entrées $6–$15.
Dinner: 6–9:30 p.m., entrées $11–$20.

There's a fairyland of lights and greenery on the spacious porch of this popular saloon facing Christiansted harbor. A surprising carnival of eclectic treats are prepared with aplomb—witness hungarian goulash and a Thai curry on the same menu. The frequently served chocolate velvet cake is wicked on the waistline and heaven on the tastebuds. Reservations recommended. Credit cards: A, MC, V.

Top Hat   **$$$**   ★ ★ ★

52 Company Street, Christiansted, ☎ *(809) 773-2346.*
Seafood cuisine. Specialties: Herring appetizers, frikadeller with red cabbage, gravlax.
Dinner: 6–10 p.m., entrées $14–$28. Closed: Sun.

Probably the only Danish restaurant on the island, Top Hat has consistently pleased visitors and residents for 20 years. The Danish owners—chef Bent Rasmussen and his wife Hanne—run a spic-and-span operation on the top floor of a charming gingerbread trimmed-house. Located above a shopping center, it's painted in muted, tasteful tones. Reservations recommended. Credit cards: A, MC, V.

Frederiksted

Blue Moon   **$$**   ★ ★ ★

17 Strand St., Frederiksted, ☎ *(809) 772-2222.*
International cuisine.
Dinner: entrées $10–$20. Closed: Mon.

Hot jazz and hot food draw folks to this restaurant and club in a quaint Victorian building in the heart of funky, laid-back Frederiksted. The place bustles Friday night for live jazz concerts and at Sunday brunch, and this bistro's creative chefs are always experimenting with different cooking styles. Some nights, specials could be Cajun, or at other times French-influenced Asian temptations. Usually there are one or more chocolate delights on the dessert menu. Closed July–September. Reservations recommended. Credit cards: A.

Le St. Tropez   **$$$**   ★ ★ ★

67 King Street, Frederiksted, ☎ *(809) 772-3000.*
French cuisine.
Lunch: entrées $10–$25.
Dinner: entrées $10–$25. Closed: Sun.

This amiable bistro is a corner of Gallic charm in the center of the West Indian town of Frederiksted. Familiar favorites like quiche, roast duck and frog legs are served on a terrace or in a romantic dining room. The woodsy bar is a little dark, but that's how many people like it. Reservations recommended. Credit cards: A, MC, V.

Not only is St. Croix a duty-free port, but U.S. citizens can bring back $1200 worth of merchandise tax-free to the States—twice that of any other Caribbean island (except the two other U.S. Virgins, St. Thomas and St. John). Among the more interesting things to look for are St. Croix's signature hook bracelet, also called a Cruzian bracelet. If you wear the U-shaped hook up, it means you are "taken," if worn upside-down, you're telling the world you're available. Also popular are hurricane bracelets, which symbolize survival.

Christiansted's quaint downtown is a good spot for shoppers; among the more interesting stores are **Tribal Threadz** *(52A Company Street,* ☎ *(809) 773-2883)*, an upscale boutique with men's and women's fashions; the **Quin House Gallery** *(51 Company Street,* ☎ *(809) 773-0404)* which features Indonesian imports, solid mahogany and hand-carved furniture and other home fashions; and **Jeltrup's Books** *(also on Company Street,* ☎ *(809) 773-1018)*, which has a great selection of works by local authors, tomes on island history and antique, used and new books. For jewelry, check out **Sonya's** *(1 Company Street,* ☎ *(809) 778-8605)*, where the popular hook bracelet originated; the **Natural Jewel** *(Queen Cross Street,* ☎ *(809) 773-3845)*, which specializes in pearl, coral, larimar and semi-precious stones; and **Little Switzerland** *(King Street,* ☎ *(809) 773-1976)*, the chain that offers high-quality pieces. For locally made crafts, try **Folk Art Traders** *(Strand Street,* ☎ *(809) 773-1900)*, **Unique Accents** *(Pan Am Pavilion,* ☎ *(809) 773-7585)*, and **America West Indian Company** *(Strand Street,* ☎ *(809) 773-7325)*.

Frederiksted has less shops than Christiansted, but there's some well worth checking out: **Frederiksted Gallery** *(King Street,* ☎ *(809) 772-1611)*, which showcases works by local artists; **Me Dundo's Place** *(Strand Street,* ☎ *(809) 772-0774)*, with a good selection of island-made crafts; and **Yemaya's** *(Inner Passage Court,* ☎ *(809) 773-1169)*, with hand-dyed silks. **Vendors' Plaza**, open on cruiseship days, is an open-air market featuring island-made goods.

The gift shop at **Estate Whim Plantation** *(*☎ *(809) 772-0598)* is one of the best in the Caribbean and highly recommended, as is the giftshop at the **Westin Carombola Resort** *(Kingshill,* ☎ *(809) 778-1682)*. For high-quality (and dearly priced) mahogany furnishings, try **St. Croix Leap** *(Mahogany Road,* ☎ *(809) 772-0421)*, located in the rainforest.

St. Croix Directory

Arrival and Departure

American Airlines offers nonstop service to St. Croix from Miami, with connecting service from NYC, Newark and Raleigh/Durham via Miami on San Juan. (Flights into San Juan connect into St. Croix on convenient commuter airlines.) **Carnival Airlines** flies nonstop from Miami, NYC, Orlando and Newark to San Juan with connecting flights on commuters. **Continental** flies direct from Newark to St. Croix, with connecting service from Boston, Chicago, Detroit and Philadelphia via Newark. **Delta** flies direct from Atlanta to St. Croix, nonstop from Atlanta to San Juan. **Trans World Airways** flies nonstop from NYC, St. Louis and Miami to San Juan. **United Airlines** flies nonstop from Dulles International (Washington, D.C.) to San Juan. **USAir** flies nonstop from Baltimore, Charlotte and Philadelphia to San Juan. Once you're in the Caribbean you might consider **Air Anguilla**, which flies direct from Anguilla to St. Croix, and returns via St. Thomas. **American Eagle** flies daily from San Juan to St. Croix and back. **LIAT** flies from St. Croix to other Caribbean islands to the south and return. **Sunaire Express** offers frequent jet-prop and daily service between St. Croix and St. Thomas, and San Juan to St. Thomas and St. Croix and return. **Virgin Air** makes passenger/freight service between San Juan and St. Croix and islands to the south. It also has a charter ambulance. One of the joys of the USVI is the ability to island hop. Inexpensive transportation via ferry is available among the **USVI** and the **BVI** as well, opening up other possibilities for day trips. Year-round Caribbean cruises from San Juan, Miami and other stateside ports go to St. Croix and return.

Business Hours

Stores open weekdays 9 a.m.–5 p.m., some later in Christiansted. Banks generally open Monday–Thursday 9 a.m.–2:30 p.m. and Friday 9 a.m.–2 p.m. and 3:30–5 p.m.

Climate

Temperatures during the summer, cooled by eastern trade winds, keep the temperature around 82 degrees F. Brief showers also keep things cool. Winter temperatures rise to 77 degrees F. Rainiest months are September–January, and about 40 inches of rain fall per year. A light sweater is needed in winter.

Documents

U.S. citizens need not carry a passport, although some proof of identity will be required upon leaving the islands. A passport is a good idea since the nearby British Virgin Islands are so accessible from St. John and St. Thomas. If you wish to dive the Rhone or snorkel amid the fantastic granite boulders at the baths on Virgin Gorda, you'll need to first clear BVI Customs with a passport and an $8 entry fee.

Electricity

Current runs at 110 volts at 60 cycles.

Getting Around

Transportation on the islands is handled either by taxi or rental cars. Remember, that driving is on the left side of the road. Many rental companies in Cuz Bay offer competitive rates. Expect to pay roughly $60 per day, plus gas and insurance for a Suzuki Sidekick (with four-wheel drive to accommodate the blind switchbacks and extreme mountain inclines).

Language

The official language is English, but the special lilt to the accent is called cruzan. Some locals speak a musical patois called English Creole—a blend of English, African and Spanish. Many people also speak good Spanish.

Medical Emergencies

St. Croix has a 250-bed **hospital** ☎ *(809) 778-6311*, with 24-hour emergency service. Ask your hotel about doctors on call when you check-in.

Money

The official currency is the U.S. dollar.

Telephone

The area code is *809*. Since USVI is an incorporated territory, toll-free numbers that operate in the U.S. work here. You can also dial direct to the mainland. Normal postage rates apply.

Time

Atlantic Standard Time, one hour later than New York City; during Daylight Saving Time, it is the same as New York.

Tipping and Taxes

Some hotels include a 10–15 percent service charge; this should include all tips for both restaurant and room service, unless the attention was extraordinary. If no service is added, leave a 15 percent tip for the waitress, $1–2 a day to the maid; bartenders and wine stewards should be tipped always. Tip the bellboy and porter at least 50 cents a bag. Taxi drivers should receive a 15 percent tip if you are satisfied with the service.

Tourist Information

The **St. Croix Tourist Office** ☎ *(809) 773-0495* is located at the Christiansted Wharf. It is open daily.

When to Go

The Fiesta Food Fair is held on Jan. 5 at the Agriculture Fair Grounds in Estate Lower Love, featuring native cooks and their cuisine, arts and crafts, and steel and quelbe bands. Organic Act Day is June 21. Oct. is one of the busiest months. The Champagne Mumm's Cup Regatta sets sail on Oct. 8–10. Columbus Day/Puerto Rican Friendship Day is celebrated on Oct. 6–10, a week-long celebration featuring parade, horse racing and native foods and music. The St. Croix Jazz & Caribbean Music & Arts Festival takes place in mid-October. The Golden Hook Challenge is slated for Oct. 21–23, a sportsfishing contest. Veterans Day is celebrated on Nov. 11, with island-style parades of steel bands, calypso and partying. The Crucian Christmas Fiesta, the traditional two-week event that features parades, pageants, food and music starts Dec. 11–Jan. 7. The Crucian Christmas Festival Food Fairs in Christiansted and Frederiksted is held in the third week of Dec. The Festival Village in Christiansted takes place on Dec. 29. Frederiksted's Village opens on Dec. 30, with nightly reggae, calypso and Latin music. A Carnival-like Christmas celebration takes place from several days before Christmas to about a week after New Year's.

St. CROIX HOTELS		RMS	RATES	PHONE	CR. CARDS
Christiansted					
★★★★★	**Buccaneer Hotel**	150	$210–$341	(800) 223-1108	A, CB, D, MC, V
★★★★★	**Westin Carambola Beach Resort**	151	$235–$330	(800) 333-3333	A, D, MC, V
★★★★	**Villa Madeleine**	43	$300–$425	(800) 548-4461	A, MC
★★★	**Cane Bay Reef Club**	9	$85–$165	(800) 253-8534	A, MC
★★★	**Club St. Croix**	54	$120–$225	(800) 635-1533	A, CB, D, MC, V
★★★	**Cormorant Beach Club**	38	$120–$230	(800) 548-4460	A, MC, V
★★★	**Cormorant Cove**	38	$105–$230	(800) 548-4460	A, MC, V
★★★	**Hibiscus Beach Hotel**	37	$120–$240	(800) 442-0121	A, D, MC, V
★★★	**Hilty House Inn**	6	$70–$110	(809) 773-2594	
★★★	**Horizons**		$1400–$5000	(609) 751-2413	
★★★	**Hotel on the Cay**	55	$95–$198	(800) 524-2035	A, MC, V
★★★	**King Christian Hotel**	39	$80–$135	(800) 524-2012	A, CB, D, MC, V
★★★	**St. Croix by the Sea**	65	$90–$145	(800) 524-5006	A, MC, V
★★★	**Tamarind Reef Hotel**	46	$145–$180	(800) 619-0014	A, MC, V
★★	**Anchor Inn**	30	$80–$145	(800) 524-2030	MC, V
★★	**Anchor Inn of St. Croix**	31	$80–$150	(800) 524-2030	A, CB, D, MC, V
★★	**Chenay Bay Beach Resort**	50	$125–$210	(800) 548-4457	A, MC
★★	**Colony Cove**	60	$130–$185	(800) 524-2025	A, D, MC
★★	**Gentle Winds Resort**	66	$230–$305	(809) 773-3400	None
★★	**Hotel Caravelle**	43	$79–$255	(800) 524-0410	A, CB, D, MC, V
★★	**Pink Fancy Hotel**	13	$65–$120	(800) 524-2045	A, MC
★★	**Schooner Bay Resort**	62	$110–$150	(800) 524-2025	A, D, MC
★★	**Sugar Beach Condominiums**	46	$110–$250	(800) 524-2049	A, MC, V
★★	**Waves at Cane Bay**	12	$85–$195	(800) 545-0603	A, D, MC

St. CROIX HOTELS	RMS	RATES	PHONE	CR. CARDS
★ Cactus Inn		$39–$45	(809) 692-9331	
★ Caribbean View All-Suites	18	$80–$120	(809) 773-3335	A, CB, D, MC, V
★ Club Comanche	42	$35–$126	(800) 524-2066	A, MC
★ Danish Manor Hotel	35	$49–$95	(800) 524-2069	A, MC, V

Frederiksted

★★ Frederiksted Hotel	40	$80–$110	(800) 524-2025	A, MC, V
★★ On the Beach Resort	20	$50–$180	(800) 524-2018	A, CB, D, MC, V
★★ Sprat Hall Plantation	16	$95–$220	(809) 772-0305	
★ Cottages by the Sea	20	$70–$110	(800) 323-7252	A, D, MC

ST. CROIX RESTAURANTS	PHONE	ENTRÉE	CR. CARDS

Christiansted

American

★★ Chart House	(809) 773-7718	$14–$26	A, DC, MC, V
★★ Saman	(809) 778-3800	$15–$20	A, MC, V
★ Mango Grove	(809) 773-0200	$5–$8	A

International

★★★★ Kendrick's	(809) 773-9199	$14–$26	A, MC, V
★★ Antoine's	(809) 773-0263	$14–$32	A, MC, V
★★ Comanche	(809) 773-2665	$9–$21	A, MC, V
★★ Tivoli Gardens	(809) 773-6782	$6–$20	A, MC, V

Italian

★★★★★ Cafe Madeleine	(809) 773-8141	$18–$26	A, DC, MC, V
★★ Picnic in Paradise	(809) 778-1212	$10–$20	A, MC, V

Latin American

★★★ Harvey's	(809) 773-3433	$8–$20	None

Mediterranean

★★ Dino's	(809) 778-8005	$14–$20	None

Seafood

★★★ Mahogany	(809) 778-3800	$26–$36	A, MC, V
★★★ Top Hat	(809) 773-2346	$14–$28	A, MC, V
★★ Banana Bay Club	(809) 778-9110	$15–$25	A, MC, V

ST. CROIX

ST. CROIX RESTAURANTS PHONE ENTRÉE CR. CARDS

Frederiksted

French

	PHONE	ENTRÉE	CR. CARDS
★★★ **Le St. Tropez**	(809) 772-3000	$10–$25	A, MC, V

International

	PHONE	ENTRÉE	CR. CARDS
★★★ **Blue Moon**	(809) 772-2222	$10–$20	A

SINT EUSTATIUS

Many Statia visitors are daytrippers from Saba and Sint Maarten.

One of the Caribbean's least-known islands, St. Eustatius—more popularly known as Statia—is located just 38 miles south of St. Maarten and is part of the Windward Islands of the Dutch Caribbean. The poorest and least populated of the three Windwards (St. Maarten and Saba are the others), life here is laid back, peaceful and friendly—though not for everyone. The beaches aren't great, shopping is limited, nightlife is mellow and accommodations are generally rustic. On the other hand, prices are very inexpensive, the hiking and diving are great, and Statia is not the kind of place where you'll be overrun by tourists.

The island is dominated by the Quill, an extinct volcano that soars up 2000 feet. Its crater is home to a thriving rainforest with breadfruit, balsam and mahogany trees, colorful orchids, giant elephant ears, tree ferns, white and pink begonias and wild cherry trees. Hikers are also rewarded with great views of Saba, St. Barts, St. Maarten, St. Kitts and Nevis.

Diving is excellent, with visibility typically at more than 100 feet and numerous coral reefs, volcanic canyons and some 250 historic shipwrecks to explore. Especially intriguing are the artifacts of the "sunken city" in Oranje Bay, where you'll see the ruins of 18th-century houses, bars and warehouses. You may even unearth some historic "litter" such as an old bottle or utensil; if so, be a good sport and donate it to the Historical Museum in Oranjestad.

Most of Statia's visitors are day trippers from Saba and St. Maarten; those who choose to spend their entire vacation here are richly rewarded with the kind of tranquillity that is fast becoming a thing of the past in the Caribbean. If you're looking to stock up on fine imported goods and boogie till dawn, look elsewhere. But if a true respite for the workaday world sounds like your idea of heaven, read on.

Bird's-Eye View

St. Eustatius totals just 11.8 square miles, measuring five miles long by two miles wide. The climate is generally dry and sunny, with an average temperature of 70 to 80 degrees Fahrenheit and constant northeast tradewinds. The island gets some 45 inches of rain each year, mostly occurring in April, June and September.

The terrain is generally quite arid, save the rainforest that fills the crater of the Quill, a perfected formed extinct volcano that is the island's highest point at nearly 2000 feet. Other extinct volcanoes line the north and south, with a central plan running along the island's midsection.

The capital city of Oranjestad is actually just a town (the island's only one, in fact) of vintage Dutch colonial structures and a fort dating back to 1636. The island's three beaches all have black or beige sand; the undertow along the Atlantic side can be quite overpowering, so swimming is not recommended.

History

Columbus discovered Sint Eustatius on his second voyage, but a Spanish settlement never followed. The Dutch founded the first settlement in 1636,

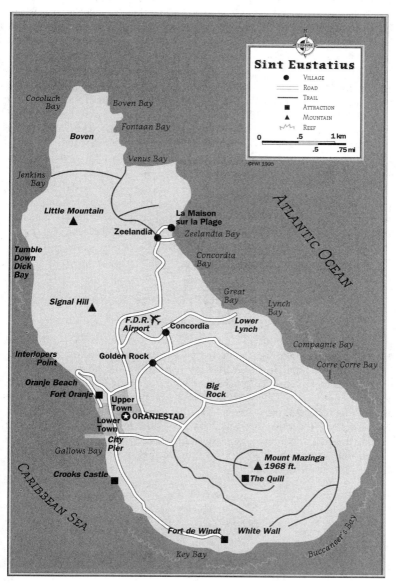

Cocoluch Bay
Boven Bay
Fontaan Bay
Boven
Venus Bay
Jenkins Bay

Sint Eustatius

● VILLAGE
ROAD
TRAIL
■ ATTRACTION
▲ MOUNTAIN
REEF

0   .5   1 km
.5   .75 mi

©FWI 1995

ATLANTIC OCEAN

Little Mountain ▲
La Maison sur la Plage
Zeelandia ●
Zeelandia Bay
Concordia Bay

Tumble Down Dick Bay

Great Bay
Lynch Bay

Signal Hill ▲
F.D.R. Airport ✈
Concordia
Lower Lynch
Compagnie Bay

Interlopers Point
Golden Rock ●
Corre Corre Bay

Oranje Beach
Fort Oranje ■
Big Rock

Upper Town
ORANJESTAD ✪
Lower Town
City Pier
Gallows Bay

Mount Mazinga 1968 ft. ▲
■ **The Quill**

Crooks Castle ■

CARIBBEAN SEA

Fort de Windt   **White Wall**
Key Bay
Buccaneer's Bay

building Fort Orange but the Dutch claim it was never finalized until 1816, after the island changed hands 22 times. During the 18th century, the island became extraordinarily prosperous, as more than 8000 swarmed to the island, half of whom were slaves. Trade became the most profitable way to make a living, and the island gained the nickname "The Golden Rock."

Statia has a long and unique relationship with the United States. At the time of the War for Independence, Statia was a major port from which arms were shipped to General Washington's troops via Boston, New York and Charleston. On Nov. 16, 1776, the island unknowingly fired the first initial salute to the just-declared nation, but the British retaliated, the port being taken in 1781 by Admiral George Brydges Rodney, who captured 150 merchant ships and 5 million pounds before the French expelled him the next year.

After that, the economy began to decline as control of the island changed power numerous times, and merchants were banished by changing rules. The Emancipation Act of 1863 significantly squashed any hope for a plantation industry. Most natives were reduced to sustenance farming and receiving monetary assistance from relatives abroad.

People

The population is about 2100, made up mainly of descendants of African slaves, forced into labor on the more than 70 plantations that once dominated Statia. More than 20 nationalities are represented on the small island. Instruction is in Dutch—the official language— though English and Spanish are also taught and widely spoken. A variety of religions are practiced on the island, including Roman Catholic, Methodist, Baptist, Anglican, Methodist, Seventh Day Adventist, Jehovah Witness, Bahai Faith, and the World of Faith Ministry. The people are extraordinarily friendly and crime is virtually nonexistent. Those not working in tourism make their living by farming, trading and at the oil refinery.

Beaches

One of the loveliest beaches is **Oranje Baai**, stretching for a mile along the coast away from the Lower Town. The strand is perfectly safe for swimming, with a large expanse of sand appearing January-July. Other times the beach narrows and even disappears. Avoid **Zeelandia** for swimming, but you can see interesting geological formations in the cliff and even nesting sea birds. (A dangerous undertow here can be deadly and there is no lifeguard to save you.) After a rain, you can find lots of shells and driftwood on the beach— hikers love it. The beach itself, however, is especially lovely and two miles long. **Lynch Beach**, also on the Windward side, is a bit safer for swimming if you do not venture far out into the surf.

Underwater

Sint Eustatius is a diver's dream with coral reefs, marine life and many shipwrecks to explore.

Still emerging from the shadow cast by her better-known little sister Saba, Sint Eustatius is possibly the best-kept dive secret in the Eastern Caribbean, and it's easy to understand why. If you're looking for an island with beaches, nightlife and resorts to complement a vivid underwater scene, you are kindly requested to skip Statia. This is a minimally developed destination visited by only a few hundred divers each year. But do head for Statia if you desire an off-the-wall vacation to an island your friends have never heard of (and all your dive buddies know of Saba by now). The payoff, for those willing to "rough it" without a disco, is pristine diving through deep volcanic canyons and fissures, over shallow reefs and plunging walls, and around a bevy of quietly disintegrating 17th- and 18th-century trading ships. And those are just the documented sites; there are a number of unexplored areas offering true virgin dive possibilities.

Statia's wrecks provided a delightful bounty to early diver visitors. So much so that, although their wooden hulls were long gone, the government eventually ruled that nonresidents may dive only when accompanied by a local dive operator; today, the occasional bottle or pewter utensil unearthed will be donated to the Oranjestad museum. Fortunately, there are still plenty of antiquities to see, but the reefs are the real star of Statia's underwater show, and you won't have to elbow your way in to do it. The spectacular and rare flying gurnard is regularly spotted on Statia, and larger pelagics frequent a number of the sites. Humpback whales cruise the area December through February. Perhaps the best snorkeling site is found 70 feet from shore at **City Wall** (in front of Dive Statia's shop), a barricade that once represented the old sea wall for Lower Town and is now inhabited by reef fish and invertebrate life; watch for sea urchins. A steep trail leads to calm **Jenkins Bay** in the northwest or to **Corre Corre Bay**, off the eastern side of the island (see "On Foot"), both providing excellent snorkeling. There's one professional dive operator on Statia at present, but rumors are swirling about competition coming to town.

On Foot

Good things come in small packages and, for hikers, Statia is a small treasure. With only 12 square miles to cover, the island realistically can be seen entirely on foot, albeit by dedicated walkers. But more sedate visitors will still want to climb **The Quill**, the classically shaped volcanic cone that dominates the island from every vantage point (although the best view is actually obtained from nearby St. Kitts). It represents one of the Caribbean's easier "high points" and rewards its guests with a lush crater rainforest (the only one on an otherwise arid island), where islanders hunt land crabs after dark. A three-hour guided tour of **Oranjestad** is easily arranged with local historians through the island museum or tourist office; they will also provide a walking map featuring a few trails and donkey tracks not listed below.

By Pedal

Judging from the fact that only Dive Statia (see "Under Water") can provide visitors with bike rentals—and only two at that!—Statia can be considered virgin mountain biking territory. The island is small, but the main roads will reward cyclists with relaxed touring. The trail to the Quill is said to be unrideable, but perhaps it's just waiting for the right pair of muscles? One caution: off-roading appears inviting, but invites stickers and thorns; carry a patch kit.

What Else to See

Statia's only town is Oranjestad, the capital "city," which is divided into Upper Town (the main center) and Lower Town. You can tour both on foot in about an hour and a half. Building around the bay in Lower Town began around the mid 1700s; you'll see lots of ruins of warehouses from the era. Lynch Plantation Museum, located on the island's northeastern side, has a good collection of household artifacts and antiques. Just outside Oranjestad, to the east, is the old Jewish Burial Ground with graves dating as far back as 1742.

Historical Sites

Fort Oranje ★★

Upper Town, Oranjestad.

This fort dates back to 1636. It was restored in honor of the U.S. Bicentennial in 1976. St. Eustatius was the first foreign entity to support the United States in the Revolutionary War, and a plaque here, presented by Franklin D. Roosevelt, gives thanks. The British retaliated by sacking the then-rich town and its harbor, and much of the rebuilding was done with U.S. funds. The tourist office out front is a good place to pick up brochures and maps and hire a guide.

Museums and Exhibits

St. Eustatius Historical Museum ★★

Wilhelmina Way, Oranjestad.
Hours open: 9 a.m.–5 p.m.

This museum is housed in a beautifully restored 18th-century building once lived in by British Admiral Rodney during the American Revolution. (Not a popular man, as he's the one who ordered the town destroyed after it acknowledged the fledgling United States as an independent country.) The museum's eclectic exhibits focus on sugar production, slave trading, 18th-century antiques, and pre-Columbian artifacts. General admission: $2.

Tours

The Quill   ★ ★ ★

Southern portion, Oranjestad.

The island's highest point at 1968 feet, the Quill is an extinct volcano with a lush rainforest in its crater. Twelve marked trails offer all level of hikes, from simple treks to strenuous trips to the summit. Pick up a brochure at the tourist office, or hire a guide to take you for about $20. Excellent birdwatching. Locals come at night to catch the large crabs that live in the crater. You can accompany them and get your hotel to cook your quarry. Inquire at the tourist office for details.

Sporting activities on Statia are confined to snorkeling, diving and hiking. Climbing to the top of the Quill is de rigeuer; pick from one of 12 trails that take you to the top, where the views are amazing and a verdant rainforest is tucked into the extinct volcano's crater. Snorkelers will find good underwater sights at Jenkins and Venus bays and Crooks Castle. Diving is excellent, with teems of historic shipwrecks and even a submerged village to explore. **Dive Statia** *(☎ 599-38-2435)* and **Golden Rock Dive Center** *(☎ 599-38-2964)* will set you up in style; it costs about $40 to $50 for a one-tank dive. Golden Rock also offers sportfishing ($350 for a half-day) and sunset cruises ($30 each).

Tennis

Rosemary Lane, Oranjestad.

St. Eustatius is not the place to come to play tennis—there's one lone court on the entire island. The concrete court at the Community Center is open every day and lit for night play, but you'll have to bring your own racquet and balls, though they do have changing rooms. The fee is about $5.

Watersports

Lower Toen, Oranjestad.

Dive Statia *(☎ 599-38-2435)* is the island's most complete (and virtually only) watersports center. They offer deep-sea fishing trips, snorkeling equipment, and scuba instruction and excursions. St. Eustatius is a diver's paradise, with all sorts of interesting undersea items to explore, including myriad sunken ships and their booty. Snorkelers can see a lot too, as the depths are often only about 10 feet.

Where to Stay

Fielding's Highest Rated Hotels in Sint Eustatius

★★★	Old Gin House	$125–$225

Fielding's Most Exclusive Hotels in Sint Eustatius

★★★	Old Gin House	$125–$225
★★	Maison sur la Plage	$60–$95
★★	Airport View Apartments	$60–$75

Fielding's Best Value Hotels in Sint Eustatius

★★	Airport View Apartments	$60–$75
★★	Talk of the Town	$57–$88
★★	Maison sur la Plage	$60–$95
★★	Golden Era	$70–$88
★★★	Old Gin House	$125–$225

You won't find fancy resorts with theme nights on St. Eustatius, and so much the better; such a property would be a true mistake on this unspoiled isle. Rates, as you'll see in the following listings, are wonderfully cheap. La Maison Sur la Plage and the Old Gin House offer the spiffiest accommodations.

Hotels and Resorts

Golden Era   **$70–$88**   ★★

Lower Town, Oranjestad, ☎ *(599) 3-82445. FAX (599) 3-82445.*
Single: $70. Double: $88.
This small hotel sits right at the water's edge, but you'll have to travel a half-mile for the beach, as the shoreline here is rocky. Guest rooms are quite basic, but comfortable with air conditioning, phones and tiny private balconies. The restaurant serves decent Caribbean cuisine. The saltwater pool is the only other facility. Acceptable for the rates, but nothing too exciting. 20 rooms. Credit cards: A, D, MC.

Maison sur la Plage   **$60–$95**   ★★

Zeelandia, Oranjestad, ☎ (599) 3-82256. FAX (599) 3-82831.
Single: $60–$80. Double: $60–$95.

Located on the northeastern coast, this small property took a real pummeling during Hurricane Hugo, and has yet to return to its predestruction days. That's not to say that all is in ruins, but some repairs have a slapdash quality. Accommodations are in cottages with basic furnishings, private terraces and bright artwork. Facilities include a gourmet French restaurant, a bar, a TV lounge (you won't find one in your room), a small library and a pool. The beach stretches for two miles, but the sea is too rough for most swimmers. The rates include continental breakfast. 10 rooms. Credit cards: A, MC.

Talk of the Town   **$57–$88**   ★★

Oranjestaad ☎ (599) 3-82236. FAX (599) 3-82640.
Single: $57–$71. Double: $72–$88.

This small hotel is set off the beach, but does have a pool. Rooms are quite basic but nice, with air conditioning, locally made furnishings, telephones, and cable TV. There are also two efficiencies with kitchenettes. The downstairs restaurant is fine. Though frills are few, this is still one of the better choices on this tiny island. Rates include breakfast. 18 rooms. Credit cards: A, MC.

Apartments and Condominiums

Ask the tourist board for help in finding just the right house or apartment for your needs. Bring your own staples from home.

Airport View Apartments   **$60–$75**   ★★

Golden Rock, Oranjestad, ☎ (599) 3-82474.
Single: $60. Double: $75.

Like the name implies, these units are indeed near the airport. Each unit is a studio with just the basics—refrigerator, coffeemaker, cable TV—but not complete kitchens, though there is a barbecue area where you can grill meals. There's also a bar and restaurant on the premises, but not much else, not even a pool. 9 rooms. Credit cards: A, MC.

Inns

Old Gin House   **$125–$225**   ★★★

Lower Town, Oranjestad, ☎ (599) 3-82319. FAX (599) 3-82555.
Single: $125–$150. Double: $175–$225.

This elegant inn is by far the nicest place to stay on St. Eustatius, and also by far the most expensive. Housed in a restored 18th-century cotton gin factory, rooms are spacious and individually decorated with good artwork, antique furnishings and ceiling fans (no air conditioning). Request one of the rooms in the original inn as they have the most character, though the ones in the newer building across the street are also quite pleasant. There's a restaurant, small pool and library on the premises, and the beach is steps away. No children under 10 permitted. 20 rooms. Credit cards: A, CB, MC, V.

Where to Eat

★★★	**Fielding's Highest Rated Restaurants in Sint Eustatius**	
★★★	La Maison Sur La Plage	$15–$25
★★★	Old Gin House	$10–$22
★★★	Talk of the Town	$5–$20

	Fielding's Most Exclusive Restaurants in Sint Eustatius	
★★★	La Maison Sur La Plage	$15–$25
★★★	Old Gin House	$10–$22
★★★	Talk of the Town	$5–$20

	Fielding's Best Value Restaurants in Sint Eustatius	
★★	Kim Cheng's Chinese	$5–$10
★★★	Talk of the Town	$5–$20
★★	Cool Corner	$8–$10
★★★	Old Gin House	$10–$22
★★★	La Maison Sur La Plage	$15–$25

Restaurants on Statia are as informal as their surroundings, though you'll find good French fare at La Maison Sur la Plage. The Old Gin House also has good food, and is a favorite with locals. Fresh fish and yummy just-baked bread are island favorites.

Cool Corner   **$**   ★★

Fort Oranjestraat, Oranjestad, ☎ *(599) 38-2523.*
International cuisine.
Lunch: 10 a.m.–4 p.m., entrées $8–$10.
Dinner: 4 p.m.–midnight, entrées $8–$10.
This hot spot (for Statia) beckons with a prime location near the local tourist office. A good place to meet the friendly townspeople, Cool Corner stays open late to serve

the needs of the few night owls who may be prowling. Fare is Caribbean-Chinese, with curry plates and Cantonese specialties available. Credit cards: not accepted.

Kim Cheng's Chinese $ ★★

Prinsesweg, Oranjestad, ☎ *(599) 30-2389.*
Chinese cuisine.
Lunch: entrées $5–$10.
Dinner: entrées $5–$10. Closed: Sun.
Sometimes called The Chinese Restaurant this tiny eatery manages to produce plates heaped with hearty food in rather cramped surroundings. The fare is actually a potpourri of dishes encompassing West Indian, creole and Chinese. Credit cards: not accepted.

L'Etoile $$ ★★

6 Van Rheeweg, Oranjestad, ☎ *(599) 38-2299.*
Latin American cuisine.
Lunch: Noon–4 p.m., entrées $7–$20.
Dinner: 4–10 p.m., entrées $7–$20.
What appears to be a roadhouse is really a warm, welcoming room proffering tasty island specialties prepared by the amiable Caren Henriquez. Its location on a hillside is a little out of the way for the average tourist, so it's mainly frequented by a crowd of regulars. Along with hamburgers, tasty spareribs and hotdogs, Henriquez prepares goat stew or stuffed crab. Reservations required. Credit cards: not accepted.

La Maison Sur La Plage $$$ ★★★

Zeelandia Beach, Oranjestad, ☎ *(599) 38-2256.*
Associated hotel: La Maison Sur La Plage.
French cuisine.
Lunch: entrées $15–$25.
Dinner: entrées $15–$25.
In what's considered to be an out-of-the-way location for Statia, La Maison sur Plage is the only fine French restaurant on Zeelandia beach, which is only a few miles from Oranjestad. Meals are served on a breezy, trellised terrace overlooking windswept sands and the Quill. Expect traditional Gallic specialties like duck breast or beef fillets with green peppercorn sauce, and crepes for dessert. Reservations required. Credit cards: MC, V.

Old Gin House $$$ ★★★

Lower Town, Oranjestad, ☎ *(599) 38-2319. Associated hotel: Old Gin House.*
American cuisine.
Lunch: Noon–2 p.m., entrées $10–$22.
Dinner: 6:30–8 p.m., prix fixe $10–$22.
Dinner at the Mooshay Bay Dining Room of this venerable hotel is one of the best deals in town. A delicious four-course meal that often includes chateaubriand or lobster and two kinds of wine is available for $22 per person. The 18th-century tavern room is spiffily decorated with burnished pewter and gleaming crystal, and it faces the pool. Across the street, the Terrace Restaurant, which has an ocean view, is a nice place for burgers or steak and chicken plates. Reservations recommended. Credit cards: A, DC, MC, V.

Stone Oven　　　　　　　**$$**　　　　　　　★★
> 16A Feaschweg, Oranjestad, ☎ (599) 38-2247.
> *Latin American cuisine.*
> *Lunch: entrées $10–$15.*
> *Dinner: entrées $10–$15.*
> This cozy, coconut-palm fringed bar and danceteria serves as a West Indian eatery depending on who's available to cook. When the burners are going, it's a good spot for goat water or conch. Check out the wild party animals swinging on Friday nights when it stays open until the last guest moseys on home. Reservations required. Credit cards: not accepted.

Talk of the Town　　　　**$$**　　　　　　★★★
> L.E. Saddlerweg, Oranjestad, ☎ (599) 38-2236. *Associated hotel: Talk of the Town.*
> *International cuisine.*
> *Lunch: 11:30 a.m.–2 p.m., entrées $5–$20.*
> *Dinner: 7–10 p.m., entrées $5–$20.*
> A Dutch family owns and operates this plant-filled, indoor-outdoor restaurant near the airport. It has a reputation for the best creole meals in town, but the cuisine jumps often from one exotic clime to the next. Specialties include lobster stew, which can be ordered in advance. Good deals include the Dutch-style breakfast buffet with some American standards thrown in—all for under $10. Reservations recommended. Credit cards: A, MC, V.

Statia is no St. Thomas. You'll find a few items imported from Holland, including cosmetics, perfumes, liquors, cigarettes and jewelry at the **Mazinga Gift Shop** in Upper Town (Fort Oranjestraat). One good native buy is **Masinga Mist** (schnapps made from soursop) which you can pick up at **Dive Statia's boutique** near the Old Gin House. The museum at Fort Oranje has a small selection of books and postcards.

Sint Eustatius Directory

Arrival and Departure
You can reach Sint Eustatius several times a day on 20-minute flights from St. Maarten on **WINAIR**. WINAIR also flies to the island from St. Kitts, which takes only 10 minutes. WINAIR also offers flights from Sint Eustatius to Saba. All flights are in small planes, but be sure you look out the window when you land and take off to get a great view of The Quill, the island's volcano. There is a departure tax of $3 if you are going to the U.S., $3 if you are going on to any other Caribbean island.

Business Hours

Shops generally open weekdays 8 a.m.–noon and 1–4 p.m. Bank (there's only one) open Monday–Thursday 8:30 a.m.–1 p.m. and Friday 8:30 a.m.–1 p.m. and 4–5 p.m.

Climate

Daytime temperatures hover in the mid-80s during the day and drop to the 70s during the evening, year-round. Only 45 inches of rain fall a year.

Documents

U.S. and Canadian citizens need to show only proof of citizenship (current passport or one that expired less than five years ago, or voter's registration card or birth certificate with raised seal and a photo ID), plus an ongoing or return ticket.

Electricity

Current runs 110 volts, 60 cycles, same as in the U.S. No converter or transformer necessary.

Getting Around

Most destinations are within walking distance, but several taxi drivers make excellent guides. A tour around the island runs about $35. Cars can be hired at the airport, but you must show your own driver's license or an international driver's license. Driving is on the right, but the cows, sheep and goats who casually graze over the roadways don't seem to know. You should drive slowly to avoid hitting them.

Language

The official language is Dutch (most of the signs are written so), but everyone speaks English. If you meet someone on the street, use the national greeting; "Awright, ok-a-a-y."

Medical Emergencies

Most emergencies are immediately flown to Sint Maarten (though you may want to charter a flight to San Juan, Puerto Rico), but there is a small hospital on the outskirts of Oranjestad.

Money

The official currency is the Netherlands Antilles florin (abbreviated NAf), also called the guilder. American dollars are generally accepted everywhere, but Canadians should change their money into florins (Barclays Bank in Wilhelminaweg) or in St. Maarten before coming. Only hotels and a few restaurants will accept credit cards. Imagine you are out in the middle of nowhere.

Telephone

The country code is *599*. To call from the States, dial *011* (international access code), plus *599* (country code) plus *38* (city code) plus 4-digit local number. You may need to use a different code when calling from another Caribbean island.

Time

Atlantic Standard Time, one hour ahead of New York, except during Daylight Saving Time, when it is the same.

Tipping and Taxes

Restaurants, hotels and bars all add a 15 percent service charge. You don't need to tip anyone on top of this. Taxi drivers should get $1–2. No porters to worry about, so be prepared to carry our own luggage.

Tourist Information

There are three tourist offices on the island: at the airport, in Lower Town opposite Roro Pier, operated by the Sint Eustatius Historical Society, and in the village center. For more information, call ☎ *(599) 3-82433.* In the U.S. ☎ *(800) 722-2394.*

When to Go

The Queen's Coronation Day on April 30 is a big island bash with fireworks, music, dancing and sports events. Carnival is celebrated in July. Statia-America Day is commemorated on Nov. 16, honoring the first salute to the American flag by a foreign government. Boxing Day is celebrated the day after Christmas on Dec. 26.

SINT EUSTATIUS HOTELS		RMS	RATES	PHONE	CR. CARDS
Oranjestad					
★★★	**Old Gin House**	20	$125–$225	(599) 3-82319	A, CB, MC, V
★★	**Airport View Apartments**	9	$60–$75	(599) 3-82474	A, MC
★★	**Golden Era**	20	$70–$88	(599) 3-82445	A, D, MC
★★	**Maison sur la Plage**	10	$60–$95	(599) 3-82256	A, MC
★★	**Talk of the Town**	18	$57–$88	(599) 3-82236	A, MC

SINT EUSTATIUS RESTAURANTS		PHONE	ENTRÉE	CR. CARDS
Oranjestad				
American				
★★★	**Old Gin House**	(599) 38-2319	$10–$22	A, DC, MC, V
Chinese				
★★	**Kim Cheng's Chinese**	(599) 30-2389	$5–$10	None
French				
★★★	**La Maison Sur La Plage**	(599) 38-2256	$15–$25	MC, V

SINT EUSTATIUS RESTAURANTS	PHONE	ENTRÉE	CR. CARDS
International			
★★★ Talk of the Town	(599) 38-2236	$5–$20	A, MC, V
★★ Cool Corner	(599) 38-2523	$8–$10	None
Latin American			
★★ L'Etoile	(599) 38-2299	$7–$20	None
★★ Stone Oven	(599) 38-2247	$10–$15	None

ST. JOHN

Maho Bay, St. John

Few places in the Caribbean are as genuinely "untouched" as St. John in the U.S. Virgin Islands, and for many environmentally sensitive travelers, the island is one of the world's great natural wonders. Indeed, St. John has more than its fair share of aquamarine bays, snow-white beaches and lushly carpeted mountains, but it is the protection of these beauties and minimal development that make St. John so special. Almost two-thirds of the island is protected by the National Park service, plus another 5600 acres of underwater territory—all part of the Virgin Islands National Park. As such, there are terrific adventures to be had both above and under water. All it takes is a good pair of boots and the park service map to mash one's way through densely packed forest or hike over well-marked nature trails that lead past

200-year-old plantation houses. Underwater, the views are just as spectacular, with rock formations, grottoes and wrecks that rate among the best in the Eastern Caribbean. The eco-sensitive accommodations on St. John are in-synch with the land, lead by the famous Maho Bay Campground and its spin-offs, created by visionary developer Stanley Selengut. But don't expect to leave creature comforts too far behind—fine dining and lively bars are clustered around the town of Cruz Bay, and the truly needy can check in to Caneel Bay Resort for a few hundred dollars a night, where the staff will cater to guest's every whim. The absence of sales tax here might drive some visitors into a frenzy, but once the shopper's dust settles, even these folks find a way to appreciate the pristine environment that beckons at every turn.

St. John took a direct hit from Hurricane Marilyn in September 1995, a storm that did enough damage to close the island's two main resorts for over a year (one of which is still closed and tangled in legal problems as we go to press). Yet because the island had little overall infrastructure, putting things back together was a process that took only a matter of months. On the other hand, the economic fallout from Marilyn, particularly with the bulk of St. John's hotel rooms temporarily unavailable, has been acute, and many shop-owners and restaurants have been clinging precariously to the campground and villa traffic to keep their businesses solvent. However, savvy travelers who vacationed on the island in 1996 found that it was in terrific shape—greener, friendlier and quieter than ever.

The smallest of the three inhabited U.S. Virgins, St. John lies a mere two miles east of St. Thomas. The island is bordered on the north and east by the British Virgin Islands just a few miles away, while the southern shore faces the Caribbean Sea. The island is nine miles end-to-end, but much further if you drive it. The ruffled topography rises to 1277 feet at Bordeaux Mountain, though the winding, up-and-down nature of the roads suggests something far more dramatic. Two main roads traverse the western portion of the island: the Northshore Road which sticks to the north coast, and the Centerline Road, which connects the island's two main towns, Cruz Bay and Coral Bay via a mountain ridge. Scenic overlooks provide glimpses of the sugary white sand lining impossibly beautiful coves; one, Trunk Bay, is among the most photographed beaches in the world. St. John has no airstrip—it is connected to St. Thomas (and nearby Tortola) by regular ferry service across the Pillsbury Sound. There are a number of uninhabited islets and outcrops surrounding St. John, or so Christopher Columbus fantasized when he named

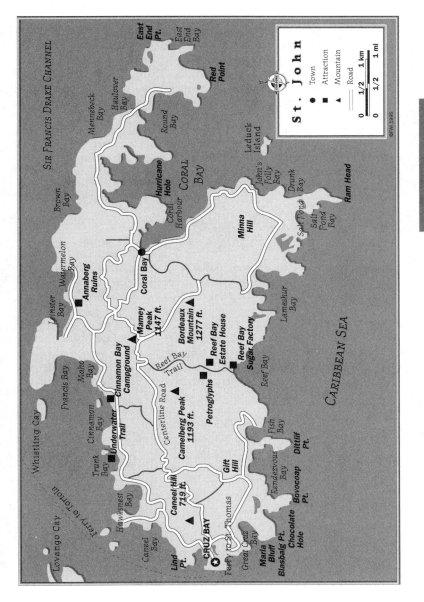

the group St. Ursula and her 11,000 virgins. Because almost two-thirds of the island has been a National Park for over three decades, the territory is still virgin, by Caribbean standards anyway, with only 3500 residents living on St. John, most of them residing in the area surrounding Cruz Bay, a tiny, ramshackle (flirting with slick) community surrounding a quaint harbor. In town, ferries and cruise-ship tenders dock, tourists shop and islanders go about their very laid-back business, but just beyond lies the dense forest of the National Park. When the ferry landing was built in Cruz Bay, opening a gateway to St. Thomas and her airport, the community of Coral Bay on the other side of the island sank slowly into seclusion. It was once the biggest town and main harbor on the island, and although there are still a few bars and restaurants in Coral Bay, the success of Cruz Bay has meant that the further one proceeds east, the further you are from tourist trappings.

History

Archaeologists have yet to decide whether the Arawaks or Caribs (the island's first pre-Columbian inhabitants), African slaves or a combination thereof were responsible for the primitive etchings along the Reef Bay trail. In 1493, Columbus discovered the islands of St. Croix, St. John and St. Thomas, and then shoved off to Puerto Rico. A hundred years later saw the arrival in of Sir Francis Drake as he prepared to confront the Spanish troops in San Juan. While St. Croix changed hands between the French and Spanish, St. John (along with St. Thomas) was appropriated by the Danish West India Company. The two Dutch-held islands became a hub of business (St. Thomas), and a magnet for sugarcane, tobacco and cotton plantations (St. John). In 1717, the Danes established St. John's Coral Bay as a permanent port. In 1733, a great slave rebellion devastated the country, when a large group of slaves, ostensibly carrying bundles of wood, were admitted to Fort Berg in Coral Bay. Once inside, they brandished cane knives and massacred hundreds of settlers and the entire Danish garrison. The rebels held the fort for nine months until the Danes, with the support of two French warships and an army from Martinique, recaptured the island and rebuilt the factories. In 1848, slavery was abolished, though planters tried to hold onto their crops until the advent of the European sugar-beet soured their profits. When the planters eventually left the island, the former slaves divided up their properties and relied on the land and the sea for sustenance. In 1917, with a view to protect its interest in the Panama Canal, the U.S.bought the Virgin Islands package—St. John, St. Thomas and St. Croix—from the Danes for a only $25 million. Starting in the '50s, tourism began to raise the standard of

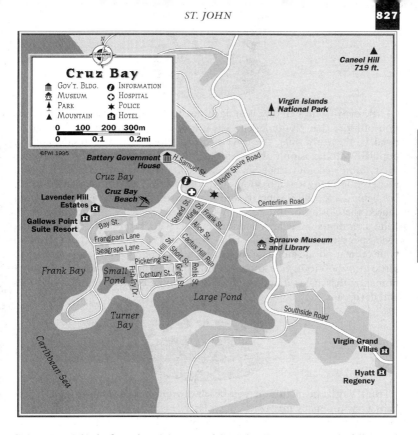

Cruz Bay

🏛	GOV'T. BLDG.	❼	INFORMATION
🏛	MUSEUM	✚	HOSPITAL
🔺	PARK	✶	POLICE
▲	MOUNTAIN	🏨	HOTEL

```
0    100   200  300m
0         0.1      0.2mi
```

©FWI 1995

Caneel Hill
719 ft.

Virgin Islands
National Park

Battery Government House

Cruz Bay

H. Samuel St.

North Shore Road

Centerline Road

Lavender Hill Estates

Cruz Bay Beach

Gallows Point Suite Resort

Bay St.

Strand St.

King St.

Alice St.

Frank St.

Frangipani Lane

Seagrape Lane

Hill St.

Short St.

Cactus Hill Run

Rells St.

Sprauve Museum and Library

Pickering St.

Frank Bay

Small Pond

Fish Fry Dr.

Century St.

Gnein St.

Large Pond

Southside Road

Turner Bay

Caribbean Sea

Virgin Grand Villas

Hyatt Regency

living. In 1952, before electricity served St. John, Lawrence Rockefeller took a shine to the island, bought 5000 acres, and built his Caneel Bay Resort, which gave well-heeled visitors a chance to enjoy the pleasures of an undeveloped backwater. He later donated most of the land to the government, which added to it, and created the nation's 29th National Park. With the advent later of the Cinnamon Bay and Maho Bay camps, more ecologically oriented travelers arrived on St. John's shores, ready to scale and sail the lush resources. A second resort, the Virgin Grand (later the Hyatt Regency St. John) opened in 1987, with a slew of high-class condos in its wake.

People

Little of St. John's culture is indigenous. In 1773 there was a slave population of more than 2000, legend has it that when Lawrence Rockefeller arrived in the early '50s, there were barely more than 400 residents. The population today is only about 3500, and although residents are protective of St. John's ecology, they are virtually 100 percent dependent on tourism for revenue. Reggae is a passion on the island, and the Rastafarian influence lies behind a few local superstitions: natives still believe the jumbies (spirits) caused the closing of the Reef Bay Sugar Factory in 1916. But most of St. John's residents today are American ex-pats who, keen to the laid-back lifestyle, spend their days casually selling wares in Cruz Bay. If you can abandon your cellular phone and datebook at home, it will take only a day or two to settle into the Virgin vibe known as "limin"—a kind of wrinkle-in-time phenomenon that makes it impossible to do anything but lounge, sip cool drinks and daydream.

Beaches

Trunk Bay is the picture-perfect beach of your dreams. Unfortunately, perhaps a few too many magazine covers later, it is almost always swamped with visitors throughout the day, many drawn to the 225-yard snorkeling trail (see "Underwater"). Not to worry, there are a couple dozen other beaches on St. John that may be a notch below Trunk Bay, but are resplendent nonetheless.

Winding east along the north coast road from Cruz Bay, the first beach you *won't* see is secluded **Salomon Bay**. Not coincidentally, it's also the nudist's choice—access is via the Lind Point Trail (which starts at the National Park Visitor Center in Cruz Bay). Nearby, beautiful **Honeymoon Beach** is on the Caneel Bay property, but there are no guest rooms here so you'll probably be left alone to your Rockefeller-primed fantasies. The Caneel Bay peninsula is wrapped by a pearly necklace of well-kept coves (theoretically off-limits to non-guests) that end with **Hawksnest Beach**, yet another splendid strand, though it receives its share of day-trippers; Hawksnest has changing rooms and picnic tables. Two of Caneel's beaches are among the Caribbean's best: **Scott Beach** and **Turtle Bay**. The next two beaches are also very popular, **Cin-**

namon Bay (backed by the campground) and **Trunk Bay**. Cozy **Maho Bay** lies juts below the tent cabin settlement of the same name, while **Francis Beach** is a memorable, less visited cove with bird-watching and nature trails nearby. On the south shore, **Great Cruz Bay**, backed by the Hyatt Regency, is also pleasant. The rest of the island's beaches take a little more effort to reach, but the payoff might be a deserted cove to call your own. Among the best are four on the remote southern coast: **Reef Bay** (see "On Foot"), **Lameshur Bay**, **Saltpond Bay** and nearby **Drunk Bay**.

Hawksnest Bay on St. John has two good reefs offshore with elkhorn coral.

Underwater

Although there's plenty of beautiful underwater life to mirror the island's lush above-ground geography, diving on St. John tends to be shallow and mild, which makes it a great place to learn, or to visit if you've just been certified. There are relatively few surface conditions to complicate matters, although the northern coast is subject to swells in the winter (which usually renders these sites inaccessible). Several USVI operators visit the wonderful wreck of the RMS Rhone off the British Virgin Islands (you'll need a passport or birth certificate; see "Underwater" in "British Virgin Islands"). Dives off eastern St. Thomas are easily accessible from Cruz and Cinnamon bays. **Trunk Bay** has a heavily-visited, 225-yard self-guiding underwater trail that will thrill first-time snorkelers, but better snorkeling lies off **Cinnamon**

Bay, **Hawksnest Beach** or in **Leinster Bay** (at nearby Waterlemon Cay). The rangers at the Park Service headquarters in Cruz Bay will help you find other locations—remember, much of the National Park lies off-shore.

If you've been looking for something to thank the Rockefellers for, look no further than St. John. After falling in love with its pristine, untouched beauty, in 1954 Lawrence Rockefeller donated 5000 acres of prime St. John real estate to the U.S. government, which turned around and created the unique Virgin Islands National Park, eventually comprising just under two-thirds of the island's above-water territory, and a decent chunk of its underwater coral reefs and offshore islands. As such, there is virtually no comparison between St. John and the other U.S. Virgins when it comes to hiking; it's where the Virgins, well... practically live up to their name. With the possible exception of Martinique and Guadeloupe, St. John has the best-developed trail system in the Caribbean, offering a variety of short jaunts. Although the two longest trails come in under two-and-a-half miles, it's possible to make a few itinerary adjustments to create memorable all-day excursions, particularly in the vicinity of Lameshur. Pick up a copy of the free trail guide available at the park's Cruz Bay Visitor Center, which outlines 22 hiking possibilities; better yet, purchase a waterproof Trails Unlimited topo map (available throughout Cruz Bay) for a more detailed look at the island's geography. If you're visiting from St. Thomas for the day, two trails leave from the vicinity of Cruz Bay leading to Caneel Hill and Lind Point, and can be combined (using the Caneel Hill Spur trail) for a shorter hike. Another enticing offering is the Park Service's guided outing which buses guests to the start of the Reef Bay Trail, near the top of Mamey Peak, for a mostly downhill and casual stroll past petroglyphs and sugar factory ruins to Reef Bay. Here hikers can swim and snorkel before being ferried back to Cruz Bay late in the afternoon. Other guided hikes are available and will provide an informative glimpse into the Caribbean ecosystem and the history of the Virgin Islands.

Other islands are bigger or taller, but few concentrate as many fierce grades into a compact area as St. John. While some residents view cycling here as a form of masochism, those who delight in steep, short hills will be delighted and challenged. Buck up, well-toned friends, and head up to **Centerline Road**, which traces the island's main east-west ridge; once you've climbed the initial hill on either side, it rolls somewhat more gently through gorgeous forests. Somewhere near the navel of the island, the dirt **Bordeaux Mountain Road** follows another ridge southeast to Bordeaux Mountain. Just east of this mountain is a steep, four-wheel-drive road that drops down to Coral Harbor; if you're at all unsure about descending extreme, gravel-washed grades, walk it. From Cruz Bay to Leinster Bay the **North Coast Road** passes one beautiful beach after another; however, this also is the most trafficked stretch on the island. Instead, head east out of Cinnamon Bay to the **Annaberg Ruins** where quieter roads visit more beaches; riding as far as Waterlemon Bay and over to Francis Bay will create a not-too-difficult half-day trip of about eight or nine miles. The best moderate ride on the island leaves from Coral Bay and follows the **Salt Pond Road** south and over to Lameshur Bay. This is about eight mile round-tip ride and, although it ascends several hills in each direction, none exceed a few hundred feet above sea level. The **East End Road** is all but impossible for cyclists: don't say we didn't warn you. Throughout St. John, watch out for the slick concrete you'll find spanning ravine crossings (The concrete is usually covered in algae). One final note: Although you may use the numerous marked dirt roads, bikes are strictly forbidden on all walking trails.

By Paddle

Sea kayaking is quickly finding a niche in the U.S. and Virgin Islands. The classic tour leaves from Virgin Gorda or Peter Island in the British Virgin Islands and heads toward St. John, the wind on your back for most of the way. En route on this idyllic trip, stops at Beef, Cooper, and Jost Van Dyke islands reward with hidden beaches and pristine snorkeling. You can stay at hotels and guest houses and sleep in a real bed—which minimizes your load factor to a change of clothes, fresh water, swimsuit, a towel, mask and snorkel, sunscreen (essential) and hat—or, play "no-see-um" on beaches by pulling onto shore late, camping and leaving early before anyone catches you. If planning such a trip, you can take a kayak on the ferry to the British Virgins, but don't forget to bring your passport or birth certificate. Keep in mind that summer sun can be intense, and is best combated with water, sunscreen and a fashionable, wide-brimmed hat. Although the trip can be done in a few days, allow a week for maximum enjoyment. Sea conditions in the Virgins are usually calm, however, an overnight trip is not suitable as a beginner's excursion; make sure you have adequate training and experience before undertaking such an adventure.

FIELDING'S CHOICE:

Sign up for the National Parks Service tour, which offers guided adventure hikes that acquaint you with native wildlife, including rippled-tail man lizards, black spiny sea urchins, and peely barked "tourist trees."

What Else to See

Although shopping and dining have gradually evolved to become a worthwhile pursuit in Cruz Bay, they still take a back seat to St. John's breathtaking natural environment. To orient yourself, begin with a stop at the **National Park Visitor Center**, a few hundred feet from the ferry dock, where park rangers will assist you in assembling an itinerary suitable for a few hours or a week. The Park Service also schedules nature walks and snorkeling trips. Take the scenic drive along **Centerline Road**—the ruins of the **Catherineberg Sugar Mill** are worth a visit, and feature a crumbling windmill yielding stupendous views. Another great roadside pullout is at the turnoff for **Bordeaux Mountain Road**, where a restaurant, **Le Chateaux de Bordeaux**, has a deck overlooking Coral Bay and the British Virgin Islands in the distance. Two peaceful spots missed by many day-trippers are **Saltpond Bay**, near the location of the environmentally sensitive **Concordia Eco-Tents** development (ask for a tour of the site), and **East End**, which has a delightful roadside restaurant serving local food. History is served up at the **Annaberg Sugar Mill Ruins**, a sugarmill and estate built in 1733 overlooking Leinster Bay, and the park service regularly schedules living history demonstrations of how islanders survived in the post-slavery era. Back in **Cruz Bay**, two small museums are worth a stop. The **Elaine Ione Sprauve Museum and Library** honors a local activist with a collection old maps, drawings and displays showing the history of the island, while the **Museum of Cultural Arts** occupies an old 18th-century plantation house that contains photos and artifacts illustrating the survival of island arts. At present, Wednesday is the big cruise-ship day on St. John—a day when Cruz Bay and the most popular beaches are best avoided.

Museums and Exhibits

Elaine Ione Sprauve Museum ★★★

Enghied Street; Cruz Bay, Cruz Bay, ☎ *(809) 776-6359.*

This small museum has exhibits on St. John's Danish West Indian history, as well as displays of locally created artwork.

Parks and Gardens

Virgin Islands National Park ★ ★ ★ ★ ★

☎ *(809) 776-6201.*
Hours: 8 a.m.–4 p.m.

No visit to St. John—or any of the U.S. Virgins—would be complete without at least a day spent at the breathtaking national park. It encompasses 12,624 acres and has 20 miles of trails to explore (see "On Foot" for additional hiking information). Stop by the Visitors Center next to the ferry dock in Cruz Bay to peruse the exhibits, pick up a map, and get details of special ranger-led events. Highlights in the park include the Annaberg Ruins, a sugar plantation and mill from the 1780s; the Reef Bay Trail, which passes plantation ruins and petroglyphs; and Trunk Bay, a picture-postcard beach and the start of a marked underwater trail well-loved by snorkelers.

Tours

Guided Tours

Cruz Bay.

The St. John Taxi Association will show you around the island for about $30 for one or two people, $13 per person for three or more. The St. John Island Tour ☎ *(809) 774-4550* lasts two hours and costs $12 per person. Ranger-led tours are popular at **Virgin Islands National Park**; call ☎ *(809) 776-6201* for details. Finally, local personality **Miss Lucy** ☎ *(809) 776-6804* tailors private tours to individual interests, while **John Abraham** ☎ *(809) 776-6177* offers a friendly, insider's look at his island.

> ### BEST VIEW:
>
> *Le Chateau de Bordeaux clings to the edge of a mountain top along Center-line Road, offering spectacular views of Bordeaux Mountain, St. John's highest peak, and the serpentine Sir Francis Drake Channel, with the British Virgin Islands scattered below. And the cuisine is superb.*

Watersports are an integral part of the St. John lifestyle. The island even has its own unique watersport: SNUBA—a hybrid of snorkeling and diving available at **Trunk Bay** (no lengthy training course or certification is necessary). In addition to the Trunk Bay underwater trail, another good snorkeling site is **Flanagan's Cay** off the southeast coast of St. John, and reached by one of the snorkel tour operators. The campgrounds offer extensive sports packages, including nature hikes and snorkeling trips. The Virgin Islands are famous for spectacular **deep-sea fishing** for blue marlin with many world records to prove it—the best fishing is found in the St. Croix Channel to the south and the Sir Francisco Drake Channel in the east. Deep sea fishing is not allowed within the National Park boundary, but you can **rod-and-reel fish** from the beaches. Anglers from all over the world head for the **Blue Marlin Fishing Tournament** in August.

Excellent sea conditions with balmy weather and numerous coves and sheltered anchorages create a superlative **sailing** environment. Every type of vessel, from sailfish to oceangoing yachts can be hired (though many do so on nearby St. Thomas or the British Virgin Islands, where the selection is even greater). **Boats** may be chartered with a full crew, but you'll need to know what you're doing if you're going to leave the crew behind. Many half- and full-day sailing excursions are available; check first with your hotel, which probably has a full and up-to-date list and can recommend what will best suit your needs. Operators on St. John are based in both Cruz Bay and Coral Bay. Because of the constant trade winds, **windsurfing** also finds a number of fans. The winds, whipping down the Sir Francis Drake Channel north of St. John, are funneled by two hills through the Narrows to the Windward Passage. Expert windsurfers can also cross the Pillsbury Sound to St. Thomas.

Constant trade winds off St. John thrill windsurfers.

Tennis courts are provided at the Caneel Bay and Hyatt Regency; both have pro shops and instructors. **Horseback riding** can be found on Bordeaux Mountain at Pony Express Riding Stables ☎ *(809) 776-6494.* A local outfit, Connections, acts as a booking service for day-sails, snorkeling and fishing trips; they're located in Cruz Bay near the ferry dock ☎ *(809) 776-6922.* Additional information on island activities can be obtained by calling the **St. John Visitors' Bureau** ☎ *(809) 776-6450.*

Watersports

Various locations, Cruz Bay.

St. John's two lavish resorts, the Hyatt Regency and Caneel Bay, have their own watersports facilities. Otherwise you're probably on your own. For general equipment rentals, try: **Coral Bay Watersports** ☎ *(809) 776-6850*, **Paradise Watersports** ☎ *(809) 693-8690*, **Low Key Watersports** ☎ *(809) 693-8999*, **Cinnamon Bay Watersports Center** ☎ *(809) 776-6330*, and **Cruz Bay Watersports** ☎ *(809) 776-6234*. For deep-sea fishing, call **Gone Ketchin** ☎ *(809) 693-8657*, **World Class Anglers** ☎ *(809) 779-4281*, and **Low Key Watersports** ☎ *(809) 693-8999*. For day-sails and snorkeling trips, try **Jolly Mon Day Sailing** ☎ *(809) 776-6239* or **Proper Yachts** ☎ *(809) 776-6256*.

FIELDING'S CHOICE:

No other sport will bring you closer to the spirit of the original Arawaks and Caribs than sea kayaking, and the best Caribbean waters for it are found among the sheltered cays and coves of the British and the U.S. Virgin Islands. Arawak Expeditions offers a challenging trip of 3 hours paddling a day, 5–6 miles a day, 5 days in a row. The tour begins in St. John, where you're briefed and supplied with paddles, sleeping bag, tents and sleeping pad. Then you and your two-person 20-foot-long kayak are taken by launch to Virgin Gorda, so you'll be paddling downwind back to St. John. Itineraries vary, depending on weather and tides, but can include stops at Ginger, Peter, Norman and Jost Van Dyke islands.

To avoid the afternoon breezes and blustery seas, you do most of the traveling before lunch, then pitch camp on a deserted beach. You don't even have to know which way to point the kayaks. The company gives you full instructions how to slip in, button up, manage the paddles, and get back in when you flip. First-timers from 14–73 have returned. Arawak Expeditions, P.O. Box 853, Cruz Bay, St. John, USVI 00831, ☎ (800) 238-8687. Five-night cruises cost $750 per person, seven days $925 year-round, including kayaks, camping equipment, meals and drinks, minimum four guests per tour.

Insider Tip:

Wednesday is cruise day, so hunker down and stay clear away from Cruz Bay.

Where to Stay

Fielding's Highest Rated Hotels in St. John

★★★★★	Caneel Bay Resort	$250–$650
★★★★	Estate Concordia	$95–$190
★★★	Concordia Eco-Tents	$60–$95
★★★	Gallows Point Suite Resort	$145–$355
★★★	Harmony Resort	$95–$180

Fielding's Most Exclusive Hotels in St. John

★★★★★	Caneel Bay Resort	$250–$650
★★	Lavender Hill Estates	$140–$290
★★★	Harmony Resort	$95–$180
★★	Raintree Inn	$65–$123
★★★	Concordia Eco-Tents	$60–$95

Fielding's Best Value Hotels in St. John

★★★	Concordia Eco-Tents	$60–$95
★★	Inn at Tamarind Court	$38–$88
★★★★	Estate Concordia	$95–$190
★★	Cinnamon Bay Campground	$48–$105
★★	Maho Bay Campground	$60–$95

Although the quantity of bunks on St. John is relatively small, there is an eclectic variety of accommodations. The island's two resorts, Caneel Bay and Hyatt Regency St. John (which may or may not be open as you read this), take care of big-spenders, while several guest houses, small inns and upscale campgrounds accommodate budget travelers. In between are a plethora of self-catering villas, apartments and condos, some of which are quite plush.

Over the past two decades, and through the dedication of a number of eco-logically minded islanders, St. John has become known as a world leader in the creation of "sustainable" resorts. Lawrence Rockefeller and Caneel Bay essentially invented tourism on St. John, but it was the elegant "camping" provided by his rustic beachfront cottages at Cinnamon Bay that really set the tone for developments. In 1976, entrepreneur Stanley Selengut, a civil engineer and carpenter, opened the Maho Bay Camps (before the term "eco-tourism" existed, he notes), starting with 18 tent cottages on a pristine hillside at the edge of the National Park, connected by a series of elevated wooden walkways. It was his goal to provide "creature comforts for all the creatures." Maho was a success that eventually grew to 114 units and spawned an increasingly eco-conscious empire of dwellings: Harmony, a condo-style site above Maho Bay; Estate Concordia, another development above remote Saltpond Bay; and the nearby Concordia Eco-Tents, which represents the current apex of Selengut's efforts to use recycled building ma-terials, minimize waste, and integrate the tourist experience closely with the land. Maho Bay Camps and its siblings have captured the eye of the press and public, and are popular throughout the year. As further testimony to their rapport with Mother Nature, the four creations suffered little at the hands of Hurricane Marilyn in 1995, and the durable structures at Maho Bay were re-ceiving guests just four days after the storm.

Hotels and Resorts

The classy Hyatt Regency St. John closed following the onslaught of Hurricane Mari-lyn in September 1995, but legal tangles (rather than hurricane damage) have kept the re-sort closed indefinitely as we went to press. For a status report, call the hotel directly for the latest ☎ *(809) 693-8000.* It's a fine property with a beautiful beach, but it is not cer-tain whether Hyatt Regency will still have a hand in the operation when it inevitably re-opens. Until then, Caneel Bay remains the only hotel on St. John, but it's a classic, chosen as the Caribbean's number three resort by readers of *Conde Nast Traveler* in 1995. Va-cations integrating a stay at both Caneel and sister property Little Dix (in the British Vir-gins) can be arranged easily.

Caneel Bay Resort   **$250–$650**   ★★★★★

Caneel Bay, ☎ *(800) 928-8889, (809) 776-6111. FAX (809) 693-8280.*
Single: $250–$650. Double: $250–$650.
Set on a 171-acre peninsular estate, this distinguished resort continues to do much right, as it has since Lawrence Rockefeller bought it in the early '50s, when the operation was a small plantation inn. The accommodations he built are scattered about in recently renovated, spacious cottages. All are quite gorgeous and include patios, minibars and coffeemakers, but are free of TV and telephones. Air condition-ing is limited solely to the breezes that flow through the property. The rooms over-looking the tennis courts and garden areas offer the most serenity and are cheaper, while those on the beaches are understandably more popular. Or you may rent Cot-tage 7, once the five-room home of the Rockefellers, but more recently the accom-

modations for some of the luminaries who have overnighted at Caneel ($450–750 per night). The extensive facilities include 11 tennis courts, three restaurants, a lounge with nightly entertainment, a small pool, and a new air-cooled exercise room. There are seven lovely beaches, with all the watersports one could want. The grounds, which abut Virgin Islands National Park, are kept in gorgeous condition year-round. You're required to dress for dinner, there's very little nightlife, and the rates keep out most young folks (though summer brings in the honeymooners). If you're going to be out past midnight, you must let them know in advance or you'll be literally locked out of the main gate. In fact, everything is a long walk at this sprawling resort, and while shuttle buses frequently ply the grounds, the impatient may feel, well, impatient with this arrangement. No, the Caneel is not for everyone, but it is ideal for those looking for a slow-paced retreat, Caneel remains one of the Caribbean's great escapes. Amenities: tennis, balcony or patio. 171 rooms. Credit cards: A, DC, MC, V.

Apartments and Condominiums

Rental properties have become extremely popular on St. John—there are almost as many of these as there are hotel rooms—and they are a particularly good buy for families or other groups. Many of the sites are first-class private homes and villas, and deluxe condos are also available, most offering fully-equipped kitchens, VCRs, stereos, patio grills; the bigger units have their own pools. There are more than 400 rental villas sprinkled throughout St. John, almost all of them within a mile or so of Cruz Bay. Most are represented by a dozen local rental firms, allowing you to shop around for exactly the arrangements and price you want. Among the bigger outfits are **Caribbean Villas** ☎ *(800) 338-0987 or (809) 776-6152;* **Villa Portfolio** ☎ *(800) 858-7989 or (809) 693-9100;* **Catered To** ☎ *(800) 424-6641 or (809) 776-6641;* **Windspree Vacation Homes** ☎ *(809) 693-5423;* **Vacation Vistas** ☎ *(809) 776-6462;* and **Destination St. John** ☎ *(800) 562-1901 or (809) 779-4647.* Prices vary considerably—in the summer it's possible to find small villas that rent for under $100 per night. Dozens of homes are represented by smaller firms (not listed above) plus many homeowners represent themselves; contact the USVI Department of Tourism for more information ☎ *(800) 372-USVI.* Remember that groceries are expensive on St. John and you'll want to procure most of your provisions on St. Thomas before ferrying over. Still, if you arrive on the island without fresh herbs, dried morels and fine wine, a quick stop at the lavishly-stocked StarFish Market in Boulon Center should help you fill your pantry with gourmet goodies.

Estate Concordia	**$95–$190**	★★★★

Saltpond Bay, ☎ *(800) 392-9004, (809) 693-5855. FAX (809) 693-5960.*
Single: $95–$190. Double: $95–$190.
Owned by the same folks who developed eco-sensitive Maho Bay Campground and Harmony, this property offers deluxe accommodations in an off-the-beaten-track setting on St. John's southeastern coast. The 51-acre estate looks out on Saltpond Bay with lovely views of the beach below. The nicest unit is the loft duplex, which has 20-foot cathedral ceilings, a wrap-around deck, two bathrooms, a full kitchen, two twin beds, ceiling fans, and a queen-size sofabed. There's also a vaulted studio with a full kitchen and efficiency suites with kitchenettes. The facilities include a 20-

by 40-foot swimming pool, laundry room, and store. The location is quite remote and a car is necessary—the nearest restaurant or shopping is 20 minutes away in Coral Bay. 10 rooms. Credit cards: MC, V.

Gallows Point Suite Resort $145–$355 ★★★

Cruz Bay, ☎ *(800) 323-7229, (809) 776-6434. FAX (809) 776-6520.*
Single: $145–$355. Double: $145–$355.

All accommodations at this oceanfront resort are suites ideally positioned on a point at the entrance to Cruz Bay's port—close enough to walk to town, but just beyond the (admittedly minimal) traffic. Garden units have sunken living rooms, while the larger upper suites have loft bedrooms and two baths. All are spacious, with quality furnishings, fully equipped kitchens, living and dining rooms, and ceiling fans (no air conditioning, but breezes generally do the job.) A restaurant and two bars can be found on the premises, and the staff will shuttle you into town (a five-minute walk) for free. The beach is too small for sunbathing (fine for snorkeling, though) but the free-form pool is large and inviting. No kids under five. Amenities: secluded garden atmosphere. 60 rooms. Credit cards: A, DC, MC, V.

Harmony Resort $95–$180 ★★★

Maho Bay, ☎ *(800) 392-9004, (809) 776-6240. FAX (809) 776-6504.*
Single: $95–$180. Double: $95–$180.

As the name implies, these cottages were built as much in harmony with nature as possible. Set high on a hill over the Maho Bay Campground (and owned by the same folks), each unit is powered by the sun and wind, and was built using recycled materials—even the nails came from recycled steel. Guests can even keep track of their energy use on computers installed in each unit. The spacious, one-room cottages are quite nicely done, with tile floors, wicker furniture, kitchenettes, living and dining areas, interesting artwork, ceiling fans, high wood-beamed ceilings, and nice decks. The shower-only baths are small but functional. No phones or TVs are available, and for some reason, all the beds are twins (easily pushed together). It's a five- to seven-minute walk to the beach down a steep road. 12 rooms. Credit cards: MC, V.

Lavender Hill Estates $140–$290 ★★

Cruz Bay, ☎ *(800) 562-1901, (809) 776-6969. FAX (809) 776-6969.*
Single: $140–$235. Double: $140–$290.

Set on a hillside within walking distance of Cruz Bay shops and restaurants, this complex offers condominium living. Each of the 12 units has full kitchens, nice views off the balconies, spacious living rooms, and one or two bedrooms. All have TVs and phones, but the two-bedroom units rely on ceiling fans instead of air conditioners. There's a good-sized pool on the premises. 12 rooms. Credit cards: D, MC, V.

Serendip Condominiums $85–$140 ★

Cruz Bay, ☎ *(809) 776-6646. FAX (809) 776-6646.*
Single: $85–$140. Double: $85–$140.

This secluded mountainside resort above Cruz Bay consists of eight one-bedroom units and two studios, each with a kitchen, limited maid service, and dining areas.

ST. JOHN

Furnishings are simple but adequate. There are no facilities on-site, but beaches and watersports can be found nearby at the national park. 10 rooms. Credit cards: MC, V.

Low Cost Lodging

There are a few decent budget properties around Cruz Bay. Another nice spot, priced $100–130 per night, is **Frank Bay Bed and Breakfast**, which opened three pleasant rooms in 1995 ☎ *(800) 561-7290 or (809) 693-8617.*

Cruz Inn   **$50–$95**   ★

Cruz Bay, ☎ *(800) 666-7688, (809) 693-8688. FAX (809) 693-8590.*
Single: $50–$85. Double: $50–$95.
Accommodations at this basic guesthouse range from simple guestrooms with shared baths to efficiencies with private baths and kitchen facilities. You'll pay $10 extra for air conditioning. Continental breakfast is served daily. Okay for the rates. 14 rooms. Credit cards: A, D, MC, V.

Inn at Tamarind Court   **$38–$88**   ★ ★

Cruz Bay, ☎ *(800) 221-1637, (809) 776-6378. FAX (809) 776-6722.*
Single: $38–$48. Double: $68–$88.
This simple spot is one of St. John's least-expensive properties with particularly good rates for singles who don't mind sharing a bathroom. Guestrooms seem to be decorated with garage sale specials, but all have air conditioning. You can choose from a few suites and a one-bedroom apartment with private bath. Despite its somewhat rundown appearance, the Tamarind Court does a brisk business with pennywatchers, and the atmosphere is friendly and fun. A bar and restaurant are on the premises and rates include a continental breakfast. 20 rooms. Credit cards: A, D, MC, V.

Raintree Inn   **$65–$123**   ★ ★

Cruz Bay, ☎ *(800) 666-7449, (809) 693-8590. FAX (809) 693-8590.*
Single: $65–$123. Double: $65–$123.
The rooms here are as simple as the rates suggest, but very comfortable and with private baths. Each room has air conditioning and a ceiling fan. There are also loft bedrooms and kitchens in three of the units—these sleep up to six. Smoking is forbidden. The restaurant serves dinner only. Not bad for the price. 11 rooms. Credit cards: A, D, MC, V.

Campgrounds

On St. John, a niche market has developed that locates a unique common ground between camping and a stay in a cottage. The first foray into this field was made in 1964 by Lawrence Rockefeller as an adjunct to Caneel Bay Resort. His creation, Cinnamon Bay Campground, used prime land along a splendid beach to create a series of bungalows, later supplemented by tent and bare sites. In 1976, conservationist Stanley Selengut created the "site-sensitive" Maho Bay Campground, which eventually gave birth to the ultimate in luxury camping, the Concordia Eco-Tents. In all three cases, it's not necessary to bring your sleeping bag and equipment. These accommodations may be simple, but you could arrive with a swimsuit, change of clothes and toothbrush and feel right at home (both Maho and Cinnamon have dining facilities on-site). You won't be pampered, but "roughing it" was never so easy for eco-sensitive travelers. Accordingly, Maho Bay in particular continues to be exceedingly popular and winter months book up early—the camp has the highest occupancy figures of any hostelry in the U.S. Virgin Islands.

Cinnamon Bay Campground $48–$105   ★★

Cinnamon Bay, ☎ (800) 539-9998, (809) 776-6330. FAX (809) 776-6458.
Single: $48–$105. Double: $48–$105.

Set in the woods just off Cinnamon Bay in the Virgin Islands National Park, this Rosewood Hotels-run campground offers everything from bare sites where you can pitch a tent ($15 per night) to rather ugly open-air cottages with electricity, simple cooking facilities, and two trundle beds. In between, there are also small tents with wooden floors that lack electricity but do have gas lanterns and stoves—a great budget choice for true campers. Four bath houses provide toilets and showers, and meals can be had in the cafeteria. There's no pool, but the nearby beach is grand—units in cottage 10 sit right on the beach (and are priced a few dollars extra per night for the privilege). Many watersports are available. This spot is prettier than the campground at Maho Bay, but its accommodations are more rustic. Two-week maximum stay. Amenities: houses, cottages or bungalows. 113 units. Credit cards: A, MC, V.

Concordia Eco-Tents $60–$95   ★★★

Saltpond Bay, ☎ (800) 392-9004, (809) 693-5855. FAX (809) 693-5960.
Single: $60–$95. Double: $60–$95.

Pushing the sustainable development envelope yet one step further, in late 1994 Stanley Selengut unveiled his fourth project on St. John, a small group of canvas eco-tents designed to maximize the ecological interaction guests experience on the island while minimizing their impact. The high-tech yet unpretentious tent cottages utilize solar and wind power, composting toilets, and have private baths with running water. Each of the units can sleep five or six on sofa beds. Guests may use Estate Concordia's pool, or hike to a beach at Saltpond Bay just a short distance away. This is the ultimate in combining simple creature comforts with a back-to-nature escape. 5 rooms. Credit cards: MC, V.

Maho Bay Campground $60–$95   ★★

Maho Bay, ☎ (800) 392-9004, (809) 776-6226. FAX (809) 776-6504.
Single: $60–$95. Double: $60–$95.

Set on 14 forested acres in the Virgin Islands National Park, this gorgeous spot is for nature lovers who like to camp without sacrificing too many creature comforts. Accommodations are in three-room tent-style cottages, with kitchenettes, a screened dining area, sofabeds, twin beds, living areas, private decks and electricity. Five communal bath houses have toilets and showers. Facilities include a sandy beach, simple restaurant and watersports. Each site is limited to two adults and two kids. The only drawback is the steep walk to the beach. Otherwise, for camping, this is quite comfortable and nice, and very popular—book early for choice winter dates. No radios allowed. 114 rooms. Credit cards: MC, V.

Where to Eat

Fielding's Highest Rated Restaurants in St. John

★★★★	Chateau de Bordeaux, Le	$20–$30
★★★★	Paradiso	$13–$23
★★★	Don Carlos	$6–$16
★★★	Ellington's	$13–$28
★★★	Fish Trap, The	$8–$23
★★★	Mongoose	$10–$50
★★★	Morgan's Mango	$7–$22
★★★	Vie's Snack Shack	$2–$6

Fielding's Most Exclusive Restaurants in St. John

★★★	Mongoose	$10–$50
★★★★	Chateau de Bordeaux, Le	$20–$30
★★★	Ellington's	$13–$28
★★★★	Paradiso	$13–$23
★★★	Fish Trap, The	$8–$23

Fielding's Best Value Restaurants in St. John

★★★	Don Carlos	$6–$16
★★★★	Paradiso	$13–$23
★★★	Morgan's Mango	$7–$22
★★★	Fish Trap, The	$8–$23
★★★★	Chateau de Bordeaux, Le	$20–$30

No doubt spurred on by the culinary delights produced on the other side of the Pillsbury Sound, the restaurant scene on St. John has blossomed in recent years into a group of first-class operations that roll out an impressive

Carnival, Trinidad

Hawksnest Beach, U.S. Virgin Islands

array of international taste sensations. There's even room for a mini-empire of fine restaurants, operated by Chris Rosbrook and Winston Bennett. In addition to the fine Le Chateau de Bordeaux and their newly acquired Italian establishment, Paradiso, the pair owns the warped Bad Art Bar (drinks only) and hopes to re-open their long-celebrated (and hurricane-damaged) Asolare, where seafood is prepared with a dynamic Asian flare, by December 1996. The Bad Art Bar hangs its velvet Elvis and other tacky contributions from the artist wannabe world in Cruz Bay, kitty-corner from the Chase Manhattan Bank. The best ice cream parlor is Luscious Licks, scooping Ben and Jerry's alongside a few vegetarian items. "Local" food—saltfish and *funghi*, conch fritters, johnnycakes, callaloo, goat water—is harder to find on St. John than elsewhere in the Caribbean, but don't miss a trip out to Vie's Snack Shack on the east end of the island.

Cafe Roma $$ ★★
Cruz Bay, ☎ *(809) 776-6524.*
Italian cuisine. Specialties: Pizza, shrimp with garlic sauce.
Dinner: 5–10 p.m., entrées $11–$16.
A touch of Italy in the tropics, this pretty trattoria overlooks the sights and sounds of Cruz Bay from a second-floor perch. No slouch on when it comes to gustatory delights, the place is noted for dynamite pizza—there's a choice of a white or traditional tomato sauce as a base for several tasty toppings. Seafood is also a standout, especially shrimp with garlic sauce. An excellent choice for a varied selection of tropical drinks. Credit cards: MC, V.

Chateau de Bordeaux, Le $$$ ★★★★
Centerline Road; Bordeaux Mountain, Bordeaux Mountain, ☎ *(809) 776-6611.*
French cuisine.
Dinner: 5:30–8:45 p.m., entrées $20–$30. Closed: Mon., Sun.
This petite dazzler clings to the cliffs of Bordeaux Mountain in the center of the island, and its terrace commands an unparalleled view of the rising moon (if you're on St. John during a full moon, dinner here is a must!). Despite its unprepossessing exterior, within is a cozy room with hand-crocheted tablecloths, flickering oil lanterns and eclectic chandeliers. It's no surprise many honeymooners end up here, as this place just oozes romance. The cuisine is as good as the atmosphere—don't miss the roasted rack of lamb with a rosemary, honey and nut crust and a port wine and shallot reduction. A wild game special is featured each evening. This is one of the Caribbean's few non-smoking restaurants, though there's a deck where smokers can slip off to for their fix. The deck area is open through the day for burgers, fish and chicken sandwiches and drinks. Features: non-smoking area. Reservations required. Credit cards: MC, V.

Don Carlos $$ ★★★
10-19 Estate Carolina; Coral Bay, ☎ *(809) 776-6866.*
Mexican cuisine.
Lunch: 11 a.m.–4 p.m., entrées $6–$16.
Dinner: 4–9 p.m., entrées $6–$16.

This upscale cantina buzzes with zingy waiters delivering foaming margaritas and zippy fajitas (this stateside chain is famous for them) to happy customers. Don Carlos also features lots of lively entertainment three nights a week. You might see island favorites like conch fritters or a few pasta dishes slipped in here and there on the menu along with south-of-the-border staples. Features: Sunday brunch. Credit cards: A, D, MC, V.

Ellington's $$$ ★★★

Gallows Point; Cruz Bay, ☎ *(809) 693-8490. Associated hotel: Gallows Point Resort.*
International cuisine.
Dinner: 6–10 p.m., entrées $13–$28.
Some of the best seafood on the island is prepared at this view spot positioned near the ferry dock. On a clear day, you can see St. Thomas from a front-row seat on the terrace. After a tasty drink, dine on hearty seafood chowder followed by the daily special, which could be blackened fish, or chicken Martinique in an exotic fruit sauce. Reservations required. Credit cards: A, MC, V.

Fish Trap, The $$$ ★★★

Cruz Bay, ☎ *(809) 693-9994. Associated hotel: Rain Tree Inn.*
Seafood cuisine.
Dinner: 4:30–9:30 p.m., entrées $8–$23. Closed: Mon.
Owned by a long-time St. John couple whose son Aaron runs the kitchen, the Fish Trap puts its effort into the food rather than on fancy trappings, which makes it a favorite with locals who enjoy the well-prepared shellfish and surf and turf offerings. The blackened jumbo shrimp are popular, and the fries are always dependable. Credit cards: MC, V.

Lime Inn, The $$ ★★

Lemon Tree Mall; Cruz Bay, ☎ *(809) 776-6425.*
International cuisine. Specialties: All-you-can-eat shrimp.
Lunch: 11:30 a.m.–3 p.m., entrées $3–$8.
Dinner: 5:30–10 p.m., entrées $3–$20. Closed: Sun.
The local practice of *limin'* is strictly adhered to here so plan on "hanging out" with a congenial group of limers that include veteran travelers as well as residents. Settle for a terrace seat to while away the hours with a steak or fish entrée cooked on the outdoor grill; the lunch salads are ambitious and varied. Hungry bargain-hunters crowd the place Wednesday nights for the well-regarded, all-you-can-eat shrimp extravaganza, but no reservations are taken, so line up early. Reservations required. Credit cards: A, MC, V.

Mongoose $$$ ★★★

Mongoose Junction; Cruz Bay, Mongoose Junction, ☎ *(809) 693-8677.*
International cuisine.
Lunch: 11:30 a.m.–5 p.m., entrées $6–$10.
Dinner: 5–10 p.m., entrées $10–$50.
A pleasant refueling spot for tired shoppers after souvenir hunting at the Tony Mongoose Junction arcade, this eatery and bar offers a bevy of cooling fruity alcoholic drinks and plates of fresh seafood. Patrons poise themselves on a tree-shaded wooden deck or at the bar, which serves light meals until midnight. Live music on

Friday and Saturday keeps the joint jumpin'. Reservations recommended. Credit cards: A, DC, MC, V.

Morgan's Mango $$ ★★★

Cruz Bay, ☎ *(809) 693-8141.*
Latin American cuisine.
Dinner: 6–10 p.m., entrées $7–$22.
There's often a crowd at this very popular dining spot in a gingerbread-trimmed house painted in pastels. One reason is an excellent bar and unusual Argentinian specialties interspersed with local seafood and chicken. Another is the woodsy patio where guests sit surrounded by trees and greenery. A plate-crowding hunk of prime beef comes accompanied by the piquant Pampas-style *chimmichurri* sauce—a spicy melding of oregano, peppers, lots of garlic and olive oil. The bar is a happening spot with a vast array of tropical libations; live music on Thursdays. Reservations recommended. Credit cards: A, MC, V.

Paradiso $$$ ★★★★

Mongoose Junction; Cruz Bay, Mongoose Junction, ☎ *(809) 693-8899.*
Italian cuisine. Specialties: Lobster fra diavolo.
Dinner: 6–9:30 p.m., entrées $13–$23. Closed: Wed.
The words "suave" and "chic" appropriately describe this Italian restaurant all dolled up in burnished woods and marble that recently changed owners. Dine in air-conditioned comfort on daily seafood and pasta specials and designer pizzas prepared with signature flare; the *osso d'agnello Milanese* is a highlight. Paradiso also has an impressive wine list and well-mixed drinks. Reservations recommended. Credit cards: MC, V.

Vie's Snack Shack $ ★★★

East End, ☎ *(809) 693-5033.*
Latin American cuisine.
Lunch: 10 a.m.–5 p.m., entrées $2–$6. Closed: Mon., Sun.
This is probably the best local cooking on St. John—but it's only open for lunch. If you're out at East End when Vie's at the stove, don't miss it for conch fritters both sweet and savory, island-style beef patties, garlic chicken with johnny cakes, and homemade fruit drinks (in season). Located four miles east of Coral Bay beneath Blackrock Hill.

Though it can hardly hold a candle to the panoply of wares offered in Charlotte Amalie across the channel, the shopping is still duty free. There is no sales tax and a $1200 per person exemption from duty applies when returning to the U.S. A small, attractive mall, **Mongoose Junction**, is the hub of most shopping activities, featuring island clothing and T-shirts, jewelry, a bookstore and a well-stocked deli. Stop by **Bamboula** for folk art, artifacts and

West Indian furniture. Liquor is also a bargain and anyone over 21 can return to the states with five bottles duty free (or six, if one is produced in the U.S. Virgin Islands).

St. John Directory

Arrival and Departure

Getting to St. John requires an extra hop as the island does not have an airport. **American**, **American Eagle**, **Delta** and **USAir** all have daily service into St. Thomas, the most convenient connection point. For information on other carriers, see "Arrival and Departure" in "St. Thomas."

Once on St. Thomas, visitors hop on one of the scheduled **ferries** that ply the link to St. John. Two routes are available: for those flying into St. Thomas, the one from downtown Charlotte Amalie is closest to the airport, while another dock is located at the eastern tip of St. Thomas at Red Hook. The ferry from Charlotte Amalie leaves almost hourly ($7 each way; about 45 minutes), while the ferry from Red Hook leaves hourly throughout the day ($3 each way; about 20 minutes). For additional information and departure times, call Transportation Services ☎ *(809) 776-6282* or Varlack Ventures ☎ *(809) 776-6412*. A car ferry is also provided by **Blue Lines** that leaves from Red Hook about every 90 minutes ($50 for car and passengers round-trip; about 25 minutes); call ahead to reserve a slot ☎ *(809) 777-6111*. The **Caneel Bay** and **Hyatt Regency** resorts have their own ferry service to transport guests from St. Thomas to St. John. Ferries also work the route between St. John and Tortola daily, with more limited service available to Jost Van Dyke and Virgin Gorda (you'll need to bring a passport or birth certificate and photo identification to enter the British Virgin Islands).

Business Hours

Shops generally open weekdays 9 a.m.–5 p.m. Banks generally open Monday–Thursday 9 a.m.–2:30 p.m. and Friday 9 a.m.–2 p.m. and 3:30–5 p.m.

Climate

Temperatures during the summer, cooled by eastern trade winds, keep the temperature around 82 degrees Fahrenheit. Brief showers also keep things cool. Winter temperatures rise to 77 degrees Fahrenheit. Rainiest months are September-January, and about 40 inches of rainfall per year. April–August are the calmest sea conditions with the best visibility, although days of stunning clarity in excess of 100 feet are not unusual in winter.

Documents

U.S. Citizens do not need a passport to enter the U.S. Virgin Islands. However, a passport or birth certificate and photo identification is necessary to visit the British Virgins. If you wish to dive the *RMS Rhone*, or snorkel amid The Baths of Virgin Gorda they are but a short ferry ride away, but you'll first need to clear British Virgin Islands customs.

Electricity

Current runs at 110 volts at 60 cycles.

Getting Around

Several car rental companies in Cruz Bay compete for the tourist trade including **Avis** and **Hertz**, but rental rates are high—expect to spend about $50 per day. Driving is on the left. Taxis meet all ferry landings, and two-hour island tours can be easily arranged through **Wesley Easley** ☎ *(809) 693-8177*. Other recommended guides are **Miss Lucy**, **George Simmonds**, **Jimmy Powell**, or **Calvin George**. Tours run $15 per person, or $12 each for a group of three or more.

Language

The official language is English. Some locals speak a musical patois called English Creole—a blend of English, African and Spanish. Many people also speak good Spanish.

Medical Emergencies

Police ☎ ext. *915*, fire ☎ ext. *921*, ambulance ☎ ext. *922*.

Money

The official currency is the U.S. dollar.

Telephone

The area code is 809. Since U.S. Virgin Islands are an incorporated territory, toll-free numbers that operate in the U.S. work here, and normal postage rates apply. You can also direct dial to the mainland.

Time

Atlantic Standard Time, one hour later than New York City; during Daylight Saving Time, it is the same as New York.

Tipping and Taxes

Some hotels include a 10–15 percent service charge; this should include all tips for both restaurant and room service, unless the attention was extraordinary. If no service is added, leave a 15 percent tip for the waitress, $1–2 a day to the maid; bartenders and wine stewards should always be tipped. Tip the bellboy and porter at least 50 cents a bag. Taxi drivers should receive a 15 percent tip if you are satisfied with the service.

Tourist Information

The **St. John Tourist Office** is located around the corner from the Cruz Bay ferry dock and is open daily ☎ *(809) 776-6450*. They will help arrange an island tour. Additional travel information can be obtained through ☎ *(800) 372-USVI*.

When to Go

St. John's Carnival events take place from June 18–July 4, including a food fair, boat races and the recreation of a carnival village. The St. John Carnival Parade takes place on July 4.

ST. JOHN HOTELS

		RMS	RATES	PHONE	CR. CARDS
Cruz Bay					
★★★★★	Caneel Bay Resort	171	$250–$650	(800) 928-8889	A, DC, MC, V
★★★★	Estate Concordia	10	$95–$190	(800) 392-9004	MC, V
★★★	Concordia Eco-Tents	5	$60–$95	(800) 392-9004	MC, V
★★★	Gallows Point Suite Resort	60	$145–$355	(800) 323-7229	A, DC, MC, V
★★★	Harmony Resort	12	$95–$180	(800) 392-9004	MC, V
★★	Cinnamon Bay Campground	113	$48–$105	(800) 539-9998	A, MC, V
★★	Inn at Tamarind Court	20	$38–$88	(800) 221-1637	A, D, MC, V
★★	Lavender Hill Estates	12	$140–$290	(800) 562-1901	D, MC, V
★★	Maho Bay Campground	114	$60–$95	(800) 392-9004	MC, V
★★	Raintree Inn	11	$65–$123	(800) 666-7449	A, D, MC, V
★	Cruz Inn	14	$50–$95	(800) 666-7688	A, D, MC, V
★	Serendip Condominiums	10	$85–$140	(809) 776-6646	MC, V

ST. JOHN RESTAURANTS

		PHONE	ENTRÉE	CR. CARDS
Coral Bay				
	French			
★★★★	Chateau de Bordeaux, Le	(809) 776-6611	$20–$30	MC, V
	International			
★★★	Ellington's	(809) 693-8490	$13–$28	A, MC, V
	Italian			
★★	Cafe Roma	(809) 776-6524	$11–$16	MC, V
	Latin American			
★★★	Vie's Snack Shack	(809) 693-5033	$2–$6	
	Mexican			
★★★	Don Carlos	(809) 776-6866	$6–$16	A, D, MC, V
Cruz Bay				
	International			
★★★	Mongoose	(809) 693-8677	$6–$50	A, DC, MC, V
★★	Lime Inn, The	(809) 776-6425	$3–$20	A, MC, V

ST. JOHN

ST. JOHN RESTAURANTS	PHONE	ENTRÉE	CR. CARDS
Italian			
★★★★ **Paradiso**	(809) 693-8899	$13–$23	MC, V
Latin American			
★★★ **Morgan's Mango**	(809) 693-8141	$7–$22	A, MC, V
Seafood			
★★★ **Fish Trap, The**	(809) 693-9994	$8–$23	MC, V

ST. JOHN

ST. KITTS

Local and international regattas are held at St. Kitts.

Boasting dark, humid rain forests presided over by colonies of vervet monkeys as well as secluded bays and luscious beaches, St. Kitts is one of the Caribbean's treasures, with a little something to please everybody. Properly (though rarely) referred to as St. Christopher, the island was part of the British Empire just over a decade ago but, along with its sister Nevis, decided to go its own way in 1983. With a mere 44,000 inhabitants (9000 of them on Nevis), the nation is today one of the Western Hemisphere's smallest—though a referendum on succession being debated over on Nevis might make St. Kitts smaller still. Sugar cane is the dominant crop on St. Kitts, but with a decline in sugar prices worldwide, tourism has been looked to as the economic force of the future. Fortunately, outside Basseterre and Frigate

Bay, unhampered tranquillity reigns, and the noisiest things you'll usually encounter will be the gentle skittering of surf across the black and blonde sands. Hikes into the rainforest or up the slopes of Mt. Liamuiga (a Carib Indian word for "fertile land") are a big attraction, as is the splendidly restored fort at Brimstone Hill. Your accommodations may be further immersed in the island's history if you overnight in one of the centuries-old plantation inns dotting the cane-covered slopes. Only about half the size of St. Kitts, Nevis hefts its bulk equally majestically out of the sea just across from its sister. The two islands are separated by a two-mile-wide channel of water, the Narrows—a proximity so close that from some vantage points the two sometimes appear joined at the hip. The quiet revolt on the Nevis side may split them apart politically in the near future but, rest assured, the blood ties on the two islands run so thick there will always be a common bond.

Untrammeled by tourism, St. Kitts is a stunning combination of volcanic mountains, rain forest and golden beaches.

Boasting dark, humid rain forests presided over by colonies of vervet monkeys and a quantity of secluded bays and beaches, St. Kitts is one of the Caribbean's treasures, with a little something to please everybody. Properly (though rarely) referred to as St. Christopher, the island was part of the British Empire just over a decade ago but, along with its sister Nevis, decided to

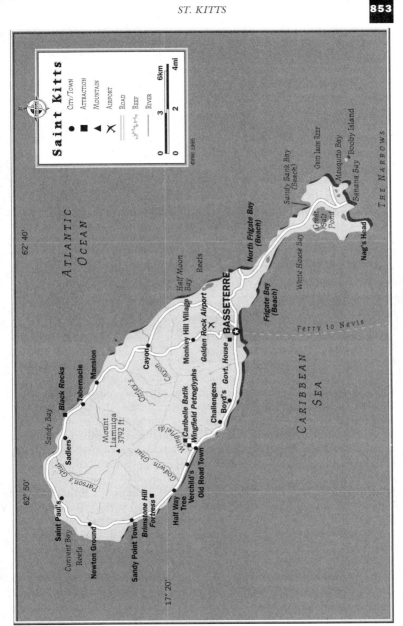

go its own way in 1983. With a mere 44,000 inhabitants (9000 of them on Nevis), the nation is today one of the Western Hemisphere's smallest—though a referendum on succession being debated over on Nevis might make them smaller communities still. Sugar cane is the dominant crop on St. Kitts, but with a decline in sugar prices worldwide, tourism has been looked to as the economic force of the future. Fortunately, outside Basseterre and Frigate Bay, unhampered tranquillity reigns in St. Kitts and the noisiest things you'll usually encounter will be the gentle skittering of surf across the black and blonde sands. Hikes into the rainforest or up the slopes of Mt. Liamuiga (a Carib Indian word for "fertile land") are a big attraction, as is the splendidly restored fort at Brimstone Hill. Your accommodations may be further immersed in the island's history if you overnight in one of the centuries-old plantation inns dotting the cane-covered slopes. Only about half the size, Nevis hefts its bulk equally majestically out of the sea just across from St. Kitts. The two islands are separated by a two-mile-wide channel of water, the Narrows—a proximity so close the two sometimes appear joined at the hip from a few vantage points. The quiet revolt on the Nevis side may split them apart politically in the near future but, rest assured, the blood ties on the two islands run so thick there will always be a common bond.

History

Columbus first sighted the island of St. Kitts, dubbing it—with a touch of self-aggrandizement—St. Christopher. The title was later shortened to St. Kitts by British tobacco planters, who ignored Spanish claims and moved in with their African slaves. For years the island remained lost in obscurity, inhabited by cohiba-smoking Carib Indians who found nourishment from the island in the form of turtles, iguanas and *mawby* liquor. In 1623, a daring group of settlers led by Sir Thomas Warner plopped themselves on the island, but were soon forced to share the beach uneasily with some French colonists. On June 20, 1690, during a French occupation, the Englishman Sir Timothy Thornhill led a party of soldiers in the dead of night through Friars Bay and over a rocky hill full of thorn bushes and spiky acacia trees to catch the French sentries off guard, who thought the British could only attack from the sea. After taking Basseterre, the island's main city, the English troops spiked the fortress cannons so that other English troops could land in safety. The hill was later named Sir Timothy in honor of Thornhill, but remains a daunting natural barrier, stretching from steep cliffs on the Atlantic to even steeper cliffs on the Caribbean. The 1783 Treaty of Versailles finally awarded sovereignty to the Brits. Independent from Britain since 1983, St.

Kitts is dealing peacefully with the challenges of economy, but still maintains affectionate ties with the mother country. In fact, Queen Elizabeth II visited St. Kitts in 1985 and her portrait continues to grace island bank notes.

Jewish communities on both islands can be traced back to the 17th century. The earliest date on the 19 tombstones in the Jewish cemetery on Nevis goes back to the 1680s, and records in England suggest that the Nevis synagogue is older than the 1732 synagogue in Curaçao. Recently, on Nevis a *mikvah*, or ritual bath, was discovered by an island historian. When large populations of Jews fled to the islands to escape the Spanish Inquisition, the majority of those who came to Nevis were from Brazil.

People

Comparing the two halves of this twin-island nation, fun-loving Kittians are more gregarious than their conservative neighbors on Nevis. The most festive event on genteel Nevis is horseback racing, while a raucous music festival was introduced on St. Kitts in 1996 to great acclaim—frequent visitor Louis Farrakhan has been among the attendees. A little fishing, some gardening, long pauses to chat—that's the pattern of a day's dally on St. Kitts, where the remains of British *haut monde* mix colorfully with the Caribbean way of life. The political tie to England may be severed, but the countries remain close, and Kittians were delighted with Queen Elizabeth's comments about the island's unspoiled beauty, an opinion shared by Christopher Columbus. Yes, the British are aground, running many of the inns and hotels on the island. There are a few local artists, including sculptor Valentine Brown who lives in Dieppe Bay and is known for his finely crafted sculptures of faces and figures out of cedar. Style in St. Kitts is casual, though visitors are advised not to wear skimpy shorts, bikinis or bare chests away from the beach.

Beaches

St. Kitts' best beaches lie in coves around the southeast peninsula, where white or golden sand faces the calm Caribbean on one side, and the choppier Atlantic on the other. **Frigate Bay** is one such divided personality, with a **North** and **South** strand on either side of the golf course and **Jack Tar Village**— they are probably the most popular on the island and possess a wide variety

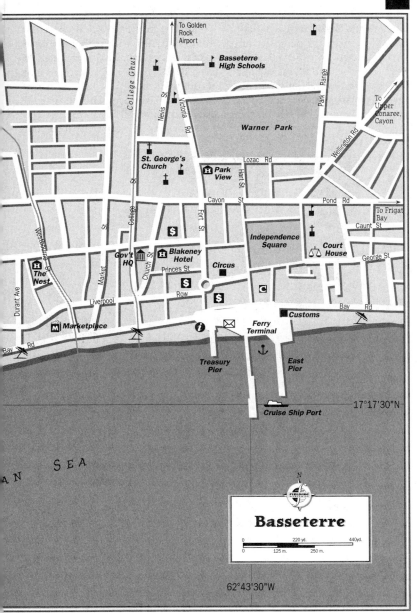

Basseterre

of watersports options. A mile southeast of Sir Timothy's Hill, **North** and **South Friar's Bay**, on either side of the peninsula, are a pair of good beaches. Near the end of the peninsula are several fine strands, each within a mile or two of one another: **Sand Bank Bay**, **Cockleshell Bay**, **Banana Bay** and **Major's Bay** are lovely, and **Mosquito Bay** (or **Turtle Beach**) has a bar, restaurant and watersports. Snorkeling can be found throughout this area. Closer to Basseterre is **Conaree Beach**, used by many islanders, but as you continue around the larger wing of the island, the beaches become smaller, less reliable and are composed of gray or black sand. Ask at the plantation inns for their sun-sea-sand suggestions.

The southern beaches of St. Kitts, Frigate Bay and Salt Pond have long been considered the "Caribbean Shangri-La."

Underwater

Hundreds of wrecks are thought to rest off the sloping reefs of St. Kitts. Few of them have been discovered, and most are presumed to be long disintegrated, yet the island continues to inspire the dedicated wreck-diver. For the rest of us, the west coast offers inviting reefs, particularly at distant Sandy Point near the island's northern end, and in the channel between St. Kitts and Nevis, **The Narrows**. Probably the best overall area is **Grid Iron**, a six-mile undersea shelf rising to within 15 feet of the surface, located on a map by drawing a line between the coastline east of the St. Kitts airport, and the coast just off the Nevis airport (tiny **Booby Island** lies almost in its path). Although there are a number of dives on this formation, the star is **Monkey Shoals** (see "Underwater" in "Nevis"). Just a few dozen divers a week visit St. Kitts, and three shops, one of them recently opened, compete for their favor.

Defined trails to notable sights on St. Kitts are difficult to locate, a situation the government seems in no hurry to change (perhaps eco-tourism has not yet been identified as a potential money-maker?). You'll be reliant on one of the several hiking outfits that have sprung up on the island. St. Kitts' big **volcano hike** is easier than those on some islands, but is sufficiently spectacular to amply reward intrepid vacationers. One attractive trek, the **Mansion Source Trail**, ascends **Verchild's Mountain**, a 3100-foot summit one mile southeast of **Mount Liamuiga** that features a pond surrounded by dense tropical vegetation. A variation, sometimes referred to as **Nine Turn Ghaut**, also ascends the area below Verchild's, but continues through a valley to Molineux on the other side of the island; trail conditions vary and may require a guide. You'll need to obtain 1:25,000 and 1:50,000 topographic maps; most of the island's trails are not detailed as the government has not yet assembled hiking information or identified and maintained major trails.

ST. KITTS

Northern St. Kitts is dominated by Mount Liamuiga and a rugged shoreline.

Bicycling has yet to be discovered on St. Kitts. Although a few ex-pats explore the island's sugarcane-covered slopes on mountain bikes, no dedicated rental outfits exist at this writing. For those importing their own wheels, an ideal ride follows the road from Frigate Bay down the southern peninsula to **Mosquito Bay**; two good-sized hills are encountered each way on the 14-mile round-trip. The main highway circling St. Kitts is a pleasant journey of about 31 miles with numerous "R-and-R" possibilities en route. Alternatively, one can construct a more demanding circuit off-road by using the maze of dirt tracks that more-or-less parallel the main highway, transecting the sugarcane fields, particularly along the Atlantic coast. These roads connect the plantations and are still used for cane harvesting, but are relatively free from thorns and stickers. It's possible to avoid the main highway on all but a few miles of this circumnavigation. Finally, Nevis is but a 45-minute ferry ride away and, if you smile nicely, you may not be charged for bringing a bike across. The all-inclusive **Jack Tar Village** has a small supply of mountain bikes for its customers; if you really want to ride and aren't staying at the resort, you can purchase a day pass for $50 which will get you one of their bikes, and all other facilities (check on the quality of the bikes provided before signing up).

Basseterre is St. Kitts' the center of business and commerce. Decimated by fire in 1867 and rebuilt in the Franco-British colonial style, Basseterre is now a bustling seaboard community of 20,000. The town boasts such delightful Caribbean nuances as high-pitched, awningless roofs (to reduce their vulnerability in storms), shutters (to lessen sun glare but retain the essential flow of air through the interior spaces), and occasional outbursts of carpenter Gothic trim. Many of the renovations are due to the efforts of the "Basseterre Beautiful" organization, which has worked hard to restore sections of the old town, opening up new stores and courtyard cafes, and keeping the frilly, high-roofed architecture. The hub of the town is **The Circus**, built in tribute to London's Piccadilly Circus, with a memorial to Thomas Berkeley at its center. The **St. Christopher Heritage Society** is located on **Bank Street** and contains a photo collection and information on the island's history and culture, while the **Tourist Board** is found in **Pelican Mall**, just opposite the Circus. Nearby **Independence Square**, where slave auctions were held for 200 years, leads to **St. George's Church** now named after the patron saint of England, but originally called Notre Dame when it was first completed by the French in 1670. Several fires burned the structure over the years. A subsequent earthquake in 1843 means the church has been rebuilt four times—the current building was completed in 1869.

The lovely southeast peninsula of St. Kitts, also known as Salt Pond Estate, extends toward the hulk of Nevis and has been the location of several unsuccessful development schemes. A seven-mile road was completed in 1990 and extends from Frigate Bay down to the tip, where a bar and restaurant, **Turtle Beach**, hosts lively Sunday brunches and rents watersports equipment—watch for playful vervet monkeys in the surrounding hills. The St. Kitts-Nevis government promises that any development of this peninsula will be limited to a few select hotels and that they will have to comply with strict ecological and preservation laws. More than one abandoned structure tells a different story, but the point and its treasured bays remain an idyllic retreat.

The 30-mile circuit of the island's mountainous northwest wing is a great day-trip. Driving up the west coast of the island from Basseterre, stop by **Romney Manor**, a 17th-century great house and plantation that suffered a major fire in 1995. The manor houses **Caribelle Batik**, which sells locally-produced batiks and currently operates out of makeshift structures while plans for rebuilding Romney are debated. Next door is **Wingfield Estate**, once the home of Carib Chief Tegreman in 1623—remnants of St. Kitts' indian population, including petroglyphs, are nearby. Just down the hill from these historical sites is **Old Road Town**, the first permanent English settlement and original capital of the island. Continuing north on the main road, you'll soon encounter 800-foot-high **Brimstone Hill Fortress**, the most photographed tourist attraction on the island, and one of the most magnificent fortresses in the Caribbean. Rounding the northern wing of the island, you'll pass two of the island's historic inns: **Rawlings Plantation** is nestled in the fields of sugarcane above St. Paul's, while the **Golden Lemon** lies a few miles further on the shore next to a fishing village, **Dieppe Bay Town**—both are fine stops for breakfast, lunch or dinner. Scenically positioned off the coast to the northwest is St. Eustatius and, on a clear day, Saba. A bit further along on the road as it heads back to Basseterre are the **Black Rocks**, coastal cliffs with a not-to-distant relationship to the summit of volcanic Mount Liamuiga above—the turnoff from the main road is not marked for northbound traffic.

Historical Sites

Brimstone Hill Fortress ★★★★★
   On the western slope of Mount Liamuiga, ☎ *(869) 465-2609.*

Hours open: 9:30 a.m.–5:30 p.m.
This national park houses one of the Caribbean's largest and best-preserved fortresses, called the "Gibraltar of the West Indies" due to its sheer size. Set on top of an 800-foot basalt outcrop, the 38-acre fort dates back to 1690. Brimstone saw several skirmishes between the French and the British, who alternated in their control of the fort. Although it was abandoned in 1850, today it is quite nicely restored, and you can see the officer's quarters, barracks, hospital and kitchen. A museum is devoted to military history. The park also includes nature trails through dense vegetation and features stunning views of neighboring islands—St. Eustatius and Nevis are reliable sights, and on a clear day you can see Montserrat, Saba, St. Maarten and St. Barthelemy. General admission: $5.

Sports

Watersports activities on St. Kitts are focused around Frigate Bay, where you can find options from **sailing** to **scuba**. **Windsurfing** is best at the end of the southeast peninsula, where breezy bays provide both shelter and challenge under the watchful eye of Nevis Peak; try Turtle Beach for board rentals. Facilities for many sports can be found at the Jack Tar Village, including **golf** at the 18-hole Frigate Bay Golf Club, though serious duffers won't want to miss the spectacular course at the Four Seasons Nevis. Tennis is available at many of the island hotels, and **horseback riding** can take the form of half-day outings into the rain forest or along rugged beaches from Trinity Stables in Conaree (it's worth checking into whether the sport has been resumed on the beautiful southeast peninsula). Greg's Safaris is the best-known and established guide for nature walks (see "On Foot"), but other outfits are riding the coattails of Greg's success.

Horseback Riding

Various locations, Basseterre.
Several outfits offer trail rides along the beach or through the rain forest: Royal Stables ☎ *(869) 465-2222* and Trinity Stables ☎ *(869) 465-2922*.

Royal St. Kitts Golf Club

Adjacent to Jack Tar Village, Frigate Bay, ☎ (869) 465-8339.
Hours open: 7 a.m.–6 p.m.
St. Kitts' lone golf outlet is an 18-hole championship course on the flats behind Jack Tar. It was designed by Peter Thomson in 1974 and opened two years later. Green fees are $25–35, cart rental (mandatory) is $30-40, and club rental runs $10-15. There is also a nine-hole course many of the locals use, Golden Rock, near the airport.

Watersports

Various locations, Basseterre.

General watersports equipment and instruction can be found at **R.G. Watersports** ☎ *(869) 465-8050* and **Pro-Divers** ☎ *(869) 465-3223.* **Tropical Tours** ☎ *(869) 465-4167* and **Pelican Cove Marina** ☎ *(869) 465-2754* offer deep-sea fishing excursions. For boating and cruising, call **Kantours** ☎ *(869) 465-2098,* **Leeward Island Charters** ☎ *(869) 465-7474,* and **Tropical Tours** ☎ *(869) 465-4039.* Leeward Island Charters also provides day sails to Nevis aboard the 70-foot catamaran, the *Spirit of St. Kitts.* **Turtle Tours** offers guided kayak and snorkeling trips along the southeast peninsula ☎ *(869) 469-9094.*

Where to Stay

Fielding's Highest Rated Hotels in St. Kitts

★★★★	Golden Lemon Inn & Villas	$140–$435
★★★★	Ottley's Plantation Inn	$175–$400
★★★★	Rawlins Plantation	$185–$390
★★★	Frigate Bay Resort	$75–$263
★★★	Ocean Terrace Inn	$76–$350
★★★	St. Christopher Club	$60–$235

Fielding's Most Exclusive Hotels in St. Kitts

★★	Casablanca Resort	$240–$355
★★★★	Ottley's Plantation Inn	$175–$400
★★	Jack Tar Village	$120–$340
★★	Island Paradise Village	$98–$285
★★★	Frigate Bay Resort	$75–$263

Fielding's Best Value Hotels in St. Kitts

★★★	St. Christopher Club	$60–$235
★★★	Frigate Bay Resort	$75–$263
★★	Fort Thomas Hotel	$100–$160
★★★	Ocean Terrace Inn	$76–$350
★★★★	Golden Lemon Inn & Villas	$140–$435

Accommodations on St. Kitts fall into two general categories—historic plantation inns, all northwest of Basseterre set amid scenic volcanic slopes, and more contemporary condo-like structures, around and just southeast of Basseterre. The two groupings offer vastly different experiences, and a sub-category—the all-inclusive vacation—is proffered by the Jack Tar Village

Beach Resort. Choose your accommodations carefully on this island, as most cater to very specific needs. If good beaches and a variety of nearby activities are important, you'll want to be in Frigate Bay; if solitude amid antiques and history is your cup of tea, choose one of the upscale inns, but you'll need a car for serious exploration. Several of the toll-free numbers listed below connect directly to the island, allowing you to speak directly with the manager or perhaps even the owner. A pair of abandoned developments lie on the southeastern tip of the island facing Nevis. One day they may be a reality; for now they're unfinished eyesores.

Hotels and Resorts

With 244 rooms and a bustling casino, the Jack Tar Village Beach Resort is by far the largest and busiest property on St. Kitts, though it has seen better days. It caters to those who want the price of their vacation—room, food, activities and, perhaps, airfare—packaged and written in stone before they step foot on the island. As one of the Caribbean's original all-inclusives, its success is such that a number of other, smaller properties have sprung up around it, leading to a fair amount of development in Frigate Bay. Most of these newer hostelries are listed under Apartments and Condominiums.

Bird Rock Beach Hotel $75–$240 ★★

Bird Rock; Basseterre, ☎ (800) 621-1270, (869) 465-8914. FAX (869) 465-1675.
Single: $75–$180. Double: $75–$240.
This small hotel is located on a bluff overlooking the sea, one mile from town. Accommodations are in one- or two-room units with air conditioning, balconies and cable TV; some have kitchens. A three-bedroom suite is also available. Two restaurants serve continental and local cuisine, and you'll find two bars a pool and a tennis court on the premises. The speck-sized beach is more for snorkeling than sunning, and a new on-site dive shop supplies watersport equipment. Amenities: tennis. 38 rooms. Credit cards: A, D, MC, V.

Casablanca Resort $240–$355 ★★

Cockleshell Bay, Basseterre, ☎ (800) 231-1945, (869) 497-6999.
FAX (869) 497-6899.
Single: $240–$355. Double: $240–$355.
This new resort is on the island's southeast peninsula, facing a white sand beach. Accommodations are in air-conditioned suites or villas, all with living rooms, minibars, VCRs, refrigerators and balconies. On-site facilities include three restaurants, two bars, a stylish lobby, pool, fitness center, and six tennis courts. 66 rooms. Credit cards: A, MC.

Fort Thomas Hotel $100–$160 ★★

Basseterre, ☎ (800) 851-7818, (869) 465-2695. FAX (869) 465-7518.
Single: $100–$140. Double: $115–$160.
Built on the site of an old fort, this former Holiday Inn reopened in 1993 after extensive renovations. It caters mainly to business travelers who don't mind the fact that the beach is four miles away (The staff will shuttle you over for free). Guestrooms are spacious but nothing special, though you can count on modern amenities and good housekeeping; otherwise rates are a bit high for what you get. The

ST. KITTS

dining room serves West Indian and international dishes. The hotel also offers a few bars and a pool. 52 rooms. Credit cards: A, MC, V.

Jack Tar Village $120–$340   ★★

Frigate Bay, Basseterre, ☎ (800) 999-9182, (869) 465-8651. FAX (869) 465-1031.
Single: $120–$185. Double: $210–$340.

Set on 20 acres on the isthmus between the Caribbean and Atlantic, this is an all-inclusive resort that is showing increasing wear-and-tear despite recent renovations. Guestrooms are scattered about the grounds in two-story buildings and are simple but comfortable and have modern conveniences. Most everything is included in the rates, from scuba lessons to tennis on four courts to nightly entertainment. Even the greens fees at a nearby golf course are covered (though the mandatory golf cart is not—go figure). You'll need your own cash in the casino. Children five and under stay and eat free at the resort (12 and under in the summer), and tykes from 3 to 11 are kept happy in supervised day-time programs. Higher rates apply at Christmas. 244 rooms. Credit cards: A, MC, V.

Ocean Terrace Inn $76–$350   ★★★

Basseterre, ☎ (800) 524-0512, (869) 465-2754. FAX (869) 465-1057.
Single: $76–$175. Double: $101–$350.

Known throughout St. Kitts as "OTI," this informal inn, set on lushly landscaped hilltop grounds, overlooks the bay and Basseterre. Great views abound from all the air-conditioned rooms, which are modern and tasteful. You can choose from several one- and two-bedroom apartments and six suites. Two restaurants and three bars keep guests sated. Facilities include two pools, a business center and free transportation to the beach at Turtle Bay, a 20-minute ride. Popular especially with business travelers, but fine for vacationers. Amenities: Jacuzzi. 57 rooms. Credit cards: A, DC, D, MC, V.

St. Christopher Club $60–$235   ★★★

Frigate Bay, Basseterre, ☎ (869) 465-4854. FAX (869) 465-6466.
Single: $60–$100. Double: $100–$235.

This oceanfront hotel is located just down the street from the Jack Tar complex. Accommodations range from traditional guestrooms to spacious studios to one- and two-bedroom suites with kitchenettes. All rooms are pleasant and comfortable and have air conditioners, phones and TV. Facilities include a restaurant, bar and pool on the premises. 32 rooms. Credit cards: MC, V.

Apartments and Condominiums

A trend that developed on St. Kitts in the '80s was a move toward condo-style properties, most of them located in (now) overbuilt Frigate Bay. What the area does have is a golf course, casino, restaurants, some nightlife and a good beach, and even better beaches along the beautiful southeast peninsula are close by. Additionally, there are good values to be found along here, none less than the Timothy Beach Resort, which overlooks Frigate Bay Beach. The swankest villas on the island are offered by the Golden Lemon (see "Inns" below).

Frigate Bay Resort $75–$263   ★★★

Frigate Bay, Basseterre, ☎ (800) 266-2185, (869) 465-8935. FAX (869) 465-7050.

Single: $75–$263. Double: $75–$263.
Set just up from the beach, this hotel consists of four three-story buildings that face either the pool or the hills. Accommodations are air-conditioned and nicely done; many, but not all, have kitchens. There's a swim-up bar in the Olympic-size pool and a bar, plus restaurant on the premises. Watersports and an 18-hole golf course (free to guests) are within easy walk. 64 rooms. Credit cards: A, MC, V.

Island Paradise Village   **$98–$285**   ★★
Frigate Bay, Basseterre, ☎ (869) 465-8035. FAX (869) 465-8236.
Single: $98–$170. Double: $155–$285.
This condominium complex on the beach consists of one- to three-bedroom units, all with fully equipped kitchens, living/dining areas, and balconies or patios. Some have TV and air conditioning, but not all, so be sure to make your reservations accordingly. A pool and Italian restaurant are located on the premises, while golf, tennis and a casino are within walking distance. 62 rooms. Credit cards: MC, V.

Leeward Cove Condominiums   **$50–$275**   ★★
Frigate Bay, Basseterre, ☎ (869) 465-8030. FAX (869) 465-3476.
Single: $50–$80. Double: $60–$275.
This condominium complex occupies five acres in the Frigate Bay area. All units are air-conditioned and have one or two bedrooms, full kitchens, living and dining areas, and patios or balconies. Some also have TVs and phones. Guests who stay a week get a free rented car—not a bad deal. All can golf for free at the municipal course. There are no facilities on the premises, but many are within an easy walk. 6 rooms. Credit cards: A, MC, V.

Sun 'n Sand Beach Resort   **$90–$270**   ★★
Frigate Bay, Basseterre, ☎ (800) 223-6510, (869) 465-8037. FAX (869) 465-6745.
Single: $90–$270. Double: $90–$270.
Located near Jack Tar, this complex consists of apartment-style one-bedroom studios and charming cottages that house two-bedroom, two-bath units. All have phones, cable TV, kitchens and patios. There are two pools on-site (one for kids), two tennis courts, and a beach bar and restaurant. The golf course is just across the street, and restaurants and shops are within walking distance. A nice combination of self-catering and resort amenities. 68 rooms. Credit cards: A, DC, D, MC, V.

Timothy Beach Resort   **$65–$265**   ★★
Frigate Beach, Basseterre, ☎ (800) 777-1700, (869) 465-8597. FAX (869) 465-7723.
Single: $65–$165. Double: $65–$265.
This basic condominium complex is just off the beach, on the opposite side of the isthmus from Jack Tar. Accommodations range from standard guestrooms to one- and two-bedroom suites, some with full kitchens. All have air conditioning, phones, private balconies, and coffeemakers. There's a good cafe and bar on-site, as well as an inviting pool and tennis court. Watersports await at the beach. One of St. Kitts' best values. 60 rooms. Credit cards: A, MC, V.

Inns

Like it's sibling, Nevis, St. Kitts has a rich history visible in the form of plantation inns set on the slopes of a verdant extinct volcano. Each has its own personality—stately Ottley's greets guests with well-tended lawns and rows of impressive royal palms, while the seaside Golden Lemon exudes eccentricity and color. With each of the four choices below, you're 20 to 40 minutes from either the airport or Basseterre, and none have beaches nearby to speak of—a car is a must if solitude keeps you awake at night. Note that Fairview has a superb location and much history, too, but has slid several notches from its former glory when it was the first of the plantation homes to welcome tourists. The future of a fifth spot, the White House, was uncertain at press time, call ☎ *(869) 465-8162* to get an update.

Fairview Inn $70–$130 ★

Palmetto Point, Basseterre, ☎ *(800) 223-9815, (869) 465-2472. FAX (869) 465-1056. Single: $70–$130. Double: $70–$130.*

Located some 10 minutes from Basseterre, this complex consists of cottages set around an 18th-century great house. Guestrooms, housed in the cottages, are small and motel-like, but decent enough if you want that "inn experience" on a budget. Only some are air-conditioned, and not all have ceiling fans, so be sure to make your requests accordingly. The site includes a pool, West Indian restaurant and a bar. You'll need a car to get around. Ask about package rates. Amenities: houses, cottages or bungalows. 27 rooms. Credit cards: A, D, MC, V.

Golden Lemon Inn & Villas $140–$435 ★★★★

Dieppe Bay Town, Basseterre, ☎ *(800) 633-7411, (869) 465-7260. FAX (869) 465-4019. Single: $140–$435. Double: $215–$435.*

Since 1961 one of the most unique inns in all the Caribbean, the Golden Lemon is located on a black-sand beach at St. Kitts' northern tip. Seven of the guestrooms are located in the 17th-century great house, beautifully restored with lots of fine antiques. The rooms are individually furnished with smashing results, sporting antiques, Oriental rugs, West Indian art, raised four-poster beds, ceiling fans (no air), and verandas—no two are alike. The site also includes 21 villas, each with a very private pool. Complementary afternoon tea is a refined treat and breakfast is included in the rates. There's a pool and tennis court, and a quaint fishing village next door, otherwise the isolated location encourages solitude and escape. No kids under 16 allowed at this very tony operation, though management will turn a blind eye in summer. Not for everyone, but those who love it keep coming back. Amenities: tennis. 28 rooms. Credit cards: A, MC, V.

Ottley's Plantation Inn $175–$400 ★★★★

Ottley's, Basseterre, ☎ *(800) 772-3039, (869) 465-7234. FAX (869) 465-4760. Single: $175–$320. Double: $200–$400.*

This grand plantation inn sits on a 35-acre estate amid sugar cane fields above the ocean. Accommodations are in the 18th-century great house or in cottages, all air-conditioned and sporting antique and wicker furniture, ceiling fans, phones, combination baths and verandas. The large pool is spring-fed and built into the ruins of a sugar mill, and there are nature trails for exploring the adjacent rain forest. They'll shuttle you to the beach, but it's so nice here that you'll hate to leave. The restaurant is wonderful—as is everything else. Room rates include breakfast; no children under 10. 12 rooms. Credit cards: A, MC, V.

ST. KITTS

Rawlins Plantation   **$185–$390**   ★ ★ ★ ★

St. Paul's, Basseterre, ☎ (800) 346-5358, (869) 465-6221. FAX (869) 465-4954.
Single: $185–$260. Double: $265–$390.

Located on 12 acres at the base of Mount Liamuiga, the scenic views from this charming inn encompass fields of sugar cane, miles of ocean and St. Eustatius in the distance. It was built around the ruins of a 17th-century sugar mill at the north end of St. Kitts on well-landscaped grounds. Guestrooms are in cottages decorated with good local artwork, nice fabrics, four-poster beds, and antiques. No air conditioning, but breezes generally do the job. Guests can relax at the small spring-fed pool, play tennis on a grass court, or enjoy croquet. Breakfast and dinner is included in the rates, and afternoon tea is a nice touch. You'll want a rental car to get around— Rawlins is quite isolated—though it's so peaceful and relaxing here you'll have to be motivated to move on. 9 rooms. Credit cards: A, MC, V.

Low Cost Lodging

Good deals can be found at some of the condo/apartment complexes in Frigate Bay listed above, particularly for families. Otherwise, among several options, head for the **Conaree Beach Cottages**, which makes up for a lack of luxury by being positioned right on the beach, just northeast of Basseterre ☎ *(869) 465-8475*. Another possibility is the **Morgan Heights Resort**, 10 minutes drive from Basseterre and a short stroll to the beach ☎ *(869) 465-8633*. **Trinity Inn Apartments** is a family-run operation located on Palmetto Point a few miles west of Basseterre ☎ *(869) 465-3226*. You can also ask around for rooms in private homes, but this option is best explored in person.

Where to Eat

ST. KITTS

Fielding's Highest Rated Restaurants in St. Kitts

★★★★★	Royal Palm, The	$50–$50
★★★★	Golden Lemon	$30–$50
★★★★	Rawlins Plantation	$35–$35
★★★	Ballahoo	$10–$21
★★★	Chef's Place	$5–$20
★★★	Fisherman's Wharf	$4–$26
★★★	Georgian House, The	$21–$27
★★★	PJ's Pizza	$10–$20
★★★	Patio, The	$26–$30
★★★	Turtle Beach Bar & Grill	

Fielding's Most Exclusive Restaurants in St. Kitts

★★★★★	Royal Palm, The	$50–$50
★★★★	Golden Lemon	$30–$50
★★★★	Rawlins Plantation	$35–$35
★★★	Patio, The	$26–$30
★★★	Georgian House, The	$21–$27

Fielding's Best Value Restaurants in St. Kitts

★★★	Chef's Place	$5–$20
★★★	PJ's Pizza	$10–$20
★★★	Fisherman's Wharf	$4–$26
★★★	Ballahoo	$10–$21
★★★	Georgian House, The	$21–$27

For such a small island, St. Kitts has a wide spectrum of dining choices, from gourmet delights in historical settings to the homey kitchens of casual local hangouts. Typical St. Kittian delicacies include goat water (an ill-named stew), fried plantain, creole bean soup, boiled saltfish, conch chowder, and poached parrotfish with grilled yams. The **plantation inns** have outdoor patios for candlelit dinners, while in Basseterre, dinner at the 400-year-old **Georgian House** is a leisurely, elegant evening in a high-ceilinged salon, with aperitifs enjoyed in the walled garden beneath the big mango tree. At the **Ocean Terrace Inn**, award-winning chef James Venterpool makes a stunning Two-Flavor Soup (pumpkin and broccoli) and a carrot cake with local sugarcane sauce. Good West Indian food can be enjoyed with street theater at **Ballahoo**, a prime location overlooking the town center. Don't miss an opportunity to try a swig of the island brew—Royal Extra Stout—or a glass of mauby, made from tree bark, or the local grapefruit soft drink, Ting.

Ballahoo $$$ ★★★

Fort Street; Basseterre, ☎ (869) 465-4197.
Latin American cuisine.
Lunch: 8 a.m.–6 p.m., entrées $2–$21.
Dinner: 6:30–10 p.m., entrées $10–$21. Closed: Sun.
This upper-level eatery overlooks the bustling downtown district that is Basseterre's version of Piccadilly Circus. The restaurant's customer base is a hodgepodge of cruise-ship passengers, businesspeople and shoppers who munch on fresh parrotfish fillets, *rotis*, burgers and yummy desserts. The place prides itself in presenting reasonably priced French wines. It's also a great location for West Indian or American-style breakfasts—be adventurous and have saltfish with your eggs instead of bacon. Reservations recommended. Credit cards: A, MC, V.

Chef's Place $$ ★★★

Church Street; Basseterre, ☎ (869) 465-6176.
Latin American cuisine. Specialties: Souse, lamb stew.
Lunch: 8 a.m.–6 p.m., entrées $5–$10.
Dinner: 6–11 p.m., entrées $5–$20. Closed: Sun.
Get friendly owner Oliver Peetes to describe the West Indian specialties on the daily blackboard—he'll probably oblige. Then settle down on picnic tables outdoors with a streetside view and await generous helpings of *souse* (pigs' feet stew with a special sauce) or lamb stew. Main dishes will be rounded out with rice, a tasty salad and island vegetables. Beverages are also homemade and may include *mauby*, a bittersweet and spicy brew made from tree bark, or fresh ginger beer for the less adventurous. Credit cards: not accepted.

Coconut Cafe $$$ ★★

Frigate Bay Beach, Basseterre, ☎ (869) 465-3020.
Associated hotel: Timothy Beach Resort.
African cuisine.
Lunch: 7 a.m.–4 p.m., entrées $3–$19.
Dinner: 4–11 p.m., entrées $13–$21.

Open to the sea breezes and steps away from the sand on the island's most popular swimming beach, this cafe dispenses three meals a day, but it's most popular for sunset cocktails and fresh seafood suppers to follow. There's steel band entertainment in season on Sunday and Wednesday evenings, and the bar stays open 'till the wee hours. Credit cards: A, D, MC, V.

Fisherman's Wharf $$ ★ ★ ★

Basseterre, ☎ (869) 465-2754. Associated hotel: Ocean Terrace Inn.
Seafood cuisine.
Dinner: 7–11 p.m., entrées $4–$26.
Eating here is like being at a beach cookout, with diners choosing meat, fish, or chicken to be grilled to order, and serving themselves from a salad and condiments buffet. Orders are taken to long wooden tables facing the oceanfront. Everything is reliably good, but the fresh lobster and shrimp are standouts. A steel band entertains on Friday. An institution. Credit cards: A, MC, V.

Georgian House, The $$$ ★ ★ ★

Independence Square; Basseterre, ☎ (869) 465-4049.
International cuisine.
Dinner: 6–10 p.m., entrées $21–$27.
This beautifully restored home, decorated with Georgian-era reproductions, is a showcase for a continental menu of seafood, chicken, and steaks, prepared with West Indian flourishes. Peas and rice accompany some of the main courses. Dinner is served nightly on a patio behind the house. Now operated by the owners of the White House. Reservations recommended. Credit cards: A, MC, V.

Golden Lemon $$$ ★ ★ ★ ★

Dieppe Bay Town, Basseterre, ☎ (869) 465-7260. Associated hotel: Golden Lemon.
International cuisine.
Lunch: 11:30 a.m.–3 p.m., entrées $6–$12.
Dinner: 7–10 p.m., entrées $30–$50.
Some returning visitors would never dream of leaving the island without at least one visit to this exquisite boutique inn's fine restaurant. The three-course dinners are rotated frequently; owner Arthur Leaman creates the internationally themed menus himself. Gleaming antiques and crystal chandeliers accentuate the dining room and a breezy patio is a gathering spot for Sunday brunch and cocktails (11:30 a.m.–3 p.m.; $20). While touring by car, stop by for lunch, which features more informal offerings, including sandwiches, salads and fish dishes. Features: Sunday brunch. Reservations required. Credit cards: A, DC, MC, V.

PJ's Pizza $$ ★ ★ ★

North Frigate Bay, Basseterre, ☎ (869) 465-8373.
Italian cuisine. Specialties: Pizza, subs.
Lunch: 10 a.m.–6 p.m., entrées $5–$20.
Dinner: 6–10:30 p.m., entrées $10–$20. Closed: Mon.
A reputation for some of the most creative pizza toppings in the Caribbean chain is putting this small place on the culinary map. Refried beans embellish the Mexican pizza and a Rastafarian-Ital pie is capped with island veggies in the Rasta colors of gold, red and green; don't miss the Garbage Pizza. The rest of the offerings are basi-

cally Italian, with hero sandwiches made on homebaked bread. Dinner plates usually include lasagne and chili. Credit cards: A, MC, V.

Patio, The   **$$$**   ★★★

Frigate Bay Beach, Basseterre, ☎ *(869) 465-8666.*
Latin American cuisine.
Dinner: 7–8:30 p.m., entrées $26–$30. Closed: Sun.
Although talented chef Helen Mallalieu has left to attend university, she trained a replacement and her father stills runs this restaurant positioned on the patio of their Frigate Bay Beach home. Diners face one of the prettiest private gardens on the island while feasting on specialties like pepper pot stew, broiled fresh seafood, and tropical desserts. Wines and liquors are complementary with dinner. Reservations advised in high season. Reservations required. Credit cards: MC, V.

Rawlins Plantation   **$$$**   ★★★★

St. Paul's, Basseterre, ☎ *(869) 465-6221. Associated hotel: Rawlins Plantation.*
International cuisine.
Lunch: 12:30–2 p.m., prix fixe $23.
Dinner: 8 p.m. Seating, prix fixe $35.
Cap off a tour of the island with lunch or dinner at this splendidly restored estate on the northwest coast. A varied buffet of creole specialties is served to diners on the terrace of the estate's great house, and offerings often include curries, fritters, salads, vegetables and several international specialties. Call before noon to make a reservation for a fixed-price dinner of four courses with soup, salad, entrée and a tantalizing dessert—possibly chocolate terrine with passion fruit sauce. Reservations required. Credit cards: A, MC, V.

Royal Palm, The   **$$$**   ★★★★★

Ottley's Estate, Basseterre, ☎ *(869) 465-7234. Associated hotel: Ottley's Plantation.*
International cuisine.
Lunch: Noon–3 p.m., entrées $8–$18.
Dinner: 8 p.m. Seating, prix fixe $50.
Possibly the most creative food on the island is served at this restaurant located in Ottley's Plantation Inn. Chef Pam Yahn's new "island cuisine" has been glossied on the pages of national magazines, including *Food and Wine*. Her ever-changing menu has included delights like lobster quesadillas and sweet treats like mango mousse with raspberry sauce. Lunches, dinners and Sunday brunch with champagne are served in a location that couldn't be lovelier—the dining room skirts a nearby rain forest. Fixed-price brunch is $20, and served from 11 a.m. to 2 p.m. Features: Sunday brunch. Reservations required. Credit cards: A, MC, V.

Turtle Beach Bar & Grill   **$$$**   ★★★

S.E. Peninsula Road, Basseterre, ☎ *(869) 469-9086.*
American cuisine.
Lunch: 8 a.m.–6 p.m., entrées $16–$24.
Combine an afternoon of snorkeling (the preferred activity), scuba diving, or just plain loafing on the beach with a notable barbecue of chicken, fish, meat, or lobster prepared at this off-the-beaten-track eatery on the southeast coast. Operated by the Ocean Terrace Inn in Fortlands, the Grill is also a cool place Sundays for a well-

ST. KITTS

regarded West Indian buffet replete with live entertainment. Dinner is served only on Saturdays, from 7:30–10 p.m. Equipment for watersports can be rented here as well. Features: Sunday brunch. Reservations recommended. Credit cards: A, V.

Where to Shop

Shopping in Basseterre is concentrated in the area around **The Circus** and **Pelican Mall**—not coincidentally, also the docking place for cruise ships. T-shirts and duty free items are found in mass quantities, but among the more unusual spots is the **Spencer Cameron Gallery** at North Independence Square which sells artwork from St. Kitts and around the world. Just below the Ballahoo Restaurant, **Island Hopper**, provides a collection of art, pottery, textiles and fabrics. Duty-free items are available at **A Slice of the Lemon** on Fort Street where you can browse through pottery, teas, spices and condiments priced lower than those in St. Maarten or the U.S. Virgin Islands. The **St. Kitts Philatelic Bureau** in Pelican Mall sells a wide variety of the island's famous and collectable stamps.

Outside Basseterre, check into the **Plantation Picture House**, a gallery at Rawlings Plantation featuring the work of Kate Spencer, known for her portraits, landscapes and still lifes, some of them found on stone-washed silk scarves; a smaller store is also located on Fort Street in Basseterre. Located inside the Golden Lemon and with another shop in Basseterre is **Lemonaid**, which sells jewelry, antiques, imported crafts and Island to Island resort wear. Surrounded by lush gardens, **Caribelle Batik** creates and sells their colorful batiks at Romney Manner, above Old Road Town.

St. Kitts Directory

Arrival and Departure

At this time, no airline service connects St. Kitts' **Robert Llewelyn Bradshaw International Airport** (formerly Golden Rock) directly with North America, although winter charter flights out of Chicago are sometimes possible. For now, most visitors travel to the island via San Juan, from where **American Eagle** provides three to five flights daily into St. Kitts. **LIAT** has daily service into St. Kitts from Anguilla, Antigua, Nevis, St. Maarten, St. Thomas and Tortola, with connecting service from a number of other islands through Antigua. The 10-minute hop between Nevis and St. Kitts is served by two local operations: **Air St. Kitts-Nevis** ☎ *(869) 465-8571* and **Nevis Express** ☎ *(869) 469-3346*. Public ferry service from Nevis, aboard the *Caribe Queen* or the

Spirit of Mount Nevis, makes the 45-minute crossing between Charlestown and Basseterre one to three times daily for $4 one way ☎ *(869) 469-9373*.

Business Hours

Shops open Monday–Saturday 8 a.m.–noon and 1–4 p.m. Most close earlier on Thursday. Banks open Monday–Thursday 8 a.m.–3 p.m. and Friday 8 a.m.–5 p.m.

Climate

The climate is pleasant and moderate, with an average temperature of 79 degrees Fahrenheit. Humidity is low and constant northeast trade winds keep the islands cool. Although there is no rainy season, annual rainfall averages 55 inches.

Documents

U.S. citizens need to present proof of citizenship (passport, voters registration or birth certificate), along with a return or ongoing ticket. There is a departure tax of $10.

Electricity

The current runs 230 volts, 60 cycles AC. While the electricity supply at some hotels is 110 volts, AC transformers and adapters are generally needed.

Getting Around

Local transportation is available via **minibuses** and **taxis**. Numerous taxi rates are set, among them: from the airport into Basseterre, $5; to Frigate Bay, $10; to Dieppe Bay, $19. From Basseterre to Frigate Bay, $7; to Ottley's, $10.50; to Rawlings, $20. There is a 25 percent surcharge between 11 p.m. and 6 a.m. Prices for island tours by taxi are based on where you begin your trip: from Basseterre, an island tour is about $45; a two-hour tour of the southeast peninsula from Basseterre is $31. **Dave Charles** is a good choice for island taxi-tours ☎ *(869) 465-4253*. **Rental car** rates start at about $35 per day; you'll need to obtain a St. Kitts-Nevis drivers license for $12 at the police station on Canyon Street in Basseterre—drive on the left. Among the firms, all located in Basseterre, are **Avis** ☎ *(869) 465-6507* and **Budget** ☎ *(869) 466-5555*. and **TDC Rentals** ☎ *(869) 465-2991*. Day-trips to Nevis are possible via air or ferry; see "Arrival and Departure" above.

Language

The official language of both St. Kits and Nevis is English.

Medical Emergencies

There is a 24-hour emergency room at **Joseph N. France General Hospital** in Buckley ☎ *(869) 465-2551*. Also ask your hotel about physicians on call.

Money

The official currency is the Eastern Caribbean dollar. The exchange rate is closely tied to the American dollar, and trades at about $2.65 for one U.S. dollar. Make sure you know which dollar is being used when your restaurant or hotel bill is calculated since both are widely accepted.

Telephone

The new St. Kitts-Nevis area code effective October 1996 is *869*. International calls, telexes and telegrams can be made from Skantel on Canyon Street in Basseterre ☎ *(869) 465-2219.*

Time

Atlantic Standard Time. That is to say, it's one hour ahead of New York time, except during Daylight Saving Time, when it is the same.

Tipping

Expect a 10 percent service charge added to most hotel and restaurant bills. If it isn't, be prepared to tip 10–15 percent.

Tourist Information

Good brochures and information can be found at the **St. Kitts Tourist Board**, *Pelican Mall, P.O Box 132, Basseterre*; ☎ *(869) 465-2620/4040*, FAX *(869) 465-8794.* In the U.S. ☎ *(212) 535-1234.*

When to Go

Carnival Celebrations take place in a week-long spectacle the last week of December, featuring calypso competitions, queen shows, street dancing and festivals. Tourism Week in Nevis is an annual fair in February. Museum Day is May 18, usually an open house at various museums. Culturama 20, in Nevis the last week of July, is a 20-year-old festival of native arts, crafts and music. Every other month the St. Kitts-Nevis Boating Club provides races and relays for residents and tourists alike. On the last Sunday of every month the Golden Rock Golf Club presents a day of fun golf played on a nine-hole fun course. The Nevis Jockey Club has scheduled nine race days throughout the year to coincide with national holidays.

ST. KITTS HOTELS	RMS	RATES	PHONE	CR. CARDS
Basseterre				
★★★★ Golden Lemon Inn & Villas	28	$140–$435	(800) 633-7411	A, MC, V
★★★★ Ottley's Plantation Inn	12	$175–$400	(800) 772-3039	A, MC, V
★★★★ Rawlins Plantation	9	$185–$390	(800) 346-5358	A, MC, V
★★★ Frigate Bay Resort	64	$75–$263	(800) 266-2185	A, MC, V
★★★ Ocean Terrace Inn	57	$76–$350	(800) 524-0512	A, D, DC, MC, V
★★★ St. Christopher Club	32	$60–$235	(869) 465-4854	MC, V
★★ Bird Rock Beach Hotel	38	$75–$240	(800) 621-1270	A, D, MC, V
★★ Casablanca Resort	66	$240–$355	(800) 231-1945	A, MC
★★ Fort Thomas Hotel	52	$100–$160	(800) 851-7818	A, MC, V
★★ Island Paradise Village	62	$98–$285	(869) 465-8035	MC, V
★★ Jack Tar Village	244	$120–$340	(800) 999-9182	A, MC, V

ST. KITTS HOTELS		RMS	RATES	PHONE	CR. CARDS
★★	Leeward Cove Condominiums	6	$50–$275	(869) 465-8030	A, MC, V
★★	Sun 'n Sand Beach Resort	68	$90–$270	(800) 223-6510	A, D, DC, MC, V
★★	Timothy Beach Resort	60	$65–$265	(800) 777-1700	A, MC, V
★	Fairview Inn	27	$70–$130	(800) 223-9815	A, D, MC, V

ST. KITTS RESTAURANTS		PHONE	ENTRÉE	CR. CARDS

Basseterre

		African		
★★	Coconut Cafe	(869) 465-3020	$3–$21	A, D, MC, V
		American		
★★★	Turtle Beach Bar & Grill	(869) 469-9086	$16–$24	A, V
		International		
★★★★★	Royal Palm, The	(869) 465-7234	$8–$50	A, MC, V
★★★★	Golden Lemon	(869) 465-7260	$6–$50	A, DC, MC, V
★★★★	Rawlins Plantation	(869) 465-6221	$23–$35	A, MC, V
★★★	Georgian House, The	(869) 465-4049	$21–$27	A, MC, V
		Italian		
★★★	PJ's Pizza	(869) 465-8373	$5–$20	A, MC, V
		Latin American		
★★★	Ballahoo	(869) 465-4197	$2–$21	A, MC, V
★★★	Chef's Place	(869) 465-6176	$5–$20	None
★★★	Patio, The	(869) 465-8666	$26–$30	MC, V
		Seafood		
★★★	Fisherman's Wharf	(869) 465-2754	$4–$26	A, MC, V

ST. KITTS

ST. LUCIA

Waterskiing and parasailing are popular activities around St. Lucia.

Though it offers most of what the Caribbean is known for, St. Lucia particularly delivers spectacle. St. Lucia is an island of lavish scenery—the dramatic profiles of the green-cloaked Pitons, the moon-like lava flows and bubbling mud pots of Mount Soufriére, and a multicolored waterfall that changes from blue-purple to yellow are only a few of the sights. Islanders are gradually catching the eco-tourism bug, finally figuring out that St. Lucia's chief draw is the wondrous natural resources—from golden beaches seductively wrapped by steep mountains, to lush highlands that are home to rare and exotic species of birds, plants and wildlife. Every visitor should drive the winding roads through the emerald peaks and valleys along the southwestern coast, where jungle flowers scent the air and giggling children soap themselves under roadside water faucets. To obtain the full Lucian experience, however, you must head out on foot, breathe in the rain forest, and even bathe in the volcano's hot mineral baths. But the spirit of St. Lucia lies not only in the land but in the people as well—spirited, musical, and forever ready to party. Festivals dominate the rhythm of life here, ranging from not one but two quaint, elaborate flower festivals—La Rose and La Marguerite—to a jazz festival in May that draws international musicians and a bevy of admirers. St. Lucia is the most developed of the British Windwards, with a bustling population of 143,000. Many are employed by the agricultural industry, but a growing number work directly or indirectly for the tourism sector, which is successfully luring an increasing faction of Americans to its shores. The island is reasonably well-connected by air to North America, and a diverse range of accommodations—from guest houses to plush hotels, all-inclusives and luxury resorts—make the island one of the region's most accessible.

Bird's-Eye View

At 238 square miles, pear-shaped St. Lucia is the second largest of the British Windwards, though its vertical heft makes it seem much larger. 27 miles long, and 14 across at its widest, the island is positioned between Martinique and St. Vincent in the Eastern Caribbean. Like its sister Windwards islands, St. Lucia has a mountainous interior crafted by volcanic activity over the centuries. This is most apparent in the southern half, where the highest mountains (topping out with Mount Gimie at 3118 feet), are overshadowed by a pair of spectacular volcanic plugs a mile-and-a-half apart, Petit Piton and Gros Piton, that rise straight up out of the ocean to 2461 and 2619 feet respectively. Most of the southern half of the island is densely forested in tropical vegetation, with an abundance of flowers such as hibiscus, frangipani, orchids, jasmine and poinciana. A 19,000-acre national forest protects much of this primal area. The bright green jacquot, St. Lucia's own rare and indigenous parrot is found here—the subject of a successful breeding and education program initiated by Paul Butler that has halted the parrot's slide toward extinction and more than doubled the population to almost 400. The northwest coast seems positively cosmopolitan by Caribbean standards, though Castries, the island's capital and victim of one too many fires (the last in 1948), is in need of a beautification project. About half of the population lives on or near the busy coast between Castries and Gros Islet. Tourism has been growing steadily, with marinas and resorts filling up the coastline north and south of Castries. St. Lucia is trying to learn from the over-development

Saint Lucia

- ✪ CAPITAL
- ● CITY/TOWN
- ✕ AIRPORT
- ═══ PRIMARY ROAD
- ━━ SECONDARY ROAD
- ▲ MOUNTAIN
- ━━ RIVER

0   3   6km
0   2   4mi

©FWI 1995

SAINT LUCIA CHANNEL

Pigeon Island
61°

Gros Islet

Gros Islet

Monchy

Bon Air

Vigie Airport

CASTRIES

Babonneau

14°

Ciceron

Forestière

Piton Flore
1871 ft.

La Croix Maingot

Dernière
Rivière

CARIBBEAN
SEA

Anse la Raye

Grand Riviere

Canaries

Millet

Dennery

Mt. Gimie
3118 ft.

Mt. Tabac
2224 ft.

Praslin

Mon Repos

Soufrière

Mt. Grand
Magazin
2022 ft.

Petit Piton
2461 ft.

Fond St. Jacques

Gros Piton
2619 ft.

Micoud

Desruisseaux

Choiseul

Laborie

Hewanorra Airport

Vieux Fort

ATLANTIC
OCEAN

SAINT VINCENT PASSAGE

ST. LUCIA

mistakes that have occurred on other islands before it's too late. For now, agriculture remains the larger industry—bananas and coconuts mostly—though marijuana is also a major crop.

History

The first inhabitants of St. Lucia were surely Arawak Indians, and later Caribs, who did not appreciate the British invasion of their island in the early 17th century; for some time they managed to successfully fend off colonization. In 1650, the French overcame the resistance and settled a colony, completing a treaty with the Caribs in 1660. Over the next 164 years, the island exchanged hands 14 times between the French and British in an almost comical seesaw play of power. It was not until the issue of the 1814 Treaty of Paris that the British finally secured all rights. During this time, the Carib Indians were played as a pawn between the two powers until the British finally—and unceremoniously—exiled them to a still-existing reservation on Dominica. Although the island gained control of its own government on Feb. 22, 1979, its official head of state still remains the British throne, represented by a Governor General, who appoints the eleven members of St. Lucia's Senate. The House of Assembly is elected by popular vote.

People

As in neighboring states, 87 percent of the inhabitants of St. Lucia are African, descendants of the slaves who were imported as plantation laborers in the 17th and 18th centuries. Almost 10 percent are mixed race; a few islanders are descended from indentured servants brought in from India and still others are of European origin. The rich mixture has produced a highly musical local patois, a combination of French, English and Spanish words utilizing a French and African grammatical structure. Although the language of tourism is English, most private conversations, jokes, street jibe and some court cases are conducted in patois. In most cases friendly and helpful, St. Lucians have retained a love of African and Caribbean rhythms—celebrated annually at Carnival, a calypso explosion held two days before Ash Wednesday. Every small town and village holds dances throughout the year, propelled by a little beer, rum, smoking weed, and music pumped out of speakers at ear-splitting volume. Friday night block parties in the village of

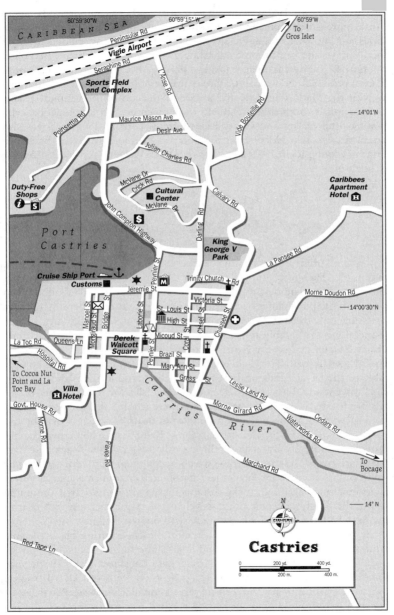

Castries

Gros Islet are especially welcoming to tourists; other neighborhoods can be a little more closed. Spurred by a less-than-ideal employment situation, some locals are known to be aggressive with visitors—offering guided tours or local wares—and can become aggravated when you refuse them. Be polite, but firm, and always ask before taking a photo. About 80 percent of the population profess to be Roman Catholics. Many of the older women continue to wear the Madras head-tie and a modern version of the panniered skirt. Occupation by both the British and the French has left a population celebrating both cricket and savory French creole cooking. St. Lucia has also given birth to two Nobel Laureates: Sir W. Arthur Lewis won the Nobel Prize in economics in 1979 and the poet Derek Walcott won the 1992 prize in literature.

St. Lucia's prime goal is to keep beaches open to the public, but as pristine as possible. Therefore, you will find only a few restrooms, changing facilities and snack bars. The best way to locate your beach is to hire a sailboat and scope out the possibilities from sea, many of them deserted because they are accessible only by boat. With a couple exceptions, all of the best beaches are found along the Caribbean coast—the first exception being relatively quiet **Cas En Bas**, located on the North tip of the island opposite Gros Islet at the end of a small road. The sheltered bay is ideal for windsurfing, and comparable to the Silver Sands on Barbados. Circling around the island counterclockwise, several busy strands surround Gros Islet, where a number of hotels are located—one wide beach heads west toward Pigeon Point and is popular with locals on weekends, and **Reduit Beach** is watched over by the Royal St. Lucian Hotel and other resorts. Reduit is usually crowded, but provides a variety of watersports through the resorts. **Choc Beach** and **Vigie Beach** are the closest to Castries, which keeps them humming, while just south of the city is **La Toc Bay**—a half-moon crescent which is fine for lunch and sunbathing, although tricky currents make swimming risky. Continuing south, the beaches become progressively more exotic, starting with charming **Anse La Raye**, a small village beach with limited facilities, but plenty of shady palm trees. **Anse Couchon** is a remote beach featuring black volcanic sand, calm waters for swimming and a romantic setting accessible only by boat. Against a backdrop of the Pitons, **Anse Chastanet** offers spectacular snorkeling and shore diving—the steep drop-off leads quickly to tropical fish, a variety of sponges and well-preserved coral life. **Anse des Pitons** lies in between the Pitons, a dramatic setting reached by boat or through the Jalousie Resort. At the southern tip of the island, immediately east of the Hewanorra Airport is **Anse de Sables**, or **Vieux Fort Beach**—you'll discover a lovely, undeveloped expanse facing the Atlantic and with miles of coconut palms.

Over the past several years, St. Lucia has emerged as one of the premier dive destinations in the Eastern Caribbean. The island has stunning, pristine reefs and vertigo-inducing walls, the latter best exemplified by a quick glance at St. Lucia's shoreside signature peaks, the Pitons, which plunge precipitously into the sea below. The resulting publicity in the dive community has created a popular product, similar to St. Lucia's neighboring attractions, Dominica and St. Vincent. Fortunately, diving was commercialized relatively recently on the island and the government has maintained a firm hand on the number of dive businesses it will license (and, therefore, limiting the number of dive visitors). The area surrounding the Pitons boasts many of the best dive sites, and is where the marine park is centered, but impressive dives are located along the entire length of the Caribbean side. A faint current runs along the coast, sometimes providing drift opportunities off Soufriére Bay, and visibility generally exceeds 75 feet. The coral is unusually clean on St. Lucia, with currents washing over shallower sites to give them an added sheen. Shore diving, among the best in the Eastern Caribbean, is available at Anse Chastanet Reef, immediately below the similarly-named hotel. It's a great place for experienced divers to start their St. Lucia adventure. A surprisingly diverse collection of unusual marine life can be found here: frogfish, sea horses, octopus, electric rays and much more. It's also an excellent night dive. Sea conditions allowing, most of the sites listed below are accessible to beginners.

St. Lucia is one of the largest of the islands dotting the Eastern Caribbean. It is also one of the most heavily populated, yet still contains extensive and marginally explored rain forest within the range of mountains which form a spine leading down the western side of the island. Mount Gimie (3118 feet) is St. Lucia's highest peak, but you'll need a guide to locate the trail lead to its summit. Peak-baggers can tackle two other points: Gros Piton, the larger of the spectacular spires rising above the town of Soufriére, and Piton Flore, a peak within easy reach of the north coast resorts. The excellent Ordnance Survey 1:50,000 topographical map of St. Lucia can be found at a few bookstores in Castries. Be forewarned, however, that the considerable network of enticing tracks displayed on the map frequently are found to be overgrown and/or impossible to follow. Paths are often muddy, particularly following rain, of which the island's interior receives an ample share. A guide is advised for the difficult ascent of Gros Piton and any other extensive explorations; the helpful staff of the Forest and Lands Department can provide trail and guide information ☎ *(758) 450-2231* or ☎ *(758) 450-2078.* Also, beware of the rare *fer de lance*, the poisonous snake that lurks in St. Lucia's back yard; bites are infrequent, but can be deadly (see "On Foot" introductory chapter). Finally, for those seeking a gentler stroll, the Union Nature Trail, offers a 45-minute gravel-paved loop through dry woodland forest; it is located in the hills beneath the community of Babonneau, east of Castries.

Hikers on St. Lucia have a choice of several beautiful, panoramic views.

St. Lucia offers extensive and challenging options for hard-core cyclists. The only problem is that the island's road network is a maze of switchbacks and indirect paths, with few obvious loop trips. An even bigger issue is hectic road traffic; the island's fledgling cycling organization nearly folded after a series of fatal biking accidents. As such, a bike rental firm has not established a footing on the island at this writing. By the time you read this, however, things may have changed.

The popular road from Castries south to Soufriére is the most appealing destination, but riders should be aware this is a serious all-day package involving major ascents along the winding coastal road; it's further than it looks and climbs to 1000 feet before reaching sea-level Canaries, then to over 1600 feet near Mount Tabac. An easier outing visits the gentler terrain north of Castries, skirting resorts, golf-courses and tony residential areas. One itinerary covering this region would head inland from Castries to Babonneau, then north to Monchy and Gros Islet, and return to Castries via the busy coastal route. This ride involves one moderate climb to about 1200 feet. But perhaps St. Lucia's nicest, most relaxed riding lies on the quieter eastern coast (which also is the area furthest removed from the tourism infrastructure). The ride from Dennery south to Vieux Fort stays below 400-foot elevation and visits less-trafficked areas, with numerous asphalt fingers climbing from the coast into the rainforest for impromptu exploration possibilities; the road from Castries to Vieux Fort (via Dennery) is about 38 miles.

What Else to See

A driving tour is the best way to see St. Lucia, but be forewarned—road conditions vary from adequate to miserable, and driving is on the left. One bit of good news: the road between **Castries** (where many of the hotels are) and **Soufriére** (where most of the scenic attractions are located) has finally been completed after a three-and-a-half year construction period. Otherwise, begin your tour in Castries, the island's densely populated capital, where the harbor is nestled within a long-extinct volcanic crater. The town was a classic West Indian port a few decades ago, but a series of fires, as well as contemporary commerce and population expansion has conspired to replace most of the old Victorian wooden architecture with buildings of glass, steel and concrete. The best opportunity to experience the old hustle-bustle is on Saturday mornings, when market takes over at the corner of Jeremie and Peynier streets, and local farmers and island artisans lay out their wares for serious barter. Stop by **Derek Walcott Square**, where a 400-year-old *samaan* tree shades the Cathedral of the Immaculate Conception, built in 1897; the late-Victorian-era **Government House** stands nearby. Above and south of the town is **Morne Fortune** and **Fort Charlotte**, where good views can be had encompassing Castries, the Pitons, and Martinique on a clear day; see if you can note the difference at the fort between the French architecture and British walls built at different stages of occupation. The area north of Castries is heavily developed for the tourist trade, and the village of **Gros Islet** comes wildly alive on Friday nights with a raging weekly street festival—the "jump-up" is noisy with *soca*, reggae and other beats of the Caribbean. The prominent peninsula just beyond Gros Ilet is **Pigeon Island**, connected by causeway to the coast and home to an 18th-century British naval garrison, a museum, and beaches for picnicking.

St. Lucia's dramatic countryside includes emerald hills, waterfalls, rain forest, volcanic mineral baths and pristine beaches.

A full day should be allotted to explore the west coast south of Castries. **Marigot Bay** is a lush and slender harbor that was where Rex Harrison talked to the animals in the 1967 film *Doctor Doolittle*, now inhabited by yachties and others who enjoy the secluded location. The tiny fishing villages of **Anse la Raye** and **Canaries** are also charming, though afternoons are the best time to visit when the colorful fishing boats come in with their daily catch. Soufriére lies at the foot of sheer **Petit Piton**, one of the most dramatic settings a village could wish for, though you'll struggle to fit the entire vision into your camera. The new marketplace at Soufriére is decorated with colorful murals and gingerbread trim; otherwise the shabby town, at one time the capital of the island until it was destroyed by a hurricane in 1780, retains a Third World aura. Stop by the **Morne Coubaril Estate** in Soufriére, a working cocoa plantation that offers a 90-minute guided tour. The road that winds up and behind the Pitons affords more great views, though you may want to pull in at the dormant and oversold **drive-in volcano** of nearby Mount Soufriére. It presents a face akin to a B-horror movie, complete with open pits of fuming sulfur and bubbling mud—guides are unnecessary but omnipresent. Also nearby is the **Diamond Mineral Baths**, constructed by order of Louis XVI when his doctors recommended the waters for French soldiers stationed in the area. At the southern tip of St. Lucia off Vieux Fort is the **Maria Islands Nature Reserve**, where a species of lizard and bird exist that are found nowhere else in the world.

BEST VIEW:

A startling panoramic view can be glimpsed from the Fort Charlotte fortress at the top of Morne Fortune, the same site used alternatively by French and British troops to defend the island. To the north is Pigeon Island, to the south the Pitons, and the entire scope of the capital's harbor and the Virgie Peninsula. While you're at the fort, notice the difference between the French architecture and the walls built by the British at different stages.

Historical Sites

Fort Charlotte   ★★★
Morne Fortune, Castries.
Set atop a hill 853 feet above sea level, this fortress was started by the French in 1764 and finished 20 years later by the British. Today it holds government and education offices, but it's worth a trip for the great views if nothing else. The grounds include a military cemetery that dates back to 1782 where French and British soldiers are buried as well as six former governors of the island.

Parks and Gardens

Maria Islands Nature Reserve   ★★★
Off Vieux Fort, Castries, ☎ *(758) 454-5014.*
Hours open: 9:30 a.m.–5 p.m.
This reserve consists of two small islands in the Atlantic—one 25 acres, the other just four. It is home to a thriving population of birds and rare snakes and lizards. Great snorkeling off the larger island, Maria Major.

Pigeon Island National Park   ★★★★
Pigeon Point, Castries, ☎ *(758) 452-5005.*
Hours open: 9 a.m.–4 p.m.
This 40-acre island is connected to the mainland by a causeway. It has a long history and was used for all sorts of things before becoming a national park—pirates hid out here in the 1600s, the French and British militaries used it as a fort, and long before any of them, the Arawak Indians lived here. Ruins from some of these days still exist on the island, but this is primarily a place to picnic and hang out on its picturesque beaches. There's also an interpretive center. General admission: $1.

Tours

Diamond Falls and Mineral Bath   ★★★★
Soufriére Estate, Soufriére.

Hours open: 10 a.m.–5 p.m.

The water in these sulfuric mineral baths average a toasty 106 defrees Fahrenheit. Louis XVI ordered them built in 1784 so French soldiers stationed in the area could soak the supposedly curative waters. Bring your suit so you, too, can "take the waters." General admission: $3.

La Soufriére   ★★★

Soufriére.

Hours open: 9 a.m.–5 p.m.

Called the world's only drive-in volcano, this spot encompasses a seven-acre crater complete with pool of boiling mud and sulfurous waters.

The Pitons   ★★★★

Soufriére.

These dramatic twin cones are St. Lucia's most identifying landmark. Formed by a prehistoric volcano eruption, Petit Piton rises to 2619 ft., Gros Piton (the fatter of the two) to 2461 ft. Most folks just admire them from the land or sea, but the truly hardy can climb through their lush foliage to the top. You'll need a permit from the Forestry Division ☎ *(758) 452-3231)*, and it's best to hire a guide for the very strenuous hike.

Watersports are available at most hotels, with **windsurfing**, **waterskiing**, **sailing** and other activities usually available. Strong windsurfers head for two spots: Anse de Sables, the bay on the southeastern tip of the island between the Hewanorra Airport and Maria Islands; or Cas en Bas, a cove on the northern tip of the island, also facing the Atlantic. Conditions for windsurfing are fine along the western coast, and particularly suitable for beginners, but more advanced windsurfers like the rougher, choppier waters of the Atlantic coast. **Tennis courts** are available at many of the island's larger resorts, and **golfers** can enjoy two moderate nine-hole courses. Half- and full-day **fishing** charters are available and can be arranged through hotels or resorts, or at the marinas at Rodney Bay and Castries. The main fishing season runs from January to June, reeling in tuna, kingfish and dolphin; the rest of the year the catch is closer to shore. St. Lucians depend on fishing for their livelihood, and you can join fishermen to use lines and pots to catch snapper, lobster and reef fish. Yachtsmen and day-trippers from Castries tend to congregate in Soufriére, beneath the wonderful Pitons. The region's major charter operator is **The Moorings**, which offers day cruises for four to six passengers with lunch and drinks—bareboat or with crew. Other day cruise operators can be found at Rodney Bay, with Stevens Yachts one of the most foremost names in the region. Horseback riding through the forest is also available.

Golf

Two locations, Castries.
The choices for duffers are limited to two, nine-hole courses. Cap Estate Golf Club ☎ *(758) 452-8523* is open to the public while the course at Sandals St. Lucia ☎ *(758) 452-3081* is only available when not fully booked by guests at the island's two Sandals resorts.

Horseback Riding

Various locations, Castries.
At least two stables await the horseman (and woman): North Point ☎ *(758) 450-8853* and Trim's ☎ *(758) 452-8273*.

Watersports

Various locations, Castries.
If your hotel doesn't offer the watersports you're seeking try one of these. Deep-sea fishing: **Mako Watersports** ☎ *(758) 452-0412* and **Captain Mike's** ☎ *(758) 452-7044*. **Mistral Windsurfing** ☎ *(758) 452-8351* specializes in board rentals and instruction. For cruises and snorkel expeditions, call **Captain Mike's** ☎ *(758) 452-0216*, **Surf Queen** ☎ *(758) 452-8351*, **Brig Unicorn** ☎ *(758) 452-6811*, and **Cat Inc.** ☎ *(758) 450-7044*. Finally, **St. Lucian Watersports** ☎ *(758) 452-8351* offers waterskiing and parasailing in addition to general equipment rentals.

Where to Stay

Fielding's Highest Rated Hotels in St. Lucia

★★★★★	LeSport	$300–$670
★★★★	Anse Chastanet Hotel	$95–$505
★★★★	Jalousie Plantation	$345–$655
★★★★	Royal St. Lucian	$310–$600
★★★★	Sandals St. Lucia	$3250–$7050 weekly
★★★★	Windjammer Landing	$150–$590
★★★	Club St. Lucia	$100–$310
★★★	Doolittle's Resort	$65–$95
★★★	Ladera Resort	$195–$650
★★★	Marigot Bay Resort	$55–$135

Fielding's Most Exclusive Hotels in St. Lucia

★★★★	Jalousie Plantation	$345–$655
★★★	East Winds Inn	$300–$625
★★★	Ladera Resort	$195–$650
★★★★	Windjammer Landing	$150–$590
★★★	Rendezvous	$380–$510

Fielding's Best Value Hotels in St. Lucia

★★★	Doolittle's Resort	$65–$95
★★★	Marigot Bay Resort	$55–$135
★★	Orange Grove Hotel	$45–$83
★★	Tapion Reef Hotel	$50–$80
★★	Auberge Seraphine	$45–$95

St. Lucia offers a full range of lodging possibilities, from all-inclusive resorts to luxurious five-star hotels to intimate inns surrounded by greenery and talcum-soft beaches; there are also numerous self-catering options in villas and apartments. Many properties offer the optional Modified American Plan (MAP), which includes breakfast and dinner. In most circumstances, you will receive a 10 percent service charge on the hotel bill, plus an eight percent government tax. Families tend to do best at the all-inclusive resorts since everything is usually right out your door and you don't have to run around finding an activity to please everybody (though neither Rendezvous nor Sandals allow kids). Note that most properties are located north of Castries, while the larger planes can only fly into Hewanorra, on the island's southern tip.

Hotels and Resorts

Sandals, the chain of all-inclusive Caribbean resorts, has two locations on the island. The original location is the most expensive of the 10 Sandals properties, with seven-night rates starting at $3720 per couple in winter; Sandals Halcyon opened in 1994 on the site of the former Halcyon Beach Club at Choc Bay, with breathtaking views from its restaurant, The Pier House, which extends out over the water. It's been said that if you stay at Ladera, which looks across (rather than up) to the Pitons, you won't want to go anywhere else, so fabulous is the setting—but then Anse Chastenet has its own special view of the Pitons, with breathtaking snorkeling and diving on the beach below as well. Special spa facilities characterize Le Sport, where the beach, tennis courts, golf course and accommodations are only steps from each other.

Anse Chastanet Hotel   **$95–$505**   ★ ★ ★ ★

Anse Chastanet Beach, Castries, ☎ *(800) 223-1108, (758) 459-7000.*
FAX (758) 459-7700.
Single: $95–$355. Double: $135–$505.
Situated on a 500-acre hillside beachfront plantation, this unique resort is located on the southwest coast, north of Soufriére. The grounds are wonderfully lush and steeply lead down to a black-sand beach. Accommodations are found on the hillside or on the beach. Guestrooms are large, individually decorated, and quite posh. The facilities include an excellent dive center (lots of scuba enthusiasts stay here), two good restaurants, two bars, and a tennis court. No pool or air conditioning, but no one's complaining. Best suited to the fit, as there are steep stairs everywhere. 48 rooms. Credit cards: A, D, MC, V.

Candyo Inn   **$75–$90**   ★ ★

Rodney Bay, Castries, ☎ *(758) 452-0712.*
Single: $75–$90. Double: $75–$90.
You can walk to the beach in five minutes from this small hotel. The four guestrooms are standard and well-kept, with modern amenities like phones, TV, and clock radios. The eight apartments have kitchens and more room to spread out; all accommodations are air-conditioned. Facilities are limited to a snack bar, mini-market and pool. There are many restaurants within walking distance, and this small operation is a good deal. 12 rooms. Credit cards: A, MC.

Club Med St. Lucia   **$520–$1300**   ★ ★ ★

Vieux Fort, Castries, ☎ (800) 258-2633, (758) 454-6546. FAX (758) 454-6017.
This Club Med is set on 95 acres at Savannes Bay, on the southeast coast—a fairly remote region, so you'll have to depend on organized tours (or rent a car) to see the island. Many of the guests here are families with children; this is not a swinging singles Club Med. Accommodations are small, with air conditioning, twin beds and balconies. As with all Club Meds, there's always tons going on, and lots of activities for the youngsters, including an intensive English riding program for kids eight and above (which, like scuba and island tours, costs extra). The recreational options include tennis on eight courts, circus workshops, all watersports, a fitness center, exercise classes, archery, rollerblading, and on and on and on. Great for families; singles may want to look elsewhere. Rates are $800 to $1300 per week per adult, and $520 to $845 per week per children 2–11. Occasionally small children (ages 2–5) can stay free; ask for details. Club Med also charges $30 for a one-time initiation fee per family and $50 per person annual dues. 265 rooms. Credit cards: A, MC.

Club St. Lucia   **$100–$310**   ★ ★ ★

Anse du Cap, Castries, ☎ (800) 777-1250, (758) 450-0551. FAX (758) 450-0281.
Single: $100–$155. Double: $200–$310.
This all-inclusive resort appeals to romantics—the hotel even offers two wedding chapels for those who get so carried away they decide to tie the knot. Guestrooms and suites are large and nicely done. Most, but not all, are air-conditioned (those without rely on ceiling fans). There are three pools, a fitness center, two restaurants, a disco, nightly entertainment, and supervised children's programs year-round; rates include access to a private tennis club with nine courts and pro lessons. Watersports await on two beaches. The rates include all activities, meals and drinks. A good deal for the price. Amenities: tennis, family plan. 312 rooms. Credit cards: A, CB, D, MC, V.

Doolittle's Resort   **$65–$95**   ★ ★ ★

Marigot Bay, Castries, ☎ (800) 322-3577, (758) 451-4974. FAX (758) 452-0802.
Single: $65–$80. Double: $80–$95.
This new hotel is perched on a verdant hillside above Marigot Bay and is accessible only by a short ride on a gingerbread-trimmed ferry. Accommodations are found in pleasant, inn-like rooms with cathedral ceilings, ceiling fans, small kitchenettes and large, screened porches. Further up the hill are 10 one- and two-bedroom villas with screened, open-air living areas and kitchens; these require a three-night minimum stay. The constant trade winds ensure you won't mind the lack of air conditioners. The hotel caters mainly to divers, with an on-site PADI shop as well as a variety of complimentary watersports, boutiques, a pool and a good bar and restaurant. Diving packages cost $975 per person per week and include accommodations, breakfast and dinner, transfers and unlimited boat dives. 22 rooms. Credit cards: A, MC, V.

Green Parrot Inn   **$70–$110**   ★

Morne Fortune, Castries, ☎ (800) 278-5824, (758) 452-3399. FAX (758) 453-2272.
Single: $70–$90. Double: $90–$110.
Located on a mountainside with nice views of Castries and the sea, this inn houses one of St. Lucia's best gourmet restaurants. Guestrooms are air-conditioned and have balconies, but won't win any prizes for decor or ambience. There's a large pool

on the premises but no other facilities. You'll want a car to get around. Okay for the rates, but you're probably better off just eating here (that's a delight) than staying overnight. 55 rooms. Credit cards: A, MC, V.

Hummingbird Beach Resort $80–$165 ★★

Soufriére, Castries, ☎ (758) 459-7232. FAX (758) 459-7033.
Single: $80–$125. Double: $105–$165.

This small resort is private and secluded. Guestrooms have ceiling fans (no air), mosquito netting over the beds, and balconies. The grounds are very nicely landscaped and open onto a public black-sand beach. Facilities are limited to a fine restaurant and a pool. Decent for the rates, and don't miss the giftshop, which has a lovely array of batik articles created by the owner. 10 rooms. Credit cards: A, D, MC.

Islander Hotel $80–$130 ★★

Rodney Bay, Castries, ☎ (800) 278-5824, (758) 452-8757. FAX (758) 452-0958.
Single: $80–$120. Double: $90–$130.

Guests at this resort can choose from standard rooms (nicely done and very comfortable) and one-bedroom apartments with fully equipped kitchens. All are air-conditioned and benefit from maid service. Amenities include a restaurant, terrace bar and pool. The beach is a 10-minute walk away, and there are lots of nearby eateries. Quite a bargain. 60 rooms. Credit cards: A, D, MC, V.

Jalousie Plantation $345–$655 ★★★★

Soufriére, Castries, ☎ (800) 392-2007, (758) 459-7666. FAX (758) 459-7667.
Single: $345–$655. Double: $485–$655.

Environmentalists with a conscience probably wouldn't consider staying at this all-inclusive resort, as it was developed in a pristine area that many believe should have been left alone. The setting is gorgeous, perched on a hillside between the Pitons on beautifully landscaped grounds. Most accommodations are in one- and two-bedroom cottages with air conditioning, refrigerators, cable TV, verandas and plunge pools. Twelve suites are housed in a former sugar mill. The extensive facilities include many dining options, four tennis courts, a spa, and private beach. The Hilton chain was rumored to be taking Jalousie over in late 1996; rates and amenities will undoubtedly change. 115 rooms. Credit cards: A, MC.

Ladera Resort $195–$650 ★★★

Soufriére, Castries, ☎ (800) 841-4145, (758) 459-7323. FAX (758) 459-5156.
Single: $195–$650. Double: $195–$650.

Set on a lush hillside 1000 feet above sea level, this romantic resort offers great views of the Pitons and beyond. Accommodations are in six, three-story, three-bedroom villas and 13 suites, all quite luxurious with four-poster beds and antique furnishings. The best feature in each is the completely open wall that affords breathtaking views, yet still provides complete privacy. Some units also have private plunge pools or Jacuzzis. The food in the restaurant is about as fine as the views; a bar and smallish communal pool round out the limited facilities. This unique spot for lovers is very unique and popular with those in search of true peace and seclusion. 19 rooms. Credit cards: A, MC, V.

Le Sport   **$300–$670**   ★★★★★

Cap Estate, Castries, ☎ *(800) 544-2883, (758) 450-8551. FAX (758) 450-0368.*
Single: $300–$410. Double: $450–$670.

Prepare to be pampered, spoiled and primped at this all-inclusive resort situated at
St. Lucia's secluded northwestern tip and encompassing some 1500 acres. The
resort's health spa, called the Oasis, is a lavish Moorish-themed facility with exercise
classes, yoga and t'ai chi programs, and wonderful treatments such as massages,
facials and body wraps. Guestrooms are as plush as everything else; there's also a
three-bedroom plantation house with private staff that goes for $850–920 for two.
Meals are wonderfully prepared, with lots of delicious dishes that are also low on
calories and—could it be true?—good for you. Tennis, watersports, nightly entertainment and bicycles; you can even obtain full PADI certification as part of your
stay. Indulge! Amenities: tennis, health club, exercise room, Jacuzzi. 102 rooms.
Credit cards: A, MC, V.

Rendezvous   **$380–$510**   ★★★

Malabar Beach, Castries, ☎ *(800) 544-2883, (758) 452-4211. FAX (758) 452-7419.*
Double: $380–$510.

Formerly known as Couples, this all-inclusive is now managed by SunSwept (the
company also operates Le Sport), though it's still open only to two-somes. Encompassing seven acres with two miles of beachfront in Castries, it houses guests in garden or oceanfront rooms in one- to three-story buildings—all feature air
conditioning, modern amenities, and balconies or patios. The rates include all
meals, drinks, and activities, and there's plenty to do: two pools, two tennis courts,
all watersports, and exercise classes in the gym. A newly instituted policy works weddings into the rate. There's daily entertainment in the Terrace Bar, and night owls
appreciate the Piano Bar, which stays open until the last guest leaves. Tipping is not
allowed. Amenities: tennis, Jacuzzi. 100 rooms. Credit cards: A, MC, V.

Rex St. Lucian Hotel   **$140–$192**   ★★★

Reduit Beach, Castries, ☎ *(800) 255-5859, (758) 452-8351. FAX (758) 452-8331.*
Single: $140–$192. Double: $140–$192.

Set on one of the island's best beaches, this sprawling Rex resort houses guests in
typical rooms that are air-conditioned and comfortable enough, but which were a
bit on the worn side—a late 1996 renovation should spruce things up. The grounds
include a restaurants, two bars, a pool, two tennis courts, and all watersports,
including a certified windsurfing school. Not the most luxurious resort on St. Lucia
by any means, but the rates are reasonable, and the active set is kept happy. Until
recently a 260-room property, 140 rooms have been split off to form the Rex Papil-
lion all-inclusive resort, opening December 1996. Amenities: tennis. 120 rooms.
Credit cards: A, CB, DC, MC, V.

Royal St. Lucian   **$310–$600**   ★★★★

Reduit Beach, Castries, ☎ *(800) 255-5859, (758) 452-9999. FAX (758) 452-9639.*
Single: $310–$600. Double: $310–$600.

Located north of Castries on the beach at Gros Islet, this all-suite resort is long on
modern conveniences, short on lived-in personality. The standard rooms are quite
luxurious, with air-conditioning, minibar, bathrobes, and expansive, marble-tiled

bathrooms. Beachfront suites have large sundecks that face the sea. The hotel's centerpiece is the tropical pool, a series of interconnected waterholes complete with swim-up bar. Two restaurants are available, and guests can spend hours whiling away the time in the gorgeous, marbled atrium lobby. Tennis and watersports await at the adjacent Rex St. Lucian, the hotel's sister property. Very elegant. Amenities: tennis, business services. 96 rooms. Credit cards: A, CB, DC, MC, V.

Sandals Halcyon $3280–$4330 ★★★

Choc Bay, Castries, ☎ *(800) 726-3257, (758) 452-5331. FAX (758) 452-5434.*
This all-inclusive resort joined the Sandals family in 1994 after a previous incarnation as the Halcyon Beach Club Hotel. Open only to opposite-sex couples, the resort is set on a nice beach four miles north of Castries. The rates cover everything from soup to nuts, with three restaurants and seven bars—theme nights, like the weekly toga party, are a big part of the scene. Recreational facilities include two tennis courts, two pools, watersports, plenty of organized tours and activities, and nine holes of golf at Sandals St. Lucia (Halcyon guests may use all the facilities at the sister property). One week rates range from $3280 to $4330 per couple; three nights is the minimum stay. Amenities: exercise room, Jacuzzi, balcony or patio. 170 rooms. Credit cards: A, MC, V.

Sandals St. Lucia $3250–$7050 ★★★★

La Toc, Castries, ☎ *(800) 726-3257, (758) 452-3081. FAX (758) 452-1012.*
This 155-are resort is set in an idyllic cove just outside Port Castries. Open only to heterosexual couples, it follows the bullet-proof all-inclusive plan that has made Sandals' Jamaica resorts so successful. Guests are housed in standard rooms done with four-poster beds and modern amenities; there are also several categories of suites with living rooms, VCRs, refrigerators, and terraces—some even have private plunge pools. Facilities include three pools (one reportedly the largest in the Caribbean), five restaurants, karaoke bar, a disco and theme nights. The rates include virtually everything, including tennis on five courts, nine holes of golf, watersports, fitness classes, and lots of activities. One week rates range from $3520 to $7050 per couple; three nights is the minimum stay. Amenities: tennis, health club, exercise room, Jacuzzi, balcony or patio. 273 rooms. Credit cards: A, MC, V.

Wyndham Morgan Bay Resort $265–$500 ★★★

Gros Islet, Castries, ☎ *(800) 822-4200, (758) 450-2511. FAX (758) 450-1050.*
Single: $265–$335. Double: $360–$500.
This all-inclusive resort is located a mile from Castries on a small beach. Guestrooms and suites are modern and attractive, with all the creature comforts associated with Wyndham. The rates include all meals, drinks and activities, and there's plenty to keep guests busy: four tennis courts, a fitness center, watersports (scuba and fishing cost extra), and nightly entertainment. Children are kept occupied in organized programs. Amenities: tennis. 238 rooms. Credit cards: A, D, MC, V.

Apartments and Condominiums

You can rent either luxurious villas, or more basic digs that come with a kitchen. Decide on whether you want to be close to the tourist hub or away from it all; an apartment in rustic Soufriére will be more secluded than a number of other options. Fruits and vegetables can be picked up at the local market, and fish can be bought right off the boats.

Harmony Suites — $75–$115 ★★

Rodney Bay, Castries, ☎ (800) 278-5824, (758) 452-0336. FAX (758) 452-8677.
Single: $75–$115. Double: $75–$115.

This all-suite hotel is set on Rodney Bay, some 200 yards from Reduit Beach. Standard suites are air-conditioned and include coffeemakers and minifridge; some also have kitchenettes. Deluxe units have four-poster beds, Jacuzzis and a private sundeck. All are serviced by maids. Amenities include a pool, mini-market, restaurant and a body therapy studio with massage and body wraps. A good value and popular with families. Amenities: health club, balcony or patio. 30 rooms. Credit cards: A, D, MC, V.

Marigot Bay Resort — $55–$135 ★★★

Marigot Bay, Castries, ☎ (800) 334-2435, (758) 451-4357. FAX (758) 451-4353.
Single: $55–$100. Double: $85–$135.

Located seven miles from Castries, this resort owned by the Moorings charter yacht company encompasses a group of cottages located at a picturesque harbor. Its marina attracts the yachting set, and the property is split in two by the lovely bay; water taxis provide transportation back and forth. Guests are put up in an inn, villas, and pretty cottages, all with nice decor and full kitchens. The grounds include a restaurant and bar, a pool, and extensive watersports—this place is home to both a windsurfing school and a dive shop. You'll need a car to get around, as it's isolated here. 16 rooms. Credit cards: A, MC, V.

Tapion Reef Hotel — $50–$80 ★★

Tapion Bay, Castries, ☎ (758) 452-7471. FAX (758) 452-7552.
Single: $50–$60. Double: $60–$80.

This cliffside hotel attracts business travelers and those carefully watching their budget. Guestrooms have twin beds, small baths, air conditioning, and kitchenettes. Facilities are limited to a restaurant, bar, pool, and TV room. You can get TV in your room for an extra $5 per night. The beach is within walking distance. Not bad for the rates. 30 rooms. Credit cards: A, MC.

Windjammer Landing — $150–$590 ★★★★

Labrelotte Bay, Castries, ☎ (800) 958-7376, (758) 452-0913. FAX (758) 452-9454.
Single: $150–$395. Double: $150–$590.

Set on 55 landscaped acres on a hillside overlooking a white sand beach, this luxurious enclave consists of Mediterranean-style villas with one to four bedrooms. All are spacious and beautifully done, with living and dining rooms, kitchenettes, air conditioners in the bedrooms, and all the modern conveniences. Two- to four-bedroom villas each have a private plunge pool. This resort combines the best of self-sufficient housing (including an on-site mini-mart) with all the pampering of a resort, including nightly turndown, four bars and restaurants, four swimming pools, two tennis courts, a fitness center, and watersports on the recently expanded beach. Parents can stash their kids in the daily supervised programs, available year-round.

A wonderful spot that, while not cheap, provides great value for the money. Amenities: tennis, business services. 131 rooms. Credit cards: A, DC, MC, V.

Inns

Staying at a smaller property affords a chance for interaction with islanders in more congenial surroundings, often well off the beaten track. **Inns of St. Lucia** is an umbrella organization that covers more than two dozen smaller properties on the island; they provide a portfolio of brochures on the inns—which range from 3 rooms to 62—through the **St. Lucia Tourist Board** ☎ *(800) 456-3984* or call the organization directly ☎ *(758) 452-4599.*

East Winds Inn $300–$625   ★★★

La Brelotte Bay, Castries, ☎ *(800) 223-9832, (758) 452-8212. FAX (758) 452-9941. Single: $300–$525. Double: $400–$625.*

This small, all-inclusive resort accommodates guests in cottages in a lush garden next to a beach. Each unit has a king-size bed and living area with a stocked mini-fridge and coffeemaker on the patio; rooms rely on ceiling fans to keep things cool. You'll find a beach bar and excellent dining room in a thatched hut, a library and pool, with kayaking and snorkeling off the beach. Stays of three nights or more earn a meal voucher for a local restaurant. Amenities: secluded garden atmosphere, balcony or patio. 26 rooms. Credit cards: MC, V.

Low Cost Lodging

There are a few budget options available on St. Lucia, some of which are covered in the portfolio created by the Inns of St. Lucia (see "Inns" above). Expect little in the way of location, air conditioning or decor at budget guest houses.

Auberge Seraphine $45–$95   ★★

Vigie Cove, Castries, ☎ *(758) 453-2073. FAX (758) 451-7001. Single: $45–$80. Double: $55–$95.*

A new Georgian-style hotel, the Auberge Seraphine overlooks the Vigie Yacht Marina, just outside Castries. Units are basic, but clean and equipped with direct-dial phones and cable TV—most have nice views of the marina and cove, some have a sundeck. A pool, giftshop and restaurant are located on-site, and a shuttle is provided for the beach. 22 rooms. Credit cards: MC, V.

Caribbees Hotel $60–$90   ★★

La Pansee, Castries, ☎ *(800) 278-5824, (758) 452-4767. FAX (758) 453-1999. Single: $60–$90. Double: $60–$90.*

This recently expanded Castries hotel offers reasonable rates for those who don't mind sacrificing a beach—the hillside location overlooks the capital. Guestrooms are air-conditioned and simple, with phones, TVs, and patios or balconies. A bar, restaurant and pool are located on the premises, but not much else. You'll want a car for mobility, though the hotel provides a daily shuttle to the beach. Amenities: Jacuzzi, balcony or patio. 57 rooms. Credit cards: A, MC, V.

Orange Grove Hotel $45–$83   ★★

Gros Islet, Castries, ☎ *(800) 777-1250, (758) 452-9040. FAX (758) 452-8094. Single: $45–$70. Double: $55–$83.*

ST. LUCIA

A recently renovated hotel near Rodney Bay, the Orange Grove is one of the island's better values, housing guests in an orange-trimmed 19th-century French colonial plantation house. Room furnishings are simple but fresh—rattan furniture, tile floors and king-size beds in all units. The hilltop location has nice views and the hotel provides a daily shuttle to the beach. 62 rooms. Credit cards: MC, V.

Where to Eat

Fielding's Highest Rated Restaurants in St. Lucia

★★★★	Dasheene Restaurant	$19–$38
★★★★	Jimmie's	$14–$25
★★★	Capones	$11–$24
★★★	Charthouse	$12–$36
★★★	Chez Paul and the Rain Bar	$10–$21
★★★	Green Parrot	$34–$34
★★★	Hummingbird	$17–$37
★★★	Key Largo	$6–$17
★★★	Piton	$35–$35
★★★	San Antoine	$15–$28

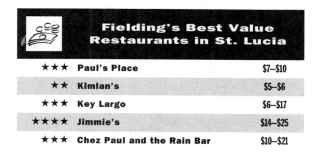

Fielding's Most Exclusive Restaurants in St. Lucia

★★★	Green Parrot	$34–$34
★★★	Piton	$35–$35
★★★★	Dasheene Restaurant	$19–$38
★★★	San Antoine	$15–$28
★★★	Charthouse	$12–$36

Fielding's Best Value Restaurants in St. Lucia

★★★	Paul's Place	$7–$10
★★	Kimlan's	$5–$6
★★★	Key Largo	$6–$17
★★★★	Jimmie's	$14–$25
★★★	Chez Paul and the Rain Bar	$10–$21

In the last decade, excellent international cuisine has appeared on St. Lucia. The fertile volcanic soil supports a cornucopia of exotic fruits and vegetables; the six types of local bananas are particularly delicious. Island chefs make inventive use of papayas, soursops, mangoes, passionfruit and coconuts. Most restaurants try to take advantage of the island's unparalleled natural beauty, so stellar views are almost commonplace. One of the most atmospheric eateries is **San Antoine**, perched in the hills overlooking Castries, which incorporates the walls of a 19th-century greathouse, with antique tableware to match. Try the delicious swordfish at **Jammer's** at Windjammer's Landing, with pole beams, table linens and bridal-white cane furniture. **Naked Virgin** in Castries is a good bet for traditional West Indian and Creole specialties such as callaloo, curry and pepper-pot stew. Excellent jerk chicken, and green fig and saltfish (a local specialty), can be had at **Jimmie's**.

A-Pub $$$ ★★

The Waterfront, Castries, ☎ *(758) 452-8725.*
International cuisine.
Lunch: entrées $15–$30.
Dinner: entrées $15–$30. Closed: Sun.

A convivial yachtie hangout and local watering hole fronting Rodney Bay, the A-Pub serves up terrific, hand-picked steaks, fish and chips, West Indian specialties, and a few international dishes. Join the crowd for a friendly happy hour each evening. Credit cards: A, MC, V.

Bistro, The $$$ ★★★

Waterfront, Castries, ☎ *(758) 452-9494.*
Seafood cuisine.
Dinner: 5–10:30 p.m., entrées $7–$24.

The British owners provide pub offerings such as steak and kidney and shepherd's pie along with a varied, extensive seafood menu, West Indian pepper-pot and pasta. Dining is on a wide, elevated deck perched on the waterfront. Nautical types and others like the 20 percent discount on food items before 6:30 p.m., sort of a Caribbean early-bird special. Closed Thursdays in summer. Reservations recommended. Credit cards: A, MC, V.

Capone's $$$ ★★★

Reduit Beach, Castries, ☎ *(758) 452-0284.*
Italian cuisine.
Lunch: 11:30 a.m.–4:30 p.m., entrées $11–$24.
Dinner: 4:30–10:30 p.m., entrées $11–$24. Closed: Mon.

Patrons are served by waitpersons dressed like 1930s mobsters who present the dinner check in a violin case. But it's all a lot of fun, and the Italian food is skillfully prepared. Dishes include fresh pasta, grilled fish, osso bucco, and juicy steaks. If the atmosphere is too heavy in the main dining room, there's a pizza parlor adjacent serving decent pies, burgers and sandwiches. Reservations recommended. Credit cards: A, MC, V.

Charthouse   **$$$**   ★★★

Reduit Beach, Castries, ☎ *(758) 452-8115.*
American cuisine.
Dinner: 6–10:30 p.m., entrées $12–$36. Closed: Sun.

The most popular dining room on the island could be this all-American chain steakhouse overlooking the yacht harbor. Guests like the attentive service by a loyal staff (very little turnover here) and the food, which is steak, lobster (in season), tangy baby back ribs, and some Caribbean specialties, all familiar and well-prepared. The restaurant is a fern-filled wood-frame house that exudes warmth. Reservations recommended. Credit cards: A, MC, V.

Chez Paul and the Rain Bar   **$$$**   ★★★

Derek Walcott Square, Castries, ☎ *(758) 451-3111.*
International cuisine.
Lunch: 9 a.m.–5 p.m., entrées $8–$10.
Dinner: 5–11 p.m., entrées $10–$21.

Chez Paul retains the romance, charm and Somerset Maugham decor of Rain, the restaurant that originally held court on this spot. The drinks are still heady and rum-based, but the food, which was never the real attraction, is now a more sophisticated melding of European, Asian and Caribbean influences. The restaurant is open for lighter meals all day long, with a dinner menu offering traditional Caribbean pepperpot, and a rich medley of prawns, shrimp and scallops in a spicy amaretto sauce. The elegant and gingerbread-fringed, tin-roofed house overlooks Derek Walcott Square, which is named after St. Lucia's distinguished Nobel Prize winner. Reservations recommended. Credit cards: A, MC, V.

Dasheene Restaurant   **$$$**   ★★★★

Ladera Resort, Castries, ☎ *(758) 459-7850. Associated hotel: Ladera Resort.*
International cuisine.
Lunch: 11:30 a.m.–2:30 p.m., entrées $11–$17.
Dinner: 6:30–9:30 p.m., entrées $19–$38.

The view from this hilltop aerie is unbeatable, nestled between the Pitons just outside Soufriére, an old French fishing community known for its sulphur springs. Located in a rustically chic villa resort, Dasheene is named after an exotic leaf used in cooking, and the menu, which changes often, incorporates locally grown produce, prime meats and seafood—all under the auspices of new chef Robert Skeete. Fish and shellfish are delivered to the restaurant daily, and the desserts are renowned. A great lunch spot for those making the trip from the Castries area to Soufriére. Reservations recommended. Credit cards: A, D, MC, V.

Eagle's Inn   **$**   ★★

Reduit Beach Road, Castries, ☎ *(758) 452-0650.*
Latin American cuisine.
Lunch: entrées $8–$10.
Dinner: entrées $8–$10. Closed: Fri., Sat.

This small, funky spot, which is one of a friendly string of similar joints in Reduit Beach, serves French-inspired West Indian food. The atmosphere is low-key and romantic, with an eagle-eye view of Gros Ilet in the distance. A good place for curry and fish dishes. Credit cards: A, MC, V.

Ginger Lily $$$ ★★

Reduit Beach, Castries, ☎ *(758) 452-8303.*
Chinese cuisine.
Lunch: 11:30 a.m.–2:30 p.m., entrées $6–$30.
Dinner: 6:30–11:30 p.m., entrées $6–$30.

Cantonese specialties are on hand at this popular restaurant near the tourist hotels in Reduit Beach. There's always a long list of familiar favorites, which pleases residents who flock here often. Combination dinners run $30 per person, and lunch specials are also available, with several courses for under $8. Lunch is served Tuesday–Saturday only. Credit cards: MC, V.

Green Parrot $$$ ★★★

Red Tape Lane, Castries, ☎ *(758) 452-3399. Associated hotel: Green Parrot.*
International cuisine.
Lunch: Noon–3 p.m., entrées $14–$30.
Dinner: 7 p.m.–midnight, prix fixe $34.

Chef Harry brought his years of culinary expertise learned at Claridge's in London home to St. Lucia, and now cooks and entertains nightly at this lively spot on a hilltop in Morne Fortune, overlooking Castries. His spiced pumpkin creation, "soup oh la la" will make you say just that when you taste it. Dinner offerings include curries, fish, and a steak called "stuffed pussy." Renowned for a scrumptious lunch buffet, Green Parrot is also a wild scene on Wednesday and Saturday nights when belly or limbo dancers (including Harry) reign. On Mondays, women with a flower in their hair dine free when accompanied by gents in jacket and tie. There's also a well-chosen wine list. Reservations recommended. Credit cards: A, MC, V.

Hummingbird $$$ ★★★

Anse Chastenet Road, Soufriére, ☎ *(758) 459-7232.*
Associated hotel: Hummingbird Resort.
French cuisine.
Lunch: 10 a.m.–4 p.m., entrées $7–$21.
Dinner: 7–10 p.m., entrées $17–$37.

Combine lunch with a plunge in the pool at this restaurant located in a rustic resort on the Soufriére waterfront with lush views of Petit Piton. Visitors flock here when the house specialty, freshwater mountain crayfish, is in season. At other times, enjoy tasty seafood dishes including offbeat choices such as whelks and octopus, along with steaks, sandwiches and rich desserts. Credit cards: A, D, MC, V.

Jimmie's $$$ ★★★★

Vigie Marina, Castries, ☎ *(758) 452-5142.*
Latin American cuisine.
Lunch: 11 a.m.–4 p.m., entrées $14–$25.
Dinner: 4–11 p.m., entrées $14–$25.

Jimmie's bar has long been known as the place to meet and greet, but the cuisine, authentic West Indian specialties prepared by a local chef who trained in fine restaurants in England, is also worth noting. Jimmie James cooks with a light touch—his crepes stuffed with vegetables and seafood are sublime—saltfish and green fig (bananas) is a respected tradition, and the Saturday night special of *bouyon* (a robust pork, chicken and bean stew), draws the locals, always a good sign. Open Sundays for dinner only, from 6 p.m. Credit cards: A, MC, V.

Key Largo $$ ★★★

The Marina, Castries, ☎ *(758) 452-0282.*
Italian cuisine.
Lunch: 11:30 a.m.–4 p.m., entrées $6–$17.
Dinner: 4–10 p.m., entrées $6–$17. Closed: Mon.
Sophisticated California-style pizzas on a patio are served at this small restaurant with its own outdoor brick oven. Try the house specialty, a pizza made with artichokes and shrimp, or make do with one of several tasty salads. All manner of Italian coffee drinks are dispensed here as well. Credit cards: MC, V.

Kimlan's $ ★★

Micoud Street, Castries, ☎ *(758) 452-1136.*
Latin American cuisine.
Lunch: 7 a.m.–4 p.m., entrées $5–$6.
Dinner: 4–11 p.m., entrées $5–$6. Closed: Sun.
A local family runs this upper-level West Indian restaurant with a terrace positioned directly across from Columbus Square. Steaming bowls of curry, fish stews or chicken *roti* are served with rice, salad and provisions. A good spot for people watching, and for lighter snacks and ice cream.

Naked Virgin $$$ ★★

Marchand Road, Castries, ☎ *(758) 452-5594.*
Latin American cuisine. Specialties: Flying fish.
Dinner: 6–10 p.m., entrées $15–$25.
This graceful West Indian building in the Castries suburb of Marchand is the home of an excellent punch that gives the restaurant its provocative name. The brew is so potent, it might encourage you to take your clothes off. Be that as it may, the Virgin also has a loyal following of regulars who admire chef/owner John Paul's traditional creole cooking, including creole shrimp and fried flying fish. Reservations recommended. Credit cards: A, MC, V.

Paul's Place $ ★★★

Bridge St., Castries, ☎ *(758) 452-3398.*
International cuisine.
Lunch: 9 a.m.–4 p.m., entrées $7–$10.
Dinner: 4–10 p.m., entrées $7–$10.
Paul's provides a tasty lunch buffet to office workers who crowd the place at noon. Those who don't want to brave the line can choose from a menu of *rotis*, sandwiches, and plate meals. Dinner is more subdued, with innovatively prepared fish, chicken, and steak dishes. The food is not always up to par, but when it is, it shines brightly. Reservations recommended. Credit cards: A, MC, V.

Piton $$$ ★★★

Anse Chastenet Road, Soufriére, ☎ *(758) 459-7354.*
Associated hotel: Anse Chastenet.
Creole cuisine.
Dinner: 7–9:30 p.m., prix fixe $35.

Great sunset views of the Pitons are served with fine creole and continental food at this lovely, greenery-enhanced dining spot. The five-course fixed-price menu changes daily, but might include a roast pork loin, grilled mahi-mahi or vegetarian *gateaux*; desserts range from light to hefty. A beachside bar at this same resort, Trou au Diable, is a great place to dine between ocean dips, with *rotis*, pepper-pot, chicken and beef *satays* or sandwiches to entice you away from snorkeling. The staff is quite welcoming at both places. Credit cards: A, DC, D, MC, V.

San Antoine $$$ ★★★

Old Morne Rd., Castries, ☎ *(758) 452-4660.*
International cuisine.
Lunch: Noon–2 p.m., entrées $15–$28.
Dinner: 6:30–12 p.m., entrées $15–$28. Closed: Sun.

The surroundings are old-fashioned and gracious, with meals served in the main house of the old San Antoine Hotel. The elegant dining room, lit by candles at night, is run by an English couple who keep things purring along smoothly. Those looking for a special night out often choose this salon, which overlooks the twinkling lights of the harbor. The menu includes French and continental specialties, including seafood in parchment, pepper steak, or filet mignon with crayfish stuffing. A five-course fixed-price dinner is available for $34. Reservations recommended. Credit cards: A, MC, V.

Where to Shop

St. Lucia is not a shopping destination, though the ardent browser will find a few treasures. In Castries, a new harborfront shopping complex, **Pointe Seraphine**, features a large variety of duty-free imports such as designer perfumes, crystal and china. You'll also find native crafts and resortwear, but avoid the complex when a cruise ship has docked. You'll find more variety of bananas than you ever knew existed on Saturday, market day, at the 100-year-old **Castries market**, which provides a chance to rub shoulders with hundreds of farmers' wives displaying luscious tropical fruits and vegetables, spices and local crafts; don't be shy about asking to sample a bite of tamarind, but keep a watch on your handbag and wallet. The **government handicraft store** at the waterfront provides a nice selection—woven fruit baskets are good buys for your kitchen back home. Other shops sell wood carvings, pottery and locally made baskets. Hand-screened clothing and colorful batik apparel are featured buys, particularly at the **Caribelle Batik** store. St. Lucia's artists tend to specialize in designs and portraits of the island's flora and fauna. More local crafts are available outside Castries—two spots that merit a visit are **Bagshaws**, a store selling silk-screened work by local artist Sydney Bagshaw, including shirts, skirts and a variety of other apparel (located across from the Sandals Halcyon); and the **Arts and Crafts Centre** near Choiseul on the southwest coast, where craftspeople are usually at work and baskets, dishes, tapestries and woodcarvings are a good buy.

St. Lucia Directory

Arrival and Departure

St. Lucia has two airports—a smaller one, **Vigie**, on the edge of Castries and a larger airstrip suitable for jets, **Hewanorra**, at the southern tip at Vieux Fort. Since most of the hotels are located close to Castries, Vigie is more convenient for most visitors, but you'll be flying in on a smaller plane. The hotels located near Soufriére or south are more convenient to Hewanorra.

American Airlines has flights into both airports daily out of their hub in San Juan, Puerto Rico. **BWIA** offers direct flights into Hewanorra several times a week out of New York's JFK and Miami. Within the Caribbean, **LIAT** provides direct or non-stop service to Vigie out of Antigua, Barbados, Caracas, Carriacou, Dominica, Grenada, Guadeloupe, Martinique, St. Kitts, St. Vincent and Trinidad, as well as connecting service from most other islands. **LIAT** also has a daily flight between Hewanorra and St. Vincent, and a daily flight between Hewanorra and Vigie. Charter service is increasingly available to St. Lucia out of major U.S. markets.

The airport departure tax is $11.

Business Hours

Shops open weekdays 8 a.m.–12:30 p.m. and 1:30–4 p.m. and Saturdays 8 a.m.–noon. Banks open Monday–Thursday 8 a.m.–3 p.m., Friday 8 a.m.–5 p.m. Some banks in Rodney Bay also open Saturday from 9 a.m.–noon.

Climate

Temperatures year-round average between 70 and 90 degrees Fahrenheit. Constant trade winds keep the air cool and the humidity from becoming oppressive.

Documents

U.S. and Canadian citizens need to show a full and valid passport. British citizens need no passport if their stay does not exceed six months. French citizens must show an ID card. An ongoing or return ticket must also be shown.

Electricity

Current runs 220 volts, 50 cycles, with a square three-pin plug. A few hotels use 110 volts, 50 cycles. Bring an adapter and converter plug.

Getting Around

Travel between Castries and other towns including Soufriére and Vieux Fort can be done in **minibuses**, usually overcrowded and stocked with local produce; you may have to share your seat with a carton of tomatoes. Buses leaving for Soufriére and Vieux Fort can be picked up in front of the department store on Bridge Street. To get to Cap Estate, take the bus near the market on Jeremy Street in Castries.

Taxis run all over the island. They have excellent experience with the small, winding roads outside the capital. Many taxi drivers are guides and have been trained in showing tourists around the city and island. Cars are unmetered, but official rates have been set by the government. Before setting off for a destination, verify the price in advance, and in what currency. When someone says dollar, you must specify whether you are talking about the American dollar or the Eastern Caribbean dollar.

Rental cars are available in St. Lucia, but roads are difficult in the countryside and driving is on the left—always a bit hazardous for drivers used to the right side of the road. A driver's license is required and may be obtained from the Immigration Office upon arrival. It remains valid for three months. Stick with the top American names in agencies. You have assurance that you can use your credit card, arrangements can be easily made in advance before you leave, and if anything goes wrong, you can easily contact the head office back home. **Budget** ☎ *(758) 452-8021*; **Avis** ☎ *(758) 353-2046*; and **Hertz** ☎ *(758) 452-0679*. Of the three, Hertz is the most expensive. It's best to get collision insurance; membership in auto clubs may lower the price in certain circumstances. Budget is the least expensive, about $300 per week for its least expensive car. All agencies can have cars waiting at the airport, or you can contact their office at the airport when you arrive. If it is the first time you are driving on the left-hand side of the road, it's a good idea to travel with a companion and allow him or her to spot the road for you. In foreign situations or one in which there are many distractions, or late at night, it is very easy to become forgetful and cross to the wrong side of the road, especially when you are turning or looking for directions.

Language

The official language is English, though a local patois is spoken.

Medical Emergencies

A 24-hour emergency room is available at **St. Jude's Hospital**, Vieux Fort ☎ *(758) 454-6041* and **Victoria Hospital**, Hospital Road, Castries ☎ *(758) 452-2421*.

Money

The official currency is the Eastern Caribbean dollar, commonly referred to as E.C. It is pegged to the American dollar and trades at about $2.65 to one U.S. dollar. American currency is accepted almost everywhere, but verify which currency is being used when you are quoted prices, particularly in smaller hotels and restaurants.

Telephone

Effective as we go to press, the new area code for St. Lucia is *(758)*. All local numbers have seven digits—to call the island from the U.S., dial *1+(758)*, then the seven-digit number. International phone calls, as well as cables, can be made at the offices of the **Cable and Wireless** in the George Gordon Building on Bridge Street in Castries ☎ *(758) 452-3301.*

Time

Atlantic Standard Time, all year round, one hour earlier than New York time. During Daylight Saving Time, however, it is the same hour.

Tipping and Taxes

The government imposes an 8 percent occupancy tax on hotel room rentals. Sometimes hotels and restaurants add a 15 percent service charge, but check your bill carefully. In restaurants it is customary to tip waiters or waitresses 10–15 percent if it has not already been added to the bill. Airport porters usually receive about 75 cents a bag.

Tourist Information

The **St. Lucia Tourist Board** is located at Point Seraphine in Castries ☎ *(758) 452-5968.* It's always worth stopping by to see if they have any brochures or suggestions for hikes, excursions, as well as to find out what is happening in the community. In the U.S. call ☎ *(800) 456-3984.*

When to Go

January 1 and 2, the local New Year's celebration, culminates in a two-day street fair offering local foods, island music, and dancing and games for children. Carnival is celebrated the two days prior to Ash Wednesday in mid-February, with elaborate costumes, dancing until dawn and national calypso contests. The annual St. Lucia Jazz Festival takes place in the middle of May, with outdoor concerts at Pigeon Island and late-night performances at hotels around the Castries area. June 29 is the Feast of St. Peter, or Fisherman's Day, where priests bless the fishermen's brightly decorated boats. August 30 is the Feast of St. Rose of Lima, a spectacular flower festival dating back to the 18th century where members of La Rose Flower Society dress in costume to sing and dance in the streets. An annual culinary competition in October, *Annou T'juit Sent Lisi*, lures judges from throughout the region to sample fare from island restaurants and hotels. The annual Billfish Tournament is also held in October, as well as the island's second flower festival, the Feast of St. Margaret Alacoque, which is based on African traditions shaped by political affiliations with France and England. November 22 is St. Cecilia's Day, celebrated by musicians who serenade through the streets of Castries. Early December brings the Atlantic Rally for Cruisers, the world's largest trans-Atlantic yacht race, when more than 100 yachts set sail for St. Lucia from the Canary Islands.

ST. LUCIA

ST. LUCIA HOTELS	RMS	RATES	PHONE	CR. CARDS
Castries				
★★★★★ **LeSport**	102	$300–$670	(800) 544-2883	A, MC, V
★★★★ **Anse Chastanet Hotel**	48	$95–$505	(800) 223-1108	A, D, MC, V
★★★★ **Jalousie Plantation**	115	$345–$655	(800) 392-2007	A, MC

ST. LUCIA HOTELS	RMS	RATES	PHONE	CR. CARDS
★★★★ Royal St. Lucian	96	$310–$600	(800) 255-5859	A, CB, DC, MC, V
★★★★ Sandals St. Lucia	273	weekly	(800) 726-3257	A, MC, V
★★★★ Windjammer Landing	131	$150–$590	(800) 958-7376	A, DC, MC, V
★★★ Club Med St. Lucia	265	weekly	(800) 258-2633	A, MC
★★★ Club St. Lucia	312	$100–$310	(800) 777-1250	A, CB, D, MC, V
★★★ Doolittle's Resort	22	$65–$95	(800) 322-3577	A, MC, V
★★★ East Winds Inn	26	$300–$625	(800) 223-9832	MC, V
★★★ Ladera Resort	19	$195–$650	(800) 841-4145	A, MC, V
★★★ Marigot Bay Resort	16	$55–$135	(800) 334-2435	A, MC, V
★★★ Rendezvous	100	$380–$510	(800) 544-2883	A, MC, V
★★★ Rex St. Lucian Hotel	120	$140–$192	(800) 255-5859	A, CB, DC, MC, V
★★★ Sandals Halcyon	170	weekly	(800) 726-3257	A, MC, V
★★★ St. Lucian Hotel	260	$59–$165	(800) 255-5859	A, MC, V
★★★ Wyndham Morgan Bay Resort	238	$265–$500	(800) 822-4200	A, D, MC, V
★★ Auberge Seraphine	22	$45–$95	(758) 453-2073	MC, V
★★ Candyo Inn	12	$75–$90	(758) 452-0712	A, MC
★★ Caribbees Hotel	57	$60–$90	(800) 278-5824	A, MC, V
★★ Harmony Suites	30	$75–$115	(800) 278-5824	A, D, MC, V
★★ Hummingbird Beach Resort	10	$80–$165	(758) 459-7232	A, D, MC
★★ Islander Hotel	60	$80–$130	(800) 278-5824	A, D, MC, V
★★ Orange Grove Hotel	62	$45–$83	(800) 777-1250	MC, V
★★ Tapion Reef Hotel	30	$50–$80	(758) 452-7471	A, MC
★ Green Parrot Inn	55	$70–$110	(800) 278-5824	A, MC, V

ST. LUCIA RESTAURANTS	PHONE	ENTRÉE	CR. CARDS
Castries			
American			
★★★ Charthouse	(758) 452-8115	$12–$36	A, MC, V
Chinese			
★★ Ginger Lily	(758) 452-8303	$6–$30	MC, V

ST. LUCIA RESTAURANTS	PHONE	ENTRÉE	CR. CARDS
International			
★★★★ **Dasheene Restaurant**	(758) 459-7850	$11–$38	A, D, MC, V
★★★ **Chez Paul and the Rain Bar**	(758) 451-3111	$8–$21	A, MC, V
★★★ **Green Parrot**	(758) 452-3399	$14–$34	A, MC, V
★★★ **Paul's Place**	(758) 452-3398	$7–$10	A, MC, V
★★★ **San Antoine**	(758) 452-4660	$15–$28	A, MC, V
★★ **A-Pub**	(758) 452-8725	$15–$30	A, MC, V
Italian			
★★★ **Capones**	(758) 452-0284	$11–$24	A, MC, V
★★★ **Key Largo**	(758) 452-0282	$6–$17	MC, V
Latin American			
★★★★ **Jimmie's**	(758) 452-5142	$14–$25	A, MC, V
★★ **Eagle's Inn**	(758) 452-0650	$8–$10	A, MC, V
★★ **Kimlan's**	(758) 452-1136	$5–$6	
★★ **Naked Virgin**	(758) 452-5594	$15–$25	A, MC, V
Seafood			
★★★ **Bistro, The**	(758) 452-9494	$7–$24	A, MC, V

Soufriére

★★★ **Piton**	(758) 459-7354	$35–$35	A, D, DC, MC, V
French			
★★★ **Hummingbird**	(758) 459-7232	$7–$37	A, D, MC, V

ST. LUCIA

SINT MAARTEN/ ST. MARTIN

Sailing excursions from St. Martin to other islands are easily arranged.

Half-Dutch, half-French, the island of Sint Maarten/St. Martin provides a unique, bi-polar Caribbean vacation for the price of one. Sint Maarten, the Dutch side, is part of the trio of islands that make up the Dutch Windwards (which includes Sint Eustatius and Saba, both visible off the island's southern coast), while St. Martin belongs to the French West Indies, a sub-prefecture of the French department of Guadeloupe, 140 miles to the southeast. A mere welcoming sign acts as the only border between the two sides—nary a customs officer in sight—and English is frequently a common denominator. The split personality doesn't end with linguistics, however, for each side of the island goes out of the way to define its own identity. Marigot, the capital of the more quiet and refined French side, is the place to go if you're looking for unique French shopping or fine creole and Gallic cooking. The Dutch capital, Philipsburg, has an excellent port providing sailing opportunities, a wide array of duty-free shops, and an upscale nightlife that includes more than a dozen casinos. Throw in a healthy dose of Caribbean cultures imported by the many nationalities that work on the island and you have a vibrant medley of not two, but at least three cultural influences. Beyond the beaches and duty-free shopping, the one thing consistent all the way around the island is massive development. It started in earnest on Sint Maarten during the 1960s, but two decades later, the French side was embarking on an equally enthusiastic game of catch-up. The upshot is that, by the '90s, more than 7000 hotel rooms had been built on the two sides of the small island and the fiscal impact of more than 1 million tourists annually had become essentially the sole economy.

Unfortunately, the island spent most of 1996 trying to reassemble its tourism infrastructure after a devastating wallop from Hurricane Luis in September 1995. The storm shuttered huge hotels for months, siphoned sand away from postcard-perfect beaches, and left thousands under- or un-employed as businesses tried to re-group. In truth, many of the problems that became prevalent after Luis—pollution, over-crowding, crime—already existed before the storm arrived. But the hurricane succeeded in lifting the roof off new issues and exacerbated the existing problems. The respective governments have been since forced to acknowledge both how dependent they are on the tourism sector, and how fragile that market is. The French side responded quickly to the clean-up and re-building, with French troops arriving on the island just hours after the storm. Sint Maarten was slower to respond, and several hotels were mired in tussles with insurance companies that delayed the reconstruction effort. But as a whole, the island should be well prepared for tourist arrivals by the advent of the 1996–97 winter season and Sint Maarten/St. Martin should soon re-emerge as one of the region's most popular destinations. Daily airline service from North America (the most comprehensive in the Eastern Caribbean), an extensive array of duty-free shopping opportunities, and some of the best, most varied dining to be found in the region will speed things along. Additionally, the island remains an excellent hub for sailing excursions or day-trips to nearby Anguilla, St. Barthélemy, Saba and Statia, all of which are but a 10- or 15-minute plane hop away.

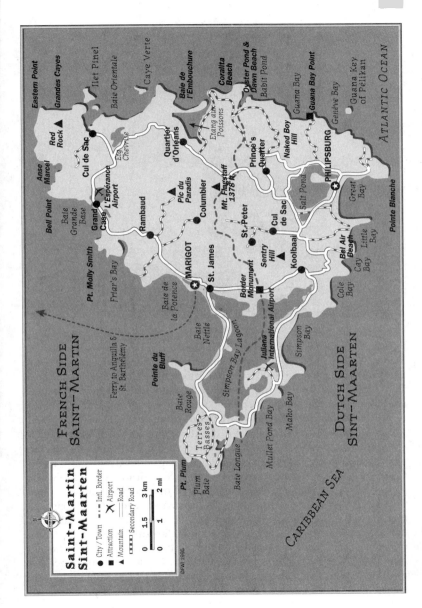

Saint-Martin / Sint-Maarten

Legend:
- ● City / Town
- ■ Attraction
- ▲ Mountain
- ·–·– Intl. Border
- ✕ Airport
- —— Road
- ▪▪▪▪ Secondary Road

| 0 | 1.5 | 3 km |
| 0 | 1 | 2 mil |

©RWI 1995

FRENCH SIDE SAINT-MARTIN

DUTCH SIDE SINT-MAARTEN

ATLANTIC OCEAN

CARIBBEAN SEA

Bird's-Eye View

Simpson's Bay lagoon is spectacular at sunset.

One of the smaller islands in the Eastern Caribbean, Sint Maarten/St. Martin's 37-square-mile territory is almost three-fifths French-owned, while a little more than two-fifths of the land is Dutch. The western side of the island is low-lying and primarily comprised of Simpson Bay Lagoon, an excellent harbor for smaller craft shared by both the French and Dutch. The rest of the island is more hilly, almost conical, rising to 1378 feet at Paradise Peak. A number of coves scallop the coastline, some of which are backed by salt ponds (salt production was once a principle industry). Though the island is relatively scrubby and dry, on the French side, a sheltered valley named Colombier, is comparatively verdant. Though Sint Maarten/St. Martin once supported sugar cane and other crops, little of the island is used for produce today, preferring instead to import the fruits and vegetables it consumes, even including the guavaberries used for the island's famed guavaberry liqueur. Sint Maarten/St. Martin was destined for tourism in some part due to the fact that Juliana Airport, an improbably large airfield on a narrow isthmus along Simpson Lagoon, was created in 1943 for military rather than touristic reasons. After the war, the airport was ideal for bringing in larger planes filled with vacationers, and tourist arrivals began to pick up in the 1960s. Today, with about 60,000 residents, the island is the most populous

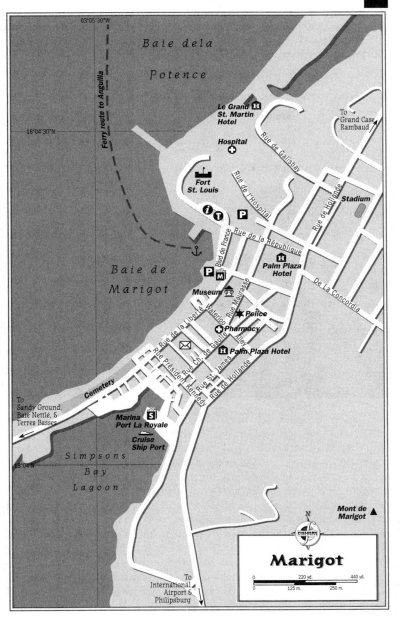

Marigot

per square mile of any in the Caribbean, particularly on the crowded Dutch side. It is surrounded by several other nearby Leeward Islands, including Anguilla, just seven miles to the north, and St. Barthélémy, 19 miles southeast. Philipsburg is the capital of the Dutch side, and Marigot the capital of the French.

A cannon on Sint Maarten recalls the days when pirates roamed the shores.

Columbus discovered and named St. Martin in 1493, and by the 1630s both the Dutch and French had settled on the island. Pirates combed the craggy shores and secret coves of the island, burying treasure and booty they had won at sea. It was in St. Martin that Peter Stuyvesant (the last Dutch governor of New York) lost his leg in a struggle with the Spanish in 1640. According to legend, the binational division of St. Martin was determined when a Dutchman and a Frenchman stood back to back, then circled the island until they encountered each other again, face to face. (Since the French side is somewhat bigger than the Dutch, leading devotees of this legend like to believe that the Dutchman was fatter and slower.) More legitimate historians tend to suppose that a small group of French and Dutch prisoners escaped their Spanish captors and drew up an agreement to divide the island between them. In 1946, Guadeloupe, of which St. Martin is a dependency, became an Overseas Department of France and in 1974, an Overseas Region of France.

People

As of a 1994 census, there were about 28,000 residents on the French side, and 32,000 on the Dutch side. But ask residents what they want to be called, and nobody knows, in part because 77 nationalities are represented on the Dutch side alone. Part of the confusion lies in the multi-linguistic nature that divides the island, as well as the genuine amiability that unites it. On the Dutch side, children in primary school study in English, while St. Martin students don't learn English until secondary school. To make matters even more confusing, there are many different accents among English speakers (one distinctly Jamaican) and even a lively street dialect called *papiamento*, a hefty, only-in-the-Caribbean mix of English, Spanish, Portuguese, Dutch and African languages. There's enough interest in *papiamento* to warrant its own newspaper (published in Curacao). Poet Lasana Sekou singularly upholds the literary tradition as the island's only published muse, with work rich in local dialects and slang.

Despite all the French sophistication and Dutch geniality, superstition and backwoods lore are still strong and thriving among long-time residents, kindled further by the many workers representing other West Indian cultures, particularly the Dominican Republic. The fervent love of calypso is also pure Caribbean, though the local lyrics lack the political bite known among more dissident communities. Calypso contests and parties are held regularly throughout the year. The island's colonial roots bore the first real signs of backlash in 1996 when a sign promoting the Sint Maarten/St. Martin Carnival had depictions of a Dutch windmill and Eiffel Tower crossed out with spray paint—the protesters stated they didn't want symbols of Europe used to represent Caribbean culture.

Beaches

One of Sint Maarten/St. Martin's chief draws has always been its beaches. In the days following the onslaught of Hurricane Luis, it was sad to hear of the toll a number of the island's beaches took from the storm. Fortunately, over time, most of the beaches have come back nicely and the island's official

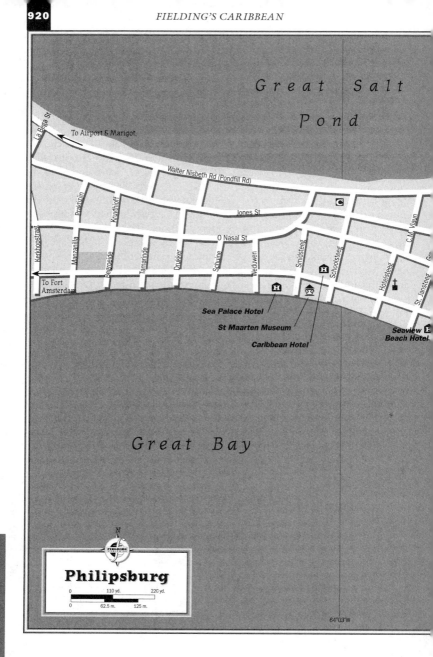

Great Salt

Pond

To Airport & Marigot.

La Bega St.

Walter Nisbeth Rd (Pondfill Rd)

Jones St

O Nasal St

Kerkhoostraat

Praktizin

Kruythoff

Manzanilla

Begneeide

Tamarinde

Drukker

Schulne

Weduwen

Smidsteeg

Schoolsteeg

C.M. Vlaun

Hotelsteeg

St. Jansteeg

To Fort
Amsterdam

Sea Palace Hotel

St Maarten Museum

Caribbean Hotel

Seaview
Beach Hotel

Great Bay

N

Philipsburg

| 0 | 110 yd. | 220 yd. |
| 0 | 62.5 m. | 125 m. |

64°03'W

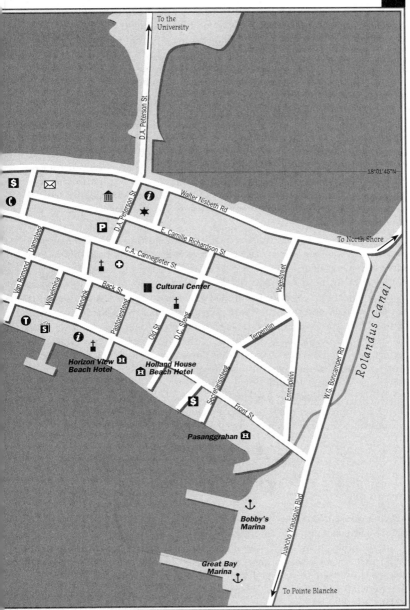

To the
University

18°01'45"N

D.A. Peterson St

Walter Nisbeth Rd

D.A. Peterson St

E. Camille Richardson St

To North Shore

C.A. Cannegieter St

Damsteeg

Van Romond

Wilhelmina

Hendrik

Back St

Pastorijesteeg

Old St

D.C. Steeg

Vogelstreet

Terpentijn

Cultural Center

Horizon View
Beach Hotel

Holland House
Beach Hotel

Secretarissteeg

Front St

Emmaplein

W.G. Boncamper Rd

Rolandus Canal

Pasanggrahan

Bobby's
Marina

Great Bay
Marina

Juancho Yrausquin Blvd

To Pointe Blanche

count of 37 beaches may once again be accurate. Beginning on Dutch Sint Maarten's east side, **Dawn Beach** is a good place to begin the day, with spectacular sunrises followed by snorkeling to the colorful depths. **Guana Bay** is one of the island's few isolated strands, but a rugged current makes it more suitable for surfing than swimming. **Great Bay** is a mile-long beach set against the backdrop of busy Philipsburg (the best swimming is at the west end near the Great Bay Beach Hotel), while just around the corner is **Little Bay**, a sheltered cove with good snorkeling. **Simpson Bay** is fine for swimming and sunning, though it lies against the Juliana airstrip (the big jets land mid-day), while **Maho Bay** is immediately under the flight path. A little further is Mullet Bay, long a favorite, and less crowded while the 600-room Mullet Bay Resort behind it is closed. A scenic beauty that is slowly recovering from the hurricane is **Cupecoy**, whose evanescent string of sand (widest in winter) is backed by eroding limestone cliffs that provide caves and smaller coves—it's the subject of a number of photos promoting Sint Maarten as a beach destination.

The sand on the French side is equally prime, starting with **Baie Longue**, a velvety strip watched over by **La Samanna**. **Baie Rouge** is a little off the beaten path, but spectacular—a picturesque swatch of sand big enough to spread out away from the crowd. **Baie Nettle** was actually expanded in some places by the hurricane; it has also sprouted several resorts in the last few years. **Friar's Bay** is small and tricky to reach, but that works to its advantage, while Grand Case is a long expanse of sand fringed by lolos, the roadside snack stands favored by the French. The calm, shallow waters of Anse Marcel are perfect for families, while nearby **Petites Cayes** is accessible only by boat or on foot. The most famous beach on the French side is lively Baie Orientale, an immensely popular clothing optional spot with a naturist resort, Club Orient. Live music, casual restaurants, beachside vendors and watersports at Orient do more to set the tone than concern over tan lines—the beach came through Luis fine and recently looks better than ever.

Diving on Sint Maarten/St. Martin is often lost within the shadows of the island's glittering nightlife and rippling canvas sails. The sport seems virtually an afterthought, most obviously displayed by the fact that day trips to Saba, St. Barthélemy and Anguilla are promoted eagerly by local dive shops. Sites close to shore have been over-fished and the coral degraded, and winds frequently whip up the seas, making access a bit bumpy. As locals will quietly explain, the island simply is not a major dive destination. And yet, there are at least two good wrecks—one ancient, the other very new—and the shallow reef structure is extensive, stretching for more than two miles off the island's coast. An excellent site, **One Step Beyond**, is not listed below; rough waters rarely make the location (seven miles southeast of Philipsburg) available to divers, but it yields large pelagics, coral arches and tunnels. The best of the rest are concentrated on the south coast around Philipsburg and visibility averages 60 to 80 feet (better in winter). Dive prices are a little steeper here than in most parts of the Eastern Caribbean. There are a few small operators on the French side, but using them requires familiarity with the French system of diving. In sum, most anyone serious about exploring the depths will visit a couple sites on this island, then beeline to nearby Saba, where the real excitement lies, but beginners and less worldly divers will be kept sufficiently happy on Sint Maarten/St. Martin. Snorkelers will find the island's coves and inlets ideal; try Mullet Bay or the waters off **Green Cay**, **Tintamarre** or **Ilet Pinel**.

On Foot

One of the better local legends has it that Sint Maarten/St. Martin's national boundaries were determined by having two statesmen, one French, one Dutch, walk the island's perimeter to establish an equal territorial claim for each nation. Whether the Frenchman was a faster walker, slimmer or, as some suggest, the Dutchman was slowed by inebriation, the French wound up with the larger chunk of land (others suggest both men were carrying a bottle, but the Dutch beer was stronger than the French wine). Since this story's origin several hundred years ago, hiking has faded into the background, while shimmering beaches have become firmly established as the island's principle outdoor attraction. It doesn't help matters that this densely populated island has little room left for explorations on foot. But there are unexpected options, which quietly appear on backcountry roads, particularly on the less densely populated French side and on Terres Basses, the peninsula west of Simpson Bay. Keep your mind open to these sporadic strolls and you will be rewarded. The **Sint Maarten National Heritage Foundation** conducts interesting guided hikes of varying difficulty every other Sunday morning; a donation of $5 is requested ☎ *(599-5) 249-17.*

By Pedal

Over the past few years, residents of Sint Maarten/St. Martin have fervently embraced bicycles, creating the latest fitness craze to strike this affluent island. On Sundays, it's not uncommon to see 100 or more cyclists tooling around **Simpson Bay Lagoon**, and although primary arteries are fast-paced, there are usually viable alternatives. The main road circling the island rolls past most of the best scenery, as well as topping nine good-sized hills; several routing possibilities are available, but figure about 35 miles (including the loop around Simpson) for the whole circuit. A shorter, relatively flat option is the 13-mile ride around Simpson Bay, while quieter dirt roads west of the lagoon lead to **Terres Basses**, a peninsula sprinkled with lovely beaches and posh residences. Off-roaders will find lovely riding along the coast immediately north of **Marigot**, and on the hillsides leading to **Paradise Peak**. In general, the best mountain biking lies on the less-crowded French side, though **Cay Bay** (near the GEB water plant) is not a bad area. The island offers little respite from heat other than bars and restaurants, so riders are well-advised to carry plenty of water for any extensive undertakings.

What Else to See

Unless you have a fort fetish, Sint Maarten/St. Martin offers little in the way of exploration and sightseeing—sticking to beaches and watersports, or shopping in **Marigot** and **Philipsburg** are your best options. If the island's forts do call to you, begin your explorations with a swing by the **Sint Maarten Museum** in Philipsburg which will help put the rich history in perspective. **Fort Amsterdam** is the most important, representing the first Dutch military outpost in the Caribbean—its ruins are found on the peninsula southwest of Philipsburg (just past the Divi Little Bay Resort). Also noteworthy on the Dutch side is **Fort Willem**, atop **Fort Hill** immediately west of Philipsburg, reached by a treacherous road that is best walked. On the French side is **Fort St. Louis** (also known as Fort de Marigot), built in 1767 and recently restored, with excellent views above Marigot and extending to Simpson Bay Lagoon and Terres Basses. You can drive part way up, but the steep climb to the top yields the best views.

Sint Maarten's shops at Simpson's Bay offer French fashions, batiks from St. Barts, jewelry, perfumes and quality gift items.

Try to visit Marigot on Wednesday or Saturday morning, when the charming town comes alive with its traditional French West Indian **market**, now housed in an elaborate new enclosure. Above the town of **Rambaud** is **Colombier**, a village in a lush valley beneath Paradise Peak—it represents St. Martin at its most quiet and rural. Further up the coast is **Grand Case**, a seaside community dotted with charming creole houses sporting gingerbread trim and whose restaurant row has earned the town the title "Gastronomique Center of St. Martin." The hustle of nudist **Baie Orientale** is worth a visit—the sand is always lively with music and food. Don't miss the pastoral hamlet of **Orleans**—also known as the French Quarter, and the oldest French settlement on the island. Here you'll find small homes set among gardens alive with tropical blossoms. **Roland Richardson**, perhaps the island's best-known artist/conservationist/historian, captures these scenes on canvas and welcomes visitors into his Orleans studio on Thursdays ☎ *(590) 87-32-24.*

Most visitors take at least one day-trip to a neighboring island. Anguilla is a 15-minute, $9 ferry ride from Marigot (see "Getting Around").

BEST VIEW:

At 1278-feet, Paradise Peak, called Pic du Paradis, offers a breathtaking view of both the French and Dutch capitals.

Historical Sites
St. Martin

Fort St. Louis ★ ★ ★

just off Rue de la Republique, Marigot.

Also known as Fort de Marigot, this ruin dates back to 1786 and is well preserved with some original cannons still intact. It's worth the very steep climb (bring water) for the splendid views of Marigot.

Museums and Exhibits
Sint Maarten

Courthouse of Sint Maarten   ★★★

Frontstreet, Philipsburg.

Located north of the town square on bustling Frontstreet, this 1793 building was recently restored with glorious results. The second floor still functions as a courthouse, while the first floor is a post office. You'll definitely want to snap a picture of this colorful edifice.

Simartn Museum   ★★★

7 Front Street, Philipsburg.
Hours open: 10 a.m.–4 p.m.

Exhibits are on a changing basis, most focusing on the island's history and culture. There are some upscale specialty boutiques on the premises. Not worth a special trip, but a pleasant way to spend an hour or two if you're in the neighborhood. General admission: $1.

St. Martin

Museum of Marigot   ★★★★

Sandy Ground Road, Marigot.
Hours open: Mon.–Sat. from 9 a.m.–1 p.m. and from 3–6 p.m.

This new museum hosts an interesting exhibit, "On the Trail of the Arawaks." The collection focuses on pre-Columbian artifacts, including remains of indigenous inhabitants dating back to 1800 B.C. and ceramics from 550 B.C. There's also a reproduction of a 1,500-year-old Indian burial site (just discovered in 1994), early 20th-century photographs of the island, and displays on the plantation and slavery periods. Located next to the Royal Marina on the lagoon side. General admission: $5.

Museum of Marigot

Sandy Ground Road.

This new museum recounts island history in an exhibit titled "On the trail of the Arawaks," which begins with the arrival of the first Native Americans. It's located next to the Royal Marina.

Nightlife
Sint Maarten

La Cage International

Casino Royale, Maho Plaza, Maho Bay.

Leave it to glittering Sint Maarten to put on the Caribbean's flashiest female impersonation spectacle. Janet Jackson, Tina Turner, Madonna, Pearl Bailey and other legends are dragged out for this revue, held nightly upstairs from Maho's Casino Royale. Admission is a steep $25

Parks and Gardens
St. Martin

Butterfly Farm ★★★★★

Le Galion Beach Road, Orient Bay.
Hours open: 9 a.m.–5 p.m.
If you're never given butterflies a second thought (or look) before, you certainly will after visiting this tranquil spot near Orient Bay. Hundreds of rare and exotic butterflies fly free in a large screened-in garden replete with fish ponds, fountains and tropical foliage. Interesting exhibits showcase egg laying, caterpillar and pupa stages, and you'll get to see butterflies emerge from their cocoons and fly off into the great beyond (or at least around their 900-square-meter home). It's truly fascinating, and a tour, offered at no additional charge, is a must to really appreciate the exhibits. Butterflies are free... but this tour costs $10 for one or two people, $25 for three and $7.50 each for a group of four.

Tours
Sint Maarten

Sint Maarten Zoo ★★★

Madame Estate, Philipsburg.
Hours open: 9 a.m.–5 p.m.
This small zoo is especially suited to children (who get in for $2), with its playground and petting zoo. The grounds include botanical gardens, two walk-through aviaries, and caged animals from the Caribbean and South America. General admission: $3.

St. Martin

Pinel Island ★★★★

Cul de Sac Bay.
Just five bucks will get you a roundtrip boat ride to this tiny island off the coast of French St. Martin. There you can snorkel (they rent equipment), sunbathe or dine in the casual restaurant.

Seaworld Explorer ★★★★

Grand Case Pier, Grande Case.
This semi-submarine has an open-air deck and underwater observatory hull that lets you view sealife in air-conditioned comfort—and without getting your hair wet. Trips depart from Grand Case Pier and explore the waters surrounding Creole Rock. A diver feeds the fishies to make sure tourists have lots to see. Tours cost $30 for adults, $20 for kids 2–12. Add $10 each ($7 for kids) for roundtrip transportation from your hotel.

Sports

Sailing is an island passion, and neophytes will receive a thorough, if all-too-brief immersion into the sport by partaking in the **Sint Maarten 12 Metre Challenge**, which uses actual America's Cup boats for races just off Great Bay. Visiting boaters have a variety of bays and marinas for mooring. On French St. Martin, **Baie Rouge** provides good anchorage, Port la Royale and Marigot Bay are good sites for shopping, while Baie de Grand Case features excellent dining at all price levels. A top-class marina can be found at Port de Lonvilliers (Anse Marcel), with docking space for up to 60 boats (up to 73 feet), and boutiques, grocery, cafe and La Capitanerie, a ship's chandlery. At Oyster Pond, Captain Oliver's Marina serves the French side, while Oyster Pond Yacht Club is on the Dutch side of the placid bay. On Dutch Sint Maarten, Bobby's Marina and Great Bay Marina are the primary access into Philipsburg, while two marinas are also positioned in Cole Bay. Large enough to accommodate virtually any yacht, passage into Simpson Bay Lagoon is available from both the windward (French) and leeward (Dutch) sides of the island.

Day-sails to other nearby islands are popular—Anguilla is a nearby favorite, but St. Barts, Saba and St. Eustatius are other possibilities. Two types of vessels are commonly used: large catamarans holding 25 or more, or smaller sailboats that hold six to 10 for excursions to secluded beaches. Boats depart from Bobby's Marina and Great Bay Marina in Philipsburg, Simpson Bay Marina, Captain Oliver's in Oyster Pond, Port la Royale in Marigot Bay and the new marina at Anse Marcel, Port de Lonvilliers. Rates for a day sail with snorkeling, open bar and picnics run between $65–75 per person. **Sport fishing** is also prominent. Half- and full-day charters with tackle, bait and snacks are readily available at Bobby's Marina, Great Bay Marina, Simpson Bay Marina and Port la Royale Marina. December to April is the season for kingfish, dolphin and barracuda; tuna is available year-round. **Windsurfing** is increasingly popular, and many resorts offer rentals and lessons.

The focus sticks primarily to the ocean, but a few other sports are popular. Although the Mullet Bay Resort is still closed from the hurricane, golf at the 18-hole Joe Lee-designed course is now possible, though serious duffers won't be enthralled with its sometimes scruffy conditions. A new miniature golf course in Marigot will keep the kids happy. Several stables on both sides of the island provide **horseback riding**, while **tennis courts** can be located at most of the island's resorts.

Sint Maarten

Golf

Mullet Bay Resort, Philipsburg.

The island's only links are an 18-hole course designed by Joe Lee, and located next to Mullet Bay Resort. It is quite scenic and very challenging, though upkeep is sometimes an issue. Greens fees are about $100.

Sint Maarten 12 Metre Challenge ★★★★★

Great Bay Marina, Philipsburg.

If you've ever wanted to try your hand at racing in the America's Cup, this unique attraction allows you the opportunity. Guests participate as crew on one of the actual America's Cup racing boats, including two incarnations of *Stars and Stripes* (the '86 and '87 winners), and several other multi-million dollar contenders. You and 17 others crew alongside three experts, racing against one or more of the other boats on a streamlined version of an actual America's Cup course. Everyone is assigned a duty, be it trimming the sails or grinding a winch, but previous sailing experience is not necessary. The two-hour adventure is not cheap ($60 per person), but for many it is the highlight of a visit to Sint Maarten. Races are held up to seven days a week in high season, but call the day before to book a seat.

St. Martin

Horseback Riding

Various locations.

On the Dutch side, horses can be rented at Crazy Acres, ☎ *(599-5) 427-93*. On the French side, try Caid and Isa, ☎ *(590) 87-45-70* and the O.K. Corral, ☎ *(590) 87-40-72*. The going rate is about $40 for a two-hour trail ride.

Watersports

Various locations.

If your hotel doesn't offer the watersports you're seeking, a slew of companies will be happy to help. **Dutch Side**: for boating and cruises, try **Swaliga**, ☎ *(599-5) 221-67*, **White Octopus**, ☎ *(599-5) 240-96*, **Caribbean Watersports**, ☎ *(599-5) 428-01*, **Bobby's Marina**, ☎ *(599-5) 223-66*, and **Bluebeard**, ☎ *(599-5) 528-98*. For deep-sea fishing, try **Wampum**, ☎ *(599-5) 223-66*, **Sea Brat**, ☎ *(599-5) 240-96*, and **Bobby's Marina** ☎ *(599-5) 223-66*. Scuba divers can call **Leeward Island Divers**, ☎ *(599-5) 428-66*, **Tradewinds**, ☎ *(599-5) 751-76*, St. Maarten Divers, ☎ *(599-5) 224-46*, and **Ocean Explorers**, ☎ *(599-5) 452-52*, which also runs a unique underwater "helmet" walk in which non-swimmers can stroll with the help of special apparatus that supply oxygen. **French side**: For boating and cruises, call **Marina de Captain Oliver**, ☎ *(590) 87-33-47*, **Marina Port la Royale**, ☎ *(590) 87-20-43*, or **Port de Lonvilliers**, ☎ *(590) 87-31-94*. General watersports, **Nettle Bay Beach Club**, ☎ *(590) 87-20-59* or **Kontiki Watersports**, ☎ *(590) 87-46-89*. For scuba diving call **Lou Scuba**, ☎ *(590) 87-16-61*, or **Meridien Dive Center**, ☎ *(590) 87-67-90*.

Where to Stay

Fielding's Highest Rated Hotels in Sint Maarten/St. Martin

	Hotel	Price
★★★★★	La Belle Creole	$205–$455
★★★★★	La Samanna	$250–$1900
★★★★	Dawn Beach Hotel	$105–$290
★★★★	Esmeralda Resort	$180–$950
★★★★	Green Cay Village	$1800–$2400
★★★★	Le Meridien l'Habitation	$160–$780
★★★★	Point Pirouette Villas	$161–$845
★★★★	Port de Plaisance	$220–$600
★★★★	Privilege Resort & Spa	$180–$640
★★★	Mullet Bay Resort	$270–$765

Fielding's Most Exclusive Hotels in Sint Maarten/St. Martin

	Hotel	Price
★★★★	Esmeralda Resort	$180–$950
★★★★	Point Pirouette Villas	$161–$845
★★★★	Privilege Resort & Spa	$180–$640
★★★	Maho Beach Hotel & Casino	$110–$590
★★★	Cupecoy Beach Club	$100–$500

Fielding's Best Value Hotels in Sint Maarten/St. Martin

	Hotel	Price
★★	Hevea	$40–$99
★★	Royale Louisiana	$66–$88
★★★	Golden Tulip St., Martin	$95–$140
★★★	Mary's Boon	$90–$150
★★	La Residence	$74–$98

Where to Stay—Sint Maarten

Almost 4000 hotel rooms are scattered across Dutch Sint Maarten, providing a bevy of options, though little room is furnished for travelers on a budget. Lodging ranges from small, family-run inns where you can make friends with the proprietors, to time-share condos where you'll never meet the owner(s). The hotels positioned around Great Bay and Philipsburg tend to be older properties, while the Lowlands immediately northwest of the Juliana Airport were developed more recently, with the huge Maho Beach Hotel and Casino dominating the landscape.

U.S. arrivals to the island were down 53 percent for the four months ending April 1996 (compared to the previous winter) and a $1 million advertising campaign was launched to promote Sint Maarten for the 1997 season. For travelers, this means hotel bargains should be prevalent for the immediate future. Although most properties were operational at press time, several of Sint Maarten's major resorts—Mullet Bay, Port de Plaisance and Dawn Beach Hotel—are suspended in limbo and closed until further notice; Divi Little Bay Beach Resort anticipates having a few dozen rooms ready by December 1996, with the rest of the room inventory phased in during 1997. Among other developments, Oyster Pond Hotel became Oyster Bay Beach and its new owners will be turning the hotel into a 200-room time-share in 1997–98. Most other properties received a spruce-up after the hurricane that left them polished and fresh.

Hotels and Resorts

The best of the luxury resorts have been opened on the French side, though Oyster Bay Beach Hotel provides frills on one of the last-to-be-developed pieces of land on Sint Maarten, and the Maho Beach Hotel satisfies those looking for an all-encompassing, neon-trimmed high-rise vacation.

Divi Little Bay Beach Resort   **$120–$300**   ★ ★ ★

Little Bay, Philipsburg, ☎ *(800) 367-3484, (599-5) 223-33. FAX (599-5) 239-11. Single: $120–$300. Double: $120–$300.*
Located a mile out of Philipsburg and set on an attractive beach, this resort dates back to 1955, making it one of the island's oldest. Accommodations run the gamut from standard guestrooms in casitas to suites with one to three bedrooms. All are quite comfortable, air-conditioned, and feature balconies or patios with nice ocean views. The facilities include a restaurant and two bars, a pool, two tennis courts, shops and watersports on the pretty, quiet beach. It's about a 20-minute walk into town. Decent for the price. Amenities: tennis, balcony or patio. 118 rooms. Credit cards: A, DC, MC, V.

Great Bay Beach Hotel   **$85–$260**   ★ ★ ★

Philipsburg ☎ *(800) 223-0757, (599-5) 224-46. FAX (599-5) 238-59. Single: $85–$250. Double: $95–$260.*
This large property sits at the end of Philipsburg and the town beach. Guestrooms are adequate, but nothing to write home about—they received a spruce-up in 1996.

The 10 junior suites have very large bathrooms with whirlpool tubs, but are not necessarily worth the bump in price. There are two restaurants and three bars, one with entertainment and shows nightly. The grounds also include two pools, a casino, a tennis court, gym, and all the usual watersports at the pleasant beach. Rates provided are European Plan, but an all-inclusive set-up is also available. Amenities: tennis, exercise room. 285 rooms. Credit cards: A, DC, MC, V.

Holland House Beach Hotel $74–$190   ★★

Philipsburg ☎ *(800) 223-9815, (599-5) 225-72. FAX (599-5) 246-73.*
Single: $74–$175. Double: $89–$190.
This hotel is right in the center of Philipsburg on the town's narrow, palm-dotted beach. Air-conditioned guestrooms have sitting areas, twin beds, TVs, and private balconies, though not all have views; most have small kitchenettes. Be sure to book a room on the beach side, or you'll suffer from the street noise. You'll find a pleasant beachfront restaurant and bar, but no other facilities—much lies within walking distance, however. This is a good in-town bet, serving both business and leisure travelers. Amenities: balcony or patio. 54 rooms. Credit cards: A, D, MC, V.

Horizon View Beach Hotel $90–$225   ★★

Philipsburg ☎ *(599-5) 321-20. FAX (599-5) 321-23.*
Single: $90–$225. Double: $90–$225.
A business hotel in the heart of Philipsburg, the five-story Horizon View is one block from the town pier. All rooms are air-conditioned and offer cable TV, direct-dial phones and fully equipped kitchenettes—half offer oceanfront balconies. Accommodations range from studios to one-bedrooms suites. Nothing special, and the beach isn't very appealing, but not bad for the rates (make sure you're quoted the lowest rate available), and plenty of shopping and restaurants are a block or two away. 30 rooms. Credit cards: A, MC, V.

Maho Beach Hotel & Casino $110–$590   ★★★

Maho Bay, Philipsburg, ☎ *(800) 223-0757, (599-5) 521-15. FAX (212) 969-9227.*
Single: $110–$415. Double: $125–$590.
Set on a rocky bluff above the beach, this bustling, nine-story resort (the island's largest) is near the airport and can suffer from the roar of jets in the afternoon. Accommodations are nice and feature private balconies and large baths, all with bidets and some with whirlpool tubs. There are also 57 efficiency units with small kitchenettes. Facilities include a number of restaurants, two cafes, a nightclub and several bars, a large casino, two pools, four tennis courts, a full-service health club, and all the usual watersports. This spot appeals to conventioneers and those who like busy resorts with all the accompanying activity. Amenities: tennis, health club, balcony or patio. 600 rooms. Credit cards: A, DC, MC, V.

Mullet Bay Resort $270–$765   ★★★

Mullet Bay, Philipsburg, ☎ *(800) 468-5538, (599-5) 528-01. FAX (599-5) 542-81.*
Single: $270–$515. Double: $270–$765.
Located seven miles from Philipsburg on 172 beachfront acres, this mega-resort is situated around the island's only 18-hole golf course. Accommodations include 300 guestrooms and 300 suites with kitchens. All are spacious and comfortable with

refrigerators, modern conveniences, and views of the ocean, lake, or golf course. Guests can choose from six restaurants, eight bars, a casino, and a host of recreational options: 14 tennis courts, two pools, aerobics classes in the fitness center, all watersports, and lots of organized programs. There's also an arcade with more than a dozen tony boutiques, so bring lots of cash. The grounds are nicely landscaped and include a boardwalk and nature path for scenic strolls. Very nice for resort lovers, but lots of conventioneers can make things crowded. Those who like large and thriving resorts will not be disappointed. 570 rooms. Credit cards: A, DC, MC, V.

Oyster Bay Beach Resort　　　**$120–$360**　　　★★★

Oyster Pond, Philipsburg, ☎ *(800) 231-8331, (599-5) 222-06. FAX (599-5) 256-95.*
Single: $120–$360. Double: $120–$360.
This intimate hideaway is located in a semi-secluded cove and surrounded on three sides by water, but new owners plan to turn it into a 200-room time-share in 1997–98. Accommodations are beautifully done in white wicker and pastel fabrics; each room is individually decorated and has ceiling fans, air conditioners, and seaview patios. The 20 suites are especially luxurious. The French restaurant is romantic and well regarded, and there's also a comfortable lounge for quiet respites. The mile-long beach is quite lovely, but not the greatest for swimming; most guests prefer the saltwater pool. The planned expansion will add a small casino and shopping area. Amenities: balcony or patio. 40 rooms. Credit cards: A, DC, D, MC, V.

Point at Burgeaux Bay　　　**$70–$395**　　　★★

Philipsburg ☎ *(599-5) 543-35. FAX (516) 466-2359.*
Single: $70–$395. Double: $70–$395.
This three-story hotel is located in a residential area, 15 minutes from downtown Philipsburg. It fronts the ocean, but the beach is a bit of a walk. Accommodations range from standard rooms to one- and two-bedroom suites with kitchens and terraces. Maids tidy up daily. Facilities are limited to a swimming pool and Jacuzzi. 14 rooms. Credit cards: not accepted.

Port de Plaisance　　　**$220–$600**　　　★★★★

Simpson Bay, Philipsburg, ☎ *(800) 732-9480, (599-5) 452-22. FAX (599-5) 423-15.*
Single: $220–$455. Double: $220–$600.
Set just to the Dutch side of the border, this hotel has a great location for those who want to experience both the French and Dutch sides of the island. The sprawling complex has junior suites and one- and two-bedroom suites with all modern amenities, plus fully equipped kitchens and large terraces with garden or marina views. The grounds include five restaurants (including a spa bar for the health-conscious), a shopping arcade, a spa and tennis center and a picturesque marina. The hotel also boasts the nicest casino on the island, a truly elegant room with a gorgeous painted ceiling, upscale chandeliers and a very professional staff. Credit cards: A, DC, MC, V.

Summit Resort Hotel　　　**$80–$190**　　　★★

Simpson Bay Lagoon, Philipsburg, ☎ *(800) 351-5656, (599-5) 521-50.*
FAX (599-5) 526-15.
Single: $80–$190. Double: $80–$190.
Perched on a bluff and overlooking the lagoon, this complex consists of ginger-bread-trimmed cottages clustered very closely (too closely) together. Accommoda-

tions are either studios or duplexes, all air-conditioned and boasting sitting areas and verandas. The more expensive rooms have kitchens. You'll find a restaurant and bar on the premises, and the large saltwater pool is very nice. The staff will shuttle you to the beach and Philipsburg, but you'll probably want a car so you can travel on your own schedule. 50 rooms. Credit cards: A, MC, V.

Apartments and Condominiums

Apartments, condos and time shares are big business on Sint Maarten. Among the nicest is the Cupecoy Beach Club, located above one of the island's most beautiful beaches.

Beach House   **$53–$100**   ★

Philipsburg ☎ *(599-5) 224-56. FAX (599-5) 303-08.*
Single: $53–$90. Double: $63–$100.
Located on Great Bay, a 10-minute walk from downtown Philipsburg, this guest-house provides air-conditioned efficiencies with maid service. All have terraces and simple furnishings, as the rates suggest. You can cook in or saunter over to one of the many restaurants in the area. 10 rooms. Credit cards: A, MC.

Beachside Villas   **$150–$295**   ★ ★ ★

Simpson Bay, Philipsburg, ☎ *(599-5) 542-94.*
Single: $150–$295. Double: $150–$295.
These elegant Mediterranean-style villas are set on the beach. All are individually owned but identically decorated, with two bedrooms, fully equipped kitchens, combination baths, living and dining areas, VCRs, and decks. Maids tidy up daily. Facilities are limited to a small pool, but there are many restaurants and shops in the area. The only downside is the proximity to the airport, which means loud roars when jets take off and land. 14 rooms. Credit cards: A, MC.

Belair Beach Hotel   **$165–$375**   ★ ★

Little Bay Beach, Philipsburg, ☎ *(599-5) 233-66. FAX (599-5) 252-95.*
Single: $165–$300. Double: $190–$375.
This all-suite hotel is situated on Little Bay Beach, next to the Divi Little Bay. The condos at this Mediterranean-style hotel are individually owned and rented out when the owners are elsewhere. Each unit has two bedrooms, two baths, full but small kitchens, living and dining rooms, VCRs, and private patios or balconies, and can sleep up to six. Facilities include a bar and restaurant and a tennis court—but the beach is right there, where watersports equipment can be rented. Request a unit on an upper floor for more privacy. Good for families. Amenities: balcony or patio. 72 rooms. Credit cards: A, MC, V.

Cupecoy Beach Club   **$100–$500**   ★ ★ ★

Cupecoy Lowlands, Philipsburg, ☎ *(215) 885-9008. FAX (215) 572-7731.*
Single: $100–$300. Double: $100–$500.
Situated on white sandstone cliffs that overlook Cupecoy Beach (whose size varies, depending on the tides), this Mediterranean-style complex offers suites with one- to three-bedrooms, all privately-owned. Each has full kitchen, air conditioning, nice decor, and spacious terraces. You'll find a pool with a swim-up bar on the premises, and the staff will help arrange other activities and watersports. A restaurant and

casino await across the street. The hotel does not have a local phone; the number shown is the management company in Pennsylvania. 126 rooms.

Horizon View Beach Hotel $90–$300 ★★

Frontstreet, Philipsburg, ☎ *(599-5) 321-20. FAX (599-5) 321-23.*
Single: $90–$300. Double: $90–$300.

If you want to be in the heart of Philipsburg—not, incidentally, one of the island's most desirable locations—this hotel will fit your needs. Each unit is air-conditioned and offers cable TV, direct-dial phones and fully equipped kitchenettes. Only half have ocean-front balconies, however. Accommodations range from studios to one- and two-bedroom suites. There's a restaurant on site, and shopping and nightlife right out the front door. The beach is small and not especially picturesque. 30 rooms.

Horny Toad Guesthouse $98–$180 ★★★

Simpson Bay, Philipsburg, ☎ *(800) 351-5656, (599-5) 543-23. FAX (599-5) 533-16.*
Single: $98–$180. Double: $98–$180.

This former governor's residence combines guest-house ambience with apartment living. It is located on a lovely beach that sometimes suffers from jet noise at the nearby airport. Each one-bedroom apartment is individually decorated and quite charming, with fully equipped kitchens, fresh flowers, and maid service. The friendly owners, Earle and Betty Vaughn, treat renters like personal guests, providing a gracious touch lacking in the fancier resorts. There are no facilities on-site, but there's plenty to do within walking distance. No kids under seven. 8 rooms.

Pelican Resort & Casino $95–$270 ★★★

Simpson Bay, Philipsburg, ☎ *(800) 626-9637, (599-5) 425-03. FAX (599-5) 421-33.*
Single: $95–$192. Double: $95–$270.

This full-service resort combines the best of both worlds: condo living with full resort amenities. The air-conditioned accommodations range from studios to two-bedroom suites, all colorfully done in tropical decor and with fully equipped kitchens with dishwashers and microwaves. Facilities include three restaurants, a large casino, a deli, a full-service health spa, six pools—two with swim-up bars—six tennis courts, and a marina. Extensive watersports include cruises aboard the property's catamaran. There's even a doctor's office! With all that going on, this resort isn't for everyone—it's not exactly an idyllic escape, more like a teeming mini-city, and to get to the beach you'll have to brave steep hillsides. Especially suited to families, the hotel offers its two kiddie pools, a playground and a daycare center. Amenities: tennis, health club, exercise room. 343 rooms. Credit cards: A, D, MC, V.

Point Pirouette Villas $161–$845 ★★★★

Simpson Bay Lagoon, Philipsburg, ☎ *(800) 365-8484, (599-5) 542-07.*
FAX (599-5) 523-38.
Single: $161–$700. Double: $161–$845.

This villa complex is situated on a private peninsula opposite the Maho Bay development. The posh Mediterranean-style villas have one to four bedrooms. All are air-conditioned and have living and dining rooms, VCRs, stereos, full kitchens, small private pools. Facilities include a tennis court and gym; restaurants, shops, and casinos are within walking distance. Amenities: tennis, exercise room. 85 rooms. Credit cards: A, MC, V.

Royal Islander Club $108–$336 ★★★

Maho Bay, Philipsburg, ☎ *(800) 223-0757, (599-5) 523-88. FAX (599-5) 525-85.*
Single: $108–$240. Double: $108–$336.

This time-share property shares the beach and facilities with its sister property, the Maho Beach Hotel & Casino. Guests, therefore, have the convenience of condo living combined with the bells and whistles of a full resort. Accommodations range from studios to one- and two-bedroom suites, all very tastefully done with kitchens and all the modern comforts. An Olympic-size pool is located on the grounds, and guests can take advantage of the restaurants, bars, tennis courts, and other extensive facilities next door. Amenities: tennis. 135 rooms. Credit cards: A, DC, D, MC, V.

Town House Villas $125–$300 ★★

Philipsburg ☎ *(800) 223-9815, (599-5) 2289-8. FAX (599-5) 224-18.*
Single: $125–$250. Double: $125–$300.

Located on the edge of Philipsburg and right on the beach, this complex consists of 11 duplex villas. Each has two bedrooms, 1.5 baths, living and dining rooms, and full kitchens. Patios are set along a nice courtyard. Maids keep things tidy. No facilities on the premises, but lots of shops and restaurants are a short stroll away. Reasonable rates and a casual atmosphere make this a popular choice. 12 rooms. Credit cards: A, MC, V.

Tradewinds Beach Inn $61–$155 ★

Simpson Bay, Philipsburg, ☎ *(599-5) 542-06.*
Single: $61–$115. Double: $61–$155.

This small inn is located on the beach at Simpson Bay. Guests can choose from studios, and one- and two-bedroom apartments, all air-conditioned and with kitchenettes and maid service. Facilities are limited to a pool. 10 rooms.

Inns

Inns are not Sint Maarten's specialty, but a couple of charmers with lots of colorful history welcome guests. The Pasanggrahan Royal Guest House is the island's oldest hotel, originally built for Queen Wilhelmina, and has the creaking hardwood floors and fluttering ceiling fans to prove it. Mary's Boon was built by a notorious, gun-toting Caribbean legend, Mary Pomeroy, who disappeared in her private plane some time in the late '70s. "All the stories you've heard about Mary are true," say those who knew her. The food at Mary's Boon, the responsibility of one chef for more than two decades, is well respected.

Mary's Boon $90–$150 ★★★

Juliana Beach, Philipsburg. ☎ *(800) 351-5656, (599-5) 542-35. FAX (599-5) 534-03.*
Single: $90–$150. Double: $90–$150.

Located next to the airport, 15 minutes from Philipsburg, this is an authentic West Indian beachcomber inn—not someone's idea of one. The long beach is quite nice, but can disappear during high tide. Accommodations are in large studios with kitchenettes, patios and ceiling fans, though a few rooms now have air conditioning. Public spaces are nicely accented with island art, tropical prints, and antiques—the owner's dogs are quite prevalent. There's a terrific restaurant, as well as an honor bar, but no other facilities. As with all the properties in this area, occasional airport noise—particularly the big jets midday—is intrusive. 12 rooms.

Pasanggrahan Royal Guest House   **$78–$158**   ★★

Philipsburg ☎ *(800) 351-5656, (599-5) 23588. FAX (599-5) 22885.*
Single: $78–$158. Double: $78–$158.

This inn (the name means "guest house" in Indonesian), is housed in a 19th-century governor's house and was the former residence of Queen Wilhelmina. Guestrooms are decorated in wicker and have balconies or patios; not all are air-conditioned and some are fairly run-down. The studios are a better bet with their superior furnishings and kitchenettes. The Guest House sits on a narrow sliver of Great Bay Beach so there is no pool, and guests forego modern amenities like phones and TV, but are rewarded with a good dose of historical charm, especially noteworthy on this modern and developed island. The bar and restaurant are popular with locals, and afternoon tea is a treat. Lots to see and do within walking distance. 30 rooms. Credit cards: A, MC.

Low Cost Lodging

Although a number of hotels drop their rates below the hundred-dollar mark in summer, there's precious little to be obtained for budget travelers on Sint Maarten during the winter. One option is to hook up with another couple and share a condo or apartment. The new **Hotel L'Esperance** located on Cay Hill has attractive apartment-style rooms ☎ *(599-5) 25355.* Another is the **Sea Breeze Hotel**, also a pleasant and inexpensive hostelry ☎ *(599-5) 26054.* Both are in a residential neighborhood a mile west of Philipsburg (you'll need a car).

Where to Stay—St. Martin

About 3500 hotel rooms have been built on St. Martin, many in the past decade during a building boom which has seemingly left no cove cement-free. The development has not reached the rampant level seen on the Dutch side, and a building moratorium recently has been debated. Although many Americans visit the island, accommodations on the French side are decidedly more European than is typically found in the Caribbean. English is spoken by most who work in the hotels.

One legendary property, La Belle Creole, was closed down by Hurricane Luis and a target re-opening date of December 1997 has been announced. A few small properties were awaiting rebuilding, including Le Pirate and Golden Tulip. The ever-popular Orient Beach nudist resort was blown away by Hurricane Luis, but was scheduled to re-open in time for the 1996–97 winter season.

Hotels and Resorts

La Samanna, a swank oasis amid St. Martin's hubbub, is one of the Caribbean's great hotels, a bastion of tasteful retreat overlooking a priceless beach, and containing some of the most seductive rooms to be found anywhere in the region. Yes, it's true: the resort's caviar sampler (Beluga, Sevruga, et al) runs $500, though a bottle of glacial vodka comes with it. The flip side of La Samanna is probably Le Meridien l'Habitation, a mammoth development on the most "remote" corner of St. Martin—though rooms are appropriately deluxe, and the on-site spa delivers the goods, it's geared for French conventions and groups as well as typical vacationers (it was the site of a Bush-Mitterrand meeting in 1989). Another spa experience in more intimate surroundings is delivered just up the hill from l'Habitation at Privilege Resort.

Anse Margot $125–$249 ★★★

Baie Nettle, Marigot, ☎ (800) 742-4276, (590) 87-92-01. FAX (590) 87-92-13.
Single: $125–$235. Double: $150–$249.

Located a mile out of Marigot and fronting Simpson Bay Lagoon, this hotel is a popular spot. Nine three-story buildings with pretty gingerbread trim house the guestrooms and suites, all quite pleasant with air conditioners, refrigerators, and private balconies. The restaurant is a beautiful spot for a romantic meal, and you can enjoy the bar, two pools, and watersports on the beach. The clientele is predominantly European. Amenities: balcony or patio. 96 rooms. Credit cards: A, DC, D, MC, V.

Coralita Beach Hotel $115–$140 ★★

Marigot, ☎ (590) 87-31-81.
Single: $115. Double: $140.

This small hotel is family run. As the name implies, it's located right on the beach, about four miles from the center of town. Rooms are pleasant and air-conditioned, but could use a little work; some boast kitchenettes. Facilities include a bar, restaurant, pool and a tennis court. The staff can arrange horseback riding, watersports and even yoga classes. 24 rooms. Credit cards: A, CB, MC, V.

Dawn Beach Hotel $105–$290 ★★★★

Oyster Pond, Marigot, ☎ (800) 351-5656, (599-5) 229-29. FAX (599-5) 244-21.
Single: $105–$290. Double: $105–$290.

This resort is located three miles from Philipsburg in a relatively remote area. Guests are accommodated in recently renovated cottages (set too close together) on the hillside or beach, each holding studios with rattan furnishings, living and dining areas, full kitchenettes, and private balconies or patios. The pretty pool is accented by a waterfall. There are also two tennis courts, a restaurant and watersports on the very nice beach. You'll need a car to get around. 155 rooms. Credit cards: A, MC, V.

Golden Tulip St. Martin $95–$140 ★★★

Cul de Sac Bay, Marigot, ☎ (800) 344-1212, (590) 87-49-19. FAX (590) 87-49-23.
Single: $95–$140. Double: $95–$140.

The on-site beach is not the greatest, but guests can easily make their way to the better sands at Orient Beach. The luxurious Golden Tulip has spacious villa-style guestrooms with all the modern amenities and ocean views off the terrace. Facilities include five pools, a bar and restaurant, daily shopping trips to Marigot and Philipsburg and watersports. Nice digs for the price. 94 rooms. Credit cards: A, D, MC, V.

Hotel Royal Beach $70–$132 ★★

Baie Nettle, Marigot, ☎ (590) 87-89-89. FAX (590) 87-89-89.
Single: $70–$111. Double: $91–$132.

St. Maarten

St. Maarten

Rooms are simple but adequate at this budget property, but several buildings took a beating from Hurricane Luis. Many rooms have a king-size bed, while some offer kitchenettes. Rates include breakfast. 113 rooms. Credit cards: A, MC, V.

La Belle Creole   **$205–$455**   ★ ★ ★ ★ ★

Marigot, ☎ (590) 87-66-00. FAX (590) 87-56-66.
Single: $205–$455. Double: $205–$455.
Designed to resemble a Mediterranean village, this resort encompasses 25 acres and has two beaches. Guestrooms are found in villas linked by picturesque pathways. All are very spacious and luxuriously appointed. The 18 suites, which run from $900 to $1320 per night, are as posh as can be (at that rate, they'd better be!). Guests can enjoy the lovely plaza, four tennis courts, a croquet lawn, pool, complete watersports including a dive center, and exercise classes in the fitness center. Dining choices range from casual to elegant and there's frequent entertainment in one of the three bars. The beaches are not the greatest, but no one seems to mind at this lovely enclave. 160 rooms. Credit cards: A, CB, MC, V.

La Samanna   **$250–$1900**   ★ ★ ★ ★ ★

Baie Longue, Marigot, ☎ (800) 854-2252, (590) 87-64-00. FAX (590) 87-87-86.
Single: $250–$1400. Double: $250–$1900.
Now operated by the Rosewood chain (which runs Little Dix and Caneel Bay in the Virgins), this stellar spot is splendidly perched on 55 beachfront acres, and designed to resemble a Moorish Mediterranean village. Accommodations are in the main building and in villas scattered about the beach. The corner Terrace Suite remains a Caribbean classic, while most of the rest are on the small side, but still very elegant, with luxurious, Spanish-tiled bathrooms. Large patios, minibars, refrigerators, and air conditioning are standard throughout; massive renovations a few years ago polished La Samanna perfectly. The resort's well-heeled guests can play tennis on three courts, partake in all watersports, and splash about in the pool. The food is grand, the extensive wine cellar is one of the best in the region. La Samanna gets high marks for seclusion and sophistication on this otherwise cluttered isle. Attentive service and extra touches like daily fresh flowers make this one of the Caribbean's premiere resorts—and one blessedly free of pretensions. Amenities: tennis, exercise room, balcony or patio. 80 rooms. Credit cards: A, MC, V.

Laguna Beach Hotel   **$88–$245**   ★ ★ ★

Baie Nettle, Marigot, ☎ (800) 333-1970, (590) 87-91-75. FAX (590) 87-81-65.
Single: $88–$176. Double: $96–$245.
This Victorian-style hotel overlooks Simpson Bay Lagoon and its beach. Guests are housed in standard rooms or studios with balconies and kitchenettes. All are air-conditioned and have modern comforts like direct-dial phones, cable TV and hair dryers. The grounds include a large pool, restaurant and bar, and three tennis courts. Watersports can be rented on the public beach. Decent for the rates. Amenities: tennis, balcony or patio. 62 rooms. Credit cards: A, MC, V.

Le Flamboyant   **$150–$395**   ★ ★ ★

Baie Nettle, Marigot, ☎ (800) 221-5333, (590) 87-60-00. FAX (590) 87-99-57.
Single: $150–$295. Double: $150–$395.

This large beach hotel houses guests in tropically decorated standard rooms; the more expensive one- and two-bedroom suites have kitchenettes. Many resort amenities are offered at this busy spot, including two pools, a tennis court, and watersports on Simpson Bay Lagoon. Sunbathers on the beach go topless. Two restaurants offer a choice of elegant or casual dining, and an all-inclusive plan is available. Amenities: tennis. 271 rooms. Credit cards: A, MC, V.

L'Esplanade Caraibe Hotel $100–$300   ★★★

Grand Case, ☎ *(800) 633-7411, (590) 87-06-55. FAX (590) 87-29-15.*
Single: $100–$250. Double: $150–$300.

This new hotel is set high on a hill overlooking Grande Case and the sea; both are an easy, five-minute walk. Accommodations are in suites with fully equipped kitchens, color TV, direct-dial phones, central air conditioning and ceiling fans, and furnished balconies. One-bedroom and loft suites have a king bed and a sleeper sofa in the living room; lofts have an additional half-bathroom downstairs. The rooms are pleasant, but don't quite live up to the splendor of the hotel's pretty facade. Facilities are limited to a small pool and a bar that's open only in the high season. The bar offers sandwiches at lunch, but that's it in terms of food service, so you'll definitely want to stock the kitchen. Friendly service and a sophisticated French ambience make this property a winner. A 10-room beachfront property, Le Petit L'Esplanade, is under construction for a December 1996 opening. 24 rooms. Credit cards: A, MC, V.

Le Meridien l'Habitation $160–$780   ★★★★

Anse Marcel, Grand Case 4, ☎ *(800) 543-4300, (590) 87-67-00. FAX (590) 87-30-38.*
Single: $160–$780. Double: $160–$780.

Situated on 170 acres, this sprawling resort consists of the 251-room l'Habitation and the 145-room Le Domaine. All the guestrooms are nicely decorated and comfortable, though those in Le Domaine are larger, have oversized tubs, making them the better choice. Many rooms have kitchenettes; be sure to ask if this is important to you. The extensive grounds cater to resort lovers, with four restaurants, three bars, two lovely pools, six tennis courts, racquetball and squash courts, a marina and full watersports at the gorgeous beach. Most activities are included in the rates. Guests can also use the adjacent Le Privilege Fitness Center and Spa, a luxurious spot to work up a sweat or get a massage. Nice, but a bit isolated. Amenities: tennis, health club, exercise room. 396 rooms. Credit cards: A, DC, MC, V.

Mont Vernon $120–$415   ★★★

Baie Orientale, Grand Case 4, ☎ *(800) 223-0888, (590) 87-62-00.*
FAX (590) 87-37-27.
Single: $120–$295. Double: $140–$415.

Situated on a mile-long beach, all accommodations here are in junior suites or larger, all spacious, comfortable and pleasant. The free-form pool is the island's largest, and there are also two tennis courts and a fitness room for energetic types. The beach has all watersports and many topless bathers. Supervised programs keep little tykes busy during holidays and high season. Lots of conventioneers congregate at this bustling resort, the biggest on the French side. Amenities: tennis, exercise room. 394 rooms. Credit cards: A, MC, V.

Pavillion Beach Hotel   **$90–$280**   ★★★

Grand Case, ☎ (800) 322-2223, (590) 87-96-46. FAX (590) 87-71-04.
Single: $90–$240. Double: $130–$280.
This small hotel is set right on the beach, with a sea view from each of its 16 rooms. Accommodations are either studios or suites, all large and inviting and boasting kitchenettes and air conditioning. Request an upper floor for more privacy. There are no on-site facilities, but the central location puts much within walking distance. 16 rooms. Credit cards: A, D, MC, V.

Privilege Resort & Spa   **$180–$640**   ★★★★

Anse Marcel, Grand Case v, ☎ (800) 874-8541, (590) 87-38-38. FAX (590) 87-44-12.
Single: $180–$640. Double: $180–$640.
Located on St. Martin's northern shore, this deluxe choice for spa lovers has creole architecture outside and luxurious rooms and suites within, with central air, mini-bars, TVs and VCRs and quality tropical furnishings. The spiffy spa offers hydro-therapy baths and every possible pampering service (most of which are not included in room rates). Other facilities include six tennis courts, four squash courts, two rac-quetball courts, aerobics classes, a high-tech exercise room, two restaurants, two bars and a disco. There's also a marina and heliport that offer excursions to neigh-boring islands. Amenities: tennis, health club, exercise room. 27 rooms. Credit cards: A, DC, MC, V.

St. Tropez   **$120–$235**   ★★★

Orient Bay Beach, Grand Case 4, ☎ (800) 476-5849, (590) 87-42-01.
FAX (590) 87-41-69.
Single: $120–$235. Double: $120–$235.
This new complex is actually three hotels operating under the St. Tropez name. Accommodations are in modern junior suites, all with air conditioning, king-size beds, sitting areas, terraces, TV, phone and refrigerator. Facilities include a pool and watersports. 84 rooms. Credit cards: A, MC, V.

Sol Hotel   **$90–$125**   ★★

Oyster Pond, Marigot, ☎ (800) 476-5849, (590) 87-38-10. FAX (590) 87-32-23.
Single: $90–$115. Double: $100–$125.
Fashioned in creole-style architecture, this little charmer overlooks Oyster Pond Marina and surrounds a pleasant pool area. Rooms are simple, but feature kitchen-ettes, air conditioning and a terrace for enjoying the view. Several rooms offer a Murphy Bed to sleep a third adult. Dawn Beach is a 15-minute hike, and a bevy of watersports are available at the nearby marina. 8 rooms. Credit cards: A, MC, V.

Apartments and Condominiums

You can actually spend as much money on a fabulous villa as you would at a chic resort on St. Martin. Two cases in point: the luxurious Esmeralda Resort and Green Cay Village, where the classification as villa complexes masks that they both provide many of the amenities of a full-service hotel. Only here you can have your own private pool. But more modest digs are also available, and may save you money, either via cooking at home, or by hooking up with another couple to split the accommodation costs. Among the villa rental companies are **Carimo** ☎ *(590) 87-57-58*, **Immobilier St. Martin Caraibes**

☎ *(590) 87-55-21*, and **West Indies Immobilier** ☎ *(590) 87-56-48*. In the U.S., call **WIMCO** toll-free ☎ *(800) 932-3222*.

Captain Oliver's Hotel $84–$225   ★★★

Oyster Pond, Marigot, ☎ *(800) 447-7462, (590) 87-40-26. FAX (590) 87-40-84.*
Single: $84–$135. Double: $140–$225.

Located on the French/Dutch border and fronting the lagoon, this charming complex gets high marks for its peaceful grounds and reasonable rates. Guests are housed in attached pink bungalows that hold junior suites with kitchenettes, rattan furnishings, air conditioners, and private balconies. The well-landscaped grounds feature two restaurants, a bar, a 100-slip marina, a dive center, and a pool. Dawn Beach can be reached via water taxi. Amenities: balcony or patio. 50 rooms. Credit cards: A, MC, V.

Club Orient Resort $115–$340   ★★

Baie Orientale, Grand Case 4, ☎ *(800) 476-5849, (590) 87-33-85.*
FAX (590) 87-33-76.
Single: $115–$288. Double: $135–$340.

This popular resort has a "clothes-optional" policy which means that most guests are closet nudists. Located on a flat and scruffy peninsula on the Atlantic side of the island, guests are housed in rustic wooden chalets that have living rooms, full kitchens and large porches, or in newer units in pine duplex cottages. Most rooms have air conditioners and ceiling fans, and facilities include a beachside restaurant, a bar and two tennis courts. No pool, but you're right on the beach. You'll need a car for mobility. Amenities: tennis, houses, cottages or bungalows. 108 rooms. Credit cards: A, CB, DC, D, MC, V.

Esmeralda Resort $180–$950   ★★★★

Baie Orientale, Grand Case 4, ☎ *(800) 622-7836, (590) 87-36-36.*
FAX (590) 87-35-18.
Single: $180–$800. Double: $180–$950.

Situated on secluded grounds overlooking Orient Bay, this property consists of 18 posh villas that can be rented in their entirety or partially as standard guest rooms. Each villa has three to five rooms, are nicely decorated and have all the modern conveniences; all units have at least a kitchenette. Each villa has its own pool, but you may be sharing it, depending on how much of the villa you rent. There are two restaurants, a bar, a large communal pool and three tennis courts. Watersports await on the mile-long beach, one of the island's best. Amenities: tennis, Jacuzzi. 65 rooms. Credit cards: A, MC, V.

Grand Case Beach Club $95–$290   ★★★

Grand Case, ☎ *(800) 423-4433, (590) 87-51-87. FAX (590) 87-59-93.*
Single: $95–$290. Double: $95–$290.

Located on a crescent beach, this apartment complex consists of six white stucco buildings that offer nice ocean views. Accommodations include studios and one- and two-bedroom suites, all air-conditioned and decorated with rattan furnishings, fully equipped kitchens. Other features include satellite TV, wet bars, and nice balconies. Facilities include a restaurant, bar, tennis court and complete watersports.

No pool, but the beach is fine for swimming. This quiet spot is a great value and very popular, so book early. Amenities: tennis. 71 rooms. Credit cards: A, DC, MC, V.

Green Cay Village   **$1800–$2400**   ★★★★

Orient Bay Beach, Grand Case 4, ☎ (800) 476-5849, (590) 87-38-63.
FAX (590) 87-39-27.
Double: $1800–$2400.
Perched atop Orient Bay, each villa at this creole-inspired complex has its own small swimming pool. The villas are quite spacious and include a large living room with an entertainment center (VCR, cable TV, CD player), a full and modern kitchen, food for your first evening and a barbecue grill. Amenities include concierge services by the professional hotel staff and a tennis court. All of the villas are three-bedroom, but you can rent one or two of the bedrooms without sharing the unit (except during high season); prices quoted are for a one-bedroom villa for seven nights. Rates include airport transfers and daily maid service. Amenities: tennis, balcony or patio. 16 rooms. Credit cards: A, DC, D, MC, V.

Hotel le Belvedere   **$85–$120**   ★★

French Cul de Sac, Grand Case 4, ☎ (590) 87-37-89. FAX (590) 87-30-52.
Single: $85–$120. Double: $85–$120.
Located on the northeast coast, all accommodations at this property are suites that are on the small side, but all offer kitchenettes and other creature comforts. A large free-form pool and a bar and restaurant are located on the premises, and guests are transported free of charge to Pinel Island, where watersports await. You'll want a car, as this place is fairly remote, but the rates are very reasonable. 130 rooms. Credit cards: A, MC, V.

Le Pirate Beach Hotel   **$110–$180**   ★★

Marigot Bay, Marigot, ☎ (800) 666-5756, (590) 87-78-37. FAX (590) 8-79567.
Single: $110–$180. Double: $110–$180.
Set on the beach just outside of Marigot, this condominium hotel houses guests in air-conditioned studios with kitchenettes and terraces; each can sleep up to four. Facilities include a bar and restaurant, as well as watersports and an activities desk for booking sightseeing excursions. Several restaurants are within walking distance, so renting a car is not as important as at some of the more remote resorts. 60 rooms. Credit cards: A, MC, V.

Marine Hotel Simson Beach   **$110–$263**   ★★

Baie Nettle, Marigot, ☎ (800) 221-4542, (590) 87-54-54. FAX (590) 87-92-11.
Single: $110–$192. Double: $122–$263.
This bay-side property combines self-catering units with resort amenities. Accommodations are found in five-story creole-style buildings, each decorated with rattan furniture and sporting kitchenettes on the balcony. There are also 45 duplex units with two bedrooms and two baths. The premises include a restaurant, bar, pool, tennis court and watersports. 165 rooms. Credit cards: A, CB, MC, V.

Nettle Bay Beach Club   **$100–$455**   ★★★

Baie Nettle, Marigot, ☎ (800) 999-3543, (590) 87-68-68. FAX (590) 87-21-51.
Single: $100–$275. Double: $100–$455.

Despite its size and location on a wide beach, Nettle Bay attempts to impart a charming French country feel. Accommodations here range from villas to garden suites, all with full kitchens. The villas are large and bright, furnished in Philippine rattan, and come in one- and two-bedroom configurations. The garden suites are one-bedroom units with smaller kitchen areas. All are air-conditioned and have private terraces or patios. The grounds include three tennis courts, five pools, and a restaurant—the beach here was generously expanded during Hurricane Luis. Amenities: tennis. 230 rooms. Credit cards: A, DC, MC, V.

Inns

As on the Dutch side, there are not many true inns on St. Martin, but La Residence offers plenty of character.

La Residence $74–$98 ★★

Rue Charles de Gaulle; Marigot ☎ *(800) 365-8484, (590) 87-70-37. FAX (590) 87-90-44.*
Single: $74–$80. Double: $92–$98.

This small hotel is in the heart of Marigot, one mile from the beach. Rooms are air-conditioned, modern, and comfortable; some have very high ceilings and a few offer kitchens. The French restaurant is quite good, and there's also a bar for unwinding. Popular with business travelers, as there is much within an easy walk, and quite reasonable rates in winter. 21 rooms. Credit cards: A, D, MC, V.

Low Cost Lodging

A few budget spots are found in Marigot, where the town's location away from a beach keeps rates low, particularly during the more expensive winter season. Hevea and La Residence (see "Inns," above) are reasonably priced year-round. A couple other possibilities are Chez Martine in Grand Case, ☎ *(590) 87-51-59* and Golfe in Belleview, just outside Marigot, ☎ *(590) 87-92-05.*

Hevea $40–$99 ★★

163, Boulevard Grande Case, Grand Case, ☎ *(590) 87-56-85. FAX (590) 87-83-88.*
Single: $40–$84. Double: $55–$99.

Located just across the street from the beach, this inn is housed in a restored creole mansion that offers two guestrooms, three studios and three suites. Five units are air-conditioned; the other three made do with ceiling fans. All are quite pleasant, and the French restaurant of the same name is highly regarded. 8 rooms.

Royale Louisiana $66–$88 ★★

Marigot, ☎ *(590) 87-86-51. FAX (590) 87-96-49.*
Single: $66. Double: $88.

Located in downtown Marigot above several shops, this hotel is a great bargain—if you don't mind the fact that a decent beach is a good 20-minute walk away (there's a small one closer, but it's nothing to brag about). Air-conditioned guestrooms are simple but comfortable, with telephones and VCRs. Facilities are limited to a restaurant and bar, but there's much within walking distance. Since the beach is not terribly convenient, it's unfortunate that this hotel does not have a pool, but it keeps the rates very low. 58 rooms. Credit cards: MC, V.

Where to Eat

Fielding's Highest Rated Restaurants in Sint Maarten/St. Martin

★★★★	Antoine's	$16–$36
★★★★	Bye Bar Brazil	$8–$19
★★★★	L'Auberge Gourmande	$15–$31
★★★★	Le Perroquet	$18–$26
★★★★	Rainbow	$18–$34
★★★★	Saratoga	$16–$26
★★★	Da Livio Ristorante	$16–$30
★★★	La Rhumerie	$16–$45
★★★	Le Bec Fin	$16–$31
★★★	Shivsager	$11–$22

Fielding's Most Exclusive Restaurants in Sint Maarten/St. Martin

★★★	La Rhumerie	$16–$45
★★★	Hevea	$22–$38
★★★★	Rainbow	$18–$34
★★★	La Maison sur le Port	$17–$34
★★★★	Antoine's	$16–$36

Fielding's Best Value Restaurants in Sint Maarten/St. Martin

★★★	Mark's Place	$3–$13
★★★	Drew's Deli	$3–$15
★★★★	Bye Bar Brazil	$8–$19
★★★	Sambuca Ristorante	$8–$13
★★★	David's	$6–$17

With its strong French influence, Sint Maarten/St. Martin has almost a legal obligation to serve world-class cuisine, and it doesn't disappoint. On the French side alone, there are more than 100 restaurants and many have top gourmet kitchens—there are also fine Italian, Indian, Indonesian and other eateries. The variety of international cuisines served here is probably more expansive than any other Caribbean island. Seafood is omnipresent, and French wines are in abundance, but it all comes with a price, and all too often the prices on menus don't reflect what is served. Before splurging on a hundred-dollar meal, ask around to see what spot is new or in fashion— many restaurants did not weather the post-hurricane fallout. In Philipsburg, good burgers and conch chowder can be had for reasonable prices at The Greenhouse, while simple but tasty Italian food is served up at Sambuca near the airport. Back Street in Philipsburg has a number of Chinese and Indian restaurants where a good meal can be had for $10–15. American food is represented in the form of Taco Bell and Burger King. On the other hand, inexpensive fast food, French Caribbean-style is proffered by the *lolos*, family-run "chicken shacks" that washed out to sea during Hurricane Luis, and are being rebuilt along the Boulevard Grand Case. Acclaimed chef Mario Tarduff, formerly of Rainbow, opened his own eatery, Mario's Bistro in Sandy Ground. Another important new spot is L'Arhawak (formerly Calanque).

Sint Maarten

Antoine's $$$ ★★★★

103 Frontstreet; Philipsburg, ☎ *(599-5) 229-64.*
French cuisine. Specialties: Fresh local crayfish.
Dinner: 4–10 p.m., entrées $16–$36. Closed: Sun.

A gorgeous, new post-hurricane setting on a breezy patio above Great Bay makes this restaurant a romantic choice for a celebration dinner. Cuisine is classic French with Italian touches. Some specialties offered bring back memories of an uncomplicated past; to wit, duck with cherries, lobster thermidor, and chocolate mousse. When in season, fresh local crayfish makes a welcome appearance. Reservations recommended. Credit cards: A, MC, V.

Cheri's Cafe $$ ★★

Cinnamon Grove Center; Maho Bay, Philipsburg, ☎ *(599-5) 533-61.*
American cuisine. Specialties: Steaks, seafood.
Lunch: 11 a.m.–4:30 p.m., entrées $6–$12.
Dinner: 4:30–1:30 p.m., entrées $12–$17.

Cheri Batson, owner of the legendary cafe and bar that bears her name, must share the honors for the success of her hugely popular eating establishment with her steak purveyor—customers are always raving about the quality and quantity of the grilled beef. A huge sirloin steak fills out a plate for a modest $10.95. A lot of customers think the place is just plain fun—nobody sits down for long when the house band, Ramon, starts to play. Great burgers are also on the menu, along with the inevitable grilled seafood. Features: late dining. Credit cards: not accepted.

Chesterfield's   **$$**   ★★★

Great Bay Marina, Philipsburg, ☎ *(5595) 234-84.*
American cuisine.
Lunch: 11:30 a.m.–2:30 p.m., entrées $7–$12.
Dinner: 5:30–10 p.m., entrées $7–$20.
Rub epaulets with the boating crowd at this pier-side restaurant that has a casual, congenial ambience. The food is well-prepared, with a host of seafood, duckling and beef dishes served with flair at lunch and dinner. A companionable group often gathers on a daily basis for happy hour. Reservations recommended. Credit cards: not accepted.

Da Livio Ristorante   **$$$**   ★★★

159 Frontstreet; Philipsburg, ☎ *(599-5) 226-90.*
Dinner: 6–10 p.m., entrées $16–$30. Closed: Sun.
Classic Italian is the focus at this charming Philipsburg restaurant offering alfresco dining on a seaside terrace. Antipasto, lobster cocktail and beef carpaccio are nice starters, while house pasta specialties include a classic manicotti with spinach and ricotta cheese, and a homemade lasagne. Lobster *fra diavolo* and several veal items round out the menu. Credit cards: DC, MC, V.

Greenhouse   **$$$**   ★★

Bobby's Marina, Philipsburg, ☎ *(599-5) 229-41.*
American cuisine.
Lunch: 11 a.m.–5 p.m., entrées $6–$10.
Dinner: 5–10 p.m., entrées $11–$25.
An all-purpose eatery that serves American favorites and exotic Indonesian specialties, the Greenhouse has a harbor location and a dining room lush with plant life. Guests can play pool, throw darts and dance as well as dine. The place jumps daily at happy hour, which actually lasts a little longer; good for twofers and gratis hors d'oeuvres. Credit cards: A, MC, V.

L'Escargot   **$$$**   ★★★

84 Frontstreet; Philipsburg, ☎ *(599-5) 224-83.*
French cuisine.
Lunch: 11 a.m.–3 p.m., entrées $8–$23.
Dinner: 6:30–11 p.m., entrées $18–$29.
Snail fanciers and others will enjoy a meal at this venerable grande dame of a restaurant, which has been in the same spot for more than 25 years. The delectable delicacy is a specialty, and it shows up stuffed in mushrooms and in various other ways. The rest of the menu is largely French, encompassing duck, seafood, and meat dishes. Reservations required. Credit cards: A, MC, V.

Le Bec Fin   **$$$**   ★★★

119 Front Street; Philipsburg, ☎ *(599-5) 229-76.*
French cuisine.
Dinner: 6–10 p.m., entrées $16–$31.
Ascend a flight of stairs to this second-floor dining salon in a pleasant courtyard. At night, the ambience is candlelit and intimate, during the day try to snag a table overlooking the sea; there are only a few of them available. The kitchen really shines with

its seafood preparations, especially lobster, served grilled or flamed in brandy. Reservations required. Credit cards: A, MC, V.

Le Perroquet   **$$$**   ★★★★

72 Airport Road, Philipsburg, ☎ *(599-5) 543-39.*
French cuisine.
Dinner: 6–10 p.m., entrées $18–$26. Closed: Mon.
Situated in a typical West Indian house near the airport, this restaurant serves very unique meals. Once seated, servers wheel a cart to your table with a choice of nightly specials—which often include filets of ostrich or boar steaks. Surprisingly, ostrich tastes more like beef, rather than the expected chicken. For less adventurous palates, fresh red snapper or beef dishes are usually available. Simpson Bay Lagoon can be viewed from the plant-filled porch. Reservations required. Credit cards: A, MC, V.

Lynette's Grill and Seafood Re   **$$$**   ★★★

Airport Road, Philipsburg, ☎ *(599-5) 528-65.*
Caribbean cuisine.
Dinner: 6–10 p.m., entrées $15–$27.
Lynette's is the spot for authentic West Indian dishes prepared with casual flair in upscale surroundings near the foot of the Julina airstrip. Grilled fish, shrimp and lobster are usually excellent, while barbecued chicken or ribs, chateau briand and rack of lamb are designed for heartier appetites. Or stick to the local specialties, conch creole, stewed goat or fish and *funchi*. The service is always friendly and local recording artist King Bobo gyrates and sings merrily on Friday evenings. Credit cards: A, MC, V.

Sambuca Ristorante   **$$**   ★★★

46 Airport Road, Simpson Bay, Philipsburg, ☎ *(599-5) 526-33.*
Italian cuisine.
Dinner: 6–11 p.m., entrées $8–$13.
An attractive new Italian ristorante near the Juliana airport, Sambuca serves up tasty and inexpensive pizzas and pastas (the fusilli with chicken and broccoli is delicious), while specialties include eggplant parmigiana, a ribeye topped with peperoncini, carmelized onions and mushrooms, and chicken Marsala. Desserts include a pretty decent Tiramisu. The Sunday champagne brunch ($19.95) is appealing. Features: Sunday brunch. Credit cards: D, MC, V.

Saratoga   **$$$**   ★★★★

Simpson Bay Yacht Club, Philipsburg, ☎ *(599-5) 424-21.*
Seafood cuisine.
Dinner: 6:30–10 p.m., entrées $16–$26. Closed: Sun.
A perennial favorite, this yacht club restaurant in a mahogany-panelled dining room features a changing menu of very fresh seafood. Although pricey, its faithful following returns for specialties like scallops ceviche or salmon in puff pastry with spinach and mushrooms. Leafy salads feature at least two kinds of greens, served with two homemade dressings. Steaks and beef dishes are also available. Reservations recommended. Credit cards: A, MC, V.

Shivsager   **$$$**   ★★★

#3 Frontstreet; Philipsburg ☎ *(599-5) 222-99.*

Dinner: 6:30–10 p.m., entrées $11–$22.
The island's best Indian food is served up at this simply decorated Philipsburg restaurant across from the Barclay's Bank. There's a tandoori oven for kebabs and chicken *tikka*, while the chicken marsala and the mutton *rogan josh* are other recommended items. Samosas, fish and shrimp curry, chicken *mankhanwalia* and a variety of *naans* help to round out an authentic Indian dining experience. Credit cards: A, MC, V.

The Grill & Ribs Co. $$ ★ ★

Old Street Shopping Center, Philipsburg, ☎ *(599-5) 277-23.*
American cuisine.
Lunch: 11 a.m.–4 p.m., entrées $5–$6.
Dinner: 4–10 p.m., entrées $5–$14.
This informal place is the island's best-known and best-loved rib-arama. For a reasonable price of $12.95, diners can chow down on an unlimited amount of baby back pork or beef ribs. The Grill & Ribs Co. has two locations—a second-story alfresco terrace eatery at the Old Street Shopping Center, or the rib place behind Pizza Hut on Simpson Bay Beach. Other offerings include chicken fajitas, burgers, chicken and sandwiches heaped with a side of fries. Reservations required. Credit cards: not accepted.

The Seafood Galley $$ ★ ★ ★

Bobby's Marina, Philipsburg, ☎ *(599-5) 232-53.*
Seafood cuisine.
Lunch: 11 a.m.–3 p.m., entrées $7–$18.
Dinner: 6–10 p.m., entrées $7–$18. Closed: Sun.
Although this pier-side establishment has a clubby restaurant offering hot plates of fresh fish and seafood, some people bypass it and head straight for the adjoining raw bar. There they can graze all night from a generous menu of oyster shooters, clams on the half shell, or crab claws. Lunchtime is popular for the view and the hearty sandwiches and egg dishes. Reservations recommended. Credit cards: A, MC, V.

The Wajang Doll $$$ ★ ★ ★

137 Frontstreet, Philipsburg, ☎ *(599-5) 226-87.*
Asian cuisine. Specialties: Rijstaffel.
Dinner: 7–10 p.m., entrées $19–$25. Closed: Sun.
It helps to come here with a big group and a healthy appetite for this restaurant's 14- to 19-item Javanese feasts. This cuisine, known as *rijstaffel* (rice table), originated in the former Dutch colony of Indonesia. Seemingly endless plates of savory and spicy seafood, meats and chicken are served over a mountain of fragrant rice. They can be embellished with "try them if you dare" hot pepper *sambals*. Couples and singles won't feel left out, as smaller and cheaper versions are available as well as à la carte dishes. Reservations recommended. Credit cards: A, MC, V.

St. Martin

Bye Bar Brazil $$ ★ ★ ★ ★

47 Boulevard Grande Case, Marigot, ☎ *(590) 87-76-49.*
Latin American cuisine.
Dinner: 7 p.m.–3 a.m., entrées $8–$19. Closed: Tue.

Locals love to hang out here and talk literature and politics with Michel, the opin-
ionated (but gracious) owner of this laid-back spot in the heart of Grande Case.
Michel is famous for his *caipirinha*—a wonderful concoction of rum, sugar and
lime—as well as his selection of 38 whiskeys, including 16 single malts from Scotland. You can try three shots for $10. The Brazilian and French food is great, too,
and the entire wine list is available by the bottle and by the glass, something we'd
like to see more restaurants offer. Save room for the *manjar*, a coconut desert, then
try the *batita de coco*, a drink of coconut milk and rum that's an excellent digestive.
This place is not to be missed! Reservations recommended. Credit cards: MC, V.

Captain Oliver's Restaurant $$$ ★ ★ ★
Oyster Pond, Grand Case, ☎ *(590) 87-30-00. Associated hotel: Captain Oliver's.*
Seafood cuisine.
Lunch: Noon–2 p.m., entrées $16–$24.
Dinner: 7–11 p.m., entrées $16–$24.
A popular outdoor restaurant/snackbar/store on a pier facing the sea, Captain
Oliver's sits across from its namesake resort. A thoroughly democratic place, the
good Captain has provided a choice of eateries to fit every budget. There's a snack
shack dispensing brochettes, Indonesian lamb chops and other inexpensive meals
(open noon to midnight daily). The centerpiece, though, is the oceanfront restaurant, where creative international cuisine, with an emphasis on seafood, is served for
lunch and dinner. Soups are delicious and different, and the fresh tuna, when available, is stellar. Reservations recommended. Credit cards: A, DC, MC, V.

Cha Cha Cha's $$$ ★ ★ ★
Boulevard de Grand Case, Marigot, ☎ *(590) 87-53-63.*
Latin American cuisine.
Dinner: 6–11 p.m., entrées $11–$20.
This colorful cafe draws the au courant set who like to behave a little outre. The
menu is a melting pot of piquant Latin and Gallic specialties that usually taste as
good as they read. Skillfully grilled or steamed fresh seafood is served with tropical
salsas. Some people never make it to the dining room, preferring to graze on a daring tapas menu while sipping a blender drink in a whimsical garden. Come before 7
p.m. to save a little money on a generous prix-fixe, three-course supper for under
$20. Credit cards: MC, V.

Claude Mini Club $$$ ★ ★
Rue de la Liberte, Marigot, ☎ *(590) 87-50-69.*
French cuisine.
Lunch: Noon–3 p.m., entrées $12–$25.
Dinner: 7:30–10 p.m., entrées $18–$35.
Locals who like to stuff themselves silly with food as good as mother makes are
grateful for the continuing success of the gargantuan French-creole buffet served
here on Wednesdays and Saturday nights. The setting is lots of fun too: a jungly,
tropical terrace suspended over the water. The popular feast includes all the wine
you can drink, so bring a friend who can help you down the stairs. On other days
sample an unparalleled lobster soufflé and other French specialties. The buffet is

$40 per person, or the fixed priced dinner is $25. Closed for lunch Sunday. Reservations required. Credit cards: A, MC, V.

Coco Beach Bar $$$ ★★★

Orient Beach, Grand Case, ☎ *(590) 87-34-62.*
International cuisine.
Dinner: 6–10 p.m., entrées $12–$36.
By day Coco Beach bar is just one of a number of plain open-air eateries competing for the tourist dollar on clothing-optional Orient Beach. But at night, it becomes a quaint, little candlelit restaurant, with tastefully set tables and a diverse menu, which includes Caesar salad, stuffed crab, filet mignon, and grilled lobster with pasta. Softly lapping ocean waves provide atmospheric background music. Despite an often full-house, service is among the best on the island. Credit cards: A, MC, V.

David's $$ ★★★

Rue de la Liberté, Marigot, ☎ *(590) 87-51-58.*
English cuisine.
Lunch: 11:30 a.m.–2:30 p.m., entrées $6–$17.
Dinner: 6–10 p.m., entrées $6–$17.
When it's crowded, David's can be a convivial place, with word games or darts providing the entertainment while waiting for light pub fare or full dinners. An interesting menu of hearty soups, meat, and pasta dishes are all reasonably priced, and freshly caught seafood is a standout. The bar stays open until the witching hour and the scene can be boisterous or dull, depending upon who shows up. Reservations recommended. Credit cards: A, MC, V.

Drew's Deli $ ★★★

French Cul-de-Sac, Marigot.
American cuisine. Specialties: Cheeseburgers, cheesecake.
Lunch: 11 a.m.–3 p.m., entrées $3–$15.
Dinner: 7–9:30 p.m., entrées $3–$15. Closed: Fri., Sat.
North of Orient Bay lies the little community of French-Cul-de-Sac, where Drew from Wisconsin, a wonderful host, grills up some of the best bacon cheeseburgers around. Cole slaw and New York-style cheesecake with the burger provides a well-balanced vacation diet. The place is a little cramped, but the friendly reception might urge you to sit a spell. Full meals are also offered. Credit cards: A, MC, V.

Hevea $$$ ★★★

Boulevard de Grand Case, Grand Case, ☎ *(590) 87-56-85. Associated hotel: Hevea.*
French cuisine.
Dinner: 6:30–10 p.m., entrées $22–$38.
Set in a restored creole-style mansion that is also an intimate inn, this 10-table French eatery is charming and romantic. The small size of the dining room ensures the consistently fine quality of the French cuisine served here. The proprietors, who hail from Nice, use only the finest ingredients and believe that simplicity is key. Sauces made with fresh herbs, wine reductions, or wild mushrooms are often used to subtly accentuate, never overpower, lamb, duck breast, or a signature red snapper en papillote. Closed Mondays from April 15–December 14. Reservations recommended. Credit cards: MC, V.

La Maison sur le Port   **$$$**   ★★★

Rue de la Republique, Marigot, ☎ *(590) 87-56-38.*
French cuisine.
Lunch: Noon–2:30 p.m., entrées $11–$14.
Dinner: 6–10:30 p.m., entrées $17–$34. Closed: Sun.

Positioned in a lovely colonial-style house overlooking the harbor, chef Christian Verdeau presents impeccably prepared but rather small portions of duck (a specialty), lobster and other prime meats and seafood. The veranda is especially popular for sunset views. You get a good value for the excellent quality of the ingredients, and a warm welcome is reserved for all comers. Closed June and September. Reservations recommended. Credit cards: A, CB, MC, V.

La Nadaillac   **$$$**   ★★★

Rue de la Liberte, Marigot, ☎ *(590) 87-53-77.*
French cuisine.
Lunch: Noon–2:30 p.m., entrées $16–$32.
Dinner: 6:30–9:30 p.m., entrées $16–$32.

This intimate gem, albeit a very dear one (as in prices), is the province of Fernand Mallard, from the Perigord. Appropriately enough, most specialties involve products from that region of France, including preserved goose. The restaurant is on an attractive patio facing the harbor, nestled among the chic clothing stores in the Galerie Perigourdine. Reservations required. Credit cards: A, DC, MC, V.

La Rhumerie   **$$$**   ★★★

route de Colombier ☎ *(590) 87-56-98.*
French-creole cuisine.
Dinner: 7–10 p.m., entrées $16–$45. Closed: Thurs.

A lovely countryside setting far from the citified pace of St. Martin is the spot for this French and creole restaurant. Avacado *farcee*, stuffed crab backs, herbed conch and smoked chicken are menu highlights. Desserts are heavenly and include bananas flambee and *profiteroles*, or simply papayas drizzled with lime. As a topper, try one of the flavored rums that sit elegantly in jars on the bar counter—passion fruit, prune, coconut and others. La Rhumerie would be the perfect escape for lunch, but it's open for dinner only. Closed September–October. Credit cards: CB, MC, V.

L'Auberge Gourmande   **$$$**   ★★★★

89 Boulevard Grand Case, Grand Case, ☎ *(590) 87-73-37.*
French cuisine.
Dinner: 6:30–10 p.m., entrées $15–$31. Closed: Wed.

The setting is a quaint, converted residence sporting jalousied windows. Guests dine by candlelight in a comfortable room, although noise on the streets of Grand Case may affect a romantic tete-a-tete. Soups are a specialty and are interestingly prepared, including a brew of mussels with orange, and a fine grouper in leek sauce. Grilled fish is reliable, although the roast pork and roast lamb were only average on one occasion and the once-impeccable service has slipped as of late. Reservations required. Credit cards: A, MC, V.

Les Lolos   **$**   ★★

Boulevard Grande Case, Grand Case.
Seafood cuisine.

The food stalls that line a section of Grande Case Bouldvard are known as *lolos*, though most were washed out to sea during Hurricane Luis. Fortunately for us, eight or 10 have been rebuilt in time for the 1996–97 season. These mom-and-pop operations offer the freshest seafood and local treats each day for amazingly low prices (at least, in comparison to the rest of this island). Most open from noon on, but it's a catch-as-catch-can type of business—the one named Talk of the Town is just that. Well worth checking out on any budget. Credit cards: not accepted.

L'ile Flottante $ ★★

Boulevard Grande Case, Grand Case, ☎ (590) 87-89-46.
French cuisine.
This open-air French bakery is just about the only place to get breakfast in Grande Case. They offer up wonderful pastries and delicious cafe au lait, but don't expect service with a smile—unless you're a local. Open daily from 6-10 a.m. Credit cards: not accepted.

Mark's Place $ ★★★

French-Cul-de-Sac, Marigot, ☎ (590) 87-34-50.
Latin American cuisine.
Lunch: 12:30–2:30 p.m., entrées $3–$13.
Dinner: 6:30–9:30 p.m., entrées $3–$13. Closed: Mon.
The West Indian food served here is hearty, plentiful, and varied—on a given night you could have lobster bisque with a curry of conch or goat, or a crab back appetizer and swordfish, but sometimes the quality is unexceptional. It's hard to quibble with the reasonable prices, but you get what you pay for. And the crowds keep coming—Mark's Place is usually jammed. Credit cards: A, MC, V.

Rainbow $$$ ★★★★

176 boulevard de Grand Case, Grand Case, ☎ (590) 87-55-80.
French cuisine.
Dinner: 6:30–10:30 p.m., entrées $18–$34. Closed: Sun.
Going on its 17th year, David and Fleur's romantic seaside eatery is not inexpensive, but the simple, blue-and-white wooden cottage belies the gastronomique delights that pour forth from the kitchen of Frederick Lecullier the restaurant's new chef. The always-evolving menu leans to French contemporary, with a succulent spicy shrimp salad and a number of grilled meat and fish dishes prepared with flair. Always fashionable, Rainbow remains a true "in" spot with locals. Closed annually from mid-September through October. Credit cards: A, MC, V.

Surf Club South $ ★★

Boulevard Grande Case, Marigot.
American cuisine.
New Jersey natives will do a double take as they come upon the Garden State Parkway, Turnpike and other highway signs prominently displayed on Boulevard Grande Case. Jersey expatriots run this funky spot, which boasts of a "New Jersey menu" (lots of burgers and cheese steaks). It's a happening spot, especially on Sunday, when they give out free drinks from 10 a.m.–2 p.m. and live music kicks in at 6 p.m. All the locals come and party, then head over to Jimbo's when the Surf Club closes at 10 p.m.

FIELDING'S CHOICE:

Little known to the outside world is the special purple and bittersweet gua-vaberry liqueur produced on the island ever since Dutch colonists settled in the 18th century. During the Christmas holidays, it's customary to go from home to home serenading for samples. Every family makes a different brew, which is usually fully consumed by the end of the Christmas season. The Sint Maarten Guavaberry Company now makes the liqueur locally, and offers shade, seating and a few samples at its midtown production area at the Gua-vaberry Shop on 10 Front St. Try a guavaberry colada (blended with cream of coconut and pineapple juice), or a guavaberry screwdriver (mixed with orange juice). A bottle of guavaberry sells for less than $15 and is considered duty-free because it is an island craft.

Where to Shop

Shopping is a major industry here, and Sint Maarten/St. Martin's duty-free port carries all of the typical products one would expect to find at 25–50 percent discounts: china, jewelry, crystal, perfumes and fashions. Prices are usually quoted in U.S. dollars and virtually all sales clerks speak English. Bargaining is not part of the culture on either side of the island, though discounts are sometimes offered to those paying by traveler's checks. Before beginning your shopping splurge, it pays to know what the prices are at home.

Marigot is the main shopping area of French St. Martin—be prepared to pay in French francs if you want a good exchange. The **Gold Mine** reputedly carries the largest diamond inventory in the Caribbean. High fashion designs can be found in the **Galerie Perigourdine** shopping complex, across from the post office, and the **Marina Royale** has another good collection of shops. **Ma Doudou** makes traditional West Indian fruit-imbued rums of coconut, orange and other flavors—the bottles make inexpensive and attractive gifts for about $10. Local art shown in galleries and studios can sometimes be reasonable and several local artists are known outside the region; besides Roland Richardson in Orleans (see "What Else to See"), seek out the work of Genevieve Curt at the **Tropical Gallery**. Other fine names are the painter Alexandre Minguet, and the Lynn family (husband, wife and two sons). There is a twice-weekly **market** in **Marigot** (Wednesday and Saturday mornings), where locals sell their spices, fruits, vegetables and handicrafts. Marigot's **Port la Royale** is a beehive of activity after dawn; hang out here if you want to meet yachties and even local schooner captains cruising in from other islands with new goods. Shopping in Grand Case is limited to the narrow main street.

Philipsburg, capital of Dutch St. Maarten, is full of shops and markets.

Philipsburg and the Dutch side is less fashion-oriented than St. Martin, and you'll need to wander past the maze of T-shirt and trinket shops, but you can find memorable leather products (**Domina**), clothes (**Maurella Senesi**) and jewelry (**Caribbean Gems**). The **Shipwreck Shop** on Frontstreet has an eclectic array of island goods, maps, and Lord & Hunter spices. Gucci, H. Stern Jewelers, Little Switzerland, Benetton and other name brands are represented in Philipsburg. **Sualouiga Festival** is an open market held on Fridays in Philipsburg, with local food, handicrafts, exhibits and music. Another area to hunt for bargains is the **Maho** complex.

On the French side, shops are generally open Monday through Friday from 9 a.m.–noon, and from 2–6 p.m. Shops on Sint Marten are typically open 8 a.m.–noon, and 2–6 p.m. Monday through Friday; most Dutch shops are also open Saturday mornings and Philipsburg stores will usually open on Sundays if a cruise ship has landed.

Sint Maarten/St. Martin Directory

Arrival and Departure

Sint Maarten's **Juliana Airport** is one of the best-connected in the Caribbean (a small airstrip on the French side, **L'Esperance**, connects St. Martin with the nearby French islands only). American Airlines has daily non-stop flights from New York's JFK and Miami, as well as several flights daily from its hub in San

Juan, Puerto Rico. **Continental** serves Sint Maarten several times weekly out of Newark, and **USAir** flies to the island several times a week from Baltimore. Of the regional carriers, **LIAT** offers direct or non-stop service from Anguilla, Antigua, St. Croix, St. Kitts, St. Thomas and Tortola. **BWIA** offers limited service to Juliana from Jamaica and Barbados. **Winair** connects Sint Maarten with Saba and Sint Eustatius, as well as other nearby islands. **ALM Antillean** flies in from Aruba, Bonaire and Curaçao. **Air Martinique**, **Air Guadeloupe** and **Air St. Barts** serve the French islands out of both Juliana and L'Esperance.

There is a departure tax from Juliana Airport of $12, or $5 if you are headed for other islands in the Netherlands Antilles.

Business Hours

On the Dutch side, shops open Monday–Saturday 8 a.m.–noon and 2–6 p.m. Banks open Monday–Thursday 8 a.m.–1 p.m. and Friday from 8:30 a.m.–1 p.m. and 4–5 p.m. On the French side, shops open Monday–Saturday 9 a.m.–12:30 p.m. and 3–7 p.m. Some shops take a longer or shorter siesta, so call ahead. Banks open weekdays 8:30 a.m.–1:30 p.m.

Climate

Sunshine prevails on the island and it is warm year-round. Temperatures during the winter average 80 degrees Fahrenheit, in the summer, it gets a little warmer. Constant trade winds keep the climate pleasant.

Documents

U.S. citizens entering via the Dutch side (Juliana Airport) for stays of up to three months need a valid passport, or one that has expired no longer than five years prior, or a notarized or original birth certificate with raised seal, or a voter's registration card. Canadian citizens must have a valid passport. U.S. residents and Canadians who are not citizens must have a green card or multiple re-entry stamp. Travelers must also show a return or onward ticket.

U.S. citizens and Canadians traveling as tourists and entering via the French side (Espérance Airport) for stays up to three weeks must have proof of citizenship in the form of a valid passport, a passport that has expired no more than five years prior, or other proof of citizenship, in the form of a birth certificate (original or official copy), or a voter's registration card, plus a government-authorized identification with photo. For stays over three weeks, or for nontourist visits, a valid passport is necessary. Resident aliens of the U.S. and Canada, and visitors from countries other than those of the Common Market (E.E.C.) and Japan, must have a valid passport and visa. A return or onward ticket is also required for all visitors.

Electricity

The Dutch side is wired for 110 volts, 60 cycles. The French side is set up for 220 AC, 50 cycles—American and Canadian appliances require French plug converters and transformers.

Getting Around

Taxis are prevalent at Juliana Airport. Rates from the airport to Philipsburg are about $10, to Marigot, about $8, and about $16 to Grand Case. Between 10 p.m. and midnight, rates rise 25 percent; after midnight, 50 percent. The taxi stand in **Marigot** is located near the tourist office ☎ *(590) 87-56-54*; in **Grand Case** ☎ *(590) 87-75-79*. **Car rentals** are easy and abundant on the island. In addition to numerous local firms, several of the name American outfits provide rentals on the French and/or Dutch side, including **Avis**, **Budget**, **Dollar**, **Hertz** and **National**.

Day-trips to neighboring islands are easy and popular. Closest and easiest to reach is Anguilla, which is a five-minute flight from Juliana, or a 15-minute **ferry ride** that leaves from the Marigot marina to Blowing Point every 30 minutes (see "Arrival and Departure" in "Anguilla"). St. Barts can be reached by plane from either Juliana or L'Esperance airport, or via boat from Marigot or Philipsburg into Gustavia (see "Arrival and Departure" in "St. Barthélémy"). You will be hit with a $12 departure tax for day trips to Anguilla, St. Barts, or other non-Dutch islands; $5 for trips to other islands in the Netherlands Antilles.

Language

French is the official language of St. Martin and Dutch is the official language of Sint Maarten. English is spoken everywhere on the Dutch side, and in virtually all establishments catering to tourists on the French side.

Medical Emergencies

There is a hospital in Marigot ☎ *(590) 29-57-57*, and another in Philipsburg ☎ *(599-5) 221-11*. Hotels can contact English-speaking physicians for you. There are about 18 doctors practicing general medicine and specialists in many fields. There are several pharmacies in St. Martin, and a medical clinic and pharmacy at Maho Bay. Serious emergencies may warrant a trip to San Juan.

Money

The official currency on the French side is the French franc, and the guilder on the Dutch side, but U.S. dollars are accepted everywhere and prices are usually quoted in U.S. dollars, particularly in Sint Maarten. The rates of exchange fluctuates, but at press time the French franc was trading at about 5 to the dollar, while Dutch guilders were about 1.80 to the dollar.

Telephone

The international country code for St. Martin is *590*. To call the Dutch side, dial the code *599-5*. French side numbers have 6 digits, the Dutch side 5. The cheapest way to make calls is with a telephone card on public phones (eight on the square in Marigot and two in Grand Case in front of the pier). It's a toll call when phoning from one side of the island to the other.

Time

St. Martin is one hour ahead of East Standard Time in New York. French St. Martin uses the 24-hour system of telling time; hence, 1 p.m. in the afternoon is 13 hours.

Tipping and Taxes

Most Sint Maarten hotels include a 5 percent tax and 10–15 percent service charge in their quoted room rates—some add an energy surcharge. If no service charge is added, feel free to leave 10–15 percent on restaurant bills.

Tourist Information

The **Dutch Sint Maarten Tourist Office** is located at Wathey Square in Philipsburg ☎ *(599-5) 223-37*. The **French St. Martin Tourist Office** is located at the waterfront in Marigot ☎ *(590) 87-57-21*. In the United States, information on Dutch Sint Maarten is obtained through ☎ *(800) STMAARTEN* or ☎ *(212) 953-2084*; for French St. Martin ☎ *(212) 529-8484*. The French side also maintains an information center at ☎ *(900) 990-0040*, but be forewarned you'll be charged.95 per minute on your phone bill.

When to Go

Mardi Gras is held on February 28, a frenzied carnival with dancing filling the streets of Marigot and Grand Case. Another carnival, with calypso, "jump ups," floats, steel bands and bright costumes takes place the last two weeks in April and early May, mostly on the Dutch side, but with some French participation. The Marlin Open de St. Martin on May 29–June 3 is an invitational organized by the Sailfish Caraibes Club. June 6 is the African Festival with arts, crafts, music and dance lectures. Bastille Day on July 14 is celebrated with fireworks, parades and sports contests. Schoelcher Day, on July 21, in honor of the French parliamentarian who led the campaign against slavery, is celebrated with boat and bike races. Halloween is a wild affair in Grande Case, when locals go crazy with exotic costumes. Concordia Day, on November 11, starts the season off with parades and ceremonies. New Year's Eve, called *Réveillon de la Saint Sylvestre*, is celebrated noisily with balloons, late-night dancing and dining at hotels and restaurants.

SINT MAARTEN/ ST. MARTIN HOTELS		RMS	RATES	PHONE	CR. CARDS
Sint Maarten					
Philipsburg					
★★★★	**Point Pirouette Villas**	85	$161–$845	(800) 365-8484	A, MC, V
★★★★	**Port de Plaisance**		$220–$600	(800) 732-9480	A, DC, MC, V
★★★	**Beachside Villas**	14	$150–$295	(599-5) 542-94	A, MC
★★★	**Cupecoy Beach Club**	126	$100–$500	(215) 885-9008	
★★★	**Divi Little Bay Beach Resort**	118	$120–$300	(800) 367-3484	A, DC, MC, V
★★★	**Great Bay Beach Hotel**	285	$85–$260	(800) 223-0757	A, DC, MC, V
★★★	**Horny Toad Guesthouse**	8	$98–$180	(800) 351-5656	

SINT MAARTEN/ ST. MARTIN HOTELS		RMS	RATES	PHONE	CR. CARDS
★★★	Maho Beach Hotel & Casino	600	$110–$590	(800) 223-0757	A, DC, MC, V
★★★	Mary's Boon	12	$90–$150	(800) 351-5656	
★★★	Mullet Bay Resort	570	$270–$765	(800) 468-5538	A, DC, MC, V
★★★	Oyster Bay Beach Resort	40	$120–$360	(800) 231-8331	A, D, DC, MC, V
★★★	Pelican Resort & Casino	343	$95–$270	(800) 626-9637	A, D, MC, V
★★★	Royal Islander Club	135	$108–$336	(800) 223-0757	A, D, DC, MC, V
★★	Belair Beach Hotel	72	$165–$375	(599-5) 233-66	A, MC, V
★★	Holland House Beach Hotel	54	$74–$190	(800) 223-9815	A, D, MC, V
★★	Horizon View Beach Hotel	30	$90–$225	(599-5) 321-20	A, MC, V
★★	Pasanggrahan Royal Guest House	30	$78–$158	(800) 351-5656	A, MC
★★	Point at Burgeaux Bay	14	$70–$395	(599-5) 543-35	None
★★	Summit Resort Hotel	50	$80–$190	(800) 351-5656	A, MC, V
★★	Town House Villas	12	$125–$300	(800) 223-9815	A, MC, V
★	Beach House	10	$53–$100	(599-5) 224-56	A, MC
★	Tradewinds Beach Inn	10	$61–$155	(599-5) 542-06	

St. Martin

Grand Case

★★★★	Esmeralda Resort	65	$180–$950	(800) 622-7836	A, MC, V
★★★★	Green Cay Village	16	$1800–$2400	(800) 476-5849	A, D, DC, MC, V
★★★★	Le Meridien l'Habitation	396	$160–$780	(800) 543-4300	A, DC, MC, V
★★★★	Privilege Resort & Spa	27	$180–$640	(800) 874-8541	A, DC, MC, V
★★★	Grand Case Beach Club	71	$95–$290	(800) 423-4433	A, DC, MC, V
★★★	L'Esplanade Caraibe Hotel	24	$100–$300	(800) 633-7411	A, MC, V
★★★	Mont Vernon	394	$120–$415	(800) 223-0888	A, MC, V
★★★	Pavillion Beach Hotel	16	$90–$280	(800) 322-2223	A, D, MC, V
★★★	St. Tropez	84	$120–$235	(800) 476-5849	A, MC, V
★★	Club Orient Resort	108	$115–$340	(800) 476-5849	A, CB, D, DC, MC, V
★★	Hevea	8	$40–$99	(590) 87-56-85	
★★	Hotel le Belvedere	130	$85–$120	(590) 87-37-89	A, MC, V

SINT MAARTEN/ ST. MARTIN HOTELS	RMS	RATES	PHONE	CR. CARDS
Marigot				
★★★★★ **La Belle Creole**	160	$205–$455	(590) 87-66-00	A, CB, MC, V
★★★★★ **La Samanna**	80	$250–$1900	(800) 854-2252	A, MC, V
★★★★ **Dawn Beach Hotel**	155	$105–$290	(800) 351-5656	A, MC, V
★★★ **Anse Margot**	96	$125–$249	(800) 742-4276	A, D, DC, MC, V
★★★ **Captain Oliver's Hotel**	50	$84–$225	(800) 447-7462	A, MC, V
★★★ **Golden Tulip St., Martin**	94	$95–$140	(800) 344-1212	A, D, MC, V
★★★ **Laguna Beach Hotel**	62	$88–$245	(800) 333-1970	A, MC, V
★★★ **Le Flamboyant**	271	$150–$395	(800) 221-5333	A, MC, V
★★★ **Nettle Bay Beach Club**	230	$100–$455	(800) 999-3543	A, DC, MC, V
★★ **Coralita Beach Hotel**	24	$115–$140	(590) 87-31-81	A, CB, MC, V
★★ **Hotel Royal Beach**	113	$70–$132	(590) 87-89-89	A, MC, V
★★ **La Residence**	21	$74–$98	(800) 365-8484	A, D, MC, V
★★ **Le Pirate Beach Hotel**	60	$110–$180	(800) 666-5756	A, MC, V
★★ **Marine Hotel Simson Beach**	165	$110–$263	(800) 221-4542	A, CB, MC, V
★★ **Royale Louisiana**	58	$66–$88	(590) 87-86-51	MC, V
★★ **Sol Hotel**	8	$90–$125	(800) 476-5849	A, MC, V

SINT MAARTEN/ ST. MARTIN RESTAURANTS	PHONE	ENTRÉE	CR. CARDS
Sint Maarten			
Philipsburg			
★★★ **Da Livio Ristorante**	(599-5) 226-90	$16–$30	DC, MC, V
★★★ **Lynette's Grill and Seafood Re**	(599-5) 528-65	$15–$27	A, MC, V
★★★ **Sambuca Ristorante**	(599-5) 526-33	$8–$13	D, MC, V
★★★ **Shivsager**	(599-5) 222-99	$11–$22	A, MC, V
American			
★★★ **Chesterfield's**	(559-5) 234-84	$7–$20	None
★★ **Cheri's Cafe**	(599-5) 533-61	$6–$17	None
★★ **Greenhouse**	(599-5) 229-41	$6–$25	A, MC, V

SINT MAARTEN/ ST. MARTIN RESTAURANTS	PHONE	ENTRÉE	CR. CARDS
★★ The Grill & Ribs Co.	(599-5) 277-23	$5–$14	None
Asian			
★★★ The Wajang Doll	(599-5) 226-87	$19–$25	A, MC, V
French			
★★★★ Antoine's	(599-5) 229-64	$16–$36	A, MC, V
★★★★ Le Perroquet	(599-5) 543-39	$18–$26	A, MC, V
★★★ L'Escargot	(599-5) 224-83	$8–$29	A, MC, V
★★★ Le Bec Fin	(599-5) 229-76	$16–$31	A, MC, V
Seafood			
★★★★ Saratoga	(599-5) 424-21	$16–$26	A, MC, V
★★★ The Seafood Galley	(599-5) 232-53	$7–$18	A, MC, V

St. Martin

Colombier

French			
★★★ La Rhumerie	(590) 87-56-98	$16–$45	CB, MC, V

Grand Case

★★★★ L'Auberge Gourmande	(590) 87-73-37	$15–$31	A, MC, V
★★★ Hevea	(590) 87-56-85	$22–$38	MC, V
★★ L'ile Flottante	(590) 87-89-46		None
International			
★★★ Coco Beach Bar	(590) 87-34-62	$12–$36	A, MC, V
Seafood			
★★★★ Rainbow	(590) 87-55-80	$18–$34	A, MC, V
★★★ Captain Oliver's Restaurant	(590) 87-30-00	$16–$24	A, DC, MC, V
★★ Les Lolos			None

Marigot

American			
★★★ Drew's Deli		$3–$15	A, MC, V
★★ Surf Club South			

SINT MAARTEN/ ST. MARTIN RESTAURANTS	PHONE	ENTRÉE	CR. CARDS
English			
★★★ **David's**	(590) 87-51-58	$6–$17	A, MC, V
French			
★★★ **La Maison sur le Port**	(590) 87-56-38	$11–$34	A, CB, MC, V
★★★ **La Nadaillac**	(590) 87-53-77	$16–$32	A, DC, MC, V
★★ **Claude Mini Club**	(590) 87-50-69	$12–$35	A, MC, V
Latin American			
★★★★ **Bye Bar Brazil**	(590) 87-76-49	$8–$19	MC, V
★★★ **Cha Cha Cha's**	(590) 87-53-63	$11–$20	MC, V
★★★ **Mark's Place**	(590) 87-34-50	$3–$13	A, MC, V

ST. THOMAS

St. Thomas has 34 dive sites and offers excellent snorkeling.

Few sights are as breathtaking as the one of St. Thomas's glittering Charlotte Amalie harbor, particularly when seen high above from Paradise Point at dusk. Enormous cruise ships ply the water, the downtown area bustles with shoppers, homes dot the verdant slopes, and comely swathes of sand can be seen in the distance. It's a seductive vision, and for many it defines the quintessential Caribbean paradise. In fact, St. Thomas is the most cosmopolitan of the U.S. Virgin Islands, and perhaps the most unabashedly commercial destination in the entire Caribbean, as well. With the capacity to dock up to 10 cruise ships in a single day, and an extensive infrastructure in hot pursuit of the tourist dollar, the island will be a serious turnoff to anyone in search of genuine retreat and tranquillity. On the other hand, if your vacation is geared toward shopping, fine dining and Americanized nightlife, St. Thomas may be exactly what you're looking for.

Not everything is perfect in paradise as we go to press. Hurricane Marilyn delivered a body blow to St. Thomas in September 1995. The "storm of the century" churned a path of destruction that, one year later, left the island still desperately trying to recover. Compounding the damage by Marilyn, several violent incidents made their way into American newspapers in 1996, as if to provide potential visitors one more reason to choose another island for their hard-earned vacation. The good news is that, at press time, almost all of the resorts are back in operation, the beaches have been cleared and cleaned, and the primary shopping area, Charlotte Amalie's Main Street, has been turned into a pedestrian street mall, a much-needed improvement to solve the grid-lock that previously plagued the town. The crime rate, however, is alarming, and some of it has been directed at tourists. Realistically, however, one need only take the kind of precautions here that one would take visiting any large American city. In the end, many islanders are choosing to see a silver lining to Marilyn—that the storm may have provided a much-needed (if costly) excuse to re-examine St. Thomas's overdevelopment and to force people to quit ignoring the need to make the hard choices for the future.

St. Thomas is about 40 miles north of St. Croix and just two miles west of St. John, the sister islands that make up the bulk of the 68 or so U.S. Virgin Islands. The island lies about 75 miles east of Puerto Rico. With an official population of 48,166 residents for its 32 square miles, St. Thomas vies with St. Martin/Sint Maarten as the most populous island in the Caribbean, and homes crawl along ridges and down valleys in every direction—only the western tip of the island remains relatively undeveloped. Sometimes referred to as "Rock City" for the way it is draped onto steep slopes, Charlotte Amalie is the hub of most non-beach activities. Although a few inns are nestled into the hills immediately behind the town, most of the island's 2000-plus rooms lie along the coastline, where a succession of pretty beaches invite sunning and relaxing. Viewed from a distance, Magens Bay is a world treasure, though by late morning the sand is covered with day-trippers fresh off the cruise ships, each one in search of the pristine beauty promised in glossy brochures. The island rolls to its apex at Crown Mountain, 1556 feet high, and a slender spine of ridges taper off east and west of this point. St. Thomas is easy to navigate by auto, but also time-consuming—there is a daily traffic jam that clogs downtown Charlotte Amalie at rush hour, particularly late af-

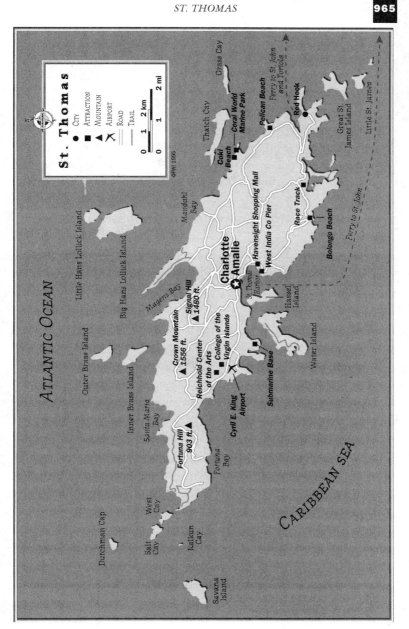

St. Thomas

- ● City
- ■ Attraction
- ▲ Mountain
- ✈ Airport
- ═══ Road
- ─── Trail

0   1   2 km
0   1   2 mi

©FW 1995

ATLANTIC OCEAN

CARIBBEAN SEA

Grass Cay
Thatch Cay
Little Hans Lollick Island
Big Hans Lollick Island
Outer Brass Island
Inner Brass Island
Dutchman Cap
West Cay
Salt Cay
Kalkun Cay
Savana Island

Pelican Beach
Ferry to St. John and Tortola
Red Hook
Great St. James Island
Little St. James

Coral World Marine Park
Coki Beach
Mandahl Bay
Havensight Shopping Mall
West India Co Pier
Race Track
Bolongo Beach
Ferry to St. John

Charlotte Amalie
St. Thomas Harbor
Hassel Island
Water Island

Signal Hill ▲ 1480 ft.
Crown Mountain ▲ 1556 ft.
Magens Bay
Santa Maria Bay
Fortuna Hill ▲ 903 ft.
Fortuna Bay
College of the Virgin Islands
Reichhold Center of the Arts
Cyril E. King Airport
Submarine Base

ternoon when a large contingent of cruise ships are loading package-laden passengers for the trip to the next port.

The tram to Paradise Point gives a bird's eye view of the St. Thomas harbor.

History

As with St. Croix and St. John, Columbus discovered these islands on his third voyage in 1493. A plan for colonizing St. Thomas was signed by Frederick III of Denmark, but the first settlement failed. Charlotte Amalie, St. Thomas's first permanent European settlement, dates back to 1671. Set on a grand circular harbor, the town was laid out by planners in Denmark who had never seen the mountainous 32-square mile island. Danish control of the Virgin Islands ended when the U.S. bought St. Croix, St. Thomas and St. John for $25 million in order to protect its interests in the Panama Canal. Today, the self-governing unincorporated territory has a nonvoting delegate to the U.S. House of Representatives.

People

For many years, the U.S. Virgin Islands have been sold to vacationers as an American Paradise, and St. Thomas is where the American flag flies most

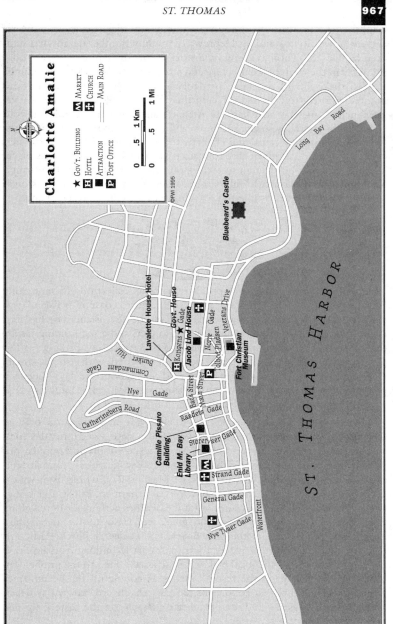

Charlotte Amalie

★ GOV'T. BUILDING   M MARKET
H HOTEL   ✝ CHURCH
■ ATTRACTION   MAIN ROAD
P POST OFFICE

0   .5   1 Km
0   .5   1 Mi

©FW 1995

Bluebeard's Castle

Lavalette House Hotel

Gov't. House Gade

Jacob Lind House

Commandant Gade

Bunker Hill

Kongens Gade

Norre Gade

Talbod Pladsen

Veterans Drive

Fort Christian Museum

Nye Gade

Catherineberg Road

Back Street

Main Street

Raadets Gade

Camille Pissaro Building

Enid M. Bay Library

Storetvaer Gade

Strand Gade

General Gade

Nye Tvaer Gade

Waterfront

ST. THOMAS HARBOR

Long Bay Road

brightly. The population, though predominantly black African, is diverse and includes a long-standing Hebrew community numbering about a hundred families. St. Thomas's lengthy history as part of Denmark is seen today primarily in the form of architecture and street names. Many islanders can be curt to the point of rudeness, particularly taxi drivers (who, some locals pointedly note, "run the island" with their considerable clout). The icy veneer melts somewhat in Charlotte Amalie's shops when you roll out your wallet for big purchases. The surliness can be excused to some degree by the fact that this island is invaded literally by thousands of cruise-ship passengers every day—although given that tourism is virtually the only business on St. Thomas, it might be prudent to receive outsiders with a little more warmth. St. Thomas also has a colorful Carnival celebration in April which is quite festive with parades, costumed Mocko Jumbies on stilts, and steel bands.

Beaches

One of St. Thomas's biggest appeals remains its collection of shimmering beaches, lead by spectacular **Magens Bay**, on the north coast of the island (opposite Charlotte Amalie). Magens is one of the few island beaches that doesn't have a chain of hotels along its perimeter, and a self-guiding nature trail adds to the attraction. Despite an admission price and parking fee ($1 per person and $1 per car), it is also the most crowded, with a steady stream of cruise-ship passengers landing on its sand throughout the day. Magens is perhaps best appreciated from the dazzling viewpoint at Mountain Top, where a bar and shopping mall are a diversion for island tours.

But there are plenty of other beaches to choose from. Among the best are **Coki Beach**, where snorkeling is excellent and a pate stand provides local snacks; **Limetree Beach**, just east of the Morningstar Resort and popular not just for swimming but iguana sightings; **Brewer's Bay**, near the University and airport runway, and **Hull Bay**, just east of Magens Bay, where calm waters greet bathers and provide anchorage for local fishermen, but winter brings swells off a long reef ideal for surfing. Of the beaches with major hotels along their length, the choice spots are **St. John's Bay** (also known as Sapphire Beach, after the resort), **Morningstar Beach**, and **Lindbergh Beach**. Although the latter suffers from the noise of jets, particularly midday (the airport is nearby), Lindbergh is the local pick. All beaches are open to the public. Watersports are available at the resort beaches. A couple off-the-beaten-track beauties where swimming conditions are less reliable are **Stumpy Bay Beach** on the island's western end, and **Bluebeard's Beach**, on the eastern tip just past the Ritz Carlton.

FIELDING'S CHOICE:

From January to April, pilot whales frequent the breeding grounds off the north end of the island. Inquire at your sports activity center about whale-watch tours.

Underwater

St. Thomas probably does more dive business than any other destination in the Eastern Caribbean, resulting in a profusion of operators. Most of the diving is easily accessible and not difficult, and certification and resort courses are very popular. Make sure the dive shop you select is not one of the cattle-drive operators geared toward massive groups of cruise-ship passengers. Locals will reluctantly point out that St. Thomas (like St. John) doesn't offer a lot of big fish and there are no real walls, but decent reef dives are available off the cays clustered around the island, particularly on its eastern half (see "Underwater" in "St. John" for some of the shared destinations in the Pillsbury Sound). Shore diving is nice from Coki Bay. Several good wrecks ornament the St. Thomas depths, and local dive shops offer weekly trips to the wreck of the *RMS Rhone* in the British Virgins; prices vary, but be sure to bring your passport or birth certificate if you want to make the trip. Visibility normally averages 80 to 100 feet. A recompression chamber is available at the St. Thomas Naval Hospital.

On Foot

Bustling St. Thomas is undeniably beautiful, but it's also one of the most heavily developed and densely populated islands in the Eastern Caribbean. Its relatively compact, 14-by-three-mile size, coupled with a population approaching 50,000, means that truly virgin territory is long gone. Paved roads lead to the island's highest point, Crown Mountain (1556 feet), and snake to the crests of other scenic vistas. So, where does a walker go? **Hassel Island** (recently adopted as part of the National Park) features nice beaches and a long-abandoned ruin, **Fort Cowell**, but is currently reachable only by private boat. Nearby **Water Island**, the fourth largest of the U.S. Virgins, was an Army base during World War II and later, its (now-closed) hotel may have served as inspiration for Herman Wouk's *Don't Stop the Carnival*. The island has a small population and a manufactured, quarter-mile strip of sand; impromptu ferry service is provided to Water Island by its residents. A St. Thomas walking itinerary also should include a tour of charming **Charlotte Amalie**, which buzzes with activity when cruise ships are docked, and even when they aren't. For ample appreciation of the capitol's history, pick up a **Historic District Guide** from the tourist office.

Of course, serious hikers need only step onto the ferry in Charlotte Amalie or Red Hook to visit **St. John**, where the national park provides 22 hiking possibilities (see "On Foot" in "St. John" for more information).

Bicycling on St. Thomas is not to be taken lightly. The island's heavily trafficked roads are complicated by steep grades and switchbacks, making cycling a brain-rattling experience, and not for the timid. No bike rental outfits exist at present, but **Island Bike Adventures** does group excursion tours to quiet Picara Point and Magens Bay for cruise ship passengers ☎ *(809) 776-1727.*

Sailboats leave Charlotte Amalie for excursions to St. John and the British Virgin Islands.

Charming, though busy, Charlotte Amalie is worth a half day of exploration and shopping. Schedule it for a rainy day if the clouds are so inclined. The Government House is a bit of a bore, while the Virgin Islands Museum, housed in Fort Christian, might harbor a few ghosts—it was the center of social and political activity on the island for several hundred years. It's a striking Danish building of red brick and the oldest structure still in use on the island. Also worth visiting in town are some of the historic churches, but particularly the St. Thomas Synagogue, which celebrated its bicentennial in 1996 with a series of very high-profile events. The steep 99 Steps that rise to the top of Government Hill were the product of over-zealous 18th-century Danish engineers who wanted the city laid out in a grid (and actually, there's 103 steps). Near the top of the steps is Blackbeard's Castle, a recently-designated National Historic Landmark, and reputedly once the haunt of pirate Edward Teach—it's now a hotel and restaurant. Just outside Charlotte Amalie, above the cruise ship dock, is Paradise Point, a terrific scenic overlook reached by aerial tram or via a winding road that begins just past the tram station. The view of the town and harbor at sunset is unbeatable.

Half of another day can be devoted to exploring the rest of the island. Tillett Gardens in the Tutu area is the site of funky and delightful arts and crafts studios, a "peaceful sanctuary of creativity and wonderment," in the words of English silk-screen artist Jim Tillett—classical and other concerts are often hosted here. Mountain Top is commercialized, but no-one can deny the spectacular view down to Magens Bay, while nearby Drake's Seat is, according to legend, the spot where Sir Francis Drake observed ships passing through the dozens of British Virgins and (what is now called) Drake's Passage. The Estate St. Peter Greathouse and Botanical Gardens sprawls over 11 lush acres on the northern slopes of the island, with an observation deck providing views of nearby islands. The meticulously landscaped gardens offer self-guided nature trails through such exotic flora as the umbrella plant from Madagascar, the cane orchid of China, and bird of paradise from South Africa. The University of the Virgin Islands (just north of the airport) is home to the Reichhold Center for the Arts, a 1200-seat amphitheater in a spectacular setting on Brewer's Bay that is host to a wide variety of performances, from classical to jazz, ballet to South African dance troupes, and more. Event and ticket information can be obtained through your hotel concierge or through ☎ *(809) 693-1559.*

Wednesday is typically the biggest day for cruise ship dockings on St. Thomas. It's a bad time for shopping, exploration of Charlotte Amalie, or visiting Magens Bay, when you'll have to compete for elbow room. It's a good day to bury yourself in a book next to your hotel's pool, or to head over to the British Virgin Islands for a daytrip away from the masses (see "Getting Around")—a cruise ship also lands on St. John on Wednesdays. A few important sights were shuttered following Hurricane Luis: Coral World, an underwater observatory at Coki Point, was heavily damaged and awaiting repairs as we went to press, while the Arboretum at Magens Bay was turned upside down by Luis just after a 1995 refurbishing.

BEST VIEW:

From the 1500-foot Mountain Top, on St. Peter's Mountain, you can see a panoramic view of both sides of the island as well as a multitude of islands stretching east to Virgin Gorda.

FIELDING'S CHOICE:

To experience the scuba thrill without getting wet, take a ride on the Atlantis Submarine, *a 46-passenger underwater craft that takes passengers for an hour's ride at depths of 50-90 feet. The sub's large windows give good views of corals reefs and a multitude of marine life. Hours are generally 10 a.m.-2 p.m., but call ahead for reservations. The boat ride leaves from the West Indies dock at Havensight Mall on the outskirts of Charlotte Amalie. For more information* ☎ *(809) 775-1555.*

Historical Sites

Fort Christian　　　　　　　　★★★★

At the harbor, ☎ *(809) 776-4566.*
Hours open: 8:30 a.m.-4:30 p.m.
This brick fortress is the oldest building still in daily use in the Virgin Islands, and a U.S. national landmark dating back to 1672. It has housed everything from the entire St. Thomas colony to a jail to a church over the years, and is now home to an art gallery, book store, and, in the former dungeons, the Virgin Islands Museum, which traces the island's history. The museum recently completed a $900,000 renovation.

Historic Churches　　　　　　　　★★★★

Various locations.
Charming Charlotte Amalie is home to several historic churches well worth a look. The Frederick Lutheran Church (Norre Gade) is the Western Hemisphere's second-oldest Lutheran church. All Saints Anglican Church on Garden Street was built in 1848 to celebrate the end of slavery. The Dutch Reformed Church on Nye Gade was built in 1844, but actually dates back to 1744 (the original was destroyed by a fire in 1804). Finally, the Cathedral of St. Peter and St. Paul in Kronprindsens Alley was built in 1848 and is enhanced by murals done in 1899 by Belgian artists.

St. Thomas Synagogue　　　　　　　　★★★★

Synagogue Hill, ☎ *(809) 774-4312.*
Hours open: 9 a.m.-4 p.m.
Founded in 1796, this is the oldest synagogue in continuous use under the American flag, and the second-oldest in the Western Hemisphere. The current structure

was built in 1833 by Sephardic Jews, and functions today for some 120 Jewish families. The floor is sand, symbolic of the desert through which Moses and the Israelis wandered for 40 years. A well-received bicentennial celebration, commemorating 200 years of Jewish life on St. Thomas, took place in 1996; an exhibit of never-before-seen artwork by St. Thomas-born Camille Pissarro will be on display December 14, 1996 through March 14, 1997. The full name, incidentally, is *Synagogue of Berecha V'Shalom V'Gemilath Chasidim*, or "Blessings and Peace and Acts of Piety."

Museums and Exhibits

Seven Arches Museum ★★★

Government Hill, ☎ *(809) 774-9259.*
Hours open: 10 a.m.–3 p.m.
This Danish house was built in 1800 and is now a private home, but they'll let you in to see its historic furnishings and antiques. The grounds include a separate kitchen and a walled garden, the perfect spot to quaff the drink included in the admission fee. General admission: $8.

Parks and Gardens

Estate St. Peter Greathouse Gardens ★★★★

Route 40 and Barrett Hill Road, Above Hull Bay, ☎ *(809) 774-4999.*
Hours open: 9 a.m.–5 p.m.
As you stroll the grounds of these new gardens, it's hard to believe this verdant spot was completely leveled by Hurricane Hugo in 1989, and again by Marilyn in 1995. Owners Sylvie and Howard DeWolfe did an amazing job restoring everything to its former glory. The gardens are perched 1000 feet above Hull Bay and Magens Bay Beach on the island's north side. Self-guided trails lead through more than 200 varieties of Caribbean plants and trees, as well as imported treasures like the tropical day lily from Asia and South African bird of paradise. There's also ponds, waterfalls and a rain forest—not to mention sweeping views from the observation deck, 1000 feet above sea level, where you can spot more than 20 other Virgin Islands. The recreated great house is filled with contemporary Caribbean furnishings and locally done artwork. A treat! General admission: $8.

Tours

Atlantis Submarine ★★★★★

Havensight Mall, Charlotte Amalie, ☎ *(809) 776-5650.*
A treat for all but the claustrophobic, this modern submarine voyage seats 46 people in air-conditioned comfort on a 65-foot sub built specifically as a tourist attraction. The 50-minute ride provides non-divers a taste of the fascinating underwater sights 90 feet down off Little Buck Island (a different one than the Buck Island near St. Croix). Regular stars of the show include a green moray eel, blue chromis and yellow-tail snapper scooting through the sea whips, brain and pillar coral. The trip is $72, or half that for kids under 12 (children under 36" are not permitted).

Coral World ★★★★

Coki Point, ☎ *(809) 775-1555.*
Hours open: 9 a.m.–6 p.m.

Non-swimmers can see what all the fuss is about at this five-acre marine park, home to 21 aquariums, a touch tank, an 80,000-gallon tank showcasing the world's largest living man-made reef, an exotic bird habitat, and semi-submarine rides. The highlight is the underwater observatory, an air-conditioned room 20 feet below sea level through which you can observe all sorts of sea life, an especially exciting sight at feeding time. The grounds also include duty-free shops, a bar and restaurant, and a pretty beach where you can rent snorkel and scuba equipment (showers and changing rooms are available). Kids get in for $10. General admission: $16.

Guided Tours

Various locations.

St. Thomas is easily explored on your own, but if you'd like to spare the expense of renting a car, take a guided tour. **Destination Virgin Islands**, ☎ *(809) 776-2424* offers walking tours, beach and shopping trips, and excursions to St. John and St. Croix; prices vary. The **St. Thomas Islands Tour**, ☎ *(809) 774-7668* explores the island in two hours for $14 per person; another excursion takes in the many splendid views and costs $20. **Tropic Tours**, ☎ *(809) 774-1855* offers various shopping and scenic tours; call for prices. Also try **Smitty Island Tour**, ☎ *(809) 775-2787*, a 3.5-hour tour in air-conditioned vans which goes to Drakes Seat, Mountain Top and Magen's Bay ($35); and **Timmy Island Tour**, ☎ *(809) 775-9529*, whose 2.5-hour tour includes Red Hook, Sapphire Beach overlook, Magen's Bay, Mountain Top, and Charlotte Amalie for $25 a person.

Paradise Point Tramway   ★★★

Havensight, ☎ *(809) 774-9809.*
Hours open: 8:30 a.m.–6:30 p.m.

When this $2.8-million tramway opened in August 1994, it brought back a popular attraction that ceased to exist in the 1970s. The 3.5-minute ride—not recommended for those afraid of heights—gives a bird's-eye view of the Charlotte Amalie harbor and stops at 697-foot-high Paradise Point, where you can wander among the shops, have a quiet drink or just soak in the scenery. When going up, try to snag the last car; when coming down, hop in the first car for the best unobstructed views. $5 for kids under 13; kids under six are free. Note that a rugged road snakes up the slope for those who want the view without buying the ride. General admission: $10.

Seaborne Seaplane Adventure   ★★★★★

Charlotte Amalie Harbor, Charlotte Amalie, ☎ *(809) 777-4491.*

Amazing views abound on this 45-minute flight aboard the twin-engine seaplane Vistaliner. Bring lots of film, because you'll be snapping away like mad as you fly over some 100 islands of the U.S. and British Virgin Islands. The entire tour takes 1.5 hours (it's exciting to take off and land from the ocean) and is greatly enhanced by extra-large windows, lively narration via headphones (which can also be plugged right into your video camera) and an interesting booklet that gives details on the islands spotted. Great fun! General admission: $79.

Sports

All manner of watersports activities are enjoyed on St. Thomas. **Sportfishing** is devoted primarily to the blue marlin—from March to June, marlin are found to the south in the Caribbean, while the fish navigate the waters of the Atlantic to the north of the island July through September. Other fish common to the area include kingfish, wahoo, dolphin, white marlin and Allison tuna, and some 21 world records have been set here in recent years. On this side of the Virgins is a 100-fathom drop-off bordering the Puerto Rico Trench, the deepest hole in the Atlantic. Because the Virgin Islands lie in the Trade Winds Belt, fishing can always be done on the leeward side. Redhook is the main center of operations for boat charters. Many operators offer half- and full-day boat excursions on a variety of craft; full-day fishing expeditions usually come equipped with equipment, picnic, beer and ice.

Surfing attracts a few fans during the winter when the waves roll in at Hull Bay, just west of Magens Bay. **Windsurfing** is best on the eastern end of the island—winds peak around noon, with Morningstar Beach offering some of the gentlest conditions. **Kayaking** is possible along the scenic coast, and can be arranged at some of the bigger resorts including Sapphire Beach. **Snorkeling** and **diving** equipment is sold by Mask and Fin (across from Fort Christian in Charlotte Amalie), and can provide good information about the best snorkeling locations.

Horse racing is a party event on St. Thomas, involving thoroughbred horses, pan-mutuel and daily double betting. Events are held approximately monthly, usually on a local holiday or Sunday. English-style **riding lessons** are offered at Rosenthal Riding Ring, which also provides trail rides. **Tennis** is available at a number of resorts, and two public courts are found at the Sub Base. St. Thomas also has a spectacular 18-hole championship **golf** course, Mahogany Run, designed by George and Tom Fazio. A desalination plant was completed in 1996 and promises to keep the greens in shape year-round. There's also a free, nine-hole course at the University of the Virgin Islands.

Mahogany Run Golf Course ★★★★

Mahogany Run Road, North Shore, ☎ (809) 775-5000.
Hours open: 7 a.m.–4:50 p.m.
St. Thomas' only golf course is an especially scenic and challenging one, a par-70 known for its dramatic 13th and 14th holes, which hug cliffs overlooking the Atlantic Ocean. If you play holes 13, 14 and 15 (the "Devil's Triangle") without a penalty shot your first time on the course, you will win a prize. A 270,000-gallon desalination plant opened in 1996 to keep everything lush and green (in the past,

the course was in a constant battle with Mother Nature). Designed by George and Tom Fazio, greens fees vary depending on the season, and range from $75 in the winter to $55 in summer. Nine holes can be played before 8 a.m. and after 3 p.m.; discount twilight rates kick in after 2 p.m. Tee times are taken 48 hours in advance and run daily from 7 a.m.–4:50 p.m. Several resorts, including Grand Palazzo, Renaissance Grand and Secret Harbour offer golf packages.

Virgin Islands Ecotours

2 Estate Nadir, ☎ *(809) 779-2155.*

A new addition to St. Thomas is this kayaking outfit providing 2.5-hour tours through the St. Thomas Marine Sanctuary and mangrove lagoon, where you" see many juvenile reef fish. The two-person ocean kayaks are stable and easy to paddle, and snorkel and safety gear is also provided. Two tours daily: 9:30 a.m. and 1 p.m. Price is $50 per person.

Watersports

Various locations.

If your hotel doesn't offer the equipment you need, these companies are happy to help out. For boat charters, try: **Regency Yacht Vacations**, ☎ *(809) 776-5950 or (800) 524-7676*; **Island Yachts**, ☎ *(809) 775-6666 or (800) 524-2019*; **Avery's Marine** ☎ *(809) 776-0113*; **Coconut Charters**, ☎ *(809) 775-5959*; **Nightwin**, ☎ *(809) 775-4110*, and **New Horizons**, ☎ *(809) 775-1171.* For scuba and snorkel instruction and excursions, try: Seahorse Div, ☎ *(809) 774-2001*; **Adventure Center**, ☎ *(809) 774-2990*; **Dean Johnston's Diving**, ☎ *(809) 775-7610*, and **Hi-Tec Water Sports**, ☎ *(809) 774-5650.* Deep-sea fishers can call **Fish Hawk**, ☎ *(809) 775-9058*, and **St. Thomas Sportfishing Center**, ☎ *(809) 775-7990.*

Where to Stay

Fielding's Highest Rated Hotels in St. Thomas

★★★★★	Ritz-Carlton St. Thomas	$400–$525
★★★★	Anchorage Beach Villas	$195–$235
★★★★	Bolongo Inclusive Beach Resort	$175–$440
★★★★	Elysian Resort	$175–$630
★★★★	Marriott's Morning Star Beach Resort	$185–$395
★★★★	Renaissance Grand Beach Resort	$225–$895
★★★★	Sapphire Beach Resort and Marina	$195–$475
★★★★	Secret Harbour Resort	$160–$295
★★★★	Sugar Bay Plantation	$180–$370
★★★★	Watergate Villas	$73–$375

Fielding's Most Exclusive Hotels in St. Thomas

★★★★	Renaissance Grand Beach Resort	$225–$895
★★★★	Elysian Resort	$175–$630
★★★	Cowpet Bay Village	$247–$420
★★★★	Marriott's Morning Star Beach Resort	$185–$395
★★★	Colony Point Pleasant Resort	$170–$380

Fielding's Best Value Hotels in St. Thomas

★★	Heritage Manor	$45–$85
★★★	Blackbeard's Castle	$75–$140
★★★	Best Western Carib Beach Resort	$89–$149
★★	Mafolie Hotel	$65–$97
★★★	Island Beachcomber	$100–$150

Bluebeard's Castle gets high marks for retaining historic touches while providing modern amenities to hotel guests/visitors.

Most of the accommodations on St. Thomas are concentrated into two areas. The first surrounds Charlotte Amalie and the island's scenic main harbor, and extends to near the airport on the west and to Bolongo Bay on the east. This hotel group is where you'll find the most variety, from the all-inclusive Bolongo to the classic island inn, Hotel 1829; from family-owned guest houses such as Villa Santana to the 516-room Marriott complex at the harbor entrance. The second area lies along the island's eastern tip facing St. John, where a group of large hotels and apartment/condo complexes dot the coastline between Coki Point and Nazareth Bay. The resorts, such as Sapphire Beach and the Renaissance Grand Beach, tend to be expensive, while Magens Point and other apartment/condo facilities can be easier on the wallet, particularly for families. This portion of the island tends to be quieter than around Charlotte Amalie, but your commute into town will be up to a half-hour each way, despite the relatively short distance.

Hurricane Marilyn did a real number on St. Thomas, and many accommodations suffered extensive damage. In addition to physical damage, the fall-out paved the way for a number of properties to change hands, led by the swank Grand Palazzo, which re-opened under the Ritz Carlton name in late 1996. Fortunately, most island hotels underwent a full makeover when the insurance monies came through, which means most of St. Thomas's properties look better than ever. All hotels listed in the following section anticipate being fully operational by Christmas 1996. It doesn't hurt to verify directly with the hotel you are considering, however, so that your 1997 vacation won't be undertaken against a backdrop of construction noise. Among the properties closed indefinitely at press time are Sugar Bay, Ramada Yacht Haven, Cowpet Bay, and Pavilions and Pools. The watchtower in front of Blackbeard's Castle, said to be the oldest structure on the island, came through the 1995 hurricane just fine, but the rooms were severely damaged and awaiting repair at press time.

Hotels and Resorts

There is no shortage of hotels and resorts to choose from on St. Thomas, in all styles, shapes, colors and sizes. Start by organizing your priorities. Do you want to be near shopping, or on a secluded beach? Do you want a smaller, more intimate property or would you prefer a full-service resort with an array of on-site activities? Remember that the view your room offers will almost always affect the price of accommodations. For instance, at Marriott's Morningstar Beach Resort, the Ocean Front rooms are terrific, but you'll save at least $50 a night by choosing a Garden View room that, in walking distance, is only about 10 seconds further from the sand.

Bolongo Bay

Bolongo Inclusive Beach Resort **$175–$440** ★ ★ ★ ★

Bolongo Bay, 802, ☎ (800) 524-4746, (809) 775-1800. FAX (809) 775-3208. Single: $175–$440. Double: $195–$440.

This busy family-owned property, also known as Club Everything, offers full resort amenities and a lovely palm-studded beach. Guestrooms have white tile floors, two double or king beds, shower-only baths and a small refrigerator. The west wing is quietest, while those in the center have the nicest views, but all are quite close to the beach. Definitely request a second-floor unit for more privacy, but remember ground-level rooms open onto the beach. The grounds include lighted tennis and volleyball courts, a new health club, a pretty pool complete with swim-up bar, two restaurants, and all the watersports one could want, including daily boat trips and a dive shop. Guests may choose from an all-inclusive or semi-inclusive plan—the latter includes all non-motorized sports, an introductory scuba dive and other amenities. Amenities: tennis, health club, balcony or patio. 116 rooms. Credit cards: A, DC, D, MC, V.

Charlotte Amalie

Best Western Carib Beach Resort **$89–$149** ★ ★ ★

Lindberg Bay, Charlotte Amalie, ☎ (800) 792-2742, (809) 774-2525. FAX (809) 777-4131. Single: $89–$149. Double: $89–$149.

This Best Western hotel is located on a very small, man-made beach where you can tan—there's no ocean access, but a better stretch of sand is nearby. Each basic room is air-conditioned and has a private balcony, cable TV, telephones, refrigerator and coffeemaker. Facilities include a pleasant restaurant and a small pool. This hotel is located just a stone's throw from the airport, so expect some noise from jets. Though this place is rather bare-bones compared to St. Thomas' many glittering resorts, there's something agreeable about it. 69 rooms. Credit cards: A, MC, V.

Best Western Emerald Beach Resort $145–$239 ★★★

Lindbergh Bay, Charlotte Amalie, ☎ *(800) 233-4936, (809) 777-8800.*
FAX (809) 776-3426.
Single: $145–$239. Double: $145–$239.

Located near the foot of the airport runway, this smaller hotel has decent guestrooms that won't win any prizes for originality, but are quite modern and comfortable nonetheless, with newly added refrigerators and coffeemakers. Facilities include a bar and restaurant, pool and tennis court. There's watersports for hire at the nice public beach, just steps away. 90 rooms. Credit cards: A, CB, DC, D, MC, V.

Blackbeard's Castle $75–$140 ★★★

Blackbeard's Hill; Charlotte Amalie, ☎ *(800) 344-5771, (809) 776-1234.*
FAX (809) 776-4321.
Single: $75–$110. Double: $95–$140.

This inn, a national historic landmark, is built around a stone tower once reportedly used by pirates and boasts an avid gay following today. Guestrooms are quite small but charming enough with simple furnishings, air conditioners, and tiny balconies. There are also several one-bedroom suites with more amenities. The grounds include a large pool, a highly regarded restaurant, and a bar with nightly cabaret bands. Wonderful views abound everywhere and downtown Charlotte Amalie is within walking distance. After extensive hurricane damage, some or all rooms were scheduled to be open by December 1996. Amenities: balcony or patio. 25 rooms. Credit cards: A, D, MC, V.

Bluebeard's Castle Hotel $140–$235 ★★★

Charlotte Amalie, ☎ *(800) 524-6599, (809) 774-1600. FAX (809) 774-5134.*
Single: $140–$235. Double: $140–$235.

Set high up on a hill with splendid views of the harbor and beyond, this venerable hotel is built around a 17th-century tower. Lodgings are found in villas and range from studios to one-bedroom suites, all air-conditioned, nicely decorated, and boasting balconies or terraces. An additional 14 suites were scheduled to open in 1997. There's nightly entertainment in the lounge, three well-regarded restaurants, a large pool, two tennis courts, and a fitness center. The staff will shuttle you over to the beach for free. Nice, but group business dominates here, so individual travelers can feel lost in the shuffle. Amenities: tennis, exercise room, balcony or patio. 184 rooms. Credit cards: A, DC, D, MC, V.

Colony Point Pleasant Resort $170–$380 ★★★

Smith Bay, Charlotte Amalie, ☎ *(800) 524-2300, (809) 775-7200.*
FAX (809) 776 5694.
Single: $170–$380. Double: $170–$380.

This property takes up 15 acres on a lush hillside overlooking Smith Bay, Coki Point and the British Virgins. Guests are put up in spacious one- or two-bedroom suites with full kitchens and living and dining areas. If you choose not to do your own cooking, two restaurants will do the job. Facilities include a small beach, tennis, three pools, and complimentary non-motorized watersports. Guests also get free use of a car for four hours each day (though insurance is mandatory). A better beach is found next door at the Renaissance Grand, which guests are welcome to use. Very nice. Amenities: tennis, exercise room, balcony or patio. 134 rooms. Credit cards: A, DC, D, MC, V.

Island Beachcomber $100–$150   ★★★

Lindbergh Bay, Charlotte Amalie, ☎ *(800) 982-9898, (809) 774-5250. FAX (809) 774-5615.*
Single: $100–$145. Double: $105–$150.

Set right on a fine beach, this hotel has a faithful clientele—the management says some 80 percent of the guests are repeat visitors who don't mind the occasional jet noise from the nearby airport. This casual spot houses guests in comfortable, air-conditioned rooms facing the lush garden or beach; all have cable TV, phones, refrigerators, and patios or porches. The restaurant is open-air and reasonably priced, and there's also a beach bar. No pool, but the sea is calm and good for swimming. Snorkeling equipment and water rafts are complimentary (other watersports cost extra), and the staff will shuttle you into town for free. A pleasantly informal spot with the kind of friendly staff we'd like to see at all Caribbean resorts. 48 rooms. Credit cards: A, CB, DC, D, MC, V.

Limetree Beach Resort $110–$195   ★★★

Frenchman Bay, Charlotte Amalie, ☎ *(800) 753-2554, (809) 776-4770. FAX (809) 776-0910.*
Single: $110–$170. Double: $135–$195.

Previously an all-inclusive resort, the Limetree draws mainly a younger crowd and was scheduled to reopen December 1996 after repairing the substantial damage from Hurricane Marilyn. Guestrooms are quite small but ingeniously built on two levels, giving a feeling of space. Each has pretty rattan furnishings, white tile floors, and small shower-only baths. The junior loft-suites, with a king bed upstairs and a sofa bed below, are quite nice. Unfortunately, all rooms lack a terrace or balcony. On the plus side, each is quite close to the beach. Facilities include two lit tennis courts, several restaurants, a pretty wedding gazebo, and a disco. Theme nights each week get guests mingling. 84 rooms. Credit cards: A, DC, MC, V.

Marriott's Frenchman's Reef $150–$298   ★★★

Overlooking Charlotte Amalie harbor, Charlotte Amalie, ☎ *(800) 524-2000, (809) 776-8500. FAX (809) 776-3054.*
Single: $150–$298. Double: $150–$298.

This full-service resort complex, which incorporates Morning Star Beach just down the hill, looks a bit like the mammoth cruise ships that busily navigate the waters of the nearby harbor. Guests are housed on a rocky promontory surrounded by water and overlooking Charlotte Amalie—rooms were scheduled for renovation in 1997. Many of the facilities are shared with Morning Star, and include a huge pool, four tennis courts, watersports on the fine beach, a dinner theater, and six restaurants, several bars and a disco. Live entertainment is frequently scheduled, as are all sorts of activities. A water taxi will whisk you into town. On the downside, the property hosts a lot of conventions—it's the largest meeting facility on the island—so you'll be sharing the facilities with name tag-wearing business folk. This is a good spot for those who covet full resorts, but if you're looking for a laid-back tropical escape, look elsewhere. Ditto if you hate long walks. Amenities: tennis, exercise room, Jacuzzi. 420 rooms. Credit cards: A, CB, DC, D, MC, V.

Marriott's Morning Star Beach Resort $185–$395   ★★★★

Morning Star Beach, Charlotte Amalie, ☎ *(800) 524-2000, (809) 776-8500. FAX (809) 776-3054.*

Single: $185–$395. Double: $185–$395.

Though it shares the same management company and facilities, Morning Star has a distinct personality from the 420-room Frenchman's Reef complex next door, starting with a separate front desk. Rooms at Morning Star are more luxurious, with balconies or patios that face a garden or open directly onto the splendid beach. Four tennis courts and a wide array of watersports are available, plus you can hike up the hill to Frenchman's for more restaurants and bars, a huge pool, or to the dock for the resort's water taxi into Charlotte Amalie. Most people, however, are content to stay put on Morning Star's half-mile stretch of velvety sand. Amenities: tennis, exercise room, balcony or patio. 96 rooms. Credit cards: A, CB, DC, D, MC, V.

Ramada Yacht Haven Hotel $90–$225   ★★★

5400 Long Bay, Charlotte Amalie, 802, ☎ *(800) 228-9898, (809) 774-9700. FAX (809) 776-3410.*

Single: $90–$200. Double: $90–$225.

Guests sacrifice a beach for the relatively reasonable rates at this so-so hotel. Located on a large marina from which you can watch the cruise ships come in, accommodations are found in six low-rise buildings. Rooms have modern amenities like VCRs but are a bit run down. The grounds include two pools (one with a swim-up bar) and two restaurants and bars. The staff will shuttle you over to the beach at the Marriott for free. 151 rooms. Credit cards: A, CB, DC, D, MC, V.

8/96: CLOSED DUE TO HURRICANE DAMAGE. REOPENING DATE TBD

Renaissance Grand Beach Resort $225–$895   ★★★★

Water Bay, Charlotte Amalie, ☎ *(800) 468-3571, (809) 775-1510. FAX (809) 775-2185.*

Single: $225–$595. Double: $225–$895.

Set on a lush hillside sloping to a small beach, this former Stouffer is another full-service resort that keeps guests pleasantly occupied. As with other large resorts, there's not a lot of true island flavor here, but no one seems to mind (or even notice). Guestrooms, just redone in 1996, are quite plush; a few hundred dollars more buys a two-story townhouse suite or a one-bedroom unit with an indoor whirlpool. Recreational options include six tennis courts, two pools, an excellent health club, and lots of watersports. You'll also find two restaurants and bars, and organized programs for the kids. Like most of St. Thomas' beaches, the one here is quite narrow and not as pretty as at some competing properties. The grounds are quite green, though—in fact, the resort is a certified botanical garden with some 500 species of plants. You'll find all you want at this large spot, but be warned the clientele is dominated by conventioneers. Amenities: tennis, health club. 297 rooms. Credit cards: A, DC, D, MC, V.

Ritz-Carlton St. Thomas   **$400–$525**   ★ ★ ★ ★ ★

Great Bay, Charlotte Amalie, ☎ (800) 241-3333, (809) 775-3333.
FAX (809) 775-5635.
Single: $400–$525. Double: $400–$525.

The rates are high, but those who can afford it will be happily impressed with this deluxe Italian Renaissance-style resort, formerly known as the Grand Palazzo and acquired by the Ritz-Carlton Hotel chain in 1996. Accommodations are in plush junior suites with expensive and luxurious furnishings and wonderful views of St. John and the British Virgin Islands off the terrace. The hotel offers a handful of one- and two-bedroom suites. Facilities include a large free-form pool, four tennis courts, a full health club with modern exercise equipment and pampering services, a 56-foot catamaran for ocean cruises, two elegant restaurants, several bars, and watersports, including a dive shop. The rates include such niceties as afternoon tea, ice delivered to your room twice daily and a weekly cocktail party. The grounds are simply gorgeous and the beach is fine. Things don't come much better! Summer 1997 rates not established at press time. Amenities: secluded garden atmosphere, tennis, balcony or patio. 150 rooms. Credit cards: A, D, MC, V.

Sapphire Beach Resort and Marina   **$195–$475**   ★ ★ ★ ★

St. John Bay, Charlotte Amalie, ☎ (800) 524-2090, (809) 775-6100.
FAX (809) 775-4024.
Single: $195–$475. Double: $195–$475.

Located on one of St. Thomas' best beaches, this well-liked resort encompasses 35 picturesque acres. It's a bit out of the way, so you'll want to rent a car to get around. The accommodations are quite posh, with large balconies, fresh flowers, and fully equipped kitchens; most are right on the beach. The largest units have two baths, two balconies, and two queen-size sofa beds in addition to the bedroom, so can sleep six. Maids tidy up daily, and room service is available. Watersports and super- vised children's programs are free. Amenities include a restaurant, a posh pool with nice views of neighboring islands, three bars, and a 67-slip marina. Kids under 12 stay and eat for free. Amenities: tennis. 171 rooms. Credit cards: A, MC, V.

Sugar Bay Plantation   **$180–$370**   ★ ★ ★

Water Bay, Charlotte Amalie, ☎ (800) 927-7100, (809) 777-7100.
FAX (809) 777 7200.
Single: $180–$370. Double: $180–$370.

Located on the island's east end, this resort opened in 1992 and has switched hands several times in the ensuing few years. A large hillside complex of nine buildings, the property has fairly standard room interiors, but they vaunt spectacular views from their rocky perch—all balconies face out to the ocean. Down below are all the usual resort diversions including three interconnected pools complete with a grotto, bar and waterfalls, seven tennis courts, a fitness room, two restaurants, four bars, and watersports at the small beach. Kids are kept busy (and parents relaxed) with super- vised programs year-round. A good, all-around resort. Amenities: tennis, exercise room, balcony or patio. 300 rooms. Credit cards: A, DC, D, MC, V.

Windward Passage   **$125–$230**   ★ ★

Charlotte Amalie, 804, ☎ (800) 524-7389, (809) 774-5200. FAX (809) 774-1231.

Single: $125–$220. Double: $135–$230.

The rates are fairly reasonable at this busy commercial hotel, located downtown in the heart of the shopping district and overlooking the harbor. Guestrooms are basic but fine, and the 11 more expensive suites offer sitting areas, hair dryers and refrigerators. You'll find a restaurant, bar and pool, but no other facilities on the property. Most of the guests are business travelers, as the beach is beyond walking distance. 151 rooms. Credit cards: A, CB, DC, MC, V.

Red Hook

Elysian Resort   **$175–$630**   ★★★★

Estate Nazareth; Red Hook, ☎ (800) 753-2554, (809) 775-1000.
FAX (809) 776-0910.
Single: $175–$375. Double: $175–$630.

This resort, set on a hill above a peaceful cove, houses guests in a variety of nicely done guestrooms or loft-units with full kitchens and one to three bedrooms. Sporting facilities include a large and elaborate pool, a tennis court, an excellent and well-equipped health club and complimentary watersports on the nice beach. Dining choices range from the elegant Palm Court to the casual Oasis outdoor grill. It's peaceful, and there's less going on here than at some island properties—a plus or minus, depending upon your preference. Amenities: tennis, exercise room, balcony or patio. 118 rooms. Credit cards: A, DC, D, MC, V.

Apartments and Condominiums

Apartments, villas and condos are numerous on St. Thomas, and the common language and the familiar U.S.-style supermarkets make self-catering a breeze. The one shock will be how high food prices are. You can always bring staples from home, soft packages of soup, etc., that will fit easily into the unused corners of a suitcase.

The largest condo agency on the island is Ocean Property Management, which oversees 65 units in four separate condominium developments: Secret Harbourview Villas, Sapphire Village, Sapphire Bay West (aka Crystal Cove), and the Anchorage. Rates for some of these units start at $115 per night for a double during the summer season, ☎ *(800) 874-7897 or (809) 775-2600.* Two other agencies handle villas and private homes: **Leisure Enterprises**, ☎ *(809) 775-9203*, and **McLaughlin Anderson Villas**, ☎ *(800) 537-6246 or (809) 776-0635.*

Bolongo Bay

Bolongo Bay Beach Villas   **$195–$390**   ★★★

Bolongo Bay, Bolongo Bay, ☎ (800) 524-4746, (809) 775-1800.
FAX (809) 775-3208.
Double: $195–$390.

Located on the grounds of Bolongo Inclusive, this villa complex offers the best of the self-catering and resort worlds. Villas are individually decorated and include full kitchens, one or two bedrooms and very large balconies. Villa guests have their own pool, and guests can also use all the facilities at Bolongo, which include lighted tennis and volleyball courts, watersports, a health club, two bars and restaurants. Amenities: tennis, health club. 39 rooms. Credit cards: A, DC, MC, V.

Charlotte Amalie

Anchorage Beach Villas   **$195–$235**   ★★★★

Cowpet Bay Point, Charlotte Amalie, ☎ *(800) 524-6599, (809) 774-1600. FAX (809) 774-5134.*
Single: $195–$235. Double: $195–$235.
Located on the beach near the island's eastern tip, this complex consists of 30 villas that are large and modern. Each has two bedrooms, two baths, full kitchens, skylights, large decks, and washer/dryers. Most sleep up to four, while the loft units can accommodate six. Maids tidy up daily. Facilities include a pool, two tennis courts, and a fitness center. There's a restaurant for those who don't feel up to cooking in. The weekly manager's cocktail party is a nice opportunity to meet your fellow guests. The beach is small but decent, and the staff will shuttle you about for a fee. 30 rooms. Credit cards: A, DC, D, MC, V.

Crystal Cove   **$126–$273**   ★★

Route 6, Charlotte Amalie, ☎ *(809) 775-6220. FAX (809) 775-4202.*
Single: $126–$205. Double: $131–$273.
This 25-year-old complex shows its age, but the rates are reasonable for self-sufficient types who want kitchen facilities. Accommodations are in condominiums that range in size from studios to one- and two-bedroom units, all with complete kitchens, balconies, and basic furnishings. Maid service is available every day but Sunday. Facilities include a saltwater pool and two tennis courts. There's no restaurant on site, so you'll want a car. 50 rooms. Credit cards: A, DC, MC, V.

Magens Point Hotel   **$100–$300**   ★★

Magens Bay Road, Charlotte Amalie, ☎ *(800) 524-2031, (809) 777-6000. FAX (809) 777-6055.*
Single: $100–$250. Double: $113–$300.
Set on a hillside next to the Mahogany Run Golf Course and overlooking the beach, this informal operation consists of motel-style guestrooms and 44 studio and one- and two-bedroom suites with cooking facilities. There's a restaurant, bar, pool, and two tennis courts on-site, and they'll shuttle you to the beach or golf course (about a half mile away) at no charge. All here is quite casual, and the property underwent a post-hurricane makeover. Good on-site restaurant with a rotating menu of sushi, Tex Mex and East Indian food. Amenities: tennis, exercise room, Jacuzzi. 54 rooms. Credit cards: A, CB, DC, D, MC, V.

Pavilions & Pools   **$180–$260**   ★★★

Charlotte Amalie, ☎ *(800) 524-2001, (809) 775-6110. FAX (809) 775-6110.*
Single: $180–$260. Double: $180–$260.
This villa resort is located seven miles from Charlotte Amalie, near Sapphire Beach. Each of the 25 air-conditioned villas has one bedroom, living/dining areas, complete kitchens, VCRs, and private, decent-sized pools. Maids tidy up daily, and the rates are quite reasonable for self-sufficient types. Enjoy the restaurant and an open-air bar that occasionally hosts live entertainment. Guests can play tennis on the courts at the nearby Sapphire Bay Beach Resort for free; watersports equipment can be rented there as well. 25 rooms. Credit cards: A, D, MC, V.

Secret Harbour Resort $160–$295   ★★★★

Nazareth Bay, Charlotte Amalie, ☎ *(800) 524-2250, (809) 775-6550. FAX (809) 775-1501.*

Single: $160–$295. Double: $160–$295.

All accommodations are in suites at this secluded resort set on a fine beach. Lodging is in spacious studios and one- and two-bedroom condos with full kitchens, quality tropical furnishings, air conditioning and ceiling fans, and enormous balconies. Facilities include an extensive watersports center, a pool and two tennis courts; the well-regarded restaurant was washed out to sea by Hurricane Marilyn. The narrow, coconut tree-dotted beach is lovely, and the sea here is so calm it sports one of the island's few swim floats. This operation combines the best of self-sufficient and resort living. 60 rooms. Credit cards: A, MC, V.

Secret Harbourview Villas $140–$360   ★★★

P.O. Box 8529, Charlotte Amalie, ☎ *(800) 874-7897, (809) 775-2600. FAX (809) 775-5901.*

Single: $140–$281. Double: $140–$360.

Set on a cliff above the beach, this condominium resort offers studios and one- and two-bedroom units, all with complete kitchens, balconies, and maid service. Facilities include a restaurant, pool, and three tennis courts. Guests can use the beach and facilities at the nearby Secret Harbour Beach Resort. While the staff can offer shuttle service into town (for a fee), you'll probably want to rent a car for independence. 30 rooms. Credit cards: DC, D, MC, V.

Villa Santana $95–$195   ★★

Denmark Hill; Charlotte Amalie, ☎ *(809) 776-1311. FAX (809) 776-1311.*

Single: $95–$195. Double: $95–$195.

Located high on a hill in a residential area of Charlotte Amalie, Villa Santana was built in 1857 and today is a sweetly atmospheric guest house. Stone-walled rooms are tastefully appointed with wooden shutters, rattan furniture, kitchenettes and ceiling fans (no air conditioning but good ventilation), and are spread over three cozy, two-story buildings with sparkling views. A small pool and lawn keeps things inviting. A tad pricey, but perfect for someone who wants easy access to town without the overload of a big hotel. 5 rooms.

Watergate Villas $73–$375   ★★★★

Route 7, Charlotte Amalie, ☎ *(800) 524-2038, (809) 775-6220. FAX (809) 775-2298.*

Single: $73–$247. Double: $142–$375.

Set on a hill on the south coast 15 minutes out of Charlotte Amalie, this complex offers individually decorated villas that are rented out in their owners' absence. Configurations range from studios to one-, two-, and three-bedroom units, all with complete kitchens, living/dining areas, maid service, balconies, and contemporary furnishings. There are three pools, two tennis courts, and a restaurant on the premises. Good for self-sufficient types, but you'll want to rent a car to get around. 100 rooms. Credit cards: A, DC, D, MC, V.

Red Hook

Cowpet Bay Village   **$247–$420**   ★ ★ ★

6222 Estate Nazareth, Red Hook, ☎ *(800) 524-2038, (809) 775-6220.*
FAX (809) 775-4202.
Single: $247–$300. Double: $247–$420.
This complex, located on the beach at Cowpet Bay, consists of 30 two- and three-bedroom villas. All are spacious and airy, with fully equipped kitchens, living/dining areas, balconies, washer/dryers, and maid service. There's a restaurant on site, and guests can borrow snorkeling equipment for free. There's no pool, but the beach is right at hand. You'll need a car for mobility. 30 rooms. Credit cards: A, DC, D, MC, V.

Inns

The number of inns available on St. Thomas is limited—the focus here has long been on larger and newer hotels. But Hotel 1829 oozes with atmosphere, providing a romantic excursion into an earlier era.

Charlotte Amalie

Admiral's Inn   **$79–$149**   ★ ★

Villa Olga; Charlotte Amalie, ☎ *(800) 544-0493, (809) 774-1376.*
FAX (809) 774-8010.
Single: $79–$149. Double: $79–$149.
This brightly-painted inn is not in one of St. Thomas' better neighborhoods, but on the other hand, the area is home to many fine restaurants. Guestrooms, located on the hillside, are air-conditioned and have private baths and satellite TV, and new furnishings following 1995's hurricanes. The inn's four acres include a Chart House restaurant, a pool, and a saltwater pool on the shore. A continental breakfast is included in the rates. Amenities: balcony or patio. 13 rooms. Credit cards: A, D, MC, V.

Hotel 1829   **$60–$230**   ★ ★ ★

Government Hill; Charlotte Amalie, ☎ *(800) 524-2002, (809) 776-1829.*
FAX (809) 776-4313.
Single: $60–$220. Double: $70–$230.
This atmospheric inn was built in (you guessed it) 1829 by a French sea captain for his bride. It's located right in the heart of the city, so you'll have to drive or take a taxi to the beach (beautiful Magen's Bay is 15 minutes away). Now a national historic site, the hotel accommodates guests in charming rooms enhanced with antiques, air conditioners, minibars and VCRs. The price you pay depends on the size of your room, which varies widely—definitely request one in the original building (the rest were added in the late 1920s and are not as nice); note that most are dark and stone-walled. The continental restaurant is well-regarded, and you'll also find a wonderful bar and a tiny pool. Not especially suited to small children or the physically challenged, as there are many steep stairs to negotiate and no elevator to help things along. 15 rooms. Credit cards: A, MC, V.

Low Cost Lodging

Lodging is not inexpensive on St. Thomas overall, but there are a few family-run budget options available, particularly if you don't mind a bathroom down the hall. One other possibility, the Bunker Hill Hotel, has rooms from $59 to $90, though it's a somewhat antiseptic property in an okay Charlotte Amalie neighborhood, ☎ *(809) 774-8056.* Additional options can be provided by the Virgin Island Tourist Office, ☎ *(800) 372-USVI.*

Charlotte Amalie

Danish Chalet Inn   **$60–$95**   ★

Charlotte Amalie, ☎ *(800) 635-1531, (809) 774-5764. FAX (809) 777-4886.*
Single: $60–$95. Double: $60–$95.

This pleasant if simple bed and breakfast is on a hill within walking distance of Charlotte Amalie. Most rooms have air conditioning, but can be a little tight; a few share a bathroom and are priced somewhat less. The $1 honor bar in front is welcoming, while the Jacuzzi in back provides a little splash. Orange Marmalade, a 13-year-old cat, "runs the hotel," and owners Mary and Frank Davis will regale you with stories about their son-in-law Tony Blankley (Newt Gingrich's press secretary). Homey and unpretentious. Amenities: Jacuzzi. 10 rooms. Credit cards: MC, V.

Galleon House   **$49–$119**   ★★

Charlotte Amalie, ☎ *(800) 524-2052, (809) 774-6952. FAX (809) 774-6952.*
Single: $49–$109. Double: $59–$119.

Delightful family-run inn has character and homey touches. Six economy rooms (two with shared bath) are in the main building, a rustic house with a player piano out on the veranda. Newer lodgings are in two apartment-style buildings up on the hillside—air conditioning, ceiling fans, coffeemaker and refrigerator are standard, as is a nice view of Charlotte Amalie. The garden is nicely kept, with iguanas crawling through the *kenip* tree and orchids that bloom in September. A dozen or more restaurants are within a short stroll. Amenities: secluded garden atmosphere. 14 rooms. Credit cards: A, D, MC, V.

Heritage Manor   **$45–$85**   ★★

Charlotte Amalie, ☎ *(800) 828-0757, (809) 774-3003. FAX (809) 776-9585.*
Single: $45–$85. Double: $45–$85.

Located in the historical district, this small inn dates back to the early 1800s and was originally the home of a Danish merchant. All rooms are air-conditioned and include such niceties as ceiling fans, refrigerators and brass beds—five of the units share a bathroom—and an apartment with a full kitchen. There's a tiny pool on site (built in an old Danish oven!) plus an honor bar, but little else, though you can walk to shops and restaurants. The neighborhood is a bit iffy, so spring for a cab at night. 8 rooms. Credit cards: A, MC, V.

Island View Guest House   **$45–$100**   ★

Charlotte Amalie, ☎ *(800) 524-2023, (809) 774-4270. FAX (809) 774-6167.*
Single: $45–$100. Double: $50–$100.

This informal guest house is five minutes out of Charlotte Amalie and perched high on a hill with great harbor views. Guestrooms are quite simple, but comfortable enough. Most, but not all, have private baths, and those who want air conditioners will pay an extra fee. The high-priced units have kitchenettes. An honor bar and small pool provide diversions, and continental breakfast is complimentary. Ask about special packages. 15 rooms. Credit cards: A, MC, V.

Mafolie Hotel $65–$97 ★★

Mafolie Hill; Charlotte Amalie, ☎ *(800) 225-7035, (809) 774-2790. FAX (809) 774-4091.*

Single: $65–$87. Double: $80–$97.

Set high on a hill overlooking Charlotte Amalie, this Mediterranean-style villa hotel is a great deal for those who can handle steep climbs. Guestrooms are simple and basic; only some have air conditioners and none sport phones. A pool and a restaurant comprise the amenities, and the views are stunning. The hotel will feed you breakfast for free, and the shuttle to Magen's Bay Beach is also gratis. 23 rooms.

Credit cards: A, MC, V.

Where to Eat

Fielding's Highest Rated Restaurants in St. Thomas

★★★★	Cafe Normandie	$25–$39
★★★★	Craig and Sally's	$12–$28
★★★★	Hotel 1829	$20–$32
★★★★	Old Stone Farmhouse	$23–$29
★★★★	Palm Court	$14–$32
★★★★	Ritz Carlton	$22–$32
★★★★	Virgilio's	$16–$39
★★★	Agave Terrace	$18–$24
★★★	Blackbeard's Castle	$18–$29
★★★	Cafesito	$4–$19

Fielding's Most Exclusive Restaurants in St. Thomas

★★★★	Cafe Normandie	$25–$39
★★★★	Virgilio's	$16–$39
★★★★	Ritz Carlton	$22–$32
★★★	Chart House	$16–$37
★★★★	Old Stone Farmhouse	$23–$29

Fielding's Best Value Restaurants in St. Thomas

★★★	Epernay Champagne Bar	$6–$18
★★★	Cafesito	$4–$19
★★★	Cuzzin's	$10–$20
★★★★	Craig and Sally's	$12–$28
★★★	Victor's New Hide Out	$11–$20

ST. THOMAS

Locals dine out almost as frequently as visitors on St. Thomas, which accounts for the extraordinary range of dining options with cuisines hailing from nearly every corner of the world. Splurging on Sunday brunch at the big resorts is a national pastime, but otherwise restaurants are pleasantly informal and frequently open-air—casual dress, even shorts, generally pass muster. Prices can edge to the expensive, but primarily this is because of the high cost of importing food rather than due to some local conspiracy. Visitors on a budget will be able to locate good food at a reasonable price.

Seafood, lobster and conch top the list at many island restaurants, but local specialties include *fungi*, a dumpling made from corn meal, and *maubi*, a foamy beverage made from bark and herbs. *Souse* is a stew made from a pig's head, tail and feet, drenched in lime juice, and traditionally served at special events. Johnny cakes (fried bread), and *pate* (turnovers plump with goat, beef or saltfish) can be found at a few roadside stands, particularly at Mavens Bay. Another "local" delicacy you should not miss are the liquor-flavored milkshakes, such as the chocolate and coconut ice cream blended with Kahlua at **Udder Delight Dairy Bar** near Magens Bay, ☎ *(809) 775-2501.*

Several noteworthy eateries were lost to Hurricane Marilyn, or through post-storm fallout. The Cafe Normandie, Lemongrass Cafe and Provence are among the casualties. The healthy appetite for fine food is such that new restaurants are sure to spring up as St. Thomas tourism picks up again. One such contender is **La Scala**, in Charlotte Amalie's Palm Passage. Created by the team responsible for Chateau de Bordeaux and others on St. John, La Scala opened in 1996 to instant acclaim. Another is **Herve**, the creation of the former manager of Hotel 1829.

Charlotte Amalie

Art Geckos   **$$**   ★

Tillet Gardens, Smith Bay Road, Charlotte Amalie, ☎ *(809) 775-4550.*
American cuisine.
Lunch: 11 a.m.–4:30 p.m., entrées $5–$8.
Dinner: 6–11:30 p.m., entrées $6–$16. Closed: Sun.
Enjoy burgers, sandwiches and salads at lunch, plus fresh seafood and grilled Jamaican jerk chicken at dinner at this casual open-air cafe in Tillett Gardens. If you're lucky, you'll get to watch the daily iguana feedings. The restaurant is a true oasis in a peaceful garden setting, though the real reason to come here is to check out the fascinating artisans' shops that surround it. Besides the famed maps and underwater seascapes by Jim Tillett, you'll find a goldsmith shop, African mahogany carvings, a tea shop and beautiful hand-painted gifts. A must! Credit cards: A, MC, V.

Blackbeard's Castle   **$$$**   ★★★

P.O. Box 6041, Charlotte Amalie, ☎ *(809) 776-1234.*
Associated hotel: Blackbeard's Castle.
American cuisine.
Lunch: 11:30 a.m.–2:30 p.m., entrées $8–$13.

Dinner: 6:30–9:30 p.m., entrées $18–$29.

Feel like Blackbeard the pirate surveying his domain from this stunning aerie with an eagle eye view of the harbor and the city. The international cuisine has won many awards from local publications several years in a row. It's hard to have a meal here without sampling from a varied array of homemade soups, salads or creative appetizers. Entrées include a choice of veal, excellent seafood, beef filets or a devilishly rich pasta. Lighter meals can be had in the lounge or by the pool, where non-guests can swim. There's a bountiful buffet Sundays from 11 a.m.–3 pm. Reservations recommended. Credit cards: A, MC, V.

Cafe Normandie $$$ ★★★★

rue de St. Barthélémy, Charlotte Amalie, ☎ *(809) 774-1622.*
French cuisine.
Dinner: 6–10 p.m., entrées $25–$39. Closed: Mon.

In an informal survey a few years ago, island residents anointed this cozy, elegant French restaurant with a bright yellow painted exterior as their favorite overall dining-out spot. Food, service and location are all exceptional, but we suspect people return again and again for the sinful chocolate fudge pie. There's a well-regarded five-course, prix-fixe supper available nightly that includes a palate-cleansing sorbet. Make sure to reserve in season, as this place is small and popular. Closed Mondays in summer. Reservations recommended. Credit cards: A, MC, V.

Cafesito $$ ★★★

21 Queens Quarter; Charlotte Amalie, ☎ *(809) 774-9574.*
Mediterranean cuisine.
Lunch: from 11 a.m., entrées $4–$19.
Dinner: to 11 p.m., entrées $4–$19.

This recently opened spot is real winner. The long dining room has wood-beamed ceilings, white-washed walls and pretty wooden cases displaying a good wine selection (featuring a $120 bottle of Dom Perignon). The cuisine is Spanish tapas, with such delicacies as sizzling shrimp in virgin olive oil with saffron and garlic, fish and chicken, and the most wonderful salad of vine-ripe tomatoes, hearts of palm and gorgonzola cheese. Most tapa plates run $5–7, and a pitcher of sangria is $15, making this a great place for a light meal, but a variety of *paellas* ($10–15) are popular. Flamenco dancing Thursday–Saturday evenings. Credit cards: A, D, MC, V.

Chart House $$$ ★★★

Villa Olga; Frenchtown, Charlotte Amalie, ☎ *(809) 774-4262.*
Associated hotel: Admiral's Inn.
American cuisine.
Dinner: 5:30–10 p.m., entrées $16–$37.

Salad-bar lovers flock here for a huge spread of many items, including passable caviar. Dinner specialties include sizzling steaks, juicy prime rib, chicken, lobster and pasta (the grilled salmon over orzo is a treat); the salad bar is included. All this bounty is consumed on a terrace overlooking the sea, situated in a 19th century building which was once home to Russian diplomats. Don't overlook the famous "mud pie" if you still have room. Reservations recommended. Credit cards: A, DC, MC, V.

Craig and Sally's $$$ ★★★★

22 Estate Honduras; Frenchtown, Charlotte Amalie, ☎ (809) 777-9949.
International cuisine.
Lunch: 11:30 a.m.–3 p.m., entrées $9–$13.
Dinner: 5:30–10:30 p.m., entrées $12–$28. Closed: Mon.

A talented husband-and-wife team combine his knowledge of fine wines and her culinary expertise in the operation of this muraled restaurant in Frenchtown. Although there are several dining areas, it's often crowded; the word is out on the creative Mediterranean and Asian specialties prepared here. The menu changes daily, but sun-kissed tomatoes, broiled peppers or salsas made with market picked fruits are used liberally on plump scallops, chicken or swordfish. Sally's desserts recall a childhood learning to bake at mother's elbow—there's key lime pie and killer chocolate cakes. The wine list received an award of excellence citation from *Wine Spectator*. Reservations required. Credit cards: A, MC, V.

Cuzzin's $$ ★★★

Back Street; Charlotte Amalie, ☎ (809) 777-4711.
Caribbean cuisine.
Lunch: 11 a.m.–4 p.m., entrées $10–$20.
Dinner: 5–9:30 p.m., entrées $10–$20. Closed: Mon., Sun.

Authentic island cuisine awaits in this local's hangout, a cute yellow brick building with wooden shutters. Specialties include stewed conch, curried chicken and other local dishes and drinks like sea moss (milk, sugar, seaweed and nutmeg). Each Entrée comes with a choice of three side dishes such as potato stuffing, rice and beans, yams and macaroni and cheese. The daring will like the homemade hot sauce that accompanies some meals. Reservations recommended. Credit cards: A, D, MC, V.

Epernay Champagne Bar $$ ★★★

24 B Honduras St.; Frenchtown, Charlotte Amalie, ☎ (809) 774-5348.
International cuisine.
Dinner: 4:30 p.m.–1 a.m., entrées $6–$18. Closed: Sun.

Before or after a night on the prowl, nestle here for champagne by the glass; sample up to six different varieties. A grazing menu of sophisticated snacks covers the *globe. There's* sushi, caviar and goat cheese. A small selection of entrées are also available. Food is served from 5 p.m.–midnight; the bar is open later on weekends. Wine and desserts are also available. Credit cards: A, MC, V.

Gladys' Cafe $$ ★★

17 Main Street; Charlotte Amalie, ☎ (809) 774-6604.
Caribbean cuisine.
Lunch: 10:30 a.m.–4 p.m., entrées $6–$13.

This spot, set in an alleyway in Charlotte Amalie, is where locals congregate for breakfast (served from 7 a.m.) and Caribbean-style lunches. Besides the standard burgers and sandwiches, the menu offers up conch in lemon butter sauce, sauteed shrimp and other West Indian favorites. On Fridays, Gladys' serves dinner with live jazz music until 1 a.m.; entrées $16–18. The brick walls, covered in murals, feature flying pigs; check out the blackboard for Gladys' thought of the day, such as the recent "the effect of hope is astounding." Credit cards: A, MC, V.

Hard Rock Cafe $$ ★★

International Plaza, Charlotte Amalie, ☎ *(809) 777-5555.*
American cuisine.
Lunch: 11 a.m.–4 p.m., entrées $7–$16.
Dinner: 4 p.m.–midnight, entrées $7–$16.
This memorabilia-laden retro-rock burger palace draws a more subdued crowd than those in mainland cities, but there's the requisite antique auto suspended over the entrance. Bob Marley mementoes are also included with the gold Beatles records behind glass frames. Among the wall exhibits is a red and gold neon sign proclaiming "No drugs or nuclear weapons allowed" inside. Good burgers barbecue ribs nachos and fajitas are served. Credit cards: A, MC, V.

Herve Restaurant and Wine Bar $$$ ★★★

Government Hill; Charlotte Amalie, ☎ *(809) 777-9703.*
International cuisine.
Dinner: 6–10 p.m., entrées $16–$26. Closed: Mon.
Pronounced "air-VAY," this new eatery is located in the historic district, next door to Hotel 1829, with generous views extending into the Charlotte Amalie harbor. The menu combines classic French with contemporary American, and specialties include lobster and coquile St. Jacques, pan-seared Norwegian salmon with tomatoes and capers, and a black sesame-crusted tuna in a ginger-raspberry sauce. Classic turn-of-the-century black-and-white prints of St. Thomas decorate the walls of the restaurant, while a separate wine bar provides hot and cold appetizers. Credit cards: A, MC, V.

Hook, Line and Sinker $$ ★★

2 The Waterfront; Frenchtown, Charlotte Amalie, ☎ *(809) 776-9708.*
International cuisine.
Lunch: 11:30 a.m.–4 p.m., entrées $5–$10.
Dinner: 6–10 p.m., entrées $6–$20.
Yachties tie up to this seaside eatery that's nothing special, but it's a good meet-and-greet place. There's a nice outdoor deck, and offerings are reasonably priced. It's a convenient stop if you're in the area, especially for a burger or steak lunch. The Sunday brunch (10 a.m –2:30 p.m.) is popular with locals. Features: Sunday brunch. Reservations recommended. Credit cards: A, MC, V.

Hotel 1829 $$$ ★★★★

Government Hill; Charlotte Amalie, ☎ *(809) 776-1829, (800) 524-2002. Associated hotel: Hotel 1829.*
American cuisine.
Dinner: 6–10 p.m., entrées $20–$32. Closed: Sun.
Streamlined service and stellar food are served in a restored Government Hill hotel. Tables on the terrace are sought after for the terrific views, while the dark brick-walled interior room is air-conditioned and offers another form of romance, but wherever you sit, the cuisine is fine, if expensive. French-American continental cuisine is the focus, with chateaubriand, shellfish and rack of lamb as some highlight. Other specialties include a wilted spinach salad and dessert soufflés—the raspberry chocolate is especially toothsome. Reservations required. Credit cards: A, MC, V.

Il Cardinale   **$$**   ★★

Back Street, Charlotte Amalie, ☎ *(809) 775-1090.*
Italian cuisine.
Lunch: until 4 p.m., entrées $11–$19.
Dinner: 5:30–11 p.m., entrées $11–$19.
This air-conditioned spot offers a quiet and dignified respite from the teeming
streets of Charlotte Amalie. Located upstairs in the Taste of Italy shopping mall, the
decor is subdued, with large oil paintings dominating the walls and tables clothed in
white linen. Among the choices are homemade crepes, salmon in champagne sauce,
a highly regarded chicken salad and *pasta e fagiolo* soup. After your meal, stroll the
adjacent gallery that spotlights local artwork. Credit cards: A, MC, V.

L'Escargot   **$$$**   ★★★

12 Submarine Base, Charlotte Amalie, ☎ *(809) 774-6565.*
Seafood cuisine.
Lunch: 11:45 a.m.–2:45 p.m., entrées $7–$15.
Dinner: 6-10 p.m., entrées $15–$27. Closed: Sun.
A long-established dining room, this classic French restaurant is one of a few eater-
ies located at a submarine base west of Charlotte Amalie, near the airport. Two din-
ing areas are available: an alfresco terrace, or a wine cellar for more formal meals.
Specialties are continental favorites like rack of lamb or lobster thermidor—all sim-
ply and impeccably prepared, but with an Italian flair that allows room for an angel
hair pasta topped with scampi and pesto. There's also a West Indian buffet added on
Thursday and Friday. Reservations recommended. Credit cards: A, MC, V.

La Scala   **$$$**   ★★★

Palm Passage; Charlotte Amalie, ☎ *(809) 774-2206.*
International cuisine.
Lunch: 11 a.m.–3 p.m., entrées $10–$17.
Dinner: 5:30 p.m.–9 p.m., entrées $13–$25. Closed: Sun.
Another fine creation from the creative team responsible for Chateau de Bordeaux
and Asolare on St. John, La Scala is a great addition to the St. Thomas restaurant
scene. Pizzas, pastas and sandwiches fill out the lunch menu, while dinner brings a
huge osso bucco of lamb, pan-seared red snapper and other items prepared with
Italian sizzle. The food is fresh and tasty, and the pleasant alfresco courtyard dining
is next to a large bar made from coral. A live jazz happy-hour is planned for Thurs-
days. Credit cards: A, MC, V.

Lemon Grass Cafe   **$$$**   ★★

Bakery Square, Back Street, Charlotte Amalie, ☎ *(809) 777-1877.*
Lunch: 11 a.m.–3:30 p.m., entrées $7–$16.
Dinner: 6–10 p.m., entrées $16–$20.
The menu changes often at this pretty spot located in a scenic courtyard. Dine outdoors next to the lily pond, or inside, where gleaming woods, stone walls and ceiling fans create a lovely atmosphere. Entrées range from salads and burgers to roast
salmon, grilled swordfish and pork and lamb dishes. Sunday brunch (10:30 a.m.–
2:30 p.m.) is followed by a "tea dance" with a mini-menu from 5–9 p.m. Credit cards:
A, MC, V.

Old Stone Farmhouse $$$ ★★★★

Mahogany Run, Charlotte Amalie, ☎ *(809) 775-1377.*
International cuisine.
Dinner: 6:30–10 p.m., entrées $23–$29. Closed: Sun.
Considered one of St. Thomas' fining dining outlets, the Old Stone is built in the ruins of a 200-year-old dairy farm near Mahogany Run Golf Course (on the north side, 20 minutes from Charlotte Amalie). A pianist lends just the right amount of ambience to this lovely room of thick stone walls and varied antiques. Entrées include such imaginative offers as filet mignon with boursin cheese and a red onion marmalade and snapper in a potato crust. Whatever you choose, you'll be well pleased. Reservations required. Credit cards: A, MC, V.

Palm Court $$$ ★★★★

Red Hook, Charlotte Amalie, ☎ *(809) 775-1000. Associated hotel: Elysian.*
International cuisine.
Dinner: 6:30–10 p.m., entrées $14–$32.
Located steps from the beach at the Elysian Resort, this fine dining spot offers tables inside or, better yet, out under the stars. Entrées run the gamut from fresh seafood to beef, lamb, poultry and pasta dishes. Such specialties as a grilled portabella mushroom served with carmelized onions and port wine sauce and swordfish in ginger lime butter with poached peaches in dark Cruzan rum keep patrons happy. Heavenly! Credit cards: A, DC, MC, V.

Palm Passage $ ★

off of Main Street, Charlotte Amalie, ☎ *(809) 779-2708.*
Italian cuisine.
Lunch: 11 a.m.–3:30 p.m., entrées $6–$12.
Located in a scenic courtyard and surrounded by art galleries, Palm Passage is a nice place for a tasty lunch of risotto, roasted garlic, pizza or grilled eggplant salad. The menu also features burgers and sandwiches. Credit cards: A.

Provence $$$ ★★★

Honduras Street, Charlotte Amalie, ☎ *(809) 777-5600.*
French cuisine. Specialties: Antipasto table.
Dinner: 6-10:30 p.m., entrées $15–$19. Closed: Sun.
Chef and restaurateur Patricia La Corte, who created the well-regarded Fiddle Leaf on Government Hill is now roosting at this country-French bistro on the second floor of a wooden building in funky Frenchtown. The warmly-decorated room, with arched doorways and potted palms, offers a wharf-side view. Specialties include lamb shank with hearty *chakerny* and rosemary sauce on a bed of mashed potatoes and oven roasted garlic chicken. Nibblers go into grazing heaven with La Corte's reasonably priced antipasto table, served daily until 11 p.m. Reservations recommended. Credit cards: A, MC, V.

Rain Forest Cafe $ ★

Mountain Top Shopping Mall, Charlotte Amalie, ☎ *(809) 774-2400.*
American cuisine.
The best reason to come to this new cafe is to check out its amazing views—probably the best on an island that abounds with sweeping vistas. The offerings are sim-

ple—deli sandwiches, salads, pastries—the better to leave room for at least one banana daiquiri. The frothy drink was reportedly invented here in 1949 by British restaurateur Conrad Graves. Cheers! Credit cards: A, MC, V.

Terrace Restaurant $$ ★

Lindbergh Bay, Charlotte Amalie, ☎ (809) 774-2525. Associated hotel: Best Western Carib Beach.
American cuisine.
Lunch: 11:30 a.m.–2:30 p.m., entrées $5–$7.
Dinner: 6-9:30 p.m., entrées $7–$19.
No need to make a special trip here (the food's merely adequate), but if you have a long wait at the airport, stroll on over to this pleasantly informal outdoor spot at the Carib Beach Resort. The menu features typical salads, burgers, steak, chicken and the catch of the day. On Friday nights from 6–9:45, a steel band helps liven things up. A great place to catch the moon rise, and it sure beats sitting in the airport. Also open for breakfast from 7–10:30 a.m.

The Frigate $$$ ★★★

P.O. Box 1506, Charlotte Amalie, ☎ (809) 774-2790, (800) 225-7035. Associated hotel: Mafolie Hotel.
Seafood cuisine.
Dinner: entrées $15–$30.
An awe-inspiring ocean view and tender steaks hot off the charcoal broiler continue to please the regulars that flock to this small, charming hotel dining room on Mafolie Hill. Non-red meat eaters will be pleased with fresh seafood, chicken and a salad bar. There's a smaller branch in Red Hook (No. 18-8) near the Marina, ☎ 775-1829. Reservations recommended. Credit cards: A, MC, V.

Victor's New Hide Out $$$ ★★★

103 Submarine Base, Charlotte Amalie, ☎ (809) 776-9379.
International cuisine.
Lunch: 11:30 a.m.–3:30 p.m., entrées $9–$11.
Dinner: 4–10 p.m., entrées $11–$20.
Chef Victor left quiet Montserrat 30 years ago for more action, and he cooks his West Indian specialties for an appreciative crowd of locals, tourists, and the occasional celebrity. The ubiquitous conch and curried chicken dishes are available, as well as his signature dish, Lobster Montserrat, cooked with fruit and cream sauce. Newcomers should probably arrive by taxi, as the hilltop hideaway is a little hard to find. No lunch served on Sunday. Reservations recommended. Credit cards: A, MC, V.

Virgilio's $$$ ★★★★

18 Dronningens Gade; Charlotte Amalie, ☎ (809) 776-4920.
Italian cuisine.
Lunch: 11:30 a.m.–4 p.m., entrées $13–$22.
Dinner: 4–10:30 p.m., entrées $16–$39. Closed: Sun.
It looks like a dump from the outside, but a true haven awaits inside this wonderful restaurant. The walls are covered with eclectic artwork, the ceilings twinkle with tiny lights and display cases proudly spotlight the Caribbean's largest wine collection—400 bottles, plus an extensive collection of cordials. The food is as good as the atmosphere. The huge menu offers up 40 kinds of homemade pastas, fish, chicken

and vegetarian specialties. Save room for a luscious dessert such as bananas foster or crepes suzette prepared tableside. You'll find few tourists among the upscale locals who regularly dine here. Features: rated wine cellar. Reservations recommended. Credit cards: A, MC, V.

Zorba's $ ★★★

Government Hill; Charlotte Amalie, ☎ *(809) 776-0444.*
Greek cuisine.

The bright whites of Greece animate this festive deli and restaurant located on Government Hill. Featuring scintillating fresh bread baked on the premises the restaurant also offers a few shrimp and fish entrées, but most dishes embrace chicken and lamb with generous appetizers of *baba ganush*, tabouli and a chilled octopus in white wine, garlic and lemon. Macrobiotic and vegetarian platters are available and the small outdoor patio is quite pleasant. Closed Sunday for lunch, but live entertainment is featured on Sunday nights. Credit cards: A, MC, V.

Red Hook

Agave Terrace $$$ ★★★

6400 Estate Smith Bay, Red Hook, ☎ *(809) 775-4142.*
Associated hotel: Point Pleasant Resort.
Seafood cuisine.
Dinner: 6–10 p.m., entrées $18–$24.

It may be a little hard to find, with a hilltop resort location on the northeastern end of the island, but even non-guests should try to make it here for a leisurely dinner on the patio while the light is still good for an unparalleled view of the Caribbean sea in the distance. The cuisine is mostly Mediterranean-style seafood, and the chef is delighted to create any dish (within reason) that a customer requests. A live steel band performs Tuesday and Thursday, and the Saturday and Sunday brunch is acclaimed. Reservations required. Credit cards: A, MC, V.

Blue Marlin, The $$$ ★★

6300 Smith Bay Road; Red Hook, ☎ *(809) 775-6350.*
International cuisine.
Lunch: 11:30 a.m.–2:30 p.m., entrées $7–$11.
Dinner: 6–10 p.m., entrées $13–$19.

Salads, sandwiches, fish and chips, fried calamari are served for lunch, with pasta and seafood taking over at night—the selection changes daily based on what's fresh. But the real reason to come is the pleasant setting overlooking the Red Hook marina and it's also a good spot to wait if you miss one of the midday ferries. Features: outside dining. Credit cards: A, MC, V.

Eunice's Terrace $$$ ★★

66-67 Smith Bay, Route 38, Red Hook, ☎ *(809) 775-3975.*
West Indies cuisine.
Lunch: 11 a.m.–5 p.m., entrées $6–$11.
Dinner: 6–10 p.m., entrées $10–$28.

Don't let the junk yard out back put you off. An island success story, Eunice's establishment grew quickly from a simple food stand to a two-story building with a popular bar on Smith Bay just west of the Renaissance Grand. The West Indian cuisine that built her reputation is possibly the best on the island. There's a daily menu, but conch fritters, broiled fish, *fungi*, and peas and rice are usually available. Don't miss Eunice's incomparable tropical rum cake (available in a gift box for $4). Closed for lunch on Sunday. Reservations recommended. Credit cards: A, MC, V.

Piccola Marina Cafe $$$ ★ ★ ★
6300 Smith Bay, Red Hook, ☎ *(809) 775-6350.*
American cuisine.
Lunch: 11 a.m.–5:30 p.m., entrées $5–$14.
Dinner: 5:30–10:30 p.m., entrées $13–$24.
This alfresco restaurant on the Red Hook Marina dock is a fun place, with a selection of pastas for your dining pleasure. Sauces range from tomato marinara to a creamy alfredo. Other options include sandwiches, chicken, fresh seafood or you can quaff a brew or two. Sunday brunch is served in the winter from 10 a.m. to 3 p.m. Reservations recommended. Credit cards: A, MC, V.

Raffles $$$ ★ ★ ★
The Marina; Compass Point, Red Hook, ☎ *(809) 775-6004.*
Seafood cuisine.
Dinner: 6:30–10:30 p.m., entrées $15–$29. Closed: Mon.
This south-seas themed restaurant is a favorite with residents, who enjoy the steaks flambeed at tableside. Relax in the high-backed peacock chairs in a salon cooled by ceiling fans and ocean breezes. Other specialties include fresh fish, conch sauteed in wine and garlic, and stuffed leg of lamb. Chocoholics will die for Peter's Paradise, a chocolate basket filled with white chocolate mousse, almonds and drizzled with raspberry puree. Reservations required. Credit cards: A, MC, V.

Ritz Carlton $$$ ★ ★ ★ ★
Red Hook, ☎ *(809) 775-3333, (800) 545-0509.*
Associated hotel: Ritz-Carlton St. Thomas.
International cuisine.
Dinner: 6:30–10 p.m., entrées $22–$32.
A chef with a background in cooking for luxury health spas in California and Florida holds court at this, the Ritz-Carlton resort's crown jewel. Weight-watchers can delight in the fact that many of the delectable meals are prepared in natural juices and infusions instead of heavy cream sauces. Alas, the calories await in the desserts, one of which is caramel ice cream encased in chocolate. The surroundings here are some of the most luxurious on the island—everything exudes a rosy glow and all is pretty in pink. A pianist helps further the romantic mod. Divine! Reservations required. Credit cards: A, MC, V.

Where to Shop

St. Thomas moves to a mercantile beat. Charlotte Amalie was declared a free port in 1755, a move that opened the island for trade with both the European powers and the growing American colonies. Today there are literally hundreds of duty free shops to tempt shoppers in and around Charlotte Amalie. Jewelry, electronics, china, linen and perfume shops crowd Main Street (also known as Dronnigens Gade) and the alleys and passageways that bisect it, with a number of stores having a second outlet at the Havensight Mall just outside town near the cruise ship dock. Reputable establishments generally avoid the sidewalk barker come-ons that grow more shrill as one moves west on Main Street.

Most visitors leave toting at least a one bottle of local rum, like Cruzan, which is priced about $3 a fifth. But U.S. residents may bring home $1200 in goods free of duty, with the next $1000 subject to a five percent duty. Members of a household may make a joint declaration, entitling a family of four to a $4800 duty-free allowance. There is no sales or luxury tax, and products manufactured in the USVI (clothing, and handicrafts like jams or local jewelry) do not count toward your duty free exemption. Unset precious gems, original paintings and binoculars are also exempt. The best buys traditionally include jewelry, fine china, crystal and perfume, while bargains can also be found in gems, watches and electronic products (verify the service warranty). However, it pays to do a little research before you arrive on island. By familiarizing yourself with prices on items you are interested in at home, you can separate the good deals from those that offer little or no savings. Finesse in bargaining also goes a long way.

Beyond the name brand stores, there are a number of specialty shops worth investigating. Artisans from Jamaica, Haiti, the Dominican Republic and Martinique are represented at several galleries, and The Gallery has a two-room studio featuring fine Caribbean folk art including work from some of the island's top primitivists. Another favorite is Down Island Traders, next to Post Office Alley on the waterfront, where you choose everything from edible delicacies such as marmalades and jellies to sweet Caribbean rum balls, fiery mustards, fruit chutneys and exotic spices. Down Island also has an extensive collection of Haitian and Jamaican wall hangings, handmade cloth and wooden dolls, including the famous Caribbean worry doll. At Mango Tango in the Al Cohen building (across the street from Havensight), you can stock up on wooden masks from Jamaica, wooden carvings from Trinidad and original and print work from the Virgin Islands. Tillett Gardens Craft Complex, located in Tutu across from the Four Winds Plaza, features the work of Jim Tillett, who creates screen-painted maps of the Caribbean, cruising maps of the Virgin Islands, and abstract paintings; other local artists are also represented. Color of Joy is a boutique that features watercolors and prints by St. Thomas painter Corinne Van Rensselaer, as well as varied gifts from the islands. A small annex, the Caribbean Enamel Guild features hand-painted jewelry, boxes and various accessories. The best time to visit Tillet

Gardens is during the popular Arts Alive arts and craft fairs, held on-site three times a year. For more information ☎ *(809) 775-1929.*

If shopping is a big part of your St. Thomas itinerary, pick up a free copy of St. Thomas This Week, a bright yellow magazine that provides shopping information and a detailed map of Charlotte Amalie's shopping district; it can be found at the St. Thomas airport, as well as in San Juan's airport. Charlotte Amalie stores are generally open 9 a.m. to 5 p.m. Monday through Saturday, though they will sometimes open on Sunday if cruise ship business warrants.

St. Thomas Directory

Arrival and Departure

The most comprehensive service to St. Thomas is via **American Airlines**, which provides daily nonstop service from Miami and New York's Kennedy Airport. **American Eagle** provides more than a dozen flights daily out of San Juan, Puerto Rico, allowing easy connections from throughout North America. American Eagle also has seven daily non-stop flights to St. Thomas out of St. Croix. **Delta** provides daily non-stop service out of Atlanta. **USAir** flies to St. Thomas nonstop from Baltimore. Low-cost start-up **Prestige Airways** handles the link between Miami and St. Thomas. **United**, **Continental** and **TWA** fly into San Juan where you may connect to American Eagle.

Inter-island service is provided by **LIAT**, which provides nonstop or direct service to St. Thomas from Anguilla, Antigua, St. Kitts, St. Maarten and Tortola, with connecting service from a number of other islands available through Antigua. Among the other regional carriers connecting St. Thomas to Caribbean destinations are **Air Anguilla** (Anguilla, St. Croix, St. Maarten), **Air St. Thomas** (San Juan, St. Barts, Virgin Gorda) and **Bohlke International Airways** (St. Croix). Scheduled seaplane service is available to and from St. Croix six times daily on **Seaborne Seaplane**; $45 one way for USVI residents, or $50 for visitors ☎ *(809) 777-4491.*

Taxis are plentiful at the **St. Thomas airport**, hovering at the far left end of the new terminal.

Business Hours

Shops generally open weekdays 9 a.m.–5 p.m. Banks generally open Monday–Thursday 9 a.m.–2:30 p.m. and Friday 9 a.m.–2 and 3:30–5 p.m.

Climate

Summer temperatures, cooled by eastern trade winds, hover around 82 degrees Fahrenheit. Winter temperatures range from 77 degrees, dipping to 69 degrees at night and rising as high as 84 degrees. The rainy season runs September–January, though the sun shines nearly every day. The average rainfall is about 40 inches per year, and showers are usually brief.

Documents

U.S. citizens need no passport. But if you plan to visit the British Virgin Islands, you must show proof of citizenship (passport, or birth certificate with photo ID). Canadians must have a valid passport.

Electricity

Current runs at 110 volts, 60 cycles.

Getting Around

Cabs are not metered but each driver must carry the current fare structure. Rates are per person, but drop if two or more are going to the same destination. Sample rates from Charlotte Amalie are: to Red Hook $9 for one, or $5 each for two or more; to the airport, $4.50 and $4; to Magens Bay, $6.50 and $4. If you are traveling between two points that aren't on the official list, negotiate firmly ahead of time. Note that when you board at a popular departure point (for instance, at Red Hook when a ferry comes in), you'll need patience while drivers try to fill the cab with other passengers headed in your general direction. There are open-air taxi buses between Charlotte Amalie and Red Hook for $3. The buses leave the Market Place every hour from 8:15 a.m. to 5:15 p.m.; buses leave Red Hook every hour from 7:15 a.m. to 4:15 p.m. A two-hour island tour for one or two passengers runs $30, with additional passengers paying $12 each.

Rental cars are easily obtained, typically from one of the name American agencies like Budget, for about $50 per day. Comparing prices and reserving your car ahead of your trip will usually net the best deals. No special license or permit is required, but driving is on the left.

Ferries are the primary transportation between St. Thomas and the Virgins to the east and daytrips are easy and popular. Ferries to Cruz Bay, St. John originate hourly from Red Hook ($3 each way; about 20 minutes) or almost hourly from Charlotte Amalie ($7, about 45 minutes). For exact schedules, call **Transportation Services**, ☎ *(809) 776-6282*, or **Varlack Ventures**, ☎ *(809) 776-6412*. Blue Lines has a **car ferry** that plies the route between Red Hook and Cruz Bay every 90 minutes ($50 round-trip for car and passengers, about 25 minutes); call to reserve, ☎ *(809) 777-6111*. For information on ferry service to West End, Road Town and Virgin Gorda, see "Arrival and Departure" in "British Virgin Islands." You'll need a passport or a birth certificate and photo identification for entry. **Per Dohm's Water Taxi** provides speedy charter service between Red Hook and St. John or the BVIs, ☎ *(809) 775-6501*. A ferry also connects downtown Charlotte Amalie with the Frenchman's Reef Hotel and Morningstar Beach hourly ($4, about 15 minutes).

Language

English is the official language. Locals also speak a native patois, a mixture of English, African and Spanish. Many people are bilingual in Spanish.

Medical Emergencies

Police ext. *915*, fire ext. *921*, ambulance ext. *922*.

St. Thomas, U.S. Virgin Islands

Fort Christian, St. Thomas, U.S. Virgin Islands

Money

The official currency is the American dollar. There is no sales tax.

Telephone

The area code is *(809)*. Since the U.S. Virgin Islands is an incorporated territory, toll-free (800) numbers on the island can be accessed from the mainland. Regular U.S. postage rates also apply.

Time

Atlantic Standard Time, which means an hour later than New York City, except during Daylight Saving Time, when it is the same.

Tipping and Taxes

Some hotels include a 10–15 percent service charge; this should include all tips for both restaurant and room service, unless the attention was extraordinary. If no service is added, leave a 15 percent tip for the waitress, $1–$2 a day to the maid; bartenders and wine stewards should always be tipped. Tip the bellboy and porter at least 50 cents a bag. Taxi drivers should receive a 15 percent tip if you are satisfied with the service.

Tourist Information

The **U.S. Virgin Islands Department of Tourism** has information booths at the airport, at Emancipation Garden in Charlotte Amalie, and in Havensight Mall near the cruise ship dock, ☎ *(809) 774-8784*. You can also pick up brochures, rest your feet, and even check shopping bags at an island-sponsored hospitality lounge in the Old Customs House next to Little Switzerland. You may write to the **St. Thomas Visitors Bureau** at *24 Tolbod Gade, St. Thomas, VI 00802*. There is also a toll-free information number for the U.S. Virgin Islands, ☎ *(800) 372-USVI*.

Water

There is ample water for showers and bathing, but you are asked to conserve water whenever possible. It's safe to drink.

When to Go

The Calypso Competition is held at the University of the Virgin Islands cafeteria on March 4. Arts Alive & Crafts Festival, where Caribbean vendors sell handmade crafts and arts, is held on March 17–19. The Caribbean Chorale, one of the most popular groups in the USVI, performs a blend of classical, West Indian and native compositions on April 2. The 10th annual Easter Bonnet Contest takes place on April 17. The Virgin Islands Carnival Events, with nightly competitions in music and costumes, takes place on April 18–22. The 22nd Annual International Rolex Cup Regatta is April 21–23 (tentative). Virgin Islands Carnival Village features local foods, drink, and rides on April 24–29. STARfest 1995, a star-studded tribute to Caribbean talent, is May 13. The 8th Annual American Yacht Harbor Billfish tournament is July 13–18. Arts Alive Arts & Crafts Festival is August 11–13. The Hebrew Congregation of St. Thomas Bicentennial Celebration Gala Opening Weekend, featuring a celebration of Jewish History, is September 15–17. Hebrew Congregation of St.

Thomas Bicentennial Celebration Interfaith Succot Service is October 6–8. The Hebrew Congregation of St. Thomas Bicentennial Celebration Jewish Musical Performance starts October 24 for four weeks. St. Thomas/St. John Agriculture Food Fair is November 18–19. Arts Alive Arts & Crafts Festival is November 24–26. The Hebrew Congregations of St. Thomas Bicentennial Celebration, featuring an authentic Sephardic Service and Chanukah Celebration is December 22.

ST. THOMAS HOTELS		RMS	RATES	PHONE	CR. CARDS
Bolongo Bay					
★★★★	**Bolongo Inclusive Beach Resort**	116	$175–$440	(800) 524-4746	A, D, DC, MC, V
★★★	**Bolongo Bay Beach Villas**	39	$195–$390	(800) 524-4746	A, DC, MC, V
Charlotte Amalie					
★★★★★	**Ritz-Carlton St. Thomas**	150	$400–$525	(800) 241-3333	A, D, MC, V
★★★★	**Anchorage Beach Villas**	30	$195–$235	(800) 524-6599	A, D, DC, MC, V
★★★★	**Marriott's Morning Star Beach Resort**	96	$185–$395	(800) 524-2000	A, CB, D, DC, MC, V
★★★★	**Renaissance Grand Beach Resort**	297	$225–$895	(800) 468-3571	A, D, DC, MC, V
★★★★	**Sapphire Beach Resort and Marina**	171	$195–$475	(800) 524-2090	A, MC, V
★★★★	**Secret Harbour Resort**	60	$160–$295	(800) 524-2250	A, MC, V
★★★★	**Sugar Bay Plantation**	300	$180–$370	(800) 927-7100	A, D, DC, MC, V
★★★★	**Watergate Villas**	100	$73–$375	(800) 524-2038	A, D, DC, MC, V
★★★	**Best Western Carib Beach Resort**	69	$89–$149	(800) 792-2742	A, MC, V
★★★	**Best Western Emerald Beach Resort**	90	$145–$239	(800) 233-4936	A, CB, D, DC, MC, V
★★★	**Blackbeard's Castle**	25	$75–$140	(800) 344-5771	A, D, MC, V
★★★	**Bluebeard's Castle Hotel**	184	$140–$235	(800) 524-6599	A, D, DC, MC, V
★★★	**Colony Point Pleasant Resort**	134	$170–$380	(800) 524-2300	A, D, DC, MC, V
★★★	**Hotel 1829**	15	$60–$230	(800) 524-2002	A, MC, V
★★★	**Island Beachcomber**	48	$100–$150	(800) 982-9898	A, CB, D, DC, MC, V
★★★	**Limetree Beach Resort**	84	$110–$195	(800) 753-2554	A, DC, MC, V
★★★	**Marriott's Frenchman's Reef**	420	$150–$298	(800) 524-2000	A, CB, D, DC, MC, V
★★★	**Pavilions & Pools**	25	$180–$260	(800) 524-2001	A, D, MC, V
★★★	**Ramada Yacht Haven Hotel**	151	$90–$225	(800) 228-9898	A, CB, D, DC, MC, V

ST. THOMAS HOTELS		RMS	RATES	PHONE	CR. CARDS
★★★	**Secret Harbourview Villas**	30	$140–$360	(800) 874-7897	D, DC, MC, V
★★	**Admiral's Inn**	13	$79–$149	(800) 544-0493	A, D, MC, V
★★	**Crystal Cove**	50	$126–$273	(809) 775-6220	A, DC, MC, V
★★	**Galleon House**	14	$49–$119	(800) 524-2052	A, D, MC, V
★★	**Heritage Manor**	8	$45–$85	(800) 828-0757	A, MC, V
★★	**Mafolie Hotel**	23	$65–$97	(800) 225-7035	A, MC, V
★★	**Magens Point Hotel**	54	$100–$300	(800) 524-2031	A, CB, D, DC, MC, V
★★	**Villa Santana**	5	$95–$195	(809) 776-1311	
★★	**Windward Passage**	151	$125–$230	(800) 524-7389	A, CB, DC, MC, V
★	**Danish Chalet Inn**	10	$60–$95	(800) 635-1531	MC, V
★	**Island View Guest House**	15	$45–$100	(800) 524-2023	A, MC, V

Red Hook

★★★★	**Elysian Resort**	118	$175–$630	(800) 753-2554	A, D, DC, MC, V
★★★	**Cowpet Bay Village**	30	$247–$420	(800) 524-2038	A, D, DC, MC, V

ST. THOMAS RESTAURANTS	PHONE	ENTRÉE	CR. CARDS
Charlotte Amalie			
★★★ **Herve Restaurant and Wine Bar**	(809) 777-9703	$16–$26	A, MC, V
★★★ **La Scala**	(809) 774-2206	$10–$25	A, MC, V
★★★ **Zorba's**	(809) 776-0444		A, MC, V
American			
★★★★ **Hotel 1829**	(809) 776-1829	$20–$32	A, MC, V
★★★ **Blackbeard's Castle**	(809) 776-1234	$8–$29	A, MC, V
★★★ **Chart House**	(809) 774-4262	$16–$37	A, DC, MC, V
★★ **Hard Rock Cafe**	(809) 777-5555	$7–$16	A, MC, V
★ **Art Geckos**	(809) 775-4550	$5–$16	A, MC, V
★ **Rain Forest Cafe**	(809) 774-2400		A, MC, V
★ **Terrace Restaurant**	(809) 774-2525	$5–$19	
Caribbean			
★★★ **Cuzzin's**	(809) 777-4711	$10–$20	A, D, MC, V
★★ **Gladys' Cafe**	(809) 774-6604	$6–$13	A, MC, V

ST. THOMAS RESTAURANTS	PHONE	ENTRÉE	CR. CARDS
Continental			
★★★★ Old Stone Farmhouse	(809) 775-1377	$23–$29	A, MC, V
★★★★ Palm Court	(809) 775-1000	$14–$32	A, DC, MC, V
★★ Lemon Grass Cafe	(809) 777-1877	$7–$20	A, MC, V
French			
★★★★ Cafe Normandie	(809) 774-1622	$25–$39	A, MC, V
★★★ Provence	(809) 777-5600	$15–$19	A, MC, V
International			
★★★★ Craig and Sally's	(809) 777-9949	$9–$28	A, MC, V
★★★ Epernay Champagne Bar	(809) 774-5348	$6–$18	A, MC, V
★★★ Victor's New Hide Out	(809) 776-9379	$9–$20	A, MC, V
★★ Hook, Line and Sinker	(809) 776-9708	$5–$20	A, MC, V
Italian			
★★★★ Virgilio's	(809) 776-4920	$13–$39	A, MC, V
★★ Il Cardinale	(809) 775-1090	$11–$19	A, MC, V
★ Palm Passage	(809) 779-2708	$6–$12	A
Mediterranean			
★★★ Cafesito	(809) 774-9574	$4–$19	A, D, MC, V
Seafood			
★★★ L'Escargot	(809) 774-6565	$7–$27	A, MC, V
★★★ The Frigate	(809) 774-2790	$15–$30	A, MC, V

Red Hook

	PHONE	ENTRÉE	CR. CARDS
★★ Blue Marlin, The	(809) 775-6350	$7–$19	A, MC, V
American			
★★★ Piccola Marina Cafe	(809) 775-6350	$5–$24	A, MC, V
Caribbean			
★★ Eunice's Terrace	(809) 775-3975	$6–$28	A, MC, V
International			
★★★★ Ritz Carlton	(809) 775-3333	$22–$32	A, MC, V
Seafood			
★★★ Agave Terrace	(809) 775-4142	$18–$24	A, MC, V
★★★ Raffles	(809) 775-6004	$15–$29	A, MC, V

ST. VINCENT AND THE GRENADINES

Picturesque St. Vincent's terrain ranges from rugged cliffs to lush valleys and beaches with golden and black sand.

This lovely chain of islands consists of St. Vincent, the largest, with runs 18 miles long by 11 miles wide; and, to the southwest, the Grenadines, some 31 cays scattered along 45 miles of the eastern Caribbean.

St. Vincent is lush and volcanic, with dramatic cliffs, steep mountain ridges, verdant valleys and the crown jewel, a 4000-foot-high volcano called La Soufrière. The Grenadines vary from uninhibited isles and rock cays to the larger islands of Bequia, Mustique, Petit St. Vincent and Union Island— some of which are privately owned.

St. Vincent

Boat excursions and hiking trails lead to cascading waterfalls and mineral springs on St. Vincent.

The largest island in the chain of 32 known as St. Vincent and the Grenadines, St. Vincent is lush and lovely, with stunning botanical gardens, awe-inspiring waterfalls and beaches of both black and gold sand. Its 150 square miles are a nature lover's dream, with excellent nature and hiking trails throughout. The Atlantic coast is wild, rugged and somewhat primitive; the leeward side along the Caribbean Sea has beaches with gentle, soothing surf. The interior is taken over by large mountains and verdant valleys punctuated by fields of bananas, breadfruit and coconut palms. The lower hills have dense forests that are home to the endangered St. Vincent parrot, the national bird.

St. Vincent offers the most cosmopolitan experience of its siblings, and the most for visitors to see and do. The capital city of Kingstown has a busy port as well as include vintage cathedrals, Carib petroglyphs and the oldest botanical garden in the Western Hemisphere (dating to 1765). Other sites around the island include the gorgeous Mesopotamia region along the windward coast, an area rich in forests, banana fields and coconut trees; and the 63-foot Falls of Baleine, reached only by boat. La Soufrière, an active volcano that last erupted in 1979, is a great climb for experienced hikers. No easy trek, plan a half-day just to reach the summit, and be sure to check the weather first, as clouds often obscure the sweeping views.

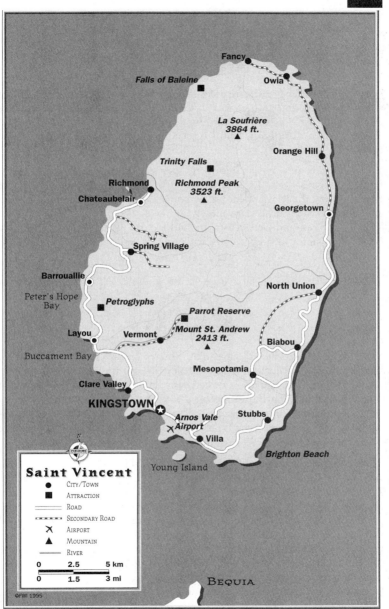

St. Vincent

Saint Vincent

- ● CITY/TOWN
- ■ ATTRACTION
- ═══ ROAD
- ┅┅┅ SECONDARY ROAD
- ✕ AIRPORT
- ▲ MOUNTAIN
- ── RIVER

| 0 | 2.5 | 5 km |
| 0 | 1.5 | 3 mi |

©FWI 1995

St. Vincent totals 133 square miles and measures 18 miles long by 11 miles wide. The Grenadines, which total 17 square miles, stretch out over 45 miles to the southeast. These Windward Islands of the Lesser Antilles are located in the Eastern Caribbean. The largest Grenadine is Bequia, located nine miles from St. Vincent.

St. Vincent is quite mountainous and sports a variety of interesting ecosystems. Its highest peak, La Soufrière, is an active volcano, and some of the beaches along the leeward side are composed of volcanic black sand. The island also has the Morne Garu mountain range, which runs southward with spurs to the east and west coasts. Its hills are deeply forested. The Atlantic coast is known for its rugged cliffs, while verdant valleys are dotted throughout the inland.

Columbus marked the presence of St. Vincent on his third voyage in 1498, but luckily didn't go ashore since the resident Carib Indians might have cannibalized him. The native tribes here were more tenacious than those on other islands, keeping the European conquistadors at bay longer than any other island. In 1763 a treaty allowed the British to take control of the island. Sixteen years later, they found themselves battling the French, but the Treaty of Versailles in 1783 gave the power back to England.

Some years later, Captain Bligh took off for Tahiti from England with his crew of the *Bounty*, only to be mutinied by them and pushed out to sea. In 1793 he finally reached St. Vincent on his own, equipped with a canoeful of breadfruit seedlings, which became the progenitors of a crop that would eventually make the island famous. In 1795, the native population sided with the French and burned down British plantations during a ferocious battle; a year later the Brits triumphantly quelled the rebellion. At that time, the Brits decided to deport the rest of the native Indians to British Honduras (now known as Belize), where their ancestors live today. Until 1979 the island was under British rule, at which time it received independent statehood, along with the other Grenadines, within the Commonwealth. It is governed

St. Vincent

by a governor-general appointed by the Crown on the advice of the prime minister. The Parliament's House of Assembly is elected every five years.

People

St. Vincent

Islanders are a friendly and open lot and visitors are made to feel most welcome; service is uniformly excellent. St. Vincent has a population of about 99,000; the other Grenadines bring total population to about 106,500. Most are of African, Carib, East Indian and Portuguese descent. The majority of islanders are Protestant, with Roman Catholics a healthy minority. Some 85 percent of the population is literate. Most work in agriculture, with construction, manufacturing, and tourism also contributing to the economy. The islands are a constitutional monarchy within the Commonwealth of Great Britain; British customs are commonplace.

Beaches

If you're looking for white-sand beaches, stay around Kingstown; the black ones are located around the rest of the island. Beautiful white sands can be found at **Villa Beach**, on the calm western coast. Also fine for swimming is the black **Questelle's Bay** and the black **Buccament Bay**. Dive shops are located at Villa beach and the CSY Yacht Club. The exposed Atlantic Coast is considered too rough for swimming, but the view of the crashing waves can be very exciting. None of the beaches here sport lifeguards, so take precautions; even experienced swimmers should have someone spotting them, particularly when the water is rough. No beach or changing facilities are located on the windward side.

Underwater

For now, diving in St. Vincent and the Grenadines still appeals to the adventurous spirit. The reefs remain pristine and new sites continue to be discovered. As on Dominica and St. Lucia, visibility is usually excellent despite significant rain runoff, because the main island's soil is mostly volcanic (and heavier), allowing it to sink quickly to the depths rather than mucking up the waters. However, unlike the aforementioned destinations, St. Vincent is not known for its walls. This is a place for reefs, which flourish on the tongues of ancient lava flows snaking into the sea, and for its extensive fish activity. There is an abundance of smaller life, including the unusual and rare frog fish, and frequent sightings of seahorses. Additionally, black coral, which usually grows deeper than recreational diving allows, is found much nearer sea level here, in some spots as close as 27 feet below the surface. Somehow, these beautiful underwater forests, whose branches come in six different colors, have not been leveled. Diving on St. Vincent is concentrated on the southwestern coast, generally close to the two main operators on the island;. With the notable exception of **St. Vincent Dive Experience**, diving does not come cheaply in this country. Four affiliated dive shops (**Dive St. Vincent**, **Dive Bequia**, **Dive Canouan** and **Grenadine Dive** on Union Island) have worked out a mix-and-match package which will appeal to island-hoppers: 10 dives spread among the four shops for $400, including all equipment. Other packages (which lock you into one location) are also available. Snorkelers comfortable in water depths of 25 feet or more can explore each of the following three prime locations.

Somehow, St. Vincent feels like a forgotten outpost in the Eastern Caribbean. Many tourists use the island simply as a jumping-off point for the exclusive resorts of the Grenadines, while briefly-glimpsed bare-boat charterers make up another transient portion of the tourism infrastructure. For an island of over 100,000 residents, surprisingly, St. Vincent still has the magical milieu of a backwater place, waiting to be discovered. There is a smoldering volcano, **La Soufrière** (up until recently the most actively-monitored in the Caribbean), treks into rain forests which are home to the few remaining St. Vincent parrots, and several splendid waterfalls worth visiting. The Forestry Department has guides to some of the island's trails, and the 1:50,000 *Ordnance Survey* map is helpful for exploration. Hikers should carry insect repellent (mosquitoes are prevalent), and be prepared for rainy weather and muddy trails.

By Pedal

Although St. Vincent's road network is hardly extensive, there are picturesque villages and coconut plantations lining the island's coasts which make for very pleasant two-wheeled excursions. A complete circuit of the island, as is possible on most other Caribbean islands, is not feasible by road (the maintained roads form the shape of a "U" on a map). However, the rugged trails to La Soufrière (see On Foot) can be ridden in parts, and completed with the bikes hoisted over your shoulders. This is a true he-man adventure, not to be taken lightly; if you originate in Kingstown, ride up one side of La Soufrière and down the other, you are undertaking a walloping loop of about 65 miles (including several on foot). Regardless of your ability—and you'll need to be in terrific shape—do not attempt this trip by yourself; an injury in the mountains would be a serious problem. A rough road travels north from Georgetown along the windward coast to the poor and isolated villages of Sandy Bay and Fancy. The coastline here is pummeled splendidly by the Atlantic and relatively few tourists visit the area. In general, if you stick to the road closest to the shoreline, the east coast offers easier riding than the leeward side. A splendid half-day loop trip would follow the east coast as far as North Union, then head inland along the Union River and into fertile Mesopotamia Valley. From here, the road climbs steadily over rolling hills toward Eyry Hill (1050 feet) before descending steeply into Kingstown. Off-roading is better on the west coast, particularly around Palmyra, in the hills above Chateaubelair.

What Else to See

The capital city of Kingston holds much of interest for the visitor. The waterfront is a good place to start; you'll see everything plying the waters from luxury yachts to commercial fishing boats. On Back Street, **St. Mary's Catholic Church**, which dates to 1893, is an interesting blend of Romanesque, Moorish and Georgian architecture. Just across the street is another house of worship, St. George's Cathedral, a Georgian structure with a vintage graveyard. Also worth checking out is the **National Museum**, ☎ *(809) 456-1787*, open just Wednesdays from 9:00 a.m. to noon and Saturdays from 3:00 to 6:00 p.m., a tiny enclave of Indian pottery that's the project of curator Dr. Earle

Kirby, a local archaeologist. If you're on the island during a Saturday, be sure to head for the **market at Bay Street**, where exotic fruits, fresh-from-the-sea fish and all sorts of vegetables are snapped up by islanders and visitors alike.

St. Mary's Catholic Church, St. Vincent

Historical Sites

Fort Charlotte   ★★

Kingston, ☎ *(809) 456-1830.*

Hours open: 6 a.m.–6 p.m.

Construction on this fort was started around 1791, and it was completed in 1812. It's mostly in ruins today, but well worth a visit for the stunning views from its perch some 650 feet above sea level of Kingston and the Grenadines. Check out the murals that tell the history of black Caribbeans.

Parks and Gardens

Botanical Gardens   ★★★

Kingston, ☎ *(809) 457-1003.*

Hours open: 7 a.m.–4 p.m.

Located on a hillside north of town, this 20-acre garden is the oldest in the Western Hemisphere, dating back to 1765. Among the teak, mahogany and cannonball trees and exotic plants and flowers are bread fruit trees descended from seedlings brought over by Captain Bligh in 1793. The lush grounds also include a pagoda, lily pond, and the Archeological Museum, located in a West Indian house and displaying artifacts from pre-Columbian days. Admission to the gardens is free, but once there, it's well worth a couple of dollars to hire a guide for an hour-long tour. Garden lovers should also checkout **Kingston's Montreal Gardens** (☎ *[809] 458-5452)*, which are not as well-tended.

Tours

Soufrière Volcano   ★★★★

The north side, Kingston.

St. Vincent's dominant feature is the Soufrière Mountains, home to a volcano that has been active for centuries. The most devastating eruption occurred in 1812 and claimed some 2000 lives. Another in 1902 created the mile-wide crater; in 1972, still another eruption created the lava rock island in the crater lake. The latest eruption, in 1979, caused thousands to evacuate but happily took no lives. Two trails climb through rainforest to the crater rim; the easiest (that's a relative term) starts 26 miles out at Kingston at Rabacca. It takes at least three hours to get to the top, though it's only a three-mile trek. Hiring a local guide is strongly advised.

Virtually every hotel can arrange watersports; diving and snorkeling are popular (especially on privately owned Young Island), as is windsurfing, thanks to the nearly constant tradewinds. But the big thing here is sailing, and the excellent conditions are what attract most visitors to the region. You can rent anything from a small catamaran to a luxurious yacht complete with crew. You can easily spend an entire week just island hopping. One firm to contact for staffed charters is **Regency Yacht Vacations**, ☎ *(800) 524-7676*.

Hiking to the summit of La Soufrière is a rugged challenge and only recommended to those in good physical shape. Less-strenuous hikes include Mt. St. Andrew, the Vermont Trail in Buccament Valley and Dorsetshire Hill.

Watersports

Various locations, Kingston.

Most watersports can be found at your hotel, and those staying on the Grenadines should be amply outfitted at the exclusive resorts. Otherwise, try one of these. For boating and cruising, call **Barefoot Yacht Charters** *(☎ [809] 456-9526)* or **Lagoon Marina** *(☎ [809] 458-4308)*, both on St. Vincent. On Bequia, call **Frangipani Yacht Services** *(☎ [809] 458-3255)*. For scuba, call **Dive St. Vincent** *(☎ [809] 457-4714)* and **St. Vincent Dive Experience** *(☎ [809] 456-9714)*, both on St. Vincent. On Bequia, call **Dive Bequia** *(☎ [809] 458-3504)* or **Sunsports** *(☎ [809] 458-3577)*. **Grenadines Dive** *(☎ [809] 458-8138)* handles diving on Union Island, while **Dive Mustique** *(☎ [809] 456-3486)* takes care of that island's needs.

St. Vincent

Where to Stay

St. Vincent

★★★★★ Fielding's Highest Rated Hotels in St. Vincent and The Grenadines	
★★★★★ Young Island Resort	$236–$596
★★★★ Canouan Beach Hotel	$108–$316
★★★★ Cotton House	$225–$730
★★★★ Petit Byahaut	$160–$290
★★★★ Petit St. Vincent Resort	$355–$710
★★★★ Plantation House	$105–$290
★★★ Mustique Villas	
★★★ Palm Island Beach Club	$165–$345
★★★ Saltwhistle Bay Club	$200–$340
★★★ Spring on Bequia	$75–$195

Fielding's Most Exclusive Hotels in St. Vincent and The Grenadines

★★★	Beaches	$1960
★★★★	Cotton House	$225–$730
★★★	Saltwhistle Bay Club	$200–$340
★★★★	Petit Byahaut	$160–$290
★★★★	Canouan Beach Hotel	$108–$316

Fielding's Best Value Hotels in St. Vincent and The Grenadines

★	Kingston Park Guest House	$25–$28
★★	Cobblestone Inn	$60–$75
★★	Frangipani Hotel	$30–$130
★★★	Spring on Bequia	$75–$195
★	Umbrella Beach Hotel	$38–$53

Most accommodations on St. Vincent are along the south coast, with the city of Kingston just a few minutes away. Many properties don't have air conditioning; ceiling fans and constant trade winds usually do a good job keeping things cool. If money is no object, consider Young Island, a perfectly wonderful resort set on its own private island.

Hotels and Resorts

St. Vincent simply hasn't gone the way of the high-rise resort. The closest is the property at Young Island, which covers the entire islet, but Sunset Shores gives off the ambience of a enclosed conclave, fortunately air-conditioned, with a family ambience running through the management.

Beachcombers Hotel $50–$75 ★

P.O. Box 126, Villa Beach, Kingston, ☎ (809) 458-4283. FAX (809) 458-4385.
Single: $50–$55. Double: $75.
This basic property accommodates guests in five different buildings, with all rooms air-conditioned and sporting TVs and private patios. Facilities are limited to a bar and restaurant, with watersports available on the beach. 12 rooms. Credit cards: A, MC, V.

Grand View Beach Hotel $100–$335 ★ ★ ★

P.O. Box 173, Villa Point, Kingston, ☎ (809) 458-4811. FAX (809) 457-4174.
Single: $100–$215. Double: $125–$335.
A former plantation house is the focal point of this quiet property, located on a promontory overlooking a small private beach. And, as the name suggests, the views here are indeed grand. Lodgings are simple yet comfortable, and while all share the splendid views, not all have air conditioners. The hotel's eight acres include tennis and squash courts, a small pool, a health club, a reading room, and a restaurant serving West Indian fare. Don't come looking for nightlife, but do come for tranquil surroundings and friendly, family-run service. 19 rooms. Credit cards: A, MC, V.

Lagoon Marina & Hotel $80–$105 ★

P.O. Box 133, Blue Lagoon, Kingston, ☎ (809) 458-4308. FAX (809) 457-4716.
Single: $80–$105. Double: $85–$105.
This simple hotel overlooks Blue Lagoon and its marina, and is often filled with sea folk. Rooms are basic and you'll pay a bit extra for air conditioning, but all have large patios nice to while away the hours on. The bar and restaurant do a brisk business with marina customers, and there's also a pool and watersports center on the black-sand beach. 19 rooms. Credit cards: A, MC, V.

Sunset Shores Beach Hotel $115–$210 ★ ★

849 Villa Street, Villa Beach, Kingston, ☎ (809) 458-4411. FAX (809) 457-4800.
Single: $115. Double: $115–$210.
The name makes it sound something like a retirement community, but in fact this motel-like property is one of St. Vincent's few commercial hotels. Guestrooms are air-conditioned and comfortable enough; they form a horseshoe around an attractive courtyard. Facilities include a small pool, a bar and restaurant favored by locals, and nearby watersports on the beach. Kingston is some 10 minutes away. 32 rooms. Credit cards: A, D, MC, V.

Villa Lodge Hotel $105–$185 ★★

P.O. Box 1191, Indian Bay, Kingston, ☎ *(809) 458-4641. FAX (809) 457-4468.*
Single: $105–$140. Double: $115–$185.

Set on a hillside and overlooking the sea, this converted home is popular, friendly, and family run. Guestrooms are air-conditioned and simply furnished; most have balconies or patios. The restaurant serves West Indian fare, and the large pool is a nice alternative to the small beach, which is easily within walking distance. The occasional poolside barbecues attract a lot of locals and are great fun, especially when steel bands liven things up. 10 rooms. Credit cards: A, D, MC, V.

Young Island Resort $236–$596 ★★★★★

Young Island, Kingston, ☎ *(800) 223-1108, (809) 458-4826. FAX (809) 457-4567.*
Single: $236–$596. Double: $275–$596.

Set on its own private island 200 yards offshore St. Vincent, this resort offers the kind of tropical pleasures most folks have in mind when they dream of a Caribbean vacation. In this case, the dream is restricted to those who can afford the high rates and honeymooners blowing the bank. Accommodations are in cottages scattered along a hillside or set on the beach, and all are spacious, cooled by ceiling fans, tropically decorated, and have private patios. Most also have unique rock showers that are open-air but very private. The lushly landscaped 25 acres include cages of exotic birds, a floating bar off the beach, and charming stone walkways and steps. This is not so much luxurious as it is the ultimate escape. 30 rooms. Credit cards: A, D, MC, V.

Apartments and Condominiums

Options are easy to find, since self-catering has long been a tradition on the island. Food is readily available in the market at Kingstown, as is fresh fish. Everyone seems to know someone who has a fishing boat. Staples that are strictly American-made should be brought from home.

Indian Bay Beach Hotel $55–$85 ★

Indian Bay, Kingston, ☎ *(809) 458-4001. FAX (809) 457-4777.*
Single: $55–$60. Double: $70–$85.

This small apartment hotel offers one- and two-bedroom units with kitchens, patios, telephones, and living and dining areas. Furnishings are simple but adequate. Indian Bay's beach is small and rocky, but the snorkeling just off the coast is good. There's a restaurant and bar on the premises, and the rates are certainly reasonable. 14 rooms. Credit cards: A, D, MC, V.

Umbrella Beach Hotel $38–$53 ★

Villa Beach, Kingston, ☎ *(809) 458-4651. FAX (809) 457-4930.*
Single: $38–$43. Double: $48–$53.

The rates are incredibly low, and the lodgings prove that you get what you pay for, but if you're on a tight budget and want the convenience (and economy) of having a kitchenette, this may be just the spot. As noted, the rooms are very basic and rely on ceiling fans for sleeping comfort, but they are clean and the location is handy, right near the beach and several restaurants. 9 rooms. Credit cards: A, DC, MC, V.

Inns

Most accommodations in St. Vincent come with an "inn" feeling about them. That's the nature of the St. Vincent life. Some can be found in Kingstown, others in the highlands away from the hustle of city life.

Cobblestone Inn $60–$75   ★★

P.O. Box 867, Kingston, ☎ *(809) 456-1937. FAX (809) 456-1938.*
Single: $60. Double: $75.
This harborside inn dates back to 1814 and was originally intended as a sugar warehouse. Guestrooms are cozy (read small) but comfortable and air-conditioned, and all have private combination baths. Request one in the back to avoid street noise, but be warned that all are rather dark. The bar and restaurant are popular, and the in-town location attracts business travelers. There's no pool, which is unfortunate since the beach is a 10-minute drive away. 19 rooms. Credit cards: A, MC, V.

Kingston Park Guest House $25–$28   ★

Kingston, ☎ *(809) 456-1532.*
Single: $25. Double: $28.
This 18th-century plantation house, a private home, is set in a garden overlooking the town and, further out, the Grenadines. As can be expected by the rates, the rooms are nothing too exciting, and many share baths. You'll need a car, which may offset the savings on your accommodations. 20 rooms. Credit cards: not accepted.

Low Cost Lodging

It is possible to find cheap lodgings in simple hotels in the Kingstown area. The style is usually West Indian, with very basic furnishings. Cleanliness is usually not a problem.

Heron Hotel $49–$65   ★

Kingston, ☎ *(809) 457-1631. FAX (809) 457-1189.*
Single: $49–$51. Double: $55–$65.
Located on the waterfront within walking distance of the town center, this is another of St. Vincent's economical and simple guesthouses. The rooms are very basic and quite old-fashioned, and lack modern amenities like TV but at least have air conditioners and private baths. The restaurant is similarly no-frills, but the reasonably priced meals are tasty enough. 15 rooms. Credit cards: D, MC, V.

Campgrounds

Petit Byahaut $160–$290   ★★★★

Petit Byahaut Bay, Kingston, ☎ *(809) 457-7008. FAX (809) 457-7008.*
Single: $160–$180. Double: $250–$290.
The rates are high for camping, but guests are pampered at this remote spot a bit more than at your typical tent site. Set in a 50-acre valley that's reached only by boat from Kingston (included in the rates), this isolated spot accepts only 14 people at a time, and kids are not allowed. Accommodations are in large tents with wooden floors, queen-size beds, decks, and sun-warmed showers. The rates include all meals and watersports off the black-sand beach. Dinner is served by candlelight overlooking the bay. Inquire about weekly and scuba packages. Not for everyone, but well-loved by those seeking an offbeat alternative, and the surrounding rainforest is just gorgeous. Credit cards: not accepted.

Where to Eat

Fielding's Highest Rated Restaurants in St. Vincent and The Grenadines

★★★★★	Mac's Pizzeria	$7–$30
★★★★★	The French Restaurant	$8–$16
★★★★	Basil's Bar & Raft	$4–$28
★★★	Basil's Bar & Restaurant	$3–$15
★★★	Cobblestone Roof Top	$5–$6
★★★	Gingerbread Cafe	$4–$18
★★★	Heron Restaurant	$5–$10

Fielding's Most Exclusive Restaurants in St. Vincent and The Grenadines

★★★★★	Mac's Pizzeria	$7–$30
★★★★	Basil's Bar & Raft	$4–$28
★★★★★	The French Restaurant	$8–$16
★★★	Gingerbread Cafe	$4–$18
★★★	Basil's Bar & Restaurant	$3–$15

Fielding's Best Value Restaurants in St. Vincent and The Grenadines

★★★★★	The French Restaurant	$8–$16
★★★	Heron Restaurant	$5–$10
★★★	Basil's Bar & Restaurant	$3–$15
★★★	Gingerbread Cafe	$4–$18
★★★★★	Mac's Pizzeria	$7–$30

You won't find much in the way of international cuisine on St. Vincent, but the local West Indian fare is consistently good. Specialties include goat stew, fresh seafood, breadfruit dishes and callaloo soup. You'll have no problem finding American-style burgers and fried chicken. The French Restaurant is *tres bon.*

Basil's Bar & Restaurant $ ★★★

Bay Street, Kingston, ☎ *(809) 457-2713. Associated hotel: Cobblestone Inn.*
International cuisine.
Lunch: 10 a.m.–4 p.m., prix fixe $11.
Dinner: 4 p.m.–midnight, entrées $3–$15. Closed: Sun.
Those who can't get to Basil Charles' Fantasy Island overwater bar in Mustique make the scene at his second namesake hangout with food on the ground floor of the Cobblestone Inn. Lunchtime buzzes with hungry diners going back and forth from a tasty all-you-can-eat buffet. The spread includes salads and desserts, and a la carte burgers, sandwiches, egg dishes, and seafood are also available. Nighttime is more romantic, with candlelit tables and simple grills on the menu, plus French wines at decent prices. There's a Chinese buffet on Friday evenings. Reservations recommended. Credit cards: A, MC, V.

Cobblestone Roof Top $ ★★★

Bay Street, Kingston, ☎ *(809) 456-1937. Associated hotel: Cobblestone Inn.*
Latin American cuisine.
Lunch: 7:30 a.m.–3 p.m., entrées $5–$6.
Whatever business is conducted on this leisurely island is usually done at breakfast or lunchtime from this eatery atop the Cobblestone Inn. Housed in a quaint, restored early 1800s-era warehouse, the restaurant serves substantial West Indian lunches along with good burgers and fish and chips. Credit cards: A, MC, V.

Heron Restaurant $ ★★★

Upper Bay Street, Kingston, ☎ *(809) 457-1631. Associated hotel: Heron Hotel.*
International cuisine.
Lunch: Noon–1:30 p.m., entrées $5–$10.
Dinner: 7–10 p.m., prix fixe $5–$10.
A friendly local couple run this budget hotel and restaurant that's popular with residents for American bacon and eggs breakfasts. Lunch features soups, salads, and sandwiches, and a soup-to-nuts supper is served daily for a set price. Market fresh vegetables are a standout. There's always a lot of action here, and reservations are required for dinner. Reservations required. Credit cards: not accepted.

The French Restaurant $$ ★★★★★

Villa Beach, Kingston, ☎ *(809) 458-4972. Associated hotel: Umbrella Beach Hotel.*
French cuisine. Specialties: Lobster.
Lunch: 7 a.m.–9 p.m., entrées $6–$14.
Dinner: 7–9:30 p.m., entrées $8–$16.
Behind a homey white picket fence lies an excellent restaurant that dazzles with its simplicity. Guests sit on plain folding chairs, feet planted on rough wooden floors in a windowless structure open to salty breezes. Succulent lobster couldn't get much fresher, retrieved as they are live from an on-site pool. The Parisian chef serves the juicy crustaceans flambeed in brandy, sliced in crepes, or broiled. All dishes are prepared with island-grown herbs and spices. The dining room overlooks Villa Beach and Young Island. Reservations recommended. Credit cards: A, MC, V.

St. Vincent

St. Vincent

St. Vincent is not a duty-free port, so don't come expecting great bargains on imported merchandise. Some things to look out for are colorful batiks and tie-died fabrics at **Batik Caribe** *(Wallilabou Bay, ☎ (809) 458-7270)*, and woven items, wood carvings, books and other locally made crafts at **St. Vincent Craftsmen** *(James Street, Kingston, ☎ (809) 457-1288)*. **Noah's Arcade** *(Bay Street, Kingston, ☎ (809) 457-1513)* has a good selection of local arts and handiworks; they also have a shop on Bequia at Port Elizabeth ☎ *(809) 458-3424)*. If you're a stamp collector, you'll love **St. Vincent Philatelic Services** *(Lower Bay Street, Kingston, ☎ (809) 457-1911)*, the Caribbean's largest bureau. Note that stores usually close from noon to 1:00 for lunch.

The Grenadines

Devil's Table

Bequia

The largest of the Grenadines at seven square miles, Bequia (BECK-we) lies nine miles south of St. Vincent. The island is relaxed and laid-back, and its 6000 residents all seem to know one another. The island was accessible only by boat until 1992, when a small airport was built. Bequia is hilly and wooded, with some good beaches at Friendship Bay, Lower Bay, Princess Margaret and Spring Bay. Boatbuilding is the main industry, and you're sure to see many craftsmen constructing sea-faring vessels by hand along the beaches.

The main village, Port Elizabeth, is known for its safe anchorage at Admiralty Bay. There is not a lot of do and see on the island, save sailing, sunning and diving. The idea behind a vacation on Bequia is one of pure relaxation—and bragging to your friends back home about your holiday in a place not many have heard of.

Bequia Underwater

With its western coast part of a marine park, Bequia features several excellent dive locations, all within a few minutes of the main boat dock. **Devil's Table** is a flat reef sitting in Bequia's harbor, with channels of sand amid the coral structure; terrific detail, including occasional frog fish and sea horses.

The Wall is a sheer, dramatic plunge from a ledge at 30 feet to a sandy floor 120 feet down, while **The Boulders** is a delightful drift dive among coral encrusted monoliths.

Dive Bequia

Port Elizabeth; ☎ *(809) 458-3504.*

Bob Sachs conducted much of the original dive exploration in and around Bequia, opening his shop in 1983. PADI and NAUI affiliated, with courses to Divemaster. Two-tank dive, $75 with your own equipment (or $85 without).

On Foot in Bequia

In Bequia, hikes from Admiralty Bay lead over unpaved roads and footpaths, but are relatively easy, and arrive at such places as **Mt. Pleasant**, where there is a spectacular view of Bequia. A favored destination also is Hope Bay, where the waves are good for body surfing. The northern part of the island is covered with gentle hills good for hiking; in the central and southern sections, more mountainous areas give hikers a chance to view incredible vistas. There are no roads or cars on Mayreau, but from the bay you can take a track to the tiny hilltop village in the center of the island; here you can see a great view of **Tobago Cays**. Tobago Cays is considered one of the most serene paradises in the Caribbean—four uninhabited islets ringed by pure white beaches and clear blue waters. From a beach anywhere here, you can walk/paddle to see clusters of tropical fish swimming through the coral gardens. **Petit Rameau**, the northernmost cay, has a short trail through heavy mangroves along a sandy beach.

Sports in Bequia

The **Frangipani** and **Plantation House** hotels have fully equipped dive facilities. You can also find windsurfing and sunfish sailing in **Admiralty Bay** and snorkeling around **Spring** and **Friendship Bays**. To find a new beach, hop on a water taxi to **Lower Bay**. Or rent a bicycle at the **Almond Tree** boutique and toot over to Spring or Friendship Bay. Evening entertainment revolves around whichever hotel is sponsoring a jump-up, a beach barbecue with bamboo bands and vigorous, sexy dancing.

Where to Stay

Lodging in Bequia is geared for total relaxation. Nearly each property is unique and exudes a certain personal ambiance. Prices for rooms are not exorbitant and many are within a reasonable range.

Hotels and Resorts

Friendship Bay Hotel	$115–$200	★ ★ ★

Friendship Bay, Bequia, ☎ *(809) 458-3222. FAX (809) 458-3840.*
Single: $115–$130. Double: $130–$200.

Set on a palm-studded cove and a sandy beach, this casual complex provides motel-like lodging in stone buildings scattered around picturesque grounds. The rooms are basic but comfortable enough, with ceiling fans, private baths, and verandas. Facilities include a bar and restaurant popular with locals, a watersports center (some rentals are complimentary), and a tennis court. The weekly barbecues and jump-ups are not to be missed, and the beach is quite fine. 27 rooms. Credit cards: A, D, MC, V.

Plantation House $105–$290 ★★★★

Admiralty Bay, Bequia, ☎ (800) 223-1108, (809) 458-3425. FAX (809) 458-3612.
Single: $105–$220. Double: $140–$290.
Located on 10 handsome acres, this property's focal point is the pretty colonial-style main house with a wide veranda on three sides, a great place for people watching and gazing at the harbor. Accommodations are in the main house, cottages, and (relatively) deluxe cabanas. Those in the main house are air-conditioned, while the rest rely on ceiling fans and sea breezes. All are nicely done and quite comfortable. There's a pool, tennis court, restaurant and beach bar on the premises, and a dive shop and watersports center on the beach. Inquire about dive and sailing packages. 27 rooms. Credit cards: A, MC, V.

Spring on Bequia $75–$195 ★★★

Spring Bay, Bequia, ☎ (809) 458-3414. FAX (809) 457-3305.
Single: $75–$180. Double: $95–$195.
Set on a hillside of the grounds on a 200-year-old working plantation, this rather isolated spot practically oozes tranquillity. Don't come here for the beach life—the nearest one is 10 minutes away and nothing great—but do come if you're looking for a true escape in pastoral surroundings. Lodging is found in three stone and shingle buildings; all rooms are clean and comfortable, and kept cool by constant breezes. There's a tennis court and pool on-site, and the Sunday curry buffet is a popular hit. 10 rooms. Credit cards: A, MC, V.

Inns

Frangipani Hotel $30–$130 ★★

Frangipani Beckway, Bequia, ☎ (809) 458-3255. FAX (805) 458-3824.
Single: $30–$130. Double: $80–$130.
This small inn dates back to 1920 and was once the childhood home of the island's current prime minister. Guestrooms are found in the main building—a New England-style house—or in superior garden units in the rear. All are simply furnished and rely on fans to keep things cool and mosquito netting over the beds to keep the pests at bay. Not all have a private bath. The beach is a 10-minute walk and there's no pool, but you can swim in the harbor. Facilities are limited to a restaurant, bar, tennis court, and watersports center. Nice for casual types. 15 rooms. Credit cards: A, D, MC, V.

Low Cost Lodging

Julie & Isola Guesthouse $36–$59 ★

P.O. Box 12, Port Elizabeth, Bequia, ☎ (809) 458-3304. FAX (809) 458-3812.
Single: $36. Double: $59.
It's as basic as basic can be, which explains the rates, but the rooms, located in two buildings, are clean, though they can be uncomfortably hot. Not all have private

baths, and showers are not always hot. Facilities are limited to a bar and small restaurant serving up good West Indian fare. 20 rooms. Credit cards: not accepted.

Where to Eat

No great claims to chefdom here, but do get ready for home-style island cooking with lots of fresh seafood. Most of the eating places are along the waterfront within walking distance of each other.

Gingerbread Cafe $$ ★★★

P.O. Box 1, Gingerbread Complex, Bequia, ☎ *(809) 458-3800.*
International cuisine.
Lunch: entrées $4–$10.
Dinner: 7:30–6:30 p.m., entrées $4–$18.

This cute Hansel and Gretelish stone cottage is the place to go for Italian coffees, puckery-fresh limeade and fruit juices, and the appropriate cakes and breads to go with them. Sit here at leisure all day at an outdoor table with a book and gaze out at the activity in the harbor. Next door, the Gingerbread Restaurant serves full meals and sandwiches, and is a nice spot for happy hour rum drinks and music. Credit cards: A, MC, V.

Mac's Pizzeria $$$ ★★★★★

Box 23, Belmont Beach, Bequia, ☎ *(809) 458-3474.*
International cuisine. Specialties: Lobster pizza.
Lunch: 11 a.m.–4 p.m., entrées $7–$30.
Dinner: 4–10 p.m., entrées $7–$30. Closed: Mon.

Bequia veterans daydream about the 15-inch lobster pizzas that this terraced restaurant is famous for. Besides the dream pies, Mac's homebakes all its scrumptious breads and bakery goods, and the banana bread, plump with raisins and flavored with rum, is especially toothsome. The menu also features East Indian samosas (fried pastries stuffed with curried vegetables or meats), crunchy conch nuggets, and chunky pita bread sandwiches. This place is a winner. Credit cards: MC, V.

Where to Shop

There are a decent number of stores for such a small island, though Bequia is hardly a shopper's paradise. **Noah's Arcade** *(Frangipani Hotel,* ☎ *(809) 458-3424)* is the place for locally crafted pieces including fine batiks, woven goods, pottery, and, of course, tee-shirts. At the **Crab Hole** *(next to Plantation House,* ☎ *(809) 458-3290)* you can watch locals silk-screen cotton fabrics, then pick out a few to your liking. **Garden Boutique** *(Port Elizabeth,* ☎ *(809) 458-3892)* has excellent women's fashions, including some stunning batik dresses. And don't miss **Sergeants Model Boat Shop** *(Port Elizabeth,* ☎ *(809) 458-3344)*, where woodcarver Lawson Sergeant makes perfectly crafted boat models. This spot is a favorite of the many yachters who frequent the island, who order up an exact-scale-model of their vessel.

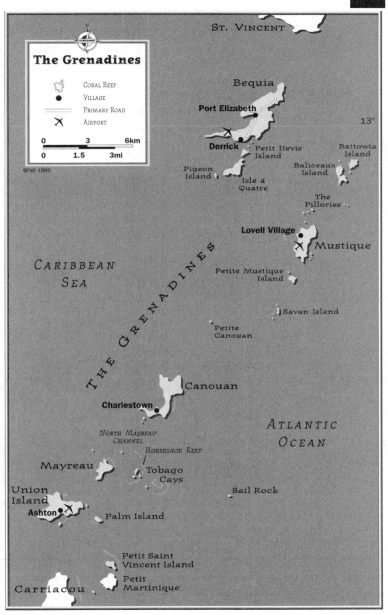

Canouan

This small islet, home to less than 1000 souls, is shaped like a crescent. Located 25 miles south of St. Vincent, it has excellent beaches, an 800-foot peak—and not much else. Fishing is the main industry; tourists are few and far between.

Where to Stay

Hotels and Resorts

Canouan Beach Hotel   **$108–$316**   ★★★★

Canouan Beach, ☎ (809) 458-8888. FAX 809 458 8875.
Single: $108–$316. Double: $249–$316.

This all-inclusive resort is located on a peninsula on the island's west side. Accommodations are in nicely furnished bungalows that have air conditioners and patios. Facilities include a very good restaurant, large bar, tennis court, and watersports. The beach is really pretty and a catamaran takes guests to neighboring islands at no extra charge. The rates include all meals, drinks and activities, but those not speaking French may feel left out. Though it has only 43 rooms, this is St. Vincent's largest and most modern resort. 43 rooms. Credit cards: A, CB, DC, MC, V.

Mayreau

This privately owned island is reached only by boat. Measuring just 1.5 square miles, it has less than 200 citizens. The Tobago Cays, which lie just offshore, are small islets with perfectly translucent water.

Where to Stay

Hotels and Resorts

Saltwhistle Bay Club   **$200–$340**   ★★★

Mayreau, ☎ (809) 493-9609.
Single: $200–$300. Double: $300–$340.

This casual hideaway is the island's only lodging choice. Guests are housed in spacious, one-bedroom stone bungalows that are rely on ceiling fans to keep things cool. The setting is idyllic—lovely tropical grounds, fine sandy beaches, and a crystal-clear sea that well-appreciated by divers. Facilities include a bar, restaurant, and most watersports free of charge, though you'll pay extra for scuba and catamaran excursions to neighboring islands. There's virtually nothing in the way of nightlife; this spot has an early-to-bed, early-to-rise charm. 10 rooms. Credit cards: not accepted.

Mustique

Measuring three miles long by one mile wide, Mustique has gorgeous beaches and verdant valleys. A favorite escape for the rich and famous, the well-manicured island is dotted with luxurious villas—one belonging to

HRH Princess Margaret, who actually rents it out when she's not gracing the island.

Where to Stay

Hotels and Resorts

Cotton House   **$225–$730**   ★★★★

☎ *(809) 456-4777. FAX (809) 456-5887.*
Single: $225–$730. Double: $225–$730.

Built on the remains of an old sugar plantation, this deluxe operation is Mustique's only hotel, and it's quite lovely (and pricey). Guests are accommodated in elegant cottages that house standard guestrooms, junior suites, or full suites, all nicely decorated and sporting balconies or patios. The grounds include a highly regarded restaurant, bar, two beaches, and most watersports at no extra charge. Horseback riding can be arranged, and there's also a pool, two tennis courts, and occasional live bands. This exclusive spot pampers guests and attracts the well-heeled set. 20 rooms. Credit cards: A, DC, MC, V.

Apartments and Condominiums

Mustique Villas   ★★★

☎ *(800) 225-4255, (809) 458-4621. FAX (809) 456-4565.*

These 46 privately owned villas are located all around the island. Several were designed by Oliver Messel, the late architect and stage designer. Each is individually decorated and has from one to six bedrooms and full kitchens. Each is staffed with a maid, cook and gardener, and the rates include free use of a vehicle. Rates are on a weekly basis and range from a low of $2500 to a high of $15,000 for the five- and six-bedroom mansions. One of the villas belongs to Princess Margaret—needless to say, rent that one far, far in advance. 46 rooms. Credit cards: A, DC, MC, V.

Where to Eat

Basil's Bar & Raft   **$$$**   ★★★★

Britannia Bay, Mustique, ☎ *(809) 458-4621.*
International cuisine.
Lunch: entrées $4–$26.
Dinner: entrées $4–$28.

Basil's is not just a bar—it's a way of life. Possibly the most beautiful watering hole in the world, this unique establishment is a thatch-roofed structure built over the turquoise waters of Britannia Bay in Mustique. Owner Basil Charles has a great thing going—this is the only nightlife spot on the island. Everyone ends up here sooner or later, including titled lords and ladies and *People* magazine cover girls and boys. There's good seafood served daily and a $28 barbecue on Wednesday nights. It's open from 10:00 am until the last guest goes home. Reservations recommended. Credit cards: A, MC, V.

Palm Island

This private isle is entirely taken up by the Palm Island Beach Club (below). Prices are high, but this spot is that Caribbean Garden of Eden you've always dreamed out.

Where to Stay

Hotels and Resorts

Palm Island Beach Club   **$165–$345**   ★ ★ ★

Palm Island, ☎ *(800) 999-7256, (809) 458-8824. FAX 809 458 8804.*
Single: $165–$230. Double: $255–$345.

Located on its own private 130-acre island, this is another of the Grenadines' paradise-on-Earth choices. It's not cheap, but the rates are much more affordable than some of the nation's other tropical resorts, and this spot remains popular for its lovely grounds and fine hospitality. Accommodations are in 12 duplex cottages and eight villas, all very comfortable and cooled by ceiling fans. The resort boasts five lovely beaches, where watersports await, including complimentary windsurfers, Sunfish and snorkel gear. There's also a good restaurant, bar, and tennis court, and supervised activities for kids. 24 rooms. Credit cards: A, D, MC, V.

Petit St. Vincent

Like Palm and Young islands, Petit St. Vincent is privately owned. Reached by boat from Union Island, it covers just 113 acres. The perfect escape for those who don't mind dropping a bundle and spending all their time in tranquil privacy.

Where to Stay

Hotels and Resorts

Petit St. Vincent Resort   **$355–$710**   ★ ★ ★ ★

Petit St. Vincent, ☎ *(800) 854-9326, (809) 458-8801.*
Single: $355–$550. Double: $450–$710.

Another of the Grenadines' private islands-turned-resorts, this deluxe property is surrounded by white, sandy beaches and an impossibly clear sea. Accommodations are in large one-bedroom wood and stone cottages with large and luxurious baths. If you want room service, hoist a yellow flag; if you prefer privacy, raise the red one. The rates include most watersports, and there's also a tennis court, fitness trail, and weekly entertainment. The emphasis here is on privacy, and those who can afford it return again and again. 22 rooms. Credit cards: not accepted.

Union Island

Lots of Europeans on this island, which measures three miles long by one mile wide. The southernmost of the Grenadines (St. Vincent is 40 miles away), Union is a lot cheaper than most of its siblings, but it's not all that great, either. Beaches are virtually nonexistent, and there's not much to see or do, though watersports are decent.

Union Island Underwater

Although Union Island offers good snorkeling and decent diving, the best sites are just a couple of miles away, off **Tobago Cays** and **Mayreau Island**. One area, named **Mayreau Gardens**, allows three different drift dives of intermediate difficulty; the strong current discourages fishermen from visiting the reef. There is an excellent wreck, the **HMS Purina**, a 140-foot English gunship which went down in 1918 just off Mayreau. Much of its superstructure is still intact, and with a maximum depth of just 40 feet, the site is terrific for beginners. For experienced divers, ten miles east of Union Island is **Sail Rock**, a dynamic and isolated location which requires very calm seas to visit; the rock outcrop draws barracudas by the dozens and a plethora of nurse sharks. **Horseshoe Reef**, which wraps around the Tobago Cays, offers superb snorkeling.

Grenadines Dive

Clifton; ☎ *(809) 458-8138.*
Owner Glenroy Adams, a NAUI instructor, has been on Union Island since 1988. His staff is all PADI, with courses to Divemaster. Two-tank dive, $90, including equipment. Dives Mayreau Island and Tobago Cays.

Where to Stay

Hotels and Resorts

Anchorage Yacht Club $95–$165   ★ ★

Union Island, ☎ *(809) 458-8221. FAX 809 458 8365.*
Single: $95–$165. Double: $95–$165.
Most who come to this motel-like property are en route to the Grenadines, though this is a decent-enough spot to while away your entire vacation. Guestrooms are spacious and air conditioned and have nice harbor views off the balconies. The twice-weekly jump-ups are well attended; the fine restaurant and bar keep guests occupied the rest of the time. The hotel sits right on a nice beach, where a dive shop handles watersports rentals. There's also a shark pool on the premises, as well as a busy marina. 10 rooms. Credit cards: D, MC, V.

St. Vincent Directory

Arrival and Departure

The departure tax from St. Vincent and the Grenadines is U.S. $6 (E.C. $15). A 5 percent government tax is added to all hotel and restaurant bills. Hotels regularly add a 10 percent service charge. If a 10 percent service charge is not added to your restaurant check, it would be very acceptable (and expected) for you to do so.

Business Hours

Most shops open weekdays 8 a.m.–noon and 1–4 p.m., Saturday 8 a.m.–noon. Banks open Monday–Thursday 8 a.m.–1 or 3 p.m. and Friday 8 a.m.–5 p.m. Some banks take a two-hour break from 1–3 p.m. on Friday.

Climate

Temperatures all year round are around 78–80 degrees Fahrenheit, cooled by gentle northeast trade window. Rain is heavier in the mountains of St. Vincent than in the Grenadines, which are generally flatter. Hurricanes can ravish the islands in the fall, while summers attract high humidity. Mosquito repellent is a must between July to November.

Documents

U.S. and Canadian citizens must have a passport; all visitors must hold return or ongoing tickets. Visas are not required.

Electricity

Current runs 220/40 v. 50 cycles.

Getting Around

Island roads are like roller coasters, so if you're not used to such challenging driving, you're probably better off hiring a taxi to get around. Potholes are everywhere and increase the possibility of accidents and car damage.

Taxis fares run about $3–$4 around Kingstown, $8 from Kingstown to Villa Beach. A good way to see the island is to hire a taxi by the hour (about $15). Rates are fixed by the government, but most drivers try to get twice as much. Public buses in the form of minivans are the cheapest way to get around; they tend to be boisterous, noisy and crowded, and full of local color. All you need to do is wave at the driver and he will stop for you. The terminal is at Market Square in Kingstown.

Rental cars run about $45–$50 a day. Driving is on the left. Since roads are not well maintained, do get as many directions as possible before you get behind the wheel. You might even take a minibus tour of the island first to get acquainted with the potholes. To rent a car, you will need a Vincentian license, unless you already have an international license.

Language

English is spoken everywhere, often with a Vincentian patois or dialect.

Medical Emergencies

The government hospital, called **General Hospital** ☎ *(809) 61185,* is located at the west end of Kingstown. There is also **Bequia Casualty Hospital** at Port Elizabeth ☎ *(809) 83294.*

Money

The official currency is the Eastern Caribbean dollar, although U.S. and Canadian dollars are accepted at all but the smallest shops. Most establishments would prefer to take the Eastern Caribbean dollar. When quoted a price, make sure you know what dollar is being referred to. You can get a slightly higher exchange rate at banks; hotels are notoriously low and sometimes charge a fee.

Telephone

The area code for St. Vincent and the Grenadines is *809*. At press time, only AT&T offered direct dial to the area, but check with the Sprint and the MCI offices in your area to verify the latest service. Before dialing other countries from St. Vincent, ask the operator; sometimes there are special codes. Also verify in advance the probable cost, surcharge and government tax; your hotel will probably also add another fee, which can send the bill sky-high. When dialing a local number from your hotel, you can drop the 45-prefix. Few hotels have phones in the rooms.

Time

Atlantic Standard Time, one hour ahead of New York time, except during Daylight Saving Time, when it is the same.

Tipping and Taxes

Hotels tend to add 10–15 percent service charge. If so, you won't be expected to tip chambermaids as well, but the gesture is always appreciated. Restaurants usually charge 10 percent for service. Tip taxi drivers 10 percent of the fare.

Tourist Information

The **St. Vincent Department of Tourism** is located at Administrative Centre, Bay St., Kingstown, ☎ *(809) 457-1502*. Stop by and pick up brochures on lodging and sightseeing options. The St. Vincent and the Grenadines tourist guide called *Escape* contains useful tips and suggestions for excursions. The office is only open Monday–Friday.

Bequia has its own office on the waterfront in Port Elizabeth, ☎ *(809) 458-3286*, closed on Saturday afternoons. In the U.S. call ☎ *(212) 687-4981*.

When to Go

Carnival is a huge week-long celebration in early July, one of the most fantastic parties in the entire eastern Caribbean. Here you'll be able to witness and participate in calypso and steel-band competitions. Do be around when the queen and king of Carnival are crowned, a spectacular event.

ST VINCENT & THE GRENADINES HOTELS	RMS	RATES	PHONE	CR. CARDS
Bequia				
★★★★ **Plantation House**	27	$105–$290	(800) 223-1108	A, MC, V
★★★ **Friendship Bay Hotel**	27	$115–$200	(809) 458-3222	A, D, MC, V
★★★ **Spring on Bequia**	10	$75–$195	(809) 458-3414	A, MC, V
★★ **Frangipani Hotel**	15	$30–$130	(809) 458-3255	A, D, MC, V
★ **Julie & Isola Guesthouse**	20	$36–$59	(809) 458-3304	None
Canouan				
★★★★ **Canouan Beach Hotel**	43	$108–$316	(809) 458-8888	A, CB, DC, MC, V

ST VINCENT & THE GRENADINES HOTELS	RMS	RATES	PHONE	CR. CARDS
Mustique				
★★★★ Cotton House	20	$225–$730	(809) 456-4777	A, DC, MC, V
★★★ Mustique Villas	46		(800) 225-4255	A, DC, MC, V
St. Vincent				
Kingston				
★★★★★ Young Island Resort	30	$236–$596	(800) 223-1108	A, D, MC, V
★★★★ Petit Byahaut		$160–$290	(809) 457-7008	None
★★★ Grand View Beach Hotel	19	$100–$335	(809) 458-4811	A, MC, V
★★ Cobblestone Inn	19	$60–$75	(809) 456-1937	A, MC, V
★★ Sunset Shores Beach Hotel	32	$115–$210	(809) 458-4411	A, D, MC, V
★★ Villa Lodge Hotel	10	$105–$185	(809) 458-4641	A, D, MC, V
★ Beachcombers Hotel	12	$50–$75	(809) 458-4283	A, MC, V
★ Heron Hotel	15	$49–$65	(809) 457-1631	D, MC, V
★ Indian Bay Beach Hotel	14	$55–$85	(809) 458-4001	A, D, MC, V
★ Kingston Park Guest House	20	$25–$28	(809) 456-1532	None
★ Lagoon Marina & Hotel	19	$80–$105	(809) 458-4308	A, MC, V
★ Umbrella Beach Hotel	9	$38–$53	(809) 458-4651	A, DC, MC, V
The Grenadines				
★★★★ Petit St. Vincent Resort	22	$355–$710	(800) 854-9326	None
★★★ Palm Island Beach Club	24	$165–$345	(800) 999-7256	A, D, MC, V
★★★ Saltwhistle Bay Club	10	$200–$340	(809) 493-9609	None
★★ Anchorage Yacht Club	10	$95–$165	(809) 458-8221	D, MC, V

ST. VINCENT & THE GRENADINES RESTAURANTS	PHONE	ENTRÉE	CR. CARDS
Bequia			
International			
★★★★★ Mac's Pizzeria	(809) 458-3474	$7–$30	MC, V
★★★ Gingerbread Cafe	(809) 458-3800	$4–$18	A, MC, V

ST. VINCENT & THE GRENADINES RESTAURANTS	PHONE	ENTRÉE	CR. CARDS

St. Vincent

Kingston

	French		
★★★★★ The French Restaurant	(809) 458-4972	$6–$16	A, MC, V
	International		
★★★ Basil's Bar & Restaurant	(809) 457-2713	$11–$15	A, MC, V
★★★ Heron Restaurant	(809) 457-1631	$5–$10	None
	Latin American		
★★★ Cobblestone Roof Top	(809) 456-1937	$5–$6	A, MC, V

Mustique

	International		
★★★★ Basil's Bar & Raft	(809) 458-4621	$4–$28	A, MC, V

The Grenadines

The Grenadines

TOBAGO

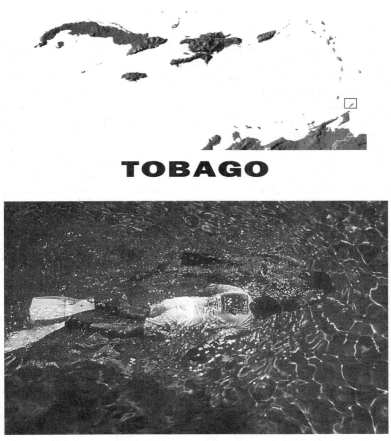

The quiet turquoise waters of Tobago are great for snorkeling.

The sister island of nearby Trinidad, Tobago is a verdant, languid jewel in the Caribbean. Of the two, Tobago is where tourism is most developed, though it remains quiet and laid-back, even by Caribbean standards. People visit these two islands for different reasons. On Trinidad, the rhythms and harmonies of steel pan bands set the pace, artists and playwrights are nurtured, and the spice of east Indian curry wafts through its restaurants. On quiet Tobago, ecological resources—gentle green hills navigated by squawking parrots, placid bays populated with manta rays—take the front seat, with cultural assets registering as an also-ran. Tobago is the destination where Trinidadians go when they want to get away from it all (particularly following Carnival). And though the smaller island's economic status continues to play catch-up with Trinidad's relatively prosperous and cosmopolitan life-style, the gap is slowly closing.

A larger percentage of Tobago's visitors are from Europe and South America than on most other Caribbean destinations—relatively few Americans (beyond the diving community) are familiar with the island. At press time, no direct airline service is available between North America and Tobago (see "Arrival and Departure"), though connections through Trinidad, Grenada or Barbados are not difficult. Yet, three expensive, new resorts were built and opened on Tobago in 1995, and a fourth, the biggest yet, promises a late 1997 debut. None of this activity seems to have severely or negatively impacted the quiet, relaxed atmosphere that dominates away from the developed southwestern tip of the island. Forays into the bucolic hills and bays beyond Scarborough and Plymouth, the island's two main population areas, are an essential part of any vacation to Tobago.

Bird's-Eye View

Located in the extreme southeastern corner of the Caribbean, just 70 miles off the Venezuelan coast of South America, Tobago is 21 miles from its larger sibling, Trinidad. The island covers 116 square miles—less than a fifteenth the size of Trinidad—and is 27 miles in length, nine miles wide at the center. Although Tobago's high point is only about 1900 feet, the eastern three-quarters of the island is consistently hilly and has very few roads or trails to access the highlands. The northeastern tip of Tobago is where the mountains are steepest and several points are dramatically scooped to provide beautiful coves of sand within the larger Tyrrel's and Man O' War bays on either side of this end of the island. The steep, jungle-like slopes between the two bays are populated by a wide variety of parrots and other birds, while below the surface of the water lie most of the island's best dive sites. The coastline on this end of the island is dotted with fishing villages that drowse in the sun— their brightly painted *pirogues* hauled up on the shore beneath coconut palms and sea grapes. Just inland are farms and plantations of brilliant green—the northern coast between Plymouth and L'Anse Fourmi is a succession of improbably-located towns high on the scenic ridges.

The other end of the island has an entirely different appearance. From a geographical standpoint, as one proceeds west from the island's capital, Scarborough, the hills roll along modestly for a few miles, then peter out as one approaches the Lowlands. Additionally, the weather tends to be drier, creating scrublands and coconut groves, rather than the dense jungle found on

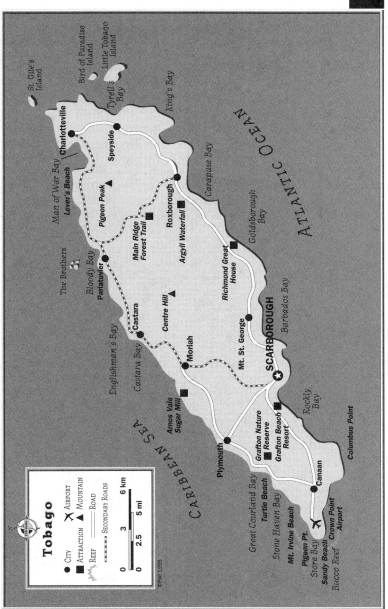

the other end. The southwestern corner is hemmed by Crown Point and Pigeon Point, and an airport bisects the peninsula. More than half of Tobago's accommodations are located here, and it's the sheer mass of population and increasing development from Scarborough and Plymouth to the west that most defines the bustling character of this end of the island. Elsewhere, Tobago moves along at an unhurried pace.

Several areas of the island have been designated as protected reserves or sanctuaries. The Tobago Forest Reserve is the oldest forest reserve in the western hemisphere, dating back to 1764. Another important sanctuary is Little Tobago Island, which lies just offshore from the fishing village of Speyside. Here can be found important nesting grounds for an enormous number of species, including Audubon's shearwater, the red-footed booby, the sooty fern, the red-billed tropic-bird and at least 600 species of butterflies—a lepidopterist's dream. The Buccoo Reef off Pigeon Point is now protected, but a fair amount of damage has been done to the coral, and enforcement of environmental laws here (and everywhere on Tobago) is somewhat haphazard.

Most historians believe Tobago was discovered by Columbus in 1498, who supposedly dubbed it "Bella Forma" (beautiful form). Its present name was derived from the word tobacco, which the native Caribs cultivated. In 1641, a Baltic duke received permission to settle a number of Courlanders on the north side of the island, but the Dutch took over in 1658, remaining in control until 1662. For the next few centuries, the island changed hands at least a dozen times among world powers who considered Tobago a treasure. Not only the Dutch, but the French and English fought each other for control, not to mention pirate invasions and settlers from Latvia. The conflicts formed the stuff of legends. Bloody Bay, on the island's west coast, earned its name after a 17th-century clash between combined French and Dutch forces against a British fleet (the latter was the victor). History records that the battle was so "sanguinary" that the water became red with blood. In another ferocious struggle, more than 1700 lives were lost in the battle of Roodklyn Bay, fought between the Dutch and the French. Eventually Tobago was declared neutral territory and promptly became a haven for pirates and treasure hunters. (In fact, rumors of treasure still buried on Pirate's Bay abound today.) During the early 19th century, Tobago was a leading contender in the British and French sugarcane industry, producing more sugar per square acre than any other island. When the sugar industry went bust, Tobago also went bankrupt, and in 1888 the island was tacked to nearby Trinidad by a British colonial government that didn't know what to do with it. In 1962, both islands gained independence from Britain and became a republic within the Commonwealth in 1976. Today Tobago has its own 12-seat House of Assembly, which runs many local services. (For more information, also read the history section in the Trinidad chapter.)

People

Tobago's population has been on the upswing over the last decade or so, as new resorts have been built and Trinidadians have come over to work them; the current population figure is about 50,000. Unlike Trinidad, where almost half the population is of East Indian background, about 90 percent of Tobagonians are of African descent. Their food, folklore, music and religion are all African-based. Although the official language on both islands is English, it's spoken with a more lilting, softer accent on Tobago. In general, islanders are extremely friendly and helpful, and perhaps because the island's economy depends on tourism, visitors seem to receive special attention. There's less crime here than on Trinidad, as everyone will tell you, but the problems on the larger island (usually tied to drugs) are frequently exaggerated, while those on Tobago are often shrugged off. Take simple precautions with valuables and you are unlikely to encounter any problems.

Trinidad has its Carnival, and Tobago has its Heritage Festival. Held the last two weeks of July, the nostalgic event taps into the history of the island, and features old-time weddings, traditional local music played with fiddles and tambourines, and showcases the complex courting rituals and codes and dances of days gone by. Each village presents one aspect of the island's heritage, showing off its own versatility in music, dance, costuming, drama, arts and cooking.

Beaches

The beach most point to as Tobago's best is **Pigeon Point**, one mile north of the Crown Point Airport. It's also where cruise ship passengers are carted to by the hundreds when they dock—hardly an attribute that contributes to making Pigeon Point the Caribbean beach of your dreams. Still, its placid turquoise waters are nice for swimming, the snorkeling on nearby **Buccoo**

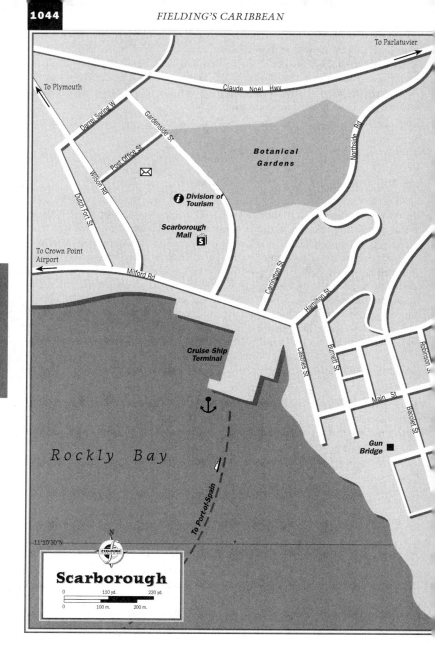

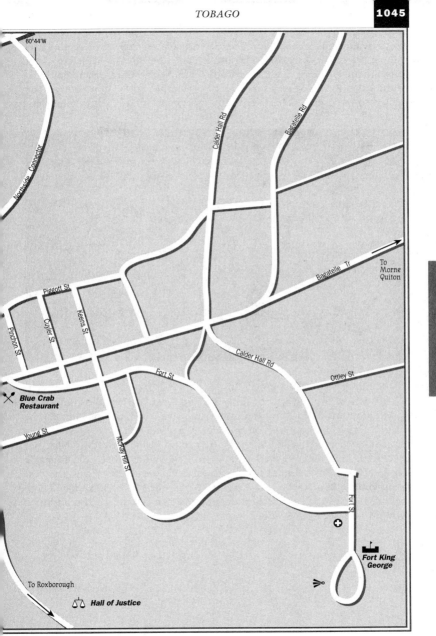

60°44'W

Northside Connector

Calder Hall Rd

Bagatelle Rd

Bagatelle Tr

To Morne Quiton

Piggott St

Cuyler St

Keens St

Pinchon St

Calder Hall Rd

Fort St

Ottley St

✕ **Blue Crab Restaurant**

Young St

McKay Hill St

Fort St

To Roxborough

⚖ **Hall of Justice**

Fort King George

Reef can be quite good, and sunsets along the coast are often terrific—there's also a quaint, photogenic pier. The peninsula is privately owned, and a fee ($2 per person) is charged for day use; there's a beach bar, picnic tables and huts and full changing facilities available. A half-mile south is **Store Bay**, next to the Coco Reef Resort, a small public beach that can be quite festive, particularly on weekends. This is Tobago's most happening beach, where young rastas sell local arts and crafts—expect the vibe to be lively.

Coco Reef, Tobago

Continuing the opposite direction along the north coast, two good beaches are watched over by resorts: **Turtle Bay** and **Great Courland Bay**. Both offer good swimming amid calm waters and are clean and well-kept, but can be relatively busy in season. As you continue east along this coast, however, the coves of sand meet fishing villages—frequently idyllic settings. Check out usually-deserted **King Peter's Bay** (accessed by a difficult road), **Englishman's Bay** and **Bloody Bay**. Around the northeastern tip are several prizes, the best being **Pirate's Bay**, reached via a half-mile trail out of Charlotteville. There are similar coves and bays along the southern coast, but the water tends to be rougher as it faces the Atlantic.

TOBAGO

FIELDING'S CHOICE:

Leatherback turtles, by the hundreds, come out of the water to nest during the months of March–June. Tobago Island is one of the few places in the Caribbean where this occurs. Organized turtle-watches allow visitors to witness the awesome spectacle while also protecting the nesting sites. Watchers help their guide measure each turtle and gather relevant statistics, which are sent to the U.S. turtle-research stations. The primary location is along the southwestern shore from Great Courland Bay to Turtle Beach. On one June night last year, 80 giant leatherbacks as much as six feet long came up on Grand Riviere beach, while tiny hatchlings, emerging from eggs laid in the sand, were making their way to the sea. For more information, contact Thalia Moolochan of the Grande Riviere Environmental Trust, ☎ *(809) 670-8458, who is in charge of the program. Trinidad and Tobago Sightseeing Tours,* ☎ *(809) 628-1051, FAX (809) 627-0856, has turtle-watching trips for $50, Caroni Swamp tours for $34, Buccoo Reef tours for $20, including hotel transport.*

Underwater

Unlike the murky reefs of Trinidad, Tobago is an excellent dive location which is only on the cusp of being discovered by Americans. Big pelagics are frequently spotted here, closer to the surface than in most of the Eastern Caribbean, including manta rays, dolphins, and even the occasional hammerhead or whale shark. As on Trinidad, Venezuela's Orinoco River filters freshwater nutrients onto Tobago's reefs, courtesy of the Guyana Current, but usually without the heavy dose of silt found off the larger island. The Orinoco can still limit visibility in the "bad water" rainy season (July through November), but the good news is that the multitude of currents that swirl around Tobago make drift-diving a dependable specialty. On the Atlantic side, currents of up to three knots are a regular occurrence, although the patterns and directions shift constantly, requiring the insight of a local dive operator.

The island's best diving is found around **Little Tobago Island** just off Speyside, and along Tobago's **north coast**, although an area referred to as **The Shallows**, in the channel between Trinidad and Tobago, features several excellent advanced dives. **Kelliston Deep** is famous as the location for the world's biggest known brain coral, some 16 feet high. Year-round visibility at Little Tobago averages 80 to 100 feet; on the southern half of the island,

Fielding TOBAGO

Wandering Robinson Crusoe's Island

"I was in an Island environ'd every Way with the Sea, no Land to be seen," wrote Daniel Defoe's hero in the classic tale. Legend has it that Tobago inspired Defoe's writings. Feel like Crusoe yourself as you explore this laid-back neighbor to more sophisticated Trinidad.

Bucco Reef Restricted Area

Situated on the leeward side of Tobago's west end, this proposed marine park is a transitional zone that includes non-Caribbean influences, such as outflow from the Orinoco River. The major reef crests a lagoon, and diving is popular along the outer reef, where depths reach 60 feet.

Arnos Vale

This rustic resort north of Grafton was once a plantation. Set on a hillside, it's a superb place to bird-watch. Look for jacamars, motmots and doves. The reefs beyond the shore are perfect for snorkelers and novice divers.

Pigeon Point

This famous beach is a Caribbean classic—azure water, white sand and a line of royal palms. Swimming is excellent, as is bird-watching in the mangrove lagoon. A fee is charged.

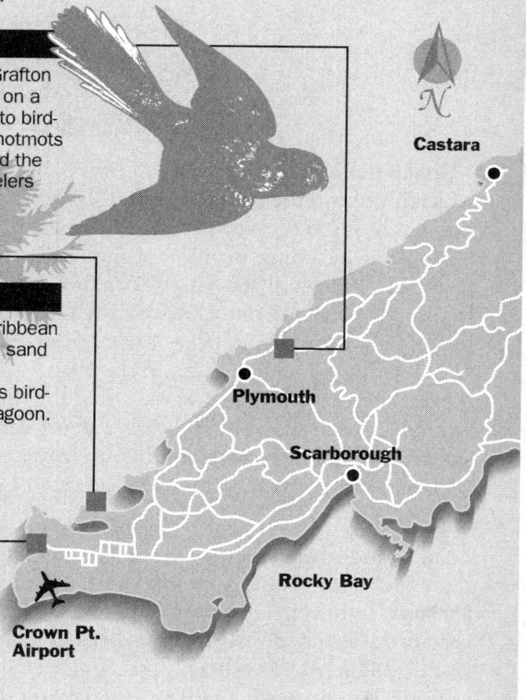

N

Castara

Plymouth

Scarborough

Rocky Bay

Crown Pt.
Airport

TOBAGO

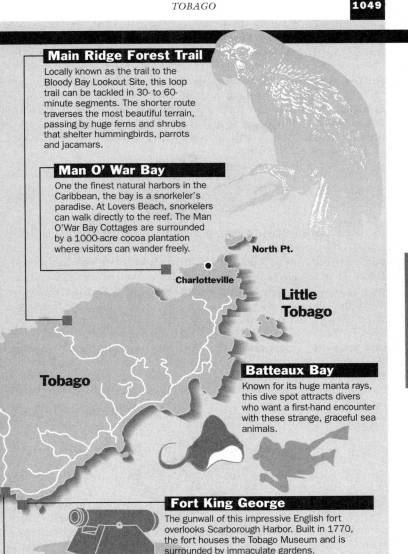

Main Ridge Forest Trail

Locally known as the trail to the Bloody Bay Lookout Site, this loop trail can be tackled in 30- to 60-minute segments. The shorter route traverses the most beautiful terrain, passing by huge ferns and shrubs that shelter hummingbirds, parrots and jacamars.

Man O' War Bay

One the finest natural harbors in the Caribbean, the bay is a snorkeler's paradise. At Lovers Beach, snorkelers can walk directly to the reef. The Man O'War Bay Cottages are surrounded by a 1000-acre cocoa plantation where visitors can wander freely.

North Pt.

Charlotteville

Little Tobago

Tobago

Batteaux Bay

Known for its huge manta rays, this dive spot attracts divers who want a first-hand encounter with these strange, graceful sea animals.

Fort King George

The gunwall of this impressive English fort overlooks Scarborough Harbor. Built in 1770, the fort houses the Tobago Museum and is surrounded by immaculate gardens.

Scarborough

No hustle, no bustle, no glitz, no glamour—this island capital exudes the feel of the old-time Caribbean. Soak up the sun and enjoy the charm of this quaint, quiet city.

TOBAGO

expect 50 to 60 feet in the dry season, and 40 or 50 during the rainy season. Sections of famed **Buccoo Reef** have been overused and abused for years, in part by glass-bottom boat operators who allow visitors to walk on the reef. The result: much of Buccoo is now a heap of dead coral attracting few fish. If you take a snorkel trip to Buccoo, make sure you're visiting its living sections or, better, head for some of the other bays that curl along the island's Caribbean coast. Pirate Bay, just north of Man O' War Bay, is a particularly lovely setting, and Tyrrel's Bay (off Speyside) also features spots accessible from the shore.

Relaxed and unspoiled, Tobago has plenty of exploration possibilities, but few identified trails at this writing. Coupled with Trinidad, the island is riding the eco-tourism boom and more trails are reportedly in the works. **Centre Hill** is Tobago's high point, 1900 feet, around which the island's forest reserve spreads. The **Argyle Waterfall**, just west of Roxborough, is well worth the 10-minute walk/wade off the main road (guides will make themselves obvious, but are not necessary). There is a book of trails available locally, and the helpful 1:50,000 map of Tobago is dependably obtained at the **Land and Survey Department** in Port of Spain, Trinidad (though it does not show trails or elevations). The Trinidad and Tobago Field Naturalists' Club, ☎ *(809) 624-3321,* has frequent field trips and welcomes outsiders. the island's complex interior, filled with diverse animal and bird life, invites exploration in the company of a naturalist, who can add greatly to your experience.

Lots of winding, hilly roads greet riders, but Tobago is an excellent island to explore by bicycle. The only level area is around the airport, with the island becoming progressively more mountainous as you travel northeast, even along the coastline. A wonderful, quiet area for mountain biking is the dirt track between Bloody Bay and Man O' War Bay, with another nice (but steep) ride cutting through the mountains via Parlatuvier Road. The roller-coaster road between Roxborough and Charlotteville is challenging. Trail riding can be sought in the hills above the Hillsborough Dam; a rough road wanders through lush rain forest to Castara or Mason Hall (good birdwatching, too).

What Else to See

The island's star attractions are mostly the natural ones. Don't miss a drive to Tobago's east-end **fishing villages**, Speyside and Charlotteville, where zinc roofs and wandering animals are the rule. Speyside is a speck of a town, but a couple good restaurants, including Jemma's, reward those who stop for lunch. A boat trip to **Little Tobago Island**, two miles offshore, is worthy, particularly for hikers or birdwatchers (see "On Foot" above). As you head out of Speyside, notice the great rusting waterwheel at the turnoff for the Blue Waters Inn. The road climbs steeply to a ridge, but before heading down into Charlotteville, watch for the dirt road that leads off to the right. After one mile, the dirt road takes you to the top of **Flagstaff Hill**, the site of an American military lookout during World War II. The view from the manicured lawns is superb, and at sunset pairs of parrots swoop madly through the jungle below. **Charlotteville** is a picture-perfect West Indian fishing village. Swimming is okay in town, or head along an obvious 20-minute path to secluded **Pirate's Bay**. Legend has it that pirate treasure is buried here, but not a single piece of gold has ever turned up.

From Charlotteville, those with a four-wheel-drive can continue along the north coast toward **Bloody Bay** on a difficult road. Or retrace your tracks back to Roxborough and take the well-paved **Parlatuvier Road** through the lush **Tobago Forest Reserve** where trails quickly deposit you into the thick of the jungle (see "On Foot" above). Rejoin the **Northside Road** at Bloody Bay and continue west past beautiful coves and more fishing villages, until the road heads into the hills where quaint villages are perched along the main ridge. In **Golden Lane**, seek out the grave of **Gang Gang Sara**, an African woman rumored to be a witch who once flew to Tobago and took up residence. When she tried to leave, we're told, she lost her power to fly because she had eaten salt while on the island. Just prior to reaching the Arnos Vale Hotel is another photo-worthy waterwheel and rusting processing plant which has been turned into a restaurant and nature preserve.

Scarborough, the eccentric capital of Tobago, is also worth a tour, but try to visit on Saturday when the market is running at full speed. The weekly market is an explosion of shouts, colors and aromas as the turbaned vendors lay out piles of fresh vegetables and fruits. Bargaining is a necessity, but don't try so hard for a good deal that you miss biting down on a delicious papaya or a ripe golden tomato. From here, you may walk or drive up to **Fort King George**, 450 feet above the sea and the island's most significant historical monument, though the museum is open only on weekdays. Just below is the **National Fine Arts Centre**, which houses a collection of local paintings and crafts.

Argyle Waterfalls ★★★

Roxborough.

This three-tiered waterfall is just outside the town of Roxborough, and plunges into a green lagoon perfect for swimming. It's only a 10-minute walk from the road and easy to find, but guides will make their presence known and can be aggressive. If the scene here (or at Rainbow Falls just inland from Goodwood) is too much, head for King's Bay a little further up the coast, where the falls are next to the road and guides don't bother offering to show you the way.

Historical Sites

Fort King George ★★

Scarborough, ☎ (809) 639-3970.
Hours open: 9 a.m.–5:30 p.m.

Tobago's best-preserved historical building is this fort perched on a hill above Scarborough. English troops built it in 1779 and over the years, it traded hands several times between the English and French. You can inspect its ruins and cannons, and on a clear day you can see forever—or at least to Trinidad. The Barrack Guard House is the site of the Tobago Museum, and has exhibits on Amerindian pottery and relics, military artifacts, and documents from the slave era. General admission: $1.

Tours

Adventure Farm and Nature Reserve ★★

Arnos Vale Road, Plymouth.

This 12-acre plantation grows mangoes, citrus, bananas and papaya, and rears sheep and goats in its pasture. You can come and pick your own fruit (they charge market prices) and for bird-watching. Open to the public every day but Saturday from 7 a.m. to 9 a.m. and 5 to 6 p.m., when a caretaker acts as guide for an extra $1. Nearby, just past the Arnos Vale Hotel, is a rusting waterwheel and machinery in the woods, which in 1996 was converted to a restaurant and museum.

Buccoo Reef ★★★★

Off Pigeon Point, ☎ (809) 639-8519.

Although much of this large, accessible reef has suffered from visitors walking on the coral, the better guides will take you to the less damaged portions—and will advise you to avoid touching the coral. The 10,000-year-old reef is spectacular and a stop at the Nylon Pool (a surreal, natural shallow pool in the lagoon) is mandatory. Two-and-a-half hour tours via glass bottomed boats available daily for $10; departure times vary by season.

BEST VIEW:

The view from the top of Fort King George is a panoramic sweep of the surrounding coastline, but for sunsets head for Flagstaff Hill on the island's northernmost tip to watch the last golden rays penetrate the deep indigo sea. Deep-sea fishing is also available, as is horseback riding, with equipment provided by the Palm Tree Village Beach Resort. The leading beachfront hotels have their own watersports facilities.

An unexpected highlight for many on Tobago is the Mount Irvine Golf Course, one of the best greens in the Caribbean. The leading beachfront hotels boast their own watersports programs. Other tour operators can be found in the vicinity of Pigeon Point; in rural areas, arrangements can frequently be made with local fishermen. Horseback riding is offered at the Palm Tree Village Resort, which has its own stables, ☎ *(809) 639-4347*. There are several professional sports associations on the island that will provide information on their respective activities.

Mount Irvine Golf Course

Mount Irvine Hotel, Scarborough, ☎ *(809) 639-8871.*
Hours open: 6:30 a.m.–3 p.m.
This 18-hole, par-72 course is among the Caribbean's most scenic, covering 125 acres of rolling hills and overlooking the sea. Great views from the clubhouse, too. Greens fees are $46, with a 30 percent discount to guests of the hotel; club rentals also available.

Watersports

Various locations.
If your hotel can't supply the necessary aqua activity, try one of these. Sailing: Viking Sail/Yacht Chartering Limited, ☎ *(809) 639-9209*. Deep-sea fishing: Gerald deSilva, ☎ *(809) 639-7108*. Surfing: Surfing Association of Trinidad and Tobago, ☎ *(809) 623-0920*. Windsurfing: Windsurfing Association of Trinidad and Tobago, ☎ *(809) 659-2457*. General watersports: Blue Waters Inn, ☎ *(809) 660-4341*, and Mount Irvine Watersports, ☎ *(809) 639-9379*.

Where to Stay

Fielding's Highest Rated Hotels in Tobago

★★★★	Coco Reef Resort	$154–$350
★★★★	Grand Courlan, Le	$200–$475
★★★	Arnos Vale Hotel	$120–$260
★★★	Grafton Beach Resort	$162–$252
★★★	Kariwak Village Hotel	$60–$90
★★★	Manta Lodge	$65–$150
★★★	Mount Irvine Bay Hotel	$165–$390
★★★	Palm Tree Village	$75–$240
★★★	Rex Turtle Beach Hotel	$110–$200

Fielding's Most Exclusive Hotels in Tobago

★★★★	Grand Courlan, Le	$200–$475
★★★★	Coco Reef Resort	$154–$350
★★★	Arnos Vale Hotel	$120–$260
★★★	Palm Tree Village	$75–$240
★★	Richmond Great House	$60–$160

Fielding's Best Value Hotels in Tobago

★★	Hampden Inn	$30–$50
★★★	Kariwak Village Hotel	$60–$90
★★	Sandy Point Beach Club	$35–$80
★★	Speyside Inn	$50–$85
★★★	Manta Lodge	$65–$150

Most of Tobago's tourist accommodations are concentrated in and around the airport, squeezed between Crown Point and Pigeon Point. All manner of rooms can be found here—resorts, condos and guest houses—though the area can sometimes become congested with activity. Most of the other moderate-to-expensive properties will be found northeast of here, near Plymouth, on or near some of the better beaches. Little is found in Scarborough or through the middle portion of the island, until you reach the northeast tip, where two fine dive properties, the Manta Lodge and Blue Waters Inn, are located.

On the hotel front, Tobago is currently suffering an embarrassment of riches. With three important new resorts that opened in late 1995, and decreased airline service to the island that limits the number of arrivals, rooms are empty, even in high season when they should be fully booked. Their loss is your gain. If you want a resort vacation, compare the rates and amenities of the various big hotels. If you're on a budget, you will find a surfeit of low-cost rooms under $75 in high season—and under $50 in low season.

Hotels and Resorts

Two major new resorts opened in 1995 and are vying for the honor of being the island's most exclusive property. The beautifully-designed Coco Reef is the creation of famed Bermudan hotelier John Jefferis, who made the resort a five-year labor of love—it replaces the old Crown Radisson that previously occupied this coral coast between Crown Point and Pigeon Point. Meanwhile, the Grafton Beach Resort empire spawned Le Grand Courlan in 1995 with the hope of luring vacationers for serious pampering and spa treatments; rooms are luxurious, but the facility leaves something to be desired. Those who want easy access to the island's golf course will want to stay at the Mount Irvine Bay, where country-club charm mingles with old-fashioned Caribbean style. Two popular spots that always stay busy are the Rex Turtle Beach and Grafton Beach—well-worn properties with good beaches, solid amenities and moderate prices that make up for what they lack in glitzy style.

Despite the current oversupply of resort rooms, at press time, construction was about to begin on a 200-room Tobago Hilton in the Lowlands area with an adjoining 18-hole golf course and condo development.

Arnos Vale Hotel   **$120–$260**   ★★★

Arnos Vale Road; Plymouth, ☎ (809) 639-2881. FAX (809) 639-4629.
Single: $120–$260. Double: $120–$260.

This self-contained resort, located in a coastal valley 15 minutes north of Scarborough, has attracted a mostly Italian clientele in the past. But a 1996 change of management will alter much of that—a promised room refurbishing is overdue, but may elevate this spot to match the beautiful landscaping. The sloping grounds include acres of fruit orchards—the bounty of which often enhances the creole, Italian and international meals served at the hotel's restaurant. Accommodations are located on the hillside or in apartment-style dwellings near the nice beach; all are air-conditioned. Facilities include two bars, a pool and a few watersports. There are lots of stairs between the beach and lobby/restaurant area. Amenities: secluded garden atmosphere. 30 rooms. Credit cards: A, DC, MC, V.

Blue Waters Inn $75–$258   ★★

Batteaux Bay, ☎ *(800) 742-4276, (809) 660-4341. FAX (809) 660-5195.*
Single: $75–$150. Double: $85–$258.

Set in a beautiful protected cove with a good beach, this diver's inn is almost 90 minutes from the airport, but offers enough escape to make the drive worthwhile. Guestrooms are basic and some rely on sea breezes to keep cool. Four self-catering efficiencies are available for those that want to cook (the nearest store is miles away), and one- and two-bedroom luxurious bungalows rent for $175–$400 per night. The surrounding rain forest keeps nature-lovers happy, but those who want to explore the island will want to rent a car—the location is truly isolated. A tennis court, kayaks, windsurfing, a restaurant and bar are located on the grounds, but no pool. Bird-watching excursions are frequently offered, but diving is the main draw and excellent sites are less than 10 minutes from your door. Amenities: balcony or patio. 38 rooms. Credit cards: A, MC, V.

Coco Reef Resort $154–$350   ★★★★

Crown Point, ☎ *(800) 221-1294, (809) 639-8571. FAX (809) 639-8574.*
Single: $154–$350. Double: $154–$350.

Guests are greeted to the sparkling new Coco Reef Resort via a subdued hallway that leads into a grand, arching, two-story lobby filled with 30-foot palms, statues and a vibrant papaya-and-white color scheme. Guest rooms feature Saltillo tile floors and wicker furnishings, and most units open onto sweeping views of the Caribbean and Pigeon Point. The Presidential Suite is situated above the lobby, but the coup de grace is a "lover's cottage" nestled on a rocky promontory next to the resort and featuring a private porch perfect for sunset ($1000–$1500 per night). The artificial sand beach and lagoon seems a little manicured, but the mosaic-tiled pool in inviting and other fine beaches are close by. A cozy and cool champagne bar, Bobster's, features undulating walls and murals of Caribbean entertainers, and an open-air gourmet restaurant provides fine food. Coco Reef is well-positioned to become Tobago's leading resort. Amenities: tennis. 135 rooms. Credit cards: A, DC, MC, V.

Grafton Beach Resort $162–$252   ★★★

Black Rock, Plymouth, ☎ *(800) 223-6510, (809) 639-0191. FAX (809) 639-0030.*
Single: $162–$252. Double: $162–$252.

This busy resort, 15 minutes out of Scarborough and practically joined at the hip with the new Grand Courlan next door, attracts a mostly European clientele. Guestrooms are nicely appointed with teak furnishings, minibars, marble baths and all the modern comforts. The two suites, which go for $300–$450 per night, also have Jacuzzis. There's lots to do: a large pool, shuffleboard, two air-conditioned squash courts, a well-equipped gym, and two restaurants and three bars. A new dive shop, Diamond Divers, takes care of sporting needs on the nice beach, and there is frequent evening entertainment. 112 rooms. Credit cards: A, DC, MC, V.

Grand Courlan, Le   **$200–$475**   ★★★★

Black Rock, Plymouth, ☎ *(800) 467-4464, (809) 639-0191. FAX (809) 639-0030.*
Single: $200–$475. Double: $200–$475.

A sibling to the popular Grafton, Le Grand Courlan shares the former property's hillside and beach bar below, but works hard to create an elegant luxury resort with the island's first full spa. During a summer 1996 visit, almost a year after opening, the resort felt unfinished—great expanses of concrete sprawled vacant and gleaming in the sun. The 12,000-square-foot spa was set to open in late 1996 and will feature cell-injection therapy—the resort also houses the largest gym on the island. Standard rooms are impressively furnished with king-size beds, Asian rugs and nice amenities like personalized stationery, seaweed loofa soap in the bathroom and a fruit tray on arrival. Some rooms also feature a semi-private Jacuzzi. The airy restaurant downstairs from the lobby features local and Guyanese teak, and the large pool has an attractive swim-up bar; the beach is a five-minute walk. A property with great potential, but overpriced until it attains it. Amenities: health club, exercise room. 78 rooms. Credit cards: A, MC, V.

Kariwak Village Hotel   **$60–$90**   ★★

Plymouth, ☎ *(809) 639-8545. FAX (809) 639-8441.*
Single: $60–$90. Double: $60–$90.

This authentic island getaway is nicely designed and is quite popular with both tourists and locals. Accommodations are in nine octagonal stucco cottages tightly configured around a swimming pool. Rooms are basic, but most guests will spend their time out at the pool, or at Store Bay Beach, a 10-minute walk. Couch potatoes can camp out in the TV lounge to get their fix. The restaurant is a local favorite, and on the weekends, this place is a popular spot to hear live music. The staff can arrange tours and watersports. Amenities: secluded garden atmosphere. 18 rooms. Credit cards: A, DC, MC, V.

Manta Lodge   **$65–$150**   ★★★

Speyside ☎ *(800) 544-7631, (809) 660-5268. FAX (809) 660-5030.*
Single: $65–$125. Double: $75–$150.

One of the three new resorts that opened on Tobago in 1995, Manta is the least prepossessing, yet it delivers a simple elegance that belies its diver's lodge concept. Delightful touches include handpainted manta ray dining tables, and a ceramic moray eel that writhes over the length of the restaurant's bar—most of these accents are created by the owner's wife and mother, both artists with a nice feel for whimsy. Rooms are spare but tasteful in design—the standard units (priced less without air conditioning) are an excellent buy. Manta is geared to divers: there's not much of a beach and you'll need a car to go just about anywhere of note. But below the water offshore, the huge manta rays of Speyside glide through the blue with inspirational grace. 22 rooms. Credit cards: A, DC, MC, V.

Mount Irvine Bay Hotel   **$165–$390**   ★★★

Mount Irvine Bay; Buccoo, Plymouth, ☎ *(800) 221-1294, (809) 639-8871. FAX (809) 639-8800.*
Single: $165–$390. Double: $165–$390.

Until recently, this north shore resort was Tobago's best. The amenities and grounds still shine, but Mt. Irvine's decor and style seems more in touch with 1960s country-club life than with the desires of many of today's Caribbean vacationers. The property is highlighted by a solid, well-maintained 18-hole golf course. There's plenty to keep travelers occupied off the greens, too, with two tennis courts, Tobago's largest pool, a health spa, and watersports on the nearby beach. Two restaurants and two bars, with frequent entertainment once the sun goes down provide other diversions. Lodging is in well-appointed guestrooms and in 46 fairly plush cottages. Six one- and two-bedroom suites are decorated with mahogany antiques and go for $510–$1000 per night. Amenities: tennis. 105 rooms. Credit cards: A, DC, MC, V.

Rex Turtle Beach Hotel   **$110–$200**   ★★★

Plymouth Local Road, Plymouth, ☎ *(800) 255-5859, (809) 639-2851. FAX (809) 639-1495.*
Single: $110–$200. Double: $110–$200.

If you're visiting this hotel between May and October, you might get a chance to see leatherback turtles laying their eggs on the beach at Courland Bay—hence the name. It's decent any time of the year here, though, with a lovely one-mile beach, full dive shop, two tennis courts, and small pool to keep guests happy. Accommodations are comfortable, though central air would be a great improvement over the individual units. Additional facilities include two restaurants and two bars at this well-run and popular spot. 125 rooms. Credit cards: A, DC, MC, V.

Apartments and Condominiums

A fair amount of variety can be found in the self-catering department; you can splurge on luxury homes and apartments (with a live-in chef and maid) or you can hole up in a cottage and do your own cooking. Most of your supplies will be best procured at the Scarborough market on Saturday, when fruits, vegetables, meats and more are put up for sale. Bring any unusual staples you think you'll need because supplies at grocery stores are limited and those you do find will be expensive. For more information and rates, contact the Tobago Villas Agency, ☎ *(809) 639-8737.* Plantation Beach Villas offers a selection of six two-story, three-bedroom villas, ☎ *(809) 639-9377.*

Crown Point Beach Hotel   **$55–$105**   ★

Store Bay Beach, Plymouth, ☎ *(809) 639-8781. FAX (809) 639-8731.*
Single: $55–$105. Double: $55–$105.

Set on seven acres, this time-share condominium resort is eight miles from Scarborough, but a two-minute walk from Store Bay Beach, one of the island's nicest coves. Accommodations are in studios and one-bedroom units with air conditioning and kitchenettes; maids tidy up daily. A restaurant, bar, two tennis courts, and a supermarket are found on the premises. Accommodations are very simple, but cheap. 100 rooms. Credit cards: A, DC, MC, V.

Man O' War Bay Cottages   **$55–$70**   ★

Charlotteville Estate, Plymouth, ☎ *(809) 660-4327. FAX (809) 660-4328.*
Single: $55–$70. Double: $60–$70.

Set on a 1000-acre cocoa plantation, these modest cottages boast an idyllic location right on the beach, just outside Charlotteville, but little else. Configurations vary from one to four bedrooms, all with kitchens, fans and verandas. Maid and cook service is available for an extra charge. This spot is especially popular with birdwatchers and those really looking to get away form it all. You'll want a car for mobility. 6 rooms. Credit cards: MC, V.

Palm Tree Village   **$75–$240**   ★ ★ ★
Little Rockly Bay, Plymouth, ☎ *(809) 639-4347. FAX (809) 639-4180.*
Single: $75–$240. Double: $75–$240.
This self-styled village is located only a five-minute-drive from Scarborough and is across the street from a public beach. Guests can choose to stay in the hotel wing with its 20 standard air-conditioned rooms; there are an additional 18 villas with two to four bedrooms, large living areas, kitchens and patios. Maid service is available, as are cooks. Facilities include a restaurant, bar, small pool, gym and tennis court—horseback riding on the beach can be arranged. Amenities: tennis, horseback riding, exercise room. 20 rooms. Credit cards: A, DC, MC, V.

Sandy Point Beach Club   **$35–$80**   ★ ★
Crown Point, Plymouth, ☎ *(800) 223-6510, (809) 639-8533. FAX (809) 639-8495.*
Single: $35–$80. Double: $35–$80.
This resort, located near the airport, sometimes suffers from the roar of jets. Accommodations are in studios and one-bedroom suites, all with air conditioners, kitchenettes, and pleasing decor. The beach is not good for swimming, so guests splash about in the pool (fine for laps) or take the free shuttle to the beach at Pigeon Point. The casual restaurant serves varied fare for those not into cooking. This friendly spot is a great bargain. 50 rooms. Credit cards: DC, MC, V.

Inns

Inns on Tobago are defined more by size than style and, accordingly, few options exist. The bright new Manta Lodge in Speyside is geared to divers and lacks a real beach, but those content with a remote retreat will be happy if they have a set of wheels at their beck and call. The Richmond Guest House vaunts a beautiful country location and courteous family management, but is well off the beaten track and almost too quiet.

Richmond Great House   **$60–$160**   ★ ★
Belle Garden, ☎ *(809) 660-4467. FAX (809) 660-4467.*
Single: $60–$130. Double: $75–$160.
Located on the coast half-way between Scarborough and Speyside on verdant hillside, this unique former plantation house brims with interesting African art, and local antiques. The 200-year-old house offers a handful of nicely decorated and colorful rooms, each individually done, with a handful of spacious newer rooms in the basement. The beach is a 10-minute drive; restaurants are further. 12 rooms. Credit cards: A, MC, V.

Speyside Inn   **$50–$85**   ★ ★
Windward Road; Speyside, ☎ *(809) 660-4852. FAX (809) 660-4852.*
Single: $50–$70. Double: $60–$85.
Just outside the fishing village of Speyside is this laid-back charmer, a seaside family-run inn with simple, but nicely decorated rooms. No air conditioning, but ceiling fans and pleasant balconies do the trick for most. No pool, but you can swim in Tyr-

rel's Bay across the street from the rocky shoreline. A restaurant and bar are located on the premises, and a couple more are within walking distance. Amenities: balcony or patio. 7 rooms. Credit cards: A, MC, V.

Low Cost Lodging

Lots of possibilities exist on Tobago, and because rooms prices on the island are generally low, some of the options are surprisingly good. Guest houses are listed by the Tobago branch of TIDCO but you may want to see them and gauge their location before committing, ☎ *(809) 639-4333.* The new German-owned Hampden Inn is a very good buy though its location is less than ideal and you'll want to lay out some cash for a car or bike rental while staying. Also worth considering for slightly more money is the Conrado Beach Resort which sits in a prime location next to Pigeon Point ☎ *(809) 639-0145.*

Arthur's by the Sea $50–$70   ★

Crown Point, ☎ *(800) 223-9815, (809) 639-0196. FAX (809) 639-4122.*
Single: $50–$70. Double: $50–$70.
This small hotel is situated on a busy street a few minutes' walk from Store Bay Beach. The air-conditioned guestrooms are simple and basic, but are kept in good shape and have private patios. All but two rooms have TVs. A restaurant (lunch and dinner by request), bar and small pool are located on the premises; 10-minute walk to the beach. 15 rooms. Credit cards: A, DC, MC, V.

Coral Reef Guest House $40–$45   ★

Milford Road; Lowlands, ☎ *(809) 639-2536. FAX (809) 639-0770.*
Single: $40. Double: $45.
This basic guesthouse is located in a quiet residential neighborhood between Scarborough and the airport has simple air-conditioned rooms with private baths. Eight apartments have one-to-three bedrooms and kitchenettes. Facilities are limited to a dining room, bar, pool and game room; 10-minute walk to o.k. beach. 24 rooms. Credit cards: A, DC, MC, V.

Golden Thistle Hotel $35–$50   ★

Store Bay Road, Plymouth, ☎ *(809) 639-8521. FAX (809) 639-8521.*
Single: $35–$40. Double: $40–$50.
This low-frills property is two minutes from the airport and houses guests in air-conditioned studios with kitchenettes, twin beds, and TV sets. The beach is walkable, but there's a pool on-site for those feeling especially lazy. A bar and restaurant complete the limited facilities. 36 rooms. Credit cards: A, DC, MC, V.

Hampden Inn $30–$50   ★★

Milford Road; Lowlands, ☎ *(809) 639-7522. FAX (809) 639-7522.*
Single: $30–$40. Double: $40–$50.
This homey guest house features a series of one-story buildings facing a thatched-rood bar and restaurant that serves good local food. Rooms are spare, and on-site activities limited, but the friendly management goes out of the way to showcase the best of Tobago to its mostly European clientele. You'll need a car to go anywhere beyond the decent beach (10-minute walk), but bicycle rentals are available. An excellent budget choice. 10 rooms. Credit cards: MC, V.

Where to Eat

	Fielding's Highest Rated Restaurants in Tobago	
★★★★★	La Tartaruga	$11–$17
★★★★	Eleven Degrees North	$15–$26
★★★★	Rouselle's	$13–$26
★★★	Dillon's Seafood	$12–$27
★★★	Jemma's Sea View Kitchen	$10–$27
★★★	Old Donkey Cart House	$20–$25
★★★	Papillon	$15–$25

	Fielding's Most Exclusive Restaurants in Tobago	
★★★	Old Donkey Cart House	$20–$25
★★★★	Eleven Degrees North	$15–$26
★★★★	Rouselle's	$13–$26
★★★	Papillon	$15–$25
★★★	Dillon's Seafood	$12–$27

	Fielding's Best Value Restaurants in Tobago	
★★★★★	La Tartaruga	$11–$17
★★★★	Rouselle's	$13–$26
★★★★	Eleven Degrees North	$15–$26
★★★	Jemma's Sea View Kitchen	$10–$27
★★★	Papillon	$15–$25

TOBAGO

Since Tobago aspires to be a resort destination, the food tends to be a
more refined than what is traditionally found on Trinidad. Continental cuisine is served in most of the resorts and at a few local restaurants—led by the
Italian at the excellent La Tartaruga. Otherwise, local cuisine centers on sea-

food, curries and traditional Caribbean fare. Although meals are slightly more expensive than the comparable food on Trinidad, prices are still reasonable by Caribbean standards. Favorites include curried crab and dumplings, and *rotis*, chicken or beef and potatoes in a curry sauce wrapped in a thin, unleavened bread. During Heritage and other island festivals, *pacro* can be found—it's reputed to hold aphrodisiacal powers. Near the Crown Point Airport, along Milford Road, there are a number of stands that prepare authentic local food. Here you'll be able to sample *roti* and conch, crab and kingfish, or *doubles*, a burrito-like package containing chickpeas, chutney and hot pepper sauce. Among the numerous small eateries that bridge the difference between roadside stand and restaurant, the better choices include Sharon and Phebe's in Charlotteville, and the Riverside Restaurant in Parlatuvier, which is run by Sharon's sister Gloria. Good cooking, in fact, seems to run in this family—another sister, Sheila, heads up the restaurant at the Hampden Inn Guesthouse.

Black Rock Cafe $$$ ★★

Black Rock, Plymouth, ☎ *(809) 639-7625.*
Lunch: Noon–4 p.m., entrées $3–$8.
Dinner: 6:30–10 p.m., entrées $13–$32.
A tin-roofed roadside house has been opened to the breeze for this pleasant low-key eatery specializing in seafood and curried dishes. Surf and turf runs $32, but crayfish, shrimp and lobster items are a better deal. Credit cards: A, MC, V.

Blue Crab $ ★★

Robinson Street; Scarborough, Plymouth, ☎ *(809) 639-2737.*
Latin American cuisine.
Lunch: 11 a.m.–3 p.m., entrées $4–$6. Closed: Sat., Sun.
The hardworking family that runs this popular spot whips up good meals that combine the cuisines of East India, Portugal and Creole. Fresh vegetables and fruits from their own gardens are used in the preparation of such delights as pumpkin soup and homemade ice cream and fruit wines. Lunches are served on the wide terrace of the traditional West Indian building and are very popular with the local business community. Only fish caught that day is used in their seafood dishes—the fresh catch might include benito, red snapper, kingfish or shark. Dinner is available by advance reservation only from Wednesday through Friday. Reservations recommended. Credit cards: A, MC, V.

Dillon's Seafood $$$ ★★★

Airport Road, Plymouth, ☎ *(809) 639-8765.*
Seafood cuisine.
Dinner: 6–10 p.m., entrées $12–$27. Closed: Mon.
This modern, air-conditioning-cooled restaurant is run be a charter captain and fisherman, which assures that all fish and seafood is so fresh it snaps back at you. There's lobster thermidor, or island kingfish in a tomato sauce, and fish soup. Some of the food though, could use a braver hand with the salt shaker or the spice rack. Reservations required. Credit cards: A, MC, V.

TOBAGO

Eleven Degrees North   **$$$**   ★★★★

Store Bay Road; Crown Point, Plymouth, ☎ *(809) 639-0996.*
Caribbean cuisine.
Dinner: 6:30–11:30 p.m., entrées $15–$26.

"New world cuisine" is celebrated at this newer Crown Point establishment, with a spicy selection originating from Mexico, Cajun country and, of course, the Caribbean—the seafood enchilada is popular. Grilled meats and a catch of the day round out the fine menu. The one-of-a-kind, lacquered tables created by the owners are lovely and local artworks are showcased on the walls of the restaurant. Stop by on a night live entertainment is scheduled. Credit cards: MC, V.

Jemma's Sea View Kitchen   **$$$**   ★★★

Windward Road, Plymouth, ☎ *(809) 660-4066.*
Latin American cuisine.
Lunch: 9 a.m.–4 p.m., entrées $10–$20.
Dinner: 4–9 p.m., entrées $10–$27. Closed: Sat.

Kids, big and small, will enjoy eating in a real treehouse overlooking Tyrell's Bay. They may have to fight for space, though, as there are only 10 tables. The emphasis is on local dishes, served in generous portions by an amiable staff. Specialties include callaloo soup, grilled seafood, and crab and dumplings. This is a great place to stop at during a circle-island tour or after a day at the beach. Open Fridays from 8 a.m. to 5 p.m. only. Reservations required. Credit cards: not accepted.

La Tartaruga   **$$**   ★★★★★

Buccoo Bay, Plymouth, ☎ *(809) 639-0940.*
Italian cuisine.
Dinner: 7–11 p.m., entrées $11–$17. Closed: Mon., Sun.

Fresh is the key word at this intimate, friendly spot. The delightful Italian owner/chef prepares delicious pasta that's homemade daily. Sauces are embellished with garden-grown herbs and fish is delivered to his door from a reliable source. The service, by a well-trained staff, is as quick as it gets on the island. Recommended dishes include spaghetti with dorado in a sauce of olive oil and pepper, served with tomatoes. Stop by for a drink, an espresso, homemade ice cream or luscious deserts such as ricotta cakes, and amaretto cheesecake. Features: rated wine cellar. Reservations recommended. Credit cards: A, MC, V.

Old Donkey Cart House   **$$$**   ★★★

Bacolet Street; Scarborough, Plymouth, ☎ *(809) 639-3551.*
International cuisine.
Lunch: Noon–3 p.m., entrées $3–$10.
Dinner: 6:30 p.m.–midnight, entrées $20–$25.

The Viennese owner of this charming restaurant in a white colonial house is the island's only authority on German wines, which are a specialty of the place. These fine vintages accompany well-prepared local fish, steaks and pastas. Start your meal with some excellent cheese. At lunch, sandwiches are served on homebaked bread (lunch weekdays only). Features: rated wine cellar. Reservations recommended. Credit cards: A, MC, V.

TOBAGO

Papillon   **$$$**   ★ ★ ★

Buccoo Bay Road, Plymouth, ☎ *(809) 639-0275. Associated hotel: Old Grange Inn.*

Seafood cuisine.

Lunch: entrées $15–$25.

Dinner: entrées $15–$25.

Chef Jakob Straessle's cuisine may not be on the cutting edge of chic, but the Swiss restaurateur always delivers reliably tasty old favorites like lobster thermidor, served with a choice of soup, rice and salad. Also featured are conch in season, cooked in coconut milk. Dine in air-conditioned comfort in a rustic, out-of-the-way lodge. Closed for lunch on Sundays. Reservations required. Credit cards: A, DC, MC, V.

Rouselle's   **$$$**   ★ ★ ★ ★

Old Windward Road; Bacolet, Plymouth, ☎ *(809) 639-4738.*

International cuisine.

Dinner: 3 p.m.–11 p.m., entrées $13–$26. Closed: Sun.

Charlene and Bopbbie, the delightful couple that runs this friendly seaview establishment, place a high priority on good vibes in a pleasant setting. Neither were cooks a few years ago when they started out, but have developed a reputation for the care they put into their menu, evidenced by a fine and cool cucumber soup and a delectable grouper (when available)—a generous usage of local herbs and spices accents most of the dishes. Reservations are a good idea for this small spot. Credit cards: MC, V.

Where to Shop

Compared to the cascade of goods available on Trinidad, Tobago's share represents a mere trickle. The Saturday **market** in Scarborough usually finds a few vendors selling leather sandals and belts, carved gourds and hand-wrought jewelry. A small area for vendors has been developed behind Store Bay; although what will be sold there isn't yet known. Two **malls** cater to the obvious and uninspiring: **Scarborough Mall** in the center of town and, slightly more fashionable, **Breeze Mall** on Milford Road. You'll find more original items in designer boutiques such as the **Cotton House** on Bacolet Street in Scarborough; it creates and sells brilliantly colored batik and tie-dye fabrics. Tobago's own fashion mavens head for **Nairobi**, above the Starting Gate Pub off Shirvan Road. A local jeweler, Jose Andres, is especially revered for his unique jewelry made from indigenous woods, bone, coral and seedpods. Finally, the large resorts have their own small gift shops, but expect the prices to be heavily inflated.

Tobago Directory

Arrival and Departure

At press time, **BWIA** (British West Indies Airlines) had discontinued service from North America to Tobago and no other carrier has stepped into the void, yet. Therefore, you have several indirect routing options. The most obvious is to fly to Port of Spain, Trinidad and connect to one of Air Caribbean's five to eight daily flights to Tobago's **Crown Point Airport**; the trip takes about 25 minutes. Port of Spain is served by **American Airlines** out of Miami and by **BWIA** out of Miami and JFK in New York (allow at least an hour for your connection as airport customs and immigrations in Port of Spain can be time-consuming when a big flight lands). Alternatively, you may fly to Grenada or Barbados (see "Arrival and Departure" in the "Grenada" and "Barbados" chapters), and connect to the daily **LIAT** flight to Tobago. A final option is too lengthy to warrant serious consideration except by those on a very tight budget: an almost-daily passenger **ferry** plies the route between Port of Spain and Scarborough, but the crossing takes about five hours and the return trip from Tobago usually leaves at 11 p.m. A round-trip tourist-class ticket is $10, or a cabin runs $28; the once-a-day departure schedule changes frequently, but there is usually no crossing on Saturday. The Port Authority in Port of Spain can be reached at ☎ *(809) 625-3055*, in Tobago ☎ *(809) 639-2416*.

Tobago's Crown Point Airport is big enough to handle wide-body jets, and located within 10 to 15 minutes of most of the island's hotels; allow 90 minutes for the drive to Speyside. There is a $15 departure tax collected when you leave the country.

Business Hours

Shops open Monday–Thursday 8 a.m.–4 p.m., Friday 8 a.m.–6 p.m. and Saturday 8 a.m.–noon. Banks open Monday–Thursday 9 a.m.–2 p.m. and Friday 9 a.m.–noon and 3–5 p.m.

Climate

Weather conditions are very comfortable, with temperatures averaging 83 degrees Fahrenheit. The wet season runs June to December, with rainfall in mostly short sharp bursts. Tobago is slightly cooler and less humid than Trinidad. A scant 11 degrees above the equator, the climate is decidedly tropical.

Documents

A passport is required for entry, as is a return or ongoing ticket. A departure tax of $15 is collected when you leave the country. An American drivers license will generally suffice for car rental.

Electricity

Current runs either 115 or 220 volts at 60 cycles. While many hotels have 115 volt current, it is advisable to travel with a small transformer just in case. These supplies are readily available at low cost.

TOBAGO

Getting Around

Although Tobago is small, you'll need a car if you want to travel outside the Crown Point area. Get one at the Crown Point Airport from **Baird's Rental**, ☎ *(809) 639-7054* or **Thrifty**, ☎ *(800) 367-2277* or *(809) 639-0357*. On the northeast tip of the island, one outfit, **Paradise Rentals**, operates out of the Blue Waters Inn, ☎ *(809) 660-4341*. Ask for a map, and remember to drive on the left. Note that the north coast road between L'Anse Fourmi and Charlotteville is rutted and suitable for four-wheel-drive vehicles only.

Taxis charge fixed fares to the major hotels from the airport. Fares from the airport to any of the nearby Crown Point hotels run about $4, while a taxi to Plymouth is $20 and to Speyside is about $40 (or $50 after 9 p.m.).

There are several good tour operators on the island. **Pioneer Journeys** works out of the Man O' War Bay Cottages in Charlotteville and does a variety of trips into the Forest Reserve ☎ *(809) 660-4327*. Fredericka at Good Time Tours is reported to be a pleasant guide ☎ *(809) 639-6816*.

Language

English is the official language and is spoken with a rich, melodious accent. The old French-based patois has almost died out; some Hindi is still used among the Indian community.

Medical Emergencies

There is a decent hospital in Scarborough, but more serious emergencies may require an air lift to Port of Spain or, in an extreme, to San Juan, Puerto Rico. There is an extensive network of health centers and clinics, both public and private. Both government and private doctors practice. The nearest decompression chamber for divers is in Trinidad.

Money

The official currency is the Trinidad and Tobago dollar (written as TT$), which floats against other currencies. At press time, the exchange rate hovered around 5.8 TT to 1 American dollar. Most prices in smaller restaurants are listed in the local currency, though all will accept U.S. dollars and all but the smallest restaurants now take credit cards. There are several banks in Scarborough that will exchange your dollars for smaller purchases.

Telephone

The country code is 809, however, a change to 869 is scheduled for 1998. If dialing Tobago from the U.S. and Canada, dial the number "1" first"; from other countries, including Cuba, Haiti, and the Dutch and French Caribbean, dial "01."

Time

Atlantic Standard Time, one hour ahead of New York City, except during Daylight Saving Time, when it is the same.

Tipping

Most hotels and restaurants add a 10 percent service charge to your bill at check-out and all but the smaller spots add a 15 percent VAT tax on top. If

Pigeon Point, Tobago

Mt. Irvine Golf Course, Tobago

the service charge is not included in your hotel or restaurant bill, be sure to leave something equivalent.

Tourist Information

Tourist information is doled out by the **Trinidad and Tobago Tourism and Industrial Development Company**, known everywhere on the islands as TIDCO. Local TIDCO offices are at the Crown Point Airport, ☎ *(809) 639-0509* and in Scarborough, ☎ *(809) 639-4333*. The TIDCO office in Port of Spain can be reached by toll-free number, ☎ *(800) 595-1TNT* or *(809) 623-6022*.

Water

Tap water is safe to drink; bottled mineral waters are widely available.

When to Go

Carnival explodes on Trinidad in February with steel bands, parades and lots of local food and drink (see "What Else to See" in "Trinidad"). The Round the Gulf Sailing Competition takes place in March. The Tobago Arts Festival occurs March–April. Goat and Crab races take place in April. The Indo-Caribbean Festival of the Arts takes place in May. The Tobago Heritage Festival is held the last two weeks of July. The Tobago Music Festival takes place in November and December. The Tobago Christmas Pageant, with local music and dance, is in December. For more information, contact TIDCO's toll-free Port of Spain number, ☎ *(800) 595-1TNT* or *(809) 639-4333* in Tobago.

TOBAGO HOTELS		RMS	RATES	PHONE	CR. CARDS
Plymouth					
★★★★	Coco Reef Resort	135	$154–$350	(800) 221-1294	A, DC, MC, V
★★★★	Grand Courlan, Le	78	$200–$475	(800) 467-4464	A, MC, V
★★★	Arnos Vale Hotel	30	$120–$260	(809) 639-2881	A, DC, MC, V
★★★	Grafton Beach Resort	112	$162–$252	(800) 223-6510	A, DC, MC, V
★★★	Kariwak Village Hotel	18	$60–$90	(809) 639-8545	A, DC, MC, V
★★★	Mount Irvine Bay Hotel	105	$165–$390	(800) 221-1294	A, DC, MC, V
★★★	Palm Tree Village	20	$75–$240	(809) 639-4347	A, DC, MC, V
★★★	Rex Turtle Beach Hotel	125	$110–$200	(800) 255-5859	A, DC, MC, V
★★	Blue Waters Inn	38	$75–$258	(800) 742-4276	A, MC, V
★★	Hampden Inn	10	$30–$50	(809) 639-7522	MC, V
★★	Richmond Great House	12	$60–$160	(809) 660-4467	A, MC, V
★★	Sandy Point Beach Club	50	$35–$80	(800) 223-6510	DC, MC, V
★	Arthur's by the Sea	15	$50–$70	(800) 223-9815	A, DC, MC, V
★	Coral Reef Guest House	24	$40–$45	(809) 639-2536	A, DC, MC, V
★	Crown Point Beach Hotel	100	$55–$105	(809) 639-8781	A, DC, MC, V

TOBAGO HOTELS		RMS	RATES	PHONE	CR. CARDS
★	Golden Thistle Hotel	36	$35–$50	(809) 639-8521	A, DC, MC, V
★	Man O' War Bay Cottages	6	$55–$70	(809) 660-4327	MC, V

Speyside

★★★	Manta Lodge	22	$65–$150	(800) 544-7631	A, DC, MC, V
★★	Speyside Inn	7	$50–$85	(809) 660-4852	A, MC, V

TOBAGO RESTAURANTS		PHONE	ENTRÉE	CR.C ARDS
Plymouth				
★★★★	Eleven Degrees North	(809) 639-0996	$15–$26	MC, V
★★★★	Rouselle's	(809) 639-4738	$13–$26	MC, V
★★	Black Rock Cafe	(809) 639-7625	$3–$32	A, MC, V
International				
★★★	Old Donkey Cart House	(809) 639-3551	$3–$25	A, MC, V
Italian				
★★★★★	La Tartaruga	(809) 639-0940	$11–$17	A, MC, V
Latin American				
★★★	Jemma's Sea View Kitchen	(809) 660-4066	$10–$27	None
★★	Blue Crab	(809) 639-2737	$4–$6	A, MC, V
Seafood				
★★★	Dillon's Seafood	(809) 639-8765	$12–$27	A, MC, V
★★★	Papillon	(809) 639-0275	$15–$25	A, DC, MC, V

TRINIDAD

One of the Magnificent Seven mansions, Trinidad

The largest and most-populated of the Lesser Antilles, yet possibly the least-touristed as well, Trinidad offers a rich smorgasbord of cultural and natural attractions set against the backdrop of the Eastern Caribbean's center of commerce and trade—Port of Spain. During the '70s, oil revenue made the two-island nation (which includes sister island Tobago) the region's wealthiest and most cosmopolitan, allowing it to eschew tourism as an un-needed intrusion. But as finances plummeted in the 1980s, the country began courting tourists on Tobago—long the spot where Trinidadians vaca-tioned—and recently has begun developing tourism on the larger island as well. Eco-tourism, in particular, is considered the best avenue for expanding the infrastructure for visitors. To its credit, the government began protecting

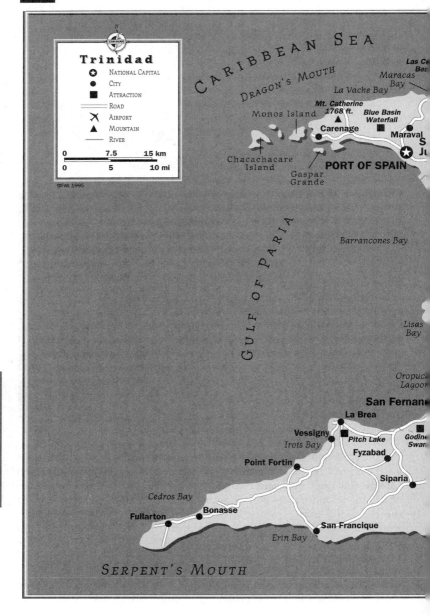

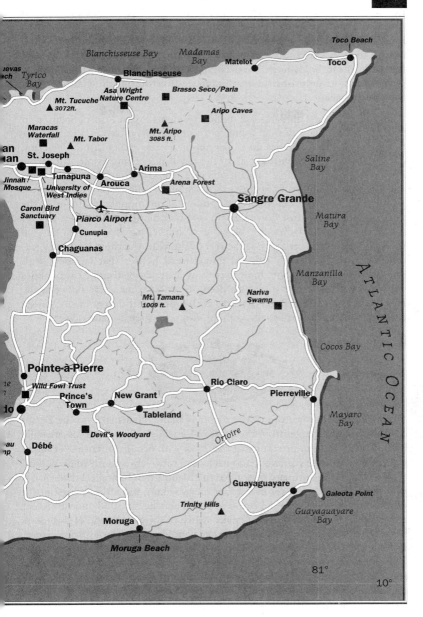

its wildlife long before it was fashionable (though illegal logging and parrot smuggling are a growing concern). Still, expanding tourist arrivals will be a long haul on Trinidad, where accommodations are primarily in small guest houses and sun-sea-sand activities have yet to be polished for the masses. But this large island holds numerous delights and deserves more than a cursory glance from adventurous travelers interested in touring the Caribbean off the beaten track.

About a third of Trinidad's 1.2 million residents live in Port of Spain, a vibrant and bustling city that contains a number of embassies and business headquarters. The city has an unfair reputation as being crime-filled and dangerous—in reality, virtually all of the few incidents involving tourists are drug-related. With simple precautions one would take in any large metro area (like avoiding Port of Spain's eastern suburbs) the city is well worth exploring for a few days before heading to one of the mountain retreats or the north coast's small inns. Port of Spain is also home to the Caribbean's best Carnival festivities, a dizzying blowout of music, parades and exotic costumes held every February. For the rest of the year, the capital is a busy waterfront town filled with colorful gingerbread houses that compete with ramshackle stalls and short high-rises as at least seven distinct nationalities stream down the streets intent on doing business somewhere between the First World and Third. Also dynamic is the food, and dinner at one of the city's best restaurants is usually unpretentious, inexpensive and delectable.

Bird's-Eye View

Trinidad is at the bottom of the string of islands that make up the Lesser Antilles, just eight miles from the coast of Venezuela. The 1864-square-mile island has more than proximity in common with South America—Trinidad was once part of the continent and broke off, relatively recently in geological terms, which is the primary reason for the island's rich biological diversity. A lush mountain range flexes its verdant muscle along the 50-mile-long north coast, climaxed by Cerro del Aripo and El Tucuche, at 3083 and 3075 feet respectively, the island's highest peaks. Much of the eastern end of this range has neither trails nor roads, only a single, winding route through the center, the Blanchisseuse Road, provides access between Arima and the north coast. The southern two-thirds of the island are a series of rolling plains, with the southeastern corner of Trinidad relatively underpopulated. On the coasts are important swamps—the Caroni is just south of Port of Spain, and the Nariva faces the Atlantic.

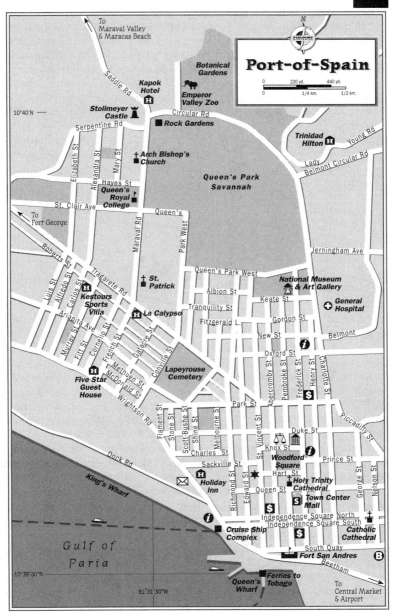

Port-of-Spain

Port of Spain is Trinidad and Tobago's capital, and it sits at the western end of the mountain range, on the Gulf of Paria, which separates the island from Venezuela. The official population of Port of Spain is about 46,000, but a series of suburbs—Diego Martin, Maraval, St. Ann's, Barataria, Tunapuna—extend into the surrounding hillsides and lowlands to create a much larger community of about 350,000. Port of Spain's unofficial hub is not its downtown, but an expansive park, the Queen's Park Savannah, and a commanding hotel, the Trinidad Hilton, looks down on the greens. The west edge of the park is faced by The Magnificent Seven, a row of impressive colonial mansions built in 1904–1910 in architectural styles embracing a French château, a Scottish castle, and more, although most are vacant now as the community attempts to find new uses for the manors. Along the park's northern perimeter is the President's House, which is surrounded by the 70-acre Botanical Gardens and the Emperor Valley Zoo. The 2.5-mile one-way drive around the park is called the world's largest roundabout; you'll encounter it often on your trips in and around the city.

History

Columbus stumbled upon Trinidad and Tobago in 1498. Since then, the two islands have been a battlefield of contention among the French, Dutch, British and Spanish. Trinidad was long viewed as a source for Amerindian slaves, so the island was fiercely guarded, in contrast to Tobago which was nearly deserted by the Spanish. In 1592, an inland capital was erected at St. Joseph, stimulating interest in the cultivation of tobacco and cocoa. During the middle of the 18th century, plagues swept through the area, decimating the settlement and forcing the Spanish governor to move to a more coastal location, less vulnerable to jungle diseases and Indian raids. Port of Spain took its time to develop, first attracting a slow stream of settlers, followed by Christian missionaries intent on civilizing the Indians. Both tobacco and cocoa production soon fell off, the former a victim of competition among the northern islands, the latter a victim of blight. In 1776, the Spanish government offered land grants and tax incentives to Roman Catholic settlers; in response, numerous French planters from French Caribbean countries poured in to establish farms. By the end of the century, prosperous Frenchmen had gained control of the government, spreading the lilt of their patois and their tasty cuisine islandwide. During the Napoleonic Wars in 1797, the British sent a fleet to Trinidad, who swiftly overcame the resident Spaniards who had been too distracted fighting off Indians. In 1815, Tobago itself came under British control and was made a ward of Trinidad in 1897.

In the 1970s, offshore petroleum discoveries propelled Trinidad to the enviable status of the wealthiest nation in the Caribbean. Literacy rose to 90 percent, roads were paved, electricity installed. Signs of abject poverty, common among West Indian nations, nearly disappeared. In 1962, Sr. Eric Williams, the father of Trinidad and Tobago's new independence from British rule, vowed to avoid what he called the mistakes of his Caribbean neighbors, which in his mind, was servile catering to tourists. As such, tourism was ignored for several decades. However, during the mid-1980s, resources plummeted, and the challenge of the Trinidadian government in this decade will be to reestablish economic stability and ensure conservation of the island's natural resources.

People

Trinidad's Carnival is the Caribbean's most celebrated annual spectacle with islanders working all year on floats and costumes.

Racially dynamic—40 percent Indian and 40 percent African for starters—Trinidad is home to about 1.2 million people who live in relative prosperity by Caribbean standards, despite the nation's oil bust. Children are kept healthy by plentiful fish and fruit, as well as by free medical care, and are taught in schools that have a higher literacy rate than those in the United States. In addition to the predominant Indian and African, the population has intermingled with Chinese, Arab, British and remnant Carib Amerindian peoples. The cultural jetsam takes its biggest influence from the conquerors who stayed the longest—Spain, France and Holland. But also important is the legacy left by the Africans who arrived as slaves, and the indentured servants from India brought in to replace the slaves after abolition. Then add in the Chinese who proved unfit to harvest sugar but adept at everything else, Syrians bearing textiles, and former British estate owners whose descendants wouldn't leave for anything. Consequently, skin color is less an issue in this country, where intercultural cooperation has received lots of elbow grease.

As many Trinidadians will passionately explain, music is the true life blood of the island, and every Trini is an expert about what's hot at any particular moment. Lyrics—sometimes bawdy, sometimes political—hold the soul of the people, and calypso has morphed into *soca* (which is faster), *kaiso* (calypso/soca), *rapso* (told in rap), and the latest is chutney, a blending of calypso with authentic Indian folk music. The importance of music on the island is more than a historical footnote. A century ago, the British outlawed African drums in Trinidad for allegedly inciting passions leading to violence. People switched to beating on bamboo, biscuit tins, hubcaps and, as local petroleum exploitation surged on, musicians began using oil drums. Someone soon figured out that the pitch changed after much pounding, particularly when dented, and the steel pan was born. The music was further legitimized when Harry Belafonte exported the calypso sound to the rest of the world (he is still considered a hero by many locals in the music industry). In the months leading up to Carnival, pan music can be heard everywhere on the island, from Sunday mass to jazz ensembles to 120-piece orchestras during Carnival's Panorama. Although Carnival is only a two-day event, the planning stage for parade floats and costumes begin months in advance, and by January, a few weeks before the festivities, Port of Spain has worked itself into a feverish pitch in delirious preparation. At the point of the actual event, the city grinds to a halt, and then collapses from exhaustion at its conclusion—usually decamping to Maracas Bay on the north coast, or to Tobago.

Because the country pursued tourism on Tobago before ever contemplating there was an audience who might enjoy Trinidad, the smaller island's beaches are better known. The reality is that Trinidad has just as many (if not more) fine beaches, though many are remote and still underpublicized. The best lie on the north coast, with **Maracas Bay** leading the pack due to its proximity to Port of Spain—it's a 35-minute drive, the closest good beach to the city. Maracas received facility upgrades in 1996 that lead to an expanded parking lot and a series of structures for food service and restrooms; the beach is the place to unwind after Carnival, but it's popular year-round, particularly on weekends (watch valuables and don't leave them in your car). Continuing east along the north coast, **Las Cuevas Bay** has partially submerged caves and is just as nice as Maracas, but the extra five miles of road keeps the crowds down—the hulking mass of El Tucuche rises majestically behind the palms. The town of Blanchisseuse has a series of small coves tucked between the rock cliffs, and at the end of the road, a long stretch of golden sand—nearby **Damier Beach** is popular with surfers.

Elsewhere, there are other beauties, though swimming conditions can be tricky—inquire locally before diving in. On the other end of the north coast are several fine coves—**Grande Riviere**, **Toco Bay** and **Salybia Bay**. **Shark River** (near Grande Riviere) is a popular local freshwater swimming spot. Although the waters are calm, Trinidad's west coast (south of Port of Spain) offers little for bathers, but on the eastern Atlantic coast, **Manzanilla Bay** or Queen's Beach is a long stretch of sand fronted by stands of coconut. Further south, **Mayaro Bay** is also lovely. Note that several of Trinidad's beaches, particularly around the northeast tip of the island at Grande Riviere and Matura, are nesting areas for leatherback turtles from March to August. Heed all signs during this period to avoid disturbing nests.

If you ask about diving on Trinidad, you'll be steered straight to Tobago in the blink of an eye. If you pry further, you'll probably be told—in no uncertain terms—"There's no diving on Trinidad." Well, they're right, but only to a degree. Tobago's stunning reefs and giant mantas are stiff competition for any neighboring island, but most particularly for Trinidad, which has a few complicating factors visiting divers need to consider. The first is the Orinoco, Venezuela's massive river, which flows straight to Trinidad. While this has the positive effect of steering rich nutrients into Trinidad's reef system, it also brings silt, reducing visibility just 20–50 feet during the January–May dry season, and a ghastly 10 or 20 feet during the June–December rainy season. Suffice to say, that "blue water" feeling one attains on most Caribbean islands simply isn't found here. To make matters worse, the Orinoco's colder waters settle into the depths below the surface and create a thermocline, which means that diving down past 35 or 40 feet is like entering a refrigerator, by Caribbean standards, anyway.

Trinidad does have some fair dive sites, mostly concentrated around the tiny islands which lie directly west of Port of Spain: Monas, Heuvos and Chacachacare islands, all part of the Gulf of Paria. Each of these sites, referred to locally as "down the islands," provide suitable beginner dives. A number of mid- to late-18th-century wrecks, including three Spanish galleons, pepper the vast northern coast. Although nothing is left of their wooden frames, divers can outline the shape of the disintegrated wrecks through cannonballs, ballast, anchors, pottery and bottles strewn around the sites, along with several cannons that are tucked against one shoreline. Shore diving is possible from a number of points along the northern coast, in Maracas Bay, and off Las Cuevas and Toco Beaches; a tender boat is recommended as entry can be rough and buddy separation is not infrequent. Additionally, currents on the north coast are sometimes tricky, making diving here a more advanced pursuit than is found off the Gulf of Paria islands. Some divers explore the oil platforms along the west coast. In sum, Trinidad remains an offbeat dive destination nurtured by locals, and visited by few outsiders, but suitable as a jumping-off point for the more dynamic sites on Tobago. Decent snorkeling is possible at Toco Beach (beware again of rough water) or around St. Peter's Bay, just west of Port of Spain.

On Foot

Trinidad is the biggest island in the Eastern Caribbean, and not just in geographical terms. The island was once part of the South American continent—some say as recently as 6000 years ago—and, as such, it has more in common with nearby Venezuela than it does with other Caribbean islands. This is most magnificently displayed by the island's diverse wildlife. A few of the highlights are the unique golden tree frog, ocelot, armadillo, peccary, porcupine, deer and red howler monkeys. In addition to the almost-extinct bush turkey and the brilliant scarlet ibis, the avian population includes over 400 species of birds, 617 types of butterflies and some 60-odd species of bat. Further, on the ground are 2300 different flowering shrubs and plants, including 700 kinds of orchids and a number of carnivorous species that grow in swampy areas. To its credit, Trinidad, richly-endowed with oil deposits, began protecting its natural resources well before "eco-tourism" became a marketing concept. At this writing, there are 13 official wildlife sanctuaries that shelter much of the island's swamps and mountain forests.

The downside, for adventurous hikers, is that much of the country's wildlife is not easily visited without a guide. Consequently, there are a growing number of tour operators who are accommodating the growing demand for wilderness exploration. Perhaps the top of the list is occupied by the famous Asa Wright Nature Center, a lodge and bird sanctuary set deep in the rain forest of the Northern Range, at an elevation of about 1200 feet.

What Else to See

Several scenic drives invite you to explore Trinidad. A common daytrip is to head out of Port of Spain via the Eastern Main Road to Arima and then into the mountains laced with *christophene* vines via the Blanchisseuse Road. A stop at **Asa Wright** is mandatory (see "On Foot"), as is a break for an afternoon dip in **Blanchisseuse** or **Maracas** before returning through Maraval. An even longer trip heads out to the northeastern point of the island, to **Toco**, **Grande Riviere** and **Matelot**—beautiful villages struggling to keep pace with the economics of modern Trinidad (allow three hours each way, plus stops for the beaches and scenery).

The island's two major **coastal swamps** can only be explored with a guide, but they are rewarding treks. The **Nariva Swamp** is the largest and most varied wetland on the island, containing many species of reptiles and amphibians, including caimans, anaconda and several varieties of poisonous snakes. The critically endangered manatee is found here, and a dazzling variety of parrots, macaws and toucans wing through regularly. The **Nariva's Bush Bush Wildlife Sanctuary** is strictly off-limits, except by permit issued by the Directory of Forestry, ☎ *(809) 662-5114.* The **Caroni Swamp** is also protected, but access is easier through one of the individuals who conducts tours (see below). Endangered leatherback turtles, the largest species of marine turtle, conduct their nocturnal egg-laying from March to August each year on several beaches around Trinidad's northeastern tip. The females deposit between 80 and 125 eggs in their laboriously dug nests—a moving event for onlookers that the Forestry Department regulates for the protection of the species, ☎ *(809) 662-5114.*

Two curious geological phenomena are found in southwest Trinidad. **Pitch Lake** is an immense reservoir of tar that supplies the island with all its resurfacing needs (excavate a truck-load and the hole fills up overnight). Disappointed visitors sometimes note the lake looks a bit like a vast parking lot. Tour guides are aggressive, but will assist in making the site interesting—try Amena Hosein, recommended by TIDCO, ☎ *(809) 648-7697.* A holy site to some Hindus, the **Devil's Woodyard** is the major of several Trinidad spots known for sputtering mud volcanoes. It's located outside Prince's Town, just east of San Fernando.

Many visitors are surprised that **pan** and **calypso** is hard to find on Trinidad outside the winter prelude to Carnival. One reliable spot is the Hilton's Tuesday night Poolside Fiesta or Sunday Brunch where live music and colorful costumes spill into the outdoor dining area ☎ *(809) 624-3211.*

City Celebrations

Carnival ★★★★★

Port of Spain, ☎ *(809) 627-1354.*

Trinidad's famous carnival officially lasts just two days, from sunrise on Monday to midnight on Tuesday before Ash Wednesday—1997 dates are February 10–11, and 1998's will be February 23–24. However the unofficial season starts right after Christmas, when creation of the colorful floats and costumes begins. Started by the French plantocracy 200 years ago, the festival was adopted by the island's blacks as a celebration of the end of slavery. Today, the joyous festival is eagerly anticipated by Trinidadians all year long. Most everyone dons elaborate costumes they've spent months making, then parades through the streets to the beat of steel bands. Tourists are welcome to join a troupe from a few hundred to literally thousands of costumed revelers. Note that Port of Spain hotel prices, particularly budget accommodations, double or triple during carnival; book rooms by Christmas.

Museums and Exhibits

National Museum ★★★

117 Frederick Street, Port of Spain, ☎ *(809) 623-5941.*
Hours open: 10 a.m.–6 p.m.

The museum's exhibits center on Trinidad's geography and history through the ages, with artifacts from pre-Columbian times. The highlight is a large art gallery with changing displays and a permanent exhibit on the works of famed 19th-century painter Michel Jean Cazabon.

Parks and Gardens

Royal Botanical Gardens ★★★

Queen's Park Savannah, Port of Spain, ☎ *(809) 622-3530.*
Hours open: 9:30 a.m.–5:30 p.m.

Located in the two-mile Queen's Park Savannah, these lush gardens cover 70 colorful acres on land that was once a sugar plantation. The grounds include the President's House, an 1875 Victorian mansion home to the president of Trinidad and Tobago, and the Emperor Valley Zoo ☎ *(809) 625-2264,* named after the huge Emperor butterflies common in the area. The gardens, laid out in 1820, showcase specimens from around the world.

Tours

Asa Wright Nature Center ★★★★★

Spring Hill Estate; Arima ☎ *(809) 667-4655.*
Hours open: 9 a.m.–5 p.m.

This 730-acre estate turned wildlife sanctuary and mountain lodge is a must for bird watchers, with more than 130 species recorded on the grounds. 13 varieties of hummingbirds alone regularly call on the feeders that dangle off the inn's veranda, and brilliant purple and green honeycreepers add another palette of color to the cool

TRINIDAD

mountain air. Three miles of trails canvas the densely-forested slopes. One trail may reveal white-bearded manikins—their exotic courtship dance is fascinating—another trail leads to caves that are home to the world's most-accessible colony of oilbirds (this one is limited to guests staying three nights or more at the lodge; see "Accommodations"). Guided tours are offered daily at 10:30 a.m. and 1:30 p.m.; reservations are suggested. Allow at least 90 minutes by car from Port of Spain. General admission: $6.

Caroni Bird Sanctuary ★★★★★

Butler Highway, Port of Spain.
Hours open: 4 p.m.–6:30 p.m.
This sanctuary comprises 40 square miles of mangrove swampland bisected by waterways, located just a few miles southeast of Port of Spain. Come at sunset to see the national bird, the scarlet ibis, come home to roost—an amazing, colorful sight that takes place daily just before sundown. Boat tours are conducted by Winston Nanon, ☎ *(809) 645-1305.* General admission: $10.

Humming Bird Tours

Frederick Street; Port of Spain, Port of Spain, ☎ *(809) 623-3300.*
Provides four different island tours, including a Port of Spain shopping tour, a North Coast Tour, a visit to Asa Wright and the Caroni Swamp Bird Sanctuary.

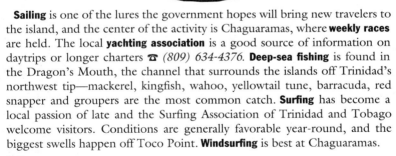

Sailing is one of the lures the government hopes will bring new travelers to the island, and the center of the activity is Chaguaramas, where **weekly races** are held. The local **yachting association** is a good source of information on daytrips or longer charters ☎ *(809) 634-4376.* **Deep-sea fishing** is found in the Dragon's Mouth, the channel that surrounds the islands off Trinidad's northwest tip—mackerel, kingfish, wahoo, yellowtail tune, barracuda, red snapper and groupers are the most common catch. **Surfing** has become a local passion of late and the Surfing Association of Trinidad and Tobago welcome visitors. Conditions are generally favorable year-round, and the biggest swells happen off Toco Point. **Windsurfing** is best at Chaguaramas.

Golf

Two locations, Port of Spain.
Trinidad has four courses for duffers; the best are also the closest to Port of Spain. The island's only 18-hole course is at St. Andrew's Golf Club in Maravel, ☎ *(809) 629-2314.* The Chaguaramas Golf Course has nine holes, ☎ *(809) 634-4349.*

Watersports

Various locations, Port of Spain.
A variety of companies are happy to assist with watersports. Deep-sea fishing: **Bayshore Charters,** ☎ *(809) 637-8711,* and **Trinidad and Tobago Game Fishing Asso-**

ciation, ☎ *(809) 624-5304*. Boating and sailing: **Island Yacht Charters,** ☎ *(809) 637-7389*. Windsurfing: **Windsurfing Association of Trinidad and Tobago,** ☎ *(809) 659-2457*. General watersports equipment and instruction: **Ron's Watersports,** ☎ *(809) 622-0459* and the **Surfing Association of Trinidad and Tobago,** ☎ *(809) 637-4355*.

Where to Stay

★★★★	Fielding's Highest Rated Hotels in Trinidad	
★★★★	Trinidad Hilton	$175–$225
★★★	Asa Wright Nature Center	$107–$210
★★★	Holiday Inn Trinidad	$99–$185
★★★	Kapok Hotel	$76–$143

	Fielding's Most Exclusive Hotels in Trinidad	
★★★★	Trinidad Hilton	$175–$225
★★★	Holiday Inn Trinidad	$99–$185
★	Chaconia Inn	$65–$110
★	Bel Air International	$56–$89
★★	Monique's Guest House	$45–$55

	Fielding's Best Value Hotels in Trinidad	
★★	Laguna Mar Resort	$35–$65
★★	Monique's Guest House	$45–$55
★★	Pax Guest House - Mt. St. Benedict	$45–$85
★★★	Kapok Hotel	$76–$143
★★	Normandie Hotel	$60–$95

Because Trinidad took a long time to recognize its tourism potential, accommodations tend to fall into two categories: business hotels (usually highrises) or quaint guest houses. All of the former establishments are in Port of Spain, while the latter, family-run outfits seem to be springing up everywhere. In both cases, accommodations are inexpensive by Caribbean standards, though the 10 percent service charge, 15 percent VAT (the heftiest hotel tax in the region) and a sometimes overlooked $1.25-per-day energy surcharge can add up to a shock when you get your final bill. The biggest plus is that high season lasts only a couple weeks on this island—during Carnival in February, when Port of Spain room rates more than double and five-night minimums become the rule. Book carnival dates by Christmas to secure the lodgings you want. Otherwise, Trinidad boasts what are easily the lowest winter room rates in the Eastern Caribbean. None of the Port of Spain or mountain hostelries are anywhere near a beach and, for the moment, Trinidad law prevents any hotel developments on the beautiful north coast beaches, though there are a few small properties nearby. In fact, Trinidad is the one major Caribbean island with no real resorts.

Trinidad's airport is a 30-minute drive from downtown Port of Spain and further still from the north coast—a few visitors opt for one of two airport hotels for their first or last night on the island. The better of these two crash pads is the 17-room Airport View Guesthouse in a three-story building above a convenience store located a mile from the terminal, but rooms are strictly spartan ☎ *(809) 664-3186.* Local tourism officials have received complaints about the nearby Bel-Air. A much better choice if you need airport-close accommodations is Pax Guest House, about a 15-minute drive from the terminal in the foothills above Tunapuna.

Hotels and Resorts

The premiere hotel is the Trinidad Hilton, an island institution since 1962 when it opened. The Hilton serves as an important meeting and social hub for many of Trinidad's business and political leaders, as well as visiting dignitaries (U.S. Secretary of State Warren Christopher in 1996, et al). Although other properties are a notch below the Hilton, what the Kapok, Normadie and others lack in amenities and service, they make up for in laid-back charm. Other island possibilities include the Valley Vue Hotel, in a curious location well away from any other Port of Spain facilities, next to a hillside water park with slides, ☎ *(809) 623-3511,* and much further south, the Farrel House Hotel, just outside San Fernando where much of the island's oil business is conducted, ☎ *(809) 659-2230.*

Laguna Mar Resort   **$35–$65**   ★★

Blanchisseuse, ☎ *(809) 628-3731. FAX (809) 628-3737.*
Single: $35–$45. Double: $55–$65.
This simple lodge lies on a 28-acre property at the end of the road outside Blanchisseuse and is a five-minute walk from a regal sweep of sand. Rooms are simple but clean and the beds are draped in mosquito netting. A small, affiliated restaurant, the Cocos Hut, sevres good food. Laguna Mar aspires to be a resort (another six rooms are under planned), but its low-key charm is a chief sales point—the lovely beach is another. 6 rooms. Credit cards: MC, V.

Chaconia Inn   **$65–$110**   ★

Maraval Valley; Port of Spain, Maraval, ☎ *(809) 628-8603. FAX (809) 628-3214.*
Single: $65–$85. Double: $75–$110.
Located three miles form Port of Spain in pleasant Maraval Valley, this hotel houses guests in air-conditioned rooms (most with TV). There are also four two-bedroom

TRINIDAD

apartments with kitchenettes for self-catering types. Facilities include a restaurant, a pool and occasional entertainment in the bar. An okay choice during Carnival when you won't be spending much time in your room, but otherwise a little pricey for the digs. 35 rooms. Credit cards: A, DC, MC, V.

Holiday Inn Trinidad $99–$185 ★★★

Wrightson Road; Port of Spain, ☎ *(800) 465-4329, (809) 625-3366. FAX (809) 625-4166. Single: $99–$175. Double: $108–$185.*

This 13-story downtown hotel overlooks the harbor and attracts mainly business travelers and conventioneers, but very few vacationers. Accommodations are standard tried-and-true Holiday Inn: modern, air-conditioned, with cable TV, and balconies offering nice views. Those staying on the executive floor pay extra for upgraded rooms and a private lounge. Facilities include La Ronde, a revolving rooftop restaurant (another HI tradition), dancing in the lounge, a nice pool with a swim-up bay and a small fitness center. Amenities: exercise room. 221 rooms. Credit cards: A, DC, MC, V.

Kapok Hotel $76–$143 ★★★

16-18 Cotton Street; Port of Spain, ☎ *(809) 922-6441. FAX (809) 622-9677. Single: $76–$130. Double: $89–$143.*

Located five minutes from downtown, near Queen's Park Savannah, the 10-story Kapok is a business-oriented hotel, but doesn't have an overly-corporate feel and the staff goes out of its way to accommodate vacationers. Most of the rattan-furnished guestrooms have a fridge, and the six suites have full kitchens; there are also some cozy studios with a kitchenette. The Tiki Village Restaurant offers Polynesian fare, and you'll also find a cocktail lounge, koi ponds and a nice tile-lined pool. Quite decent for the rates, but beware—the south-facing lower floors which can suffer from traffic noise. 71 rooms. Credit cards: A, DC, MC, V.

Normandie Hotel $60–$95 ★★

St. Anns; Port of Spain, ☎ *(809) 624-1181. FAX (809) 624-1184. Single: $60–$85. Double: $70–$95.*

This two-story hotel is located in St. Ann's Valley, near the botanical gardens. Taking a cue from the gardens, the mixed-use complex includes a restaurant, disco, pool, art gallery and shopping arcade with well-made local wares. Guestrooms are air-conditioned and comfortable, but on the dark side. The loft-style rooms cost a little more money, but perfect for families. A nice inexpensive alternative to Port of Spain's business hotels, and in a good neighborhood near the Presidents House. 53 rooms. Credit cards: A, CB, DC, MC, V.

Trinidad Hilton $175–$225 ★★★★

Lady Young Road; Port of Spain, Belmont Hill, ☎ *(800) 445-8667, (809) 624-3211. Single: $175–$205. Double: $195–$225.*

This commercial hotel is located a mile from downtown and receives few travelers on vacation, but remains the best-run property on the island—which is important for some Port of Spain visitors. The 12-floor hotel sits on a hillside overlooking Queen's Park Savannah, and is entered via the top floor—it's known locally as the "upside-down hotel." The main lobby area is always buzzing with activity, and the

Tuesday Night Poolside Fiesta and Sunday Brunch are the island's most dependable year-round spots for steel band entertainment. The air-conditioned guestrooms and suites have all the modern conveniences, and some include fax and computer hookups. Facilities include two restaurants, three bars, a pool, and two tennis courts. Guests are mainly American, and more than 90 percent of the rooms are occupied by business travelers who appreciate the nice trappings. What the Hilton lacks in local color it makes up through attentive service. Amenities: exercise room. 394 rooms. Credit cards: A, DC, MC, V.

Inns

Trinidad's two mountain inns are special retreats, each with its own unique flavor. Both are well away from Port of Spain and other conveniences, but deliver hiking, birdwatching and eco-tourism at their unrefined best. Complete meal service is available at both locations.

Asa Wright Nature Center $107–$210 ★★★

Arima Valley, ☎ *(800) 426-7781, (809) 667-4655. FAX (809) 623-8560.*
Single: $107–$139. Double: $162–$210.

This special spot is devoted to preserving nature. Located two hours out of Port of Spain some 1200 feet up, it is a former coffee, cocoa and citrus plantation converted into a 730-acre wildlife sanctuary. Two tall-ceilinged guestrooms are in the main house, which dates to 1908, and are quite romantic and furnished with antiques. The rest are located in cottages; all are basic but quite peaceful. The lush grounds and neighboring rain forest attract birders from around the world. The rates include afternoon tea and rum punch, and three meals a day—a good thing, since this spot is way off on its own. Amenities: houses, cottages or bungalows, balcony or patio. 25 rooms.

Pax Guest House–Mount St. Benedict $45–$85 ★★

Mt. St. Benedict; Tunapuna, ☎ *(809) 662-4084. FAX (809) 662-4084.*
Single: $45–$55. Double: $75–$85.

Located on a 600-acre monastery complex amid forested slopes, Pax Guest House was bought by Gerard and Oda Ramsawak in 1993 and they have spent the ensuing years upgrading and polishing the weathered guest facilities—the property was "the most luxurious on the island" when it opened in 1932, though the building dates to 1916. The result is simple, somewhat rustic accommodations, peacefully situated among the Caribbean's largest Benedictine settlement (monastery tours are available). Most rooms share bathroom facilities, but six have private baths. Daytime activities focus on bird-watching and hiking, and the afternoon tea is an island institution. Rates include full breakfast and three-course dinner, a must if you're overnighting without a car (Port of Spain is 40-minutes away). Pax is also an excellent place to begin or end a trip to Trinidad—the airport is only a short drive away. 18 rooms.

Low Cost Lodging

As the government has worked to develop a tourism infrastructure for Trinidad during the past decade, it has encouraged bed-and-breakfasts and guest houses, particularly during Carnival when rooms at hotels become scarce. The choices are endless, even within

Port of Spain, and the Trinidad and Tobago Bed and Breakfast Society maintains a list of properties they have inspected and approved for public consumption, ☎ *(809) 627-BEDS.* Among the small hostelries that we saw and liked were **Carnetta's House** in Maraval Valley, ☎ *(809) 628-2732,* **Alcazar Guest House** near Queen's Park Savannah, ☎ *(809) 628-8612,* and **Second Spring**, on the rocky coast at Blanchisseuse, ☎ *(809) 664-3909.* All of these locations have common areas shared by guests and owners.

Alicia's House   **$30–$58**   ★

St. Ann's; Port of Spain, ☎ *(809) 623-2802. FAX (809) 623-8560.*
Single: $30–$40. Double: $50–$58.

One of Port of Spain's small budget inns, Alica's is a five-minute walk from the Presidents House and the Hilton in a pleasant residential area, St. Ann's. Four different room types, each named after flowers are available, but the best is the Admiral Rodney which features mahogany antique furnishings, an oval bathtub and ample space; Fleur is a little smaller, but has more light and views across the valley. All units have air conditioning and refrigerators. The small dining room serves breakfast, and a pool is available. 17 rooms. Credit cards: A, MC, V.

Bel Air International   **$56–$89**   ★

Piarco, ☎ *(809) 664-4771. FAX (809) 664-4771.*
Single: $56–$89. Double: $75–$89.

This hotel is three minutes from the airport, so it attracts mainly travelers in transit. The air-conditioned guestrooms are rather simple and dated, and could use soundproofing to reduce airport noise. Facilities are limited to a pool and decent restaurant. There's no reason to stay here unless you're enroute to someplace else. 56 rooms. Credit cards: A, DC, MC, V.

Monique's Guest House   **$45–$55**   ★★

Maraval Valley; Port of Spain, ☎ *(809) 628-3334. FAX (809) 622-3232.*
Single: $45–$55. Double: $45–$55.

This small hotel is run by the friendly Mike and Monique Charbonne, who opened it in 1973 as the first guest house on the island. It's located in Maravel Valley, an affluent suburb amid lush hills a couple miles from downtown Port of Spain. Rooms are nicely furnished, air-conditioned, and spotless. The small restaurant serves bargain fare, and guests can splash about in a nearby pool. But the best reason for staying here is the Charbonne's attentive hospitality; they love their country and do all they can to expose visitors to its highlights. An excellent value. 11 rooms. Credit cards: A, MC, V.

Par-May-La's   **$30–$50**   ★

53 Picton Street; Port of Spain, ☎ *(809) 628-2008. FAX (809) 628-4707.*
Single: $30. Double: $50.

Simple accommodations in a good neighborhood near the French, German and American embassies. The apartment-style building was built in 1993 and most of the spare but clean rooms are on the second floor and feature air conditioning and lock boxes. Popular with Europeans and backpackers; rates include breakfast. 14 rooms. Credit cards: V.

TRINIDAD

Where to Eat

Fielding's Highest Rated Restaurants in Trinidad

★★★★	Chateau de Poisson, Le	$9–$26
★★★★	Veni Mange	$8–$10
★★★	Chaconia Inn	$12–$19
★★★	Hong Kong City	$8–$20
★★★	Monsoon	$4–$5
★★★	Rafters	$6–$21
★★★	Singho	$7–$12
★★★	Surf's Country Inn	$9–$17
★★★	Wazo Deyzeel	$4–$11
★★★	Woodford Cafe	$3

Fielding's Most Exclusive Restaurants in Trinidad

★★★★	Chateau de Poisson, Le	$9–$26
★★★	Chaconia Inn	$12–$19
★★★	Rafters	$6–$21
★★★	Hong Kong City	$8–$20
★★★	Tiki Village	$6–$13

Fielding's Best Value Restaurants in Trinidad

★★★	Monsoon	$4–$5
★★★	Wazo Deyzeel	$4–$11
★★★	Tiki Village	$6–$13
★★★	Singho	$7–$12
★★★★	Chateau de Poisson, Le	$9–$26

Though far from gourmet, food is a highlight of a trip to Trinidad. Seven distinct cultures have influenced the cuisine of Trinidad. Spanish settlers cooked up *pastelles*, tamales concocted by placing meats, raisins, capers and fresh herbs atop grated corn or cornmeal and folded in bright green leaves instead of the usual corn husks. The French introduced herbs such as broad-leaved thyme and basil. Tamarind was brought in by the British from the East Indies for sauces still used today in red snapper. Otherwise, in many restaurants, the influence of both India and South America is more prominent that on most other Caribbean islands. But some of the best specialties are found at street vendors, from *doubles*, the local equivalent of a burrito, to shark-and-bake, the ubiquitous Maracas Bay specialty of fried shark wrapped in bread. The Breakfast Shed is a colorful scene for tasty bowls of hot fish soup, all prepared fresh on the premises by one of a dozen or so counters. On the other end of the spectrum, the recently opened Chateau de Poisson deserves the fast acclaim it has built for its careful preparations of memorable seafood dishes. One holdover from the British is afternoon tea; in town, try La Maison Rustique, where Maureen Chin Asiong serves freshly baked pastries and cakes with tea Monday–Friday from 2–6 p.m., ☎ *(809) 622-1512.* The tea at Pax Guest House is one of the oldest traditions on the island, served daily from 3–6 p.m. and taken in by a number of visiting diplomats as well as the guests of the hotel ☎ *(809) 662-4084.*

Breakfast Shed $ ★★

Waterfront; Port of Spain, Wrightson Road, ☎ (809) 627-2337.
Latin American cuisine.
Lunch: 5 a.m.–3 p.m., entrées $2–$3. Closed: Sun.
Join the wharf rats at this colorful Trinidad institution near the cruise-ship dock, across the street from the Holiday Inn. Fellow diners are working people and early-risers who like the breakfasts served from 5 a.m. The two principle offerings from the shed's female cooks (who each have their own counter) are hot and pungent fish soup—about $2 for a large bowl, which is immense—and fish-and-bake, a few cents less and served with pepper sauce, crushed fresh on the premises. Lunch (the only other meal served) is accompanied by plantains, rice and peas and other plate stretchers. So down home, the hall-like room is called the "Holiday Out" by regulars. A must-see on any budget.

Chaconia Inn $$$ ★★★

106 Saddle Road, Maraval, ☎ (809) 628-8603. Associated hotel: Chaconia Inn.
Latin American cuisine.
Lunch: 11 a.m.–2 p.m., entrées $12–$19.
Dinner: 7–11 p.m., entrées $12–$19.
The dining rooms of this motel-like resort in a Port of Spain suburb serve a double purpose: at lunch in the Lounge, business folk gather for a no-frills lunch of fish, pasta, pork and some vegetarian offerings. Sandwiches are tasty and moderately priced. And once a week, a West Indian barbecue is the attraction at the modern,

plant-filled alfresco Roof Garden atop the hotel. A bar serves drinks until 2 p.m. Reservations recommended. Credit cards: A, DC, MC, V.

Chateau de Poisson, Le $$$ ★★★★

Corner of Ariapita and Cornelio; Port of Spain, ☎ *(809) 622-6087.*
Seafood cuisine. Specialties: Spanish crawfish, seafood curries.
Lunch: 11:30 a.m.–2:30 p.m., entrées $6–$22.
Dinner: 7 p.m.–10 p.m., entrées $9–$26. Closed: Sun.
An excellent new seafood restaurant located in a quaint gingerbread cottage in the Woodbrook neighborhood. Though lobster selections are priced as high as $26, the extensive menu features many other succulent fish preparations. Try one with the *Moqueca*, a Brazilian curry that makes a vibrant sauce for several dishes, or the Spanish crawfish, a local favorite. Seafood-lovers should aim for the Thursday night buffet ($16); a lunch buffet is also served on Wednesday and Friday for a bargain $7. Credit cards: A, MC, V.

Hong Kong City $$ ★★★

86 Tragarete Road, Newtown, ☎ *(809) 622-3949.*
Chinese cuisine.
Lunch: entrées $8–$20.
Dinner: entrées $8–$20.
Spicy, creative Tri-Chi food is served amidst gaudy red and gold trappings. Bright Oriental lanterns hang from an intricately decorated ceiling. Chinese-food loving Trinidadians favor pepper shrimp, pork with dasheen and other delights. Karaoke nights are sometimes offered, for those who enjoy that sort of thing. For more Chinese food around town, try: New Shay-Shay Ten, *81 Cipriani Blvd.,* ☎ *(809) 627-8089,* and in San Fernando area Soong's Great Wall, *97 Circular Road,* ☎ *(809) 652-2583.* Credit cards: A, DC, MC, V.

Monsoon $ ★★★

72 Tragarete Road; Port of Spain, ☎ *(809) 628-7684.*
Indian cuisine.
Lunch: 11 a.m.–4 p.m., entrées $4–$5.
Dinner: 4–10 p.m., entrées $4–$5. Closed: Sun.
This brisk, but stylish East/West Indian restaurant is probably the most popular in town for curries and flatbread *(paratha).* Lunch is a fast-paced affair, and very busy; many people take advantage of the take-out service. Complete meals built around shrimp, chicken, and fish include several veggies, lentils and rice. There are great *rotis*, dough wrapped around spiced conch or chicken, and fresh squeezed, exotic drinks. The Wednesday night buffets are a good bet for a well-rounded feast in quieter surroundings—the seven-course meal is about $11. Reservations recommended. Credit cards: A, DC, MC, V.

Rafters $$ ★★★

6A Warner Street, Newtown, ☎ *(809) 628-9258.*
Seafood cuisine.
Lunch: 11:30 a.m.–4 p.m., entrées $6–$21.
Dinner: 4–11 p.m., entrées $6–$21. Closed: Sun.
Meat-and-potatoes people and seafood-lovers all get their culinary kicks here: On Wednesday, a buffet of fresh local sea creatures is featured. Thursdays, Fridays and

Saturdays, chefs carve hunks of roast beef and other meats nonstop until it's all gone. In an adjacent lounge, snacks and sandwiches are available for folks with more prudent appetites and pocketbooks. The restaurant resides in a lovely old restored dry goods store. Reservations recommended. Credit cards: A, DC, MC, V.

Singho $$ ★★★

Long Circular Mall, Port of Spain, ☎ *(809) 628-2077.*
Chinese cuisine.
Lunch: 11:30 a.m.–7 p.m., entrées $5–$7.
Dinner: 7:30–11 p.m., entrées $7–$12.
Solidly good Cantonese food is the star at this tony eatery in the gargantuan Long Circular Mall. Decor features an aquarium, and meals run on the lines of cashew chicken, spareribs in black bean sauce, and curries. Regulars and tourists like to stop in Wednesday nights for the Chinese buffet. Credit cards: A, MC, V.

Surf's Country Inn $$ ★★★

Lower Village; Blanchisseuse, ☎ *(809) 669-2475.*
Continental cuisine. Specialties: Snapper en papillote, poached red snapper.
Lunch: 10 a.m.–6 p.m., entrées $9–$17.
Perched on a series of decks that overlooks the undulating north coast, this father and son operation is very popular for Sunday brunch, when Port of Spain families make the 90-minute drive to Blanchisseuse for a meal at this scenic spot. The food is good too—snapper en papillote is the signature dish, but the king fish poached in spicy garlic sauce is also tasty. Reservations essential for Sunday brunch. Features: Sunday brunch. Credit cards: A, MC, V.

Tiki Village $$ ★★★

16–18 Cotton Hill, St. Clair, ☎ *(809) 622-6441. Associated hotel: Kapok Hotel.*
Chinese cuisine.
Lunch: 11:30 a.m.–7 p.m., entrées $6–$13.
Dinner: 7:30–9 p.m., entrées $6–$13.
The island's version of Trader Vic's sits atop the plush Kapok Hotel, with a night vista of the glittering city lights; at lunch, Queens Park Savannah is spread out in all its glory. Food is good to average, with a dim sum lunch served from 11 a.m.–3 p.m. on weekends and holidays. Management thoughtfully provides cards for diners to mark their choices on. The regular menu features Polynesian-style fish, steaks and chicken. Reservations recommended. Credit cards: A, DC, MC, V.

Veni Mange $ ★★★★

67 Ariapita Avenue; Port of Spain, ☎ *(809) 624-4597.*
Latin American cuisine.
Lunch: 11:30 a.m.–2:30 p.m., entrées $8–$10. Closed: Sat., Sun.
Come and eat, say local media star Allyson Hennesey and co-owner and sister Rosemary Hezekiah, in the local lingo. A cross between Julia Child and Oprah Winfrey, Allyson manages to run the best West Indian lunch-spot in town and she also hosts her own TV talk-show. Specialties include tasty crab backs, hollowed out crab shells filled with peppered meat and a spicy mix of peppers and tomatoes. Hearty soups, including pumpkin and callaloo, are also recommended. Reservations required. Credit cards: not accepted.

Wazo Deyzeel   **$**   ★★★

Carib Way; St. Ann's, ☎ *(809) 623-0115.*
African cuisine. Specialties: Soups and sandwiches.
Dinner: 4 p.m.–2 midnight, entrées $4–$11. Closed: Mon., Tue.

Perched high on a hill above Port of Spain, Wazo Deyzeel is a cafe that boasts a wonderful view; visit at sunset for maximum effect. The Thursday night buffet is a good value (under $11) with a diverse array of traditional West Indian dishes—a great way to sample local cuisine. Other nights feature a lighter, bistro-style menu of items under $5 including soups, chicken dishes, a vegetarian platter and home-made ice cream. There's usually live entertainment on Fridays and the spot draws artists and other creative types for socializing 'til the wee hours (open until 1 a.m. on Friday and Saturday nights). If you're not going via taxi, call for directions—it's a little hard to find. Features: late dining. Credit cards: MC, V.

Woodford Cafe   **$**   ★★★

62 Tragarete Road; Port of Spain, ☎ *(809) 623-2233.*
African cuisine. Specialties: Guyanese pepper pot, stewed meat dishes.
Lunch: 11 a.m.–4 p.m., entrées $3–$6.
Dinner: 4 p.m.–10 p.m., entrées from $3.

Opened in 1995 by the proprietors of Monsoon at the other end of the block, this Port of Spain diner was an immediate hit with the local business community at lunch, but dinners are equally good. The stewed and creole dishes are served with sides of callaloo, steamed pumpkin, dasheen and other West Indian specialties. The Guyanese pepper pot served on Fridays is highly recommended ($5). Credit cards: A, MC, V.

Where to Shop

Relative prosperity has kept the number of local crafts to a minimum, on the other hand its allowed for artisans to develop their trade and flourish without the assistance of tourists. The latest in island-inspired jewelry, hand-painted T-shirts and batiks can be found at the extensive shopping area connected to the Normandie Hotel, on **Nook Avenue** in St. Ann's (behind the Presidents House). The pleasant mall shelters art galleries, crafts stores, a newsstand and more. Art Creators is just around the corner on **St. Ann's Road** and features the best local artists. The **Drag Mall** located on Charlotte Street just east of downtown is a good spot for inexpensive local handicrafts and leather goods (visit the spot with someone who knows the area).

For residents, Port of Spain's principle shopping area is eight-block-long **Frederick Street**, a humming scene any day of the week when the avenue bustles with activity. Calypso and **soca** music is always a great buy—ask for a disc highlighting the best of the most recent Carnival. **Rhyner's Record Shop** on

Prince Street sells the new along with the old; **Metronome**, on the Western Main Road is another good music source.

Trinidad Directory

Arrival and Departure

Piarco Airport is located some 30 miles east of Port of Spain and serves as the island's main point of entry. **American Airlines** provides daily non-stop jet service out of Miami. **BWIA** offers daily nonstop flights to Piarco Airport from Miami, New York's Kennedy Airport and Toronto. **Air Canada** also provides service to the island. **LIAT** and **BWIA** offer nonstop inter-island flights to Barbados, Grenada and St. Lucia. **Air Caribbean** connects Trinidad with Tobago and there is also a **ferry** between the two islands (see "Arrival and Departure" in "Tobago"). Customs and immigration at Piarco is lengthy when a large jet lands.

Taxis are plentiful at the airport when you land and run about $20 into Port of Spain. **Buses** (or Maxi Taxis) run on the hour from the airport to the city's South Quay Bus Terminal; the price is about $1, but you'll then need a taxi to get to any Port of Spain accommodations. The airport departure tax is $15.

Business Hours

Shops open Monday–Thursday 8 a.m.–4 p.m., Friday 8 a.m.–6 p.m. and Saturday 8 a.m.–noon. Banks open Monday–Thursday 9 a.m.–2 p.m. and Friday 9 a.m.–noon and 3–5 p.m.

Climate

Trinidad has a tropical climate, with a dry season that runs from January–June, and a wet season the for rest of the year. Temperatures are uniformly high year-round. In Port-of-Spain, average temperature in January is 78 degrees Fahrenheit, in July 79 degrees Fahrenheit. Annual rainfall is around 60 inches.

Documents

U.S. and Canadian citizens, as well as those of the United Kingdom, may enter the country with a valid passport if they only plan to stay less than two months. An ongoing or return ticket is also required. An immigration card is handed to you upon arrival (or on the plane) which must be filled out and handed in as you depart. Do not lose it. A visa is required for longer stays. Long delays in clearing customs have often been reported. Visitors may bring in 200 cigarettes or 50 cigars, plus one quart of "spirits." To facilitate customs, pack as lightly and unostentatiously as possible.

Electricity

Current runs 110 or 220 volts, AC 60 cycles. Always inquire of your hotel when you are making reservations what kind of transformer or adapter you will need.

Getting Around

On a country this big and diverse, you'll want to explore, and gas is inexpensive by Caribbean standards, though rental cars are not. One American firm is represented at the airport—**Thrifty's**, ☎ *(800) 367-2277* or *(809) 669-0602*—or you can use a local firm which is usually cheaper. Try **Kalloo's Auto Rentals**, ☎ *(809) 669-5673* or **Singh's Auto Rentals**, ☎ *(809) 664-5417*, both have locations at the airport and in Port of Spain. In any case, you will obtain a well-used set of wheels for your journeys—inspect your car's condition carefully on pick-up; the numerous dings and dents will be laboriously tallied when you return. Port of Spain is full of crazy drivers who taunt each other into dangerous maneuvers. Do your best to avoid driving yourself around in the city, or at least downtown. Conditions are usually less unsettling in the country, though potholes are not uncommon in less-visited areas and driving after dark requires a lot of nerve on the dark and windy roads.

Private **taxis** do not pick up any other passengers and take you straight to your destination. Take one for longer trips or destinations not on the public route. Rates are not usually observed during Carnival, when anything goes since the demand is so high. Adjust and go with the flow or you will drive yourself crazy arguing. You can explore the north coast by taxi, but always negotiate a fixed price and in advance. Public transportation around the island is good, if initially a little bewildering to outsiders. **Route (shared) taxis** and **maxi taxis** (color-coded minibuses) provide rapid transit at a reasonable cost. Yellow stripes operate within Port of Spain, red stripes are for eastern Trinidad, etc. Destinations within Port of Spain are under $1; Port of Spain to Maracas Bay is $3, to Toco, $5. The maxi taxi terminus in Port of Spain is on South Quay.

Language

The official language is English, spiced with a rich slew of local idioms. There is also some facility in Chinese, Hindi, Spanish and French, due to the large amount of immigrants.

Medical Emergencies

There are several adequate hospitals in Port of Spain, including the **St. Clair Medical Center** and **Mount Hope**, a large teaching facility. There is also an extensive network of health centers and clinics, both public and private; both government and private doctors practice. Serious emergencies, however, require an airlift to San Juan, Puerto Rico. Ask your hotel to suggest the nearest pharmacy, though carrying your own prescription medicine is advised in case you lose your luggage.

Money

The Trinidad and Tobago dollar (written as TT$) has been devalued twice in the past few years. At press time, the exchange rate was about 5.8 "TT" to 1 American dollar. You can exchange money in most major hotels, though banks usually offer a slightly better rate. Most shops, restaurant sand hotels will accept American dollars if you run out of "TT", but generally all prices are listed in the local currency. Traveler's checks are accepted in major businesses, as are all major credit cards.

Telephone

The area code for the two islands is *809*. Telegraphs, telefax, teletype, and tel-ex, can be sent through the textel office at *1 Edward St., Port-of-Spain;* ☎ *(809) 625-4431*. Cables can be sent from the Tourism office and major hotels. To place an intra-island call, dial the local seven-digit number. To reach the U.S., dial 1, the area code, then the local number.

Time

Atlantic Standard Time.

Tipping and Taxes

Restaurants and hotels usually add a 15 percent Value Added Tax (called VAT). Most also add an additional 10 percent service charge. If they have not (check your bill carefully), add your own comparable tip if you find the service satisfactory.

Tourist Information

Trinidad and Tobago's Tourism and Industrial Development Company (TID-CO) is the political unit responsible for luring visitors to island shores, and a toll-free number is provided to Americans looking for vacation brochures or other resources, ☎ *(800) 595-1TNT* or *(809) 623-6022*. TIDCO is located in Port of Spain at 10-14 Phillips Street. They are well-staffed, eager to pro-mote tourism in Trinidad, and can provide maps, brochures and assistance in finding bed-and-breakfast situations. They are particularly helpful in securing accommodations during Carnival, when beds become scarce.

When to Go

The Kaiso House calypso tent opens in January. Carnival and many associated events take place in February (see "What Else to See"). Leatherback turtle nesting season goes from March until August. The four-day Muslim Hosay festival takes place in June. Steelband Week takes place in August. The Pan Jazz Festival takes place in November. The Hindu Divali Festival is celebrated in November.

Fielding's Choice:

Don't miss Divali, the Hindu Festival of Lights, usually celebrated in October. The beauty of pan music is epitomized by the world steel-band festivals. The festival, called Pan Is Beautiful, is held in the last week of October. Check with the tourist board for exact dates.

TRINIDAD HOTELS	RMS	RATES	PHONE	CR. CARDS
Port of Spain				
★★★★ **Trinidad Hilton**	394	$175–$225	(800) 445-8667	A, DC, MC, V
★★★ **Asa Wright Nature Center**	25	$107–$210	(800) 426-7781	

TRINIDAD

TRINIDAD HOTELS		RMS	RATES	PHONE	CR. CARDS
★★★	Holiday Inn Trinidad	221	$99–$185	(800) 465-4329	A, DC, MC, V
★★★	Kapok Hotel	71	$76–$143	(809) 922-6441	A, DC, MC, V
★★	Laguna Mar Resort	6	$35–$65	(809) 628-3731	MC, V
★★	Monique's Guest House	11	$45–$55	(809) 628-3334	A, MC, V
★★	Normandie Hotel	53	$60–$95	(809) 624-1181	A, CB, DC, MC, V
★★	Pax Guest House - Mt. St. Benedict	18	$45–$85	(809) 662-4084	
★	Alicia's House	17	$30–$58	(809) 623-2802	A, MC, V
★	Bel Air International	56	$56–$89	(809) 664-4771	A, DC, MC, V
★	Chaconia Inn	35	$65–$110	(809) 628-8603	A, DC, MC, V
★	Par-May-La's	14	$30–$50	(809) 628-2008	V

TRINIDAD RESTAURANTS		PHONE	ENTRÉE	CR.C ARDS
Blanchisseuse				
★★★	Surf's Country Inn	(809) 669-2475	$9–$17	A, MC, V
Port of Spain				
African				
★★★	Wazo Deyzeel	(809) 623-0115	$4–$11	MC, V
★★★	Woodford Cafe	(809) 623-2233	$3–$6	A, MC, V
Chinese				
★★★	Hong Kong City	(809) 622-3949	$8–$20	A, DC, MC, V
★★★	Singho	(809) 628-2077	$5–$12	A, MC, V
★★★	Tiki Village	(809) 622-6441	$6–$13	A, DC, MC, V
Indian				
★★★	Monsoon	(809) 628-7684	$4–$5	A, DC, MC, V
Latin American				
★★★★	Veni Mange	(809) 624-4597	$8–$10	None
★★★	Chaconia Inn	(809) 628-8603	$12–$19	A, DC, MC, V
★★	Breakfast Shed	(809) 627-2337	$2–$3	
Seafood				
★★★★	Chateau de Poisson, Le	(809) 622-6087	$6–$26	A, MC, V
★★★	Rafters	(809) 628-9258	$6–$21	A, DC, MC, V

TURKS & CAICOS ISLANDS

The Caicos feature extensive caverns and caves.

With many islands in the Caribbean already overdeveloped or well on their way to becoming so, Turks and Caicos (KAY-Kos) remain a breath of fresh air. The region is an archipelago of eight inhabited islands and nearly three dozen smaller cays at the southwestern tip of the Bahamas, some 90 miles north of Havana. Though tourism is the principal source of revenue, the islands have yet to—and hopefully never will—succumb to the overdevelopment that has plagued destinations such as St. Maarten and Jamaica. That's not to say you'll be roughing it; the islands that cater to tourists manage nicely to combine pleasant accommodations with natural beauty without the ubiquitous array of tee-shirt shops and duty-free shops seen all too often.

Turks and Caicos, two island groups separated by a 22-mile passage, together total 193 square miles; Providenciales (more commonly known as Provo), the most popular for visitors, claims 37.5 of those. Grand Turk, which totals just seven square miles, also accommodates those on holiday, with a few properties on some of the smaller islands. Most hotels have less than 20 rooms; even the largest, Club Med Turkoise, has less than 300.

Grand Turk is the capital, with about 4300 residents. The major spot for tourists, however, is Providenciales, which has an international airport, an excellent golf course and even a casino. North Caicos, called the "garden island" due to its relatively high rainfall, has some interesting caves and a pond frequented by pink flamingos. There is also a good cave network on Middle Caicos, the largest of the chain but the least developed, while South Caicos is a fishing center for spiny lobster, bonefish and queen conch. Salt Cay, once the world's largest producer of salt, today has less than 300 residents. It is something of a living museum on its once-thriving industry. Pine Cay is privately owned, while East and West Caicos are uninhabited.

Throughout the islands, much emphasis is put on the preservation of its rich sealife (the diving here is among the Caribbean's best). The islands even have an unofficial mascot, JoJo, an Atlantic bottlenose dolphin who has made these waters home since 1980. Declared a "national treasure" by the Ministry of Natural Resources in 1989, JoJo is so beloved he even has his own warden who looks after him and tends his wounds.

Bird's-Eye View

The Turks and Caicos are part of the same geological structures that make up the Bahamas. In fact, they were actually the same country until 1874, when Great Britain divided the territories to make governing easier. Located 575 miles southeast of Miami, the islands are arrayed around the edges of two large limestone platforms. Caicos, the westernmost bank, is the base of six primary islands—West Caicos, Provo, North Caicos, Middle Caicos, East Caicos and South Caicos—as well as 30 smaller cays. The Caicos are encircled by a barrier reef lying one to two miles offshore. A 22-mile passage more than 7,000 feet deep, called the Christopher Columbus Passage, separates the Caicos from the Turks.

The Turk islands get about 21 inches of rain each year, while the lusher Caicos receive some 40 inches. Temperatures average 90 degrees Fahrenheit in

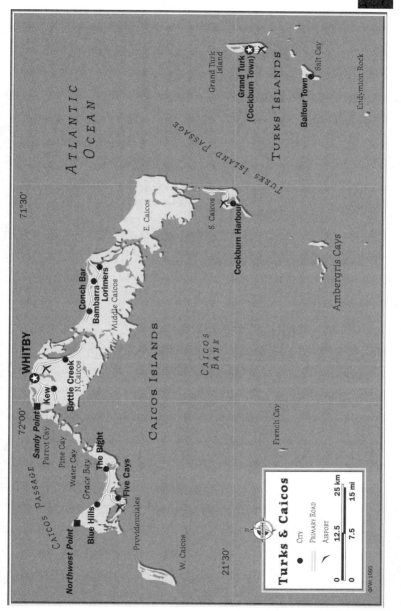

the summer and 77 degrees in the winter. The islands are known for their gorgeous beaches—230 miles in all—and excellent diving, with abundant marine life and visibility of 200 feet.

Serious evidence suggests that Grand Turk was the first landfall made by Columbus in 1492. Since the islands had no riches, however, the fleet quickly moved on. For 900 years prior, the Taino and Lucayan Amerindians had occupied these islands, having originated in the Orinocco region in South America—peace-loving tribes who had survived by fishing, farming and trading dried conch meat and conch pearls in Hispaniola to the south. Only 40 years after their first European contact, the native tribes were totally wiped out by enslavement, disease and abuse. With the exception of an odd shipwrecked sailor, the islands remained uninhabited for more than 200 years.

In the mid-1600s, Bermudian salt rakers arrived and their influence is still felt. They divided the tidal lakes on Salt Cay, Grand Turk and South Caicos into salt pans (called *slainas*), controlled the flooding and evaporating of the sea water and raked out the salt, creating an industry that was the mainstay of the economy for the next 275 years. Even today, broken windmills stand, ghostly sentinels over the salinas. Simultaneously, buccaneers hiding out in the Caicos preyed on treasure vessels passing through the Caicos Passage. Colorful legends still abound about Calico Jack Rackman and the two women pirates Bonnie Anne and Mary Reid. In the late 1700s, British patriots departing from the newly formed United States arrived, taking up the role in the growing plantocracy of sisal and cotton—a valiant but frustrating attempt doomed to failure. The most extensive ruins of plantations may be seen at Yankeetown on West Caicos and Wade's Green on North Caicos.

Today with the exception of Provo, time stands still here. History is found in every cove on the Turks and Caicos. The outlines of wrecked vessels in the shallow sand, the Loyalist plantation homes and workhouses abandoned to weather lie rusting and in ruins. The history is peppered with tales of explorers and adventurers, indentured servants, slaves, fishermen, pirates, salt rakers and shipbuilders.

People

"Belongers," as the residents of Turks and Caicos are called, are a welcoming and friendly lot. Most are descendants of Africans or Bermudian salt rakers, with a sprinkling of Americans, Brits, Canadians, Frenchmen and Swedish expatriates thrown in for good measure. The islands are a British Dependent Territory. Besides tourism, the principal source of employment, locals work in the fishing and financial services industries. Crime is generally quite low, but use common sense on Provo, where more development inevitably leads to pickpocketing and other petty crimes. Social life revolves around the church, whose choirs are magnificent. Visitors are more than welcome to drop into a Sunday service—if for not other reason than to enjoy the music.

Underwater

Providenciales

Although its walls are comparable in many ways to those of the world renowned Cayman Islands, diving amid the Turks and Caicos Islands still feels a little like an insider's secret. But the reality is that one dive shop has been established for over a quarter-century now, and the number of divers visiting the islands has skyrocketed over the past decade. You may not be touring virgin reefs and walls, but the undersea display is still quite wild and pristine, with magnificent visibility (almost always exceeding 100 feet, and approaching 200 feet during the summer months), and you won't have to deal with the crowds who pack the Caymans year-round.

The archipelago is actually two separate geological structures divided by the Turk Island Passage, a 22-mile undersea trench, 7000 feet deep, which connects the Caribbean Sea with the Atlantic Ocean. Each of the island groups, the Caicos to the west and the smaller Turks to the east, are essentially great mesas rising from either side of the passage, with a water depth rarely exceeding 20 feet. Most of the barrier reef surrounding the islands is undistinguished. But two great wall formations, both running roughly southwest to northeast, provide the impressive diving: one drops into the Turks Passage immediately west of Grand Turk and Salt Cay (discussed in

Beautiful By Nature

"Beautiful by nature" is the official motto of this cluster of islands and cays, where it is said that Columbus made his first landfall. Ignored (for now) by the resort-set, favored (in growing numbers) by international bankers, and beloved (with good reason) by divers, this chain of islands offers 230 miles of powder-white beaches, innumerable dive spots and landscapes that range from tropical forest to salt ponds.

North Caicos

West Caicos

Caicos Islands

Governor's Beach

Located on the west coast of the island, this long stretch of white sand beckons sun-worshippers and beach-combers.

The Black Forest

On the island's leeward side, just a seven-minute boat ride from shore, this underwater "forest" of black coral is located at a depth of 35 feet. Novice-to-intermediate divers will sight fairy basslets and brilliantly colored corals.

Grand Turk Wall

At this famous dive site, divers of all levels can get up close and personal with the Wall, which drops 7000 ft. into the ocean. Along its upper reaches divers can see gorgonians and other corals.

Grand Turk

This island serves as the administrative headquarters for the colony, but life is far from urban-hectic. Dotted with caves that invite exploration, the island was once a major salt producer, and the remnants of the industry can still be seen today.

Turks and Caicos National Museum

Sixteenth-century cannons line the entrance to this superb museum, which includes extensive displays of the Molasses Reef wreck of 1513, the oldest authenticated European shipwreck in the Caribbean.

East Caicos

Cockburn Town

The capital is a small town of narrow streets lined with low stone walls. Houses reflect typical Bermudian-style architecture, with red roofs and long verandas.

South Caicos

Turks Islands

Salt Cay

Encompassing only 2.5 square miles, this tiny island was once the world's largest salt producer. The diving is excellent. Stroll the beaches, or watch for windmills, salt sheds and ponds.

the Turks section below), the other wall abuts the Caicos Passage, just west of Provo and West Caicos.

Feather Duster worm, Providenciales, Turks/Caicos

The Provo dive shops typically visit four different areas. **Grace Bay**, the long sweep of water immediately north of The Bight, features a tapered spur-and-groove barrier reef from 30 feet down to 60, where a mini-wall starts and drops to about 100 feet below the surface; these sites are close to most of the Provo operators. To the north, **Pine Cay** also features a spur-and-groove reef system of rolling undersea mountains that drop from 50 feet down to 150; two easier sites are usually frequented here, **Football Field** and **Meridian Club Reef**. **Northwest Point**, about a 45-minute boat ride from Grace Bay, overlooks the wall, which lies about a third-mile off the Provo west coast. The wall starts 45 to 50 feet below the surface, descends another hundred feet to a ledge or platform only a few feet wide in some places, and then drops for thousands of feet into the abyss. The fourth area lies off uninhabited **West Caicos**, where the wall parallels the island as close as 500 feet from the shore; these sites are over an hour away from the dive shops on Provo, but yield some of the very best diving in the island chain. In winter months, when winds blow from the northeast, the wall sites offer the best visibility, while the barrier reefs are best during the summer as winds come in from the southeast.

There are some sites along **South Caicos**, 40 miles east of Provo, as well as idyllic diving off remote, uninhabited **French Cay**, but these are generally visited only by the several live-aboard boats which troll the waters, and only sporadically at that. Otherwise, neither the Provo operations nor the Turks dive shops visit their counterparts' sites; the distances by sea are much too far for day trips. There are several wreck sites, but the most famous, the W.E., was churned around in a recent storm and slid down the slope it was resting on to a depth below safe diving limits; the other wrecks on the Provo side are mere distractions from the real star of Caicos diving, the splendid wall. A recompression chamber is available at Menzies Medical Practice on Provo.

Grand Turk

If Provo is an escape from well-known destinations, Grand Turk, which has been dived for only the past decade, is quieter still. The Turks Island Passage serves as a conduit between the Caribbean and Atlantic, providing much of the rich marine life into the region. Summer months draw mantas to the passage, and January through March brings humpback whales that swim quite close to Grand Turk and actually hover off Salt Cay on their annual trek to and from their winter breeding grounds off the Dominican Republic. The massive wall plunges from a point only a quarter-mile off Grand Turk's shoreline, and the crest of the wall sits at an average of just 30 to 40 feet below the surface. There are virtually no currents, and the minimal rain run-off allows visibility to average 120 feet year-round, but it can extend much further in the calm summer months. Weather permitting, the Grand Turk dive shops sometimes make the long trip to **Salt Cay**, which features lovely sites, but only Porpoise Divers makes the occasional haul even further south to the **H.M.S. Endymion**. Salt Cay is, for now, the last frontier of Turks and Caicos destinations, averaging under 500 dive visitors a year; spectacular snorkeling amid giant coral formations in 15 feet of water is available at **Point Pleasant**.

By Pedal

Cycling is definitely a sport in search of an audience, but Provo provides the best and most varied road network, allowing some touring possibilities. From the Grace Bay area, **North West Point** is about 15 miles, and the road travels through a few of the smaller villages on the island on its way to remote and relatively unvisited territory. The **Lower Bight Road**, which runs along the north coast to the Leeward Marina, is a shorter trip, under five miles to the eastern tip of the island.

What Else to See

Turks and Caicos National Museum, a must-see under the direction of Brian Riggs, gives you a glimpse into the early days of the islands, reaching back to the tribal population. A special exhibit on the **Molasses Reef** wreck, found on the southern reaches of the Caicos Bank, is fascinating. The wreck, dating from the early days of the 16th century, is the first recorded European wreck in the New World.

Museums and Exhibits

Island Sea Center　　　　　　　　　　　　　　　　　★★
Blue Hills, ☎ *(809) 946-5330.*
Visitors can learn about the ocean and its creatures at this spot, highlighted by the Caicos Conch Farm, where the tasty critters are bred from tiny eggs. You can watch a video on their production and a touch tank allows for up-close inspections. The admission is $6.00 for Adults and $3.00 for Children.

Turks & Caicos National Museum　　　　　　　　　　　★★
Guinep House, Cockburn Town, ☎ *(809) 946-2160.*
Hours open: 9 a.m.–4 p.m.
This small museum, housed in an old stone building, centers on the nation's people and natural history. The highlight is the wreck of a caravel that sank on Molasses Reef in 1513, believed to be the earliest shipwreck found in the Americas. General admission: $5.

Sports

Provo Golf Club

Blue Hills, ☎ *(809) 946-5591.*
Hours open: 7 a.m.–7 p.m.
This challenging course, designed by Karl Litten, just opened in 1991. It has 18 holes and a par of 72. There's a club house, driving range, and pro shop on the premises. Greens fees are about $80, cart included.

Watersports

Various locations, Cockburn Town.
These islands are especially known for their excellent beaches and wonderful scuba diving. If your hotel lacks the necessary equipment, try one of these. Grand Turk: Blue Water Divers *(FAX: [809] 946-2432)* and Sea Divers *(☎ [809] 946-1407).* Diving on Providenciales can be found at Dive Provo *(☎ [809] 946-5040),* Provo Turtle Divers *(☎ [809] 946-4232),* and Flamingo Divers *(☎ [809] 946-4193).* Boats can be rented at Provo at Dive Provo *(☎ [809] 946-5040).*

Providenciales

Provo is the most developed island in the archipelago for tourists. Its 44 square miles include a 12-mile beach and 6000 residents, many of whom are American and Canadian expats. Though it did not even have a single wheeled vehicle until 1964, today Provo has a good infrastructure for visitors, with many accommodations on Grace Bay.

Things to do include a visit to the Island Sea Center and its Caicos Conch Farm, a mariculture project where conchs are bred in an underwater egg farm. The farm has some 2.5 million of the tasty creatures in stock and plans to start importing to Florida soon. You can also learn all about JoJo the dolphin at this interesting spot. Duffers enjoy the well-regarded Provo Golf Club, considered one of the Caribbean's finest.

Grand Turk

Cockburn Town, the seat of government and capital city, is a little charmer with its narrow streets, 19th-century Bermudian-style buildings and vintage churches. Don't miss the Turks and Caicos National Museum at the beautifully restored Guinep House, and the Odd Fellows Lodge on Front Street, one of the island's oldest buildings and the place where it is believed slavery was proclaimed abolished in 1832. Also of interest is recent archaeological work that has uncovered what appears to be the oldest Lucayan Indian site in the Bahamian archipelago, dating to 750 A.D. Recovered artifacts such as pottery, tools, beads, fireplaces and midden mounds (trash heaps) are on display at the National Museum.

Wild donkeys and horses roam the island at will, seeming outnumbering Grand Turk's 3700 residents. Birders will find the watching good at Gibb and Round Cay Bird Sanctuaries.

Pine Cay

This private isle, measuring just 800 square acres, is home to the Meridian Club, which has a wonderful two-mile beach. Just off the north coast are the ruins of a British fort and ruins of pre-Columbian settlements at Fort George Cay National Park. Nine miles of nature trails make this special spot a great day trip for hikers.

North Caicos

The most northerly of the chain of Caicos, this island is ringed by spectacular beaches and punctuated by thriving fruit trees. Flamingo Pond is the place to come to see the pink birds in all their glory. This is the lushest of all the islands, with a mangrove swamp along the south coast and several nature reserves.

Middle Caicos

Middle Caicos, also called Grand Caicos in tribute to the fact that it is the largest in the chain, is quite lovely and, despite its size, barely developed. Giant caves with underground lakes await exploration; these were once the haunt of Lucayan Indians, so keep your eyes peeled for artifacts. You'll also find ruins of an Arawak and Lucayan Indian settlement.

South Caicos

Located 22 miles from Grand Turk, this island was once a large producer of salt, though it is now a major fishing port thanks to its fine natural harbor, which yields scads of conch and spiny lobster. Cockburn Harbour, the main town, is a favorite spot for yachters to drop anchor and spend the night. If you're interested in the processing of fish, you're welcome to tour one of the island's four plants. The Sail Rock Hills (elevation 150 feet) make for a nice hike, and the diving around the island is outstanding.

Salt Cay

Just a few hundred residents grace Salt Cay, a major producer of its namesake from 1673 to 1971. Tools still lie about as if workers will soon be returning to harvest the spice. There's not much to see except the quaint village of Balfour Town, though snorkeling and diving is consistently excellent. Come January through March to see humpback whales migrate through the channel.

FIELDING'S CHOICE:

Both Grand Turk and Salt Cay, down to the Mouchoir and Silver Banks off Hispaniola, are the southern terminus of the migrational route of the Atlantic herd of some 2500 humpback whales. Sightings happen daily from December–April and divers frequently have a chance encounter both in water and from the boat.

Where to Stay

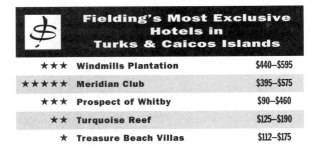

Fielding's Highest Rated Hotels in Turks & Caicos Islands		
★★★★★	Club Med Turkoise	
★★★★★	Meridian Club	$395–$575
★★★★	Grace Bay Club	$255–$725
★★★	Le Deck Hotel	$95–$175
★★★	Prospect of Whitby	$90–$460
★★★	Ramada Turquoise Reef	$125–$460
★★★	Windmills Plantation	$440–$595

Fielding's Most Exclusive Hotels in Turks & Caicos Islands		
★★★	Windmills Plantation	$440–$595
★★★★★	Meridian Club	$395–$575
★★★	Prospect of Whitby	$90–$460
★★	Turquoise Reef	$125–$190
★	Treasure Beach Villas	$112–$175

Fielding's Best Value Hotels in Turks & Caicos Islands		
★★★	Le Deck Hotel	$95–$175
★★	Sunworshippers Pelican Beach Club	$70–$120
★★	Coral Reef Beach Club	$65–$135
★★	Erebus Inn	$80–$150
★★	Turtle Cove Inn	$90–$180

Most tourists head for Provo, which has the largest number of accommodations, including a smashing Club Med and the new Beaches, another all-inclusive. Grand Turk also has facilities for visitors. The Meridian Club, on

Pine Cay, is a deluxe choice that never fails to please. On Salt Cay, Windmills Plantation is ideal for relaxing getaways; you don't even have to bring your own reading material, as their library has more than 1000 books. If you're looking for something completely different, charter a live-aboard yacht complete with pampering staff and diving equipment. For rates and information, contact: **Island Diver**, ☎ *(809) 941-5810*, **M/V Sea Dancer**, ☎ *(800) 932-6237*, or **Turks & Caicos Aggressor**, (fax inquiries to ☎ *[809] 946-5390*).

Hotels and Resorts
Blue Hills

Club Med Turkoise	$850–$1650 per week	★ ★ ★ ★ ★

Blue Hills, ☎ (800) 258-2633, (809) 946-4491.

This large Club Med is one of the best in the chain. It is set on 70 acres with a mile-long beach and attracts mainly couples and singles devoted to scuba diving—as well as the pleasures of a tropical vacation. Lodging is found in low-rise buildings lining the beach, all with two double beds and ceiling fans. The extensive facilities include three restaurants, a theater complex, a pool, eight tennis courts, a fitness center and a nightclub. The rates include all activities, meals and watersports, though you'll pay extra for diving and golf at a nearby course. Children from age 12 and teens are welcome, though unlike the family-oriented Club Meds, there are no special facilities for them. Rates range from $850 to $1650 per person per week, plus a one-time $30 membership fee and a $50 annual fee. 400 rooms. Credit cards: A, DC, MC, V.

Turtle Cove Inn	$90–$180	★ ★

Blue Hills, ☎ (800) 633-7411, (809) 946-4203.
Single: $90–$180. Double: $90–$180.

This hotel, located at the marina, houses guests in air-conditioned rooms with TV, VCRs, small refrigerators and phones. Sporting facilities include a pool, two clay tennis courts, bike rentals, and watersports, including diving. Snorkelers can take advantage of free boat service to a reef and beach. Ramada's casino is nearby and there's lots within walking distance. 30 rooms. Credit cards: A, D, MC, V.

Cockburn Town

Guanahani Beach Hotel	$120–$165	★ ★

P.O. Box 178, Guanahani Beach, Cockburn Town, ☎ (800) 468-8752, (809) 946-2135. FAX (809) 946-1460.
Single: $120–$165. Double: $120–$165.

This small hotel is a 20-minute walk from Cockburn Town. Guestrooms are simple and rely on ceiling fans to keep cool. This property attracts mainly divers, and has an excellent dive shop and resident instructor. There's also great snorkeling right off the beach. Facilities include a restaurant, bar and pool at this casual spot. 16 rooms. Credit cards: A, MC, V.

Prospect of Whitby	$90–$460	★ ★ ★

North Beach, Cockburn Town, ☎ (809) 946-7119. FAX (809) 946-7114.
Single: $90–$195. Double: $145–$460.

Situated on seven miles of beach, this isolated hotel bills itself as perfect for escaping the outside world. Rooms are spacious and air conditioned, with basic but comfortable furnishings. There's a pool, tennis court, bar and restaurant on the premises, and they'll handle watersports requests. 28 rooms. Credit cards: A, MC, V.

Sitting Pretty Hotel $75–$220   ★★

Duke Street, Cockburn Town, ☎ *(809) 946-2666. FAX (809) 946-2668.*
Single: $75–$215. Double: $95–$220.
Located on the west side, five minutes from town, this family-owned hotel, formerly called Kittina, is across the street from the beach. It was completely refurbished in 1996. Guestrooms are generally pleasant with local art, ceiling fans, and balconies; most are air conditioned. The newer beachfront suites also have kitchenettes. The grounds include a dive shop, two bars, a restaurant, and scooter rentals. The Friday night barbecues, held around the pool, are great fun, and you can walk to town in just a few minutes. 28 rooms. Credit cards: A, MC, V.

Sunworshippers Pelican Beach Club $70–$120   ★★

Sapodilla Bay, Cockburn Town, ☎ *(809) 946-4488. FAX (809) 946-4488.*
Single: $70–$95. Double: $70–$120.
Located at this island's south end and overlooking a pretty bay, this small hotel is unique for its wonderful pastry shop, baked fresh each day by the owner himself. Guestrooms are simple and airy with ceiling fans and ocean views. There's a dive shop on the pleasant beach, a bar and restaurant, and a small pool. 25 rooms. Credit cards: A, MC, V.

Grace Bay

Grace Bay Club $255–$725   ★★★★

Grace Bay, ☎ *(800) 946-5758, (809) 946-5757. FAX (809) 946-5758.*
Single: $255–$555. Double: $355–$725.
Situated on a 12-mile sandy beach and designed to resemble a Mediterranean village, this deluxe choice pampers guests nicely. Lodging choices range from studios to one- and two-bedroom suites and penthouses, all air conditioned, elegantly appointed, and with kitchens and all the latest creature comforts. On-premise facilities include a gourmet restaurant, bar, pool, two tennis courts and most watersports. 22 rooms. Credit cards: A, MC, V.

Le Deck Hotel $95–$175   ★★★

Grace Bay, ☎ *(809) 946-5547. FAX (809) 946-5547.*
Single: $95–$175. Double: $95–$175.
This two-story hotel is located on Grace Bay's lovely sandy beach. The air-conditioned guestrooms are clean and simple. Facilities include a pool, watersports and a popular bar and restaurant. Lots of young singles and couples at this informal and popular spot. 27 rooms. Credit cards: A, D, MC, V.

Pine Cay

Meridian Club $395–$575   ★★★★★

Pine Cay, Cockburn Town, ☎ *(800) 331-9154, (809) 946-5128. FAX (809) 946-5128.*
Single: $395–$520. Double: $400–$575.
This deluxe operation is located on its own 800-acre private island with a very spectacular beach. Accommodations are in colorful and quite pleasant beachfront rooms; 15 more expensive cottages supply sitting areas, screened porches, and

kitchenettes. The idea here is pure escapism—no TV, newspapers, or radios to remind guests that there is a world out there. Ceiling fans and trade winds make up nicely for the lack of air conditioners. There's a bar and restaurant, and active types are kept happy with a pool, tennis court, watersports and nature trails. Nice. 28 rooms. Credit cards: not accepted.

Providenciales

Beaches   **$1730–$1960**   ★★★

Grace Bay Beach, Providenciales, ☎ (800) 726-3257, (809) 946-8000.
FAX (809) 946-8001.
Double: $1730–$1960.

This resort, formerly called Royal Bay, is a new concept from the Sandals chain, which operates successful couples-only all-inclusives in Jamaica and other Caribbean islands. Beaches is still all inclusive, but the couples-only designation is gone, meaning it's open to everyone. Facilities at this busy site include a free-form pool two restaurants, a bar and grill, a cocktail lounge, even a pastry shop. Guestrooms come equipped with satellite TV, minibar, coffeemaker and hairdryer. Recreational facilities include a dive shop, fitness center and lighted tennis courts. The rates quoted are double occupancy for the minimum three-night stay. And no, that's not a typo—a two-bedroom villa really does cost $11,000 for three nights. 200 rooms. Credit cards: A, MC, V.

Turquoise Reef   **$125–$190**   ★★

Grace Bay, Providenciales, ☎ (800) 223-6510, (809) 946-5555. FAX (809) 946-5629.
Single: $125–$160. Double: $155–$190.

This low-rise resort overlooks 12 miles of white sandy beach that is part of the Princess Alexandra National Marine Park. Accommodations are outfitted with balcony or patio, cable TV, air conditioning and tile floors. Facilities include a PADI dive shop and watersports center, a fitness club, two lit tennis courts, three restaurants and the Provo Golf Course. There's also nightly entertainment, weekly theme parties and the island's only casino. Inquire about dive and golf packages. 228 rooms. Credit cards: A, MC, V.

Salt Cay

Windmills Plantation   **$440–$595**   ★★★

North Beach Road, ☎ (800) 822-7715, (809) 946-6962. FAX (410) 820-9179.
Single: $440–$595. Double: $440–$595.

This all-inclusive resort is located on Salt Cay, nine miles south of Grand Turk. Set on a 2.5-mile sandy beach, this recreated colonial plantation is a colorful and eclectic mix of architectural styles and facades that is as inviting as it is comfortable. Each lovely guestroom is uniquely decorated with four-poster beds, antiques, and porches or verandas. Dinner is served by candlelight in the fine restaurant, and three bars keep thirsty throats at bay. There's also a pool and watersports, included in the rates. Horseback riding and nature trails are nearby. Wonderful! 8 rooms. Credit cards: A, V.

TURKS & CAICOS ISLANDS

Apartments and Condominiums
Cockburn Town

Coral Reef Beach Club   **$65–$135**   ★ ★

The Ridge, Cockburn Town, ☎ *(809) 946-2055. FAX (809) 946-2503.*
Single: $65–$135. Double: $65–$135.

This beachfront property accommodates guests in one- and two-bedroom apartments with motel-like furnishings and air conditioners. Recreational amenities include a dive shop, watersports, a pool and a tennis court. There's also a bar and restaurant for those not up to cooking in. A good combination of efficiency living and hotel facilities. 21 rooms. Credit cards: A, D, MC, V.

Treasure Beach Villas   **$112–$175**   ★

Bight, Cockburn Town, ☎ *(809) 946-4211. FAX (809) 946-4108.*
Single: $112–$175. Double: $112–$175.

This complex offers one- and two-bedroom villas sitting on the beach, each with living and dining areas, full kitchens, and ceiling fans in lieu of air conditioners. There's a pool and tennis court on the premises, and restaurants are within a five-minute walk, though you're best off renting a car for true mobility. They'll help arrange watersports and deep-sea fishing. 18 rooms. Credit cards: A, MC, V.

Grace Bay

Ocean Club   **$205–$339**   ★ ★

Grace Bay, ☎ *(800) 825-8703, (809) 946-5880. FAX (809) 946-5845.*
Single: $205–$295. Double: $239–$339.

This deluxe condominium complex sits on nicely landscaped grounds fronting a gorgeous beach. Accommodations are found in five buildings housing studios and units of one to three bedrooms, all air conditioned and quite luxuriously appointed with modern amenities and full kitchens. There's a bar and grill on-site, as well as a pool and lighted tennis court. You can walk to the casino at the Ramada and area restaurants. Very nice. 32 rooms. Credit cards: A, D, MC, V.

North Caicos

Ocean Beach Hotel/Condos   **$94–$175**   ★

Whitby, North Caicos, ☎ *(809) 946-7113.*
Single: $94–$145. Double: $105–$175.

This complex on North Caicos is set right on the beach. The ocean here is calm and inviting thanks to a protective reef. Guests can choose from standard rooms or apartments with kitchens, all done in rattan furnishings and with ocean views. Ceiling fans do the job in lieu of air conditioners. Facilities include a bar, restaurant and pool, and they'll help arrange watersports and island tours. 10 rooms. Credit cards: MC, V.

Inns
Cockburn Town

Erebus Inn   **$80–$150**   ★ ★

Turtle Cove Marina, Cockburn Town, ☎ *(809) 946-4240. FAX (809) 946-4704.*
Single: $80–$150. Double: $80–$150.

Set on a cliff with wonderful views, this cheerful spot accommodates guests in comfortable rooms, bungalows and chalets. All have telephones and TV, and 22 are air-conditioned. There's a restaurant, bar, two pools and two tennis courts on the premises, and they'll shuttle you over to a nearby beach. Unless your heart is set on being right on the sea, this property fills most needs very nicely. 30 rooms. Credit cards: A, D, MC, V.

Turks Head Inn $55–$80 ★

Cockburn Town, ☎ (809) 946-2466. FAX (809) 946 2825.
Single: $55. Double: $80.

This Bermuda-style inn, surrounded by gardens, dates back to 1849 and was a government guest house and American Consulate in prior years. Guestrooms are simple but very pleasant with original antique furnishings such as four-poster beds and rocking chairs, air conditioners, TV and private baths. There's also an apartment with kitchenette for rent. Facilities are limited to a bar and restaurant. 7 rooms. Credit cards: A, MC, V.

Where to Eat

★★★★★	**Fielding's Highest Rated Restaurants in Turks & Caicos Islands**	
★★★★★	Anacaona	$28–$32
★★★★	Alfred's Place	$10–$25
★★★★	Hey, Jose	$8–$14
★★★	Top o' the Cove	$5–$12

	Fielding's Most Exclusive Restaurants in Turks & Caicos Islands	
★★★★★	Anacaona	$28–$32
★★★★	Alfred's Place	$10–$25
★★★★	Hey, Jose	$8–$14
★★★	Top o' the Cove	$5–$12

	Fielding's Budget Restaurants in Turks & Caicos Islands	
★★★★	Hey, Jose	$8–$14
★★★★	Alfred's Place	$10–$25
★★★★★	Anacaona	$28–$32

Restaurants are as casual as everything else on the islands, but since virtually all foodstuffs are imported, prices can be high. Obviously, seafood is a staple, and you're apt to see grouper, tuna, reef-dwelling hogfish (a local favorite), conch and spiny lobster on the menu. Goat roti (an East Indian curried dish) and turtle are also widely available. Foods are often heavily seasoned with tangy or biting spices, and Cajun blackening and Jamaican jerking are popular ways of preparing white-meat fish, shellfish and chicken. For nightlife, head to the islands' sole casino, the Port Royale at the Ramada Turquoise Reef Hotel on Provo Though life here is quite informal, you'll notice that locals like to dress up for an evening out.

Alfred's Place $$$ ★★★★

Turtle Cove, Blue Hills, ☎ *(809) 946-4679.*
International cuisine.
Lunch: Noon–4 p.m., entrées $12–$19.
Dinner: 4–11 p.m., entrées $10–$25. Closed: Mon.

A French chef and Austrian owner dish out mostly American meals and stiff drinks to an appreciative crowd. Diners schmooze and munch on a deck set above Turtle Cove. Prime rib, swordfish, lobster, salads and sandwiches are on the bill of fare. Reservations required. Credit cards: A, MC, V.

Anacaona $$$ ★★★★★

Grace Bay Club, Blue Hills, ☎ *(809) 946-5950. Associated hotel: Grace Bay Club.*
International cuisine.
Lunch: entrées $10–$25.
Dinner: entrées $28–$32.

It's hard not to feel like a god or goddess while dining indolently under one of the stunningly decorated thatched roofed huts fronting the ocean. Each of the discreetly spaced tables within display pristine napery and gleaming glassware and a single candle encased in a hurricane lamp. Ceiling fans cool the air and torches enhance the glow from the star-filled night sky. Succulent seafood straight off the fishing boats are often served tasting redolently of the in-house smoker. Terrific wine list, homemade desserts and Italian coffee drinks. Reservations required. Credit cards: A, MC, V.

Hey, Jose $$ ★★★★

Atlas House, Blue Hills, ☎ *(809) 946-4812.*
Mexican cuisine.
Lunch: Noon–3 p.m., entrées $8–$13.
Dinner: 6–10 p.m., entrées $8–$14. Closed: Sun.

This airport area restaurant has a whiz behind the bar who makes the frothiest margaritas on the island. The chef keeps tasty platters of tacos and sizzling fajitas coming out of the kitchen at all hours of the day and night. Housed in a shopping center, it isn't very intimate, but that's not what the boisterous crowds come for. Pizza, burgers and chicken are also available. Reservations recommended. Credit cards: A, MC, V.

Top o' the Cove $ ★★★

Leeward Highway, Blue Hills, ☎ *(809) 946-4694.*
American cuisine.
Lunch: 6:30 a.m.–4 p.m., entrées $5–$12.

Homesick New Yorkers and other big city dwellers appreciate the bagels and deli fare provided by this cozy spot. The mean cups of eye-opening espressos and foamy cappuccinos wake everybody else out of a midday stupor. There's a nice atmosphere despite its location next to an auto parts store. Mostly take-out, but there are a few tables to park the body for an hour or two. Credit cards: not accepted. Credit cards: A, MC, V.

There's not much in the way of shopping here, though Provo has a few outlets worth mentioning. Baskets woven from fresh grass and rag rugs are craft specialties; you'll find both at **Greensleeves**, ☎ *(809) 946-4147)*. For Caribbean artworks, try **Bamboo Gallery**, ☎ *(809) 946-4748)* and **Local Color**, ☎ *(809) 946-5547)*. You'll find other shops at Market Place, Plantation Hills and Central Square along Provo's Leeward Highway. The post office is a good place to pick up colorful stamps that make good, inexpensive souvenirs.

Turks and Caicos Directory

Arrival and Departure

Travel to and from the Turks and Caicos is made easy by **American Airlines**, the country's primary carrier, which flies into Provo from Miami seven times a week. Transfers to Grand Turk are handled by **Turks and Caicos Airways**, with small, six-passenger planes. TCA also flies a 19-passenger jet, offering alternative service from Nassau and Miami as well as other destinations. Air travel to all other inhabited islands is also offered by TCA as well as several small carriers such as Interisland.

A departure tax of $15 is collected at the airport.

Business Hours

Shops generally open weekdays 8 a.m.–4 p.m. Banks open Monday–Thursday 8:30 a.m.–2:30 p.m. and Friday 8:30 a.m.–12:30 p.m. and 2:30–4:30 p.m.

Climate

Temperatures range from 75–85 degrees F. from November -May, spiraling up to the 90s in June through October. Constant trade winds keep the heat bearable. There is no marked rainy season. Hurricane season runs June-October.

Documents

Visitors are required to write a valid passport (or proof of citizenship in the form of a birth certificate, voter's registration card plus a photo ID).

Electricity

Current runs 100 volts, 60 cycles, the same as in the United States.

Getting Around

Those who've come to the Turks and Caicos for watersports and trekking will find that a cab to and from the airport is probably the only transportation they will need. Major hotels are within walking distance of a beach; those that aren't offer a shuttle service. However, restaurants and most attractions to Provo are located about a $10 taxi trip from most hotels, making a scooter or rental car necessary.

Taxis are unmetered, and rates, posted in the taxis, are regulated by the government. A trip between Provo's airport and most major hotels runs $15. On Grand Turk, a trip from the airport to town is about $4.; from the airport to the hotels outside town $5–$10.

Rental cars are available on the island. On Provo, **Budget** ☎ *(809) 94-64079* and **Highway** ☎ *(809) 94-52623* offer the lowest rates, which average $40–$50 per day. Scooters are available at **The Honda Shop** ☎ *(809) 94-65585* and **Scooter Rental** ☎ *(809) 94-65585* and ☎ *(809) 94-64684* for $25 per 24-hour day.

Ferry service is available with the **Caicos Express** ☎ *(809) 94-67111* or *(809) 94-67258* with two scheduled interisland ferries between Provo, Pine Cay, Middle Caicos, Parrot Cay and North Caicos daily except Sunday. Tickets cost $15 each way. Caicos Express also offers various guided tours to the out islands.

A bus runs into town from most hotels on Providenciales, running about $2–$4 one-way. A new public bus system on Grand Turk charges 50 cents one-way to any scheduled stop.

Language

The official language of the Turks and Caicos is English.

Medical Emergencies

Emergency medical care is provided at the **Provo Health Medical Centre** downtown ☎ *(809) 946-4201*, including eye and dentalwork. The government **Blue Hills Clinic** has a doctor and midwife on call ☎ *(809) 946-4228*. Grand Turk has a hospital on the north side of town. Other islands organize emergency air service to the closest hospital available.

Money

The official currency of the Turks and Caicos is the U.S. dollar.

Telephone

The area code is *809*. To dial direct from the U.S., dial *011* (international access) + *809* (country code) +local number. To make international calls from the Turks and Caicos, it's best to go to the Cable & Wireless office in Provo ☎ *(809) 94-64499* and Grand Turk ☎ *(809) 94-62200*. These offices are open Monday-Thursday 800 a.m.–4:30 p.m., Friday 8 a.m.–4 p.m. You can make calls from local phones with the use of a credit card purchased in increments of $5, $10 and $20.

Time

Atlantic Standard Time, meaning one hour earlier than New York. During daylight saving time, it is the same time as New York.

Tipping and Taxes

Hotels charge a seven percent government tax and add a 10–15 percent service charge to your bill. In a restaurant, it's appropriate to leave a 10–15 percent tip if it is not added already; check so you don't duplicate efforts. Taxi drivers expect a small tip.

Tourist Information

The **Turks and Caicos Islands Tourist Board** has a toll-free number on the islands ☎ *(800) 241-00824.* For hotel information, contact **The Turks & Caicos Resort Association** ☎ *(800) 2 TC-ISLES.*

Water

Outside of Providenciales, where desalinators have transformed much of the island into a riot of flowers, water remains a precious commodity. Drink only from the decanter of fresh water provided by the hotel, but tap water is safe for brushing your teeth and other hygienic purposes.

When to Go

Late April to the end of November is off-season, when you can save 15–20 percent on hotel rates.

TURKS & CAICOS ISLANDS HOTELS		RMS	RATES	PHONE	CR. CARDS
Providenciales					
Blue Hills					
★★★★★	Club Med Turkoise	400	All-Inclusive	(800) 258-2633	A, DC, MC, V
★★★	Beaches	200	$1730–$1960	(800) 726-3257	A, MC, V
★★	Turquoise Reef	228	$125–$190	(800) 223-6510	A, MC, V
★★	Turtle Cove Inn	30	$90–$180	(800) 633-7411	A, D, MC, V
Grace Bay					
★★★★	Grace Bay Club	22	$255–$725	(800) 946-5758	A, MC, V
★★★	Le Deck Hotel	27	$95–$175	(809) 946-5547	A, D, MC, V
★★	Ocean Club	32	$205–$339	(800) 825-8703	A, D, MC, V
Turks					
Cockburn Town					
★★★★★	Meridian Club	28	$395–$575	(800) 331-9154	None
★★★	Prospect of Whitby	28	$90–$460	(809) 946-7119	A, MC, V
★★★	Ramada Turquoise Reef	228	$125–$460	(800) 228-9898	A, MC, V
★★★	Windmills Plantation	8	$440–$595	(800) 822-7715	A, V
★★	Coral Reef Beach Club	21	$65–$135	(809) 946-2055	A, D, MC, V

TURKS & CAICOS ISLANDS HOTELS		RMS	RATES	PHONE	CR. CARDS
★★	Erebus Inn	30	$80–$150	(809) 946-4240	A, D, MC, V
★★	Guanahani Beach Hotel	16	$120–$165	(800) 468-8752	A, MC, V
★★	Sitting Pretty Hotel	28	$75–$220	(809) 946-2666	A, MC, V
★★	Sunworshippers Pelican Beach Club	25	$70–$120	(809) 946-4488	A, MC, V
★	Ocean Beach Hotel/ Condos	10	$94–$175	(809) 946-7113	MC, V
★	Treasure Beach Villas	18	$112–$175	(809) 946-4211	A, MC, V
★	Turks Head Inn	7	$55–$80	(809) 946-2466	A, MC, V

TURKS & CAICOS ISLANDS RESTAURANTS		PHONE	ENTRÉE	CR. CARDS
Providenciales				
Blue Hills				
American				
★★★	Top o' the Cove	(809) 946-4694	$5–$12	A, MC, V
International				
★★★★★	Anacaona	(809) 946-5950	$10–$32	A, MC, V
★★★★	Alfred's Place	(809) 946-4679	$12–$25	A, MC, V
Mexican				
★★★★	Hey, Jose	(809) 946-4812	$8–$14	A, MC, V

INDEX

Order Your Guide to Travel and Adventure

Title	Price	Title	Price
Fielding's Alaska Cruises and the Inside Passage	$18.95	Fielding's London Agenda	$14.95
Fielding's The Amazon	$16.95	Fielding's Los Angeles	$16.95
Fielding's Asia's Top Dive Sites	$19.95	Fielding's Malaysia & Singapore	$16.95
Fielding's Australia	$16.95	Fielding's Mexico	$18.95
Fielding's Bahamas	$16.95	Fielding's New Orleans Agenda	$16.95
Fielding's Baja	$18.95	Fielding's New York Agenda	$16.95
Fielding's Bermuda	$16.95	Fielding's New Zealand	$16.95
Fielding's Borneo	$18.95	Fielding's Paris Agenda	$14.95
Fielding's Budget Europe	$17.95	Fielding's Portugal	$16.95
Fielding's Caribbean	$18.95	Fielding's Paradors, Pousadas and Charming Villages	$18.95
Fielding's Caribbean Cruises	$18.95	Fielding's Rome Agenda	$14.95
Fielding's Disney World and Orlando	$18.95	Fielding's San Diego Agenda	$14.95
Fielding's Diving Indonesia	$19.95	Fielding's Southeast Asia	$18.95
Fielding's Eastern Caribbean	$17.95	Fielding's Southern Vietnam on 2 Wheels	$15.95
Fielding's England	$17.95	Fielding's Spain	$18.95
Fielding's Europe	$18.95	Fielding's Surfing Indonesia	$19.95
Fielding's European Cruises	$18.95	Fielding's Sydney Agenda	$16.95
Fielding's Far East	$18.95	Fielding's Thailand, Cambodia, Laos and Myanmar	$18.95
Fielding's France	$18.95	Fielding's Vacation Places Rated	$19.95
Fielding's Freewheelin' USA	$18.95	Fielding's Vietnam	$17.95
Fielding's Hawaii	$18.95	Fielding's Western Caribbean	$18.95
Fielding's Italy	$18.95	Fielding's The World's Most Dangerous Places	$19.95
Fielding's Kenya	$16.95	Fielding's Worldwide Cruises	$19.95
Fielding's Las Vegas Agenda	$14.95		

To place an order: call toll-free 1-800-FW-2-GUIDE
(VISA, MasterCard and American Express accepted)
or send your check or money order to:
Fielding Worldwide, Inc., 308 S. Catalina Avenue, Redondo Beach, CA 90277
http://www.fieldingtravel.com
Add $2.00 per book for shipping & handling (sorry, no COD's), allow 2–6 weeks for delivery

FIELDING'S CARIBBEAN CRUISES

Frank, in-depth reviews of every major ship that sails the Caribbean.

The most comprehensive guide to the ships that ply the Caribbean and all 35 ports of call. Written in a descriptive, entertaining style, it contains all the facts the reader needs to choose the right ship and the right destinations.

Filled with hundreds of helpful hints, loads of charts and tables, plus 43 maps, 150 b/w photos and 868 restaurant and attraction listings.

- *Comprehensive reviews:* Profiles of 87 ships, from luxury liners to chartered yachts and sailing vessels, including facilities, features and star-ratings.
- *Ship comparisons:* Which ships are best for singles, families, seniors, adventurers or honeymooners—plus theme cruises.
- *Essential info:* From how to reserve a cabin, book a table, pack the right stuff, to even avoid seasickness—plus how much to tip and safety measures at sea.
- *Ideas for things to do in the various ports of call:* Such as explore bustling Fort-de-France on Martinique and tour the colorful gabled houses in Willemstad.

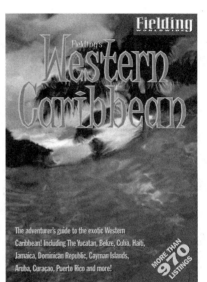

FIELDING'S EASTERN CARIBBEAN

Fielding's guide to the best Eastern Caribbean escapes!

Fielding's updated guidebook to the Eastern Caribbean reveals the secrets of this tropical paradise. Here, readers will discover the hidden and little-known attractions of 23 islands. With hundreds of insider tips, this is the ultimate guide to the region.

Twenty-three 3-D tour guides, 94 maps and b/w photos are included.

- *Island snapshots:* Descriptions of the history, culture and special features of each island, plus how to choose the destinations that best suit you.

- *Rated hotels and restaurants:* More than 800 in-depth reviews, along with 138 helpful comparison charts.

- *Tips on an array of watersports:* Where to explore coral reefs, wrecks and secret coves; the best spots for night dives, wall diving and snorkeling, as well as windsurfing, deep-sea fishing, sailing, parasailing and surfing; plus 60 listings of dive shops and classes.

- *Ideas for high adventure on land:* Hiking through rain forests, climbing volcanoes, cycling hills and valleys, exploring wildlife preserves.

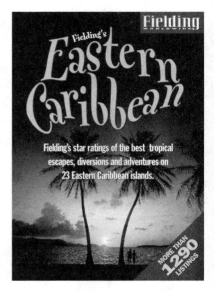

Fielding's star ratings of the best tropical escapes, diversions and adventures on 23 Eastern Caribbean islands.

MORE THAN 1290 LISTINGS

800 pages, 5" x 7-1/4", 30 b/w photos
94 maps, 23 3-D tour guides

$17.95
UK £13.95 CAN $22.95 AUS $24.95
ISBN 1-56952-120-4

To order:
1-800-FW-2-GUIDE
1-310-372-4474
FAX: 1-310-376-8064
E-mail: fielding@fieldingtravel.c